Anthropology
Ninth Edition

Carol R. Ember

HUMAN RELATIONS AREA FILES

Melvin Ember

HUMAN RELATIONS AREA FILES

Prentice Hall, Upper Saddle River, New Jersey 07458

Library of Congress Cataloging-in-Publication Data

Ember, Carol R.
   Anthropology / Carol R. Ember, Melvin Ember. —9th ed.
     p.   cm.
   Includes bibliographical references and index.
   ISBN 0–13–791526–8
    1. Anthropology. I. Ember, Melvin. II. Title.
GN25.E46 1999   98-38298
301—dc21   CIP

Editorial Director: Charlyce Jones Owen
Editor in Chief: Nancy Roberts
Managing Editor: Sharon Chambliss
Marketing Manager: Christopher DeJohn
Production Editor: Serena Hoffman
AVP, Director of Production and Manufacturing: Barbara Kittle
Manufacturing Manager: Nick Sklitsis
Buyer: Lynn Pearlman
Creative Design Director: Leslie Osher
Interior and Cover Design: Diana McKnight, Joseph Rattan Design
Art Director: Anne Bonanno Nieglos
Electronic Graphic Assistance: James Bruce Killmer
Line Art Coordinator: Guy Ruggiero
Illustrator: Maria Piper
Executive Manager, New Media: Alison Pendergast
New Media Assistant: Maurice Murdock
New Media Buyer: Diane Hynes
New Media Testing: David Moles
Photo Researcher: Linda Sykes
Director, Image Resource Center: Lori Morris-Nantz
Photo Research Supervisor: Melinda Lee Reo
Image Permission Supervisor: Kay Dellosa
Cover art: "Masks," Sonya McQueen/Superstock

This book was set in 10/11.5 Minion
by The Clarinda Company and was
printed and bound by World Color.
The cover was printed by The Lehigh Press, Inc.

 © 1999, 1996, 1993, 1990, 1988, 1985,
1981, 1977, 1973 by Prentice-Hall, Inc.
Simon & Schuster/ A Viacom Company
Upper Saddle River, New Jersey 07458

Printed in the United States of America

10 9 8 7 6 5 4 3 2

ISBN 0-13-791526-8

Prentice-Hall International (UK) Limited, *London*
Prentice-Hall of Australia Pty. Limited, *Sydney*
Prentice-Hall Canada Inc., *Toronto*
Prentice-Hall Hispanoamericana, S.A., *Mexico*
Prentice-Hall of India Private Limited, *New Delhi*
Prentice-Hall of Japan, Inc., *Tokyo*
Simon & Schuster Asia Pte. Ltd., *Singapore*
Editora Prentice-Hall do Brasil, Ltda., *Rio de Janeiro*

Brief Contents

Contents

Part III   Cultural Variation

Part IV   Culture and Anthropology in the Modern World

Boxes

Current Issues

New Perspectives on Gender

 # Research Frontiers

 # Applied Anthropology

Preface

One out of two anthropologists in this country is now employed outside of academia. This situation reflects an increasing realization that anthropology, and what it has discovered about humans, is useful. Why else would so many anthropologists be hired to help solve practical problems? It is appropriate therefore that this edition focus more on applied and practicing anthropology than in the past. We do so in many of the chapters, particularly in a new set of boxes that highlight how anthropological knowledge has been used to solve problems in the real world.

As always, in updating this book, we go beyond descriptions. We are interested not only in *what* humans were and are like; we are also interested in *why* humans are the way they are, why they got to be that way, and why they vary. When there are alternative explanations, we try to communicate the necessity to evaluate them on logical grounds as well as on the basis of the available evidence. The chapter now titled "Theory and Evidence in Cultural Anthropology" is designed to help students see how explanations can be and have been tested. Throughout the book, we note when the available evidence is still lacking or is not clear. We would be pleased if we succeeded in helping students understand that no idea, including ideas put forward in textbooks, should be accepted simply as authority.

NEW FEATURES

CD-ROM

A CD-ROM accompanies every book. Developed by Object Learning Environment, Inc., **Anthropology: Culture and Diversity** has been adapted to coincide with the book's chapters and provides quizzes, exercises, Internet links, and links to portions of the text for definitions.

INTERNET EXERCISES

With the help of Ramesh Krishnamurthy of Oregon State University, Internet exercises have been developed to provide students with Web-based resources on topics covered in each chapter. Students are encouraged to use the Internet addresses (URLs) provided to discover more about the dynamic changes that are occurring in the field of anthropology.

APPLIED ANTHROPOLOGY BOXES

The new boxes on Applied Anthropology describe how anthropology and applied anthropologists have worked to put anthropological knowledge to use in dealing with practical problems (examples: getting development programs to notice women farmers; analyzing why Bedouin do not readily settle down; finding a way to reforest Haiti; and impact of the world-system—deforestation of the Amazon).

HIGHLIGHTS OF THE CHAPTERS AND WHAT IS NEW IN THIS EDITION

CHAPTER 1: WHAT IS ANTHROPOLOGY?

Chapter 1 introduces the student to anthropology. We discuss what we think is special and distinctive about anthropology in general, and about each of its subfields in particular. We outline how each of the subfields is related to other disciplines such as biology, psychology, and sociology. We direct attention to the increasing importance of applied anthropology by expanding the section on applied anthropology with a revised Figure 1-1 to show how applied anthropology relates to other subfields, and adding a box on an applied anthropologist at work.

CHAPTER 2: EVOLUTION

This chapter discusses evolutionary theory as it applies to all forms of life, including humans. Following an extensive review of natural selection and what it means, we discuss how natural selection may operate on behavioral traits and how cultural evolution differs from biological evolution. We consider the ethical issues posed by the possibility of genetic engineering. The first box examines the evidence suggesting that evolution proceeds abruptly rather than slowly and steadily. The second box discusses whether genetic engineering should be feared.

CHAPTER 3: THE LIVING PRIMATES

This chapter describes the living nonhuman primates and their variable adaptations as background for understanding the evolution of primates in general and humans in particular. After describing the various species, we discuss some possible explanations of how the primates differ—in body and brain size, size of social group, and female sexuality. The chapter ends with a discussion of the distinctive features of humans in comparison with the other primates. The first box deals with how and why many primates are endangered and how they might be protected. The second box describes a primatologist and some of her work.

CHAPTER 4: PRIMATE EVOLUTION: FROM EARLY PRIMATES TO HOMINOIDS

This chapter begins with the emergence of the early primates and ends with what we know or suspect about the Miocene apes, one of whom (known or unknown) was ancestral to bipedal hominids. We describe ways of dating fossils and the molecular clock. To highlight how theory is generated and revised, the first box deals with how a paleoanthropologist has reexamined his own theory of primate origins. The second box describes a giant ape that overlapped with *Homo erectus,* and why the ape became extinct.

CHAPTER 5: EARLY HOMINIDS AND THEIR CULTURES

This chapter starts with the emergence of the first bipedal hominids. Before getting to the available fossil evidence, we first discuss trends in, and possible explanations of, the distinctive developments in the hominid line—bipedalism, the expansion of the brain, and the reduction of the face, teeth, and jaws. We update and discuss the latest fossil finds, including the recent finds of australopithecines and a possible precursor, namely, *Ardipithecus ramidus* from 4.5 million years ago, who may have been mostly or intermittently bipedal. The first box discusses the puzzle posed by similarities between the robust australopithecines and *Homo.* The second box discusses research evaluating the claim that *Homo erectus* should be divided into two species. We discuss how the earliest dating of *Homo erectus* may affect ideas about when hominids first moved out of Africa.

CHAPTER 6: THE EMERGENCE OF *HOMO SAPIENS* AND THEIR CULTURES

This chapter discusses the transition between *Homo erectus* and *Homo sapiens* and the emergence of modern-looking humans. In keeping with our global orientation, we discuss fossil and archaeological evidence from many areas of the world, not just Europe and the Near East. We discuss the new evidence—preserved wooden spears—indicating that people were hunting big game at least 400,000 years ago. The first box describes the evidence from mitochondrial DNA regarding the "Out of Africa" theory of modern human origins. A second box describes the latest evidence from South America indicating that modern humans moved into the New World south of Canada at least 12,500 years ago.

CHAPTER 7: HUMAN VARIATION

This chapter brings the discussion of human evolution into the present, dealing with biological variation in living human populations and how biological anthropologists study such variation. In a much revised section on race and racism, we discuss why many anthropologists think that the concept of race as applied to humans is not scientifically useful. In this view, human variation is more usefully studied in terms of clinal variation in particular traits. For example, we indicate how differences between populations—in body build, skin color, height, susceptibility to disease, lactase deficiency, etc.—can be explained as adaptations to differences in the physical and cultural environment. We discuss the myths of racism and how race is largely a social category in humans. One of the boxes deals with differences in average I.Q. scores and what they mean. The other box deals with biological factors affecting the capacity to have offspring.

CHAPTER 8: ORIGINS OF FOOD PRODUCTION AND SETTLED LIFE

This chapter deals with the emergence of broad-spectrum collecting and settled life, and the domestication of plants and animals in various parts of the world. Our discussion focuses mainly on the possible causes and consequences of these developments in southeast Asia, Africa, the Andes, and eastern North America, as well as the Near East and Europe. We discuss puzzles such as why much of Native North America switched to a dependence on corn even though the earlier agricultural diet was apparently adequate. The first box discusses the domestication of dogs and cats, and the second box discusses how researchers are finding out about ancient diets from chemical analysis of bones and teeth.

CHAPTER 9: ORIGINS OF CITIES AND STATES

This chapter deals with the rise of civilizations in various areas of the world and the theories that have been offered to explain the development of state-type political systems. The chapter concludes with a discussion of the decline and collapse of states. For example, environmental degradation may at least partly account for the fall of the Akkadian empire and other civilizations not far away after 2300 A.D. Environmental degradation may be due to events in the natural world, but the behavior of humans may sometimes be responsible. Civilizations may also decline because human behavior has increased the incidence of disease. One box discusses the links between imperialism, colonialism, and the state. The other box discusses the consequences of ancient imperialism for women's status.

CHAPTER 10: THE CONCEPT OF CULTURE

This chapter introduces the concept of culture. We first try to convey a feeling for what culture is before dealing more explicitly with the concept and some assumptions about it. We have added a new section on cultural relativism, putting the concept in its historical context and discussing recent thinking on the subject. We discuss the fact that individual behavior varies in all societies and how such variation may be the beginning of new cultural patterns. The first box, which asks whether Western countries are ethnocentric in their ideas about human rights, has been extensively revised to incorporate the debate within anthropology about cultural relativism. The second box shows how an anthropologist, Dawn Chatty, enabled the government of Oman to evaluate the needs of the Bedouin.

CHAPTER 11: THEORY AND EVIDENCE IN CULTURAL ANTHROPOLOGY

This chapter now combines what used to be two separate chapters on schools of thought in cultural anthropology and explanation and evidence. In combining the two, we focus first on those theoretical orientations that remain popular in cultural anthropology. Then we discuss what it means to explain and what kinds of evidence are needed to evaluate an explanation. We end with a discussion of the major types of study in cultural anthropology— ethnography, ethnohistory, within-culture comparisons, regional comparisons, and worldwide cross-cultural comparisons. The first box uses a research question about the Abelam of New Guinea to illustrate how different theoretical orientations suggest different types of answers. The second box explores the differences between scientific and humanistic understanding and points out that the different approaches are not really incompatible. In the third box, we have two purposes. One is to give a feeling for the experience of fieldwork; the second is to use the Mead-Freeman controversy to explore the issue of how we can know that an ethnographer is accurate.

In most of the chapters that follow, we try to convey the range of cultural variation with ethnographic examples from all over the world. Wherever we can, we discuss possible explanations of why societies may be similar or different in regard to some aspect of culture. If anthropologists have no explanation as yet for the variation, we say so. But if we have some idea of the conditions that may be related to a particular kind of variation, even if we do not know yet why they are related, we discuss that too. If we are to train students to go beyond what we know now, we have to tell them what we do not know, as well as what we think we know.

CHAPTER 12: COMMUNICATION AND LANGUAGE

We begin by discussing communication in humans and other animals. We have added new information on human nonverbal communication. After discussing the origins of language and how creoles and children's language acquisition may help us understand the origins, we move on to structural linguistics and the processes of linguistic divergence. After discussing the interrelationships between language and other aspects of culture, we end with the ethnography of speaking, including differences in speech by status, gender, and ethnicity.

We have greatly revised the sections on phonology and morphology, including new research on consonant-vowel syllables, and have added a new discussion of research on linguistic relativity. The first box deals with the problem of language extinction and what some anthropologists are doing about it. To stimulate thinking about the possible impact of language on thought, we ask in the second box whether the English language promotes sexist thinking, referring to new research on the subject.

CHAPTER 13: GETTING FOOD

Chapter 13 discusses how societies vary in getting their food, how they have changed over time, and how such variation seems to affect other kinds of cultural variation—including variation in economic systems, social stratification, and political life. We include a discussion of "market foragers" to emphasize that most people in a modern market economy are not in fact producers of food. The first box deals with the change from "Man the Hunter" to "Woman the Gatherer," and we raise the question of whether either view is accurate. Although it is commonly thought that industrialization is mainly to blame for negative developments in the environment, our second box deals with the negative effects in preindustrial times of irrigation, animal grazing, and overhunting.

CHAPTER 14: ECONOMIC SYSTEMS

Chapter 14 discusses how societies vary in the ways they allocate resources (what is "property" and what ownership may mean), convert or transform resources through labor into usable goods, and distribute and perhaps exchange goods and services. We discuss the effects of political systems (including colonialism) on land ownership and use, and we distinguish between gift and commodity exchanges. We have added a discussion of why children in some foraging societies do more work than in others. The first box addresses the controversy over whether communal ownership leads to economic disaster. After the discussion of commercialization, the second box illustrates the impact of the world-system on local economies, with special reference to the deforestation of the Amazon.

CHAPTER 15: SOCIAL STRATIFICATION

Chapter 15 deals with variation in degree of social stratification and how the various forms of social inequality (rank, class, caste, slavery) may develop. We discuss new research on how egalitarian societies keep leaders from dominating others, and how rank societies might have more inequality than previously thought, judging by research on Ifaluk. The section on class systems has been extensively revised. We now include a community study in Canada that describes differing perceptions of social class by different individuals and how the class system became more open with in-migration. In the first of the boxes in this chapter, we discuss recent changes in the United States, particularly the widening of the gap between rich and poor, and how people feel about the changes. In the second box, we discuss social stratification on the global level—how the gap between rich and poor countries has been widening, and what may account for that trend.

CHAPTER 16: SEX, GENDER, AND CULTURE

In the first part of Chapter 16 we discuss how and why sex and gender differences vary cross-culturally; in the second part we discuss variation in sexual attitudes and practices. We explain how the concepts of gender do not always involve just two genders. We emphasize all the ways women contribute to work, and how conclusions about contributions by gender depend on how you measure "work." We have added a discussion of female aggression in an Australian aborigine community. In the first box, we discuss research on why women's political participation may be increasing in some Coast Salish communities of western Washington State and British Columbia, now that they have elected councils. A second box examines cross-cultural research about why some societies allow women to participate in combat. Finally, we have incorporated new survey results on the United States in the section on variation in sexual attitudes and practices.

CHAPTER 17: MARRIAGE AND THE FAMILY

After discussing various theories about why marriage might be universal, we move on to discuss variation in how one marries, restrictions on marriage, whom one should marry, and how many one should marry. We close with a discussion of variation in family form. To introduce topics regarding the husband-wife relationship that are only beginning to be investigated, we have added a box on variation in love, intimacy, and sexual jealousy. The box in the section on family organization discusses why one-parent families are on the increase in countries like ours.

CHAPTER 18: MARITAL RESIDENCE AND KINSHIP

In addition to explaining the variation that exists in marital residence, kinship structure, and kinship terminology, this chapter emphasizes how understanding residence is important for understanding social life. One of the boxes discusses the possible relationship between neolocality and adolescent rebellion. The second box is on how variation in residence and kinship affects the lives of women.

CHAPTER 19: ASSOCIATIONS AND INTEREST GROUPS

We discuss the importance of associations in many parts of the world, particularly nonvoluntary associations such as age sets, and the increasing importance of voluntary associations in the modern world. We have added a new section on a special kind of mutual aid association—rotating-credit associations. We discuss how they work to provide lump sums of money to individuals, how they are especially important to women, and how they become even more important when people move to new places. The first box addresses the question of whether separate women's associations increase women's status and power; the second box discusses why street gangs develop and why they often become violent.

CHAPTER 20: POLITICAL LIFE

We look at how societies have varied in their levels of political organization, the various ways people become leaders, the degree to which they participate in the political process, and the peaceful and violent methods of resolving conflict. We discuss how colonialization has transformed legal systems and ways of making decisions. We have expanded the discussion of peaceful resolution of conflict and now discuss research that casts doubt on the notion that wars are fought over women. The first box deals with how new local courts among the Abelam of New Guinea are allowing women to address sexual grievances. The second box deals with the cross-national and cross-cultural relationship between economic development and democracy.

CHAPTER 21: PSYCHOLOGY AND CULTURE

Chapter 21 discusses some of the universals of psychological development, some psychological differences between societies and what might account for them, how people in different societies conceive of personality differently (e.g., the concept of self), and how knowledge of psychological processes may help us understand cultural variation. We have added a new discussion on research indicating that even the concept of love, as mysterious and as culturally variable as it seems, may be similar in different cultures. We also discuss research showing that schizophrenic individuals in different cultures seem to have the same patterns of distinctive eye movements. The first box in this chapter discusses the idea that women have a different sense of themselves than men have, and therefore a different sense of morality. The second box, which refers to a recent comparison of preschools in Japan, China, and the United States, discusses how schools may consciously and unconsciously teach values.

CHAPTER 22: RELIGION AND MAGIC

After discussing why religion may be culturally universal, we discuss variation in religious belief and practice with extensive examples. We have added a discussion on revitalization movements and a dis-

cussion of how humans tend to anthropomorphize in the face of unpredictable events. The first box discusses research on New England fishermen that suggests how their taboos, or "rituals of avoidance," may be anxiety reducing. The second box discusses the emergence of new religions or cults and points out that nearly all the major churches or religions in the world began as minority sects or cults.

CHAPTER 23: THE ARTS

After discussing how art might be defined, we discuss variation in the visual arts, music, and folklore, and review how some of those variations might be explained. In regard to how the arts change over time, we discuss the myth that the art of "simpler" peoples is timeless, and we have added a section on changes in art as a result of European contact. We address the role of ethnocentrism in studies of art with a section on how Western museums and art critics look at the visual art of less complex cultures. One box discusses how art varies with different kinds of political systems. The second box, dealing with universal symbolism in art, reviews recent research on the emotions displayed in masks.

CHAPTER 24: CULTURE CHANGE

After discussing the ultimate sources of culture change—discovery and innovation—we discuss some of what is known about the conditions under which people are likely to accept innovations. We have added a new section on costs and benefits of innovations. We discuss external and internal pressures for culture change and the likelihood of cultural diversity in the future. One of the boxes examines what has happened in Communist China—what has changed because of goverment intervention and what has persisted nevertheless. To convey that culture change often has biological consequences, we have added a new box on obesity, hypertension, and diabetes as health consequences of modernization.

CHAPTER 25: APPLIED ANTHROPOLOGY AND SOCIAL PROBLEMS

After pointing out that about half of our profession is now engaged in applied and practicing anthropology, the first part of this extensively revised chapter reviews the interaction between basic and applied research, the types of jobs outside of academia, the history and types of applied anthropology in the United States, the ethical issues involved in trying to improve people's lives, the difficulties in evaluating whether a program is beneficial, and ways of implementing planned changes. We point out how applied anthropologists are playing more of a role in planning, rather than as peripheral advisers to change programs already in place. The three boxes show how anthropologists have been able to help in a variety of domains—in business, in medical anthropology, and in reforestation. We have added a section on colloborative applied anthropology in which the target population is involved in planning and carrying out projects. Finally, we discuss how research may suggest possible solutions to various global social problems, including AIDS, disasters, homelessness, crime, family violence, and war. The section on famine pays increased attention to social factors involved in producing famine.

CONTINUING FEATURES

BOXES IN EACH CHAPTER

In addition to the new boxes on applied anthropology, we provide three other kinds of boxes:

CURRENT ISSUES. These boxes deal with topics students may have heard about in the news (examples: the increase in single-parent families; the widening gap between rich and poor in the United States) or topics that are currently the subject of debate in the profession (examples: science versus humanism; human rights and cultural relativity).

RESEARCH FRONTIERS. These boxes look at researchers at work or take an in-depth look at new research or a research controversy (examples: love, intimacy, and sexual jealousy; the universality of emotions expressed in masks).

NEW PERSPECTIVES ON GENDER. These boxes involve issues pertaining to sex and gender, both in anthropology and everyday life (examples: sexism in language; separate women's associations and women's status and power; morality in women versus men).

READABILITY

We derive a lot of pleasure from trying to describe research findings, especially complicated ones, in ways that introductory students can understand. Thus, we try to minimize technical jargon, using only those terms students must know to appreciate the achievements of anthropology and to take advanced courses. We think readability is important, not only because it may enhance the reader's understanding of what we write, but also because it should make learning about

anthropology more enjoyable! When new terms are introduced, which of course must happen sometimes, they are set off in boldface type and defined.

GLOSSARY TERMS

At the end of each chapter we list the new terms that have been introduced; these terms were identified by boldface type and defined in the text. We deliberately do not repeat the definitions at the end of the chapter to allow students to test themselves against the definitions provided in the Glossary at the end of the book.

CRITICAL QUESTIONS

We also provide three or four questions at the end of each chapter that may stimulate thinking about the implications of the chapter. The questions do not ask for repetition of what is in the text. We want students to imagine, to go beyond what we know or think we know.

SUMMARIES AND SUGGESTED READING

In addition to the outline provided at the beginning of each chapter, there is a detailed summary at the end of each chapter that will help the student review the major concepts and findings discussed. Suggested Reading provides general or more extensive references on the subject matter of the chapter.

A COMPLETE GLOSSARY AT THE END OF THE BOOK

As noted above, important glossary terms for each chapter are listed (without definitions) at the end of each chapter, so students can readily check their understanding after they have read the chapter. A complete Glossary is provided at the back of the book to review all terms in the book and serve as a convenient reference for the student.

NOTES AT THE END OF THE BOOK

Because we believe firmly in the importance of documentation, we think it essential to tell our readers, both professional and student, what our conclusions are based on. Usually the basis is published research. References to the relevant studies are provided in complete notes by chapter at the end of the book and an Index to the Notes.

SUPPLEMENTS

The supplement package for this textbook has been carefully crafted to amplify and illuminate materials in the text itself.

CUSTOM ONDEMAND RESOURCES (CORE): CUSTOMIZED ORIGINAL CHAPTERS. The authors have commissioned three series of original chapters from which instructors can choose supplemental readings to accompany this text: *Portraits of Culture: Ethnographic Originals; Research Frontiers in Anthropology;* and *Cross-Cultural Research for Social Science.* The instructor can mix and match chapters from one or more of these series. (Many of these chapters are referred to in this edition.) Please see your local Prentice Hall representative or telephone 1-888-847-1737 or e-mail CORE_Anthropology@prenhall.com to receive more information about these series.

INSTRUCTOR'S RESOURCE MANUAL. For each chapter of the text, this manual provides learning objectives, chapter outlines, teaching tips, suggestions for classroom activities, topics for class discussion, written assignments, and additional Internet exercises.

TEST ITEM FILE. This carefully prepared manual contains over 1500 multiple-choice, true-false, and essay questions that are keyed to the text.

PRENTICE HALL CUSTOM TEST. This computerized version of the Test Item File allows instructors to construct tests, create alternative versions of the same test, edit existing questions, and add their own questions. Available for DOS, Windows, and Macintosh computers.

VIDEOS. A selection of high-quality, award-winning videos from *Filmmaker's Library* and *Films for the Humanities and Sciences* is available to qualified adopters upon adoption. Please contact your Prentice Hall sales representative for more information.

THE NEW YORK TIMES/ PRENTICE HALL THEMES OF THE TIMES. Through this program, the core subject matter provided in the text is supplemented by a collection of timely articles from one of the world's most distinguished newspapers, *The New York Times.* These articles demonstrate vital ongoing connections between what is learned in the classroom and what is happening in the world around us.

ANTHROPOLOGY ON THE INTERNET. This brief guide introduces students to the origin of and innovations behind the Internet and provides clear strategies for navigating the complexity of the Internet and World Wide Web. Exercises at the end of the chapters allow students to practice searching for the myriad resources available to the student of anthropology. This 96-page supplementary book is **free** to students when packaged with *Anthropology, 9/e.*

PRENTICE HALL ANTHROPOLOGY POWER-POINT SLIDE PRESENTATION, VERSION I. Created by Roger J. Eich of Hawkeye Community College, this PowerPoint slide set combines graphics and text in a colorful format to help convey anthropological principles in a new and exciting way. Created in PowerPoint, an easy-to-use, widely available software program, this set contains over 300 content slides.

PRENTICE HALL COLOR TRANSPARENCIES, ANTHROPOLOGY. Taken from graphs, diagrams, and tables in this text and other sources, over 50 full-color transparencies offer an effective means of amplifying lecture topics.

WORLD WIDE WEBSITE. Students can now take full advantage of the World Wide Web to enrich their study of anthropology through the *Anthropology, 9/e* Website. This study resource will correlate the text with related material available on the Internet. Features of the Website include chapter objectives, study questions, news updates, as well as links to interesting material and information from other sites on the Web that reinforce and enhance the content of each chapter. Address **http://www. prenhall.com/ember**.

STUDENT STUDY GUIDE. This carefully written guide helps students better understand the material presented in the text. Each chapter consists of chapter outlines, chapter summaries, definition of key concepts, self tests, and applied exercises.

ACKNOWLEDGMENTS

We thank the people at Prentice Hall for various kinds of help: Nancy Roberts, editor-in-chief for the social sciences; Sharon Chambliss, managing editor; Serena Hoffman for seeing the manuscript through the production process; Linda Sykes for photo research; and Ramesh Krishnamurthy for help in developing the Internet exercises.

We are grateful to a number of people, including a few who wish to remain anonymous, for agreeing to review our chapters and make suggestions. These reviewers include:

Ben G. Blount, University of Georgia
Daniel E. Brown, University of Hawaii at Hilo
Audrey Choh, SUNY at Albany

Heather Edgar, The Ohio State University
Ralph L. Holloway, Columbia University
S. Homes Hogue, Mississippi State University
Lyle W. Konigsberg, University of Tennessee
Gilbert Kushner, University of South Florida
Leila Monaghan, University of California at Los
  Angeles
Pia Nystrom, University of Sheffield
Shawn Phillips, SUNY at Albany
Jeffrey H. Schwartz, University of Pittsburgh
Andris Skreija, University of Nebraska–Omaha

Suzanne Strait, Marshall University
John H. Steinbring, Ripon College
Susan R. Trencher, George Mason University
William Wedenoja, Southwest Missouri State
  University
Sharon R. Williams, The Ohio State University

We thank all of you, named and unnamed, who
gave us advice.

Carol R. Ember and Melvin Ember

About the Authors

Carol R. Ember started at Antioch College as a chemistry major. She began taking social science courses because some were required, but she soon found herself intrigued. There were lots of questions without answers, and she became excited about the possibility of a research career in social science. She spent a year in graduate school at Cornell studying sociology before continuing on to Harvard, where she studied anthropology primarily with John and Beatrice Whiting.

For her Ph.D. dissertation she worked among the Luo of Kenya. While there she noticed that many boys were assigned "girls work," such as babysitting and household chores, because their mothers (who did most of the agriculture) did not have enough girls to help out. She decided to study the possible effects of task assignment on the social behavior of boys. Using systematic behavior observations, she compared girls, boys who did a great deal of girls' work, and boys who did little such work. She found that boys assigned girls' work were intermediate in many social behaviors, compared with the other boys and girls. Later, she did cross-cultural research on variation in marriage, family, descent groups, and war and peace, mainly in collaboration with Melvin Ember, whom she married in 1970. All of these cross-cultural studies tested theories on data for worldwide samples of societies.

From 1970 to 1996, she taught at Hunter College of the City University of New York. She has also served as president of the Society of Cross-Cultural Research and is one of the directors of the Summer Institutes in Comparative Anthropological Research, which are funded by the National Science Foundation. She is now executive director at the Human Relations Area Files, Inc., a nonprofit research agency of Yale University.

After graduating from Columbia College, Melvin Ember went to Yale University for his Ph.D. His mentor at Yale was George Peter Murdock, an anthropologist who was instrumental in promoting cross-cultural research and building a full-text database on the cultures of the world to facilitate cross-cultural hypothesis testing. This database came to be known as the Human Relations Area Files (HRAF) because it was originally sponsored by the Institute of Human Relations at Yale. Growing in annual installments and now distributed in electronic format, the HRAF database currently covers more than 355 cultures, past and present, all over the world.

Melvin Ember did fieldwork for his dissertation in American Samoa, where he conducted a comparison of three villages to study the effects of commercialization on political life. In addition, he did research on descent groups and how they changed with the increase of buying and selling. His cross-cultural studies focused originally on variation in marital residence and descent groups. He has also done cross-cultural research on the relationship between economic and political development, the origin and extension of the incest taboo, the causes of polygyny, and how archaeological correlates of social customs can help us draw inferences about the past.

After four years of research at the National Institute of Mental Health, he taught at Antioch College and then Hunter College of the City University of New York. He has served as president of the Society for Cross-Cultural Research and has been president since 1987 of the Human Relations Area Files., Inc., a nonprofit research agency of Yale University.

What Is Anthropology?

*A*nthropology, by definition, is a discipline of infinite curiosity about human beings. The term comes from the Greek *anthropos* for "man, human" and *logos* for "study." Anthropologists seek answers to an enormous variety of questions about humans. They are interested in discovering when, where, and why humans appeared on the earth, how and why they have changed since then, and how and why modern human populations vary in certain physical features. Anthropologists are also interested in how and why societies in the past and present have varied in their customary ideas and practices. There is a practical side to anthropology too. Applied and practicing anthropologists put anthropological methods, information, and results to use, in efforts to solve practical problems.

But defining anthropology as the study of human beings is not complete, for such a definition would appear to incorporate a whole catalog of disciplines: sociology, psychology, political science, economics, history, human biology, and perhaps even the humanistic disciplines of philosophy and literature. Needless to say, practitioners of the many other disciplines concerned with humans would not be happy to be regarded as being in subbranches of anthropology. After all, most of those disciplines have existed longer than anthropology, and each is somewhat distinctive. There must, then, be something unique about anthropology—a reason for its having developed as a separate discipline and for its having retained a separate identity over the last 100 years.

THE SCOPE OF ANTHROPOLOGY

Anthropologists are generally thought of as individuals who travel to little-known corners of the world to study exotic peoples or who dig deep into the earth to uncover the fossil remains or the tools and pots of people who lived long ago. These views, though clearly stereotyped, do indicate how anthropology differs from other disciplines concerned with humans. Anthropology is broader in scope, both geographically and historically. Anthropology is concerned explicitly and directly with all varieties of people throughout the world, not just those close at hand or within a limited area. It is also interested in people of all periods. Beginning with the immedi-

ate ancestors of humans, who lived a few million years ago, anthropology traces the development of humans until the present. Every part of the world that has ever contained a human population is of interest to anthropologists.

Anthropologists have not always been as global and comprehensive in their concerns as they are today. Traditionally, they concentrated on non-Western cultures and left the study of Western civilization and similarly complex societies, with their recorded histories, to other disciplines. In recent years, however, this division of labor among the disciplines has begun to disappear. Now anthropologists work in their own and other complex societies.

What induces anthropologists to choose so broad a subject for study? In part, they are motivated by the belief that any suggested generalization about human beings, any possible explanation of some characteristic of human culture or biology, should be shown to apply to many times and places of human existence. If a generalization or explanation does not prove to apply widely, we are entitled or even obliged to be skeptical about it. The skeptical attitude, in the absence of persuasive evidence, is our best protection against accepting invalid ideas about humans.

For example, when American educators discovered in the 1960s that African American schoolchildren rarely drank milk, they assumed that lack of money or education was the cause. But evidence from anthropology suggested a different explanation. Anthropologists had known for years that in many parts of the world where milking animals are kept, people do not drink fresh milk; rather, they sour it before they drink it, or they make it into cheese. Why they do so is now clear. Many people lack an enzyme, lactase, that is necessary for breaking down lactose, the sugar in milk. When such people drink regular milk, it actually interferes with digestion. Not only is the lactose in milk not digested but other nutrients are less likely to be digested as well; in many cases, drinking milk will cause cramps, stomach gas, diarrhea, and nausea. Studies indicate that milk intolerance is found in many parts of the world.[1] The condition is common in adulthood among Asians, southern Europeans, Arabs and Jews, West Africans, Inuit (Eskimos), and North and South American Indians, as well as African Americans. Because anthropologists are acquainted with human life in an enormous variety of geographic and historical settings, they are often able to correct mistaken beliefs about different groups of people.

THE HOLISTIC APPROACH

In addition to the worldwide as well as historical scope of anthropology, another distinguishing feature of the discipline is its **holistic,** or multifaceted, approach to the study of human beings. Anthropologists study not only all varieties of people but many aspects of human experience as well. For example, when describing a group of people, an anthropologist might discuss the history of the area in which the people live, the physical environment, the organization of family life, the general features of their language, the group's settlement patterns, political and economic systems, religion, and styles of art and dress.

In the past, individual anthropologists tried to be holistic and cover all aspects of a subject. Today, as in many other disciplines, so much information has been accumulated that anthropologists tend to specialize in one topic or area. Thus, one anthropologist may investigate the physical characteristics of some of our prehistoric ancestors. Another may study the biological effect of the environment on a human population over time. Still another will concentrate on the customs of a particular group of people. Despite this specialization, however, the discipline of anthropology retains its holistic orientation in that its many different specialties, taken together, describe many aspects of human existence, both past and present.

THE ANTHROPOLOGICAL CURIOSITY

Thus far we have described anthropology as being broader in scope, both historically and geographically, and more holistic in approach than other disciplines concerned with human beings. But this statement again implies that anthropology is the all-inclusive human science. How, then, is anthropology really different from those other disciplines? We suggest that anthropology's distinctiveness lies principally in the kind of curiosity it arouses.

Anthropologists are concerned with many types of questions: Where, when, and why did people first begin living in cities? Why do some peoples have darker skin than others? Why do some languages contain more terms for color than other languages? Why do women have more of a voice in politics in some societies than in others? Why do populations differ in their acceptance of birth control? Although these questions deal with very different aspects of human existence, they have at least one thing in common: They all deal with *typical characteristics* (traits, customs) of particular populations. The typical characteristic of a people might be relatively dark skin, a language with many color terms, female participation in politics, or acceptance of birth control. This concern with typical characteristics of populations is perhaps the most distinguishing feature of anthropology. For example, whereas economists take a monetary system for granted and study how it operates, anthropologists ask why only some societies during the last few thousand years used money. In short, anthropologists are curious about the typical characteristics of human populations—how and why such populations and their characteristics have varied throughout the ages.

FIELDS OF ANTHROPOLOGY

Different anthropologists concentrate on different typical characteristics of societies. Some are concerned primarily with *biological,* or *physical, characteristics* of human populations; others are interested principally in what we call *cultural characteristics.* Hence, there are two broad classifications of subject matter in anthropology: **biological (physical) anthropology** and **cultural anthropology.** Biological anthropology is one major field of anthropology. Cultural anthropology is divided into three major subfields—archaeology, linguistics, and ethnology. Ethnology, the study of recent cultures, is often referred to by the parent name, cultural anthropology (see Figure 1–1).

BIOLOGICAL ANTHROPOLOGY

Biological (physical) anthropology seeks to answer two distinct sets of questions. The first set includes questions about the emergence of humans and their later evolution (this focus is called **human paleontology,** or **paleoanthropology**). The second set includes questions about how and why contemporary human populations vary biologically (this focus is called **human variation**).

In order to reconstruct human evolution, human paleontologists search for and study the buried, hardened remains or impressions—known as **fossils**—of humans, prehumans, and related animals. Paleontologists working in East Africa, for instance, have excavated the fossil remains of hu-

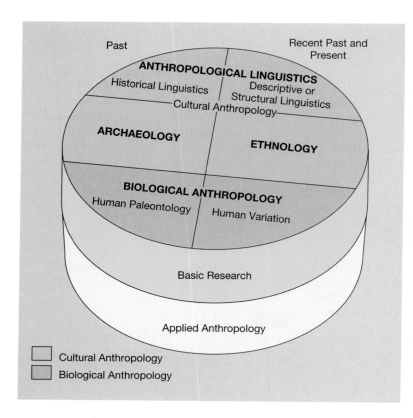

Past   Recent Past and Present

ANTHROPOLOGICAL LINGUISTICS
Historical Linguistics   Descriptive or Structural Linguistics
Cultural Anthropology

ARCHAEOLOGY   **ETHNOLOGY**

BIOLOGICAL ANTHROPOLOGY
Human Paleontology   Human Variation

Basic Research

Applied Anthropology

☐ Cultural Anthropology
▨ Biological Anthropology

FIGURE 1-1
The Subdivisions of Anthropology

The four major subdisciplines of anthropology (in bold letters) may be classified according to subject matter (biological or cultural) and according to the period with which each is concerned (distant past versus recent past and present). There are applications of anthropology in all four subdisciplines.

manlike beings who lived more than 3 million years ago. These findings have suggested the approximate dates when our ancestors began to develop two-legged walking, very flexible hands, and a larger brain.

In attempting to clarify evolutionary relationships, human paleontologists may use not only the fossil record but also geological information on the succession of climates, environments, and plant and animal populations. Moreover, when reconstructing the past of humans, paleontologists are also interested in the behavior and evolution of our closest relatives among the mammals—the prosimians, monkeys, and apes, which, like ourselves, are members of the order of **Primates.** Anthropologists, psychologists, and biologists who specialize in the study of primates are called **primatologists.** The various species of primates are observed in the wild and in the laboratory. One especially popular subject of study is the chimpanzee, which bears a close resemblance to humans in behavior and physical appearance, has a similar blood chemistry, and is susceptible to many of the same diseases.

From primate studies, biological anthropologists try to discover characteristics that are distinctly human, as opposed to those that might be part of the primate heritage. With this information, they

may be able to infer what our prehistoric ancestors were like. The inferences from primate studies are checked against the fossil record. The evidence from the earth, collected in bits and pieces, is correlated with scientific observations of our closest relatives. In short, biological anthropologists piece together bits of information obtained from different sources. They construct theories that explain the changes observed in the fossil record and then attempt to evaluate their theories by checking one kind of evidence against another. Human paleontology thus overlaps disciplines such as geology, general vertebrate (and particularly primate) paleontology, comparative anatomy, and the study of comparative primate behavior.

The second major focus of biological anthropology, the study of human variation, investigates how and why contemporary human populations differ in biological or physical characteristics. All living people belong to one species, **Homo sapiens,** for all can successfully interbreed. Yet there is much that varies among human populations. Investigators of human variation ask such questions as: Why are some peoples taller than others? How have human populations adapted physically to their environmental conditions? Are some peoples, such as Inuit (Eskimos), better equipped than other peoples to

Nadine Peacock, a biological anthropologist, studying reproduction and health among the Efe-Ituri Pygmies of Zaire.

endure cold? Does darker skin pigmentation offer special protection against the tropical sun?

To better understand the biological variations observable among contemporary human populations, biological anthropologists use the principles, concepts, and techniques of at least three other disciplines: human genetics (the study of human traits that are inherited), population biology (the study of environmental effects on, and interaction with, population characteristics), and epidemiology (the study of how and why diseases affect different populations in different ways). Research on human variation, therefore, overlaps with research in other fields. Biological anthropologists, however, are concerned most with human populations and how they vary biologically.

CULTURAL ANTHROPOLOGY

Cultural anthropologists are interested in how populations or societies vary in their cultural features. But what is culture? Because the concept of culture is so central to anthropology, we devote a whole chapter to it. To an anthropologist, the term **culture** refers to the customary ways of thinking and behaving of a particular population or society. The culture of a social group includes many things—its language, religious beliefs, food preferences, music, work habits, gender roles, how they rear their children, how they construct their houses, and many other learned behaviors and ideas that have come to be widely shared or customary among the group. The three main branches of cultural anthropology are **archaeology** (the study of past cultures, primar-

ily through their material remains); **anthropological linguistics** (the anthropological study of languages), and **ethnology** (the study of existing and recent cultures).

ARCHAEOLOGY. The archaeologist seeks not only to reconstruct the daily life and customs of peoples who lived in the past but also to trace cultural changes and to offer possible explanations of those changes. This concern is similar to that of the historian, but the archaeologist reaches much farther back in time. The historian deals only with societies that left written records and is therefore limited to the last 5,000 years of human history. Human societies, however, have existed for more than a million years, and only a small proportion in the last 5,000 years had writing. For all those past societies lacking a written record, the archaeologist serves as historian. Lacking written records for study, archaeologists must try to reconstruct history from the remains of human cultures. Some of these remains are as grand as the Mayan temples discovered at Chichén Itzá in Yucatán, Mexico. More often they are as ordinary as bits of broken pottery, stone tools, and garbage heaps.

Most archaeologists deal with **prehistory,** the time before written records. But there is a specialty within archaeology, called **historical archaeology,** that studies the remains of recent peoples who left written records. This specialty, as its name implies, employs the methods of both archaeologists and historians to study recent societies for which there is both archaeological and historical information.

Research Frontiers

RESEARCHER AT WORK: ELIZABETH M. BRUMFIEL

Now a professor of anthropology at Albion College, Elizabeth Brumfiel became interested in the origins of social inequality when she was an undergraduate. Archaeologists had known for some time that substantial wealth differences between families developed only recently (archaeologically speaking), that is, only after about 6,000 years ago. The archaeological indicators of inequality are fairly clear—elaborate burials with valuable goods for some families and large differences in houses and possessions. But *why* the transformation occurred was not so clear. When she was in graduate school at the University of Michigan, Brumfiel says, she didn't accept the then-current explanation, that inequality provided benefits to the society (for example, the standard of living of most people improved as the leaders got richer). Consequently, for her Ph.D. research in central Mexico, she began to test the "benefit" explanation in an area that had been independent politically at first and then became part of the Aztec Empire. She studied the surface material remains in the area and historical documents written by Europeans and Aztec nobility.

Her findings contradicted the benefit explanation of social inequality; she found little improvement in the standard of living of the local people after the Aztec Empire had absorbed them.

Another important part of her research agenda was understanding the lives of women. How were they affected by the expansion of the Aztec Empire? Did their work change? How were women portrayed in art? In the Aztec capital of Tenochtitlán, images of militarism and masculinity became increasingly important with the growth of the empire, and sculptures showed women in subordinate positions (for example, kneeling). But the images of women in the area of Brumfiel's fieldwork did not change. For example, most of the sculptures after the Aztecs had taken over still showed women standing, not kneeling.

Like many anthropologists, Brumfiel asked herself how she could contribute to the community in which she did her fieldwork. She decided to design an exhibit to display the successes of the people who had lived in the area for 1,200 years. The exhibit tells the people of Xalto-

Elizabeth Brumfiel

can what she found out from her studies.

As she continues to explore issues about the origins of inequality and the position of women, Brumfiel is quite comfortable with knowing that someone will think that she has "gotten it wrong, and will set out on a lifetime of archaeological research to find her own answers."

Source: Elizabeth M. Brumfiel, "Origins of Social Inequality," in Carol R. Ember, Melvin Ember, and Peter N. Peregrine, eds., *Research Frontiers in Anthropology* (Upper Saddle River, NJ: Prentice Hall, 1998). Prentice Hall/Simon & Schuster Custom Publishing.

In trying to understand how and why ways of life have changed through time in different parts of the world, archaeologists collect materials from sites of human occupation. Usually, these sites must be unearthed. On the basis of materials they have excavated and otherwise collected, they then ask various questions: Where, when, and why did the distinctive human characteristic of toolmaking first emerge? Where, when, and why did agriculture first develop?

Where, when, and why did people first begin to live in cities?

To collect the data they need in order to suggest answers to these and other questions, archaeologists use techniques and findings borrowed from other disciplines as well as what they can infer from anthropological studies of recent and contemporary cultures. For example, to guess where to dig for evidence of early toolmaking, archaeologists rely on geology to tell them where sites of early human occupation are likely to be found, because of erosion and uplifting, near the surface of the earth. To infer when agriculture first developed, archaeologists date the relevant excavated materials by a process originally developed by chemists. And to try to understand why cities first emerged, archaeologists may use information from historians, geographers, and others about how recent and contemporary cities are related economically and politically to their hinterlands. If we can discover what recent and contemporary cities have in common, we can speculate on why cities developed originally. Thus, archaeologists use information from the present and recent past in trying to understand the distant past.

ANTHROPOLOGICAL LINGUISTICS. A second branch of cultural anthropology is anthropological linguistics. *Linguistics,* or the study of languages, is a somewhat older discipline than anthropology, but the early linguists concentrated on the study of languages that had been written for a long time—languages such as English that had been written for nearly a thousand years. Anthropological linguists began to do fieldwork in places where the language was not yet written. This meant that anthropologists could not consult a dictionary or grammar to help them learn the language. Instead, they first had to construct a dictionary and grammar. Then they could study the structure and history of the language.

Like biological anthropologists, linguists study changes that have taken place over time, as well as contemporary variation. Some anthropological linguists are concerned with the emergence of language and also with the divergence of languages over thousands of years. The study of how languages change over time and how they may be related is known as **historical linguistics.** Anthropological linguists are also interested in how contemporary languages differ, especially in their construction. This focus of linguistics is generally called **structural** or **descriptive linguistics.** The study of how language is used in social contexts is called **sociolinguistics.**

In contrast with the human paleontologist and archaeologist, who have physical remains to help them reconstruct change over time, the historical linguist deals only with languages—and usually unwritten ones at that. (Remember that writing is only about 5,000 years old, and most languages since then have not been written.) Because an unwritten language must be heard in order to be studied, it does not leave any traces once its speakers have died. Linguists interested in reconstructing the history of unwritten languages must begin in the present, with comparisons of contemporary languages. On the basis of these comparisons, they draw inferences about the kinds of change in language that may have occurred in the past and that may account for similarities and differences observed in the present. The historical linguist typically asks such questions as these: Did two or more contemporary languages diverge from a common ancestral language? If they are related, how far back in time did they begin to differ?

Unlike the historical linguist, the descriptive (or structural) linguist is typically concerned with discovering and recording the principles that determine how sounds and words are put together in speech. For example, a structural description of a particular language might tell us that the sounds *t* and *k* are interchangeable in a word without causing a difference in meaning. In American Samoa, one could say *Tutuila* or *Kukuila* as the name of the largest island, and everyone, except perhaps the newly arrived anthropologist, would understand that the same island was being mentioned.

The sociolinguist is interested in the social aspects of language, including what people speak about and how they interact conversationally, their attitudes toward speakers of other dialects or languages, and how people speak differently in different social contexts. In English, for example, we do not address everyone we meet in the same way. "Hi, Sandy" may be the customary way a person greets a friend. But we would probably feel uncomfortable addressing a doctor by first name; instead, we would probably say, "Good morning, Dr. Brown." Such variations in language use, which are determined by the social status of the persons being addressed, are significant for the sociolinguist.

ETHNOLOGY. Ethnologists seek to understand how and why peoples today and in the recent past differ in their customary ways of thinking and acting. Ethnology, then, is concerned with patterns of thought and behavior, such as marriage customs, kinship organization, political and economic systems, religion, folk art, and music, and with the ways in which these patterns differ in contemporary societies. Ethnologists also study the dynamics of culture—that is, how various cultures develop and change. In addition, they are interested in the relationship between beliefs and practices within a culture. Thus, the aim of ethnologists is largely the same as that of archaeologists. Ethnologists, however, generally use data collected through observation and interviewing of living peoples. Archaeologists, on the other hand, must work with fragmentary remains of past cultures, on the basis of which they can only make inferences about the customs of prehistoric peoples.

One type of ethnologist, the **ethnographer,** usually spends a year or so living with, talking to, and observing the people whose customs he or she is studying. This fieldwork provides the data for a detailed description (an **ethnography**) of many aspects of the customary behavior and thought of those people. The ethnographer not only tries to describe the general patterns of their life but also may suggest answers to such questions as: How are economic and political behavior related? How may the customs of people be adapted to environmental conditions? Is there any relationship between beliefs about the supernatural and beliefs or practices about the natural world? In other words, the ethnographer depicts the way of life of a particular group of people and may suggest explanations for some of the customs observed.

Because so many cultures have undergone extensive change in the recent past, it is fortunate that another type of ethnologist, the **ethnohistorian,** is prepared to study how the ways of life of a particular group of people have changed over time. Ethnohistorians investigate written documents (which may or may not have been produced by anthropologists). They may spend many years going through documents, such as missionary accounts, reports by traders and explorers, and government records, to try to establish the cultural changes that have occurred. Unlike ethnographers, who rely mostly on their own observations, ethnohistorians rely on the reports of others. Often, they must attempt to piece together and make sense of widely scattered, and even apparently contradictory, information. Thus, the ethnohistorian's research is very much like that of the historian, except that the ethnohistorian is usually concerned with the history of a people who did not themselves leave written records. The ethnohistorian tries to reconstruct the recent history of a people and may also suggest why certain changes in their way of life took place.

With the data collected and analyzed by the ethnographer and ethnohistorian, the work of a third type of ethnologist, the **cross-cultural researcher,** can be done. The cross-cultural researcher is interested in discovering why certain cultural characteristics may be found in some societies but not in others. Why, for example, do some societies have plural marriages (one spouse of one sex and two or more spouses of the other sex), circumcision of adolescent boys, or belief in a high god or supreme being? In testing possible answers to such questions, cross-cultural researchers use data from samples of cultures to try to arrive at general explanations of cultural variation.

Because ethnologists may be interested in many aspects of customary behavior and thought—from economic behavior to political behavior to styles of art, music, and religion—ethnology overlaps with disciplines that concentrate on some particular aspect of human existence, such as sociology, psychology, economics, political science, art, music, and comparative religion. But the distinctive feature of cultural anthropology is its interest in how all these aspects of human existence vary from society to society, in all historical periods, and in all parts of the world.

SPECIALIZATION

As disciplines grow, they tend to develop more and more specialties. This trend is probably inevitable because, as knowledge accumulates and methods become more advanced, there is a limit to what any one person can reasonably keep track of. So, in addition to the general divisions we have outlined already, particular anthropologists tend to identify themselves with a variety of specializations. It is common for anthropologists to have a geographic specialty, which may be as broad as Old World or New World or as narrow as the southwestern United States. And those who study the past (archaeologists or human paleontologists) may also specialize in different time periods. Ethnologists often specialize in more specific subject matters in addition to one or two cultural areas. Just as most of the chapters in this book refer to broad subject specialties, so some ethnologists identify themselves as *economic anthropologists,* or *political anthropologists,* or *psychological anthropologists.* Others may identify themselves by theoretical orientations, such as *cultural ecologists,* who are concerned with the relationship between culture and the physical and social environments. These specialties are not mutually exclusive, however. A cultural ecologist, for example, might be interested in the effects of the environment on economic behavior, or political behavior, or how people bring up their children.

Does specialization isolate an anthropologist from other kinds of research? Not necessarily. Some

Research Frontiers

RESEARCHER AT WORK: TERENCE E. HAYS

Books and articles often report research in a straightforward manner. Here's the problem; here's the answer—that kind of thing. But many researchers know from experience that knowledge does not always come in a straightforward manner. Now a professor at Rhode Island College, Terence Hays has reflected on the twists and turns in his fieldwork among the Ndumba in the Eastern Highlands Province of Papua New Guinea. He first started out studying whether different types of people (for example, women and men) had different types of plant knowledge and whether they classified plants differently. (The interest in plant and animal classification, *ethnobiology,* is closely connected with linguistic research.) In the course of his first fieldwork, in 1972, he witnessed an initiation ceremony for 10- to 12-year-old males—a dramatic and traumatic rite of passage ceremony that included the physical trauma of nose-bleeding as well as the social traumas of "attacks" by women and seclusion in the forest. The ceremony was full of symbolism of why the sexes needed to avoid each other. And while he collected stories and myths about plants for his research on ethnobiology, he kept uncovering themes in the stories about the danger of men's associating with women.

Hays's curiosity was aroused about these ceremonies and myths. How important are myths in perpetuating cultural themes? Do other societies that have separate men's houses have similar myths? He realized when he returned home from the field that many societies have similar stories. Are these stories generally linked to initiation rites and to physical segregation of the sexes? Answering these questions required comparison, so he embarked on collecting myths and folktales from colleagues who worked in other New Guinea highland societies. In the course of collecting these comparative materials, he realized he didn't have all the ethnographic information he needed, so he went back to the field to get it. As Hays remarked, "As an ethnographer I was continually faced with the question, How do you know it's true? But even when I could reach a (hard-won) conviction that something was true for the Ndumba, the second question awaited: How do you know it's generally true, which you can't know without comparison?"

Source: Terence E. Hays, "From Ethnographer to Comparativist and Back Again," in Carol R. Ember, Melvin Ember, and Peter N. Peregrine, eds., *Research Frontiers in Anthropology* (Upper Saddle River, NJ: Prentice Hall, 1998). Prentice Hall/Simon & Schuster Custom Publishing.

Terence Hays

specialties have to draw on information from several fields, inside and outside anthropology. For example, *medical anthropologists* study the cultural and biological contexts of human health and illness. Thus, they need to understand the economy, diet, and patterns of social interaction, as well as attitudes and beliefs regarding illness and health. In addition, they may need to draw on research in human genetics, public health, and medicine.

APPLIED ANTHROPOLOGY

All knowledge may turn out to be useful. In the physical and biological sciences it is well understood that technological breakthroughs like DNA splicing, spacecraft docking in outer space, and the development of miniscule computer chips could not have taken place without an enormous amount of basic research to uncover the laws of nature in the physical and biological worlds. If we did not understand fundamental principles, the technological achieve-

Applied Anthropology

GETTING DEVELOPMENT PROGRAMS TO NOTICE WOMEN'S CONTRIBUTIONS TO AGRICULTURE

When Anita Spring first did fieldwork in Zambia in the 1970s, she was not particularly interested in agriculture. Rather, medical anthropology was her interest. Her work focused on customary healing practices, particularly involving women and children. She was surprised at the end of the year when a delegation of women came to tell her that she didn't understand what it meant to be a woman. "To be a woman is to be a farmer," they said. She admits that it took her a while to pay attention to women as farmers, but then she began to participate in efforts to provide technical assistance to them. Like many others interested in women in development, Spring realized that all too often development agents downplay women's contributions to agriculture.

How does one bring about change in male-centered attitudes and practices? One way is to document how much women actually contribute to agriculture. Beginning with the influential writing of Ester Boserup in *Woman's Role in Economic Development* (1970), scholars began to report that in Africa south of the Sahara, in the Caribbean, and in parts of Southeast Asia, women were the principal farmers or agricultural laborers. Moreover, as agriculture became more complex, it required more work time in the fields, so the women's contribution to agriculture increased. In addition, men increasingly went away to work, so women had to do much of what used to be men's work on the farms.

In the 1980s, Anita Spring designed and directed the Women in Agricultural Development Project in Malawi, funded by the Office of Women in the U.S. Agency for International Development. Rather than focusing just on women, the project aimed to collect data on both women and men agriculturalists and how they were treated by development agents. The project did more than collect information; mini-pro- jects were set up and evaluated so that successful training techniques could be passed on to development agents in other regions. Spring points out that the success of the program was due not just to the design of the project. Much of the success depended on the interest and willingness of Malawi itself to change. And it didn't hurt that the United Nations and other donor organizations increasingly focused attention on women. It takes the efforts of many to bring about change. Increasingly, applied anthropologists like Anita Spring are involved in these efforts from beginning to end, from the design stage to implementation and evaluation.

Source: Anita Spring, *Agricultural Development and Gender Issues in Malawi* (Lanham, MD: University Press of America, 1995).

Anthropologist Anita Spring demonstrates the technical aspects of growing soybeans to women farmers in Malawi.

ments we are so proud of would not be possible. Researchers are often simply driven by curiosity, with no thought to where the research might lead, which is why such research is sometimes called *basic research*. The same is true of the social sciences. If a researcher finds out that societies with combative sports tend to have more wars, it may lead to other inquiries about the relationships between one kind of aggression and another. The knowledge aquired may ultimately lead to discovering ways to correct social problems such as family violence and war.

Whereas basic research may ultimately help to solve practical problems, applied research is more explicit in its practical goals. Today about half of all professional anthropologists are *applied,* or *practicing, anthropologists.* **Applied** or **practicing anthropology** is explicit in its concern with making anthropological knowledge useful.[2] Applied anthropologists may be trained in any or all of the subfields of anthropology. In contrast to basic researchers, who are almost always employed in colleges, universities, and museums, applied anthropologists are usually employed in settings outside of traditional academia, including government agencies, international development agencies, private consulting firms, businesses, public health organizations, medical schools, law offices, community development agencies, and charitable foundations.

Biological anthropologists may be called upon to give forensic evidence in court, or they may work in public health, or design clothes and equipment to fit human anatomy. Archaeologists may be involved in preserving and exhibiting artifacts for museums and in doing contract work to find and preserve cultural sites that might be damaged by construction or excavation. Linguists may work in bilingual educational training programs or may work on ways to improve communication. Ethnologists may work in a wide variety of applied projects ranging from community development, urban planning, health care, and agricultural improvement to personnel and organizational management and assessment of the impact of change programs on people's lives.[3] We discuss applied anthropology more fully in the chapter on applied anthropology and social problems.

THE RELEVANCE OF ANTHROPOLOGY

Anthropology is a comparatively young discipline. It was only in the late 1800s that anthropologists began to go to live with people in far-away places. Compared to our knowledge of the physical laws of nature, we know much less about people, about how and why they behave as they do. That anthropology and other sciences dealing with humans began to develop only relatively recently is not in itself a sufficient reason for our knowing less than in the physical sciences. Why, in our quest for knowledge of all kinds, did we wait so long to study ourselves? Leslie White suggests that those phenomena most remote from us and least significant as determinants of human behavior were the first to be studied. The reason, he surmises, is that humans like to think of themselves as citadels of free will, subject to no laws of nature. Hence, there is no need to see ourselves as objects to be explained.[4]

The idea that it is impossible to account for human behavior scientifically, either because our actions and beliefs are too individualistic and complex or because human beings are understandable only in otherworldly terms, is a self-fulfilling notion. We cannot discover principles explaining human behavior if we neither believe such principles exist nor bother to look for them. The result is assured from the beginning. Persons who do not believe in principles of human behavior will be reinforced by their finding none. If we are to increase our understanding of human beings, we first have to believe it is possible to do so.

If we aim to understand humans, it is essential that we study humans in all times and places. How else can we understand what is true of humans generally or how they are capable of varying? If we study just our own society, we may come up only with explanations that are culture-bound, not general or applicable to most or all humans. Anthropology is useful, then, to the degree that it contributes to our understanding of human beings everywhere.

In addition, anthropology is relevant because it helps us avoid misunderstandings between peoples. If we can understand why other groups are different from ourselves, we might have less reason to condemn them for behavior that appears strange to us. We may then come to realize that many differences between peoples are products of physical and cultural adaptations to different environments. For example, someone who first finds out about the !Kung as they lived in the Kalahari Desert of southern Africa in the 1950s might think that the !Kung were savages.[5] The !Kung wore little clothing, had few possessions, lived in meager shelters, and enjoyed none of our technological niceties. But let us reflect on how a typical North American community might react if it awoke to find itself in an environment similar to that in which the !Kung lived. The people would find that the arid land makes both

Tourism is one way to learn about other cultures, as here in Asmat country of western New Guinea. But anthropology is a better way. It tells us not just how cultures are different, but helps us to understand why.

agriculture and animal husbandry impossible, and they might have to think about adopting a nomadic existence. They might then discard many of their material possessions so that they could travel easily, in order to take advantage of changing water and food supplies. Because of the extreme heat and the lack of extra water for laundry, they might find it more practical to be almost naked than to wear clothes. They would undoubtedly find it impossible to build elaborate homes. For social security, they might start to share the food brought into the group. Thus, if they survived at all, they might end up looking and acting far more like the !Kung looked than like typical North Americans.

Physical differences, too, may be seen as results of adaptations to the environment. For example, in our society we admire people who are tall and slim. If these same individuals were forced to live above the Arctic Circle, however, they might wish they could trade their tall, slim bodies for short, compact ones, because stocky physiques conserve body heat more effectively and may therefore be more adaptive in cold climates.

Exposure to anthropology might help to alleviate some of the misunderstandings that arise between people of different cultural groups from subtle causes operating below the level of consciousness. For example, different cultures have different conceptions of the gestures and interpersonal distances

that are appropriate under various circumstances. Arabs consider it proper to stand close enough to other people to smell them.[6] On the basis of the popularity of deodorants in our culture, we can deduce that Americans prefer to keep the olfactory dimension out of interpersonal relations. We may feel that a person who comes too close is being too intimate. We should remember, however, that this person may only be acting according to a culturally conditioned conception of what is proper in a given situation. If our intolerance for others results in part from a lack of understanding of why peoples vary, then the knowledge accumulated by anthropologists may help lessen that intolerance.

Knowledge of our past may also bring both a feeling of humility and a sense of accomplishment. If we are to attempt to deal with the problems of our world, we must be aware of our vulnerability so that we do not think that our problems will solve themselves. But we also have to think enough of our accomplishments to believe that we can find solutions to our problems. Much of the trouble we get into may be a result of feelings of self-importance and invulnerability—in short, our lack of humility. Knowing something about our evolutionary past may help us to understand and accept our place in the biological world. Just as for any other form of life, there is no guarantee that any particular human population, or even the entire human species, will

Simplicity of technology should not be taken to imply backwardness. The Inuit have very ingenious ways of dealing with their extremely difficult environment. Constructing an igloo out of specially shaped blocks of ice, as shown here in the Canadian Arctic, is not easy.

perpetuate itself indefinitely. The earth changes, the environment changes, and humanity itself changes. What survives and flourishes in the present might not do so in the future.

Yet our vulnerability should not make us feel powerless. There are many reasons to feel confident about the future. Consider what we have accomplished so far. By means of tools and weapons fashioned from sticks and stones, we were able to hunt animals larger and more powerful than ourselves. We discovered how to make fire, and we learned to use it to keep ourselves warm and to cook our food. As we domesticated plants and animals, we gained greater control over our food supply and were able to establish more permanent settlements. We mined and smelted ores to fashion more durable tools. We built cities and irrigation systems, monuments and ships. We made it possible to travel from one continent to another in a single day. We conquered illnesses and prolonged human life.

In short, human beings and their cultures have changed considerably over the course of history. Human populations have often been able to adapt to changing circumstances. Let us hope that humans continue to adapt to the challenges of the present and future.

SUMMARY

1. Anthropology is literally the study of human beings. It differs from other disciplines concerned with people in that it is broader in scope. It is concerned with humans in all places of the world (not simply those places close to us), and it traces human evolution and cultural development from millions of years ago to the present day.

2. Another distinguishing feature of anthropology is its holistic approach to the study of human beings. Anthropologists study not only all varieties of people but also all aspects of those peoples' experiences.

3. Anthropologists are concerned with identifying and explaining typical characteristics (traits, customs) of particular human populations.

4. Biological or physical anthropology is one of the major fields of the discipline. Biological anthropology studies the emergence of humans and their later physical evolution (the focus called human paleontology). It also studies how and why contemporary human populations vary biologically (the focus called human variation).

5. Another broad area of concern to anthropology is cultural anthropology. Its three subfields—archaeology, anthropological linguistics, and ethnology—all deal with aspects of human culture, that is, with the customary ways of thinking and behaving of a particular society.

6. Archaeologists seek not only to reconstruct the daily life and customs of prehistoric peoples but also to trace cultural changes and offer possible explanations of those changes. Therefore, archaeologists try to reconstruct history from the remains of human cultures.

7. Anthropological linguists are concerned with the emergence of language and with the divergence of languages over time (a subject known as historical linguistics). They also study how contemporary languages differ, both in construction (structural or descriptive linguistics) and in actual speech (sociolinguistics).

8. The ethnologist seeks to understand how and why peoples of today and the recent past differ in their customary ways of thinking and acting. One

type of ethnologist, the ethnographer, usually spends a year or so living with and talking to a particular population and observing their customs. Later, she or he may prepare a detailed report of the group's behavior, which is called an ethnography. Another type of ethnologist, the ethnohistorian, investigates written documents to determine how the ways of life of a particular group of people have changed over time. A third type of ethnologist, the cross-cultural researcher, studies data collected by ethnographers and ethnohistorians for a sample of cultures and attempts to discover which explanations of particular customs may be generally applicable.

9. In all four major subdisciplines of anthropology, there are applied anthropologists, people who apply anthropological knowledge to achieve more practical goals, usually in the service of an agency outside the traditional academic setting.

10. Anthropology may help people to be more tolerant. Anthropological studies can show us why other people are the way they are, both culturally and physically. Customs or actions that appear improper or offensive to us may be other people's adaptations to particular environmental and social conditions.

11. Anthropology is also valuable in that knowledge of our past may bring us both a feeling of humility and a sense of accomplishment. Like any other form of life, we have no guarantee that any particular human population will perpetuate itself indefinitely. Yet knowledge of our achievements in the past may give us confidence in our ability to solve the problems of the future.

GLOSSARY TERMS

anthropological
  linguistics
anthropology
applied (practicing)
  anthropology
archaeology
biological (physical)
  anthropology
cross-cultural
  researcher
cultural anthropology
culture
ethnographer
ethnography
ethnohistorian
ethnology

fossils
historical archaeology
historical linguistics
holistic
Homo sapiens
human paleontology
human variation
paleoanthropology
prehistory
Primates
primatologists
sociolinguistics
structural (or
  descriptive)
  linguistics

CRITICAL QUESTIONS

1. Why study anthropology?
2. How does anthropology differ from other fields of study you've encountered?
3. What do you think about the suggestion that anthropology is the fundamental discipline concerned with humans?

INTERNET EXERCISES

1. Many of you may keep up with the news and weather on the Internet. But have you ever tried to keep up with the latest news in anthropology? Check out the latest on what is happening in anthropology at **http://www.tamu.edu/anthropology/news.html**. What are the two latest news items?

2. Have you ever gone to a virtual museum? Check out one of these virtual museums. For a visit to the Canadian Museum of Civilization (**http://www.civilization.ca/membrs/lobby.html/**) click on the elevator and go to Level 1. Visit the First Peoples Hall or the Archaeology Hall. For a virtual museum experience whose content is created by students, visit the Mankato State University Museum at **http://www.anthro.mankato.msus.edu/**. Other museums can be accessed from **http://www.lib.uconn.edu/ArchNet/Museums/**. Write a brief summary of your findings.

3. Anthropology is an interdisciplinary subject. Researchers in the field of anthropology employ various tools and techniques to learn about the interaction of humans and their environment. Explore one such study in which robots are used in anthropology. Learn all about the use of the latest techniques to study anthropology at **http://www.usc.edu/dept/raiders/story/fmi.html**. What are your thoughts on the application of these techniques?

SUGGESTED READING

Boaz, N. T., and Almquist, A. J. *Biological Anthropology: A Synthetic Approach to Human Evolution.* Upper Saddle River, NJ: Prentice Hall, 1997. After briefly reviewing the principles and sequences of biological evolution, the authors review human evolution from earliest times to the present. The book also includes chapters on human variation, human growth and adaptability, and applied biological anthropology.

Ember, C. R., Ember, M., and Peregrine P. N., eds. *Research Frontiers in Anthropology.* Upper Saddle River, NJ: Prentice Hall, 1998. Prentice Hall/Simon

& Schuster Custom Publishing. Particularly appropriate to this chapter are pieces written by 10 researchers from different subfields of anthropology about their careers and personal research experiences ("Researchers at Work"). They are biological anthropologists Timothy Bromage and Katharine Milton, archaeologists Richard Blanton and Elizabeth Brumfiel, linguists Benjamin Blount and Susan Philips, ethnologists Carol Ember and Terence Hays, and applied anthropologists Andrew Miracle and Susan Weller.

FAGAN, B. M. *People of the Earth: An Introduction to World Prehistory,* 7th ed. New York: HarperCollins, 1992. A survey of world prehistory, describing what we know from archaeology about hunters and gatherers, farmers, and cities and civilizations in all areas of the world.

FOLEY, W. A. *Anthropological Linguistics: An Introduction.* Malden, MA: Blackwell, 1997. An overview of anthropological linguistics including the evolution of language, linguistic universals, linguistic relativism, and the ethnography of speaking.

HOWELLS, W. *Getting Here: The Story of Human Evolution.* Washington, DC: Compass Press, 1993. An accessible introduction to the study of human evolution.

KONNER, M. *The Tangled Wing: Biological Constraints on the Human Spirit.* New York: Harper & Row, 1987. A biological anthropologist discusses the biological and cultural roots of human behavior and emotions.

VAN WILLIGEN, J. *Applied Anthropology: An Introduction,* rev. ed. Westport, CT: Bergin and Garvey, 1993. A survey of applied anthropology that includes a history of the discipline, research techniques, examples of applied projects, and a discussion of ethics.

2

Evolution

Astronomers estimate that the universe has been in existence for some 15 billion years, plus or minus a few billion. To make this awesome history more understandable, Carl Sagan devised a calendar that condenses this span into a single year.[1] Using as a scale 24 days for every billion years and 1 second for every 475 years, Sagan moves from the "Big Bang," or beginning of the universe, on January 1 to the origin of the Milky Way on May 1. September 9 marks the beginning of our solar system, and September 25 the origin of life on earth. At 10:30 in the evening of December 31, the first human-like primates appear. Sagan's compression of history provides us with a manageable way to compare the short span of human existence with the total time span of the universe. Human-like beings have been around for only about 90 minutes out of a 12-month period! In this book we are concerned with what has happened in the last few hours of that year.

Some 55 million to 65 million years ago, the first primates may have appeared. They were ancestral to all living primates, including monkeys, apes, and humans. The early primates may or may not have lived in trees, but they had flexible digits and could grasp things. Later, about 35 million years ago, the first monkeys and apes appeared. About 15 million years ago, some 20 million years after the appearance of monkeys and apes, the immediate apelike ancestors of humans probably emerged. About 4 million years ago the first human-like beings appeared. Modern-looking humans evolved only about 100,000 years ago.

How do we account for the biological and cultural evolution of humans? The details of the emergence of primates and the evolution of humans and their cultures are covered in subsequent chapters. In this chapter we focus on how the modern theory of evolution developed and how it accounts for change over time.

THE EVOLUTION OF EVOLUTION

Traditional Western ideas about nature's creatures were very different from Charles Darwin's theory of *evolution,* which suggested that different species developed, one from another, over long periods of time. In the fifth millennium B.C., the Greek philosophers Plato and Aristotle believed that animals and plants form a single, graded continuum going from more perfection to less perfection. Humans, of course, were at the top of this scale. Later Greek philosophers added the idea that the creator gave life or "radiance" first to humans, but at each subsequent creation some of that essence was lost.[2] Macrobius, summarizing the thinking of Plotinus, used an image that was to persist for centuries, the image of what came to be called the "chain of being": "The attentive observer will

The history of the earth, and the plant and animal forms that evolved on it, is often revealed to us by rock formations that become visible because of uplifting and erosion. The emergence of geology—the study of the earth's structure and history—stimulated evolutionary thinking.

discover a connection of parts, from the Supreme God down to the last dregs of things, mutually linked together and without a break. And this is Homer's golden chain, which God, he says, bade hand down from heaven to earth."[3]

Belief in the chain of being was accompanied by the conviction that an animal or plant species could not become extinct. In fact, all things were linked to each other in a chain, and all links were necessary. Moreover, the notion of extinction threatened people's trust in God; it was unthinkable that a whole group of God's creations could simply disappear.

The idea of the chain of being persisted through the years, but it was not discussed extensively by philosophers, scientists, poets, and theologians until the eighteenth century.[4] Those discussions prepared the way for evolutionary theory. It is ironic that, although the chain of being did not allow for evolution, its idea that there was an order of things in nature encouraged studies of natural history and comparative anatomical studies, which stimulated the development of the idea of evolution. People were also now motivated to look for previously unknown creatures. Moreover, humans were not shocked when naturalists suggested that humans were close to apes. This notion was perfectly consistent with the idea of a chain of being; apes were simply thought to have been created with less perfection.

Early in the eighteenth century, an influential scientist, Carolus Linnaeus (1707–1778), classified plants and animals in a *systema naturae,* which placed humans in the same order (Primates) as apes and monkeys. Linnaeus did not suggest an evolutionary relationship between humans and apes; he mostly accepted the notion that all species were created by God and fixed in their form. Not surprisingly, then, Linnaeus is often viewed as an anti-evolutionist. But Linnaeus's hierarchical classification scheme, in descending order going from kingdom to class, order, genus, and species, provided a framework for the idea that humans, apes, and monkeys had a common ancestor.[5] See Figure 2–1.

Others did not believe that species were fixed in their form. According to Jean Baptiste Lamarck (1744–1829), acquired characteristics could be inherited and therefore species could evolve; individuals who in their lifetime developed characteristics helpful to survival would pass those characteristics on to future generations, thereby changing the physical makeup of the species. For example, Lamarck explained the long neck of the giraffe as the result of

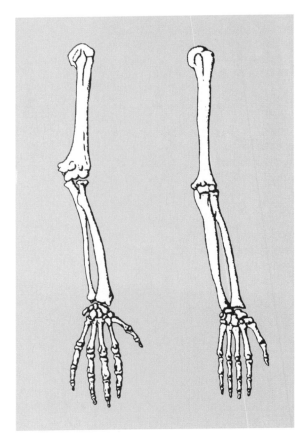

FIGURE 2–1

The idea that chimpanzees and humans descend from a common ancestor is suggested by anatomical similarities, such as in their forelimbs. Chimpanzee forelimb skeleton (left): human forelimb skeleton (right).

successive generations of giraffes stretching their necks to reach the high leaves of trees. The stretched muscles and bones of the necks were somehow transmitted to the offspring of the neck-stretching giraffes, and eventually all giraffes came to have long necks. But because Lamarck and later biologists failed to produce evidence to support the hypothesis that acquired characteristics can be inherited, this explanation of evolution is now generally dismissed.[6]

By the nineteenth century, some thinkers were beginning to accept evolution while others were trying to refute it.[7] For example, Georges Cuvier (1769–1832) was a leading opponent of evolution. Cuvier's theory of *catastrophism* proposed that a quick series of catastrophes accounted for changes in the earth and the fossil record. Cataclysms and upheavals such as Noah's flood had killed off previous sets of living creatures, which each time were replaced by new creations.

Major changes in geological thinking occurred in the nineteenth century. Earlier, the geologist James Hutton (1726–1797) had questioned catastrophism, but his work was largely ignored. In contrast, Sir Charles Lyell's (1797–1875) volumes of the *Principles of Geology* (1830–1833), which built on Hutton's earlier work, received immediate acclaim. Their concept of *uniformitarianism* suggested that the earth is constantly being shaped and reshaped by natural forces that have operated over a vast stretch of time. Lyell also discussed the formation of geological strata and paleontology. He used fossilized fauna to define different geological epochs. Lyell's works were read avidly by Charles Darwin before Darwin's now-famous voyage on the *Beagle*. The two corresponded and subsequently became friends.

After studying changes in plants, fossil animals, and varieties of domestic and wild pigeons, Charles Darwin (1809–1882) rejected the notion that each species was created at one time in a fixed form. The results of his investigations pointed clearly, he thought, to the evolution of species through the mechanism of *natural selection*. While Darwin was completing his book on the subject, Lyell sent him a manuscript by Alfred Russel Wallace (1823–1913), a naturalist who had independently reached conclusions about the evolution of species that matched Darwin's own.[8] In 1858, the two men presented the astonishing theory of natural selection to their colleagues at a meeting of the Linnaean Society of London.[9]

In 1859, when Darwin published *The Origin of Species by Means of Natural Selection,*[10] he wrote, "I am fully convinced that species are not immutable; but that those belonging to what are called the same genera are lineal descendants of some other and generally extinct species, in the same manner as the acknowledged varieties of any one species."[11] His conclusions outraged those who believed in the biblical account of creation, and the result was years of bitter controversy.

Until 1871, when his *The Descent of Man* was published, Darwin avoided stating categorically that humans were descended from nonhuman forms, but the implications of his theory were clear. People immediately began to take sides. In June 1860, at the annual meeting of the British Association for the Advancement of Science, Bishop Wilberforce saw an opportunity to attack the Darwinists. Concluding his speech, he faced Thomas Huxley, one of the Darwinists' chief advocates, and inquired, "Was it through his grandfather or his grandmother that he claimed descent from a monkey?" Huxley responded,

> If . . . the question is put to me would I rather have a miserable ape for a grandfather than a man highly endowed by nature and possessing great means and influence and yet who employs those faculties and that influence for the mere purpose of introducing ridicule into a grave scientific discussion—I unhesitatingly affirm my preference for the ape.[12]

THE PRINCIPLES OF NATURAL SELECTION

Darwin was not the first person to view the creation of new species in evolutionary terms, but he was the first to provide a comprehensive, well-documented explanation—**natural selection**—for the way evolution had occurred. Natural selection is the main process that increases the frequency of adaptive traits through time. The operation of natural selection involves three conditions or principles.[13] The first is *variation:* Every species is composed of a great variety of individuals, some of which are better adapted to their environment than others. The existence of variety is important. Without it, natural selection has nothing on which to operate; without variation, one kind of characteristic could not be favored over another. The second principle of natural selection is *heritability:* Offspring inherit traits from their parents, at least to some degree and in some way. The third principle of natural selection is *differential reproductive success:* Since better adapted individuals generally produce more offspring over the generations than the poorer adapted, the frequency of adaptive traits gradually increases in subsequent generations. A new species emerges when changes in traits or geographic barriers result in the reproductive isolation of the population.

When we say that certain traits are adaptive or advantageous, we mean that they result in greater reproductive success in a particular environment. The phrase *particular environment* is very important. Even though a species may become more adapted to a particular environment over time, we cannot say that one species adapted to its environment is "better" than another species adapted to a different environment. For example, we may like to think of ourselves as "better" than other animals, but humans are clearly less adapted than fish for living under water, than bats for catching flying insects, than raccoons for living on suburban garbage.

Although the theory of natural selection suggests that disadvantageous or maladaptive traits will generally decline in frequency or even disappear eventually, it does not necessarily follow that all such traits will do so. After all, species derive from prior forms that have certain structures. This means that not all changes are possible; it also means that some traits are linked to others that might have advantages that outweigh the disadvantages. Choking may be very maladaptive for any animal, yet all vertebrates are capable of choking because their digestive and respiratory systems cross in the throat. This trait is a genetic legacy, probably from the time when the respiratory system developed from tissue in the digestive system of some ancestral organism. Apparently, the propensity to choke has not been correctable evolutionarily.[14]

Changes in a species can be expected to occur as the environment changes or as some members of the species move into a new environment. With environmental change, different traits become adaptive. The forms of the species that possess the more

Current Issues

IS EVOLUTION SLOW AND STEADY OR FAST AND ABRUPT?

Darwin's evolutionary theory suggested that new species emerge gradually over time. Through the process of natural selection, frequencies of traits would slowly change, and eventually a new species would appear. But Darwin did not explain why *so much* speciation has occurred. If trait frequencies change only gradually over time, wouldn't descendant populations retain their ability to interbreed and wouldn't they, therefore, continue to belong to the same species?

In the 1930s and 1940s, Theodosius Dobzhansky, Julian Huxley, Ernst Mayr, George Simpson, and others advanced what came to be called the "modern synthesis" in evolutionary theory, adding what was known from genetics about heredity. Mutation and the recombination of genes now provided for genetic variety. The driving force of change was still adaptation to environments through natural selection; gene frequencies of a population presumably changed slowly as adaptive traits (because of existing genes or mutations) increased in prevalence and maladaptive traits decreased. As for speciation, the development and divergence of different species, the modern synthesis postulated that it would occur when subpopulations became isolated by geographic barriers or when different subpopulations encountered different climatic conditions or moved into new ecological niches; those environmental isolating processes would eventually result in the development of reproductive isolation and therefore new species.

This gradualist view of evolution was challenged in 1972 by Niles Eldredge and Stephen Jay Gould. Their alternative model of evolution is referred to as "punctuated equilibrium." They still assume that natural selection is the primary mechanism of evolutionary change, but they see the pace of evolution quite differently. In their view, new species evolve quickly; but once a successful species emerges, its characteristics are likely to change very little over long periods of time. Thus, in contrast to the modern synthesis, Eldredge and Gould do not think it is common for the world's species to change gradually into descendant species. Rather, species are born more or less abruptly, they have lifetimes during which they do not change much, and they become extinct. As examples, Eldredge and Gould cite the history of North American trilobites and Bermudan land snails. In both groups of animals, it looks as if the different species did not change for a long period of time—millions of years for some species—but then certain species seem to have been quickly replaced by related species from nearby areas. In short, Eldredge and Gould believe that the succession of one species after another involves replacement from outside more often than gradual change over time.

Evolution may or may not occur as the model of punctuated equilibrium specifies, but most evolutionists today agree that change could occur relatively quickly. Recent research suggests that some relatively quick climate changes in the earth's history helped bring about massive extinctions of species and families of species and exponential increases

adaptive traits will become more frequent, whereas those forms whose characteristics make continued existence more difficult or impossible in the modified environment will eventually become extinct.

Consider how the theory of natural selection would explain why giraffes became long-necked. Originally, the necks of giraffes varied in length, as happens with virtually any physical characteristic in a population. During a period when food was scarce, those giraffes with longer necks, who could reach higher tree leaves, might be better able to survive and suckle their offspring, and thus they would leave more offspring than shorter-necked giraffes. Because of heredity, the offspring of long-necked giraffes are more likely to have long necks. Eventually, the shorter-necked giraffes would diminish in number and the longer-necked giraffes would increase. The resultant population of giraffes would still have variation in neck length but on the average would be longer-necked than earlier forms.

Natural selection does not account for all variation in the frequencies of traits. In particular, it does in the subsequent number of new families. For example, there is considerable evidence that a large meteorite collided with the earth at the end of the Cretaceous geological period, about 65 million years ago. Louis Alvarez and his colleagues proposed that so much dust was sent into the atmosphere by the collision that the earth was shrouded in darkness for months, if not longer. Some investigators now think that the meteorite impact may also have triggered a great deal of volcanic activity, even on the opposite side of the world, which would also have reduced solar radiation to the earth's surface. Not only the dinosaurs disappeared about 65 million years ago, so also did many sea animals and plants. Afterward, the earth saw the proliferation of many other kinds of animals, such as fish, lizards, birds, and mammals, as well as flowering trees. As we shall see in the chapter on primate evolution, our own biological order, the Primates, is believed to have emerged around that time.

Peter Grant has recently studied the same finches on the Galápagos Islands that partially inspired Darwin's theory. But unlike Darwin, Grant had the chance to see natural selection in action. And it was surprisingly quick. Central to the project was the attachment of colored bands to each individual bird, which allowed each bird to be identified at a distance. In the midst of the project, in 1977, when half the birds had been banded, there was a serious drought. Of the two main species of finch on one island, the cactus finch and the medium finch, only the cactus finches were able to breed, but they had no surviving offspring. During the next 18 months, 85 percent of the adult medium finches disappeared. Those finches that survived tended to be larger and to have larger beaks than the ones that died. Why larger beaks? Both species of finch eat seeds, but small seeds produced by grasses and herbs are scarce in a drought; bigger seeds are more available. So it seems that natural selection under conditions of drought favored finches with bigger beaks, which are better at cracking the husks of large seeds.

If it were not for the fact that wet years, which favor smaller finches, occur between years of drought, we might see the quick evolution of new finch species. It is estimated that 20 drought episodes would be sufficient to produce a new species of finch. Darwin's (and Grant's) finches do not really provide an example of punctuated equilibrium (no replacement from outside occurred), but they do suggest that evolutionary change could be a lot quicker than Darwin imagined.

Controversy continues over whether evolution is slow and steady or fast and abrupt. But many scholars, including Gould, point out that there is no need to pit one model against the other. Both may be correct in different instances. In any case much more investigation of evolutionary sequences is needed to help us evaluate the competing theoretical models.

Sources: Ian Tattersall, "Paleoanthropology and Evolutionary Theory," in Carol R. Ember, Melvin Ember, and Peter N. Peregrine, eds. *Research Frontiers in Anthropology* (Upper Saddle River, NJ: Prentice Hall, 1998), Prentice Hall/Simon & Schuster Custom Publishing; Charles Devillers and Jean Chaline, *Evolution: An Evolving Theory* (New York: Springer-Verlag, 1993); Peter R. Grant, "Natural Selection and Darwin's Finches," *Scientific American*, October 1991, 82–87.

The giraffe's long neck is adaptive for eating tree leaves high off the ground. When food is scarce, longer-necked giraffes would get more food and reproduce more successfully than shorter-necked giraffes; in this environment, natural selection would favor giraffes with longer necks.

The changes that occurred in the moth population in different areas of England show natural selection in action. Before industrialization, tree trunks were lighter, and light-colored moths predominated. (Rural areas today, with little or no industrial air pollution, show that natural selection in unpolluted areas still favors light-colored moths.) But with industrial pollution and the darkening of tree trunks, light-colored moths became more visible to predators. Darker-colored moths quickly increased in number in the new industrial environment.

not account for variation in the frequencies of neutral traits—that is, those traits that do not seem to confer any advantages or disadvantages on their carriers. Changes in the frequencies of neutral traits may result rather from random processes that affect gene frequencies in isolated populations—genetic drift—or from matings between populations—gene flow. We discuss these other processes in the chapter on human variation.

OBSERVED EXAMPLES OF EVOLUTION

Because the process of evolution may involve nearly imperceptible gradations over generations, it is usually difficult to observe directly. Nevertheless, because some life forms reproduce rapidly, some examples of natural selection have been observed over relatively short periods in changing environments.

For example, scientists think they have observed natural selection in action in British moths. In 1850, an almost black moth was spotted for the first time in Manchester. That was quite unusual, for most of the moths were speckled gray. A century later, 95 percent of the moths in industrial parts of Britain were black; only in the rural areas were the moths mostly gray. How is this to be explained? It seems that in the rural areas, the gray-speckled moth is hard to spot by bird predators against the lichen growing on the bark of trees. But in industrial areas, lichen is killed by pollution. The gray-speckled moths, formerly well adapted to blend into their environment, became clearly visible against the darker background of the lichen-free trees and were easier prey for birds. In contrast, the black moths, which previously would have had a disadvantage against the lighter bark, were now better adapted for survival. Their dark color was an advantage, and subsequently the darker moths became the predominant variety in industrial regions.

How can we be sure that natural selection was the mechanism accounting for the change? Consistent evidence comes from a series of experiments performed by H. B. D. Kettlewell. He deliberately released specially marked moths, black and gray, into two areas of England—one urban industrial and one rural—and then set light traps to recapture them subsequently. The proportions of the two kinds of moths recovered tell us about differential survival. Kettlewell found that proportionately more black moths compared with gray moths were recovered in the urban industrial area. Just the reverse happened in the rural area; proportionately more gray-speckled moths were recovered.[15] The same transformation—the switch to darker color—

occurred in 70 other species of moth, as well as in a beetle and a millipede. It did not occur just in Britain; it also happened in other highly polluted areas, the Ruhr area of Germany and in the Pittsburgh area of the United States. Moreover, in the Pittsburgh area, antipollution measures in the last 30 years have apparently caused the black moth to dwindle in number once again.[16]

Another well-known example of observed natural selection is the acquired resistance of houseflies to the insecticide DDT. When DDT was first used to kill insects, beginning in the 1940s, several new, DDT-resistant strains of housefly evolved. In the early DDT environment, many houseflies were killed, but the few that survived were the ones that reproduced, and their resistant characteristics became common to the housefly populations. To the chagrin of medical practitioners, similar resistances develop in bacteria. A particular antibiotic may lose its effectiveness after it comes into wide use because new, resistant bacterial strains emerge. These new strains will become more frequent than the original ones because of natural selection. In the United States now, a few strains are resistant to *all* antibiotics on the market, a fact that worries medical practitioners. One possible way to deal with the problem is to stop using antibiotics for a few years, so resistance to those antibiotics might not develop or develop only slowly.

The theory of natural selection answered many questions, but it also raised at least one whose answer eluded Darwin and others. The appearance of a beneficial trait may assist the survival of an organism, but what happens when the organism reproduces by mating with members that do not possess this new variation? Will not the new adaptive trait eventually disappear if subsequent generations mate with individuals that lack this trait? Darwin knew variations were transmitted through heredity, but he did not have a clear model of the mode of inheritance. Gregor Mendel's pioneering studies in the science of genetics provided the foundation for such a model, but his discoveries did not become widely known until 1900.

HEREDITY

GREGOR MENDEL'S EXPERIMENTS

Mendel (1822–1884), a monk and amateur botanist who lived in what is now the Czech Republic, bred several varieties of pea plants and made detailed observations of their offspring. He chose as breeding partners plants that differed by only one observable trait. Tall plants were crossed with short ones, and yellow ones with green, for example.

When the pollen from a yellow pea plant was transferred to a green pea plant, Mendel observed a curious phenomenon: All of the first-generation offspring bore yellow peas. It seemed that the green trait had disappeared. But when seeds from this first generation were crossed, they produced both yellow and green pea plants in a ratio of three yellow to one green pea plant (see Figure 2–2). Apparently, Mendel reasoned, the green trait had not been lost or altered; the yellow trait was simply **dominant** and the green trait was **recessive.** Mendel observed similar results with other traits. Tallness dominated shortness, and the factor for smooth-skinned peas dominated the factor for wrinkled ones. In each cross, the 3-to-1 ratio appeared in the second generation. Self-fertilization,

---

FIGURE 2–2

When Mendel crossed a plant having two genes for yellow peas (YY) with a plant having two genes for green peas (yy), each offspring pea was yellow but carried one gene for yellow and one gene for green (Yy). The peas were yellow because the gene for yellow is dominant over the recessive gene for green. Crossing the first generation yielded three yellow pea plants for each green pea plant.

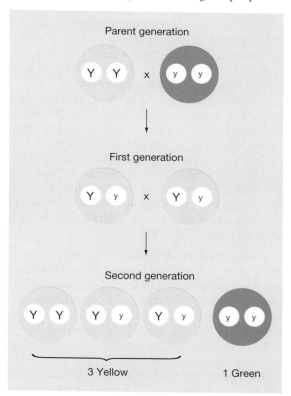

however, produced different results. Green pea plants always yielded green pea plants, and short plants always produced short plants.

From his numerical results, Mendel concluded that some yellow pea plants were pure for that trait, whereas others also possessed a green factor. That is, although two plants might both have yellow peas, one of them might produce offspring with green peas. In such cases, the genetic makeup, the **genotype,** differed from the observable appearance, or **phenotype.**

GENES: THE CONVEYORS OF INHERITED TRAITS

Mendel's units of heredity were what we now call **genes.** He concluded that these units occurred in pairs for each trait and that offspring inherited one unit of the pair from each parent. Each member of a gene pair or group is called an **allele.** If the two genes, or alleles, for a trait are the same, the organism is **homozygous** for that trait; if the two genes for a characteristic differ, the organism is **heterozygous** for that trait. A pea plant that contains a pair of genes for yellow is homozygous for the trait. A yellow pea plant with a dominant gene for yellow and a recessive gene for green, although phenotypically yellow, has a heterozygous genotype. As Mendel demonstrated, the recessive green gene can reappear in subsequent generations. But Mendel knew nothing of the composition of genes or the processes that transmit them from parent to offspring. Many years of scientific research have yielded much of the missing information.

The genes of higher organisms (not including bacteria and primitive plants such as green-blue algae) are located on ropelike bodies called **chromosomes** within the nucleus of every one of the organism's cells. Chromosomes, like genes, usually occur in pairs. Each allele for a given trait is carried in the identical position on corresponding chromosomes. The two genes that determined the color of Mendel's peas, for example, were opposite each other on a pair of chromosomes.

MITOSIS AND MEIOSIS. The body cells of every plant or animal carry chromosome pairs in a number appropriate for its species. Humans have 23 pairs, or a total of 46 chromosomes, each carrying many times that number of genes. Each new body cell receives this number of chromosomes during cellular reproduction, or **mitosis,** as each pair of chromosomes duplicates itself.

But what happens when a sperm cell and an egg cell unite to form a new organism? What prevents the human baby from receiving twice the number of chromosomes characteristic of its species—23 pairs from the sperm and 23 pairs from the egg? The process by which the reproductive cells are formed, **meiosis,** ensures that this will not happen. Each reproductive cell contains *half* the number of chromosomes appropriate for the species. Only one member of each chromosome pair is carried in every egg or sperm. At fertilization, the human embryo normally receives 23 *separate* chromosomes from its mother and the same number from its father, which add up to the 23 pairs.

DNA. As we have said, genes are located on chromosomes. Each gene carries a set of instructions encoded in its chemical structure. It is from this coded information carried in genes that a cell makes all the rest of its structural parts and chemical machinery. It appears that in most living organisms, heredity is controlled by the same chemical substance, **DNA**—deoxyribonucleic acid. An enormous amount of research has been directed toward understanding DNA—what its structure is, how it duplicates itself in reproduction, and how it conveys or instructs the formation of a complete organism.

One of the most important keys to understanding human development and genetics is the structure and function of DNA. In 1953, the American biologist James Watson, with the British molecular biologist Francis Crick, proposed that DNA is a long, two-stranded molecule shaped like a double helix[17] (see Figure 2–3). Genetic information is stored in the linear sequences of the bases; different species have different sequences, and every individual is slightly different from every other individual. Notice that in the DNA molecule each base always has the same opposite base; adenine and thymine are paired, as are cytosine and guanine. The importance of this pattern is that the two strands carry the same information, so that when the double helix unwinds each strand can form a template for a new strand of complementary bases.[18] Because DNA stores the information required to make up the cells of an organism, it has been called the language of life. As George and Muriel Beadle put it,

> the deciphering of the DNA code has revealed our possession of a language much older than hieroglyphics, a language as old as life itself, a language that is the most living language of all—even if its letters are invisible and its words are buried deep in the cells of our bodies.[19]

Once it was understood that genes are made of DNA, concerted efforts were begun to map DNA

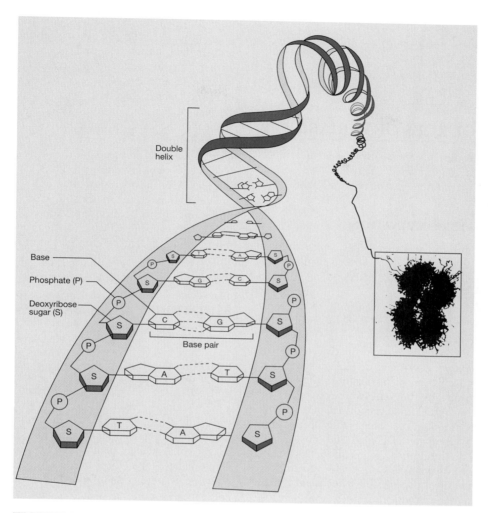

FIGURE 2–3

The DNA molecule consists of two spiral sugar-phosphate strands. The strands are linked by the nitrogenous bases adenine (A), guanine (G), thymine (T), and cytosine (C). When the DNA molecule reproduces, the bases separate and the spiral strands unwind. Each original strand serves as a mold along which a new complementary chain is formed. *Source:* From Paul Berg and Maxine Singer, *Dealing with Genes: The Language of Heredity* (Mill Valley, CA: University Science Books, 1992).

sequences and their locations on the chromosomes of different organisms. A project known as the human genome project set out to assemble a complete genetic map for humans. Much progress has already been made, but it may take many years and an enormous amount of research to finish this task.[20]

MESSENGER RNA. DNA stores the information to make cells, but it does not directly affect the formation of cells. One type of ribonucleic acid (RNA), messenger RNA (mRNA), is copied from a portion of DNA and moves outside the cell nucleus to direct the formation of proteins.[21] Proteins have so many functions that they are considered to be responsible for most of the characteristics of an organism. They act as catalysts for synthesizing DNA and RNA and for the activities of cells; they also contribute many of the structural elements that determine the shape and movement of cells.[22] Messenger RNA is like DNA in that it has a linear sequence of bases attached to a sugar-phosphate backbone, but it is slightly different chemically. One difference is that messenger RNA has the base uracil instead of the base thymine. Messenger RNA also has a different sugar-phosphate backbone and is single- rather than double-stranded. Messenger RNA is formed when a double-stranded DNA molecule unwinds and forms a template for the mRNA. After a section of DNA is copied, the RNA releases from the DNA and leaves the nucleus, and the double helix of the DNA is re-formed.[23]

▰▰▰ SOURCES OF VARIABILITY

Natural selection proceeds only when individuals within a population vary. There are two genetic sources of variation: genetic recombination and mutation.

GENETIC RECOMBINATION

The distribution of traits from parents to children varies from one offspring to another. Brothers and sisters, after all, do not look exactly alike, nor does each child resemble 50 percent of the mother and 50 percent of the father. This variation occurs because when a sperm cell or an egg is formed, the single member of each chromosome pair it receives is a matter of chance. Each reproductive cell, then, carries a *random assortment* of chromosomes and their respective genes. At fertilization, the egg and sperm that unite are different from every other egg carried by the mother and every other sperm carried by the father. A *unique* offspring is thus produced by a shuffling of the parents' genes. One cause of this shuffling is the random **segregation,** or sorting, of chromosomes in meiosis. Conceivably, an individual could get any of the possible assortments of the paternal and maternal chromosomes. Another cause of the shuffling of parental genes is **crossing-over,** the exchange of sections of chromosomes between one chromosome and another.[24] Thus, after meiosis, the egg and sperm do not receive just a random mixture of complete paternal and maternal chromosomes; because of crossing-over they also receive chromosomes in which some of the sections may have been replaced.

The traits displayed by each organism are not simply the result of combinations of dominant and recessive genes, as Mendel had hypothesized. In humans, most traits are influenced by the activity of many genes. Skin color, for example, is the result of several inherited characteristics. A brownish shade results from the presence of a pigment known as *melanin;* the degree of darkness in the hue depends largely on the amount of melanin present and how it is distributed in the layers of the skin. Another factor contributing to the color of all human skin is the blood that flows in blood vessels located in the outer layers of the skin. Humans carry at least five different genes for the manufacture of melanin and many other genes for the other components of skin hue. In fact, almost all physical characteristics in humans are the result of the concerted action of many genes. Some traits are sex-linked. The X chromosome, which together with the presence or absence of a Y chromosome determines sex, may also carry the gene for hemophilia or the gene for color blindness. The expression of these two characteristics depends on the sex of the organism.

Genetic recombination produces variety, which is essential for the operation of natural selection. Ultimately, however, the major source of variability is mutation. This is because mutation replenishes the supply of variability, which is constantly being reduced by the selective elimination of less fit variants. Mutation also produces variety in organisms that reproduce asexually.

MUTATION

A **mutation** is a change in the DNA sequence. Such a change produces an altered gene. The majority of mutations are thought to occur because of occasional mismating of the chemical bases that make up DNA. Just as a typist will make errors in copying a manuscript, so will DNA, in duplicating itself, occasionally change its code.[25] A mutation will result from such an error. Some mutations have more drastic consequences than others. Suppose the error is in one base on a DNA strand. The effect depends on what that portion of the DNA controls. The effect may be minimal if the product hardly affects the organism. On the other hand, if the change occurs at a place where the DNA regulates the production of many proteins, the effect on the organism can be serious.[26]

Although it is very difficult to estimate the proportions of mutations that are harmful, neutral, or beneficial, there is no doubt that some mutations have lethal consequences. We can discuss the relative merits or disadvantages of a mutant gene *only* in terms of the physical, cultural, and genetic environment of that gene.[27] Galactosemia, for example, is caused by a recessive mutant gene and usually results in mental retardation and blindness. But it can be prevented by dietary restrictions begun at an early age. In this instance, the intervention of human culture counteracts the mutant gene and allows the afflicted individual to lead a normal life. Thus, some cultural factors can modify the effects of natural selection by helping to perpetuate a harmful mutant gene. People with the galactosemia trait who are enabled to function normally can reproduce and pass on one of the recessive genes to their children. Without cultural interference, natural selection would prevent such reproduction. Usually, natural selection acts to retain only those mutations that aid survival.

Even though most mutations may not be adaptive, those that are will multiply in a population relatively quickly, by natural selection. As Theodosius Dobzhansky has suggested:

> Consistently useful mutants are like needles in a haystack of harmful ones. A needle in a haystack is hard to find, even though one may be sure it is there. But if the needle is valuable, the task of finding it is facilitated by setting the haystack on fire and looking for the needle among the ashes. The role of the fire in this parable is played in biological evolution by natural selection.[28]

The black moth that was spotted in Manchester in 1850 probably resulted from a mutation. If the tree trunks had been light colored, that moth or its offspring probably would have died out. But as industrialization increased and the tree trunks became darker, a trait that was once maladaptive became adaptive.

THE ORIGIN OF SPECIES

One of the most controversial aspects of Darwin's theory was the suggestion that one species could, over time, evolve into another. A **species** is a population that consists of organisms able to interbreed and produce fertile and viable offspring. In general, individuals from one species cannot successfully mate with members of a different species because of genetic and behavioral differences. If members of different species did mate, it is unlikely that the egg would be fertilized, or, if it were, that the embryo would survive. If the offspring were born, it would soon die or be infertile. But how could one species evolve into another? What is the explanation for this differentiation? How does one group of organisms become so unlike another group with the same ancestry that it forms a totally new species?

Speciation, or the development of a new species, may occur if one subgroup of a species finds itself in a radically different environment. In adapting to their separate environments, the two populations may undergo enough genetic changes to prevent them from interbreeding, should they renew contact. Numerous factors can prevent the exchange of genes. Two species living in the same area may breed at different times of the year, or their behavior during breeding—their courtship rituals—may be

distinct. The difference in body structure of closely related forms may in itself bar interbreeding. Geographic barriers may be the most common barriers to interbreeding.

Once species differentiation does occur, the evolutionary process cannot be reversed; the new species can no longer mate with other species related to its parent population. Humans and gorillas, for example, have the same distant ancestors, but their evolutionary paths have diverged irreversibly.

NATURAL SELECTION OF BEHAVIORAL TRAITS

Until now we have discussed how natural selection might operate to change a population's physical traits, such as the color of moths or the neck length of giraffes. But natural selection can also operate on the behavioral characteristics of populations. Although this idea is not new, it is now receiving more attention. The approaches called **sociobiology**[29] and **behavioral ecology**[30] involve the application of evolutionary principles to the behavior of animals. Behavioral ecology is interested in how all kinds of behavior are related to the environment; sociobiology is particularly interested in social organization and social behavior. The typical behaviors of a species are assumed to be adaptive and to have evolved by natural selection. For example, why do related species exhibit different social behaviors even though they derive from a common ancestral species?

Consider the lion, as compared with other cats. Although members of the cat family are normally solitary creatures, lions live in social groups called *prides.* Why? George Schaller has suggested that lion social groups may have evolved primarily because group hunting is a more successful way to catch large mammals in open terrain. He has observed that not only are several lions more successful in catching prey than are solitary lions, but several lions are more likely to catch and kill large and dangerous prey such as giraffes. Then, too, cubs are generally safer from predators when in a social group than when alone with their mothers. Thus, the social behavior of lions may have evolved primarily because it provided selective advantages in the lions' open-country environment.[31]

It is important to remember that natural selection operates on expressed characteristics, or the phenotype, of an individual. In the moth example, the color of the moth is part of its phenotype, subject to natural selection. Behavior is also an expressed characteristic. If hunting in groups, a behavioral trait, gets you more food, then individuals who hunt in groups will do better. But we must also remember that natural selection requires traits to be heritable. Can the concept of heritability be applied to learned behavior, not just genetically transmitted behavior? And, even more controversially, if the concept of heritability can include learning, can it also include cultural learning?

Early theorizing in sociobiology and behavioral ecology appeared to emphasize the genetic component of behavior. For example, Edward O. Wilson, in his book *Sociobiology*, defined sociobiology as "the systematic study of the biological causes of behav-ior."[32] But Bobbi Low points out that, although the term *biology* may have been interpreted to mean "genetic," most biologists understand that expressed or observable characteristics are the results of genes and environment and life history, all interacting. Behavior is a product of all three. If we say that some behavior is heritable, we mean that the child's behavior is more likely to resemble the parents' behavior than the behavior of others.[33] Learning from a parent could be an important part of why the offspring is like the parent. If the child is more like the parent than like others, then the likeness is heritable, even if it is entirely learned from the parent.

Current Issues

DO WE NEED TO FEAR GENETIC ENGINEERING?

So much is known about molecular genetics that it is now possible to alter individual genes and even whole organisms in very precise ways. The revolution occurred very quickly after the structure of DNA was first identified in 1953 by James Watson and Francis Crick. Particular genetic traits could then be linked to particular sequences of DNA messages. In the 1970s, the development of *recombinant DNA techniques* allowed researchers to splice pieces of DNA from one organism into the DNA of another, in precise locations. Researchers learned how to make copies by putting these "recombined" strands into host organisms such as bacteria, which reproduce by cloning. The applications of these techniques are potentially enormous. *Biotechnology* companies are already doing genetic engineering to manufacture medicines (such as insulin and a vaccine against hepatitis B) and to produce more desirable plant and animal products (for example, a strain of tomato that can be shipped when it's ripe without spoiling). They are also working on how to reintroduce altered cells into organisms to fix genetic defects. As of now about 4,000 human disorders are known to be caused by defects in a few genes; theoretically they should be fixable some day by genetic engineering. As more becomes known about the precise location of genes and the DNA sequences that convey particular information, much more engineering will be possible. Already some imagine that genetic therapy will eventually cure various cancers and heart disease.

Might there be risks associated with such interventions? Some fear that recombinant DNA engineering may have disastrous consequences. Could a dangerous runaway strain of bacteria or virus be produced in the lab? Might a kind of Frankenstein be produced? Could unscrupulous governments mandate certain kinds of alterations? Do we have reason to entertain such fears?

It is important to remind ourselves that although DNA al-teration by recombinant techniques is new, genetic engineering is not new. Humans have genetically altered plants and animals for thousands of years. We usually do not call it genetic engineering—we call it domestication or breeding. To be sure, the mechanism of traditional genetic engineering, selective breeding, is different from DNA splicing, but the effect is genetic alteration nonetheless. By breeding for preferred traits, humans are able to produce breeds of horses, dogs, cattle, varieties of corn and beans, and all of the other animals and plants we depend on for food, fiber, and other materials and chemicals. All of them are different, often very different, from their wild progenitors. Humans have also domesticated microorganisms. An example that goes back thousands of years is the yeast used for brewing beer and baking bread; a more recent example is a particular mold used to produce penicillin. And live vaccines that are deliberately weakened viruses, as, for example, in the vaccine against

The sociobiological approach has aroused considerable controversy in cultural anthropology, probably because of its apparent emphasis on genes, rather than experience and learning, as determinants of human behavior. In the chapter titled "Theory and Evidence in Cultural Anthropology," we discuss the controversy over sociobiology in more detail. As we shall see, cultural ecologists have argued that the customs of a society may be more or less adaptive because cultural behaviors also have reproductive consequences. It is not just an individual's behavior that may have reproductive consequences. So does natural selection also operate in the evolution of culture? Most biologists think not. They say there are substantial differences between biological and cultural evolution. How do cultural evolution and biological evolution compare? To answer this question, we must remember that the operation of natural selection requires three conditions, as we aleady noted: variation, heritability or mechanisms that duplicate traits in offspring, and differential reproduction because of heritable differences. Do these three requirements apply to cultural behavior?

In biological evolution, variability comes from genetic recombination and mutation. In cultural evolution, it comes from recombination of learned

polio, have already been widely used to prevent illness.

So what does our past engineering tell us about the risks of future engineering? In general, the past suggests that no serious harm is attributable to domestication. In fact, domesticated animals and plants are *less* likely to do well if reintroduced into the wild than their wild cousins. They usually need human help to eat, to get shelter from the elements, and to care for their offspring. So why should genetic engineering be any different? It has basically the same purpose as selective breeding—humans want organisms, large or small or microscopic, to be useful to humans. So far, the available evidence indicates that organisms altered genetically to satisfy human needs are no threat to humans because they are unlikely to survive without human assistance. Needless to say, that does not obviate the need to test for risks. It is reassuring that DNA in nature can cross over from one organism to another and that such natural genetic alteration is not generally harmful to us.

People may mostly be afraid that a dangerous microbe could be accidentally released from a laboratory and multiply uncontrollably. But, as already noted, any microbe or new genetic form is unlikely to be as hardy as its wild cousins. If a bacterium is mistakenly released, it is not going into an artificially empty environment like a sterile petri dish. The natural environment is already filled with bacteria (most of them beneficial to humans), as well as other organisms that attack bacteria. In short, it is not so easy to produce a harmful microbe.

The improbability of making destructive organisms does not mean that humans should not guard against the possibility. That is why we have government agencies to certify new products, along with guidelines for testing procedures and oversight panels. A new product of recombinant DNA research has to be approved before it can be widely used.

Can humans use such technology for eugenic purposes, such as creating superhumans or for biological warfare? Possibly. But recombinant DNA techniques are not the problem. After all, the lack of such technology has not prevented genocide, ethnic cleansing, sterilization, and rape. The absence of recombinant technology did not prevent the use of natural biological weapons (such as smallpox-infected blankets given to Native Americans in the nineteenth century) or the manufacture and use of poison gas in World War I and since. It is not technology or the absence of it that explains evil; it is other things. If we want to reduce the risk of human violence, we have to understand why it occurs. Only more research can make us safer.

Sources: Allan M. Campbell, "Microbes: The Laboratory and the Field," Bernard D. Davis, "The Issues: Prospects versus Perceptions" and "Summary and Comments: The Scientific Chapters," and Henry I. Miller, "Regulation," in Bernard D. Davis, ed., *The Genetic Revolution: Scientific Prospects and Public Perceptions* (Baltimore: Johns Hopkins University Press, 1991), pp. 28–44, 1–8, 239–65, 196–211; Paul Berg and Maxine Singer, *Dealing with Genes: The Language of Heredity* (Mill Valley, CA: University Science Books, 1992), pp. 221–44.

Prides of lions who live in open country are more successful in catching large animals than are solitary lions. This social behavior may have evolved because it provided selective advantages in the lion's open-country environment.

behaviors and from invention.[34] Cultures are not closed or reproductively isolated, as species are. A species cannot borrow genetic traits from another species, but a culture can borrow new things and behaviors from other cultures. The custom of growing corn, which has spread from the New World to many other areas, is an example of this phenomenon. As for the requirement of heritability, although learned traits obviously are not passed to offspring through purely genetic inheritance, parents who exhibit adaptive behavioral traits are more likely to "reproduce" those traits in their children, who may learn them by imitation or by parental instruction. Children and adults may also copy adaptive traits they see in people outside the family. Finally, as for the requirement of differential reproduction, it does not matter whether the trait in question is genetic or learned or both. As Henry Nissen emphasized, "be-havioral incompetence leads to extinction as surely as does morphological disproportion or deficiency in any vital organ. Behavior is subject to selection as much as bodily size or resistance to disease."[35]

Many theorists are comfortable with the idea of applying the theory of natural selection to cultural evolution, but others prefer to use other terminology when dealing with traits that do not depend on purely genetic transmission from one generation to the next. For example, Robert Boyd and Peter Richerson discuss human behavior as involving "dual inheritance." They distinguish cultural transmission, by learning and imitation, from genetic transmission, but they emphasize the importance of understanding both and the interaction between them.[36] William Durham also deals separately with cultural transmission, using the term *meme* (analogous to the term *gene*) for the unit of cultural transmission.

Mountain lions live in wooded environments and hunt individually. Here we see one that has killed a mule deer in western Montana.

He directs our attention to the interaction between genes and culture, calling that interaction "coevolution," and provides examples of how genetic evolution and cultural evolution may lead to changes in each other, how they may enhance each other, and how they may even oppose each other.[37]

So biological and cultural evolution in humans may not be completely separate processes. As we will discuss, some of the most important biological features of humans—such as two-legged walking and relatively large brains—may have been favored by natural selection because our ancestors made tools, a cultural trait. Conversely, the cultural trait of informal and formal education may have been favored by natural selection because humans have a long period of immaturity, a biological trait.

As long as the human species continues to exist and the social and physical environment continues to change, there is reason to think that natural selection of biological and cultural traits will also continue. However, as humans learn more and more about genetic structure they will become more and more capable of curing genetically caused disorders and even altering the way evolution proceeds. Today, genetic researchers are capable of diagnosing genetic defects in developing fetuses, and parents can and do decide often whether to terminate a pregnancy. Soon genetic engineering will probably allow humans to fix defects and even try to "improve" the genetic code of a growing fetus. Whether and to what extent humans should alter genes will undoubtedly be the subject of continuing debate. Whatever the decisions we eventually make about genetic engineering, they will affect the course of human biological and cultural evolution.

SUMMARY

1. If we think of the history of the universe in terms of 12 months, the history of human-like primates would take up only about one and a half hours. The universe is some 15 billion years old; modern-looking humans have existed for about 100,000 years.

2. Ideas about evolution took a long time to take hold because they contradicted the biblical view of events; species were viewed as fixed in their form by the creator. But in the eighteenth and early nineteenth centuries increasing evidence suggested that evolution was a viable theory. In geology, the concept of *uniformitarianism* suggested that the earth is constantly subject to shaping and reshaping by natural forces working over vast stretches of time.

A number of thinkers during this period began to discuss evolution and how it might occur.

3. Charles Darwin and Alfred Wallace proposed the mechanism of natural selection to account for the evolution of species. Basic principles of the theory of natural selection are that (1) every species is composed of a great variety of individuals, some of which are better adapted to their environment than others; (2) offspring inherit traits from their parents at least to some degree and in some way; and (3) since better adapted individuals generally produce more offspring over the generations than the poorer adapted, the frequency of adaptive traits increases in subsequent generations. In this way, natural selection results in increasing proportions of individuals with advantageous traits.

4. Mendel's and subsequent research in genetics and our understanding of the structure and function of DNA and mRNA help us to understand the biological mechanisms by which traits may be passed from one generation to the next.

5. Natural selection depends on variation within a population. The two sources of biological variation are genetic recombination and mutation.

6. Speciation, the development of a new species, may occur if one subgroup becomes separated from other subgroups. In adapting to different environments, these subpopulations may undergo enough genetic changes to prevent interbreeding, even if they reestablish contact. Once species differentiation occurs, it is believed that the evolutionary process cannot be reversed.

7. Natural selection can also operate on the behavioral characteristics of populations. The approaches called sociobiology and behavioral ecology involve the application of evolutionary principles to the behavior of animals. Much controversy surrounds the degree to which the theory of natural selection can be applied to human behavior, particularly cultural behavior. There is more agreement that biological and cultural evolution in humans may influence each other.

GLOSSARY TERMS

allele	heterozygous
behavioral ecology	homozygous
chromosome	meiosis
crossing-over	mitosis
DNA	mutation
dominant	natural selection
gene	phenotype
genotype	recessive

segregation   speciation
sociobiology   species

 CRITICAL QUESTIONS

1. Do you think the theory of natural selection is compatible with religious beliefs? Explain your reasoning.

2. How might the discovery of genetic cures and the use of genetic engineering affect the future of evolution?

3. Why do you think humans have remained one species?

 INTERNET EXERCISES

1. Explore the Human Behavior and Evolution Society at **http://psych.lmu.edu/hbes.htm**. Select the Evolution and Science News Reports and summarize at least two recent articles related to human evolution.

2. Visit the home page of *Evolution (International Journal of Organic Evolution)* at **http://lsvl.la. asu.edu/evolution/**. By looking at the table of contents, provide bibliography of at least 15 articles related to human evolution.

3. Read the article on speciation as it relates to Darwinian evolution at **http://www.santarosa.edu/ lifesciences/ensatina.htm**. Summarize your findings.

 SUGGESTED READING

BOYD, R., AND RICHERSON, P. J. *Culture and the Evolutionary Process.* Chicago: University of Chicago Press, 1985. The authors develop mathematical models to analyze how biology and culture interact under the influence of evolutionary processes.

BRANDON, R. N. *Adaptation and Environment.* Princeton, NJ: Princeton University Press, 1990. After defining basic concepts regarding adaptation and the theory of natural selection, the author emphasizes that the process of adaptation and its outcomes cannot be understood without analysis of the environment.

CHIRAS, D. D. *Human Biology: Health, Homeostasis, and the Environment,* 2nd ed. St. Paul, MN: West, 1995. An introductory textbook in human biology. See chapters 3–5 for a detailed discussion of chromosomes, DNA, RNA, principles of heredity, and genetic engineering.

DEVILLERS, C., AND CHALINE, J. *Evolution: An Evolving Theory.* New York: Springer-Verlag, 1993. Aimed at the general audience, this book addresses the questions: What is the place of humans in the living world? What is evolution? How can the observed data be explained? Appendixes give more detailed information.

DOBZHANSKY, T. *Mankind Evolving: The Evolution of the Human Species.* New Haven, CT: Yale University Press, 1962. A classic demonstration that the mechanisms of evolution, primarily natural selection, are still active.

DURHAM, W. H. *Coevolution: Genes, Culture, and Human Diversity.* Stanford, CA: Stanford University Press, 1991. A discussion of the evolution of culture that considers how theory and research point to the interaction of genes and culture in human populations.

MAYR, E. *The Growth of Biological Thought: Diversity, Evolution, and Inheritance.* Cambridge, MA: Belknap Press of Harvard University Press, 1982. A history of ideas that discusses the successful and unsuccessful attempts to understand problems in the study of evolution.

3

The Living Primates

*T*he goal of *primatology,* the study of primates, is to understand how different primates have adapted anatomically and behaviorally to their environments. The results of such studies may help us to understand the behavior and evolution of the human primate.

But how can living primates such as chimpanzees tell us anything about humans or the primates that were our ancestors? After all, each living primate species has its own history of evolutionary divergence from the earliest primate forms. All living primates, including humans, evolved from earlier primates that are now extinct. Nonetheless, by observing how humans and other primates differ from and resemble each other, we may be able to infer how and why humans diverged from the other primates.

In conjunction with fossil evidence, anatomical and behavioral comparisons of living primates may help us reconstruct what early primates were like. For example, if we know that modern primates that swing through the trees have a particular kind of shoulder bone structure, we can infer that similar fossil bones probably belonged to an animal that also swung through the trees. Differing adaptations of living primates may also suggest why certain divergences occurred in primate evolution. If we know what traits belong to humans, and to humans alone, this knowledge may suggest why the line of primates that led to humans branched away from the line leading to chimpanzees and gorillas.

In this chapter we first examine the common features of the living primates. Next we introduce the different animals that belong to the order Primates, focusing on the distinctive characteristics of each major type. Then we discuss possible explanations of some of the varying adaptations exhibited by the different primate species. We close with a look at the traits that make humans different from all other primates. The purpose of this chapter is to help us understand more about humans. Therefore, we emphasize the features of primate anatomy and behavior that perhaps have the greatest bearing on human evolution.

COMMON PRIMATE TRAITS

All primates belong to the class Mammalia, and they share all the common features of mammals. Except for humans, the bodies of primates are covered with dense hair or fur, which provides insulation. Even humans have hair in various places, though perhaps not always for insulation. Mammals are *warm-blooded;* that is, their body temperature is more or less constantly warm and usually higher than that of the air around them. Almost all mammals give birth to live young that develop to a considerable size within the mother and are nourished by suckling from the mother's mammary glands. The young have a relatively long period of dependence on adults after birth. This period is also a time of learning, for a great deal of adult mammal behavior is learned rather than instinctive. Play is a learning technique common to mammal young and is especially important to primates, as we shall see later in this chapter.

In addition to their mammalian features, the primates have a number of physical and social traits that set them apart from other mammals.

PHYSICAL FEATURES

No one of the primates' physical features is unique to primates; animals from other orders share one or more of the characteristics described below. But the complex of all these physical traits *is* unique to primates.[1]

Many skeletal features of the primates reflect an **arboreal** (tree-living) existence. All primate hind limbs are structured principally to provide support, but the "feet" in most primates can also grasp things. Some primates—orangutans, for instance—can suspend themselves from their hind limbs. The forelimbs are especially flexible, built to withstand both pushing and pulling forces. Each of the hind limbs and forelimbs has one bone in the upper portion and two bones in the lower portion (with the exception of the tarsier). This feature has little changed since the time of the earliest primate ancestors. It has remained in modern primates (although many other mammals have lost it) because the double bones give great mobility for rotating arms and legs. Another characteristic structure of primates is the clavicle, or collarbone. The clavicle also gives primates great freedom of movement, allowing them to move the shoulders both up and down and back and forth. Although humans obviously do not use this flexibility for arboreal activity, they do use it for other activities. Without a clavicle we could not throw a spear or a ball; no fine tools could be made and no doorknobs turned if we did not have rotatable forearms.

Primates generally are **omnivorous;** that is, they eat all kinds of food, including insects and small animals, as well as fruits, seeds, leaves, and roots. The teeth of primates reflect this omnivorous diet. The chewing teeth—the **molars** and **premolars**—are very unspecialized, particularly in comparison with those of other groups of animals, such as the grazers. The front teeth—the **incisors** and **canines**—are often very specialized, principally in the lower primates. For example, in many prosimians the slender, tightly packed lower incisors and canines form a "dental comb" the animals use in grooming or for scraping hardened gum (which is a food for them) from tree trunks.[2] Primate hands are extremely flexible. As Figure 3–1 indicates, all primates have **prehensile**—grasping—hands, which can be wrapped around an object. Primates have five digits on both hands and feet (in some cases, one digit may be reduced to a stub), and their nails, with few exceptions, are broad and flat, not clawlike. This

structure allows them to grip objects; the hairless, sensitive pads on their fingers, toes, heels, and palms also help them to grip. Most primates have **opposable thumbs,** a feature that allows an even more precise and powerful grip.

Vision is extremely important to primate life. Compared with other mammals, primates have a relatively larger portion of the brain devoted to vision rather than smell. Primates are characterized by *stereoscopic,* or depth, *vision.* Their eyes are directed forward rather than sideways, as in other animals—a trait that allows them to focus on an object (insects or other food or a distant branch) with both eyes at once. Most primates also have color vision, perhaps to recognize when plant foods are ready to eat. By and large, these characteristics are more developed in anthropoids than in prosimians.

FIGURE 3–1 *Some Common Primate Traits*

Source: (A) From Ronald G. Wolff, *Functional Chordate Anatomy* (Lexington, MA: D. C. Heath and Company, 1991), p. 255. Reprinted with permission of D. C. Heath. (B, C) From Terrence Deacon, "Primate Brains and Senses," in Stephen Jones, Robert Martin, and David Pilbeam, eds., *The Cambridge Encyclopedia of Human Evolution* (New York: Cambridge University Press, 1992), p. 110. (D) From Matt Cartmill, "Non-Human Primates," in ibid., p. 25. (E, F) From ibid., p. 24. Reprinted with permission of Cambridge University Press.

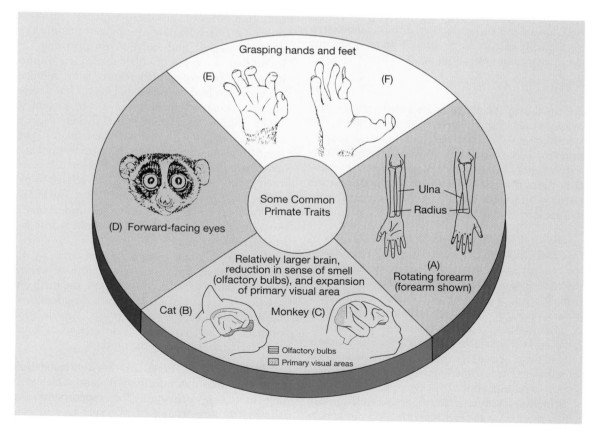

Another important primate feature is a large brain relative to body size. That is, primates generally have larger brains than animals of similar size, perhaps because their survival depends on an enormous amount of learning, as we discuss later. In general, animals with large brains seem to mature more slowly and to live longer than animals with small brains.[3] The more slowly an animal grows up and the longer it lives, the more it can learn.

Finally, the primate reproductive system sets this order of animals apart from other mammals. Males of most primate species have a pendulous penis that is not attached to the abdomen by skin, a trait shared by a few other animals, including bats and bears. Females of most primate species have two nipples on the chest (a few prosimians have more than two nipples). The uterus is usually constructed to hold a single fetus (only the marmosets and tamarins typically give birth to twins), not a litter, as with most other animals. This reproductive system can be seen as emphasizing quality over quantity—an adaptation possibly related to the dangers of life in the trees.[4] Primate infants tend to be relatively well developed at birth, although humans, apes, and some monkeys have helpless infants. Most infant primates, except for humans, can cling to their mothers from birth. Primates typically take a long time to mature. For example, the rhesus monkey is not sexually mature until about 3 years of age, the chimpanzee not until about age 9.

SOCIAL FEATURES

For the most part, primates are social animals. And just as physical traits such as grasping hands and stereoscopic vision may have developed as adaptations to the environment, so may have many patterns of social behavior. For most primates, particularly those that are **diurnal**—that is, active during the day—group life may be crucial to survival, as we will see later in this chapter.

DEPENDENCY AND DEVELOPMENT IN A SOCIAL CONTEXT. Social relationships begin with the mother and other adults during the fairly long dependency period of primates. (For the dependency period of primates, the infancy and juvenile phases, see Figure 3–2.) The prolonged dependency of infant monkeys and apes probably offers an evolutionary advantage in that it allows infants more time to observe and learn the complex behaviors essential to survival while enjoying the care and protection of mature adults.

Primates without a warm, social relationship with a mother or another individual do not appear

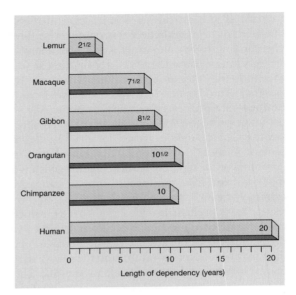

FIGURE 3–2   *A Comparison of the Dependency Periods of Primate Offspring*

Source: Data from Alison Jolly, *The Evolution of Primate Behavior,* 2nd ed. (New York: Macmillan, 1985), p. 292.

to develop appropriate patterns of social interaction. In a series of classic experiments with rhesus monkeys, Harry Harlow investigated the effects of maternal neglect and isolation on offspring.[5] He found that as a result of either inadequate mothering or isolation from other infants, some monkeys are unable to lead normal social lives. They develop aberrant sexual activities and may even become juvenile delinquents. Harlow mated socially deprived female monkeys with well-adjusted males. When these females gave birth, their behavior was not at all motherly, and they often rejected their babies entirely. Their abnormal behavior was offered as evidence that mothering is more than instinctive. Harlow's experiments underline the importance of maternal care and attention for monkeys and, as a corollary, for humans.

In many primate groups the mother is not the only individual providing care to the dependent young. Among gray langur monkeys, the birth and subsequent rearing of a baby absorb the attention of most female members of the troop.[6] And in some primate species, the father may expend as much time caring for infants as the mother.[7]

PRIMATES AT PLAY. Harlow's investigations have provided other information about social learning in young primates. The experiments that showed the importance of maternal care to baby rhesus monkeys also revealed that play is another crucial ingredient of normal development during the dependency period. Just as monkeys raised without mothers showed abnormal behavior as adults, so did monkeys raised with mothers but that lacked peers to play with. In fact, when some of the monkeys raised without mothers were allowed a regular playtime with peers, many of them behaved more normally. Subsequent work has supported Harlow's findings.[8]

Play is important for learning.[9] It provides practice for the physical skills necessary or useful in adulthood. For example, young monkeys racing through the trees at top speed are gaining coordi-nation that may save their lives if they are chased by predators later on. Play is also a way of learn-ing social skills, particularly in interacting and communicating with other members of the group. Some dominance relationships seem to be es-tablished partly through the rough-and-tumble games that older juveniles play, where winning depends on such factors as size, strength, and agility. These qualities, or the lack of them, may in-fluence the individual's status throughout adult life. (Other factors also help determine an individ-ual's status. For instance, the mother's status has been shown to be very important in some pri-mates.[10])

Applied Anthropology

ENDANGERED PRIMATES

In contrast to many human pop-ulations that are too numerous for their resources, many popula-tions of nonhuman primates face extinction because they are not numerous enough. The two trends—human overpopulation and nonhuman primate extinc-tions—are related. Were it not for human expansion in many parts of the world, the nonhu-man primates living in those habitats would not be endan-gered. Various lemur and other prosimian species of Madagas-car, the mountain gorilla and red colubus monkeys of Africa, and the lion tamarin monkeys of Brazil are among the species most at risk. Many factors are re-sponsible for the difficulties faced by nonhuman primates, but most of them are directly or indirectly the result of human activity. Perhaps the biggest problem is the destruction of tropical rain forest, the habitat of most nonhuman primates, because of encroaching agricul-ture and cattle ranching and the felling of trees for wood prod-ucts. The people who live in these areas are partly responsible for the threats to nonhuman pri-mates—population pressure in the human populations increases the likelihood that more forest will be cleared and burned for agriculture, and in some areas nonhuman primates are an im-portant source of hunted food. But world market forces are probably more important. The increasing need for "American" hamburger in fast food restau-rants has accelerated the search for places to raise beef inexpen-sively. There is also enormous demand for wood products from tropical forests; Japan imports half of all the timber from rain forests to use for plywood, card-board, paper, and furniture.

Some would argue that it is important to preserve all species. Primatologists remind us that it is especially important to preserve primate diversity. One reason is the scientific one of needing those populations to study and under-stand how humans are similar and different and how they came to be that way. Another reason is the usefulness of nonhuman pri-mates in biomedical research on human diseases; we share many of our diseases, and most of our genes, with many of our primate relatives. The film *The Planet of the Apes,* in which the humans are subordinate to the apes, tells us that the primates in zoos could have been us.

So how can nonhuman pri-mates be protected from us? There really are only two major ways: Either human population growth in many places has to be curtailed, or we have to preserve substantial populations of non-human primates in protected parks and zoos. Both are difficult but humanly possible.

Sources: Russell A. Mittermeier and Eleanor J. Sterling, "Conservation of Pri-mates," in Steve Jones, Robert Martin, and David Pilbeam, eds., *The Cambridge Encyclopedia of Human Evolution* (Cam-bridge: Cambridge University Press, 1992), pp. 33–36; Toshisada Nishida, "In-troduction to the Conservation Sympo-sium," in Naosuke Itoigawa, Yukimaru Sugiyama, Gene P. Sackett, and Roger K. R. Thompson, *Topics in Primatology,* vol. 2 (Tokyo: University of Tokyo Press, 1992), pp. 303–304.

LEARNING FROM OTHERS. We know that primates, nonhuman and human alike, learn many things in social groups. Among humans, children often imitate others, and adults often deliberately teach the young. In English we say, "Isn't it cute how Tommy 'apes' his father." But do apes (and monkeys) imitate others, or do they just learn to do similar things whether or not a model is observed? There is controversy among researchers as to how much imitation versus independent learning occurs in nonhuman primates. Even more arguable is whether deliberate teaching occurs among nonhuman primates.[11]

Primates can learn from direct teaching, but they learn mostly by imitation and trial-and-error.

Some fieldworkers have suggested that chimpanzees may learn by imitation to use tools. For example, Jane Goodall cited an occasion when a female with diarrhea picked up a handful of leaves to wipe her bottom. Her 2-year-old infant watched closely, and then twice picked up leaves to wipe its own clean behind.[12] Termite "fishing," using a grass stalk to withdraw termites from a termite mound, is probably the best known example of chimpanzee tool use. Immature chimpanzees in the wild have been observed to watch attentively and pick up stalks while others are "fishing." And mothers let their infants hold on to the stalks while the mothers "fish." But some observers do not think these reports provide clear evidence of imitation or teaching. Even though the mother lets the infant hold on to the "fishing" stalk, the infant is doing the activity with her, not watching it and then independently repeating it soon after.[13]

CLASSIFICATION OF PRIMATES

Classification provides a useful way to refer to groups of species that are similar in biologically important ways. Sometimes classification schemes vary because the classifiers emphasize somewhat different aspects of similarity and difference. For instance, one type of classification stresses the evolutionary branching that led to the primates of today; another the quantity of shared features. A third approach considers the evolutionary lines as well as similarity and difference of features, but not all features are equally weighted. More "advanced" and specialized features that develop in an evolutionary line are emphasized.[14] Figure 3–3 gives a classification scheme that follows this last approach, but this is not the only way to classify the primates.[15]

Despite the different ways to classify, there is generally little disagreement about how the various primates should be classified. Most of the disagreement, as we shall see when we discuss the various primates, revolves around the classification of tarsiers and humans.

The order Primates is often divided into two suborders: the **prosimians**—literally, premonkeys— and the **anthropoids.** The prosimians include lemurs, lorises, tarsiers. The anthropoid suborder includes New World monkeys, Old World monkeys, the lesser apes (gibbons, siamangs), the great apes (orangutans, gorillas, chimpanzees), and humans.

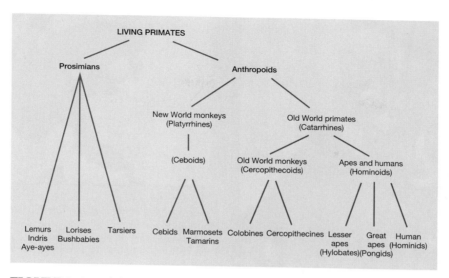

FIGURE 3–3 *A Simplified Classification of the Living Primates*

![icon] THE VARIOUS PRIMATES

Now that we have discussed their common features, let us focus on some of the ways in which the primates living in the world today vary.

PROSIMIANS

The prosimians resemble other mammals more than the anthropoid primates do. For example, the prosimians depend much more on smell for information than do anthropoids. Also in contrast with the anthropoids, they typically have more mobile ears, whiskers, longer snouts, and relatively fixed facial expressions. The prosimians also exhibit many traits shared by all primates, including grasping hands, stereoscopic vision, and enlarged visual centers in the brain.

LEMUR-LIKE FORMS. Lemurs and their relatives, the indris and the aye-ayes, are found only on two island areas off the southeastern coast of Africa: Madagascar and the Comoro Islands. These primates range in size from the mouse lemur to the 4-foot-long indri. Members of the lemur group usually produce single offspring, although twins and even triplets are common in some species. Many of the species in this group are **quadrupeds**—animals that move on all fours; they walk on all fours in the trees as well as on the ground. Some species, such as the indris, use their hind limbs alone to push off from one vertical position to another in a mode of locomotion called **vertical clinging and leaping.** Lemurs are mostly vegetarians, eating fruit, leaves, bark, and flowers. Lemur species vary greatly in their group size. Many lemur species, particularly those that are **nocturnal** (active during the night), are solitary during their active hours. Others are much more social, living in groups ranging in size from a small family to as many as 60 members.[16] An unusual feature of the lemur-like primates is that females often dominate males, particularly over access to food. In most primates, and in most other mammals, female dominance is rarely observed.[17]

LORIS-LIKE FORMS. Representatives of the loris group, found in both Southeast Asia and sub-Saharan Africa, are all nocturnal and arboreal. They eat fruit, tree gum, and insects, and usually give birth to single infants.[18] There are two major sub-families, the lorises and the bushbabies (galagos), and they show wide behavioral differences. Bushbabies are quick, active animals that hop between branches and tree trunks in the vertical-clinging-and-leaping pattern. On the ground they often resort to a kangaroo-like hop. Lorises are much slower, walking sedately along branches hand over hand in the quadrupedal fashion. With the use of searchlights and technical aids such as radio tracking, field researchers have learned a good deal about these nocturnal primates. For example, we now know that among bushbabies, females, particularly mothers and young adult daughters, stay together in small groups, whereas the males disperse. Newborns

Prosimians such as these ring-tailed lemurs depend much more on smell than do anthropoids. Prosimians also have more mobile ears, whiskers, longer snouts, and relatively fixed facial expressions.

Nocturnal tree-living tarsiers, like this one in the Philippines, are the only primates that depend completely on animal foods. Their enormous eyes equip them to find insects and other prey in the night. Their elongated ankle bones (tarsals) make them very good at vertical clinging and leaping.

are born in nests or hollows of trees (which related females may share), and mothers return to nurse them regularly. A few days after birth, a mother may carry her infant in her mouth to nearby trees, "parking" it while she eats.[19]

TARSIERS. The nocturnal, tree-living tarsiers, found now only on the islands of the Philippines and Indonesia, are the only primates that depend completely on animal foods. They are usually insect-eaters, but they sometimes capture and eat other small animals. They are well equipped for night vision, possessing enormous eyes, extraordinary eyesight, and enlarged visual centers in the brain. The tarsiers get their name from their elongated tarsal bones (the bones of the ankle), which give them tremendous leverage for their long jumps. Tarsiers are very skilled at vertical clinging and leaping. They live in family groups composed of a mated pair and their offspring. Like some higher primates, male and female tarsiers sing together each evening to advertise their territories.[20]

The classification of tarsiers is somewhat controversial. Instead of placing them with the suborder prosimians, as we have done here, some classifiers group tarsiers with anthropoids. In this other classification scheme the suborders of primates are labeled *strepsirhines* (which includes lemurs and lorises) and *haplorhines* (which includes tarsiers and anthropoids). Tarsiers have chromosomes similar to other prosimians; they also have claws for grooming on some of their toes, more than two nipples, and a uterus shaped like the uterus of other prosimians (two-horned). Like bushbabies, tarsiers move about through vertical clinging and leaping. In other respects tarsiers are more like the anthropoids. They have a reduced dependence on smell; not only are their noses smaller, but they lack the wet, doglike snout of lemurs. In common with the anthropoids, their eyes are closer together and are protected by bony orbits. Reproductively, the tarsier, like anthropoids, has a placenta that allows contact between the mother's blood and that of the fetus.[21]

ANTHROPOIDS

The anthropoid suborder includes humans, apes, and monkeys. Most anthropoids share several traits in varying degree. They have rounded braincases; reduced, nonmobile outer ears; and relatively small, flat faces instead of muzzles. They have highly efficient reproductive systems, including a placenta that is formed more fully than in any prosimian. They also have highly dextrous hands.[22] The anthropoid order is divided into two main groups: **platyrrhines** and **catarrhines.** These groups take their names from the nose shape of the different anthropoids, but as we shall see they differ in other features as well. Platyrrhines have broad, flat-bridged noses, with nostrils facing outward; these monkeys are found only in the New World, in Central and South America. Catarrhines have narrow noses with nostrils facing downward. Catarrhines include monkeys of the Old World (Africa, Asia, and Europe), as well as apes and humans.

NEW WORLD MONKEYS. Besides the shape of the nose and position of the nostrils, other anatomical features distinguish the New World monkeys (platyrrhines) from the catarrhine anthropoids. The New World species have three premolars, whereas the Old World species have two. Some New World monkeys have a prehensile (grasping) tail; no Old World monkeys do. All the New World monkeys are completely arboreal; they vary a lot in the size of their groups; and their food ranges from insects to nectar and sap to fruits and leaves.[23]

There are two main families of New World monkeys; one family contains marmosets and tamarins, the other cebid monkeys. The marmosets and tamarins are very small, have claws instead of

---

This howler monkey, like all platyrrhines, has a broad, flat-bridged nose. Platyrrhines live wild only in Central and South America and are arboreal.

fingernails, and give birth to twins who mature in about two years. Perhaps because twinning is so common and the infants have to be carried, marmoset and tamarin mothers cannot take care of them alone. Fathers and older siblings have often been observed carrying infants. Indeed, males may do more carrying than females. Marmoset and tamarin groups may contain a mated pair (monogamy) or a female mated to more than one male (polyandry). The marmosets and tamarins eat a lot of fruit and tree sap, but like other very small primates, they obtain a large portion of their protein requirements from insects.[24]

Cebids are generally larger than marmosets, take about twice as long to mature, and tend to bear only one offspring at a time.[25] The cebids vary widely in size, group composition, and diet. For example, squirrel monkeys weigh about 2 pounds, whereas woolly spider monkeys weigh more than 16 pounds. Some cebids have small groups with one male-female pair, others have groups of up to 50 individuals. Some of the smallest cebids have a diet of leaves, insects, flowers, and fruits, whereas others are mostly fruit-eaters with lesser dependence on seeds, leaves, or insects.[26]

OLD WORLD MONKEYS. The Old World monkeys, or **cercopithecoids,** are related more closely to humans than to New World monkeys. They have the same number of teeth as apes and humans. The Old World monkey species are not as diverse as their New World cousins, but they live in a greater variety of habitats. Some live both in trees and on the ground; others, such as the gelada baboon, are completely **terrestrial,** or ground-living. Macaques are found both in tropical jungles and on snow-covered mountains, and they range from the Rock of Gibraltar to Africa to northern India, Pakistan, and Japan. There are two major subfamilies of Old World monkeys.

COLOBINE MONKEYS. The colobine group includes Asian langurs, the African colobus monkeys, and several other species. These monkeys live mostly in trees, and their diet consists principally of leaves and seeds. Their digestive tracts are equipped to obtain maximum nutrition from a high-cellulose diet; they have pouched stomachs, which provide a large surface area for breaking down plant food, and very large intestinal tracts.

One of the most noticeable features of colobines is the flamboyant color typical of newborns. For example, in one species dusky gray mothers give birth to brilliant orange babies.[27] Observational studies suggest that the colobines are also unusual among the primates (except for humans) in that mothers let other group members take care of their infants shortly after birth. But males who are not members of the group are dangerous for infants; males trying to enter and take over a group have been observed to kill infants. Although this description may suggest that a one-male group is the typical group structure, there does not appear to be a typical pattern for a given species. When more than one site of a species has been studied, both one-male and multiple-male groups have been found.[28]

CERCOPITHECINE MONKEYS. The cercopithecine subfamily of monkeys includes more terrestrial species than any other subfamily of Old World monkeys. Many of these species are characterized by a great deal of **sexual dimorphism** (the sexes look very different); the males are larger, have longer canines, and are more aggressive than the females. Cercopithecines depend more on fruit than do colobines. They are also more capable of surviving in arid and seasonal environments.[29] Pouches inside the cheeks allow cercopithecines to store food for later eating and digestion. An unusual physical feature of these monkeys is the *ischial callosities,* or callouses, on their bottoms—an adaptation that enables them to sit comfortably in trees or on the ground for long periods of time.[30]

Studies of baboons and macaques suggest that closely related females form the core of a local group, or *troop.* In large groups, which are common among rhesus monkeys, many social behaviors seem to be determined by degree of biological relatedness. For example, an individual is most likely to sit next to, groom, or help an individual who is closely related maternally.[31] Moreover, a closely related subgroup is likely to stay together when a large troop divides.[32]

THE HOMINOIDS: APES AND HUMANS. The **hominoid** group includes three separate families: the lesser apes, or **hylobates** (gibbons and siamangs); the great apes, or **pongids** (orangutans, gorillas, and chimpanzees); and humans, or **hominids.** Several characteristics distinguish the hominoids from the other primates. Their brains are relatively large, especially the areas of the cerebral cortex associated with the ability to integrate data. The hominoids have several skeletal and muscular traits that point toward their common ancestry. All have fairly long arms, short, broad trunks, and no tails. Their blood proteins show many similarities, too. This blood likeness is particularly strong among chimpanzees, gorillas, and humans. For this reason, primatologists think chimpanzees and gorillas are evo-

A troop of baboons in Kenya spends most of its time on the ground.

lutionarily closer to humans than are the lesser apes and orangutans, which probably branched off at some earlier point.

GIBBONS AND SIAMANGS. The agile gibbons and their close relatives the siamangs are found in the jungles of Southeast Asia. The gibbons are small, weighing only about 11 to 15 pounds. The siamangs are somewhat larger, no more than 25 pounds. Both are mostly fruit-eaters, although they also eat leaves and insects. They are spectacular **brachiators;** their long arms and fingers let them swing hand over hand through the trees.[33] A gibbon can move more than 30 feet in a single forward swing.

Gibbons and siamangs live in small family groups consisting of an adult pair, who appear to mate for life, and one or two immature offspring. When the young reach adulthood, they are driven from home by the adults. There is little sexual dimorphism—males and females do not differ in size or appearance—nor is there any clear pattern of dominance by either sex. These lesser apes are also highly territorial; an adult pair advertises its territory by singing and defends it by chasing others away.[34]

ORANGUTANS. Orangutans survive only on the islands of Borneo and Sumatra. Unlike gibbons and siamangs, they are clearly recognizable as males or females. Males not only weigh almost twice as much as females (up to 200 pounds), but they also have large cheek pads, throat pouches, beards, and long hair.[35] Like gibbons and siamangs, orangutans are primarily fruit-eaters and arboreal. They are the heaviest of the arboreal primates, and perhaps for this reason they move slowly and laboriously through the trees. Orangutans are unusual among the higher primates in living basically solitary lives, except for mothers and their young; however, a recent field study of orangutans on Sumatra found that groups of as many as 10 adults fed together in the same tree.[36]

Different ideas have been proposed about the solitary habit of the orangutans that live in the mountainous areas of Borneo. One is that there may be insufficient food in any one tree or home range to support more than a single adult orangutan, a pretty large animal, as animals go. To obtain sufficient food each day without having to travel over a huge area, orangutans may therefore live alone rather than in groups.[37] Another idea is that animals live in groups when they are subject to heavy predation; the large size of orangutans may make them immune to attacks from most animals, so living alone may be a viable option.[38] A third idea, which on the face of it seems opposite to the second, is that living alone may be an adaptation to heavy predation by humans. The orangutan's best defense against humans with guns may be to hide alone in the trees.[39]

Except for mothers and their young, orangutans are unusual among the higher primates in living basically solitary lives.

GORILLAS. Gorillas are found in the lowland areas of western equatorial Africa and in the mountain areas of Congo, Uganda, and Rwanda.[40] Unlike the other apes, who are mostly fruit-eaters, gorillas mostly eat other parts of plants—stems, shoots (for example, bamboo), pith, leaves, roots, and flowers. The amount of fruit eaten by gorillas varies greatly. In many populations fruit-eating is rare; in some, however, fruit is a common part of the diet.[41] Gorillas are by far the largest of the surviving apes. In their natural habitats, adult males weigh up to 450 pounds and females up to 250 pounds. To support the weight of massive chests, gorillas travel mostly on the ground on all fours in a form of locomotion known as **knuckle walking:** They walk on the thickly padded middle joints of their fingers. Gorillas' arms and legs, especially those of the young, are well suited for climbing. As adults, their heavier bodies make climbing more precarious.[42] They sleep on the ground or in tub-shaped nests they make from nonfood plants each time they bed down.[43]

Gorillas tend to live in groups consisting of a dominant male, called a *silverback,* other adult males, adult females, and immature offspring. Both males and females, when mature, seem to leave the groups into which they were born to join other groups. The dominant male is very much the center of attention; he acts as the main protector of the group and the leader in deciding where the group will go next.[44]

CHIMPANZEES. Perhaps because they are more sociable and easier to find, chimpanzees have been studied far more than gorillas. Chimpanzees live in the forested areas in Africa, from Sierra Leone in the west to Tanzania in the east.

Although they are primarily fruit-eaters, chimpanzees show many similarities to their close relatives, the gorillas. Both are arboreal and terrestrial. Like gorillas, chimpanzees are good climbers, especially when young, and they spend many hours in the trees. But they move best on the ground, and when they want to cover long distances they come down from the trees and move by knuckle walking. Occasionally, they stand and walk upright, usually when they are traveling through tall grass or are trying to see long distances. Chimpanzees sleep in tree nests that they carefully prepare anew, complete with a bunch of leaves as a pillow, each time they bed down.[45]

Chimpanzees are only slightly sexually dimorphic. Males weigh a little more than 100 pounds on the average, females somewhat less. But males have longer canines. For some time it was thought that

Chimps in the wild, as in Ivory Coast, use tools—in this case, a stone to crack nuts. But as far as we know, they don't use tools to make other tools, as humans do.

that chimpanzees come together and drift apart depending upon circumstances such as the availability of food and the risk of predation.[50]

HOMINIDS. According to the classification we use here, the hominoids we call hominids include only one living species—modern humans. Humans have many distinctive characteristics that set them apart from other anthropoids and other hominoids, which lead many to place humans in a category separate from the pongids. These traits will be discussed later in this chapter and also throughout much of the rest of the book. However, others believe that the differences are not so great as to justify a separate hominid category for humans. For example, humans, chimpanzees, and gorillas are very similar in their proteins and DNA. And it is widely agreed that the lines leading to humans, chimpanzees, and gorillas diverged from a common ancestor perhaps 5 million to 6 million years ago.[51] Whether we stress the similarities or differences between humans and apes does not matter that much; what does matter is that we try to understand the reasons for those similarities and differences.

EXPLANATIONS OF VARIABLE PRIMATE ADAPTATIONS

Thus far we have discussed the common features of primates and introduced the different primates that survive in the world today. Now let us examine possible explanations, suggested by research, of some of the ways in which the surviving primates vary.

BODY SIZE

Surviving primates vary enormously in body size, ranging from the 2 or so ounces of the average gray mouse lemur to the 350 pounds of the average male gorilla. What accounts for this sizable variation? Three factors seem to predict body size—the time of day the species is active, where it is active (in the trees or on the ground), and the kinds of food eaten.[52] All the nocturnal primates are small. Among the primates active during the day, the arboreal ones tend to be smaller than the terrestrial ones. Finally, species that eat mostly leaves tend to be larger than species that eat mostly fruits and seeds.

Why do these factors predict size? One important consideration is the general relationship in mammals between body weight and energy needs. In general, larger animals require more absolute energy, but smaller animals require much more energy for their body weight. That being so, smaller

chimpanzees ate only plant food. Although most of their diet is vegetarian, a significant amount comes from meat. After three decades of studies at Gombe Park in Tanzania and elsewhere, researchers have found that chimpanzees not only eat insects, small lizards, and birds, but they actively hunt and kill larger animals.[46] They have been observed hunting and eating monkeys, young baboons, and bushbucks in addition to smaller prey. At Gombe, the red colobus monkey is by far the most often hunted animal. So it is not only humans who endanger other primates (see the box titled "Endangered Primates"); the red colobus monkey population is quite small in areas of intense chimpanzee hunting. Hunting appears to be undertaken more often during the dry season when food is scarce.[47] Prey is caught mostly by the males, which hunt either alone or in small groups. It is then shared with—or perhaps more accurately begged by—as many as 15 other chimpanzees in friendly social gatherings that may last up to nine hours.[48]

Despite considerable observation, the organization of chimpanzee social groups is still not clear. Groups usually are multimale and multifemale, but the size may range considerably from a few to 100 or so members. In Gombe, males typically remain in their natal group throughout life, and females often move to a neighboring group; but males in Guinea do not tend to stay in their natal groups.[49] It appears

animals (and small primates) need more energy-rich food. Insects, fruits, gum, and sap are full of calories and tend to be more important in the diet of small primates. Leaves are relatively low in energy, so leaf-eaters have to consume a lot of food to get enough energy. They also need large stomachs and intestines to extract the nutrients they need, and a bigger gut in turn requires a bigger skeleton and body.[53] Small primates, which eat insects and other rich foods, probably would compete with birds for food. However, most very small primates are nocturnal, whereas most forest-living birds are diurnal. Energy requirements may also explain why arboreal primates are usually smaller. Moving about in trees usually requires both vertical and horizontal motion. The energy required to climb vertically is proportional to weight, so larger animals require more energy to climb. But the energy for traveling horizontally, as on the ground, is not proportionate to weight, so larger animals use energy more efficiently on the ground than in the trees.[54] An addi-tional consideration is the amount of weight that can be supported by small tree branches, where foods such as fruits are mostly located. Small animals can go out to small branches more safely than large animals. Also, ground dwellers might be bigger because large size is a protection against predation.[55]

RELATIVE BRAIN SIZE

Larger primates usually have larger brains, but larger animals of all types generally have larger brains (see Figure 3–4). Thus primatologists are interested in *relative brain size,* that is, the ratio of brain size to body size.

Perhaps because human primates have the largest brain relatively of any primate, we tend to think a larger brain is "better." However, a large brain does have "costs." From an energy perspective, the development of a large brain requires a great deal of metabolic energy; therefore it should not be favored

FIGURE 3–4

As this graph shows, larger animals generally have larger brains. Primates generally have even larger brains than we would expect from their body weight. Note that most of the primates (as indicated by the colored circles) fall above the line showing the relationship between brain weight and body weight. The brains in primates are about twice as heavy as the brains of nonprimate mammals of the same body weight. *Source:* From Terrence W. Deacon, "Primate Brains and Senses" in Stephen Jones, Robert Martin, and David Pilbeam, eds., *The Cambridge Encyclopedia of Human Evolution* (New York: Cambridge University Press, 1992), p. 111. Copyright © 1992. Reprinted with permission of Cambridge University Press.

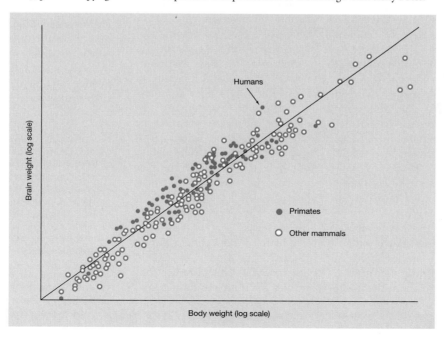

by natural selection unless the benefits outweigh the costs.[56]

Fruit-eating primates tend to have relatively larger brains than leaf-eating primates. This difference may be due to natural selection in favor of more capacity for memory, and therefore relatively larger brains, in fruit-eaters. Leaf-eaters may not need as much memory, because they depend on food that is more readily available in time and space, and therefore they may not have to remember where food might be found. In contrast, fruit-eaters may need greater memory and brain capacity because their foods ripen at different times and in separate places that have to be remembered to be found.[57] The brain requires large supplies of oxygen and glucose. Because leaf-eating primates do not have as much glucose in their diets as fruit-eating primates, they may also not have the energy reserves to support relatively large brains.[58]

GROUP SIZE

Primate groups vary in size from solitary males and females with young (in orangutans) to a few individuals and young (as in gibbons) to the 100 or so individuals in some Old World monkey troops.[59] What factors might account for such variation?

Nocturnal activity is an important predictor not only of small body size but also of small group size. Nocturnal primates feed either alone or in pairs.[60] John Terborgh has noted that most nocturnal predators hunt by sound, so a nocturnal animal might best avoid attack by being silent.[61] Groups are noisy, and therefore nocturnal animals might be more likely to survive by living alone or in pairs.

On the other hand, a large group might provide advantages in the daytime. The more eyes, ears, and noses a group has, the more quickly a would-be predator might be detected—and perhaps

Research Frontiers

RESEARCHER AT WORK: KATHARINE MILTON

Katharine Milton is Professor of Anthropology at the University of California, Berkeley, with an avid interest in the scientific study of monkeys. But that is far from how she started out. Born in Alabama, Katharine Milton went to Sweet Briar College in Virginia. She was an English major in college and went on to receive her M.A. in that subject at the University of Iowa. It wasn't until later, while she was living in Argentina, that she discovered her great interest in animal behavior and primates in particular. After receiving her Ph.D. from New York University, with a dissertation on the "economics" of the howler monkeys of Panama, she was fortunate to be able to study the woolly spider monkey—a little-known endangered monkey species living in southeastern Brazil. Because so little was known about them, she

started out doing a basic review of their diet and behavior. Woolly spider monkeys look like spider monkeys, so they were assumed also to be fruit eaters as are the spider monkeys. But Milton discovered through systematic observation over a year's time that this "commonsense" view was wrong. As she put it: "Apparently no one ever connected the short lifespan of captive woolly spider monkeys with the fact that perhaps, just perhaps, they were being fed the wrong food. Zoos, listen up—if you are ever fortunate enough to obtain a woolly spider monkey or two, be sure to give them leafy matter as their major dietary component, not ripe sugary fruits!"

Much of Katharine Milton's research has been devoted to understanding the implications of diet for both nonhuman and

human primates. Compared with fruit-eaters, leaf-eating primates are generally larger, require relatively less area to feed in, and have relatively smaller brains. Why? Milton suggested that despite the energy costs of a larger brain, the greater intellectual difficulties of remembering locations of dispersed high-quality food (for example, fruit, which provides more nutrients by weight than leaves) favored greater mental development in such primates.

Sources: Katharine Milton, "The Evolution of a Physical Anthropologist," in Carol R. Ember, Melvin Ember, and Peter N. Peregrine, eds., *Research Frontiers in Anthropology* (Upper Saddle River, NJ: Prentice Hall, 1998). Prentice Hall/Simon & Schuster Custom Publishing. Katharine Milton, "Foraging Behaviour and the Evolution of Primate Intelligence," in Richard W. Bryne and Andrew Whiten, eds., *Machiavellian Intelligence: Social Expertise and the Evolution of Intellect in Monkeys, Apes, and Humans* (Oxford: Clarendon Press, 1988), pp. 285–305.

avoided—and a larger group would have more teeth and strength to frighten or mob a predator that actually attacked.[62] But this line of reasoning would lead us to expect that all diurnal terrestrial species would have large groups. Yet not all do. Other factors must be operating. One seems to be the amount and density of food. If food resources occur in small amounts and in separate places, only small groups can get enough to eat; if food occurs in large patches, there will be enough to support large groups.[63] An additional factor may be competition over resources. One suggestion is that substantial but separated patches of resources are likely to be fought over, and therefore individuals living in larger groups might be more likely to obtain access to them.[64]

DISTINCTIVE HUMAN TRAITS

We turn now to some of the features that distinguish us—humans—from the other primates. Although we like to think of ourselves as unique, many of the traits we discuss here are at the extreme of a continuum that can be traced from the prosimians through the apes.

PHYSICAL TRAITS

Of all the primates, only humans consistently walk erect on two feet. Gibbons, chimpanzees, and gorillas (and some monkeys too) may stand or walk on two feet some of the time, but only for very short periods. All other primates require thick, heavy musculature to hold their heads erect; this structure is missing in humans, for our heads are more or less balanced on top of our spinal columns. A dish-shaped pelvis (peculiar to humans), straight lower limbs, and arched, nonprehensile feet are all related to human **bipedalism.** Because we are fully bipedal, we can carry objects without impairing our locomotor efficiency. (In Chapter 5 we consider the effects bipedalism may have had on such diverse traits as toolmaking, prolonged infant dependency, and the division of labor by gender.) Although many primates have opposable thumbs that enable them to grasp and examine objects, the greater length and flexibility of the human thumb allow us to handle objects with more firmness and precision.

The human brain is large and complex, particularly the **cerebral cortex,** the center of speech and other higher mental activities. The brain of the average adult human measures more than 1,300 cubic centimeters, compared with 525 cubic cen-

timeters for the gorilla, the primate with the next largest brain. The frontal areas of the human brain are also larger than those of other primates, so that humans have more prominent foreheads than monkeys or gorillas. Human teeth reflect our completely omnivorous diet and are not very specialized, which may reflect the fact that we use tools and cooking to prepare our food. Many other primates have long lower canines, which are accommodated by a space in the upper jaw; in humans, the canines both look and act very much like incisors, and there are no spaces between the teeth. The human jaw is shaped like a parabolic arch, rather than a U shape, as in the apes, and is composed of relatively thin bones and light muscles. Humans have chins; other primates do not. Humans are relatively hairless; other primates are not.

One other distinctive human trait is the sexuality of human females, who may engage in intercourse at any time throughout the year; most other primate females engage in sex only periodically, just around the time they can conceive.[65] Humans are also unusual among the primates in having female-male bonding.[66] Later, in the chapter on marriage and the family, we discuss some theories suggesting why male-female bonding, which in humans we call "marriage," may have developed. It used to be thought that more or less continuous female sexuality may be related to female-male bonding, but comparative research on mammals and birds contradicts this idea. Those mammals and birds that have more frequent sex are not more likely to have male-female bonding.[67]

Why, then, does human female sexuality differ from that of most other primates? One suggestion is that more or less continuous female sexuality became selectively advantageous in humans after female-male bonding developed in conjunction with local groups consisting of at least several adult males and adult females.[68] More specifically, the combination of group living *and* male-female bonding—a combination unique to humans among the primates—may have favored a switch from the common higher-primate pattern of periodic female sexuality to the pattern of more or less continuous female sexuality. Such a switch may have been favored in humans because periodic rather than continuous female sexuality would undermine female-male bonding in multimale/multifemale groups.

Field research on nonhuman primates strongly suggests that males usually attempt to mate with any females ready to mate. If the female (or females) a male was bonded to was not interested in sex at certain times, but other females in the group were, it seems likely that the male would try to mate with those other females. Frequent "extramarital affairs" might jeopardize the male-female bond and thereby presumably reduce the reproductive success of both males and females. Hence natural selection may have favored more or less continuous sexuality in human females if humans already had the combination of group living (and the possibility of "extramarital affairs") and marriage. If bonded adults lived alone, as do gibbons, noncontinuous female sexuality would not threaten bonding, because "extramarital" sex would not be likely to occur. Similarly, seasonal breeding would also pose little threat to male-female bonds, because all females would be sexually active at more or less the same time.[69] So the fact that the combination of group living and male-female bonding occurs only in humans may explain why continuous female sexuality developed in humans. The bonobo, or pygmy chimpanzee, female engages in intercourse throughout the year, but bonobos do not have male-female bonding and the females are not interested in sex as often as human females.[70]

Behavioral Abilities

In comparison with other primates, a much greater proportion of human behavior is learned and culturally patterned. As with many physical traits, we can trace a continuum in the learning abilities of all primates. The great apes, including orangutans, gorillas, and chimpanzees, are probably about equal in learning ability.[71] Old and New World monkeys do much less well in learning tests, and, surprisingly, gibbons perform more poorly than most monkeys.

TOOLMAKING. The same kind of continuum is evident in inventiveness and toolmaking. There is no evidence that any nonhuman primates except great apes use tools, although several species of monkeys use "weapons"—branches, stones, or fruit dropped onto predators below them on the ground. Chimpanzees both fashion and use tools in the wild. As we have noted, they strip leaves from sticks and then use the sticks to "fish" termites from their mound-shaped nests. They use leaves to mop up termites, to sponge up water, or to wipe themselves clean.

One example of chimpanzee tool use suggests planning. In Guinea, West Africa, observers watched a number of chimpanzees crack oil palm nuts with two stones. The "platform" stone had a hollow depression; the other stone was used for pounding. The observers assumed that the stones had been brought by the chimpanzees to the palm trees, because no stones like them were nearby and the chimps were observed to leave the pounding stone on top of or near the platform stone when they were finished.[72] Observers in other areas of West Africa have also reported that chimpanzees use stones to crack nuts. In one location in Liberia, an innovative female appeared to have started the practice; it seems to have been imitated within a few months by 13 others who previously showed no interest in the practice.[73]

In captivity, chimpanzees have also been observed to be inventive toolmakers. One mother chimpanzee was seen examining and cleaning her son's teeth, using tools she had fashioned from twigs. She even extracted a baby tooth he was about to lose.[74]

Humans have usually been considered the only toolmaking animal, but observations such as these call for modification of the definition of toolmaking. If we define toolmaking as adapting a natural object for a specific purpose, then at least some of the great apes are toolmakers too. As far as we know, though, humans are unique in their ability to use one tool to make another.

LANGUAGE. Only humans have spoken, symbolic language. But, as with toolmaking abilities, the line between human language and the communications of other primates is not as sharp as we once thought. In the wild, vervet monkeys make different alarm calls to warn of different predators. Observers playing back tape recordings of these calls found that monkeys responded to them differently, depending on the call. If the monkeys heard an "eagle" call, they looked up; if they heard a "leopard" call, they ran high into the trees.[75]

Common chimpanzees are also communicative, using gestures and many vocalizations in the wild. Researchers have used this "natural talent" to teach chimpanzees symbolic language in experimental settings. In their pioneering work, Beatrice T. Gardner and R. Allen Gardner raised a female chimpanzee named Washoe and trained her to communicate with startling effectiveness by means of American Sign Language hand gestures.[76] After a year of training, she was able to associate gestures with specific activities. For example, if thirsty, Washoe would make the signal for "give me" followed by the one for "drink." As she learned, the instructions grew more detailed. If all she wanted was water, she would merely signal for "drink." But if she craved soda pop, as she did more and more, she prefaced the drink signal with the sweet signal—a quick touching of the tongue with her fingers. Later, the Gardners had even more success in training four other chimpanzees, who were taught by fluent deaf users of American Sign Language.[77]

Bonobos, or pygmy chimpanzees, have recently provided strong evidence that they understand simple grammatical "rules," very much like 2-year-old humans. Pointing to graphic symbols for different particular meanings, a bonobo named Kanzi regularly communicated sequences of types of symbols; for example, he would point to a symbol for a verb ("bite") and then point to a symbol for an object ("ball," "cherry," "food").[78]

In the chapter on communication and language, we discuss the teaching of language to nonhuman primates (chimpanzees, gorillas) in more detail.

OTHER HUMAN TRAITS. Although many primates are omnivores, eating insects and small reptiles in addition to plants—some even hunt small mammals—only humans hunt very large animals. Also, humans are one of the few primates that are completely terrestrial. We do not even sleep in trees, as many other ground-living primates do. Perhaps our ancestors lost their perches when the forests receded, or cultural advances such as weapons or fire may have eliminated the need to seek nightly shelter in the trees. In addition, as we have noted, we have the longest dependency period of any of the primates, requiring extensive parental care for up to 20 years or so.

Finally, humans are unlike almost all other primates in having a division of labor by gender in food-getting and food sharing in adulthood. Among nonhuman primates, both females and males forage for themselves after infancy. Humans have more gender-role specialization, perhaps because men, unencumbered by infants and small children, were freer to hunt and chase large animals. We consider the possible causes and consequences of the gender division of labor among humans in the chapter on sex, gender, and culture.

Having examined our distinctive traits and the traits we share with other primates, we need to ask what selective forces may have favored the emergence of primates, and then what forces may have favored the line of divergence leading to humans. These questions are the subjects of the next two chapters.

SUMMARY

1. Although no living primate can be a direct ancestor of humans, we do share a common evolutionary history with the other surviving primates. Studying the behavioral and anatomical features of our closest living relatives may help us make infer-

ences about primate evolution. Studying distinctive human traits may help us understand why the line of primates that led to humans branched away from the line leading to chimpanzees and gorillas.

2. No one trait is unique to primates. However, primates do share the following features: two bones in the lower part of the leg and in the forearm, a collarbone, flexible prehensile (grasping) hands, stereoscopic vision, a relatively large brain, only one (or sometimes two) offspring at a time, long maturation of the young, and a high degree of dependence on social life and learning.

3. The order Primates is divided into two suborders: the prosimians and the anthropoids. Compared with the anthropoids, prosimians depend more on smell for information. They have mobile ears, whiskers, longer snouts typically, and relatively fixed facial expressions. Anthropoids have rounded braincases; reduced, nonmobile outer ears; and relatively small, flat faces instead of muzzles. They have highly dextrous hands.

4. The anthropoid order is divided into two main groups: platyrrhines (monkeys of the New World) and catarrhines. The catarrhines are subdivided into cercopithecoids (Old World monkeys) and hominoids (apes and humans). The anthropoid apes consist of the hylobates, or lesser apes (gibbons and siamangs), and the pongids, or great apes (orangutans, gorillas, and chimpanzees).

5. Along with the gorilla, the chimpanzee has proteins and DNA remarkably similar to that of humans, as well as anatomical and behavioral similarities to humans. Wild chimpanzees have been seen to create and use tools, modifying a natural object to fulfill a specific purpose. High conceptual ability is also demonstrated by both the chimpanzee's and the gorilla's facility in learning sign language.

6. Variable aspects of the environment, differences in activity patterns, and variation in diet may explain many of the traits that vary in the primates. Nocturnal primates tend to be small and to live alone or in very small groups. Among diurnal species, the arboreal primates tend to be smaller and to live in smaller social groups than terrestrial primates. Fruit-eaters have relatively larger brains than leaf-eaters.

7. The differences between humans and the other anthropoids show us what makes humans distinctive as a species. Humans are totally bipedal; they walk on two legs and do not need the arms for locomotion. The human brain, particularly the cerebral cortex, is the largest and most complex. In contrast to females of almost all other primates, human females may engage in sexual intercourse at any time throughout the year. Human offspring have a pro-

portionately longer dependency stage. And in comparison with other primates, more human behavior is learned and culturally patterned. Spoken, symbolic language and the use of tools to make other tools are uniquely human behavioral traits. Humans also generally have a division of labor in food-getting and food sharing in adulthood.

GLOSSARY TERMS

anthropoids	molars
arboreal	nocturnal
bipedalism	omnivorous
brachiators	opposable thumbs
canines	platyrrhines
catarrhines	pongids
cercopithecoids	prehensile
cerebral cortex	premolars
diurnal	prosimians
hominids	quadrupeds
hominoid	sexual dimorphism
hylobates	terrestrial
incisors	vertical clinging
knuckle walking	and leaping

CRITICAL QUESTIONS

1. How could you infer that a fossil primate lived in the trees?
2. Why are primates so smart?
3. Under what conditions would the ability to communicate be adaptive?
4. Why are humans immature for so long?

INTERNET EXERCISES

1. The Duke University Primate Center (**http://www.duke.edu/web/primate/index.html**) is devoted to research on and conservation of prosimians. Click on the Animals button and read about how prosimians differ from primates and the differences between lemurs, lorises, galagos, pottos, and tarsiers. Also use this site to find out which prosimians are most endangered.
2. Visit the Primate Gallery site at **http://www. selu. com/~bio/PrimateGallery/main.html** and read about the primate of the week. Look at the new images at **http://www.selu.com/~bio/PrimateGallery/new/images.html**.
3. Visit the *Great Ape Project* at **http://www. envirolink.org/arrs/gap/gaphome.html** and click

on the latest news reports. Read one of the reports of interest to you and summarize the article.
4. Want to hear some primate vocalizations? Go to the Web site at **http://www.indiana.edu/~primate/primates.html** and listen to vocalizations from a number of different primates.

SUGGESTED READING

GRAY, J. P. *Primate Sociobiology.* New Haven, CT: HRAF Press, 1985. A survey and discussion of empirical studies that tested 396 possible explanations, mostly derived from sociobiological theory, of many aspects of variation in primate behavior.

JONES, S., MARTIN, R., AND PILBEAM, D., EDS. *The Cambridge Encyclopedia of Human Evolution.* Cambridge: Cambridge University Press, 1992. About a third of this comprehensive book reviews current information about primate classification, conservation, aspects of and variation in physique, physiology, behavior, and cognitive abilities of the living primates.

MILTON, K. "The Evolution of a Physical Anthropologist." In C. R. Ember, M. Ember, and P. N. Peregrine, eds., *Research Frontiers in Anthropology* (Upper Saddle River, NJ: Prentice Hall, 1998). Prentice Hall/Simon & Schuster Custom Publishing. A personal account of how the author's interest in primatology emerged and developed over time.

PARKER, S. T., AND GIBSON, K. R., EDS. *"Language" and Intelligence in Monkeys and Apes: Comparative Developmental Perspectives.* New York: Cambridge University Press, 1990. A volume of 20 papers that apply frameworks from human developmental psychology and evolutionary biology to comparative studies of primate abilities.

ROWE, N. *The Pictorial Guide to the Living Primates.* East Hampton, NY: Pogonias Press, 1996. A beautiful successor to J. R. Napier and P. H. Napier's *Handbook of Living Primates* (New York: Academic Press, 1967), with a photograph or illustration of each of the living primates. This is the most complete collection of images yet published in a single source.

SMUTS, B. B., CHENEY, D. L., SEYFARTH, R. M., WRANGHAM, R. W., AND STRUHSAKER, T. T., EDS. *Primate Societies.* Chicago: University of Chicago Press, 1987. An extensive review, by some 50 primatologists, of primate species that have been studied in the wild.

STANFORD, C. "Chimpanzee Hunting Behavior and Human Evolution." In C. R. Ember, M. Ember, and P. N. Peregrine, EDS., *Research Frontiers in Anthropology* (Upper Saddle River, NJ: Prentice Hall, 1998). Prentice Hall/Simon & Schuster Custom Publishing. An in-depth look at chimpanzee hunting—what goes on, what predicts it, and what implications it has for understanding human evolution.

Primate Evolution: From Early Primates to Hominoids

CHAPTER OUTLINE

*P*rimate paleontologists and paleoanthropologists focus on various questions about primate evolution. How far back in time did the primates emerge? What did they look like? What conditions favored them? How did the early primates diverge after that point? What kinds of niches did the different primates occupy? Although our concern as anthropologists is largely with the emergence of humans, and with the primates that are in the ancestral line leading to humans, we must remember that evolution does not proceed with a purpose or to give rise to any particular species; rather, organisms adapt, or fail to adapt, to the environments in which they find themselves. Thus, the primate fossil record is full of diversity; it is also full of apparent extinctions. Probably most of the primate lineages of the past never left any descendants at all.[1]

The reconstruction of primate evolution requires the finding of fossil remains. Although many fossils have been discovered and continue to be discovered, the fossil record is still very incomplete. If geological strata are not uplifted, exposed by erosion, or otherwise accessible in the areas where ancient primates lived, paleoanthropologists cannot recover their fossils. The fossils that are found are usually fragmented or damaged, and judgments about what the organism looked like may be based on one or just a few pieces. As we shall see, piecing together the evolutionary history of the primates requires much more than recovering fossil remains. The knowledge gained from anatomical studies of living species can allow us to make inferences about physical and behavioral traits that are likely to have been associated with the fossil features. Dating techniques developed in geology, chemistry, and physics are used to estimate the age of fossil remains. And studies of ancient plants and animals, geography, and climate help us reconstruct the environments of ancient primates.

Although much of primate evolution is not yet known or is still controversial, there is a lot we do know. We know that as of the early Eocene epoch, which began about 55 million years ago, primates with some of the features of modern prosimians had already emerged (see Figure 4–1). Primates with monkey- and apelike features appeared in the Oligocene epoch, beginning about 34 million years ago. The Miocene epoch, beginning about 24 million years ago, saw the appearance of many different kinds of apes. The ancient primates we know

from fossils had some of the features of today's primates, but none of the ancient primates looked like the primates of today.

In this and the next two chapters we describe the main features of current theory and evidence about primate evolution, from the origin of primates to the origin of modern humans. In this chapter we deal with that part of the story before the emergence of definite bipedal hominids. Our overview covers the period from about 65 million years ago to the end of the Miocene, a little over 5 million years ago.

INTERPRETING THE FOSSIL RECORD

How can paleoanthropologists know about what may have happened millions of years ago? There is no written record from that period from which to draw inferences. But we do have another kind of evidence for primate evolution: the fossil record. And we have ways of "reading" the record left by fossils and of telling how old fossils are.

WHAT ARE FOSSILS?

A **fossil** may be an impression of an insect or leaf on a muddy or other surface that now is stone. Or it may consist of the actual hardened remains of an animal's skeletal structure. It is this second type of fossil—bone turned to stone—that has given paleoanthropologists the most information about primate evolution.

When an animal dies, the organic matter that made up its body quickly begins to deteriorate. The teeth and skeletal structure are composed largely of inorganic mineral salts, and soon they are all that remains. Under most conditions, these parts eventually deteriorate too. But once in a great while conditions are favorable for preservation—for instance, when volcanic ash, limestone, or highly mineralized groundwater is present to form a high-mineral environment. If the remains are buried under such circumstances, the minerals in the ground may become bound into the structure of the teeth or bone, hardening and thus making them less likely to deteriorate.

But we have fossil remains only of some species and sometimes only fragments from one or a few individuals. So the fossil record is very incomplete. Robert Martin estimates that the earth has probably seen 6,000 primate species; and remains of only 3 percent of those species have been found. It is hardly surprising that primate paleontologists cannot identify most of the evolutionary connections between

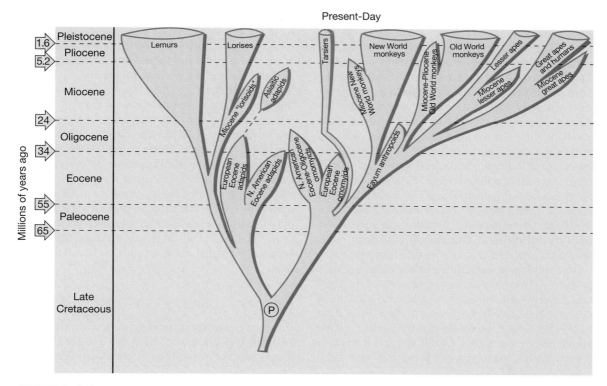

FIGURE 4–1

A view of the evolutionary relationships between early primates and living primates, adapted from one suggested by R. D. Martin. The primate lineages that do not extend to the present day indicate presumed extinctions. Branching from a common "stalk" suggests divergence from a common ancestor. Ⓟ represents the unknown common ancestor of all primates. *Source:* From Robert D. Martin, *Primate Origins and Evolution: A Phylogenetic Reconstruction* (Princeton, NJ: Princeton University Press, 1990). The dates for the Paleocene, Eocene, Oligocene, and the beginning of the Miocene are from William A. Berggren, Dennis V. Kent, John D. Obradovich, and Carl C. Swisher III, "Toward a Revised Paleogene Geochronology," in Donald R. Prothero and William A. Berggren, eds., *Eocene-Oligocene Climatic and Biotic Evolution* (Princeton, NJ: Princeton University Press, 1992), pp. 29–45. The dates for the end of the Miocene, Pliocene, and Pleistocene are from Steve Jones, Robert Martin, and David Pilbeam, eds., *The Cambridge Encyclopedia of Human Evolution* (New York: Cambridge University Press, 1992), p. 469.

early and later forms. The task is particularly difficult with small mammals, such as the early primates, which are less likely to be preserved in the fossil record than are large animals.[2]

WHAT CAN WE LEARN FROM FOSSILS?

Paleontologists can tell a great deal about an extinct animal from its fossilized bones or teeth, but that knowledge is based on much more than just the fossil record itself. Paleontologists rely on comparative anatomy to help reconstruct missing skeletal pieces as well as the soft tissues attached to bone. New techniques, such as electron microscopy, CAT scans, and computer-assisted biomechanical modeling, provide much information about how the organism may

have moved, the microstructure of bone and teeth, and how the organism developed. Chemical analysis of fossilized bone can suggest what the animal typically ate. Paleontologists are also interested in the surroundings of the fossil finds. With methods developed in geology, chemistry, and physics, paleontologists use the surrounding rocks to identify the time period in which the organism died. In addition, the study of associated fauna and flora can suggest what the ancient climate and habitat were like.[3]

Much of the evidence for primate evolution comes from teeth, which along with jaws are the most common animal parts to be preserved as fossils. Animals vary in *dentition*—the number and kinds of teeth they have, their size, and their arrangement in the mouth. Dentition provides clues to evolutionary relationships because animals with similar evolutionary histories often have similar teeth. For example, no primate, living or extinct, has more than two incisors in each quarter of the jaw. That feature, along with others, distinguishes the primates from earlier mammals, which had three incisors in each quarter. Dentition also suggests the relative size of an animal and often offers clues about its diet. For example, comparisons of living primates suggest that fruit-eaters have flattened, rounded tooth cusps, unlike leaf- and insect-eaters, which have more pointed cusps.[4] CAT scan methodology has helped paleontologists image the internal parts of teeth, such as the thickness of enamel, which can also suggest the diet. Electron microscopy has revealed different patterns of growth in bones and teeth; different species have different patterns.[5]

Paleontologists can tell much about an animal's posture and locomotion from fragments of its skeleton. Arboreal quadrupeds have front and back limbs of about the same length; because their limbs tend to be short, their center of gravity is close to the branches on which they move. They also tend to have long grasping fingers and toes (see Figure 4–2).

Terrestrial quadrupeds are more adapted for speed, so they have longer limbs and shorter fingers and toes. Disproportionate limbs are more characteristic of vertical clingers and leapers and brachiators. Vertical clingers and leapers have longer, more powerful hind limbs; brachiators have longer forelimbs.[6] Even though soft tissues are not preserved, much can be inferred from the fossils themselves. For example, the form and size of muscles can be estimated by marks found on the bones to which the muscles were attached. And the underside of the cranium may provide information about the proportions of the brain devoted to vision, smell, or memory. The skull also reveals information about characteristics of smell and vision. For example, animals that rely more on smell than on vision tend to have large snouts. Nocturnal animals tend to have large eye sockets.

DATING FOSSILS

In order to reconstruct the evolutionary history of the primates, one must know how old the primate fossils are. For some time *relative dating* methods

---

FIGURE 4–2

The forelimbs and hind limbs of *Proconsul africanus* (dating from about 20 million years ago) are about the same length, suggesting that it moved on all fours on the tops of branches. *Proconsul africanus* was the smallest of the *Proconsul* species, weighing about 22 to 26 pounds. *Source:* From A. Walker and M. Pickford, "New Postcranial Fossils of Proconsul Afficannus and Proconsul Nyananzae," *New Interpretation of Ape and Human Ancestry*, R. Ciochon and R. Corruccina (eds.), pp. 325–352, 1983. Reprinted with permission of Plenum Publishing Corporation.

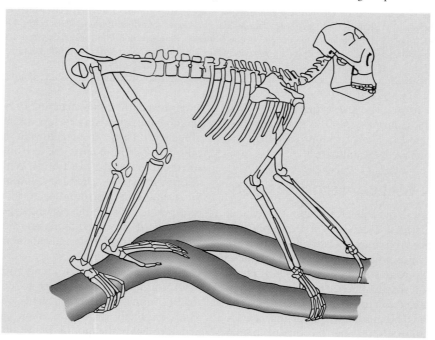

were the only methods available. The last 45 years have seen important advances in *absolute dating,* including techniques that allow the dating of the earliest phases of primate evolution.[7] **Relative dating** is used to determine the age of a specimen or deposit relative to another specimen or deposit. **Absolute dating,** or **chronometric dating,** is used to measure how old a specimen or deposit is in years.

RELATIVE DATING METHODS. The earliest and still the most commonly used method of relative dating is based on **stratigraphy,** the study of how different rock formations and fossils are laid down in successive layers, or strata. Older layers are generally deeper or lower than more recent layers. The most suitable indicator fossils for establishing a stratigraphic sequence for the relative dating of new finds are from animals *(fauna)* and plants *(flora)* that spread widely over short periods of time, or that died out fairly rapidly, or that evolved rapidly. Different animals and plants are used as indicators of relative age in different areas of the world. In Africa, elephants, pigs, and horses have been particularly important in establishing stratigraphic sequences. Once the stratigraphy of an area is established, the relative ages of two different fossils in the same or different sites are indicated by the associated flora and fauna.[8] Major transitions in flora and fauna define the epochs and larger units of geologic time. The dates of the boundaries between such units are estimated by absolute dating, described below.

If a site has been disturbed, stratigraphy will not be a satisfactory way of determining relative age. For instance, remains from different periods may be washed or blown together by water or wind. Or a landslide may superimpose an earlier on a later layer. Still, it may be possible using chemical methods to estimate the relative age of the different fossils found together in a disturbed site.

Three of the chemical methods used to date fossil bones relatively are the fluorine, uranium, and nitrogen tests, sometimes known as the **F-U-N trio.**[9] All are based on the same general principle: Bones and teeth undergo a slow transformation in chemical composition when they remain buried for long periods, and this transformation reflects the mineral content of the groundwater in the area in which they are buried. Fluorine is one mineral present in groundwater; therefore, the older a fossil is, the higher its fluorine content will be. Uranium, like fluorine, is also present in groundwater, so the longer bones or teeth remain in the ground, the greater their uranium content. The proportions are re-versed for nitrogen: The older the fossil is, the smaller the amount of nitrogen present in it. Thus, older bones have relatively higher concentrations of fluorine and uranium and less nitrogen than recent bones do.

But a problem can arise with the F-U-N tests because the mineral content of bones reflects the mineral content of the groundwater in the area. A 30-million-year-old fossil from a high-mineral area may have the same fluorine content as a 50-million-year-old fossil from a low-mineral site. So these chemical relative dating methods cannot be used to find the relative ages of specimens from widely separated sites. The F-U-N tests are restricted, then, to specimens from the same site or from neighboring sites.

Each of the chemical relative dating methods, used alone, can give only tentative evidence. But when the three methods are combined and confirm—that is, corroborate—one another, they are very effective. Of the three methods we have discussed, the uranium test is by far the most reliable when used alone. It is not strictly a relative dating method. There seems to be some consistency in the increase in radioactivity with age, even in bones from different deposits. The uranium test has another distinct advantage over the other tests. Because uranium is radioactive, measuring the radioactivity does not require the destruction of any part of the sample in testing.

ABSOLUTE, OR CHRONOMETRIC, DATING METHODS. Many of the absolute dating methods are based on the decay of a radioactive isotope. Because the rate of decay is known, the age of the specimen can be estimated, within a range of possible error. Radiocarbon, or carbon-14 (^{14}C), dating is perhaps the most popularly known method of determining the absolute age of a specimen. However, radiocarbon dating is not used to study early phases in primate evolution, for one important reason: The **half-life,** or rate of deterioration, of ^{14}C is relatively short. This means that radiocarbon dating usually is not accurate for anything more than 50,000 years old—and the primate paleontologist is interested in fossils as early as the late Cretaceous period, over 65 million years ago. The potassium-argon and argon-argon dating methods are more useful for studying primate evolution.

POTASSIUM-ARGON DATING AND ARGON-ARGON DATING. Potassium-40 (^{40}K), a radioactive form of potassium, decays at an established rate and forms argon-40 (^{40}Ar). The half-life of ^{40}K is a known quantity, so the age of a material containing potassium can be measured by the amount of ^{40}K compared with the amount of ^{40}Ar it contains.[10] Radioactive potassium's (^{40}K's) half-life is very long—1,330 million years. This means that **potassium-argon (K-Ar) dating** may be used to date samples from 5,000 years old up to 3 billion years old.

The K-Ar method is used to date potassium-rich minerals in rock, not the fossils that may be found in the rock. A very high temperature, such as occurs in a volcanic event, drives off any original argon in the material. Therefore, the amount of argon that accumulates afterward from the decay of radioactive potassium is directly related to the amount of time since the volcanic event. This type of dating has been extremely useful in east Africa, where volcanic events have occurred frequently since the Miocene.[11] If the material to be dated is not rich in potassium, or the area did not experience any high-temperature events, other methods of absolute dating are required.

One problem with the K-Ar method is that the amounts of potassium and argon must be measured on different rock samples; researchers must assume that the potassium and argon are evenly distributed in all the rock samples from a particular stratum. Researchers got around this problem by developing the ^{40}Ar-^{39}Ar **dating method.** After measuring the amount of ^{40}Ar, a nuclear reactor is used to convert another kind of argon, ^{39}Ar, to potassium so that the potassium/argon ratio can be measured from the same sample.[12]

FISSION-TRACK DATING. The **fission-track dating method** is another way to determine the absolute age of fossil deposits.[13] Like the K-Ar method, it dates minerals contemporaneous with the deposit in which fossils are found and it also requires the prior occurrence of a high-temperature event, as a volcanic eruption. But the kinds of samples it can be used to date—such as crystal, glass, and many uranium-rich minerals—include a much wider variety than those that can be dated by the K-Ar method. The age range of fission-track dating, like that of K-Ar dating, is extensive—20 years to 5 billion years.[14]

How does it work? This method is basically the simplest of all the methods discussed here. It entails counting the number of paths or tracks etched in the sample by the fission—explosive division—of uranium atoms as they disintegrate. Scientists know that ^{238}U, the most common uranium isotope, decays at a slow, steady rate. This decay takes the form of spontaneous fission, and each separate fission leaves a scar or track on the sample, which can be seen when chemically treated through a mi-

croscope. To find out how old a sample is, one counts the tracks, then measures their ratio to the uranium content of the sample.

The fission-track method was used to date Bed I at Olduvai Gorge in Tanzania, East Africa, where some early hominids were found.[15] It was able to corroborate earlier K-Ar estimates that the site dated back close to 2 million years. That the K-Ar and fission-track methods use different techniques and have different sources of error makes them effective as checks on each other. When the two methods support each other, they provide very reliable evidence.

PALEOMAGNETIC DATING. Most fossils of interest to anthropologists occur in sedimentary rocks, but the potassium-argon and argon-argon methods are suitable only for igneous rocks. When rock of any kind forms, it records the ancient magnetic field of the earth. When this knowledge is put together with the fact that the earth's magnetic field has reversed itself many times, the geomagnetic patterns in rocks can be used to date the fossils within those rocks. Strictly speaking, paleomagnetic dating is not an absolute dating method, but geomagnetic time periods have been dated absolutely in conjunction with potassium-argon dating. Paleomagnetic dating has dated primate finds from the Eocene and Miocene.[16]

In later chapters we discuss other methods of relative and absolute dating that are used for more recent finds.

THE EMERGENCE OF PRIMATES

When did the primates first emerge? This question turns out to be hard to answer from the current fossil record. Some paleoanthropologists have suggested that fossil finds from the **Paleocene** epoch, which began about 65 million years ago, are archaic primates. These are the *plesiadapiforms.* But other paleoanthropologists find so few similarities between them and later obvious primates that they do not include the plesiadapiforms in the order of primates.[17] There is no dispute, however, about fossils dating from the early **Eocene,** about 55 million years ago. These oldest definite primates appear in two major groups of prosimians—*adapids* and *omomyids.* Because these two kinds of primate are different from each other in major ways, and because they both appeared rather abruptly at the border of the Paleocene and Eocene, there presumably was an earlier common primate ancestor. But what it was is not yet known, or at least there is no

A reconstruction of smilodectes, *a primate found in western North America from 50 million years ago.*

consensus about it yet among paleoanthropologists. Even if we do not know exactly what the earliest primate looked like, the presence of the prosimians in the Eocene tells us that we need to look to an earlier time to explain the emergence of the primates. The circled *P* in Figure 4–1 represents the unknown common ancestor, which Robert D. Martin suggests lived in the late Cretaceous. Others think the common ancestor emerged in the Paleocene.

Now we turn to the conditions that may have favored the emergence of the primates.

THE ENVIRONMENT

It is generally agreed that the earliest primate may have emerged by the Paleocene, 65 million years to 55 million years ago, and perhaps earlier, in the late **Cretaceous.** What was the environment like in those times? The beginning of the Paleocene marked a major geological transition, what geologists call the transition from the Mesozoic to the Cenozoic era. About 75 percent of all animal and plant life that lived in the last part of the Cenozoic (the late Cretaceous) vanished by the early Paleocene. The extinction of the dinosaurs is the most famous of these disappearances.[18] (See the chapter on evolution for a discussion of these extinctions.)

The climate of the Cretaceous period was almost uniformly damp and mild, but temperatures began falling at the end of the Cretaceous. Around the beginning of the Paleocene epoch, both seasonal and geographic fluctuations in temperature began to develop. The climate became much drier in many areas, and vast swamplands disappeared. The climate of the Paleocene was generally somewhat cooler than in the late Cretaceous, but by no means cold. Forests and savannas thrived in fairly high latitudes. Subtropical climates existed as far north as latitude 62 in Alaska.[19] With changes in climate came changes in vegetation. Although the first deciduous (not evergreen) trees and flowering plants arose during the Cretaceous, it was during the late Paleocene and early Eocene that large trees with large fruits and seeds became common.[20]

Although some mammals date from the Cretaceous, the Paleocene saw the evolution and diversification of many different types of mammal. Primate paleontologists think primates evolved from one of these *radiations,* or extensive diversifications, probably from the **insectivore** order of mammals, including modern shrews and moles, that is adapted to eating insects.

The new kinds of plant life opened up sources of food and protection for new animal forms. In other words, new habitats became exploitable. Of most interest to us is that the new deciduous plant life provided an abundant food supply for insects. The result was that insects proliferated in both number and variety, and in turn there was an increase in insectivores—the mammals that ate the insects. The insectivores were very adaptable and were able to take advantage of many different habitats—under the ground, in water, on the ground, and above the ground, including the woody habitat of bushes, shrubs, vines, and trees. It was the last kind of adaptation, above the ground, that may have been the most important for primate evolution. The woody habitat had been exploited only partially in earlier periods. But then several different kinds, or *taxa,* of small animals, one of which may have been the archaic primate, began to take advantage of the woody habitat.

WHAT IN PARTICULAR MAY HAVE FAVORED THE EMERGENCE OF PRIMATES?

The traditional explanation of primate origins is called the *arboreal theory.* According to this view, the primates evolved from insectivores that took to the trees. Different paleoanthropologists emphasized different possible adaptations to life in the trees. In 1912, G. Elliot Smith suggested that taking to the trees favored vision over smell. Searching for food by sniffing and feeling with the snout might suit terrestrial insectivores, but vision would be more useful in an animal that searched for food in the maze of tree branches. With smaller snouts and the declining importance of the sense of smell, the eyes of the early primates would have come to face forward. In 1916, Frederic Wood Jones emphasized changes in the hand and foot. He thought that tree climbing would favor grasping hands and feet, with the hind limbs becoming more specialized for support and propulsion. In 1921, Treacher Collins suggested that the eyes of the early primates came to face forward not just because the snout got smaller. Rather, he thought that three-dimensional binocular vision would be favored because an animal jumping from branch to branch would be more likely to survive if it could accurately judge distances across open space.[21] In 1968, Frederick Szalay suggested that a shift in diet—from insects to seeds, fruits, and leaves—might have been important in the differentiation of primates from insectivores.[22]

Arboreal theory still has some proponents, but in 1974 Matt Cartmill highlighted some crucial weaknesses in the theory.[23] He argued that tree living is not a good explanation for many of the primate features because there are living mammals that dwell in trees but seem to do very well without primatelike characteristics. One of the best examples, Cartmill says, is the tree squirrel. Its eyes are not front-facing, its sense of smell is not reduced in comparison with other rodents, it has claws rather than nails, and it lacks an opposable thumb. Yet these squirrels are very successful in the trees. They can leap accurately from tree to tree, they can walk over or under small branches, they can go up and down vertical surfaces, and they can even hang from their hind legs to get food below them. Furthermore, other animals have some primate traits but do not live in trees or do not move around in trees as primates do. For example, carnivores, such as cats, hawks, and owls, have forward-facing eyes, and the chameleon, a reptile, and some Australian marsupial mammals that prey on insects in bushes and shrubs have grasping hands and feet.

Cartmill thinks, then, that some factor other than moving about in trees may account for the emergence of the primates. He proposes that the early primates may have been basically insect-eaters, and that three-dimensional vision, grasping hands and feet, and reduced claws may have been selectively advantageous for hunting insects on the slender vines and branches that filled the undergrowth of tropical forests. Three-dimensional vision would allow the insect hunter to gauge the prey's distance accurately. Grasping feet would allow the predator to move quietly up narrow supports to reach the prey, which could then be grabbed with the hands. Claws, Cartmill argues, would make it difficult to grasp very slender branches. And the sense of smell would have become reduced, not so much because it was no longer useful, but because the location of the eyes at the front of the face would leave less room for a snout. (See the box titled " Matt Cartmill Reexamines His Own Theory" for a discussion of his recent revision in response to criticisms.)

Robert Sussman's theory builds on Cartmill's *visual predation theory* and on Szalay's idea about a dietary shift.[24] Sussman accepts Cartmill's point that the early primates were likely to eat and move about mostly on small branches, not on large trunks and branches (as do squirrels). If they did, grasping hands and feet, and nails rather than claws (as squirrels have) would have been advantageous. Sussman also accepts Szalay's point that the early primates probably ate the new types of plant food (flowers, seeds, and fruits) that were beginning to become abundant at the time, as flowering trees and plants spread throughout the world. But Sussman asks an important question: If the early primates ate mostly plant foods rather than quick-moving insects, why did they become more reliant on vision than on smell? Sussman suggests it was because the early primates were probably nocturnal (as many prosimians still are): If they were to locate and manipulate small food items at the ends of slender branches in dim light, they would need improved vision.

We still have very little fossil evidence of the earliest primates. When additional fossils become available we may be better able to evaluate the various explanations that have been suggested for the emergence of primates.

THE EARLY PRIMATES: WHAT THEY LOOKED LIKE

The earliest definite (undisputed) primates, dating back to the Eocene epoch, appear abruptly in North America, Europe, and Asia about 55 million years ago. At that time many landmasses that are now separate were connected by land bridges. North America and Europe were connected by Iceland, Greenland, and the Faeroe Islands. Europe and North America became disconnected later in the Eocene. The beginning of the Eocene was warmer and less seasonal than the Paleocene, and vast tropical forests abounded.[25]

MATT CARTMILL REEXAMINES HIS OWN THEORY OF PRIMATE ORIGINS

Matt Cartmill originally conceived his visual predation theory to explain primate origins because he thought that the arboreal theory did not explain enough. Why do other animals, such as tree squirrels, manage very well in the trees, even though they don't have primate traits? Cartmill's theory attracted some criticism. How did he respond?

One criticism, by J. Allman, is that if visual predation is such an important predictor of forward-facing eyes, then why don't some visual predators have such eyes? Cats and owls have forward-facing eyes, but mongooses and robins do not. A second criticism, by Paul Garber, is that if claws were disadvantageous for moving on slender branches, why does at least one small primate—the Panamanian tamarin—feed on insects among small twigs and vines but have claws on four of its five digits? And Robert Sussman pointed out that most small nocturnal prosimians eat more fruit than insects. Sussman suggests that the need for precise finger manipulation to grasp small fruits and flowers at the ends of small branches, while hanging on by the hind feet, might favor both clawless digits and grasping extremities.

Cartmill acknowledged these problems and responded to them by revising his theory. He also suggests how new research could test some of the implications of his revised theory.

In regard to the problem of forward-facing eyes, Cartmill says that Allman's own research suggests a solution: namely, that forward-facing eyes are advantageous for seeing something in front more clearly in dim light. Daytime predators have eye pupils that constrict to see ahead more clearly, so fully forward-facing eyes are not necessary for daytime predation. Nocturnal predators relying on sight are more likely to have forward-facing eyes because constricting pupils would be disadvantageous. So Cartmill now believes that the earliest primates were probably nocturnal. And he now thinks that they also probably ate fruit (in addition to insects), as Sussman suggests, just as many contemporary nocturnal prosimians do. If they ate fruit and insects at the ends of small branches and twigs, claws may have been disadvantageous. The Panamanian tamarin is not a case to the contrary; it has claws, to be sure, but it also eats gum on the tree trunks to which it clings, using its claws as a tree squirrel does.

Cartmill thinks that his modified theory explains the changes in primate vision better than Sussman's theory. For example, how can we explain stereoscopic, forward-facing eyes in the early primates? Sussman says that the early primates were fruit-eaters, but Cartmill points out that, although stereoscopic, forward-facing eyes are not necessary for getting nonmoving fruit, they might be essential for catching insects.

Cartmill suggests how future research on other arboreal mammals may help us answer some of the remaining questions about the origins of primates. Arboreal marsupials, for instance, tend to have grasping hind feet with clawless divergent first toes, and many have reduced claws on some other toes and fingers. The eyes of arboreal marsupials are also somewhat convergent (not as much, of course, as the eyes of primates). One genus of marsupial, an opposum in South America (Caluromys), has many additional primatelike features, including a relatively large brain, more forward-facing eyes, a short snout, and a small number of offspring at one time. Studies by Tab Rasmussen suggest that Caluromys fits both Cartmill's theory and Sussman's because it eats fruit on terminal branches and catches insect prey with its hands. More field research on marsupials and other animals with some primatelike habits or features could tell us a lot more. So would new fossil finds.

Sources: Matt Cartmill, "Explaining Primate Origins," in Carol R. Ember, Melvin Ember, and Peter N. Peregrine, eds., *Research Frontiers in Anthropology* (Upper Saddle River, NJ: Prentice Hall, 1998). Prentice Hall/Simon & Schuster Custom Publishing. Matt Cartmill, "New Views on Primate Origins," *Evolutionary Anthropology,* 1 (1992): 105–11; Robert Sussman, "Primate Origins and the Evolution of Angiosperms," *American Journal of Primatology,* 23 (1991): 209–23; D. Tab Rasmussen, "Primate Origins: Lessons from a Neotropical Marsupial," *American Journal of Primatology,* 22 (1990): 263–77.

The anatomy of the diverse Eocene primates suggests that they already had many of the features of modern primates—for example, nails rather than claws, a grasping, opposable first toe, and a bony bar around the side of the eye socket.[26] Vertical clinging and leaping was probably a common method of locomotion. Eocene prosimians not only moved around the way modern prosimians do; some were similar skeletally to living prosimians.

Two groups of prosimians appear in the early Eocene. One group, called **omomyids,** has many tarsierlike features; the other group, **adapids,** has many lemurlike features. The omomyids were very small, no bigger than squirrels; the adapids were kitten- and cat-sized.

Omomyids are considered tarsierlike because of their large eyes, long tarsal bones, and very small size. The large eyes suggest that they were active at night; the smaller-sized omomyids may have been insect-eaters and the larger ones may have relied more on fruit.[27] Most of the omomyids have dental formulas characteristic of modern prosimians: two incisors and three premolars on each side of the lower jaw rather than the three incisors and four premolars of early mammals.[28] The importance of vision is apparent in a fossilized skull of the Eocene omomyid *Tetonius*. Imprints in the skull show that the brain had large occipital and temporal lobes—the regions associated with perception and the integration of visual memory.[29]

The lemurlike adapids were more active during the day and relied more on leaf and fruit vegetation. In contrast to the omomyids, adapid remains show considerable sexual dimorphism in the canines. And they retain the four premolars characteristic of

earlier mammals (although there are fewer incisors).[30] One adapid known from its abundant fossil finds is *Notharctus*. It has a small, broad face with full stereoscopic vision and a reduced muzzle. It appears to have lived in the forest and had long and powerful hind legs for leaping from tree to tree.[31]

There was a great deal of diversity among all mammals during the Eocene epoch, and the primates were no exception. Evolution seems to have proceeded rapidly during those years. Both the omomyids and adapids have a few features that suggest links between them and the anthropoids that appear later, in the Oligocene, but there is no agreement that either group gave rise to the anthropoids. Although the omomyids had some resemblances to modern tarsiers and the adapids had some resemblances to lemurs and lorises, paleoanthropologists are not sure that either group is ancestral to modern prosimians. But it is generally thought that the populations ancestral to lemurs and lorises as well as tarsiers did emerge in the Eocene or even earlier, in the late Paleocene.[32]

THE EMERGENCE OF ANTHROPOIDS

The anthropoids of today—monkeys, apes, and humans—are the most successful living primates and include well over 150 species. Unfortunately, the fossil record documenting the emergence of the anthropoids is extremely spotty, and there is no clear fossil record of the Old World forms (the catarrhines) in the two areas where they are most abundant today—the rain forests of sub-Saharan Africa and Southeast Asia.[33] Some paleoanthropologists think that recent Eocene primate finds from China, Southeast Asia, and Algeria have anthropoid affinities, but there is no clear agreement on their evolutionary status.[34] Undisputed remains of early anthropoids date from a somewhat later period, the early Oligocene, about 34 million years ago, in the Fayum area, southwest of Cairo, Egypt.

THE FAYUM OLIGOCENE ANTHROPOIDS

The Fayum is an uninviting area of desert badlands, but during the **Oligocene** epoch, 34 million to 24 million years ago, it was a tropical rain forest very close to the shores of the Mediterranean Sea. The area had a warm climate, and it contained many rivers and lakes. The Fayum, in fact, was far more inviting than the northern continents then, for the climates of both North America and Eurasia were

A reconstruction of Amphipithecus, *a primate from the later Eocene in Asia. Some paleoanthropologists consider it the earliest anthropoid, but its status is somewhat controversial. Definite anthropoids appear in the Oligocene.*

beginning to cool during the Oligocene. The general cooling seems to have resulted in the virtual disappearance of primates from the northern areas, at least for a time.

In addition to a prosimian family related to tarsiers, the Fayum yielded two main types of anthropoid: the monkeylike **parapithecids** and the apelike **propliopithecids.** Dating from 35 million to 31 million years ago,[35] the parapithecids and the propliopithecids had enough features to be classified as anthropoids.

The monkeylike parapithecids had three premolars (in each quarter), as do most prosimians and the New World monkeys. They are similar to modern anthropoids in the presence of a bony partition behind the eye socket, broad incisors, projecting canines, and low, rounded cusps on their molars. But they have prosimian-like premolars and relatively small brains. The parapithecids were small, generally weighing under 3 pounds; they resembled the squirrel monkeys living now in South and Central America.[36] Their relatively small eye sockets suggest that they were not nocturnal. Their teeth suggest that they ate mostly fruits and seeds. Locomotion is best known from one of the parapithecids, *Apidium,* an arboreal quadruped that also did a considerable amount of leaping.[37] There is still disagreement among paleoanthropologists as to whether the parapithecids preceded or followed the split between the New World monkeys (platyrrhines) and the Old World monkeys and apes (catarrhines). In any case, the parapithecids are the most primitive known anthropoids.[38]

The other type of anthropoid found in the Fayum, the propliopithecids, had the dental formula of modern catarrhines. This trait clearly places the propliopithecids with the catarrhines.[39] In contrast with the parapithecids, which had three premolars, the propliopithecids had only two premolars, as do modern apes, humans, and Old World monkeys. Propliopithecids shared with the parapithecids the anthropoid dental characteristics of broad lower incisors, projecting canines, and lower molars with low, rounded cusps. And, like parapithecids, propliopithecids had a bony partition behind the eye socket.

Aegyptopithecus, the best-known propliopithecid, probably moved around quadrupedally in the trees, weighed about 13 pounds, and ate mostly fruit. It had a long muzzle and a relatively small brain and showed considerable sexual dimorphism. Although its teeth and jaws are apelike, the rest of *Aegyptopithecus*'s skeleton is similar to that of the modern South American howler monkey.[40]

Because the propliopithecids lack the specialized characteristics of living Old World monkeys and apes (catarrhines), but share the dental formula of the catarrhines, some paleoanthropologists think that the propliopithecids included the ancestor of both the Old World monkeys and the hominoids (apes and humans).[41]

THE MIOCENE ANTHROPOIDS: MONKEYS, APES, AND HOMINIDS(?)

During the **Miocene** epoch, 24 million to 5.2 million years ago, monkeys and apes clearly diverged in appearance, and numerous kinds of apes appeared in Europe, Asia, and Africa. In the early Miocene, the temperatures were considerably warmer than the temperatures in the Oligocene. From early to late Miocene, conditions became drier.[42] We can infer that late in the Miocene, between about 8 million and 5 million years ago, the direct ancestor of humans—the first hominid—may have emerged in Africa. The inference about *where* hominids emerged is based on the fact that undisputed hominids lived in East Africa after about 5 million years ago. The inference about *when* hominids emerged is based not on fossil evidence but on comparative molecular and biochemical analyses of modern apes and humans.

One of the Miocene apes (known or unknown) was ancestral to hominids, so our discussion here deals mostly with the *proto-apes*—anthropoids with some apelike characteristics—of the early Miocene and the definite apes of the middle and late Miocene. But before we get to the apes, we should say something about monkeys and prosimians in the Miocene. Unfortunately, monkey fossils from the early Miocene are rare. In the New World, the whole Miocene fossil record is quite empty. There are only a few primate fossils found in Colombia and Argentina; they show close affinities with present-day South American monkeys. In the Old World, early Miocene monkey fossils have been found only in northern Africa. The situation is different for the middle and late Miocene: Old World monkey fossils become much more abundant than ape fossils.[43] As for prosimians, fossils from the Miocene are scarce, but we know that at least some adapids survived into the middle Miocene in India and the late Miocene in China.[44] Some lorislike prosimians appear in East Africa, Pakistan, and India during the Miocene.[45]

EARLY MIOCENE PROTO-APES

Most of the fossils from the early Miocene are described as proto-apes. They have been found mostly in Africa. The best-known genus is **Proconsul**, found in sites in Kenya and Uganda that are about 20 million years old.[46]

All of the various *Proconsul* species that have been found were much bigger than any of the anthropoids of the Oligocene, ranging from about the size of a gibbon to that of a female gorilla.[47] They lacked a tail. That lack is one of the most definitive features of hominoids, and most paleoanthropologists now agree that *Proconsul* was definitely hominoid, but quite unlike any ape living today. Modern hominoids have many anatomical features of the shoulder, elbow, wrists, and fingers that are adapted for locomotion by suspension (brachiation). Suspension was apparently not *Proconsul*'s method of getting around. Its elbows, wrists, and fingers may have permitted brachiation,[48] but, like the Oligocene anthropoids, *Proconsul* was primarily an arboreal quadruped (see Figure 4–2). Some of the larger forms may have sometimes moved on the ground. Most *Proconsul* species appear to have been fruit-eaters, but larger species may have also consumed leaves.[49]

If *Proconsul* is the best-known group of the many kinds of primates with some hominoid features from the early Miocene, some recent finds from East Africa suggest that other types of proto-ape were also on the scene. But these other finds are quite

Research Frontiers

WHAT HAPPENED TO *GIGANTOPITHECUS?*

In studying human evolution we tend to focus on the primate lineages that presumably are ancestral to modern humans and our closest primate cousins. There were, however, other primate lineages that left no apparent descendants but were very successful in the sense that they persisted for millions of years. The first definite primates, the omomyids and the adapids, first appeared early in the Eocene and stayed for more than 20 million years, much longer than bipedal hominids have been around! Why some primates were successful for so long is an important question; so is why they became extinct. To understand evolution, we need to investigate not only why some form may have survived for a while; we need also to investigate why it died out. For example, what happened to the largest primate, *Gigantopithecus*, that ever lived?

A paleoanthropologist, Russell Ciochon, and an archaeologist, John Olsen, have searched for clues to understanding the extinction of "Giganto," as they call it, who apparently left no descendants living in the world today. Ciochon and Olsen think that the largest form of *Gigantopithecus, G. blacki,* persisted for at least 5 million years and did not become extinct until about 250,000 years ago. And if you count earlier *Gigantopithecus* forms, the genus may have been around for nearly 10 million years. Ciochon and Olsen think it likely that Giganto and *Homo erectus,* a hominid that looked very much like modern humans from the head down, met up about a quarter of a million years ago in at least two Asian locations—now parts of China and Vietnam. The possible contact with *H. erectus* may have been partly responsible for the demise of Giganto.

What did Giganto look like? Reconstruction requires some guesswork, particularly with Giganto, because the only remains we have are teeth and jaw fragments. But we can reasonably infer some of Giganto's features and measurements from the body proportions of existing apes and the more complete fossil remains of extinct apes. Thus, it is estimated that Giganto was 10 feet tall and weighed about 1,200 pounds.

What did Giganto eat? Ciochon's guess is that Giganto mostly ate bamboo from the then-plentiful bamboo forests. The large size of the jaw, the wear patterns on the teeth, and the fact that large primates eat mostly foods with a lot of cellulose all suggest a diet of bamboo or something like it. Another kind of evidence suggests the same conclusion. A student had suggested to Ciochon that he look for phytoliths on the fossil teeth of Giganto. Phytoliths are microscopic granules of silicon dioxide that enter a plant's cells and take their shape. When the plants decompose, the phytoliths remain.

fragmentary and not clearly classifiable. *Proconsul* may or may not have been ancestral to later apes and humans, but given its combination of monkeylike and apelike features it may have looked a lot like the common ancestor of apes and humans.[50] (See also the chapter opener for a reconstruction of *Proconsul africanus*.)

MIDDLE MIOCENE APES

The first definitely apelike finds come from East Africa in the middle Miocene, 16 million to 10 million years ago. The fossils, on Maboko Island and nearby locations in Kenya, include several kinds of primate—a prosimian, several types of Old World monkeys, and a definite hominoid, **Kenyapithecus.**[51]

Kenyapithecus has many of *Proconsul*'s features, but its molars resemble those of more modern hominoids. And, in contrast to *Proconsul*, *Kenyapithecus* was probably more terrestrial. It also had very thickly enameled teeth and robust jaws, suggesting a diet of hard, tough foods, or possibly a great deal of grit in the food because it was found on the ground. Finds similar to *Kenyapithecus* appear in Europe and Turkey. Whether *Kenyapithecus* is ancestral to the later apes and humans is something of a puzzle. Its molars are more modern, but its limbs do not show the capacity for brachiation that is characteristic of all the later apes.[52] Then again, perhaps Sue Savage-Rumbaugh is correct in suggesting that the common ancestor of apes and humans was essentially a biped. According to her argument, knuckle

---

Different plants have phytoliths of different shapes. So, on the chance that phytoliths were on the fossil teeth from Giganto, the researchers looked microscopically at the teeth. They found phytoliths that belong to a family of grasses as well as phytoliths from a kind of fruit. Bamboo is a kind of grass, so the phytoliths found on the Giganto teeth are consistent with both bamboo- and fruit-eating. The teeth revealed something else too. Many of the teeth show pitting of the tooth enamel (hypoplasias), which suggests that Giganto suffered periodically from malnutrition. (Hypoplasias are produced by dietary insufficiencies.)

Bamboo forests are found almost everywhere in China and Southeast Asia, but for reasons not yet understood they dwindle every 20 years or so. If Giganto ate bamboo, it would have had a serious problem every so often, which is consistent with the hypoplasias. Could the extinction of Giganto be linked to something

that happened to the bamboo forests? Perhaps. Giant pandas, which are bamboo-eaters almost exclusively, are now at risk of extinction because of the spread of humans throughout China and Southeast Asia. Bamboo is used by humans for shelter, boats, tools, and food (bamboo shoots), and the bamboo forests are now drastically reduced. In their time, *H. erectus* may also have reduced the bamboo forests, thus contributing to the demise of Giganto. It is also possible that *H. erectus* hunted Giganto for food. This possibility is very speculative, but nonhuman primates have been hunted for food by many recent human societies. Like the giant panda, Giganto was probably very slow-moving and easy to hunt, as are most megaherbivores.

Humans in different places tell stories about huge, hairy, humanlike creatures—"Bigfoot" or Sasquatch in northwestern North America, the "Abominable Snowman" or Yeti of the Hima-

layas. Is it possible that Giganto is still around? Ciochon and Olsen point out that no recent Giganto bones have been found, so it is very unlikely that Giganto is still out there. But perhaps humans continue to believe it because they encountered Giganto in the not-so-distant past. After all, Australian aborigines still tell stories referring to events that happened more than 30,000 years ago.

What we do know is that *Gigantopithecus* persisted for a very long time, until humans came on the scene. Researchers have learned a lot about Giganto from very fragmentary remains. If more fossils are found in the future, we can expect that more will come to be known about the gigantic ape.

Source: Russell Ciochon, John Olsen, and Jamie James, *Other Origins: The Search for the Giant Ape in Human Prehistory* (New York: Bantam, 1990), pp 99–102. Used by permission of Bantam Books, a division of Bantam Doubleday Dell Publishing Group.

walking may have evolved as a mode of terrestrial lo-comotion only in later apes. Because they are knuckle walkers, living apes cannot make a snapping motion with the hand (which is called "abducting the wrist"), as humans uniquely can.[53] This last ability, along with other things hands can do if they are not in-volved in locomotion, may have been crucial in making complete bipedalism adaptive in the earliest humans, as we will discuss in the next chapter.

LATE MIOCENE APES

From the end of the middle Miocene into the late Miocene, the apes diversified and moved into many areas. Fossils are abundant in Europe and Asia, less so in Africa. This does not mean that apes were more numerous than monkeys. In fact, the fossil record suggests that monkeys in the Old World became more and more numerous than apes toward the end of the Miocene, and this trend continues to the present day. There are many more monkey than ape species now. The climate throughout the Miocene was turning cooler and drier, which proba-bly favored more drought-resistant plants with thicker cell walls. Modern monkeys tend to be more adapted than apes for eating leaves, so monkeys may have had an advantage in the changing environment toward the end of the Miocene, and since.[54]

Most paleoanthropologists divide the later Miocene apes into at least two main groups: *Siva-pithecus,* found primarily in western and southern Asia, and *Dryopithecus,* found primarily in Europe.[55]

Sivapithecus, known for its thickly enameled teeth, was remarkably similar to the modern orang-utan in the face, and is now thought to be ancestral to the orangutan. Its teeth, like those of *Kenyapithe-cus,* suggest a diet of hard, tough, or gritty items. The closely related *Gigantopithecus* was similar in its teeth, but, as its name suggests, it was huge, perhaps 10 feet tall if it stood up.[56] Some paleoanthropolo-gists suggest that *Gigantopithecus* weighed over 600 pounds and got even larger over the nearly 10 million years of its existence.[57] (See the box titled "What Happened to *Gigantopithecus?*")

Dryopithecus had thin tooth enamel, lighter jaws, and pointed molar cusps. In the palate, jaw, and midface, *Dryopithecus* looked like the African apes and humans. In contrast to later hominoids, however, *Dryopithecus* had a very short face and a relatively small brow ridge.[58]

The fingers and elbows of *Dryopithecus* and *Siva-pithecus* suggest that they were quite a bit more capable of suspending themselves than were earlier hominoids, but they did not have as much of that

Gigantopithecus probably lived mostly on bamboo. It is the largest primate known to us. The genus survived for about 10 million years and only became extinct 250,000 years ago. Bill Munns is shown here with the model of "Giganto" reconstructed by him and Russell Ciochon.

capacity as modern hominoids. *Sivapithecus* may have moved about more on the ground than *Dryo-pithecus,* but both were probably mostly arboreal.[59]

It is still very difficult to identify the evolutionary lines leading from the Miocene apes to modern apes and humans. Only the orangutans have been linked to a Late Miocene ape genus, *Sivapithecus,* so pre-sumably that lineage continued into modern times.[60] *Dryopithecus* disappears from the fossil record after about 10 million years ago, leaving no descendants, perhaps because less rainfall and more seasonality reduced the forests where they lived.[61]

THE DIVERGENCE OF HOMINIDS FROM THE OTHER HOMINOIDS

The later Miocene apes are best known from Europe and Asia. There is almost a complete gap in the African fossil record between 13.5 million and 5 million years ago.[62] This gap is unfortunate for our understanding of human evolution because the earliest known bipedal primates (hominids) appear in Africa near the beginning of the Pliocene, after 5 million years ago. To understand the evolutionary links between the apes of the Miocene and the hominids of Africa, we need more fossil evidence from late Miocene times in Africa.

However, we do have some idea about the transition to hominids. The molecular biology of the various modern primates suggests when the last common ancestor of humans and our closest primate relatives, chimpanzees, probably lived.

THE MOLECULAR CLOCK

In 1966, on the basis of biochemical comparisons of blood proteins in the different surviving primates, Vincent Sarich and Allan Wilson estimated that gibbons diverged from the other hominoids about 12 million years ago, orangutans 10 million years ago, and the other apes (gorillas and chimps) from hominids only 4.5 million years ago. These estimates depended on the assumption that the more similar in chemistry the blood proteins of different primates are—for instance, comparing chimpanzees and humans—the closer those primates are in evolutionary time. In other words, the more similar the blood proteins of related species, the more recently they diverged.[63]

But knowing that species are close molecularly does not translate into evolutionary time unless it is assumed that molecular changes occur at a constant rate. After all, a reliable "molecular clock" should not slow down or speed up from one period of time to another. To maximize the likelihood of molecular change at a constant rate, researchers try to examine molecular characteristics that are probably neutral in terms of adaptation. (Natural selection can speed up the rate of molecular change in the case of a characteristic that is very advantageous or very disadvantageous.) The rate of change in a neutral characteristic is calculated from the time of some divergence that is absolutely dated. For example, if we know that two lineages split 20 million years ago, and we know the degree of molecular difference between a contemporary representative of each, we can estimate the rate of change that produced that degree of difference. Given such an estimated rate of change (in a particular characteristic), we can estimate the amount of time that has elapsed since other pairs of related species diverged from each other.[64]

Subsequent comparative studies of the living primates have employed a variety of techniques, including comparisons of amino acid sequences, chromosomal structures, and the degree of matching of DNA strands from different species. These studies have confirmed the probable recency of the hominid divergence from chimpanzees and gorillas. Although the different techniques yield slightly different estimates, the results are not that divergent. Most of the recent comparisons place the split somewhat earlier than the Sarich and Wilson estimates, but not by much. The common ancestor of chimpanzees and hominids is estimated to have lived 5 million to 6 million years ago, the common ancestor of gorillas and hominids a little farther back.[65]

So what does the fossil evidence tell us about where and when hominids first emerged? Unfortunately, the answer is nothing as yet. For we still do not have any definitely hominid fossils in Africa from the end of the Miocene, 8 million to 5 million years ago, the presumed place and time hominids emerged. And definitely hominid fossils dating from the late Miocene have not been found anywhere else as yet. All we know for sure now is that primates with undisputably hominid characteristics lived about 4 million years ago in East Africa. We turn to these undisputed hominids in the next chapter.

SUMMARY

1. We cannot know with certainty how primates evolved. But fossils, a knowledge of ancient environments, and an understanding of comparative anatomy and behavior give us enough clues to have a tentative idea of when, where, and why primates emerged and diverged.

2. There are two general ways to date fossils. Relative dating methods, using stratigraphy and associated fauna and flora and certain chemical tests within sites, tell whether one find is about the same age (or older or younger) than another find. Absolute dating methods, such as potassium-argon, give the approximate age (in years ago) of a fossil or deposit.

3. The surviving primates—prosimians, New World monkeys, Old World monkeys, apes, and humans—are thought to be descendants of small, originally terrestrial insectivores (the order, or major grouping, of mammals, including modern shrews and moles, that is adapted to feeding on insects). However, exactly who the common ancestor was and when it emerged are not yet known.

4. Fossils dating from the early Eocene, about 55 million years ago, are definitely primates. They

appear to fall into two major groups of prosimians—adapids and omomyids. These two kinds of primate are different from each other in major ways, and they both appeared rather abruptly at the border of the Paleocene and Eocene, so their common ancestor would have had to emerge earlier, probably in the Paleocene.

5. What conditions may have favored the emergence of the primates? The proliferation of insects led to an increase in insectivores—the mammals that ate the insects, some of which lived above ground, in the woody habitat of bushes, shrubs, vines, and trees. Eventually, trees with large flowers and fruits evolved. The exploitation of resources in the woody habitat was probably the key adaptation in the emergence of the primates.

6. The traditional view of primate evolution was that arboreal (tree) life would have favored many of the common primate features, including distinctive dentition, greater reliance on vision over smell, three-dimensional binocular vision, and grasping hands and feet. A second theory proposes that some of the distinctive primate characteristics were selectively advantageous for hunting insects on the slender vines and branches that filled the undergrowth of forests. A third theory suggests that the distinctive features of primates (including reliance more on vision than on smell) were favored because the early primates were nocturnal and ate flowers, fruits, and seeds, which they had to locate on slender branches in dim light.

7. Undisputed remains of early anthropoids unearthed in Egypt date from the early Oligocene (after 34 million years ago). They include the monkeylike parapithecids and the propliopithecids with apelike teeth.

8. During the Miocene epoch (24 million to 5.2 million years ago), monkeys and apes clearly diverged in appearance, and numerous kinds of apes appeared in Europe, Asia, and Africa. Most of the fossils from the Early Miocene are described as proto-apes. From the end of the middle Miocene into the late Miocene, the apes diversified and spread geographically. Most paleoanthropologists divide the later Miocene apes into at least two main groups: *Dryopithecus,* found primarily in Europe, and *Sivapithecus,* found primarily in western and southern Asia.

9. The fossil record does not yet tell us who the first hominid was, but biochemical and genetic analyses of modern apes and humans suggest that the hominid-ape split occurred during the late Miocene (after about 6 million years ago). Because undisputed hominids lived in East Africa after about 4 million years ago, the first hominid probably emerged in Africa.

GLOSSARY TERMS

absolute dating or
  chronometric dating
adapids
^{40}Ar-^{39}Ar dating
  method
Cretaceous
Dryopithecus
Eocene
fission-track dating
  method
fossil
F-U-N trio
half-life
insectivore

Kenyapithecus
Miocene
Oligocene
omomyid
Paleocene
parapithecids
potassium-argon (K-
  Ar) dating method
Proconsul
propliopithecids
relative dating
Sivapithecus
stratigraphy

CRITICAL QUESTIONS

1. What an animal eats and how it gets its food are suggested by its skeletal anatomy. Discuss possible examples in the evolution of the primates.

2. Why do you suppose there are more monkey than ape species?

3. We like to think of the human lineage as biologically unique, which of course it is (like all evolutionary lineages). But some paleoanthropologists say that humans, chimpanzees, and gorillas are so similar that all three should be grouped as hominids. What do you think, and why do you think so?

INTERNET EXERCISES

1. Read at least one example from relative dating and absolute dating at **http://www.anthro. mankato.msus.edu/DATING/index.htm** and briefly describe how they can be used in anthropology.

2. Mary Leakey is best known for her work at Olduvai Gorge, where early hominids were found. But she also played a role in discoveries of anthropoids from the Miocene. Read the article about her at **http://www.sciam.com/explorations/ 121696explorations.html** and summarize what those discoveries were.

3. Go to **http://www.cruzio.com/~cscp/beard. htm** and read the article Searching for Our Primate Ancestors in China.

SUGGESTED READING

ANDREWS, P., AND STRINGER, C. *Human Evolution: An Illustrated Guide.* London: British Museum, 1989. A brief introduction to primate and human evolution, illustrated by reconstructions in color of many fossil finds.

BEGUN, D., "Miocene Apes." In C. R. Ember, M. Ember, and P. Peregrine, eds., *Research Frontiers in Anthropology* (Upper Saddle River, NJ: Prentice Hall, 1998). Prentice Hall/Simon & Schuster Custom Publishing. An up-to-date survey of the diversity among Miocene hominoids. Suggests that humans evolved from knuckle walkers.

CARTMILL, M. "Explaining Primate Origins." In C. R. Ember, M. Ember, and P. Peregrine, eds., *Research Frontiers in Anthropology* (Upper Saddle River, NJ: Prentice Hall, 1998). Prentice Hall/Simon & Schuster Custom Publishing. A review of the major theories of primate origins with a close look at criticisms of his own theory.

CONROY, G. C. *Primate Evolution.* New York: Norton, 1990. Conveys both the consensus and the points of disagreement in theories of primate evolution. Assumes some basic knowledge of physical anthropology or biology.

FLEAGLE, J. G. *Primate Adaptation and Evolution.* San Diego: Academic Press, 1988. A textbook that examines the comparative anatomy, behavioral ecology, and paleontology of humans and their nearest relatives. Chapters 9–14 are particularly relevant to this chapter.

FLEAGLE, J. G., AND KAY, R. F., EDS. *Anthropoid Origins.* New York: Plenum, 1994. Based on a conference, this book brings together technical information about recent discoveries and current theories concerning the origin and early evolution of anthropoid primates—monkeys, apes, and humans.

MARTIN, R. D. *Primate Origins and Evolution: A Phylogenetic Reconstruction.* Princeton, NJ: Princeton University Press, 1990. The author draws together findings from comparisons of living primates, the fossil record, and molecular evidence to make a provisional synthesis of primate phylogeny.

5

Early Hominids and Their Cultures

*U*ndisputed bipedal hominids lived in East Africa about 4 million years ago. These hominids, and some others who lived later in East and South Africa, are generally classified in the genus *Australopithecus.* And some East African hominids that are nearly 2.5 million years old are classified in our own genus, *Homo* (see Figure 5–1). In this chapter we discuss what we know or suspect about the emergence and relationship of the australopithecines and *Homo.* We also discuss the life-styles or cultures of the hominids from about 4 million until about 300,000–500,000 years ago, when the first members of our own species, *Homo sapiens,* may have emerged.

TRENDS IN HOMINID EVOLUTION

Perhaps the most crucial change in early hominid evolution was the development of bipedal locomotion, or walking on two legs (see Figure 5–2). We know from the fossil record that other important

physical changes—including the expansion of the brain, modification of the female pelvis to allow bigger-brained babies to be born, and reduction of the face, teeth, and jaws—did not occur until about 2 million years after the emergence of bipedalism. Other human characteristics, including an extended period of infant and child dependency and increased meat-eating, may also have developed after that time.

BIPEDALISM

We do not know whether bipedalism developed quickly or gradually, because the fossil record for the period between 8 million and 4 million years ago is very skimpy. We do know that many of the Miocene anthropoids, on the basis of the skeletal anatomy, were capable of assuming an upright posture. For example, brachiation, swinging by the arms through the trees, puts an animal in an upright position; so does climbing up and down trees with the use of grasping hands and feet. It is also likely that the protohominids were capable of occasional bipedalism, just as many modern monkeys and apes are.[1]

As we noted at the end of the last chapter, definitely bipedal hominids apparently emerged first in

---

FIGURE 5–1   *An Evolutionary Time Line*

Source: Stephen Jones, Robert Martin, and David Pilbeam, eds., *The Cambridge Encyclopedia of Human Evolution* (New York: Cambridge University Press, 1992), p. 454. Reprinted by permission of Cambridge University Press.

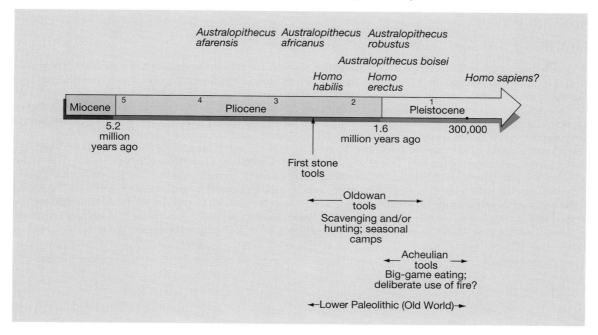

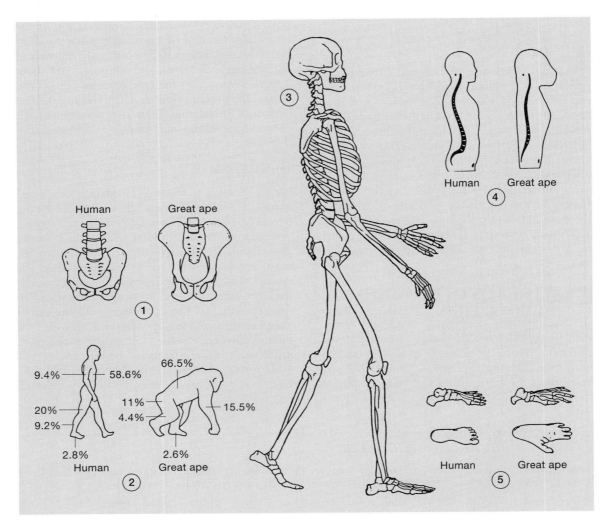

FIGURE 5–2 *Skeletal Evidence of Bipedalism*

Because humans move about on their legs only, the human skeleton differs from the skeleton of the great ape. The human head is more or less balanced on the backbone (see the feature marked 3 in the figure). There is no need for powerful muscles at the back of the neck, as in the great ape. The human vertebral column (see 4 in the figure) has a forward curvature in the neck and lower back regions. These two extra curves, along with the curvature in the middle back region, allow the backbone to act more like a spring, which is advantageous given that the legs have to bear all the weight and given the need to balance on one leg with each stride. Bipedal locomotion has favored a human pelvis (see 1 in the figure) that is lower and broader than the ape pelvis. In contrast to the apes, the legs in humans are longer than the arms and represent a larger proportion of the body weight (see 2 in the figure); this change lowers the body's center of gravity and is advantageous with bipedalism. The most obvious adaptation to bipedalism is the human foot (see 5 in the figure). The big toe is not opposed to the other toes, as in the other primates, and the foot can no longer grasp. When we walk, the big toe is the last point of contact with the ground before the leg swings forward, which explains why the big toe has become aligned with the other toes.   *Source:* From Stephen Jones, Robert Martin, and David Pilbeam, eds., *The Cambridge Encyclopedia of Human Evolution* (New York: Cambridge University Press, 1992), p. 78. Reprinted by permission of Cambridge University Press.

Africa. The physical environment in Africa was changing from extensive tropical forest cover to more discontinuous patches of forest and open country.[2] About 16 million to 11 million years ago, a drying trend set in that continued into the Pliocene. Gradually, the African rain forests, deprived of intense humidity and rainfall, dwindled in extent; areas of **savanna** (grasslands) and scattered deciduous woodlands became more common. The tree-dwelling primates did not completely lose their customary habitats, because some tropical forests remained in wetter regions, and natural selection continued to favor the better adapted tree dwellers in those forested areas. But the new, more open country probably favored characteristics adapted to ground living in some primates as well as other animals. In the evolutionary line leading to humans, these adaptations included bipedalism.

So what in particular may have favored the emergence of bipedal hominids? There are several possible explanations for this development. One idea is that bipedalism was adaptive for life amid the tall grasses of the savannas because an erect posture may have made it easier to spot ground predators as well as potential prey.[3] This theory does not adequately account for the development of bipedalism, however. Baboons and some other Old World monkeys also live in savanna environments, yet, although they can stand erect, and occasionally do so, they have not evolved fully bipedal locomotion. And recent evidence suggests that the area where early hominids lived in East Africa was not predominantly savanna; rather, it seems to have had a mix of woodland and open country.[4]

Other theories stress the importance of freeing the hands. If some hand activity is critical while an animal is moving, selection may favor bipedalism because it frees the hands to perform other activities at the same time. What hand activities might have been so critical?

Gordon Hewes suggested that carrying food in the hands was the critical activity; if it were necessary to carry food from one locale to another, moving about only on the hind limbs would have been adaptive.[5] Hewes emphasized the importance of carrying hunted or scavenged meat, but many paleoanthropologists now question whether early hominids hunted or even scavenged.[6] However, the ability to carry any food to a place safe from predators may have been one of the more important advantages of bipedalism. C. Owen Lovejoy has suggested that food carrying might have been important for another reason. If males provisioned females and their babies by carrying food back to a home base, the females

would have been able to conserve energy by not traveling and therefore might have been able to produce and care for more babies.[7] Thus, whatever the advantages of carrying food, the more bipedal a protohominid was, the more it might reproduce.

Bipedalism might also have been favored by natural selection because the freeing of the hands would allow protohominids to use, and perhaps even make, tools that they could carry with them as they moved about. Consider how advantageous such tool use might have been. Sherwood Washburn noted that some contemporary ground-living primates dig for roots to eat, "and if they could use a stone or a stick they might easily double their food supply."[8] David Pilbeam also suggests why tool use by the more open-country primates may have appreciably increased the number and amount of plant foods they could eat: In order to be eaten, many of the plant foods in the grassy areas probably had to be chopped, crushed, or otherwise prepared with the aid of tools.[9] Tools may also have been used to kill and butcher animals for food. Without tools, primates in general are not well equipped physically for regular hunting. Their teeth and jaws are not sharp and strong enough, and their speed afoot is not fast enough. So the use of tools to kill and butcher game might have enlarged even further their ability to exploit the available food supply.

Finally, tools may have been used as weapons against predators, which would have been a great threat to the relatively defenseless ground-dwelling protohominids. In Milford Wolpoff's opinion, it was the advantage of carrying weapons *continuously* that was responsible for transforming occasional bipedalism to completely bipedal locomotion.[10] In particular, Sue Savage-Rumbaugh has suggested that the ability to abduct the wrist would have permitted early humans "to perfect both throwing and rock-striking skills [for tool-making] and consequently to develop throwing as a much more effective predator defense system than apes could ever manage."[11]

But some anthropologists question the idea that tool use and toolmaking favored bipedalism. They point out that our first evidence of stone tools appears perhaps a million years *after* the emergence of bipedalism. So how could toolmaking be responsible for bipedalism? Wolpoff suggests an answer. Even though bipedalism appears to be at least a million years older than stone tools, it is not unlikely that protohominids used tools made of wood and bone, neither of which would be as likely as stone to survive in the archaeological record. Moreover, unmodified stone tools present in the archaeological record might not be recognizable as tools.[12]

Some researchers have taken a closer look at the mechanics of bipedal locomotion to see if it might be a more efficient form of locomotion in the savanna-woodland environment, where resources are likely to be scattered. Compared with the quadrapedal locomotion of primates such as chimpanzees, bipedalism appears to be more efficient for long-distance travel. But why travel long distances? If the ancestors of humans had the manipulative ability and tool-using capability of modern chimpanzees (for example, using stones to crack nuts) *and* those ancestors had to move around in a more open environment, then those individuals who could more efficiently travel longer distances to exploit those resources might do better.[13]

All theories about the origin of bipedalism are speculative. We do not yet have direct evidence that any of the factors we have discussed were actually responsible for bipedalism. Any or all of these factors—being able to see far, carrying food back to a home base, carrying tools that included weapons, or more efficient long-distance traveling—may explain the transformation of an occasionally bipedal protohominid to a completely bipedal hominid.

We must remember that there are also "costs" to bipedal walking. Bipedalism makes it harder to overcome gravity to supply the brain with sufficient blood,[14] and the weight of the body above the pelvis and lower limbs puts greater stress on the hips,

---

We do not know what the common ancestor of humans and chimpanzees looked like, but this computerized image of a hybrid between a modern human and a modern chimpanzee face hauntingly reminds us that we are not that far apart.

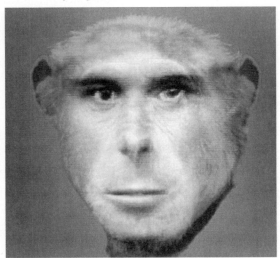

lower back, knees, and feet. As Adrienne Zihlman points out, the stresses on the lower body are even greater for females. Females have to support extra weight during pregnancy, and as mothers they usually are responsible for carrying nursing infants. So whatever the advantages of bipedalism, they must be greater than the disadvantages—or our ancestors never would have become bipedal.[15]

EXPANSION OF THE BRAIN

The first definitely bipedal hominids, the australopithecines, had relatively small cranial capacities, ranging from about 380 to 530 cubic centimeters (cc)—not much larger than that of chimpanzees. But around 2 million years ago, half a million years after stone tools appear, some hominids showed evidence of enlarged brain capacity. These hominids, classified as early members of our genus, *Homo (H. habilis),* had cranial capacities averaging about 630–640 cc, which is about 50 percent of the brain capacity of modern humans (average slightly more than 1,300 cc). (See Figure 5–3.) A later member of our genus, *Homo erectus,* which may have first appeared about 1.8 million years ago, had a cranial capacity averaging about 895–1,040 cc, or about 70 percent of the brain capacity of modern humans.[16]

The australopithecines were small, and the earliest *Homo* finds were hardly bigger, so much of the increase in brain size over time might have been a result of later hominids' bigger bodies. When we correct for body size, however, it turns out that brain size increased not only absolutely but also relatively after 2 million years ago. Between about 4 million and 2 million years ago, relative brain size remained just about the same. Only in the last 2 million years has the hominid brain doubled in relative size, and tripled in absolute size.[17]

What may have favored the increase in brain size? Many anthropologists think that the increase is linked to the emergence of stone toolmaking about 2.5 million years ago. The reasoning is that stone toolmaking was important for the survival of our ancestors, and therefore natural selection would have favored bigger-brained individuals because they had motor and conceptual skills that enabled them to be better toolmakers. According to this view, the expansion of the brain and more and more sophisticated toolmaking would have developed together. Other anthropologists think that the expansion of the brain may have been favored by other factors, such as warfare, hunting, longer life, and language.[18]

Whatever the factors selecting for bigger brains, natural selection also favored the widening of the

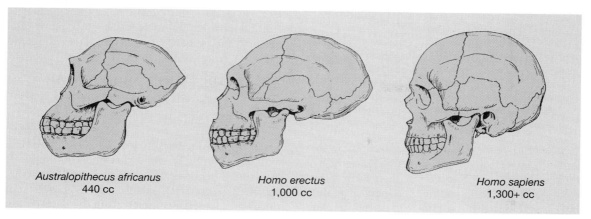

FIGURE 5–3

Comparison of the estimated cranial capacities of *Australopithecus africanus*, *Homo erectus*, and *Homo sapiens*, demonstrating the expansion of the brain in hominid evolution. *Source:* Estimated cranial capacities from Ian Tattersall, Eric Delson, and John van Couvering, eds., *Encyclopedia of Human Evolution and Prehistory* (New York: Garland, 1988), pp. 80, 263, 268.

female pelvis to allow larger-brained babies to be born. But there was probably a limit to how far the pelvis could widen and still be adapted to bipedalism. Something had to give, and that something was the degree of physical development of the human infant at birth—for instance, the human infant is born with cranial bones so plastic that they can overlap. Because birth takes place before the cranial bones have hardened, the human infant with its relatively large brain can pass through the opening in the mother's pelvis.

REDUCTION OF THE FACE, TEETH, AND JAWS

As in the case of the brain, substantial changes in the face, teeth, and jaws do not appear in hominid evolution until after about 2 million years ago. The australopithecines all have cheek teeth that are very large relative to their estimated body weight. The diet of the australopithecines may have been especially high in plant foods,[19] including small, tough objects such as seeds, roots, and tubers. The australopithecines have thick jawbones, probably also related to their chewing needs. The earlier australopithecines have relatively large faces that project forward below the eyes. It is particularly in the *Homo* forms that we see reduction in the size of the face, cheek teeth, and jaws. It would seem that natural selection in favor of a bigger and stronger chewing apparatus was relaxed, perhaps because human control over fire and the development of cooking made various kinds of food easier to chew. If food is cooked and easy to chew, individual

humans with smaller jaws and teeth would not be disadvantaged, and therefore the face, cheek teeth, and jaw would get smaller on average over time.

OTHER EVOLVED TRAITS

The fossil evidence, which we discuss shortly, suggests when, and in which hominids, changes occurred in brain size and in the face, teeth, and jaws. Other changes in the evolution of hominids cannot yet be confidently dated with regard to time and particular hominid. For example, we know that modern humans are relatively hairless compared with the other surviving primates. But we do not know when hominids became relatively hairless, because fossilized bones do not tell us whether their owners were hairy. On the other hand, we suspect that most of the other characteristically human traits developed after the brain began to increase in size, during the evolution of the genus *Homo*. These changes include the extension of the period of infant and child dependency, the scavenging and hunting of meat, the development of a division of labor by gender, and the sharing of food.

One of the possible consequences of brain expansion was the lessening of maturity at birth, as we have noted. That babies were born more immature may at least partly explain the lengthening of the period of infant and child dependency in hominids. Compared with other animals, we spend not only a longer proportion of our life span, but also the longest absolute period, in a dependent state. Prolonged infant dependency has probably been of great significance in human cultural evolution. According to Theodosius Dobzhansky,

> it is this helplessness and prolonged dependence on the ministrations of the parents and other persons that favors . . . the socialization and learning process on which the transmission of culture wholly depends. This may have been an overwhelming advantage of the human growth pattern in the process of evolution.[20]

It used to be thought that the australopithecines had a long period of infant dependency, just as modern humans do, but the way their teeth apparently developed suggests that the early australopithecines followed an apelike pattern of development. Thus, prolonged maturation may be relatively recent, but just how recent is not yet known.[21]

Although some use of tools for digging, defense, scavenging, or hunting may have influenced the development of bipedalism, full bipedalism may have made possible more efficient toolmaking and consequently more efficient scavenging and hunting. As we shall see, there are archaeological signs that early hominids may have been scavenging and hunting animals at least as far back as Lower Pleistocene times. We have fairly good evidence that *Homo erectus* was butchering and presumably eating big game after a million years ago. Whether the big game were hunted is not clear.

Whenever it was that hominids began to hunt regularly, the development of hunting, combined with longer infant and child dependency, may have fostered a division of labor by gender. The demands of nursing might have made it difficult for women to hunt. Certainly, it would have been awkward, if not impossible, for a mother carrying a nursing child to chase animals. Alternatively, if she left the child at home, she would not have been able to travel very far to hunt. Because the men would have been freer to roam farther from home, they probably became the hunters. While the men were away hunting, the women may have gathered wild plants within an area that could be covered in a few hours.

The division of labor by gender may have increased the likelihood of food-sharing. If men primarily hunted and women primarily gathered plant foods, the only way each gender could obtain a complete diet would have been to share the results of their respective labors.

What is the evidence that the physical and cultural changes we have been discussing occurred during the evolution of the hominids? We shall now trace the sequence of known hominid fossils and how they are associated with the development of bipedalism, brain expansion, and reduction of the face, jaws, and teeth. We also trace the sequence of cultural changes in toolmaking, scavenging and hunting, and other aspects of cultural development.

AUSTRALOPITHECINES: THE EARLIEST DEFINITE HOMINIDS

Fossil finds from East Africa—Ethiopia, Tanzania, and Kenya—clearly show that bipedal hominids lived there between 4 million and 3 million years ago, perhaps even earlier. Since the 1960s, important discoveries have come mostly from the East African Rift system, an area where the underlying plates of the earth are pulling away from each other. In many places the Rift Valley drops precipitously from the rim, exposing layers and layers of older rock. See Figure 5–4 for some sites where australopithecines have been found. The current environment of a fossil site may hardly resemble the reconstructed environment of millions of years ago. For example, Hadar, in the Afar Depression of north-central Ethiopia, has yielded a large number of fossil hominids. It is now one of the hottest and driest places on earth, but Hadar used to be a slightly to fully wooded area[22] on the margin of an extensive lake.[23]

At Laetoli, Tanzania, more than 50 hardened humanlike footprints from about 3.6 million years old give striking confirmation that the hominids there were fully bipedal. But their bipedalism does not mean that these earliest definite hominids were completely terrestrial. All of the australopithecines, including the later ones, seem to have been capable of climbing and moving in trees, judging by arm versus leg lengths and other skeletal features.[24]

The australopithecines of Africa show considerable variability, and paleoanthropologists divide the genus *Australopithecus* into at least four species.[25] And there may have been six different species. One called **Australopithecus anamensis** (east of Lake Turkana in Kenya) may be 4.2 million years old. The hominids found in East Africa from 4 million to 3 million years ago are classified by most paleoanthropologists as belonging to the species **Australopithecus afarensis.** Some paleoanthropologists do not think that these hominids should be placed in a separate species, because they resemble the later hominid species **Australopithecus africanus,** which lived between about 3 million and 2 million years ago. And then there were the robust australopithecines who lived between 2.5 million and 1 million years ago. Most paleoanthropologists think that the robust australopithecines consist of two

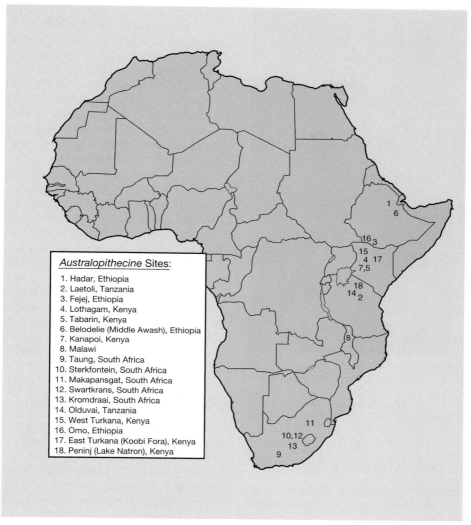

FIGURE 5–4 *Australopithecine Sites*

Source: From Russell L. Ciochon and John G. Fleagle, eds., *The Human Evolution Source Book* (Englewood Cliffs, NJ: Prentice Hall, 1993), p. ix.

species: the East African species *Australopithecus boisei* and the South African species *Australopithecus robustus.* And there may have been an even earlier robust australopithecine, *A. aethiopicus.*

Recently, Ethiopia has yielded a fossil find from 4.5 million years ago that has paleoanthropologists intrigued.[26] Is it a link between a Miocene ape and the australopithecines who lived about 4 million years ago? Or is it an australopithecine? Some paleoanthropologists have classified the new find as an early australopithecine, *A. ramidus;* others put it in a different genus, *Ardipithecus ramidus.* But it is difficult to tell from the few available bones whether

ramidus was mostly or only intermittently bipedal. So we will have to wait to see how far back bipedalism goes.

Which of the australopithecines was ancestral to our own genus, *Homo?* Here, too, there is controversy, as we shall see. Whatever the ancestry of *Homo,* fossils so classified date from about 2 million years ago.

Although the oldest australopithecine fossils come from East Africa, they were not the first australopithecine discoveries. The first finds called *Australopithecus* were discovered in caves in South Africa in the 1920s.

Mary Leakey's expedition discovered a trail about 70 yards long of 3.6 million-year-old fossilized footprints at Laetoli, Tanzania. Shown here is one of the footprints that were left by two adults who were clearly upright walkers. The footprint shows a well-developed arch and forward-facing big toe.

RAYMOND DART'S TAUNG CHILD

In 1925, Raymond Dart, professor of anatomy at the University of Witwatersrand in Johannesburg, South Africa, presented the first evidence that an erect bipedal hominid existed in the Pliocene epoch. As he separated bones from a matrix of material found in the Taung cave on the edge of the Kalahari Desert, Dart realized he was looking at more than the remains of an ape. He described the experience:

> On December 23, [1924,] the rock parted. I could view the face from the front, although the right side was still embedded. The creature that had contained this massive brain was no giant anthropoid such as a gorilla. What emerged was a baby's face, an infant with a full set of milk teeth and its permanent molars just in the process of erupting.[27]

By the teeth Dart identified the fossil as the remains of a 5- to 7-year-old child (although recent analysis by electron microscope suggests that the child was no more than three and a half[28]). He named the specimen *Australopithecus africanus*, which means "southern ape of Africa." Dart was certain the skull was that of a bipedal animal. He based his conclusion on the fact that the **foramen magnum,** the hole in the base of the skull through which the spinal cord passes en route to the brain, faced downward, indicating that the head was carried directly over the spine. (In monkeys and apes, this passageway is near the back of the skull, in a position more appropriate to a less erect head posture.) Furthermore, the Taung child's incisors and canine teeth were short, and therefore definitely more human- than apelike.

Dart's conclusion met with widespread skepticism and opposition. Not the least of the problems was that scientists at the time believed hominids had originated in Asia. But there were probably other reasons: Dart had found only one fossil; it was an infant rather than an adult; and no other hominid fossils had yet been found in Africa. Other australopithecines were not discovered until the 1930s, when Robert Broom recovered some fossils from the Sterkfontein cave near Johannesburg. Dart's and Broom's conclusions did not begin to be accepted until after 1945, when Wilfred Le Gros Clark, a professor of anatomy at Oxford, supported the hominid status of their finds.[29]

Australopithecus africanus

Since the Taung child's discovery more than 70 years ago, the remains of hundreds of other similar australopithecines have been unearthed from the caves at Sterkfontein and Makapansgat in South Africa. From this abundant evidence a fairly complete picture of *Australopithecus africanus* can be drawn: "The brain case is rounded with a relatively well-developed forehead. Moderate brow ridges surmount a rather projecting face."[30] The estimated cranial capacity for the various finds from Taung and Sterkfontein is between 428 and 485 cc. In contrast, modern humans have a cranial capacity of between 1,000 and 2,000 cc.[31] *Australopithecus africanus* was very small; the adults were only about 3.5 to 4.5 feet tall and weighed about 45 to 90 pounds.[32]

Australopithecus africanus retained the large, chinless jaw of the Miocene apes, but some of the dental features of *A. africanus* were similar to those of modern humans—broad incisors and short canines. And, although the premolars and molars were larger than in modern humans, their form was very similar. Presumably, function and use were also similar.

The broad, bowl-shaped pelvis, which is very similar to the human pelvis in form and in areas for muscle attachments, provides corroborating evidence for bipedalism. The australopithecine spine also suggests that the australopithecines walked erect. The bottom part of the vertebral column forms a curve, causing the spinal column to be S-shaped (seen from the side). This **lumbar curve** and an S-shaped spinal column are found only in hominids (see Figure 5–2). Analysis of hip-joint and femoral-bone fossils also indicates that the australopithecines walked fully upright and that at least the later ones walked with the same direct, striding gait observed in modern humans.[33]

Dating of the australopithecine finds from the South African limestone caves is somewhat difficult because none of the absolute dating techniques can be applied. But relative dating is possible. Comparisons of the fauna found in the strata with fauna found elsewhere suggest that the South African *A. africanus* lived between 3 million and 2 million years ago. The climate was probably semiarid, not too different from the climate of today.[34]

Australopithecus afarensis

It appears that other bipedal australopithecines lived earlier in East Africa, before 3 million years ago. The fossils showing the clearest evidence of bipedalism come from Laetoli, Tanzania, and Hadar, Ethiopia. Do the finds of Hadar and Laetoli, dated between 4 million and 3 million years ago, represent an earlier species of *Australopithecus* different from *A. africanus*? Most paleoanthropologists now think yes; they classify the Hadar and Laetoli hominids, as well as those from some other East African sites, as *A. afarensis*. Other paleoanthropologists think that the finds labeled *afarensis* by some are not different enough from *africanus* to merit a separate species designation. The paleoanthropologists who think that *A. afarensis* was a separate species go not only by its apparently earlier dating; they also think that the finds they designate as *afarensis* are different in some anatomical features.

Remains from at least two dozen hominids were unearthed at Laetoli, Tanzania.[35] Although the remains there consisted largely of teeth and jaws, there is no question that the Laetoli hominids were bipedal, because it was at the Laetoli site that the now famous trail of footprints was found. Two hominids walking erect and side by side left their tracks in the ground 3.6 million years ago. The remains of at least 35 individuals have been found at another site, Hadar, in Ethiopia. The Hadar finds are remarkable for their completeness. Whereas paleoanthropologists often find just parts of the cranium and jaws, many parts of the skeleton were

A reconstruction of Australopithecus afarensis *of about 3 million years ago.*

also found at Hadar. For example, paleoanthropologists found 40 percent of the skeleton of a female hominid they named Lucy, after the Beatles' song "Lucy in the Sky with Diamonds."[36] An analysis of Lucy's pelvis indicates clearly that she was a bipedal walker.[37] But she probably also climbed a lot in the trees, if we judge by her leg bones and joints; they are not as large proportionally as those of modern humans.[38]

Dating of the hominid remains at Laetoli suggests that the hominids there lived between 3.8 million and 3.6 million years ago.[39] Although Lucy and the other hominids at Hadar were once thought to be about as old as those at Laetoli, recent dating suggests that they are somewhat younger—less than 3.2 million years old. Lucy probably lived 2.9 million years ago.[40] The Laetoli environment when Lucy lived there was semiarid, upland savanna with rainy and dry seasons.[41]

Those paleoanthropologists, such as Donald Johanson and Tim White, who believe the Laetoli and Hadar hominids should be given the separate species name *A. afarensis* base their decision primarily on some features of the skull, teeth, and jaws that they feel are more apelike than those of the later hominids classified as *A. africanus*. For example, the incisors and canines of the Laetoli and Hadar hominids are rather large, their tooth rows converge slightly at the back of the jaw, and the palate (roof of the mouth) is flat and narrow. The *A. afarensis* skull tends also to have a crest across the lower back.[42]

In some other respects, the Laetoli and Hadar fossils resemble *A. africanus*. Like *A. africanus*, individuals are very small. Lucy, for example, was about 3.5 feet tall, and the largest individuals at these sites, presumably males, were about 5 feet tall.[43] The brains of the Laetoli and Hadar hominids also tend to be small; cranial capacity is estimated at 415 cc, just slightly less than that of *A. africanus.*[44]

Australopithecus robustus and *boisei*

Paleoanthropologists may disagree about whether *A. afarensis* is separate from *A. africanus.* But there is little disagreement that other species of australopithecines, called the "robust" australopithecines,

lived in East Africa and in South Africa from about 2.5 million to 1 million years ago. Indeed, some paleoanthropologists think these fossils are so different that they deserve to be classified in a different genus, which they call *Paranthropus,* literally "beside humans." Robust australopithecines were found first in South African caves, in Kromdraai and in Swartkrans, and later in East Africa, in the Omo Basin in Ethiopia, the east and west sides of Lake Turkana in Kenya, and Olduvai Gorge in Tanzania.[45] Most paleoanthropologists classify the South African robust australopithecines from about 1.8 million to 1 million years ago as *A. robustus* and the East African robust forms from 2.2 million to 1.3

Research Frontiers

NEW FINDS OF EARLY "ROBUST" AUSTRALOPITHECINES ARE PUZZLING

Where do the robust australopithecines, with their big jaws and bony skull ridges, fit into the evolution of humans? Paleoanthropologists agree that the robust australopithecines are a side branch of human evolution, but when did they diverge from the *Homo* line? The very early date of some robust australopithecine fossils in East Africa presents a puzzle, according to paleoanthropologist Henry McHenry. (These fossils, classified by some as belonging to a new species, *Australopithecus aethiopicus,* date apparently from about 2.5 million years ago.) If the late robust forms *(A. robustus* and *A. boisei)* descend from *A. aethiopicus* and if the line leading to *Homo* had already split off from an earlier australopithecine, then why do the late robust australopithecines resemble *Homo erectus* more than they resemble the australopithecines, who were their presumed ancestors?

The late robust australopithecines are like *H. erectus* in

having a relatively large brain (as compared with *A. africanus*), reduced prognathism (lower face projection), and a deep jaw joint. If they diverged earlier from the *Homo* line, similarity to *Homo* would not present a puzzle. But if the robust line diverged much earlier, as the 2.5-million-year-old *A. aethiopicus* suggests, the late robust forms should be much more divergent from *Homo.* After all, the further back in time two lines diverge, the more you would expect the later examples in each to differ.

What could explain some of the similarities between the late robust australopithecines and the *Homo* line? McHenry suggests two possible explanations, both involving convergence. McHenry points out that convergence, the independent appearance of similar structures in different lines of descent, can obscure the issue of how far back there was common ancestry. Bats, birds, and butterflies have wings, but they are not closely

related—their common ancestor is way back in evolutionary time. One possible explanation of the similarities between the late robust australopithecines and the *Homo* line is that the late robust forms descend from the early robust forms but resemble *H. erectus* because of convergence. A second possibility is that the late robust forms and *Homo* share a recent, not yet found ancestor; if they do, then the early robust forms were not ancestral to the late robust forms. Convergence, not close common ancestry, might then explain the resemblance between the late and early robust forms.

McHenry prefers the second possibility. On the basis of his analysis of trait similarities, McHenry thinks that the two late robust australopithecine species *(A. robustus* and *A. boisei)* share a common ancestor but that ancestor was not the early robust form, *A. aethiopicus.* In many ways, the late robust forms are not that similar to *A. aethiopicus.* One of the best examples of *A. aethiopicus* is a nearly complete

million years ago as *A. boisei*.[46] There may have been another robust species even earlier, dating back more than 2.5 million years ago (see the box titled "New Finds of Early 'Robust' Australopithecines"), but many paleoanthropologists classify this earlier find as *A. boisei*. And even earlier than that, another species, called *Australopithecus aethiopicus,* may have been ancestral to *A. boisei*.

In contrast to *A. africanus,* the robust australopithecines generally had thicker jaws, with larger molars and premolars but smaller incisors, more massive muscle attachments for chewing, and well-developed cranial crests and ridges to support heavy chewing.[47] In addition, *A. robustus* and *A. boisei* have somewhat larger cranial capacities (about 490–530 cc) than *A. africanus*. Compared with *A. robustus, A. boisei* has even more extreme features that reflect a huge chewing apparatus—enormous molar teeth and expanded premolars that look like molars, a massive thick and deep jaw, thick cheek bones, and a more pronounced cranial crest.[48]

It used to be thought that the robust australopithecines were substantially bigger than the other australopithecines—hence the use of the word *robust.* But recent calculations suggest that these australopithecines were *not* substantially different in body weight or height as compared with the other australopithecines. The robustness is primarily in skull (the "Black Skull"). It is no doubt robust. It has huge premolars and molars and a cranial crest. But in other ways it resembles *A. afarensis:* protruding muzzle, shallow jaw joint, and small braincase. McHenry thinks that convergent evolution produced the resemblances between the early and late robust australopithecines and the convergence happened because of strong selective pressure for heavy chewing. Features good for heavy chewing have evolved in other primates as well, in evolutionary lines far removed from the human line—*Gigantopithecus,* with its enormous premolars and molars, was one such primate. Thus, although McHenry still considers the late robust australopithecines to constitute a side branch to the *Homo* line, his analysis suggests that *A. robustus* and *A. boisei* were not as far from *Homo* as previously thought.

Timothy Bromage, who has studied fossil facial growth, and Randall Susman, who has studied the hominid thumb, have other suggestions about the robust australopithecines. Bromage has used the scanning electron microscope to study images of fossil faces, particularly to see how the face would have grown from infancy to adulthood. The maturing face changes in shape by a combination of deposition of bone in some locations and resorption of bone in other locations. So, for instance, a jaw becomes more protruding when bone deposits on the forward-facing surfaces and resorbs on the opposite surfaces. Scanning electron microscopy can reveal whether bone is deposited or resorbed. Bromage found differences between the growth patterns of the robust australopithecines and *A. africanus. Australopithecus africanus* and even early *Homo* finds are more apelike in their growth pattern than the later robust australopithecines.

Susman has studied thumb bones and attached musculature to see what traits would be needed to make tools. Modern humans have longer but stouter thumbs than apes, so they can perform the kind of precision grasping needed for toolmaking. Did any early hominids have such precision-grasping ability? Susman thinks that all the australopithecines after about 2.5 million years ago, including the robust ones, had toolmaking hand capabilities. This doesn't mean that they made tools, only that they could have.

The robust australopithecines with their small foreheads, extremely flat cheeks, and enormous jaws may have looked very different from the forms in the *Homo* line, but they could be closer to us evolutionarily than we once thought.

Sources: Henry M. McHenry, "'Robust' Australopithecines, Our Family Tree, and Homoplasy," and Timothy G. Bromage, "Paleoanthropology and Life History, and Life History of a Paleoanthropologist," in Carol R. Ember, Melvin Ember, and Peter N. Peregrine, eds., *Research Frontiers in Anthropology* (Upper Saddle River, NJ: Prentice Hall, 1998); Prentice Hall/Simon & Schuster Custom Publishing. Randall L. Susman, "Fossil Evidence for Early Hominid Tool Use," *Science,* September 9, 1994, 1570–73.

the skull and jaw, most strikingly in the teeth. If the robust forms were larger in body size, their slightly bigger brain capacity would not be surprising, since larger animals generally have larger brains. However, the body of the robust forms is similar to that of *A. africanus,* so the brain of the robust australopithecines was relatively larger than the brain of *A. africanus.*[49]

In 1954, John T. Robinson proposed that *A. africanus* and *A. robustus* had different dietary adaptations—*africanus* being an omnivore (dependent on meat and plants) and *robustus* a vegetarian with a need for heavy chewing. Robinson's view was hotly debated for many years. Evidence from electron microscopy supports Robinson's view that *A. robustus* ate mostly small hard objects such as seeds, nuts, and tubers. But how different was *A. africanus* in this respect? Recent analyses suggest that *A. africanus* also had to withstand fairly heavy chewing.[50]

The idea that *A. robustus* was just a vegetarian is also questioned by a relatively new chemical technique that analyzes strontium-calcium ratios in teeth and bones to estimate the proportions of plant versus animal food in the diet. This new kind of analysis suggests that *A. robustus* was an omnivore.[51] Thus *A. robustus* may have needed large teeth and jaws to chew seeds, nuts, and tubers, but that doesn't mean that it didn't eat other things too.

Was *A. robustus* adapted then to a drier, more open environment than *A. africanus?* This is a possibility, but the evidence is somewhat controversial. At any rate, most paleoanthropologists think that *A. robustus* died out shortly after 1 million years ago[52] and therefore could not be ancestral to our own genus, *Homo.*[53]

ONE MODEL OF HUMAN EVOLUTION

Figure 5–5 shows one model entertained by paleoanthropologists about how the known fossils may be related. The main disagreement among paleontologists concerns which species of *Australopithecus* were ancestral to the line leading to modern humans. For example, the model shown in Figure 5–5 suggests that *A. africanus* is not ancestral to *Homo,* only to one line of robust australopithecines. *Australopithecus afarensis* is viewed as ancestral to both lines of robust australopithecines and to the line leading to modern humans. Those who think that *A. afarensis* was the last common ancestor of all the hominid lines shown in Figure 5–5 think the split to *Homo* occurred over 3 million years ago.[54] Despite the uncertainty and disagreements about what species was ancestral to the *Homo* line, there is widespread agreement among pa-

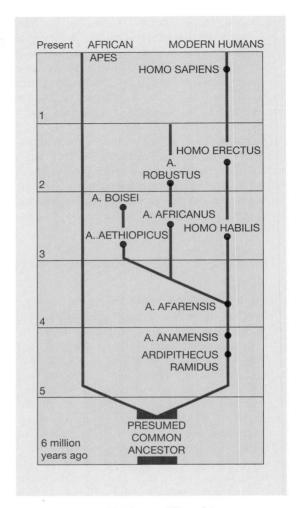

FIGURE 5–5 *Evolution Time Lines*

Sources: Copyright © 1995 by The New York Times. Reprinted by permission.

leoanthropologists about other aspects of early hominid evolution: (1) There were at least two separate hominid lines between 3 million and 1 million years ago; (2) the robust australopithecines were not ancestral to modern humans but became extinct after 2 million years ago; and (3) *Homo habilis* (and successive *Homo* species) were in the direct ancestral line to modern humans.

EARLY SPECIES OF *HOMO*

Hominids with a brain absolutely and relatively larger than that of the australopithecines appear about 2.5 million years ago. These hominids, classified in our own genus, *Homo,* are generally called *Homo habilis,* after the fossils found in Olduvai Gorge, Tanzania, and named by Louis Leakey, Phillip Tobias, and John Napier. (Less than a million years later, a larger-brained species, *Homo erectus,* appears in East Africa.) **Homo habilis** apparently lived in the same place and time as the robust australopithecine, *A. boisei,* which was also found in Olduvai Gorge.[55] Other *H. habilis* finds come from the eastern area of Lake Turkana in Kenya, the Omo Basin of Ethiopia, and the Sterkfontein cave in South Africa.[56] Compared with the australopithecines, *Homo habilis* had a significantly larger brain, averaging 630–640 cc,[57] and reduced molars and premolars.[58]

Because stone tools are found at various sites in East Africa around the time of *H. habilis,* some anthropologists surmise that *H. habilis,* rather than the australopithecines, made those tools. After all, *H. habilis* had the greater brain capacity. But the fact is that none of the earliest stone tools are clearly associated with *H. habilis,* so it is impossible as yet to know who made them. As we noted in the box about the robust lines, all the hominids found after 2.5 million years had a thumb capable of toolmaking, so all of them may have been toolmakers.[59] We turn now to those tools and what archaeologists infer about the life-styles of their makers, the hominids (whoever they were) who lived between about 2.5 million and 1.5 million years ago.

EARLY HOMINID CULTURES

TOOL TRADITIONS

The earliest identifiable stone tools found so far come from various sites in East Africa and date from about 2.5 million years ago,[60] and maybe earlier. The oldest tools, some 3,000 in number, were discovered recently at Gona, Ethiopia. The tools range from very small flakes (thumb-size) to cobble or core tools that were fist-size.[61] These early tools were apparently made by striking a stone with another stone, a technique called **percussion flaking.** Both the sharp-edged flakes and the sharp-edged cores (the pieces of stone left after flakes are removed) were probably used as tools. Archaeologists consider a pattern of behavior, such as a particular way to make a tool that is shared and learned by a group of individuals, to be a sign of some cultural behavior. (We discuss the concept of culture more fully in a later chapter.) To be sure, toolmaking does not imply that early humans had anything like the complex cultures of humans today. As we noted in the chapter on living primates, chimpanzees have patterns of tool use and toolmaking that appear to be shared and learned, but they do not have that much in the way of cultural behavior. On the basis of their toolmaking, early hominids had some cultural behavior, but we cannot tell yet how much culture they had.

What were those earliest stone tools used for? What do they tell us about early hominid culture? Unfortunately, little can be inferred about life-styles from the earliest tool sites because little else was found with the tools. In contrast, finds of later tool assemblages at Olduvai Gorge in Tanzania have yielded a rich harvest of cultural information. The Olduvai site was uncovered accidentally in 1911, when a German entomologist followed a butterfly into the gorge and found fossil remains. Beginning in the 1930s, Louis and Mary Leakey searched the gorge for clues to the evolution of early humans. Of the Olduvai site, Louis Leakey wrote,

> [It] is a fossil hunter's dream, for it shears 300 feet through stratum after stratum of earth's history as through a gigantic layer cake. Here, within reach, lie countless fossils and artifacts which but for the faulting and erosion would have remained sealed under thick layers of consolidated rock.[62]

The oldest cultural materials from Olduvai (Bed I) date from Lower Pleistocene times. The stone *artifacts* (things made by humans) include core tools and sharp-edged flakes. Flake tools predominate. Among the core tools, so-called *choppers* are common. Choppers are cores that have been partially flaked and have a side that might have been used for chopping. Other core tools, with flaking along one side and a flat edge, are called *scrapers.* Whenever a stone has facets removed from only one side of the cutting edge, we call it a **unifacial tool.** If the stone has facets removed from both sides, we call it a **bifacial tool.** Although there are some bifacial tools in the early stone tool assemblages, they are not as plentiful or as elaborated as in later tool traditions. The kind of tool assemblage found in Bed I and to some extent in later (higher) layers is referred to as **Oldowan** (see Figure 5–6).[63]

LIFE-STYLES

Archaeologists have speculated about the life-styles of early hominids from Olduvai and other sites. Some of these speculations come from analysis of what can be done with the tools, microscopic analysis of wear on the tools, and examination of the

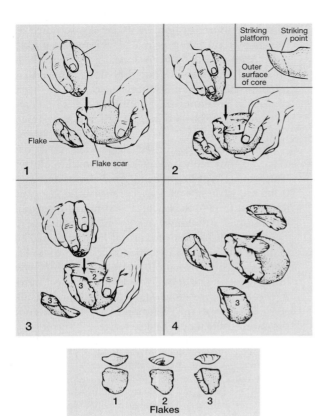

FIGURE 5–6 *The Production of a Simple Oldowan Chopper Core and the Resultant Flakes*

Source: Drawing by R. Freyman adapted from "The First Technology," © Scientific American, Inc. Reprinted by permission of Ed Hanson, artist.

marks the tools make on bones; other speculations are based on what is found with the tools.

Archaeologists have experimented with what can be done with Oldowan tools. The flakes appear to be very versatile; they can be used for slitting the hides of animals, dismembering animals, and whittling wood into sharp-pointed sticks (wooden spears or digging sticks). The larger stone tools (choppers and scrapers) can be used to hack off branches or cut and chop tough animal joints.[64] Those who have made and tried to use stone tools for various purposes are so impressed by the sharpness and versatility of flakes that they wonder whether most of the core tools were really used as tools. The cores could mainly be what remained after wanted flakes were struck off.[65] Archaeologists surmise that many early tools were also made of wood and bone, but these do not survive in the archaeological record. For example, present-day populations use sharp-pointed digging sticks for extracting roots and tubers from the ground; stone flakes are very effective for sharpening wood to a very fine point.[66]

None of the early flaked stone tools can plausibly be thought of as a weapon. So, if the toolmaking hominids were hunting or defending themselves

with weapons, they had to have used wooden spears, clubs, or unmodified stones as missiles. Later Oldowan tool assemblages also include stones that were flaked and battered into a rounded shape. The unmodified stones and the shaped stones might have been lethal projectiles.[67]

Experiments may tell us what can be done with tools, but they cannot tell us what was actually done with them. Other techniques, such as microscopic analysis of the wear on tools, are more informative. Early studies looked at the microscopic scratches formed when a tool was used in different ways. Scratches parallel to the edge of a tool often occur when a tool is used in a sawing motion; perpendicular scratches suggest whittling or scraping.[68] Lawrence Keeley used high-powered microscopes in his experimental investigations of tools and found that different kinds of "polish" develop on tools when they are used on different materials. The polish on tools used for cutting meat is different from the polish on tools used for woodworking. On the basis of microscopic investigation of the 1.5-million-year-old tools from the eastern side of Lake Turkana, Keeley and his colleagues concluded that at least some of the early tools were probably used for cutting meat, others for cutting or whittling wood, and others for cutting plant stems.[69]

In the 1950s and 1960s, Olduvai Gorge revealed the presence of both Oldowan tools and the remains of broken bones and teeth from many different animal species. For many years it seemed plausible to assume that hominids were the hunters and the animals their prey. But archaeologists had to reexamine this assumption with the emergence of the field of *taphonomy,* which studies the processes that can alter and distort an assemblage of bones. So, for example, flowing water can bring bones and artifacts together, which may have happened at Olduvai Gorge about 1.8 million years ago. (The area of what is now the gorge bordered the shores of a shallow lake at that time.) And other animals such as hyenas could have brought carcasses to some of the same places that hominids spent time. Taphonomy requires archaeologists to consider all the possible reasons things may be found together.[70]

But there is little doubt that hominids shortly after 2 million years ago were cutting up animal carcasses for meat. Microscopic analyses show that cut marks on animal bones were unambiguously created by stone flake tools, and microscopic analyses of polish on stone tools show the polish to be consistent with butchering. We still do not know for sure whether the hominids around Olduvai Gorge were just scavenging meat (taking meat from the kills of other animals) or hunting the animals. On the basis of her analysis of cut marks on bone from Bed I in Olduvai Gorge, Pat Shipman suggested that scavenging, not hunting, was the major meat-getting activity of the hominids living there between 2 million and 1.7 million years ago. For example, the fact that cut marks made by stone tools usually (but not always) overlie teeth marks made by carnivores suggests that the hominids were often scavenging the meat of animals killed and partially eaten by nonhominid predators. The fact that the cut marks were sometimes made first, however, suggested to Shipman that the hominids were also sometimes the hunters.[71] On the other hand, prior cut marks may indicate only that the hominids scavenged before carnivores had a chance to.

The artifact and animal remains from Bed I and the lower part of Bed II at Olduvai suggest a few other things about the life-styles of the hominids there. First, it seems that the hominids moved around during the year; most of the sites in what is now the Olduvai Gorge appear to have been used only in the dry season, as indicated by an analysis of the kinds of animal bones found there.[72] Second, whether the early Olduvai hominids were hunters or scavengers, they apparently exploited a wide range of animals. Although most of the bones are from medium-sized antelopes and wild pigs, even large animals such as elephants and giraffes seem to have been eaten.[73] It is clear, then, that the Olduvai hominids scavenged or hunted for meat, but we cannot tell yet how important meat was in their diet.

There is also no consensus yet about how to characterize the Olduvai sites. In the 1970s, there was a tendency to think of these sites (which contain tools and animal bones) as home bases to which hominids (presumably male) brought meat to share with others (presumably nursing mothers and young children). In short, the scenario involved a home base, a division of labor by gender, and food-sharing. But archaeologists now are not so sure. For one thing, carnivores also frequented these sites. Places with meaty bones lying around may not have been so safe for hominids to use as home bases. Second, the animal remains at the sites had not been completely dismembered and butchered. If the sites had been hominid home bases, we would expect more complete processing of carcasses.[74]

If these sites were not home bases, what were they? Some archaeologists are beginning to think that these early sites with many animal bones and tools may just have been places where hominids processed food but did not live. Why would the hominids return to a particular site? Richard Potts suggests one possible reason—that hominids left caches of stone tools and stones for toolmaking at various locations to facilitate their food-collecting and processing activities.[75] Future research may tell us more about early hominid life. Did they have home bases, or did they just move from one processing site to another? How did they protect themselves from predators? They apparently did not have fire to keep the predators away. Did they climb trees to get away or to sleep?

HOMO ERECTUS

We know from many finds that **Homo erectus** was the first hominid species to be widely distributed in the Old World (see Figure 5–7). Examples of *H. erectus* were found first in Java, later in China, and still later in Africa. Most paleoanthropologists agree that some human ancestor moved from Africa to Asia at some point. Until recently it was assumed that it was *H. erectus* who moved, because *H. erectus* lived in East Africa about 1.6 million years ago but not until after about 1 million years ago in Asia.[76] Recent re-dating, however, suggests that *H. erectus* in Java may be somewhat older, dating to perhaps

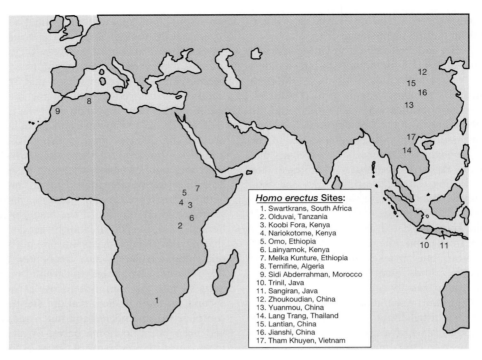

FIGURE 5–7 *Homo erectus Sites*

Source: From Russell L. Ciochon and John G. Fleagle, eds., *The Human Evolution Source Book* (Englewood Cliffs, NJ: Prentice Hall, 1993), p. x.

1.8 million years ago.[77] If this dating is accurate, early hominids may have moved out of Africa earlier, or *H. erectus* may have emerged elsewhere.

Homo erectus may have spread to Europe. However, some paleoanthropologists think that the finds in Europe thought to be *H. erectus* are actually early examples of *H. sapiens,* as are some of the finds in southern Africa and the Near East that were previously thought to be *H. erectus.*[78]

THE DISCOVERY IN JAVA AND LATER FINDS

In 1891, Eugene Dubois, a Dutch anatomist digging in Java, found what he called *Pithecanthropus erectus,* meaning "erect ape man." (We now refer to this hominid as *Homo erectus.*) The discovery was not the first humanlike fossil found; Neandertals, which we discuss in the next chapter, were known many years earlier. But no one was certain, not even Dubois himself, whether the fossil he found in Java was an ape or a human.

The actual find consisted of a cranium and a thighbone. For many years it was thought that the fragments were not even from the same animal. The skull was too large to be that of a modern ape but was smaller than that of an average human, having a cranial capacity between the average ape's 500 cc and the average modern human's 1,300+ cc. The thighbone, however, matched that of a modern human. Did the two fragments in fact belong together? The question was resolved many years later by fluorine analysis. As we saw in Chapter 4, if fossils from the same deposit contain the same amount of fluorine, they are the same age. The skull fragment and thighbone found by Dubois were tested for fluorine content and found to be the same age.

A discovery by G. H. R. von Koenigswald in the mid-1930s, also in Java, not only confirmed Dubois' earlier speculations and extended our knowledge of the physical characteristics of *Homo erectus* but also gave us a better understanding of this early human's place in time. Since then, many more *H. erectus* fossils have been found in Java. These *H. erectus* in Java were thought not to be more than 1 million years old;[79] now argon-argon dating puts some of the Java specimens back to a time 1.8 million years ago.[80]

Between the times of Dubois' and von Koenigswald's discoveries, Davidson Black, a Canadian

Homo erectus, *seen in this skull and facial reconstruction, had prominent brow ridges, a thickly walled skull, and a low forehead. Its brain capacity was about 70 percent of that of modern humans.* H. erectus *was hardly distinguishable from modern humans.*

anatomy professor teaching in Peking (Beijing), China, set out to investigate a large cave at nearby Zhoukoudian where a fossilized tooth had been found. Confident that the tooth came from a hitherto unknown hominid genus, he obtained funds to excavate the area extensively. After two years of excavation, he and his colleagues found a skull in limestone whose owner was dubbed "Peking man." Black died in 1934, and his work was carried on by Franz Weidenreich.

It was not until the 1950s that *H. erectus* fossils were uncovered in northern Africa. Many finds since then come from East Africa, particularly two sites—Olduvai Gorge in Tanzania and the Lake Turkana region of Kenya. An almost complete skeleton of a boy was found at Nariokotome, on the western side of Lake Turkana, dating from about 1.6 million years ago. The Olduvai finds are from about 1.2 million years ago.[81]

PHYSICAL CHARACTERISTICS OF *Homo erectus*

The *Homo erectus* skull generally was long, low, and thickly walled, with a flat frontal area and prominent brow ridges. Compared with *H. habilis, H. erectus* had relatively small teeth. The brain, averaging 895–1,040 cc, was larger than that found in any of the australopithecines or *H. habilis* but smaller than the average brain of a modern human.[82]

Homo erectus had a prominent, projecting nose, in contrast to the australopithecines' flat, nonprojecting noses.[83] From the neck down, *H. erectus* was practically indistinguishable from *H. sapiens*. In contrast to the much smaller australopithecines and *H. habilis,* who lived in East Africa around the same

time, *H. erectus* was comparable to modern humans in size. The almost complete skeleton of the boy at Nariokotome suggests that he was 5′3″ tall when he died, at about 11 years of age; the researchers estimate that he would have been 6′1″ had he lived to maturity. About 1.6 million years ago, the Nariokotome region was probably open grassland, with trees mostly along rivers.[84] *Homo erectus* in East Africa was similar in size to Africans today who live in a similarly open, dry environment.[85]

HOMO ERECTUS CULTURES

The archaeological finds of tools and other cultural artifacts dating from 1.5 million years ago to about 200,000 years ago are assumed to have been produced by *Homo erectus*. But fossils are not usually associated with these materials. Therefore it is possible that some of the tools during this period were produced by hominids other than *H. erectus,* such as australopithecines earlier and *H. sapiens* later. The so-called Acheulian tool assemblages dating from 1.5 million years ago to more than a million years later are very similar to each other, and *H. erectus* is the only hominid that spans the entire period, so it is conventionally assumed that *H. erectus* was responsible for most if not all of the Acheulian tool assemblages we describe below.[86]

THE ACHEULIAN TOOL TRADITION

A stone toolmaking tradition known as the **Acheulian** was named after the site at St. Acheul, France, where the first examples were found. But the oldest Acheulian tools recovered are from East Africa, on

Research Frontiers

HOMO ERECTUS: ONE OR MORE SPECIES?

In living populations it is possible to tell whether two different primates belong to different species. Can they interbreed? And are the offspring fertile? If the answer to either question is no, we are dealing with different species. But how can we tell species apart in the fossil record? Paleoanthropologists must judge by degree of difference between them. Once two populations stop interbreeding, they will begin to develop divergent traits. But how different do they have to be for us to call them different species?

Because the fossil record does not reveal mating patterns, it is not surprising that paleoanthropologists have differences of opinion about whether two fossils represent the same species or not. And paleoanthropologists have different predispositions; some tend to be "splitters," identifying more different species; and others tend to be "lumpers," identifying fewer different species. In the 1920s and 1930s, splitting was common; almost every new find of what we now call *Homo erectus* was assigned to a different species or even a different genus. For example, *Pithecanthropus erectus* is now called *H. erectus* from Java, and *Sinanthropus pekinensis* is now *H. erectus* from near Peking (now Beijing). Franz Weidenreich in the 1940s suggested this lumping, which dominated classification through the 1960s and 1970s. But, in the 1980s, Peter Andrews, Christopher Stringer, and Bernard Wood proposed that the Asian and African fossils

previously grouped as *H. erectus* were different enough to be split into two separate species—one Asian and one African. So once again there were opposing hypotheses about those fossils. Was *H. erectus* one or two species?

To discover which hypothesis is more likely to be correct, Andrew Kramer analyzed various skull measurements for the Asian and African fossils and two other groups—modern humans, who we know belong to the same species, and a mixed set of early hominids, who are conventionally classified as belonging to two or three different species. Kramer reasoned that if the African and Asian fossils are not more variable than the modern humans, we can conclude that those fossils belong to one species, *H. erectus*. And the mixed set of ancient hominids should be more variable than the modern humans.

The 16 Asian and African skulls in Kramer's analysis (that might or might not be from a single species, *H. erectus*) were the ones available that could provide the required measurements. They ranged in dating from 1.8 million to 500,000 years ago; other things being equal, such a great range in dating should make for more variability and therefore more likelihood that the 16 supposed *H. erectus* skulls would show more variability than the sample of modern humans. Kramer wanted to compare the 16 with the same number of modern skulls. But how does one choose 16 modern skulls from the many available?

(He had measurements from 2,533 skulls.) One random sample would not be sufficient. One can never know for sure how representative a particular random sample of 16 is. So Kramer used 1,000 different random samples of 16 each from the 2,533 modern skulls available. For each trait compared, he computed a measure of variability for the sample of 16. What were the results of the comparisons? The 16 supposed *H. erectus* skulls were *not* more variable than most of the modern human samples, strongly suggesting that they did come from the same species. To test this conclusion further, Kramer compared the modern samples with the mixed sample of ancient hominids (the skulls used were again ones that allowed the required measurements). Because the mixed ancient sample presumably came from more than one species, it should look *more* variable than the modern human samples. And it did. Almost all of the modern human samples were less variable than the mixed ancient sample.

So Kramer's research strongly suggests that the hominids in Asia and Africa between 1.8 million years and 500,000 years ago were all *Homo erectus.*

Source: Andrew Kramer, "The Natural History and Evolutionary Fate of *Homo erectus*" in Carol R. Ember, Melvin Ember, and Peter N. Peregrine, eds., *Research Frontiers in Anthropology,* Vol. 3, *Physical Anthropology* (Upper Saddle River, NJ: Prentice Hall, 1998), pp. 133–150. Prentice Hall/Simon & Schuster Custom Publishing.

the Peninj River, Tanzania, dating back about 1.5 million years.[87] In contrast to Oldowan, Acheulian assemblages have more large tools created according to standardized designs or shapes. Oldowan tools have sharp edges made by a few blows. Acheulian toolmakers shaped the stone by knocking more flakes off most of the edges. Many of these tools were made from very large flakes that had been struck from very large cores or boulders. One of the most characteristic and prevalent tools in the Acheulian tool kit is the so-called handaxe, which is a teardrop-shaped bifacially flaked tool with a thinned sharp tip. Other large tools resemble cleavers and picks. There were also many other kinds of flake tools, such as scrapers with a wide edge. Early Acheulian tools appeared to have been made by blows with a hard stone, but later tools are wider and flatter and may have been made with a soft "hammer" of bone or antler.[88]

Were handaxes made for chopping trees, as their name suggests? We cannot be sure what they were used for, but experiments with Acheulian handaxes suggest that they are not good for cutting trees; they seem more suited for butchering large animals.[89] Lawrence Keeley microscopically examined some Acheulian handaxes, and the wear on them is consistent with animal butchery. The picks may have been used for woodworking, particularly hollowing and shaping wood, and they are also good for digging.[90]

Acheulian tools are found widely in Africa, Europe, and western Asia, but bifacial handaxes, cleavers, and picks are not found as commonly in eastern and southeastern Asia. Because H. erectus has been found in all areas of the Old World, it is puzzling why the tool traditions seem to differ from west to east. Recently, some archaeologists have suggested that large bifacial tools may be lacking in eastern and southeastern Asia because H. erectus there had a better material to make tools out of—bamboo. Bamboo is used today in Southeast Asia for many purposes, including incredibly sharp arrows and sticks for digging and cutting. Geoffrey Pope showed that bamboo is found in those areas of Asia where handaxes and other large bifacial tools are missing.[91]

BIG-GAME EATING

Some of the Acheulian sites have produced evidence of big-game eating. F. Clark Howell, who excavated sites at Torralba and Ambrona, Spain, found a substantial number of elephant remains and unmistakable evidence of human presence in the form of tools. Howell suggests that the humans at those sites used fire to frighten elephants into muddy bogs, from which they would be unable to escape.[92] To hunt elephants in this way, the humans would have had to plan and work cooperatively in fairly large groups.

But do these finds of bones of large and medium-sized animals, in association with tools, tell us that the humans definitely were big-game hunters? Some archaeologists who have reanalyzed the evidence from Torralba think that the big game may have been scavenged. Because the Torralba and Ambrona sites are near ancient streams, many of the elephants could have died naturally, their bones accumulating in certain spots because of the flow of water.[93] What seems fairly clear is that the humans did deliberately butcher different kinds of game—different types of tools are found with different types of animal.[94] Thus, whether the humans hunted big game at Torralba and Ambrona is debatable; all we can be sure of, as of now, is that they consumed big game and probably hunted smaller game.

CONTROL OF FIRE

Because H. erectus was the first hominid to be found throughout the Old World and in areas with freezing winters, most anthropologists presume that H. erectus had learned to control fire, at least for warmth. There is archaeological evidence of fire in some early sites, but fires can be natural events. Thus, whether fire was under deliberate control by H. erectus is difficult to establish.

Suggestive but not conclusive evidence of the deliberate use of fire comes from Kenya in East Africa and is over 1.4 million years old.[95] More persuasive, but still not definite, evidence of human control of fire, dating from nearly 500,000 years ago, comes from the cave at Zhoukoudian in China where H. erectus fossils have been found.[96] In that cave are thousands of splintered and charred animal bones, apparently the remains of meals. There are also layers of ash, suggesting human control of fire.

But recent analysis raises questions about these finds. The most serious problem is that human remains, tools, and ash rarely occur together in the same layers. In addition, there are no hearths at the Zhoukoudian site. Fires can spontaneously occur with heavy accumulation of organic matter, so clear evidence of human control of fire is still not definitely attested. Even the inference that humans brought the animals to the cave for butchering is only possibly a correct guess. Throughout the cave there is evidence of hyenas and wolves, and they, not the humans, may have brought many of the animal parts to the cave.[97]

Better evidence of the deliberate use of fire comes from Europe somewhat later. Unfortunately, the evidence of control of fire at these European sites is not associated with *H. erectus* fossils either, so the link between deliberate use of fire and *H. erectus* cannot be definitely established yet. The lack of clear evidence does not, of course, mean that *H. erectus* did not use fire. After all, *H. erectus* did move into cold areas of the world, and it is hard to imagine how that could have happened without the deliberate use of fire.

Fire would be important not only for warmth; cooking would also be possible. The control of fire was a major step in increasing the energy under human control. Cooking made all kinds of possible food (not just meat) more safely digestible and therefore more usable. Fires would also have kept predators away, a not inconsiderable advantage given that there were a lot of them around.

CAMPSITES

Acheulian sites were usually located close to water sources, lush vegetation, and large stocks of herbivorous animals. Some camps have been found in caves, but most were in open areas surrounded by rudimentary fortifications or windbreaks. Several African sites are marked by stony rubble brought there by *H. erectus,* possibly for the dual purpose of securing the windbreaks and providing ammunition in case of a sudden attack.[98]

The presumed base campsites display a wide variety of tools, indicating that the camp was the center of many group functions. More specialized sites away from camp have also been found. These are marked by the predominance of a particular type of tool. For example, a butchering site in Tanzania contained dismembered hippopotamus carcasses and rare heavy-duty smashing and cutting tools. Workshops are another kind of specialized site encountered with some regularity. They are characterized by tool debris and are located close to a source of natural stone suitable for toolmaking.[99]

FIGURE 5–8 *A Reconstruction of the Oval Huts Built at Terra Amata*

These huts were approximately 30 by 15 feet. *Source:* From Henry de Lumley, "A Paleolithic Camp at Nice." Copyright © 1969 by Scientific American, Inc. All rights reserved.

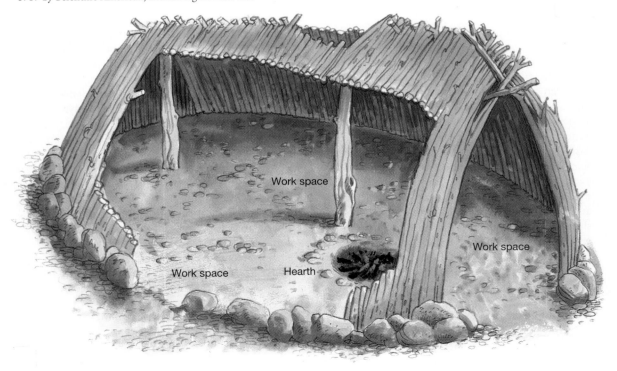

A camp has been excavated at the Terra Amata site near Nice, on the French Riviera. The camp appears to have been occupied in the late spring or early summer, judging by the pollen found in fossilized human feces. The excavator describes stake holes driven into the sand, paralleled by lines of stones, presumably marking the spots where the people constructed huts of roughly 30 by 15 feet (Figure 5–8). A basic feature of each hut was a central hearth that seems to have been protected from drafts by a small wall built just outside the northeast corner of the hearth. The evidence suggests that the Terra Amata occupants gathered seafood such as oysters and mussels, did some fishing, and hunted in the surrounding area. The animal remains suggest that they obtained both small and large animals but mostly got the young of larger animals such as stags, elephants, boars, rhinoceroses, and wild oxen. Some of the huts contain recognizable toolmakers' areas, scattered with tool debris; occasionally, the impression of an animal skin shows where the toolmaker actually sat.[100]

The cultures of early hominids are traditionally classified as Lower Paleolithic or early Stone Age. In the next chapter we discuss the emergence of *Homo sapiens* and cultural developments in the middle and Upper Paleolithic periods.

SUMMARY

1. The drying trend in climate that began about 16 million to 11 million years ago diminished the extent of African rain forests and gave rise to areas of savanna (grasslands) and scattered deciduous woodlands. The new, more open country probably favored characteristics adapted to ground living in some primates. In the evolutionary line leading to humans, these adaptations included bipedalism.

2. One of the crucial changes in early hominid evolution was the development of bipedalism. There are several theories for this development: It may have increased the emerging hominid's ability to see predators and potential prey while moving through the tall grasses of the savanna; by freeing the hands for carrying, it may have facilitated transferring food from one place to another; tool use, which requires free hands, may have favored two-legged walking; and bipedalism may have made long-distance traveling more efficient.

3. Other important physical changes—including the expansion of the brain, modification of the female pelvis to allow bigger-brained babies to be born, and reduction of the face, teeth, and jaws—did not begin until about 2 million years after the emergence of bipedalism. By that time (about 2 million years ago) hominids had come to depend to some extent on scavenging and possibly hunting meat.

4. Undisputed hominids dating back to between 4 million and 3 million years ago have been found in East Africa. These definitely bipedal hominids are now generally classified in the genus *Australopithecus*. Most paleoanthropologists divide the genus *Australopithecus* into at least four species. Some East African hominids nearly 2 million years old are classified as *Homo habilis,* an early species of our own genus, *Homo.*

5. The earliest stone tools found so far come from various sites in East Africa and date from about 2.5 million years ago. We do not yet know who made them. These tools were made by striking a stone with another stone to remove sharp-edged flakes. Both the flakes and the sharp-edged cores were used as tools. This early tool tradition is named Oldowan.

6. *Homo erectus,* with a larger brain capacity than *Homo habilis,* emerged about 1.8 million to 1.6 million years ago. *Homo erectus* was the first hominid species to be widely distributed in the Old World. The tools and other cultural artifacts from about 1.6 million to about 200,000 years ago were probably produced by *H. erectus;* Acheulian is the name given to the tool tradition of this period. Acheulian tools include both small flake tools and large tools, but handaxes and other large bifacial tools are characteristic. Although it is presumed that *H. erectus* had learned to use fire to survive in areas with cold winters, there is no definite evidence of the control of fire by *H. erectus.* There is evidence in some sites of big-game eating, but whether *H. erectus* hunted those animals is debated.

GLOSSARY TERMS

Acheulian	foramen magnum
Australopithecus	*Homo*
Australopithecus afarensis	*Homo erectus*
Australopithecus africanus	*Homo habilis*
	lumbar curve
Australopithecus boisei	Oldowan
Australopithecus robustus	percussion flaking
	savanna
bifacial tool	unifacial tool

CRITICAL QUESTIONS

1. How could there have been more than one species of hominid living in East Africa at the same time?

2. What may have enabled australopithecines to survive in the face of many ground predators?

3. *Homo erectus* lived in many places in the Old World. What enabled them to spread so widely?

INTERNET EXERCISES

1. Visit **http://www.talkorigins.org/faqs/homs/specimen.html** to view some of the prominent hominid fossils. Based on the web site, write a brief summary of your findings pertaining to *Australopithecus afarensis* and Donald Johanson.

2. Go to **http://www.cruzio.com/~cscp/maps.htm** to view sites where fossil hominids have been found in China.

3. Explore a site devoted to stone tool technology at **http://www.hf.uio.no/iakn/roger/lithic/sarc.html**. Look in particular for earlier stone tool technologies.

SUGGESTED READING

CONROY, G. C. *Primate Evolution.* New York: Norton, 1990. Chapter 6 summarizes the fossil record for the australopithecines and early *Homo,* discusses the geography and climate of the early sites, and explains the biomechanical principles of bipedalism.

EMBER, C. R., EMBER M., AND PEREGRINE, P. N., EDS. *Research Frontiers in Anthropology.* Upper Saddle River, NJ: Prentice Hall, 1998. Prentice Hall/Simon & Schuster Custom Publishing. Several chapters in this series deal with the evolution of early hominids and their cultures: T. G. Bromage, "Paleoanthropology and Life History, and Life History of a Paleoanthropologist"; A. Kramer, "The Natural History and Evolutionary Fate of *Homo erectus*"; H. M. McHenry, "'Robust' Australopithecines, Our Family Tree, and Homoplasy"; S. W. Simpson, "*Australopithecus afarensis* and Human Evolution"; and J. D. Speth, "Were Our Ancestors Hunters or Scavengers?"

GRINE, F. E., ED. *Evolutionary History of the "Robust" Australopithecines.* New York: Aldine, 1988. A great deal of controversy has surrounded the "robust" australopithecines. In a 1987 workshop, participants from many different fields were asked to summarize recent knowledge of this group of australopithecines.

PHILLIPSON, D. W. *African Archaeology,* 2nd ed. Cambridge: Cambridge University Press, 1993. A summary and interpretation of the archaeological evidence in Africa and what it tells us about human history from its beginnings to historic times. Chapters 2 and 3 are particularly relevant to this chapter.

RIGHTMIRE, G. P. *The Evolution of Homo erectus: Comparative Anatomical Studies of an Extinct Human Species.* Cambridge: Cambridge University Press, 1990. A review of the anatomical features of *Homo erectus* and how they changed over time.

SCHICK, K., AND TOTH, N. *Making Silent Stones Speak.* New York: Simon & Schuster, 1993. A large part of understanding past tool traditions is making them and using them. The authors describe their experimental work and relate it to the archaeologically recovered tool traditions of the past.

The Emergence of *Homo sapiens* and Their Cultures

CHAPTER OUTLINE

*U*ntil recently, paleoanthropologists thought that modern-looking people evolved about 50,000 years ago. Now we know that they appeared earlier. The date of about 50,000 years ago is for Europe, but recent finds in southern Africa and elsewhere indicate the presence of modern-looking people perhaps as much as 100,000 or even 200,000 years ago. The skeletal resemblances between those humans and recent people are so great that most paleoanthropologists consider them all to be "modern humans," *Homo sapiens sapiens.* One paleoanthropologist, Christopher Stringer, characterizes the modern human, *Homo sapiens sapiens,* as having "a domed skull, a chin, small eyebrows, brow ridges, and a rather puny skeleton."[1] Some of us might not like to be called puny, but except for our larger brain, most modern humans definitely are puny compared with *Homo erectus* and even with earlier forms of our own species, *H. sapiens.* We are relatively puny in several respects, including our thinner and lighter bones as well as our smaller teeth and jaws.

In this chapter we discuss the fossil evidence as well as the controversies about the transition from *H. erectus* to modern humans, which may have begun 500,000 years ago. We also discuss what we know archaeologically about the Middle and Upper Paleolithic cultures of the early *H. sapiens* who lived between about 300,000 and 15,000 years ago.

THE TRANSITION FROM *HOMO ERECTUS* TO *HOMO SAPIENS*

Most paleoanthropologists agree that *H. erectus* evolved into *H. sapiens,* but they disagree about how and where the transition occurred. There is also disagreement about how to classify some fossils from 500,000 to about 200,000 years ago that have a mix of *H. erectus* and *H. sapiens* traits.[2] A particular fossil might be called *H. erectus* by some anthropologists and "archaic" *Homo sapiens* by others. And, as we shall see, still other anthropologists see so much continuity between *H. erectus* and *H. sapiens* that they think it is completely arbitrary to call them different species. According to these anthropologists, *H. erectus* and *H. sapiens* may just be earlier and later varieties of the same species and therefore all should be called *H. sapiens.* (*H. erectus* would then be *H. sapiens erectus*).

Fossils with mixed traits have been found in Africa, Europe, and Asia. For example, a specimen from the Broken Hill mine in Zambia, central Africa, dates from about 200,000 years ago. Its mixed traits include a cranial capacity of over 1,200 cc (well within the range of modern *H. sapiens*), together with a low forehead and large brow ridges, which are characteristic of earlier *H. erectus* specimens.[3] Other fossils with mixed traits have been found at Bodo, Hopefield, Ndutu, Elandsfontein, and Rabat in Africa; Heidelberg, Bilzingsleben, Petralona, Arago, Steinheim, and Swanscombe in Europe; and Dali and Solo in Asia.

NEANDERTALS AND OTHER DEFINITE *HOMO SAPIENS*

There may be disagreement about how to classify the mixed-trait fossils from 500,000 to 200,000 years ago, but there is hardly any disagreement about the fossils that are less than 200,000 years old. Nearly all anthropologists agree that they were definitely *Homo sapiens.* Mind you, these early definite *H. sapiens* did not look completely like modern humans, but they were not so different from us either—not even the ones called Neandertals, after the valley in Germany where the first evidence of them was found. Somehow through the years the Neandertals have become the victims of their cartoon image, which usually misrepresents them as burly and more ape than human. Actually, they might go unnoticed in a cross section of the world's population today.

In 1856, three years before Darwin's publication of *The Origin of Species,* a skullcap and other fossilized bones were discovered in a cave in the Neander Valley (*tal* is the German word for "valley"), near Düsseldorf, Germany. The fossils in the Neander Valley were the first that scholars could tentatively consider as an early hominid. (The fossils classified as *Homo erectus* were not found until later in the nineteenth century, and the fossils belonging to the genus *Australopithecus* not until the twentieth century.) After Darwin's revolutionary work was published, the Neandertal find aroused considerable controversy. A few evolutionist scholars, such as Thomas Huxley, thought that the Neandertal was not that different from modern humans. Others dismissed the Neandertal as irrelevant to human evolution; they saw it as a pathological freak, a peculiar, disease-ridden individual. However, similar fossils turned up later in Belgium, Yugoslavia, France, and elsewhere in Europe, which meant that the original Neandertal find could not be dismissed as an oddity.[4]

The predominant reaction to the original and subsequent Neandertal-like finds was that the Neandertals were too "brutish" and "primitive" to have been ancestral to modern humans. This view prevailed in the scholarly community until well into the 1950s. A major proponent of this view was Marcellin Boule, who claimed between 1908 and 1913 that the Neandertals would not have been capable of complete bipedalism. Boule and others may have been misled by the bowed leg bones, due to the vitamin-deficiency disease called rickets, in some Neandertal specimens. Since the 1950s, however, a number of studies have disputed Boule's claim, and it is now generally agreed that the skeletal traits of the Neandertals are completely consistent with bipedalism. Perhaps more important, when the much more ancient australopithecine and *H. erectus* fossils were accepted as hominids in the 1940s and 1950s, anthropologists realized that the Neandertals did not look that different from modern humans—despite their sloping foreheads, large brow ridges, flattened braincases, large jaws, and nearly absent chins.[5] After all, they did have larger brains (averaging more than 1,450 cc) than modern humans (slightly more than 1,300 cc).[6] Some scholars believe that the large brain capacity of Neandertals suggests that they were capable of the full range of behavior characteristic of modern humans. Their skeletons did, however, attest to one behavioral trait markedly different from behaviors of most modern humans: Neandertals apparently made very strenuous use of their bodies.[7]

It took almost 100 years for scholars to accept the idea that Neandertals were not that different from modern humans and therefore should be classified as ***Homo sapiens neanderthalensis.*** But, as we shall see, there still is debate over whether the Neandertals in western Europe were ancestral to modern-looking people who lived later in western Europe, after about 40,000 years ago. In any case, Neandertals lived in other places besides western Europe. A large number of fossils from central Europe strongly resemble those from western Europe, although some features, such as a projecting midface, are less pronounced.[8] Neandertals have also been found in southwestern Asia (Israel, Iraq) and Central Asia (Uzbekistan). One of the largest collections of Neandertal fossils comes from Shanidar Cave in the mountains of northeastern Iraq, where Ralph Solecki unearthed the skeletons of nine individuals (see site 31 in Figure 6–1).[9]

The Neandertals have received a great deal of scholarly and popular attention, probably because they were the first premodern humans to be found. But we now know that other premodern *H. sapiens,* some perhaps older than Neandertals, lived elsewhere in the Old World—in East, South, and North Africa, as well as in Java and China.[10] These other premodern but definite *H. sapiens* are sometimes considered Neandertal-like, but more often they are named after the places where they were first found, as indeed the original Neandertal was. For example, the cranium from China called *Homo sapiens daliensis* was named after the Chinese locality, Dali, in which it was found in 1978.[11]

The Neandertal on the left has bigger brow ridges and a more sloping forehead than the Cro-Magnon on the right. The Neandertal brain was larger on average than the Cro-Magnon brain.

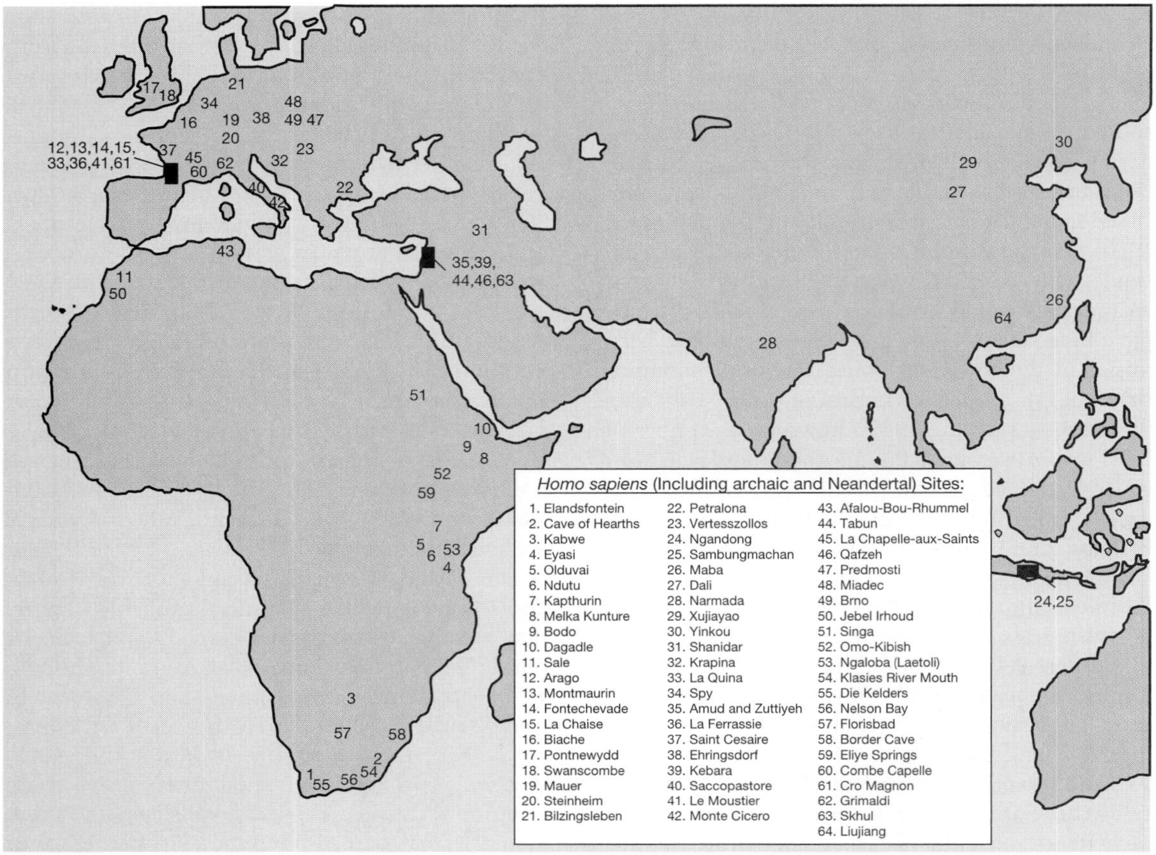
Homo sapiens (Including archaic and Neandertal) Sites:
1. Elandsfontein
2. Cave of Hearths
3. Kabwe
4. Eyasi
5. Olduvai
6. Ndutu
7. Kapthurin
8. Melka Kunture
9. Bodo
10. Dagadle
11. Sale
12. Arago
13. Montmaurin
14. Fontechevade
15. La Chaise
16. Biache
17. Pontnewydd
18. Swanscombe
19. Mauer
20. Steinheim
21. Bilzingsleben
22. Petralona
23. Vertesszollos
24. Ngandong
25. Sambungmachan
26. Maba
27. Dali
28. Narmada
29. Xujiayao
30. Yinkou
31. Shanidar
32. Krapina
33. La Quina
34. Spy
35. Amud and Zuttiyeh
36. La Ferrassie
37. Saint Cesaire
38. Ehringsdorf
39. Kebara
40. Saccopastore
41. Le Moustier
42. Monte Cicero
43. Afalou-Bou-Rhummel
44. Tabun
45. La Chapelle-aux-Saints
46. Qafzeh
47. Predmosti
48. Miadec
49. Brno
50. Jebel Irhoud
51. Singa
52. Omo-Kibish
53. Ngaloba (Laetoli)
54. Klasies River Mouth
55. Die Kelders
56. Nelson Bay
57. Florisbad
58. Border Cave
59. Eliye Springs
60. Combe Capelle
61. Cro Magnon
62. Grimaldi
63. Skhul
64. Liujiang
12,13,14,15,
33,36,41,61
35,39,
44,46,63
24,25

FIGURE 6–1 ***Homo sapiens Sites***

Source: From Russell L. Ciochon and John G. Fleagle, eds., *The Human Evolution Source Book* (Englewood Cliffs, NJ: Prentice Hall, 1993), p. xi.

MIDDLE PALEOLITHIC CULTURES

The period of cultural history associated with the Neandertals is traditionally called the Middle Paleolithic in Europe and the Near East and dates from about 300,000 years ago to about 40,000 years ago.[12] For Africa, the term *Middle Stone Age* is used instead of *Middle Paleolithic.* The tool assemblages from this period are generally referred to as *Mousterian* in Europe and the Near East and as *post-Acheulian* in Africa. (See the time line in Figure 6–2.)

Tool Assemblages

THE MOUSTERIAN. The Mousterian type of tool complex is named after the tool assemblage found in a rock shelter at Le Moustier in the Dordogne region of southwestern France. Compared with an Acheulian assemblage, a **Mousterian tool assemblage** has a smaller proportion of large core tools such as handaxes and cleavers and a bigger proportion of small flake tools such as scrapers.[13] Although many flakes struck off from a core were used "as is," the Mousterian is also characterized by flakes that were often altered or "retouched" by striking small flakes or chips from one or more edges (see Figure 6–3).[14] Studies of the wear on scrapers suggest that many were used for scraping hides or working wood. The fact that some of the tools, particularly points, were thinned or shaped on one side suggests that they were hafted or attached to a shaft or handle.[15]

Toward the end of the Acheulian period, a technique developed that enabled the toolmaker to produce flake tools of a predetermined size instead of simply chipping flakes away from the core at random. In this **Levalloisian method,** the toolmaker

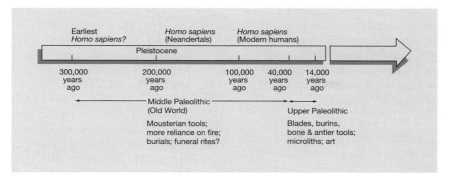

FIGURE 6–2 *An Evolutionary Time Line*

first shaped the core and prepared a "striking platform" at one end. Flakes of predetermined and standard sizes could then be knocked off. Although some Levallois flakes date as far back as 400,000 years ago, they are found more frequently in Mousterian tool kits.[16]

The tool assemblages in particular sites may be characterized as Mousterian, but one site may have more or fewer scrapers, points, and so forth, than another site. A number of archaeologists have suggested possible reasons for this variation. For example, Sally Binford and Lewis Binford suggested

FIGURE 6–3 *A Typical Mousterian Tool Kit*

A Mousterian tool kit emphasized sidescrapers (1–4), notches (5), points (6), and saw-toothed denticulates (7). How these stone artifacts were actually used is not known, but the points may have been joined to wood shafts, and denticulates could have been used to work wood. The tools illustrated here are from Mousterian sites in western Europe. *Source:* From Richard G. Klein, "Ice-Age Hunters of the Ukraine." Reprinted with permission of Nelson H. Prentiss.

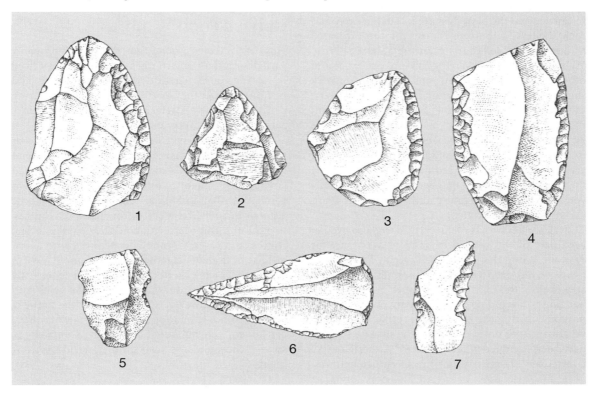

that different activities may have occurred in different sites. Some sites may have been used for butchering and other sites may have been base camps; hence the kinds of tools found in different sites should vary.[17] And Paul Fish has suggested that some sites may have more tools produced by the Levalloisian technique because larger pieces of flint were available.[18]

THE POST-ACHEULIAN IN AFRICA. Like Mousterian tools, many of the post-Acheulian tools in Africa during the Middle Stone Age were struck off prepared cores in the Levalloisian way. The assemblages consist mostly of various types of flake tools. A well-described sequence of such tools comes from the area around the mouth of the Klasies River on the southern coast of South Africa. This area contains rock shelters and small caves in which early and later *Homo sapiens* lived. The oldest cultural remains in one of the caves may date back 120,000 years.[19] These earliest tools include parallel-sided flake blades (probably used as knives), pointed flakes (possibly spearpoints), burins or gravers (chisel-like tools), and scrapers. Similar tools discovered at Border Cave, South Africa, may have been used almost 200,000 years ago.[20]

HOMESITES

Most of the excavated Middle Paleolithic homesites in Europe and the Near East are located in caves and rock shelters. The same is true for the excavated Middle Stone Age homesites in sub-Saharan Africa. We might conclude, therefore, that Neandertals and other early *H. sapiens* lived mostly in caves or rock shelters. But that conclusion could be incorrect. Caves and rock shelters may be overrepresented in the archaeological record because they are more likely to be found than are sites that originally were in the open but now are hidden by thousands of years, and many feet, of sediment. **Sediment** is the dust, debris, and decay that accumulates over time; when we dust the furniture and vacuum the floor, we are removing sediment.

Still, we know that many early *H. sapiens* lived at least part of the year in caves. This was true, for example, along the Dordogne River in France. The river gouged deep valleys in the limestone of that area. Below the cliffs are rock shelters with overhanging roofs and deep caves, many of which were occupied during the Middle Paleolithic. Even if the inhabitants did not stay all year, the sites do seem to have been occupied year after year.[21] Although there is evidence of some use of fire in earlier cultures,

Middle Paleolithic humans seem to have relied more on fire. There are thick layers of ash in many rock shelters and caves and evidence that hearths were used to increase the efficiency of the fires.[22]

Quite a few homesites of early *H. sapiens* were in the open. In Africa, open-air sites were located on floodplains, at the edges of lakes, and near springs.[23] Many open-air sites have been found in Europe, particularly eastern Europe. The occupants of the well-known site at Moldova in western Russia lived in river-valley houses framed with wood and covered with animal skins. Bones of mammoths, huge elephants now extinct, surround the remains of hearths and were apparently used to help hold the animal skins in place. Even though the winter climate near the edge of the glacier nearby was cold at that time, there would still have been animals to hunt because the plant food for the game was not buried under deep snow.

The hunters probably moved away in the summer to higher land between the river valleys. In all likelihood, the higher ground was grazing land for the large herds of animals the Moldova hunters depended on for meat. In the winter river-valley sites archaeologists have found skeletons of wolf, arctic fox, and hare with their paws missing. These animals probably were skinned for pelts that were made into clothing.[24]

GETTING FOOD

How early *Homo sapiens* got their food probably varied with their environment. In Africa, they lived in savanna and semiarid desert. In western and eastern Europe, they had to adapt to cold; during periods of increased glaciation, much of the environment was steppe grassland and tundra.

The European environment during this time was much richer in animal resources than the tundra of northern countries is today. Indeed, the European environment inhabited by Neandertals abounded in game, both big and small. The tundra and alpine animals included reindeer, bison, wild oxen, horses, mammoths, rhinoceroses, and deer, as well as bears, wolves, and foxes.[25] Some European sites have also yielded bird and fish remains. For example, people in a summer camp in northern Germany apparently hunted swans and ducks and fished for perch and pike.[26] Little, however, is known about the particular plant foods the European Neandertals may have consumed; the remains of plants are unlikely to survive thousands of years in a nonarid environment.

Archaeologist Hilary Deacon at the mouth of the Klasies River in South Africa, where early modern humans have been found.

In Africa, too, early *H. sapiens* varied in how they got food. For example, we know that the people living at the mouth of the Klasies River in South Africa ate shellfish as well as meat from small grazers such as antelopes and large grazers such as eland and buffalo.[27] But archaeologists disagree about how the Klasies River people got their meat when they began to occupy the caves in the area.

Richard Klein thinks they hunted the large as well as small game. Klein speculates that because the remains of eland of all ages have been found in Cave 1 at this site, the people there probably hunted the eland by driving them into corrals or other traps, where animals of all ages could be killed. Klein thinks that buffalo were hunted differently. Buffalo tend to charge attackers, which would make it difficult to drive them into traps. Klein believes that, because bones from mostly very young and very old buffalo are found in the cave, the hunters were able to stalk and kill only the most vulnerable animals.[28]

Lewis Binford thinks the Klasies River people hunted only small grazers and scavenged the eland and buffalo meat from the kills of large carnivores. He argues that sites should contain all or almost all of the bones from animals that were hunted. According to Binford, since more or less complete skeletons are found only from small animals, the

Klasies River people were not at first hunting all the animals they used for food.[29]

But there is new evidence suggesting that people were hunting big game as much as 400,000 years ago. Wooden spears that old were recently found in Germany in association with stone tools and the butchered remains of more than 10 wild horses. The heavy spears resemble modern aerodynamic javelins, which suggests they would have been thrown at large animals such as horses, not at small animals. This new evidence strongly suggests that hunting, not just scavenging, may be older than archaeologists used to think.[30]

FUNERAL RITUALS?

Some Neandertals were deliberately buried. At Le Moustier, the skeleton of a boy 15 or 16 years old was found with a beautifully fashioned stone ax near his hand. Near Le Moustier, graves of five other children and two adults, apparently interred together in a family plot, were discovered. These finds, along with one at Shanidar Cave in Iraq, have aroused speculation about the possibility of funeral rituals.

The evidence at Shanidar consists of pollen around and on top of a man's body. Pollen analysis suggests that the flowers included ancestral forms of modern grape hyacinths, bachelor's buttons, hollyhocks, and yellow flowering groundsels. John Pfeiffer speculated about this find:

A man with a badly crushed skull was buried deep in the cave with special ceremony. One spring day about 60,000 years ago members of his family went out into the hills, picked masses of wild flowers, and made a bed of them on the ground, a resting place for the deceased. Other flowers were probably laid on top of his grave; still others seem to have been woven together with the branches of a pinelike shrub to form a wreath.[31]

Can we be sure? Not really. All we really know is that there was pollen near and on top of the body. It could have gotten there because humans put flowers in the grave, or it could have gotten there for other, even accidental, reasons.

THE EMERGENCE OF MODERN HUMANS

Cro-Magnon humans, who appear in western Europe about 35,000 years ago, were once thought to be the earliest specimens of modern humans, or *Homo sapiens sapiens*. (The Cro-Magnons are named after the rock shelter in France where they were first found in 1868.[32]) But we now know that modern-looking humans appeared earlier outside of Europe. As of now, the oldest known fossils classified as *H. sapiens sapiens* come from Africa. Some of these fossils, discovered in one of the Klasies River Mouth caves, are possibly as old as 100,000 years.[33] Other modern-looking fossils of about the same age have been found in Border Cave in South Africa, and a find at Omo in Ethiopia may be an early *H. sapiens sapiens*.[34] Remains of anatomically modern humans found at two sites in Israel, at Skhul and Qafzeh, which used to be thought to date back 40,000 to 50,000 years, may be 90,000 years old.[35] There are also anatomically modern human finds in Borneo, at Niah, from about 40,000 years ago and in Australia, at Lake Mungo, from about 30,000 years ago.[36]

These modern-looking humans differed from the Neandertals and other early *H. sapiens* in that they had higher, more bulging foreheads, thinner and lighter bones, smaller faces and jaws, chins (the bony protuberances that remain after projecting faces recede), and slight bone ridges (or no ridges at all) over the eyes and at the back of the head.

THEORIES ABOUT THE ORIGINS OF MODERN HUMANS

Two theories about the origins of modern humans continue to be debated among anthropologists. One, which can be called the *single-origin* theory, suggests that modern humans emerged in just one part of the Old World and then spread to other parts, replacing Neandertals and other premodern *Homo sapiens*. (Africa is generally thought to be the place of modern humans' origin.) The second theory, which has been called the *multiregional theory,* suggests that modern humans evolved in various parts of the Old World after *Homo erectus* spread out of Africa.[37]

According to the single-origin theory, most of the Neandertals and other premodern *H. sapiens* did not evolve into modern humans. Rather, according to this view, Neandertals became extinct after 35,000 years ago because they were replaced by modern humans. The presumed place of origin of the first modern humans has varied over the years as new fossils have been discovered. In the 1950s the source population was presumed to be the Neandertals in the Near East, who were referred to as "generalized" or "progressive" Neandertals. Later, when earlier *Homo sapiens sapiens* were found in Africa, paleoan-

thropologists postulated that modern humans emerged first in Africa and then moved to the Near East and from there to Europe and Asia. Single-origin theorists think that the originally small population of *H. sapiens sapiens* had some biological or cultural advantage, or both, that allowed them to spread and replace premodern *Homo sapiens.*

According to the multiregional theory, *Homo erectus* populations in various parts of the Old World gradually evolved into anatomically modern-looking humans. The theorists espousing this view believe that the "transitional" or "archaic" *H. sapiens* and the Neandertals and other definite *H. sapiens* represent phases in the gradual development of more "modern" anatomical features. Indeed, as we have noted, some of these theorists see so much continuity between *Homo erectus* and modern humans that they classify *Homo erectus* as *Homo sapiens erectus.*

To explain why human evolution would proceed gradually and in the same direction in various parts of the Old World, multiregional theorists point to cultural improvements in cutting-tool and cooking technology that occurred all over the Old World. These cultural improvements may have relaxed the prior natural selection for heavy bones and musculature in the skull. The argument is that unless many plant and animal foods were cut into small pieces and thoroughly cooked in hearths or pits that were efficient thermally, they would be hard to chew and digest. Thus people previously would have needed robust jaws and thick skull bones to support the large muscles that enabled them to cut and chew their food. But robust bone and muscle would no longer be needed after people began to cut and cook more effectively.[38]

The single-origin and multiregional theories are not the only possible interpretations of the available fossil record. There is also the intermediate interpretation that there may have been some replacement of one population by another, some local continuous evolution, and some interbreeding between early modern humans, who spread out of Africa, and populations encountered in North Africa, Europe, and Asia.[39] As the biologist Alan Templeton has noted, the debates over a single-origin versus multiregional evolution of *Homo sapiens* "are based on the myth that replacement of one physical feature in a fossil series with another feature can only be created by one population replacing another (by exterminating them, for example), but such fossil patterns could be a reflection of one genotype replacing another through gene flow and natural selection. Morphological replacement should not be equated with population replacement when one is dealing with populations that can interbreed."[40] The next chapter discusses how modern human populations may also vary in physical features because natural selection favors different features in different environments.

DATING SKELETAL AND ARCHAEOLOGICAL REMAINS OF MODERN HUMANS

RADIOCARBON DATING. **Radiocarbon dating** (discussed briefly in Chapter 4) is a reliable method for dating remains up to 50,000 years old.[41] It is based on the principle that all living matter possesses a certain amount of a radioactive form of carbon (carbon-14, or ^{14}C). Radioactive carbon, produced when nitrogen-14 is bombarded by cosmic rays, is absorbed from the air by plants and then ingested by animals that eat the plants. After an organism dies, it no longer takes in any of the radioactive carbon. Carbon-14 decays at a slow but steady pace and reverts to nitrogen-14. (By "decays," we mean that the ^{14}C gives off a certain number of beta radiations per minute.) The rate at which the carbon decays (its half-life) is known: ^{14}C has a half-life of 5,730 years. In other words, half of the original amount of ^{14}C in organic matter will have disintegrated 5,730 years after the organism's death; half of the remaining ^{14}C will have disintegrated after another 5,730 years; and so on. After about 50,000 years, the amount of ^{14}C remaining in the organic matter is too small to permit reliable dating.

To discover how long an organism has been dead—that is, to determine how much ^{14}C is left in the organism and therefore how old it is—we count the number of beta radiations given off per minute per gram of material. Modern ^{14}C emits about 15 beta radiations per minute per gram of material, but ^{14}C that is 5,730 years old emits only half that amount (the half-life of ^{14}C) per minute per gram. So if a sample of some organism gives off 7.5 radiations a minute per gram, which is only half the amount given off by modern ^{14}C, the organism must be 5,730 years old.[42]

The accuracy of radiocarbon dating was tested by using it to judge the age of parts of the Dead Sea Scrolls and some wood from an Egyptian tomb, the dates of which were already known from historical records. The results based on ^{14}C analysis agreed very well with the historical information.

Because the ^{14}C method is not accurate for samples more than 50,000 years old, a particle accelerator can allow researchers to assess the actual amount of ^{14}C, not just its radioactive emissions, in some material; this new method provides a way to date specimens that are up to 80,000 years old.[43]

URANIUM-SERIES DATING. The decay of two kinds of uranium, ^{235}U and ^{238}U, into other isotopes (such as ^{230}Th, thorium) has also proved useful for dating *Homo sapiens* sites, particularly in caves where stalagmites and other calcite formations form. Because water that seeps into caves usually contains uranium but not thorium, the calcite formations trap uranium. Uranium starts decaying at a known rate into other isotopes (such as thorium-230, or ^{230}Th), and the ratio of those isotopes to uranium isotopes can be used to estimate the time elapsed. The thorium-uranium ratio is useful for dating cave sites less than 300,000 years old where there are no volcanic rocks suitable for the potassium-argon method. Early *H. sapiens* from European cave sites in Germany, Hungary, and Wales were dated this way.[44]

There are different varieties of **uranium-series dating**, depending on the specific isotope ratios used.

THERMOLUMINESCENCE DATING. Many minerals emit light when they are heated (thermoluminescence), even before they become red hot. This cold light comes from the release under heat of "outside" electrons trapped in the crystal structure. **Thermoluminescence dating**[45] makes use of the principle that if an object is heated at some point to a high temperature, as when clay is baked to form a pot, it will release all the trapped electrons it held previously. Over time, the object will continue to trap electrons from radioactive elements (potassium, thorium, uranium) around it. The amount of thermoluminescence emitted when the object is heated during testing allows researchers to calculate the age of the object, if it is known what kind of radiation the object has been exposed to in its surroundings (for example, the surrounding soil in which a clay pot is found).

Thermoluminescence dating is well suited to samples of ancient pottery, brick, tile, or terra cotta that were originally heated to a high temperature when they were made. This method can also be applied to burnt flint tools, hearth stones, lava or lava-covered objects, meteorites, and meteor craters.[46]

Research Frontiers

DNA EVIDENCE AND THE "OUT-OF-AFRICA" THEORY OF MODERN HUMAN ORIGINS

Paleoanthropologists used to believe that the humans (hominids) diverged from apes (pongids) more than 10 million years ago. Then molecular biologists started comparing the blood proteins and DNA of living primate species. These comparisons indicated that the probable time of divergence should be pushed up to 5–6 million years ago. Molecular biology now has entered another paleoanthropological debate—this time about the origin of modern-looking humans. On the basis of comparisons of mitochondrial DNA in various populations of living humans, molecular biologists generally support the "out-of-Africa" theory—the view that modern-looking humans emerged first in Africa and then spread throughout the world, replacing premodern *Homo sapiens.*

Mitochondrial DNA (mtDNA) is found in the mitochondrion, a part of the cell that converts food into energy for the cell. There are three advantages to using mtDNA over other kinds of DNA found in cell nuclei. The first is that mtDNA comprises only 37 genes; the fewer the genes, the easier the comparisons. Second, many neutral mutations accumulate rapidly and steadily in mtDNA, making it easier to find markers of similarity and difference in recent populations. (The more similar the mutations, the closer are two populations to a common ancestor.) The third advantage of mitochrondrial DNA is that it is inherited only from the mother, making it less complicated to trace evolutionary lines. Because mtDNA is passed on through the maternal line, molecular biologists refer to the ancestor of all modern humans as "Eve." Of course, there wasn't just one "Eve"; there must have been more than one of her generation with similar mtDNA.

Comparing the mtDNA of humans from different geographic regions and using computer software to create branching "tree" diagrams, the molecular researchers claim that the simplest or most parsimonious of the obtained solutions traces modern human mtDNA back to females who lived some 200,000 years ago. They also suggest that the mtDNA evidence is consistent with paleoanthropological evidence indicating that modern-looking humans appeared first in Africa, somewhat later in the Near East, and later still in Europe and Asia.

Critics of the out-of-Africa theory point out that the acceptability of the model depends on dubious assumptions. Perhaps the most telling criticism is that the solutions obtained so far are not the only ones possible. Actually, there are thousands of solutions possible in constructing tree diagrams from mtDNA data. The solutions obtained so far may point to an African origin of modern humans, but other possible solutions may suggest other scenarios. Why should we assume that the solutions obtained so far cover all the reasonable possibilities?

A second criticism of the out-of-Africa theory points to fossil evidence suggesting continuous

---

ELECTRON SPIN RESONANCE DATING. **Electron spin resonance dating** is a technique that, like thermoluminescence dating, measures trapped electrons from surrounding radioactive material. But the method in this case is different. The material to be dated is exposed to varying magnetic fields, and a spectrum of the microwaves absorbed by the tested material is obtained. Because no heating is required for this technique, electron spin resonance is especially useful for dating organic material such as bone and shell, which decompose if heated.[47]

 UPPER PALEOLITHIC CULTURES

The period of cultural history in Europe, the Near East, and Asia known as the Upper Paleolithic (see Figure 6–2) dates from about 40,000 years ago to the period known as the Mesolithic (about 14,000 to about 10,000 years ago, depending on the area). In Africa, the cultural period comparable to the Upper Paleolithic is known as the Later Stone Age and may have begun much earlier. To simplify terminology, we use the term *Upper Paleolithic* in referring to cul-

evolution toward modern-looking traits in various regions of the world. In other words, the fossil record is not consistent with the idea that modern-looking traits were introduced from outside those regions. The out-of-Africa theory must be wrong, critics argue, if physical traits persist in even just one region other than Africa, from the time of early humans to modern humans. For the out-of-Africa theory assumes that humans from southern Africa completely *replaced* early *H. sapiens*, with no gene flow between them. If this is what happened, the fossil record should show some discontinuity over time. But in Southeast Asia and Australia the fossils spanning 700,000 years (from *Homo erectus* to modern-looking humans) have similar features throughout that span of time. For instance, they have sloping rather than vertical frontal bones (foreheads), in contrast to early modern skulls in South Africa (such as at Border Cave), which have more vertical foreheads. In China there are shovel-shaped incisors from an-

cient times to modern times; African populations, early and late, lack this trait. So the persistence of distinctive traits in different regions (shovel-shaped incisors in China and sloping foreheads in Southeast Asia and Australia) is not consistent with the idea that modern-looking humans completely replaced previous *H. sapiens* in those regions.

There is also a lack of archaeological evidence to support the idea that an invading modern population came out of southern Africa. An invading population might have a very different tool kit, but in the Near East, where both Neandertal and modern human fossils are found with tools, the two have similar tool kits. In Asia, too, there is no discontinuity in technology, as we might expect with an invading population.

We would expect an invading population that replaced all other *H. sapiens* populations to have had some significant superiority. If not technological, then what? Some out-of-Africa theorists have suggested that the

earliest modern humans had language, whereas previous *H. sapiens* did not. But the evidence from anatomy regarding capacity for spoken language is still controversial.

As with most controversies, this one may be resolved with additional fossil evidence and more deliberate hypothesis tests of alternative interpretations.

Sources: For support of the out-of-Africa theory, see Linda Vigilant, Mark Stoneking, Henry Harpending, Kristen Hawkes, and Allan C. Wilson, "African Populations and the Evolution of Human Mitochondrial DNA," *Science,* September 27, 1991, 1503; and Allan C. Wilson and Rebecca L. Cann, "The Recent African Genesis of Humans," *Scientific American,* April 1992, 68–73. For critiques of the out-of-Africa theory, see David W. Frayer, "Testing Theories and Hypotheses about Human Origins," and Susan Weller, "The Research Process," in Carol R. Ember, Melvin Ember, Peter N. Peregrine, eds., *Research Frontiers in Anthropology* (Upper Saddle River, NJ: Prentice Hall, 1998), Prentice Hall/Simon & Schuster Custom Publishing; and Alan G. Thorne and Milford H. Wolpoff, "The Multiregional Evolution of Humans," *Scientific American,* April 1992, 76–83.

tural developments in all areas of the Old World during this period.

In many respects, life-styles during the Upper Paleolithic were similar to life-styles before. People were still mainly hunters and gatherers and fishers who probably lived in highly mobile bands. They made their camps out in the open in skin-covered huts and in caves and rock shelters. And they continued to produce smaller and smaller stone tools.

But the Upper Paleolithic is also characterized by a variety of new developments. One of the most striking is the emergence of art—painting on cave

walls and stone slabs and carving tools, decorative objects, and personal ornaments out of bone, antler, shell, and stone. (Perhaps for this as well as other purposes, people began to obtain materials from distant sources.) Because more archaeological sites date from the Upper Paleolithic than from any previous period and some Upper Paleolithic sites seem larger than any before, many archaeologists think that the human population increased considerably during the Upper Paleolithic.[48] And new inventions, such as the bow and arrow, the spear-thrower, and tiny replaceable blades that could be fitted into handles, appear for the first time.[49]

HOMESITES

As was the case in the known Middle Paleolithic sites, most of the Upper Paleolithic remains that have been excavated were situated in caves and rock shelters. In southwestern France, some groups seem to have paved parts of the floor of the shelter with stones. Tentlike structures were built in some caves, apparently to keep out the cold.[50] Some open-air sites have also been excavated.

The site at Dolni Vestonice in what is now the Czech Republic, dated to around 25,000 years ago, is one of the first for which there is an entire settlement plan.[51] The settlement seems to have consisted of four tentlike huts, probably made from animal skins, with a great open hearth in the center. Around the outside were mammoth bones, some rammed into the ground, which suggests that the huts were surrounded by a wall. All told, there were bone heaps from about 100 mammoths. Each hut probably housed a group of related families—about 20 to 25 people. (One hut was approximately 27 by 45 feet and had five hearths distributed inside it, presumably one for each family.) With 20 to 25 people per hut, and assuming that all four huts were occupied at the same time, the population of the settlement would have been 100 to 125.

Up a hill from the settlement was a fifth and different kind of hut. It was dug into the ground and contained a bake oven and more than 2,300 small, fired fragments of animal figurines. There were also some hollow bones that may have been musical instruments. Another interesting feature of the settlement was a burial find, of a woman with a disfigured face. She may have been a particularly important personage, because her face was found engraved on an ivory plaque near the central hearth of the settlement.

TOOLS: NEW TECHNIQUES

Upper Paleolithic toolmaking appears to have had its roots in the Mousterian and post-Acheulian traditions, because flake tools are found in many Upper Paleolithic sites. But the Upper Paleolithic is characterized by a preponderance of blades; there were also *burins*, bone and antler tools, and microliths. In addition, two new techniques of toolmaking appeared—*indirect percussion* and *pressure flaking*. Blades were found in Middle Paleolithic assemblages, but they were not widely used until the Upper Paleolithic. Although blades can be made in a variety

of ways, **indirect percussion** using a hammer-struck punch was commonly used in the Upper Paleolithic. After shaping a core into a pyramidal or cylindrical form, the toolmaker put a punch of antler or wood or another hard material into position and struck it with a hammer. Because the force is readily directed, the toolmaker was able to strike off consistently shaped **blades,** which are more than twice as long as they are wide[52] (see Figure 6–4).

The Upper Paleolithic is also noted for the production of large numbers of bone, antler, and ivory tools; needles, awls, and harpoons made of bone appear for the first time.[53] The manufacture of these implements may have been made easier by the development of many varieties of burins. **Burins** are chisel-like stone tools used for carving (see Figure 6–5); bone and antler needles, awls, and projectile points could be produced with them.[54] Burins have been found in Middle and Lower Paleolithic sites

---

FIGURE 6–4

One way to remove blades from a core is to hit them with a punch using indirect percussion. The object being struck is the punch, which is made of bone or horn. *Source:* From Brian M. Fagan, *In the Beginning* (Boston: Little, Brown, 1972), p. 195.

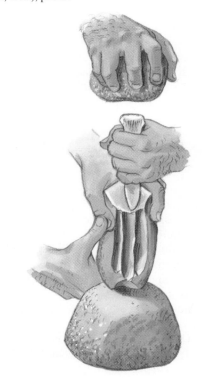

but are present in great number and variety only in the Upper Paleolithic.

Pressure flaking also appeared during the Upper Paleolithic. Rather than using percussion to strike off flakes as in previous technologies, pressure flaking works by employing pressure with a bone, wood, or antler tool at the edge of the tool to remove small flakes. Pressure flaking would usually be used in the final stages of retouching a tool.[55]

As time went on, all over the Old World smaller and smaller blade tools were produced. The very tiny ones, called **microliths,** were often hafted or fitted into handles, one blade at a time or several blades together, to serve as spears, adzes, knives, and sickles. The hafting required inventing a way to trim the blade's back edge so that it would be blunt rather than sharp. In this way the blades would not split the handles into which they might be inserted; the blunting would also prevent the users of an unhafted blade from cutting themselves.[56]

Some archaeologists think that the blade technique was adopted because it made for more economical use of flint. André Leroi-Gourhan of the Musée de l'Homme in Paris calculated that with the old Acheulian technique, a 2-pound lump of flint yielded 16 inches of working edge and produced only two handaxes. If the more advanced Mousterian technique were used, a lump of equal size would yield 2 yards of working edge. The indirect percussion method of the Upper Paleolithic would yield as

FIGURE 6–5

Upper Paleolithic tool kit from Hungary and Czechoslovakia. Burin (1), burin scraper (2), multiple burin (3), end-scraper on retouched blade (4), denticulated-backed bladelets (5, 6), pointed retouched blade (8), gravette points (9, 10), and bifacial points (7, 11). *Source:* From François Bordes, *The Old Stone Age,* trans. J. E. Anderson (New York: World University Library, 1968).

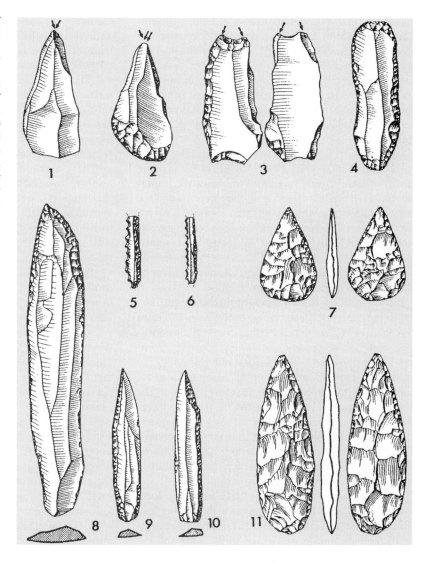

much as 25 yards of working edge.[57] With the same amount of material, a significantly greater number of tools could be produced. Getting the most out of a valuable resource may have been particularly important in areas lacking large flint deposits.

Jacques Bordaz suggested that the evolution of toolmaking techniques, which continually increased the amount of usable edge that could be gotten out of a lump of flint, was significant because people could then spend more time in regions where flint was unavailable. Another reason for adopting the blade toolmaking technique may have been that it made for easy repair of tools. For example, the cutting edge of a tool might consist of a line of razorlike microliths set into a piece of wood. The tool would not be usable if just one of the cutting edge's microliths broke off or was chipped. But if the user carried a small prepared core of flint from which an identical-sized microlith could be struck off, the tool could be repaired easily by replacing the lost or broken microlith. A spear whose point was lost could be repaired similarly. Thus, the main purpose of the blade toolmaking technique may not have been to make more economical use of flint, but rather to allow easy replacement of damaged blades.[58]

HOW WERE THE TOOLS USED? Ideally, the study of tools should reveal not only how the implements were made but also how they were used. One way of suggesting what a particular tool was used for in the past is to observe the manner in which similar tools are used by members of recent or contemporary societies, preferably societies with subsistence activities and environments similar to those of the ancient toolmakers. This method of study is called reasoning from **ethnographic analogy.** The problem with such reasoning, however, is obvious: We cannot be sure that the original use of a tool was the same as the present use. When selecting recent or contemporary cultures that may provide the most informative and accurate comparisons, we should try to choose those that derive from the ancient culture we are interested in. If the cultures being compared are historically related—prehistoric and recent Pueblo cultures in the southwestern United States, for example—there is a greater likelihood that the two groups used a particular kind of tool in similar ways and for similar purposes.[59]

Another way of suggesting what a particular kind of tool was used for is to compare the visible and microscopic wear marks on the prehistoric tools with the wear marks on similar tools made and ex-perimentally used by contemporary researchers. The idea behind this approach is that different uses leave different wear marks. A pioneer in this research was S. A. Semenov, who re-created prehistoric stone tools and used them in a variety of ways to find out which uses left which kinds of wear marks. For example, by cutting into meat with his re-created stone knives, he produced a polish on the edges that was like the polish found on blades from a prehistoric site in Siberia. This finding led Semenov to infer that the Siberian blades were probably also used to cut meat.[60]

The tools made by Upper Paleolithic people suggest that they were much more effective hunters and fishers than their predecessors.[61] During the Upper Paleolithic, and probably for the first time, spears were shot from a spear-thrower rather than thrown with the arm. We know this because bone and antler **atlatls** (the Aztec word for "spear-thrower") have been found in some sites. A spear propelled off a grooved board could be sent through the air with increased force, causing it to travel farther and hit harder, and with less effort by the thrower. The bow and arrow was also used in various places during the Upper Paleolithic; and harpoons, used for fishing and perhaps for hunting reindeer, were invented at this time.

These new tools and weapons for more effective hunting and fishing do not rule out the possibility that Upper Paleolithic people were still scavenging animal remains. Olga Soffer suggests that Upper Paleolithic people may have located their settlements near places where many mammoths died naturally in order to make use of the bones for building (see Figure 6–6). For example, in Moravia the mammoths may have come to lick deposits of calcite and other sources of magnesium and calcium, particularly during the late spring and early summer when resources were short and mortality was high. Consistent with the idea that humans may not have killed so many of the enormous mammoths is the fact that in some places there are few human-made cut marks on mammoth bones. For example, at Dolni Vestonice, where bones of 100 mammoths were found, few bones show cut marks from butchering and few bones were found inside the huts. In contrast, the living floors are littered with bison, horse, and reindeer bones, suggesting that these other animals were deliberately killed and eaten by humans. If the people had been able to kill all the mammoths we find the remains of, why would they have hunted so many other animals?[62]

FIGURE 6–6

Here we see the type of mammoth-bone shelters constructed about 15,000 years ago on the East European Plain. Often mammoth skulls formed part of the foundation for the tusk, long bone, and wooden frame, covered with hide. As many as 95 mammoth mandibles were arranged around the outside in a herringbone pattern. Ten men and women could have constructed this elaborate shelter of 258 square feet in six days, using 46,000 pounds of bone.

ART

The earliest discovered traces of art are beads and carvings, and then paintings, from Upper Paleolithic sites. We might expect that early artistic efforts were crude, but the cave paintings of Spain and southern France show a marked degree of skill. So do the naturalistic paintings on slabs of stone excavated in southern Africa. Some of those slabs appear to have been painted as much as 28,000 years ago, which suggests that painting in Africa is as old as painting in Europe.[63] But painting may be even older than that. The early Australians may have painted on the walls of rock shelters and cliff faces at least 30,000 years ago and maybe as much as 60,000 years ago.[64]

Peter Ucko and Andrée Rosenfeld identified three principal locations of paintings in the caves of western Europe: (1) in obviously inhabited rock shelters and cave entrances—art as decoration or "art for art's sake"; (2) in "galleries" immediately off the inhabited areas of caves; and (3) in the inner reaches of caves, whose difficulty of access has been interpreted by some as a sign that magical-religious activities were performed there.[65]

The subjects of the paintings are mostly animals. The paintings rest on bare walls, with no backdrops or environmental trappings. Perhaps, like many contemporary peoples, Upper Paleolithic men and women believed that the drawing of a human image could cause death or injury. If that were indeed their belief, it might explain why human figures are rarely depicted in cave art. Another explanation for the focus on animals might be that these people sought to improve their luck at hunting. This theory is suggested by evidence of chips in the painted figures, perhaps made by spears thrown at the drawings. But if hunting magic was the chief motivation for the paintings, it is difficult to explain why only a few show signs of having been speared. Perhaps the paintings were inspired by the need to increase the supply of animals. Cave art seems to have reached a peak toward the end of the Upper Paleolithic period, when the herds of game were decreasing.

The particular symbolic significance of the cave paintings in southwestern France is more explicitly revealed, perhaps, by the results of Patricia Rice and Ann Paterson's statistical study.[66] The data suggest that the animals portrayed in the cave paintings were mostly the ones that the painters preferred for meat and for materials such as hides. For example, wild cattle (bovines) and horses are portrayed more often than we would expect by chance, probably because they were larger and heavier (meatier) than the other animals in the environment. In addition, the paintings mostly portray animals that the painters may have feared the most because of their size, speed, natural weapons such as tusks and horns, and unpredictability of behavior. That is,

Cave paintings from the Upper Paleolithic discovered in 1995 in a grotto in Vallon-Pont-D'Arc, Ardech, France. Statistical research on cave paintings suggests that artists tended to portray animals that were meatier as well as more fearsome.

mammoths, bovines, and horses are portrayed more often than deer and reindeer. Thus, the paintings are consistent with the idea that "the art is related to the importance of hunting in the economy of Upper Paleolithic people."[67] Consistent with this idea, according to the investigators, is the fact that the art of the cultural period that followed the Upper Paleolithic also seems to reflect how people got their food. But in that period, when getting food no longer depended on hunting large game (because they were becoming extinct), the art ceased to focus on portrayals of animals.

Upper Paleolithic art was not confined to cave paintings. Many shafts of spears and similar objects were decorated with figures of animals. Alexander Marshack has an interesting interpretation of some of the engravings made during the Upper Paleolithic. He believes that as far back as 30,000 B.C., hunters may have used a system of notation, engraved on bone and stone, to mark the phases of the moon. If this is true, it would mean that Upper Paleolithic people were capable of complex thought and were consciously aware of their environment.[68] In addition, figurines representing the human female in exaggerated form have been found at Upper Paleolithic sites. Called *Venuses,* these figurines portray women with broad hips and large breasts and abdomens. It has been suggested that the figurines were an ideal type or an expression of a desire for fertility.

What the Venus figurines symbolized is still controversial. As is usually the case in current scholarly controversies, there is little or no evidence available now that might allow us to accept or reject a particular interpretation. But not all controversies in anthropology continue because of lack of evidence. Sometimes a controversy continues because there is some, usually disputed evidence on all sides. This was the case until recently with the controversy to which we now turn—whether there were people in the Americas before about 11,500 years ago.

THE EARLIEST HUMANS AND THEIR CULTURES IN THE NEW WORLD

So far in this chapter we have dealt only with the Old World—Africa, Europe, and Asia. What about the New World—North and South America? How long have humans lived there, and what were their earliest cultures like?

Because only *Homo sapiens sapiens* fossils have been found in North and South America, migrations of humans to the New World had to have taken place sometime after the emergence of *H. sapiens sapiens*. But exactly when these migrations occurred is subject to debate, particularly about when people got to areas south of Alaska. Until recently, the prevailing view was that humans were not present south of Alaska until after 11,500 years ago. Now it appears from an archaeological site called Monte Verde in Chile that modern humans got to southern South America by at least 12,500 years ago, and maybe as much as 33,000 years ago. (See the box "When and How Did Humans Populate the New World?") The Monte Verde site contains more than 700 stone tools, the remains of hide-covered huts, and a child's footprint next to a hearth.[69]

The people there may or may not have hunted big game, but just a little while later there were

A jury of visiting archaeologists at the Monte Verde site in Chile confirmed that modern humans arrived in southern South America at least 12,500 years ago.

people living in the Amazon jungle of what is now Brazil who were definitely not hunters of mammoths and other big game, as the contemporaneous Clovis people of North America were. In other words, it looks like the earliest inhabitants of the New World—in Chile, Brazil, North America—varied in culture. The people in the Amazon lived by collecting fruits and nuts, fishing, and hunting small game. They lived in caves with painted art on the walls and left 30,000 stone chips from making tips of spears, darts, or harpoons).[70]

According to the comparative linguists Joseph Greenberg and Merritt Ruhlen, there were three waves of migration into the New World.[71] They compared hundreds of languages in North and South America, grouping them into three different language families. Because each of these language families has a closer relationship to an Asian language family than to the other New World language families, it would appear that three different migrations came out of Asia. The first arrivals spoke a language that diverged over time into most of the languages found in the New World—the Amerind family of languages; the speakers of these related languages came to occupy all of South and Central America as well as most of North America. Next came the ancestors of the people who speak languages belonging to the Na-Dené family, which today includes Navaho and Apache in the southwestern United States and the various Athapaskan languages of northern California, coastal Oregon, northwestern Canada, and Alaska. Finally, perhaps 4,000 years ago, came the ancestors of the Inuit (Eskimo) and Aleut (the latter came to occupy the islands southwest of Alaska and the adjacent mainland), who speak languages belonging to the Inuit-Aleut family.

Christy Turner's study of New World teeth supports the Greenberg and Ruhlen proposal of three separate migrations. Turner looked at the proportions of shovel-shaped incisors, a common Asian trait, in New World populations. The varying proportions fall into three distinct groupings, the same three suggested by the linguists.[72] (see Figure 6–7). But a recent genetic analysis suggests that Inuit-Aleut may have split from Na-Dené in the New World.[73] The peopling of the New World may have even been more complicated. There could have been four separate migrations from the Old World, from different regions of Asia; this was recently suggested by researchers who presented new evidence at the 1998 annual meeting of the American Association for the Advancement of Science.[74]

Research Frontiers

WHEN AND HOW DID HUMANS POPULATE THE NEW WORLD?

On the basis of similarities in biological traits such as tooth forms and blood types, and on possible linguistic relationships, anthropologists agree that Native Americans originally came from Asia. The traditional assumption is that they came to North America from Siberia, walking across a land bridge (Beringia) that is now under water (the Bering Strait) between Siberia and Alaska. The ice sheets or glaciers that periodically covered most of the high latitudes of the world contained so much of the world's water (the ice sheets were thousands of feet thick in some places) that Beringia was dry land in various periods. For example, there was a land bridge for a while until the last 10,000 years or so. Since then, the glaciers have mostly melted, and the Bering "bridge" has been completely covered by a higher sea level. We now know that the Monte Verde site in Chile was occupied 12,500 years ago, so it would seem that there was at least one wave of human migration into the New World before then, by walking and/or perhaps in boats. Even when the last glaciers were at their fullest extent, there was a small ice-free corridor through which

people could have walked (see the diagram in this box). And there were ice-free corridors earlier.

It was geologically possible then for humans to have walked into the New World at various times, and they could have traveled by boat too. Parts of the Beringia land bridge were exposed from about 60,000 to 25,000 years ago. It wasn't until between 20,000 and 18,000 years ago that the land bridge was at its maximum. When did the last land bridge disappear? Until recently, it was widely believed that the land bridge was flooded around 14,000 years ago, but recent evidence suggests that walking across Beringia was still

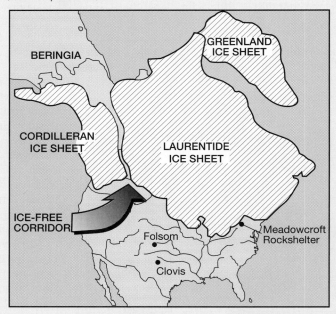

Beringia and the Ice Sheets   *Source:* David K. Meltzer, "Pleistocene Peopling of the Americas," *Evolutionary Anthropology,* Vol. 1, 1993. Copyright © 1993. Reprinted by permission of Wiley-Liss, Inc. a subsidiary of John Wiley and Sons, Inc.

Archaeological remains of early New World hunters have been found in the United States, Mexico, and Canada. For example, just south of the farthest reaches of the last glaciation, the area east of the Rockies known as the High Plains abounded with mammoths, bison, wild camels, and wild horses. The tools found with mammoth kills are

known as the *Clovis complex,* which includes the Clovis projectile point as well as stone scrapers and knives and bone tools. The Clovis projectile point is large and leaf-shaped, flaked on both sides. It has a broad groove in the middle, presumably so that the point could be attached to a wooden spear shaft.[75] Because one mammoth was found with eight Clovis

possible until about 10,000 years ago. An ice-free corridor between the Laurentide and Cordilleran ice sheets may have been present after 25,000 years ago, but that corridor is not likely to have supported big game, and permitted humans to hunt enough, until after about 14,000 years ago. So some investigators suggest that moving through the ice-free corridor to what is now south of Canada was not likely until after that time.

There is no disagreement that humans were living south of Canada around 11,000 years ago. The Clovis people, as they are called (after an archaeological site near Clovis, New Mexico), left finely shaped spear points in many locations in North America. And we have human skeletal remains from after 11,000 years ago. Now that the Monte Verde site has been reliably dated, we know that there were people south of Canada earlier than the Clovis people were in New Mexico. And there are other possible sites of pre-Clovis occupation, although many archaeologists do not agree that the presumed tools at these sites were made by humans (they could have been made by rockfalls or other natural forces) or that the sites are accurately dated. One site that

may be another pre-Clovis site is the Meadowcroft Rockshelter in western Pennsylvania.

In the bottom third of a stratum that seems to date from 19,600 to 8,000 years ago, the Meadowcroft site shows clear signs of human occupation—a small fragment of human bone, a spearpoint, and chipped knives and scrapers. If the dating is accurate, the tools would be about 12,800 years old. William Parry suggests we need to date the human bone found in the site. If the bone turns out to date from before 12,000 years ago, few anthropologists would question the conclusion that humans occupied the Meadowcroft site before the time of the Clovis people.

People now cross the Bering Strait by water. Could earlier humans have come to the New World the same way, before a land bridge existed? If they had come by water, instead of by walking over a land bridge and down through an ice-free corridor, there would be coastal sites with evidence of humans who traveled by water. Such sites would now be covered by water because sea level is higher now. It is conceivable then that humans came very early to the New World by water, but there is as yet no evidence of that under water along

the coast. Even if people did come early to the New World by water, they might not have survived long enough and spread widely enough to give archaeologists a chance to find their remains. There might be some remains somewhere, but that has not yet been definitely established.

Exactly when humans first came into the New World, how many migrations were there, and how they spread south of Canada are questions to which we still have only tentative answers. But new relevant evidence surfaces regularly, mainly because investigation actively continues. So we should have firmer answers to these questions before too long. That is part of what makes research exciting. There is always something new to look for.

Sources: Kim A. McDonald, "New Evidence Challenges Traditional Model of How the New World Was Settled," *Chronicle of Higher Education,* March 13, 1998, A22ff; John F. Hoffecker, W. Roger Powers, and Ted Goebel, "The Colonization of Beringia and the Peopling of the New World," *Science,* January 1, 1993, 46–53; and William J. Parry, "When and How Did Humans Populate the New World?" in Carol R. Ember, Melvin Ember, and Peter N. Peregrine, eds., *Research Frontiers in Anthropology* (Upper Saddle River, NJ: Prentice Hall, 1998). Prentice Hall/Simon & Schuster Custom Publishing.

points in it, there is little dispute that Clovis people hunted large game such as the mammoth.[76] Recent dating places most Clovis sites in the range of 11,200 to 10,900 years ago.[77]

The mammoth disappeared about 10,000 years ago (for possible reasons, see Chapter 8), and the largest game animal became the now-extinct large,

straight-horned bison. The hunters of that bison used a projectile point called the Folsom point, which was much smaller than the Clovis point. Tools are also found with many other kinds of animal remains, including wolf, turtle, rabbit, horse, fox, deer, and camel, so the bison hunters obviously depended on other animals as well.[78] In the Rio

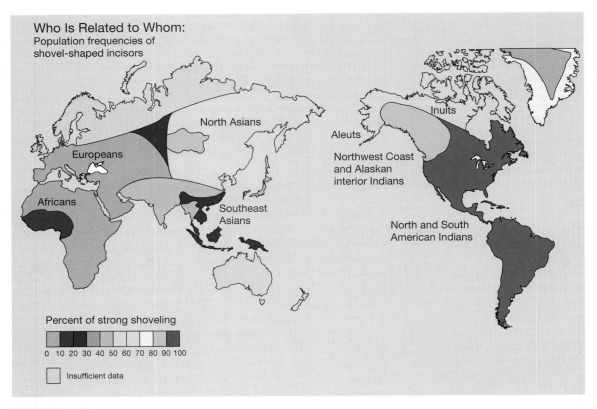

Who Is Related to Whom:
Population frequencies of
shovel-shaped incisors

North Asians

Europeans

Africans

Southeast
Asians

Aleuts

Inuits

Northwest Coast
and Alaskan
interior Indians

North and South
American Indians

Percent of strong shoveling

0 10 20 30 40 50 60 70 80 90 100

Insufficient data

FIGURE 6–7

Inuit (Eskimos) and Aleuts, speakers of Na-Dené languages, and other Native American language groups differ in the frequency of shovel-shaped incisors. These genetic differences seem to reflect three waves of migration into the New World. *Source:* From Christy G. Turner II, "Telltale Teeth," *Natural History*, January 1987, p. 8. Courtesy of *Natural History* magazine.

Grande valley, the Folsom toolmakers characteristically established a base camp on low dune ridges overlooking both a large pond and broad, open grazing areas. If we assume that the pond provided water for the grazing herds, the people in the camp would have been in an excellent position to watch the herds.[79]

As the climate of what is now the American Southwest became drier, the animals and the cultural adaptations changed somewhat. About 9,000 years ago the smaller modern bison replaced the earlier straight-horned variety.[80] Base camps began to be located farther from ponds and grazing areas and closer to streams. If the ponds were no longer reliable sources of water during these drier times, the animals probably no longer frequented them, which would explain why the hunters had to change the sites of their base camps. Not that much is known about the plant foods these people may have exploited, but on the desert fringes plant gathering

may have been vital. In Nevada and Utah, archaeologists have found milling stones and other artifacts for processing plant food.[81]

The Olsen-Chubbuck site, a kill site excavated in Colorado, shows the organization that may have been involved in hunting bison.[82] In a dry gulch dated to 6500 B.C. were the remains of 200 bison. At the bottom were complete skeletons and at the top, completely butchered animals. This find clearly suggests that hunters deliberately stampeded the animals into a natural trap—an arroyo, or steep-sided dry gully. The animals in front were probably pushed by the ones behind into the arroyo. Joe Wheat estimated that the hunters may have obtained 55,000 pounds of meat from this one kill. If we judge from nineteenth century Plains Indians, who could prepare bison meat to last a month, and estimate that each person would eat a pound a day, the kill at the Olsen-Chubbuck site could have fed more than 1,800 people for a month (they probably did not all live together throughout the year). The hunters must have been highly organized not only for the stampede itself but also for butchering. It seems that the enormous carcasses had to be carried to flat ground for that job. In addition, the 55,000 pounds of meat and hides had to be carried back to camp.[83]

Although big game may have been most important on the High Plains, other areas show different adaptations. For example, people in woodland regions of what is now the United States seem to have depended more heavily on plant food and smaller game. In some woodland areas, fish and shellfish may have been a vital part of the diet.[84] On the Pacific coast, some people developed food-getting strategies more dependent on fish.[85] And in other areas, the lower Illinois River valley being one example, people who depended on game and wild vegetable foods managed to get enough food to live in permanent villages of perhaps 100 to 150 people.[86]

In recent and modern times, too, the peoples of the world have varied culturally. In the next chapter we discuss how they vary physically.

SUMMARY

1. Most anthropologists agree that *Homo erectus* began to evolve into *Homo sapiens* after about 500,000 years ago. But there is disagreement about how and where the transition occurred. The mixed traits of the transitional fossils include large cranial capacities (well within the range of modern humans), together with low foreheads and large brow ridges, which are characteristic of *H. erectus* specimens. The earliest definite *H. sapiens,* who did not look completely like modern humans, appeared after about 200,000 years ago.

2. Premodern *Homo sapiens* have been found in many parts of the Old World—in Africa and Asia as well as in Europe. Some of these *H. sapiens* may have lived earlier than the Neandertals of Europe, who were the first premodern humans to be found. There is still debate over whether the Neandertals in western Europe became extinct or survived and were ancestral to the modern-looking people who lived in western Europe after about 40,000 years ago.

3. The period of cultural history associated with the Neandertals is traditionally called the Middle Paleolithic in Europe and the Near East and dates from about 300,000 to about 40,000 years ago. For Africa, the term *Middle Stone Age* is used. The assemblages of flake tools from this period are gener-

ally referred to as *Mousterian* in Europe and the Near East and as *post-Acheulian* in Africa. Compared with an Acheulian assemblage, a Mousterian tool assemblage has a smaller proportion of large handaxes and cleavers and a larger proportion of small flake tools such as scrapers. Some Mousterian sites show signs of intentional burial.

4. Fossil remains of fully modern-looking humans have been found in Africa, the Near East, Asia, and Australia, as well as in Europe. The oldest of these fossils have been found in South Africa and may be 100,000 years old.

5. Two theories about the origins of modern humans continue to be debated among anthropologists. One, which can be called the *single-origin* theory, suggests that modern humans emerged in just one part of the Old World—the Near East and, more recently, Africa have been the postulated places of origin—and spread to other parts of the Old World, superseding Neandertals and other premodern *Homo sapiens.* The second theory, which has been called the *multiregional theory,* suggests that modern humans emerged in various parts of the Old World, becoming the varieties of humans we see today.

6. The period of cultural history known as the Upper Paleolithic in Europe, the Near East, and Asia or the Later Stone Age in Africa dates from about 40,000 years ago to about 14,000 to 10,000 years ago. The Upper Paleolithic is characterized by the preponderance of blades; there were also burins, bone and antler tools, and (later) microliths. In many respects, life-styles were similar to life-styles before. People were still mainly hunters and gatherers and fishers who probably lived in highly mobile bands. They made their camps out in the open and in caves and rock shelters.

7. The Upper Paleolithic is also characterized by a variety of new developments: new techniques of toolmaking, the emergence of art, population growth, and new inventions such as the bow and arrow, the spear-thrower (atlatl), and the harpoon.

8. Only *Homo sapiens* remains have been found in the New World. The prevailing opinion is that humans migrated to the New World over a land bridge between Siberia and Alaska in the area of what is now the Bering Strait. The prevailing view until recently was that humans were not present south of Alaska until after 11,500 years ago. Now it appears from an archaeological site called Monte Verde in Chile that modern humans got to southern South America by at least 12,500 years ago, and perhaps as much as 33,000 years ago.

GLOSSARY TERMS

atlatls
blades
burins
Cro-Magnon
electron spin resonance
    dating
ethnographic analogy
*Homo sapiens
    neanderthalensis*
Homo sapiens sapiens
indirect percussion

Levalloisian method
microliths
Mousterian tool
    assemblage
pressure flaking
radiocarbon dating
sediment
thermoluminescence
    dating
uranium-series dating

CRITICAL QUESTIONS

1. If the single-origin or "out-of-Africa" theory were correct, by what mechanisms could one group of *Homo sapiens* have been able to replace another?

2. If modern human traits emerged in *Homo erectus* populations in different areas more or less at the same time, what mechanisms would account for similar traits emerging in different regions?

3. Upper Paleolithic cave paintings arouse our imaginations. We have described some research that tested ideas about what these paintings might mean. Can you think of other ways to understand the significance of cave art?

INTERNET EXERCISES

1. Learn about some of the archaeological remains of the native cultures of Arizona and their 6,000-year-old paintings. Visit **http://aztec.asu.edu/ aznha/palatki/palatki.html** and briefly interpret your findings as they relate to this chapter.

2. Reconstructions of fossil hominids are often collaborations of artists and biological anthropologists. For a reconstruction of a Neandertal family, review the steps shown at **http://www.bvl.uic.edu/ bvl/ng/.**

3. A team of experts has accepted the findings from a site in Chile named Monte Verde suggesting that humans were in the New World earlier than traditionally thought. Look at the press release at **http://www.nationalgeographic.com/ society/ngo/events/97/monteverde/dallas.html.** Also visit the site **http://www.unl.edu/anthro/ Hames/MonteVerde.htm** to read more about the findings and what they mean.

4. Stone tools played an important role in human cultural evolution. Visit **http://rubens.anu. edu.au/student.projects/tools/homepage.html** to see the various forms of Australian stone tools and summarize your findings.

SUGGESTED READING

CIOCHON, R. L., AND FLEAGLE, J. G., EDS. *The Human Evolution Source Book.* Upper Saddle , NJ: Prentice Hall, 1993. A collection of original articles about human evolution. Parts VI and VII are particularly relevant to this chapter.

DIBBLE, H. L., AND MELLARS, P., EDS. *The Middle Paleolithic: Adaptation, Behavior, and Variability* (Philadelphia: University Museum, 1992). A collection of papers that presents new data and provides rethinking about the variability in behavior during the Middle Paleolithic. The focus is on Europe and the Near East.

EMBER, C. R., EMBER, M., AND PEREGRINE, P., EDS. *Research Frontiers in Anthropology.* Upper Saddle River, NJ: Prentice Hall, 1998: Simon & Schuster Custom Publishing. Especially relevant to this chapter are D. W. Frayer, "Testing Theories and Hypotheses about Modern Human Origins"; A. Kramer, "The Natural History and Evolutionary Fate of *Homo erectus*"; N. Minugh-Purvis, "Neandertal Growth: Examining Developmental Adaptations in Earlier *Homo sapiens*"; W. J. Parry, "When and How Did Humans Populate the New World?"; and I. Tattersall, "Paleoanthropology and Evolutionary Theory."

FAGAN, B. M. *People of the Earth: An Introduction to World Prehistory,* 6th ed. Glenview, IL: Scott, Foresman, 1989. Chapters 5–8 survey the fossil and archaeological evidence on *Homo sapiens* in different parts of the world.

TRINKAUS, E., ED. *The Emergence of Modern Humans: Biocultural Adaptations in the Later Pleistocene.* Cambridge: Cambridge University Press, 1989. Physical anthropologists and archaeologists review and debate what is known and not known about the Neandertals and the transition to modern humans.

WENKE, R. J. *Patterns in Prehistory: Humankind's First Three Million Years,* 3rd ed. New York: Oxford University Press, 1990. A summary of cultural development that focuses on why various crucial changes may have occurred. Chapter 4 is particularly relevant to this chapter.

7

Human Variation

*I*n the preceding chapter we discussed the emergence of people like ourselves, *Homo sapiens sapiens.* Just as the cultures of those human beings differed in some respects, so do the cultures of peoples in recent times, as we will see in the chapters that follow. But anthropologists are also concerned with how recent human populations physically resemble or differ from each other, and why.

In any given human population, individuals vary in external features such as skin color or height and in internal features such as blood type or susceptibility to a disease. If you measure the frequencies of such features in different populations, you will typically find differences on average from one population to another. So, for example, some populations are typically darker in skin color than other populations.

Why do these physical differences exist? They may be largely the product of differences in genes. Or they may be largely due to growing up in a particular environment, physical and cultural. Or perhaps they are the result of an interaction between environmental factors and genes.

We turn first to the processes that may singly or jointly produce the varying frequencies of physical traits in different human populations. Then we discuss specific differences in external and internal characteristics and how they might be explained. Finally, we close with a critical examination of racial classification and whether it helps or hinders the study of human variation.

PROCESSES IN HUMAN VARIATION

NATURAL SELECTION

Mutations, or changes in the structure of a gene, are the ultimate source of all genetic variation. Because different genes make for greater or lesser chances of survival and reproduction, natural selection results in more favorable genes becoming more frequent in a population over time. How adaptive a gene or trait is depends on the environment; what is adaptive in one environment may not be adaptive in another. For example, in the chapter on evolution, we discussed the advantage that dark moths had over light moths when certain areas of England became industrialized. Predators could not easily see the darker moths against the newly darkened trees, and these

moths soon outnumbered the lighter variety. Similarly, human populations live in a great variety of environments, so we would expect natural selection to favor different genes and traits in those different environments. As we shall see, variations in skin color and body build are among the many features that may be at least partly explainable by how natural selection works in different environments.

The type of natural selection in the moth example is called **directional selection** because a particular trait seems to be positively favored and the average value shifts over time toward the adaptive trait. Figure 7–1 shows the effects of directional selection over time. But there can also be **normalizing selection.** In this type of selection the average value does not change, but natural selection removes the extremes.[1] An example is the birthweight of babies. Both very low birthweights and very high birthweights are disadvantageous and would be selected against. Directional and normalizing selection both assume that natural selection will either favor or disfavor genes, but there is a third possibility—balancing selection.[2] **Balancing selection** occurs when a heterozygous combination of alleles is positively favored even though a homozygous combination is disfavored. Later in this chapter we discuss a trait that apparently involves balancing selection—sickle-cell anemia—which is found in persons of West African ancestry, among other populations.

Natural selection does not account for variation in frequencies of neutral traits—that is, traits that do not seem to confer any advantages or disadvantages on their carriers. The sometimes different and sometimes similar frequencies of neutral traits in human populations may result, then, from genetic drift or gene flow.

GENETIC DRIFT

The term **genetic drift** is used to refer to various random processes that affect gene frequencies in small, relatively isolated populations. Genetic drift is also known as the *Wright effect,* after the geneticist Sewall Wright who first directed attention to this process. Over time in a small population, genetic drift may result in a neutral or nearly neutral gene becoming more or less frequent just by chance.[3]

One variety of genetic drift, called the *founder principle,* occurs when a small group recently derived from a larger population migrates to a relatively isolated location.[4] If a particular gene is absent just by chance in the migrant group, the descendants are likely also to lack that gene, assuming

FIGURE 7–1

Directional selection shifts the average value of a continuous trait (such as darkness of skin color) in a population over time. The shaded gray area represents the individuals who are selected against in a particular environment; the blue represents the individuals who are selected for in that same environment. So, for example, in a very sunny environment, light skin color would be selected against and dark skin color would be selected for. Gradually, darker skin would become more common. *Source:* From John Relethford, *The Human Species: An Introduction to Biological Anthropology* (Mountain View, CA: Mayfield, 1990), pp. 130, 132.

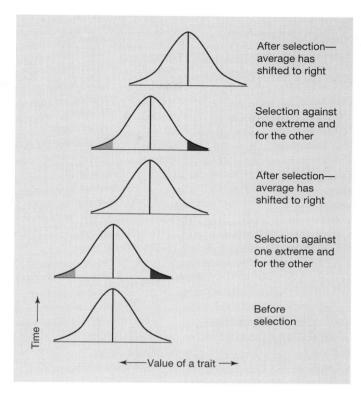

that the group remains isolated. Similarly, if all members of the original migrant group just by chance carried a particular gene, their descendants would also be likely to share that gene. Isolation can occur for physical reasons, such as when a group moves to a previously uninhabited place and does not return. The populations that traveled over the Bering land bridge from Asia to North America could not readily return when the sea level rose. Or the isolation can occur for social reasons. A religious sect of Dunkers emigrated from Germany to the United States in the early 1700s. The fact that the 50 original families kept to themselves probably explains why some of their gene frequencies differ from what is found in both the German and general U.S. populations.[5]

GENE FLOW

Gene flow is the process whereby genes pass from one population to another through mating and reproduction. Unlike the other processes of natural selection and genetic drift, which generally increase the differences between populations in different environments, gene flow tends to work in the opposite direction—it decreases differences between populations. Two populations at opposite ends of a region may have different frequencies of a particular gene,

but the populations located between them have an intermediate gene frequency because of gene flow between them. The variation in gene frequency from one end of the region to the other is called a **cline.** In Europe, for example, there is a cline in the distribution of blood type B, which gradually diminishes in frequency from east to west.[6]

Gene flow may occur between distant as well as close populations. Long-range movements of people, to trade or raid or settle, may result in gene flow. But they do not always do so.

INFLUENCE OF THE PHYSICAL ENVIRONMENT

Natural selection may favor certain genes because of certain physical environmental conditions, as in the case of the moths in England. But the physical environment can sometimes produce variation even in the absence of genetic change. As we shall see, climate may influence the way the human body grows and develops, and therefore some kinds of human variation may be explainable largely as a function of environmental variation. Moreover, access to certain nutrients and exposure to certain diseases may vary from one physical environment to another, and this variation may also influence how one population differs physically from another. But the influence of the physical environment might be modified by the cultural environment.

INFLUENCE OF THE CULTURAL ENVIRONMENT

Culture may allow humans to modify their environments to some extent, and such modifications may lessen the likelihood of genetic adaptation. For example, the effects of cold may be modified by the culture traits of living in houses, harnessing energy to create heat, and clothing the body to insulate it. In these cultural ways, we alter our "microenvironments." Iron deficiency may be overcome by the culture trait of cooking in iron pots. If a physical environment lacks certain nutrients, people may get them by the culture trait of trading for them; trading for salt has been common in world history. Culture can also influence the direction of natural selection. As we shall see, the culture of dairying seems to have increased the frequency of genes that allow adults to digest milk.[7]

In the next section we discuss some aspects of human (physical) variation for which we have explanations that involve one or more of the processes responsible for human variation.

PHYSICAL VARIATION IN HUMAN POPULATIONS

The most noticeable physical variations among populations are those that are external, on the surface—body build, facial features, skin color, and height. No

less important are those variations that are internal, such as variation in susceptibility to different diseases and differences in the ability to produce certain enzymes.

We begin our survey with some physical features that appear to be strongly linked to variation in climate, particularly variation in temperature, sunlight, and altitude.

BODY BUILD AND FACIAL CONSTRUCTION

Scientists have suggested that the body build of many birds and mammals may vary according to the temperature of the environment in which they live. Bergmann and Allen, two nineteenth-century naturalists, suggested some general rules for animals, but it was not until the 1950s that researchers began to examine whether these rules applied to human populations.[8] **Bergmann's rule** describes what seems to be a general relationship between body size and temperature: The slenderer populations of a species inhabit the warmer parts of its geographic range, and the more robust populations inhabit the cooler areas.

D. F. Roberts' studies of variation in mean body weight of human populations in regions with widely differing temperatures have provided support for Bergmann's rule.[9] Roberts discovered that the lowest body weights were found among residents of areas with the highest mean annual temperatures, and vice versa. Figure 7–2 shows the relationship between body weight of males and average annual

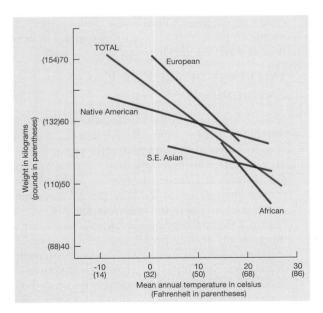

FIGURE 7–2 *Relationship between Body Weight of Males and Average Annual Temperature for Four Major Population Groups*

Source: From D. F. Roberts, "Body Weight, Race, and Climate," *American Journal of Physical Anthropology,* 11(1953): 553–38, Fig. 2, reproduced in Stephen Jones, Robert Martin, and David Pilbeam, *The Cambridge Encyclopedia of Human Evolution* (New York: Cambridge University Press, 1992), p. 47. Reprinted with the permission of Cambridge University Press.

Jumping Samburu dancers in northern Kenya have the long-limbed, lean body type that is often found in equatorial regions. Such a body type provides more surface area in relation to body mass, and thus may facilitate the dissipation of body heat.

temperature for four different geographic populations. Although the slope of the relationship is slightly different for each group, the trend is the same—with colder temperatures, weight is greater. Looking at the general trend across populations (see the "Total" line), we see that where the mean annual temperatures are about freezing (0°C; 32°F), the average weight for males is about 65 kilograms (143 pounds); where the mean annual temperatures are about 25°C (77°F), men weigh, on the average, about 50 kilograms (110 pounds).

Allen's rule refers to another kind of variation in body build among birds and mammals: Protruding body parts (e.g., limbs) are relatively shorter in the cooler areas of a species' range than in the warmer areas. Research comparing human populations tends to support Allen's rule.[10]

The rationale behind these theories is that the long-limbed, lean body type often found in equatorial regions provides more surface area in relation to body mass and thus facilitates the dissipation of

body heat. In contrast, the chunkier, shorter-limbed body type found among residents of cold regions promotes retention of body heat because the amount of surface area relative to body mass is lessened. The build of the Inuit (Eskimo) appears to exemplify Bergmann's and Allen's rules. The relatively large bodies and short legs of the Inuit may be adapted to the cold temperatures in which they live.

It is not clear whether differences in body build between populations are due solely to natural selection of different genes under different conditions of cold or heat. Some of the variation may be induced during the life span of individuals.[11] Alphonse Riesenfeld provided experimental evidence that extreme cold can affect body proportions during growth and development. Rats raised under conditions of extreme cold generally showed changes that resemble characteristics of humans in cold environments. These cold-related changes included shortening of the long bones, consistent with Allen's rule.[12]

Like body build, facial structure may also be affected by environment. Riesenfeld found that the facial width of rats increased in cold temperatures and their nasal openings grew smaller.[13] Because the rats raised in cold environments were genetically similar to those raised in warmer environments, we can confidently conclude that environment, not genes, brought about these changes in the rats. How much the environment directly affects variation in the human face is not clear. We do know that variation in climate is associated with facial variation. For example, people living in the humid tropics tend to have broad, short, flat noses, whereas people living in climates with low humidity (with cold or hot temperatures) tend to have long, thin noses. A narrow nose may be a more efficient humidifier of drier air than a broad nose.[14]

SKIN COLOR

Human populations obviously differ in average skin color. Many people consider skin color the most important indicator of "race" and sometimes treat others differently solely on this basis. But anthropologists, in addition to being critical of prejudice, also note that skin color is not a good indicator of ancestry. For example, extremely dark skin is found most commonly in Africa. However, there are natives of southern India whose skin is as dark as or darker than that of many Africans. Yet these people are not closely related to Africans, either genetically or historically.

How can we explain the wide range of skin colors among the peoples of the world? The color of a person's skin depends on both the amount of dark pigment, or melanin, in the skin and the amount of blood in the small blood vessels of the skin.[15] Despite the fact that there is still much to understand about the genetics of skin color, we do have some theories that may partly account for variation in skin color.

The amount of melanin in the skin seems to be related to the climate in which a person lives. **Gloger's rule** states that populations of birds and mammals living in warmer climates have more melanin, and therefore darker skin, fur, or feathers, than do populations of the same species living in cooler areas. On the whole, this association with climate holds true for people as well as for other mammals and birds.

The populations of darker-skinned humans do live mostly in warm climates, particularly sunny climates. Dark pigmentation seems to have at least one specific advantage in sunny climates. Melanin protects the sensitive inner layers of the skin from the sun's damaging ultraviolet rays; therefore, dark-skinned people living in sunny areas are safer from sunburn and skin cancers than are light-skinned people. Dark skin may also confer other important biological advantages in tropical environments, such as greater resistance to tropical diseases.[16]

What, then, might be the advantages of light-colored skin? Presumably, there must be some benefits in some environments; otherwise, human populations would all tend to have relatively dark skin. Although light-skinned people are more susceptible to sunburn and skin cancers, the ultraviolet radiation that light skin absorbs also facilitates the body's production of vitamin D. Vitamin D helps the body incorporate calcium and thus is necessary for the proper growth and maintenance of bones. Too much vitamin D, however, can cause illness. Thus, the light-colored skin of people in temperate latitudes maximizes ultraviolet penetration, perhaps ensuring production of sufficient amounts of vitamin D for good health, whereas the darker skin of people in tropical latitudes minimizes ultraviolet penetration, perhaps thereby preventing illness from too much vitamin D.[17] Light skin may also confer another advantage in colder environments: It is less likely to be damaged by frostbite.[18]

ADAPTATION TO HIGH ALTITUDE

Oxygen constitutes 21 percent of the air we breathe at sea level. At high altitudes, the percentage of oxygen in the air is the same, but because the barometric pressure is lower, we take in less oxygen with each breath.[19] We breathe more rapidly, our hearts beat faster, and all activity is more difficult. The net effects are discomfort and a condition known as **hypoxia,** or oxygen deficiency.

If high altitude presents such difficulties for many human beings, how is it that populations numbering in the millions can live out their lives, healthy and productive, at altitudes of 6,000, 12,000, or even 17,000 feet? Populations in the Himalayas and the Andes have adapted to their environments and do not display the symptoms suffered by low-altitude dwellers if and when they are exposed to high altitudes. Moreover, high-altitude dwellers have also come to terms physiologically with extreme cold, deficient nutrition, strong winds, rough countryside, and intense solar radiation.[20]

Early studies of Andean high-altitude dwellers found that they differed in certain physical ways from low-altitude dwellers. Compared with low-altitude dwellers, high-altitude Andean Indians had larger chests and greater lung capacity, as well as more surface area in the capillaries of the lungs (which was believed to facilitate the transfer of oxygen to the blood).[21] Early researchers thought that genetic changes had allowed the Andeans to maximize their ability to take in oxygen at the lower barometric pressure of their high-altitude environment. Recent research, however, has cast some doubt on this conclusion. It appears now that other populations living at high altitudes do not show the Andean pattern of physical differences. In the Himalayas, for example, low-altitude dwellers and

These women in Kerala, India, have a great deal of melanin in their skin. Similar skin coloring is found in much of Africa and the Pacific, areas close to the equator. This suggests that skin color is an adaptation to the amount of sunlight in the locality.

high-altitude dwellers do not differ in chest size or lung size, even though both groups show adequate lung functioning.[22]

Thus, current research does not suggest that high-altitude living requires biological adaptations that are purely genetic. In fact, some evidence suggests that humans who grow up in a high-altitude environment may adapt to hypoxia during their lifetimes, as they mature. For example, Peruvians who were born at sea level but who grew up at high altitudes developed the same amount of lung capacity as people who spent their entire lives at high altitudes.[23] Consistent with a presumed environmental effect, the children of high-altitude Peruvians who grow up in the lowlands do not develop larger chests. As with other traits that have been studied, it appears that life experiences can have profound effects on how the body grows.

HEIGHT

Studies of identical twins and comparisons of the height of parents and children suggest that heredity plays a considerable role in determining height,[24] so genetic differences must at least partly explain differences between populations in average height. But if average height can increase dramatically in a few decades, as in Japan between 1950 and 1980 and in many other countries in recent times,[25] then environmental influences are also likely to be important.

The considerable variation in average height among human populations may be partly explained by temperature differences. The Dutch of Europe are among the tallest populations in the world on average, and the Mbuti of Zaire in central Africa are among the shortest.[26] We already know that weight is related to mean annual temperature (Bergmann's rule). Weight is also related to height (taller people are likely to be heavier). So, since the taller (heavier) Dutch live in a cooler climate, some of the population variation in height would appear to involve adaptation to heat and cold.[27] Other factors besides heat and cold must also be operating, however, because tall and short peoples can be found in most areas of the world.

Many researchers think that poor nutrition and disease lead to reduced height and weight. In many parts of the world, children in higher social classes are taller on the average than children in lower social classes,[28] and this difference is more marked in economically poorer countries,[29] where the wealth and health differences between the classes are particularly large. During times of war and poor nutrition, children's stature often decreases. For example, in Germany during World War II, the stature of children 7 to 17 years of age declined as compared with previous time periods, despite the fact that stature had generally increased over time.[30]

More persuasive evidence for the effects of poor nutrition and disease comes out of longitudinal studies of the same individuals over time. For example, Reynaldo Martorell found that children in Guatemala who had frequent bouts of diarrhea were on the average over an inch shorter at age 7 than children without frequent diarrhea.[31] Although malnourished or diseased children can catch up in their growth, follow-up research on Guatemalan children suggests that if stunting occurs before 3 years of age, stature at age 18 will still be reduced.[32]

A controversial set of studies links a very different environmental factor to variation in height in human populations. The factor at issue is stress, physical and emotional, in infancy.[33] Contrary to the view that any kind of stress is harmful, it appears that some presumably stressful experiences in infancy are associated with greater height and weight. Experimental studies with rats provided the original stimulus for the studies investigating the possible effect of stress on height. The experiments showed that rats that were physically handled ("petted") by the experimenters grew to be longer and heavier than rats not petted. Researchers originally thought that this was because the petted rats had received "tender loving care." But someone noticed that the petted rats seemed terrified (they urinated and defecated) when petted by humans, which suggested that the petting might have been stressful. It turned out in subsequent studies that even more obviously stressful experiences such as electric shock, vibration, and temperature extremes also produced rats with longer skeletons as compared with unstressed rats.

Thomas Landauer and John Whiting thought that stress in human infants might similarly produce greater adult height. Many cultures have customs for treating infants that could be physically stressful, including circumcision, branding of the skin with sharp objects, piercing the nose, ears, or lips for the insertion of ornaments, molding and stretching the head and limbs for cosmetic purposes, and vaccination. In addition, Shulamith Gunders and John Whiting suggested that separating the baby from its mother right after birth is another kind of stress. In cross-cultural comparisons by Whiting and his colleagues,[34] it seems that *both* physical stress and mother-infant separation *if practiced before 2 years of age* predict greater adult height; males are on the average 2 inches taller in such societies. (It is important to note that the stresses being discussed are short in duration, often a one-time occurrence, and do not constitute prolonged stress or abuse, which can have opposite effects.)

Because the cross-cultural evidence is associational, not experimental, it is possible that the results are due to some factor confounded with infant stress. Perhaps societies with infant stress have better nutrition or have climates that favor tallness. Recently, using new cross-cultural comparisons, J. Patrick Gray and Linda Wolfe attempted to assess possible predictors of height differences between populations. The predictors compared were nutrition, climate, geography, physical stress, and mother-infant separation. Gray and Wolfe's analysis indicated which of those factors predicted adult height independently of the others. It turned out that geographic region, climatic zone, and customs of infant stress were all significant independent predictors of height.[35] So the results now available clearly show that the effect of infant stress cannot be discounted.

Persuasive evidence for the stress hypothesis also comes from an experimental study conducted in Kenya.[36] Landauer and Whiting arranged for a randomly selected sample of children to be vaccinated before they were 2 years old. Other children were vaccinated soon after they were 2. At 7 years of age the two groups were compared with respect to height. Consistent with the cross-cultural evidence on the possible effect of stress on height, the children vaccinated before the age of 2 were significantly taller than the children vaccinated later. The children vaccinated before the age of 2 were selected *randomly* for early vaccination, so it is unlikely that nutritional or other differences between the two groups account for the difference between them in height.

As we noted earlier, in several areas of the world, people have been getting taller. What accounts for this recent trend toward greater height? Several factors may be involved. Some researchers think that it may be the result of improved nutrition and lower incidence of infectious diseases.[37] But it might also be that infant stress has increased as a result of giving birth in hospitals, which usually separate babies from mothers and also subject the newborns to medical tests, including the taking of blood. And various kinds of vaccinations have also become more common in infancy.[38]

In short, both genetic and environmental factors seem to be responsible for differences in human size.

In recent times there has been a dramatic increase in average height, which may be due to one or more environmental factors. Here we see a Chinese American girl who is taller than her mother and almost as tall as her father.

SUSCEPTIBILITY TO INFECTIOUS DISEASES

Certain populations seem to have developed inherited resistances to certain infectious diseases. That is, populations repeatedly decimated by certain diseases in the past now have a high frequency of genetic characteristics that ameliorate the effects of these diseases. As Arno Motulsky pointed out, if there are genes that protect people from dying when they are infected by one of the diseases prevalent in their area, these genes will tend to become more common in succeeding generations.[39]

A field study of the infectious disease myxomatosis in rabbits supports this theory. When the virus responsible for the disease was first introduced into the Australian rabbit population, more than 95 percent of the infected animals died. But among the offspring of animals exposed to successive epidemics of myxomatosis, the percentage of animals that died from the disease decreased from year to year. The more epidemics the animals' ancestors had lived through, the smaller the percentage of current animals that died of the disease. Thus, the data suggested that the rabbits had developed a genetic resistance to myxomatosis.[40]

Infectious diseases seem to follow a similar pattern among human populations. When tuberculosis first strikes a population that has had no previous contact with it, the disease is usually fatal. But some populations seem to have inherited a resistance to death from tuberculosis. For example, the Ashkenazi Jews in America (those whose ancestors came from central and eastern Europe) are one of several populations whose ancestors survived many years of exposure to tuberculosis in the crowded European ghettos where they had previously lived. Although the rate of tuberculosis infection is identical among American Jews and non-Jews, the rate of tuberculosis mortality is significantly lower among Jews than among non-Jews in the United States.[41] After reviewing other data on this subject, Motulsky thought it likely "that the present relatively high resistance of Western populations to tuberculosis is genetically conditioned through natural selection during long contact with the disease."[42]

We tend to think of measles as a childhood disease that kills virtually no one, and we now have a vaccine against it. But when first introduced into populations, the measles virus can kill large numbers of people. In 1949, the Tupari Indians of Brazil numbered about 200 people. By 1955, two-thirds of the Tupari had died of measles introduced into the tribe by rubber gatherers in the area.[43] Large numbers of people died of measles in epidemics in the Faeroe Islands in 1846, in Hawaii in 1848, in the Fiji Islands in 1874, and among the Canadian Inuit very recently. It is possible that where mortality rates from measles are low, populations have acquired a genetic resistance to death from this disease.[44]

But why is a population susceptible to a disease in the first place? The epidemiologist Francis Black suggests that lack of genes for resistance is not the whole answer. A high degree of genetic homogeneity in the population may also increase susceptibility.[45] A virus grown in one host is preadapted to a genetically similar new host and is therefore likely to be more virulent in the new host. For example, the measles virus adapts to a host individual; when it replicates, the forms that the host cannot kill are those most likely to survive and continue replicating. When the virus passes to a new host *with similar genes,* the preadapted virus is likely to kill the new host. If, on the other hand, the next host is very different genetically, the adaptation process starts all over; the virus is not so virulent at first because the host can kill it. Populations that recently came to an area, and that had a small group of founders (as was probably true for the first Native Americans and the Polynesian seafarers who first settled many islands in the Pacific), tended to have a high degree of genetic homogeneity. Therefore, epidemic diseases introduced by Europeans (such as measles) would be likely to kill many of the natives within the first few years after contact. It is estimated that 56 million people died in the New World after contact with Europeans, mostly because of introduced diseases such as smallpox and measles. Similarly caused depopulation occurred widely in the Pacific.

Some researchers suggest that nongenetic factors may also partly explain differential resistance to infectious disease. For example, cultural practices may partly explain the epidemics of measles among the Yanomamö Indians of Venezuela and Brazil. The Yanomamö frequently visit other villages, and that, together with the nonisolation of sick individuals, promoted a very rapid spread of the disease. Because many individuals were sick at the same time, there were not enough healthy people to feed and care for the sick; mothers down with measles could not even nurse their babies. Thus, cultural factors may increase exposure to a disease and worsen its effect on a population.[46]

Epidemics of infectious disease may occur only if many people live near each other. Food collectors, who usually live in small dispersed bands, do not have enough people in and near the community to keep an epidemic going. Without enough people to infect, short-lived microorganisms that cause or carry diseases die out. In contrast, among agriculturalists, there are larger numbers of people in and around the community to whom a disease can spread. Permanent settlements, particularly urban settlements, also are likely to have poor sanitation and contaminated water.[47] Tuberculosis is an example of an infectious disease that, although very old, began to kill large numbers of people only after the emergence of sedentary, larger communities.[48]

SICKLE-CELL ANEMIA

Another biological variation is an abnormality of the red blood cells known as **sickle-cell anemia,** or **sicklemia.** This is a condition in which normal, disk-shaped red blood cells assume a crescent (sickle) shape when deprived of oxygen. The sickle-shaped red blood cells do not move through the body as readily as normal cells, and thus cause more oxygen deficiency and damage to the heart, lungs, brain, and other vital organs. In addition, the red blood cells tend to "die" more rapidly, and the anemia worsens still more.[49]

Sickle-cell anemia is caused by a variant form of the genetic instructions for hemoglobin, the protein that carries oxygen in the red blood cells.[50] Individuals who have sickle-cell anemia have inherited the same allele (Hb^S) from both parents and are therefore homozygous for that gene. Individuals who receive this allele from only one parent are heterozygous; they have one Hb^S allele and one allele for normal hemoglobin (Hb^A). Heterozygotes generally will not show the full-blown symptoms of sickle-cell disease, although in some cases a heterozygous individual may have a mild case of anemia. A heterozygous person has a 50 percent chance of passing on the sickle-cell allele to a child. And if the child later mates with another person who is also a carrier of the sickle-cell allele, the statistical probability is that 25 percent of their children will develop sickle-cell anemia. Without advanced medical care, most individuals with two Hb^S alleles are unlikely to live more than a few years.[51]

Why has the allele for sickle-cell persisted in various populations? If people with sickle-cell anemia do not usually live to reproduce, we would expect a reduction in the frequency of Hb^S to near zero through the process of *normalizing selection*. But the sickle-cell allele occurs fairly often in some parts of the world, particularly in the wet tropical belt of Africa, where frequencies may be between 20

Research Frontiers

FACTORS AFFECTING FECUNDITY

Fertility—that is, how many children women have—ranges widely from one human population to another. There are places where it is not uncommon for women to have ten or more children; there are others where the norm is less than two. Until relatively recently it was widely assumed that the variation was due entirely to social and cultural factors—the later people marry, the less sex couples have, and the more they practice contraception, the fewer babies should be born. It was also widely assumed that if people did not exert restraint, fertility would naturally be very high. But now researchers are considering it likely that variation in human fertility may also be due to biological factors. In other words, human fecundity—the biological capacity to have offspring—may also vary in different populations.

In the next chapter we discuss how breast-feeding can affect fecundity. The physiological mechanisms are not yet fully understood, but we know that nursing somehow impedes the resumption of ovulation and hence increases the interval between births. We are also now beginning to understand the effects of nutrition and activity on fecundity, of individuals as well as populations. It appears that insufficient caloric intake—when activity increases dramatically but the diet remains the same, or when the amount of food consumed drops considerably—reduces the capacity to conceive and carry a baby to successful birth. But why should this be? Reproduction requires a substantial amount of extra energy. Since a mother may not survive a pregnancy or birth if she loses too many calories or nutrients to the fetus, natural selection should favor mechanisms that turn off reproductive capacity if a mother, fetus, or both have a reduced chance to survive. Insufficient caloric intake should activate such mechanisms.

To investigate the possible effects of nutrition and activity on fecundity, researchers need to measure reproductive potential (the likelihood of successful pregnancy). Lack of menstruation for months in the absence of pregnancy is a clear sign that a woman is not ovulating, but the presence of menstrual periods by itself does not indicate a high likelihood of successful pregnancy. A better indicator of the likelihood of successful pregnancy is a measure of the rise in levels of progesterone in the second half of the menstrual cycle: The more progesterone levels rise after ovulation, the more likely a fertilized egg will be viable. In the past, researchers had to rely on expensive and intrusive blood tests to measure progesterone levels, but now researchers have tests that can evaluate progesterone levels from saliva samples.

Research on women in industrial societies who engage in strenuous exercise (athletes and ballet dancers) has shown that

and 30 percent, and in Greece, Sicily, and southern India.[52]

Because the sickle-cell gene occurs in these places much more often than expected, researchers in the 1940s and the 1950s began to suspect that heterozygous individuals (who carry one Hb^S allele) might have a reproductive advantage in a malarial environment.[53] If the heterozygotes were more resistant to attacks of malaria than the homozygotes for normal hemoglobin (who get the Hb^A allele from both parents), the heterozygotes would be more likely to survive and reproduce, and therefore the recessive Hb^S allele would persist at a higher than expected frequency in the population. This kind of outcome is an example of *balancing selection*.[54]

A number of pieces of evidence support the "malaria theory." First, geographic comparisons show that the sickle-cell allele tends to be found where the incidence of malaria is high (see Figure 7–3). Second, as land in the tropics is opened to yam and rice agriculture, the incidence of the sickle-cell allele also increases. The reason seems to be that malaria, carried principally by the *Anopheles gambiae* mosquito, becomes more prevalent as tropical forest gives way to more open land where mosquitoes can thrive in warm, sunlit ponds. Indeed, even among peoples of similar cultural backgrounds, the incidence of the sickle-cell allele increases with greater rainfall and surpluses of water. Third, children who are heterozygous for the

---

such women are less likely to menstruate and therefore are less likely to ovulate than are less active women. With saliva tests, researchers can assess the effects of moderate levels of exercise and diet on reproductive potential, even in women who are menstruating. So, for example, researchers have discovered that women of normal weight who jog for recreation or go on moderate diets have lower levels of progesterone than do women who don't exercise or diet. Therefore the chances to give birth successfully are reduced for joggers and dieters.

We also have studies of ovarian function in nonindustrial societies. One study among the Tamang of Nepal by Catherine Panter-Brick, Deborah Lotstein, and Peter Ellison has documented that during the monsoon season when women work hard at agriculture, many women lose weight and show evidence of reduced reproductive function. Nadine Peacock and Robert Bailey found that Lese women of

Zaire tended to lose weight particularly during the later part of the "hungry" season (April, May, and June) before the new crops come in. The Lese had significantly fewer births nine months after the later part of the "hungry" season (January, February, March), suggesting that malnutrition reduces reproductive function. It is possible that the decline in reproduction was due to changes in behavior, such as avoidance of sex during the "hungry" months, but Peter Ellison's study of progesterone levels confirmed that it was nutrition that affected reproductive function—80 percent of the Lese women ovulated in April (a less "hungry" month), but only 65 percent ovulated in June (a more "hungry" month).

Much still needs to be studied, but the available research suggests that reproduction is finely tuned to the needs of the nursing baby and to the caloric surpluses available to the mother. Voluntary behavior such as avoidance,

abstinence, or contraception can reduce fertility. But fecundity can be reduced by physiological changes that occur in response to breast-feeding, exercise, and nutritional deficiency. These conditions can vary a lot from individual to individual and from one population to another, and hence reproductive function and fecundity also vary.

Sources: Peter T. Ellison, "Natural Variation in Human Fecundity," in Carol R. Ember, Melvin Ember, and Peter N. Peregrine, eds., *Research Frontiers in Anthropology* (Upper Saddle River, NJ: Prentice Hall, 1998), Prentice Hall/Simon & Schuster Custom Publishing; Catherine Panter-Brick, Deborah S. Lotstein, and Peter T. Ellison, "Seasonality of Reproductive Function and Weight Loss in Rural Nepali Women," *Human Reproduction*, 8 (1993): 684–90; and Nadine Peacock and Robert Bailey, "Efe: Investigating Food and Fertility in the Ituri Forest," in Melvin Ember, Carol R. Ember, and David Levinson, eds., *Portraits of Culture: Ethnographic Originals* (Upper Saddle River, NJ: Prentice Hall, 1998), Prentice Hall/ Simon & Schuster Custom Publishing.

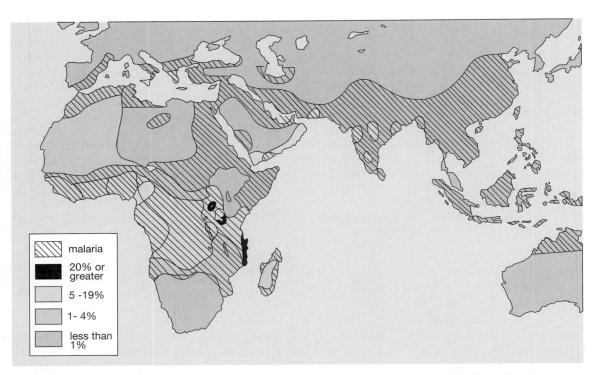

FIGURE 7–3 *Geographic Distribution of Sicklemia and Its Relationship to the Distribution of Malaria*

Source: From John Buettner-Janusch, *Physical Anthropology: A Perspective.* © 1973 by John Wiley & Sons, Inc. Reprinted by permission of John Wiley & Sons, Inc.

sickle-cell trait tend to have fewer malarial parasites in their bodies than do homozygous normal individuals, and they are more likely to survive.[55] The sickling trait does not necessarily keep people from contracting malaria, but it greatly decreases the rate of mortality from malaria—and in evolutionary terms, the overall effect is the same.[56] Fourth, if there is no balancing selection because malaria is no longer present, we should find a rapid decline in the incidence of the sickle-cell allele. Indeed, we find such a decline in populations with African ancestry. Those who live in malaria-free zones of the New World have a much lower incidence of sicklemia than do those who live in malarial regions of the New World.[57]

Hb^S is not the only abnormal hemoglobin to have a distribution related to malaria. It seems that a number of abnormal hemoglobins may be much more widespread because of the advantage heterozygotes have against the disease. For example, another abnormal hemoglobin, Hb^E, occurs in populations from India, through Southeast Asia and New Guinea where malaria occurs, but Hb^S is not that common. Why should heterozygotes have resis-

tance to malaria? One possibility is that malarial parasites are less able to survive in an individual's blood with some normal and some abnormal hemoglobin. Abnormal hemoglobin cells are more delicate and live less long, so they cannot readily support malarial parasites.[58]

LACTASE DEFICIENCY

When American educators discovered that African American schoolchildren very often did not drink milk, they assumed that lack of money or of education was the reason. These assumptions provided the impetus for establishing the school milk programs prevalent around the country. However, it now appears that after infancy many people lack an enzyme, lactase I, that is necessary for breaking down the sugar in milk, lactose, into simpler sugars that can be absorbed into the bloodstream.[59] Thus, a person without lactase cannot digest milk properly, and drinking it may cause bloating, cramps, stomach gas, and diarrhea. A study conducted in Baltimore among 312 "black" and 221 "white" children in grades 1 through 6 in two elementary schools indicated that 85 percent of the "black" children *and* 17 percent of the "white" children were milk-intolerant.[60]

More recent studies indicate that lactose intolerance occurs frequently in adults in many parts of the world.[61] The condition is common in Southeast and East Asia, India, the Mediterranean and the Near East, sub-Saharan Africa, and among Native North and South Americans. The widespread incidence of lactose intolerance should not be surprising. After infancy, mammals normally stop producing lactase.[62]

If lactose intolerance in adulthood in mammals is normal, we need to understand why only some human populations have the ability to make lactase I in adulthood and digest lactose. Why would selection favor this genetic ability in some populations but not in others? In the late 1960s F. J. Simoons and Robert McCracken noted a relationship between lactose absorption and dairying (raising cows for milk). They suggested that with the advent of dairying, individuals with the genetic ability to produce lactase in adulthood would have greater reproductive success, and hence dairying populations would come to have a high proportion of individuals with the ability to break down lactose.[63]

But people in some dairying societies do not produce lactase in adulthood. Rather, they seem to have developed a cultural solution to the problem of lactase deficiency; they transform their milk into cheese, yogurt, sour cream, and other milk products that are low in lactose. To make these low-lactose products, people separate the lactose-rich whey from the curds or treat the milk with a bacterium *(Lactobacillus)* that breaks down the lactose, thus making the milk product digestible by a lactase-deficient person.[64]

So why in some dairying societies did natural selection favor a biological solution (the production in adulthood of the enzyme lactase) rather than the cultural solution? William Durham has collected evidence that natural selection may favor the biological solution in dairying societies farther from the equator. The theory is that lactose behaves biochemically like vitamin D, facilitating the absorption of calcium—but only in people who produce lactase so that they can absorb the lactose. Because people in more temperate latitudes are not exposed to that much sunlight, particularly in the winter, and therefore make less vitamin D in their skin, natural selection may have favored the lactase way of absorbing dietary calcium.[65] In other words, natural selection may favor

(Top) Milking a cow in Barnstable, Massachusetts. Natural selection may favor production of the enzyme lactase, a genetic way of making milk digestible in dairying populations far from the equator. (Bottom) A Masai woman milking a cow in Kenya. Natural selection may favor the souring of milk, a cultural way of making it digestible in dairying populations close to the equator.

lactase production in adulthood, as well as lighter skin, at higher latitudes (where there is less sunlight).

This is an example of how culture may influence the way natural selection favors some genes over others. Without dairying, natural selection may not have favored the genetic propensity to produce lactase.

RACE AND RACISM

Fortunately, internal variations such as lactase deficiency have never been associated with intergroup tensions—perhaps because such differences are not immediately obvious. Unfortunately, the same cannot be said for some of the more obvious external human differences such as skin color.

For as long as any of us can remember, countless aggressive actions—from fistfights to large-scale riots and civil wars—have stemmed from tensions and misunderstandings between various groups commonly referred to by many as races. Race has become such a common term that most of us take the concept for granted, not bothering to consider what it does, and does not, mean. We may talk about the "human race," which means that all humans belong to the same breeding population. Yet we are often asked to check a box to identify our particular "race." We discuss first how biologists sometimes use the term *race;* then we turn to why many biological anthropologists and others now conclude that the concept of race does not usefully apply to humans. We discuss how racial classifications are largely social constructions that have been used to justify the exploitation and even execution of certain categories of people.

RACE AS A CONSTRUCT IN BIOLOGY

Biological variation is not uniformly distributed in any species. While all members of a species can potentially interbreed with others, most matings take place within smaller groups or breeding populations. Through the processes of natural selection and genetic drift, populations inhabiting different geographic regions will exhibit some differences in biological traits. When differences within a species become sufficiently noticeable, biologists may classify different populations into different *varieties,* or **races.** If the term *race* is understood to be just a shorthand or classificatory way that biologists describe slight population variants within a species, the concept of race would probably not be controversial. Unfortunately, as applied to humans, racial classifications have often been confounded with **racism,** the belief that some races are innately inferior to others. The misuse and misunderstanding of the term *race* and its association with racist thinking is one reason that many biological anthropologists and others have suggested that the term should not be applied to human biological differences.

A second reason for not applying racial classification to humans is that humans have exhibited so much interbreeding that different populations are not clearly classifiable into discrete groups that can be defined in terms of the presence or absence of particular biological traits.[66] Therefore, many argue that race is not scientifically useful for describing human biological variation. The difficulty of employing racial classification is evident by comparing the number of races that classifiers come up with. The number of racial categories has varied from as little as 3 to more than 37.[67]

How can groups be clearly divided into races if most adaptive biological traits show clinal or gradual differences from one region to another?[68] Skin color is a good example of clinal variation. In the area around Egypt, there is a gradient of skin color as one moves from north to south in the Nile Valley. Skin generally becomes darker closer to the equator (south) and lighter closer to the Mediterranean. But other adaptive traits may not have north-south clines, because the environmental predictors may be distributed differently. Nose shape varies with humidity, but clines in humidity do not particularly correspond to variation in latitude. So the gradient for skin color would not be the same as the gradient for nose shape. Because adaptive traits tend to be clinally distributed, there is no line you could draw on a world map that would separate "white" from "black" people, or "whites" from "Asians."[69] Only traits that are neutral in terms of natural selection will tend (because of genetic drift) to cluster in regions.[70]

Racial classification is problematic also because there is sometimes more physical, physiological, and genetic diversity *within* a single geographic group that might be called a race (e.g., Africans) than there is *between* supposed racial groups. Africans vary more among themselves than they do in comparison with people elsewhere.[71]

RACE AS A SOCIAL CATEGORY

If race, in the opinion of many biological anthropologists, is not a useful device for classifying humans, why is it so widely used? Racial classifications should be recognized for what they mostly are—social categories to which individuals are assigned, by themselves and others, on the basis of supposedly shared biological traits.

If racial categories are mostly just social categories, we need to ask why they were invented. Part of the answer may be a desire to separate "my" group from others. We will see later, in the chapter on the concept of culture, that people tend to be ethnocentric, to view their culture as better than other cultures. Racial classifications may reflect the same tendency to divide "us" from "them," except that the divisions are supposedly based on biological differences.[72]

We do know that racial classifications have often been, and still are, used by certain groups to justify discrimination, exploitation, or genocide. The "Aryan race" was supposed to be the group of blond-haired, blue-eyed, white-skinned people whom Adolf Hitler wanted to dominate the world, to which end he and others attempted to destroy as many members of the Jewish "race" as they could. (It is estimated that 6 million Jews and others were murdered in what is now called the Holocaust.[73]) But who are the Aryans? Technically, Aryans are any people, including the German-speaking Jews in Hitler's Germany, who speak one of the Indo-European languages. The Indo-European languages include such disparate modern tongues as Greek, Spanish, Hindi, Polish, French, Icelandic, German, Gaelic, and English. And many Aryans speaking these languages have neither blond hair nor blue eyes. Similarly, all kinds of people may be Jews, whether or not they descend from the ancient Near Eastern population that spoke the Hebrew language. There are light-skinned Danish Jews and darker Jewish Arabs. One of the most orthodox Jewish groups in the United States is based in New York City and is composed entirely of African Americans.

The arbitrary and social basis of most racial classifications becomes apparent when you compare how they differ from one place to another. Consider, for example, what used to be thought about the races in South Africa. Under apartheid, the system of racial segregation and discrimination, someone with mixed "white" and "black" ancestry was considered "colored." However, when important people of African ancestry from other countries would visit South Africa, they were often considered "white." Chinese were considered "Asian"; but the Japanese, who were important economically to South Africa, were considered "white."[74] In some parts of the United States, laws against interracial marriage continued in force through the 1960s. You would be considered a "negro" if you had an eighth or more "negro" ancestry (if one or more of your eight grandparents were "negro"). So only a small amount of "negro" ancestry made a person "negro," but a small amount of "white" ancestry did not make a person "white." Biologically speaking, this makes no sense, but socially it was another story.[75]

THE MYTHS OF RACISM

RACE AND CIVILIZATION. Many persons hold the racist viewpoint that the biological inferiority of certain groups, which they call "races," is reflected in the supposedly "primitive" quality of their cultures. They will argue that the "developed" nations are "white" and the "underdeveloped" nations are not. (We put terms like "white," which are used as racial categories, in quotes to indicate the problematic nature of the categories.) But to make such an argument ignores much of history. Many of today's so-called underdeveloped nations—primarily in Asia, Africa, and South America—had developed complex and sophisticated civilizations long before European nations expanded and acquired considerable power. The advanced societies of the Shang dynasty in China, the Mayans in Mesoamerica, and the African empire of Ghana were all founded and developed by "nonwhites."

Between 1523 and 1028 B.C., China had a complex form of government, armies, metal tools and weapons, and production and storage facilities for large quantities of grain. The early Chinese civilization also had writing and elaborate religious rituals.[76] From A.D. 300 to 900, the Mayans were a

"We don't consider ours to be an underdeveloped country so much as we think of yours as an overdeveloped country."
Courtesy of *Saturday Review*, January 10, 1970.

Current Issues

DIFFERENCES IN AVERAGE IQ SCORES— WHAT DO THEY MEAN?

In late 1994, a new book reignited controversy about the relationship between "race" and intelligence. Once again people thought they now had evidence of African American "inferiority." But once again there were problems with the evidence. The book was *The Bell Curve*, by Richard Herrnstein and Charles Murray. It purported to show that the intelligence of an individual was largely inherited and unchangeable throughout the life span, that an individual's success was largely based on intelligence, and that African Americans were likely to remain at the bottom of society because they had less intelligence than European Americans. Herrnstein and Murray appealed to a lot of studies to buttress their argument. But their argument was still faulty.

If you look at the average scores on many standard intelligence tests, you might conclude, as racists have, that African Americans are less intelligent than European Americans. The averages *are* different between the two groups; African Americans typically have lower scores. But what does this average difference mean? Herrnstein and Murray, like many before them, fail to distinguish between a *measure,* such as a particular IQ test, and what is supposedly being measured, intelligence. If a test only imperfectly measures what it purports to measure, lower average IQ scores merely mean lower scores on that particular IQ test; they do not necessarily reflect lower intelligence. There are many reasons why some smart people might not do well on particular kinds of IQ tests. For example, the way the tests are administered may affect performance, as may lack of familiarity with the format or the experiences and objects referred to. The test might also not measure particular kinds of intelligence such as social "smarts" and creativity.

If African Americans were really less intelligent, more than their average IQ scores would be lower. The whole frequency distribution of their individual scores should also be lower—they should have fewer geniuses and more retarded individuals. That is, the bell-shaped curve showing how their scores are distributed should range lower than the curve for other Americans, and African Americans should also have proportionately fewer scores at the very high end of the scale. *But neither expectation is confirmed.* According to research by Henry Grubb, the proportion of African Americans at the low end of the scale is not significantly different from the proportion of European Americans. And Grubb and Andrea Barthwell report that, on the basis of IQ tests administered by Mensa (a high-IQ society), the proportion of African Americans at the high end of the scale is not different from the proportion of European Americans. So the available evidence suggests that

large population with a thriving economy. They built many large and beautiful cities in which were centered great pyramids and luxurious palaces.[77] According to legend, the West African civilization of Ghana was founded during the second century A.D. By A.D. 770, the time of the Sonniki rulers, Ghana had developed two capital cities—one Muslim and the other non-Muslim—each with its own ruler and both supported largely by Ghana's lucrative gold market.[78]

Considering how recently northern Europeans developed cities and central governments, it seems odd that some "whites" should label Africans, Native Americans, and others backward in terms of historical achievement, or biologically inferior in terms of capacity for civilization. But racists, both "white" and "nonwhite," choose to ignore the fact that many populations have achieved remarkable advances in civilization. Most significant, racists refuse to believe that they can acknowledge the achievements of another group without in any way downgrading the achievements of their own.

RACE, CONQUEST, AND THE ROLE OF INFECTIOUS DISEASE. There are those who would argue that Europeans' superiority accounted for their ability to colonize much of the world during the last few hundred years. But it now appears that

African Americans have lower average test scores, but not fewer very high scores or more very low scores (proportionately). Why, then, might their average scores be lower?

Grubb and Barthwell point out that the average scores are *not* lower on all IQ tests. One test that shows no significant difference is an *untimed* version of an intelligence test using pictures (the pictorial reasoning test). You can administer the pictorial reasoning test in one of two ways—timed or untimed. A person must finish the test by the end of a prescribed, relatively short time period; or the test-taker can respond to the questions with-out any time limit. African Americans have lower average scores than European Americans on the timed version of the pictorial reasoning test (although not as much lower as on other tests) but *not* on the untimed version. This finding suggests that a timed test measures or reflects more than just intelligence. What else besides intelligence might affect performance on a timed IQ test?

Familiarity with a particular format or the content could increase performance on a timed test. So could familiarity or comfort with *speed*. Although they do not have evidence for how African Americans feel about speed, Grubb and Barthwell cite a study that shows that discomfort with speed can affect performance on an IQ test. The study cited was conducted by A. Lieblich and S. Kugelmass and compared Jewish and Arab children in Israel. The Arab children scored lower than the Jewish children on the parts of a standard Wechsler intelligence test that were timed, but the Arab children scored the same or even higher on the parts that were untimed. Lieblich and Kugelmass concluded that the Arabs' poorer performance on the timed tests may reflect a cultural abhorrence of speed; "Time is of the Devil" is an Arab saying. Speed is not highly valued in some cultures. If unfamiliarity or discomfort with speed can affect performance on an IQ test, then clearly the test is not measuring intelligence only.

Critics have pointed to many other problems with the evidence presented in *The Bell Curve*. But the fundamental problem is the same as with all attempts to use differences in average IQ scores to make judgments about the capability of different groups. IQ tests may not adequately measure what they purport to measure. If they do not—and there are good reasons to think they do not—it is scientifically and morally incorrect to conclude that differences in average scores are caused by genetic differences in intelligence.

Sources: Richard J. Herrnstein and Charles Murray, *The Bell Curve: Intelligence and Class Structure in American Life* (New York: Free Press, 1994); Henry J. Grubb and Andrea G. Barthwell, "Superior Intelligence and Racial Equivalence: A Look at Mensa," paper presented at 1996 annual meeting of the Society for Cross-Cultural Research; Henry J. Grubb, "Intelligence at the Low End of the Curve: Where Are the Racial Differences?" *Journal of Black Psychology*, 14 (1987): 25–34; and Leon J. Kamin, "Behind the Curve," *Scientific American*, February 1995, 99–103.

Europeans were able to dominate at least partly because many native peoples were susceptible to diseases brought by the Europeans.[79] Earlier, we discussed how continued exposure to epidemics of infectious diseases, such as tuberculosis and measles, can cause succeeding generations to acquire a genetic resistance to death from such diseases. Smallpox had a long history in Europe and Africa; genetic resistence eventually made it mostly a survivable childhood disease. But in the New World it was quite another story. Cortez and the conquistadores were inadvertently aided by smallpox in their attempt to defeat the Aztecs of Mexico. In 1520, a member of Cortez's army unwittingly transmitted smallpox to the natives. The disease spread rapidly, killing at least 50 percent of the population, and so the Aztecs were at a considerable disadvantage in their battling with the Spanish.[80]

Outbreaks of smallpox repeatedly decimated many Native American populations in North America a century or two later. In the early nineteenth century, the Massachusetts and Narragansett Indians, with populations of 30,000 and 9,000, respectively, were reduced by smallpox to a few hundred members. Extremely high mortality rates were also noted among the Crow, the Blackfoot, and other Native American groups during the nineteenth century. The germ theory alone may not

The stone walls of Great Zimbabwe in southeast Africa, which date from the twelfth to the fifteenth century, are evidence of a complex culture at a time when Europe was still in the Dark Ages.

completely explain these epidemics; Europeans may have deliberately encouraged the spread of one new disease, smallpox, by purposely distributing infected blankets to the natives. Motulsky calls the spread of smallpox "one of the first examples of biological warfare."[81]

RACE AND INTELLIGENCE. Attempts to document differences in intelligence among the so-called races has a fairly long history. One of the latest attempts is a 1994 book, titled *The Bell Curve*, by Charles Murray and Richard Herrnstein (see the box titled "Differences in Average IQ Scores").

In the nineteenth century, European white supremacists tried to find scientific justification for what they felt was the genetically inherited mental inferiority of "blacks." They did this by measuring skulls. It was believed that the larger the skull, the greater the cranial capacity and the bigger (hence, also better) the brain. Although the skull-measuring mania quickly disappeared and is no longer considered seriously as a way to measure intelligence, other "facts" may be used to demonstrate the presumed intellectual superiority of "white" people—namely, statistics from intelligence tests.

The first large-scale intelligence testing in the United States began with our entry into World War I. Thousands of draftees were given the so-called Alpha and Beta IQ tests to determine military assignments. Later, psychologists arranged the test results according to the racial categories of "white" and "black" and found what they had expected— "blacks" scored consistently lower than "whites." This result was viewed as scientific proof of the innate intellectual inferiority of "blacks" and was used to justify further discrimination against them, both in and out of the army.[82]

Otto Klineberg's subsequent statistical analyses of IQ-test results demonstrated that "blacks" from northern states scored higher than "blacks" from the South. Although dedicated racists explained that this difference was due to the northward migration of innately intelligent "blacks," most academics attributed the result to the influence of superior education and more stimulating environments in the North. When further studies showed that northern "blacks" scored higher than southern "whites," the better-education-in-the-North theory gained support—but again racists insisted such results were due to northward migration by all innately intelligent "whites."

As a further test of his conclusions, Klineberg gave IQ tests to "black" schoolgirls born and partly raised in the South who had spent varying lengths of time in New York City. He found that the longer the girls had been in the North, the higher their average IQ. In addition to providing support for the belief that "blacks" are not inherently inferior to "whites," these findings suggested that cultural factors can and do influence IQ scores, and that IQ is not a fixed quantity.

The controversy about race and intelligence was fueled again in 1969 by Arthur Jensen.[83] He suggested that although the IQ scores of American "blacks" overlapped considerably with the IQ scores of "whites," the average score for "blacks" was 15 points lower than the average for "whites." IQ scores presumably have a large genetic component, so the lower average score for "blacks" implied to Jensen that "blacks" were genetically inferior to "whites."

Until all people have an equal education and opportunities to achieve, there is no way we can say that some people are smarter than others.

But others contend that the evidence presented by Jensen and more recently by Murray and Herrnstein implies no such thing.

The critics of the genetic interpretation point to at least two problems. First, there is widespread recognition now that IQ tests are probably not accurate measures of "intelligence" because they are probably biased in favor of the subculture of those who construct the tests. That is, many of the questions on the test refer to things that "white," middle-class children are familiar with, thus giving such children an advantage.[84] So far, no one has come up with a "culture-fair," or bias-free, test. There is more agreement that, although the IQ test may not measure "intelligence" well, it may predict scholastic success or how well a child will do in the primarily "white"-oriented school system.[85]

A second major problem with a purely genetic interpretation of the IQ difference is that many studies also show that IQ scores can be influenced by the social environment. Economically deprived children, whether "black" or "white," will generally score lower than affluent "white" or "black" children. And training of children with low IQ scores clearly improves their test scores.[86] More dramatic evidence is provided by Sandra Scarr and her colleagues. "Black" children adopted by well-off "white" families have IQ scores above the average for "whites." And those "blacks" with more European ancestry do not have higher IQ scores.[87] So the average difference between "blacks" and "whites" in IQ cannot be attributed to a presumed genetic difference. For all we know, the 15-point average difference may be due completely to differences in environment or to test bias.

The geneticist Theodosius Dobzhansky reminded us that conclusions about the causes of different levels of achievement on IQ tests cannot be drawn until all people have equal opportunities to develop their potentials. He stressed the need for an open society operating under the democratic ideal, where all persons are given an equal opportunity to develop whatever gifts or aptitudes they possess and choose to develop.[88]

THE FUTURE OF HUMAN VARIATION

Laboratory fertilization, subsequent transplantation of the embryo, and successful birth have been accomplished with humans and nonhumans. *Cloning*—the exact reproduction of an individual from cellular tissue—has been achieved with frogs and sheep. And *genetic engineering*—the substitution of some genes for others—is increasingly practiced in nonhuman organisms. Indeed, as we discussed in the chapter on evolution, genetic engineering is now used in humans to eliminate certain disorders that are produced by defective genes. What are the implications of such practices for the genetic future of humans? Will it really be possible someday to control the genetic makeup of our species? If so, will the effects be positive or negative?

It is interesting to speculate on the development of a "perfect human." Aside from the serious ethical question of who would decide what the perfect human should be like, there is the serious biological question of whether such a development might in the long run be detrimental to the human species, for what is perfectly suited to one physical or social environment may be totally unsuited to another. The collection of physical, emotional, and intellectual attributes that might be "perfect" in the late twentieth century might be inappropriate in the twenty-first.[89] Even defects such as the sickle-cell trait may confer advantages under certain conditions, as we have seen.

In the long run, the perpetuation of genetic variability is probably more advantageous than the creation of a "perfect" and invariable human being. In the event of dramatic changes in the world environment, absolute uniformity in the human species might be an evolutionary dead end. Such uniformity might lead to the extinction of the human species if new conditions favored genetic or cultural variations that were no longer present in the species. Perhaps our best hope for maximizing our chances of survival is to tolerate, and even encourage, the persistence of many aspects of human variation, both biological and cultural.[90]

SUMMARY

1. Physical variation—variation in the frequencies of physical traits—from one human population to another is the result of one or more of the following factors: natural selection, genetic drift, gene flow, the influence of the physical environment, and the influence of the social or cultural environment.

2. Some physical variations in human populations involve genetic variation; other variations, including body build, facial construction, and skin color, may be adapted to variation in climate. Still other variations, such as the ability to make lactase, may be adapted partially to variation in cultural environment.

3. Most biological anthropologists today agree that race is *not* a useful way of referring to human biological variation because human populations do not unambiguously fall into discrete groups defined by a particular set of biological traits. Physical traits that are adaptive vary clinally, which makes it meaningless to divide humans into discrete racial entities. Rather it is suggested that racial classifications are mostly social categories that *are presumed* to have a biological basis.

4. Perhaps the most controversial aspect of racial discrimination is the relationship supposed between racial categories and intelligence. Attempts have been made to show, by IQ tests and other means, the innate intellectual superiority of one racial category over another. But there is doubt that IQ tests measure intelligence fairly. Because evidence indicates that IQ scores are influenced by both genes and environment, conclusions about the causes of differences in IQ scores cannot be drawn until all the people being compared have equal opportunities to develop their potentials.

GLOSSARY TERMS

Allen's rule	Gloger's rule
balancing selection	hypoxia
Bergmann's rule	normalizing selection
cline	race
directional selection	racism
gene flow	sickle-cell anemia
genetic drift	(sicklemia)

CRITICAL QUESTIONS

1. Why is skin color used more often than hair or eye color or body proportions in "racial" classifications?

2. If Europeans had been more susceptible to New World and Pacific diseases, would the world be different today?

3. How might studies of natural selection help increase tolerance of other populations?

INTERNET EXERCISES

1. Explore **http://www.emory.edu/PEDS/SICKLE/sicklept.htm** to find out what groups are most likely to have sickle-cell anemia (a group of inherited red blood cell disorders). Briefly discuss the cause and symptoms of this inherited disorder.

2. The site on Genetics and Public Issues (**http://www.ncgr.org/gpi/**) contains information on current issues. If humans were cloned, how similar do you think the clones would be to each other? Using the search words "nature" and "nurture," find an article that explores this question and summarize its position.

3. Use the Human Genome Site at **http://www.ornl.gov/TechResources/Human_Genome/home.html** to either review your knowledge of molecular genetics or explore some of the ethical issues that may arise.

SUGGESTED READING

DOBZHANSKY, T. *Mankind Evolving: The Evolution of the Human Species.* New Haven, CT: Yale University Press, 1962. A now-classic introduction to the interaction between cultural and biological components of human evolution. Keeping the technical details and vocabulary of genetics to a minimum, Dobzhansky discusses natural selection and biological fitness in human populations.

DURHAM, W. H. *Coevolution: Genes, Culture, and Human Diversity.* Stanford, CA: Stanford University Press, 1991. Intended as an update of Dobzhansky's *Mankind Evolving,* this book discusses recent theory and research on how the interaction of genes and culture helps determine human diversity.

EMBER, C. R., EMBER, M., AND PEREGRINE, P. N. *Research Frontiers in Anthropology.* Upper Saddle River, NJ: Prentice Hall, 1998. Prentice Hall/Simon & Schuster Custom Publishing. Several chapters in this series deal with the physical aspects of human variation and racism. They include P. T. Ellison, "Natural Variation in Human Fecundity"; J. P. Gray and L. Wolfe, "What Accounts for Population Variation in Height?"; M. A. Little, "Growth and Development of Turkana Pastoralists"; and M. D. Williams, "Racism: The Production, Reproduction, and Obsolescence of Social Inferiority."

FRISANCHO, A. R. *Human Adaptation and Accommodation,* rev. ed. Ann Arbor: University of Michigan Press, 1993. A survey of research on human adaptations to heat, cold, humidity, high altitude, solar radiation, under- and overnutrition, and the Westernization of dietary habits.

MASCIE-TAYLOR, C. G. N., AND LASKER, G. W. *Applications of Biological Anthropology to Human Affairs.* New York: Cambridge University Press, 1991. This book discusses how biological anthropologists study fertility, childhood development, adult health, degenerative diseases, and aging.

MOLNAR, S. *Human Variation: Races, Types, and Ethnic Groups,* 4th ed. Upper Saddle River, NJ: Prentice Hall, 1998. A basic text on human biological diversity. Considers the biological principles underlying human variation and various aspects of that variation.

SHANKLIN, E. *Anthropology and Race.* Belmont, CA: Wadsworth Publishing, 1994. This book is about the scientific uselessness of the concept of "race" and its abuses. The author thinks that anthropologists have a moral responsibility to combat racism.

Origins of Food Production and Settled Life

oward the end of the period known as the Upper Paleolithic, people seem to have gotten most of their food from hunting migratory herds of large animals, such as wild cattle, antelope, bison, and mammoths. These hunter-gatherers were probably highly mobile in order to follow the migrations of the animals. Beginning about 14,000 years ago, people in some regions began to depend less on big-game hunting and more on relatively stationary food resources, such as fish, shellfish, small game, and wild plants. In some areas, particularly Europe and the Near East, the exploitation of local, relatively permanent resources may account for an increasingly settled way of life. The cultural period in Europe and the Near East during which these developments took place is called the **Mesolithic**. Other areas of the world show a similar switch to what is called *broad-spectrum* food-collecting, but they do not always show an increasingly settled life-style.

We see the first clear evidence of a changeover to food production—the cultivation and domestication of plants and animals—in the Near East, about 8000 B.C.[1] This shift, called the "Neolithic revolution," occurred, probably independently, in other areas of the Old and New Worlds within the next few thousand years. In the Old World there were independent centers of domestication in China, Southeast Asia (what is now Malaysia, Thailand, Cambodia, and Vietnam), and Africa around 6000 B.C.[2] In the New World there were centers of cultivation and domestication in the highlands of Mesoamerica (about 7000 B.C.), the central Andes around Peru (about 7000 B.C.), and the Eastern Woodlands of North America (about 2000 B.C.).[3] Most of the world's major food plants and animals were domesticated well before 2000 B.C. Also developed by that time were techniques of plowing, fertilizing, fallowing, and irrigation.[4] Figure 8–1 shows

FIGURE 8–1 *Original Locations of the World's Main Food Crops*

The world's main food crops were originally domesticated in different regions: (A1) barley, wheat, peas, lentils, and chickpeas in the Near East; (A2) various millets, sorghum, groundnuts, yams, dates, coffee, and melons in Africa; (B1) various millets and rice in North China; (B2) rice, bananas, sugar cane, citrus fruits, coconuts, taro, and yams in Southeast Asia; (C1) maize or corn, squash, beans, and pumpkins in Mesoamerica; (C2) lima beans, potatoes, sweet potatoes, manioc, and peanuts in lowland and highland South America. There was also independent domestication in North America, but (except for sunflower) the plants domesticated there are not common crops today. *Source:* From Frank Hole, "Origins of Agriculture," in Stephen Jones, Robert Martin, and David Pilbeam, eds., *The Cambridge Encyclopedia of Human Evolution* (New York: Cambridge University Press, 1992) p. 376. Reprinted with permission of Cambridge University Press.

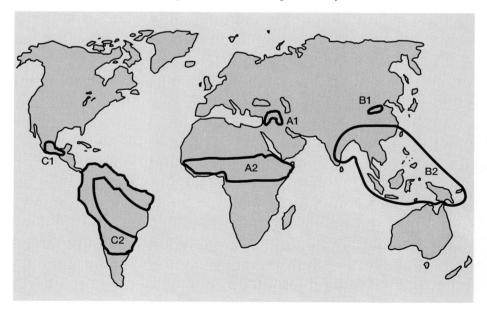

the regions of the world that domesticated today's main food crops.

In this chapter we discuss what is believed about the origins of food production and settled life, called **sedentarism**—how and why people in different places may have come to cultivate and domesticate plants and animals and to live in permanent villages. Agriculture and a sedentary life did not necessarily go together. In some regions of the world, people began to live in permanent villages before they cultivated and domesticated plants and animals, whereas in other places people planted crops without settling down permanently. Much of our discussion focuses on the Near East and Europe, the areas we know best archaeologically for the developments leading to food production and settled life. As much as we can, however, we try to indicate how data from other areas appear to suggest patterns different from, or similar to, those in Europe and the Near East.

 PREAGRICULTURAL DEVELOPMENTS

EUROPE

After about 10,000 years ago in Europe, the glaciers began to disappear. With their disappearance came other environmental changes. The melting of the glacial ice caused the oceans to rise, and, as the seas moved inland, the waters inundated some of the richest fodder-producing coastal plains, creating islands, inlets, and bays. Other areas, particularly in Scandinavia, were opened up for human occupation as the glaciers retreated and the temperatures rose.[5] The cold, treeless plains, **tundras,** and grasslands eventually gave way to dense mixed forests, mostly birch, oak, and pine, and the mammoths became extinct. The warming waterways began to be filled with fish and other aquatic resources.[6]

Archaeologists believe that these environmental changes induced some populations in Europe to alter their food-getting strategies. When the tundras and grasslands disappeared, hunters could no longer obtain large quantities of meat simply by remaining close to large migratory herds of animals, as they probably did during Upper Paleolithic times. Even though deer and other game were available, the number of animals per square mile (density) had decreased, and it became difficult to stalk and kill animals sheltered in the thick woods. Thus, in many areas of Mesolithic Europe people seemed to have turned from a reliance on big-game hunting to the intensive collecting of wild plants, mollusks, fish, and small game to make up for the extinction of the mammoths and the northward migration of the reindeer.

THE MAGLEMOSIAN CULTURE OF NORTHERN EUROPE. Some adaptations to the changing environment can be seen in the cultural remains of the settlers in northern Europe who are called Maglemosians by archaeologists. Their name derives from the peat bogs (*magle mose* in Danish means "great bog") where their remains have been found.

With the disappearance of mammoths in the Northern Hemisphere, hunter-gatherers had to change how they got their food. They began to rely more on smaller game and marine resources.

To deal with the new, more forested environment, the Maglemosians made stone axes and adzes to chop down trees and form them into various objects. Large timbers appear to have been split for houses; trees were hollowed out for canoes; and smaller pieces of wood were made into paddles. The canoes presumably were built for travel and perhaps for fishing on the lakes and rivers that abounded in the postglacial environment.

We do not know to what extent the Maglemosians relied on wild plant foods, but there were a lot of different kinds available such as hazelnuts. However, we do know many other things about the Maglemosians' way of life. Although fishing was fairly important, as suggested by the frequent occurrence of bones from pike and other fish, as well as fishhooks, these people apparently depended mainly on hunting for food. Game included elk, wild ox, deer, and wild pig. In addition to many fishing implements and the adzes and axes, the Maglemosians' tool kit included the bow and arrow. Some of their tools were ornamented with finely engraved designs. Ornamentation independent of tools also appears in amber and stone pendants and small figurines such as the head of an elk.[7]

Like the Maglemosian finds, many of the European Mesolithic sites are along lakes, rivers, and oceanfronts. But these sites probably were not inhabited year-round; there is evidence that at least some groups moved seasonally from one place of settlement to another, perhaps between the coast and inland areas.[8] Finds such as **kitchen middens** (piles of shells) that centuries of Mesolithic seafood-eaters had discarded and remains of fishing equipment, canoes, and boats indicate that Mesolithic people depended much more heavily on fishing than had their ancestors in Upper Paleolithic times.

THE NEAR EAST

Cultural developments in the Near East seem to have paralleled those in Europe.[9] Here, too, there seems to have been a shift from mobile big-game hunting to the utilization of a broad spectrum of natural resources. There is evidence that people subsisted on a variety of resources, including fish, mollusks, and other water life; wild deer, sheep, and goats; and wild grains, nuts, and legumes.[10] The increased utilization of stationary food sources such as wild grain may partly explain why some people in the Near East began to lead more sedentary lives during the Mesolithic.

Even today, a traveler passing through the Anatolian highlands of Turkey and other mountainous regions in the Near East may see thick stands of wild wheat and barley growing as densely as if they had been cultivated. Wielding flint sickles, Mesolithic people could easily have harvested a bountiful crop from such wild stands. Just how productive these resources can be was demonstrated in a field experiment duplicating prehistoric conditions. Using the kind of flint-blade sickle a Mesolithic worker would have used, researchers were able to harvest a little over two pounds of wild grain in an hour. A Mesolithic family of four, working only during the few weeks of the harvest season, probably could have reaped more wheat and barley than they needed for the entire year.[11]

The amount of wild wheat harvested in the experiment prompted Kent Flannery to conclude, "Such a harvest would almost necessitate some degree of sedentism—after all, where could they go with an estimated metric ton of clean wheat?"[12] Moreover, the stone equipment used for grinding would have been a clumsy burden to carry. Part of the harvest would probably have been set aside for immediate consumption, ground, and then cooked either by roasting or boiling. The rest of the harvest would have been stored to supply food for the remainder of the year. A grain diet, then, could have been the impetus for the construction of roasters, grinders, and storage pits by some Mesolithic people, as well as for the construction of solid, fairly permanent housing. Once a village was built, people may have been reluctant to abandon it. We can visualize the earliest preagricultural settlements clustered around such naturally rich regions, as archaeological evidence indeed suggests they were.

THE NATUFIANS OF THE NEAR EAST. Eleven thousand years ago the Natufians, a people living in the area that is now Israel and Jordan, inhabited caves and rock shelters and built villages on the slopes of Mount Carmel in Israel. At the front of their rock shelters they hollowed out basin-shaped depressions in the rock, possibly for storage pits. Examples of Natufian villages are also found at the Eynan site in Israel.

Eynan is a stratified site containing the remains of three villages in sequence, one atop another. Each village consisted of about 50 circular *pit houses*. The floor of each house was sunk a few feet into the ground, so that the walls of the house consisted partly of earth, below ground level, and partly of stone, above ground level. Pit houses had the advantage of retaining heat longer than houses built above the ground. The villages appear to have had stone-paved walks; circular stone pavements ringed what seem to be permanent hearths; and the dead were interred in village cemeteries.

The tools suggest that the Natufians harvested wild grain intensively. Sickles recovered from their villages have a specific sheen, which experiments have shown to be the effect of flint striking grass stems, as the sickles would have been used in the cutting of grain. The Natufians are the earliest Mesolithic people known to have stored surplus crops. Beneath the floors of their stone-walled houses they constructed plastered storage pits. In addition to wild grains, the Natufians exploited a wide range of other resources.[13] The remains of many wild animals are found in Natufian sites; Natufians appear to have concentrated on hunting gazelle, which they would take by surrounding whole herds.[14]

The Natufians, as well as food collectors in other areas at the time, show many differences as compared with food collectors in earlier periods.[15] Not only was Natufian food collection based on a more intensive use of stationary resources such as wild grain, but the archaeological evidence suggests increasing social complexity. Natufian sites on the average were five times larger than those of their predecessors. Communities were now occupied for most of the year, if not year-round. Burial patterns suggest more social differences between people. Although wild cereal resources appear to have enabled the Natufians to live in relatively permanent villages, their diet seems to have suffered. Their tooth enamel shows signs of nutritional deficiency, and their stature declined over time.[16]

OTHER AREAS

People in other areas in the world also shifted from hunting big game to collecting many types of food before they apparently began to practice agriculture. The still-sparse archaeological record suggests that such a change occurred in Southeast Asia, which may have been one of the important centers of original plant and animal domestication. The faunal remains in inland sites there indicate that many different sources of food were being exploited from the same base camps. For example, at these base camps we find the remains of animals from high mountain ridges as well as lowland river valleys, birds and primates from nearby forests, bats from caves, and fish from streams. The few coastal sites indicate that many kinds of fish and shellfish were collected and that animals such as deer, wild cattle, and rhinoceros were hunted.[17] As in Europe, the preagricultural de-

velopments in Southeast Asia probably were responses to changes in the climate and environment, including a warming trend, more moisture, and a higher sea level.[18]

In Africa, too, the preagricultural period was marked by a warmer, wetter environment. The now-numerous lakes, rivers, and other bodies of water provided fish, shellfish, and other resources that apparently allowed people to settle more permanently than they had before. For example, there were lakes in what is now the southern and central Sahara desert, where people fished and hunted hippopotamuses and crocodiles. This pattern of broad-spectrum food-collecting seems also to have been characteristic of the areas both south and north of the Sahara.[19] One area showing increased sedentism is the Dakhleh Oasis in the Western Desert of Egypt. Between 9,000 and 8,500 years ago, the inhabitants lived in circular stone huts on the shores of rivers and lakes. Bone harpoons and pottery are found there and in other areas from the Nile Valley through the central and southern Sahara westward to what is now Mali. Fishing seems to have allowed people to remain along the rivers and lakes for much of the year.[20]

At about the same time in the Americas, people were beginning to exploit a wide variety of wild food resources. For example, evidence from Alabama and Kentucky shows that, by about 5000 B.C., people had begun to collect freshwater mussels as well as wild plants and small game. In the Great Basin of what is now the United States, people were beginning to spend longer and longer periods each year collecting the wild resources around and in the rivers and glacial lakes.[21]

WHY DID BROAD-SPECTRUM COLLECTING DEVELOP?

It is apparent that the preagricultural switch to broad-spectrum collecting was fairly common throughout the world. Climate change was probably at least partly responsible for the exploitation of new sources of food. For example, the worldwide rise in sea level may have increased the availability of fish and shellfish. Changes in climate may have also been partly responsible for the decline in the availability of big game, particularly the large herd animals. In addition, it has been suggested that another possible cause of that decline was human activity, specifically overkilling of some of these animals. The evidence suggesting overkill is that the extinction in the New World of many of the large Pleistocene animals, such as the mammoth, coincided with the movement of humans from the Bering Strait region to the southern tip of South America.[22]

The overkill hypothesis has been questioned on the basis of bird as well as mammal extinctions in the New World. An enormous number of bird species also became extinct during the last few thousand years of the North American Pleistocene, and it is difficult to argue that human hunters caused all of those extinctions. Because the bird and mammal extinctions occurred simultaneously, it is likely that most or nearly all the extinctions were due to climatic and other environmental changes.[23]

The decreasing availability of big game may have stimulated people to exploit new food resources. But they may have turned to a broader spectrum of resources for another reason—population growth (see Figure 8–2). As Mark Cohen has noted, hunter-gatherers were "filling up" the world, and they may have had to seek new, possibly less desirable sources of food.[24] (We might think of shellfish as more desirable than mammoths, but only because we don't have to do the work to get such food. A lot of shell-fish have to be collected, shelled, and cooked to produce the animal protein obtainable from one large animal.) Consistent with the idea that the world was filling up around this time is the fact that not until after 30,000 years ago did hunter-gatherers begin to move into previously uninhabited parts of the world, such as Australia and the New World.[25]

Broad-spectrum collecting may have involved exploitation of new sources of food, but that does not necessarily mean that people were eating better. A decline in stature often indicates a poorer diet. During the Mesolithic, height apparently declined by as much as two inches in many parts of the Old World (Greece, Israel, India, and northern and western Europe).[26] This decline may have been a result of decreasing nutrition, but it could also be that natural selection for greater height was relaxed because leverage for throwing projectiles such as spears was not so favored after the decline of big-game hunting. (Greater limb-bone length, and therefore greater height, would enable you to throw a spear with more force and farther.[27]) In other areas of the world, such as Australia and what is now

---

FIGURE 8–2 *Reconstructed Increases in World Population and Carrying Capacity for Humans during the Pleistocene*

Estimates of human population suggest that substantial increases preceded the movement of humans into more marginal areas. Further population increase preceded the emergence of broad spectrum collecting. *Source:* Adapted from Fekri A. Hassan, *Demographic Archaeology* (New York: Academic Press, 1981), p. 207.

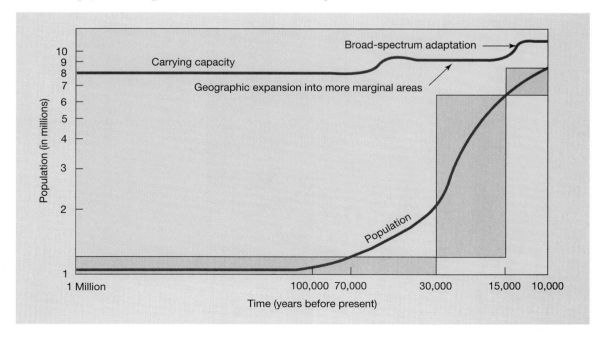

the midwestern United States, skeletal evidence also suggests a decline in the general level of health with the rise of broad-spectrum collecting.[28]

BROAD-SPECTRUM COLLECTING AND SEDENTARISM

Does the switch to broad-spectrum collecting explain the increasingly sedentary way of life we see in various parts of the world in preagricultural times? The answer seems to be both yes and no. In some areas of the world—some sites in Europe, the Near East, Africa, and Peru—settlements became more permanent. In other areas, such as the semiarid highlands of Mesoamerica, the switch to broad-spectrum collecting was not associated with increasing sedentarism. Even after the highland Mesoamericans began to cultivate plants, they still did not live in permanent villages.[29] Why?

It would seem that it is not simply the switch to broad-spectrum collecting that accounts for increasing sedentarism in many areas. Rather, a comparison of settlements on the Peruvian coast suggests that the more permanent settlements were located nearer, within three and a half miles, to most, if not all, of the diverse food resources exploited during the year than were temporary settlements. The community that did not have a year-round settlement seems to have depended on more widely distributed resources. What accounts for sedentarism may thus be the nearness[30] or the high reliability and yield[31] of the broad-spectrum resources, rather than the broad spectrum itself.

SEDENTARISM AND POPULATION GROWTH

Although some population growth undoubtedly occurred throughout the hunting and gathering phase of world history, some anthropologists have suggested that populations would have increased dramatically when people began to settle down. The evidence for this suggestion comes largely from a comparison of recent nomadic and sedentary !Kung populations.

The settling down of a nomadic group may reduce the typical spacing between births.[32] Nomadic !Kung have children spaced four years apart on the average; in contrast, recently sedentarized !Kung have children about three years apart. Why might birth spacing change with settling down? There are several possibilities.

The spacing of children far apart can occur in a number of ways. One way, if effective contraceptives are not available, is prolonged sexual abstinence after the birth of a child—the postpartum sex taboo—which is common in recent human societies. Another way is abortion or infanticide.[33] Nomadic groups may be motivated to have children farther apart because of the problem of carrying small children. Carrying one small child is difficult enough; carrying two might be too burdensome.

The !Kung of the Kalahari Desert on the move. Spacing births an average of four years apart helps to ensure that a woman will not have to carry more than two children at a time. The woman in front is carrying both a large and a small child.

Thus, sedentary populations could have their children spaced more closely because carrying children would not always be necessary.

Although some nomadic groups may have deliberately spaced births by abstinence or infanticide, there is no evidence that such practices explain why four years separate births among nomadic !Kung. There may be another explanation, involving an unintended effect of how babies are fed. Nancy Howell and Richard Lee have suggested that the presence of baby foods other than mother's milk may be responsible for the decreased birth spacing in sedentary agricultural !Kung groups.[34] It is now well established that the longer a mother nurses her baby without supplementary foods, the longer it is likely to be before she starts ovulating again. Nomadic !Kung women have little to give their babies in the way of soft, digestible food, and the babies depend largely on mother's milk for two to three years. But sedentary !Kung mothers can give their babies soft foods such as cereal (made from cultivated grain) and milk from domesticated animals. Such changes in feeding practices may shorten birth spacing by shortening the interval between birth and the resumption of ovulation. In preagricultural sedentary communities, it is possible that baby foods made from wild grains might have had the same effect. For this reason alone, therefore, populations may have grown even before people started to farm or herd.

Another reason sedentary !Kung women may have more babies than nomadic !Kung women has to do with the ratio of body fat to body weight. Some investigators suspect that a critical minimum of fat in the body may be necessary for ovulation. A sedentary !Kung woman may have more fatty tissue than a nomadic !Kung woman, who walks many miles daily to gather wild plant foods, often carrying a child around with her. Thus, sedentary !Kung women might resume ovulating sooner after the birth of a baby and so may be likely for that reason alone to have more closely spaced children. If some critical amount of fat is necessary for ovulation, that would explain why in our own society many women who have little body fat—long-distance runners, gymnasts, and ballet dancers are examples—do not ovulate regularly.[35]

MESOLITHIC TECHNOLOGY

Technologically, Mesolithic cultures did not differ radically from Upper Paleolithic cultures.[36] (Mesolithic, like the term Upper Paleolithic, properly applies only to cultural developments in the Old World. However, we use the term Mesolithic here for some general preagricultural trends.) The trend toward smaller and lighter tools continued. Microliths, small blades half an inch to two inches long, which were made in late Upper Paleolithic times, were now used in quantity. In place of the one-piece flint implement, Mesolithic peoples in Europe, Asia, and Africa equipped themselves with composite tools—that is, tools made of more than one material.

Microliths, too small to be used one at a time, could be fitted into grooves in bone or wood to form arrows, harpoons, daggers, and sickles. A sickle, for example, was made by inserting several microliths into a groove in a wooden or bone handle. The blades were held in place by resin. A broken microlith could be replaced like a blade in a modern razor. Besides being adaptable for many uses, microliths could be made from many varieties of available stone; Mesolithic people were no longer limited to flint. Since they did not need the large flint nodules to make large core and flake tools, they could use small pebbles of flint to make the small blades.[37]

THE DOMESTICATION OF PLANTS AND ANIMALS

Neolithic means "of the new stone age"; the term originally signified the cultural stage in which humans invented pottery and ground-stone tools. We now know, however, that both were present in earlier times, so we cannot define a Neolithic state of culture on the basis of the presence of pottery and ground-stone tools. At present, archaeologists generally define the **Neolithic** in terms of the presence of domesticated plants and animals. In this type of culture, people began to produce food rather than merely collect it.

The line between food-collecting and food-producing occurs when people begin to plant crops and to keep and breed animals. How do we know when this transition occurred? In fact, archaeologically we do not see the beginning of food production; we can see signs of it only after plants and animals show differences from their wild varieties. When people plant crops, we refer to the process as cultivation. It is only when the crops cultivated and the animals raised are modified—different from wild varieties—that we speak of plant and animal **domestication.**

We know, in a particular site, that domestication occurred if plant remains have characteristics different from those of wild plants of the same types. For example, wild grains of barley and wheat have a fragile **rachis**—the seed-bearing part of the stem—which shatters easily, releasing the seeds. Domesticated grains have a tough rachis, which does not shatter easily.

How did the domesticated plants get to be different from the wild varieties? Artificial or human selection, deliberate or accidental, obviously was required. Consider how the rachis of wheat and barley may have changed. As we said, when wild grain ripens in the field, the rachis shatters easily, scattering the seed. This trait is selectively advantageous under wild conditions; it is nature's method of propagating the species. Plants with a tough rachis, therefore, have only a slight chance of reproducing themselves under natural conditions, but they are more desirable for planting. When humans arrived with sickles and flails to collect the wild stands of grain, the seeds harvested probably contained a high proportion of tough-rachis mutants, because these could best withstand the rough treatment of harvest processing. If planted, the harvested seeds would be likely to produce tough-rachis plants. If in each successive harvest seeds from tough-rachis plants were the least likely to be lost, tough-rachis plants would come to predominate.[38]

Domesticated species of animals also differ from the wild varieties. For example, the horns of wild goats in the Near East are shaped differently from

Research Frontiers

DID DOGS (AND CATS) DOMESTICATE THEMSELVES?

Early evidence of a close relationship between dogs and people comes from an archaeological site in northern Israel dating to nearly 12,000 years ago. At that site, archaeologists found the grave of an elderly woman, lying on her right side with her legs folded up, with a dog under her left hand. Our dog is always happy to greet us when we come home. She also is a retriever, an alarm system, can follow a scent, and eats up everything we drop on the floor. Do any of these attributes explain why humans all over the world have had domesticated descendants of wolves around the house for the last 10,000 to 15,000 years?

Dogs were probably the first animals domesticated by humans, some thousands of years before plants, sheep, and goats were domesticated in the Near East. Humans were starting to settle down in semipermanent camps and villages, as they began to depend less on big game (which they had to follow over big distances) and more on relatively stationary food resources, such as fish, shellfish, small game, and wild plants rich in carbohydrates, proteins, and oils.

Why would humans have been interested in taming wolves at that time? One theory is that humans were shifting their prey from large animals to small, and they needed dogs for tracking wounded game or for retrieving killed game from bodies of water or underbrush. Dogs might also have been useful as alarm-givers in case predators came close. Finally, dogs might have helped to keep a camp clean, by scavenging garbage.

The authors of this book think that this last use of dogs suggests an alternative theory of dog domestication. Perhaps it wasn't so much that humans domesticated dogs, but that some wolves domesticated themselves by hanging around human camps. Why would wolves be interested in those humans who were first settling down? It couldn't have been the possibility of a human dinner, because that would have been a possibility for millions of years before. So perhaps something else lured wolves to those early settled camps and villages. What was different about those early settlements? For the first time in human history, people were staying put for considerable periods of time—months at a time, *year after year*—because they could count on being able to "harvest" and live on the wild resources of the area for long periods of time. If they lived there for years, even if only seasonally, they would eventually have had a problem with garbage.

The residues of meals, in particular, would have been a problem. They might not only come to stink; they might also attract rodents and bigger threats to health and children. What could the people do about this problem? Well, as any camper nowadays realizes, they could have buried the garbage so that its scent would not attract unwelcome visitors. But eventually they would have run out of room for garbage pits in or close to the settlement. Of course, they could have moved the settlement. But

those of domesticated goats.[39] But differences in physical characteristics may not be the only indicators of domestication. Some archaeologists believe that imbalances in the sex and age ratios of animal remains at particular sites also suggest that domestication had occurred. For example, at Zawi Chemi Shanidar in Iraq, the proportion of young to mature sheep remains was much higher than the ratio of young to mature sheep in wild herds. One possible inference to be drawn is that the animals were domesticated, the adult sheep being saved for breeding purposes while the young were eaten. (If mostly young animals were eaten, and only a few animals were allowed to grow old, most of the bones found in a site would be from the young animals that were killed regularly for food.[40])

DOMESTICATION IN THE NEAR EAST

For some time most archaeologists have thought that the Fertile Crescent (see Figure 8–3), the arc of land stretching up from Israel and the Jordan Valley through southern Turkey and then downward to the western slopes of the Zagros Mountains in Iran, was one of the earliest centers of plant and animal domestication. We know that several varieties of domesticated wheat were being grown there after about 8000 B.C., as were oats, rye, barley, lentils,

maybe they didn't want to. After all, they had spent a lot of time and effort building a permanent house that was warm in the winter and dry in the rains. And they had a lot of things stored there. So what *could* they do?

Maybe people didn't have to do anything. Maybe those wolves hanging around the neighborhood solved the problem for our ancestors. How? By scavenging, which is something most dogs (particularly larger ones, like the first domesticated dogs) do quite naturally and efficiently. Our own dog eats anything (except maybe undressed lettuce). So even a few tame wolves or domesticated dogs could have kept a garbage pit or pile from stinking and growing. And the people "feeding" that pit or pile could stay put in one place for a long time, safe from smells, vermin, and disease. Dogs may have mostly domesticated themselves because it was good for some of them as well as for those Mesolithic humans.

A similar theory may explain the domestication of cats. Cats are especially good at catching and killing mice. Masses of mice skeletons (of the house mouse) begin to appear in basements of Near East dwellings after the emergence of agriculture. It is possible that humans purposely tried to domesticate cats to catch mice, but it is more likely that cats would have domesticated themselves by adapting to life near or in a granary or storage cellar. Of course, humans might have helped the process of domestication a little, by killing the more ferocious wild cats that were attracted to the settlement. The same was probably true for the wolves attracted to garbage. Even if you didn't at first want to "pet" the canids or felids who were hanging around, you wouldn't want them to attack humans. Wolves in the wild have a dominance-submission hierarchy, so they would be preadapted to heeding a "dominant" human; those that were not sufficiently submissive could be killed.

How could these theories of dog and cat domestication be tested? If dogs domesticated themselves as scavengers, archaeologists should find evidence of dog domestication (for example, changes in anatomy) only in sites that were occupied for a good part of the year over a period of years. Only under those circumstances would garbage be a problem and dogs a solution. Similarly, evidence of cat domestication should be found only in sites that show signs of year-to-year storage of grain. Only then would rodents be a problem and cats a solution. We hope archaeologists will make these tests in the future.

Sources: Juliet Clutton-Brock, "Domestication of Animals," and Frank Hole, "Origins of Agriculture," in Steve Jones, Robert Martin, and David Pilbeam, eds., *The Cambridge Encyclopedia of Human Evolution* (New York: Cambridge University Press, 1992), pp. 380–85, 373–79; Juliet Clutton-Brock, "Dog," and Roy Robinson, "Cat," in Ian L. Mason, *Evolution of Domesticated Animals* (New York: Longman, 1984), pp. 198–210, 217–25; Stephen Budiansky, *The Covenant of the Wild: Why Animals Chose Domestication* (New York: William Morrow, 1992).

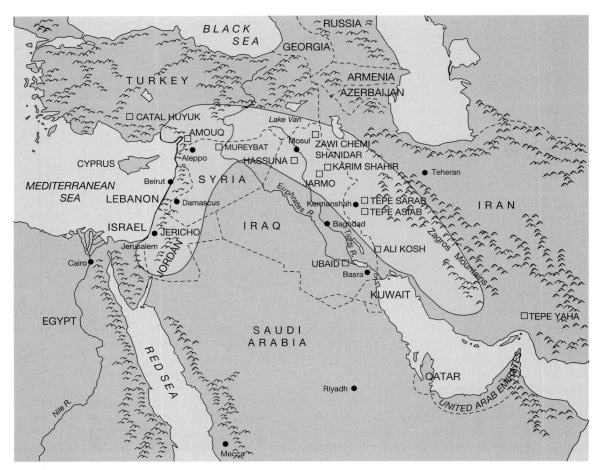

FIGURE 8–3 *Early Agricultural Settlements in the Near East*

Modern cities are represented by a dot, early settlements by a square. The green color indicates the area known as the Fertile Crescent.

peas, and various fruits and nuts (apricots, pears, pomegranates, dates, figs, olives, almonds, and pistachios).[41] It appears that the first animals were domesticated in the Near East. Dogs were first domesticated before the rise of agriculture, around 10,000 B.C. (see the box titled "Did Dogs (and Cats) Domesticate Themselves?"), goats and sheep around 7000 B.C., and cattle and pigs around 6000 B.C.[42]

Let us look at two early Neolithic sites in the Near East to see what life there may have been like after people began to depend on domesticated plants and animals for food.

ALI KOSH. At the stratified site of Ali Kosh in what is now southwestern Iran (see Figure 8–3), we see the remains of a community that started out about 7500 B.C. living mostly on wild plants and

animals. Over the next 2,000 years, until about 5500 B.C., agriculture and herding became increasingly important. After 5500 B.C. we see the appearance of two innovations—irrigation and the use of domesticated cattle—that seem to have stimulated a minor population explosion during the following millennium.

From 7500 to 6750 B.C., the people at Ali Kosh cut little slabs of raw clay out of the ground to build small multiroom structures. The rooms excavated by archaeologists are small, seldom more than 7 by 10 feet, and there is no evidence that the structures were definitely houses where people actually spent time or slept. Instead they may have been storage rooms. On the other hand, house rooms of even smaller size are known in other areas of the world, so it is possible that the people at Ali Kosh in its earliest phase were actually living in those tiny unbaked "brick" houses. There is a bit of evidence that the people at Ali Kosh may have moved for the summer (with their goats) to the grassier mountain valleys nearby, which were just a few days' walk away.

We have a lot of evidence about what the people at Ali Kosh ate. They got some of their food from cultivated emmer wheat and a kind of barley and a considerable amount from domesticated goats. We know the goats were domesticated because wild goats do not seem to have lived in the area. Also, the fact that virtually no bones from elderly goats were found in the site suggests that the goats were domesticated and herded rather than hunted. Moreover, it would seem from the horn cores found in the site that mostly young male goats were eaten, so the females probably were kept for breeding and milking. But with all these signs of deliberate food production, there is an enormous amount of evidence—literally tens of thousands of seeds and bone fragments—that the people at the beginning of Ali Kosh depended mostly on wild plants (legumes and grasses) and wild animals (including gazelles, wild oxen, and wild pigs). They also collected fish, such as carp and catfish, and shellfish, such as mussels, as well as waterfowl that visited the area during part of the year.

The flint tools used during this earliest phase at Ali Kosh were varied and abundant. Finds from this period include tens of thousands of tiny flint blades, some only a few millimeters wide. About 1 percent of the chipped stone found by archaeologists was **obsidian,** or volcanic glass, which came from what is now eastern Turkey, several hundred miles away. Thus, the people at Ali Kosh during its earliest phase definitely had some kind of contact with people elsewhere. This contact is also suggested by the fact that the emmer wheat they cultivated did not have a wild relative in the area.

From 6750 to 6000 B.C., the people increased their consumption of cultivated food plants; 40 percent of the seed remains in the hearths and refuse areas were now from emmer wheat and barley. The proportion of the diet coming from wild plants was much reduced, probably because the cultivated plants have the same growing season and grow in the same kind of soil as the wild plants. Grazing by the goats and sheep that were kept may also have contributed to the reduction of wild plant foods in the area and in the diet. The village may or may not have gotten larger, but the multiroom houses definitely had. The rooms were now larger than 10 by 10 feet; the walls were much thicker; and the clay-slab bricks were now held together by a mud mortar.

Also, the walls now often had a coat of smooth mud plaster on both sides. The stamped-mud house floors were apparently covered with rush or reed mats (you can see the imprints of them). There were courtyards with domed brick ovens and brick-lined roasting pits. Understandably, considering the summer heat in the area, none of the ovens found were inside a house.

Even though the village probably contained no more than 100 individuals, it participated in an extensive trading network. Seashells were probably obtained from the Persian Gulf, which is some distance to the south; copper may have come from what is now central Iran; obsidian was still coming from eastern Turkey; and turquoise somehow made its way from what is now the border between Iran and Afghanistan. Some of these materials were used as ornaments worn by both sexes—or so it seems from the remains of bodies found buried under the floors of houses.

After about 5500 B.C., the area around Ali Kosh begins to show signs of a much larger population, apparently made possible by a more complex agriculture employing irrigation and plows drawn by domesticated cattle. In the next thousand years, by 4500 B.C., the population of the area probably tripled. This population growth was apparently part of the cultural developments that culminated in the rise of urban civilizations in the Near East,[43] as we will see in the next chapter.

Population growth may have occurred in and around Ali Kosh but did not continue in all areas of the Near East after domestication. For example, one of the largest early villages in the Near East, 'Ain Ghazal (on the outskirts of what is now Amman, Jordan), suffered a decline in population and standard of living over time, perhaps because the environment around 'Ain Ghazal could not permanently support a large village.[44]

CATAL HÜYÜK. On a wind-swept plateau in the rugged, mountainous region of southern Turkey stand the remains of a mud-brick town known as Catal Hüyük (see Figure 8–3). Hüyük is the Turkish word for a mound formed by a succession of settlements, one built on top of another.

About 5600 B.C., Catal Hüyük was an adobe town. Some 200 houses have been excavated, and they are interconnected in *pueblo fashion* (each flat-roofed structure housed a number of families). The inhabitants decorated the walls of the houses with imaginative murals, and their shrines with symbolic statuary. The murals depict what seem to be religious scenes and everyday events. Archaeologists peeling away frescoes found layer upon layer of murals, indicating that old murals were plastered over to make way for fresh paintings. Several rooms are believed to have been shrine rooms. They contain many large bull murals and clay bull figurines and have full-sized clay heads of cattle on the walls. Other "shrine-room" murals depict scenes of life and death, painted in red and black, respectively. Clay statuettes of a pregnant woman and of a bearded man seated on a bull have also been found in these rooms.

Farming was well advanced at Catal Hüyük. Lentils, wheat, barley, and peas were grown in quantities that produced a surplus. Archaeologists were astonished at the richly varied handicrafts, including beautifully carved wooden bowls and boxes, that the people of the town produced. These people also had obsidian and flint daggers, spearheads, lance heads, scrapers, awls, and sickle blades. Bowls, spatulas, knives, ladles, and spoons were made from bone. The houses contained belt hooks, toggles, and pins carved from bone. Evidence also suggests that men and women wore jewelry fashioned from bone, shell, and copper and that they used obsidian mirrors.[45] (See Figure 8–4 for similar tools and ornaments in Neolithic Switzerland.)

Because Catal Hüyük is located in a region with few raw materials, the town evidently depended on exchange with other areas to secure the rich variety of materials it used. Shells were procured from the Mediterranean, timber from the hills, obsidian from 50 miles away, and marble from western Turkey.

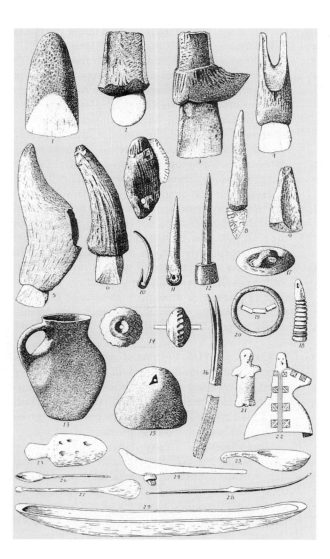

FIGURE 8–4

Neolithic implements from Switzerland, including axes (1–5, 24), chisels made of stone and bone (6, 9), awls made of bone (11, 12), fling knives (7, 8), weaving implements made of clay and bone (14–16), and ornaments (18–22).

DOMESTICATION ELSEWHERE IN THE OLD WORLD

The archaeological record for the domestication of seed crops is better known than for soft-flesh crops because the latter do not preserve well. The earliest clear evidence of cereal cultivation outside the Near East is from China. Late in the sixth millennium B.C. in North China there were sites where foxtail millet was cultivated. Storage pits, storage pots, and large numbers of grinding stones suggest that millet was an enormously important item in the diet. The wild-animal bones and the hunting and fishing tools that have been found suggest that people still depended on hunting and fishing somewhat, even though domesticated pigs (as well as dogs) were present. In South China, from about the same time, archaeologists have found a village by the edge of a small lake where people cultivated rice, bottle gourds, water chestnuts, and the datelike fruit called jujube. The people in South China also raised water buffalo, pigs, and dogs. And, as in the North China sites, some of their food came from hunting and fishing.[46]

Mainland Southeast Asia may have been a place of domestication as early as the Near East was. The dating of domestication in Southeast Asia is not yet clear; the dates of the oldest site with probable domesticates—Spirit Cave in northwest Thailand—range from about 9500 B.C. to 5500 B.C. Some of the plants found at Spirit Cave are not clearly distinguishable from wild varieties, but others, such as gourds, betel nut, betel leaf, and water chestnut, were probably domesticates.[47]

Most of the early cultivation in mainland Southeast Asia seems to have occurred in the plains and low terraces around rivers, although the main subsistence foods of early cultivators were probably the fish and shellfish in nearby waters. The first plants to be domesticated probably were not cereal grains, as they were in the Near East. Indeed, some early cultivated crops may not have been used for food at all. In particular, bamboo may have been used to make cutting tools and for a variety of building purposes, and gourds were probably used as containers or bowls. We do not know yet exactly when rice was first domesticated, but there is definite evidence of cultivated rice in Thailand after 4000 B.C. Other major food plants were domesticated first in Southeast Asia, including root crops, such as taro and yams, and tree crops, such as breadfruit, coconuts, and bananas.[48]

Some plants and animals were domesticated first in Africa. Most of the early domestications probably occurred in the wide, broad belt of woodland-savanna country south of the Sahara and north of the equator. Among the cereal grains, sorghum was probably first domesticated in the central or eastern part of this belt, bulrush millet and a kind of rice (different from Asian rice) in the western part, and finger millet in the east. Groundnuts and yams were first domesticated in West Africa.[49] We do know that farming became widespread in the northern half of Africa after 6000 B.C.; investigators continue to debate whether the earliest crops grown there were indigenous or borrowed from the Near East. There is little doubt, however, that some of the plant foods were first domesticated in sub-Saharan Africa because the wild varieties occur there.[50] Many of the important domestic animals in Africa today—cattle, sheep, and goats—probably were domesticated first in the Near East; most likely the donkey and guinea fowl were first domesticated in Africa.[51]

DOMESTICATION IN THE NEW WORLD

In the New World, evidence of independent domestication of plants comes from at least three areas: Mexico, South America, and the eastern United States. Possibly the first plants to be domesticated in the New World were members of the cucurbit family; they included a variety of the bottle gourd, summer squash, and pumpkins. Although probably not an important source of food anywhere, the woody bottle gourd could have been used as a water jug or cut into bowls. People may also have made musical instruments and art objects out of the bottle gourd. It is difficult to establish exactly when and where the New World variety of bottle gourd was first domesticated. Some suspect it is native to Africa and floated to the New World like a runaway buoy.[52] Fragments and seeds of bottle gourd do date from as far back as 7400 B.C. in Oaxaca, Mexico. Summer squash was probably domesticated in Mexico between 7400 and 6700 B.C.[53]

Although the origins of maize (corn) are controversial, an early domesticated form dating from about 5000 B.C. has been found in Tehuacán, Mexico. Until 1970, the most widely accepted view was that maize was cultivated from a now-extinct "wild maize" that had tiny cobs topped by small tassels. Now other views are considered: that maize was domesticated from teosinte, a tall, wild grass that still grows widely in Mexico, or that it resulted from a cross between a perennial variety of teosinte and a wild corn.[54]

Domesticated corn from about 7,000 years ago appears first in central Mexico. One possible wild ancestor is teosinte, a tall wild grass that still grows widely in Mexico. Here we see kernels of dent corn, the most important corn in the United States, and kernels of teosinte.

People who lived in Mesoamerica, Mexico and Central America, are often credited with the invention of planting maize, beans, and squash together in the same field. This planting strategy provides some important advantages. Maize takes nitrogen from the soil; beans, like all legumes, put nitrogen back into the soil. The maize stalk provides a natural pole for the bean plant to twine around, and the low-growing squash can grow around the base of the tall maize plant. Beans supply people with the amino acid lysine, which is missing in maize. Thus, maize and beans together provide all the essential amino acids that humans need to obtain from food. Whether teosinte was or was not the ancestor of maize, it may have provided the model for this unique combination since wild runner beans and wild squash occur naturally where teosinte grows.[55]

We can trace more than 200 domesticated plants to the Andes in South America, including potatoes, lima beans, peanuts, amaranth, and quinoa. The first clear domesticate was the chili pepper, dating back to about 7300 B.C., which makes domestication in the Andes about as old as in Mexico. The origins of the root crops manioc and sweet potato are less certain, but those crops probably originated in lowland tropical forest regions of South America.[56]

Many of the plants grown in North America, such as corn, beans, and squash, were apparently introduced from Mesoamerica. However, at least three seed plants were probably domesticated independently in North America at an earlier time—sunflowers, sumpweed, and goosefoot. Sunflowers and sumpweed contain seeds that are highly nutritious in terms of protein and fat; goosefoot is high in starch and similar to corn in food value.[57] Sumpweed is an unusually good source of calcium, rivaled only by greens, mussels, and bones. It is also a very good source of iron (better than beef liver) and thiamine.[58] These plants may have been cultivated in the area of Kentucky, Tennessee, and southern Illinois beginning around 2000 B.C. (Corn was introduced about A.D. 200.)

All of the pre-corn domesticates are nutritionally superior to corn, so why did North American agriculturalists switch to a reliance on corn in the last 1,000 years?[59] In the archaeologist Bruce Smith's words, "With the exception of the sunflower, North American seed crops are not exactly household words."[60] Crop yields of corn would have had to be quite high to surpass the yields of those other crops, so perhaps the crucial factors were the time of harvest and the amount of effort required. Goosefoot, for example, was comparable to corn nutritionally. But harvesting and preparing it for storage took a lot of work and had to be done during the fall, the time of year when deer could be hunted intensively. So perhaps the incompatibility of goosefoot production and deer hunting, and the ease of harvesting corn and preparing it for storage, explain the switch to corn.[61]

On the whole, domestic animals were less important economically in the New World than they were in many parts of the Old World. In North America, dogs and turkeys were the main domesticated animals before the arrival of the Spanish. Dogs in North and South America probably descended from the North American wolf and were domesticated relatively early. Domesticated turkeys from about A.D. 500 have been found in pueblos in the American Southwest.[62] Their feathers were used for arrows, ornaments, and weaving, and their bones for tools; but they do not seem to have been used frequently for food. However, turkeys were an important food in Mexico, where they may have been independently domesticated, and in Central America. When Cortes came to Mexico in 1519, he found domesticated turkeys in great quantities.[63]

The central Andes was the only part of the New World where animals were a significant part of the economy. Used for meat, transportation, and wool, llamas and alpacas (members of the camel family) were domesticated as early as 5000 B.C. in the Andes.[64] Guinea pigs, misnamed because they are neither pigs nor from Guinea, are rodents that were domesticated in the Andes sometime later. They were an important source of food even before domestication.[65] Since they were domesticated, they have been raised in people's dwellings.

Animal domestication in the New World differed from that in the Old World because different wild species were found in the two hemispheres. The Old World plains and forests were the homes for the wild ancestors of the cattle, sheep, goats, pigs, and horses we know today. In the New World, the Pleistocene herds of horses, mastodons, mammoths, and other large animals were long extinct, allowing few opportunities for domestication of large animals.[66]

Although there is evidence from Mexico and other parts of the Americas that cultivation was under way between the fifth and third millennia B.C., permanent villages probably were not established in Peru until about 2500 B.C. and in areas of Mesoamerica until about 1500 B.C.[67] Archaeologists once thought that settled village life followed as a matter of course as soon as people had learned to domesticate plants. But evidence from the arid highlands of Mesoamerica contradicts that assumption. In highland Mesoamerica resources were widely distributed and relatively scarce in the dry season. Richard MacNeish has suggested that the early cultivators depended mostly on hunting during the winter and on seed collecting and podpicking in the spring. In addition to their food-collecting activities, in the summer they planted and harvested crops such as squash, and in the fall they collected fruit and harvested the avocados they had planted. These varied activities seem to have required people to spend most of the year in small groups, gathering into larger groups only in the summer and only in moister areas.[68]

WHY DID FOOD PRODUCTION DEVELOP?

We know that an economic transformation occurred in widely separate areas of the world beginning after about 10,000 years ago, as people began to domesticate plants and animals. But why did domestication occur? And why did it occur independently in many different places within a period of a few thousand years? Considering that people depended only on wild plants and animals for millions of years, the differences in exactly when domestication first occurred in different parts of the world seem small. The spread of domesticated plants seems to have been more rapid in the Old World than in the New World, perhaps because the Old World spread was more along an east-west axis (except for the spread to sub-Saharan Africa),

whereas the New World spread was more north-south. Spreading north and south may have required more time to adapt to variation in day lengths, climates, and diseases.[69] Figure 8–5 shows a time line for domestication of plants and animals in the Old and New Worlds.

There are many theories of why food production developed; most have tried to explain the origin of domestication in the area of the Fertile Crescent. Gordon Childe's theory, popular in the 1950s, was that a drastic change in climate caused domestication in the Near East.[70] According to Childe, the postglacial period was marked by a decline in summer rainfall in the Near East and northern Africa. As the rains decreased, people were forced to retreat into shrinking pockets, or *oases,* of food resources surrounded by desert. The lessened availability of wild resources provided an incentive for people to cultivate grains and to domesticate animals, according to Childe.

Robert Braidwood criticized Childe's theory for two reasons. First, Braidwood believed that the climate changes may not have been as dramatic as Childe had assumed, and therefore the "oasis incentive" may not have existed. Second, the climatic changes that occurred in the Near East after the retreat of the last glaciers had probably occurred at earlier interglacial periods too, but there had never been a similar food-producing revolution before. Hence, according to Braidwood, there must be more to the explanation of why people began to produce food than simply changes in climate.[71]

Braidwood and Gordon Willey claimed that people did not undertake domestication until they had learned a great deal about their environment and until their culture had evolved enough for them to handle such an undertaking: "Why did incipient food production not come earlier? Our only answer at the moment is that culture was not ready to achieve it."[72]

But most archaeologists now think we should try to explain why people were not "ready" earlier to achieve domestication. Both Lewis Binford and Kent Flannery suggested that *some change* in external circumstances must have induced or favored the changeover to food production.[73] As Flannery pointed out, there is no evidence of a great economic incentive for hunter-gatherers to become food producers. In fact, as we shall see in the chapter on getting food, some contemporary hunter-gatherers may actually obtain adequate nutrition with far *less* work than many agriculturalists. So what might push food collectors to become food producers?

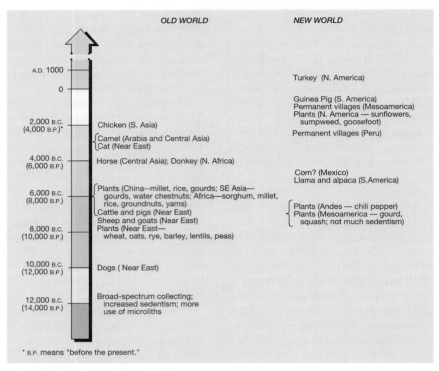

FIGURE 8–5 *The Evolution of Domestication*

Source: Dates for animal domestication are from Juliet Clutton-Brock, "Domestication of Animals," in Stephen Jones, Robert Martin, and David Pilbeam, eds., *The Cambridge Encyclopedia of Human Evolution* (New York: Cambridge University Press, 1992) p. 384. Reprinted with permission of Cambridge University Press.

Binford and Flannery thought that the incentive to domesticate animals and plants may have been a desire to reproduce what was wildly abundant in the most bountiful or optimum hunting and gathering areas. Because of population growth in the optimum areas, people might have moved to surrounding areas containing fewer wild resources. It would have been in those marginal areas that people might have first turned to food production in order to reproduce what they used to have.

The Binford-Flannery model seems to fit the archaeological record in the Levant, the southwestern part of the Fertile Crescent, where population increase did precede the first signs of domestication.[74] But as Flannery admitted, in some regions, such as southwestern Iran, the optimum hunting-gathering areas do not show population increase before the emergence of domestication.[75]

The Binford-Flannery model focuses on population pressure in a small area as the incentive to turn to food production. Mark Cohen theorizes it was population pressure on a global scale that explains

why so many of the world's peoples adopted agriculture within the span of a few thousand years.[76] He argues that hunter-gatherers all over the world gradually increased in population so that by about 10,000 years ago the world was more or less filled with food collectors. Thus people could no longer relieve population pressure by moving to uninhabited areas. To support their increasing populations, they would have had to exploit a broader range of less desirable wild foods; that is, they would have had to switch to broad-spectrum collecting, or they would have had to increase the yields of the most desirable wild plants by weeding, protecting them from animal pests, and perhaps deliberately planting the most productive among them. Cohen thinks that people might have tried a variety of these strategies but would generally have ended up depending on cultivation because that would have been the most efficient way to allow more people to live in one place.

Recently, some archaeologists have returned to the idea that climatic change (not the extreme variety that Childe envisaged) might have played a role in the emergence of agriculture. It seems clear from the evidence now available that the climate of the Near East about 13,000 to 12,000 years ago became more seasonal: The summers got hotter and drier than before and the winters became colder. These climatic changes may have favored the emergence of annual species of wild grain, which archaeologically we see proliferating in many areas of the Near East.[77] People such as the Natufians intensively exploited the seasonal grains, developing an elaborate technology for storing and processing the grains and giving up their previous nomadic existence to do so. The transition to agriculture may have occurred when sedentary foraging no longer provided sufficient resources for the population. This could have happened because sedentarization led to population increase and therefore resource scarcity,[78] or because local wild resources became depleted after people settled down in permanent villages.[79] In the area of Israel and Jordan where the Natufians lived, some of the people apparently turned to agriculture, probably to increase the supply of grain, whereas other people returned to nomadic food collection because of the decreasing availability of wild grain.[80]

Change to a more seasonal climate might also have led to a shortage of certain nutrients for food collectors. In the dry seasons certain nutrients would have been less available. For example, grazing animals get lean when grasses are not plentiful, so meat from hunting would have been in short supply in the dry seasons. Although it may seem surprising, some recent hunter-gatherers have starved when they had to rely on lean meat. If they could have somehow increased their carbohydrate or fat intake, they might have been more likely to get through the periods of lean game.[81] So it is possible that some wild-food collectors in the past thought of planting crops to get them through the dry seasons when hunting, fishing, and gathering did not provide enough carbohydrates and fat for them to avoid starvation.

CONSEQUENCES OF THE RISE OF FOOD PRODUCTION

We know that intensive agriculture (permanent rather than shifting cultivation) probably developed in response to population pressure, as we will see later in the chapter on getting food. But we do not know for sure that population pressure was even partly responsible for plant and animal domestication in the first place. Still, population growth certainly accelerated after the rise of food production (see Figure 8–6). There were other consequences too. Paradoxically, perhaps, health seems to have declined. Material possessions, though, became more elaborate.

ACCELERATED POPULATION GROWTH

As we have seen, settling down (even before the rise of food production) may have increased the rate of human population growth. But population growth definitely accelerated after the emergence of farming and herding, possibly because the spacing between

FIGURE 8–6 *Population Growth since 10,000 Years Ago*

The rate of population growth accelerated after the emergence of farming and herding 10,000 years ago. The rate of growth accelerated even more dramatically in recent times. *Source:* Adapted from Ansley J. Coale, *"The History of the Human Population."* Copyright © 1974 by Scientific American, Inc. All rights reserved. By permission of Allen Beechel, artist.

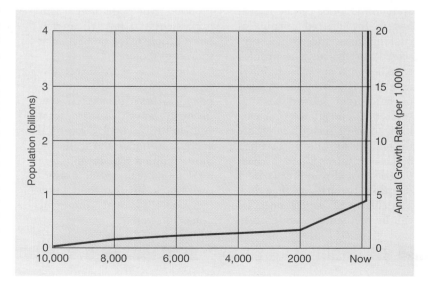

births was reduced further and therefore fertility (the number of births per mother) increased. Increased fertility may have been advantageous because of the greater value of children in farming and herding economies; there is evidence from recent population studies that fertility rates are higher where children contribute more to the economy.[82] Not only may parents desire more children to help with chores; the increased workload of mothers may also (but inadvertently) decrease birth spacing. The busier a mother is, the less frequently she may nurse and the more likely her baby will be given supplementary food by other caretakers such as older siblings.[83] Less frequent nursing[84] and greater reliance on food other than mother's milk may result in an earlier resumption of ovulation after the birth of a baby. (Farmers and herders are likely to have animal milk to feed to babies, and also cereals that have been transformed by cooking into soft, mushy porridges.) Therefore the spacing between births may have decreased (and the number of births per mother, in turn, increased) when mothers got busier after the rise of food production.

DECLINING HEALTH

Although the rise of food production may have led to increased fertility, this does not mean that health generally improved. In fact, it appears that health declined at least sometimes with the transition to food production. The two trends may seem paradoxical, but rapid population growth can occur if each mother gives birth to a large number of babies, even if many of them die early because of disease or poor nutrition.

The evidence that health may have declined sometimes after the rise of food production comes from studies of the bones and teeth of some prehistoric populations, before and after the emergence of

Research Frontiers

YOU ARE WHAT YOU EAT: CHEMICAL ANALYSES OF BONES AND TEETH

Archaeologists study ancient diets in several ways, most of them indirect. They can indirectly infer some of what ancient people ate from recovered food wastes. For example, if you find a lot of corncobs, chances are that the people ate a lot of corn. Plant and animal foods can be identified in the charred remains of cooking fires and (when preserved) in the ancient people's feces, or *coprolites*. Such inferences are usually biased in favor of hard food sources such as seeds, nuts, and grains (which are likely to be preserved); rarely are the remains of soft plants such as bananas or tubers found. Archaeologists can also indirectly infer diet from the artifacts they find, particularly of course ones we can be pretty sure were used in

obtaining or processing food. So, for example, if you find a stone with a flat or concave surface that looks like what people use in some places to grind corn, it is very likely that the ancient people also ground grain (or other hard things such as seeds) for food. But plant remains or implements do not tell us *how much* people relied on particular sources of food.

There is a more direct way to study ancient diets. Anthropologists have discovered that in many ways "you are what you eat." In particular, chemical analyses of bones and teeth, the most common remains found in excavations, can reveal distinctive traces of the foods that metabolically went into the bones and teeth.

One kind of informative chemical analysis involves the ratio of strontium to calcium in bone. This analysis can indicate the relative amounts of plant and animal food in the diet. So, for example, we know from strontium analysis of bones that just before the beginnings of cereal agriculture in the Near East, people were eating a lot of plant food, probably wild cereals that were intensively collected. Then there was a temporary decline in such collecting, suggesting overexploitation of the wild resources, or at least their decreasing availability. This problem was presumably solved by the cultivation and domestication (modification) of cereals.

Carbon isotope ratios also can tell us what types of plants people were eating. Trees, shrubs, and temperate-zone grasses (for

food production. Nutritional and disease problems are indicated by such features as incomplete formation of tooth enamel, nonaccidental bone lesions (incompletely filled-in bone), reduction in stature, and decreased life expectancy. Many of the studied prehistoric populations that relied heavily on agriculture seem to show less adequate nutrition and higher infection rates than populations living in the same areas before agriculture. Some of the agricultural populations are shorter and had lower life expectancies.[85]

The reasons for a decline in health in those populations are not yet clear. Greater malnutrition can result from an overdependence on a few dietary staples that lack some necessary nutrients. Overdependence on a few sources of food may also increase the risk of famine because the fewer the staple crops, the greater the danger to the food supply posed by a weather-caused crop failure. But some or most nutritional problems may be the result of social and political factors, particularly the rise of different socioeconomic classes of people and unequal access, between and within communities, to food and other resources.[86]

As we will see in the next chapter, social stratification or considerable socioeconomic inequality seems likely to develop after the rise of food production. The effects of stratification and political dominance from afar on the general level of health may be reflected in the skeletal remains of prehistoric Native Americans who died in what is now Illinois between A.D. 950 and 1300, the period spanning the changeover in that region from hunting and gathering to agriculture. The agricultural people living in the area of Dickson's Mounds—burial sites named after the doctor who first excavated them—were apparently in much worse health than their hunter-gatherer ancestors. But curiously, archaeological evidence suggests that they were still also hunting and fishing. A balanced diet was apparently available,

example, rice) have carbon isotope ratios that are different from those of tropical and subtropical grasses (such as millet and corn). People in China were relying heavily on cereals about 7,000 to 8,000 years ago, but the cereals were not the same in the north and south. Contrary to what we might expect, the carbon isotope ratios tell us that an originally temperate-zone cereal (rice) was the staple in subtropical southern China; in the more temperate north, an originally tropical or subtropical grass (millet) was most important. The dependence on millet in the north was enormous. It is estimated that 50 to 80 percent of the diet between 5000 and 500 B.C. came from millet.

In the New World, seed crops such as sunflower, sumpweed, and goosefoot were domesticated in eastern North America long before corn, introduced from Mexico, became the staple. We know this partly from the archaeology; the remains of the early seed crops are older than the remains of corn. Corn, an originally subtropical plant, has a carbon isotope ratio that is different from the ratio for the earlier, temperate-zone seed crops. Thus, the shift in carbon isotope ratios after A.D. 800–900 tells us that corn had become the staple.

Traditionally, nonchemical analyses of human bones and teeth were used by physical anthropologists and archaeologists to study similarities and differences between peoples in different geographic regions, between living humans and possible fossil ancestors, and between living humans and other surviving primates. Much of the research involved surface measurements, particularly of the skull (outside and inside). In recent years, physical anthropologists and archaeologists have begun to study the "insides" of bones and teeth. The new kinds of chemical analysis mentioned here are part of that trend. In N. J. van der Merwe's pithy words: "The emphasis in studies of human evolution has . . . shifted from a preoccupation with the brain to an equal interest in the stomach."

Sources: N. J. van der Merwe, "Reconstructing Prehistoric Diet," in Stephen Jones, Robert Martin, and David Pilbeam, eds., The Cambridge Encyclopedia of Human Evolution (New York: Cambridge University Press, 1992), pp. 369–72; Clark Spenser Larsen, "Bare Bones Anthropology: The Bioarchaeology of Human Remains," in Carol R. Ember, Melvin Ember, and Peter N. Peregrine, eds., Research Frontiers in Anthropology (Upper Saddle River, NJ: Prentice Hall, 1998), Prentice Hall/Simon & Schuster Custom Publishing.

As this reconstruction shows, transforming grain into flour was a "daily grind," putting a great deal of stress on the lower back and knees of women. Studies of Neolithic skeletons of women show marks of stress on bone and arthritis, probably reflecting their long hours of work at the grinding stone.

but who was getting it? Possibly it was the elite at Cahokia, 110 miles away, where perhaps 15,000–30,000 people lived, who were getting most of the meat and fish. The individuals near Dickson's Mounds who collected the meat and fish may have gotten luxury items such as shell necklaces from the Cahokia elite, but many of the people buried at Dickson's Mounds were clearly not benefiting nutritionally from the relationship with Cahokia.[87]

THE ELABORATION OF MATERIAL POSSESSIONS

In the more permanent villages that were established after the rise of food production about 10,000 years ago, houses became more elaborate and comfortable, and construction methods improved. The materials used in construction depended on whether timber or stone was locally available or whether a strong sun could dry mud bricks. Modern architects might find to their surprise that bubble-shaped houses were known long ago in Neolithic Cyprus. Families in the island's town of Khirokitia made their homes in large, domed, circular dwellings shaped like beehives and featuring stone foundations and mud-brick walls. Often, more space was created by dividing the interior horizontally and firmly propping a second floor on limestone pillars.

Sizable villages of solidly constructed, gabled wood houses were built in Europe on the banks of the Danube and along the rims of Alpine lakes.[88]

Many of the gabled wooden houses in the Danube region were long, rectangular structures that apparently sheltered several family units. In Neolithic times these longhouses had doors, beds, tables, and other furniture that closely resembled those in modern-day societies. We know the people had furniture because miniature clay models have been found at their sites. Several of the chairs and couches seem to be models of padded and upholstered furniture with wooden frames, indicating that Neolithic European artisans were creating fairly sophisticated furnishings.[89] Such furnishings are the result of an advanced tool technology put to use by a people who, because they were staying in one area, could take time to make and use furniture.

For the first time, apparel made of woven textile appeared. This development was not simply the result of the domestication of flax (for linen), cotton, and wool-growing sheep. These sources of fiber alone could not produce cloth. It was the development by Neolithic society of the spindle and loom for spinning and weaving that made textiles possible. True, textiles can be woven by hand without a loom, but to do so is a slow, laborious process, impractical for producing garments.

The pottery of the early Neolithic was similar to the plain earthenware made by some Mesolithic groups and included large urns for grain storage, mugs, cooking pots, and dishes. To improve the retention of liquid, potters in the Near East may have been the first to glaze the earthenware's porous surface. Later, Neolithic ceramics became more artistic. Designers shaped the clay into graceful forms and painted colorful patterns on the vessels.

It is probable that virtually none of these architectural and technological innovations could have occurred until humans became fully sedentary. Nomadic hunting and gathering peoples would have found it difficult to carry many material goods, especially fragile items such as pottery. It was only when humans became fully sedentary that these goods would have provided advantages, enabling villagers to cook and store food more effectively and to house themselves more comfortably.

There is also evidence of long-distance trade in the Neolithic, as we have noted. Obsidian from southern Turkey was being exported to sites in the Zagros Mountains of Iran and to what are now Israel, Jordan, and Syria in the Levant. Great amounts of obsidian were exported to sites about 190 miles from the source of supply; more than 80 percent of the tools used by residents of those areas were made of this material.[90] Marble was being sent from western to eastern Turkey, and seashells from the coast were traded to distant inland regions. Such trade suggests a considerable amount of contact among various Neolithic communities.

About 3500 B.C., cities first appeared in the Near East. These cities had political assemblies, kings, scribes, and specialized workshops. The specialized production of goods and services was supported by surrounding farming villages, which sent their produce to the urban centers. A dazzling transformation had taken place in a relatively short time. People had not only settled down, but they had also become "civilized," or urbanized. (The word *civilized* literally means to make "citified."[91]) Urban societies seem to have developed first in the Near East and somewhat later around the eastern Mediterranean, in the Indus Valley of northwestern India, in northern China, and in Mexico and Peru. In the next chapter we turn to the rise of these earliest civilizations.

SUMMARY

1. In the period before plants and animals were domesticated (called the Mesolithic period in regard to Europe and the Near East), there seems to have been a shift in many areas of the world to less dependence on big-game hunting and greater dependence on what is called broad-spectrum collecting. The broad spectrum of available resources frequently included aquatic resources such as fish and shellfish and a variety of wild plants and deer and other game. Climatic changes may have been partly responsible for the change to broad-spectrum collecting.

2. In some sites in Europe, the Near East, Africa, and Peru, the switch to broad-spectrum collecting seems to be associated with the development of more permanent communities. In other areas, such as the semiarid highlands of Mesoamerica, permanent settlements may have emerged only after the domestication of plants and animals.

3. The shift to the cultivation and domestication of plants and animals has been referred to as the Neolithic revolution, and it occurred, probably independently, in a number of areas. To date, the earliest evidence of domestication comes from the Near East about 8000 B.C. Dating for the earliest domestication in other areas of the Old World is not so clear, but the presence of different domesticated crops in different regions suggests that there were independent centers of domestication in China, Southeast Asia (what is now Malaysia, Thailand, Cambodia, and Vietnam), and Africa sometime around or after 6000 B.C. In the New World, there appear to have been several early areas of cultivation and domestication: the highlands of Mesoamerica (about 7000 B.C.), the central Andes around Peru (about the same time), and the Eastern Woodlands of North America (about 2000 B.C.).

4. Theories about why food production originated remain controversial, but most archaeologists think that certain conditions must have pushed people to switch from collecting to producing food. Some possible causal factors include (1) population growth in regions of bountiful wild resources (which may have pushed people to move to marginal areas where they tried to reproduce their former abundance); (2) global population growth (which filled most of the world's habitable regions and may have forced people to utilize a broader spectrum of wild resources and to domesticate plants and animals); and (3) the emergence of hotter and drier summers and colder winters (which may have favored sedentarism near seasonal stands of wild grain; population growth in such areas may have forced people to plant crops and raise animals to support themselves).

5. Regardless of why food production originated, it seems to have had important consequences for human life. Populations generally increased substantially *after* plant and animal domestication. Even though not all early cultivators were sedentary, sedentarism did increase with greater reliance on agriculture. Somewhat surprisingly, some prehistoric populations that relied heavily on agriculture

seem to have been less healthy than prior populations that relied on food collection. In the more permanent villages that were established after the rise of food production, houses and furnishings became more elaborate, and people began to make textiles and to paint pottery. These villages have also yielded evidence of increased long-distance trade.

 ## GLOSSARY TERMS

domestication	obsidian
kitchen middens	rachis
Mesolithic	sedentarism
Neolithic	tundra

 ## CRITICAL QUESTIONS

1. What might cause people to work harder to get food?

2. How might people have domesticated sheep, goats, and cattle?

3. Do the various theories of the rise of food production explain why domestication occurred in many areas of the world within a few thousand years?

 ## INTERNET EXERCISES

1. Write a brief summary of mesolithic and neolithic sites pertaining to Italian archaeology. Browse **http://dns.unife.it/notes/engl.htm** to find the articles. Limit your observation and interpretation to human settlement in the region.

2. Domestication of wild plants is not without its difficulties. Look at the description of attempts to cultivate wild rice at **http://www.hort.purdue.edu/ newcrop/proceedings1993/v2-235.html**. Explore the problems of shattering seed casings and increased disease with cultivation.

3. Explore animal domestication at **http://www. ag.usask.ca/cofa/displays/college/what/what.html**. Pick a domestic animal you are interested in and find out when and where it was domesticated.

SUGGESTED READING

COHEN, M. N. "Were Early Agriculturalists Less Healthy Than Food Collectors?" IN C. R. Ember, M. Ember, and P. N. Peregrine, eds., *Research Frontiers in Cultural Anthropology.* Upper Saddle River, NJ: Prentice Hall, 1998. Prentice Hall/Simon & Schuster Custom Publishing. A specially written chapter for an undergraduate audience, reviewing the evidence for a decline in health with the advent of agriculture.

COWAN, C. W., AND WATSON, P. J., EDS. *The Origins of Agriculture: An International Perspective.* Washington, DC: Smithsonian Institution Press, 1992. Summarizes the geography, climate, botany, and archaeology of the events associated with the emergence of plant cultivation in different parts of the Old and New Worlds.

HENRY, D. O. *From Foraging to Agriculture: The Levant at the End of the Ice Age.* Philadelphia: University of Pennsylvania Press, 1989. An examination and discussion of theories about the origins of agriculture, with particular reference to the areas bordering the eastern Mediterranean.

MACNEISH, R. S. *The Origins of Agriculture and Settled Life.* Norman: University of Oklahoma Press, 1991. After reviewing previous theories about the origins of agriculture, the author puts forward his own model and reviews the archaeological sequences in each of the early regions of domestication in order to evaluate his theory.

PRICE, T. D., AND BROWN, J. A., EDS. *Prehistoric Hunter-Gatherers: The Emergence of Cultural Complexity.* Orlando, FL: Academic Press, 1985. A volume of papers by archaeologists on the beginnings of social complexity among hunter-gatherers. The scope is global; most of the chapters deal comparatively or cross-archaeologically with the various adaptations of hunter-gatherers in the past.

Origins of Cities and States

*F*rom the time agriculture first developed until about 6000 B.C., people in the Near East lived in fairly small villages. There were few differences in wealth and status from household to household, and apparently there was no governmental authority beyond the village. There is no evidence that these villages had any public buildings or craft specialists or that one community was very different in size from its neighbors. In short, these settlements had none of the characteristics we commonly associate with "civilization."

But sometime around 6000 B.C., in parts of the Near East—and at later times in other places—a great transformation in the quality and scale of human life seems to have begun. For the first time we can see evidence of differences in status among households. For example, some are much bigger than others. Communities began to differ in size and to specialize in certain crafts. And there are signs that some political officials had acquired authority over several communities, that what anthropologists call "chiefdoms" had emerged.

Somewhat later, by about 3500 B.C., we can see many, if not all, of the conventional characteristics of **civilization:** the first inscriptions, or writing; cities; many kinds of full-time craft specialists; monumental architecture; great differences in wealth and status; and the kind of strong, hierarchical, centralized political system we call the **state.**

This type of transformation has occurred many times and in many places in human history. The most ancient civilizations arose in the Near East around 3500 B.C., in northwestern India after 2500 B.C., in northern China around 1750 B.C., in the New World (Mexico and Peru) a few hundred years before the time of Christ, and in tropical Africa somewhat later.[1] At least some of these civilizations evolved independently of the others—for example, those in the New World and those in the Old World. Why did they do so? What conditions favored the emergence of centralized, statelike political systems? What conditions favored the establishment of cities? We ask this last question separately, because archaeologists are not yet certain that all the ancient state societies had cities when they first developed centralized government. In this chapter we discuss some of the things archaeologists have learned or suspect about the growth of ancient civilizations. Our discussion focuses primarily on the Near East and Mexico because archaeologists know the most about the sequences of cultural development in those two areas (see Figure 9–1).

ARCHAEOLOGICAL INFERENCES ABOUT CIVILIZATION

The most ancient civilizations have been studied by archaeologists rather than historians because those civilizations evolved before the advent of writing. How do archaeologists infer that a particular people in the preliterate past had social classes, cities, or a centralized government?

As we have noted, it appears that the earliest Neolithic societies were *egalitarian;* that is, people did not differ much in wealth, prestige, or power. Some later societies show signs of social inequality, indicated by burial finds. Archaeologists generally assume that inequality in death reflects inequality in life, at least in status and perhaps also in wealth and power. Thus, we can be fairly sure that a society had differences in status if only some people were buried with special objects, such as jewelry or pots filled with food. And we can be fairly sure that high status was assigned at birth rather than achieved in later life if we find noticeable differences in children's tombs. For example, some (but not all) child burials from as early as 5500 to 5000 B.C. at Tell es-Sawwan in Iraq, and from about 800 B.C. at La Venta in Mexico, are filled with statues and ornaments, suggesting that some children had high status from birth.[2] But burials indicating differences in status do not necessarily mean a society had significant differences in wealth. It is only when archaeologists find other substantial differences, as in house size and furnishings, that we can be sure the society had different socioeconomic classes of people.

Some archaeologists think that states first evolved around 3500 B.C. in Greater Mesopotamia, the area now shared by southern Iraq and southwestern Iran. Archaeologists do not always agree on how a state should be defined, but most think that hierarchical and centralized decision making affecting a substantial population is the key criterion. Other characteristics are usually, but not always, found in these first states. They usually have cities with a substantial part of the population not involved directly in the collection or production of food (which means that people in cities are heavily dependent on people elsewhere); full-time religious

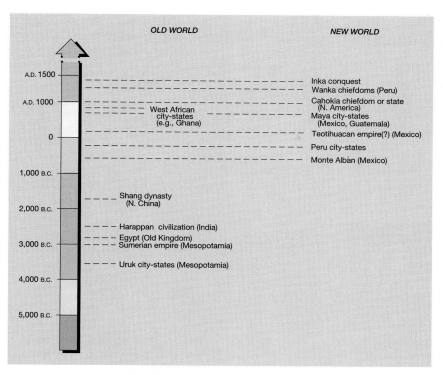

FIGURE 9–1 *The Emergence of Civilization*

and craft specialists; public buildings; and often an official art style. There is a hierarchical social structure topped by an elite class from which the leaders are drawn. The government tries to claim a monopoly on the use of force. (Our own state society says that citizens do not have the right "to take the law into their own hands.") The state uses its force or threat of force to tax its population and to draft people for work or war.[3]

How can archaeologists tell, from the information provided by material remains, whether a society was a state or not? This depends in part on what is used as the criterion for a state. For example, Henry Wright and Gregory Johnson defined a state as a centralized political hierarchy with at least three levels of administration.[4] But how might archaeologists infer that such a hierarchy existed in some area? Wright and Johnson suggested that the way settlement sites differ in size is one indication of how many levels of administration there were in an area.

During the early Uruk period (just before 3500 B.C.) in what is now southwestern Iran, there were some 50 settlements that seem to fall into three groups in terms of size.[5] There were about 45 small villages, 3 or 4 "towns," and one large center, Susa. These three types of settlements seem to have been part of a three-level administration hierarchy, since many small villages could not trade with Susa without passing through a settlement intermediate in size. Because a three-level hierarchy is Wright and Johnson's criterion of a state, they think a state had emerged in the area by early Uruk times.

Evidence from the next period, middle Uruk, suggests more definitely that a state had emerged. This evidence takes the form of clay seals that were apparently used in trading.[6] *Commodity sealings* were used to keep a shipment of goods tightly closed until it reached its destination, and *message sealings* were used to keep track of goods sent and received. The clay seals found in Susa include many message seals and *bullae*, clay containers that served as bills of lading for goods received. The villages, in contrast, had few message seals and bullae. Again, this finding suggests that Susa administered the regional movement of goods and that Susa was the "capital" of the state.

Let us turn now to the major features of the cultural sequences leading to the first states in southern Iraq.

CITIES AND STATES IN SOUTHERN IRAQ

Farming communities older than the first states have not been found in the arid lowland plains of southern Iraq—the area known as Sumer, where some of the earliest cities and states developed. Perhaps silt from the Tigris and Euphrates rivers has covered them. Or, as has been suggested, Sumer may not have been settled by agriculturalists until people learned how to drain and irrigate river-valley soils otherwise too wet or too dry for cultivation. At any rate, small communities depending partly on agriculture had emerged in the hilly areas north and east of Sumer early in the Neolithic. Later, by about 6000 B.C., a mixed herding-farming economy developed in those areas.

THE FORMATIVE ERA

Elman Service called the period from about 5000 to 3500 B.C. the *formative era,* for it saw the coming together of many changes that seem to have played a part in the development of cities and states. Service

Research Frontiers

IMPERIALISM, COLONIALISM, AND THE STATE

The first city-states in the world seem to have emerged during the Uruk period, roughly the fourth millennium B.C., in the river valleys of southern Mesopotamia, now southern Iraq. From their very beginnings, these first city-states had "foreign trade." This trade may have been indispensable; the riverine environment, though fertile when drained and irrigated, lacked necessary raw materials such as hardwood and stone. The trade with other areas could have been peaceful and balanced, as between equals. After all, it is possible that when one area has something that another wants, and vice versa, the people on both sides could voluntarily arrange to satisfy each other's needs by bargaining and negotiating. But the archaeological evidence available from the preliterate Uruk period, as well as the documentary evidence available for shortly afterward, suggests that the first city-states in Mesopotamia were engaged in imperialism and colonialism from their very beginnings.

Just like the British and French, who first came to North America to explore and trade and often used force to protect their settlements and access to trade items, the Uruk city-states seem also to have dominated their peripheral, less developed trading "partners." For example, before 3000 B.C. there were fortified towns with Uruk-style pottery and administrative artifacts at river junctions in the north of Mesopotamia. Why did the Uruk people go there? One possibility is that they deliberately built outposts to secure their access to needed trade goods, including hides and dried meat.

There was no single state involved in this imperialism and colonialism. Not until after 3000 B.C. was southern Mesopotamia (Sumer) politically unified. Rather, the various Uruk-period polities of the Tigris and Euphrates river valleys seem to have been intensely competitive. The walls around the cities indicate that they were probably subject to attack by their rivals at any time. The picture is reminiscent of the Greek city-states described by Thucydides. It is also like the picture we get from the hiero-glyphic writings of the Maya city-states in and around southern Mexico (A.D. 300–800), which, in a mixture of history and propaganda, extol the triumphs of the various rivalrous rulers. And, of course, we all are familiar with how Britain and Spain and Holland and France were rivalrous before and after the New World was discovered.

We know that the Greek city-states were imperialistic colonizers because we have historical evidence of the fact. Greek-speakers, from Athens and other polities, established colonies all over the Mediterranean—Syracuse in Sicily and Marseilles in France, for example. But what about the Uruk city-states? Why should we think they too were imperialistic colonizers? The archaeologist Guillermo Algaze recently reviewed the evidence. First there was the colonization of the plains of southwestern Iran, which people could get to from southern Mesopotamia in seven to ten days by foot or donkey caravan. Then, and maybe overlapping with the expansion into southwestern Iran, the Uruk polities established outposts or took over

suggested that with the development of small-scale irrigation, lowland river areas began to attract settlers. The rivers provided not only water for irrigation but also mollusks, fish, and water birds for food. And they provided routes by which to import needed raw materials, such as hardwood and stone, that were lacking in Sumer.

Changes during this period suggest an increasingly complex social and political life. Differences in status are reflected in the burial of statues and ornaments with children. Different villages specialized in the production of different goods—pottery in some, copper and stone tools in others.[7] Temples were built in certain places that may have been centers of political as well as religious authority for several communities.[8] Furthermore, some anthropologists think that chiefdoms, each having authority over several villages, had developed by this time.[9]

SUMERIAN CIVILIZATION

By about 3500 B.C., there were quite a few cities in the area of Sumer. Most were enclosed in a fortress wall and surrounded by an agricultural area. About

already-existing settlements to the north and northwest, on the plains of what are now northern Iraq and Syria; these latter settlements were apparently all located at intersections of the important waterways and overland routes.

According to Algaze, the Uruk enclaves and outposts outside southern Mesopotamia fit what the comparative historian Philip Curtin calls "trade diaspora." Curtin thinks that such movements develop after the emergence of cities, with their vulnerable populations. (An urban population is vulnerable because a city, by definition, is inhabited mostly by people who are dependent for their food on people who live outside the city.) Diaspora have taken various forms, but they all represent ways to organize exchange between areas with different but complementary resources. At one end of the range of possibilities—involving little or no political organization—commercial specialists remove themselves from their own society and settle as aliens somewhere else. At the other end of the range of variation—the most politically organized end—the ex-

panding polity is involved from the beginning in the founding of outposts that secure the required trade.

Algaze thinks that the Uruk expansion was motivated by a lack of resources in southern Mesopotamia. But is that a complete explanation? Other areas of the world, at the time and since, have lacked resources, but they did not all become imperialistic colonizers. So what else, in addition to the need for external resources, might explain the Uruk expansion? And how can we explain why it eventually stopped? Algaze notes that when the Uruk settlers moved into southwestern Iran, they were entering an area that was not so densely settled, so they may have encountered only minimal resistance. Indeed, the various Uruk-period enclaves and outposts outside southern Mesopotamia were apparently larger and more complex than any previous communities in the peripheral areas. Perhaps, then, imperialism and colonialism are possible only in a world of unequals.

Years ago, the anthropologist Stanley Diamond argued that

"imperialism and colonialism are as old as the State." Does this mean that states are likely to practice imperialism and colonialism if they can get away with it? Or are only some conditions likely to predispose states to imperialism and colonialism? How strongly are imperialism and colonialism linked to state organization anyway? What makes a humane state possible? Perhaps future research, particularly cross-cultural and cross-historical research, will tell us.

Sources: Guillermo Algaze, *The Uruk World System: The Dynamics of Expansion of Early Mesopotamian Civilization* (Chicago: University of Chicago Press, 1993); Melinda A. Zeder, "After the Revolution: Post-Neolithic Subsistence in Northern Mesopotamia," *American Anthropologist*, 96 (1994): 97–126; Philip D. Curtin, *Cross-Cultural Trade in World History* (Cambridge: Cambridge University Press, 1984); Stanley Diamond, *In Search of the Primitive: A Critique of Civilization* (New Brunswick, NJ: Transaction Books, 1974); and Joyce Marcus, "Maya Hieroglyphs: History or Propaganda?" in Carol R. Ember, Melvin Ember, and Peter N. Peregrine, eds., *Research Frontiers in Anthropology* (Upper Saddle River, NJ: Prentice Hall, 1998), Prentice Hall/Simon & Schuster Custom Publishing.

A partially restored ziggurat, or temple tower, in what was the Sumerian city of Ur, in 2100 B.C.

3000 B.C. all of Sumer was unified under a single government. After that time, Sumer became an empire. It had great urban centers. Imposing temples, commonly set on artificial mounds, dominated the cities. In the city of Warka the temple mound was about 150 feet high. The empire was very complex and included an elaborate system for the administration of justice, codified laws, specialized government officials, a professional standing army, and even sewer systems in the cities. Among the many specialized crafts were brickmaking, pottery, carpentry, jewelry making, leatherworking, metallurgy, basketmaking, stonecutting, and sculpture. Sumerians learned to construct and use wheeled wagons, sailboats, horse-drawn chariots, and spears, swords, and armor of bronze.[10]

As economic specialization developed, social stratification became more elaborate. Sumerian documents describe a system of social classes: nobles, priests, merchants, craftworkers, metallurgists, bureaucrats, soldiers, farmers, free citizens, and slaves. Slaves were common in Sumer; they often were captives, brought back as the spoils of war.

We see the first evidence of writing around 3000 B.C. The earliest Sumerian writings were in the form of ledgers containing inventories of items stored in the temples and records of livestock or other items owned or managed by the temples. Sumerian writing was wedge-shaped, or **cuneiform,** formed by pressing a stylus against a damp clay tablet. For contracts and other important documents, the tablet was fired to create a virtually permanent

One of the cities of the Harappan civilization in the Indus Valley was Mohenjodaro. Seen here is an excavated large "bath" with surrounding rooms. Columns originally surrounded the pool. (Modern buildings appear in the background.) In contrast to other early civilizations, there was little display of grandeur. All Harappan cities were laid out according to the same plan.

record. Egyptian writing, or **hieroglyphics,** appeared about the same time. Hieroglyphics were written on rolls woven from papyrus reeds, from which our word *paper* derives.

CITIES AND STATES IN MESOAMERICA

Cities and states emerged in Mesoamerica—Mexico and Central America—later than they did in the Near East. The later appearance of civilization in Mesoamerica may be linked to the later emergence of agriculture in the New World, as we saw in the last chapter, and possibly to the near-absence of large animals such as cattle and horses that could be domesticated.[11] We focus primarily on the developments that led to the rise of the city-state of Teotihuacán, which reached its height shortly after the time of Christ. Teotihuacán is located in a valley of the same name, which is the northeastern part of the larger Valley of Mexico.

THE FORMATIVE PERIOD

The formative period in the area around Teotihuacán (1000–300 B.C.) was characterized initially by small, scattered farming villages on the hilly slopes just south of the Teotihuacán Valley. There were probably a few hundred people in each hamlet, and each of these scattered groups was probably politically autonomous. After about 500 B.C., there seems to have been a population shift to settlements on the valley floor, probably in association with the use of irrigation. Between about 300 and 200 B.C. small "elite" centers emerged in the valley; each had an earthen or stone raised platform. Residences or small temples of poles and thatch originally stood on these platforms. That some individuals, particularly those in the elite centers, were buried in special tombs supplied with ornaments, headdresses, carved bowls, and a good deal of food indicates some social inequality.[12] The various elite centers may indicate the presence of chiefdoms.

THE CITY AND STATE OF TEOTIHUACÁN

About 150 years before the time of Christ, no more than a few thousand people lived in scattered villages in the Teotihuacán Valley. In A.D. 100 there was a city of 80,000. By A.D. 500, well over 100,000 people, or approximately 90 percent of the entire valley population, seem to have been drawn or coerced into Teotihuacán.[13]

The layout of the city of Teotihuacán, which shows a tremendous amount of planning, suggests that from its beginning the valley was politically unified under a centralized state. Mapping has revealed that the streets and most of the buildings are laid out in a grid pattern following a basic modular unit of 57 square meters. Residential structures are often squares of this size, and many streets are spaced according to multiples of the basic unit. Even the river that ran through the center of the city was channeled to conform to the grid pattern. Perhaps the most outstanding feature of the city is the colossal scale of its architecture. Two pyramids dominate the metropolis, the so-called Pyramid of the Moon and the Pyramid of the Sun. At its base the latter is as big as the great Pyramid of Cheops in Egypt.

The thousands of residential structures built after A.D. 300 follow a standard pattern. Narrow streets separate the one-story buildings, each of

The city of Teotihuacán, which had its peak in 500 A.D., was a planned city built on a grid pattern. At the center was the Pyramid of the Sun shown here.

which has high, windowless walls. Patios and shafts provide interior light. The layout of rooms suggests that each building consisted of several apartments; more than 100 people may have lived in one of these apartment compounds. There is variation from compound to compound in the size of rooms and the elaborateness of interior decoration, suggesting considerable variation in wealth.[14]

At the height of its power (A.D. 200–500), the metropolis of Teotihuacán encompassed an area larger than imperial Rome.[15] Much of Mesoamerica seems to have been influenced by Teotihuacán. Archaeologically, its influence is suggested by the extensive spread of Teotihuacán-style pottery and architectural elements. Undoubtedly, large numbers of people in Teotihuacán were engaged in production for, and the conduct of, long-distance trade. Perhaps 25 percent of the city's population worked at various specialized crafts, including the manufacture of projectile points and cutting and scraping tools from volcanic obsidian. Teotihuacán was close to major deposits of obsidian, which was apparently in some demand over much of Mesoamerica. Materials found in graves indicate that there was an enormous flow of foreign goods into the city, including precious stones, feathers from colorful birds in the tropical lowlands, and cotton.[16]

THE CITY OF MONTE ALBÁN

Teotihuacán probably was not the earliest city-state in Mesoamerica: there is evidence of political unification somewhat earlier, about 500 B.C., in the Valley of Oaxaca, in southern Mexico, with the city of Monte Albán at its center. Monte Albán presents an interesting contrast to Teotihuacán. Whereas Teotihuacán seems to have completely dominated its valley, containing almost all its inhabitants and craftspeople, Monte Albán did not. The various villages in the Valley of Oaxaca seem to have specialized in different crafts, and Monte Albán did not monopolize craft production. After the political unification of the valley, cities and towns other than Monte Albán remained important; the population of Monte Albán grew only to 30,000 or so. Unlike Teotihuacán, Monte Albán was not an important commercial or market center, it was not laid out in a grid pattern, and its architecture was not much different from that of other settlements in the valley in which it was located.[17]

Monte Albán did not have the kinds of resources that Teotihuacán had. It was located on top of a mountain in the center of the valley, far from either good soil or permanent water supplies that could have been used for irrigation. Even finding drinking water must have been difficult. No natural resources for trade were nearby, nor is there much evidence that Monte Albán was used as a ceremonial center. Because the city was at the top of a steep mountain, it is unlikely that it could have been a central marketplace for valleywide trade.

Why, then, did Monte Albán rise to become one of the early centers of Mesoamerican civilization? Richard Blanton suggested it may have originally been founded in the late formative period (500–400 B.C.) as a neutral place where representatives of the different political units in the valley could reside to coordinate activities affecting the whole valley. Thus Monte Albán may have been like the cities of Brasília, Washington, D.C., and Athens, all of which were originally founded in "neutral," nonproductive areas. Such a center, lacking obvious resources, would not, at least initially, threaten the various political units around it. Later it might become a metropolis dominating a more politically unified region, as Monte Albán came to do in the Valley of Oaxaca.[18]

OTHER CENTERS OF MESOAMERICAN CIVILIZATION

In addition to Teotihuacán and Oaxaca, there were other Mesoamerican state societies, which developed somewhat later. For example, there are a number of centers with monumental architecture, presumably built by speakers of Mayan languages, in the highlands and lowlands of modern-day Guatemala and the Yucatán Peninsula of modern-day Mexico. On the basis of surface appearances, the Mayan centers do not appear to have been as densely populated as Teotihuacán or Monte Albán. But it is now evident that the Mayan centers were more densely populated and more dependent on intensive agriculture than was once thought,[19] and recent translations of Mayan picture writing indicate a much more developed form of writing than previously thought.[20] It is apparent now that Mayan urbanization and cultural complexity were underestimated because of the dense tropical forest that now covers much of the area of Mayan civilization.

THE FIRST CITIES AND STATES IN OTHER AREAS

So far we have discussed the emergence of cities and states in southern Iraq and Mesoamerica whose development is best, if only imperfectly, known archaeologically. But other state societies probably arose more or less independently in many other areas of the world as well (see Figure 9–2). We say "independently," because such states seem to have emerged without colonization or conquest by other states.

Almost at the same time as the Sumerian empire, the great dynastic age was beginning in the Nile Valley in Egypt. The Old Kingdom, or early dynastic period, began about 3100 B.C., with a capital at Memphis. The archaeological evidence from the early centuries is limited, but most of the population appears to have lived in largely self-sufficient villages. Many of the great pyramids and palaces were built around 2500 B.C.[21]

In the Indus Valley of northwestern India, a large state society had developed by 2300 B.C. This Harappan civilization did not have much in the way of monumental architecture, such as pyramids and palaces, and it was also unusual in other respects. The state apparently controlled an enormous territory—over a million square kilometers. There was not just one major city but many, each built according to a similar pattern and with a municipal water and sewage system.[22]

The Shang dynasty in northern China (1750 B.C.) has long been cited as the earliest state society in the Far East. But recent research suggests that an even earlier one, the Xia dynasty, may have emerged in the same general area by 2200 B.C.[23] In any case, the Shang dynasty had all the earmarks of statehood: a stratified, specialized society; religious, economic, and administrative unification; and a distinctive art style.[24]

In South America, state societies may have emerged after 200 B.C. in the area of modern-day Peru.[25] In sub-Saharan Africa, by A.D. 800, the western Sudan had a succession of city-states. One of them was called Ghana, and it became a major source of gold for the Mediterranean world.[26] And in North America there is some evidence that a complex chiefdom, and possibly a state-level society, existed in the area around present-day St. Louis by A.D. 1050. Huge mounds of earth 100 feet high mark the site there called Cahokia.[27]

THEORIES ABOUT THE ORIGIN OF THE STATE

We have seen that states developed in many parts of the world. Why did they evolve when and where they did? A number of theories have been proposed. We consider those that have been discussed frequently by archaeologists.[28]

FIGURE 9–2 *Six Early Civilizations*

Source: Adapted from Elman R. Service, *Origins of the State and Civilization: The Process of Cultural Evolution.* By permission of W. W. Norton & Company, Inc. Copyright © 1975 by W. W. Norton & Company, Inc.

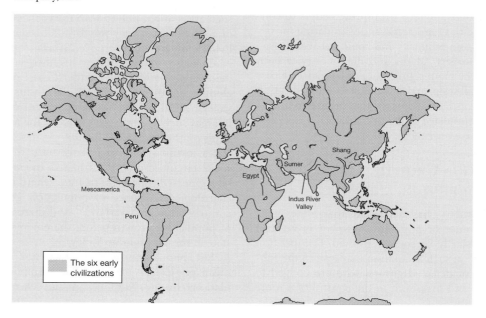

IRRIGATION

Irrigation seems to have been important in many of the areas in which early state societies developed. Irrigation made the land habitable or productive in parts of Mesoamerica, southern Iraq, the Nile Valley, and other areas. It has been suggested that the labor and management needed for the upkeep of an irrigation system led to the formation of a political elite, the overseers of the system, who eventually became the governors of the society.[29] Proponents of this view believe that both the city and civilization were outgrowths of the administrative requirements of an irrigation system.

Critics note that this theory does not seem to apply to all areas where cities and states may have emerged independently. For example, in southern Iraq, the irrigation systems serving the early cities were generally small and probably did not require extensive labor and management. Large-scale irrigation works were not constructed until after cities had been fully established.[30] Thus, irrigation could not have been the main stimulus for the development of cities and states in Sumer. Even in China, for which the irrigation theory was first formulated, there is no evidence of large-scale irrigation as early as Shang times.[31]

Although large-scale irrigation may not always have preceded the emergence of the first cities and states, even small-scale irrigation systems could have resulted in unequal access to productive land and so may have contributed to the development of a stratified society.[32] In addition, irrigation systems may have given rise to border and other disputes between adjacent groups, thereby prompting people to concentrate in cities for defense and stimulating the development of military and political controls.[33] Finally, as Robert Adams and Elman Service both suggested, the main significance of irrigation, either large or small scale, may have been its intensification of production, a development that in turn may have indirectly stimulated craft specialization, trade, and administrative bureaucracy.[34]

POPULATION GROWTH, CIRCUMSCRIPTION, AND WAR

Robert Carneiro has suggested that states may emerge because of population growth in an area that is physically or socially limited. Competition and warfare in such a situation may lead to the subordination of defeated groups, who are obliged to pay tribute and to submit to the control of a more powerful group.[35] Carneiro illustrated his theory by describing how states may have emerged on the northern coast of Peru.

After the people of that area first settled into an agricultural village life, population grew at a slow, steady rate. Initially, new villages were formed as population grew. But in the narrow coastal valleys—blocked by high mountains, fronted by the sea, and surrounded by desert—this splintering-off process could not continue indefinitely. The result, according to Carneiro, was increasing land shortage and warfare between villages as they competed for land. Since the high mountains, the sea, and the desert blocked any escape for losers, the defeated villagers had no choice but to submit to political domination. In this way, chiefdoms may have become kingdoms as the most powerful villages grew to control entire valleys. As chiefs' power expanded over several valleys, states and empires may have been born.

Carneiro noted that physical or environmental circumscription may not be the only kind of barrier that gives rise to a state. Social circumscription may be just as important. People living at the center of a high-density area may find that their migration is blocked by surrounding settlements just as effectively as it could be by mountains, sea, and desert.

Marvin Harris suggested a somewhat different form of circumscription. He argued that the first states with their coercive authority could emerge only in areas that supported intensive grain agriculture (and the possibility of high food production) and were surrounded by areas that could *not* support intensive grain agriculture. So people in such areas might put up with the coercive authority of a state because they would suffer a sharp drop in living standards if they moved away.[36]

Carneiro suggested that his theory applies to many areas besides the northern coast of Peru, including southern Iraq and the Indus and Nile valleys. Although there were no geographic barriers in areas such as northern China or the Mayan lowlands on the Yucatán Peninsula, the development of states in those areas may have been the result of social circumscription. Carneiro's theory seems to be supported for southern Iraq, where there is archaeological evidence of population growth, circumscription, and warfare.[37] And there is evidence of population growth before the emergence of the state in the Teotihuacán Valley.[38]

But population growth does not necessarily mean population pressure. For example, the populations in the Teotihuacán and Oaxaca valleys apparently did increase prior to state development, but there is no evidence that they had even begun to approach the limits of their resources. More people could have lived in both places.[39] Nor is population growth definitely associated with state formation in all areas where early states arose. For example, according to Wright and Johnson, there was population growth long before states emerged in southwestern Iran, but the population apparently declined just before the states emerged.[40]

In addition, Carneiro's circumscription theory leaves an important logical question unanswered: Why would the victors in war let the defeated populations remain and pay tribute? If the victors wanted the land so much in the first place, why wouldn't they try to exterminate the defeated and occupy the land themselves, which has happened many times in history?

LOCAL AND LONG-DISTANCE TRADE

It has been suggested that trade was a factor in the emergence of the earliest states.[41] Wright and Johnson theorized that the organizational requirements of producing items for export, redistributing the items imported, and defending trading parties would foster state formation.[42] Does the archaeological evidence support such a theory?

In southern Iraq and the Mayan lowlands, long-distance trade routes may indeed have stimulated bureaucratic growth. In the lowlands of southern Iraq, as we have seen, people needed wood and stone for building, and they traded with highland people for those items. In the Mayan lowlands, the development of civilization seems to have been preceded by long-distance trade. Farmers in the lowland regions traded with faraway places in order to obtain salt, obsidian for cutting blades, and hard stone for grinding tools.[43] In southwestern Iran, long-distance trade did not become very important until after Susa became the center of a state society, but short-distance trade may have played the same kind of role in the formation of states. The situation in other areas is not yet known.

THE VARIOUS THEORIES:
AN EVALUATION

Why do states form? As of now, no one theory seems to fit all the known situations. The reason may be that different conditions in different places may have favored the emergence of centralized government. After all, the state, by definition, implies an ability to organize large populations for a collective purpose. In some areas, this purpose may have been the need to organize trade with local or far-off regions. In other cases, the state may have emerged as a way to control defeated populations in circumscribed areas. In still other instances, a combination of factors may have fostered the development of the state type of political system.[44]

THE DECLINE AND COLLAPSE OF STATES

All of the most ancient states collapsed eventually. None of them maintained their power and influence into historic times. Why? Might the reasons for their fall tell us something about why they rose in the first place? For example, if a particular factor was partly responsible for the rise of an ancient state, its disappearance or deterioration may partly explain the decline of that state. Then again, the reasons for the decline of states may be quite different from the reasons for the growth of states.

One suggested explanation for the decline and collapse of states, environmental degradation, is perhaps relevant to state development. If states originally arose where the environment was conducive to intensive agriculture and harvests big enough to support social stratification, political officials, and a state type of political system, then perhaps environmental degradation—declining soil productivity, persistent drought, and the like—contributed to the collapse of ancient states. The archaeologist Harvey Weiss has suggested that persistent drought helped to bring about the fall of the ancient Akkadian empire, in the Near East. By 2300 B.C., the Akkadians had established an empire stretching 1,300 kilometers from the Persian Gulf in what is now Iraq to the headwaters of the Euphrates River in what is now Turkey. But a century later the empire collapsed. Weiss thinks that a long-term drought brought the empire down, as well as other civilizations around at that time too. Many archaeologists doubted there was such a widespread drought, but evidence recently presented at a meeting of the American Geophysical Union indicates that the worst dry spell of the past 10,000 years began just as the Akkadians' northern stronghold was being abandoned. The evidence of the drought, windblown dust in sediment retrieved from the bottom of the Persian Gulf, indicates that the dry spell lasted 300 years. Other geophysical evidence suggests that the drought was worldwide.[45]

Environmental degradation may occur for other reasons than natural events. The behavior of humans may sometimes be responsible. Consider the collapse of Cahokia, a city of at least 15,000 people that thrived for a while in the area where the Missouri and Mississippi rivers converge. In the twelfth century A.D., Cahokia had large public plazas, a city wall constructed from some 20,000 logs, and massive mounds. But within 300 years only the mounds were left. Silt from flooding covered former croplands and settled areas. The geographer Bill Woods thinks that overuse of woodlands for fuel, construction, and defense led to deforestation, flooding, and persistent crop failure.

The result was the abandonment of Cahokia. Timber depletion is also indicated by studies of charcoal from excavations in the area. Apparently the quality of wood used in construction declined over time, suggesting that choice trees got scarcer. Cahokia is just one example of degradation that may have been caused by human behavior. Another example is the increasing saltiness of soils caused by evaporation of water from fields that have been irrigated over long periods of time, as in what is now southern Iraq.[46]

New Perspectives on Gender

EFFECTS OF IMPERIALISM ON WOMEN'S STATUS

Archaeologists, particularly those who are women, have begun to pay attention to the gender implications of archaeological materials. Do the findings from excavated houses imply anything about what women and men did where they lived? What do the findings in houses and other places suggest about the division of labor by gender? Can archaeology tell us about women's status in the culture and how it may have changed over time? Recent research suggests that if you look for gender-related results, you often can find some. As the title of a recent book indicated, new kinds of archaeology can be "engendered." For example, the archaeologist Cathy Costin has studied the effects of Inka (Inca) imperialism on women's status in a conquered area.

Costin participated in a research project that studied culture change in the Yanamarca Valley of highland Peru. The project focused on the development of chiefdoms among the indigenous Wanka ethnic group between A.D. 1300 and 1470 and on the effects of the Inka con-

quest at the end of that period. According to the archaeology, most people before the Inka conquest were farmers, but some households specialized part time in the production of pottery, stone tools, and perhaps textiles. Documents written after the arrival of the Spanish suggest that the Wanka had developed chiefdoms at about A.D. 1300, possibly as a result of intensified warfare among the various communities. A high level of conflict is inferred from the locations and configurations of the settlements: most people lived in fortified (walled) communities located on hills above the valley floor. According to the documentary sources, the Wanka chiefs had achieved their positions because of success as war leaders.

We know from documents that the Wanka were conquered by the Inka during the reign of the emperor Pachakuti (about A.D. 1470). The Wanka region became a province within the Inka empire, and bureaucrats from the capital at Cuzco came to govern the Wanka. The Inka conquerors, including military personnel,

formed the highest class in the valley. The Wanka chiefs became vassals of the Inka state and imitators of Inka ways, using Inka-like pottery and building Inka-style additions to their homes. The economy of the valley became more specialized, apparently to meet the needs of the Inka. People in some villages still mostly farmed, but in other villages most households specialized in the production of pottery, stone tools, and other crafts. Skeletal remains indicate that the commoners became healthier and lived longer after the Inka conquest.

How did the Inka conquest affect the status of women? One key to an answer was suggested by the presence in the excavations of several thousand perforated round ceramic objects. They were spindle whorls, weights used in spinning to keep the thread tight and even. The thread (from llama and alpaca wool) was made into cloth, which became the major form of tax payment after the Inka took over. Each village had to produce a certain amount of cloth for the state tax collectors. The cloth collected was used to

Civilizations may sometimes decline because human behavior has increased the incidence of disease. For example, many lowland Mayan cities were abandoned between 800 and 1000 A.D. Explanations of this collapse have ranged from overpopulation to resource depletion. But another factor may have been increasing incidence of yellow fever. The clearing of forests and the consequent increase of breeding sites for mosquitoes may have favored the spread of the disease from areas farther south in Central America. Or the planting of particular trees by the Mayans in their urban areas may have increased the populations of co-resident monkeys who carried the disease (which mosquitoes transmitted to people). It should be noted that a disease explanation of the collapse of a state does not help us understand why the state arose in the first place.[47]

It is still not clear what specific conditions led to the emergence, or collapse, of the state in each of the early centers of civilization. But the question of why states form and decline is a lively focus of research

clothe men serving in the army and to "pay" other government personnel. The burden of producing the cloth fell on the traditional spinners and weavers, who we know from the post-Spanish documents were females of all ages.

Just before the Inka conquest, all households excavated had spindle whorls, indicating that the female occupants in all households spun and made cloth. More whorls were found the farther up the mountain the house was located, indicating that women who lived closer to the high grasslands, where the flocks of llamas and alpacas were kept, spun more thread than did women who lived farther down from the pastures. We might expect that elite women would do less work. But, to the contrary, the women in elite households seem to have produced more cloth than the women in commoner households; the elite households had twice as many whorls on average as the commoner households had.

After the Inka conquest, households appear to have produced twice the amount of thread they did before, because there are twice the number of recovered spindle whorls. There is no indication, archaeological or documentary, that the women were freed from other tasks to make more time for spinning, so it would appear that women had to work harder under Inka domination to produce thread and cloth. But the producers do not appear to have benefited from the increased cloth production. Much if not most of the cloth produced was removed from the villages and taken to Inka storage facilities in the capital and redistributed from there.

In addition to working harder for the Inka, women seem to have fared worse than the men when it came to nutrition. Christine Hastorf's chemical analysis of bones from Inka-period graves suggests that women ate less maize (corn) than did men. It seems that the men were "eating out" more than women. Maize was often consumed as *chicha* beer, a key component of state-sponsored feasts, which were probably attended more by men than women. Men also worked more in state-organized agricultural and production projects, where they probably were rewarded with meat, maize, and *chicha* for their service to the state.

So, under Inka domination, Wanka women had to produce more and received less. In a later chapter—on sex, gender, and culture—we discuss how Western colonialism has often been detrimental to women's status, as Inka colonialism seems to have been for the Wanka women. Is this a general effect of imperialism? And if so, why?

Sources: Elizabeth M. Brumfiel, "Distinguished Lecture in Archeology: Breaking and Entering the Ecosystem—Gender, Class, and Faction Steal the Show," *American Anthropologist,* 94 (1992): 551–67; Joan M. Gero and Margaret W. Conkey, eds., *Engendering Archaeology: An Introduction to Women and Prehistory* (Oxford: Basil Blackwell, 1991); Cathy Lynne Costin, "Cloth Production and Gender Relations in the Inka Empire," in Carol R. Ember, Melvin Ember, Peter N. Peregrine, eds., *Research Frontiers in Anthropology* (Upper Saddle River, NJ: Prentice Hall, 1998), Prentice Hall/Simon & Schuster Custom Publishing; and Christine Hastorf, "Gender, Space, and Food in Prehistory," in Gero and Conkey, eds., *Engendering Archaeology.*

The history of Ephesus, a former city lying in ruins in what is now western Turkey, illustrates the waxing and waning of states and empires. From about 1000 B.C. to 100 B.C., it was controlled by the Greeks, Lydians, Persians, Macedonians, and Romans, among others.

today, so more satisfactory answers may come out of ongoing and future investigations.

SUMMARY

1. Archaeologists do not always agree on how a state should be defined, but most seem to agree that hierarchical and centralized decision making affecting a substantial population is the key criterion. Most states have cities with public buildings, full-time craft and religious specialists, an official art style, and a hierarchical social structure topped by an elite class from which the leaders are drawn. Most states maintain power with a monopoly on the use of force. Force or the threat of force is used by the state to tax its population and to draft people for work or war.

2. Early state societies arose within the Near East in what is now southern Iraq and southwestern Iran. Southern Iraq, or Sumer, was unified under a single government just after 3000 B.C. It had writing, large urban centers, imposing temples, codified laws, a standing army, wide trade networks, a complex irrigation system, and a high degree of craft specialization.

3. Probably the earliest city-state in Mesoamerica developed around 500 B.C. in the Valley of Oaxaca, with a capital at Monte Albán. Somewhat later, in the northeastern section of the Valley of Mexico, Teotihuacán developed. At the height of its power, A.D. 200–500, the city-state of Teotihuacán appears to have influenced much of Mesoamerica.

4. City-states arose early in other parts of the New World: in Guatemala, the Yucatán Peninsula of Mexico, Peru, and possibly near St. Louis. In the Old World, early states developed in Egypt, the Indus Valley of India, northern China, and West Africa.

5. There are several theories of why states arose. The irrigation theory suggests that the administrative needs of maintaining extensive irrigation systems may have been the impetus for state formation. The circumscription theory suggests that states emerge when competition and warfare in circumscribed areas lead to the subordination of defeated groups, who are obliged to submit to the control of the most powerful group. Theories involving trade suggest that the organizational requirements of producing exportable items, redistributing imported items, and defending trading parties would foster state formation. Which is correct? At this point, no one theory is able to explain the formation of every state. Perhaps different organizational requirements in different areas all favored centralized government.

GLOSSARY TERMS

civilization   hieroglyphics
cuneiform   state

CRITICAL QUESTIONS

1. Cities and states did not appear until after the emergence of food production. Why might food production be necessary, but not sufficient, for cities and states to develop?

2. Like the emergence of food production, the earliest cities and states developed within a few thousand years of each other. What might be the reasons?

3. Can you imagine a future world without states? What conditions might lead to that "state" of the world?

INTERNET EXERCISES

1. The Egyptian pyramids are often thought of as monuments associated with early cities and states. Visit the pyramids at the web site **http://www.pbs.org/wgbh/nova/pyramid/** and summarize your findings.

2. Teotihuacan was one of the earliest city-states in Mesoamerica. Explore **http://archaeology.la. asu.edu/VM/mesoam/Teo/intro/Intrteo.htm** or the site describing Monte Albán, **http://www. mexconnect.com/mex_/hclassic2.html**.

3. How does Olmec culture compare with Mayan culture? Compare **http://udgftp.cencar. udg.mx/ingles/Precolombina/Maya/intromaya. html** with **http://udgftp.cencar.udg.mx/ingles/ Precolombina/Olmecas/docs/olmin.html**.

SUGGESTED READING

BLANTON, R. E., KOWALEWSKI, S. A., FEINMAN, G., AND APPEL, J. *Ancient Mesoamerica: A Comparison of Change in Three Regions,* 2nd ed. Cambridge: Cambridge University Press, 1993. A comparison and analysis of cultural development, and particularly the development of states, in three regions of Mesoamerica—the Valley of Oaxaca, the Valley of Mexico, and the eastern (Mayan) lowlands.

BURENHULT, G., ED. *Old World Civilizations: The Rise of Cities and States.* St. Lucia, Queensland, Australia: University of Queensland Press, 1994. A gorgeous book of color photographs surveying many of the ancient civilizations in Asia, Africa, and Europe.

COHEN, R., AND SERVICE, E. R., EDS. *Origins of the State: The Anthropology of Political Evolution.* Philadelphia: Institute for the Study of Human Issues, 1978. A collection of theoretical and empirical papers on the possible origins of states.

FEINMAN, G. M., AND MARCUS, J., EDS. *Archaic States.* Santa Fe, NM: School of American Research Press, 1998. This collection of papers discusses the rise and fall of the ancient states in the Near East, India and Pakistan, Egypt, Mesoamerica, and the Andes, and presents some key questions for future research.

SANDERS, W. T., PARSONS, J. R., AND SANTLEY, R. S. *The Basin of Mexico: Ecological Processes in the Evolution of a Civilization.* New York: Academic Press, 1979. A description of a long-term archaeological project that investigated the evolution of civilization in the Valley of Mexico from 1500 B.C. to A.D. 1500, particularly as reflected in the history of its settlement.

WENKE, R. J. *Patterns in Prehistory: Humankind's First Three Million Years,* 3rd ed. New York: Oxford University Press, 1990. Chapters 7–15 provide an up-to-date review of what is known and what is controversial about the origins of cities and states around the world.

The Concept of Culture

We all consider ourselves to be unique individuals with our own set of personal opinions, preferences, habits, and quirks. Indeed, all of us *are* unique individuals; and yet most of us share the feeling that it is wrong to eat dogs, the belief that bacteria or viruses cause illness, the habit of sleeping on a bed. We share many such feelings, beliefs, and habits with most of the people who live in our society. We hardly ever think about the ideas and customs we share, but they constitute what anthropologists refer to as "North American culture."

We tend not to think about our culture because it is so much a part of us that we take it for granted. But when we become aware that other peoples have different feelings from ours, different beliefs, and different habits, we begin to think of how we share certain ideas and customs. We would never even think of the possibility of eating dog meat if we were not aware that people in some other societies commonly do so. We would not realize that our belief in germs was cultural if we were not aware that people in some societies think that illness is caused by witchcraft or evil spirits. We could not become aware that it is our custom to sleep on beds if we were not aware that people in many societies sleep on the floor or on the ground. It is only when we compare ourselves with people in other societies that we become aware of cultural differences and similarities. This is, in fact, the way that anthropology as a profession began. When Europeans began to explore and move to faraway places, they were forced to confront the sometimes striking facts of cultural variation.

DEFINING FEATURES OF CULTURE

In everyday usage, the word *culture* refers to a desirable quality we can acquire by attending a sufficient number of plays and concerts and visiting art museums and galleries. The anthropologist, however, has a different definition, as Ralph Linton explained:

> *Culture* refers to the total way of life of any society, not simply to those parts of this way which the society regards as higher or more desirable. Thus culture, when applied to our own way of life, has nothing to do with playing the piano or reading Browning. For the social scientist such activities are simply elements within the totality of our culture. This totality also includes such mundane activities as washing dishes or driving an automobile, and for the purposes of cultural studies these stand quite on a par with "the finer things of life." It follows that for the social scientist there are no uncultured societies or even individuals. Every society has a culture, no matter how simple this culture may be, and every human being is cultured, in the sense of participating in some culture or other.[1]

Culture, then, refers to innumerable aspects of life. Some anthropologists think of culture as the rules or ideas behind behavior.[2] Most anthropologists define **culture** as the set of learned behaviors, beliefs, attitudes, values, and ideals that are characteristic of a particular society or population.

CULTURE IS COMMONLY SHARED

If only one person thinks or does a certain thing, that thought or action represents a personal habit, *not* a pattern of culture. For a thought or action to be considered cultural, it must be commonly shared by some population or group of individuals. Even if some behavior is not commonly practiced, it is cultural if most people think it is appropriate. The idea that marriage should involve only one man and only one woman is cultural in our society. Most North Americans share this idea and act accordingly when they marry. The role of president or prime minister is not widely shared—after all, there is only one such person at a time—but the role is cultural because most inhabitants of a country with such a position agree that it should exist, and its occupant is generally expected to exhibit certain behaviors. We usually share many values, beliefs, and behaviors with our families and friends (although anthropologists are not particularly concerned with this type of cultural group). We commonly share cultural characteristics with segments of our population whose ethnic or regional origins, religious affiliations, and occupations are the same as or similar to our own. We have certain practices, beliefs, and feelings in common with most North Americans, and we share certain characteristics with people beyond our society who have similar interests (such as rules for international sporting events) or similar roots (as do the various English-speaking nations).

When we talk about the commonly shared customs of a society, which constitute the central concern of cultural anthropology, we are referring to a culture. When we talk about the commonly shared customs of a group within a society, which are a central concern of sociology, we are referring to a **subculture.** And when we study the commonly shared customs of some group that includes different societies, we are talking about a phenomenon for which we do not have a single word—for example, as when we refer to *Western culture* (the cultural characteristics of societies in or derived from Western Europe) or the *culture of poverty* (the presumed cultural characteristics of poor people the world over).

We must remember that even when anthropologists refer to something as cultural, there is always individual variation, which means that not everyone in a society shares a particular cultural characteristic of that society. For example, it is cultural in North American society for adults to live apart from their parents. But not all adults in our society do so, nor do all adults wish to do so. The custom of living apart from parents is considered cultural because most adults practice that custom. As Edward Sapir noted in the late 1930s, in every society studied by anthropologists—in the simplest as well as the most complex—individuals do not *all* think and act the same.[3] As we discuss later, individual variation is the source of new culture.[4]

CULTURE IS LEARNED

Not all things shared generally by a population are cultural. The typical hair color of a population is not cultural, nor is eating. For something to be considered cultural, it must be learned as well as shared. A typical hair color (unless dyed) is not cultural because it is genetically determined. Humans eat because they must; but what and when and how they eat are learned and vary from culture to culture. Most North Americans do not consider dog meat edible, and indeed the idea of eating dogs horrifies us. But in China, as in some other societies, dog meat is considered delicious. In our society, many people consider a baked ham to be a holiday dish. In several societies of the Middle East, however, including those of Egypt and Israel, eating the meat of a pig is forbidden by sacred writings.

To some extent, all animals exhibit learned behaviors, some of which may be shared by most individuals in a population and may therefore be considered cultural. But different animal species vary in the degree to which their shared behaviors are learned or are instinctive. The sociable ants, for instance, despite all their patterned social behavior, do not appear to have much, if any, culture. They divide their labor, construct their nests, form their raiding columns, and carry off their dead—all without having been taught to do so and without imitating the behavior of other ants. In contrast, much of the behavior of humans appears to be culturally patterned.

We are increasingly discovering that our closest biological relatives, the monkeys and the apes, learn a wide variety of behaviors. Some of their learned responses are as basic as those involved in maternal care; others are as frivolous as the taste for candy. When shared, some of these learned behaviors could be described as cultural. For example, as we discuss

When children play at adult roles, they are often imitating what the culture allows or prefers.

in more detail in the chapter on communication and language, vervet monkeys learn to use a certain call in the presence of circling eagles, who prey on the monkeys. The call seems to mean "Watch out—there are eagles around!" Its meaning seems to be shared or understood by the group, because they all respond similarly—they look up—when one individual sounds the call.

The proportion of an animal's life span occupied by childhood seems to reflect the degree to which the animal depends on learned behavior for survival. Monkeys and apes have relatively long childhoods compared to other animals. Humans have by far the longest childhood of any animal, reflecting our great dependence on learned behavior. Although humans may acquire much learned behavior by trial and error and imitation, as do monkeys and apes, most human learned behavior is probably acquired with the aid of spoken, symbolic language.

LANGUAGE. All people known to anthropologists, regardless of their kind of society, have had a complex system of spoken, symbolic communication, what we call *language.* Language is *symbolic* in that a word or phrase can represent what it stands for *whether or not that thing is present.*

This symbolic quality of language has tremendous implications for the transmission of culture. It means that a human parent can tell a child that a snake, for example, is dangerous and should be avoided. The parent can then describe the snake in great detail—its length, diameter, color, texture, shape, and means of locomotion. The parent can also predict the kinds of places where the child is likely to encounter snakes and explain how the child can avoid them. Should the child encounter a snake, then, he or she will probably recall the symbolic word for the animal, remember as well the related information, and so avoid danger. If symbolic language did not exist, the parent would have to wait until the child actually saw a snake and then, through example, show the child that such a creature is to be avoided. Without language we probably could not transmit or receive information so efficiently and rapidly, and thus would not be heir to so rich and varied a culture.

To sum up, we may say that something is cultural if it is a learned behavior, belief, attitude, value, or ideal generally shared by the members of a group. Traditionally, anthropologists have usually been concerned with the cultural characteristics of a **society,** by which they mean a group of people who occupy a particular territory and speak a common language not generally understood by neighboring

peoples. By this definition, societies do not necessarily correspond to nations. There are many nations, particularly the new ones that have within their boundaries different peoples speaking mutually unintelligible languages. By our definition of society, such nations are composed of many different societies and cultures. Also, by our definition of society, some societies may even include more than one nation. For example, we would have to say that Canada and the United States form a single society because the two groups generally speak English, live next to each other, and share many common beliefs, values, and practices. That is why we refer to "North American culture" in this chapter. Not everyone would agree that Canada and the United States form a single society; some would prefer to consider the United States and Canada two different societies because they are separate political entities.

Given that a society refers to a group of people who occupy a particular territory and speak a common language not generally understood by neighboring peoples, when an anthropologist speaks about *a* culture, she or he is usually referring to that set of learned and shared beliefs, values, and behaviors generally characteristic of a particular society.

ATTITUDES THAT HINDER THE STUDY OF CULTURES

Many of the Europeans who first traveled to faraway places were revolted or shocked by customs they observed. Such reactions are not surprising. People commonly feel that their own behaviors and attitudes are the correct ones and that people who do not share those patterns are immoral or inferior. The person who judges other cultures solely in terms of his or her own culture is **ethnocentric—** that is, he or she holds an attitude called **ethnocentrism.** Most North Americans would think that eating dogs or insects is disgusting, but they clearly do not feel the same way about eating beef. Similarly, they would react negatively to child betrothal, lip plugs, or digging up the bones of the dead.

Our own customs and ideas may appear bizarre or barbaric to an observer from another society. Hindus in India, for example, would consider our custom of eating beef both primitive and disgusting. In their culture, the cow is a sacred animal and may not be slaughtered for food. In many societies a baby is almost constantly carried by someone, in someone's lap, or asleep next to others.[5] People in such societies may think it is cruel of us to leave babies alone for long periods of time, often in devices that resemble cages (cribs and playpens). Even our most ordinary customs—the daily rituals we take for granted—might seem thoroughly absurd when viewed from an outside perspective. An observer of our society might justifiably take notes on certain strange behaviors that seem quite ordinary to us, as the following description shows:

> The daily body ritual performed by everyone includes a mouth-rite. Despite the fact that these people are so punctilious about the care of the mouth, this rite involves a practice which strikes the uninitiated stranger as revolting. It was reported to me that the ritual consists of inserting a small bundle of hog hairs into the mouth, along with certain magical powders, and then moving the bundle in a highly formalized series of gestures. In addition to the private mouth-rite, the people seek out a holy-mouth man once or twice a year. These practitioners have an impressive set of paraphernalia, consisting of a variety of augers, awls, probes, and prods. The use of these objects in the exorcism of the evils of the mouth involves almost unbelievable ritual torture of the client. The holy-mouth man opens the client's mouth and, using the above mentioned tools, enlarges any holes which decay may have created in teeth. Magical materials are put into these holes. If there are no naturally occurring holes in the teeth, large sections of one or more teeth are gouged out so that the supernatural substance can be applied. In the client's view, the purpose of these ministrations is to arrest decay and to draw friends. The extremely sacred and traditional character of the rite is evident in the fact that the natives return to the holy-mouth man year after year, despite the fact that their teeth continue to decay.[6]

We are likely to protest that to understand the behaviors of a particular society—in this case, our own—the observer must try to find out what the people in that society say about why they do things. For example, the observer might find out that periodic visits to the "holy-mouth man" are for medical, not magical, purposes. Indeed, the observer, after some questioning, might discover that the "mouth-rite" has no sacred or religious connotations whatsoever. Ethnocentrism hinders our understanding of the customs of other people and, at the same time, keeps us from understanding our own customs. If we think that everything we do is best, we are not likely to ask why we do what we do or why "they" do what "they" do.

Because we are ethnocentric about many things, it is often difficult to criticize our own customs, some of which might be shocking to a member of another society. The elderly in America often spend their days alone. In contrast, the elderly in Japan often live in a three-generational family.

Ethnocentrism is common, but we may not always glorify our own culture. Other ways of life may sometimes seem more appealing. Whenever we are weary of the complexities of civilization, we may long for a way of life that is "closer to nature" or "simpler" than our own. For instance, a young North American whose parent is holding two or three jobs just to provide the family with bare necessities might briefly be attracted to the life-style of the !Kung of the Kalahari Desert in the 1950s. The !Kung shared their food and therefore were often free to engage in leisure activities during the greater part of the day. They obtained all their food by men hunting animals and women gathering wild plants. They had no facilities for refrigeration, so sharing a large freshly killed animal was clearly more sensible than hoarding meat that would soon rot. Moreover, the sharing provided a kind of social security system for the !Kung. If a hunter was unable to catch an animal on a certain day, he could obtain food for himself and his family from someone else in his band. Then, at some later date the game he caught would provide food for the family of another, unsuccessful hunter. This system of sharing also ensured that persons too young or too old to help with the collecting of food would still be fed.

Could we learn from the !Kung? Perhaps we could in some respects, but we must not glorify their way of life either or think that their way of life might be easily imported into our own society. Other aspects of !Kung life would not appeal to many North Americans. For example, when the nomadic !Kung decided to move their camps, they had to carry all the family possessions, substantial amounts of food and water, and all young children below age 4 or 5. This is a sizable burden to carry for any distance. The !Kung traveled about 1,500 miles in a single year.[7] Thus, for them being nomadic meant that families could not have many possessions. It is unlikely that most North Americans would find the !Kung way of life enviable in all respects.

Both ethnocentrism and its opposite, the glorification of other cultures, hinder effective anthropological study.

CULTURAL RELATIVISM

In the 1870s, the early days of anthropology, the prevailing view was that culture develops in a uniform and progressive manner; this belief is called **early evolutionism.** For example, Lewis Henry Morgan postulated that the family evolved in six stages. The first was a "horde living in promiscuity"; the highest,

or last, stage was the monogamous family. In almost every evolutionary sequence postulated by Morgan and other early evolutionists, the traits of Western cultures were thought to be at the highest, most progressive stage, and many non-Western cultures were thought to represent earlier stages of evolution. Not only were these early ideas based on very poor evidence of the details of ethnography (for example, the custom of marriage turns out to be universal), they were also based on a good deal of ethnocentrism.

One of the leading opponents of evolutionism in the early twentieth century was Franz Boas. He and many of his students—like Ruth Benedict, Melville Herskovits, and Margaret Mead—stressed that the early evolutionists did not sufficiently understand the details of the cultures they theorized about, nor did they understand the context in which these customs appeared. They challenged the attitude that Western cultures were obviously superior.[8]

The anthropological attitude that a society's customs and ideas should be described objectively and understood in the context of that society's problems and opportunities became known as **cultural relativism.** Does cultural relativism mean that the actions of another society, or of our own, should not be judged? Does our insistence on objectivity mean that anthropologists should not make moral judgments about the cultural phenomena they observe and try to explain? Does it mean that anthropologists should not try to bring about change? Not necessarily. While the concept of cultural relativism remains an important anthropological tenet, anthropologists differ in their interpretation of the principle of cultural relativism.

Many anthropologists are now uncomfortable with the strong form of cultural relativism advocated by Benedict and Herskovits in the 1930s and 1940s that morality differs in every society and that all patterns of culture are equally valid. What if the people practice slavery, torture, or genocide? If the strong doctrine of relativism is adhered to, then cultural practices such as these are not to be judged, and we should not try to eliminate them. A weaker form of cultural relativism asserts that anthropologists should strive for objectivity in describing a people, and in their attempts to understand the reasons for cultural behavior they should be wary of superficial or quick judgment. Tolerance should be the basic mode unless there is strong reason to behave otherwise.[9] The weak version of cultural relativity does not preclude anthropologists from making judgments or from trying to change behavior they think is harmful. But judgments need not,

Current Issues

HUMAN RIGHTS AND CULTURAL RELATIVITY

The news increasingly reports what we consider violations of human rights the world over. Examples range from jailing people for expressing political ideas to ethnic massacre. But faced with criticism from the West, people in other countries are saying that the West should not dictate its ideas about human rights to the rest of the world. Indeed, many countries say they have different codes of ethics. Are we in the Western countries being ethnocentric by taking our own cultural ideas and applying them to the rest of the world? Should we instead employ the strong version of the concept of cultural relativism, considering each culture on its own terms? But if we do that, it may not be possible to have a universal standard of human rights.

What we do know is that *all* cultures have ethical standards, but they do not always emphasize the same things. So, for example, some cultures emphasize individual political rights; others emphasize political order. Some cultures emphasize protection of individual property; others emphasize the sharing or equitable distribution of resources. People in the United States may have freedom to dissent and the right not to have

property taken away, but they can be deprived of health insurance or of food if they lack the money to buy them. Cultures also vary markedly in the degree to which they have equal rights for minorities and women. In some societies women are killed when a husband dies or when they disobey a father or brother.

A strong case against the concept of cultural relativism is made by Elizabeth Zechenter. She points out that cultural relativists claim there are no universal principles of morality, but insist on tolerance for all cultures. If tolerance is one universal principle, why shouldn't there be others? She also suggests that the concept of cultural relativism is often used to justify traditions desired by the dominant and powerful. She points to a case in 1996 in Algeria where two teenage girls were raped and murdered because they violated the fundamentalist edict against attending school. Are those girls any less a part of the culture than the fundamentalists? Would it make any difference if most Algerian women supported the murders? Would it then make it right? Zechenter does not believe that international treaties such as the Universal Declaration of Human Rights impose uniformity among

diverse cultures. Rather, they seek to create a floor below which no society is supposed to fall.

Can the concept of cultural relativism be reconciled with the concept of an international code of human rights? Probably not completely. Paul Rosenblatt recognizes the dilemma but nonetheless thinks that something has to be done to stop torture and "ethnic cleansing," among other practices. He makes the case that "to the extent that it is easier to persuade people whose viewpoints and values one understands, relativism can be a tool for change . . . a relativist's awareness of the values and understanding of the elite makes it easier to know what arguments would be persuasive. (For example, in a society in which the group rather than the individual has great primacy, it might be persuasive to try to show how respect for individual rights benefits the group.)" What do you think?

Sources: Elizabeth M. Zechenter, "In the Name of Culture: Cultural Relativism and the Abuse of the Individual," *Journal of Anthropological Research,* 53 (1997): 319–47; Paul C. Rosenblatt, "Human Rights Violations across Cultures," in Carol R. Ember, Melvin Ember, and Peter N. Peregrine, eds., *Research Frontiers in Anthropology* (Upper Saddle River, NJ: Prentice Hall, 1998). Prentice Hall/Simon & Schuster Custom Publishing.

and should not, preclude accurate description and explanation in spite of any judgments we might have.

But now that we have defined what is cultural, we must ask a further question: How does an anthropologist go about deciding which particular behaviors, values, and beliefs of individuals are cultural?

 DESCRIBING A CULTURE

INDIVIDUAL VARIATION

Describing a particular culture might seem relatively uncomplicated at first. You simply observe what the people in that society do and then record their behavior. But consider the substantial difficulties you might encounter. How would you decide which people to observe? And what would you conclude if each of the first dozen people you observed or talked to behaved quite differently in the same situation? Admittedly, you would be unlikely to encounter such extreme divergence of behaviors. Yet there would tend to be significant individual variation in the actual behaviors observed, even when individuals were responding to the same generalized situation and conforming to cultural expectations.

To better understand how an anthropologist might make sense of diverse behaviors, let us examine the diversity at a professional football game in the United States. When people attend a football game, various members of the crowd behave differently while "The Star-Spangled Banner" is being played. As they stand and listen, some people remove their hats; a child munches popcorn; a veteran of the armed forces stands at attention; a teenager searches the crowd for a friend; and the coaches take a final opportunity to intone secret chants and spells designed to sap the strength of the opposing team. Yet, despite these individual variations, most of the people at the game respond in a basically similar manner: Nearly everyone stands silently, facing the flag. Moreover, if you go to several football games, you will observe that many aspects of the event are notably similar. Although the plays will vary from game to game, the rules of the game are never different, and although the colors of the uniforms of the teams are different, the players never appear on the field dressed in swimsuits.

Although the variations in individual reactions to a given stimulus are theoretically limitless, in fact they tend to fall within easily recognizable limits. The child listening to the anthem may continue to eat popcorn but will probably not do a rain dance. Similarly, it is unlikely that the coaches will react to that same stimulus by running onto the field and embracing the singer. Variations in behavior, then, are confined within socially acceptable limits, and it is part of the anthropologist's goal to find out what those limits are. She or he may note, for example, that some limitations on behavior have a practical purpose: A spectator who disrupts the game by wandering onto the field would be required to leave. Other limitations are purely traditional. In our society it is considered proper for a man to remove his overcoat if he becomes overheated, but others would undoubtedly frown upon his removing his trousers even if the weather was

In deciding what is cultural behavior, anthropologists look for commonalities, but there is always individual variation. Here, during the playing of the national anthem before the start of a game, most of the crowd, but not all, are facing forward and placing a hand over the heart.

quite warm. Using such observations, the anthropologist discovers the customs and the ranges of acceptable behavior that characterize the society under study.

By focusing on the range of customary behavior, discovered by observing or asking about individual variation, the anthropologist is able to describe cultural characteristics of a group. For example, an anthropologist interested in describing courtship and marriage in our society would initially encounter a variety of behaviors. The anthropologist may note that one couple prefers to go to a movie on a first date, whereas another couple chooses to go bowling; some couples have very long engagements, and others never become engaged at all; some couples emphasize religious rituals in the marriage ceremony, but others are married by civil authorities; and so on. Despite this variability, the anthropologist, after further observation and interviewing, might begin to detect certain regularities in courting practices. Although couples may do many different things on their first and subsequent dates, they nearly always arrange the dates by themselves;

they try to avoid their parents when on dates; they often manage to find themselves alone at the end of a date; they put their lips together frequently; and so forth. After a series of more and more closely spaced encounters, a man and woman may decide to declare themselves publicly as a couple, either by announcing that they are engaged or by revealing that they are living together or intend to do so. Finally, if the two of them decide to marry, they must in some way have their union recorded by the civil authorities.

In our society a person who wishes to marry cannot completely disregard the customary patterns of courtship. If a man saw a woman on the street and decided he wanted to marry her, he could conceivably choose a quicker and more direct form of action than the usual dating procedure. He could get on a horse, ride to the woman's home, snatch her up in his arms, and gallop away with her. In Sicily, until the last few decades such a couple would have been considered legally married, even if the woman had never met the man before or had no intention of marrying. But in our society, any man who acted in such a fashion would be arrested and jailed for kidnapping and would probably have his sanity challenged. Such behavior would not be acceptable in our society. Although individual behaviors may vary, most social behavior falls within culturally acceptable limits.

CULTURAL CONSTRAINTS

A primary limit on range of individual behavior variations is the culture itself. The noted French sociologist Emile Durkheim stressed that culture is something *outside* us exerting a strong coercive power on us. We do not always feel the constraints of our culture because we generally conform to the types of conduct and thought it requires. Standards or rules about what is acceptable behavior are referred to by social scientists as **norms.** The importance of a norm usually can be judged by how members of a society respond when the norm is violated.

Cultural constraints are of two basic types, *direct* and *indirect.* Naturally, the direct constraints are the more obvious. For example, if you choose to wear a casual shorts outfit to a wedding, you will probably be subject to some ridicule and a certain amount of social isolation. But if you choose to wear nothing, you may be exposed to a stronger, more direct cultural constraint—arrest for indecent exposure.

Although indirect forms of cultural constraint are less obvious than direct ones, they are no less effective. Durkheim illustrated this point when he wrote, "I am not obliged to speak French with my fellow-countrymen, nor to use the legal currency, but I cannot possibly do otherwise. If I tried to

There may be individual variation in dress, but the variation has limits. In our society men typically wear pants and a shirt.

  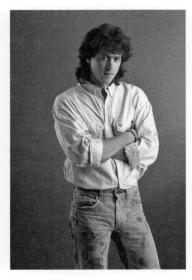

escape this necessity, my attempt would fail miserably."[10] In other words, if Durkheim had decided he would rather speak Serbo-Croatian than French, nobody would have tried to stop him. But no one would have understood him either. And although he would not have been put into prison for trying to buy groceries with Icelandic money, he would have had difficulty convincing the local merchants to sell him food.

In a series of classic experiments on conformity, Solomon Asch revealed how strong cultural constraints can be. Asch coached the majority of a group of college students to give deliberately incorrect answers to questions involving visual stimuli. A "critical subject," the one student in the room who was not so coached, had no idea that the other participants would purposely misinterpret the evidence presented to them. Asch found that in one-third of the experiments, the critical subjects *consistently* allowed their own correct perceptions to be distorted by the obviously incorrect statements of the others. And in another 40 percent of the experiments, the critical subject yielded to the opinion of the group some of the time.[11]

The existence of social or cultural constraints, however, is not necessarily incompatible with individuality. Cultural constraints are usually exercised most forcefully around the limits of acceptable behavior. Thus, there is often a broad range of behavior within which individuals can exercise their uniqueness. And individuals do not always give in to the wishes of the majority. In the Asch experiments, many individuals, about one-fourth of the critical subjects, consistently retained their independent opinions in the face of complete disagreement with the majority.

IDEAL VERSUS ACTUAL CULTURAL PATTERNS

Every society has ideas (values and norms) about how people in particular situations ought to feel and behave. In everyday terms we speak of these ideas as *ideals;* in anthropology we refer to them as *ideal cultural patterns.* These patterns tend to be reinforced through cultural constraints. But we all know that people do not always behave according to the standards they express. If they did, there would be no need for direct or indirect constraints. Some of our ideal patterns differ from actual behavior because the ideal is outmoded—that is, it is based on the way a society used to be. (Consider the ideal of "free enterprise," that industry should be totally free of gov-

ernmental regulation.) Other ideal patterns may never have been actual patterns and may represent merely what people would like to see as correct behavior.

To illustrate the difference between ideal and actual culture, consider the idealized belief, long cherished in North America, that everybody is "equal before the law," that everybody should be treated in the same way by the police and courts. Of course, we know that this is not always true. The rich, for example, may receive less jail time and be sent to nicer prisons. Nevertheless, the ideal is still part of our culture; most of us continue to believe that the law *should* be applied equally to all.

HOW TO DISCOVER CULTURAL PATTERNS

There are two basic ways in which an anthropologist can discover cultural patterns. When dealing with customs that are overt or highly visible within a society—for example, our custom of sending children to school—the investigator can determine the existence of such practices and study them with the aid of a few knowledgeable persons. When dealing with a particular sphere of behavior that encompasses many individual variations, or when the people studied are unaware of their pattern of behavior, the anthropologist should collect information from a sample of individuals in order to establish what the cultural pattern is.

One example of a cultural pattern that most people in a society are not aware of is how far apart people stand when they are having a conversation. Yet there is considerable reason to believe that unconscious cultural rules govern such behavior. These rules become obvious when we interact with people who have different rules. We may experience considerable discomfort when another person stands too close (indicating too much intimacy) or too far (indicating unfriendliness). Edward Hall reported that Arabs customarily stand quite close to others, close enough, in fact, to be able to smell the other person. In interactions between Arabs and North Americans, then, the Arabs will move closer at the same time that the North Americans back away.[12]

If we wanted to arrive at the cultural rule for conversational distance between casual acquaintances, we could study a sample of individuals from a society and determine the *modal response,* or *mode.* The mode is a statistical term that refers to the most frequently encountered response in a given series of responses. So, for the North American pattern of casual conversational distance, we would plot the actual distance for many observed pairs of people. Some pairs may be 2 feet apart, some 2.5, and some 4 feet apart. If we count the number of times every particular distance is observed, these counts provide what we call a *frequency distribution*. The distance with the highest frequency is the *modal pattern*. Very often the frequency distribution takes the form of a *bell-shaped curve,* as shown in Figure 10–1. There the characteristic being measured is plotted on the horizontal axis (in this case, the distance between conversational pairs), and the number of times each distance is observed (its frequency) is plotted on the vertical axis. If we were to plot how a sample of North American casual conversational pairs is distributed, we would probably get a bell-shaped curve that peaks at around 3 feet.[13] Is it any wonder, then, that we sometimes speak of keeping others "at arm's length"?

Frequency distributions may be calculated on the basis of behaviors exhibited or responses given by all the members of a particular population. But studying everybody is rarely necessary. Instead, most social scientists rely on a subset, or *sample,* that is believed to be representative of the larger population. The best way to ensure that a sample is representative is to choose a **random sample**—that is, give all individuals an equal chance of being selected for study. If a sample is random, it probably will include examples of all frequent variations of behavior or response exhibited in the society or community in roughly the proportions in which they actually occur.

Because it is relatively easy to make generalizations about public aspects of a culture, such as the ex-

istence of executive, legislative, and judicial branches in the U.S. government, or about widely shared norms or behaviors, which almost anyone can identify correctly, random sampling is often not necessary. But in dealing with aspects of culture that are more private, difficult to put into words, or unconscious, the investigator may have to observe or interview a random sample of people in order to generalize correctly about whether or not there are cultural patterns. The reason is that most people may not be aware of others' private behavior and thoughts, such as sexual attitudes and behavior, nor are they aware of unconscious cultural patterns, such as conversational distance. The fact that something is less readily observed publicly or harder to put into words does not imply that it is less likely to be shared. However, it is harder to discover those aspects of culture.

Although we may be able to discover by interviews and observation that a behavior, thought, or feeling is widely shared within a society, how do we establish that something commonly shared is learned, so that we can call it cultural? Establishing that something is or is not learned may be difficult. Because children are not reared apart from adult caretakers, the behaviors they exhibit as part of their genetic inheritance are not clearly separated from those they learn from others around them. We suspect that particular behaviors and ideas are learned if they vary from society to society. And we suspect purely genetic determinism when particular behaviors or ideas are found in all societies. For example, as we will see in the chapter on language, children the world over seem to acquire language at about the same age, and the structure of their early utterances seems to be similar. These facts suggest that human children are born with an innate grammar. However, although early childhood language seems similar the world over, the particular languages spoken by adults in different societies show considerable variability. This variability suggests that particular languages have to be learned. Similarly, if the courtship patterns of one society differ markedly from those of another, we can be fairly certain that those courtship patterns are learned and therefore cultural.

 SOME ASSUMPTIONS ABOUT CULTURE

CULTURE IS GENERALLY ADAPTIVE

There are some cultural behaviors that, if carried to an extreme, would decrease the chances of survival of a particular society. For example, certain tribes in

FIGURE 10–1 *Frequency Distribution Curve*

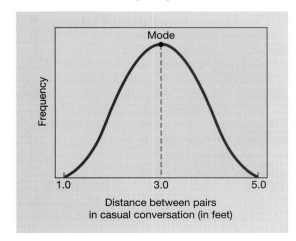

New Guinea view women as essentially unclean and dangerous individuals with whom physical contact should be as limited as possible. Suppose the men in one such tribe decided to avoid contact, including sexual contact, with women completely. Clearly, we would not expect such a society to survive for long. Although this example may appear extreme, it indicates that customs that diminish the survival chances of a society are not likely to persist. Either the people clinging to those customs will become extinct, taking the customs with them, or the customs will be replaced, thereby possibly helping the people to survive. By either process, **maladaptive** customs—those that diminish the chances of survival and reproduction—are likely to disappear. The customs of a society that enhance survival and reproductive success are **adaptive** and are likely to persist. Hence, we assume that if a society has survived long enough to be described in the annals of anthropology (the "ethnographic record"), much, if not most, of its cultural repertoire is adaptive, or was at one time.

When we say that a custom is adaptive, however, we mean it is adaptive only with respect to a specific physical and social environment. What may be adaptive in one environment may not be adaptive in another. Therefore, when we ask why a society may have a particular custom, we really are asking if that custom makes sense as an adaptation to that society's particular environmental conditions.

Many cultural behaviors that would otherwise appear incomprehensible to us may be understandable as a society's response to its environment. For example, we might express surprise at certain societies' postpartum sex taboos that prohibit women from engaging in sexual intercourse until their 2-year-olds are ready to be weaned. But in the tropical areas where such taboos exist, they may represent a people's way of adjusting to their physical environment. If there were no such taboo and a mother had another baby soon, she could no longer continue to nurse the older baby. Without its mother's milk, the older child might succumb to *kwashiorkor,* a severe protein-deficiency disease that is common in those tropical areas. The taboo, then, may serve to give infants a better chance to survive.[14] Thus, the long postpartum sex taboo may be an adaptive custom. In nontropical areas where kwashiorkor is not a problem, the same taboo may not be advantageous.

Just as culture represents an adjustment to the physical environment and to biological demands, it may also represent an adjustment to the social environment, that is, to neighboring peoples. For example, we do not know for sure why the Hopi

Indians of what is now the state of Arizona began building their settlements on the tops of mesas. They must have had strong reasons for doing so, because there are many difficulties in building on such sites—the problem of hauling water long distances to the settlements, for instance. It is possible that the Hopi chose to locate their villages on mesa tops for defensive reasons when Athapaskan-speaking groups of Indians (the Navaho and Apache) moved into the Hopi area. In other words, the Hopi may have adjusted their living habits to their social environment.

A given custom represents one society's adaptation to its environment; it does not represent all possible adaptations. Different societies may choose different means of adjusting to the same situation. Thus, among some South American Indian societies where people's diets are low in protein, there is no long postpartum sex taboo, but induced abortion is reported to be a common practice. This practice may serve the same function of spacing out live births and thereby preventing too early weaning of children. The Hopi Indians, when suddenly confronted by the Navaho and Apache, clearly had to take some action to protect themselves. But instead of building their settlements on easily defended mesa tops, they could conceivably have developed a standing army.

Why a society develops a particular response to a problem always requires explanation. The choice may depend largely on whether a particular response is possible, given the existing cultural repertoire. For example, in the Hopi case, a standing army would not have been a likely response to the problem of invaders because the Hopi economy probably could not have supported any large group of full-time specialists such as soldiers. As we shall see in the chapter on food-getting, full-time specialists have to be fed by the regular production of more food than the people involved in food production generally need, and such a level of food production did not exist among the Hopi. The strategy of moving their dwellings to easily defended mesa tops may have been the easiest option.

Although we may assume that societies surviving long enough to be described have had many more adaptive culture traits than maladaptive traits, that does not mean that all culture traits are adaptive. Some, if not many, traits may be neutral in terms of adaptation. That is, they may have no direct relationship to reproductive success. Consider, for example, rules about what to wear at weddings and funerals, how to set the table, and how far to stand from someone. Perhaps someone will uncover

Applied Anthropology

WHY THE BEDOUIN DO NOT READILY SETTLE DOWN

Most countries of the world today want to "develop." They want to increase their crop yields and their exports, build major roads and irrigation projects, and industrialize. Anthropologists interested in development have pointed out that many development schemes have failed in part because they do not adequately consider the culture of the people whose lives they affect. Thus, the international agencies that lend money have increasingly turned for advice to anthropologists to help plan and evaluate development projects.

Governments often view traditional ways of life negatively and fail to recognize that the old ways of life may be adaptive. Because culture is integrated, people cannot be expected to change an aspect of culture that is central to their lives. It is not that people do not want to change, but change is unlikely if it doesn't integrate well with other aspects of their life-style.

In many countries of the Middle East, governments want the Bedouin—people who herd animals over vast stretches of semiarid grassland—to settle down. Governments have tried to settle them by force or by enticements, but time after time settlement schemes have failed. In retrospect, such failures are not surprising. The Bedouin continue to try to herd animals near newly constructed settlements, but such grazing often results in human-made deserts near the settlements, so the settlements are abandoned. The traditional Bedouin pattern of herding animals depends on mobility. When the animals eat the tops of the grasses in a particular place, the people need to move on. When water starts drying up in one location, the herds need to be moved. Overgrazing near a settlement and plowing land in a semiarid environment can lead to quick erosion of the soil and the loss of plant cover. After the failure of many settlement schemes, governments may try to encourage a return to more traditional methods of grazing.

It is not that the Bedouin are reluctant to change in all respects. Many Bedouin readily gave up relying on camels for transport in favor of trucks. Trucks are a modern adaptation, yet they still allow mobility. Now the Bedouin are able to get water from wells and transport water to their animals by truck. The adoption of trucks led to other changes in Bedouin life. Small animals can be more readily transported to new pastures by truck, so many Bedouin have given up their dependence on camels and shifted to sheep and goat herding. Money is required to buy trucks and pay for gasoline and repairs, so more time is spent working for wages in temporary jobs.

In the 1980s, Dawn Chatty was asked by the government of Oman to help design a project to extend basic social services to the Bedouin without coercing them to alter their way of life. It isn't often that governments fund in-depth studies to understand the needs of the people being affected, but Chatty was able to persuade the Oman government that such a study was necessary as a first step. With United Nations funding, she began to survey the people to evaluate their needs. The government wanted some action right away, so the project soon incorporated a mobile health unit that could begin a program of primary care as well as immunization against measles, whooping cough, and polio. After a period of evaluation, the project team also recommended an annual distribution of tents, the establishment of dormitories so children could live at schools, a new system of water delivery, and veterinary and marketing assistance.

Unfortunately, a development project often ends without any guarantee that health and other services will continue to be provided. As Chatty found out, long-term change is not as easy to achieve as short-term change. Along with other applied anthropologists, she continues to push for what Michael Cernea called "putting people first."

Sources: Dawn Chatty, *Mobile Pastoralists: Development Planning and Social Change in Oman* (New York: Columbia University Press, 1996); Michael M. Cernea, ed., *Putting People First: Sociological Variables in Development,* 2nd ed. (New York: Oxford University Press, 1991), p. 7.

survival and reproductive consequences of these shared behaviors, but probably they are neutral in terms of survival. Such neutral traits may once have had adaptive consequences, or they may never have had any.

We must remember that a society is not forced to adapt its culture to changing environmental circumstances. Even in the face of changed circumstances, people may choose not to change their customs. For example, the Tapirapé of central Brazil did not alter their customs limiting the number of births, even though they suffered severe population losses after contact with Europeans and their diseases. The Tapirapé population fell to fewer than 100 people from over 1,000. Clearly they were on the way to extinction, yet they continued to value small families. Not only did they believe that a woman should have no more than three children, but they took specific steps to achieve this limitation. They practiced infanticide if twins were born, if the third child was of the same sex as the first two children, and if the possible fathers broke certain taboos during pregnancy or in the child's infancy.[15]

Of course, it is also possible that a people will behave maladaptively even if they try to alter their behavior. After all, although people may alter their behavior according to what they perceive will be helpful to them, what they perceive to be helpful may not prove to be adaptive.

CULTURE IS MOSTLY INTEGRATED

When we hear of an unfamiliar cultural pattern, our natural response is to try to imagine how that pattern would work in our own society. We might wonder, for example, what would happen if North American women adopted a long postpartum sex taboo—say, one year of abstinence after the birth of a baby. Such a question is purely whimsical, for the customs of one culture cannot easily be grafted onto another culture. A long postpartum sex taboo presupposes a lack of effective birth-control methods, but our society already has many such methods. Moreover, a long postpartum sex taboo could conceivably affect important aspects of our culture, such as the idea that a happy marriage is a sexy one. The point is that with such a taboo imposed on it, our culture would no longer be the same. Too many aspects of the culture would have to be changed to accommodate the new behavior. This is so because our culture is mostly integrated.

In saying that a culture is mostly *integrated,* we mean that the elements or traits that make up that culture are not just a random assortment of customs but are mostly adjusted to or consistent with one another. One reason anthropologists believe that culture tends to be integrated is that culture is generally adaptive. If certain customs are more adaptive in particular settings, then those "bundles" of traits will generally be found together under similar conditions. For example, the !Kung, as we have mentioned, subsisted by hunting wild animals and gathering wild plants. They were also nomadic, had very small communities, had few material possessions, and shared food within their bands. As we will see, these cultural traits usually occur together when people depend on hunting and gathering for their food.

A culture may also tend to be integrated for psychological reasons. The *traits* of a culture—attitudes, values, ideals, and rules for behavior—are stored, after all, in the brains of individuals. Research in social psychology has suggested that people tend to modify beliefs or behaviors that are not cognitively or conceptually consistent with other information.[16] We do not expect cultures to be completely integrated, just as we do not expect individuals to be completely consistent. But if a tendency toward cognitive consistency is found in humans, we might expect that at least some aspects of a culture would tend to be integrated for that reason.

How this pressure for consistency works is not hard to imagine. Children, for example, seem to be very good at remembering *all* the things their parents say. If they ask for something and the parents say no, they may say, "But you said I could yesterday." This pressure for consistency may even make parents change their minds! Of course, not everything one wants to do is consistent with the rest of one's desires, but there surely is pressure from within and without to make it so.

Humans are also capable of rational decision making; they can usually figure out that certain things are not easy to do because of other things they do. For example, if a society has a long postpartum sex taboo, we might expect that most people in the society could figure out that it would be easier to observe the taboo if husband and wife did not sleep in the same bed. Or if people drive on the left side of the road, as in England, it is easier and less dangerous to drive a car with a steering wheel on the right because that placement allows you to judge more accurately how close you are to cars coming at you from the opposite direction.

Consistency or integration of culture traits may also be produced by less conscious psychological processes. As we discuss in the chapters on psychology and culture, religion and magic, and the arts, people may generalize (transfer) their experiences from one area of life to another. For example, where children are taught that it is wrong to express anger toward family and friends, it turns out that folktales parallel the child rearing; anger and aggression in the folktales tend to be directed only toward strangers, not toward family and friends. It seems as if the expression of anger is too frightening, or maladaptive, to be expressed close to home, even in folktales.

The tendency for a culture to be integrated, then, may be cognitively and emotionally, as well as adaptively, induced.

CULTURE IS ALWAYS CHANGING

When you examine the history of a society, it is obvious that its culture has changed over time. Some of the shared behaviors, beliefs, and values that were common at one time are modified or replaced at another time. In North American society, we only have to consider our attitudes toward sex and marriage to realize that a lot of our culture has changed recently. The impetus for change may come from within the society or from without. From within, the unconscious or conscious pressure for consistency will produce culture change if enough people adjust old behavior and thinking to new. Change can also occur if people try to invent better ways of doing things. Michael Chibnik suggests that people who confront a new problem conduct mental or small "experiments" to decide how to behave. These experiments may give rise to new cultural traits.[17]

A good deal of culture change may be stimulated by changes in the external environment. For example, if people move into an arid area, they will either have to give up farming or develop a system of irrigation. In the modern world, changes in the social environment are probably more frequent stimuli for culture change than changes in the physical environment. Many North Americans, for example, started to think seriously about conserving energy and about using sources of energy other than oil only after oil supplies from the Near East were curtailed in 1973 and 1974. Different societies have often affected each other, and a significant amount of the radical and rapid culture change that has occurred in the last few hundred years has been due to the colonial expansion of Western societies into other areas of the world. Native Americans, for instance, were forced to alter their life-styles drastically when they were driven off their lands and confined to reservations. In the chapter on culture change, we discuss the major patterns of culture change in the modern world, much of it affected by the expansion of the West.

If we assume that cultures are more than random collections of behaviors, beliefs, and values—that they tend to be adaptive, integrated, and changing—then the similarities and differences between them should be understandable. That is, we can expect that similar circumstances within or outside the culture will give rise to, or favor, similar cultural responses. Although we may assume that cultural variation is understandable, the task of discovering which particular circumstances favor which particular patterns is a large and difficult one. In the chapters that follow, we hope to convey the main points of what anthropologists think they know about aspects of cultural variation and what they do not know. We frequently describe particular cultures to illustrate aspects of cultural variation. When we do so, the reader should understand that the culture described is probably not the same now, since the sources of our material always refer to some previous time.[18] The !Kung of the 1990s are not necessarily like the !Kung of the 1950s.

SUMMARY

1. Despite very strong individual differences, the members of a particular society closely agree in their responses to certain phenomena because they share common beliefs, attitudes, values, ideals, and behaviors, which constitute their culture.

2. Culture may be defined as the learned behaviors, beliefs, attitudes, values, and ideals generally shared by the members of a group.

3. The size of the group within which cultural traits are shared can vary from a particular society or a segment of that society to a group that transcends national boundaries. When anthropologists refer to a culture, they usually are referring to the cultural patterns of a particular society—that is, a particular territorial population speaking a language not generally understood by neighboring territorial populations.

4. A defining feature of culture is that it is learned. Although other animals exhibit some cultural behavior, humans are unusual in the number and complexity of the learned patterns that they transmit to their young. And they have a unique way of transmitting their culture: through spoken, symbolic language.

5. Ethnocentrism and its opposite—the glorification of other cultures—impede anthropological

inquiry. An important tenet in anthropology is the principle of cultural relativism: the attitude that a society's customs and ideas should be studied objectively and understood in the context of that society's culture. But when it comes to some cultural practices such as torture, slavery, or genocide, most anthropologists can no longer adhere to the strong form of cultural relativism that asserts that all cultural practices are equally valid.

6. Anthropologists seek to discover the customs and ranges of acceptable behavior that constitute the culture of a society under study. In doing so, they focus on general or shared patterns of behavior rather than on individual variations. When dealing with practices that are highly visible, or with beliefs that are almost unanimous, the investigator can rely on observation or on a few knowledgeable persons. With less obvious behaviors or attitudes, the anthropologist must collect information from a sample of individuals. The mode of a frequency distribution can then be used to express the cultural pattern.

7. Every society develops a series of ideal cultural patterns that represent what most members of the society believe to be the correct behavior in particular situations. A society's ideal cultural patterns, however, do not always agree with its actual cultural patterns.

8. One important factor that limits the range of individual variation is the culture itself, which acts directly or indirectly as a constraint on behavior. The existence of cultural constraints, however, is not necessarily incompatible with individuality.

9. Several assumptions are frequently made about culture. First, culture is generally adaptive to the particular conditions of its physical and social environment. What may be adaptive in one environment may not be adaptive in another. Some cultural traits may be neutral in terms of adaptation, some may merely have been adaptive in the past, and still others may be maladaptive. Second, culture is mostly integrated, in that the elements or traits that make up the culture are mostly adjusted to or consistent with one another. Third, culture is always changing.

GLOSSARY TERMS

adaptive	maladaptive
cultural relativism	norms
culture	random sample
early evolutionism	society
ethnocentric	subculture
ethnocentrism	

CRITICAL QUESTIONS

1. Would it be adaptive for a society to have everyone adhere to the cultural norms?

2. Why does culture change more rapidly in some societies than in others?

3. Does the concept of cultural relativism promote international understanding, or does it hinder attempts to have international agreement on acceptable behavior, such as human rights?

INTERNET EXERCISES

1. Have you ever wondered how the behavior of people changes in different cultural settings? Arab culture is a case in point. Learn some of the Arab cultural norms and practices at **http://www.tele-port.com/~iexportc/culture.htm**. This site offers rich insight into the daily lives of Arabs. Write about at least two body gestures and their meaning in Arab culture.

2. What are your thoughts on cultural relativism and human rights? If you would like to know what one anthropologist thinks, check out an article and other related sites at **http://www.cs.org/cs%20website/LevelFour/LevelFour-FluehrLobban**.

3. An important part of anthropological knowledge is understanding how people view their own culture. With the World Wide Web, it is now possible for people to make information about their own culture available. Visit the site of the Hopi Tribe Cultural Preservation Office: **http://www.nau.edu/~hcpo-p/**. What does this site tell you about what the Hopi consider important?

SUGGESTED READING

DE VITA, P., AND ARMSTRONG, D. *Distant Mirrors: America as a Foreign Culture.* Belmont, CA: Wadsworth, 1993. Several foreign scholars look at the culture of the United States. Their perceptions challenge persons who were born in the United States to look at their culture from a new perspective.

EMBER, M., EMBER, C. R., AND LEVINSON, D. *Portraits of Culture: Ethnographic Originals.* Upper Saddle River, NJ: Prentice Hall, 1998. Prentice Hall/Simon & Schuster Custom Publishing. A series of original mini-ethnographies, each describing a different culture and written by someone with firsthand experience in that culture. Each piece provides a portrait of the culture, including how it has recently changed.

FREILICH, M., ED. *The Meaning of Culture.* Lexington, MA: Xerox, 1972. Several views of culture are presented. See especially Chapters 7–21.

HALL, E. T., AND HALL, M. R. *Hidden Differences: Doing Business with the Japanese.* Garden City, NY: Anchor (Doubleday), 1987. When people from different cultures interact, their difficulties often stem from hidden, unstated cultural rules of how to behave. On the basis of extensive interviews in the United States and Japan, the authors analyze these hidden communications.

KROEBER, A. L. *The Nature of Culture.* Chicago: University of Chicago Press, 1952. A collection of papers on the nature of culture by a distinguished pioneer in North American anthropology.

SPIRO, M. "On the Strange and the Familiar in Recent Anthropological Thought." In C. R. Ember, M. Ember, and P. N. Peregrine, eds., *Research Frontiers in Anthropology* (Upper Saddle River, NJ: Prentice Hall, 1998). Prentice Hall/Simon & Schuster Custom Publishing. The author discusses the controversy about whether it is possible in anthropology to make "the strange familiar." Are cultures so diverse and so fundamentally different that it is not really possible for an outsider to understand or describe them?

WERNER, O., AND SCHOEPFLE, G. M. *Systematic Fieldwork. Volume 1: Foundations of Ethnography and Interviewing.* Newbury Park, CA: Sage, 1987. A detailed presentation and discussion of the methods used to discover patterns of culture on the basis of fieldwork.

11

Theory and Evidence in Cultural Anthropology

Anthropologists have been going to live in other societies for nearly a hundred years. At first, there were only a few such hardy (some would say foolhardy) souls. But their number slowly increased over the years as more and more individuals became interested in the challenge of spending a year or so in some usually distant place, without the comforts of home, to learn how other people lived and thought. The idea was to add to our knowledge so that we might someday come to understand how human cultural behavior could vary so much and yet be so much the same at different times and in different places.

Close to 2,000 societies have now been described in the literature of anthropology. This enormous wealth of information constitutes our data bank of cultural variation. However, if we are to understand how and why cultures differ and are similar, we must do more than simply inspect this mass of information. We must have ideas about what we should look for. Just as a photographer must aim and focus a camera in order to capture a scene, so an anthropologist must focus on what she or he considers important in order to describe and possibly explain some particular aspect of a culture. Even the most thorough observer must concentrate on certain aspects of life and neglect others.

Which aspects of life an individual anthropologist concentrates on usually reflects his or her theoretical orientation, subject interest, or preferred method of research. A *theoretical orientation* is a general attitude about how cultural phenomena are to be explained. In this chapter we first describe some of the major theoretical orientations that are currently popular among cultural anthropologists. Then we discuss what explanation means and what kinds of evidence are needed to evaluate an explanation. Finally, we discuss the various types of research that are conducted in cultural anthropology, from ethnography and ethnohistory to cross-cultural comparisons.

THEORETICAL ORIENTATIONS

In anthropology, as in any discipline, there is a continual ebb and flow of ideas. One theoretical orientation will arise and grow in popularity until another is proposed in opposition to it. Often one orientation will capitalize on those aspects of a problem that a previous orientation ignored or played down. As we discuss orientations, we will indicate what kinds of information or phenomena they emphasize as explanatory factors.

CULTURAL ECOLOGY

Some anthropologists are concerned mostly with the influence of environment on culture. Julian Steward was one of the first to advocate the study of **cultural ecology**—the analysis of the relationship between a culture and its environment. Steward felt that the explanation for some aspects of cultural variation could be found in the adaptation of societies to their particular environments. But rather than merely hypothesize that the environment did or did not determine cultural variation, Steward wished to resolve the question *empirically*—that is, he wanted to carry out investigations to evaluate his viewpoint.[1]

Steward felt, however, that cultural ecology must be separated from *biological ecology,* the study of the relationships between organisms and their environment. Later cultural ecologists, such as Andrew Vayda and Roy Rappaport, wished to incorporate principles of biological ecology into the study of cultural ecology in order to make a single science of ecology.[2] In their view, cultural traits, just like biological traits, can be considered adaptive or maladaptive. Cultural ecologists assume that cultural adaptation involves the mechanism of *natural selection*—the more frequent survival and reproduction of the better adapted. Environment, including the physical and social environment, affects the development of culture traits in that "individuals or populations behaving in certain different ways have different degrees of success in survival and reproduction and, consequently, in the transmission of their ways of behaving from generation to generation."[3]

Consider how culture and environment may interact among the Tsembaga, who live in the interior of New Guinea.[4] The Tsembaga are horticulturalists, living mainly on the root crops and greens they grow in home gardens. They also raise pigs. The pigs are seldom eaten; instead, they serve other useful functions. They keep residential areas clean by consuming garbage, and they help prepare the soil for planting by rooting in it. Small numbers of pigs are easy to keep; they run free all day, returning at night to eat whatever substandard tubers are found in the course of their owners' harvesting of their daily rations. Thus pigs, which require a minimum of maintenance, serve the Tsembaga both as janitors and as cultivating machines.

But problems arise when the pig herd grows large. Often there are not enough substandard tubers, and then the pigs must be fed human rations. Also, although a small number of pigs will clean up yards and soften the soil in the gardens, a large herd is likely to intrude upon garden crops. Pigs can even break up communities. If one person's pig invades a neighbor's garden, the garden owner often retaliates by killing the offending pig. In turn, the dead animal's owner may kill the garden owner, the garden owner's wife, or one of his pigs. As the number of such feuds increases, people begin to put as much distance as possible between their pigs and other people's gardens.

Rappaport suggests that to cope with the problem of pig overpopulation, the Tsembaga developed an elaborate cycle of rituals involving the slaughter of large numbers of surplus pigs. The cultural practice of ritual pig feasts can be viewed as a possible adaptation to environmental factors that produce a surplus pig population. But it is hard to know if the ritual pig feasts are more adaptive than other possible solutions to the problem of pig overpopulation. For example, it might be more adaptive to slaughter and eat pigs regularly so that pig herds never get too large. Without being able to contrast the effects of alternative solutions, a cultural ecologist studying a single society may find it difficult to

obtain evidence that a custom already in place is more adaptive than other possible solutions to the problem.

POLITICAL ECONOMY: WORLD-SYSTEM THEORY

Like cultural ecology, the school of thought known as **political economy** assumes that external forces explain the way a society changes and adapts. But it is not the natural environment, or the social environment in general, that is central to the approach of political economy. What is central is the social and political impact of those powerful state societies (principally Spain, Portugal, Britain, and France) that transformed the world by colonialism and imperialism after the mid-1400s and fostered the development of a worldwide economy or world system.[5] Scholars now realize that imperialism is at least, 5,000 years old; most if not all of the first civilizations were imperialistic. Imperialistic expansion of the first state societies was linked to expanding commercialization, the growth of buying and selling.[6] Today, of course, the entire world is linked commercially.

Some of the earliest figures associated with the political economy approach in anthropology were trained at Columbia University when Julian Steward

Sometimes you can have too many pigs. A pig feast solves this problem and maintains or creates close ties between groups. Here we see preparations for a pig feast on the island of Tanna in the New Hebrides.

was a professor there. For those students, Steward's cultural ecology was insufficiently attentive to recent world history. For example, Eric Wolf and Sidney Mintz argued that the communities they studied in Puerto Rico developed as they did because of colonialism and the establishment of plantations to supply sugar and coffee to Europe and North America.[7] And Eleanor Leacock, who studied the Montagnais-Naskapi Indians of Labrador, suggested that their system of family hunting territories was not an old characteristic, present before European contact, but developed instead out of the Indians' early involvement in the European-introduced fur trade.[8]

Central to the later and continuing intellectual development of political economy in anthropology are the writings, published in the 1960s and 1970s, of two political sociologists, André Gunder Frank and Immanuel Wallerstein. Gunder Frank suggested that the development of a region (Europe, for example) depended on the suppression of development or underdevelopment of other regions (the New World, Africa). He argued that if we want to understand why a country remains underdeveloped, we must understand how it is exploited by developed nations.[9] Frank is concerned with what happened in the underdeveloped world. Wallerstein is more concerned with how capitalism developed in the privileged countries and how the expansionist requirements of the capitalist countries led to the emergence of the world system.[10]

The political economy or world-system view has inspired many anthropologists to study history more explicitly and to explore the impact of external political and economic processes on local events and cultures in the underdeveloped world. In the past, when anthropologists first started doing fieldwork in the far corners of the world, they could imagine that the cultures they were studying or reconstructing could be investigated as if those cultures were more or less isolated from external influences and forces. In the modern world, such isolation hardly exists. The political economy approach has reminded us that the world, every part of it, is interconnected for better or worse.

SOCIOBIOLOGY AND BEHAVIORAL ECOLOGY

The idea that natural selection can operate on the behavioral or social characteristics of populations and not just on their physical traits is shared by cultural ecology and another, more recent, theoretical orientation called **behavioral ecology** (or, earlier, **sociobiology**). Developed mainly by biologists, particularly those who concentrated on the social insects, the behavioral ecology or sociobiological orientation involves the application of biological

Chokwe villages in Africa draw water from a pump manufactured by a corporation in India.

evolutionary principles to the social behavior of animals, including humans. Some cultural anthropologists have employed behavioral ecology theory to explain some aspects of cultural variation.[11]

How is behavioral ecology different from cultural ecology? Although both orientations assume the importance of natural selection in cultural evolution, they differ in important ways. Cultural ecology focuses mostly on what biologists would call **group selection.** Cultural ecologists talk mostly about how a certain behavioral or social characteristic may be adaptive for a group or society in a given environment; a newly emergent behavioral or social trait that is adaptive is likely to be passed on to future generations by cultural transmission. In contrast, behavioral ecology focuses mostly on what biologists call **individual selection.** Behavioral ecologists talk mostly about how a certain characteristic may be adaptive for an individual in a given environment.[12] By *adaptive* is meant the ability of an individual to get her or his genes into future generations. Does this viewpoint imply that behavior is transmitted only through genes? No, say behavioral ecologists. What matters is that behavior is *heritable*—transmitted in some way, by genes or learning, to persons (usually offspring) who share one's genes.[13] If a certain behavior is adaptive for individuals in a particular environment, it should become more widespread in future generations as the number of individuals with those traits increases.

Whereas a cultural ecologist such as Rappaport might consider how ritual pig feasts were adaptive for the Tsembaga as a whole, behavioral ecologists would insist that to speak of adaptation it must be shown how the pig feasts benefited individuals and their closest kin. Behavioral ecologists might raise the following possibilities regarding pig feasts: Do the people who organize pig feasts have more children? If so, then pig feasts may benefit an individual reproductively. Are people who have excess pigs more likely to be killed because their pigs destroy others' gardens? If so, then finding a way to cut down on the number of pigs benefits the survival chances and hence the reproductive chances of individual pig owners. We do not know of a direct comparison of the predictions of cultural ecology and behavioral ecology, but these questions convey how the behavioral ecology approach is different.

In general, behavioral ecological theory does not expect that "social good" will prevail unless "individual good" underlies it. Take the idea of conserving the earth's resources for the long-term benefit of others. If individuals and families are seeking to maximize their own benefits, behavioral ecology would not expect conservation to succeed unless an individual or family saw short-term negative effects of their not conserving. Indeed, Bobbi Low finds cross-culturally that conservation ideas—reasons to leave resources untouched—are very rare, occurring in only 5 percent of the societies surveyed.[14]

This is not to say that behavioral ecology cannot explain some kinds of *altruism*—when a person does something apparently for the good of another person. Adopting or caring for a child of a relative may help perpetuate one's own genes. Sharing food with others today may increase one's own food intake in the future. But behavioral ecology has difficulty explaining human behaviors that appear to be completely altruistic with no apparent gain for the altruist. How can we explain why so many people in the United States and other countries believe in the value of conservation? And why did some people in Nazi Germany, at risk to their own safety, hide people from the Nazis?

INTERPRETIVE APPROACHES

Since about the 1960s, writers in the field of literary criticism have influenced the development of a variety of "interpretive" approaches in cultural anthropology, particularly with respect to ethnography.[15] Clifford Geertz popularized the idea that a culture is like a literary text that can be analyzed for meaning, as the ethnographer interprets it. According to Geertz, ethnographers choose to interpret the meaning of things in their field cultures that are of interest to themselves. Then they try to convey their interpretations of cultural meaning to people of their own culture. Thus, according to Geertz, the ethnographer is a kind of selective "intercultural translator."[16]

Some anthropologists think that interpretation is the only achievable goal in cultural anthropology, because they do not believe it is possible to describe or measure cultural phenomena, and other things involving humans, in objective or unbiased ways.[17] Scientific anthropologists do not agree. To be sure, interpretive ethnographies might provide insights. But we do not have to believe what an interpretation suggests, no matter how eloquently it is stated. (We are rarely given objective evidence to support an interpretation.) Scientific researchers have developed many techniques for minimizing bias and increasing the objectivity of measurement. Thus, interpretive anthropologists who deny the possibility of scientific understanding of human behavior and thinking may not know how much has been achieved so far by scientific studies of cultural phenomena, which we try to convey in the chapters that follow.

As Dan Sperber has suggested, the task of interpretation in cultural anthropology is clearly different from the task of explanation.[18] The goal of interpretation is to convey intuitive understanding of human experience in a *particular* culture (intuitive in the sense of not requiring conscious reasoning or systematic methods of inquiry). Thus the interpretive ethnographer is like a novelist or literary critic. In contrast, the goal of explanation is to provide causal and general understanding of cultural phenomena—causal in the sense of mechanisms that account for why something comes to be shared in a population, and general in the sense of applying to a number of similar cases.

Does one goal—interpretation versus explanation—preclude or invalidate the other? We don't think so. We share Sperber's view that interpretation and explanation are not contradictory goals; they just are different kinds of understanding. Indeed, an intuitive interpretation described in causal and general terms might turn out, when scientifically tested, to be a powerful explanation.

EXPLANATION

Anthropologists in the field try to arrive at accurate answers to descriptive questions. How do the people organize labor? How do they marry? What gods do they believe in? But as important as accurate description is, it is not the ultimate goal of anthropology. Anthropologists want to *understand*—to know *why* people have certain customs or beliefs, not just to see that they *do* have them. As difficult as the *how* and *what* questions are to answer, the *why* questions are even harder. *Why* questions deal with explanations, which are harder to generate and harder to evaluate. In science, to understand is to explain, and so the major goal of science is to arrive at trustworthy explanations.[19]

For many anthropologists, the plausibility or persuasiveness of an explanation cannot be considered a sufficient reason to accept it; the explanation must be tested and supported. And even when it is supported, there still may be grounds for skepticism. According to the scientific orientation, all knowledge is uncertain and therefore subject to increasing or decreasing confirmation as new tests are made. If this is true—and it may be uncomfortable to acknowledge—it means that we will never arrive at absolute truth. On the other hand, and this is encouraging, we should be able to achieve a more reliable understanding if we keep testing our theories.

An **explanation** is an answer to a *why* question. There are many types of explanation, some more satisfying than others. For example, suppose we ask why a society has a long postpartum sex taboo. We could guess that the people in that society want to abstain from sex for a year or so after the birth of a baby. Is this an explanation? Yes, because it does suggest that people have a purpose in practicing the custom; it therefore partly answers the *why* question. But such an explanation would not be very satisfying because it does not specify what the purpose of the custom might be. How about the idea that people have a long postpartum sex taboo because it is their tradition? Yes, that too is an explanation, but it is not satisfactory for a different reason. It is a *tautology*; that is, the thing to be explained (the taboo) is being explained by itself, by its prior existence. To explain something in terms of tradition is to say that people do it because they already do it, which is not informative. What kinds of explanations are more satisfactory, then? In science, there are two kinds of explanation that investigators try to achieve, associations and theories.

ASSOCIATIONS OR RELATIONSHIPS

One way of explaining something (an observation, an action, a custom) is to say how it conforms to a general principle or relationship. So to explain why the water left outside in the basin froze, we say that it was cold last night and that water freezes at 32° F. The statement that water solidifies (becomes ice) at 32° is a statement of a relationship or association between two **variables**—things or quantities that vary. In this case, variation in the state of water (liquid versus solid) is related to variation in the temperature of the air (above versus below 32° F). The truth of the relationship is suggested by repeated observations. In the physical sciences, such relationships are called **laws** when they are accepted by almost all scientists. We find such explanations satisfactory because they allow us to predict what will happen in the future or to understand something that has happened regularly in the past.

In the social sciences, associations are usually stated *probabilistically;* that is, we say that two or more variables *tend* to be related in a predictable way, which means that there are usually some exceptions. For example, to explain why a society has a long postpartum sex taboo, we can point to the association (or correlation) that John Whiting found in a worldwide sample of societies: Societies with apparently low-protein diets tend to have long postpartum sex taboos.[20] We call the relationship

Current Issues

SCIENCE AND HUMANISM

This chapter deals largely with the scientific view of understanding, but there are anthropologists who question whether the scientific approach is desirable or possible. They often describe themselves as humanists who use the human capacity to intuit, empathize, evoke, interpret, and illuminate as ways to understand. This orientation offers a very different kind of understanding because, compared with that offered by science, it does not insist on objectivity, nor does it insist on putting insights to empirical tests as science does. This is not to say that scientists do not intuit or interpret. They often do in the process of deriving theories, which involves creative leaps of imagination. And scientists, like anyone else, may empathize with the plight of the people they study. But the crucial difference between the humanistic and scientific orientations lies in the end result. For humanists, interpretation or evocation is the goal; for scientists, the goal is testing interpretations to see if they may be wrong.

Is objectivity possible? Or, because we are humans observing other humans, can we only be subjective? Objectivity requires trying to get at the truth despite the observer's subjective desires or needs. Is that possible? Can any human be unbiased? In an absolute sense, no one can be completely free of bias. But science has ways to strive for objectivity; it does not need to assume that every human is completely unbiased. Remember that even

when humans engage in physical science, they are often the observers or the creators of the instruments that do the observation. When an instrument points to a number, two persons may get slightly different readings because they look at the instrument from different angles. But neither person will be far off the mark, and the average of readings by two or more individuals will be very close to the "true" score.

But do we see other people objectively? Undoubtedly, some things about them are harder to "see" than others. It is easier to know objectively that wives and husbands usually sit down to dinner together, harder to "see" how they feel about one another. Suppose you are in a society where you never observe any obvious expression of affection between husbands and wives. At first, your own cultural bias might lead you to think that such couples don't care for each other much. Such an observation might indeed be biased (and not objective) if it turned out that couples privately express affection to each other but avoid public expressions. Or it might be that couples communicate their affection for each other in ways you didn't notice. But that doesn't mean that you wouldn't be able to figure this out eventually. In trying to understand the meaning of female-male relationships, you might very well try to establish close, personal relationships with some families. You might then ask people to tell you stories to try to see how they portrayed relations

between husband and wife. In short, a humanistic approach might help you understand how couples really feel about each other. But a scientist might go through the same procedure too in order to come to a tentative understanding.

As this example illustrates, humanistic understanding and science are really not incompatible. Both the scientist and the humanist would agree on the need to convey what a culture is like (for example, with regard to how couples feel about each other). But scientists would insist on more. First, they would try to verify, perhaps by systematic interviewing, how commonly a feeling is shared in the culture; second, they would want to explain why this feeling is common in some cultures but not in others. Therefore, they would have to create a theory to explain the variation and then collect evidence to test the theory to see if it might be wrong.

If humans are always biased observers, how can humanists convey the meaning behind other cultures? Aren't humanists trying to get close to the "truth" too? The poet Marianne Moore wrote that poetry gives us "imaginary gardens with real toads in them." Can imagination, humanistic or scientific, be meaningful without at least some real toads?

Sources: James Lett, "Scientific Anthropology," in David Levinson and Melvin Ember, eds., *Encyclopedia of Cultural Anthropology,* 4 vols. (New York: Henry Holt, 1995). The quote from Marianne Moore is from John Timpane, "Essay: The Poetry of Science," *Scientific American,* July 1991, 128.

between low-protein diets and the sex taboo a **statistical association,** which means that the observed relationship is unlikely to be due to chance.

THEORIES

Even though laws and statistical associations explain by relating what is to be explained to other things, we want to know more: why those laws or associations exist. Why does water freeze at 32° F? Why do societies with low-protein diets tend to have long postpartum sex taboos? Therefore, scientists try to formulate theories that will explain the observed relationships (laws and statistical associations).[21]

Theories—explanations of laws and statistical associations—are more complicated than the observed relationships they are intended to explain. It is difficult to be precise about what a theory is. By way of example, let us return to the question of why some societies have long postpartum sex taboos. We have already seen that a known statistical association can be used to help explain it. In general (but not always), if a society has a low-protein diet, it will have a long postpartum sex taboo. But most people would ask additional questions: Why does a low-protein diet explain the taboo? What is the mechanism by which a society with such a diet develops the custom of a long postpartum sex taboo? A theory is intended to answer such questions. In the chapter on the concept of culture, we briefly discussed John Whiting's theory that a long postpartum sex taboo may be an adaptation to certain conditions. Particularly in tropical areas, where the major food staples are low in protein, babies are vulnerable to the protein-deficiency disease called okwashiorkor. But if a baby could continue to nurse for a long time, it might have more of a chance to survive. The postpartum sex taboo might be adaptive, Whiting's theory suggests, because it increases the likelihood of a baby's survival. That is, if a mother puts off having another baby for a while, the first baby might have a better chance to survive because it can be fed mother's milk for a longer time. Whiting suggests that parents may be aware, whether unconsciously or consciously, that having another baby too soon might jeopardize the survival of the first baby, and so they might decide that it would be a good idea to abstain from intercourse for more than a year after the birth of the first baby.

As this example of a theory illustrates, there are differences between a theory and an association. A theory is more complicated, containing a series of statements. An association usually states quite simply that there is a relationship between two or more measured variables. Another difference is that, although a theory may mention some things that are observable, such as the presence of a long postpartum sex taboo, parts of it are difficult or impossible to observe directly. For example, with regard to Whiting's theory, it would be difficult to find out if people had deliberately or unconsciously decided to practice a long postpartum sex taboo because they recognized that babies would thereby have a better chance to survive. Then, too, the concept of adaptation—that some characteristic promotes greater reproductive success—is difficult to verify because it is difficult to find out whether different individuals or groups have different rates of reproduction because they do or do not practice the supposedly adaptive custom. Thus, some concepts or implications in a theory are unobservable (at least at the present time), and only some aspects may be observable. In contrast, statistical associations or laws are based entirely on observations.[22]

WHY THEORIES CANNOT BE PROVED

Many people think that the theories they learned in physics or chemistry courses have been proved. Unfortunately, many students get that impression because their teachers present "lessons" in an authoritative manner. It is now generally agreed by scientists and philosophers of science that although some theories may have considerable evidence supporting them, no theory can be said to be proved or unquestionably true. This is because many of the concepts and ideas in theories are not directly observable and therefore not directly verifiable. For example, scientists may try to explain how light behaves by postulating that it consists of particles called photons, but photons cannot be observed, even with the most powerful microscope. So exactly what a photon looks like and exactly how it works remain in the realm of the unprovable. The photon is a **theoretical construct,** something that cannot be observed or verified directly. Because all theories contain such constructs, theories cannot be proved entirely or with absolute certainty.[23]

Why should we bother with theories, then, if we cannot prove that they are true? Perhaps the main advantage of a theory as a kind of explanation is that it may lead to new understanding or knowledge. A theory can suggest new relationships or imply new predictions that might be supported or confirmed by new research. For example, Whiting's theory about long postpartum sex taboos has implications that could be investigated by researchers. Because the theory discusses how a long postpartum sex taboo might be adaptive, we would expect that certain changes would result in the taboo's disappearance. For example, suppose people adopted either mechanical birth-control devices or began to give supplementary high-protein foods to babies. With birth control, a family could space births without abstaining from sex, so we would expect the custom of postpartum abstinence to disappear. So, too, we would expect it to disappear with protein supplements for babies, because kwashiorkor would then be less likely to afflict the babies. Whiting's ideas might also prompt investigators to try to find out whether parents are consciously or unconsciously aware of the problem of close birth spacing in areas with low supplies of protein.

Although theories cannot be proved, they are rejectable. The method of **falsification,** which shows that a theory seems to be wrong, is the main way that theories are judged.[24] Scientists derive implications or predictions that should be true *if* the theory is correct. So, for example, Whiting predicted that societies with long postpartum sex taboos would be found more often in the tropics than in temperate regions and that they would be likely to have low-protein food supplies. Such predictions of what might be found are called **hypotheses.** If the predictions turn out *not* to be correct, the researcher is obliged to conclude that there may be something wrong with the theory or something wrong with the test of the theory. Theories that are not falsified are accepted for the time being because the available evidence seems to be consistent with them. But remember that no matter how much the available evidence seems to support a theory, we can never be certain it is true. There is always the possibility that some implication of it, some hypothesis derivable from it, will not be confirmed in the future.

GENERATING THEORIES

Earlier in this chapter we discussed theoretical orientations that are popular in cultural anthropology. Most orientations merely suggest where to look for answers to questions; they do not by themselves suggest particular explanations for particular phenomena. You cannot directly deduce a theory from a theoretical orientation. For example, an anthropologist with an ecological theoretical orientation is likely to say that some particular custom exists because it is or used to be adaptive. But exactly how a particular custom may be adaptive must still be specified; the mechanism of its adaptiveness is not automatically suggested by the theoretical orientation. Whiting's theory suggests specific conditions under which the long postpartum sex taboo might be adaptive. The theory does not just say that the taboo is adaptive. How, then, does an anthropologist develop an explanation or theory for some particular phenomenon?

It is difficult to specify any one procedure that is guaranteed to produce a theory, because developing a theory requires creative imagination, and no discovery procedure by itself necessarily generates creativity. Too much dependence on a particular theoretical orientation may, in fact, be detrimental, because it may blind the investigator to other possibilities. A more important factor in generating a theory may be the investigator's belief that it is possible to do so. A person who believes that something is explainable will be more apt to notice possibly connected facts, as well as to recall possibly relevant considerations, and put them all together in some explanatory way.

We can point to two types of procedures that have helped anthropologists produce explanations of cultural phenomena: *single-case analysis* and a *comparative study.* In analyzing a single case, the anthropologist may be interested in explaining a particular custom. While in the field, he or she may ask informants why they practice (or think they practice) the custom. Sometimes such inquiries will elicit a plausible explanation. But more often than not, the informants merely answer, "We have always done it that way." The investigator may then make a kind of mental search through other features of the society or its environment that may be connected with the custom. If possible, the anthropologist may try to view the situation historically, to see if the custom appeared rather recently. If it did, what possible explanatory conditions appeared just before the custom?

An anthropologist may also generate an explanation by comparing different societies that share this characteristic, in order to determine what other characteristics regularly occur along with it. Societies in which the characteristic is lacking would also be considered, because a possible cause of that characteristic should be absent in those societies. If the anthropologist discovers that a characteristic occurs regularly in different cultures along with certain other features, she or he may be reasonably certain that the possible causes of that characteristic have been narrowed down. It must be remembered, however, that the investigator is not a computer. It is not necessary to search through all the characteristics that might be shared by different cultures. The

Research Frontiers

EVALUATING ALTERNATIVE THEORIES

In working among the Abelam of New Guinea, Richard Scaglion was puzzled why they invest so much energy in growing giant ceremonial yams, sometimes more than 10 feet long. And why do they abstain from sex for six months while they grow them? Of course, to try to understand, we need to know much more about the Abelam way of life. Scaglion had read about them, lived among them, and talked to them, but, as many ethnographers have discovered, answers to *why* questions don't just leap out at you. Answers, at least tentative ones, often come from theoretical orientations that suggest how or where to look for answers. Scaglion considers several possibilities. As Donald Tuzin had suggested for a nearby group, the Plains Arapesh, yams may be *symbols* of, or stand for, shared cultural understandings. (Looking for the meanings of symbols is a kind of interpretative approach to ethnographic data.)

The Abelam think of yams as having souls that appreciate tranquillity. Yams also have family lines; at marriage, the joining of family lines is symbolized by planting different yam lines in the same garden. During the yam-growing cycle (remember that yams appreciate tranquillity), lethal warfare and conflict become channeled mostly into competitive but nonlethal yam-growing contests. So yam growing may be functional in the sense that it helps to foster harmony.

Then again, ceremonial yam growing may have adaptive *ecological* consequences. Just as the Tsembaga pig feasts seemed to keep human population in line with resources, Scaglion thinks that ceremonial yam growing did too. Growing pig populations damage gardens and create conflicts, but during competitive yam ceremonies pigs are also given away, so the pig population declines. Wild animals that are hunted also have a chance to re-plenish themselves because hunting is frowned upon during the yam-growing cycle.

As Scaglion's discussion illustrates, theoretical orientations help researchers derive explanations. They do not have to be "rival" explanations, in the sense that one has to be right and others wrong; more than one theory may help explain some phenomenon. But we can't assume that just because a theory sounds good, it *is* correct and helps us to understand. The important point is that we need something more to evaluate theory. As we discuss in this chapter, we have to find ways to *test* a theory against evidence. Until we do that, we really don't know how many, or if indeed *any*, of the theories available are helpful.

Source: Richard Scaglion, "Abelam: Giant Yams and Cycles of Sex, Warfare and Ritual," in Melvin Ember, Carol R. Ember, and David Levinson, eds., *Portraits of Culture: Ethnographic Originals* (Upper Saddle River, NJ: Prentice Hall, 1998). Prentice Hall/Simon & Schuster Custom Publishing.

investigator usually looks only at those traits that can plausibly be connected. Here is where an individual's theoretical orientation generally comes into play, since that orientation usually points to the possible importance of one particular set of factors over others.

EVIDENCE: TESTING EXPLANATIONS

In any field of investigation, theories are generally the most plentiful commodity, apparently because of the human predisposition to try to make sense of the world. It is necessary, then, for us to have procedures that enable us to select from among the many available theories those that are more likely to be correct.

"Just as mutations arise naturally but are not all beneficial, so hypotheses [theories] emerge naturally but are not all correct. If progress is to occur, therefore, we require a superfluity of hypotheses and also a mechanism of selection."[25] In other words, generating a theory or interpretation is not enough. We need some reliable method of testing whether or not that interpretation is likely to be correct. If an interpretation is not correct, it may detract from our efforts to achieve understanding by misleading us into thinking the problem is already solved.

The strategy in all kinds of testing in science is to predict what one would expect to find if a particular interpretation were correct, and then to conduct an investigation to see if the prediction is generally consistent with the data. If the prediction is not supported, the investigator is obliged to accept the possibility that the interpretation is wrong. If, however, the prediction holds true, then the investigator is entitled to say that there is evidence to support the theory. Thus, conducting research designed to test expectations derived from theory allows researchers to eliminate some interpretations and to accept others, at least tentatively.

OPERATIONALIZATION AND MEASUREMENT

We test predictions derived from a theory to see if the theory may be correct, to see if it is consistent with observable events or conditions in the real world. A theory and the predictions derived from it are not useful if there is no way to measure the events or conditions mentioned in the predictions. If there is no way of relating the theory to observable events, it does not matter how good the theory sounds, it is still not a useful scientific theory.[26] To transform theoretical predictions into statements that might be verified, a researcher provides an operational definition of each of the concepts or variables mentioned in the prediction. An **operational definition** is a description of the procedure that is followed to measure the variable.[27]

Whiting predicted that societies with a low-protein diet would have a long postpartum sex taboo. Amount of protein in the diet is a variable; some societies have more, others have less. Length of the postpartum sex taboo is a variable; a society may have a short taboo or a long taboo. Whiting operationally defined the first variable, *amount of protein,* in terms of staple foods.[28] For example, if a society depended mostly on root and tree crops (cassava, bananas), Whiting rated the society as

having low protein. If the society depended mostly on cereal crops (wheat, barley, corn, oats), he rated it as having moderate protein, because cereal crops have more protein by weight than root and tree crops. If the society depended mostly on hunting, fishing, or herding for food, he rated it as having high protein. The other variable in Whiting's prediction, *length of postpartum sex taboo,* was operationalized as follows: a society was rated as having a long taboo if couples customarily abstained from sex for more than a year after the birth of a baby; abstention for a year or less was considered a short taboo.

Specifying an operational definition for each variable is extremely important because it allows other investigators to check on a researcher's results.[29] Science depends on *replication,* the repetition of results. Only when many researchers observe a particular association can we call that association or relationship a law. Providing operational definitions is also extremely important because it allows others to evaluate whether a measure is appropriate. Only when we are told exactly how something was measured can we judge whether the measure reflects what it is supposed to reflect. Specifying measures publicly is so important in science that we are obliged to be skeptical of any conclusions offered by a researcher who fails to say how variables were measured.

To **measure** something is to say how it compares with other things on some scale of variation.[30] People often assume that a measuring device is always a physical instrument, such as a scale or a ruler, but physical devices are not the only way to measure something. *Classification* is also a form of measurement. When we classify persons as male or female, or employed versus unemployed, we are dividing them into *sets.* Deciding which set they belong to is a kind of measurement because doing

The Yanomamö Indians of Brazil depend mostly on root crops. The Masai pastoralists of Kenya depend largely on milk and other products of their cattle.

so allows us to compare them. We can also measure things by deciding which cases or examples have more or less of something (for instance, more or less protein in the diet). The measures employed in physical science are usually based on scales that allow us to assign numbers to each case; we measure height in meters and weight in grams, for example. However we measure our variables, the fact that we *can* measure them means that we can test our hypotheses to see if the predicted relationships actually exist, at least most of the time.

SAMPLING

After an investigator decides how to measure the variables in some predicted relationship, she or he must decide how to select which cases to investigate to see if the predicted relationship holds. If the prediction is about the behavior of people, the sampling decision involves which people to observe. If the prediction is about an association between societal customs, the sampling decision involves which societies to study. Investigators must decide not only which cases to choose but also how many to choose. No researcher can investigate all the possible cases, so choices must be made. Some choices are better than others. In the chapter on the concept of culture, we talked about the advantages of random sampling. A random sample is one in which all cases selected had an equal chance of being included in the sample. Almost all statistical tests used to evaluate the results of research require random sampling, because only results based on a random sample can be assumed to be probably true for some larger set or universe of cases.

Before a researcher can sample randomly, he or she must specify the **sampling universe,** that is, the list of cases to be sampled from. Suppose an anthropologist is doing fieldwork in a society. Unless the society is very small, it is usually not practical to use the whole society as the sampling universe. Because most fieldworkers want to remain in a community for a considerable length of time, the community usually becomes the sampling universe. If a cross-cultural researcher wants to test an explanation, he or she needs to sample the world's societies. But we do not have descriptions of all the societies, past and present, that have existed in the world. So samples are usually drawn from published lists of described societies that have been classified or coded according to standard cultural variables,[31] or they are drawn from the *Human Relations Area Files (HRAF),* an indexed, annually growing collection of original ethnographic books and articles on more

than 370 societies past and present around the world.[32]

Random sampling is still not employed that often in anthropology, but a nonrandom sample might still be fairly representative if the investigator has not personally chosen the cases for study. We should be particularly suspicious of any sample that may reflect the investigator's own biases or interests. For example, if an investigator picks only the people with whom she or he is friendly, the sample is suspicious. If cross-cultural researchers select sample societies because ethnographies on them happen to be on their own bookshelves, such samples are also suspicious. A sampling procedure should be designed to get a fair representation of the sampling universe, not a biased selection. If we want to increase our chances of getting a representative sample, we have to use a random-sampling procedure. To do so, we conventionally number the cases in the statistical universe and then use a table of random numbers to draw our sample cases.

STATISTICAL EVALUATION

When the researcher has measured the variables of interest for all the sample cases, he or she is ready to see if the predicted relationship actually exists in the data. Remember, the results may not turn out to be what the theory predicts. Sometimes the researcher constructs a *contingency table,* like that shown in Table 11–1, to see if the variables are associated as predicted. In Whiting's sample of 172 societies, each

---

TABLE 11–1 *Association between Availability of Protein and Duration of Postpartum Sex Taboo*

AVAILABILITY OF PROTEIN	DURATION OF POSTPARTUM SEX TABOO		
	Short (0–1 Year)	Long (More Than 1 Year)	TOTAL
High	47	15	62
Medium	38	25	63
Low	20	27	47
Total	105	67	172

Source: Adapted from John W. M. Whiting, "Effects of Climate on Certain Cultural Practices," in Ward H. Goodenough, ed., *Explorations in Cultural Anthropology* (New York: McGraw-Hill, 1964), p. 520.

case is assigned to a box, or *cell,* in the table, depending on how the society is measured on the two variables of interest. For example, a society that has a long postpartum sex taboo and a low-protein diet is placed in the lowest right-hand cell of the Duration column. (In Whiting's sample [see Table 11–1] there are 27 such societies.) A society that has a short postpartum sex taboo and a low-protein diet is placed in the lowest left-hand cell. (There are 20 such societies in the sample.) The statistical question is: Does the way the cases are distributed in the six cells of the table generally support Whiting's prediction? If we looked just at the table, we might not know what to answer. Many cases appear to be in the expected places. For example, most of the high-protein cases (47 of 62) have short taboos, and most of the low-protein cases (27 of 47) have long taboos. But there are also many exceptions (for example, 20 cases have low protein and a short taboo). So, although many cases appear to be in the expected places, there are also many exceptions. Do the exceptions invalidate the prediction? How many exceptions would compel us to reject the hypothesis? Here is where we resort to statistical *tests of significance.*

Statisticians have devised various tests that tell us how "perfect" a result has to be for us to believe that there is probably an association between the variables of interest, that one variable generally predicts the other. Essentially, every statistical result is evaluated in the same objective way. We ask: What is the chance that this result is purely accidental, that there is no association at all between the two variables? Although some of the mathematical ways of answering this question are complicated, the answer always involves a **probability value** (or *p*-**value**)—the likelihood that the observed result or a stronger one could have occurred by chance. The statistical test used by Whiting gives a *p*-value of less than .01 ($p < .01$) for the observed result. In other words, there is less than 1 chance out of 100 that the relationship observed is purely accidental. A *p*-value of less than .01 is a fairly low probability; most social scientists conventionally agree to call any result with a *p*-value of .05 or less (5 or fewer chances out of 100) a **statistically significant** or probably true result. When we describe relationships or associations in the rest of this book, we are almost always referring to results that have been found to be statistically significant.

But why should a probably true relationship have any exceptions? If a theory is really correct, shouldn't *all* the cases fit? There are many reasons why we can never expect a perfect result. First, even if a theory is correct (for example, if a low-protein diet really does favor the adoption of a long postpartum sex taboo), there may still be other causes that we have not investigated. Some of the societies could have a long taboo even though they have high protein. For example, societies that depend mostly on hunting for their food, and would therefore be classified as having a high-protein diet, may have a problem carrying infants from one campsite to another and may practice a long postpartum sex taboo so that two infants will not have to be carried at the same time. Exceptions to the predicted relationship might also occur because of *cultural lag.*[33] Suppose that a society recently changed crops and is now no longer a low-protein society but still practices the taboo. This society would be an exception to the predicted relationship, but it might fit the theory if it stopped practicing the taboo in a few years. Measurement inaccuracy is another source of exceptions. Whiting's measure of protein, which is based on the major sources of food, is not a very precise measure of protein in the diet. It does not take into account the possibility that a "tree-crop" society might get a lot of protein from fishing or raising pigs. So it might turn out that some supposedly low-protein societies have been misclassified, which may be one reason why there are 20 cases in the lowest cell in the left-hand column of Table 11–1. Measurement error usually produces exceptions.

Significant statistical associations that are predictable from a theory offer tentative support for the theory. But much more is needed before we can be fairly confident about the theory. Replication is needed to confirm whether the predictions can be reproduced by other researchers using other samples. Other predictions should be derived from the theory to see if they too are supported. The theory should be pitted against alternative explanations to see which theory works better. We may have to combine theories if the alternative explanations also predict the relationship in question. The research process in science thus requires time and patience. Perhaps most important, it requires that researchers be humble. No matter how wonderful one's own theory seems, it is important to acknowledge that it may be wrong. If we don't acknowledge that possibility, we can't be motivated to test our theories. If we don't test our theories, we can never tell the difference between a better or worse theory, and we will be saddled forever with our present ignorance. In science, knowledge or understanding is explained variation. Thus, if we want to understand more, we have to keep testing our beliefs against sets of objective evidence that could contradict our beliefs.

TYPES OF RESEARCH IN CULTURAL ANTHROPOLOGY

Cultural anthropologists use several methods to conduct research. Each has certain advantages and disadvantages in generating and testing explanations. The types of research in cultural anthropology can be classified according to two criteria. One is the *spatial* scope of the study—analysis of a single society, analysis of societies in a region, or analysis of a worldwide sample of societies. The other criterion is the *temporal* scope of the study—historical versus nonhistorical. Combinations of these criteria are shown in Table 11–2.

ETHNOGRAPHY

Around the beginning of the twentieth century, anthropologists realized that if they were to produce anything of scientific value, they would have to study their subject in depth. To describe cultures more accurately, they started to live among the people they were studying. They observed, and even took part in, the important events of those societies and carefully questioned the people about their native customs. This method is known as **participant-observation.** Participant-observation always involves **fieldwork,** which is firsthand experience with the people you are studying, but fieldwork may also involve other methods, such as conducting a census or a survey.[34]

Fieldwork, the cornerstone of modern anthropology, is the means by which most anthropological information is obtained. Regardless of other methods that anthropologists may use, participant-observation, usually for a year or more, is regarded as fundamental. In contrast to the casual descriptions of travelers and adventurers, anthropologists' descriptions record, describe, analyze, and eventually formulate a picture of the culture, or at least part of it.[35] After doing fieldwork, an anthropologist

Anthropologist Robert Tonkinson talking to an informant in the Asmat region of West New Guinea.

may prepare an *ethnography,* a description and analysis of a single society.

How an anthropologist goes about doing long-term participant-observation in another culture—and, more important, doing it well—is not so straightforward. Much of it depends on the person, the culture, and the interaction between the two. Without doubt, the experience is physically and psychologically demanding, comparable often to a rite of passage. Although it helps enormously to learn the local language before one goes, often it is not possible to do so, and so most anthropologists find themselves struggling to communicate in addition to trying to figure out how to behave properly. Participant-observation carries its own dilemma. Participation implies living like the people you have come to study, trying to understand subjectively what they think and feel by doing what they do, whereas observation implies a certain amount of objectivity and detachment.[36] Because participant-observation is such a personal experience, it is not surprising that anthropologists have begun to realize that *reflecting* on their experiences and their personal interaction with the people they live with is an important part of understanding the enterprise.

TABLE 11–2   *Types of Research in Cultural Anthropology*

	NONHISTORICAL	HISTORICAL
Single society	Ethnography Within-culture comparison	Ethnohistory Within-culture comparison
Region	Controlled comparison	Controlled comparison
Worldwide sample	Cross-cultural research	Cross-historical research

Margaret Mead in Bali

An essential part of the participant-observation process is taking notes, jotting down things observed, questions asked and answers obtained, and things to check out later. Often these notes cannot be extensive or may not be legible later, so it is important to set aside time each day to go over and elaborate on the information and classify it somehow, so that it can be referred to later.[37]

Participant-observation is valuable for understanding some aspects of culture, particularly the things that are the most public, readily talked about, and most widely agreed upon. But more systematic methods are important too: mapping, house-to-house censuses, behavior observations (for example, to determine how people spend their time), as well as focused interviews with a sample of informants.

Ethnographies and ethnographic articles on particular topics provide much of the essential data for all kinds of studies in cultural anthropology. To make a comparison of societies in a given region, or worldwide, an anthropologist would require ethnographic data on many societies. With regard to the goal of generating theory, ethnography, with its in-depth, firsthand, long-term observation, provides an investigator with a wealth of descriptive material covering a wide range of phenomena. Thus, it may stimulate interpretations about the way different aspects of the culture are related to each other and

to features of the environment. The ethnographer in the field has the opportunity to get to know the context of a society's customs by directly asking the people about those customs and by observing the phenomena that appear to be associated with those practices. In addition, the ethnographer who develops a possible explanation for some custom can test that hunch by collecting new information related to it. In this sense, the ethnographer is similar to a physician who is trying to understand why a patient has certain symptoms of illness.

Although ethnography is extremely useful for generating explanations, a field study of a single site does not generally provide sufficient data to test a hypothesis. For example, an ethnographer may think that a particular society practices *polygyny* (one man married to two or more women simultaneously) because it has more women than men. But the ethnographer could not be reasonably sure that this explanation was correct unless the results of a comparative study of a sample of societies showed that most polygynous societies have more women than men. After all, the fact that one society has both these conditions could be a historical accident rather than a result of some necessary connection between the two conditions.

WITHIN-CULTURE COMPARISONS

An ethnographer could test a theory within one society if she or he decides to compare individuals, families, households, communities, or districts. The natural variability that exists can be used to create a comparison. Suppose we want to verify Whiting's assumption that in a society with a low-protein diet, longer postpartum taboos enhance the survival of babies. Although almost all couples might practice a long postpartum sex taboo because it is customary, some couples might not adhere to the taboo consistently and some couples might not conceive quickly after the taboo is lifted. So we would expect some variation in spacing between births. If we collected information on the births of each mother and the survival outcome of each birth, we would be able to compare the survival rates of children born a short time after the mother's last pregnancy with those of children born after longer intervals. A significantly higher survival rate for the births after longer intervals would support Whiting's theory. What if some communities within the society had access to more protein than others? If Whiting's theory is correct, those communities with more protein should also have a higher survival rate for babies. If there were

Current Issues

FIELDWORK: HOW CAN WE KNOW WHAT IS TRUE?

Hardly any cultural anthropologist disputes the value of fieldwork in another culture, both for what it contributes to understanding others and for what it contributes to understanding yourself and your own culture. Probably it is the immersion that does it. Living with other people (participant-observation) allows you to see things you would not otherwise notice. At the same time, you cannot help but realize how the smallest habitual things you do, which you may have thought were just natural, are just wrong in your field site. At the beginning, there is culture shock because there is so much you don't comprehend. And at the end, there is culture shock when you return home. All of a sudden, many things in your own society now feel strange. Indeed, the experience is so profound that most cultural anthropologists feel that fieldwork provides them with the "deepest" kind of knowledge. Not just deep, but real.

Although few people doubt the value of fieldwork, there have been challenges about its veracity. Consider the controversy over the fieldwork of Margaret Mead, who lived on a small island in American Samoa in the 1920s and wrote about the sexual freedom of adolescents in *Coming of Age in Samoa*. Derek Freeman, who worked in Western Samoa largely in the 1960s, wrote a scathing critique of Mead's fieldwork in his *Margaret Mead and Samoa: The Making and Unmaking of*

an Anthropological Myth. Essentially, Freeman said that Mead got most things wrong. For example, he stated that the Samoans are puritanical in their sexuality. If both did fieldwork, and fieldwork gives us real, deep knowledge, shouldn't they both be right? But how can they be? Was one a good fieldworker and the other not? How can we know what is true?

Paul Shankman suggests that both might be partly right if we recognize several things. First, he points out that we can speak of sexual permissiveness and sexual restrictiveness only in comparative terms. We need to understand that Mead did her fieldwork at a time when premarital sex was uncommon in the United States, but sex patterns changed subsequently. So, in contrast with American girls during Mead's time, Samoan girls may have seemed more sexually free. Second, Samoa changed a great deal over time with missionization, colonialization, World War II, and commercialization. Third, Samoa was variable—American Samoa versus Western Samoa, rural versus urban. So what the two fieldworkers experienced may have been quite different, and therefore they could both be right. But, in fact, Shankman suggests that if we ignore Mead's and Freeman's conclusions about permissive or restrictive sexuality, if we separate *ideal* from *actual* behavior, and if we look at actual data on individual sexual behav-

ior as collected by both Mead and Freeman, the two fieldworkers are not all that different: Samoans are in the middle of the worldwide range of cultures in regard to the occurrence of premarital sex.

What do we conclude from this controversy? As many anthropologists are now pointing out, it is important to reflect on the possible influences of the context of the fieldwork, the qualities of the person doing it, how that person interacts with the people she or he lives with, and the kinds of methods used to try to verify conclusions. Others point out that reflection, although important, is not enough. If we want to be more sure that we are understanding correctly, it is not sufficient to assume that the traditional style of fieldwork (participant-observation and interviewing of a few selected informants) can always discover the truth in a field situation. Particularly for those behaviors that are private, or more variable, or not easily verbalized, anthropological fieldworkers should consider interviewing a representative sample of people and using tests of informant accuracy.

Sources: Paul Shankman, "Sex, Lies, and Anthropologists: Margaret Mead, Derek Freeman, and Samoa," in Carol R. Ember, Melvin Ember, and Peter N. Peregrine, eds., *Research Frontiers in Anthropology* (Upper Saddle River, NJ: Prentice Hall, 1998), Prentice Hall/Simon & Schuster Custom Publishing; Melvin Ember, "Evidence and Science in Ethnography: Reflections on the Freeman-Mead Controversy," *American Anthropologist,* 87 (1985): 906–909.

variation in the length of the postpartum sex taboo, the communities with more protein should have shorter taboos.

Whether or not we can design intracultural tests of hypotheses depends on whether we have sufficient variability in the variables in our hypotheses. More often than not we do, and we can make use of that variation to test hypotheses within a culture.

REGIONAL CONTROLLED COMPARISONS

In a regional controlled comparison, the anthropologist compares ethnographic information obtained from societies found in a particular region—societies that presumably have similar histories and occupy similar environments. The anthropologist who conducts a regional comparison is apt to be familiar with the complex of cultural features associated with that region. These features may provide a good understanding of the context of the phenomenon that is to be explained. An anthropologist's knowledge of the region under study, however, is probably not as great as the ethnographer's knowledge of a single society. Still, the anthropologist's understanding of local details is greater in a regional comparison than in a worldwide comparison. The worldwide comparison is necessarily so broad that the investigator is unlikely to know a great deal about any of the societies being compared.

The regional controlled comparison is useful not only for generating explanations but also for testing them. Because some of the societies being compared will have the characteristic that is to be explained and some will not, the anthropologist can determine whether the conditions hypothesized to be related are in fact related, at least in that region. We must remember, however, that two or more conditions may be related in one region for reasons peculiar to that region. Therefore, an explanation supported in one region may not fit others.

CROSS-CULTURAL RESEARCH

Anthropologists can generate interpretations on the basis of worldwide comparisons by looking for differences between those societies having and those lacking a particular characteristic. But the most common use of worldwide comparisons has been to test explanations. The cross-cultural researcher first identifies conditions that should generally be associated if a particular theory is correct. Then she or he looks at a worldwide sample of societies to see if the expected association generally holds true. The advantage of cross-cultural research is that the conclu-

sion drawn from it is probably applicable to most societies, *if* the sample used for testing has been more or less randomly selected and therefore is representative of the world. In other words, in contrast with the results of a regional comparison, which may or may not be applicable to other regions, the results of a cross-cultural study are probably applicable to most societies and most regions.

As we have noted, the greater the number of societies examined in a study, the less likely it is that the investigator will have detailed knowledge of the societies involved. So if a cross-cultural test does not support a particular explanation, the investigator may not know enough about the sample societies to know how to modify the interpretation or come up with a new one. In this situation, the anthropologist may reexamine the details of one or more particular societies in order to stimulate fresh thinking on the subject. Another limitation of cross-cultural research, as a means of both generating and testing explanations, is that only those explanations for which the required information is generally available in ethnographies can be tested. An investigator interested in explaining something that has not been generally described must resort to some other research strategy to collect data.

HISTORICAL RESEARCH

Ethnohistory consists of studies based on descriptive materials about a single society at more than one point in time. It provides the essential data for historical studies of all types, just as ethnography provides the essential data for all nonhistorical types of research. Ethnohistorical data may consist of sources other than the ethnographic reports prepared by anthropologists—accounts by explorers, missionaries, traders, and government officials. Ethnohistorians, like historians, cannot simply assume that all the documents they find are simply descriptions of fact; they were written by very different kinds of people with very different goals and purposes. So they need to separate carefully what may be fact from what may be speculative interpretation. In terms of generating and testing hypotheses, studies of single societies over time tend to be subject to the same limitations as studies of single societies confined to a single period. Like their nonhistorical counterparts, studies that concentrate on a single society observed through time are likely to generate more than one hypothesis, but they do not generally provide the opportunity to establish with reasonable certainty which of those hypotheses is correct. Cross-cultural historical studies (of which we have only a few examples thus far) suffer from the opposite limitation. They provide ample means of testing hypotheses through comparison, but they are severely constrained, because of the necessity of working with secondhand data, in their ability to generate hypotheses derived from the available data.

There is, however, one advantage to historical studies of any type. The goal of theory in cultural anthropology is to explain variation in cultural patterns, that is, to specify what conditions will favor one cultural pattern rather than another. Such specification requires us to assume that the supposed causal, or favoring, conditions antedated the pattern to be explained. Theories or explanations, then, imply a *sequence* of changes over time, which are the stuff of history. Therefore, if we want to come closer to an understanding of the reasons for the cultural variations we are investigating, we should examine historical sequences. They will help us determine whether the conditions we think caused various phenomena truly antedated those phenomena and thus might more reliably be said to have caused them. If we can examine historical sequences, we may be able to make sure that we do not put the cart before the horse.

The major impediment to historical research is that collecting and analyzing historical data—particularly when they come from the scattered accounts of explorers, missionaries, and traders—is a tedious and exasperating task. It may be more efficient to test explanations nonhistorically first, in order to eliminate some interpretations. Only when an interpretation survives a nonhistorical test should we look to historical data to test the presumed sequence.

In the chapters that follow, we discuss not only what we strongly suspect about the determinants of cultural variation but also what we do not know or only dimly suspect. We devote a lot of our discussion to what we do not know—what has not yet been the subject of research that tests hypotheses and theories—because we want to convey a sense of what cultural anthropology might discover in the future.

SUMMARY

1. Which aspects of life an individual anthropologist concentrates on usually reflects his or her theoretical orientation, subject interest, or preferred method of research. Interpretation and explanation are not opposed goals; they just are different kinds of understanding.

2. Scientists try to achieve two kinds of explanation—associations (observed relationships between two or more variables) and theories (explanations of associations).

3. A theory is more complicated than an association. Some concepts or implications in a theory are unobservable; an association is based entirely on observations.

4. Theories can never be proved with absolute certainty. There is always the possibility that some implication, some derivable hypothesis, will not be confirmed by future research.

5. A theory may be rejectable through the method of falsification. Scientists derive predictions that should be true *if* the theory is correct. If the predictions turn out to be incorrect, scientists are obliged to conclude that there may be something wrong with the theory.

6. To make a satisfactory test, we have to specify operationally how we measure the variables involved in the relationships we expect to exist, so that other researchers can try to replicate, or repeat, our results.

7. Tests of predictions should employ samples that are representative. The most objective way to obtain a representative sample is to select the sample cases randomly.

8. The results of tests are evaluated by statistical methods that assign probability values to the results. These values allow us to distinguish between probably true and probably accidental results.

9. Cultural anthropologists use several different methods to conduct research. Each has certain advantages and disadvantages in generating and testing explanations. The types of research in cultural anthropology can be classified according to two criteria: the spatial scope of the study (analysis of a single society, analysis of several or more societies in a region, or analysis of a worldwide sample of societies) and the temporal scope of the study (historical versus nonhistorical). The basic research methods, then, are ethnography and ethnohistory, historical and nonhistorical regional-controlled comparisons, and historical and nonhistorical cross-cultural research.

GLOSSARY TERMS

behavioral ecology	falsification
cultural ecology	fieldwork
explanation	group selection

hypotheses
individual selection
laws
measure
operational definition
participant-observation
political economy
probability value
    (*p*-value)

sampling universe
sociobiology
statistical association
statistically significant
theoretical construct
theories
variable

CRITICAL QUESTIONS

1. Does a theoretical orientation enhance one's way of looking at the world, or does it blind one to other possibilities?

2. Can a unique event be explained?

3. How does measurement go beyond observation?

4. Why is scientific understanding always uncertain?

5. If two ethnographers describing the same culture disagree, how do we decide who's right?

INTERNET EXERCISES

1. Some of the important pioneers in cultural anthropology are Franz Boas, Ruth Benedict, Margaret Mead, Bronislaw Malinowski, A. R. Radcliffe-Brown, Leslie White, and Claude Levi-Strauss. Pick two of these names and try to find out about them using any search engine. Write a brief summary of what you've found.

2. Fieldwork using participant observation is one of the most important anthropological methods. Check out one anthropologist's Web site describing her fieldwork in New Guinea: **http://www.truman.edu/academics/ss/faculty/tamakoshil/index.html**.

3. Statistics have to be used carefully so as not to misrepresent information. Go to **www.unicef.org/pon96/nutale.htm** for an example of how a comparison must be done carefully. What are some of the potential problems that can occur when analyzing information?

4. The Collection of Ethnography by the Human Relations Area Files is a major resource for cross-cultural comparisons that is found at over 400 universities and colleges. Go to HRAF's home page at **http://www.yale.edu/hraf**. Name some of the cultures included in the HRAF Collection of Ethnography.

SUGGESTED READING

BERNARD, H. R. *Research Methods in Cultural Anthropology: Qualitative and Quantitative Approaches,* 2nd ed. Walnut Creek, CA: Alta Mira Press, 1994. Proceeding step by step through the research process, this book surveys how to prepare for a field study and how to collect and analyze the data produced.

"Cross-Cultural and Comparative Research: Theory and Method." *Behavior Science Research,* 25 (1991): 1–270. This book-length special issue provides an extensive state-of-the-art coverage of the goals, achievements, and problems in the various kinds of cross-cultural and comparative research.

EMBER, C. R., EMBER, M., AND PEREGRINE, P. N., EDS. *Research Frontiers in Anthropology.* Upper Saddle River, NJ: Prentice Hall, 1998. Prentice Hall/Simon & Schuster Custom Publishing. This series contains four types of articles about ongoing and future research: anthropologists at work, the state of current understanding of classic research questions and controversies, the newest research methods, and research on social problems.

KUZNAR, L. A. *Reclaiming a Scientific Anthropology.* Walnut Creek, CA: Alta Mira Press, 1997. This book reviews many of the anti-science arguments in anthropology and how they have been answered by philosophers of science.

LETT, J. *Science, Reason, and Anthropology: The Principles of Rational Inquiry,* Lanham, MD: Rowman & Littlefield, 1997. Cultural anthropology has had difficulty integrating its humanistic and scientific aspects. The author reviews the philosophical foundations of anthropology, particularly with regard to scientific anthropology and shows that science and humanism are not incompatible.

POGGIE, J. J., JR., DEWALT, B. R., AND DRESSLER, W. W., EDS. *Anthropological Research: Process and Application.* Albany: State University of New York Press, 1992. The chapters in this volume illustrate how a research question is translated into operational research. Also stressed is the importance of blending qualitative and quantitative methods, variability within cultures, and the practical application of answers to research questions.

STOCKING, G. W., JR., ED. *History of Anthropology,* vols. 1–6. Madison: University of Wisconsin, 1983–1989. A series of volumes on various topics in the history of anthropology, including the beginnings of fieldwork in anthropology (vol. 1, *Observers Observed: Essays on Ethnographic Fieldwork*) and romantic motives that may have driven people to become anthropologists (vol. 6, *Romantic Motives: Essays on Anthropological Sensibility*).

12

Communication and Language

*F*ew of us can remember when we first became aware that words signified something. Yet that moment was a milestone for us, not just in the acquisition of language but in becoming acquainted with all the complex, elaborate behavior that constitutes our culture. Without language, the transmission of complex traditions would be virtually impossible, and each person would be trapped within his or her own world of private sensations.

Helen Keller, left deaf and blind by illness at the age of 19 months, gives a moving account of the afternoon she first established contact with another human being through words:

> [My teacher] brought me my hat, and I knew I was going out into the warm sunshine. This thought, if a wordless sensation may be called a thought, made me hop and skip with pleasure.
>
> We walked down the path to the well house, attracted by the fragrance of the honeysuckle with which it was covered. Someone was drawing water and my teacher placed my hand under the spout. As the cool stream gushed over one hand she spelled into the other the word *water,* first slowly, then rapidly. Suddenly I felt a misty consciousness as of something forgotten—a thrill of returning thought; and somehow the mystery of language was revealed to me. I knew then that w-a-t-e-r meant the wonderful cool something that was flowing over my hand. That living word awakened my soul, gave it light, hope, joy, set it free! There were barriers still, it is true, barriers that could in time be swept away.
>
> I left the well house eager to learn. Everything had a name, and each name gave birth to a new thought. As we returned to the house every object which I touched seemed to quiver with life. That was because I saw everything with the strange, new sight that had come to me.[1]

▦ COMMUNICATION

Against all odds, Helen Keller had come to understand the essential function that language plays in all societies—namely, that of communication. The word *communicate* comes from the Latin verb *communicare,* "to share," "to impart that which is common."* We communicate by agreeing, consciously or unconsciously, to call an object, a movement, or an abstract concept by a common name. For example, speakers of English have agreed to call the color of grass green, even though we have no way of comparing precisely how two persons actually experience this color. What we share is the agreement to call similar sensations *green.* Any system of language consists of publicly accepted symbols by which individuals try to share private experiences.

Obviously, our communication is not limited to spoken language. We communicate directly through facial expression, body stance, gesture, and tone of voice and indirectly through systems of signs and symbols, such as writing, algebraic equations, musical scores, painting, code flags, and road signs. As we all know from experience, the spoken word does not communicate all that we know about a social situation. We can usually tell when someone says, "It was good to meet you," whether they really mean it. We can tell if they are sad from their demeanor, even if they just said, "I'm fine," in response to a question "How are you?" The cues are sometimes tone of voice, and sometimes they are not sound cues at all, but facial expressions, eye contact, or other body language.

There is an increasing amount of research on nonlinguistic communication. Much of this communication may be universal. For instance, humans the world over appear to understand facial expressions in the same way; that is, they are able to recognize a happy, sad, surprised, angry, disgusted, or afraid face. But much of this communication is also culturally variable. In the chapter on the concept of culture, we discussed how the distance between people standing together is culturally variable. In the realm of facial expression, different cultures have different rules about the emotions that are acceptable to express. One study compared how Japanese and Americans express emotion. Individuals from both groups were videotaped while they were shown films intended to evoke feelings of fear and disgust. When the subjects saw the films by themselves,

It is easy to recognize basic human emotions cross-culturally, as is clear in this South Indian woman's face.

without other people present, they showed the same kinds of facial expressions of fear and disgust. But there was a cultural effect too. When an authority figure was present during the videotaping, the Japanese subjects tried to mask their negative feelings with a half-smile more often than did the Americans.[2]

Despite all the various systems of communication available to us, we must recognize the overriding importance of spoken language. It is probably the major transmitter of culture, allowing us to share and pass on our complex configuration of attitudes, beliefs, and patterns of behavior.

NONHUMAN COMMUNICATION

Systems of communication are not unique to human beings. Other animal species communicate in a variety of ways. One way is by sound. A bird may communicate by a call that "this is my territory"; a squirrel may utter a cry that leads other squirrels to flee from danger. Another means of animal communication is odor. An ant releases a chemical when it dies, and its fellows then carry it away to the compost heap. Apparently the communication is highly effective; a healthy ant painted with the death chemical will be dragged to the funeral heap again and again. Another means of communication, body movement, is used by bees to convey the location of food sources. Karl von Frisch discovered that the black Austrian honey bee—by choosing a round dance, a wagging dance, or a short, straight run—can communicate not only the precise direction of the source of food but also its distance from the hive.[3]

Although primates use all three methods of communication—sound, odor, and body movement—sound is the method that most concerns us in this chapter because spoken language is human beings' major means of communication. Nonhuman primates communicate vocally too, making various kinds of calls (but not very many of them). In the past, only human communication was thought to be symbolic. Recent research suggests that some monkey and ape calls in the wild are also symbolic.

When we say that a communication (call, word, sentence) is *symbolic,* we mean at least two things. First, the communication has meaning even when its referent (whatever is referred to) is not present. Second, the meaning is arbitrary; the receiver of the message could not guess its meaning just from the sound(s) and does not know the meaning instinctively. In other words, symbols have to be learned. There is no compelling or "natural" reason that the

word *dog* in English should refer to a smallish four-legged omnivore that is the bane of letter carriers.

Vervet monkeys in Africa are not as closely related to humans as are African apes. Nevertheless, scientists who have observed vervet monkeys in their natural environment consider at least three of their alarm calls to be symbolic because each of them *means* (refers to) a different kind of predator—eagles, pythons, or leopards—and monkeys react differently to each call. For example, they look up when they hear the "eagle" call. Experimentally, in the absence of the referent, investigators have been able to evoke the normal reaction to a call by playing it back electronically. Another indication that the vervet alarm calls are symbolic is that infant vervets appear to need some time to learn the referent for each. When they are very young, infants apply a particular call to more animals than adult vervets apply the call to. So, for example, infant vervets will often make the eagle warning call when they see any flying bird. The infants learn the appropriate referent apparently through adult vervets' repetition of infants' "correct" calls; in any case, the infants gradually learn to restrict the call to eagles. This process is probably not too different from the way a North American infant in an English-speaking family first applies the "word" *dada* to all adult males and gradually learns to restrict it to one person.[4]

All of the nonhuman vocalizations we have described so far enable individual animals to convey messages. The sender gives a signal that is received and "decoded" by the receiver, who usually responds with a specific action or reply. How is human vocalization different? Since monkeys and apes appear to use symbols at least some of the time, it is not appropriate to emphasize symbolism as the distinctive feature of human language. However, there is a significant quantitative difference between human language and other primates' systems of vocal communication. All human languages employ a much larger set of symbols. Another and perhaps more important difference is that the other primates' vocal systems tend to be *closed;* different calls are not often combined to produce new, meaningful utterances. In contrast, human languages are *open* systems, governed by complex rules about how sounds and sequences of sounds can be combined to produce an infinite variety of new meanings.[5]

The idea that humans can transmit many more complex messages than any other animal does not begin to convey how different human language is from other communication systems. No chimpanzee could say the equivalent of "I'm going to the ball game next Wednesday with my friend Jim if it's not raining." Humans not only can talk (and think) with language about things completely out of context; they also can be deliberately or unconsciously ambiguous in their messages. If a person asks you for help, you could say, "Sure, I'll do it when I have time," leaving the other person uncertain about whether your help is ever going to materialize.

Primates in the wild do not exhibit anything close to human language. But recent successful attempts to teach apes to communicate with humans and with each other using human-created signs have led some scholars to question the traditional assumption that the gap between human and other animal communication is enormous. Even the bird brain of a parrot named Alex seems to be capable of some symbolic communication. When he is not willing to continue a training session, Alex says: "I'm sorry . . . Wanna go back."[6] Chimpanzees Washoe and Nim and the gorilla Koko were taught hand signs based on American Sign Language (ASL; used by the hearing impaired in the United States). The chimpanzee Sarah was trained with plastic symbols, but more recently Lana, Sherman, Austin, and a pygmy chimpanzee, Kanzi, have been trained on symbol keyboards connected to computers. Sherman and Austin began to communicate with each other about actions they were intending to do, such as the types of tools they needed to solve a problem. And they were able to classify items into categories, such as "food" and "tools." In contrast to other apes, Kanzi learned symbols just

by seeing humans point to them when they spoke to him. He did not need rewards or to have his hands put in the right position. And he understood a great deal of what was spoken to him. For example, when he was 5 years old, Kanzi heard someone talk about throwing a ball in the river, and he turned around and did so. Kanzi has come closest of all the "students" to having a primitive English grammar when he strings symbols together.[7] If chimpanzees and other primates have the capacity to *use* nonspoken language and even to understand spoken language, then the difference between humans and nonhumans may not be as great as people used to think.

Are these apes really using language? There is a lot of agreement among investigators that nonhuman primates have the ability to "symbol"—to refer to something (or a class of things) with an arbitrary "label" (gesture or sequence of sounds).[8] For example, the gorilla Koko (with a repertoire of about 375 signs) extended the sign for *drinking straw* to plastic tubing, hoses, cigarettes, and radio antennae. Washoe originally learned the sign *dirty* to refer to feces and other soil and then began to use it insultingly, as in "dirty Roger," when her trainer Roger Fouts refused to give her things she wanted. Even the mistakes made by the apes suggest that they are using signs symbolically, just as words are used in spoken language. For example, the sign *cat* may be used for dog if the animal learned *cat* first (just as our daughter Kathy said "dog" to all pictures of four-footed animals, including elephants, when she was 18 months old).

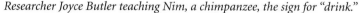

Researcher Joyce Butler teaching Nim, a chimpanzee, the sign for "drink."

In spite of the new evidence, Jane Hill believes that the answer about whether apes use language is still controversial because language is not one unitary thing. For instance, when we discuss the structure of sounds (phonology) later in this chapter, we will see that every human language has certain ways of combining sounds and ways of *not* combining those sounds. Although apes do not use sounds, the combination of symbols can be thought of as analogous to the combining of sound elements. Yet there does not appear to be anything comparable to linguistic rules for allowed and not allowed combinations. Another major difference is that humans have many kinds of discourse. Humans may make lists and speeches, tell stories, argue, and recite poetry. Apes do none of those things. But apes do have some of the capacities for some of the elements of human language. Therefore, understanding their capacities may help us better understand the evolution of human language.[9]

THE ORIGINS OF LANGUAGE

How long humans have had spoken language is not known. Some think that the earliest *Homo sapiens,* perhaps 100,000 years ago, may have had the beginnings of language. Others believe that language developed more recently. Most speculation about the origins of language has centered on the question of how natural selection may have favored the open quality of language. All known human languages are "open" in the sense that utterances can be combined in various ways to produce new meanings.[10] Somehow a call system of communication was eventually changed to a system based on small units of sound that can be put together in many different ways to form meaningful utterances. For example, an English speaker can combine *care* and *full* (*careful*) to mean one thing, then use each of the two elements in other combinations to mean different things. *Care* can be used to make *carefree, careless,* or *caretaker; full* can be used to make *powerful* or *wonderful.* And because language is a system of shared symbols, it can be re-formed into an infinite variety of expressions and be understood by all who share these symbols. In this way, for example, T. S. Eliot could form a sentence never before formed— "In the room the women come and go/talking of Michelangelo"[11]—and the sense of his sentence, though not necessarily his private meaning, could be understood by all speakers of English.

One set of theoreticians of grammar suggests that there may be a *language-acquisition device* in the brain, as innate to humans as call systems are to other animals.[12] As the forebrain evolved, this device may have become part of our biological inheritance. Whether the device in fact exists is not clear. But we do know that the actual development of individual language is not completely biologically determined; if it were, all human beings would speak the same brain-generated language. Instead, about 4,000 to 5,000 mutually unintelligible languages have been identified. More than 2,000 of them were still spoken as of recently, most by peoples who did not traditionally have a system of writing. Indeed, the earliest writing systems are not that old; they appeared only about 5,000 years ago.[13]

Can we learn anything about the origins of language by studying the languages of nonliterate and technologically simpler societies? The answer is no, because such languages are not simpler or less developed than ours. The sound systems, vocabularies, and grammars of technologically simpler peoples are in no way inferior to those of peoples with more complex technology.[14] Of course, people in other societies, and even some people in our own society, will not be able to name the sophisticated machines used in our society. All languages, however, have the potential for doing so. As we will see later in this chapter, all languages possess the amount of vocabulary their speakers need, and all languages expand in response to cultural changes. A language that lacks terminology for some of our conveniences may have a rich vocabulary for events or natural phenomena that are of particular importance to the people in that society.

If there are no primitive languages, and if the earliest languages have left no traces that would allow us to reconstruct them, does that mean we cannot investigate the origins of language? Some linguists think that understanding the way children acquire language, which we discuss shortly, can help us understand the origins of language. Recently, other linguists have suggested that an understanding of how *creole* languages develop will also tell us something about the origins of language.

CREOLE LANGUAGES

Some languages developed in various areas where European colonial powers established commercial enterprises that relied on imported labor, generally slaves. The laborers in one place often came from several different societies and in the beginning would speak with their masters and with each other in some kind of *pidgin* (simplified) version of the masters' language. Pidgin languages lack many of

Applied Anthropology

CAN LANGUAGES BE KEPT FROM EXTINCTION?

Not only animal and plant species are endangered; many peoples and their languages are too. In the last few hundred years, and continuing in some places today, Western expansion and colonization have led to the depopulation and extinction of many native societies, mainly as a result of introduced disease and campaigns of extermination. Thus, many languages disappeared with the peoples that spoke them. More than 50 aboriginal languages in Australia of approximately 200 disappeared relatively quickly as a result of massacre and disease.

Today native languages are endangered more by the fact that they are not being passed on to children. Political and economic dominance by speakers of Western languages undoubtedly plays an enormous role in this process. First, schooling is usually conducted in the dominant language. Second, when another culture is dominant, the children themselves may prefer to speak in the language perceived to have higher prestige; indeed, parents sometimes encourage this ten-

dency. It is estimated that by the year 2000 almost all the languages of aboriginal Australia will be gone. This is a worldwide trend. Michael Krauss, a linguist who tracks disappearing languages, estimates that 90 percent of the world's languages are endangered. Here is another example: Only 2 of the 20 native Alaskan languages are currently being taught to children, who therefore speak English only.

What can be done? Krauss, who is particularly interested in native Alaskan languages, is trying to do something. With help from the state government of Alaska, Krauss is developing materials on native languages to help teachers promote bilingual education as a way of preserving native languages. A very different approach has been taken by H. Russell Bernard, who believes that "to keep a language truly alive we must produce authors." With the help of computer technology, which allows reconfiguring a keyboard to produce special characters for sounds, Bernard has taught native speakers to

write their native languages directly on computers. These texts then become the basis for dictionaries. So far, more than 80 people, speaking 12 endangered languages, have become authors in Mexico and South America. Although these authors may not be using the standardized characters used by linguists to represent sounds, they are producing "written" materials that might otherwise be lost forever. These texts provide more than just information about language. In their works the authors convey ideas about curing illness, acquiring food, raising children, and settling disputes.

We are not sure when humans first developed spoken language. But the enormous linguistic diversity on this planet took a long time to develop. Unfortunately, it may take only a short time for that diversity to become a thing of the past.

Sources: Seth Shulman, "Nurturing Native Tongues," *Technology Review,* May/June 1993, 16; Janet Holmes, *An Introduction to Sociolinguistics* (London: Longman, 1992), pp. 61–62.

---

the building blocks found in the languages of whole societies, building blocks such as prepositions (*to, on,* and so forth) and auxiliary verbs (designating future and other tenses). Many pidgin languages developed into and were replaced by so-called *creole languages,* which incorporate much of the vocabulary of the masters' language but also have a grammar that differs from it and from the grammars of the laborers' native languages.[15]

Derek Bickerton argues that there are striking grammatical similarities in creole languages throughout the world. This similarity, he thinks, is consistent with the idea that there is a universal

grammar inherited by all humans. Creole languages, therefore, may resemble early human languages. All creoles use intonation instead of a change in word order to ask a question. The creole equivalent of the question "Can you fix this?" would be "You can fix this?" The creole version puts a rising inflection at the end; in contrast, the English version reverses the subject and verb without much inflection at the end. All creoles express the future and the past in the same grammatical way, by the use of particles (such as the English *shall*) between subject and verb, and they all employ double negatives, as in the Guyana English creole "Nobody no like me."[16]

It is possible that there are many things about language that are universal, that all languages are similar in many respects, because of the way humans are "wired" or because people in all societies have similar experiences. For example, names for frogs may usually contain *r* sounds because frogs make them.[17]

CHILDREN'S ACQUISITION OF LANGUAGE

Apparently a child is equipped from birth with the capacity to reproduce all the sounds used by the world's languages and to learn any system of grammar. The language the child learns is the one spoken by the parents or caretakers.

Children's acquisition of the structure and meaning of language has been called the most difficult intellectual achievement in life. If that is so, it is pleasing to note that they accomplish it with relative ease and vast enjoyment. This "difficult intellectual achievement" may in reality be a natural response to the capacity for language that is one of humans' genetic characteristics. All over the world children begin to learn language at about the same age, and in no culture do children wait until they are 7 or 10 years old. By 12 or 13 months of age, children are able to name a few objects and actions, and by 18 to 20 months they can make one key word stand for a whole sentence: "Out!" for "Take me out for a walk right now"; "Juice!" for "I want some juice now." Evidence suggests that children acquire the concept of a word as a whole, learning sequences of sounds that are stressed or at the ends of words (for example, "raffe" for giraffe). Even hearing impaired children learning signs in ASL tend to acquire and use signs in a similar fashion.[18]

Children the world over tend to progress to two-word sentences at the age of about 18 to 24 months. In their sentences they express themselves in "telegraph" form—using nounlike words and verblike words but leaving out the seemingly less important words. So a two-word sentence such as "Shoes off" may stand for "Take my shoes off" or "More milk" may stand for "Give me more milk, please."[19] They do not utter their two words in random order, sometimes saying "off " first, other times saying "shoes" first. If a child says "Shoes off," then he or she will also say "Clothes off " and "Hat off." They seem to select an order that fits the conventions of adult language, so they are likely to say "Daddy eat," not "Eat Daddy." In other words, they tend to put the subject first, as adults do. And they tend to say "Mommy coat" rather than "Coat Mommy" to indi-

A young girl displays her knowledge of words by pointing at pictures.

cate "Mommy's coat."[20] Parents do not utter sentences such as "Daddy eat," so children seem to know a lot about how to put words together with little or no direct teaching from their parents. Consider the 5-year-old who, confronted with the unfamiliar "Gloria in Excelsis," sings quite happily, "Gloria eats eggshells." To make the words fit the structure of English grammar is more important than to make the words fit the meaning of the Christmas pageant.

If there is a basic grammar imprinted in the human mind, we should not be surprised that children's early and later speech patterns seem to be similar in different languages. We might also expect children's later speech to be similar to the structure of creole languages. And it is, according to Derek Bickerton.[21] The "errors" children make in speaking are consistent with the grammar of creoles. For example, English-speaking children 3 to 4 years old tend to ask questions by intonation alone, and they tend to use double negatives, such as "I don't see no dog," even though the adults around them do not speak that way and consider the children's speech "wrong."

Future research on children's acquisition of language and on the structure of creole languages may bring us closer to understanding the origins of human language. But even if there is a universal grammar, we still need to understand how and why the thousands of languages in the world vary, which brings us to the conceptual tools linguists have had to invent in order to study languages.

STRUCTURAL LINGUISTICS

In every society children do not need to be taught "grammar" to learn how to speak. They begin to grasp the essential structure of their language at a very early age, without direct instruction. If you show English-speaking children a picture of one "gork" and then a picture of two of these creatures, they will say there are two "gorks." Somehow they know that adding an *s* to a noun means more than one. But they do not know this consciously, and adults may not either. One of the most surprising features of human language is that meaningful sounds and sound sequences are combined according to rules that often are not consciously known by the speakers.

These rules should not be equated with the "rules of grammar" you were taught in school so that you would speak "correctly." Rather, when linguists talk about rules, they are referring to the patterns of speaking that are discoverable in actual speech. Needless to say, there is some overlap between the actual rules of speaking and the rules taught in school. But there are rules that children never hear about in school, because their teachers are not linguists and are not aware of them. When linguists use the term *grammar,* they are *not* referring to the prescriptive rules that people are supposed to follow in speaking. Rather, *grammar* to the linguist consists of the actual, often unconscious principles that predict how most people talk. As we have noted, young children may speak two-word sentences that conform to a linguistic rule, but their speech is hardly considered "correct."

Discovering the mostly unconscious rules operating in a language is a very difficult task. Linguists have had to invent special concepts and methods of transcription (writing) to permit them to describe: (1) what the rules or principles are that predict how sounds are made and how they are used (often, slightly varying sounds are used interchangeably in words without creating a difference in meaning); (2) how sound sequences (and sometimes even individual sounds) convey meaning and how meaningful sound sequences are strung together to form words; and (3) how words are strung together to form phrases and sentences. Thus, **structural, or descriptive, linguistics** tries to discover the rules of **phonology**—the patterning of sounds—

morphology—the patterning of sound sequences to form meaningful units—and **syntax**—the patterning of phrases and sentences—that predict how most speakers of a language talk.

Understanding the language of another people is an essential part of understanding the culture of that people. Although sometimes what people say is contradicted by their observed behavior, there is little doubt that it is hard to understand the beliefs, attitudes, values, and worldview of a people without understanding their language and the nuances of how that language is used. Even behavior, which theoretically one can observe without understanding language, usually cannot be readily understood without interpretation. Imagine that you see people go by a certain rock and seemingly walk out of their way to avoid it. Suppose they believe that an evil spirit resides there. How could you possibly know that without being able to ask and to understand their answer?

PHONOLOGY

Most of us have had the experience of trying to learn another language and finding that some sounds are exceedingly difficult to make. Although the human vocal tract theoretically can make a very large number of different sounds—**phones** to linguists—each language uses only some of them. It is not that we cannot make the sounds that are strange to us; we just have not acquired the habit of making those sounds. And until the sounds become habitual for us, they continue to be difficult to form.

Finding it difficult to make certain sounds is only one of the reasons we have trouble learning a "foreign" language. Another problem is that we may not be used to combining certain sounds or making a certain sound in a particular position in a word. Thus, English speakers find it difficult to combine *z* and *d,* as Russian speakers often do (because we never do so in English), or to pronounce words in Samoan, a South Pacific language, that begin with the sound English speakers write as *ng,* even though we have no trouble putting that sound at the end of words, as in the English *sing* and *hitting.*

In order to study the patterning of sounds, linguists who are interested in *phonology* have to write down speech utterances as sequences of sound. This task would be almost impossible if linguists were restricted to using their own alphabet (say, the one we use to write English), because other languages use sounds that are difficult to represent with the English alphabet or because the alphabet we use in English can represent a particular sound in different ways. (English writing represents the sound *f* by *f* as in *food*, but also as *gh* in *tough* and *ph* in *phone*.) In addition, in English different sounds may be represented by the same letter. English has 26 letters but more than 40 significant sounds (sounds that can change the meaning of a word).[22] To overcome these difficulties in writing sounds with the letters of existing writing systems, linguists have developed systems of transcription with special alphabets in which each symbol represents only one particular sound.

Once linguists have identified the sounds or phones used in a language, they try to identify which sounds affect meaning and which sounds do not. One way is to start with a simple word like *lake* and change the first sound to *r* to make the word *rake*. The linguist will ask if this new combination of sounds means the same thing. An English speaker would say *lake* means something completely different from *rake*. These minimal contrasts enable linguists to identify a **phoneme** in a language—a sound or set of sounds that makes a difference in meaning in that language.[23] So the sound *l* in *lake* is different phonemically from the the sound *r* in *rake*. The ways in which sounds are grouped together into phonemes vary from language to language. We are so used to phonemes in our own language that it may be hard to believe that the contrast between *r* and *l* may not make a difference in meaning in some languages. For example, in Samoan, *l* and *r* can be used interchangeably in a word without changing the meaning (therefore, these two sounds belong to the same phoneme in Samoan.) So Samoan speakers may say "Leupena" sometimes and "Reupena" at other times when they are referring to someone who in English would be called "Reuben."

English speakers may joke about languages that "confuse" *l* and *r*, but they are not usually aware that we do the same thing with other sets of sounds. For example, in English, the word we spell *and* may be pronounced quite differently by two different English speakers without changing the meaning, and no one would think that a different word was spoken. We can pronounce the *a* in *and* as in the beginning of the word *air*, or we can pronounce it as the *a* in *bat*. If you say those varying *a* sounds and try to think about how you are forming them in your mouth, you will realize that they are two different sounds. English speakers might recognize a slight difference in pronunciation but pay little or no attention to it because the two ways to pronounce the *a* in *and* do not change the meaning. Now think about *l* and *r*. If you form them in your mouth, you will notice that they are only slightly dif-

ferent with respect to how far the tongue is from the ridge behind the upper front teeth. Languages do tend to group sounds that are close into the same phoneme, but why they choose some sounds and not others to group together is not yet fully understood.

Some recent research suggests that infants may learn early to ignore meaningless variations of sound (those that are part of the same phoneme) in the language they hear at home. It turns out that as early as 6 months of age, infants "ignore" sound shifts within the same phoneme of their own language, but they "hear" a sound shift within the phoneme of another language. Researchers are not sure how babies learn to make the distinction, but they seem to acquire much of the phonology of their language very early indeed.[24]

After discovering which sounds are grouped into phonemes, linguists can begin to discover the sound sequences that are allowed in a language and the usually unconscious rules that predict those sequences. For example, words in English rarely start with three nonvowel sounds. But when they do, the first sound or phone is always an *s*, as in *strike* and *scratch*.[25] (Some other words in English may start with three consonants but only two sounds are involved, as in *chrome* where the *ch* stands for the sound in *k*.) Linguists' descriptions of the patterning of sounds (phonology) in different languages may allow them to investigate why languages vary in their sound rules.

Why, for example, are two or more consonants strung together in some languages, whereas in other languages vowels are always put between consonants? The Samoan language now has a word for "Christmas" borrowed from English, but the borrowed word has been changed to fit the rules of Samoan. In the English word, two consonants come first, *k* and *r*, which we spell as *ch* and *r*. The Samoan word is *Kerisimasi* (pronounced as if it were spelled Keh-ree-see-mah-see). It has a vowel after each consonant, or five consonant-vowel syllables.

Why do some languages like Samoan alternate consonants and vowels more or less regularly? Recent cross-cultural research suggests three predictors of this variation. One predictor is a warmer climate. Where people live in warmer climates, the typical syllable is likely to be a consonant-vowel syllable. Linguists have found that consonant-vowel syllables provide the most contrast in speech. Perhaps when people converse outdoors at a distance, which they are likely to do in a warmer climate, they need more contrast between sounds to be understood. A second predictor of consonant-vowel alternation is literacy. Languages that are written have fewer consonant-vowel syllables. If communication is often in written form, meaning does not have to depend so much on contrast between adjacent sounds. A third predictor of consonant-vowel alternation is the degree to which babies are held by others. Societies with a great deal of baby-holding have a lot of consonant-vowel syllables. Later, in the chapter on the arts, you will read about research that relates baby-holding to a societal preference for regular rhythm in music. The theory is that when babies are held much of the day on a person, they begin to associate regular rhythm with pleasurable experiences. The baby senses the regular rhythm of the caretaker's heartbeats or the caretaker's rhythmic work, and the reward value of that experience generalizes to a preference for all regular rhythms in adult life, including regular consonant-vowel alternation in adult speech. Compare the rhythm of the Samoan word *Kerisimasi* with the English word *Christmas*.[26]

MORPHOLOGY

A phoneme in a language usually does not mean something by itself. Usually phonemes are combined with other phonemes to form a meaningful set of sounds. *Morphology* is the study of meaningful sets of sounds in a language. Often these meaningful sets of sounds make up what we call *words*, but words may be composed of a number of smaller meaningful units. We take our words so much for granted that we do not realize how complicated it is to say what words are. People do not usually pause between words when they speak; if we did not know our language, a sentence would seem like a continuous stream of sounds. This is how we first hear a foreign language. It is only when we understand the language and write down what we say that we separate (by spaces) what we call *words*. But a word is really only an arbitrary sequence of sounds that has a meaning; we would not "hear" words as separate units if we did not understand the language spoken.

Because anthropological linguists traditionally investigated unwritten languages, sometimes without the aid of interpreters, they had to figure out which sequences of sounds conveyed meaning. And because words in many languages can often be broken down into smaller meaningful units, linguists had to invent special words to refer to those units. Linguists call the smallest unit of language that has a meaning a **morph.** Just as a phoneme may have one or more phones, one or more morphs with

the same meaning may make up a **morpheme.** For example, the prefix *in-*, as in *indefinite*, and the prefix *un-*, as in *unclear*, are morphs that belong to the morpheme meaning *not*. Although some words are single morphs or morphemes (for example, *for* and *giraffe* in English), many words are built on a combination of morphs, generally prefixes, roots, and suffixes. Thus *cow* is one word, but the word *cows* contains two meaningful units—a root *(cow)* and a suffix (pronounced like *z*) meaning more than one. The **lexicon** of a language, which a dictionary approximates, consists of words and morphs and their meanings.

It seems likely that the intuitive grasp children have of the structure of their language includes a recognition of morphology. Once they learn that the morph */-z/* added to a noun-type word indicates more than one, they plow ahead with *mans, childs;* once they grasp that the morpheme class pronounced */-t/* or */-d/* or */-ed/* added to the end of a verb indicates that the action took place in the past, they apply that concept generally and invent *runned, drinked, costed*. They see a ball roll near*er* and near*er*, and they transfer that concept to a kite, which goes upp*er* and upp*er*. From their mistakes as well as their successes, we can see that they understand the regular uses of morphemes. By the age of 7, they have mastered many of the irregular forms as well—that is, they learn which morphs of a morpheme are used when.

The child's intuitive grasp of the dependence of some morphemes on others corresponds to the linguist's recognition of free morphemes and bound morphemes. A *free* morpheme has meaning standing alone—that is, it can be a separate word. A *bound* morpheme displays its meaning only when attached to another morpheme. The morph pronounced */-t/* of the bound morpheme meaning *past tense* is attached to the root *walk* to produce *walked;* but the */-t/* cannot stand alone or have meaning by itself.

In English, the meaning of an utterance (containing a subject, verb, object, and so forth) usually depends on the order of the words. "The dog bit the child" is different in meaning from "The child bit the dog." But in many other languages, the grammatical meaning of an utterance does not depend much, if at all, on the order of the words. Rather, meaning may be determined by how the morphs in a word are ordered. For example, in Luo, a language of East Africa, the same bound morpheme may mean the subject or object of an action. If the morpheme is the prefix to a verb, it means the subject; if it is the suffix to a verb, it means the object. Another way that grammatical meaning may be conveyed is by altering or adding a bound morpheme to a word to indicate what part of speech it is. For example, in Russian, the word for "mail" when it is the subject of a sentence is pronounced something like "pawchtah." When "mail" is used as the object of a verb, as in "I gave her the mail," the ending of the word changes to "pawchtoo." And if I say, "What was in the mail?" the word becomes "pawchtyeh."

Some languages have so many bound morphemes that they might express as a complex but single word what is considered a sentence in English. For example, the English sentence "He will give it to you" can be expressed in Wishram, a Chinookan dialect that was spoken along the Columbia River in the Pacific Northwest, as *acimluda* (a-c-i-m-l-ud-a, literally "will-he-him-thee-to-give-will"). Note that the pronoun *it* in English is gender-neutral; Wishram requires that *it* be given a gender, in this case, "him."[27]

SYNTAX

Because language is an open system, we can make up meaningful utterances that we have never heard before. We are constantly creating new phrases and sentences. Just as they do for morphology, speakers of a language seem to have an intuitive grasp of *syntax*—the rules that predict how phrases and sentences are generally formed. These "rules" may be partly learned in school, but children know many of them even before they get to school. In adulthood, our understanding of morphology and syntax is so intuitive that we can even understand a nonsense sentence, such as this famous one from Lewis Carroll's *Through the Looking Glass:*

> 'Twas brillig, and the slithy toves
> Did gyre and gimble in the wabe

Simply from the ordering of the words in the sentence, we can surmise which part of speech a word is, as well as its function in the sentence. *Brillig* is an adjective; *slithy* an adjective; *toves* a noun and the subject of the sentence; *gyre* and *gimble* verbs; and *wabe* a noun and the object of a prepositional phrase. Of course, an understanding of morphology helps too. The *-y* ending in *slithy* is an indication that the latter is an adjective, and the *-s* ending in *toves* tells us that we most probably have more than one of these creatures.

In addition to producing and understanding an infinite variety of sentences, speakers of a language can tell when a sentence is not "correct" without consulting grammar books. For example, an English speaker can tell that "Child the dog the hit" is not an acceptable sentence but "The child hit the dog" is fine. There must, then, be a set of rules underlying how phrases and sentences are constructed in a language.[28] Speakers of a language know these implicit rules of syntax but are not usually consciously aware of them. The linguist's description of the syntax of a language tries to make these rules explicit.

HISTORICAL LINGUISTICS

The field of **historical linguistics** focuses on how languages change over time. Written works provide the best data for establishing such changes. For example, the following passage from Chaucer's *Canterbury Tales,* written in the English of the fourteenth century, has recognizable elements but is different enough from modern English to require a translation.

> A Frere ther was, a wantowne and a merye,
> A lymytour, a ful solempne man.
> In alle the ordres foure is noon that kan
> So muche of daliaunce and fair language.
> He hadde maad ful many a mariage
> Of yonge wommen at his owene cost.
> Unto his ordre he was a noble post.
> Ful wel biloued and famulier was he
> With frankeleyns ouer al in his contree,
> And with worthy wommen of the toun;
> For he hadde power of confessioun,
> As seyde hymself, moore than a curat,
> For of his ordre he was licenciat.

> A Friar there was, wanton and merry,
> A limiter [a friar limited to certain districts], a full solemn [very important] man.
> In all the orders four there is none that knows
> So much of dalliance [flirting] and fair [engaging] language.
> He had made [arranged] many a marriage
> Of young women at his own cost.
> Unto his order he was a noble post [pillar].
> Full well beloved and familiar was he
> With franklins [wealthy landowners] all over his country
> And also with worthy women of the town;
> For he had power of confession,
> As he said himself, more than a curate,
> For of his order, he was a licentiate [licensed by the Pope].[29]

In this passage we can recognize several changes. Many words are spelled differently today, and in some cases, meaning has changed: *Full,* for example, would be translated today as *very.* What is less evident is that changes in pronunciation have occurred. For example, the g in *mariage* (marriage) was pronounced *zh,* as in the French from which it was borrowed, whereas now it is pronounced like either g in *George.*

Because languages spoken in the past leave no traces unless they were written, and most of the languages known to anthropology were not written by their speakers, you might guess that historical linguists can study linguistic change only by studying written languages such as English. But that is not the case. Linguists can reconstruct changes that have occurred by comparing contemporary languages that are very similar. Such languages show phonological, morphological, and syntactical similarities because they usually derive from a common ancestral language. For example, Romanian, Italian, French, Spanish, and Portuguese have many similarities. On the basis of these similarities, linguists can reconstruct what the ancestral language was like and how it changed into what we call the Romance languages. Of course, these reconstructions can easily be tested and confirmed because we know from many surviving writings what the ancestral language, Latin, was like; and we know from documents how Latin diversified as the Roman Empire expanded. Thus, common ancestry is frequently the reason why neighboring, and sometimes even separated, languages show patterns of similarity.

But languages can be similar for other reasons too. Contact between speech communities, often with one group dominant over another, may lead one language to borrow from the other. For example, English borrowed a lot of vocabulary from French after England was conquered by the French-speaking Normans in A.D. 1066. Languages may also show similarities even though they do not derive from a common ancestral language and even though there has been no contact or borrowing between them. Such similarities may reflect common or universal features of human cultures or human brains or both. (As we noted earlier in the chapter, the grammatical similarities exhibited by creole languages may reflect how the human brain is "wired.") Finally, even unrelated and separated languages may show some similarities because of the phenomenon of convergence; similarities can develop because some processes of linguistic change may have only a few possible outcomes.

Phonology and other elements of language, not just spelling, may change over time. The English written in the sixth century A.D., as in this Old English poem about a warrior named Beowulf, is hardly recognizable.

LANGUAGE FAMILIES AND CULTURE HISTORY

Latin is the ancestral language of the Romance languages. We know this from documentary (written) records. But if the ancestral language of a set of similar languages is not known from written records, linguists still can reconstruct many features of that language by comparing the derived languages. (Such a reconstructed language is called a **protolanguage.**) That is, by comparing presumably related languages, linguists can become aware of the features that many of them have in common, features that were probably found in the common ancestral language. The languages that derive from the same protolanguage are called a *language family.* Most languages spoken today can be grouped into fewer than 30 families. The language family English belongs to is called *Indo-European,* because it includes most of the languages of Europe and some of the languages of India. About 50 percent of the world's more than 4 billion people speak Indo-European languages.[30] Another very large language family, now spoken by more than a billion people, is Sino-Tibetan, which includes the languages of northern and southern China as well as those of Tibet and Burma.

The field of historical linguistics got its start in 1786 when a British scholar living in India, Sir William Jones, noticed similarities between Sanskrit, a language spoken and written in ancient India, and classical Greek, Latin, and more recent European languages.[31] In 1822, Jakob Grimm, one of the brothers Grimm of fairy-tale fame, formulated rules to describe the sound shifts that had occurred when the various Indo-European languages diverged from each other. So, for example, in English and the other languages in the Germanic branch of the Indo-European family, *d* regularly shifted to *t* (compare the English *two* and *ten* with the Latin *duo* and *decem*) and *p* regularly shifted to *f* (English *father* and *foot,* Latin *pater* and *pes*). Scholars generally agree that the Indo-European languages derive from a language spoken 5,000 to 6,000 years ago.[32] The ancestral Indo-European language, many of whose features have now been reconstructed, is called *proto-Indo-European,* or *PIE* for short. Table 12–1 shows the branches and existing languages of the family.

Where did PIE originate? Some linguists believe that the approximate location of a protolanguage is suggested by the words for plants and animals in the derived languages. More specifically, among these different languages, the words that are **cognates**— that is, words that are similar in sound and meaning—presumably refer to plants and animals that were present in the original homeland. So if we know where those animals and plants were located 5,000 to 6,000 years ago, we can guess where PIE people lived. Among all the cognates for trees in the Indo-European languages, Paul Friedrich has identified 18 that he believes were present in the eastern Ukraine in 3000 B.C. On this basis he suggests that the eastern Ukraine was the PIE homeland.[33] Also consistent with this hypothesis is the fact that the Balto-Slavic subfamily of Indo-European, which includes most of the languages in and around the former Soviet Union, has the most tree names (compared with other subfamilies) that are similar to the reconstructed form in proto-Indo-European.[34]

Marija Gimbutas thinks we can even identify the proto-Indo-Europeans archaeologically. She believes that the PIE people were probably the people associated with what is known as the Kurgan culture (5000–2000 B.C.), which spread out from the Ukraine around 3000 B.C. The Kurgan people were herders, raising horses, cattle, sheep, and pigs. They also relied on hunting and grain cultivation. Burials suggest differences in wealth and special status for men.[35] Why the Kurgan and linguistically similar people were able to expand to many places in Europe and the Near East is not yet clear. Some have suggested that horses and horse-drawn wagons and perhaps horseback riding provided important military advantages.[36] In any case, it is clear that many Kurgan cultural elements were distributed after 3000 B.C. over a wide area of the Old World.

Colin Renfrew disagrees with the notion that the Ukraine was the homeland of PIE. He thinks that PIE is 2,000–3,000 years older than Kurgan culture and that the PIE people lived in a different place. Renfrew locates the PIE homeland in eastern Anatolia (Turkey) in 6000–7000 B.C., and he suggests, on the basis of archaeological evidence, that the spread of Indo-European to Europe and what is now Iran, Afghanistan, and India accompanied the spread of farming to those areas.[37]

Just as some historical linguists and archaeologists have suggested when and where the PIE people may have lived originally and how they may have spread, other linguists and archaeologists have suggested culture histories for other language families. For example, the Bantu languages in Africa (spoken by perhaps 100 million people) form a subfamily of the larger Niger-Congo family of languages. Bantu speakers currently live in a wide band across the center of Africa and down the eastern and western sides of southern Africa. All of the Bantu languages presumably derive from people who spoke proto-Bantu. But where was their homeland?

LANGUAGE	BRANCH	LANGUAGE	BRANCH
Albanian	Albanian	Greek	Greek
Armenian	Armenian	Balachi	Indo-Iranian
Bulgarian	Balto-Slavic	Bengali	
Czech		Farsi (Persian)	
Latvian		Gujarati	
Lithuanian		Hindi	
Polish		Kati	
Russian		Kurdish	
Serbo-Croatian		Marathi	
Ukrainian		Pashto	
Breton	Celtic	Punjabi	
Irish (Gaelic)		Romany	
Welsh		Sinhalese	
Africaans	Germanic	Shina	
Danish		Urdu	
Dutch		Catalan	Italic
English		French	
German		Italian	
Icelandic		Portuguese	
Norwegian		Provençal	
Swedish		Romanian	
Yiddish		Sardinian	
		Spanish	

TABLE 12–1 *Branches and Existing Languages of the Indo-European Language Family*

Source: Adapted with permission of the publishers from Merritt Ruhlen, *A Guide to the World's Languages, Volume I: Classification* (Stanford, CA: Stanford University Press, 1987), pp. 293–94. © 1978, 1991 by the Board of Trustees of the Leland Stanford Junior University. Also with the permission of Edward Arnold Publishers.

As in the case of proto-Indo-European, different theories have been proposed. But most historical linguists now agree with Joseph Greenberg's suggestion that the origin of Bantu was in what is now the Middle Benue area of eastern Nigeria.[38] The point of origin is presumably where there is the greatest diversity of related languages and **dialects** (varying forms of a language); it is assumed that the place of origin has had the most time for linguistic diversity to develop, compared with an area only recently occupied by a related language. For example, England has more dialect diversity than New Zealand or Australia.

Why were the Bantu able to spread so widely over the last few thousand years? Anthropologists have only begun to guess.[39] Initially, the Bantu probably kept goats and practiced some form of agriculture and thereby were able to spread, displacing hunter-gatherers in the area. As the Bantu speakers expanded, they began to cultivate certain cereal crops and herd sheep and cattle. Around this time, after 1000 B.C., they also began to use and make iron tools, which may have given them significant advantages. In any case, by 1,500 to 2,000 years ago, Bantu speakers had spread throughout central Africa and into the northern reaches of southern Africa. But speakers of non-Bantu languages still live in eastern, southern, and southwestern Africa.

 THE PROCESSES OF LINGUISTIC DIVERGENCE

The historical or comparative linguist hopes to do more than record and date linguistic divergence. Just as the physical anthropologist may attempt to develop explanations for human variation, so the linguist investigates the possible causes of linguistic variation. Some of the divergence undoubtedly comes about gradually. When groups of people speaking the same language lose communication with one another because they become separated, either physically or socially, they begin to accumulate small changes in phonology, morphology, and syntax (which occur continuously in any language).

Eventually, if the separation continues, the former dialects of the same language will become separate languages; that is, they will become mutually unintelligible, as German and English now are.

Geographic barriers, such as large bodies of water, deserts, and mountains, may separate speakers of what was once the same language, but distance by itself can also produce divergence. For example, if we compare dialects of English in the British Isles, it is clear that the regions farthest away from each other are the most different linguistically (compare the northeast of Scotland and London).[40] In northern India, hundreds of semi-isolated villages and regions developed hundreds of local dialects. Today, the inhabitants of each village understand the dialects of the surrounding villages and, with a little more difficulty, the dialects of the next circle of villages. But slight dialect shifts accumulate village by village, and it seems as if different languages are being spoken at the opposite ends of the region, which are separated by more than a thousand miles.[41]

Even where there is little geographic separation there may still be a great deal of dialect differentiation because of social distance. So, for example, the spread of a linguistic feature may be halted by racial, religious, or social class differences that inhibit communication.[42] In the village of Khalapur in northern India, John Gumperz found substantial differences in speech between the Untouchables and other groups. Members of the Untouchables have work contacts with members of other groups, but no friendships.[43] Without friendships and the easy communication between friends, dialect differentiation can readily develop.

Whereas isolation brings gradual divergence between speech communities, contact results in greater resemblance. This effect is particularly evident when contact between mutually unintelligible languages introduces *borrowed* words, which usually name some new item borrowed from the other culture—*tomato, canoe, sushi*, and so on. Bilingual groups within a culture may also introduce foreign words, especially when the mainstream language has no real equivalent. Thus, *salsa* has come into English, and *le weekend* into French.

Conquest and colonization often result in extensive and rapid borrowing, if not linguistic replacement. The Norman conquest of England introduced French as the language of the new aristocracy. It was 300 years before the educated classes began to write in English. During this time the English borrowed words from French and Latin, and the two languages—English and French—became more alike than they would otherwise have been. About 50 percent of the English general vocabulary originated in French. As this example suggests, different social classes may react to language contact differentially. For example, English aristocrats eventually called their meat "pork" and "beef" (derived from the French words), but the people who raised the animals and prepared them for eating continued (at least for a while) to refer to the meat as "pig" and "bull," the original Anglo-Saxon words.

In those 300 years of extensive contact, the grammar of English remained relatively stable. English lost most of its inflections or case endings, but it adopted little of the French grammar. In general, the borrowing of words, particularly free morphemes,[44] is much more common than the borrowing of grammar.[45] As we might expect, borrowing by one language from another can make the borrowing language more different from its *sibling languages* (those derived from a common ancestral language) than it would otherwise be. Partly as a result of the French influence, the English vocabulary looks quite different from the languages to which it is actually most similar in terms of phonology and grammar—German, Dutch, and the Scandinavian languages.

If languages simply diverged gradually, we would expect to find many language families and many languages in small areas. Such appears to be the case among the aboriginal languages of northern Australia. But in some areas of the world there are very widespread language families. How, for example, did Indo-European languages become so widespread? Although we cannot be sure what happened in the Indo-European case, it is possible that the ancestral population (and descendants of that population) did expand by military means.[46] Military expansion and conquest can have profound linguistic consequences, much more than simply borrowing some vocabulary, as English did from French. For one population may replace another, effectively killing off a language. Conquest can also result in enormous pressure on the conquered to learn and use the language of the superiors. Once children stop being taught their native language, that language cannot survive for long.

RELATIONSHIPS BETWEEN LANGUAGE AND CULTURE

Some attempts to explain the diversity of languages have focused on the possible interactions between language and other aspects of culture. On the one hand, if it can be shown that a culture can affect the structure and content of its language, then it would follow that linguistic diversity derives at least in part from cultural diversity. On the other hand, the direction of influence between culture and language might work in reverse: Linguistic features and structures might affect other aspects of the culture.

CULTURAL INFLUENCES ON LANGUAGE

One way a society's language may reflect its corresponding culture is in **lexical content,** or vocabulary. Which experiences, events, or objects are singled out and given words may be a result of cultural characteristics.

BASIC WORDS FOR COLORS, PLANTS, AND ANIMALS. Early in this century many linguists pointed to the lexical domain (vocabulary) of color words to illustrate the supposed truth that languages vary arbitrarily or without apparent reason. Different languages not only had different numbers of basic color words (from 2 to 12 or so; for example, the words red, green, and blue in English), but they also, it was thought, had no consistency in the way they classified or divided the colors of the spectrum. But findings from a comparative (cross-linguistic) study contradicted these traditional presumptions about variation in the number and meaning of basic color words. On the basis of their study of at first 20 and later over 100 languages, Brent Berlin and Paul Kay found that languages did not encode color in completely arbitrary ways.[47]

Although different languages do have different numbers of basic color words, most speakers of any language are very likely to point to the same color chips as the best representatives of particular colors. For example, people the world over mean more or less the same color when they are asked to select the best "red." Moreover, there appears to be a nearly universal sequence by which basic color words are added to a language.[48] If a language has just two basic color words, its speakers will always refer to "black" (or dark) hues and "white" (or light) hues. If a language has three basic color words, the third word will nearly always be "red." The next category to appear is either "yellow" or "grue" (green/blue); then different words for green and blue; and so on. To be sure, we usually do not see the process by which basic color words are added to a language. But we can infer the usual sequence because, for example, if a language has a word for "yellow," it will almost always have a word for "red," whereas having a word for "red" does not mean that the language will have a word for "yellow."

What exactly is a *basic* color word? All languages, even the ones with only two basic color terms, have many different ways of expressing how color varies. For example, in English we have words such as turquoise, blue-green, scarlet, crimson, and sky blue. Linguists do not consider these to be basic color words. In English the basic color words are *white, black, red, green, yellow, blue, brown, pink, purple, orange,* and *gray.* One feature of a basic color word is that it consists of a single morph; it cannot include two or more units of meaning. This feature eliminates combinations such as *blue-green* and *sky blue.* A second feature of a basic color word is that the color it represents is not generally included in a higher-order color term. For example, scarlet and crimson are usually considered variants of red, turquoise a variant of blue. A third feature is that basic terms tend to be the first-named words when people are asked for color words. Finally, for a word to be considered a basic color word, many individual speakers of the language have to agree on the central meaning (in the color spectrum) of the word.[49]

Why do different societies (languages) vary in number of basic color terms? Berlin and Kay suggest that the number of basic color terms in a language increases with technological specialization as color is used to decorate and distinguish objects.[50] Cross-linguistic variation in the number of basic color terms does not mean that some languages make more color distinctions than others. Every language could make a particular distinction by combining words (for example, "fresh leaf" for green); a language need not have a separate basic term for that color.

There may also be many basic color terms because of a biological factor.[51] Peoples with darker (more pigmented) eyes seem to have more trouble distinguishing colors at the dark (blue-green) end of the spectrum than do peoples with lighter eyes. It might be expected, then, that peoples who live nearer the equator (who tend to have darker eyes, presumably for protection against damaging ultraviolet radiation) would tend to have fewer basic color terms. And they do.[52] Moreover, it seems that both cultural and biological factors are required to account for cross-linguistic variation in the number of basic color terms. Societies tend to have six or more such terms (with separate terms for blue and green) only when they are relatively far from the equator and only when their cultures are more technologically specialized.[53] As we will see in later chapters, technological specialization tends to go with larger communities, more centralized governments, occupational specialization, and more social inequality. Societies with such traits are often referred to in a shorthand way as more "complex," which should not be taken to mean "better."

Echoing Berlin and Kay's finding that basic color terms seem to be added in a more or less universal sequence, other researchers have found what seem to be developmental sequences in other lexical domains. Two such domains are general, or *life-form,* terms for plants and for animals. Life-form terms are higher-order classifications. All languages have lower-order terms for specific plants and animals. For example, English has words such as *oak* and *pine, sparrow* and *salmon.* English speakers make finer distinctions too—*pin oak* and *white pine, white-throated sparrow* and *red salmon.* But why in some languages do people have a larger number of general terms such as *tree, bird,* and *fish?* It seems that these general terms show a universal developmental sequence too. That is, general terms seem to be added in a somewhat consistent order. After "plant" comes a term for "tree"; then one for "grerb" (small, green, leafy, nonwoody plant); then "bush" (for plants between tree and grerb in size); then "grass"; then "vine."[54] The life-form terms for animals seem also to be added in sequence; after "animal" comes a term for "fish," then "bird," then "snake," then "wug" (for small creatures other than fish, birds, and snakes—for example, worms and bugs), then "mammal."[55]

More complex societies tend to have a larger number of general, or life-form, terms for plants and animals than do simpler societies, just as they tend to have a larger number of basic color terms. Why? And do all realms or domains of vocabulary increase in size as social complexity increases? If we look at the total vocabulary of a language (as can be counted in a dictionary), more complex societies do have larger vocabularies.[56] But we have to remember that complex societies have many kinds of specialists, and dictionaries will include the terms used by such specialists. If we look instead at the nonspecialist **core vocabulary** of languages, it seems that all languages have a core vocabulary of about the same size.[57] Indeed, although some domains increase in size with social complexity, some remain the same and still others decrease. An example of a smaller vocabulary domain in complex societies is that of specific names for plants. Urban North Americans may know general terms for plants, but they know relatively few names for specific plants. The typical individual in a small-scale society can commonly name 400 to 800 plant species; a typical person in our own and similar societies may be able to name only 40 to 80.[58] The number of life-form terms is larger in societies in which ordinary people know less about particular plants and animals.[59]

The evidence now available strongly supports the idea that the vocabulary of a language reflects the everyday distinctions that are important in the society. Those aspects of environment or culture that are of special importance will receive greater attention in the language.

GRAMMAR. Most of the examples we could accumulate would show that a culture influences the names of things visible in its environment. Evidence for cultural influence on the grammatical structure of a language is less extensive. Harry Hoijer draws attention to the verb categories in the language of the Navaho, a traditionally nomadic people. These categories center mainly in the reporting of events, or "eventings", as he calls them. Hoijer notes that in "the reporting of actions and events, and the framing of substantive concepts, Navaho emphasizes movement and specifies the nature, direction, and status of such movement in considerable detail."[60] For example, Navaho has one category for eventings that are in motion and another for eventings that have ceased moving. Hoijer concludes that the emphasis on events in the process of occurring reflects the Navaho's nomadic experience over the centuries, an experience also reflected in their myths and folklore.

A linguistic emphasis on events may or may not be generally characteristic of nomadic peoples; as yet, no one has investigated the matter cross-culturally or comparatively. But there are indications that systematic comparative research would turn up other grammatical features that are related to cultural characteristics. For example, many languages lack the possessive transitive verb we write as "have," as in "I have." Instead, the language may say something such as "it is to me." A cross-cultural study has suggested that a language may develop the verb "have" after the speakers of that language have developed a system of private property or personal ownership of resources.[61] As we shall see later in the chapter on economic systems, the concept of private property is far from universal and tends to occur only in complex societies with social inequality. In contrast, many societies have some kind of communal ownership, by kin groups or communities. How people talk about owning seems to reflect how they own; societies that lack a concept of private property also lack the verb "have."

LINGUISTIC INFLUENCES ON CULTURE: THE SAPIR-WHORF HYPOTHESIS

There is general agreement that culture influences language. But there is less agreement about the opposite possibility—that language influences other aspects of culture. Edward Sapir and Benjamin Lee Whorf suggested that language is a force in its own right, that it affects how individuals in a society perceive and conceive reality. This suggestion is known as the *Sapir-Whorf hypothesis.*[62] In comparing the English language with Hopi, Whorf pointed out that English-language categories convey discreteness with regard to time and space, but Hopi does not. English has a discrete past, present, and future, and things occur at a definite time. Hopi expresses things with more of an idea of ongoing processes without time being apportioned into fixed segments. According to Richard Wardhaugh, Whorf believed that these language differences lead Hopi and English speakers to see the world differently.[63]

As intriguing as that idea is, the relevant evidence is mixed. Linguists today do not generally accept the view that language coerces thought, but some suspect that particular features of language may facilitate certain patterns of thought.[64] The influences may be clearest in poetry and metaphors, where words and phrases are applied to other than their ordinary subjects, as in "all the world's a stage."[65] One of the serious problems in testing the Sapir-Whorf hypothesis is that researchers need to figure out how to separate the effects of other aspects of culture from the effects of language.

One approach that may reveal the direction of influence between language and culture is to study how children in different cultures (speaking different languages) develop concepts as they grow up. If language influences the formation of a particular concept, we might expect that children will acquire that concept earlier in societies where the languages emphasize that concept. For example, some languages make more of gender differences than others. Do children develop gender identity earlier when their language emphasizes gender? (Very young girls and boys seem to believe they can switch genders by dressing in opposite-sex clothes, suggesting that they have not yet developed a stable sense that they are unchangeably girls or boys.) Alexander Guiora and his colleagues have studied children growing up in Hebrew-speaking homes (Israel), English-speaking homes (the United States), and Finnish-speaking homes (Finland). Hebrew has the most gender emphasis of the three languages; all nouns are either masculine or feminine, and even second-person and plural pronouns are differentiated by gender. English emphasizes gender less, differentiating by gender only in the third-person singular (she or her or hers, he or him or his). Finnish emphasizes gender the least; although some words, such as *man* and *woman,* convey gender, differentiation by gender is otherwise lacking in the language. Consistent with the idea that language may influence thought, Hebrew-speaking children acquire the concept of stable gender identity the earliest on the average, Finnish-speaking children the latest.[66]

Another approach is to predict from language differences how people may be expected to perform in experiments. Comparing the Yucatec Mayan language and English, John Lucy predicted that English speakers might recall the *number* of things presented more than Yucatec Mayan speakers. For most classes of nouns, English requires a linguistic way of indicating whether something is singular or plural. You cannot say "I have dog" (no indication of number), but must say "I have a dog," "I have dogs," or "I have one (two, three, several, many) dogs." Yucatec Maya, like English, can indicate a plural, but allows the noun to be neutral with regard to number. For example, the translated phrase there-is-dog-over-there (yàan pèek té'elo') can be left ambiguous about whether there is one or more than one dog. In English, the same ambiguity would occur in the sentence "I saw deer over there," but English does not often allow ambiguity for animate or inanimate nouns.[67] In a number of experiments, Yucatec Mayan and American English speakers were equally likely to recall the objects in a picture, but they differed in how often they described the number of a particular object in the picture. Yucatec Mayan speakers did so less often, consistent with their language's lack of insistence on indicating number.[68] So the salience of number in the experiments was probably a consequence of how the languages differ. Of course, it is possible that salience of number is created by some other cultural feature, such as dependence on money in the economy.

THE ETHNOGRAPHY OF SPEAKING

Traditionally, linguists concentrated on trying to understand the structure of a language, the usually unconscious rules that predict how the people of a given society typically speak. In recent years, many linguists have begun to study how people in a society vary in how they speak. This type of linguistic

Strangers shake hands when they meet; friends touch each other more warmly. How we speak to others also differs according to the degree of friendship.

study, *sociolinguistics*, is concerned with the *ethnography of speaking*—that is, with cultural and subcultural patterns of speech variation in different social contexts.[69] The sociolinguist might ask, for example, what kinds of things one talks about in casual conversation with a stranger. A foreigner may know English vocabulary and grammar well but may not know that one typically chats with a stranger about the weather or where one comes from, and not about what one ate that day or how much money one earns. A foreigner may be familiar with much of the culture of a North American city, but if that person divulges the real state of his or her health and feelings to the first person who says "How are you?" he or she has much to learn about "small talk" in North American English.

Similarly, North Americans tend to get confused in societies where greetings are quite different from ours. People in some other societies may ask as a greeting, "Where are you going?" or "What are you cooking?" Some Americans may think such questions are rude; others may try to answer in excruciating detail, not realizing that only vague answers are expected, just as we don't really expect a detailed answer when we ask people how they are.

SOCIAL STATUS AND SPEECH

That a foreign speaker of a language may know little about the small talk of that language is but one example of the sociolinguistic principle that what we say and how we say it are not wholly predictable by the rules of our language. Who we are socially and whom we are talking to may greatly affect what we say and how we say it.

In a study interviewing children in a New England town, John Fischer noted that in formal interviews, children were likely to pronounce the ending in words such as *singing* and *fishing*, but in informal conversations they said "singin'" and "fishin'." Moreover, he noted that the phenomenon also appeared to be related to social class; children from higher-status families were less likely to drop the ending than were children from lower-status families. Subsequent studies in English-speaking areas tend to support Fischer's observations with regard to this speech pattern. Other patterns are observed as well. For example, in Norwich, England, lower classes tend to drop the *h* in words such as *hammer*, but in all classes the pattern of dropping the *h* increases in casual situations.[70]

Research has shown that English people from higher-class backgrounds tend to have more *homogeneous* speech, conforming more to what is considered standard English (the type of speech heard on television or radio), whereas people from lower-class backgrounds have very *heterogeneous* speech, varying in their speaking according to the local or dialect area they come from.[71] In some societies, social status differences may be associated with more marked differentiation of words. Clifford Geertz, in his study of Javanese, showed that the vocabularies of the three rather sharply divided groups in Javanese society—peasants, townspeople, and aristocrats—reflect their separate positions. For example, the concept *now* is expressed differently in these three groups. A peasant will use *saiki* (considered the lowest and roughest form of the word); a townsman will use *saniki* (considered somewhat more elegant); and an aristocrat will use *samenika* (the most elegant form).[72]

Status relationships between people can also influence the way they speak to each other. Terms of address are a good example. In English, forms of address are relatively simple. One is called either by a first name or by a title (such as *Doctor*, or *Professor*,

Ms., Mister) followed by a last name. A study by Roger Brown and Marguerite Ford indicates that terms of address in English vary with the nature of the relationship between the speakers.[73] The reciprocal use of first names generally signifies an informal or intimate relationship between two persons. A title and last name used reciprocally usually indicates a more formal or businesslike relationship between individuals who are roughly equal in status. Nonreciprocal use of first names and titles in English is reserved for speakers who recognize a marked difference in status between them. This status difference can be a function of age, as when a child refers to her mother's friend as Mrs. Miller and is in turn addressed as Sally, or can be due to occupational hierarchy, as when a person refers to his boss as Ms. Ramirez and is in turn addressed as Joe. In some cases, generally between boys and between men, the use of the last name alone represents a middle ground between the intimate and the formal usages.

GENDER DIFFERENCES IN SPEECH

In many societies the speech of men differs from the speech of women. The variation can be slight, as in our own society, or more extreme, as with the Carib Indians in the Lesser Antilles of the West Indies, among whom women and men use different words for the same concepts.[74] In Japan, males and females use entirely different words for numerous concepts (for example, the male word for water is *mizu*, the female version is *ohiya*), and females often add the polite prefix *o-* (females will tend to say *ohasi* for chopsticks; males will tend to say *hasi*).[75] In the United States and other Western societies, there are differences in the speech of females and males, but they are not as dramatic as in the Carib and Japanese cases. For example, earlier we noted the tendency for the *g* to be dropped in words such as *singing* when the situation is informal and when the social class background is lower. But there is also a gender difference. Women are more likely than men to keep the *g* sound and less likely than men to drop the *h* in words such as *happy*. In Montreal, women are less likely than men to drop the *l* in phrases such as *il fait* ("he does") or in the idiom *il y a* ("there is/are").

Gender differences occur in intonation and in phrasing of sentences as well. Robin Lakoff found that in English women tend to answer questions with sentences that have rising inflections at the end instead of a falling intonation associated with a firm answer. Women also tend to add questions to statements, such as "They caught the robber last week, didn't they?"[76]

One explanation for the gender differences, particularly with regard to pronunciation, is that women in many societies may be more concerned than men with being "correct."[77] (Not in the linguist's sense; it is important to remember that linguists do not consider one form of speech more correct than another, just as they do not consider one dialect superior to another. All are equally capable of expressing a complex variety of thoughts and ideas.) In societies with social classes, what is considered more correct by the average person may be what is associated with the upper class. In other societies, what is older may be considered more correct. For example, in the Native American language of Koasati, which used to be spoken in Louisiana, males and females used different endings in certain verbs. The differences seemed to be disappearing in the 1930s, when the research on Koasati was done. Young girls had begun to use the male forms and only older women still used the female forms. Koasati men said that the women's speech was a "better" form of speech.[78] Gender differences in speech may parallel some of the gender differences noted in other social behavior (as we will see in the chapter on sex, gender, and culture): Girls are more likely than boys to behave in ways that are acceptable to adults.

There are not enough studies to know just how common it is for women to exhibit more linguistic "correctness." We do know of some instances where it is not the case. For example, in a community in Madagascar where people speak Merina, a dialect of Malagasy, it is considered socially correct to avoid explicit directives. So instead of directly ordering an action, a Merina speaker will try to say it indirectly. Also, it is polite to avoid negative remarks, such as expressing anger toward someone. In this community, however, it is women, not men, who often break the rules; women speak more directly and express anger more often.[79] This difference may be related to the fact that women are more involved in buying and selling in the marketplace.

Some researchers have questioned whether it is correctness that is at issue. Rather, we may be dealing in these examples with unequal prestige and power. Women may try to raise their status by conforming more to standard speech. When they answer a question with a rising inflection, they may be expressing uncertainty and a lack of power. Alternatively, perhaps women want to be more cooperative conversationalists. Speaking in a more "standard" fashion is consistent with being more likely to be understood by others. Answering a question with another question leads to continued conversation.[80]

New Perspectives on Gender

DOES THE ENGLISH LANGUAGE PROMOTE SEXIST THINKING?

Does English promote sexist thinking, or does the language merely reflect gender inequalities that already exist? For those who wish to promote gender equality, the answers to these questions are important because if language influences thoughts (along the lines put forward by Edward Sapir and Benjamin Whorf), then linguistic change will be necessary in order to bring about change in the culture of gender. If it is the other way around, that is, if language reflects inequality, then social, economic, and political changes have to come before we can expect substantial linguistic change to occur.

Leaving aside for the moment which changes first, how does English represent gender inequity? Consider the following written by Benjamin Lee Whorf: "Speech is the best show man puts on. . . . Language helps man in his thinking." While *man* in English technically refers to all humans and *his* technically refers to the thinking of a single person of either gender, the frequent use of such words could convey that males are more important. Similarly, do the words *chairman, policeman, businessman, salesman* convey that males are supposed to have those jobs? What is conveyed when there are two words for the two genders, as in *actor* and *actress* and *hero* and *heroine*? Usually the base word is male and the suffix is added for the female form. Does the suffix convey that the female form is an afterthought or less important?

It is not just the structure of the language that may convey gender inequity. There are also differences in usage and metaphor. Although there is a female and male form for someone who has lost a spouse *(widow* and *widower)*, many people will say "Sally is Henry's widow" but hardly anyone would say "Henry is Sally's widower." Why? Is it considered more important that a woman was formerly attached to a man than that a man was formerly attached to a woman? Given this usage, it is not surprising that *widow* (the female form) is the basic term in this case, *widower* (the male form) the derived term. And how come in the pairs *sir/madam, master/mistress, wizard/witch,* the female version has acquired negative connotations? Why are so many animal images applied to women? They may be described as *chicks, henpeckers, cows, dogs, bitches, kittens, birds.*

Coming back to the original questions, how would we know whether language promotes sexism or sexism influences language? One way to find out is to do experimental studies, such as the one conducted by Fatemeh Khosroshashi. Some individuals were asked to read texts written with *man* and *he* and *his* referring to people; others were asked to read texts with more gender-neutral phrasing. Indi-

MULTILINGUALISM AND CODESWITCHING

For many people the ability to speak more than one language is a normal part of life. One language may be spoken at home and another in school, the marketplace, or government. Or more than one language may be spoken at home if family members come from different cultures and still other languages are spoken outside. Some countries explicitly promote multilingualism. For example, Singapore has four official languages—English, Mandarin (one of the Chinese languages), Tamil, and Malay. English is stressed for trade, Mandarin as the language of communication with most of China, Malay as the language of the general region, and Tamil as the language of an important ethnic group. Moreover, most of the population speak Hokkien, another Chinese language. Education is likely to be in English and Mandarin.[81]

What happens when people who know two or more languages communicate with each other? Very often you find them **codeswitching,** using more than one language in the course of conversing.[82] Switching can occur in the middle of a Spanish-English bilingual sentence, as in *"No van a* bring it up in the meeting" ("They are not going to bring it up in the meeting").[83] Or switching can occur when the topic or situation changes, such as from social talk to schoolwork. Why do speakers of more than one language sometimes switch? Although speakers switch for a lot of different reasons, what is clear is

viduals were subsequently asked to draw pictures to go with the texts. The ones who read the texts with more male terminology drew more accompanying pictures of men, strongly suggesting that the use of the terms *man, he,* and *his* conveyed the thought that the people in the text were men, not women, *because* of the vocabulary used. We need more such studies to help address the intellectual question of which comes first, linguistic or nonlinguistic culture.

It would be important to know whether societies with more "male-oriented" language *are* more male-dominated than are societies without such distinctions. We don't have that kind of comparative research yet. But one study by Robert and Ruth Munroe looked at the *proportion* of female and male nouns in ten languages (six Indo-European, four other than Indo-European) in which nouns have gender. Although none of those societies could be described as having a

female bias, the Munroes were able to ask whether those societies with less male bias in social customs (for example, all children are equally likely to inherit property) have a higher proportion of female nouns than male nouns (more female than male nouns). The answer appears to be yes. Although this study does not reveal what came first, studies like it are important if we want to discover how language differences may be related to other aspects of culture. If male-oriented languages are not related to male dominance, then it is not likely that sexist thinking is a consequence of language.

On the assumption that language may influence thought, many are pushing for changes in the way English is used, if not structured. It is hard to get English speakers to adopt a gender-neutral singular pronoun to replace *he.* Attempts to do so go back to the eighteenth century and include suggestions of *tey, thon, per,* and *s/he.* Although

these efforts have not succeeded, the way English is written and spoken has begun to change. Words or phrases such as *chair* (or *chairperson*), *police officer, sales assistant (salesperson)* have begun to replace their former *man* versions. If Whorf were writing his sentence now, it probably would be written: "Speech is the best show humans put on. . . . Language helps people think."

Sources: Janet Holmes, *An Introduction to Sociolinguistics* (London: Longman, 1992), pp. 336–43; Suzanne Romaine, *Language in Society: An Introduction to Sociolinguistics* (Oxford: Oxford University Press, 1994), pp. 105–16; Richard Wardhaugh, *An Introduction to Sociolinguistics,* 2nd ed. (Oxford: Blackwell, 1992), pp. 315–17; Robin Lakoff, "Language and Woman's Place," *Language in Society,* 2(1973): 45–80; Fatemeh Khosroshashi, "Penguins Don't Care, but Women Do: A Social Identity Analysis of a Whorfian Problem," *Language in Society,* 18 (1989): 505–25; Robert L. Munroe and Ruth H. Munroe, "A Cross-Cultural Study of Sex Gender and Social Structure," *Ethnology,* 8 (1969): 206–11.

that the switching is not a haphazard mix that comes from laziness or ignorance. Codeswitching involves a great deal of knowledge of two or more languages and an awareness of what is considered appropriate or inappropriate in the community. For example, in the Puerto Rican community in New York City, codeswitching within the same sentence seems to be common in speech among friends, but if a stranger who looks like a Spanish speaker approaches, the language will shift entirely to Spanish.[84]

Although each community may have its own rules for codeswitching, variations in practice may need to be understood in terms of the broader political and historical context. For example, German speakers in Transylvania, where Romanian is the national language, hardly ever codeswitch to Roman-

ian. Perhaps the reason is that, before the end of World War II, German speakers were a privileged economic group who looked down upon landless Romanians and their language. Under socialism, the German speakers lost their economic privilege, but they continued to speak German among themselves. In the rare cases that Romanian is used among German speakers, it tends to be associated with low-status speech, such as singing bawdy songs. The opposite situation occurred in a Hungarian region of German-speaking Austria. The people of this agricultural region, annexed to Austria in 1921, were fairly poor peasant farmers. After World War II, business expansion began to attract labor from rural areas, so many Hungarians eagerly moved into jobs in industry. German was seen by the younger generations as a symbol of higher status and upward mobility; not surprisingly, codeswitching between Hungarian and German became part of their conversations. Indeed, in the third generation, German has become the language of choice, except when speaking to the oldest Hungarians. The Hungarian-Austrian situation is fairly common in many parts of the world, where the language of the politically dominant group ends up being "linguistically dominant."[85]

INTERETHNIC COMMUNICATION

Even when they speak the same language, people from different ethnic groups may have some misunderstandings in communication because of the different unconscious rules they have about *how* to have a conversation. For example, English-speaking Athapaskan Indians in Canada seem to think that conversation with a white Canadian should be avoided except when they think they know the point of view of the white (who is generally more powerful politically). On the other hand, white English speakers think they should use conversation to get to know others (as at a cocktail party). So they pause a certain amount of time to let the other person talk, but they pause a much shorter time than an Athapaskan English speaker would. If the other person doesn't respond, the white English speaker, feeling awkward, will say something else. By the time an Athapaskan Indian is ready to talk, the white is already talking and the Athapaskan Indian considers it impolite to interrupt. It is easy to see how whites and Athapaskan Indians can misunderstand each other. Athapaskan Indians think white English speakers talk too much and don't let Indians express their views, and whites think Athapaskan Indians do not want to talk or get to know whites.[86]

The field of sociolinguistics is a relatively new specialty in linguistics. At present, sociolinguists seem to be interested primarily in describing variation in the use of language. An understanding of why language varies in different contexts might partly suggest why structural aspects of language change over time. For as social contexts in a society change, the structure of the language might also tend to change.

SUMMARY

1. The essential function language plays in all societies is that of communication. Although human communication is not limited to spoken language, such language is of overriding importance because it is the primary vehicle through which culture is shared and transmitted.

2. Systems of communication are not unique to humans. Other animal species communicate in a variety of ways—by sound, odor, body movement, and so forth. The ability of chimpanzees and gorillas to learn and use sign language suggests that symbolic communication is not unique to humans. Still, human language is distinctive as a communication system in that its spoken and symbolic nature permits an infinite number of combinations and recombinations of meaning.

3. Structural (or descriptive) linguists try to discover the rules of phonology (the patterning of sounds), morphology (the patterning of sound sequences and words), and syntax (the patterning of phrases and sentences) that predict how most speakers of a language talk.

4. By comparative analysis of cognates and grammar, historical linguists test the notion that certain languages derive from a common ancestral language, or protolanguage. The goals are to reconstruct the features of the protolanguage, to hypothesize how the offspring languages separated from the protolanguage or from each other, and to establish the approximate dates of such separations.

5. When two groups of people speaking the same language lose communication with each other because they become separated either physically or socially, they begin to accumulate small changes in phonology, morphology, and syntax. If the separation continues, the two former dialects of the same language will eventually become separate languages—that is, they will become mutually unintelligible.

6. Whereas isolation brings about divergence between speech communities, contact results in greater resemblance. This effect is particularly evident when contact between mutually unintelligible languages introduces borrowed words, most of which name some new item borrowed from the other culture.

7. Some attempts to explain the diversity of languages have focused on the possible interaction between language and other aspects of culture. On the one hand, if it can be shown that a culture can affect the structure and content of its language, then it would follow that linguistic diversity derives at least in part from cultural diversity. On the other hand, the direction of influence between culture and language might work in reverse; the linguistic structures might affect other aspects of the culture.

8. In recent years, some linguists have begun to study variations in how people actually use language

when speaking. This type of linguistic study, called sociolinguistics, is concerned with the ethnography of speaking—that is, with cultural and subcultural patterns of speaking in different social contexts.

GLOSSARY TERMS

codeswitching
cognates
core vocabulary
dialects
historical linguistics
lexical content
lexicon
morph
morpheme

morphology
phone
phoneme
phonology
protolanguage
structural (or descriptive) linguistics
syntax

CRITICAL QUESTIONS

1. Why might natural selection have favored the development of true language in humans but not in apes?

2. Would the world be better off with many different languages spoken or with just one universal language?

3. Can you think of some new behavior or way of thinking that led people to adopt or invent new vocabulary or some new pattern of speech?

INTERNET EXERCISES

1. Explore **http://www.bucknell.edu/~rbeard/ diction.html** to find over 400 dictionaries covering some 130 different languages. See whether you can obtain the English equivalent of "name" in the following languages: Hawaiian, Basque, and Welsh.

2. Explore **http://www.friesian.com/egypt.htm** to learn the pronunciation of some ancient Egyptian language. Based on what you discover on this site,

provide a brief description of the terms *ideogram* and *pictogram*.

3. There are thousands of languages in the world today. To find out which ten languages are spoken by the most people, go to **http://www.sil.org/ethnologue/top100.html**.

SUGGESTED READING

AKMAJIAN, A., DEMERS, R. A., AND HARNISH, R. M. *Linguistics: An Introduction to Language and Communication,* 3rd ed. Cambridge, MA: MIT Press, 1990. A survey of many varieties of research in linguistics.

BROWN, C. H., AND WITKOWSKI, S. R. "Language Universals," Appendix B, in D. Levinson and M. J. Malone, eds., *Toward Explaining Human Culture: A Critical Review of the Findings of Worldwide Cross-Cultural Research.* New Haven, CT: HRAF Press, 1980. A review of studies of universals in human languages, including universals in phonology and grammar. Focuses especially on developmental sequences in the lexicon or vocabulary.

FOLEY, W. A. *Anthropological Linguistics: An Introduction.* Malden, MA: Blackwell, 1997. A broad introduction to the particular concerns of linguistic studies in anthropology.

HILL, J. "Do Apes Have Language?" in C. R. Ember, M. Ember, and P. N. Peregrine, eds. *Research Frontiers in Anthropology.* Upper Saddle River, NJ: Prentice Hall, 1998. Prentice Hall/Simon & Schuster Custom Publishing. A discussion of the differences and similarities between human and ape language.

SAPIR, E. *Language: An Introduction to the Study of Speech.* New York: Harcourt Brace Jovanovich, 1949 [originally published 1921]. A classic nontechnical introduction to the study of human languages and how they vary. Also discusses the relations between language and thought.

WARDHAUGH, R. *An Introduction to Sociolinguistics,* 2nd ed. Oxford: Blackwell, 1992. This introduction to sociolinguistics covers, among other topics, language change, multilingualism, regional and social variation, and language and gender.

13

Getting Food

*F*or most people in our society, getting food consists of a trip to the supermarket. Within an hour, we can gather enough food from the shelves to last us a week. Seasons don't daunt us. Week after week, we know food will be there. But we do not think of what would happen if the food were not delivered to the supermarket. We wouldn't be able to eat, and without eating for a while, we would die. Despite the old adage "Man [or woman] does not live by bread alone," without bread or the equivalent we could not live at all. Food-getting activities, then, take precedence over other activities important to survival. Reproduction, social control (the maintenance of peace and order within a group), defense against external threat, and the transmission of knowledge and skills to future generations—none could take place without energy derived from food. But it is not merely energy that is required for survival and long-term reproduction. Food-getting strategies need to provide the appropriate combination of nutrients throughout varying seasons and changing environmental conditions. Food-getting activities are also important because the way a society gets its food strongly predicts other aspects of a culture, from community size and permanence of settlement to type of economy and degree of inequality and type of political system, and even art styles and religious beliefs and practices.

In contrast with our own and similar societies, most societies have not had food-getting specialists. Rather, almost all able-bodied adults were engaged in getting food. During the 2 million to 5 million years that humans have been on earth, 99 percent of the time they have obtained food by gathering wild plants, hunting wild animals, and fishing. Agriculture is a relatively recent phenomenon, dating back only about 10,000 years. And industrial or mechanized agriculture is hardly more than a century old. Harvesting machines have been used a little bit longer, but self-propelled machines had to wait for the internal combustion engine and the rise of the oil industry.

In this chapter we look at the ways different societies get food and discuss some of the features associated with the different patterns. We ask why societies vary in their food-getting strategies. We shall see that the physical environment by itself has only a limited or restraining effect on how a society gets most of its food. To explain the variation more fully, we need to ask why societies in the prehistoric past switched from collecting wild food resources to cultivating plants and raising animals.

FOOD COLLECTION

Food collection may be generally defined as all forms of **subsistence technology** in which food-getting is dependent on naturally occurring resources, that is, wild plants and animals. Although this was the way humans got their food for most of human history, the few remaining food collectors in the world today, also referred to as **foragers,** live in what have been called the *marginal areas* of the earth—deserts, the Arctic, and dense tropical forests—habitats that do not allow easy exploitation by modern agricultural technologies.

Anthropologists are interested in studying the relatively few food-collecting societies still available for observation because these groups may help us understand some aspects of human life in the past, when all people were foragers. But we must be cautious in drawing inferences about the past from our observations of contemporary food collectors, for three reasons. First, early foragers lived in almost all types of environments, including some very bountiful ones. Therefore, what we observe among recent and contemporary food collectors, who generally live in deserts, the Arctic, and tropical forests, may not be comparable to what would have been observable in more favorable environments in the past.[1] Second, contemporary foragers are not relics of the past. Like all contemporary societies, they have evolved and are still evolving. Indeed, recent research suggests considerable variation in economic behavior as well as in social structure in foraging groups that share common ancestry; this implies that recent foragers have responded to differences in local environmental conditions.[2] Third, recent and contemporary foragers have been interacting with kinds of societies that did not exist until after 10,000 years ago—agriculturalists, pastoralists, and intrusive powerful state societies.[3] So what we see in intersociety relations recently may be different from intersociety relations in the past.

Let us now examine two areas of the world with very different environments where recent food collectors lived: Australia and the North American Arctic.

AUSTRALIAN ABORIGINES

Before Europeans came to the Australian continent, all the aboriginal people who lived there depended on food collection. Although the way of life of Australian aborigines is now considerably altered, we consider the life of the Ngatatjara as described by Richard Gould in the 1960s, when they still lived by gathering wild plants and hunting wild animals in the Gibson Desert of western Australia.[4] (We mostly use the present tense in our discussion because that is the custom in ethnographic writing, but the reader should remember that we are referring to aboriginal life in the 1960s.)

The Ngatatjara desert environment averages less than 8 inches of rain per year, and the temperature in summer may rise to 118°F. The few permanent waterholes are separated by hundreds of square miles of sand, scrub, and rock. Even before Europeans arrived in Australia, the area was sparsely populated—fewer than one person per 35 to 40 square miles. Now there are even fewer people, because the aboriginal population was decimated by introduced diseases and mistreatment after the Europeans arrived.

On a typical day, the camp begins to stir just before sunrise, while it is still dark. Children are sent to fetch water, and the people breakfast on water and food left over from the night before. In the cool of the early morning, the adults talk and make plans for the day. The talking goes on for a while. Where should they go for food—to places they have been to recently or to new places? Sometimes there are other considerations. For example, one woman may want to search for plants whose bark she needs to make new sandals. When the women decide which plants they want to collect and where they think those plants are most likely to be found, they take up their digging sticks and set out with large wooden bowls of drinking water on their heads. Their children ride on their hips or walk alongside. Meanwhile, the men may have decided to hunt emus, 6-foot-tall ostrichlike birds that do not fly. The men go to a creekbed where they will wait to ambush any game that may come along. They lie patiently behind a screen of brush they have set up, hoping for a chance to throw a spear at an emu or even a kangaroo. They can throw only once, because if they miss, the game will run away.

By noon, the men and women are usually back at camp, the women with their wooden bowls each filled with up to 15 pounds of fruit or other plant foods, the men more often than not with only some small game, such as lizards and rabbits. The men's food-getting is less certain of success than the women's, so most of the Ngatatjara aborigines' diet is plant food. The daily cooked meal is eaten toward evening, after an afternoon spent resting, gossiping, and making or repairing tools.

The aborigines traditionally were nomadic, moving their campsites fairly frequently. The camp-

sites were isolated and inhabited by only a small number of people, or they were clusters of groups including as many as 80 persons. The aborigines never established a campsite right next to a place with water. If they were too close, their presence would frighten game away and might cause tension with neighboring bands, who also would wait for game to come to the scarce watering spots.

Today many aborigines live in small settled villages. For example, in the 1980s, Victoria Burbank worked in a village she calls "Mangrove" in the Northern Territory of Australia. The once-nomadic aborigines now live in a village of about 600, which was founded in the 1950s around a Protestant mission. Their houses have stoves, refrigerators, toilets, washing machines, and even television sets. Their children attend school full time, and there is a health clinic for their medical needs. They still do some foraging, but most of their food comes from the store. Some earn wages, but many subsist on government welfare checks.[5]

THE INUIT (ESKIMO)

The diet of the Australian aborigines was mainly wild plant foods. But for the Inuit (Eskimo) peoples, who live year-round in the North American Arctic, plants are too scarce to be the most important part of the diet. From Greenland and Labrador in the east to Alaska in the west, the Inuit used to depend almost entirely on sea and land mammals and fish. (The term *Eskimo* is used widely in the West, but it is not a word in any of the native languages in that area. Many of the native Arctic groups, particularly those now living in Canada, prefer to be called Inuit.) We focus here on the traditional life of the north Alaskan Inupiaq as described by Ernest Burch for the beginning of the nineteenth century (the

A modern Inuit hunter, wearing a Caribou parka and sealskin boots, aims a rifle while sitting behind the camouflage of an umbrella on Ellesmere Island.

"ethnographic present" in the following discussion).[6] Northern Alaska is relatively "warm" for its latitude but not for most of us farther south; little sun and below-zero temperatures for a month or so in the winter are hardly warm. Rivers and lakes freeze in October and do not thaw until May. Even the ocean freezes for part of the winter.

What the Inupiaq collect for food depends mostly on the season, but the critical resources are sea mammals (ranging in size from whales to seals), fish, and caribou or wild reindeer. The usual technique for hunting sea mammals is to hurl a toggle harpoon into a sea mammal from a kayak. It is very difficult to kill a moving sea mammal, so hunters attach a line to the animal with the harpoon; on the other end of the line is a sealskin float that indicates where the harpooned sea mammal can be located. The sea mammal gets more and more tired pulling the float until the hunter is able to kill it with a lance. One man can manage alone to hunt smaller sea mammals, but groups of men are needed to hunt whales. In the winter, when the sea ice is frozen, a different hunting technique is used. A hunter must locate a breathing hole and then wait, immobile and attentive, for hours or sometimes days until a seal comes up for air. The instant the

New Perspectives on Gender

FROM MAN THE HUNTER, TO WOMAN THE GATHERER, TO . . .?

Anthropologists know it is important to understand the food-collecting way of life, for all humans were food collectors until 10,000 years ago. An important conference was held in 1966 to bring together anthropologists of all types to discuss what was known about food collectors. Organized by Richard B. Lee and Irven DeVore, the conference and the resulting book were called *Man the Hunter*. At the time, the word *man* was used widely in anthropology as a way of referring to humans in general. But referring to "man the hunter" appeared to ignore women, since women rarely do the hunting among recent foragers. It was not that women's contribution was entirely ignored by the participants in the conference. Indeed, Richard Lee pointed out that some food collectors such as the !Kung of southwest Africa depended mostly on gathering, which was mainly women's work. Even so, the title of the conference and of the resulting book conveyed that hunting and the work of men were most important among food collectors.

With the growing women's movement in the United States, thinking in anthropology subsequently began to change. New questions began to be asked. What were women doing? How much did they contribute to subsistence and to other essential economic activities? How much time did they work? What were their views of the world? What kinds of mate choices do women have? What kinds of decisions did they make? How much influence did women have?

In 1981, a book edited by Frances Dahlberg appeared. It was titled *Woman the Gatherer*. The editor was well aware that gathering is not usually the most important subsistence activity among food collectors. It may be more important among contemporary foragers such as the !Kung and Australian aborigines, who live in warmer climates, but gathering is less important in colder climates, where most recent foragers have lived. Indeed, if we look at a large sample of recent foragers, we discover that fishing is more often the most important subsistence activity, more important (providing more calories) than either gathering or hunting. Why the title *Woman the Gatherer* then? Although the editor did not say so explicitly, we suggest that the title was intended to raise consciousness about the importance of women.

We now know that food-collecting societies show considerable variability in how they get their food, so neither "Man the Hunter" nor "Woman the Gatherer" describes most foragers accurately. A book title such as *Food Collectors* or *Foraging Humans* may not as be as catchy as *Man the Hunter* or *Woman the Gatherer*, but it would be more gender-fair.

Sources: Richard B. Lee and Irven DeVore, eds., *Man the Hunter* (Chicago: Aldine, 1968); Frances Dahlberg, ed., *Woman the Gatherer* (New Haven, CT: Yale University Press, 1981); Carol R. Ember, "Myths about Hunter-Gatherers," *Ethnology,* 18 (1978): 439–48, reprinted in Melvin Ember and Carol R. Ember, *Marriage, Family, and Kinship: Comparative Studies of Social Organization* (New Haven, CT: HRAF Press, 1983), pp. 313–31.

seal surfaces, the hunter must aim perfectly with the harpoon. The women butcher the animal, prepare it for eating or storage, and process the skin. All of the skin clothing is sewn by women. They also hunt small animals, such as hares, and do much of the fishing. Various techniques are used for fishing—hook and line, spearing, and ambushing with nets and dams. Women make the fishing nets, and it takes the better part of a year to make one. Although there are not many plants to gather, the women do that too.

Related families usually live together and move camp by boat or sled to be in the best place to intercept the migratory animals and fish. For instance, caribou migrate, so the Inupiaq try to catch them by building a corral in a place through which they are expected to pass. A network of interrelated families lives and moves in a territory of thousands of square miles, moving outside it only when they have made arrangements with other groups to do so.

Much has changed since the time just described. Now the Inupiaq live in villages or towns with many modern conveniences. In the village of Kivalina there are permanent houses with electricity, telephones, and television sets. Dog teams have been replaced by all-terrain vehicles and snowmobiles. There are powerful outboard motors rather than skin boats. Many men and women have full-time wage-paying jobs. But even though the people may buy most of their food, there is still a preference for traditional foods, so the Inupiaq still hunt and fish on the weekends.

GENERAL FEATURES OF FOOD COLLECTORS

Despite the differences in terrain and climate under which they live and the different food-collecting technologies they use, Australian aborigines, Inuit, and most other recent foragers traditionally have certain characteristic cultural patterns (see Table 13–1). Most live in small communities in sparsely populated territories and follow a nomadic life-style, forming no permanent settlements. As a rule, they do not recognize individual land rights. Their communities generally do not have different classes of people and tend to have no specialized or full-time political officials.[7] But food collectors who depend heavily on fishing are more likely to have bigger and more permanent communities and somewhat more social inequality than

TABLE 13–1 *Variation in Food-Getting and Associated Features*

	FOOD COLLECTORS	FOOD PRODUCERS		
	Foragers	*Horticulturalists*	*Pastoralists*	*Intensive Agriculturalists*
Population density	Lowest	Low–moderate	Low	Highest
Maximum community size	Small	Small–moderate	Small	Large (towns and cities)
Nomadism/ permanence of settlements	Generally nomadic or seminomadic	More sedentary: communities may move after several years	Generally nomadic or seminomadic	Permanent communities
Food shortages	Infrequent	Infrequent	Frequent	Frequent
Trade	Minimal	Minimal	Very important	Very important
Full-time craft specialists	None	None or few	Some	Many (high degree of craft specialization)
Individual differences in wealth	Generally none	Generally minimal	Moderate	Considerable
Political leadership	Informal	Some part-time political officials	Part- and full-time political officials	Many full-time political officials

do those who forage for game and plants.[8] Division of labor in food-collecting societies is based largely on age and gender: Men exclusively hunt large marine and land animals and usually do most of the fishing, and women usually gather wild plant foods.[9]

Is there a typical pattern of food-getting among food collectors? Many anthropologists have assumed that foragers typically get their food more from gathering than from hunting, and that women contribute more than men to subsistence, because women generally do the gathering.[10] Although gathering is the most important food-getting activity for some food collectors (for example, the Ngatatjara aborigines and the !Kung of southern Africa), this is not true for most recent food-collecting societies. A survey of 180 such societies indicates that there is a lot of variation with regard to which food-getting activity is most important to the society. Gathering is the most important activity for 30 percent of the surveyed societies, hunting for 25 percent, and fishing for 38 percent. (Perhaps, then, we should call most recent food collectors fisher-gatherer-hunters.) In any case, because men generally do the fishing as well as the hunting, the men usually contribute more to food-getting than do the women among recent food collectors.[11]

Because food collectors move their camps often and walk great distances, it may seem that the food-collecting way of life is difficult. Although we do not have enough quantitative studies to tell us what is typical of most food collectors, studies of two Australian aborigine groups[12] and of one !Kung group[13] indicate that those food collectors do not spend many hours getting food. For example, !Kung adults spend an average of about 17 hours per week collecting food. Even when you add the time spent making tools (about 6 hours a week) and doing housework (about 19 hours a week), the !Kung seem to have more leisure time than many agriculturalists, as we discuss later.

▰▰▰ FOOD PRODUCTION

Beginning about 10,000 years ago, certain peoples in widely separated geographic locations made the revolutionary changeover to **food production.** That is, they began to cultivate and then domesticate plants and animals. (Domesticated plants and animals are different from the ancestral wild forms.) With domestication of these food sources, people acquired control over certain natural processes, such as animal breeding and plant seeding. Today, most peoples in the world depend for their food on some combination of domesticated plants and animals.

Anthropologists generally distinguish three major types of food-production systems—horticulture, intensive agriculture, and pastoralism.

HORTICULTURE

The word **horticulture** may conjure up visions of people with "green thumbs" growing orchids and other flowers in greenhouses. But to anthropologists, the word means the growing of crops of all kinds with relatively simple tools and methods, in the absence of permanently cultivated fields. The tools are usually hand tools, such as the digging stick or hoe, not plows or other equipment pulled by animals or tractors. And the methods used do not include fertilization, irrigation, or other ways to restore soil fertility after a growing season.

There are two kinds of horticulture. The more common one involves a dependence on **extensive** or **shifting cultivation.** The land is worked for short periods and then left idle for some years. During the years when the land is not cultivated, wild plants and brush grow up; when the fields are later cleared by *slash-and-burn techniques,* nutrients are returned to the soil. The other kind of horticulture involves a dependence on long-growing tree crops. The two kinds of horticulture may be practiced in the same society, but in neither case is there permanent cultivation of field crops.

Most horticultural societies do not rely on crops alone for food. Many also hunt or fish; a few are nomadic for part of the year. For example, the northern Kayapo of the Brazilian Amazon leave their villages for as long as three months at a time to trek through the forest in search of game. The entire village participates in a trek, carrying large quantities of garden produce and moving their camp every day.[14] Other horticulturalists raise domestic animals, but these are usually not large animals, such as cattle and camels.[15] More often than not, the animals raised by horticulturalists are smaller ones, such as pigs, chickens, goats, and sheep.

Let us look now at two horticultural societies, the Yanomamö of the Brazilian-Venezuelan Amazon and the Samoans of the South Pacific.

THE YANOMAMÖ. Dense tropical forest covers most of Yanomamö territory. From the air, the typical village is located in a forest clearing and looks like a single large circular lean-to with its inner side open to the central plaza. Each individual family has its own portion of the lean-to under the common roof. Each family's portion of the lean-to has a back wall (part of the closed back wall around the circular village structure), but the portions are open on the sides to each other as well as onto the central plaza of the village. The Yanomamö get most of their calories from garden produce, but according to Raymond Hames, the Yanomamö actually spend most of their time foraging.[16]

Before the people can plant, the forest must be cleared of trees and brush. Like most shifting cultivators, the Yanomamö use a combination of techniques: slashing the undergrowth, felling trees, and using controlled burning to clear a garden spot—in other words, **slash-and-burn** horticulture. Before the 1950s, the Yanomamö had only stone axes, so felling trees was quite difficult. Now they have steel machetes and axes given or traded to them by missionaries.

Because of the work involved in clearing a garden, the Yanomamö prefer to make use of forest patches that have little thorny brush and not too many large trees.[17] After the ground is cleared, the Yanomamö plant plantains, manioc, sweet potatoes, taro, and a variety of plants for medicine, condiments, and craft materials. Men do the heavy clearing work to prepare a garden, and they as well as women plant the crops. Women usually go to the gardens daily to weed and harvest. After two or three years the yields diminish and the forest starts growing back, making continued cultivation less desirable and more difficult, so they abandon the garden and clear a new one. If they can, they clear adjacent forest, but if gardens are far from the village they will move the village to a new location. Villages are moved about every five years because of gardening needs and warfare. There is a great deal of intervillage raiding, so villages are often forced to flee to another location.

Extensive cultivation requires a lot of territory because new gardens are not cleared until the forest grows back. What is often misunderstood is why it is so important to shift gardens. Not only is a burned field easier to plant, but the organic matter that is burned provides necessary nutrients for a good yield. If horticulturalists come back too quickly to a spot with little plant cover, a garden made there will not produce a satisfactory yield.

The Yanomamö crops do not provide much protein, so hunting and fishing are important to their diet. Men hunt birds, peccaries, monkeys, and tapir with bows and arrows. Fishing is enjoyed by women, men, and children. They catch fish by hand, with small bows and arrows, and by stream poisoning. Everybody gathers honey, hearts of palm, Brazil nuts, and cashews, although the men usually climb trees to shake down the nuts. Much of the foraging is done from the village base, but the Yanomamö, like the Kayapo, may go on treks to forage from time to time.

THE SAMOANS. The Samoans numbered about 56,000 persons in 1839, soon after European missionaries arrived.[18] The islands of Samoa, which are about 2,300 miles south of the Hawaiian Islands, are volcanic in origin, with central ridges and peaks as high as 4,000 feet. Though the land is generally steep, the islands have a lush plant cover watered by up to 200 inches of rain a year (about five times the amount of rain that falls on New York City in a year). All that rain does not interfere much with outdoor activity, because the torrential showers do not last long and the water disappears quickly into the porous volcanic soil. The temperature is relatively constant, rarely falling below 70° or rising above 88°F. Strong cooling trade winds blow most of the year, generally from the east or southeast, and on the coasts one hears a continuous low rumble from the huge Pacific swells that break upon the fringing coral reefs offshore.

Samoan horticulture involves mostly three tree crops requiring little work except in harvesting. Once planted, and with hardly more than a few years of waiting, the breadfruit tree continues to produce about two crops a year for up to half a century. Coconut trees may continue to produce for a hundred years. And banana trees make new stalks of fruit, each weighing more than 50 pounds, for many years; merely cutting down one stalk induces the plant to grow another. Young men do most of the harvesting of tree crops. Women do the occasional weeding.

The Samoans also practice some shifting cultivation; men periodically clear small patches of land for taro, a root crop that is a staple food. The taro patches can produce a few crops before they must be allowed to revert to bush so that soil fertility can be restored. But even taro cultivation does not require much work; planting requires nothing more than slightly burying the top sliced off a root just harvested. Young men do most of the planting and harvesting. The taro patches are weeded infrequently, mostly by women. This kind of casual farming behavior prompted Captain Bligh, of *Mutiny on the Bounty* fame, to describe the Tahitians as lazy.[19] Captain Bligh's attitude was ethnocentric. South Pacific islanders such as the Samoans and Tahitians cannot weed as often as European farmers without risking the erosion of their soil, because, in contrast with European farmlands, which are generally flat or only slightly sloping, the land of Samoa and Tahiti is mostly steep. The Samoan and Tahitian practice of not weeding crops and growing them in glorious and messy confusion enables the deep and shallow root structures of the various plants growing

The islands of American Samoa have very little flat land for cultivation. To prevent soil erosion, crops are interspersed amongst the naturally occurring brush. If land were completely cleared and single-cropped, the frequent torrential rains would quickly wash away the loose volcanic topsoil.

together to prevent the loose volcanic soil from being washed away by the torrential showers.

The Samoans keep chickens and pigs, which they eat only occasionally. The major source of animal protein in the Samoan diet is fish, caught inside and outside the reef. Younger men may swim in the deep sea outside the reef and use a sling to spear fish; older men are more likely to stand on the reef and throw a four-pointed spear at fish swimming inside the reef. For many years, people in the villages of Samoa have sold copra, the sun-dried meat of the ripe coconut, to the world market for coconut oil. Men generally cut the copra from the shells after the ripe coconuts fall by themselves to the ground. With the cash earned from the sale of copra, people buy imported items such as machetes, kerosene, and flour. People in most villages still produce most of the foods they eat, but many have migrated to towns on the bigger islands and to cities in Hawaii and on the U.S. mainland to find wage-paying jobs.

GENERAL FEATURES OF HORTICULTURAL-ISTS. In most horticultural societies, simple farming techniques have tended to yield more food from a given area than is generally available to food collectors. Consequently, horticulture is able to support larger, more densely populated communities. The way of life of horticulturalists is more sedentary than that of food collectors, although communities may move after some years to farm a new series of plots. (Some horticulturalists have permanent villages because they depend mostly on food from trees that keep producing for a long time.) In contrast with most recent food-collecting groups, horticultural societies exhibit the beginnings of social differentiation. For example, some individuals may be part-time craftworkers or part-time political officials, and certain members of a kin group may have more status than other individuals in the society.

INTENSIVE AGRICULTURE

People engaged in **intensive agriculture** use techniques that enable them to cultivate fields permanently. Essential nutrients may be put back in the soil through the use of fertilizers, which may be organic material (most commonly dung from humans or other animals) or inorganic (chemical) fertilizers. But there are other ways to restore nutrients. The Luo of western Kenya plant beans around corn plants. Bacteria growing around the roots of the bean plant replace lost nitrogen, and the corn plant conveniently provides a pole for the bean plant to wind around as it grows. Some intensive agriculturalists use irrigation from streams and rivers to ensure an adequate supply of waterborne nutrients. Crop rotation and plant stubble that has been plowed under also restore nutrients to the soil.

In general, the technology of intensive agriculturalists is more complex than that of horticulturalists. Plows rather than digging sticks are generally employed. But there is enormous variation in the degree to which intensive agriculturalists rely on mechanization rather than hand labor. In some societies the most complex machine is an animal-drawn plow; in the corn and wheat belts of the United States, huge tractors till, seed, and fertilize 12 rows at a time.[20]

Let's look now at two groups of intensive agriculturalists, those of rural Greece and those of the Mekong Delta in Vietnam.

RURAL GREECE. The village of Vasilika is situated at the foot of Mount Parnassus on the Boeotian plain. As described by Ernestine Friedl in the 1950s, its population was about 220 inhabitants.[21] Grapevines and wheat are cultivated for domestic use. The agricultural year begins in March with pruning of the vines and hoeing of the fields, tasks regarded as men's work. Wine making begins in September, after the grain harvest, and involves the whole family. Men, women, and children talk and joke as they pick the grapes and put them into large baskets. After the leaves and stems are removed, the fruit is trampled by the men, and the newly pressed grape juice, or *must,* is transferred to barrels. After adding whatever sugar and alcohol are needed, farmers also add resin to give the wine its characteristic flavor.

The villagers use horses to plow their wheat fields in October, and in November they sow the seed by hand. The wheat crop is harvested the following summer, usually by machine. Wheat constitutes the staple village food and is eaten as bread, as a cereal (called *trakhana*), or as noodles. It is also commonly bartered for other food items, such as fish, olive oil, and coffee.

Cotton and tobacco are the main **cash crops**— that is, crops raised for sale. In this dry plains country, the success of the cotton crop depends on irrigation, and the villagers use efficient diesel pumps to distribute water. The real work in the cotton fields begins after the spring plowing and seeding have been completed. Then the young plants must be hoed and mulched, a task done mostly by women. The season of cotton cultivation is especially hard on women, who must do all the cooking and household chores in addition to working in the cotton fields. Irrigation, which begins in July, is men's work. It is usually done three times a season and involves the clearing of shallow ditches, the mounting of pumps, and the channeling of the water. Cotton picking, which starts in October, is considered women's work. For picking, as well as hoeing and harvesting, a farmer owning more than five acres usually hires women from the same village or neighboring villages and sometimes even from distant towns. The cotton ginning is carried out by centrally located contractors, who are paid on the spot with 6 percent of each farmer's crop. Most of the seed reclaimed in the ginning is used for the next year's planting. The remainder is pressed into cakes to serve as supplementary food for ewes at lambing time. Tobacco yields a larger cash income than cotton, and the tobacco crop fits well into what would otherwise be slack periods in cultivation.

Raising animals plays a relatively minor role in the villagers' economic life. Each farmer has a horse or two for heavy draft work, a mule or donkey, about two dozen sheep, and some fowl.

Farmers at Vasilika are responsive to modern developments; they are prepared to experiment to a certain extent, especially with mechanization. Where the amount of acreage under cultivation warrants the expense, tractors are hired for plowing. Specialists are regularly called in to handle harvesting, cotton ginning, and similar tasks. Indeed, the Greek farmer is content to be a farmer and to rely on the skills of others to repair his roof, maintain his water pump, or provide the mechanical know-how for crop production.

RURAL VIETNAM: THE MEKONG DELTA. The village of Khanh Hau, situated along the flat Mekong Delta, comprised about 600 families when it was described by Gerald Hickey in the late 1950s before the Vietnam War.[22] The delta area has a tropical climate, with a rainy season that lasts from May to November. As a whole, the area has been made habitable only through extensive drainage.

Wet rice cultivation is the principal agricultural activity of Khanh Hau. It is part of a complex, specialized arrangement that involves three interacting components: (1) a complex system of irrigation and water control; (2) a variety of specialized equipment, including plows, waterwheels, threshing sledges, and winnowing machines; and (3) a clearly defined set of socioeconomic roles—from those of landlord, tenant, and laborer to those of rice miller and rice merchant.

In the dry season, the farmer decides what sort of rice crop to plant, whether of long (120 days) or short (90 days) maturation. The choice depends on the capital at his disposal, the current cost of fertilizer, and the anticipated demand for rice. The seedbeds are prepared as soon as the rains have softened the ground in May. The soil is turned over (plowed) and broken up (harrowed) as many as six separate times, with two-day intervals for "airing" between operations. During this time, the rice seeds are soaked in water for at least two days to stimulate sprouting. Before the seedlings are planted, the paddy is plowed once more and harrowed twice in two directions at right angles.

Planting is a delicate, specialized operation that must be done quickly and is performed most often by hired male laborers. But efficient planting is not enough to guarantee a good crop. Proper fertilization and irrigation are equally important. In the irrigating, steps must be taken to ensure that the water

Vietnamese villages cultivate rice intensively in irrigated fields, using water buffalo to plow the fields.

level remains at exactly the proper depth over the entire paddy. Water is distributed by means of scoops, wheels, and mechanical pumps. Successive crops of rice ripen from late September to May; all members of the family may be called upon to help with the harvest. After each crop is harvested, it is threshed, winnowed, and dried. Normally, the rice is sorted into three portions: one is set aside for use by the household in the following year; one is for payment of hired labor and other services (such as loans from agricultural banks); and one is for cash sale on the market. Aside from the harvesting, women do little work in the fields, spending most of their time on household chores. In families with little land, however, young daughters help in the fields and older daughters may hire themselves out to other farmers.

The villagers also cultivate vegetables, raise pigs, chickens, and the like and frequently engage in fishing. The village economy usually supports three or four implement makers and a much larger number of carpenters.

GENERAL FEATURES OF INTENSIVE AGRICULTURAL SOCIETIES. Societies with intensive agriculture are more likely than horticulturalists to have towns and cities, a high degree of craft specialization, complex political organization, and large differences in wealth and power. Studies suggest that intensive agriculturalists work longer hours than simpler agriculturalists.[23] For example, men engaged

in intensive agriculture average nine hours of work a day, seven days a week; women average almost eleven hours of work per day. Most of the work for women in intensive agricultural societies involves food processing and work in and around the home, but they also spend a lot of time working in the fields. We discuss some of the implications of the work patterns for women in the chapter on sex, gender, and culture.

Intensive agricultural societies are more likely than horticultural societies to face famines and food shortages, even though intensive agriculture is generally more productive than horticulture.[24] Why, if more food can be produced per acre, is there more risk of shortage among intensive agriculturalists? Intensive agriculturalists may be more likely to face food shortages because they are often producing crops for a market. Producing for a market pushes farmers to cultivate plants that give them the highest yield rather than cultivating plants that are drought-resistant or that require fewer nutrients. Farmers producing for a market also tend to concentrate on one crop. Crop diversity is often a protection against total crop failure because fluctuations in weather, plant diseases, or insect pests are not likely to affect all the crops. There are also fluctuations in market demand. If the market demand drops and the price falls for a particular crop, farmers may not have enough cash to buy the other food they need.[25]

THE COMMERCIALIZATION AND MECHANIZATION OF AGRICULTURE. Some intensive agriculturalists produce very little for sale; most of what they produce is for their own use. But there is a worldwide trend for intensive agriculturalists to produce more and more for a market. This trend is called **commercialization,** which may occur in any area of life and which involves increasing dependence on buying and selling, usually with money as the medium of exchange.

The increasing commercialization of agriculture is associated with several other trends. One is that farm work is becoming more and more mechanized as hand labor becomes scarce, because of migration to industrial and service jobs in towns and cities, or too expensive. A second trend is the emergence and spread of *agribusiness,* large corporation-owned farms that may be operated by multinational companies and worked by hired, as opposed to family, labor. For example, consider how cotton farming has changed in the southeastern United States. In the 1930s, mules and horses used in plowing were replaced by tractors. This change allowed some landowners to evict their sharecroppers and expand their holdings. After World War II, mechanical cotton pickers replaced most of the harvest laborers. But a farmer had to have a good deal of money or be a corporation to acquire those machines, each of which cost many tens of thousands of dollars.[26] So the mechanization of cotton farming sent many rural farm laborers off to the cities of the North in search of employment, and the agricultural sector increasingly became big business. A third trend associated with the commercialization of agriculture, including animal raising, is a reduction in the proportion of the population engaged in food production. In the United States today, for example, less than 2 percent of the total population work on farms.[27]

In the next chapter, on economics, and later in the chapter on culture change, we discuss more fully some of the apparent consequences of the worldwide changeover to commercial or market economies.

"MARKET FORAGING" IN INDUSTRIAL SOCIETIES. Food in countries such as the United States and Canada comes largely from intensive agriculture and animal husbandry practiced by a small proportion of the population. Those food specialists make their living by selling animal and plant products to marketers, distributors, and food processors. Indeed, most people know very little about how to grow crops or raise animals. Food appears in markets or supermarkets already processed by other specialists. It comes in paper or plastic packages, looking far different from how it originally looked in the field or on the feedlot. Thus, most of us are "market foragers," collecting our food from stores. In some ways, as we shall see in the chapter on psychology and culture, we behave very much like foragers of wild plants and animals. But there are also enormous differences between our kind of foraging and the original kind. If our society did not have very productive intensive agriculture and animal husbandry, we would not have towns and cities, thousands of different full-time occupations (hardly any of which are involved in food-getting), a centralized government, or many of our other characteristics.

PASTORALISM

Most agriculturalists raise animals (practice animal husbandry), but a small number of societies depend directly or indirectly on domesticated herds of animals for their living. We call such a system **pastoralism.** We might assume that pastoralists breed animals to eat their meat, but most do not. Pastoral-

ists more often get their animal protein from live animals in the form of milk, and some pastoralists regularly take blood, which is rich in protein, from their animals to mix with other foods. The herds also indirectly provide food because pastoralists trade animal products for plant foods and other necessities. In fact, a large proportion of their food may actually come from trade with agricultural groups.[28] For example, some pastoral groups in the Middle East derive much of their livelihood from the sale of what we call oriental rugs, which are made from the wool of their sheep on hand looms. Two pastoral societies we shall examine are the Basseri of southern Iran and the Lapps of Scandinavia.

THE BASSERI. The Basseri, described by Fredrik Barth as of the 1960s, are a tribe of about 16,000 tent-dwelling nomads.[29] Their herds consist principally of sheep and goats, though donkeys and camels are raised for pulling or carrying, and the wealthier men have horses for riding. Theirs is a dry, arid habitat, with rainfall averaging no more than 10 inches a year. The Basseri's pastoral way of life is based on a regular, migratory exploitation of the grazing lands within their territory, which measures about 15,000 square miles in all. In winter, when the mountains to the north are covered with snow, the plains and foothills to the south offer extensive pasturage. During the spring, grazing is excellent on a plateau near the center of the territory. By summer, when most of the lower-lying pastures have dried up, sufficient food for the herds can be found in the mountains at an altitude of nearly 6,000 feet.

Annual migrations are so important to the economies of the Basseri and other pastoralist societies of that region that they have developed the concept of *il-rah*, or "tribal road." A major pastoral tribe such as the Basseri has a traditional route and schedule. The route, consisting of the localities in the order in which each is visited, follows existing passes and lines of communication. The schedule, which regulates the length of time each location will be occupied, depends on the maturation of different pastures and the movements of other tribes. The *il-rah* is regarded, in effect, as the property of the tribe. Local populations and authorities recognize the tribe's right to pass along roads and cultivated lands, to draw water from the public wells, and to pasture flocks on public land.

The Basseri herd sheep and goats together, with one shepherd (a boy or unmarried man) responsible for a flock of 300 to 400 animals. Children of both sexes are usually responsible for herding the baby animals (lambs and kids). Milk and its by-products are the most important commodities, but wool, hides, and meat are also important to the economy of the Basseri. Both wool and hides are traded, but they are even more useful within the tribe. The Basseri, especially the women, are skilled spinners and weavers, and much of their time is spent at these activities. Saddlebags and pack bags are woven on horizontal looms from homespun wool and hair, as are carpets, sleeping rugs, and the characteristic black tents made of panels of woven goat hair. Woven goat hair provides an exceptionally versatile cloth. For winter use, it retains heat and repels water; in the summer, it insulates against heat and permits free circulation of air. Lambskin hides also serve many purposes. When plucked and turned inside out, they are made into storage bags to hold water, buttermilk, sour milk, and other liquids.

Most of the Basseri must trade for the necessities and luxury items they do not produce within the community. The staple items they sell are butter, wool, lambskins, rope, and occasionally livestock.

THE LAPPS. The Lapps practice reindeer herding in northwestern Scandinavia where Finland, Sweden, and Norway share common frontiers. It is a typical Arctic habitat: cold, windswept, with long, dark days for half the year. Considerable change has occurred recently, so we first discuss the food-getting strategy in the 1950s, as described by Ian Whitaker and T. I. Itkonen.[30]

The Lapps herd their reindeer either intensively or, more often, extensively. In the *intensive system*, the herd is constantly under observation within a fenced area for the whole year. Intensively herded reindeer and other animals are accustomed to human contact. Hence, the summer corralling of the females for milking and the breaking in of the ox-reindeer for use as work animals are not difficult tasks. The *extensive system* involves allowing the animals to migrate over a large area. It requires little surveillance and encompasses large herds. Under this system, the reindeer are allowed to move through their seasonal feeding cycles watched by only one or two scouts. The other Lapps stay with the herd only when it has settled in its summer or winter habitat. But milking, breaking in, and corralling are harder in the extensive than in the intensive system because the animals are less accustomed to humans.

Even under the extensive system, which theoretically permits Lapps to engage in subsidiary economic activities such as hunting and fishing, the reindeer herd is the essential, if not the only, source of income. A family might possess as many as 1,000 reindeer, but usually the figure is half that number. Studies show

Lapps now use snowmobiles for herding and other purposes.

200 to be the minimum number of reindeer needed to provide for a family of four or five adults. Women may have shared the herding chores in the past under the intensive system, but now under the extensive system men do the herding. Women still do the milking. The Lapps eat the meat of the bull reindeer; the female reindeer are kept for breeding purposes. Bulls are slaughtered in the fall, after the mating season. Meat and hides are frequently sold or bartered for other food and necessities.

Reindeer are still herded nowadays, but instead of sleds, snowmobiles, all-terrain vehicles, and even helicopters are used for herding. Ferries move reindeer to and from different pastures, and the herders communicate by field telephones. With faster transportation, many Lapps now live in permanent homes and can still get to their herds in hours. Lapp children spend much of their time in school and, consequently, do not learn much of the herding ways. The Norwegian government now regulates pastoralism, licensing pastoralists and trying to limit the number of reindeer they can herd.[31]

GENERAL FEATURES OF PASTORALISM. In recent times, pastoralism has been practiced mainly in grassland and other semiarid habitats that are not especially suitable for cultivation without some significant technological input such as irrigation. Most pastoralists are nomadic, moving camp fairly frequently to find water and new pasture for their herds. But other pastoralists have somewhat more sedentary lives. They may move from one settlement to another in different seasons, or they may send some people out to travel with the herds in different seasons. Pastoral communities are usually small, consisting of a group of related families.[32] Individuals or families may own their own animals, but decisions about when and where to move the herds are made by the community.

As we have noted, there is a great deal of interdependence between pastoral and agricultural groups. That is, trade is usually necessary for pastoral groups to survive. Like agriculturalists, pastoralists are more vulnerable than foragers and horticulturalists to famine and food shortages. Pastoralists usually inhabit drought-prone regions, but recent pastoralists have had their access to grazing lands reduced, and political pressures have pushed them to decrease their movement over large areas. Mobility kept the risk of overgrazing to a minimum, but overgrazing in smaller territories has increased the risk of desertification.[33]

ENVIRONMENTAL RESTRAINTS ON FOOD-GETTING

Of great interest to anthropologists is why different societies have different methods of getting food. Archaeological evidence suggests that major changes in food-getting, such as the domestication of plants and animals, have been independently invented in at least several areas of the world. Yet, despite these comparable inventions and their subsequent spread by diffusion and migration, there is still wide diversity in the means by which people obtain food.

How much does the physical environment affect food-getting? Anthropologists have concluded that the physical environment by itself has a restraining, rather than a determining, effect on the major types of subsistence. Because they have very short growing seasons, cold regions of the earth are not particularly conducive to the growing of plants. No society we know of has practiced agriculture in the Arctic; instead, people who live there rely primarily on animals for food. But both food collection (as among the Inuit) and food production (as among the Lapps) can be practiced in cold areas. Indeed, cross-cultural evidence indicates that neither food collection nor food production is significantly associated with any particular type of habitat.[34]

We know that food collection has been practiced at one time or another in almost all areas of the earth. The physical environment does seem to have some effect on what kind of food collection is practiced, that is, on the extent to which food collectors will depend on plants, animals, or fish. Farther away from the equator, food collectors depend much less on plants for food and much more on animals and fish.[35] Lewis Binford argues that fishing becomes increasingly important in cold climates because food collectors need nonportable housing in severe

winters to protect themselves from the cold. Therefore, they cannot rely on large animals, which usually have to feed themselves by moving over considerable distances in the winter. Fishing is more localized than hunting, and therefore food collectors who rely on fishing can stay in their nonportable houses in winter.[36]

There is one habitat that may have precluded food collection until recent times. If it were not for the nearness of food producers, particularly agriculturalists, recent food collectors such as the Mbuti of central Africa could probably not have supported themselves in the tropical forest habitats where they now live.[37] Tropical forests are lush in plants, but they do not provide much in the way of reachable fruits, seeds, and flowers that can be eaten by humans. Animals are available in tropical forests, but typically they are lean and do not provide humans with sufficient carbohydrates or fat. Like the Mbuti groups who hunt and gather in the forest, many tropical food collectors trade for agricultural products; other collectors cultivate some crops in addition to hunting and gathering. It would seem, then, that food collectors could not survive in tropical forests were it not for the carbohydrates they obtain from agriculturalists (whoever they are).

When we contrast horticulture and intensive agriculture, the physical environment appears to explain some of the variation. Approximately 80 percent of all societies that practice horticulture or simple agriculture are in the tropics, whereas 75 percent of all societies that practice intensive agriculture are *not* in tropical forest environments.[38] Tropical forests have abundant rainfall. But despite the attractiveness of lush vegetation and brilliant coloring, tropical forestlands do not usually offer favorable environments for intensive agriculture. Perhaps the heavy rainfall quickly washes away certain minerals from cleared land. Also, the difficulty of controlling insect pests and weeds, which abound in tropical forests,[39] may make intensive agriculture less productive.

But difficulty is not impossibility. Today, there are some areas, for instance, the Mekong Delta in Vietnam, whose tropical forests have been cleared and prevented from growing again by the intensive cultivation of rice in paddies. And, although cultivation is not normally possible in dry lands, because of insufficient natural rainfall to sustain crops, agriculture can be practiced where there are oases—small, naturally watered areas where crops can be grown with a simple technology—or rivers that can be tapped by irrigation, one of the techniques used with intensive agriculture.

Current Issues

THE EFFECT OF FOOD-GETTING ON THE ENVIRONMENT

Many people are now aware of industrial pollution—the dumping of industrial wastes in the ground or into rivers, the spewing of chemicals into the air through smokestacks—but we don't often realize how much humans have altered the environment by the ways they collect and produce food. Consider irrigation. There are various ways to capture water for irrigation. Water can be channeled from rivers; rainwater can be caught in terraces carved out of hillsides; ancient water can be pumped up from vast underground reservoirs called aquifers. But not all of the water drawn for irrigation seeps into the ground. Much of it evaporates, leaving behind minerals and salts. And the more a piece of land has been irrigated, the saltier the ground becomes. Eventually, the soil becomes too salty to grow crops effectively.

Some archaeologists have suggested that the accumulation of toxic salts in the soil at least partly explains the doom or decline of various groups in the past. For example, salinization may have contributed to the decline of the earliest city-states in Mesopotamia, present-day southern Iraq and southwestern Iran. The Hohokam farmers who lived in Arizona had about 150 miles of canals for irrigation; some of their ditches were 15 feet deep and 25 feet wide. In fact, their irrigation networks were comparable to those that served the Aztecs in pre-Columbian Mexico City.

The Hohokam seem to have vanished around A.D. 1400, perhaps because the salty soil poisoned their crops. Today much of the soil is still too salty for cultivation.

The lessons of history may not have been learned yet. The San Joaquin Valley of California, perhaps the most productive agricultural area in the world, now has a serious salinization problem. One solution in many of the areas of the Great American Desert is to pump water up from underground. Indeed, in many places there is a great deal of water underground. For example, the Ogallala aquifer, which underlies parts of Nebraska, Kansas, Texas, Oklahoma, Colorado, and New Mexico, contains water left from the Ice Ages. But the pumping solution, if it is a solution, is only a short-term fix, for the huge Ogallala aquifer is also the fastest-disappearing aquifer. The only question is how long it will take to disappear totally.

Too many people raising too many animals can also have serious effects on the environment. We can easily imagine how the possibility of profit might inspire people to try to raise more animals than the land will support. For example, 300 years ago the Great American Desert looked like a vast grassland. It supported large herds of buffalo, which in the next 200 years were all but exterminated by overhunting. The white settlers soon discovered they could raise cattle and sheep on this grassland, but many parts of it were overgrazed. It took the swirling dust storms of the 1930s to make people realize that overgrazing as well as poor farming practices could be disastrous. The problems are not just recent ones. The Norse colonized Greenland and Iceland around A.D. 800; but overgrazing of pasture undoubtedly contributed to soil erosion and the disappearance or decline of the colonies by A.D. 1500.

Are environmental problems associated only with food production? Although food producers may be the worst offenders, there is reason to think that foragers may also have sometimes overfished, overgathered, or overhunted. For example, some scholars suspect that the movement of humans into the New World was mainly responsible for the disappearance of the mammoth. Unfortunately, there is little evidence that humans have been good conservers in the past. That does not mean that humans cannot do better in the future—but they have to want to.

Sources: "Plundering Earth Is Nothing New," Los Angeles Times News Service as reported in the *New Haven Register*, June 12, 1994, pp. A18–19; Marc Reisner, *Cadillac Desert: The American West and Its Disappearing Water*, rev. ed. (New York: Penguin, 1993); Robert Dirks, "Hunger and Famine," in Carol R. Ember, Melvin Ember, and Peter N. Peregrine, eds., *Research Frontiers in Anthropology* (Upper Saddle River, NJ: Prentice Hall, 1998). Prentice Hall/Simon & Schuster Custom Publishing.

The animals raised by pastoralists depend primarily on grass for food, so it is not surprising that pastoralism is typically practiced in grassland regions of the earth. These regions may be **steppes** (dry, low grass cover), **prairies** (taller, better-watered grass), or **savannas** (tropical grasslands). The grassland habitat favors large game and hence supports both hunting and pastoral technologies, except where a machine technology makes intensive agriculture possible, as in parts of the United States, Canada, and Ukraine.

Very different strategies of food-getting have been practiced in the same environment over time. A dramatic illustration is the history of the Imperial Valley in California. The complex systems of irrigation now used in that dry-land area have made it a very productive region. Yet about 400 years ago, this same valley supported only hunting and gathering groups who subsisted on wild plants and animals.

It is evident from the Imperial Valley example and many others like it that the physical environment does not by itself account for the system of food-getting in an area. Even a polar environment could have agriculture with heated greenhouses, though it would be too expensive. Technological advances as well as enormous capital investment in irrigation, labor, and equipment have made intensive agriculture possible in the Imperial Valley. But the agriculture there is precarious, depending on sources of water and power from elsewhere. In a prolonged drought, it may be difficult or too expensive to obtain the needed water. And should the prices for vegetables fall, the farming businesses in the Imperial Valley could find themselves unable to finance the investment and borrowing they need to continue. So technological and social and political factors rather than environmental factors mostly determine what kind of food-getting can be practiced in a given environment.

THE ORIGIN, SPREAD, AND INTENSIFICATION OF FOOD PRODUCTION

To understand why most people today are food producers rather than food collectors, we need to consider why plant and animal domestication may have emerged in the first place. In the chapter on the origins of food production and settled life, we examined some theories that suggested why people started to produce food, even though doing so may have involved more work and more risk of famine than did collecting food. All the theories currently considered suggest that people made the changeover because they were pushed into it. The possible reasons include:

1. Population growth in regions of bountiful wild resources pushed people to move to marginal areas, where they tried to reproduce their former abundance.

2. Global population growth filled up most of the world's habitable regions and forced people to utilize a broader spectrum of wild resources and to domesticate plants and animals.

3. Climatic change—hotter, drier summers and colder winters—favored settling near seasonal stands of wild grain; population growth in such areas would force people to plant crops and raise animals.

Whatever the reasons for the switch to food production, we still need to explain why food production has supplanted food collection as the primary mode of subsistence. We cannot assume that collectors would automatically adopt production as a superior way of life once they understood the process of domestication. After all, as we have noted, domestication may entail more work and provide less security than the food-collecting way of life.

The spread of agriculture may be linked to the need for territorial expansion. As a sedentary, food-producing population grew, it may have been forced to expand into new territory. Some of this territory may have been vacant, but much of it was probably already occupied by food collectors. Although food production is not necessarily easier than collection, it is generally more productive per unit of land. Greater productivity enables more people to be supported in a given territory. In the competition for land between the faster-expanding food producers and the food collectors, the food producers may have had a significant advantage: They had more people in a given area. Thus, the foraging groups may have been more likely to lose out in the competition for land. Some groups may have adopted cultivation, abandoning the foraging way of life in order to survive. Other groups, continuing as food collectors, may have been forced to retreat into areas not desired by the cultivators. Today, as we have seen, the small number of remaining food collectors inhabit areas not particularly suitable for cultivation—dry lands, dense tropical forests, and polar regions.

Just as prior population growth might account for the origins of domestication, so at later periods further population growth and ensuing pressure on

In parts of Israel today, agriculture is not possible without irrigation. Note the water in the ditches.

resources might at least partly explain the transformation of horticultural systems into intensive agricultural systems. Ester Boserup suggested that intensification of agriculture, with a consequent increase in yield per acre, is not likely to develop naturally out of horticulture because intensification requires much more work.[40] She argued that people will be willing to intensify their labor only if they have to. Where emigration is not feasible, the prime mover behind intensification may be prior population growth. The need to pay taxes or tribute to a politcal authority may also stimulate intensification.

Intensive agriculture has not yet spread to every part of the world. Horticulture continues to be practiced in certain tropical regions, and there still are some pastoralists and food collectors. Some environments may make it difficult to adopt certain subsistence practices. For example, intensive agriculture cannot supplant horticulture in some tropical environments without tremendous investments in chemical fertilizers and pesticides, not to mention the additional labor required.[41] And enormous amounts of water may be required to make agriculturalists out of foragers and pastoralists who now exploit semiarid environments. Hence, the different kinds of food-getting practices we observe throughout the world today are likely to be with us for some time to come.

▮▮▮▮ SUMMARY

1. Food collection or foraging—hunting, gathering, and fishing—depends on wild plants and animals and is the oldest human food-getting technology. Today, however, only a small number of societies practice it, and they tend to inhabit marginal environments.

2. Food collectors can be found in various physical habitats. Most food collectors are nomadic, and population density is low. Usually, the small bands consist of related families, with the division of labor along age and gender lines only. Personal possessions are limited, individual land rights are seldom recognized, and people are not differentiated by class.

3. Beginning about 10,000 years ago, certain peoples in widely separated geographic locations began to make the revolutionary changeover to food production—the cultivation and raising of plants and animals. Over the centuries, food production began to supplant food collection as the predominant mode of subsistence.

4. Horticulturalists farm with relatively simple tools and methods and do not cultivate fields permanently. Their food supply is sufficient to support larger, more densely populated communities than can be fed by food collection. Their way of life is sedentary, although communities may move after some years to farm a new series of plots.

5. Intensive agriculture is characterized by techniques such as fertilization and irrigation that allow fields to be cultivated permanently. In contrast with horticultural societies, intensive agriculturalists are more likely to have towns and cities, a high degree of craft specialization, large differences in wealth and power, and more complex political organization. They are also more likely to face food shortages. In the modern world, intensive agriculture is increasingly mechanized and geared to production for a market.

6. Pastoralism is a subsistence technology involving principally the raising of large herds of animals. It is generally found in low-rainfall areas. Pastoralists tend to be nomadic, to have small communities consisting of related families, and to depend significantly on trade because they do not produce items (including certain types of food) they need.

7. Anthropologists generally agree that the physical environment normally exercises a restraining rather than a determining influence on how people in an area get their food; technology and social and political factors may be more important.

8. Because food producers can support more people in a given territory than food collectors can, they may have had a competitive advantage in confrontations with food collectors.

GLOSSARY TERMS

cash crops
commercialization
extensive or shifting
    cultivation
food collection
food production
foragers
horticulture

intensive agriculture
pastoralism
prairie
savanna
slash-and-burn
steppe
subsistence technology

CRITICAL QUESTIONS

1. Why might meat be valued more than plant foods in many societies?

2. Why might foragers be less likely than intensive agriculturalists to suffer from food shortages?

3. Why do certain foods in a society come to be preferred?

INTERNET EXERCISES

1. The Food and Agriculture Organization of the United Nations maintains a comprehensive Web site devoted to global agricultural production at **http://www.fao.org**. Go to the section on FactFile and check on some facts related to food-getting. For example, which continent has received the largest amount of cereals through the world food aid program?

2. Food-getting depends upon a great deal of knowledge about the environment. Visit **http://www.ankn.uaf.edu/iks.html** and explore some indigenous knowledge about the environment in Alaska.

3. Based on your visit to the culture section of **http://www.bigmedicine.com/suquamish**, write a brief summary of the food and sustenance of Suquamish tribes.

SUGGESTED READING

BOSERUP, E. *The Conditions of Agricultural Growth: The Economics of Agrarian Change under Population Pressure.* Chicago: Aldine, 1965. The classic discussion of the theory that prior population growth is the major cause of agricultural development, at least in recent times.

BURCH, E. S., JR., AND ELLANNA, L. J. *Key Issues in Hunter-Gatherer Research* (Oxford: Berg, 1994). Research on hunter-gatherers has expanded greatly in recent decades and this edited collection deals with gender issues, concepts of territoriality, the notion of affluence, the effects of culture contact and government intervention, and native perspectives.

EMBER, M., EMBER, C. R., AND LEVINSON, D., EDS. *Portraits of Culture: Ethnographic Originals.* Upper Saddle River, NJ: Prentice Hall, 1998. Prentice Hall/Simon & Schuster Custom Publishing. This series includes more than 40 ethnographic portraits of, among others, foragers, horticulturalists, and intensive agriculturalists.

HARRIS, M., AND ROSS, E. B., EDS. *Food and Evolution: Toward a Theory of Human Food Habits.* Philadelphia: Temple University Press, 1987. A collection of original papers on why humans in different times and places eat what they do. The perspectives of several disciplines are represented, including primatology, nutrition, biological anthropology, archaeology, psychology, and agricultural economics.

JOACHIM, M. "Hunting and Gathering Societies." In D. Levinson and M. Ember, eds., *Encyclopedia of Cultural Anthropology,* 4 vols. New York: Henry Holt, 1995. A discussion of the cultural variability of recent foraging societies in subsistence, settlement pattern, political organization, economics, conflict, and changes.

KENT, S., ED. *Cultural Diversity among Twentieth-century Foragers: An African Perspective* (Cambridge: Cambridge University Press, 1996). Past research on hunter-gatherers has tended to stress the commonalities of hunter-gatherers. This book seeks to be a corrective, by exploring in its various chapters the differences within and among hunter-gatherer societies in Africa.

SALZMAN, P. "Pastoralism." In D. Levinson and M. Ember, eds., *Encyclopedia of Cultural Anthropology,* 4 vols. New York: Henry Holt, 1995. An up-to-date review and discussion of how pastoralists have adjusted to the modern world of industrialized and developing states.

TURNER, B. L., AND BRUSH, S. B. *Comparative Farming Systems.* New York: Guilford, 1987. The contributors to this volume, including anthropologists, economists, geographers, and rural sociologists, discuss the major types of agricultural systems throughout the world and the forces of change acting on them.

14

Economic Systems

*W*hen we think of economics, we think of things and activities involving money. We think of the costs of goods and services, such as food, rent, haircuts, and movie tickets. We may also think of factories, farms, and other enterprises that produce the goods and services we need or think we need. In industrial societies, workers may stand before a moving belt for eight hours, tightening identical bolts that glide by. For this task they are given bits of paper that may be exchanged for food, shelter, and other goods or services. But many societies—indeed, most that are known to anthropology—did not have money or the equivalent of the factory worker. Still, all societies have economic systems, whether or not they involve money. All societies have customs specifying how people gain access to natural resources; customary ways of transforming or converting those resources, through labor, into necessities and other desired goods and services; and customs for distributing and perhaps exchanging goods and services.

As we shall see in this chapter, a great deal of the cross-cultural variation in economic systems is predicted by how a society gets its food. However, other aspects of the culture also affect the economic system. These other influences, which we cover in subsequent chapters, include the presence or absence of social (class and gender) inequality, family and kinship groups, and the political system.

THE ALLOCATION OF RESOURCES

NATURAL RESOURCES: LAND

Every society has access to natural resources—land, water, plants, animals, minerals—and every society has cultural rules for determining who has access to particular resources and what can be done with them. In societies like the United States, where land and many other things may be bought and sold, land is divided into precisely measurable units, the borders of which may be visible or invisible. Relatively small plots of land and the resources on them are usually owned by individuals. Large plots of land are generally owned collectively. The owner may be a government agency, such as the National Park Service, which owns land on behalf of the entire population of the United States. Or the owner may

be a corporation—a private collective of shareholders. In the United States, property ownership entails a more or less exclusive right to use land or other resources (called *usufruct*) in whatever ways the owner wishes, including the right to withhold or prevent use by others. In the United States and many other societies, property ownership also includes the right to "alienate" property—that is, to sell, give away, bequeath, or destroy the resources owned. This type of property ownership is often referred to as a *private property* system.

Private property in regard to land is unknown to most food collectors and most horticulturalists. There is no individual ownership of land or ownership by a group of unrelated people. If there is collective ownership, it is always by groups of related people (kinship groups) or by territorial groups (bands or villages). Land is not bought and sold.

Society specifies what is considered property and the rights and duties associated with that property.[1] These specifications are social in nature, for they may be changed over time. For example, France declared all its beaches to be public, thereby stating, in effect, that the ocean shore is not a resource that can be owned by an individual. As a result, all the hotels and individuals that had fenced off portions of the best beaches for their exclusive use had to remove the barriers. Even in countries with private property, such as the United States, people cannot do anything that they want with their property. Federal, state, and local governments have adopted legislation to prevent the pollution of the air and the water supply. Such regulation may be new, but the rights of ownership in the United States have been limited for some time. For example, land may be taken by the government for use in the construction of a highway; compensation is paid, but the individual cannot prevent confiscation. Similarly, people are not allowed to burn their houses or to use them as brothels or munitions arsenals. In short, even with an individualistic system of ownership, property is not entirely private.

How societies differ in their rules for access to land and other natural resources seems to be related in part to how they differ in food-getting. Let us now examine how food collectors, horticulturalists, pastoralists, and intensive agriculturalists structure rights to land in different ways. We look at traditional patterns first. As we shall note later, traditional rights to land have been considerably affected by state societies that have spread to and colonized native societies in the New World, Africa, and Asia.

FOOD COLLECTORS. As we have noted, members of food-collecting societies generally do not own land individually. The reason is probably that land itself has no intrinsic value for food collectors; what is of value is the presence of game and wild plant life on the land. If game moves away or food resources become less plentiful, the land is less valuable. Therefore, the greater the possibility that the wild food supply in a particular locale will fluctuate, the less desirable it is to parcel out small areas of land to individuals and the more advantageous it is to make land ownership communal. The Hadza of Tanzania, for example, do not believe that they have exclusive rights over the land on which they hunt. Any member of the group can hunt, gather, or draw water wherever he or she likes.[2]

Although food collectors rarely practice anything resembling individual ownership of land or other resources, there is considerable variation in the extent of communal ownership. In some societies, such as the Hadza, groups do not claim or defend particular territories. In fact, the Hadza do not even restrict use of their land to members of their own language group. But the Hadza are somewhat unusual. It is more common in food-collecting societies for a group of individuals, usually kin, to "own" land. To be sure, such ownership is not usually exclusive; typically some degree of access is provided to members of neighboring bands.[3]

At the other extreme, local groups in some foraging societies try to maintain exclusive rights to particular territories. The Owens Valley Paiute in the California part of the Great Basin lived all year in permanent villages along streams. A group of villagers claimed and defended a particular territory against intruders, who may or may not have been other Owens Valley Paiute.

Why have some food collectors been more territorial than others? One suggestion is that when the plants and animals collected are predictably located and abundant, groups are more likely to be sedentary and to try to maintain exclusive control over territories. In contrast, when plant and animal resources are unpredictable in location or amount, territoriality will tend to be minimal.[4] Territorial food collectors appear to have predictably located resources *and* more permanent villages, so it is hard to know which is more important in determining whether territory will be defended.

HORTICULTURALISTS. Like food collectors, most horticulturalists do not have individual or family ownership of land. This may be because

rapid depletion of the soil necessitates letting some of the land lie fallow for a period of years or abandoning an area after a few years and moving to a new location. There is no reason for individuals or families to claim permanent access to land that, given available technology, is not usable permanently. But, unlike food collectors, horticulturalists do allocate particular plots of land to individuals or families for their use, although these individuals or families do not own the land in our sense of potentially permanent ownership.

Among the Mundurucu of Brazil, the village controls the rights to use land. People in the community can hunt and fish where they like, and they have the right to clear a garden plot wherever land belonging to the community is not being used. Gardens can be cultivated for only two years before the soil is exhausted; then the land reverts to the community. The Mundurucu distinguish between the land and the produce on the land, so that a person who cultivates the land owns the produce. Similarly, the person who kills an animal or catches a fish owns it, no matter where it was obtained. But because all food is shared with others, it does not really matter who owns it. Rights to land became more individualized when Mundurucu men began to tap rubber trees for sale. Rights to a particular path in the forest where trees were tapped could not be bought and sold, but the rights could be inherited by a son or son-in-law.[5]

PASTORALISTS. The territory of pastoral nomads far exceeds that of most horticultural societies. Since their wealth ultimately depends on two elements, mobile herds and fixed pasturage and water, pastoralists must combine the adaptive potential of both food collectors and horticulturalists. Like food collectors, they must know the potential of their territory, which can extend as much as 1,000 miles, so that they are assured supplies of grass and water. And, like horticulturalists, after their herds graze an area clean, they must move on and let that land lie fallow until the grass renews itself. Also like horticulturalists, they depend for subsistence on human manipulation of a natural resource— animals—as opposed to the horticulturalists' land.

Although grazing land tends to be communally held, it is customary among pastoralists for animals to be owned by individuals.[6] Fredrik Barth argued that if animals were not so owned, the whole group might be in trouble because the members might be tempted to eat up their productive capital—their animals—in bad times. When animals are owned

Current Issues

DOES COMMUNAL OWNERSHIP LEAD TO ECONOMIC DISASTER?

A common idea in Western thought is that when land or other resources are held in common, serious damage results because individuals do not see it in their own interest to protect those resources. In a paper called "The Tragedy of the Commons," Garrett Hardin suggested that if animals are grazed on common land, it is economically rational for individual animal owners to graze as many animals as possible, since they do not incur the pasture costs. According to Hardin, tragedy results because pasture is degraded by overgrazing, and productivity falls. Similarly, why shouldn't a fisher take as much fish as possible from the ocean, a kind of commons, and not worry about the consequences? On the other hand, if the resource is privately owned, individuals might try to conserve their resources because degrading those resources will cost

them in the long run by decreasing their yields. The theory, then, is that in order to minimize costs and maximize yields, private owners will find it rational to conserve their resources.

Is it really true that communal ownership tends to result in overexploitation of resources and lower yields, and private ownership tends to result in conservation of resources and higher yields? We do not have enough studies yet to generalize, but we do know about instances where communal grazing lands have been more productive than private grazing lands in comparable climates. For example, the Borana of Ethiopia, who have communal grazing, produce more animal protein per acre at lower cost than Australian cattle ranches, although the climates are similar. And there are instances, such as the overgrazing in the Great American Desert

(described in the box titled "The Effect of Food-Getting on the Environment" in the preceding chapter), where private ownership did lead to degradation of the environment.

We have to remember that communal ownership does not mean that anyone can graze their animals or fish at any time. Communities and kin groups often govern rights to pasturage or fishing, and only members of the group have rights of access and use. As we saw in the last chapter, pastoralists such as the Basseri have well-defined, socially arranged travel routes, moving their herds when conditions demand. For traditional pastoralists, mobility is often the key to prevent overgrazing. Similarly, many groups that fish have strict rules regulating access to fishing grounds, and some have conservation rules as well. For example, the Palauans of Micronesia usually allow only members of a cluster of villages to fish in

individually, a family whose herd drops below the minimum number of animals necessary for survival can drop out of nomadic life, at least temporarily, and work for wages in sedentary agricultural communities. But in so doing, such a family does not jeopardize other pastoral families. On the other hand, if the fortunate were to share their herds with the unfortunate, all might approach bankruptcy. Thus, Barth argued, individual ownership is adaptive for a pastoral way of life.[7]

John Dowling questioned that interpretation. As he pointed out, pastoral nomads are not the only ones who have to save some of their "crop" for future production. Horticulturalists must save some of their crop, in the form of seeds or tubers, for future planting. But horticulturalists generally lack private ownership of productive resources, so the

necessity to save for future production cannot explain private ownership of animals in pastoral societies. Dowling suggested that private ownership will develop only in pastoral societies that depend on selling their products to nonpastoralists.[8] Thus, it may be the opportunity to sell their products as well as their labor that explains both the possibility of dropping out of nomadic life and the private ownership of animals among most pastoralists.

INTENSIVE AGRICULTURALISTS. Individual ownership of land resources—including the right to use the resources and the right to sell or otherwise dispose of them—is common among intensive agriculturalists. The development of such ownership is partly a result of the possibility of using land season after season, which gives the land more or less

the adjacent lagoon waters inside the fringing reef. Traditionally, people took only what they could eat, and there were "laws" governing the times that people could fish for certain species.

Restricted access to communal property may be the main way that pastoralists and fishers prevent degradation of their environment. Some groups, such as the Palauans, clearly have conservation rules. But we do not know how many pastoralists and fishers have such rules. For example, the Ponam of New Guinea do not appear to conserve fish resources, even though they restrict access to their communal fishing territories. They do value the prestige associated with generosity, and consequently they try to collect more fish than they need in order to give some away.

Development and commercialization may be more important than private versus communal ownership in leading to

overgrazing or overfishing, at least initially. In Palau, which had traditional conservation practices, serious overfishing became a problem apparently only when people started to sell fish to Japanese colonists for imported trade goods. Some of those goods (nets and motors) helped to make fishing easier. Eventually, overfishing resulted in reduced catches and increased costs of fishing, and the Palauans had to buy much of their fish in imported cans. In arid areas of the Sahel in Africa, development may have led to pastoral overgrazing. Boreholes were built by development agencies to increase the water supply, but this practice often made people reluctant to move to new grazing land, so local land was overgrazed. In addition, the development of irrigation agriculture nearby decreased the amount of land available for pasturage.

So which is more likely in general to lead to conservation,

communal ownership or private ownership? We cannot say yet. We need more systematic comparisons of many cases of the two types of system to tell us.

Sources: Garrett Hardin, "The Tragedy of the Commons," *Science,* 162 (1968): 1243–48; Bonnie M. McCay and James M. Acheson, "Introduction," and James G. Carrier, "Marine Tenure and Conservation in Papua New Guinea," in Bonnie M. McCay and James M. Acheson, eds., *The Question of Commons: The Culture and Ecology of Communal Resources* (Tucson: University of Arizona Press, 1987); Michael M. Horowitz, "Donors and Deserts: The Political Ecology of Destructive Development in the Sahel," in Rebecca Huss-Ashmore and Solomon H. Katz, eds., *African Food Systems in Crisis. Part Two. Contending with Change* (New York: Gordon and Breach, 1990); R. E. Johannes, *Words of the Lagoon: Fishing and Marine Lore in the Palau District of Micronesia* (Berkeley: University of California Press, 1981); Robert Dirks, "Hunger and Famine," in Carol R. Ember, Melvin Ember, and Peter N. Peregrine, eds., *Research Frontiers in Anthropology* (Upper Saddle River, NJ: Prentice Hall, 1998), Prentice Hall/Simon & Schuster Custom Publishing; John J. Poggie, personal communication, 1994.

permanent value. But the concept of individual ownership is also partly a political and social matter. So, for example, the occupation and cultivation of frontier land in the United States was transformed by law into individual ownership. Under the Homestead Act of 1862, if a person cleared a 160-acre piece of land and farmed it for five years, the federal government would consider that person the owner of the land. This practice is similar to the custom in some societies by which a kin group, a chief, or a community is obligated to assign a parcel of land to anyone who wishes to farm it. The difference is that once the American homesteader had become the owner of the land, the laws of the country gave the homesteader the right to dispose of it at will by selling or giving it away. Once individual ownership of land has become established, property owners

may use their economic, and hence political, power to pass laws that favor themselves. In the early years of the United States, only property owners could vote.

Private individual ownership is usually associated with intensive agriculture, but not always. As we mentioned in the preceding chapter, intensive agriculture is usually associated with more complex political systems and with differences in wealth and power, so we need to understand the larger political and social context in order to understand fully particular systems of land allocation. For example, under the feudal and manor system in much of medieval Europe, land and protection were granted by a higher aristocrat to a lower aristocrat (vassal) in exchange for military service and other obligations. If the vassal had no heirs, the land reverted to the

In societies with intensive agriculture, private ownership of land is common. The boundaries, as on this Idaho farm, are usually clearly marked.

higher aristocrat. Most of the farming was done by commoners—tenants and serfs. Tenants were granted land by the lord of a manor in return for labor, a portion of the crops, and military service when needed. Tenancy could be passed on to the children, and tenants technically were free to leave, but it was not easy to leave. Serfs, who had similar obligations to the lord of the manor, were bound to the land and could not leave, but neither could they be ejected.

In recent times, some communist and socialist nations with intensive agriculture formed agricultural collectives. For example, after World War II, the small farm holdings in a village in Bulgaria named Zamfirovo were incorporated into a village cooperative. Most of the villagers worked as laborers on the new cooperative, but every household was allocated a small plot by the cooperative on which to grow its own grain, vegetables, and grapes. These plots were fairly productive, and Westerners often attributed their productivity to private enterprise. But the cooperative provided much of the labor needed to plant and plow these plots, so they could hardly be considered private property. In 1989, after the overthrow of the communist regime, the cooperative was dissolved, and the land was divided and sold to private owners.[9]

COLONIALISM AND NATIVES' CONTROL OVER LAND. Almost universally around the world, colonial conquerors and settlers have taken land away from the natives or aborigines. Even if the natives were given other land in exchange, as in Brazil and the United States, these reservations were often, if not always, poorer in potential than the original land. (If the reservation land hadn't been poorer in quality, the settlers would have taken it for themselves.) In addition, the new centralized governments often tried to change how land was owned

by the natives, almost always in the direction of individual or private ownership. If kin groups or larger social entities owned the land, it would be more difficult for the settlers to get the natives to give it up, either by sale or threat. Individual owners could be dispossessed more easily.[10]

The newcomers who benefitted from these forced changes were not always people of European background, but they were always people from expanding state societies. Beginning in the late fifteenth century, the expanding groups came mostly from Western Europe. But in recent times, as well as in the millennia before and after the time of Christ, conquerors and settlers have come from India, China, Japan, Arabia, Scandinavia, Russia, and other countries. This is not to say that native peoples in Africa, Asia, and the New World were never guilty of conquering and exploiting others on their continents or elsewhere. They were. The Aztecs in Mexico and Central America, the native kingdoms in West Africa after about 800 years ago, and the Arabs after the rise of Islam were just some of the expanding state societies of the past, before the rise of the West. Wherever there have been "civilized" (urban) societies, there have been imperialism and colonialism.

In North America, the British recognized the principle that lands not ceded to the crown would be Indian hunting grounds, but such recognition of rights by the British and then by the United States remained in force only as long as the various Indian groups remained numerous enough to constitute a threat to the settlers. President Andrew Jackson, for example, called for removal of all eastern Native American groups to "permanent" settlements west of the Mississippi. Some 90,000 people were removed. But as settlers moved west, the reservations were often reduced in size. Government agents usually assumed that communal forms of ownership were detrimental to progress and enacted laws to assign land to individuals.[11] In much of colonial Africa, governments ceded land to European-owned companies for development. Reserves were established for large native populations, who then were invariably forced to work as laborers on European-owned plantations and in European-owned mines. In Kenya, for example, Europeans who constituted less than 1 percent of the population acquired access to or control of 20 percent of the land, mostly in the highlands, where there was the greatest potential for commercial production of tea and coffee.[12]

TECHNOLOGY

In order to convert resources to food and other goods, every society makes use of a technology, which includes tools, constructions (such as fish traps), and required skills (such as how and where to set up a fish trap). Societies vary considerably in their technologies and in the way access to technology is allocated. For example, food collectors and pastoralists typically have fairly small tool kits. They must limit their tools, and their material possessions in general, to what they can comfortably carry with them. As for access to technology, food collectors and horticulturalists generally allow equal opportunity. In the absence of specialization, most individuals have the skills to make what they need. But in an industrial society like our own, the opportunity to acquire or use a particular technology (which may be enormously expensive as well as complex) is hardly available to all. Most of us may be able to buy a drill or a hammer, but few of us can buy the factory that makes it.

The tools most needed by food collectors are weapons for the hunt, digging sticks, and receptacles for gathering and carrying. Andaman Islanders used bows and arrows for hunting game and large fish. Australian aborigines developed two types of boomerangs: a heavy one for a straight throw in killing game and a light, returning one for playing games or for scaring birds into nets strung between trees. The Semang of Malaya used poisoned darts and blowguns. The Mbuti Pygmies of the Congo still trap elephants and buffalo in deadfalls and nets. Of all food collectors, the Inuit probably had the most sophisticated weapons, including harpoons, compound bows, and ivory fishhooks. Yet the Inuit also had relatively fixed settlements with available storage space and dog teams and sleds for transportation.[13]

Among food collectors, tools are considered to belong to the person who made them. There is no way of gaining superiority over others through possession of tools, because whatever resources for toolmaking are available to one are available to all. In addition, the custom of sharing applies to tools as well as to food. For example, Elizabeth Thomas, speaking of the !Kung, said, "The few possessions that Bushmen have are constantly circulating among the members of their groups."[14]

Pastoralists, like food collectors, are somewhat limited in their possessions, for they too are nomadic. But pastoralists can use their animals to carry some possessions. Each family owns its own tools, clothes, and perhaps a tent, as well as its own livestock. The livestock are the source of other needed articles, for the pastoralists often trade their herd products for the products of the townspeople. Horticulturalists, on the other hand, are more self-sufficient than pastoralists. The knife for slashing and the hoe or stick for digging are their principal farming tools. What a person makes is considered his or her own, yet everyone is often obligated to lend tools to others. In Truk society, the owner of a canoe has first use of it; the same is true for farming implements. Yet if a close relative needs the canoe and finds it unused, the canoe may be taken without permission. A distant relative or neighbor must ask permission to borrow any tools, but the owner may not refuse. If owners were to refuse, they would risk being scorned and refused if they were to need tools later.

Societies with intensive agriculture and industrialized societies are likely to have tools made by specialists, which means that tools must be acquired by trade or purchase. Probably because complex tools cost a considerable amount of money, they are less likely than simple tools to be shared except by those who contributed to the purchase price. For example, a diesel-powered combine requires a large amount of capital for its purchase and upkeep. The person who has supplied the capital is likely to regard the machine as individual private property and to regulate its use and disposal. Farmers may not have the capital to purchase the machine they need, so they may have to borrow from a bank. The owner must then use the machine to produce enough surplus to pay for its cost and upkeep as well as for its replacement. The owner may rent the machine to neighboring farmers during slack periods to obtain a maximum return on the investment.

Expensive equipment, however, is not always individually owned in societies with intensive agriculture or industrialized economies. Even in capitalist countries, there may be collective ownership of machines by cooperatives or co-ownership with neighbors.[15] Governments often own very expensive equipment or facilities that benefit some productive group as well as the public: Airports benefit airlines and travelers; highways benefit truckers, commuters, and travelers; dams benefit power and water companies as well as the consumers of water. Such resources are owned collectively by the whole society. Rights of use depend on the facility. Anyone can use a highway, but only contributing municipalities can draw upon the water in a dam. Other productive resources in industrial societies, such as factories or service companies, may be owned jointly by shareholders, who purchase a portion of a corporation's assets in return for a proportionate share of its earnings. The proportion of technology and facilities owned by various levels of government also reflects the type of political-economic system—socialist and communist countries have more public ownership than do capitalist countries.

THE CONVERSION OF RESOURCES

In all societies, resources have to be transformed or converted through labor into food, tools, and other goods. These activities constitute what economists call *production*. In this section, after briefly reviewing different types of production, we examine what motivates people to work, how societies divide up the work to be done, and how they organize work. As we shall see, some aspects of the conversion of natural resources are culturally universal, but there is also an enormous amount of cultural variation.

TYPES OF ECONOMIC PRODUCTION

At least at the times they were first described, most of the societies known to anthropology had a *domestic*—family or kinship—mode of production. People labored to get food and to produce shelter and implements for themselves and their kin. Usually families had the right to exploit productive resources and control the products of their labor. Even part-time specialists, such as potters, could still support themselves without that craft if they needed to. At the other extreme are *industrial* societies, where much of the work is based on mechanized production, as in factories but also in mechanized agriculture. Because machines and materials are costly, only some individuals (capitalists), corporations, or governments can afford the expenses of production. Therefore, most people in industrial societies labor for others as wage earners. Although wages can buy food, people out of work lose their

ability to support themselves, unless they are protected by welfare payments or unemployment insurance. Then there is the *tributary* type of production system, found in nonindustrial societies in which most people still produce their own food, but an elite or aristocracy controls a portion of production (including the products of specialized crafts). The feudal societies of medieval Western Europe were examples of tributary production, as was czarist Russia under serfdom.[16]

Many people have suggested that our own and other developed economies are now moving from *industrialism* to *postindustrialism*. In many areas of commerce, computers have radically transformed the workplace. Computers "drive" machines and robots, and much of the manual work required in industry is disappearing. Businesses are now more knowledge- and service-oriented. Information is more accessible with telecommunication, so much so that *telecommuting* has entered our vocabulary to describe how people can now work (for wages) at home. This economic transformation has important implications for both home life and the workplace. With inexpensive home computers and speedy data transmission by telephone and other means, more and more people are able to work at home. In addition, when information and knowledge become more important than capital equipment, more and more people can own and have access to the productive resources of society.[17] If "who owns what" partly determines who has political and other influence, the wider ownership of resources that is possible in postindustrial society may eventually translate into new, more democratic political forms and processes.

INCENTIVES FOR LABOR

Why do people work? Probably all of us have asked ourselves this question. Our concern may not be why other people are working, but why *we* have to work. Clearly, part of the answer is that work is necessary for survival. Although there are always some able-bodied adults who do not work as much as they should and rely on the labor of others, no society would survive if most able-bodied adults were like that. In fact, most societies probably succeed in motivating most people to want to do (and even enjoy) what they have to do. But are the incentives for labor the same in all societies? Anthropologists think the answer is both yes and no. One reason people may work is because they must. But why do people in some societies apparently work *more* than they must?

We can be fairly certain that a particular and often-cited motive—the profit motive, or the desire to exchange something for more than it costs—is not universal or always the dominant motive. There can be no profit motive among people who produce food and other goods primarily for their own consumption, as do most food collectors, most horticulturalists, and even some intensive agriculturalists. Such societies have what we call a *subsistence economy*, not a money or commercial economy. Anthropologists have noticed that people in subsistence economies (with a domestic mode of production) often work less than people in commercial economies (with tributary or industrial modes of production). Indeed, food collectors appear to have a considerable amount of leisure time, as do many horticulturalists. It has been estimated, for example, that the men of the horticultural Kuikuru tribe in central Brazil spent about three and a half hours a day on subsistence. It appears that the Kuikuru could have produced a substantial surplus of manioc, their staple food, by working 30 minutes more a day.[18] Yet they and many other peoples do not produce more than they need. Why should they? They cannot store a surplus for long because it would rot; they cannot sell it because there is no market nearby; and they do not have a political authority that might collect it for some purpose. Although we often think "more is better," a food-getting strategy with such a goal might even be disastrous, especially for food collectors. The killing of more animals than a group could eat might seriously jeopardize the food supply in the future, because overhunting could reduce reproduction among the hunted animals.[19] Horticulturalists might do well to plant a little extra, just in case part of the crop failed, but a great deal extra would be a tremendous waste of time and effort.

It has been suggested that when resources are converted primarily for household consumption, people will work harder if they have more consumers in the household. That is, when there are few able-bodied workers and a proportionately large number of consumers (perhaps because there are many young children and old people), the workers have to work harder. But when there are proportionately more workers, they can work less. This idea is called *Chayanov's rule*.[20] Alexander Chayanov found this relationship in data on rural Russians before the Communist revolution.[21] But it appears to work in other places too. For example, Michael Chibnik found support for Chayanov's rule when he compared data from 12 communities in 5 areas of the world. The communities ranged in complexity from New Guinea horticulturalists to commercial Swiss farmers. Although Chayanov restricted his theory to farmers who mostly produce food for their own consumption and do not hire labor, Chibnik's analysis suggests that Chayanov's rule applies even for hired labor.[22]

But there appear to be many societies, even with subsistence economies, in which some people work harder than they need to just for their own families' subsistence. What motivates them to work harder? It turns out that many subsistence economies are not oriented just to household consumption. Rather, sharing and other transfers of food and goods often go well beyond the household, sometimes including the whole community or even groups of communities, as we will see later in this chapter. In such societies, social rewards come to those who are generous, who give things away. Thus, people who work harder than they have to for subsistence may be motivated to do so because they gain respect or esteem thereby.[23] In many societies too, as we shall see in subsequent chapters, extra food and goods may be needed at times for special purposes and occasions; goods and services may be needed to arrange and celebrate marriages, to form alliances, and to perform rituals and ceremonies (including what we would call sporting events). Thus, how the culture defines what one works for and what is needed may go beyond what is necessary.

In commercial economies such as our own—where foods, other goods, and services are sold and bought—people seem to be motivated to keep any extra income for themselves and their families. Extra income is converted into bigger dwellings, more expensive furnishings and food, and other elements of a "higher" standard of living. But the desire to improve one's standard of living is probably not the only motive operating. Some people may work partly to satisfy a need for achievement,[24] or because they find their work enjoyable. In addition, just as in precommercial societies, some people may work partly to gain respect or influence by giving some of their income away. Not only do we respect philanthropists and movie stars for giving to charities; our society encourages such giving by making it an allowable tax deduction. Still, the emphasis on giving in commercial societies is clearly less developed than in subsistence economies. We consider charity by the religious or rich appropriate and even admirable, but we would think it foolish or crazy for people to give so much away that they became poverty-stricken.

FORCED LABOR

Thus far we have mostly discussed *voluntary labor*—voluntary in the sense that no formal organization within the society compels people to work and punishes them for not working. Social training and social pressure are powerful enough to persuade an individual to perform some useful task. In both food-collecting and horticultural societies, individuals who can stand being the butt of jokes about laziness will still be fed. At most, they will be ignored by the other members of the group. There is no reason to punish them and no way to coerce them to do the work expected of them.

More complex societies have ways of forcing people to work for the authorities, whether those authorities be kings or presidents. An indirect form of forced labor is taxation. The average tax in the United States (local, state, and federal) is about 33 percent of income, which means that the average person works four months out of the year for the government. If a person decides not to pay the tax, the money will be taken forcibly or the person may be put in prison.

Money is the customary form of tax payment in a commercial society. In a politically complex but nonmonetary society, persons may pay their taxes in other ways—by performing a certain number of hours of labor or by giving up a certain percentage of what they produce. The **corvée,** a system of required labor, existed in the Inca Empire in the central Andes before the Spanish conquest. Each male commoner was assigned three plots of land to work: a temple plot, a state plot, and his own plot. The enormous stores of food that went into state warehouses were used to supply the nobles, the army, the artisans, and all other state employees. If labor became overabundant, the people were still kept occupied; it is said that one ruler had a hill moved to keep some laborers busy. In addition to subsistence work for the state, Inca commoners were subject to military service, to duty as personal servants for the nobility, and to other "public" service.[25]

The draft or compulsory military service is also a form of corvée, in that a certain period of service is required, and failure to serve can be punished by a prison term or involuntary exile. Emperors of China had soldiers drafted to defend their territory and to build the Great Wall along the northern borders of the empire. The wall extends over 1,500 miles, and thousands were drafted to work on it. Slavery is the most extreme form of forced work, in that slaves

The Great Wall of China, like many monumental works in ancient societies, was built with forced labor.

have little control over their labor. Because slaves constitute a category or class of persons in many societies, we discuss slavery more fully in the chapter on social stratification.

DIVISION OF LABOR

All societies have some division of labor, some customary assignment of different kinds of work to different kinds of people. Universally, males and females and adults and children do not do the same kinds of work. In a sense, then, division of labor by gender and age is a kind of universal specialization of labor. Many societies known to anthropology divide labor only by gender and age; other societies have more complex specialization.

BY GENDER AND AGE. All societies make use of gender differences to some extent in their customary assignment of labor. In the chapter on sex, gender, and culture, we discuss the division of labor by gender in detail.

Age is also a universal basis for division of labor. Clearly, children cannot do work that requires a great deal of strength. But in many societies girls and boys contribute much more in labor than do children in our own society. For example, they help in animal tending, weeding, and harvesting and do a variety of domestic chores such as child care, fetching water and firewood, and cooking and cleaning. Indeed, in some societies a child 6 years old is considered old enough to be responsible for a younger sibling for a good part of the day.[26] Animal tending is often important work for children. Children in some societies spend more time at this task than adults.[27]

Why do children do so much work in some societies? If adults, particularly mothers, have heavy workloads, and children are physically and mentally able to do the work, a good part of the work is likely to be assigned to children.[28] As we have seen, food producers probably have more work than food collectors, so we would expect that children would be likely to work more where there is herding and farming. Consistent with this expectation, Patricia Draper and Elizabeth Cashdan found differences in children's work between nomadic and settled !Kung. Even though recently settled !Kung have not switched completely from food collection to food production, children's as well as adults' activities have changed considerably. The children living in nomadic camps had virtually no work at all; adults did all the gathering and hunting. But the settled children were given lots of chores, ranging from helping with animals to helping with the harvest and food processing.[29]

What we have said about the !Kung should not imply that children in foraging societies always do little work. For example, among the Hadza of Tanzania, children between the ages of 5 and 10 are able to get one-third to one-half of their calories as they forage with their mothers. The Hadza also have more children than the !Kung.[30] Is there a relationship between children's work and fertility? When children in a society do a great deal of work, parents may value them more and may consciously want to have more children.[31] This may be one of the reasons why birth rates are especially high in intensive agricultural societies where work loads are very high.[32]

In some societies, work groups are formally organized on the basis of age. Among the Nyakyusa of southeastern Africa, for example, cattle are the principal form of wealth, and boys 6 to 11 years old herd the cattle for their parents' village. The boys join together in herding groups to tend the cattle of their fathers and of any neighboring families that do not have a son of herding age.[33]

BEYOND GENDER AND AGE. In societies with relatively simple technologies, there is little specialization of labor beyond that of gender and age. But as a society's technology becomes more complex and it is able to produce large quantities of food, more of its people are freed from subsistence work to become specialists in some other tasks—canoe builders, weavers, priests, potters, artists, and the like.

In contrast with food collectors, horticultural societies may have some part-time specialists. Some people may devote special effort to perfecting a particular skill or craft—pottery making, weaving, house building, doctoring—and in return for their products or services be given food or other gifts. Among some horticultural groups, the entire village may specialize part-time in making a particular product, which can then be traded to neighboring people.

With the development of intensive agriculture, full-time specialists—potters, weavers, blacksmiths—begin to appear. The trend toward greater specialization reaches its peak in industrialized societies, where workers develop skills in one small area of the economic system. The meaninglessness and dehumanizing effect of much of industrialized work was depicted by Charlie Chaplin in the film *Modern Times.* When his character left the factory after repeatedly tightening the same kind of bolt all day long, he could not stop his arms from moving, as if they were still tightening bolts. In societies with full-time occupational specialization, different jobs are usually associated with differences in prestige, wealth, and power, as we shall see in the chapter on social stratification.

In many societies, children do a great deal of work. Here a young Mamvu girl in Zaire minds her two year-old brother.

Specialization is more likely in a society that practices intensive agriculture, as here in Scotland.

THE ORGANIZATION OF LABOR

The degree to which labor has to be organized reaches its peak in industrial societies, which have great occupational specialization and complex political organization. The coordination required to produce an automobile on an assembly line is obvious; so is the coordination required to collect taxes from every wage earner.

In many food-collecting and horticultural societies there is little formal organization of work. Work groups tend to be organized only when productive work requires it and to dissolve when they are no longer needed. Furthermore, the groups so organized often have changing composition and leadership; participation tends to be individualistic and voluntary.[34] Perhaps this flexibility is possible because when virtually everyone has the same work to do, little instruction is needed, and almost anyone can assume leadership. Still, some types of work require more organization than others. Hunting big game usually requires coordinated efforts by a large number of hunters; so might catching fish in large nets. For example, on Moala, a Fijian island in the

Pacific, net fishing is a group affair. Saturday is the most popular day for communal netting. A party of 20 to 30 women wade out on the reef and make a semicircle of nets. At a signal from an experienced woman, usually the chief's wife, the women move together at the ends, forming a circle. After the fish are caught in the nets, the women bite them on the backs of their heads to kill them and put them in baskets that they carry ashore. A larger fish drive is undertaken by the village, or several villages, around Christmas. The day before, more than 100 people make a "sweep," some 1,600 yards long, from coconut fronds. The next day, the men, women, and children all participate in the surround, catching thousands of fish.[35]

Kinship ties are an important basis for work organization, particularly in nonindustrial societies. For example, among the horticultural Kapauku of western New Guinea, the male members of a village are a kin group, and all work together to build drainage ditches, large fences, and bridges.[36] With increasing technological complexity, the basis of work organization begins to shift to more formally organized groups.[37] In modern industrial societies, the predominant basis of organization is the *contract*—the agreement between employers and employees whereby the latter perform a specified amount of work for a specified amount of wages. Although the arrangement may be entered into voluntarily, laws and the power of the state enforce the obligation of the parties to abide by the contract.

MAKING DECISIONS ABOUT WORK

Food collectors ignore many of the plant and animal species in their environment, choosing to go after only some. Why? The people may say that some animals are taboo whereas others are delicious. But where do such customary beliefs come from? Are they adaptive? And if there are no customary preferences for certain plants and animals, how can we explain why a food collector will go after certain foods and ignore others on a particular day? Food producers also make choices constantly. For example, a farmer has to decide when to plant, what to plant, how much to plant, when to harvest, how much to store, how much to give away or sell. Researchers have recently tried to explain why certain economic decisions become customary and why individuals make certain economic choices in their everyday lives.

A frequent source of ideas about choices is **optimal foraging theory,** which was developed originally by students of animal behavior and which has been applied to decision making by food collectors. Optimal foraging theory assumes that individuals seek to maximize the returns, in calories and nutrients, on their labor in deciding which animals and plants to hunt or collect. Natural selection should favor optimal foraging because "good" decisions would increase the chances of survival and reproduction. Research in different food-collecting societies supports the optimal foraging model.[38] For example, the Aché of eastern Paraguay consistently prefer to hunt peccaries (wild piglike mammals) rather than armadillos. Although peccaries take much longer to find and are harder to kill than armadillos, a day spent hunting peccaries yields more than 4,600 calories per hour of work, whereas hunting armadillos yields only about 1,800 calories an hour.[39] Other factors in addition to calorie yield, such as predictability of resources, may also influence which foods are collected. For example, the !Kung of the Kalahari Desert depend largely on mongongo nuts, even though these nuts yield fewer calories per hour of work than does meat. But mongongo nuts in season are more dependable than game is. Once a group of !Kung hikes to a grove of ripe mongongo nuts, they know they can obtain food there until the supply is exhausted; they are not as certain of getting game when they seek it.[40]

How does a farmer decide whether to plant a particular crop and how much land and labor to devote to it? Christina Gladwin and others suggested that farmers make decisions in steps, with each choice point involving a yes or no answer. For example, in the high-altitude region of Guatemala, farmers could choose to plant about eight crops, or combinations of them, such as corn and beans, which grow together well. A farmer will quickly exclude some choices because of the answers to certain questions: Can I afford the seed and fertilizer? Can this crop be watered adequately? Is the altitude appropriate? And so on. If any of the answers is no, the crop is not planted. By a further series of yes or no decisions, farmers presumably decide which of the remaining possibilities will be planted.[41]

Individuals may not always be able to state clearly their rules for making decisions, nor do they always have complete knowledge about the various possibilities, particularly when some of the possibilities are new. That does not mean, however, that economic choices cannot be predicted or explained by researchers. For example, Michael Chibnik found that men in two villages in Belize, in Central America, were not able to say why they devoted more or less time to working for wages versus growing crops. But their behavior was still pre-

dictable. Older men grew crops because wage labor was more physically demanding; and in the village with a higher cost of living, men were more likely to work for wages.[42]

THE DISTRIBUTION OF GOODS AND SERVICES

Goods and services are distributed in all societies by systems that, however varied, can be classified under three general types: reciprocity, redistribution, and market or commercial exchange.[43] The three systems often coexist in a society, but one system usually predominates. The predominant system seems to be associated with the society's food-getting technology and, more specifically, its level of economic development.

RECIPROCITY

Reciprocity consists of giving and taking without the use of money; it ranges from pure gift giving to equal exchanges to cheating. Technically, then, reciprocity may take three forms: generalized reciprocity, balanced reciprocity, and negative reciprocity.[44]

GENERALIZED RECIPROCITY. When goods or services are given to another, without any apparent expectation of a return gift, we call it **generalized reciprocity.** Generalized reciprocity sustains the family in all societies. Parents give food, clothing, and labor to children because they want to or perhaps feel obliged to, but they do not usually calculate exactly how their children will reciprocate years later. In this sense, all societies have some kind of generalized reciprocity. But some societies depend on it almost entirely to distribute goods and services.

Lorna Marshall recounted how the !Kung divided an eland brought to a site where five bands and several visitors were camping—more than 100 people in all. The owner of the arrow that had first penetrated the eland was, by custom, the owner of the meat. He first distributed the forequarters to the two hunters who had aided him in the kill. After that, the distribution depended on kinship: Each hunter shared with his wives' parents, wives, children, parents, and siblings, and they in turn shared with their kin. Sixty-three gifts of raw meat were recorded, after which further sharing of raw and cooked meat was begun. The !Kung distribution of large game—clearly, generalized reciprocity—is common among foragers. But giving away is not limited to game. For example, when Marshall left the band that had sponsored her in 1951, she gave

Alaskan Eskimo share the meat from whale hunting. Most foragers share game, which is less predictable than gathering.

each woman in the band a present of enough cowrie shells to make a necklace—one large shell and 20 small ones. When she returned in 1952, there were no cowrie-shell necklaces and hardly a single shell among the people in the band. Instead, the shells appeared by ones and twos in the ornaments of the people of neighboring bands.[45]

Although generalized reciprocity may seem altruistic or unselfish, researchers have suggested that giving may in fact benefit the givers in various ways. For example, parents who help their children may not only perpetuate their genes (the ultimate biological benefit) but may also be likely to receive care and affection from their grown-up children when the parents are old. And giving parents may be happier and enjoy life more than nongiving parents. So, in the shorter as well as the longer run, givers may derive economic and psychological benefits, in addition to reproductive benefits.

Parent-child giving may seem easy to understand, but giving beyond the family is more of a problem. Why do some societies rely more on generalized reciprocity than others, particularly beyond the family? Sharing may be most likely when people are not sure they can get the food and water they need. In other words, sharing may be most likely if resources are unpredictable. So a !Kung band may share its water with other bands because they may have water now but not in the future. A related group in the Kalahari, the G//ana,[46] has been observed to share less than other groups. It turns out that the resources available to the G//ana are more

predictable, because the G//ana supplement their hunting and gathering with plant cultivation and goat herding. Cultivated melons (which store water) appear to buffer the G//ana against water shortages, and goats to buffer them against shortages of game. Thus, whereas the !Kung distribute the meat right after a kill, the G//ana dry it and then store it in their houses.[47]

The idea that unpredictability favors sharing may also explain why some foods are more often shared than others. Wild game, for example, is usually unpredictable; when hunters go out to hunt, they cannot be sure that they will come back with meat. Wild plants, on the other hand, are more predictable; gatherers can be sure when they go out that they will come back with at least some plant foods. In any case, it does appear that game tends to be shared by food collectors much more than wild plant foods.[48] Even among people who depend largely on horticulture, such as the Yanomamö of Venezuela and Brazil, food items that are less predictably obtained (hunted game and fish) are shared more often than the more predictably obtained garden produce.[49]

Does food sharing increase the food supply for an individual? Calculations for the Aché of eastern Paraguay, who get most of their food from hunting when they go on food-collecting trips, suggest that the average individual gets more food when food is shared. Even the males who actually do the hunting get more, although the benefits are greater for the females and children on the trip.[50] Mathematically, the risk that an individual food collector will not find enough food on a particular day will be appreciably reduced if at least six to eight adult collectors share the food they collect. Food-collecting bands may often contain only 25 to 30 people, which is about the size that is needed to ensure that there are six to eight adult collectors.[51]

Although giving things to others may be expected in some societies, this does not necessarily mean that everyone does so willingly or without some social pressure. For example, the !Kung call "far-hearted" anyone who does not give gifts, and they express their disapproval openly. The necessity to reduce tensions, to avoid envy and anger, and to keep all social relations peaceful, not only within their own band but among all !Kung bands, creates continuing cross-currents of obligation and friendship. These are maintained, renewed, or established through the generalized reciprocity of gift giving. In a sense, one can say that in exchange for a gift, one gains prestige or perhaps "social credit" for a potential return at some indefinite time in the future. But this gain clearly is not based on explicit return considerations. Among the !Kung as well as other foraging groups, a person who does not hunt will still get a share of meat.

Day-to-day unpredictability is one thing; more prolonged scarcity is another. What happens to a system of generalized reciprocity when resources are scarce because of a drought or other disaster? Does the ethic of giving break down? Evidence from a few societies suggests that the degree of sharing may actually *increase* during the period of food shortage.[52] For example, in describing the Netsilik Inuit, Asen Balikci said, "Whenever game was abundant, sharing among non-relatives was avoided, since every family was supposedly capable of obtaining the necessary catch. In situations of scarcity, however, caribou meat was more evenly distributed throughout camp."[53] Sharing may increase during mild scarcity because people can minimize their deprivation, but generalized reciprocity may be strained by extreme scarcity. Ethnographic evidence from a few societies suggests that during famine, when individuals are actually dying from hunger, sharing may be limited to the household.[54]

BALANCED RECIPROCITY. Balanced reciprocity is explicit and short term in its expectations of return. It involves either an immediate exchange of goods or services or an agreed-upon exchange over a limited period of time. The !Kung, for instance, trade with the Tswana Bantu: a gemsbok hide for a pile of tobacco, five strings of beads made from ostrich eggshells for a spear, three small skins for a good-sized knife.[55] In the 1600s, the Iroquois of the North American Northeast traded deerskin to Europeans for brass kettles, iron hinges, steel axes, woven textiles, and guns.[56] The !Kung and Iroquois acquired trade goods by balanced reciprocity, but such exchanges were not crucial to their economies.

In contrast, some societies depend much more heavily on balanced reciprocity. For example, the Efe, who hunt and gather in the Ituri forest of central Africa, get most of their calories from manioc, peanuts, rice, and plaintains grown by another group—the agricultural Lese. Efe men and women provide labor to the Lese, and in exchange receive a portion of the harvest as well as goods such as metal pots and spears.[57] Pastoralists, too, are rarely self-sufficient, as we mentioned in the preceding chapter. They have to trade their pastoral products to agriculturalists to get the grain and other things they need.

Balanced reciprocity may mostly involve labor. Cooperative work parties exchange or balance gifts of labor. A cooperative work party, or *kuu,* among the Kpelle of Liberia may number from 6 to 40 persons, all of whom are generally relatives or friends. In addition to promising return work on a particular date, each farmer rewards the work party's hard day's labor by providing a feast and sometimes rhythmic music to work by.[58]

When we say that an exchange is balanced, we do not mean to imply that the things exchanged are exactly equivalent in value or that the exchange is purely economic. In the absence of a money economy, where there is no explicit standard by which value can be judged, there is no way to assess value objectively. The point is that the parties in balanced reciprocity are freely giving each other the respective goods and services they each want; they are not coerced into doing so, so presumably they are not conceiving of the exchange as unbalanced.[59] And when something is valued, it may be valued for other than economic reasons. The exchange itself may also be fun, adventuresome, or aesthetically pleasing, or it may enhance social relationships.

Because exchanges can have different motivations, they can have different meanings. Consequently, some economic anthropologists now want to distinguish between gift and commodity exchanges. *Gift exchanges* are personal and involve the creation or perpetuation of some kind of enduring relationship between people and groups. In our society, the exchange of dinner invitations or Christmas gifts is motivated by social considerations; we are not interested only in the actual food or objects received. As we shall see shortly, some of the exchanges involved in the famous *kula* ring seem mostly to be motivated by the desire to establish or cement trade partnerships. In contrast, *commodity exchanges,* which can occur even in the absence of money, focus on the objects or services received— the transaction itself is the motive. When the transaction is completed, the relationship between the parties involved usually ends.[60]

The Kula Ring. The horticultural Trobriand Islanders, who live off the eastern coast of New Guinea, have worked out an elaborate scheme for trading food and other items with the people of neighboring islands. Such trade is essential, for some of the islands are small and rocky and cannot produce enough food to sustain their inhabitants, who specialize instead in canoe building, pottery making, and other crafts. Other islands produce far more yams, taro, and pigs than they need. Yet the trade of such necessary items is carefully hidden beneath the panoply of the **kula ring,** a ceremonial exchange of valued shell ornaments.[61]

Two kinds of ornaments are involved in the ceremony of exchanges—white shell armbands *(mwali),* which travel around the circle of islands in a counterclockwise direction, and red shell necklaces *(soulava),* which travel in a clockwise direction (see Figure 14–1). The possession of one or more of these ornaments allows a man to organize an expedition to the home of one of his trading partners on another island. The high point of an expedition is the ceremonial giving of the valued *kula* ornaments. Each member of the expedition receives a shell ornament from his trading partner and then remains on the island for two or three days as the guest of that person. During the visit the real trading goes on. Some of the exchange takes the form of gift giving between trading partners. There is also exchange or barter between expedition members and others on the island. By the time the visitors leave, they have accomplished a year's trading, without seeming to do so.

But the practical advantages of the *kula* ring are not the only gains. There may be purely social ones, for goods are traded with ease and enjoyment. A trading expedition takes on the flavor of adventure rather than business. Many of the traditions of the islands are kept alive: Myth, romance, ritual, and history are linked to the circulating ornaments, especially the larger, finer pieces, which are well known and recognized as heirlooms. The *kula* ring also permits wide ownership of valuables. Instead of possessing one valued object permanently, a man is able to possess many valued things within his lifetime, each for a year or so. Each object, when it is received, arouses enthusiasm in a way that one lifelong possession could not.[62]

Whatever the reasons for the origin of the *kula* ring, which may date back nearly 2,000 years, it continued to be an important institution after Papua New Guinea became an independent country. For example, active participation in the *kula* ring helped candidates in the 1960s and the 1970s to be elected to the national parliament.[63]

The *kula* is not the only form of exchange in Trobriand life. For example, on the two days following a burial, the kin of the deceased give yams, taro, and valuables to those who helped care for the deceased before death, to those who participated in the burial ceremonies, and to those who came to mourn the deceased. After these initial exchanges, the hamlet settles into mourning. Women from other hamlets bring food to the people in mourning, and the mourning women prepare bundles of banana leaves

---

FIGURE 14–1 *The Kula Ring*

In the *kula* ring, red shell necklaces *(soulava)* travel in a clockwise direction; white shell armbands *(mwali)* travel counterclockwise. The solid lines show the overseas trade routes. The dashed circles identify the *(kula)* communities, and the dashed rectangles show the areas indirectly affected by the *kula.*

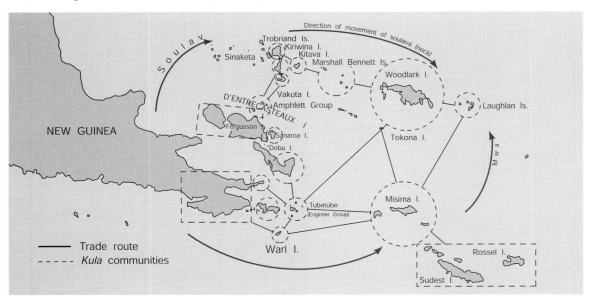

and weave skirts of banana fiber for later distribution. Husbands help their wives accumulate valuables to "buy" extra bundles of banana leaves. Then the women's mortuary ceremony is held. It is very competitive—each of the mourning women tries to distribute the most bundles and skirts. As many as 5,000 bundles and 30 skirts might be distributed by one mourning woman in a single day. Each of these giveaways completes a balanced reciprocity: The giver is reciprocating for gifts of goods and services received in the past. A woman's brothers gave her yams and taro during the year. She gives her brothers' wives bundles or skirts, which are also given to those who helped make the special mourning skirts and to those who brought or cooked food during the mourning period.[64]

Sometimes the line between generalized and balanced reciprocity is not so clear. Consider our gift giving at Christmas. Although such gift giving may appear to be generalized reciprocity, there may be strong expectations of balance. Two friends or relatives may try to exchange presents of fairly equal value, based on calculations of what last year's gift cost. If a person receives a $5 present when he or she gave a $25 present, that person will be hurt and perhaps angry. On the other hand, a person who receives a $500 present when he or she gave a $25 present may well be dismayed.

NEGATIVE RECIPROCITY. Taking without thought of a fair return is to take advantage of another, to get something for nothing or for less than its worth. A mild form is deceitful bargaining; extreme forms are theft and other varieties of seizure. In other words, **negative reciprocity** ranges from "various degrees of cunning, guile, stealth, and violence to the finesse of a well-conducted horse-raid."[65]

KINSHIP DISTANCE AND TYPE OF RECIPROCITY. Most food-collecting and horticultural societies depend on some form of reciprocity for the distribution of goods and labor. Marshall Sahlins suggested that whether the reciprocity is generalized, balanced, or negative depends largely on the kinship distance between persons. Generalized reciprocity may be the rule for family members and close kinsmen. Balanced reciprocity may be practiced among equals who are not closely related. Persons who would consider it inappropriate to trade with their own families will trade with neighboring groups. Negative reciprocity may be practiced against strangers and enemies.[66] In general, the importance of reciprocity declines with economic development.[67] In societies with intensive agriculture, and even more so in industrialized societies, reciprocity distributes only a small proportion of goods and services.

RECIPROCITY AS A LEVELING DEVICE. Reciprocal gift giving may do more than equalize the distribution of goods within a community, as in the !Kung's sharing. It may also tend to equalize the distribution of goods between communities.

Many Melanesian societies in and near New Guinea have the custom of holding pig feasts in which 50, 100, or even 2,000 pigs are slaughtered. Andrew Vayda, Anthony Leeds, and David Smith suggested that these enormous feasts, though apparently wasteful, are just one of the outcomes of a complex of cultural practices that are highly advantageous. The people of these societies cannot accurately predict how much food they will produce during the year. Some years there will be bumper crops, other years very poor crops, because of fluctuations in the weather. So it might be wise to overplant just in case the yield is poor. Yet overplanting results in overproduction during average and exceptionally good years. What can be done with this extra food? Root crops such as yams and taro do not keep well over long periods, so any surplus is fed to pigs, which become, in effect, food-storing repositories. Pigs are then available for needed food during lean times. But if there are several years of surpluses, pigs can become too much of a good thing. Pigs wanting food can destroy yam and taro patches. When the pig population grows to menacing proportions, a village may invite other villages to a gigantic feast that results in a sharp reduction of the pig population and keeps the fields from being overrun. Over the years the pig feasts serve to equalize the food consumption, and especially the protein consumption, of all the villages that participate in the feasts.[68] Thus, the custom of pig feasts may be a way for villages to "bank" surplus food by storing up "social credit" with other villages, which will return that credit in subsequent feasts.

In some Melanesian societies, the pig feasts foster an element of competition among the men who give them. "Big men" may try to bolster their status and prestige by the size of their feasts. A reputation is enhanced not by keeping wealth but by giving it away. A similar situation existed among many Native American groups of the Northwest Coast, where a chief might attempt to enhance his status by holding a **potlatch.** At a potlatch, a chief and his group would give away blankets, pieces of copper, canoes, large quantities of food, and other items to their

A man on the Northwest Pacific coast (southeastern Alaska) wears a "potlatch hat" showing how many potlatches he has had.

guests. The host chief and his group would later be invited to other potlatches.

The competitive element in the potlatch appears to have intensified after contact with whites. Because of the fur trade, the number of trade goods increased, and so more items could be given away. Possibly more important was the population decline among the Indians, caused by diseases such as smallpox that were introduced by European traders. Distant relatives of chiefs who had no direct heirs might compete for the right to the title, each attempting to give away more than the others.[69] Chiefs may also have attempted to attract men to their half-empty villages by spectacular giveaways.[70] Decimated groups might have coalesced in order to maintain the potlatching. For example, when the Tlingit population declined to a low in the 1910s, kin groups coalesced in order to assemble enough resources for a potlatch.[71] Although the potlatch system seems wasteful in that goods were often destroyed in the competition, the system probably also served to equalize the distribution of goods among competing groups.

The Pomo Indians of central California had another way to bank credit for previous generosity.

A village with an overabundance of fish or acorns might invite another village to a feast. In return for surplus fish or acorns, the guests would give the host village a certain number of beads. Before beginning the journey to the feast, the chief of the guest village would obtain from each family as many strings of beads as possible. After a few days of feasting at the host village, the chief would trade the beads for the supply of surplus fish or acorns. Each member of the visiting village would be given an equal share of the food, regardless of how many beads had been contributed. But the members of a village would not be invited to a feast unless they brought beads to trade, and they could not obtain beads unless they had given food away themselves sometime in the past. Thus, giving away food and receiving beads in return served as a means of storing social credit for times of scarcity. Later, if food was scarce in the former host village, the villagers could use the beads they had acquired by giving in the past to obtain food from another village with a surplus. The trade feasts, then, had the effect of equalizing the consumption of food not only within a village but over a fairly widespread area.[72]

On one level of analysis, the Melanesian pig feasts, the Northwest Coast potlatches, and the Pomo trade feasts were all reciprocal exchanges between communities or villages. But these exchanges were not just intercommunity versions of reciprocal gift giving between individuals. Because these feasts were organized by people who collected goods, they also involved another mode of distribution, which anthropologists call *redistribution*.

REDISTRIBUTION

Redistribution is the accumulation of goods or labor by a particular person, or in a particular place, for the purpose of subsequent distribution. Although redistribution is found in all societies, it becomes an important mechanism only in societies that have political hierarchies—that is, chiefs or other specialized officials and agencies. In all societies, there is some redistribution, at least within the family. Members of the family pool their labor or products or income for the common good. But in many societies, there is little or no redistribution beyond the family. It seems that redistribution on a territorial basis emerges when there is a political apparatus to coordinate centralized collection and distribution of goods or to mobilize labor for some public purpose.

In the African state of Bunyoro, in western Uganda, for example, the king (called the *mukama*) retained much of the wealth for himself and his close kin. The *mukama* had the authority to grant the use of land and all other natural resources to his subordinate chiefs, and they in turn granted it to the common people. In return, everyone was required to give the *mukama* large quantities of food, crafts, and even labor services. The *mukama* then redistributed these goods and services, in theory at least, to all the people. The *mukama* was praised with names that emphasized his generosity: *Agutamba* ("he who relieves distress") and *Mwebingwa* ("he to whom the people run for help"). But it is clear that much of what the king redistributed did not find its way back to the common people, who produced the bulk of the goods. Instead, the wealth was distributed largely according to rank within the state.[73]

Other redistribution systems are more equal. For example, among the Buin of Melanesia, "the chief is housed, dressed, and fed exactly like his bondsman."[74] Even though the chief owns most of the pigs, everyone shares equally in the consumption of the wealth. In general, where redistribution is important, as in societies with higher levels of productivity, the wealthy are more likely than the poor to benefit from the redistributions.[75]

Why do redistribution systems develop? Elman Service suggested that they develop in agricultural societies that contain subregions suited to different kinds of crops or natural resources. Food collectors can take advantage of environmental variation by moving to different areas. With agriculture, the task is more difficult; it might be easier to move different products across different regions.[76] If the demand for different resources or products becomes too great, reciprocity between individuals might become awkward. So it might be more efficient to have someone—a chief, perhaps—coordinate the exchanges. We saw in the Pomo trade feasts that, although whole communities appeared to be engaged in reciprocal exchanges, the collection of surplus food and beads was handled by village chiefs.

Marvin Harris agreed that redistribution becomes more likely with agriculture, but for a somewhat different reason. He argued that competitive feasting, as in New Guinea, is adaptive because it encourages people to work harder to produce somewhat more than they need. Why would this feature be adaptive? Harris argued that with agriculture, people really have to produce more than they need so that they can protect themselves against crises such as crop failure. The groups that make feasts may be indirectly ensuring themselves against crises by storing up social credit with other villages, who will reciprocate by making feasts for them in the future. On the other hand, inducements to collect more than they need may not be advantageous to food-collecting groups, who might lose in the long run by overcollecting.[77]

MARKET OR COMMERCIAL EXCHANGE

When we think of markets we usually think of bustling colorful places in other parts of the world where goods are bought and sold. In our own society we seldom use the word *market,* although we have supermarkets and the stock market and other places for buying and selling that we call shops, stores, and malls. In referring to **market** or **commercial exchange,** economists and economic anthropologists are referring to exchanges or transactions in which the "prices" are subject to supply and demand, whether or not the transactions actually occur in a marketplace.[78] Market exchange involves not only the exchange (buying and selling) of goods but also transactions of labor, land, rentals, and credit.

On the surface, many market exchanges resemble balanced reciprocity. One person gives something and receives something in return. How, then, does market exchange differ from balanced reciprocity? It is easy to distinguish market exchange from balanced reciprocity when money is involved, since reciprocity is defined as not involving money. But market exchange need not always involve money.[79] For example, a landowner grants a tenant farmer the right to use the land in exchange for a portion of the crop. So, to call a transaction market exchange, we have to ask whether supply and demand determine the price. If a tenant farmer gave only a token gift to the landowner, we would not call it market exchange, just as a Christmas gift to a teacher is not payment for teaching. If tenants, however, were charged a large portion of their crops when the supply of land is short, or if landowners lowered their demands when few people wanted to tenant-farm, then we would call the transactions market or commercial exchange.

KINDS OF MONEY. Although market exchange need not involve money, most commercial transactions, particularly nowadays, do involve what we call money. Some anthropologists define money according to the functions and characteristics of the **general-purpose money** used in our own and other complex societies, for which nearly all goods, resources, and services can be exchanged. According to this definition, money performs the basic functions of serving as an accepted medium of exchange, a standard of value, and a store of wealth. As a

Applied Anthropology

IMPACT OF THE WORLD SYSTEM— DEFORESTATION OF THE AMAZON

When we speak of the economic system of a people, we must keep in mind that probably no group has ever been completely isolated from outside economic, political, social, or environmental events. In the modern world, with the expanding demand and opportunity of a growing world market economy, even the most self-sufficient groups cannot avoid the effects of their connections to the outside world.

Consider the great rain forest drained by the Amazon River and its tributaries. Covering more than a billion acres, it is not only the home to many largely self-sufficient indigenous cultures; it also supports about 50 percent of all the earth's plants and animals. Yet the Amazon forest and other tropical forests are disappearing at an alarming rate because of their increased use. Some have suggested that the world demand for wood, hamburger, and gold is largely responsible for the diminution of the Amazon forest.

Like many tropical forests, the Amazon has large numbers of desirable hardwood trees. Forests in Africa and Asia are already largely depleted, so the demand for wood from the Amazon has grown considerably. In addition, the Amazon Development Agency in Brazil has offered incentives to clear forest for cattle ranching, which can provide hamburger to fast-food restaurants. There is little concern that a few seasons of overgrazing can make it impossible even for grasses to grow in the soils of the former forest.

The indigenous people often find themselves in a land squeeze, with loggers, cattle ranchers, and miners trying to encroach on their territory. With less land, food-getting and traditional economic practices are in jeopardy. But it is naive to assume that the indigenous people are interested only in maintaining their traditional economies. They often accept the dilemma of economic development: They might lose some land, but selling rights to loggers and miners brings in money, which they can use to buy things they need and want. Development experts and applied anthropologists are searching for ways to achieve development without destroying or degrading the environment. For example, indigenous groups are encouraged to gather Brazil nuts, a wild but renewable resource, for sale. Others are encouraged to harvest latex (natural rubber) and hearts of palm. Medicinal plants have economic value to multinational pharmaceutical and biotechnical companies, which have discovered that the conservation of bio-diversity may be economically advantageous to themselves as well as to the local people and to scientists who want to study the diversity.

Can development be sustainable? That is, are resources (such as hardwoods) renewable, so that both economic productivity and the environment can be protected? Even if some kind of sustainable development is possible, organizing it may require concerted effort by all involved, which requires participation by all in decision making. Whether we like it or not, economic development and the desire for it are not going to go away. But we need to do more than applaud or bemoan economic development. In particular, we need research that reveals what impact particular changes will have on people, other animals, plants, and the environment. Most of all, for the sake of human rights, we need to listen to the people whose lives will be most affected, to understand their needs as well as those of the developers.

Sources: Marguerite Holloway, "Sustaining the Amazon," *Scientific American,* July 1993, 91–99; Emilio F. Moran, *Through Amazon Eyes: The Human Ecology of Amazonian Populations* (Iowa City: University of Iowa Press, 1993); Robert Winterbottom, "The Tropical Forestry Plan: Is It Working?" in Pamela J. Puntenney, ed., *Global Ecosystems: Creating Options through Anthropological Perspectives, NAPA Bulletin 15* (1995): 60–70.

medium of exchange, it allows all goods and services to be valued in the same objective way; we say that an object or service is worth so much money. Also, money is nonperishable, and therefore savable or storable, and almost always transportable and divisible, so transactions can involve the buying and selling of goods and services that differ in value.

Although money can technically be anything, the first money systems used rare metals such as gold and silver. These metals are relatively soft and therefore can be melted and shaped into standard sizes and weights. The earliest standardized coins we know of are said to have been made by the Lydians in Asia Minor and the Chinese, in the seventh century A.D. It is important to realize that money has little or no intrinsic value; rather, it is society that determines its value. In the United States today, paper bills, bank checks, and credit and debit cards are fully accepted as money, and money is increasingly transferred electronically.

General-purpose money is used both for commercial transactions (buying and selling) and for noncommercial transactions (payment of taxes or fines, personal gifts, contributions to religious and other charities). General-purpose money provides a way of condensing wealth: Gold dust or nuggets are easier to carry around than bushels of wheat; paper bills, a checkbook, and plastic cards are handier than a herd of sheep or goats.

In many societies, money is not an all-purpose medium of exchange. Many peoples whose food production per capita is not sufficient to support a large population of nonproducers of food have **special-purpose money.** This consists of objects of value for which only some goods and services can be exchanged on the spot or through balanced reciprocity. In some parts of Melanesia, pigs are assigned value in terms of shell money—lengths of shells strung together in units each roughly as long as the distance covered by a man's outstretched arms. According to its size, a pig will be assigned a value in tens of such units up to 100.[80] But shell money cannot be exchanged for all the goods or services a person might need. Similarly, a Northwest Coast native could exchange food, but not most other goods and services, for a "gift of wealth," such as blankets. The gift was a "receipt" that entitled the person to receive an equal amount of food, but little else, later.

DEGREES OF COMMERCIALIZATION. Most societies were not commercialized at all, or only barely so, when first described in the ethnographic record by explorers, missionaries, and anthropologists. That is, most societies as first described did not rely on market or commercial exchange to distribute goods and services. But commercial exchange has become the dominant form of distribution in the modern world. Most societies of the ethnographic past are now incorporated into larger nation-states; for example, the Trobriand Islanders and other societies in Melanesia are now districts in the nation of Papua New Guinea. Selling today goes far beyond the nation-state. The world is now a multinational market.[81]

But there is considerable variation in the degree to which societies today depend on market or commercial exchange. Many societies still allocate land without purchase and distribute food and other goods primarily by reciprocity and redistribution, participating only peripherally in market exchange. These are societies in transition; their traditional subsistence economies are becoming commercialized. Among the Luo of western Kenya, for example, most rural families still have land that was allocated to them by their kin groups. The food they eat they mostly produce themselves. But many men also work for wages—some nearby, others far away in towns and cities, where they spend a year or two. These wages are used to pay government taxes, to pay for children's schooling, and to buy commercially produced items, such as clothes, kerosene lamps, radios, fish from Lake Nyanza, tea, sugar, and coffee. Occasionally, families sell agricultural surpluses or craft items such as reed mats. Economies such as that of the Luo are not fully commercialized, but they may become so in the future. In the chapter on culture change, we discuss some of the implications and effects of this transition to a more commercialized economy—a transition that is a worldwide phenomenon.

What anthropologists call *peasant economies* are somewhat more commercialized than transitional subsistence economies such as that of the Luo. Although peasants also produce food largely for their own consumption, they regularly sell part of their surplus (food, other goods, or labor) to others, and land is one of the commodities they buy, rent, and sell. But, although their production is somewhat commercialized, peasants still are not like the fully commercialized farmers in industrialized societies,

---

Market exchange only develops when people regularly have surpluses they want to exchange for other items or for money. This market is in the Cape Verde Islands off the West African coast.

who rely on the market to exchange all or almost all of their crops for all or almost all of the goods and services they need.

In fully commercialized societies such as our own, market or commercial exchange dominates the economy; prices and wages are regulated, or at least significantly affected, by the forces of supply and demand. A modern industrial or postindustrial economy may involve international as well as national markets in which everything has a price, stated in the same money terms—natural resources, labor, goods, services, prestige items, religious and ceremonial items. Reciprocity is reserved for family members and friends or remains behind the scene in business transactions. Redistribution, however, is an important mechanism. It is practiced in the form of taxation and the use of public revenue for transfer payments and other benefits to low-income families—welfare, social security, health care, and so on. But commercial exchange is the major way goods and services are distributed.

WHY DO MONEY AND MARKET EXCHANGE DEVELOP? Most economists think that money is invented in a society, or copied from another society, when trade increases and barter becomes increasingly inefficient. The more important trade is, the more difficult it is to find a person who can give something you want and wants something you have to give. Money is a valuable that can be exchanged for *anything,* and so it is an efficient medium of exchange when trade becomes important. In contrast, many anthropologists do not link the origins of money or market exchange to the necessities of trade. Instead they link the origins of money to various noncommercial "payments," such as the kula valuables, the Pomo beads, and the taxes that have to be paid to a political authority. All of the available explanations of money suggest that money will be found mostly in societies at higher levels of economic development; and indeed it is. When simpler societies have money, dominant and more complex societies have usually introduced it.[82]

Most theories about the development of money and market exchange assume that producers have regular surpluses they want to exchange. But why do people produce surpluses in the first place? Perhaps they are motivated to produce extra only when they want to obtain goods from a distance and the suppliers of such goods are not well known to them, making reciprocity less likely as a way to obtain those goods. Some theorists suggest that market exchange begins with external, or intersocietal, trade; kin would not likely be involved, so transactions would involve bargaining, and therefore market exchange, by definition. Finally, some argue that as societies become more complex and more densely populated, social bonds between individuals become less kinlike and friendly, and therefore reciprocity becomes less likely.[83] Perhaps this is why traders in developing areas are often foreigners or recent immigrants.[84]

In any case, Frederic Pryor's cross-cultural research supports the notion that all types of market exchange—goods, labor, land, and credit—are more likely with higher levels of economic productivity. Pryor also found that market exchange of goods appears at lower levels of economic development than market exchange of labor and credit; market exchange of land, probably because it is associated with private property (individual ownership), appears mostly at the highest levels of productivity. Perhaps surprisingly, smaller societies tend to have more market exchange or trade with other societies. Larger societies can presumably get more of what they need from inside the society; for example, China has had relatively little foreign trade throughout much of its history.[85]

POSSIBLE LEVELING DEVICES IN COMMERCIAL ECONOMIES. As we will see in the next chapter, societies that depend substantially on market or commercial exchange tend to have marked differences in wealth among the people. Nonetheless, there may be mechanisms that lessen the inequality, that act at least partially as leveling devices. Some anthropologists have suggested that the *fiesta complex* in highland Indian communities of Latin America may be a mechanism that tends to equalize income.[86] In these peasant villages, fiestas are held each year to celebrate important village saints. The outstanding feature of this system is the extraordinary amount of money and labor a sponsoring family must contribute. Sponsors must hire ritual specialists, pay for church services, musicians, and costumes for dancers, and cover the complete cost of food and drink for the entire community. The costs incurred can very easily amount to a year's wages.[87]

Some anthropologists have suggested that, although the richer Indians who sponsor fiestas are clearly distributing a good deal of wealth to the poorer members of their own and other communities, the fiestas do not really level wealth at all. First, true economic leveling would entail the redistribution of important productive resources such as land or animals; the fiesta only temporarily increases the general level of consumption. Second,

Fiesta sponsors spend a great deal of money for food and drink as well as for musicians and dancers. Here we see a fiesta in Oaxaca, Mexico.

the resources expended by the sponsors are usually extra resources that have been accumulated specifically for the fiesta, which is why the sponsors are always appointed in advance. Third, and perhaps most important, the fiestas do not seem to have reduced long-term wealth distinctions within the villages.[88]

In nations such as ours, can the income tax and the social-assistance programs it pays for, such as welfare and disaster relief, be thought of as leveling devices? Theoretically, our tax system is supposed to work that way, by taxing higher incomes at higher rates. But we know that in fact it doesn't. Those in higher income brackets can often deduct an appreciable amount from their taxable incomes and therefore pay taxes at a relatively low rate. Our tax system may help some to escape extreme poverty, but, like the fiesta system, it has not eliminated marked distinctions in wealth.

SUMMARY

1. All societies have economic systems, whether or not these involve the use of money. All societies have customs specifying access to natural resources; customary ways of transforming or converting those resources, through labor, into necessities and other desired goods and services; and customs for distributing and perhaps exchanging goods and services.

2. Regulation of access to natural resources is a basic factor in all economic systems. The concept of individual or private ownership of land—including the right to use its resources and the right to sell or otherwise dispose of them—is common among intensive agriculturalists. In contrast, food collectors, horticulturalists, and pastoralists generally lack individual ownership of land. Among pastoral nomads, however, animals are considered family property and are not usually shared.

3. Every society makes use of a technology, which includes tools, constructions, and required skills. Even though food collectors and horticulturalists tend to think of tools as "owned" by the individuals who made them, the sharing of tools is so extensive that individual ownership does not have much meaning. Among intensive agriculturalists, toolmaking tends to be a specialized activity. Tools tend not be shared, except mainly by those who have purchased them together.

4. Incentives for labor vary cross-culturally. Many societies produce just for household consumption; if there are more consumers, producers work harder. In some subsistence economies, people may work harder to obtain the social rewards that

come from giving to others. Forced labor generally occurs only in complex societies.

5. Division of labor by gender is universal. In many nonindustrial societies, large tasks are often accomplished through the cooperative efforts of a kinship group. Such cooperation is not as prevalent in industrialized societies. In general, the more technically advanced a society is, the more surplus food it produces and the more some of its members engage in specialized work.

6. The organization of labor reaches its peak in complex societies; work groups tend to be formally organized, and sometimes there is an enforced obligation to participate. In food-collecting and horticultural societies, in contrast, there is little formal organization of work.

7. Goods and services are distributed in all societies by systems that can be classified under three types: reciprocity, redistribution, and market or commercial exchange. Reciprocity is giving and taking without the use of money and may assume three forms: generalized reciprocity, balanced reciprocity, and negative reciprocity. Generalized reciprocity is gift giving without any immediate or planned return. In balanced reciprocity, individuals exchange goods and services immediately or in the short term. Negative reciprocity is generally practiced with strangers or enemies; one individual attempts to steal from another or to cheat in trading.

8. Redistribution is the accumulation of goods or labor by a particular person, or in a particular place, for the purpose of subsequent distribution. It becomes an important mechanism of distribution only in societies with political hierarchies.

9. Market or commercial exchange, where "prices" depend on supply and demand, tends to occur with increasing levels of economic productivity. Especially nowadays, market exchange usually involves an all-purpose medium of exchange—money. Most societies today are at least partly commercialized; the world is becoming a single market system.

GLOSSARY TERMS

balanced reciprocity	optimal foraging
corvée	theory
generalized reciprocity	peasants
general-purpose	potlatch
money	reciprocity
kula ring	redistribution
market or commercial	special-purpose money
exchange	
negative reciprocity	

CRITICAL QUESTIONS

1. What conditions might enable us to achieve a world of sustainable resources?

2. What are the possible effects of a postindustrial economy in which a large proportion of the population has inexpensive access to computers and information?

3. Do you expect any appreciable change in the amount of resources privately owned in the future? State your reasons.

INTERNET EXERCISES

1. For an introduction to economic anthropology, visit one of the organizations devoted exclusively to this field at **http://www.lawrence.edu/ ~peregrip/seahome.html**. Briefly narrate your findings.

2. The issue of sustainable development is a complex one. Explore some of the current thoughts and ongoing debates on the subject at **http:// www.un.org/esa/sustdev/**. Visit the 1998 meeting of the United Nations Commission on Sustainable Development at **http://www.un.org/esa/sustdev/csd6-pw.htm**. What are some of the topics the Commission discussed that are of direct relevance to this chapter?

3. Find at least four labor-related sources on Africa on the Internet. Briefly summarize your findings. For example, **http://www-sul.stanford.edu/ depts/ssrg/africa/labor.html**.

4. Money is an important concept. Visit **http:// www.ex.ac.uk/~RDavies/arian/llyfr.html** to learn about the monetary systems of ancient times. Find out the role of money during 1 and 499 A.D. in the Roman Empire (**http://www.ex.ac.uk/~RDavies/ arian/amser/chrono2.html**) and write a brief report.

SUGGESTED READING

BLANTON, R. E. "Variation in Economy." In C. R. Ember and M. Ember, eds., *Cross-Cultural Research for Social Science.* Upper Saddle River, NJ: Prentice Hall, 1998. Prentice Hall/Simon & Schuster Custom Publishing. A brief survey for undergraduates of the concepts and challenges involved in cross-cultural comparisons of variations in economic systems.

BLANTON, R. E., P. N. PEREGRINE, D. WINSLOW, AND T. D. HALL, EDS. *Economic Analysis beyond the Local System.* Lanham, MD: University Press of America, 1997. The papers in this volume explore the connections between global and local economic processes.

CASHDAN, E., ED. *Risk and Uncertainty in Tribal and Peasant Economies.* Boulder, CO: Westview Press, 1990. The contributors to this volume discuss the various ways people in nonindustrial societies respond to unpredictable variation in the environment.

MACLACHLAN, M. D., ED. *Household Economies and Their Transformations.* Monographs in Economic Anthropology No. 3. Lanham, MD: University Press of America, 1987. The papers in this volume deal with the intensification and transformation of agriculture in many societies of the modern world.

PLATTNER, S., ED. *Economic Anthropology.* Stanford, CA: Stanford University Press, 1989. Covers economic behavior among foragers, horticulturalists, peasants, and industrialized societies, as well as such issues as gender roles, communal ownership, and mass marketing in urban areas.

PRYOR, F. L. *The Origins of the Economy: A Comparative Study of Distribution in Primitive and Peasant Economies.* New York: Academic Press, 1977. A large cross-cultural study of variation in distribution systems and their possible determinants.

15

Social Stratification

A long-enduring value in the United States is the belief that "all men are created equal." These famous words from the U.S. Declaration of Independence do not mean that all people are equal in wealth or status but rather that all (including women nowadays) are supposed to be equal before the law. In fact, modern industrial societies such as our own are *socially stratified*—that is, they contain social groups that have unequal access to important advantages, such as economic resources, power, and prestige.

Many sociologists say that all societies are stratified; anthropologists disagree. But the disagreement is really a matter of definition, because sociologists and anthropologists do not usually mean the same thing by the term *stratification*. When sociologists speak of the "universality of stratification," they mean that all societies show some inequality from one *individual* to another. The sociological definition of stratification derives from the observation that in even the simplest societies there are usually differences in advantages based on age or ability or gender—adults have higher status than children, the skilled more than the unskilled, men more than women. (We discuss gender stratification in the next chapter.) When anthropologists say that stratification is not universal and that egalitarian societies exist, they mean that there are some societies known to anthropology in which all *social groups* (for example, families) have more or less the same access or right to advantages. It is not a question of deciding whether sociologists or anthropologists are correct; both are. For anthropologists, then, human inequality may be universal; social stratification is not.

Systems of social stratification are strongly linked to the customary ways in which economic resources are allocated, distributed, and converted through labor into goods and services. So we would not expect substantial inequality if all people had relatively equal access to economic resources. But stratification cannot be understood solely in terms of economic resources; there are other benefits, such as prestige and power, that may be unequally distributed. After examining how societies vary in their systems of stratification, we then turn to possible explanations of why they vary.

VARIATION IN DEGREE OF SOCIAL INEQUALITY

Societies vary in the extent to which social groups, as well as individuals, have unequal access to advantages. In this chapter we are concerned with differential or unequal access to three types of advantages: wealth or economic resources, power, and prestige. As we saw in the preceding chapter, *economic resources* may range from hunting or fishing grounds to farmland to money; the different social groups in a society may or may not have unequal access to these resources. *Power*, a second but related advantage, is the ability to make others do what they do not want to do; power is influence based on the threat of force. When groups in a society have rules or customs that give them unequal access to wealth or resources, they generally also have unequal access to power. So, for example, when we speak of a "company town" in the United States, we are referring

Sharing can occur even in a socially stratified society. Here we see men in a village in Yunnan, China, cutting the meat from a steer into 72 portions for the families of the village.

	SOME SOCIAL GROUPS HAVE GREATER ACCESS TO:			
Type of Society	Economic Resources	Power	Prestige	Examples
Egalitarian	No	No	No	!Kung, Mbuti, Australian Aborigines, Inuit, Aché, Yanomamö
Rank	No	No	Yes	Samoans, Tahiti, Trobriand Islands, Ifaluk
Class/caste	Yes	Yes	Yes	United States, Canada, Greece, India, Inca

TABLE 15–1 *Stratification in Three Types of Societies*

to the fact that the company that employs most of the residents of the town usually has considerable control over them. Finally, there is the advantage of prestige. When we speak of *prestige,* we mean that someone or some group is accorded particular respect or honor. Even if it is true that there is always unequal access by individuals to prestige (because of differences in age, gender, or ability), there are some societies in the ethnographic record that have no social groups with unequal access to prestige.

Thus, anthropologists conventionally distinguish three types of society in terms of the degree to which different social groups have unequal access to advantages: *egalitarian, rank,* and *class societies* (see Table 15–1). Some societies in the ethnographic record do not fit easily into any of these three types; as with any classification scheme, some cases seem to straddle the line between types.[1] **Egalitarian societies** contain no social groups with greater or lesser access to economic resources, power, or prestige. **Rank societies** do not have very unequal access to economic resources or to power, but they do contain social groups with unequal access to prestige. Rank societies, then, are partly stratified. **Class societies** have unequal access to all three advantages—economic resources, power, and prestige.

EGALITARIAN SOCIETIES

Egalitarian societies can be found not only among foragers such as the !Kung, Mbuti, Australian Aborigines, Inuit, and Aché, but also among horticulturalists such as the Yanomamö and pastoralists such as the Lapps. An important point to keep in mind is that egalitarian does not mean that all people within such societies are the same. There will always be differences among individuals in age and gender and in such abilities or traits as hunting skill, perception, health, creativity, physical prowess, attractiveness,

and intelligence. According to Morton Fried, egalitarian means that within a given society "there are as many positions of prestige in any given age/sex grade as there are persons capable of filling them."[2] For instance, if a person can achieve high status by fashioning fine spears, and if many persons in the society fashion such spears, then many acquire high status as spear makers. If high status is also acquired by carving bones into artifacts, and if only three people are considered expert carvers of bones, then only those three achieve high status as carvers. But the next generation might produce eight spear makers and twenty carvers. In an egalitarian society, the number of prestigious positions is adjusted to fit the number of qualified candidates. We would say, therefore, that such a society is not socially stratified.

There are, of course, differences in position and prestige arising out of differences in ability. Even in an egalitarian society, differential prestige exists. But, although some persons may be better hunters or more skilled artists than others, there is still *equal access* to status positions for people of the same ability. Any prestige gained by achieving high status as a great hunter, for instance, is neither transferable nor inheritable. Because a man is a great hunter, it is not assumed that his sons are also great hunters. There also may be individuals with more influence, but it cannot be inherited, and there are no groups with appreciably more influence over time. An egalitarian society keeps inequality at a minimal level.

Any differences in prestige that do exist are not related to economic differences. Egalitarian groups depend heavily on *sharing,* which ensures equal access to economic resources despite differences in acquired prestige. For instance, in some egalitarian communities, some members achieve higher status through hunting. But even before the hunt begins, how the animal will be divided and distributed among the members of the band has already been decided according to custom. The culture works to separate the status achieved by members—recognition as great hunters—from actual possession of the wealth, which in this case would be the slain animal.

Just as egalitarian societies do not have social groups with unequal access to economic resources, they also do not have social groups with unequal access to power. As we will see later in the chapter on political organization, unequal access to power by social groups seems to occur only in state societies, which have full-time political officials and marked differences in wealth. Egalitarian societies use a number of customs to keep leaders from dominating others. Criticism and ridicule can be very effective. The Mbuti of central Africa shout down an overassertive leader. When a Hadza man tried to get people to work for him, other Hadza made fun of him. Disobedience is another strategy. If a leader tries to command, people just ignore the command. In extreme cases, a particularly domineering leader may be killed by community agreement; this behavior was reported among the !Kung and the Hadza. Finally, particularly among more nomadic groups, people may just move away from a leader they don't like.[3]

The Mbuti provide an example of a society almost totally equal: "Neither in ritual, hunting, kinship nor band relations do they exhibit any discernable inequalities of rank or advantage."[4] Their hunting bands have no leaders, and recognition of the achievement of one person is not accompanied by privilege of any sort. Economic resources such as food are communally shared, and even tools and weapons are frequently passed from person to person. Only within the family are rights and privileges differentiated.

RANK SOCIETIES

Most societies with social *ranking* practice agriculture or herding, but not all agricultural or pastoral societies are ranked. Ranking is characterized by social groups with unequal access to prestige or status but *not* significantly unequal access to economic resources or power. Unequal access to prestige is often reflected in the position of chief, a rank to which only some members of a specified group in the society can succeed.

Unusual among rank societies were the nineteenth-century Native Americans who lived along the northwestern coast of the United States and the southwestern coast of Canada. An example were the Nimpkish, a Kwakiutl group.[5] These societies were unusual because their economy was based on food collecting. But huge catches of salmon—which were preserved for year-round consumption—enabled them to support fairly large and permanent communities. In many ways, these societies were similar to food-producing societies, even in their development of social ranking. Still, the principal means of proving one's high status was to give wealth away. The tribal chiefs celebrated solemn rites by grand feasts called potlatches at which they gave gifts to every guest.[6]

In rank societies, the position of chief is at least partly hereditary. The criterion of superior rank in some Polynesian societies, for example, was genealogical. Usually the eldest son succeeded to the position of chief, and different kinship groups were differentially ranked according to their genealogical distance from the chiefly line. In rank societies, chiefs are often treated with deference by people of lower rank. For example, among the Trobriand Islanders of Melanesia, people of lower rank must keep their heads lower than a person of higher rank. So, when a chief is standing, commoners must bend low. When commoners have to walk past a chief who happens to be sitting, he may rise and they will bend. If the chief chooses to remain seated, they must crawl.[7]

While there is no question that chiefs in a rank society enjoy special prestige, there is some controversy over whether they really do not also have material advantages. Chiefs may sometimes look as if they are substantially richer than commoners, for they may receive many gifts and have larger storehouses. In some instances, the chief may even be called the "owner" of the land. However, Marshall Sahlins maintains that the chief's storehouses may only house temporary accumulations for feasts or other redistributions. And although the chief may be designated the "owner" of the land, others have the right to use the land. Furthermore, Sahlins suggests that the chief in a rank society lacks power because he usually cannot make people give him gifts or force them to work on communal projects. Often the chief can encourage production only by working furiously on his own cultivation.[8]

This picture of economic equality is beginning to be questioned. Laura Betzig studied patterns of food sharing and labor on Ifaluk, a small atoll in the Western Carolines.[9] Chiefly status is inherited genealogically in the female line, although most chiefs are male. (In the sex, gender, and culture chapter we discuss why political leaders are usually male, even in societies structured around women.) As in other chiefly societies, Ifaluk chiefs are accorded

In societies with rank and class, deference is usually shown to political leaders, as in the case of this Fon chief in Cameroon, Africa.

deference. For example, during collective meals prepared by all the island women, chiefs were served first and were bowed to. The Ifaluk chiefs are said to control the fishing areas. Were the catches equitably distributed? Betzig measured the amount of fish each household got. All the commoners received an equal share, but the chiefs got extra fish; their households got twice as much per person as other households. Did the chiefs give away more later?

Theoretically, it is generosity that is supposed to even things out, but Betzig found that the gifts from chiefs to other households did not equal the amount the chiefs received from others. Furthermore, while everyone gave to the chiefs, the chiefs gave mostly to their close relatives. On Ifaluk, the chiefs did not work harder than others; in fact, they worked less. Is this true in other societies conventionally considered to be rank societies? We do not know. However, we need to keep in mind that the chiefs in Ifaluk were not noticeably better off either. If they lived in palaces with servants, had elaborate meals, or were dressed in fine clothes and jewelry, we would not need measures of food received or a special study to see if the chiefs had greater access to economic re-

sources because their wealth would be obvious. But rank societies may not have had as much economic equality as we used to think.

CLASS SOCIETIES

In class societies, as in rank societies, there is unequal access to prestige. But, unlike rank societies, class societies are characterized by groups that have substantially greater or lesser access to economic resources and power. That is, not every social group has the same opportunity to obtain land, animals, money, or other economic benefits or the same opportunity to exercise power that other groups have. Fully stratified or class societies range from somewhat open to virtually closed class, or *caste,* systems.

OPEN CLASS SYSTEMS

A **class** is a category of persons who all have about the same opportunity to obtain economic resources, power, and prestige. Different classes have differing opportunities. We call class systems *open* if there is some possibility of moving from one class to another. Since the 1920s, there have been many studies of classes in towns and cities in the United States. Researchers have produced profiles of these different communities—known variously as Yankee City, Middletown, Jonesville, and Old City—all of which support the premise that the United States has distinguishable, though somewhat open, social classes. Both W. Lloyd Warner and Paul Lunt's Yankee City study[10] and Robert and Helen Lynd's Middletown study[11] concluded that the social status or prestige of a family is generally correlated with the occupation and wealth of the head of the family. Class systems are by no means confined to the United States. They are found in all nations of the modern world.

Although class status is not fully determined at birth in open class societies, there is a high probability that most people will stay close to the class into which they were born and will marry within that class. Classes tend to perpetuate themselves through the inheritance of wealth. John Brittain suggested that, in the United States, the transfer of money through bequests accounts for much of the wealth of the next generation. As we might expect, the importance of inheritance seems to increase at higher levels of wealth. That is, the wealth of richer people comes more from inheritance than does the wealth of not-so-rich people.[12]

Other mechanisms of class perpetuation may be more subtle, but they are still powerful. In the United States there are many institutions that make it possible for an upper-class person to have little contact with other classes. Private day and boarding schools put upper-class children in close contact mostly with others of their class. Attending these schools makes it more likely they will get into universities with higher prestige. Debutante balls and exclusive private parties ensure that young people meet "the right people." Country clubs, exclusive city clubs, and service in particular charities continue the process of limited association. People of the same class also tend to live in the same neighborhood. Before 1948, explicit restrictions kept certain groups out of particular neighborhoods, but after the U.S. Supreme Court ruled such discrimination unconstitutional, more subtle methods were developed. For instance, zoning restrictions may prohibit multiple-family dwellings in a town or neighborhood and lots below a certain acreage.[13]

Identification with a social class begins early in life. In addition to differences in occupation, wealth, and prestige, social classes vary in many other ways, including religious affiliation, closeness to kin, ideas about child rearing, job satisfaction, leisure-time activities, style of clothes and furniture, and (as noted in the chapter on communication and language) even in styles of speech.[14] People from each class tend to be more comfortable with those from the same class; they talk similarly and are more likely to have similar interests and tastes.

Expensive restaurants are only found in stratified societies, and only the wealthy can afford to eat often in them.

Current Issues

THE WIDENING GAP BETWEEN RICH AND POOR IN THE UNITED STATES

In the 1950s and 1960s, the U.S. economy expanded enormously. Many people grew up during those years assuming that their standard of living could only get better. Their parents may have lived through the Great Depression of the 1930s, but they did not believe that such a calamity would occur in their lifetimes. They would have bigger incomes and bigger houses and live the American Dream. But from the mid-1970s through the early 1990s something went wrong. The anthropologist Katherine Newman spent two years interviewing ordinary people in a suburban town she calls "Pleasanton." Lauren's comments are typical: "I'll never have what my parents had. I can't even dream of that. . . . I worked all those years and then I didn't get to candyland." It is not that Lauren didn't follow the rules. She worked hard to get good grades, she went to college, and she has a respectable job. Yet, even though both she and her husband work, they still cannot afford a house and they are not doing as well as her parents did

How Wealthy the Wealthy: A History

The purple line shows the percentage of the national wealth held by the richest one percent of Americans, from 1774 to 1989.

The country has gone through several cycles of concentration and redistribution of wealth. Only once before were the rich as rich as they were in 1989 — but that took 150 years to achieve.

The chart data are from estimates by three economists — Claudia Goldin and Bradford DeLong at Harvard University and Edward Wolff at New York University.

1865 Emancipation. Vast "wealth" - in the form of slaves - is lost to Southern landowners and "transferred" to the poor - the freedmen themselves.

AGRARIAN SOCIETY

Colonial era to 1820. Land on frontiers is essentially free for the taking, and the population is small. Labor is expensive, compared to Europe, and industry negligible.

29
27

1862 Homestead Act opens rest of public lands to settlers.

14.6%

1787 Under the Northwest Ordinance, new land is distributed as small plots, not huge fiefs.

EARLY INDUSTRIAL REVOLUTION
1820-1850. Rise of railroads and textiles creates fortunes, concentrating wealth.

WAVES OF IMMIGRANTS
1870s-1920s. The ranks of labor are swelled by millions, holding down wage growth. Laws restricting immigration are passed in 1921, 1924, and 1929.

| 1770s | 1780s | 1790s | 1800s | 1810s | 1820s | 1830s | 1840s | 1850s | 1860s | 1870s | 1880s |

Source: Adapted by Sylvia Nasar, "The Rich Get Richer, but Never the Same Way Twice," *New York Times,* August 16, 1992, p. E3.

on just one salary. Not only is housing more expensive; jobs are less secure and harder to find, and the credentials needed for those jobs are harder to achieve.

The squeeze on the people in the middle is only a small part of the economic picture. Not all segments of society did worse since the mid-1970s. While middle- and working-class people got poorer, the rich got richer. By the end of the 1980s, the richest 1 percent of all Americans owned over 36 percent of all the wealth (assets minus debts) in the United States. The only time the very rich owned more was at the end of the 1920s, just before the Great Depression (see the graph). The same trend occurred in the distribution of income. The wealthiest 20 percent of the population earned over 44 percent of all the income in 1991, which was the highest percentage since 1949.

As the graph shows, the degree of economic inequality has fluctuated throughout U.S. history, so the recent increase in inequality may not continue. Change over time in the degree of inequality sometimes has economic causes; for example, the stock market crash in 1929 made the wealthy less wealthy. Some of the change over time is due to shifts in public policy. During the New Deal of the 1930s, tax changes and work programs shifted more income to ordinary people; in the 1980s, tax cuts for the wealthy helped the rich get richer. In the 1990s, the rich have continued to get richer.

Will the gap between rich and poor continue to widen? Only the future will tell. But whatever happens, political events, such as which interest groups can most influence Congress, are likely to be as crucial as the competitive position of the United States in the world economy.

Sources: Katherine S. Newman, *Declining Fortunes: The Withering of the American Dream* (New York: Basic Books, 1993), quotation from p. 3; Kevin Phillips, *The Politics of Rich and Poor: Wealth and the American Electorate in the Reagan Aftermath* (New York: Random House, 1990); U.S. Bureau of the Census, *Statistical Abstract of the United States: 1993,* 113th ed. (Washington, DC: U.S. Government Printing Office, 1993); *New York Times International,* Tuesday, September 30, 1997, p. A26.

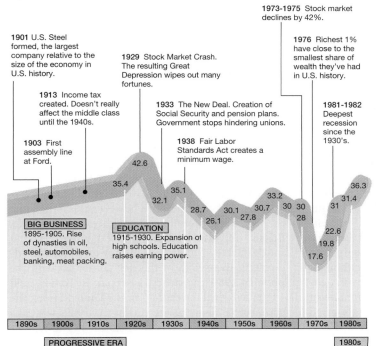

1901 U.S. Steel formed, the largest company relative to the size of the economy in U.S. history.

1913 Income tax created. Doesn't really affect the middle class until the 1940s.

1903 First assembly line at Ford.

1929 Stock Market Crash. The resulting Great Depression wipes out many fortunes.

1933 The New Deal. Creation of Social Security and pension plans. Government stops hindering unions.

1938 Fair Labor Standards Act creates a minimum wage.

1973-1975 Stock market declines by 42%.

1976 Richest 1% have close to the smallest share of wealth they've had in U.S. history.

1981-1982 Deepest recession since the 1930's.

BIG BUSINESS
1895-1905. Rise of dynasties in oil, steel, automobiles, banking, meat packing.

EDUCATION
1915-1930. Expansion of high schools. Education raises earning power.

42.6 35.4 35.1 32.1 28.7 26.1 30.1 27.8 30.7 33.2 30 30 28 31 22.6 19.8 17.6 31.4 36.3

| 1890s | 1900s | 1910s | 1920s | 1930s | 1940s | 1950s | 1960s | 1970s | 1980s |

PROGRESSIVE ERA
1900-1914. Inequality of wealth becomes a national political issue. Child labor laws, wage and hour laws, railroad rate controls created.

ROARING TWENTIES
1923-1929. Stock market boom expands richest people's fortunes.

WORLD WAR II
1941-1945. The draft dries up the labor supply, putting upward pressure on wages.

RAPID GROWTH
1950-1970. Helped by G.I. bill, many Americans got college educations.

1980s
Top tax rate slashed from 70% to less than 30%, shifting tax burden to the middle class. Federal Reserve's anti-inflation stance buoys stocks and bonds. Fluctuating dollar sends manufacturing jobs overseas.

Class boundaries, though vague, have been established by custom and tradition; sometimes they have been reinforced by the enactment of laws. Many of our laws serve to protect property and thus tend to favor the upper and upper-middle classes. The poor, in contrast, seem to be disadvantaged in our legal system. The crimes the poor are most likely to commit are dealt with harshly by the courts, and poor people rarely have the money to secure effective legal counsel.

Not all people are satisfied with their class status. In an open class society, mobility upward (as well as downward) is possible. Obtaining more education, particularly a university education, is one of the most effective ways to move upward in contemporary societies. In fact, in many countries educational attainment predicts one's social class better than parents' occupation does.[15] Lower-class persons may become "resocialized" at the university. Resocialization separates them from their parents and enables them to learn the skills, speech, attitudes, and manners characteristic of the higher class they wish to join. So successful is this process that students from a lower class who move into a higher class may find themselves ashamed to take their new friends to their parents' homes.

The determinants of class status can change over time. For example, in 1776, the middle class in the United States consisted of the families of self-employed craftspeople, shopkeepers, and farmers. By 1985, only about 8 percent of the population were self-employed, but many more people thought of themselves as belonging to the middle class. Self-employment is now a less important determinant of middle-class status than working with one's mind and having authority over others on the job.[16] Political changes may radically alter class systems. Such changes may come about from tax breaks or tax hikes, or they may be more extreme, as in revolutions. In Mexico, land reform after the revolution of 1910 effectively ended the aristocratic class; after just a few generations, most of the aristocracy fell to upper-middle class status.[17]

How open a class system is, how possible it is to move into a class that is different from the one you were born into, may also vary over time. In a study of a small rural town in Ontario, Canada, nicknamed "Paradise," Stanley Barrett found that the rigid stratification system of the 1950s opened up considerably as new people moved into the community. No one disputed who belonged to the elite in the past. They were of British background, lived in the largest houses, had new cars, and vacationed in Florida. Moreover, they controlled all the leadership positions in the town. By the 1980s, though, the leaders came mostly from the middle and working classes.[18]

In open class systems it is not always clear how many classes there are. In Paradise, Ontario, some people thought that in the past there were only two classes. One person said, "There was the hierarchy, and the rest of us." Another said that there were three classes: "The people with money, the in-between, and the ones who didn't have anything." Many said there were four: "The wealthy businessmen, the middle class, blue collar workers, and the guys that were just existing."[19] A few insisted that there were five classes. With the breakdown of the old rigid class structure, there are more people in the middle. As in the United States, there is now an ideology of "classlessness"—most people tend to put themselves in the middle. However, objective evidence indicates a continuing class system.[20]

How do the United States and Canada compare with other countries in degree of class mobility? Canada and Sweden have more mobility than the United States, France, and Britain. Japan and Italy have less mobility. If we focus on the ease of moving into the highest class, Italy, France, Spain, Germany, and Japan are more difficult than Britain and the United States.[21]

Degree of class mobility, however, is not the same as degree of economic inequality. For example, Britain and the United States do not differ that much in rate of mobility, but they do differ considerably in the wealth of the rich compared with the poor. In 1989, the richest 1 percent in Britain held 18 percent of the wealth;[22] in the United States, the comparable figure at the end of the 1980s was 36.3 percent (see the graph in the box titled "The Widening Gap between Rich and Poor in the United States"). The degree of inequality in Britain has declined greatly since the early 1900s: In 1911–1913, the wealthiest 1 percent held 69 percent of the nation's wealth.[23]

Another way to calculate the disparity between rich and poor is to use the ratio of income held by the top fifth of the population divided by the income held by the bottom fifth. Comparatively speaking, the United States has the biggest discrepancy of any of the developed countries (see Figure 15–1), with a ratio of about 10 to 1. That is, the top 20 percent of the U.S. population controls 10 times the wealth controlled by the bottom 20 percent. Among the developing countries, Brazil is the most unequal, with a ratio of 30 to 1, but the United States has more inequality than such developing countries as India, Ghana, Pakistan, and the Philippines.[24]

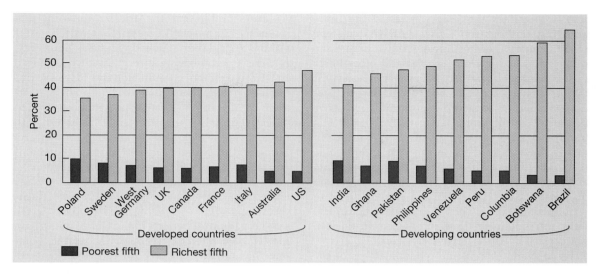

FIGURE 15–1 *Patterns of Income Distribution within Selected Countries*

Percentage of total national income received by one fifth of the population. Dates vary: most are in the late 1980s; the United States data are for 1990. *Source:* From Ruth Leger Sivard, *World Military and Social Expenditures* 1993, 15th ed. (Washington, DC: World Priorities, 1993).

CASTE SYSTEMS

Some societies have classes that are virtually closed called *castes*. A **caste** is a ranked group in which membership is determined at birth, and marriage is restricted to members of one's own caste. The only way you can belong is by being born into the group; and since you cannot marry outside the group, your children cannot acquire another caste status either. In India, for example, there are several thousand hereditary castes. Although the precise ranking of these thousands of groups is not completely clear, there appear to be four main levels of hierarchy. The castes in India are often thought to be associated with different occupations, but that is not quite true. Most Indians live in rural areas and have agricultural occupations, but their castes vary widely.[25]

Castes may exist in conjunction with a more open class system. Indeed, in India today, members of a low caste who can get wage-paying jobs, chiefly those in urban areas, may improve their social standing in the same ways available to people in other class societies. In general, however, they still cannot marry someone in a higher caste, so the caste system is perpetuated.

Questions basic to all stratified societies, and particularly to a caste society, were posed by John Ruskin, a nineteenth-century British essayist: "Which of us . . . is to do the hard and dirty work for the rest—and for what pay? Who is to do the pleasant and clean work, and for what pay?"[26] In India those questions have been answered by the caste system, which mainly dictates how goods and services are exchanged, particularly in rural areas.[27] Who is to do the hard and dirty work for the rest of society is clearly established: A large group of Untouchables forms the bottom of the hierarchy. Among the Untouchables are subcastes such as the Camars, or leatherworkers, and the Bhangis, who traditionally are sweepers. At the top of the hierarchy, performing the pleasant and clean work of priests, are the Brahmans. Between the two extremes are thousands of castes and subcastes. In a typical village, the potter makes clay drinking cups and large water vessels for the entire village population. In return, the principal landowner gives him a house site and supplies him twice yearly with grain. Some other castes owe the potter their services: The barber cuts his hair; the sweeper carries away his rubbish; the washer washes his clothes; the Brahman performs his children's weddings. The barber serves every caste in the village except the Untouchables; he, in turn, is served by half of the others. He has inherited the families he works for, along with his father's occupation. All castes help at harvest and at weddings for additional payment, which sometimes includes a money payment.

This description is, in fact, an idealized picture of the caste system of India. In reality, the system operates to the advantage of the principal landowning caste—sometimes the Brahmans and sometimes other castes. Also, it is not carried on without some resentment; signs of hostility are shown toward the ruling caste by the Untouchables and other lower castes. The resentment does not appear to be against the caste system as such. Instead, the lower castes exhibit bitterness at their own low status and strive for greater equality. For instance, one of the Camars' traditional services is to remove dead cattle; in return, they can have the meat to eat and the hide to tan for their leatherworking. Because handling dead animals and eating beef are regarded as unclean acts, the Camars of one village refused to continue this service. Thus, they lost a source of free hides and food in a vain attempt to escape unclean status.

Since World War II, the economic basis of the caste system in India has been undermined somewhat by the growing practice of giving cash payment for services. For instance, the son of a barber may be a teacher during the week, earning a cash salary, and confine his haircutting to weekends. But he still remains in the barber caste (Nai) and must marry within that caste.

Perpetuation of the caste system is ensured by the power of those in the upper castes, who derive three main advantages from their position: economic, prestige, and sexual gains. The economic gain is the most immediately apparent. An ample supply of cheap labor and free services is maintained by the threat of sanctions. Lower-caste members may have their use of a house site withdrawn; they may be refused access to the village well or to common grazing land for animals; or they may be expelled from the village. Prestige is also maintained by the threat of sanctions; the higher castes expect deference and servility from the lower castes. The sexual gain is less apparent but equally real. The high-caste male has access to two groups of females, those of his own caste and those of lower castes. High-caste females are kept free of the "contaminating" touch of low-caste males because low-caste males are allowed access only to low-caste women. Moreover, the constant reminders of ritual uncleanness serve to keep the lower castes "in their place." Higher castes do not accept water from Untouchables, sit next to them, or eat at the same table with them.

Although few areas of the world have developed a caste system like that of India, there are castelike features in some other societies. For example, African Americans in the United States used to have a caste-like status determined partly by the inherited characteristic of skin color. Until recently, some states had laws prohibiting an African American from marrying a European American. Even when interracial marriage did occur, children of the union were often regarded as having lower status than European American children, even though they may have had blonde hair and light skin. In the South, where treatment of African Americans as a caste was most apparent, European Americans refused to eat with blacks or to sit next to them at lunch counters, on buses, and in schools. Separate drinking fountains and toilets reinforced the idea of ritual uncleanness. The economic advantages and gains in prestige enjoyed by European Americans are well documented.[28]

The traditional barriers in the United States have mostly been lifted in recent years, but the "color line" has not disappeared. African Americans are found in all social classes, but they remain underrepresented in the wealthiest group and overrepresented at the bottom. Life expectancy for African Americans is substantially lower than for European Americans.[29] There still is racism, the belief that African Americans are inferior. Thus, they may have to be better to get promoted, or it may be assumed that they got ahead just because they were African American. European Americans often expect them to be "ambassadors," to be called on mainly for knowledge about how to handle situations involving other African Americans. They may work with others, but go home to African American neighborhoods. Or they may live in mixed neighborhoods and experience considerable isolation. Few African Americans can avoid the anguish of racism.[30]

Japan also had a caste group within a class society. Now called *burakumin* (instead of the pejorative *Eta*), this group traditionally had occupations that were considered unclean.[31] Comparable to India's Untouchables, they were a hereditary, endogamous (in-marrying) group. Their occupations were traditionally those of farm laborer, leatherworker, and basket weaver; their standard of living was very low. Unlike blacks in America, the burakumin were physically indistinguishable from other Japanese.[32] Discrimination against the burakumin was officially abolished by the Japanese government in 1871, but it was not until the twentieth century that the burakumin began organizing to bring about change. These movements appear to be paying off as more active steps have been taken recently by the Japanese government to alleviate discrimination and poverty. As of 1995, 73 percent of burakumin marriages are now with non-burakumin. In public opinion polls, two-thirds of burakumin now say they have not encountered discrimination.

Caste differences are not always associated with distinguishable physical differences, as in the case of these burakumin *children in Japan.*

However, most burakumin still live in segregated neighborhoods where unemployment, crime, and alcoholism rates are high.[33]

In Rwanda, a country in east-central Africa, a longtime caste system was overthrown, first by an election and then by a revolution in 1959–1960. Three castes had existed, each distinguished from the others by physical appearance and occupation.[34] The ruling caste, the Tutsi, constituted about 15 percent of the population. They were the landlords and practiced the prestigious occupation of herding. The agricultural caste, the Hutu, made up about 85 percent of the population. As tenants of the Tutsi, they produced most of the country's food. The Twa, accounting for less than 1 percent of the population, were foragers who formed the lowest caste. It is believed that the three castes derived from three different language groups who came together through migration and conquest. Later, however, they began to use a common language, although remaining endogamous and segregated by hereditary occupations.

Colonial rule, first by the Germans and then by the Belgians after World War I, strengthened Tutsi power. When the Hutu united to demand more of the rewards of their labor in 1959, the king and many of the Tutsi ruling caste were driven out of the country. The Hutu then established a republican form of government and declared independence from Belgium in 1962. In this new government, however, the forest-dwelling Twa were generally excluded from full citizenship. In 1990, Tutsi rebels invaded from Uganda, and attempts were made to negotiate a multiparty government. However, civil war continued, and in 1994 alone over a million people, mostly Tutsi, were killed. Almost 2 million refugees, mostly Hutu, fled to Zaire as the Tutsi-led rebels established a new government.[35]

SLAVERY

Slaves are persons who do not own their own labor, and as such they represent a class. We may associate slavery with a few well-known examples, such as ancient Egypt, Greece, and Rome or the southern United States, but slavery has existed in some form in almost every part of the world at one time or another, in simpler as well as in more complex societies. Slaves are often obtained from other cultures directly: kidnapped, captured in war, or given as tribute. Or they may be obtained indirectly as payment in barter or trade. Slaves sometimes come from the same culture; one became a slave as payment of a debt, as a punishment for a crime, or even as a chosen alternative to poverty. Slave societies vary in the degree to which it is possible to become freed from slavery.[36] Sometimes the slavery system has been a closed class, or caste, system, sometimes a relatively open class system. In different slave-owning societies, slaves have had different, but always some, legal rights.[37]

In ancient Greece, slaves often were conquered enemies. Because city-states were constantly conquering one another or rebelling against former conquerors, slavery was a threat to everyone. After the Trojan War, the transition of Hecuba from queen to slave was marked by her cry, "Count no one happy, however fortunate, before he dies."[38] Nevertheless, Greek slaves were considered human beings, and they could even acquire some higher-class status along with freedom. Andromache, Hecuba's daughter-in-law, was taken as slave and concubine by one of the Greek heroes. When his legal wife produced no children, Andromache's slave son became heir to his father's throne. Although slaves had no rights under law, once they were freed, either by the will of their master or by purchase, they and their descendants could become assimilated into the dominant group. In other words, slavery in Greece was not seen as the justified position of inferior people. It was regarded, rather, as an act of fate—"the luck of the draw"—that relegated one to the lowest class in society.

Among the Nupe, a society in central Nigeria, slavery was of quite another type.[39] The methods of obtaining slaves—as part of the booty of warfare, and later by purchase—were similar to those of Europeans, but the position of the slaves was very different. Mistreatment was rare. Male slaves were given the same opportunities to earn money as other dependent males in the household—younger brothers, sons, or other relatives. A slave might be given a garden plot of his own to cultivate, or he might be given a commission if his master was a craftsman or a tradesman. Slaves could acquire property, wealth, and even slaves of their own. But all of a slave's belongings went to the master at the slave's death.

Manumission—the granting of freedom to slaves—was built into the Nupe system. If a male slave could afford the marriage payment for a free woman, the children of the resulting marriage were free; the man himself, however, remained a slave. Marriage and concubinage were the easiest ways out of bondage for a slave woman. Once she had produced a child by her master, both she and the child had free status. The woman, however, was only figuratively free; if a concubine, she had to remain in that role. As might be expected, the family trees of the nobility and the wealthy were liberally grafted with branches descended from slave concubines.

The most fortunate slaves among the Nupe were the house slaves. They could rise to positions of power in the household as overseers and bailiffs,

Current Issues

IS INEQUALITY BETWEEN COUNTRIES INCREASING?

When people support themselves by what they collect and produce themselves, as most people did until a few thousand years ago, it is difficult to compare the standards of living of different societies because we cannot translate what people have into market or monetary value. It is only where people are at least partly involved in the world market economy that we can measure the standard of living in monetary terms. Today this comparison is possible for most of the world. Many people in most societies depend on buying and selling for a living; and the more people who depend on international exchange, the more possible it is to compare them in terms of standard economic indicators. We do not have such indicators for all the different societies, but we do have them for many countries. Those indicators suggest that the degree of economic inequality in the world is not only very substantial but is increasing.

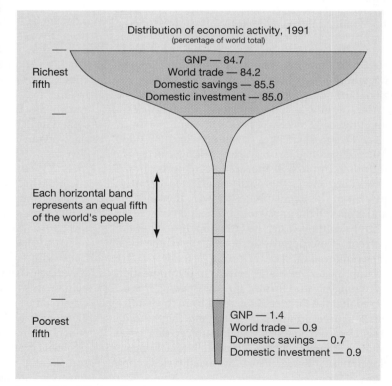

Source: United Nations Development Program, *Human Development Report, 1994* (New York: Oxford University Press, 1994).

charged with law-enforcement and judicial duties. (Recall the Old Testament story of Joseph, who was sold into slavery by his brothers. Joseph became a household slave of the pharaoh and rose to the position of second in the kingdom because he devised an ingenious system of taxation.) There was even a titled group of Nupe slaves, the Order of Court Slaves, who were trusted officers of the king and members of an elite. Slave status in general, though, placed one at the bottom of the social ladder. In the Nupe system, few slaves, mainly princes from their own societies, ever achieved membership in the titled group.

In the United States, slavery originated as a means of obtaining cheap labor, but the slaves soon came to be regarded as deserving of their low status because of their alleged inherent inferiority. Because the slaves were black, some whites justified slavery and belief in black people's inferiority by quoting Scripture out of context ("They shall be hewers of wood and drawers of water"). Slaves could not marry or make any other contracts, nor could they own property. In addition, their children were also slaves, and the master had sexual rights over the female slaves. Because the status of slavery was determined by birth in the United States, slaves constituted a caste. During the days of slavery, therefore, the United States had both a caste and a class system. And even after the abolition of slavery, as we have noted, some castelike elements remained.

As for why slavery may have developed in the first place, the cross-cultural evidence is as yet

The "champagne-glass" figure conveys how unequal are the rich and poor of the world. If you consider gross national product (GNP), which is a measure for each country of how much is produced (in U.S. dollars), and compare it across countries, the richest fifth (20 percent) of the world's population controls 84.7 percent of the world's total gross national product. The poorest fifth (20 percent) controls only 1.4 percent of the world's output. As the figure shows, similar disparities exist if you compare trade, domestic savings, or domestic investment.

To evaluate changes, we can compare the ratio between the richest and poorest fifths over time. In 1991, the ratio was 60.5 to 1, which is calculated by dividing the 84.7 percent for the top fifth by 1.4 for the bottom fifth. That ratio has increased since the 1960s. In 1960 the ratio was 30 to 1; in 1970 it was 32 to 1; in 1980 it was 45 to 1.

If the world as a whole is seeing improvements in technology and economic development, why is inequality in the world increasing? As we shall see later, in the chapter on culture change, it is often the rich within a society who benefit most from new technology, at least initially. They are not only the most likely to be able to afford it; they also are the only ones who can afford to take the risks that it involves. The same may be true for nations. Those that already have capital are more likely than the poorer nations to take advantage of improvements in technology. In addition, the poorer countries generally have the highest rates of population growth, so income per capita can fall if population increases faster than the rate of economic development. Economists tell us that a developing country may, at least initially, experience an increase in inequality, but inequality often decreases over time. Will the inequalities among countries also decrease as the world economy develops further?

The picture is not entirely bleak. It is true that the disparity between rich and poor countries has increased in recent years, but it is also true that the world economy has improved in some respects. The United Nations has computed a "human development index" for 114 countries, combining measures of life expectancy, literacy, and a measure of per capita purchasing power. According to this index, all countries have improved over a period of 30 years, many of them substantially. If this trend continues, there might be less inequality among countries in the future.

Sources: *Human Development Report 1994*, published for the United Nations Development Programme (New York: Oxford University Press, 1994), pp. 90–106; *State of the World 1994: A Worldwatch Institute Report on Progress toward a Sustainable Society* (New York: Norton, 1994), pp. 1–8; Peter Donaldson, *Worlds Apart: The Economic Gulf between Nations* (London: British Broadcasting Corporation, 1971); Philips Foster, *The World Food Problem: Tackling the Causes of Undernutrition in the Third World* (Boulder, CO: Lynne Rienner, 1992), pp. 149–51.

inconclusive. We do know, however, that slavery is not an inevitable stage in economic development, contrary to what some have assumed. In other words, slavery is *not* found mainly in certain economies, such as those dependent on intensive agriculture. Unlike the United States until the Civil War, many societies with intensive agriculture did not develop any variety of slavery. Also, the hypothesis that slavery develops where available resources are plentiful but labor is scarce is not supported by the cross-cultural evidence. All we can say definitely is that slavery does not occur in developed or industrial economies; either it disappears or it was never present in them.[40]

THE EMERGENCE OF STRATIFICATION

Anthropologists are not certain why social stratification developed. Nevertheless, they are reasonably sure that higher levels of stratification emerged relatively recently in human history. Archaeological sites dating before about 8,000 years ago do not show extensive evidence of inequality. Houses do not appear to vary much in size or content, and different communities of the same culture are similar in size and otherwise. Signs of inequality appear first in the Near East, about 2,000 years after agriculture emerged in that region. Inequality in burial suggests inequality in life. Particularly telling are unequal child burials. It is unlikely that children could achieve high status by their own achievements. So when archaeologists find statues and ornaments only in some children's tombs, as at the 7500-year-old site of Tell es-Sawwan in Iraq,[41] the grave goods suggest that those children belonged to a higher ranking family or a higher class.

Another indication that stratification is a relatively recent development in human history is the fact that certain cultural features associated with stratification also developed relatively recently. For example, most societies that depend primarily on agriculture or herding have social classes.[42] Agriculture and herding developed within the past 10,000 years, so we may assume that most food collectors in the distant past lacked social classes. Other recently developed cultural features associated with class stratification include fixed settlements, political integration beyond the community level, the use of money as a medium of exchange, and the presence of at least some full-time specialization.[43]

In 1966, the comparative sociologist Gerhard Lenski suggested that the trend since 8,000 years ago toward increasing inequality was reversing. He argued that inequalities of power and privilege in industrial societies—measured in terms of the concentration of political power and the distribution of income—are less pronounced than inequalities in complex preindustrial societies. Technology in industrialized societies is so complex, he suggested, that those in power are compelled to delegate some authority to subordinates if the system is to work. In addition, a decline in the birth rate in industrialized societies, coupled with the need for skilled labor, has pushed the average wage of workers far above the subsistence level, resulting in greater equality in the distribution of income. Finally, Lenski also suggested that the spread of the democratic ideology, and particularly its acceptance by elites, has significantly broadened the political power of the lower classes.[44] A few studies have tested and supported Lenski's hypothesis that inequality has decreased with industrialization. In general, nations that are highly industrialized exhibit a lower level of inequality than nations that are only somewhat industrialized.[45] But, as we have seen, even the most industrialized societies may still have an enormous degree of inequality.

Why did social stratification develop in the first place? On the basis of his study of Polynesian societies, Marshall Sahlins suggested that an increase in agricultural productivity results in social stratification.[46] According to Sahlins, the degree of stratification is directly related to the production of a surplus, which is made possible by greater technological efficiency. The higher the level of productivity and the larger the agricultural surplus, the greater the scope and complexity of the distribution system. The status of the chief, who serves as redistributing agent, is enhanced. Sahlins argued that the differentiation between distributor and producer inevitably gives rise to differentiation in other aspects of life:

> First, there would be a tendency for the regulator of distribution to exert some authority over production itself—especially over productive activities which necessitate subsidization, such as communal labor or specialist labor. A degree of control of production implies a degree of control over the utilization of resources, or, in other words, some preeminent property rights. In turn, regulation of these economic processes necessitates the exercise of authority in interpersonal affairs; differences in social power emerge.[47]

Sahlins later rejected the idea that a surplus leads to chiefships, postulating instead that the relationship may be the other way around—that is, leaders encourage the development of a surplus so as to enhance their prestige through feasts, potlatches, and other redistributive events.[48] Of course, both trajectories are possible—surpluses may generate stratification, and stratification may generate surpluses; they are not mutually exclusive.

Lenski's theory of the causes of stratification is similar to Sahlins's original idea. Lenski, too, argued that production of a surplus is the stimulus in the development of stratification, but he focused primarily on the conflict that arises over control of that surplus. Lenski concluded that the distribution of the surplus will be determined on the basis of power. Thus, inequalities in power promote unequal access to economic resources and simultaneously give rise to inequalities in privilege and prestige.[49]

The "surplus" theories of Sahlins and Lenski do not really address the question of why the redistributors or leaders will want, or be able, to acquire greater control over resources. After all, the redistributors or leaders in many rank societies do not have greater wealth than others, and custom seems to keep things that way. One suggestion is that as long as followers have mobility, they can vote with their feet by moving away from leaders they do not like. But when people start to make more permanent "investments" in land or technology (for example, irrigation systems or weirs for fishing), they are more likely to put up with a leader's aggrandizement in exchange for protection.[50] Another suggestion is that access to economic resources becomes unequal only when there is population pressure on resources in rank or chiefdom societies.[51] Such pressure may be what induces redistributors to try to keep more land and other resources for themselves and their families.

C. K. Meek offered an example of how population pressure in northern Nigeria may have led to economic stratification. At one time, a tribal member could obtain the right to use land by asking permission of the chief and presenting him with a token gift in recognition of his higher status. But by 1921, the reduction in the amount of available land had led to a system under which applicants offered the chief large payments for scarce land. As a result of these payments, farms came to be regarded as private property, and differential access to such property became institutionalized.[52]

Future research by archaeologists, sociologists, historians, and anthropologists should provide more understanding of the emergence of social stratification in human societies and how and why it may vary in degree.

SUMMARY

1. Sociologists contend that social stratification is universal because individual inequalities exist in all societies; anthropologists argue that egalitarian societies exist in the sense that there are societies in which access to advantages is equally available to all social groups.

2. The presence or absence of customs or rules that give certain groups unequal access to economic resources, power, and prestige can be used to distinguish three types of societies. In egalitarian societies, social groups do not have unequal access to economic resources, power, or prestige; they are unstratified. In rank societies, social groups do not have very unequal access to economic resources or power, but they do have unequal access to prestige. Rank societies, then, are partially stratified. In class societies, social groups have unequal access to economic resources, power, and prestige. They are more completely stratified than are rank societies.

3. Stratified societies range from somewhat open class systems to caste systems, which are extremely rigid, since caste membership is fixed permanently at birth.

4. Slaves are persons who do not own their own labor; as such, they represent a class and sometimes even a caste. Slavery has existed in various forms in many times and places, regardless of race and culture. Sometimes slavery is a rigid and closed, or caste, system; sometimes it is a relatively open class system.

5. Social stratification appears to have emerged relatively recently in human history, after 8,000 years ago. This conclusion is based on archaeological evidence and on the fact that certain cultural features associated with stratification developed relatively recently.

6. One theory suggests that social stratification developed as productivity increased and surpluses were produced. Another suggestion is that stratification can develop only when people have "investments" in land or technology and therefore cannot move away from leaders they do not like. A third theory suggests that stratification emerges only when there is population pressure on resources in rank societies.

GLOSSARY TERMS

caste	manumission
class	rank societies
class societies	slaves
egalitarian societies	

CRITICAL QUESTIONS

1. What might be the social consequences of large differences in wealth?

2. Is an industrial or a developed economy incompatible with a more egalitarian distribution of resources?

3. Why do you suppose the degree of inequality has decreased in some countries in recent years?

INTERNET EXERCISES

1. Go to **http://www.spiritweb.org/Hinduism Today/94-08-Caste_Point_Counterpoint.html** and read a debate on the pros and cons of a caste system. What do you think?

2. Go to the Web site of the U.S. Census Bureau and look at the text and graphs on changes in income inequality over time: **http://www.census.gov/hhes/www/incineq.html**. What conclusions can you draw from this information?

3. Read the accounts of a few people who were traded as slaves. Go to **http://odur.let.rug.nl/~usa/D/1826-1850/slavery/fugit02.htm**. Summarize the narrative on Edward Hicks. What are your thoughts?

SUGGESTED READING

BENJAMIN, L. *The Black Elite: Facing the Color Line in the Twilight of the Twentieth Century.* Chicago: Nelson-Hall, 1991. On the basis of interviews with 100 successful African Americans, the author documents how the "color line" continues to affect their lives.

BERREMAN, G. D., ED. *Social Inequality: Comparative and Developmental Approaches.* New York: Aca-demic Press, 1981. Chapters in this book discuss inequality in different societies, unstratified and stratified. Inequality is examined in relation to degree of economic development, colonialism, and education, among other factors.

FRIED, M. H. *The Evolution of Political Society: An Essay in Political Anthropology.* New York: Random House, 1967. Beginning with definitions of commonly used terms and drawing from several disciplines, this classic work suggests a theoretical approach to questions about the origins of ranking, social stratification, and the state.

KLASS, M. "Is There 'Caste' Outside of India?" In Carol R. Ember and Melvin Ember, eds., *Cross-Cultural Research for Social Science.* Upper Saddle River, NJ: Prentice Hall, 1998. Prentice Hall/Simon & Schuster Custom Publishing. A discussion of what caste is like in contemporary Hindu India and whether anything like it is found in other societies.

NEWMAN, K. S. *Declining Fortunes: The Withering of the American Dream.* New York: Basic Books, 1993. An in-depth study of ordinary Americans in a suburban town who are trying to understand why they are not better off than their parents.

PEREGRINE, P. N. "Variation in Stratification." In Carol R. Ember and Melvin Ember, eds., *Cross-Cultural Research for Social Science.* Upper Saddle River, NJ: Prentice Hall, 1998. Prentice Hall/Simon & Schuster Custom Publishing. A discussion, with examples, of egalitarian, rank, and class-stratified societies, and what may account for the variation.

PRYOR, F. L. *The Origins of the Economy: A Comparative Study of Distribution in Primitive and Peasant Economies.* New York: Academic Press, 1977. A large cross-cultural study of variation in distribution systems and their possible determinants. Chapter 8, on the varieties of slavery, is particularly relevant to this chapter.

16

Sex, Gender, and Culture

We all know that humans come in two major varieties—female and male. The contrast between them is one of the facts of life we share with most animal species. But the fact that males and females always have different organs of reproduction does not explain why males and females may also differ in other physical ways. After all, there are many animal species—such as pigeons, gulls, and laboratory rats—in which the two sexes differ little in appearance.[1] Thus, the fact that we are a species with two sexes does not really explain why human females and males typically look different. Also, the fact that humans reproduce sexually does not explain why human males and females should differ in behavior or be treated differently by society. Yet no society we know of treats females and males in exactly the same way; indeed, females usually have fewer advantages than males. That is why in the last chapter we were careful to say that egalitarian societies have no *social groups* with unequal access to resources, power, and prestige. But within social groups (for example, families), even egalitarian societies usually allow males greater access to economic resources, power, and prestige.

Because many of the differences between females and males may reflect cultural expectations and experiences, many researchers now prefer to speak of **gender differences,** reserving the term **sex differences** for purely biological differences.[2] Unfortunately, biological and cultural influences are not always clearly separable, so it is sometimes hard to know which term to use. As long as societies treat males and females differently, we may not be able to separate the effects of biology from the effects of culture, and both may be present. As we focus our discussion on differences and similarities between females and males, keep in mind that not all cultures conceive of gender as including just two categories. Sometimes "maleness" and "femaleness" are thought of as opposite ends of a continuum, or there might be three or more categories of gender, such as "female," "male," and "other".[3]

In this chapter we discuss what we know cross-culturally about how and why females and males may differ physically, in gender roles, and in personality. We also discuss how and why sexual behavior and attitudes about sex vary from culture to culture.

PHYSIQUE AND PHYSIOLOGY

As we noted at the outset, males and females of many animal species cannot readily be distinguished. Although they differ in chromosome makeup and in their external and internal organs of reproduction, they do not differ otherwise. In contrast, humans are **sexually dimorphic**—that is, the females and males of our species are generally different in size and appearance. Females have proportionately wider pelvises. Males typically are taller and have heavier skeletons. Females have a larger proportion of their body weight in fat; males have a larger proportion of body weight in muscle. Males typically have greater grip strength, proportionately larger hearts and lungs, and greater aerobic capacity (greater intake of oxygen during strenuous activity).

There is a tendency in our society to view "taller" and "more muscled" as better, which may reflect the bias toward males in our culture. Natural selection may have favored these traits in males but different ones in females. For example, because females bear children, selection may have favored earlier cessation of growth, and therefore less ultimate height, in females so that the nutritional needs of a fetus would not compete with a growing mother's needs.[4]

Training and practice can increase muscle strength and aerobic work capacity.

(Females achieve their ultimate height shortly after puberty, but boys continue to grow for years after puberty.) Similarly, there is some evidence that females are less affected than males by nutritional shortages, presumably because they tend to be shorter and have proportionately more fat.[5] Natural selection may have favored those traits in females because they resulted in greater reproductive success.

Both female and male athletes can build up their muscle strength and increase their aerobic work capacity through training. Given that fact, then, cultural factors, such as how much a society expects and allows males and females to engage in muscular activity, could influence the degree to which females and males differ muscularly and in aerobic capacity. Similar training may account for the recent trend toward decreasing differences between females and males in certain athletic events, such as marathons and swim meets. Even when it comes to female and male physique and physiology, then, what we see may be the result of both culture and genes.[6]

 GENER ROLES

PRODUCTIVE AND DOMESTIC ACTIVITIES

In the chapter on economic systems, we noted that all societies assign or divide labor somewhat differently between females and males. Because role assignments have a clear cultural component, we speak of them as **gender roles.** What is of particular interest here about the gender division of labor is not so much that every society has different work for males and females but rather that so many societies divide up work in similar ways. The question, then, is why there are universal or near-universal patterns in such assignments.

Table 16–1 summarizes the worldwide patterns. We note which activities are performed by which gender in all or almost all societies, which activities are usually performed by one gender, and which activities are commonly assigned to either gender or both. Does the distribution of activities in the table suggest why females and males generally do different things?

One possible explanation may be labeled the **strength theory.** The greater strength of males and their superior capacity to mobilize their strength in quick bursts of energy (because of their greater aerobic work capacity) have commonly been cited as the reason for the universal or near-universal pat-

terns in the division of labor by gender. Certainly, activities that require lifting heavy objects (hunting large animals, butchering, clearing land, working with stone, metal, or lumber), throwing weapons, and running with great speed (as in hunting) may generally be performed best by males. And none of the activities females usually perform, with the possible exception of collecting firewood, seems to require the same degree of physical strength or quick bursts of energy. But the strength theory is not completely convincing, if only because it cannot readily explain all the observed patterns. For example, it is not clear that the male activities of trapping small animals, collecting wild honey, or making musical instruments require much physical strength.

Another possible explanation of the worldwide patterns in division of labor can be called the **compatibility-with-child-care theory.** The argument here is that women's tasks tend to be those that are compatible with child care. Although males can take care of infants, most traditional societies rely on breast-feeding of infants, which men cannot do. (In most societies, women breast-feed their children for two years on the average.) Women's tasks may be those that do not take them far from home for long

---

Certain tasks are compatible with child care. Although tilling a field and carrying a child are not easy tasks, this peasant woman in Chikoku, Japan, is clearly managing to do both at the same time.

TYPE OF ACTIVITY	MALES ALMOST ALWAYS	MALES USUALLY	EITHER GENDER OR BOTH	FEMALES USUALLY	FEMALES ALMOST ALWAYS
Primary subsistence activities	Hunt and trap animals, large and small	Fish Herd large animals Collect wild honey Clear land and prepare soil for planting	Collect shellfish Care for small animals Plant crops Tend crops Harvest crops Milk animals	Gather wild plants	
Secondary subsistence and household activities		Butcher animals	Preserve meat and fish	Care for children Cook Prepare vegetable food drinks dairy products Launder Fetch water Collect fuel	Care for infants
Other	Lumber Mine and quarry Make boats musical instruments bone, horn, and shell objects Engage in combat	Build houses Make nets rope Exercise political leadership	Prepare skins Make leather products baskets mats clothing pottery	Spin yarn	

TABLE 16–1 *Worldwide Patterns in the Division of Labor by Gender*

Sources: Mostly adapted from George P. Murdock and Caterina Provost, "Factors in the Division of Labor by Sex: A Cross-Cultural Analysis," *Ethnology,* 12 (1973): 203–25. The information on political leadership and warfare comes from Martin K. Whyte, "Cross-Cultural Codes Dealing with the Relative Status of Women," *Ethnology,* 17 (1978): 217. The information on child care comes from Thomas S. Weisner and Ronald Gallimore, "My Brother's Keeper: Child and Sibling Caretaking," *Current Anthropology,* 18 (1977): 169–80.

periods, that do not place children in potential danger if they are taken along, and that can be stopped and resumed if an infant needs care.[7]

The compatibility theory may explain why *no ac-tivities* other than infant care are listed in the right-hand column of Table 16–1. That is, it may be that there are practically no universal or near-universal women-only activities because until recently most women have had to devote much of their time to nursing and caring for infants, as well as caring for other children. The compatibility theory may also explain why men usually perform tasks such as hunting, trapping, fishing, collecting honey, lumbering, and mining. Those tasks are dangerous for infants to be around and in any case would be difficult to coordinate with infant care.[8]

Finally, the compatibility theory may also explain why men seem to take over certain crafts in societies with full-time specialization. Although the distinction is not shown in Table 16–1, crafts such as making baskets, mats, and pottery are women's activities in noncommercial societies but tend to be men's activities in societies with full-time craft specialists.[9] Cooking is a good example in our own society. Women may be fine cooks, but chefs and bakers tend to be men, even though women traditionally do most of the cooking at home. Women might be more likely to work as cooks and chefs if they could leave their babies and young children in safe places to be cared for by other people.

But the compatibility theory does not explain why men usually prepare soil for planting, make objects out of wood, or work bone, horn, and shell. All of those tasks could probably be stopped to tend to a child, and none of them is any more dangerous to children nearby than is cooking. Why, then, do males tend to do them? The **economy-of-effort theory** may help explain patterns that cannot readily be explained by the strength and compatibility theories. For example, it may be advantageous for men to make musical instruments because men generally collect the hard materials involved (for example, by lumbering).[10] And because they collect those materials, men may be more knowledgeable about the materials' physical properties and so more likely to know how to work with them. The economy-of-effort interpretation also suggests that it would be advantageous for one gender to perform tasks that are located near each other. Thus, if women have to be near home to take care of young children, it would be economical for them to perform other chores that are located in or near the home.

A fourth explanation of division of labor is the **expendability theory.** This theory suggests that men, rather than women, will tend to do the dangerous work in a society because men are more expendable, because the loss of men is less disadvantageous reproductively than the loss of women. If some men lose their lives in hunting, deep-water fishing, mining, quarrying, lumbering, and the like, reproduction need not suffer as long as most fertile women have sexual access to men—for example, if the society permits two or more women to be married to the same man.[11] When would anybody, male or female, be willing to do dangerous work? Perhaps only when society glorifies those roles and endows them with high prestige and other rewards.

Although the various theories, singly or in combination, seem to explain much of the division of labor by gender, there are some unresolved problems. Critics of the strength theory have pointed out that in some societies women do engage in very heavy labor.[12] If women in some societies can develop the strength to do such work, perhaps strength is more a function of training than traditionally has been believed.

The compatibility theory also has some problems. It suggests that labor is divided to conform to the requirements of child care. But sometimes it seems the other way around. For example, women who spend a good deal of time in agricultural work outside the home often ask others to watch and feed their infants while they are unavailable to nurse.[13] Consider, too, the mountain areas of Nepal, where agricultural work is incompatible with child care; heavy loads must be carried up and down steep slopes, fields are far apart, and labor takes up most of the day. Yet women do this work anyway and leave their infants with others for long stretches of time.[14]

Furthermore, in some societies women hunt—one of the activities most incompatible with child care and generally not done by women. For example, many Agta women of the Philippines regularly hunt wild pig and deer; women alone or in groups kill almost 30 percent of the large game.[15] The women's hunting does not seem to be incompatible with child care. Women take nursing babies on hunting trips, and the women who hunt do not have lower reproductive rates than the women who choose not to hunt. Agta women may find it possible to hunt because the hunting grounds are only about a half-hour from camp, the dogs that accompany the women assist in the hunting and protect the women and babies, and the women generally hunt in groups, so others can help carry babies as well as carcasses.

As the cases just described suggest, we need to know a lot more about labor requirements. More precisely, we need to know exactly how much strength is required in particular tasks, exactly how dangerous those tasks are, and whether a person could stop working at a task to care for a child. So far, we have mostly guesses. When there is more systematically collected evidence on such aspects of particular tasks, we will be in a better position to evaluate the theories we have discussed. In any case, it should be noted that none of the available theories implies that the worldwide patterns of division of labor shown in Table 16–1 will persist. As we know from our own and other industrial societies, when machines replace human strength, when women have fewer children, and when women can assign child care to others, a strict gender division of labor begins to disappear.

RELATIVE CONTRIBUTIONS TO SUBSISTENCE

In our society, the stereotype of the husband is that he is the breadwinner in the family; the wife is the manager of the house and children. As we know, the stereotype is becoming more myth than reality. In addition to the many women who are single parents, many married women—in the United States, more than 50 percent—now work outside the home. Among married women with children 6 to 17 years old, more than 70 percent are employed.[16] The concept of "breadwinner" in our society emphasizes the person—traditionally, the male—who "brings in the bread" (food or money to buy it) from the outside. In focusing on the breadwinner, however, we may minimize the contributions of the person who works primarily inside the home.

How should we judge who contributes more to subsistence? Most anthropologists distinguish between **primary subsistence activities** and **secondary subsistence activities** (see Table 16–1). The primary activities are the food-getting activities: gathering, hunting, fishing, herding, and agriculture. Many of the secondary activities involve preparing and processing food for eating or storing. We know a considerable amount about how, and possibly why, women's and men's relative contributions to primary subsistence activities vary cross-culturally. We know much less about contributions to secondary subsistence activities. Researchers have focused mostly on primary subsistence activities, and they usually measure how much each gender's work in these activities contributes to the diet, in terms of caloric intake. Alternatively, contribution to primary subsistence activities—generally outside activities, away from the home—can be measured in terms of time spent doing them. Measures of caloric versus time contribution, however, can yield very different results. As we saw in the chapter on getting food, more time is spent by the Yanomamö in hunting than in horticulture, but horticulture yields more calories.

In some societies women have traditionally contributed more to the economy than men by any measure. For example, among the Tchambuli of New Guinea in the 1930s the women did all the fishing—going out early in the morning by canoe to their fish traps and returning when the sun was hot. Some of the catch was traded for sago (a starch) and sugarcane, and it was the women who went on the long canoe trips to do the trading.[17]

The stereotype of husband as breadwinner no longer fits our society, but it does fit the Toda of India. As they were described early in the twentieth century, they depended for subsistence almost entirely on the dairy products of their water buffalo, either by using the products directly or by selling them for grain. Women were not allowed to have anything to do with dairy work; only men tended the buffalo and prepared the dairy products. Women's work was largely household work. Women prepared the purchased grain for cooking, cleaned house, and decorated clothing.[18]

A survey of a wide variety of societies has revealed that both women and men typically contribute to primary food-getting activities, but men usually contribute more in terms of calories.[19] Women are almost always occupied with infant- and child-care responsibilities in most societies, so it is not surprising that men usually do most of the primary food-getting work, which generally has to be done away from the home.

In societies that depend on hunting, fishing, and herding—generally male activities—for most of their calories, men usually contribute more than women.[20] For example, among the Inuit, who traditionally depended mostly on hunting and fishing, and among the Toda, who depended mostly on herding, men did most of the primary subsistence work. But the predominant type of food-getting is not always predictive. Among the Tchambuli, who

Even when women and men both contribute labor to an activity, they may not necessarily work together. But this Ndumba man and woman in Papua New Guinea are sharing in the digging out of an earth oven for a village feast.

depended mostly on fishing, women did most of the work. In societies that depend on gathering, primarily women's work, women tend to do most of the food-getting, in terms of calories. The !Kung are an example. But most societies known to anthropology depend primarily on agriculture, not on hunting or gathering, for their calories. And, with the exception of clearing land and preparing the soil, which are usually men's tasks, the work of planting, crop tending (weeding, irrigating), and harvesting crops is done by men *or* women or both (see Table 16–1). So we need some explanation of why women do most of the agricultural work in some societies and men in others. Different patterns predominate in different areas of the world. In Africa south of the Sahara, women generally do most of the agricultural work. But in much of Asia and Europe and the areas around the Mediterranean, men do more.[21] In some societies women contribute more, in the caloric sense, to primary subsistence activities than do men.

One explanatory factor is the kind of agriculture. Many writers have pointed out that with intensive agriculture, particularly plow agriculture, men's caloric contribution to primary subsistence tends to be much higher than women's. In horticultural societies, in contrast, women's contribution is relatively high compared with men's. Figure 16–1 shows the relationship between women's relative contribution to primary subsistence and the type of cultivation

practiced. As the graph indicates, women contribute the most when horticulture is practiced, either root and tree crop horticulture (labeled Horticulture) or shifting/slash-and-burn cultivation (labeled Extensive or Shifting Agriculture). According to Ester Boserup, when population increases and there is pressure to make more intensive use of the land, cultivators begin to use the plow and irrigation, and males start to do more.[22] But it is not clear why.

Why should women not continue to contribute a lot to agriculture just because plows are used? In trying to answer this question, most researchers shift to considering how much time males and females spend in various agricultural tasks, rather than estimating the total caloric contribution of females versus males. The reason for this shift is that gender contribution to agriculture varies substantially over the various phases of the production sequence, as well as from one crop to another. Thus, the total amount of time females versus males work at agricultural tasks is easier to estimate than how much each gender contributes to the diet in terms of calories. How would caloric contribution be judged, for example, if men do the clearing and plowing, women do the planting and weeding, and both do the harvesting?

One suggestion about why males contribute more to agriculture when the plow is used is that plow agriculture involves a great deal of labor input

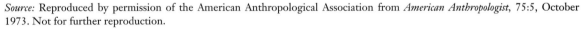

FIGURE 16–1 *Relationship between Type and Intensity of Agriculture and Average Percentage of Women's Contribution to Subsistence*

Source: Reproduced by permission of the American Anthropological Association from *American Anthropologist*, 75:5, October 1973. Not for further reproduction.

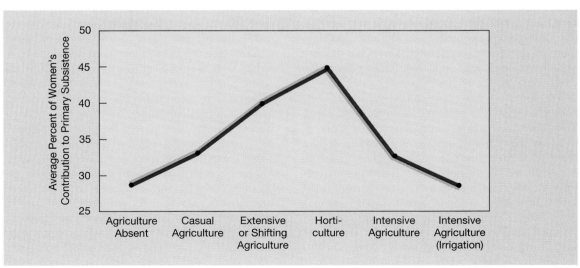

in the clearing and preparation phases of cultivation and at the same time minimizes subsequent weeding time. Men usually clear land anyway, but clearing is a more time-consuming process if intensive agriculture is practiced. It has been estimated that in one district in Nigeria, 100 days of work are required to clear one acre of virgin land for plowing by tractor; only 20 days are required to prepare the land for shifting cultivation. Weeding is a task that probably can be combined with child care, and perhaps for that reason it may have been performed mostly by women previously.[23] But the fact that men do the plowing, which may take a lot of time, does not explain why women do relatively fewer agricultural tasks, including weeding, in societies that have the plow.[24]

Another explanation for why women contribute less time than men to intensive agriculture is that household chores increase with intensive agriculture and thus limit the time women can spend in the fields. Intensive agriculturalists typically rely heavily on grain crops, which take much more work to make edible. Cereal grains (corn, wheat, oats) are usually dried before storing and thus take a long time to cook if they are left whole. More cooking requires more time to collect water and firewood (usually women's work) and more time to clean pots and utensils. A variety of techniques can reduce cooking time (such as soaking, grinding, or pounding), but the process that speeds up cooking the most—grinding—is itself time-consuming (unless done by machine). Finally, household work may increase substantially with intensive agriculture because women in such societies have more children than women in horticultural societies. If household work increases in these ways, it is easy to understand why women cannot contribute more time than men, or as much time as men, to intensive agriculture. But women's contribution, although less than men's, is nonetheless substantial; they seem to work outside the home four and a half hours a day, seven days a week, on the average.[25]

We still have not explained why women contribute so much to horticulture in the first place. They may not have as much household work as intensive-agricultural women, but neither do the men. Why, then, don't men do relatively more in horticulture also? One possibility is that in horticultural societies men are often drawn away from cultivation into other types of activities. There is evidence that if males are engaged in warfare when primary subsistence work has to be done, the women must take care of that work.[26] Men may also be withdrawn from primary subsistence work if they have to work in distant towns and cities for wages or if they periodically go on long-distance trading trips.[27]

When women contribute a lot to primary food-getting activities, we might expect their behavior and attitudes concerning children to be affected. Several cross-cultural studies suggest that this expectation is correct. In societies with a high female contribution to primary subsistence (in terms of contributing calories), infants are fed solid foods earlier (so that other persons besides mothers can feed them) than in societies with a low female contribution.[28] Girls are likely to be trained to be industrious (probably to help their mothers), and girl babies are more valued.[29]

It is important to realize that what we conclude about gender contribution to subsistence depends largely on how we measure it. Most of our discussion until now has focused on contribution to primary subsistence activities. If we change our perspective for a moment and count all kinds of work, we see a different picture of men's versus women's contribution to making a living. Adding up all work time, including activities outside the home (mostly food-getting activities) and activities inside the home (mostly preparing and cooking food), women typically work more total hours per day than men in both intensive agricultural and horticultural societies.[30]

POLITICAL LEADERSHIP AND WARFARE

In almost every known society, men rather than women are the leaders in the political arena. One cross-cultural survey found that, in about 85 percent of the surveyed societies, only men were leaders. In the societies in which some women occupied leadership positions, the women were either outnumbered by or less powerful than the men leaders.[31] If we look at countries, not cultures, women on the average make up only around 10 percent of the representatives in national parliaments or legislative bodies.[32] Whether or not we consider warfare to be part of the political sphere of life, we find an almost universal dominance of males in that arena. In 87 percent of the world's societies, women never participate actively in war.[33] (See the box titled "Why Do Some Societies Allow Women to Participate in Combat?" for a discussion of women in combat in the remaining 13 percent of societies.)

Even in *matrilineal* societies, which seem to be oriented around women (see the chapter on marital residence and kinship), men usually occupy political

New Perspectives on Gender

WHY DO SOME SOCIETIES ALLOW WOMEN TO PARTICIPATE IN COMBAT?

U.S. women can serve in the military but are usually excluded from combat. Some women feel that such exclusion is unfair and decreases their chances of promotion in the military. Other people, including some women, insist that female participation in combat would be detrimental to military performance or is inappropriate for women.

Why, then, do some societies allow women to be warriors? The psychologist David Adams compared about 70 societies studied by anthropologists to try to answer that question. Although most societies exclude women from war, Adams found that women are active warriors, at least occasionally, in 13 percent of the sample societies. In native North America, such societies included the Comanche, Crow, Delaware, Fox, Gros Ventre, and Navaho. In the Pacific, there were active warrior women among the Maori of New Zealand, on Majuro in the Marshall Islands, and among the Orokaiva of New Guinea. In none of these societies were the warriors usually women, but women were allowed to engage in combat if they wanted to.

How are the societies with women warriors different from those that exclude women from combat? They differ in one of two ways. Either they conduct war only against people in other societies (this is called "purely external" war) or they marry within their own community. Adams argues that these two conditions, which are not particularly common, preclude the possibility of conflicts of interest between wives and husbands, and therefore women can be permitted to engage in combat because their interests are the same as their husbands'. Because marriages in most cases involve individuals from the same society, husbands and wives will have the same loyalties if the society has purely external war. And even if war occurs between communities and larger groups in the same society (what we call "internal" war), there will be no conflict of interest between husband and wife if they both grew up in the same community. In contrast, there is internal war at least occasionally in most societies, and wives usually marry in from other communities. In this situation, there may often be a conflict of interest between husband and wife; if women were to engage in combat, they might have to fight against their fathers, paternal uncles, and brothers. And wouldn't we expect the wives to try to warn kin in their home communities if the husbands planned to attack them? Indeed, the men's likely fear of their wives' disloyalty would explain why women in these societies are forbidden to make or handle weapons or go near meetings in which war plans are discussed.

Many countries today engage in purely external war; so other things being equal, we would not expect conflicts of interest to impede women's participation in combat. Therefore, extrapolating from Adams's findings, we might expect that the barriers against female participation in combat will disappear completely. But other conditions may have to be present before women and men participate equally in combat. In Adams's study, not all societies with purely external war or intracommunity marriage had women warriors. So we may also have to consider the degree to which the society seeks to maximize reproduction (and therefore protect women from danger) and the degree to which the society depends on women for subsistence during wartime.

There are other related questions to explore: Does military participation by women increase women's participation in politics? Does the presence of war in a society decrease or increase women's political participation? Does women's participation in politics or in the military change the nature of war?

Source: David B. Adams, "Why There Are So Few Women Warriors," *Journal of Applied Behavior Science Research*, 18 (1983): 196–212. Reprinted by permission of Sage Publications, Inc.

Women as well as men serve on political councils in many Coast Salish communities. Here we see a swearing-in ceremony for the Special Chief's Council in Sardis, British Columbia.

positions. For example, among the Iroquois of what is now New York State, women had control over resources and a great deal of influence, but men, not women, held political office. The highest political body among the League of the Iroquois, which comprised five tribal groups, was a council of 50 male chiefs. Although women could not serve on the council, they could nominate, elect, and impeach their male representatives. Women also could decide between life and death for prisoners of war, forbid the men of their households to go to war, and intervene to bring about peace.[34]

Why have men (at least so far) almost always dominated the political sphere of life? Some scholars have suggested that men's role in warfare gives them the edge in all kinds of political leadership, particularly because they control weapons, an important resource.[35] But evidence suggests that force is rarely used to obtain leadership positions;[36] superior strength is not the deciding factor. Still, warfare may be related to political leadership for another reason. Warfare clearly affects survival, and it occurs regularly in most societies. Therefore, decision making about war may be among the most important kinds of politics in most societies. If so, then the persons

who know the most about warfare should be making the decisions about it.

To explain why males and not females usually engage in fighting, let us refer to three of the possible explanations of the worldwide patterns in the gender division of labor. Warfare, like hunting, probably requires strength (for throwing weapons) and quick bursts of energy (for running). And certainly combat is one of the most dangerous and uninterruptible activities imaginable, hardly compatible with child care. Also, even if they do not at the time have children, women may generally be kept out of combat because their potential fertility is more important to a population's reproduction and survival than their potential usefulness as warriors.[37] So, the strength theory, the compatibility theory, and the expendability theory might all explain the predominance of men in warfare.

Two other factors may be involved in male predominance in politics. One is the generally greater height of men. Why height should be a factor in leadership is unclear, but studies suggest that taller persons are more likely to be leaders.[38] Finally, there is the possibility that men dominate politics because they get around more in the outside world than do women. Men's activities typically take them farther from home; women tend to work more around the home. If societies choose leaders at least in part because of what they know about the larger world, then men will generally have some advantage. In support of this reasoning, Patricia Draper found that in !Kung bands that had settled down, women no longer engaged in long-distance gathering, and they lost much of their former influence in making decisions.[39] Involvement in child care may also detract

from such influence. In a study of village leadership among the Kayapo of Brazil, Dennis Werner found that women with heavy child-care burdens were less influential than women not as involved in child care; perhaps they had fewer friends and missed many details of what was going on in the village.[40]

These various explanations suggest why men generally dominate politics, but we still need to explain why women participate in politics more in some societies than in others. Marc Ross investigated

New Perspectives on Gender

WOMEN'S ELECTORAL SUCCESS ON THE NORTHWEST COAST

Political life has changed dramatically since first contact with Europeans for most Native American groups, including the Coast Salish of western Washington State and British Columbia. With impetus from the U.S. and Canadian governments, each of the recognized Coast Salish communities now has an elected council. But who is getting elected? Even though women did not have much of a role in traditional politics, now the Coast Salish groups are electing a lot of women. From the 1960s to the 1980s, women held over 40 percent of the council seats in the 12 Washington State groups, and in the 1990s women held 28 percent of the seats in the 50 British Columbian groups. The proportion of women on the councils varies from 6 percent among the Tulalip to 62 percent among the Stillaguamish. What accounts for the women's electoral success? And why does that success vary from one group to another, even though the groups are closely related culturally?

According to Bruce Miller, who did a comparative study

of women's electoral success in Coast Salish communities, women generally have more of a political role now perhaps because new economic opportunities in the service and technical sectors allow women to contribute more to the household economy. But why do women win proportionately more council seats in some communities than in others? Miller found that women win proportionately more seats in communities with less income, the least income derived from fishing, and the smallest populations. Why should lower household income predict more electoral success for women? Miller suggests that it is not so much the amount of income but rather the degree to which women (compared with men) contribute to household income. In groups with economic difficulties, the jobs women are able to get play a vital role in the household. Women were helped by federally funded programs such as the War on Poverty to acquire technical skills and jobs. Simultaneously, many men in some communities lost their jobs in logging and agriculture.

But a high dependence on fishing income seems to favor men politically. Families that operate vessels with a large drawstring net to catch fish at sea can make hundreds of thousands of dollars a year. Such fishing is predominantly done by men, and where there is such lucrative fishing, the successful men dominate the councils. Even though women may have jobs too, their income is not as great as the successful fisherman's.

Why should women be more successful politically in smaller communities? Miller suggests that women have a better chance to be known personally when the community is small, even though working outside the home in technical or service jobs cuts down on the time women can devote to tribal ceremonials and other public events.

Does female income relative to male and community size help explain the relative political success of women elsewhere? We do not know yet, but subsequent research may help us find out.

Source: Bruce G. Miller, "Women and Politics: Comparative Evidence from the Northwest Coast," *Ethnology,* 31 (1992): 367–82.

this question in a cross-cultural survey of 90 societies.[41] In that sample, the degree of female participation in politics varied considerably. For example, among the Mende of Sierra Leone women regularly held high office, but among the Azande of Zaire women took no part in public life. One factor that appeared to predict the exclusion of women from politics was the organization of communities around male kin. As we will see later, when they marry, women usually have to leave their communities and move to their husband's place. If women are "strangers" in a community with many related males, then the males will have political advantages because of their knowledge of community members and past events.

THE RELATIVE STATUS OF WOMEN

There are probably as many definitions of status as there are researchers interested in the topic. To some, the relative status of the sexes means how much importance society confers on females versus males. To others, it means how much power and authority men and women have relative to each other. And to still others, it means what kinds of rights women and men possess to do what they want to do. In any case, many social scientists are asking why the status of women appears to vary from one society to another. Why do women have few rights and little influence in some societies and more of each in other societies? In other words, why is there variation in degree of **gender stratification?**

In the small Iraqi town of Daghara, women and men live very separate lives.[42] In many respects, women appear to have very little status. Like women in much of the Islamic world, women in Daghara live their lives mostly in seclusion, staying in their houses and interior courtyards. If women must go out, which they can do only with male approval, they must shroud their faces and bodies in long black cloaks. These cloaks must be worn in mixed company, even at home. Women are essentially excluded from political activities. Legally, they are considered to be under the authority of their fathers and husbands. Even the sexuality of women is controlled. There is strict emphasis on virginity before marriage. Because women are not permitted even casual conversations with strange men, the possibilities for extramarital or even premarital relationships are very slight. In contrast, hardly any sexual restrictions are imposed on men.

But some societies, such as the Mbuti Pygmies, seem to approach equal status for males and females. Like most food collectors, the Mbuti have no formal political organization to make decisions or to settle disputes. Public disputes occur, and both women and men take part in the uproar that is part of such disputes. Not only do women make their positions known, but their opinions are often heeded. Even in domestic quarrels involving physical violence between husband and wife, others usually intervene to stop them, regardless of who hit whom first.[43] Women control the use of dwellings; they usually have equal say over the disposal of resources they or the men collect, over the upbringing of their children, and about whom their children should marry. One of the few signs of inequality is that women are somewhat more restricted than men with respect to extramarital sex.[44]

There are many theories about why women have relatively high or low status. One of the most common is that women's status will be high when they contribute substantially to primary subsistence activities. According to this theory, then, women should have very little status when food-getting depends largely on hunting, herding, or intensive agriculture. A second theory suggests that where warfare is especially important, men will be more valued and esteemed than women. A third theory suggests that where there are centralized political hierarchies, men will have higher status. The reasoning in the last theory is essentially the same as that in the warfare theory: Men usually play the dominant role in political behavior, so men's status should be higher wherever political behavior is more important or frequent. Finally, there is the theory that women will have higher status where kin groups and couples' place of residence after marriage are organized around women.

One of the problems in evaluating these theories is that decisions have to be made about the meaning of status. Does it mean value? Rights? Influence? And do all these aspects of status vary together? Cross-cultural research by Martin Whyte suggests that they do not. For each sample society in his study, Whyte rated 52 items that might be used to define the relative status of the sexes. These items included such things as which sex can inherit property, who has final authority over disciplining unmarried children, and whether the gods in the society are male, female, or both. The results of the study indicate that very few of these items are related. Therefore, Whyte concluded, we cannot talk about status as a single concept. Rather, it seems more appropriate to talk about the relative status of women in different spheres of life.[45]

Even though Whyte found no necessary connection between one aspect of status and another, he decided to ask whether some of the theories correctly predict why some societies have many, as opposed to few, areas in which the status of women is high. Let us turn first to the ideas that are *not* supported by the available cross-cultural evidence. The idea that generally high status derives from a greater caloric contribution to primary subsistence activities is not supported at all.[46] Women in intensive-agricultural societies (who contribute less than men to primary subsistence) do tend to have lower status in many areas of life, just as in the Iraqi case described earlier. But in societies that depend mostly on hunting (where women also do little of the primary subsistence work), women seem to have higher status, which contradicts the theoretical expectation. Similarly, there is no consistent evidence that a high frequency of warfare generally lowers women's status in different spheres of life.[47]

What does predict higher status for women in many areas of life? Although the results are not strong, there is some support in Whyte's study for the theory that where kin groups and marital residence are organized around women, women have somewhat higher status. (We discuss these features of society more fully in the chapter on marital residence and kinship.) The Iroquois are a good example. Even though Iroquois women could not hold political office, they had considerable authority within and beyond the household. Related women lived together in longhouses with husbands who belonged to other kin groups. In the longhouse, the women's authority was clear, and they could ask objectionable men to leave. The women controlled the allocation of the food they produced. Allocation could influence the timing of war parties, since men could not undertake a raid without provisions. Women were involved in the selection of religious leaders, half of whom were women. Even in politics, although women could not speak or serve on the council, they largely controlled the selection of councilmen and could institute impeachment proceedings against those to whom they objected.[48]

A generally lower status for women does appear to be found in societies with political hierarchies.[49] Lower status for women appears to be associated with other indicators of cultural complexity as well as with political hierarchies. Societies with social stratification, plow and irrigation agriculture, large settlements, private property, and craft specialization tend to have lower status for women. One type of influence for women increases with cultural complexity—informal influence. But as Whyte

pointed out, informal influence may simply reflect a lack of *real* influence.[50] Why cultural complexity is associated with women having less authority in the home, less control over property, and more restricted sexual lives is not yet understood.

Western colonialism also appears to have been generally detrimental to women's status, perhaps because Westerners have been accustomed to dealing with men. There are plenty of examples of Europeans restructuring land ownership around men and teaching men modern farming techniques, even in places where women were usually the farmers. In addition, men more often than women could earn cash through wage labor or through sales of goods (such as furs) to Europeans.[51] Although the relative status of men and women may not have been equal before the Europeans arrived, colonial influences seem generally to have undermined the position of women.

We are beginning to understand some of the conditions that may enhance or decrease certain aspects of women's status. If we can understand which of these conditions are most important, society may, if it wants to, be able to reduce gender inequality.[52]

PERSONALITY DIFFERENCES

Reporting on three tribes in New Guinea, Margaret Mead said that "many, if not all, of the personality traits we have called masculine or feminine are as lightly linked to sex as are the clothing, the manners, and the form of head-dress that a society at a given period assigns to either sex."[53] In other words, she suggested that there were *no* universal or near-universal personality differences between the sexes. Rather, societies were free to create any such differences. She described Arapesh females and males as essentially alike: Both sexes were gentle, cooperative, and nurturing. She also described the Mundugumor males and females as similar, but in this case both sexes exhibited violence and aggression. Finally, she described the Tchambuli as having substantial female-male differences in temperament, but opposite to what we might expect. The women were domineering, practical, and impersonal and were the chief economic providers; the men were sensitive and delicate and devoted their time to their appearance and to artistic pursuits.

But research conducted in recent years does not support Mead's view that there are no consistent sex differences in temperament. On the contrary, some sex differences in behavior occur consistently and in diverse societies. This does not mean that Mead was wrong about the three New Guinea societies she studied. It is possible that they were unusual cases. Nancy McDowell reanalyzed Mead's Mundugumor notes and studied a group of related neighboring people; she found no reason to doubt Mead's conclusion that female and male temperaments were similar.[54] It is also possible that Mead might have found some gender differences if she had employed the kinds of observation techniques that have been used in recent field studies. Such studies systematically record the minute details of behavior of a substantial number of males and females. Any conclusions about female-male differences in aggressiveness, for example, are based on actual counts of the number of times a particular individual tried to hurt or injure another person in a fixed amount of observation time. Almost all of these differences are subtle and a matter of degree, not a matter of a behavior being present or absent in females or males.

Which differences in personality are suggested by these systematic studies? Most of them have observed children in different cultural settings. The most consistent difference is in the area of aggression; boys try to hurt others more frequently than girls do. In an extensive comparative study of children's behavior, the Six Cultures project, this difference showed up as early as 3 to 6 years of age.[55] Research done in the United States is consistent with the cross-cultural findings.[56] In a large number of observational and experimental studies, boys exhibited more aggression than girls.

Other female-male differences have turned up with considerable consistency, but we have to be cautious in accepting them, either because they have not been documented as well or because there are more exceptions. There seems to be a tendency for girls to exhibit more responsible behavior, including nurturance (trying to help others). Girls seem more likely to conform to adult wishes and commands. Boys try more often to exert dominance over others in order to get their own way. In play, boys and girls show a preference for their own gender. Boys seem to play in large groups, girls in small ones. And boys seem to maintain more distance between each other than girls do.[57]

If we assume that these differences are consistent across cultures, how can we explain them? Many writers and researchers believe that because certain female-male differences are so consistent, they are probably rooted in the biological differences between the two sexes. Aggression is one of the traits talked about most often in this connection, particularly because this male-female difference appears so

When a society has different role expectations for boys and girls, it is difficult to know how much of the sex difference in aggression is due to biology and how much is due to learning. This Yanomamö boy, as in many societies, starts to learn about weapons for hunting and war at a very early age.

early in life.[58] But an alternative argument is that societies bring up boys and girls differently because they almost universally require adult males and females to perform different types of roles. If most societies expect adult males to be warriors or to be prepared to be warriors, shouldn't we expect most societies to encourage or idealize aggression in males? And if females are almost always the caretakers of infants, shouldn't we also expect societies generally to encourage nurturant behaviors in females?

Researchers tend to adopt either the biological or the socialization view, but it is possible that both kinds of causes are important in the development of gender differences. For example, parents might turn a slight genetic difference into a large gender difference by maximizing that difference in the way they socialize boys versus girls.

It is difficult for researchers to distinguish the influence of genes and other biological conditions from the influence of socialization. We have research indicating that as early as birth, parents treat boy and girl infants differently.[59] In spite of the fact that objective observers can see no major "personality" differences between girl and boy infants, parents often claim to.[60] But parents may unconsciously want to see differences and may therefore produce them in socialization. So even early differences could be learned rather than genetic. Remember, too, that researchers cannot do experiments with people; for example, parents' behavior cannot be manipulated to find out what would happen if boys and girls were treated in exactly the same way.

However, there is considerable experimental research on aggression in nonhuman animals. These experiments suggest that the hormone androgen is partly responsible for higher levels of aggression. For example, in some experiments, females injected with androgen at about the time the sexual organs develop (before or shortly after birth) behave more aggressively when they are older than do females without the hormone. These results may or may not apply to humans of course, but some researchers have investigated human females who were "androgenized" in the womb because of drugs given to their mothers to prevent miscarriage. By and large the results of these studies are similar to the experi-

mental studies—androgenized human females show similar patterns of higher aggression.[61] Some scholars take these results to indicate that biological differences between males and females are responsible for the male-female difference in aggression;[62] others suggest that even these results are not conclusive, because females who get more androgen show generally disturbed metabolic systems, and general metabolic disturbance may itself increase aggressiveness. Furthermore, androgen-injected females may look more like males because they develop male-like genitals; therefore, they may be treated like males.[63]

Is there any evidence that socialization differences may account for differences in aggression? Although a cross-cultural survey of ethnographers' reports on 101 societies does show that more societies encourage aggression in boys than in girls, most societies show no difference in aggression training.[64] The few societies that do show differences in aggression training can hardly account for the widespread sex differences in actual aggressiveness. But the survey does not necessarily mean that there are no consistent differences in aggression training for boys and girls. All it shows is that there are no *obvious* differences. For all we know, the learning of aggression and other "masculine" traits by boys could be produced by subtle types of socialization.

One possible type of subtle socialization that could create gender differences in behavior is the chores children are assigned. It is possible that little boys and girls learn to behave differently because their parents ask them to do different kinds of work. Beatrice and John Whiting reported from the Six Cultures project that in societies where children were asked to do a great deal of work, they generally showed more responsible and nurturant behavior. Because girls are almost always asked to do more work than boys, they may be more responsible and nurturant for that reason alone.[65] If this reasoning is correct, we should find that if boys are asked to do girls' work, they will learn to behave more like girls.

A study of Luo children in Kenya supports that view.[66] Girls were usually asked to baby-sit, cook, clean house, and fetch water and firewood. Boys were usually asked to do very little because boys' traditional work was herding cattle, and most families in the community studied had few cattle. But for some reason more boys than girls had been born, and many mothers without girls at home asked their sons to do girls' chores. Systematic behavior observations showed that much of the behavior of the boys who did girls' work was intermediary between

"It's a guy thing."

Source: Drawing by Donald Reilly. © 1995 from *The New Yorker Collection*. All rights reserved.

the behavior of other boys and the behavior of girls. The boys who did girls' work were more like girls in that they were less aggressive, less domineering, and more responsible than other boys, even when they weren't working. So it is possible that task assignment has an important influence on how boys and girls learn to behave. These and other subtle forms of socialization need to be investigated more thoroughly.

MISCONCEPTIONS ABOUT DIFFERENCES IN BEHAVIOR

Before we leave the subject of behavior differences, we should note some widespread beliefs about them that are not supported by research. Some of these mistaken beliefs are that girls are more dependent than boys, that girls are more sociable, and that girls are more passive. The results obtained by the Six Cultures project cast doubt on all these notions.[67] First, if we think of dependency as seeking help and emotional support from others, girls are generally no more likely to behave this way than boys. To be sure, the results do indicate that boys and girls have somewhat different styles of dependency. Girls more often seek help and contact; boys more often seek attention and approval. As for sociability, which means seeking and offering friendship, the Six Cultures results showed no reliable differences between the sexes. Of course, boys and girls may be sociable in different ways because boys generally play in larger groups than girls. As for the supposed passivity of girls, the evidence is also not particularly convincing. Girls in the Six Cultures project did not consistently withdraw from aggressive attacks or comply with unreasonable demands. The only thing that emerged as a female-male difference was that older girls were less likely than boys to respond to aggression with aggression. But this finding may not reflect passivity as much as the fact that girls are less aggressive than boys, which we already knew.

So some of our common ideas about female-male differences are unfounded. Others, such as those dealing with aggression and responsibility, cannot be readily dismissed and should be investigated further.

As we noted, an observed difference in aggression does not mean that males are aggressive and females are not. Perhaps because males are generally more aggressive, aggression in females has been studied less often. For that reason, Victoria Burbank focused on female aggression in an Australian aborigine community she calls Mangrove. During the 18 months that she was there, Burbank observed some act of aggression almost every other day. Consistent with the cross-cultural evidence, men initiated aggression more often than women, but women were initiators about 43 percent of the time. The women of Mangrove engaged in almost all the same kinds of aggression as men did, including fighting, except that it tended not to be as lethal as male violence. Lethal weapons were most often used by men; when women fought with weapons, they mostly used sticks, not spears, guns, or knives. Burbank points out that, in contrast to Western cultures, female aggression is not viewed as unnatural or deviant, but rather as a natural expression of anger.[68]

SEXUALITY

In view of the way the human species reproduces, it is not surprising that sexuality is part of our nature. But no society we know of leaves sexuality to nature; all have at least some rules governing "proper" conduct. There is much variation from one society to another in the degree of sexual activity permitted or encouraged before marriage, outside marriage, and even within marriage. And societies vary markedly in their tolerance of nonheterosexual sexuality.

CULTURAL REGULATION OF SEXUALITY: PERMISSIVENESS VERSUS RESTRICTIVENESS

All societies seek to regulate sexual activity to some degree, and there is a lot of variation cross-culturally. Some societies allow premarital sex; others forbid it. The same is true for extramarital sex. In addition, a society's degree of restrictiveness is not always consistent throughout the life span or for all aspects of sex. For example, a number of societies ease sexual restrictions somewhat for adolescents, and many become more restrictive for adults.[69] Then, too, societies change over time. Our own society has traditionally been restrictive, but until recently—before the emergence of the AIDS epidemic—more permissive attitudes were gaining acceptance.

PREMARITAL SEX. The degree to which sex before marriage is approved or disapproved of varies greatly from society to society. The Trobriand Islanders, for example, approved of and encouraged premarital sex, seeing it as an important preparation for later marriage roles. Both girls and boys were given complete instruction in all forms of sexual expression at the onset of puberty and were allowed plenty of opportunity for intimacy. Some societies not only allow premarital sex on a casual basis but specifically encourage trial marriages between adolescents. Among the Ila-speaking peoples of central Africa, at harvest time girls were given houses of their own where they could play at being wife with the boys of their choice. It is said that among these people virginity did not exist beyond the age of 10.[70]

On the other hand, in many societies premarital sex was discouraged. For example, among the Tepoztlan Indians of Mexico, a girl's life became "crabbed, cribbed, confined" from the time of her first menstruation. She was not to speak to or encourage boys in the least way. To do so would be to court disgrace, to show herself to be crazy. The responsibility of guarding the chastity and reputation of one or more daughters of marriageable age was often a burden for the mother. One mother said she wished her 15-year-old daughter would marry soon because it was inconvenient to "spy" on her all the time.[71] In many Muslim societies, a girl's premarital chastity was tested after her marriage. After the wedding night, blood-stained sheets were displayed as proof of the bride's virginity.

Cultures do not remain the same; attitudes and practices can change markedly over time, as in the United States. In the past, sex was generally delayed until after marriage; in the 1990s, most Americans accepted or approved of premarital sex.[72]

EXTRAMARITAL SEX. Extramarital sex is not uncommon in many societies. In about 69 percent of the world's societies men have extramarital sex more than occasionally, and in about 57 percent so do women. The frequency of such sexual activity is higher than we might expect, given that only a slight majority of societies (54 percent) say they allow extramarital sex for men, and only a small number (11 percent) say they allow it for women.[73]

In several societies, then, there is quite a difference between the restrictive code and actual practice. The Navaho of the 1940s were said to forbid adultery, but young married men under the age of 30 had 27 percent of their heterosexual contacts with women other than their wives.[74] And although people in the United States in the 1970s almost overwhelmingly rejected extramarital sex, 41 percent of married men and about 18 percent of married women had had extramarital sex. In the 1990s, proportionately more men and women reported that they had been faithful to their spouses.[75] Cross-culturally, most societies have a double standard with regard to men and women, with restrictions considerably greater for women.[76] A substantial number of societies openly accept extramarital relationships. The Chukchee of Siberia, who often traveled long distances, allowed a married man to engage in sex with his host's wife, with the understanding that he would offer the same hospitality when the host visited him.[77]

SEX WITHIN MARRIAGE. There is as much variety in the way coitus is performed as there is in sexual attitudes in general. Privacy is a nearly universal requirement. But, whereas a North American will usually find privacy in the bedroom, many other peoples are obliged to go out into the bush. The Siriono of Bolivia, for example, had as many as 50 hammocks 10 feet apart in their small huts.[78] In some cultures coitus often occurs in the presence of others, who may be sleeping or simply looking the other way.

Time and frequency of coitus also vary. Night is generally preferred, but some peoples, such as the Rucuyen of Brazil and the Yapese of the Pacific Caroline Islands, specifically opted for day. The Chenchu of India believed that a child conceived at night might be born blind. People in most societies abstain from intercourse during menstruation, during at least part of pregnancy, and for a period after childbirth. The Lesu, a people of New Ireland, an island off New Guinea, prohibited all members of the community from engaging in sex between the death of any member and burial.[79] Some societies prohibit sexual relations before various activities, such as hunting, fighting, planting, brewing, and iron smelting. Our own society is among the most lenient regarding restrictions on coitus within marriage, imposing only rather loose restraints during mourning, menstruation, and pregnancy.

HOMOSEXUALITY. The range in permissiveness or restrictiveness toward homosexual relations is as great as that for any other kind of sexual activity. Among the Lepcha of the Himalayas, a man was believed to become homosexual if he ate the flesh of an uncastrated pig. But the Lepcha said that homosexual behavior was practically unheard of, and they viewed it with disgust.[80] Perhaps because many societies deny that homosexuality exists, little is known about homosexual practices in the restrictive societies. Among the permissive ones, there is variation in the pervasiveness of homosexuality. In some societies homosexuality is accepted but limited to certain times and certain individuals. For example, among the Papago of the southwestern United States there were "nights of saturnalia" in which homosexual tendencies could be expressed. The Papago also had many male transvestites, who wore women's clothing, did women's chores, and, if not married, could be visited by men.[81] A woman did not have the same freedom of expression. She could participate in the saturnalia feasts but only with her husband's permission, and female transvestites were nonexistent.

Homosexuality occurs even more widely in other societies. The Siwans of North Africa expected all males to engage in homosexual relations. In fact, fathers made arrangements for their unmarried sons to be given to an older man in a homosexual arrangement. Siwan custom limited a man to one boy. Fear of the government made this a secret matter, but before 1909 such arrangements were made openly. Almost all men were reported to have engaged in a homosexual relationship as boys; later, when they were between 16 and 20, they married girls.[82] Among the most extremely prohomosexual societies, the Etoro of New Guinea preferred homosexuality to heterosexuality. Heterosexuality was prohibited as many as 260 days a year and was forbidden in or near the house and gardens. Male homosexuality, on the other hand, was not prohibited at any time and was believed to make crops flourish and boys become strong.[83]

REASONS FOR RESTRICTIVENESS

Before we deal with the question of why some societies are more restrictive than others, we must first ask whether all forms of restrictiveness go together. The research to date suggests that societies that are restrictive with regard to one aspect of heterosexual sex tend to be restrictive with regard to other aspects. Thus, societies that frown on sexual expression by young children also punish premarital and extramarital sex.[84] Furthermore, such societies tend to insist on modesty in clothing and are constrained in their talk about sex.[85] But societies that are gener-

Ideas about sexual modesty vary by culture and time. One of these women who work for an oil company in Kuwait is dressed traditionally; the other is not.

ally restrictive about heterosexuality are not necessarily restrictive about homosexuality. Societies restrictive about premarital sex are neither more nor less likely to restrict homosexuality. In the case of extramarital sex, the situation is somewhat different. Societies that have a considerable amount of male homosexuality tend to disapprove of males having extramarital heterosexual relationships.[86] If we are going to explain restrictiveness, then, it appears we have to consider heterosexual and homosexual restrictiveness separately.

Let us consider homosexual restrictiveness first. Why do homosexual relationships occur more frequently in some societies, and why are some societies intolerant of such relationships? There are many psychological interpretations of why some people become interested in homosexual relationships, and many of these interpretations relate the phenomenon to early parent-child relationships. So far the research has not yielded any clear-cut predictions, although several cross-cultural predictors about male homosexuality are intriguing.

One such finding is that societies that forbid abortion and infanticide for married women (most societies permit these practices for illegitimate births) are likely to be intolerant of male homosexuality. This and other findings are consistent with the point of view that homosexuality is less tolerated in societies that would like to increase population. Such societies may be intolerant of all kinds of behaviors that minimize population growth. Homosexuality would have this effect, if we assume that a higher frequency of homosexual relations is associated with a lower frequency of heterosexual relations. The less frequently heterosexual relations occur, the lower the number of conceptions there might be. Another indication that intolerance may be related to a desire for population growth is that societies with famines and severe food shortages are more likely to allow homosexuality. Famines and food shortages suggest population pressure on resources; under these conditions, homosexuality and other practices that minimize population growth may be tolerated or even encouraged.[87]

The history of the Soviet Union may provide some other relevant evidence. In 1917, in the turmoil of revolution, laws prohibiting abortion and homosexuality were revoked and reproduction was discouraged. But in the period 1934–1936 the policy was reversed. Abortion and homosexuality were again declared illegal, and homosexuals were arrested. At the same time, awards were given to mothers who had more children.[88] Population pressure may also explain why our own society has become somewhat more tolerant of homosexuality recently. Of course, population pressure does not explain why certain individuals become homosexual or why most individuals in some societies engage in such behavior, but it might explain why some societies view such behavior more or less permissively.

Let us turn now to heterosexual behavior. What kinds of societies are more permissive than others? Although we do not as yet understand the reasons, we do know that greater restrictiveness toward premarital sex tends to occur in more complex societies—societies that have hierarchies of political officials, part-time or full-time craft specialists, cities and towns, and class stratification.[89] It may be that as social inequality increases and various groups come to have differential wealth, parents become more concerned with preventing their children from marrying "beneath them." Permissiveness toward premarital sexual relationships might lead a person to become attached to someone not considered a desirable marriage partner. Even worse, from the family's point of view, such "unsuitable" sexual liaisons might result in a pregnancy that could make it impossible for a girl to marry "well." Controlling mating, then, may be a way of trying to control property. Consistent with this view is the finding that virginity is emphasized in rank and stratified societies, in which families are likely to exchange goods and money in the course of arranging marriages.[90]

The biological fact that humans depend on sexual reproduction does not by itself help explain why females and males differ in so many ways across cultures, or why societies vary in the way they handle male and female roles. We are only beginning to investigate these questions. When we eventually understand more about how and why females and males are different or the same in roles, personality, and sexuality, we may be better able to decide how much we want the biology of sex to shape our lives.

▌▐▐▌▌ SUMMARY

1. That humans reproduce sexually does not explain why males and females tend to differ in appearance and behavior, and to be treated differently, in all societies.

2. All or nearly all societies assign certain activities to females and other activities to males. These worldwide gender patterns of division of labor may be explained by male-female differences in strength, by differences in compatibility of tasks with child care, or by economy-of-effort considerations and/or the expendability of men.

3. Perhaps because women almost always have infant- and child-care responsibilities, men in most societies contribute more to primary subsistence activities, in terms of calories. But women contribute substantially to primary subsistence activities in societies that depend heavily on gathering and horticulture and in which warfare occurs while primary subsistence work has to be done. When primary and secondary subsistence work are counted, women typically work more hours than men. In most societies men are the leaders in the political arena, and warfare is almost exclusively a male activity.

4. The relative status of women compared with that of men seems to vary from one area of life to another. Whether women have relatively high status in one area does not necessarily indicate that they will have high status in another. Less complex societies, however, seem to approach more equal status for males and females in a variety of areas of life.

5. Recent field studies have suggested some consistent female-male differences in personality: Boys tend to be more aggressive than girls, and girls seem to be more responsible and helpful than boys.

6. Although all societies regulate sexual activity to some extent, societies vary considerably in the degree to which various kinds of sexuality are permitted. Some societies allow both masturbation and sex play among children, whereas others forbid such acts. Some societies allow premarital sex; others do not. Some allow extramarital sex in certain situations; others forbid it generally.

7. Societies that are restrictive toward one aspect of heterosexual sex tend to be restrictive with regard to other aspects. And more complex societies tend to be more restrictive toward premarital heterosexual sex than less complex societies.

8. Societal attitudes toward homosexuality are not completely consistent with attitudes toward sexual relationships between the sexes. Societal tolerance of homosexuality is associated with tolerance of abortion and infanticide and with famines and food shortages.

▌▐▐▌▌ GLOSSARY TERMS

compatibility-with-child-care theory
economy-of-effort theory
expendability theory
gender differences
gender roles
gender stratification

primary subsistence activities
secondary subsistence activities
sex differences
sexually dimorphic
strength theory

CRITICAL QUESTIONS

1. Would you expect female-male differences in personality to disappear in a society with complete gender equality in the workplace?

2. Under what circumstances would you expect male-female differences in athletic performance to disappear?

3. What conditions make the election of a female head of state most likely?

INTERNET EXERCISES

1. Check out women's work in Sierra Leone at **http://www.fao.org/NEWS/FACTFILE/FF9719-E.HTM** or **http://www.fao.org/NEWS/FACTFILE/FF9718-E.HTM**. What impressed you most?

2. The global gender gap is addressed in a 1995 United Nations report. Go to **http://www.undp.org/undp/hdr/1995/english.htm** and explore one of the first three topics under Measuring the Global Gender Gap. Write a brief summary of what you found.

3. Visit **http://www.swc-cfc.gc.ca/direct.html** to learn about the status of women and their changing role in Canada. Write a brief summary on the current issues this Web page addresses (**http://www.swc-cfc.gc.ca/research/indexe.html**).

SUGGESTED READING

BROUDE, G. J. "Variations in Sexual Attitudes, Norms and Practices." In C. R. Ember and M. Ember, eds., *Cross-Cultural Research for Social Science.* Upper Saddle River, NJ: Prentice Hall, 1998. Prentice Hall/Simon & Schuster Custom Publishing. An exploration of the ways in which cultures vary in their sexual attitudes and practices and the possible reasons for the variation.

EMBER, C. R. "Universal and Variable Patterns of Gender Difference." In C. R. Ember and M. Ember, eds., *Cross-Cultural Research for Social Science.* Upper Saddle River, NJ: Prentice Hall, 1998. Prentice Hall/Simon & Schuster Custom Publishing. A review of what we know and do not know about sex and gender differences cross-culturally and a critical evaluation of the theories that might explain the universal and variable patterns.

MORGEN, S., ED. *Gender and Anthropology: Critical Reviews for Research and Teaching.* Washington, DC: American Anthropological Association, 1989. Designed to bring the insights of feminist anthropology to all four subfields of anthropology. Most relevant here are the chapters on different culture areas.

SANDAY, P. R., AND GOODENOUGH, R. G., EDS. *Beyond the Second Sex: New Directions in the Anthropology of Gender.* Philadelphia: University of Pennsylvania Press, 1990. The authors of the chapters in this volume reexamine theoretical notions about gender symbolism, gender roles, and male-female relationships in particular reference to the societies they have studied.

SCHLEGEL, A. "The Status of Women." In C. R. Ember and M. Ember, eds., *Cross-Cultural Research for Social Science.* Upper Saddle River, NJ: Prentice Hall, 1998. Prentice Hall/Simon & Schuster Custom Publishing. A critical discussion of the comparative research on variation in women's status with an analysis of different kinds of equality and inequality in four ethnographic cases.

WOMACK, M., AND MARTI, J. *The Other Fifty Percent: Multicultural Perspectives on Gender Relations.* Prospect Heights, IL: Waveland Press, 1993. A collection of 24 readings about women in different societies—their roles in marriage, economic decision making, politics, and religion.

Marriage and the Family

Whatever a society's attitudes toward male-female relationships, one such relationship is found in all societies—marriage. Why marriage is customary in every society we know of is a classic and perplexing question, and one we attempt to deal with in this chapter.

The universality of marriage does not mean that everyone in every society gets married. It means only that most, usually nearly all, people in every society get married at least once in their lifetime. In addition, when we say that marriage is universal, we do not mean that marriage and family customs are the same in all societies. On the contrary, there is much variation from society to society in how one marries, whom one marries, and even how many persons one marries. The only cultural universal about marriage is that no society permits people to marry parents, brothers, or sisters.

Families also are universal. All societies have parent-child social groups, although the form and size of family may vary from one society to another. Some societies have large extended families with two or more related parent-child groups; others have smaller independent families. Today, marriage is not always the basis for family life. One-parent families are becoming increasingly common in our own and other societies. Marriage has not disappeared in these places—it is still customary to marry—but more individuals are choosing now to have children without being married.

MARRIAGE

When anthropologists speak of marriage, they do not mean to imply that couples everywhere must get marriage certificates or have wedding ceremonies, as in our own society. **Marriage** merely means a socially approved sexual and economic union usually between a woman and a man. It is presumed, by both the couple and others, to be more or less permanent, and it subsumes reciprocal rights and obligations between the two spouses and between spouses and their future children.[1]

It is a socially approved sexual union in that a married couple does not have to hide the sexual nature of their relationship. A woman might say, "I want you to meet my husband," but she could not say, "I want you to meet my lover" without causing some embarrassment in most societies. Although the union may ultimately be dissolved by divorce,

couples in all societies begin marriage with some idea of permanence in mind. Implicit too in marriage are reciprocal rights and obligations. These may be more or less specific and formalized regarding matters of property, finances, and child rearing.

Marriage entails both a sexual and an economic relationship:

> As George Peter Murdock noted, "Sexual relations can occur without economic cooperation, and there can be a division of labor between men and women without sex. But marriage unites the economic and the sexual."[2]

As we will see, the event that marks the commencement of marriage varies in different societies. A Winnebago bride, for example, knew no formal ritual such as a wedding ceremony. She went with her groom to his parents' house, took off her "wedding" clothes and finery, gave them to her mother-in-law, received plain clothes in exchange, and that was that.[3]

THE NAYAR "EXCEPTION"

There is one group of people in the ethnographic literature that did not have marriage, as we have defined it. In the nineteenth century, a caste group in southern India called the Nayar seems to have treated sex and economic relations between men and women as things separate from marriage. About the time of puberty, Nayar girls took ritual husbands. The union was publicly established in a ceremony during which the husband tied a gold ornament around the neck of his bride. But from that time on, he had no more responsibility for her. Usually, he never saw her again.

The bride lived in a large household with her family, where she was visited over the subsequent years by other "husbands." One might be a passing guest, another a more regular visitor; it did not matter, providing the "husband" met the caste restrictions and was approved by her kin group. He came at night and left the following day. If a regular visitor, he was expected to make small gifts of cloth, betel nuts, and hair and bath oil. If the father of her child, or one of a group who might be, he was expected to pay the cost of the midwife. But at no time was he responsible for the support of the woman or her child, nor did he have any say in the upbringing of his biological children. Rather, her blood relatives retained such responsibilities.[4]

Whether or not the Nayar had marriage depends, of course, on how we choose to define marriage. Certainly, Nayar marital unions involved no regular sexual component or economic cooperation, nor did they involve important reciprocal rights and obligations. According to our definition, then, the Nayar did not have marriage. But the Nayar were not a separate society—only a caste group whose men specialized in soldiering. The Nayar situation seems to have been a special response to the problem of extended male absence during military service. In more recent times, military service has ceased to be a common occupation of the Nayars, and stable married relationships have become the norm.[5] Because the Nayar were not a separate society, they are not really an exception to our statement that marriage, as we have defined it, has been customary in all societies known to anthropology.

RARE TYPES OF MARRIAGE

In addition to the usual male-female marriages, some societies recognize marriages between persons of the same biological sex. But such marriages are not typical in any known society and do not fit the usual type of marriage. First, the unions are not between a male and a female. Second, they are not necessarily sexual unions, as we will see. But these "marriages" are socially approved unions, usually modeled after regular marriages, and they often entail a considerable number of reciprocal rights and obligations. Sometimes the marriages involve an individual who is considered a "woman" or "man" even though "she" or "he" is not that sex biologically. For example, the Cheyenne Indians allowed married men to take **berdaches,** or male transvestites, as second wives.[6] (The term *two-spirits* is often used now instead of *berdache*.)

Although it is not clear that the Cheyenne male-male marriages involved homosexual relationships, it is clear that temporary homosexual marriages did occur among the Azande of Africa. Before the British took control over what is now Sudan, Azande warriors who could not afford wives often married "boy-wives" to satisfy their sexual needs. As in normal marriages, gifts (although not as substantial) were given by the "husband" to the parents of his boy-wife. The husband performed services for the boy's parents and could sue any other lover in court for adultery. The boy-wives not only had sexual relations with their husbands but also performed many of the chores female wives traditionally performed for their husbands.[7]

Female-female marriages are reported to have occurred in many African societies, but there is no evidence of any sexual relationship between the partners. It seems, rather, that female-female marriages were a socially approved way for a woman to take on the legal and social roles of a father and husband.[8] For example, among the Nandi, a pastoral and agricultural society of Kenya, about 3 percent of the marriages are female-female marriages. Such marriages appear to be a Nandi solution to the problem of a regular marriage's failure to produce a male heir to property. The Nandi solution is to have the woman, even if her husband is still alive, become a "husband" to a younger female and "father" the younger woman's children. The female husband provides the marriage payments required for obtaining a wife, renounces female work, and takes on the obligations of the husband to that woman. Although no sexual relations are permitted between the female husband and the new wife (or between the female husband and her own husband), the female husband arranges a male consort so that the new wife can have children. Those children, however, consider the female husband to be their father because she (or more aptly the gender role "he") is the socially designated father. If asked who their father is, a child of such a marriage will name the female who is the husband.[9]

WHY IS MARRIAGE UNIVERSAL?

Because all societies practice female-male marriage as we have defined it, we can assume that the custom is adaptive. But saying that does not specify exactly how it may be adaptive. Several interpretations have traditionally been offered to explain why all human societies have the custom of marriage. Each suggests that marriage solves problems found in all societies—how to share the products of a gender division of labor; how to care for infants, who are dependent for a long time; and how to minimize sexual competition. To evaluate the plausibility of these interpretations, we must ask whether marriage provides the best or the only reasonable solution to each problem. After all, we are trying to explain a custom that is presumably a universal solution. The comparative study of other animals, some of which have something like marriage, may help us to evaluate these explanations.

GENDER DIVISION OF LABOR

We noted in the preceding chapter that every society known to anthropology has had a gender division of labor. Males and females in every society perform different economic activities. This gender division of labor has often been cited as a reason for marriage.[10] As long as there is a division of labor by gender, society has to have some mechanism by

Some societies have ceremonies marking the onset of marriage and some do not. Here we see a Sikh wedding.

which women and men share the products of their labor. Marriage would be one way to solve that problem. But it seems unlikely that marriage is the only possible solution. The hunter-gatherer rule of sharing could be extended to include all the products brought in by both women and men. Or a small group of men and women, such as brothers and sisters, might be pledged to cooperate economically. Thus, although marriage may solve the problem of sharing the fruits of a division of labor, it clearly is not the only possible solution.

PROLONGED INFANT DEPENDENCY

Humans exhibit the longest period of infant dependency of any primate. The child's prolonged dependence places the greatest burden on the mother, who is the main child tender in most societies. The burden of prolonged child care by human females may limit the kinds of work they can do. They may need the help of a man to do certain types of work, such as hunting, that are incompatible with child care. Because of this prolonged dependency, it has been suggested, marriage is necessary.[11] But here the argument becomes essentially the same as the division-of-labor argument, and it has the same logical weakness. It is not clear why a group of women and men, such as a hunter-gatherer band, could not cooperate in providing for dependent children without marriage.

SEXUAL COMPETITION

Unlike most other female primates, the human female may engage in intercourse at any time throughout the year. Some scholars have suggested that more or less continuous female sexuality may

have created a serious problem—considerable sexual competition between males for females. It is argued that society had to prevent such competition in order to survive, that it had to develop some way of minimizing the rivalry among males for females in order to reduce the chance of lethal and destructive conflict.[12]

There are several problems with this argument. First, why should continuous female sexuality make for more sexual competition in the first place? One might argue the other way around. There might be more competition over the scarcer resources that would be available if females were less frequently interested in sex. Second, males of many animal species, even some that have relatively frequent female sexuality (as do many of our close primate relatives), do not show much aggression over females. Third, why couldn't sexual competition, even if it existed, be regulated by cultural rules other than marriage? For instance, society might have adopted a rule whereby men and women circulated among all the opposite-sex members of the group, each person staying a specified length of time with each partner. Such a system presumably would solve the problem of sexual competition. On the other hand, such a system might not work particularly well if individuals came to prefer certain other individuals. Jealousies attending those attachments might give rise to even more competition.

OTHER MAMMALS AND BIRDS: POSTPARTUM REQUIREMENTS

None of the theories we have discussed explains convincingly why marriage is the only or the best solution to a particular problem. Also, we now have

"I do love you. But, to be perfectly honest, I would have loved any other lovebird who happened to turn up."
(©1978 Punch/Rothco)

some comparative evidence on mammals and birds that casts doubt on those theories.[13] How can evidence from other animals help us evaluate theories about human marriage? If we look at the animals that, like humans, have some sort of stable female-male mating, as compared with those that are completely promiscuous, we can perhaps see what sorts of factors may predict male-female bonding in the warm-blooded animal species. Most species of birds, and some mammals such as wolves and beavers, have "marriage." Among 40 mammal and bird species, none of the three factors discussed above—division of labor, prolonged infant dependency, and greater female sexuality—predicts or is correlated strongly with male-female bonding. With respect to division of labor by sex, most other animals have nothing comparable to a humanlike division of labor, but many have stable female-male matings anyway. The two other supposed factors—prolonged infant dependency and female sexuality—predict just the opposite of what we might expect. Mammal and bird species that have longer dependency periods or more female sexuality are *less* likely to have stable matings.

Does anything predict male-female bonding? One factor does among mammals and birds, and it may also help explain human marriage. Animal species in which females can simultaneously feed themselves and their babies after birth *(postpartum)* tend not to have stable matings; species in which postpartum mothers cannot feed themselves and their babies at the same time tend to have stable matings. Among the typical bird species, a mother would have difficulty feeding herself and her babies simultaneously. Because the young cannot fly for a

while and must be protected in a nest, the mother risks losing them to other animals if she goes off to obtain food. But if she has a male bonded to her (as most bird species do), he can bring back food or take a turn watching the nest. Among animal species that have no postpartum feeding problem, babies almost immediately after birth are able to travel with the mother as she moves about to eat (as do grazers such as horses), or the mother can transport the babies as she moves about to eat (as do baboons and kangaroos). We think the human female has a postpartum feeding problem. When humans lost most of their body hair, babies could not readily travel with the mother by clinging to her fur. And when humans began to depend on certain kinds of food-getting that could be dangerous (such as hunting), mothers could not engage in such work with their infants along.

Even if we assume that human mothers have a postpartum feeding problem, we still have to ask if marriage is the most likely solution to the problem. We think so, because other conceivable solutions probably would not work as well. For example, if a mother took turns baby-sitting with another mother, neither might be able to collect enough food for both mothers and the two sets of children dependent on them. But a mother and father share the *same* set of children, and therefore it would be easier for them to feed themselves and their children adequately. Another possible solution is no pair bonding at all, just a promiscuous group of males and females. But in that kind of arrangement, we think, a particular mother probably would not always be able to count on some male to watch her baby when she had to go out for food or to bring her food when she had to watch her baby. Thus, it seems to us that the problem of postpartum feeding by itself helps to explain why some animals, including humans, have relatively stable male-female bonds. Of course, there is still the question of whether research on other animals can be applied to human beings. We think it can, but not everybody will agree.

HOW DOES ONE MARRY?

When we say that marriage is a socially approved sexual and economic union, we mean that all societies have some way of marking the onset of a marriage, but the ways of doing so vary considerably. For reasons that we don't fully understand, some cultures mark marriages by elaborate rites and celebrations; others mark marriages in much more informal ways. And most societies have economic transactions before, during, or even after the onset of the marriages.

MARKING THE ONSET OF MARRIAGE

Many societies have ceremonies marking the beginning of marriage. But others, such as the Taramiut Inuit, the Trobriand Islanders of the South Pacific, and the Kwoma of New Guinea, use different social signals to indicate that a marriage has taken place. Among the Taramiut Inuit, the betrothal is considered extremely important and is arranged between the parents at or before the time their children reach puberty. Later, when the youth is ready, he moves in with his betrothed's family for a trial period. If all goes well—that is, if the girl gives birth to a baby within a year or so—the couple are considered married. At this time, the wife goes with her husband to his camp.[14]

In keeping with the general openness of their society's attitudes toward sexual matters, a Trobriand couple advertise their desire to marry "by sleeping together regularly, by showing themselves together in public, and by remaining with each other for long periods at a time."[15] When a girl accepts a small gift from a boy, she demonstrates that her parents favor the match. Before long, she moves to the boy's house, takes her meals there, and accompanies her husband all day. Then the word goes around that the two are married.[16]

The Kwoma of New Guinea practice a trial marriage followed by a ceremony that makes the couple husband and wife. The girl lives for a while in the boy's home. When the boy's mother is satisfied with the match and knows that her son is too, she waits for a day when he is away from the house. Until that time, the girl has been cooking only for herself, and the boy's food has been prepared by his womenfolk. Now the mother has the girl prepare his meal. The young man returns and begins to eat his soup. When the first bowl is nearly finished, his mother tells him that his betrothed cooked the meal, and his eating it means that he is now married. At this news, the boy customarily rushes out of the house, spits out the soup, and shouts, "Faugh! It tastes bad! It is cooked terribly!" A ceremony then makes the marriage official.[17]

Among those societies that have ceremonies marking the onset of marriage, feasting is a common element. It expresses publicly the unification of the two families by marriage. The Reindeer Tungus of Siberia set a wedding date after protracted negotiations between the two families and their larger kin groups. Go-betweens assume most of the responsibility for the negotiating. The wedding day opens with the two kin groups, probably numbering as many as 150 people, pitching their lodges in separate areas and offering a great feast. After the groom's gifts have been presented, the bride's dowry is loaded onto reindeer and carried to the groom's lodge. There the climax of the ceremony takes place. The bride takes the wife's place—that is, at the right side of the entrance of the lodge—and members of both families sit in a circle. The groom enters and follows the bride around the circle, greeting each guest, while the guests, in their turn, kiss the bride on the mouth and hands. Finally, the go-betweens spit three times on the bride's hands, and the couple are formally husband and wife. More feasting and revelry bring the day to a close.[18]

In many cultures, marriage includes ceremonial expressions of hostility. One form of this custom is the trading of insults between kin groups, such as occurs on the Polynesian atoll of Pukapuka. Mock fights are staged in many societies. On occasion, hostility can have genuinely aggressive overtones, as among the Gusii of Kenya:

> Five young clansmen of the groom come to take the bride and two immediately find the girl and post themselves at her side to prevent her escape, while the others receive the final permission of her parents. When it has been granted the bride holds onto the house posts and must be dragged outside by the young men. Finally she goes along with them, crying and with her hands on her head.[19]

But the battle is not yet over. Mutual antagonism continues right onto the marriage bed, even up to and beyond coitus. The groom is determined to display his virility; the bride is equally determined to test it. "Brides," Robert and Barbara LeVine remarked, "are said to take pride in the length of time they can hold off their mates." Men can also win acclaim. If the bride is unable to walk the following day, the groom is considered a "real man."[20] Such expressions of hostility usually occur in societies in which the two sets of kin are actual or potential rivals or enemies. In many societies, it is common to marry women from "enemy" villages.

As this example suggests, marriage ceremonies often symbolize important elements of the culture. Whereas the Gusii ceremony may symbolize hostility between the two families, in other societies the ceremony may promote harmony between the families. For example, on the Polynesian island of Rotuma, a female clown is an important part of the ceremony. She is responsible for creating an enjoyable, joking atmosphere that facilitates interaction between the two sides.[21]

ECONOMIC ASPECTS OF MARRIAGE

"It's not man that marries maid, but field marries field, vineyard marries vineyard, cattle marry cattle." In its down-to-earth way, this German peasant saying indicates that in many societies marriage involves economic considerations. In our culture, economic considerations may or may not be explicit. However, in about 75 percent of the societies known to anthropology,[22] one or more explicit economic transactions take place before or after the marriage. The economic transaction may take several forms: bride price, bride service, exchange of females, gift exchange, dowry, or indirect dowry. The distribution of those forms among societies that have economic marriage transactions is shown in Figure 17–1.

BRIDE PRICE. Bride price or **bride wealth** is a gift of money or goods from the groom or his kin to the bride's kin. The gift usually grants the groom the right to marry the bride and the right to her children. Of all the forms of economic transaction involved in marriage, bride price is the most common. In one cross-cultural sample, 44 percent of the societies with economic transactions at marriage practiced bride price; in almost all of those societies the bride price was substantial.[23] Bride price occurs all over the world but is especially common in Africa and Oceania. Payment can be made in different currencies; livestock and food are two of the more common. With the increased importance of commercial exchange, money has increasingly become part of the bride price payments. Among the Nandi, the bride price consists of about five to seven cattle, one or two sheep and goats, cowrie shells, and money equivalent to the value of one cow. Even in unusual female-female marriages, the female "husband" must pay a bride price to arrange the marriage and be considered the "father."[24]

The Subanun of the Philippines have an expensive bride price—several times the annual income of the groom *plus* three to five years of bride service (described in the next section).[25] Among the Manus of the Admiralty Islands off New Guinea, a groom requires an economic backer, usually an older brother or an uncle, if he is to marry, but it will be years before he can pay off his debts. Depending on the final bride price, payments may be concluded at the time of the marriage, or they may continue for years afterward.[26]

Despite the connotations that bride price may have for us, the practice does not reduce a woman to the position of slave—although it is associated, as we shall see, with relatively low status for women. The bride price may be important to the woman and her family. Indeed, the fee they receive can serve as a security. If the marriage fails through no fault of hers and the wife returns to her kin, the family might not return the bride price to the groom. On the other hand, the wife's kin may pressure her to remain with her husband, even though she does not wish to, because they do not want to return the bride price or are unable to do so.

What kinds of societies are likely to have the custom of bride price? Cross-culturally, societies with bride price are likely to practice horticulture and lack social stratification. Bride price is also likely where women contribute a great deal to primary subsistence activities[27] and where they contribute more than men to all kinds of economic activities.[28] Although these findings might suggest that women are highly valued in such societies, recall that the status of women relative to men is *not* higher in societies in which women contribute a lot to primary subsistence activities. Indeed, bride price is likely to occur in societies in which men make most of the

---

FIGURE 17-1 *Distribution of Economic Marriage Transactions among Societies That Have Them*

Twenty-five percent of the societies in the ethnographic record lack any substantial economic transactions at marriage. *Source:* Based on data from Alice Schlegel and Rohn Eloul, "Marriage Transactions: Labor, Property, and Status," *American Anthropologist* 90 (1988): 291–309.

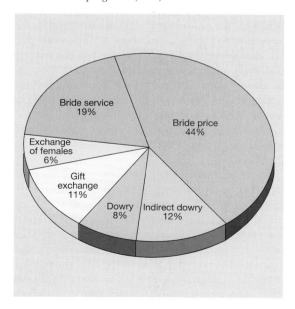

Bride service 19%
Bride price 44%
Exchange of females 6%
Gift exchange 11%
Dowry 8%
Indirect dowry 12%

The bride's brother at a wedding in Baghdad, Iraq, shows the dowry to the groom.

decisions in the household,[29] and decision making by men is one indicator of lower status for women.

BRIDE SERVICE. **Bride service,** which is the next most common type of economic transaction at marriage—occurs in about 19 percent of the societies with economic transactions—requires the groom to work for the bride's family, sometimes before the marriage begins, sometimes after. Bride service varies in duration. In some societies it lasts for only a few months; in others, as long as several years. Among the North Alaskan Eskimo, for example, the boy works for his in-laws after the marriage is arranged. To fulfill his obligation, he may simply catch a seal for them. The marriage may be consummated at any time while he is in service.[30] In some societies, bride service sometimes substitutes for bride price. An individual might give bride service in order to reduce the amount of bride price required. Native North and South American societies were likely to practice bride service, particularly if they were egalitarian food collectors.[31]

EXCHANGE OF FEMALES. Of the societies that have economic transactions at marriage, 6 percent have the custom whereby a sister or female relative of the groom is exchanged for the bride. Among these societies are the Tiv of West Africa and the Yanomamö of Venezuela-Brazil. These societies tend to be horticultural, egalitarian, and to have a relatively high contribution of women to primary subsistence.[32]

GIFT EXCHANGE. Gift exchange, which involves the exchange of gifts of about equal value by the two kin groups about to be linked by marriage, occurs somewhat more often than the exchange of females (about 11 percent of those with economic transactions).[33] For example, among the Andaman Islanders, as soon as a boy and girl indicate their intention to marry, their respective sets of parents cease all communication and begin sending gifts of food and other objects to each other through a third party. This arrangement continues until the marriage is completed and the two kin groups are united.[34]

DOWRY. A **dowry** is usually a substantial transfer of goods or money from the bride's family to the bride.[35] Unlike the types of transactions we have discussed so far, the dowry, which occurs in about 8 percent of the societies with economic transactions, is usually not a transaction between the kin of the bride and the kin of the groom. A family has to have wealth to give a dowry, but because the goods go to the bride, no wealth comes back to the family that gave the dowry. Payment of dowries was common in medieval and Renaissance Europe, where the size of the dowry often determined the desirability of the daughter. The custom is still practiced in parts of eastern Europe and in sections of southern Italy and France, where land is often the major item provided by the bride's family. Parts of India also practice the dowry.

In contrast to societies with bride price, societies with dowry tend to be those in which women contribute relatively little to primary subsistence activities, there is a high degree of social stratification, and a man is not allowed to be married to more than one woman simultaneously.[36] Why does dowry tend to occur in these types of societies? One theory suggests that the dowry is intended to guarantee future support for a woman and her children, even though she will not do much primary subsistence work. Another theory is that the dowry is intended to attract the best bridegroom for a daughter in monogamous societies with a high degree of social inequality. The dowry strategy is presumed to increase the likelihood that the daughter and her children will do well reproductively. Both theories are supported by recent cross-cultural research, with the second predicting dowry better.[37] But many stratified societies (including our own) in which women and men have only one spouse at a time do not practice dowry. Why this is so still needs to be explained.

INDIRECT DOWRY. The dowry is provided by the bride's family to the bride. But sometimes the payments to the bride originate from the groom's family. Because the goods are sometimes first given to the bride's father who passes most if not all of them to her, this kind of transaction is called **indirect dowry.**[38] Indirect dowry occurs in about 12 percent of the societies in which marriage involves an economic transaction. For example, among the Basseri of southern Iran, the groom's father assumes the expense of setting up the couple's new household. He gives cash to the bride's father, who uses at least some of the money to buy his daughter household utensils, blankets, and rugs.[39]

RESTRICTIONS ON MARRIAGE: THE UNIVERSAL INCEST TABOO

Hollywood and its press agents notwithstanding, marriage is not always based solely on mutual love, independently discovered and expressed by the two life-partners-to-be. Nor is it based on sex or wealth alone. Even when love, sex, and economics are contributing factors, regulations specify whom one may or may not marry. Perhaps the most rigid regulation, found in *all* cultures, is the **incest taboo,** which prohibits sexual intercourse or marriage between some categories of kin.

The most universal aspect of the incest taboo is the prohibition of sexual intercourse or marriage between mother and son, father and daughter, and brother and sister. No society in recent times has permitted either sexual intercourse or marriage between those pairs. A few societies in the past, however, did permit incest, mostly within the royal and aristocratic families, though generally it was forbidden to the rest of the population. For example, the Incan and Hawaiian royal families

allowed marriage within the family. Probably the best-known example of allowed incest involved Cleopatra of Egypt.

It seems clear that the Egyptian aristocracy and royalty indulged in father-daughter and brother-sister marriages. Cleopatra was married to two of her younger brothers at different times.[40] The reasons seem to have been partly religious—a member of the family of the pharaoh, who was considered a god, could not marry any "ordinary" human—and partly economic, for marriage within the family kept the royal property undivided. In the Egyptian case, between 30 B.C. and A.D. 324, incest was allowed not just in the royal family; an estimated 8 percent of commoner marriages were brother-sister marriages.[41]

But, despite these exceptions, the fact remains that no culture we know of today permits or accepts incest within the nuclear family. Why is the familial incest taboo universal? Several explanations have been suggested.

CHILDHOOD-FAMILIARITY THEORY

The childhood-familiarity theory, suggested by Edward Westermarck, was given a wide hearing in the early 1920s. Westermarck argued that persons who have been closely associated with each other since earliest childhood, such as siblings, are not sexually attracted to each other and therefore would avoid marriage with each other.[42] This theory was subsequently rejected because of evidence that some children were sexually interested in their parents and siblings. Studies have suggested, however, that there might be something to Westermarck's theory.

Yonina Talmon investigated marriage patterns among the second generation of three well-established collective communities *(kibbutzim)* in Israel. In these collectives, children live with many members of their peer group in quarters separate from their families. They are in constant interaction with their peers, from birth to maturity. The study revealed that among 125 couples, there was "not one instance in which both mates were reared from birth in the same peer group,"[43] despite parental encouragement of marriage within the peer group. Children reared in common not only avoided marriage, they also avoided any sexual relations among themselves.

Talmon stated that the people reared together firmly believed that overfamiliarity breeds sexual disinterest. As one of them told her, "We are like an open book to each other. We have read the story in the book over and over again and know all about it."[44] Talmon's evidence reveals not only the onset of disinterest and even sexual antipathy among children reared together, but a correspondingly heightened fascination with newcomers or outsiders, particularly for their "mystery."

Arthur Wolf's study of the Chinese in northern Taiwan also supports the idea that something about being reared together produces sexual disinterest. Wolf focused on a community still practicing the Chinese custom of *t'ung-yang-hsi,* or "daughter-in-law raised from childhood."

> When a girl is born in a poor family . . . she is often given away or sold when but a few weeks or months old, or one or two years old, to be the future wife of a son in the family of a friend or relative which has a little son not betrothed in marriage. . . . The girl is called a "little bride" and taken home and brought up in the family together with her future husband.[45]

Wolf's evidence indicates that this arrangement is associated with sexual difficulties when the childhood "couple" later marry. Informants implied that familiarity results in disinterest and lack of stimulation. As an indication of their disinterest, these couples produce fewer offspring than spouses not raised together, they are more likely to seek extramarital sexual relationships, and they are more likely to get divorced.[46]

The Talmon and Wolf studies suggest, then, that children raised together are not likely to be sexually interested in each other when they grow up. Such disinterest is consistent with Westermarck's notion that the incest taboo may be more an avoidance of certain matings than a prohibition of them. There is one other piece of evidence consistent with this explanation of the incest taboo. Hilda and Seymour Parker compared two samples of fathers: those who had sexually abused their daughters and those who supposedly had not.[47] To maximize their similarities otherwise, the Parkers selected the two samples of fathers from the same prisons and psychiatric facilities. The Parkers found that the fathers who had committed incest with their daughters were much more likely than the other sample of fathers to have had little to do with bringing up their daughters, because they were not at home or hardly at home during the daughters' first three years of life. In other words, the fathers who avoided incest had been more closely associated with their daughters in childhood. That finding is consistent with Westermarck's suggestion that the incest taboo is a result of familiarity in childhood.

Although Westermarck was talking about the development of sexual aversion during early childhood, some researchers have asked how the childhood-familiarity theory could explain the extension of incest taboos to first cousins. The familiarity argument implies that first-cousin marriage should be prohibited in societies in which first cousins grow up together in the same community. But that is not the case. Such societies are not more likely to prohibit first-cousin marriage.[48]

Even if there is something about familiarity in childhood that normally leads to sexual disinterest,[49] we still are left with the question of why societies have to prohibit marriages that would voluntarily be avoided because of disinterest.

FREUD'S PSYCHOANALYTIC THEORY

Sigmund Freud proposed that the incest taboo is a reaction against unconscious, unacceptable desires.[50] He suggested that the son is attracted to his mother (as the daughter is to her father) and as a result feels jealousy and hostility toward his father. But the son knows that these feelings cannot continue, for they might lead the father to retaliate against him; therefore, they must be renounced or repressed. Usually the feelings are repressed and retreat into the unconscious. But the desire to possess the mother continues to exist in the unconscious, and, according to Freud, the horror of incest is a reaction to, or a defense against, the forbidden unconscious impulse.

Although Freud's theory may account for the aversion felt toward incest, or at least the aversion toward parent-child incest, it does not explain why society needs an explicit taboo, particularly on brother-sister incest. Nor does it account for the findings of sexual disinterest we discussed in connection with the Westermarck hypothesis.

FAMILY-DISRUPTION THEORY

The family-disruption theory, often associated with Bronislaw Malinowski,[51] can best be summed up as follows: Sexual competition among family members would create so much rivalry and tension that the family could not function as an effective unit. Because the family must function effectively for society to survive, society has to curtail competition within the family. The familial incest taboo is thus imposed to keep the family intact.

But there are inconsistencies in this approach. Society could have shaped other rules about the sexual access of one member of the family to another that would also eliminate potentially disruptive competition. Also, why would brother-sister incest be so disruptive? As we noted, such marriages did exist in ancient Egypt. Brother-sister incest would not disrupt the authority of the parents if the children were allowed to marry when mature. The family-disruption theory, then, does not explain the origin of the incest taboo.

COOPERATION THEORY

The cooperation theory was proposed by the early anthropologist Edward B. Tylor and was elaborated by Leslie A. White and Claude Lévi-Strauss. It emphasizes the value of the incest taboo in promoting cooperation among family groups and thus helping communities to survive. As Tylor saw it, certain operations necessary for the welfare of the community can be accomplished only by large numbers of people working together. In order to break down suspicion and hostility between family groups and make such cooperation possible, early humans developed the incest taboo to ensure that individuals would marry members of other families. The ties created by intermarriage would serve to hold the community together. Thus, Tylor explained the incest taboo as an answer to the choice "between marrying out and being killed out."[52]

The idea that marriage with other groups promotes cooperation sounds plausible, but is there evidence to support it? After all, there are societies such as the Gusii in which marriage is often between hostile groups. But is that society an exception? Does marriage promote cooperation? Because

Arranged marriages were typical in royal families in the past.

people in all recent societies marry outside the family, we cannot test the idea that such marriages promote cooperation more than marriages within the family. We can, however, ask whether other kinds of out-marriage, such as marriage with other communities, promote cooperation with those communities. The evidence on that question does not support the cooperation theory. There is no greater peacefulness between communities when marriages are forbidden within the community and always arranged with other communities, than when they are not.[53]

But even if marriage outside the family promoted cooperation with other groups, why would it be necessary to prohibit all marriages within the family? Couldn't families have required some of their members to marry outside the family if they thought it necessary for survival but permitted incestuous marriages when such alliances were not needed? Although the incest taboo might enhance cooperation between families, the need for cooperation does not adequately explain the existence of the incest taboo in all societies; other customs might also promote alliances. Furthermore, the cooperation theory does not explain the sexual aspect of the incest taboo. Societies could conceivably allow incestuous sex and still insist that children marry outside the family.

INBREEDING THEORY

One of the oldest explanations for the incest taboo, the inbreeding theory, focuses on the potentially damaging consequences of inbreeding, or marrying within the family. People within the same family are likely to carry the same harmful recessive genes. Inbreeding, then, will tend to produce offspring who are more likely to die early of genetic disorders than are the offspring of unrelated spouses. For many years this theory was rejected because, on the basis of dog-breeding practices, it was thought that inbreeding need not be harmful. The inbreeding practiced to produce prize-winning dogs, however, is not a good guide to whether inbreeding is harmful; dog breeders don't count the runts they cull when they try to breed for success in dog shows. We now have a good deal of evidence, from humans as well as other animals, that the closer the degree of inbreeding, the more harmful the genetic effects.[54]

Genetic mutations occur frequently. Although many pose no harm to the individuals who carry a single recessive gene, matings between two persons who carry the same gene often produce offspring with a harmful or lethal condition. Close blood relatives are much more likely than unrelated individuals to carry the same harmful recessive gene. So if close relatives mate, their offspring have a higher probability than the offspring of nonrelatives of inheriting the harmful trait.

One study compared children produced by familial incest with children of the same mothers produced by nonincestuous unions. About 40 percent of the incestuously produced children had serious abnormalities, compared with about 5 percent of the other children.[55] Matings between other kinds of relatives not as closely related also show harmful, but not as harmful, effects of inbreeding. These results are consistent with inbreeding theory. The likelihood that a child will inherit a double dose of a harmful recessive gene is lower the more distantly the child's parents are related. Also consistent with inbreeding theory is the fact that rates of abnormality are consistently higher in the offspring of uncle-niece marriages (which are allowed in some societies) than in the offspring of cousin marriages; for the offspring of uncle-niece marriages, the likelihood of inheriting a double dose of a harmful recessive is twice that for the offspring of first cousins.[56]

Although most scholars acknowledge the harmful effects of inbreeding, some question whether people in former days would have deliberately invented or borrowed the incest taboo because they knew that inbreeding was biologically harmful. William Durham's recent cross-cultural survey suggests that they did. Ethnographers do not always report the perceived consequences of incest, but in 50 percent of the reports Durham found, biological harm to the offspring was mentioned.[57] For example, Raymond Firth reported on the Tikopia, who live on an island in the South Pacific:

> The idea is firmly held that unions of close kin bear with them their own doom, their *mara*. . . . The idea [*mara*] essentially concerns barrenness. . . . The peculiar barrenness of an incestuous union consists not in the absence of children, but in their illness or death, or some other mishap. . . . The idea that the offspring of a marriage between near kin are weakly and likely to die young is stoutly held by these natives and examples are adduced to prove it.[58]

So, if the harm of inbreeding was widely recognized, people may have deliberately invented or borrowed the incest taboo.[59] But whether or not people actually recognized the harmfulness of inbreeding, the demographic consequences of the incest taboo would account for its universality, since reproductive and hence competitive advantages probably accrued to groups practicing the taboo. Thus, although cultural solutions other than the incest taboo might provide the desired effects assumed by the family-disruption theory and the cooperation theory, the incest taboo is the only possible solution to the problem of inbreeding.

As is discussed toward the end of the next section, a society may or may not extend the incest taboo to first cousins. That variation is also predictable from inbreeding theory, which provides additional support for the idea that the incest taboo was invented or borrowed to avoid the harmful consequences of inbreeding.

WHOM SHOULD ONE MARRY?

Probably every child in our society knows the story of Cinderella—the poor, downtrodden, but lovely girl who accidentally meets, falls in love with, and eventually marries a prince. It is a charming tale, but as a guide to mate choice in our society it is misleading. The majority of marriages simply do not occur in so free and coincidental a way in any society. In addition to the incest taboo, societies often have rules restricting marriage with other persons, as well as preferences about which other persons are the most desirable mates.

Even in a modern, urbanized society such as ours, where theoretically mate choice is free, people tend to marry within their own class and geographic area. For example, studies in the United States consistently indicate that a person is likely to marry someone who lives close by.[60] Neighborhoods are frequently made up of people from similar class backgrounds, so it is unlikely that many of these alliances are Cinderella stories.

ARRANGED MARRIAGES

In an appreciable number of societies, marriages are arranged; negotiations are handled by the immediate families or by go-betweens. Sometimes betrothals are completed while the future partners are still children. This was formerly the custom in much of Hindu India, China, Japan, and eastern and southern Europe. Implicit in the arranged marriage is the conviction that the joining together of two kin groups to form new social and economic ties is too important to be left to free choice and romantic love.

An example of a marriage arranged for reasons of prestige comes from Clellan Ford's study of the

The female clown at a wedding ceremony on Rotuma tries to create an enjoyable atmosphere, which increases the likelihood that the two sides will get along.

Kwakiutl of British Columbia. Ford's informant described his marriage as follows:

> When I was old enough to get a wife—I was about 25—my brothers looked for a girl in the same position that I and my brothers had. Without my consent, they picked a wife for me—Lagius' daughter. The one I wanted was prettier than the one they chose for me, but she was in a lower position than me, so they wouldn't let me marry her.[61]

In many places arranged marriages are beginning to disappear, and couples are beginning to have more say about their marriage partners. As recently as 1960, marriages were still arranged on the Pacific island of Rotuma, and sometimes the bride and groom did not meet until the wedding day. Today weddings are much the same, but couples are allowed to "go out" and have a say about whom they wish to marry.[62] In a small Moroccan town, arranged marriages are still the norm, although a young man may ask his mother to make a marriage offer to a particular girl's parents, who may ask her whether she wants to accept the marriage offer. But dating is still not acceptable, so getting acquainted is hard to arrange.[63]

EXOGAMY AND ENDOGAMY

Marriage partners often must be chosen from *outside* one's own kin group or community; this is known as a rule of **exogamy.** Exogamy can take many forms. It may mean marrying outside a particular group of kin or outside a particular village or group of villages. Often, then, spouses come from a distance. For example, in Rani Khera, a village in India, 266 married women had come from about 200 different villages averaging between 12 and 24 miles away; 220 local women had gone to 200 other villages to marry. As a result of these exogamous marriages, Rani Khera, a village of 150 households, was linked to 400 other nearby villages.[64] When there are rules of exogamy, violations are often believed to cause harm. On the islands of Yap in Micronesia, people who are related through women are referred to as "people of one belly." The elders say that if two people from the same kinship group married, they would not have any female children and the group would die out.[65]

A rule of **endogamy** obliges a person to marry *within* some group. The caste groups of India traditionally have been endogamous. The higher castes believed that marriage with lower castes would "pollute" them, and such unions were forbidden. Caste endogamy is also found in some parts of Africa. In East Africa, a Masai warrior would never stoop to marry the daughter of an ironworker, nor would a former ruling-caste Tutsi in Rwanda, in central Africa, think of marrying a person from the hunting caste Twa.

COUSIN MARRIAGES

Kinship terminology for most people in the United States does not differentiate between types of cousins. In some other societies such distinctions may be important, particularly with regard to first cousins; the terms for the different kinds of first cousin may indicate which cousins are suitable marriage partners (sometimes even preferred mates) and which are not. Although most societies prohibit marriage with all types of first cousins,[66] some

Research Frontiers

THE HUSBAND-WIFE RELATIONSHIP: VARIATION IN LOVE, INTIMACY, AND SEXUAL JEALOUSY

Americans believe that love should be a basis of marriage. Does this ideal characterize most societies? We know the answer to that question: No. In fact, in many places romantic love is believed to be a poor basis for marriage and is strongly discouraged. However, even though romantic love may not be a basis for marriage everywhere, it does occur almost everywhere. A recent cross-cultural survey suggests that about 88 percent of the world's societies show signs of romantic love—accounts of personal longing, love songs or love depicted in folklore, elopement because of affection, and passionate love described by informants quoted in ethnographies. So if love is nearly universal, why is it often discouraged as a basis for marriage?

Two conditions appear to predict such discouragement. One is that the husband and wife live in an extended family. In this situation, people seem more concerned with how the person marrying into the family gets along with others, and less concerned with whether the husband and wife love each other. A second condition predicting the discouragement of romantic love as a basis for marriage is that one of the spouses does most of the primary subsistence work or earns most of the couple's income. In this situation too, marrying for love appears to be

Some cultures emphasize romantic love as a basis for marriage.

societies allow and even prefer particular kinds of cousin marriage.

Cross-cousins are children of siblings of the opposite sex; that is, a person's cross-cousins are father's sisters' children and mother's brothers' children. **Parallel cousins** are children of siblings of the same sex; a person's parallel cousins, then, are father's brothers' children and mother's sisters' children. The Chippewa Indians used to practice cross-cousin marriage, as well as cross-cousin joking. With his female cross-cousins, a Chippewa man was expected to exchange broad, risqué jokes, but he would not do so with his parallel cousins, with whom severe propriety was the rule. In general, in any society in which cross-cousin marriage is allowed but parallel-cousin is not, there is a joking relationship between a man and his female cross-cousins. This attitude contrasts with the formal and very respectful relationship the man maintains with female parallel cousins. Apparently, the joking relationship signifies the possibility of marriage,

whereas the respectful relationship signifies the extension of the incest taboo to parallel cousins.

When first-cousin marriage is allowed or preferred, it is usually with some kind of cross-cousin. Parallel-cousin marriage is fairly rare, but Muslim societies usually prefer such marriages, allowing other cousin marriages as well. The Kurds, who are mostly Sunni Muslims, prefer a young man to marry his father's brother's daughter (for the young woman this would be her father's brother's son). The father and his brother usually live near each other, so the woman will stay close to home in such a marriage. The bride and groom are also in the same kin group, so marriage in this case also entails kin group endogamy.[67]

What kinds of societies allow or prefer first-cousin marriage? There is evidence from cross-cultural research that cousin marriages are most apt to be permitted in relatively large and densely populated societies. Perhaps this is because the likelihood of such marriages, and therefore the risks of

discouraged. In general, then, romantic love is discouraged as a basis for marriage if one of the spouses is highly dependent on the other or the other's kin.

Intimacy is different from romantic love. It refers to how close the married couple are to each other—eating together, sleeping in the same bed, spending their leisure time together, as well as having frequent sex. In some societies couples are together a lot; in others they spend very little time together. Foraging societies seem on average to have more intimacy between couples than more complex herding and agricultural societies, but the reason is not entirely clear. A high involvement in war also seems to detract from intimacy between couples.

When it comes to sexual jealousy, men are far more likely to be violent than women. Anthropologists with a biological orientation point out that fathers always have some uncertainty about whether their children are theirs, so males are much more likely for that reason alone to try to guard against rival males. But how can we account for the considerable variation in jealousy from one society to another? It does seem that the more a society emphasizes the importance of getting married, the more it limits sex to the marriage relationship, the more it emphasizes property, and the more its males appear to exhibit sexual jealousy.

How are these various aspects of marriage related to each other? Does romantic love as a basis for marriage increase or decrease sexual jealousy? Does romantic love predict intimacy, or is romantic love more likely with less frequent contact between the spouses? We are still far from understanding how these different aspects are related. All we know is that an emphasis on love and intimacy does not preclude marital violence or marital dissolution.

Sources: Lewellyn Hendrix, "Varieties of Marital Relationships," in Carol R. Ember and Melvin Ember, eds., *Cross-Cultural Research for Social Science* (Upper Saddle River, NJ: Prentice Hall, 1998), Prentice Hall/Simon & Schuster Custom Publishing; William R. Jankowiak and Edward F. Fischer, "A Cross-Cultural Perspective on Romantic Love," *Ethnology,* 31 (1992): 149–55.

inbreeding, are minimal in those societies. Many small, sparsely populated societies, however, permit or even sometimes prefer cousin marriage. How can these cases be explained? They seem to cast doubt on the interpretation that cousin marriage should be prohibited in sparsely populated societies, in which marriages between close relatives are more likely just by chance and the risks of inbreeding should be greatest. It turns out that most of the small societies that permit cousin marriage have lost a lot of people to epidemics. Many peoples around the world, particularly in the Pacific and in North and South America, suffered severe depopulation in the first generation or two after contact with Europeans, who introduced diseases (such as measles, pneumonia, and smallpox) to which the native populations had little or no resistance. Such societies may have had to permit cousin marriage in order to provide enough mating possibilities among the reduced population of eligible mates.[68]

LEVIRATE AND SORORATE

In many societies, cultural rules oblige individuals to marry the spouse of deceased relatives. **Levirate** is a custom whereby a man is obliged to marry his brother's widow. **Sororate** obliges a woman to marry her deceased sister's husband. Both customs are exceedingly common, being the obligatory form of second marriage in a majority of societies known to anthropology.[69]

Among the Chukchee of Siberia, levirate obliges the next oldest brother to become the successor husband. He cares for the widow and children, assumes the sexual privileges of the husband, and unites the deceased's reindeer herd with his own, keeping it in the name of his brother's children. If there are no brothers, the widow is married to a cousin of her first husband. The Chukchee regard the custom more as a duty than as a right. The nearest relative is obliged to care for a woman left with children and a herd.[70]

HOW MANY DOES ONE MARRY?

We are accustomed to thinking of marriage as involving just one man and one woman at a time—**monogamy**—but most societies known to anthropology have allowed a man to be married to more than one woman at the same time—**polygyny.** At any given time, however, the majority of men in societies permitting polygyny are married monogamously; few or no societies have enough women to permit most men to have at least two wives. Polygyny's mirror image—one woman being married to more than one man at the same time, called **polyandry**—is practiced in very few societies. Polygyny and polyandry are the two types of **polygamy,** or plural marriage. **Group marriage,** in which more than one man is married to more than one woman at the same time, sometimes occurs but is not customary in any known society. The four possible forms of marriage are illustrated in Table 17–1.

POLYGYNY

The Old Testament has many references to men with more than one wife simultaneously: King David and King Solomon are just two examples of men polygynously married. Just as in the society described in the Old Testament, polygyny in many societies is a mark of a man's great wealth or high status. In such societies only the very wealthy can, and are expected to, support more than one wife. Some Muslim societies, especially Arabic-speaking ones, still view polygyny in this light. But a man does not always have to be wealthy to be polygynous; indeed, in some societies in which women are important contributors to the economy, it seems that men try to have more than one wife in order to become wealthier.

TABLE 17–1 *Four Possible Forms of Marriage*

FORM OF MARRIAGE	MALES	FEMALES
Monogamy	△	= ○
Polygamy		
Polygyny	△	= ○ + ○ +
Polyandry	△ + △ +	= ○
Group marriage	△ + △ +	= ○ + ○ +

△ represents male; ○, female; and =, marriage.

Polygyny is practiced by some in this country, even though it is prohibited by law.

Among the Siwai, a society in the South Pacific, status is achieved through feast giving. Pork is the main dish at these feasts, so the Siwai associate pig raising with prestige. This great interest in pigs sparks an interest in wives, because in Siwai society, women raise the food needed to raise pigs. Thus, although having many wives does not in itself confer status among the Siwai, the increase in pig herds that may result from polygyny is a source of prestige for the owner.[71]

Polygynously married Siwai men do seem to have greater prestige, but they complain that a household with multiple wives is difficult. Sinu, a Siwai, described his plight:

> There is never peace for a long time in a polygynous family. If the husband sleeps in the house of one wife, the other one sulks all the next day. If the man is so stupid as to sleep two consecutive nights in the house of one wife, the other one will refuse to cook for him, saying, "So-and-so is your wife; go to her for food. Since I am not good enough for you to sleep with, then my food is not good enough for you to eat." Frequently the co-wives will quarrel and fight. My uncle formerly had five wives at one time and the youngest one was always raging and fighting the others. Once she knocked an older wife senseless and then ran away and had to be forcibly returned.[72]

Jealousy between co-wives is reported in many polygynous societies, but it seems not to be present in some. For example, Margaret Mead reported that married life among the Arapesh of New Guinea, even in the polygynous marriages, was "so even and contented that there is nothing to relate of it at all."[73] Why might there be little or no jealousy between co-wives in a society? One possible reason is that a man is married to two or more sisters—**sororal polygyny;** it seems that sisters, having grown up together, are more likely to get along and cooperate as co-wives than are co-wives who are not also sisters—**nonsororal polygyny.** Other customs may also lessen jealousy between co-wives:

1. Co-wives who are not sisters tend to have separate living quarters; sororal co-wives almost always live together. Among the Plateau Tonga in Africa, who practice nonsororal polygyny, the husband shares his personal goods and his favors among his wives, who live in separate dwellings, according to principles of strict equality. The Crow Indians practiced sororal polygyny, and co-wives usually shared a tepee.

2. Co-wives have clearly defined equal rights in matters of sex, economics, and personal possessions. For example, the Tanala of Madagascar require the husband to spend a day with each co-wife in succession. Failure to do so constitutes adultery and entitles the slighted wife to sue for divorce and alimony of up to one-third of the husband's property. Furthermore, the land is shared equally among all the women, who expect the husband to help with its cultivation when he visits them.

3. Senior wives often have special prestige. The Tonga of Polynesia, for example, grant to the first wife the status of "chief wife." Her house is to the right of her husband's and is called "the house of the father." The other wives are called "small wives," and their houses are to the left of the husband's. The chief wife has the right to be consulted before the small wives, and her husband is expected to sleep under her roof before and after a journey. Although this rule might seem to enhance the jealousy of the secondary wives, later wives are usually favored somewhat because they tend to be younger and more attractive. By this custom, then, the first wife may be compensated for her loss of physical attractiveness by increased prestige.[74]

We must remember that, although jealousy is commonly mentioned in polygynous marriages, people who practice polygyny think it has considerable advantages. In a study conducted by Philip and Janet Kilbride in Kenya, female as well as male married people agreed that polygyny had economic and political advantages. Because they tend to be large, polygynous families provide plenty of farm labor and extra food that can be marketed. They also tend to be influential in their communities and are

likely to produce individuals who become government officials.[75]

How can we account for the fact that polygyny is allowed and often preferred in most of the societies known to anthropology? Ralph Linton suggested that polygyny derives from the general primate urge to collect females.[76] But if that were so, then why wouldn't all societies allow polygyny? Other explanations of polygyny have been suggested. We restrict our discussion here to those that statistically and strongly predict polygyny in worldwide samples of societies.

One theory is that polygyny will be permitted in societies that have a long **postpartum sex taboo.**[77] In these societies, a couple must abstain from intercourse until their child is at least a year old. John Whiting suggested that couples abstain from sexual intercourse for a long time after their child is born for health reasons. A Hausa woman reported:

> A mother should not go to her husband while she has a child she is suckling. If she does, the child gets thin; he dries up, he won't be strong, he won't be healthy. If she goes after two years it is nothing, he is already strong before that, it does not matter if she conceives again after two years.[78]

The symptoms the woman described seem to be those of *kwashiorkor*. Common in tropical areas, kwashiorkor is a protein-deficiency disease that occurs particularly in children suffering from intestinal parasites or diarrhea. By observing a long postpartum sex taboo, and thereby ensuring that her children are widely spaced, a woman can nurse each child longer. If a child gets protein from mother's milk during its first few years, the likelihood of contracting kwashiorkor may be greatly reduced. Consistent with Whiting's interpretation is the fact that societies with low-protein staples (those whose principal foods are root and tree crops such as taro, sweet potatoes, bananas, and breadfruit) tend to have a long postpartum sex taboo. Societies with long postpartum sex taboos also tend to be polygynous. Perhaps, then, a man's having more than one wife is a cultural adjustment to the taboo. As a Yoruba woman said,

> When we abstain from having sexual intercourse with our husband for the two years we nurse our babies, we know he will seek some other woman. We would rather have her under our control as a co-wife so he is not spending money outside the family.[79]

Even if we agree that men will seek other sexual relationships during the period of a long postpartum sex taboo, it is not clear why polygyny is the only possible solution to the problem. After all, it is conceivable that all of a man's wives might be subject to the postpartum sex taboo at the same time. Furthermore, there may be sexual outlets outside marriage.

Another explanation of polygyny is that it is a response to an excess of women over men. Such an imbalanced sex ratio may occur because of the prevalence of warfare in a society. Because men and not women are generally the warriors, warfare almost always takes a greater toll of men's lives. Given that almost all adults in noncommercial societies are married, polygyny may be a way of providing spouses for surplus women. Indeed, there is evidence that societies with imbalanced sex ratios in favor of women tend to have both polygyny and high male mortality in warfare. Conversely, societies with balanced sex ratios tend to have both monogamy and low male mortality in warfare.[80]

A third explanation is that a society will allow polygyny when men marry at an older age than women. The argument is similar to the sex ratio interpretation. Delaying the age of marriage for men would produce an artificial, though not an actual, excess of marriageable women. Why marriage for men is delayed is not clear, but the delay does predict polygyny.[81]

Is one of these explanations better than the others, or are all three factors—long postpartum sex taboo, an imbalanced sex ratio in favor of women, and delayed age of marriage for men—important in explaining polygyny? One way of trying to decide among alternative explanations is to do what is called a *statistical-control analysis,* which allows us to see if a particular factor still predicts when the effects of other possible factors are removed. In this case, when the possible effect of sex ratio is removed, a long postpartum sex taboo no longer predicts polygyny and hence is probably not a cause of polygyny.[82] But both an actual excess of women and a late age of marriage for men seem to be strong predictors of polygyny. Added together, these two factors predict even more strongly.[83]

POLYANDRY

George Peter Murdock's "World Ethnographic Sample" included only four societies (less than 1 percent of the total) in which polyandry, or the marriage of several men to one woman, was practiced.[84] When the husbands are brothers we call it **fraternal polyandry;** if they are not brothers, it is **nonfrater-**

nal polyandry. Some Tibetans, the Toda of India, and the Sinhalese of Sri Lanka have practiced fraternal polyandry. Among the Tibetans who practice fraternal polyandry, biological paternity seems to be of no particular concern; there is no attempt to link children biologically to a particular brother, and all children are treated the same.[85]

One possible explanation for the practice of polyandry is a shortage of women. The Toda practiced female infanticide;[86] the Sinhalese had a shortage of women but denied the practice of female infanticide.[87] A correlation between shortage of women and polyandry would account for why polyandry is so rare in the ethnographic record; an excess of men is rare cross-culturally.

Another possible explanation is that polyandry is an adaptive response to severely limited resources. Melvyn Goldstein studied Tibetans who live in the northwestern corner of Nepal, above 12,000 feet in elevation. Cultivable land is extremely scarce there, with most families having less than an acre. The people say they practice fraternal polyandry in order to prevent the division of a family's farm and animals. Instead of dividing up their land among them and each taking a wife, brothers preserve the family farm by sharing a wife. Although not recognized by the Tibetans, their practice of polyandry minimizes population growth. There are as many women as men of marriageable age. But about 30 percent of the women do not marry, and, although these women do have some children, they have far fewer than married women. Thus, the practice of polyandry minimizes the number of mouths to feed and therefore maximizes the standard of living of the polyandrous family. In contrast, if the Tibetans practiced monogamy and almost all women married, the birth rate would be much higher and there would be more mouths to feed with the severely limited resources.[88]

THE FAMILY

Although family form varies from one society to another and even within societies, all societies have families. A **family** is a social and economic unit consisting minimally of one or more parents and their children. Members of a family always have certain reciprocal rights and obligations, particularly economic ones. Family members usually live in one household, but common residence is not a defining feature of families. In our society, children may live away while they go to college. Some members of a family may deliberately set up separate households in order to manage multiple business enterprises while maintaining economic unity.[89] In simpler societies, the family and the household tend to be indistinguishable; it is only in more complex societies, and in societies becoming dependent on commercial exchange, that some members of a family may live elsewhere.[90]

The family provides a learning environment for children. Although some animals, such as fish, do take care of themselves after birth or hatching, no mammal is able to care for itself at birth, and a human is exceptional in that he or she is unable to do so for many years afterward. Since humans mature late biologically, they have few if any inborn or instinctive responses that will simplify adjustment to their surroundings. Consequently, they have to learn a repertoire of beliefs and habits (most of which are cultural) in order to become functioning adults in society. A family cares for and protects children while they acquire the cultural behavior, beliefs, and values necessary for their own, and their society's, survival.

VARIATION IN FAMILY FORM

Most societies have families that are larger than the single-parent family (the parent in such families is usually the mother, in which case the unit is called the **matrifocal family**), the monogamous (single-couple) family (called the **nuclear family**), or the polygamous (usually polygynous) family. The **extended family** is the prevailing form of family in more than half the societies known to anthropology.[91] It may consist of two or more single-parent, monogamous, polygynous, or polyandrous families linked by a blood tie. Most commonly, the extended family consists of a married couple and one or more of the married children, all living in the same house or household. The constituent nuclear families are normally linked through the parent-child tie. An extended family, however, is sometimes composed of families linked through a sibling tie. Such a family might consist of two married brothers, their wives, and their children. Extended families may be very large, containing many relatives and including three or four generations.

EXTENDED-FAMILY HOUSEHOLDS

In a society composed of extended-family households, marriage does not bring as pronounced a change in life-style as it does in our culture, where the couple typically moves to a new residence and forms a new, and basically independent, family unit.

In extended families, the newlyweds are assimilated into an existing family unit. Margaret Mead described such a situation in Samoa:

> In most marriages there is no sense of setting up a new and separate establishment. The change is felt in the change of residence for either husband or wife and in the reciprocal relations which spring up between the two families. But the young couple live in the main household, simply receiving a bamboo pillow, a mosquito net and a pile of mats for their bed. . . . The wife works with all the women of the household and waits on all the men. The husband shares the enterprises of the other men and boys. Neither in personal service given or received are the two marked off as a unit.[92]

A young couple in Samoa, as in other societies with extended families, generally has little decision-making power over the governing of the household. Often the responsibility of running the household rests with the senior male. Nor can the new family accumulate its own property and become independent; it is a part of the larger corporate structure:

> So the young people bide their time. Eventually, when the old man dies or retires, *they* will own the homestead, *they* will run things. When their son grows up and marries, he will create a new subsidiary family, to live with them, work for the greater glory of *their* extended family homestead, and wait for them to die.[93]

The extended family is more likely than the independent nuclear family to perpetuate itself as a social unit. In contrast with the independent nuclear family, which by definition disintegrates with the death of the senior members (the parents), the extended family is always adding junior families (monogamous or polygamous or both), whose members eventually become the senior members when their elders die.

A Slovakian extended family.

Current Issues

ONE-PARENT FAMILIES: WHY THE RECENT INCREASE?

Not only is the custom of marriage almost universal, but in most societies known to anthropology most people marry. And they usually remarry if they divorce. This means that, except for the death of a spouse or temporarily during times of divorce or separation, one-parent families are relatively uncommon in most societies.

In many Western countries, however, there has been a dramatic increase recently in the percentage of families that are one-parent families, most of which (about 90 percent) are female-headed families. For example, in the 1960s about 9 percent of families in the United States were one-parent families, but in the mid-1980s the figure jumped to about 24 percent. Whereas Sweden once led the Western countries in percentage of one-parent families—about 13 percent in the 1970s—the United States now has the highest percentage.

Before we try to examine the reasons for the increase, we need to consider that there are a variety of ways to become a one-parent family. First, many one-parent families result from the divorce or separation of two-parent families. Second, many one-parent families result from births out of wedlock. In addition, some result from the death of a spouse and others from the decision by a single person to adopt a child.

Many researchers suggest that the ease of divorce is largely responsible for the increase in one-parent families. On the face of it, this explanation seems plausible. But it is flawed. In many countries during the late 1960s and early 1970s, changes in the law made getting a divorce much easier, and the percentage of one-parent families did rise after that. But why did so many countries ease divorce restrictions at the same time? Did attitudes about marriage change first? A high divorce rate by itself will make for a higher percentage of one-parent households only *if* individuals do not remarry quickly. In the United States, for example, remarriage rates did decline sharply in the mid-1960s, particularly among younger, better educated women, and so the percentage of one-parent households may have risen for that reason. In many other countries, divorce rates stabilized in the 1980s, but the percentage of one-parent families still increased. Thus, easier divorce does not fully explain the increase in number of one-parent families.

Although some parents are clearly choosing to stay single, many might prefer to marry if they could find an appropriate spouse. In some countries, and among some ethnic groups within some countries, there are many fewer males than females, and sometimes a high proportion of the males have poor economic prospects. In the former Soviet Union, there are many more women than men because males are more likely to have died from war, alcoholism, and accidents. The United States does not have such a skewed sex ratio, but in some neighborhoods, particularly poor neighborhoods, there are very high mortality rates for young males. And many males in such neighborhoods do not have

POSSIBLE REASONS FOR EXTENDED-FAMILY HOUSEHOLDS

Why do most societies known to anthropology commonly have extended-family households? Extended-family households are found most frequently in societies with sedentary agricultural economies, so economic factors may play a role in determining household type. M. F. Nimkoff and Russell Middleton suggested how agricultural life, as opposed to hunting-gathering life, may favor extended families among agriculturalists. The extended family may be a social mechanism that prevents the economically ruinous division of family property in societies in which property such as cultivated land is important. Conversely, the need for mobility in hunter-gatherer societies may make it difficult to maintain extended-family households. During certain seasons, the hunter-gatherers may be obliged to divide into nuclear families that scatter into other areas.[94]

But agriculture is only a weak predictor of extended-family households. Many agriculturalists lack them, and many nonagricultural societies have them. A different theory is that extended-family

work. One study by Daniel Lichter and his colleagues estimated that for every 100 African American women between the ages of 21 and 28, there were fewer than 80 available African American men. If we count only men who are employed full or part time, the number of available men per 100 women drops below 50. So there may be considerable merit to the argument that one-parent families (usually headed by women) will be likely when a spouse (particularly an employed one) is hard to find.

Another popular explanation for the rise in number of one-parent families is that, in contrast to the past, women can manage without husbands because of support from the state. This scenario seems to fit Sweden, where unmarried and divorced mothers receive many social supports and allowances for maternity and educational leave. But Iceland has few social supports from the government and yet has the highest rate of out-of-wedlock births of all the Scandinavian countries. In the United States, the welfare argument fails to predict changes

over time. The program called Aid to Families with Dependent Children provided aid largely to single mothers. If the theory about government help were correct, increases in such aid would generally predict increases in the percentage of mother-headed households. But, in fact, during the 1970s the percentage of families receiving aid and the value of aid decreased, while the percentage of mother-headed households increased. In the 1980s it was more difficult to go "on welfare," but the percentage of mother-headed households increased anyway.

Women might be more able to manage alone if they have high-paying employment, and therefore we might expect more one-parent families by choice, as more women enter the job market. But, although this may explain the choices of some women, recent research finds that employed women generally are *more* rather than less likely to marry.

In any case, there seems to be a general association between commercial economies and the possibility of one-parent fami-

lies. Is there something about subsistence economies that promotes marriage and something about commercial economies that detracts from it? Although marriage is not universally based on love or companionship, it entails a great deal of economic and other kinds of interdependence, particularly in not-so-commercial economies. Market economies allow other possibilities; goods and services can be bought and sold, and governments may take over functions normally handled by kin and family. So the one-parent family is likely to remain an option—either a choice or a necessity—for some people.

Sources: Alisa Burns and Cath Scott, *Mother-Headed Families and Why They Have Increased* (Hillsdale, NJ: Lawrence Erlbaum Associates, 1994); David Popenoe, *Disturbing the Nest: Family Change and Decline in Modern Societies* (New York: Aldine de Gruyter, 1988); Daniel T. Lichter, Diane K. McLaughlin, George Kephart, and David J. Landry, "Race and the Retreat from Marriage: A Shortage of Marriageable Men?" *American Sociological Review,* 57 (1992): 781–99.

households come to prevail in societies that have incompatible activity requirements—that is, requirements that cannot be met by a mother or a father in a one-family household. In other words, extended-family households are generally favored when the work a mother has to do outside the home (cultivating fields or gathering foods far away) makes it difficult for her also to care for her children and do other household tasks. Similarly, extended families may be favored when the required outside activities of a father (warfare, trading trips, or wage labor far away) make it difficult for him to do the

subsistence work required of males. There is cross-cultural evidence that societies with such incompatible activity requirements are more likely to have extended-family households than societies with compatible activity requirements, *regardless* of whether or not the society is agricultural. Even though they have incompatible activity requirements, however, societies with commercial or monetary exchange may not have extended-family households. In commercial societies, a family may be able to obtain the necessary help by "buying" the required services.[95]

Of course, even in societies with money economies, not everyone can buy required services. Those who are poor may need to live in extended families, and extended-family living may become more common even in the middle class when the economy is depressed. As a popular magazine noted,

> Whatever happened to the all-American nuclear family—Mom, Pop, two kids and a cuddly dog, nestled under one cozy, mortgaged roof? What happened was an economic squeeze: layoffs, fewer jobs for young people, more working mothers, a shortage of afford-able housing and a high cost of living. Those factors, along with a rising divorce rate, a trend toward later marriages and an increase in the over sixty-five popu-lation, all hitting at once, are forcing thousands of Americans into living in multigenerational families.[96]

In many societies there are kin groups even larger than extended families. The next chapter discusses the varieties of such groupings.

SUMMARY

1. All societies known today have the custom of marriage. Marriage is a socially approved sexual and economic union usually between a man and a woman that is presumed to be more or less perma-nent and that subsumes reciprocal rights and oblig-ations between the two spouses and between the spouses and their children.

2. The way marriage is socially recognized varies greatly; it may involve an elaborate ceremony or none at all. Variations include childhood betrothals, trial-marriage periods, feasting, and the birth of a baby.

3. Marriage arrangements often include an eco-nomic element. The most common form is the bride price, in which the groom or his family gives an agreed-upon amount of money or goods to the bride's family. Bride service exists when the groom works for the bride's family for a specified period. In some societies, a female from the groom's family is exchanged for the bride; in others, gifts are ex-changed between the two families. A dowry is a payment of goods or money by the bride's family, usually to the bride. Indirect dowry is provided by the groom's family to the bride, sometimes through the bride's father.

4. No society in recent times has allowed sex or marriage between brothers and sisters, mothers and sons, or fathers and daughters.

5. Every society tells people whom they cannot marry, whom they can marry, and sometimes even whom they should marry. In quite a few societies, marriages are arranged by the couple's kin groups. Implicit in arranged marriages is the conviction that the joining of two kin groups to form new social and economic ties is too important to be left to free choice and romantic love. Some societies have rules of exogamy, which require marriage outside one's own kin group or community; others have rules of endogamy, requiring marriage within one's group. Although most societies prohibit all first-cousin marriages, some permit or prefer marriage with cross-cousins (children of siblings of the opposite sex) and parallel cousins (children of siblings of the same sex). Many societies have customs providing for the remarriage of widowed persons. Levirate is a custom whereby a man marries his brother's widow. Sororate is the practice whereby a woman marries her deceased sister's husband.

6. We think of marriage as involving just one man and one woman at a time (monogamy), but most societies allow a man to be married to more than one woman at a time (polygyny). Polyandry, the marriage of one woman to several husbands, is rare.

7. The prevailing form of family in most soci-eties is the extended family. It consists of two or more single-parent, monogamous (nuclear), polyg-ynous, or polyandrous families linked by blood ties.

GLOSSARY TERMS

berdaches
bride price (or bride
  wealth)
bride service
cross-cousins
dowry
endogamy
exogamy
extended family
family
fraternal polyandry
group marriage
incest taboo
indirect dowry

levirate
marriage
matrifocal family
monogamy
nonfraternal polyandry
nonsororal polygyny
nuclear family
parallel cousins
polyandry
polygamy
polygyny
postpartum sex taboo
sororal polygyny
sororate

CRITICAL QUESTIONS

1. Will it remain customary in our society to marry? Why do you think it will or will not?

2. Do you think extended-family households will become more frequent in this society? Why?

3. Why is polyandry so much less frequent than polygyny?

INTERNET EXERCISES

1. Explore how extended family life may help children in the United Kingdom. See **www.nspcc.org.uk/press-releases/index-36.htm**.

2. Go to **http://www.census.gov/apsd/www/statbrief** and look at Who's Minding the Kids? How might child care in the United States be different if people mostly lived in extended family households? Also read the article, "Housing in Metropolitan Areas-Single Parent Families." Summarize some of the main points.

3. Explore marriage patterns in one of the ethnographic examples given in the Kinship and Social Organization tutorial at **http://www.umanitoba.ca/faculties/arts/anthropology/tutor**.

SUGGESTED READING

EMBER, M., AND EMBER, C. R. *Marriage, Family, and Kinship: Comparative Studies of Social Organization.* New Haven, CT: HRAF Press, 1983. A collection of reprinted cross-cultural and cross-species studies testing possible explanations of some aspects of human social organization. Relevant to this chapter are the studies of male-female bonding, the incest taboo, polygyny, and the extended family.

HENDRIX, L. "Varieties of Marital Relationships." In C. R. Ember and M. Ember, eds., *Cross-Cultural Research for Social Science.* Upper Saddle River, NJ: Prentice Hall, 1998. Prentice Hall/Simon & Schuster Custom Publishing. A recent review of what is known cross-culturally about love, intimacy, jealousy, violence, and fear of sex within the marital relationship, as well as the circumstances under which divorce rates are high.

MURDOCK, G. P. *Social Structure.* New York: Macmillan, 1949. A classic cross-cultural analysis of variation in social organization. Chapters 1, 2, 9, and 10—on the nuclear family, composite forms of the family, the regulation of sex, and incest taboos and their extensions—are particularly relevant.

PASTERNAK, B. "Family and Household: Who Lives Where, Why Does It Vary, and Why Is It Important?" In C. R. Ember and M. Ember, eds., *Cross-Cultural Research for Social Science.* Upper Saddle River, NJ: Prentice Hall, 1998. Prentice Hall/Simon & Schuster Custom Publishing.

PASTERNAK, B., EMBER, C.R., AND EMBER, M. *Sex, Gender and Kinship: A Cross-Cultural Perspective.* Upper Saddle River, NJ: Prentice Hall, 1997. An up-to-date review and discussion of cross-cultural studies of sex, gender, marriage, family and kinship. See particularly Chapters 4–9 and 11.

18

Marital Residence and Kinship

*I*n the United States and Canada, as well as in many other industrial societies, a young man and woman usually establish a place of residence apart from their parents or other relatives when they marry, if they have not already moved away before that. Our society is so oriented toward this pattern of marital residence—*neolocal (new-place) residence*—that it seems to be the obvious and natural one to follow. Some upper-income families begin earlier than others to train their children to live away from home by sending them to boarding schools at age 13 or 14, or to sleep-away summer camps. Young adults of all income levels learn to live away from home most of the year if they join the army or attend an out-of-town college. In any case, when a young person marries, he or she generally lives apart from family.

So familiar is neolocal residence to us that we tend to assume that all societies practice the same pattern. On the contrary, of the 565 societies in George Peter Murdock's "World Ethnographic Sample," only about 5 percent followed this practice.[1] About 95 percent of the world's societies have some pattern of residence whereby a new couple settles within, or very close to, the household of the parents or some other close relative of either the groom or the bride. When married couples live near kin, it stands to reason that kinship relationships will figure prominently in the social life of the society. Marital residence largely predicts the types of kin groups found in a society, as well as how people refer to and classify their various relatives.

As we will see, kin groups that include several or many families and hundreds or even thousands of people are found in many societies and structure many areas of social life. Kin groups may have important economic, social, political, and religious functions.

PATTERNS OF MARITAL RESIDENCE

In societies in which newly married couples customarily live with or close to their kin, several residence patterns may be established. Children in all societies are required to marry outside the nuclear family, because of the incest taboo, and, with few exceptions, couples in almost all societies live together after they are married. Therefore some children have

to leave home when they marry. But which married children remain at home and which reside elsewhere? Societies vary in the way they deal with this question, but there are not many different patterns. Actually, only four occur with any sizable frequency (the percentages in the discussion do not sum to 100 because of rounding):

1. **Patrilocal residence.** The son stays and the daughter leaves, so that the married couple lives with or near the husband's parents (67 percent of all societies).
2. **Matrilocal residence.** The daughter stays and the son leaves, so that the married couple lives with or near the wife's parents (15 percent of all societies).
3. **Bilocal residence.** Either the son or the daughter leaves, so that the married couple lives with or near either the wife's or the husband's parents (7 percent of all societies).
4. **Avunculocal residence.** Both son and daughter normally leave, but the son and his wife settle with or near his mother's brother (4 percent of all societies).[2]

In these definitions, we use the phrase "the married couple lives *with or near*" a particular set of in-laws. When couples live with or near the kin of a spouse, the couple may live in the same household with those kin, creating an *extended-family* household, or they may live separately in an *independent-family* household, but nearby.

A fifth pattern of residence is neolocal, in which the newly married couple does not live with or near kin.

5. **Neolocal residence.** Both son and daughter leave; married couples live apart from the relatives of both spouses (5 percent of all societies).

Figure 18–1 graphically shows the percentage of societies in the ethnographic record that practice each of the five marital residence patterns.

How does place of residence affect the social life of the couple? Because the pattern of residence governs with whom or near whom individuals live, it largely determines which people those individuals interact with and have to depend on. If a married couple is surrounded by the kin of the husband, for example, the chances are that those relatives will figure importantly in the couple's future. Whether the couple lives with or near the husband's or the wife's kin can also be expected to have important consequences for the status of the husband or wife.

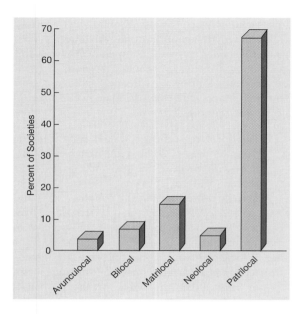

FIGURE 18–1 *Percentage of Societies in the Ethnographic Record with Various Marital Residence Patterns*

Source: Calculated from Allan D. Coult and Robert W. Habenstein, *Cross Tabulations of Murdock's World Ethnographic Sample* (Columbia: University of Missouri Press, 1965).

If married couples live patrilocally, as occurs in most societies, the wife may be far from her own kin. In any case, she will be an outsider among a group of male relatives who have grown up together. The feeling of being an outsider is particularly strong when the wife has moved into a patrilocal extended-family household.

Among the Tiv of central Nigeria,[3] the patrilocal extended family consists of the "great father," who is the head of the household, and his younger brothers, his sons, and his younger brothers' sons. Also included are the in-marrying wives and all unmarried children. (The sisters and daughters of the household head who have married would have gone to live where their husbands lived.) Authority is strongly vested in the male line, particularly the oldest of the household, who has authority over bride price, disputes, punishment, and plans for new buildings.

A somewhat different situation exists if the husband comes to live with or near his wife's parents. In this case, the wife and her kin take on somewhat greater importance, and the husband is the outsider. As we shall see, however, the matrilocal situation is not quite the mirror image of the patrilocal, because in matrilocal societies the husband's kin often are not far away. Moreover, even though

In most societies known to anthropology, the bride leaves her home to live with or near her husband's parents when she marries. A Korean bride was traditionally carried in a litter to the home of the groom.

residence is matrilocal, women often do not have as much to say in decision making as their brothers do.

If the married couple does not live with or near the parents or close kin of either spouse, the situation is again quite different. It should not be surprising that relatives and kinship connections do not figure very largely in everyday life in neolocal residence situations.

EXPLANATIONS OF VARIATION IN RESIDENCE

Questions can be raised as to why different societies have different patterns of residence. If in most societies married couples live with or near kin, as in patrilocal, matrilocal, bilocal, and avunculocal residence, then why in some societies, such as our own, do couples typically live apart from kin? And, among the societies in which couples live with or near kin, why do most choose the husband's side (patrilocal residence), but some the wife's side (matrilocal residence)? Why do some nonneolocal societies allow a married couple to go to either the wife's or the husband's kin (bilocal residence), whereas most others do not allow a choice? (Because matrilocal, patrilocal, and avunculocal residence specify just one pattern, they are often called nonoptional, or **unilocal residence,** patterns.)

NEOLOCAL RESIDENCE

Many anthropologists have suggested that neolocal residence is somehow related to the presence of a money or commercial economy. They argue that when people can sell their labor or their products for money, they can buy what they need to live, without having to depend on kin. Because money is not perishable, unlike crops and other foods in a world largely lacking refrigeration, it can be stored for exchange at a later time. Thus, a money-earning family can resort to its own savings during periods of unemployment or disability, or it might be able to rely on monetary aid from the government, as in our own society. This strategy is impossible in non-money economies, where people must depend on relatives for food and other necessities if for some reason they cannot provide their own.

There is some cross-cultural evidence to support this interpretation. Neolocal residence tends to occur in societies with monetary or commercial exchange, whereas societies without money tend to have patterns of residence that locate a couple near or with kin.[4] The presence of money, then, appears to be related to neolocal residence: Money seems to *allow* couples to live on their own. Still, this fact does not quite explain why they choose to do so.

One reason may be that in commercial societies, couples do better on their own because the jobs available require physical or social mobility. Or perhaps couples prefer to live apart from kin because they want to avoid some of the interpersonal tensions and demands that may be generated by living with or near kin. But why couples, when given money, should *prefer* to live on their own is not completely understood.

MATRILOCAL VERSUS PATRILOCAL RESIDENCE

Traditionally, it has been assumed that in societies in which married children live near or with kin, residence will tend to be patrilocal if males contribute more to the economy and matrilocal if women contribute more. However plausible that assumption may seem, the cross-cultural evidence does not support it. Where men do most of the primary subsistence work, residence is patrilocal no more often than would be expected by chance. Conversely, where women do an equal amount or more of the subsistence work, residence is no more likely to be matrilocal than patrilocal.[5] And if we counted all work in and outside the home, most societies should be matrilocal because women usually do more. But that is not true either; most societies are not matrilocal.

We can predict whether residence will be matrilocal or patrilocal, however, from the type of warfare practiced in a society. In most societies known to anthropology, neighboring communities or districts are enemies. The type of warfare that breaks out periodically between such groups is called *internal,* because the fighting occurs between groups that speak the same language. In other societies, the warfare is never within the same society but only with other language groups. This pattern of warfare is referred to as purely *external.* Cross-cultural evidence suggests that in societies where warfare is at least sometimes internal, residence is almost always patrilocal rather than matrilocal. In contrast, residence is usually matrilocal when warfare is purely external.[6]

How can we explain this relationship between type of warfare and matrilocal versus patrilocal residence? One theory is that patrilocal residence tends to occur with internal warfare because there may be concern over keeping sons close to home to help with defense. Because women do not usually

NEOLOCALITY AND ADOLESCENT REBELLION: ARE THEY RELATED?

In our society it is taken for granted that adolescence means turmoil and parent-child conflict. Teenagers, parents, and educators worry about how to reduce the conflict. But few in our society ask why the conflict occurs in the first place. Is it "natural" for adolescents to be rebellious? Are they rebellious in all cultures? If not, why do we have conflict in our society?

This issue was first raised by Margaret Mead. In her bestselling *Coming of Age in Samoa* (originally published in 1928), she said that conflict during adolescence was minimal in Samoa. Some researchers have recently criticized her analysis (see the discussion in the chapter on psychology and culture), but many field and comparative studies by anthropologists have since found that adolescence is not experienced in the same way in all societies. For example, in their systematic cross-cultural study of adolescence, Alice Schlegel and Herbert Barry concluded that relations between adolescents and their families were generally harmonious around the world. They suggested that when family members need each other throughout their lives, independence, as expressed in adolescent rebelliousness, would be foolhardy. Indeed, Schlegel and Barry found that adolescents are likely to be rebellious only in societies, like our own, that have *neolocal* residence and considerable job and geographic mobility.

Why should this be? We might speculate that adolescent rebellion is an elaborate psychodrama played out by both parents and children to prepare themselves for separation. Children spend a considerable part of their lives being dependent on their parents. But they know they must move away, and that prospect may arouse anxiety. Children want to be independent, but independence is scary. Dependence is nice in some ways—at least it can make life easier (someone else cooks for you and so on)—but it is also less grown-up than independence. So what pushes a child to leave? Perhaps the conflict itself propels the departure. Teenagers ask for things they want, but they may know, at least unconsciously, that their parents will say no. And parents often do say no, so the teenagers get angry and can't wait to be on their own. Parents are also ambivalent. They want their children to grow up, but they miss them when they leave. After a period of conflict, it may be a relief for all concerned when parents and children go their separate ways.

What if our social structure were different? What if parents and children knew that some of the children were going to spend the rest of their lives with or near the parents? And even those children who moved away, as some would have to in societies practicing matrilocal, patrilocal, avunculocal, or bilocal residence, would know they were going to spend the rest of their lives with or near their in-laws. Could teenagers in nonneolocal societies afford to have serious conflict with their parents? Could the parents afford to have serious conflict with the teenagers who will be staying put after their marriages? We think not. We suggest that adolescent conflict would be very disadvantageous in a nonneolocal society, and therefore we would expect its

constitute the fighting force in any society, having sons reside at home after marriage might be favored as a means of maintaining a loyal and quickly mobilized fighting force in case of surprise attack from nearby. If warfare is purely external, however, people may not be so concerned about keeping their sons at home because families need not fear attack from neighboring communities or districts.

With purely external warfare, then, residence may be determined by other considerations, especially economic ones. If in societies with purely external warfare the women do most of the primary subsistence work, families might want their daughters to remain at home after marriage, so the pattern of residence might become matrilocal. If warfare is purely external but men still do more of the primary subsistence work, residence should still be patrilocal. Thus, the need to keep sons at home after marriage when there is internal warfare may take precedence over any considerations

minimization or suppression when the residence pattern is other than neolocal.

There is another reason why rebelliousness might be associated with neolocality; it has to do with the fact that neolocality is predicted by commercial exchange. In the modern world, commercial societies are likely to have a great deal of occupational specialization and people with many different values. Thus children are presented with a great many choices in a rapidly changing culture. Let us consider the effect of a rapidly changing technology. If children have to know and do things that the parents do not know about, how can we expect the children to want to follow in their parents' footsteps?

But a rapidly changing culture is not necessarily accompanied by parent-child conflict. Other conditions are probably also necessary to generate the conflict, if the situation in a Moroccan town is any guide. As part of a comparative research project on adolescence, Susan and Douglas Davis interviewed young people in a small town in Morocco. The culture had changed a lot recently. Parents mostly worked at

jobs in and related to agriculture; children aspired to white-collar jobs. Grandparents rarely saw a car; teenagers took trains to the capital. Only a few parents went to school; most teenagers did. Yet the Davises reported little serious parent-child conflict, despite the cultural changes. For example, 40 percent of the teenagers said that they had never disagreed with their mothers. Perhaps we need to consider other facets of the culture. For one thing, Morocco has an authoritarian political structure with a monarchy and a clear pyramid of offices; perhaps parent-child conflict is unlikely in such a political system because it emphasizes and requires obedience. A second possible consideration is that group life is more important than the individual. The family is the most important social group, and as such cannot tolerate adolescent rebelliousness. A third possible consideration is that adults are supposed to avoid open conflict. The study by the Davises implies that adolescent rebelliousness is likely only in societies like the United States that emphasize individuality, personal autonomy, and individual achievement.

What we need is research that tries to untangle the various causal possibilities. To discover the possible effect of neolocality, or rapid change, or cultural emphasis on individual autonomy, or an authoritarian political system, we need to study samples of cultures that have different combinations of those traits. It is possible that they all are influential, or that some are more important than others, or that some *cause* the others. Whatever we discover in the future about the causality, we know now that adolescent rebelliousness is not inevitable or natural, that it is probably linked to some other aspects of cultural variation—as Margaret Mead suggested many years ago.

Sources: Margaret Mead, *Coming of Age in Samoa* (New York: Morrow, 1928); Alice Schlegel and Herbert Barry III, *Adolescence: An Anthropological Inquiry* (New York: Free Press, 1991); Susan Schaefer Davis, "Rebellious Teens? A Moroccan Instance," paper presented at annual meeting of the Middle East Studies Association, November 1993; Susan Schaefer Davis, "Morocco: Adolescents in a Small Town," in Melvin Ember, Carol R. Ember, and David Levinson, eds., *Portraits of Culture: Ethnographic Originals* (Upper Saddle River, NJ: Prentice Hall, 1998). Prentice Hall/Simon & Schuster Custom Publishing.

based on division of labor. It is perhaps only when internal warfare is nonexistent that a female-dominant division of labor may give rise to matrilocal residence.[7]

The frequent absence of men because of long-distance trade or wage labor in distant places may also provide an impetus for matrilocal residence even after warfare ceases. For example, among the Miskito of eastern Central America, matrilocality allowed domestic and village life to continue

without interruption when men were away from home for long periods of time, working as lumberers, miners, and river transporters. These jobs were not always available, but when they were the men went away to work at them in order to earn money. Even though some men would always be away from home, the Miskito continued to get food in their traditional ways, from farming (done mostly by the women) and from hunting and fishing (which was mostly men's work).[8]

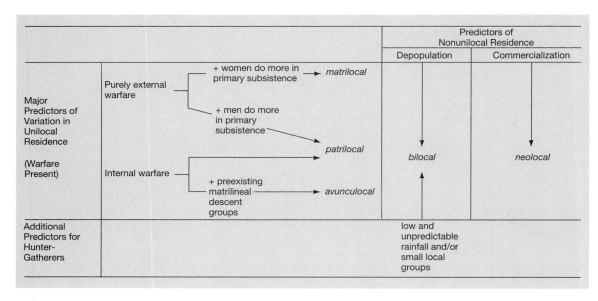

| | | | | Predictors of Nonunilocal Residence | |
				Depopulation	Commercialization
Major Predictors of Variation in Unilocal Residence (Warfare Present)	Purely external warfare	+ women do more in primary subsistence → *matrilocal*			
		+ men do more in primary subsistence ↘		*bilocal*	*neolocal*
	Internal warfare	↗	*patrilocal*		
		+ preexisting matrilineal descent groups → *avunculocal*			
Additional Predictors for Hunter-Gatherers				low and unpredictable rainfall and/or small local groups	

FIGURE 18–2   *The Main Predictors of Marital Residence Patterns*

An arrow indicates the suggested causal direction.   *Source:* Adapted from Melvin Ember and Carol R. Ember, *Marriage, Family, and Kinship: Comparative Studies of Social Organization* (New Haven, CT: HRAF Press, 1983).

BILOCAL RESIDENCE

In societies that practice bilocal residence, a married couple goes to live with or near either the husband's or the wife's parents. Although this pattern seems to involve a choice for the married couple, theory and research suggest that bilocal residence may occur out of necessity instead. Elman Service suggested that bilocal residence is likely to occur in societies that have recently suffered a severe and drastic loss of population because of the introduction of new infectious diseases.[9] Over the last 400 years, contact with Europeans in many parts of the world has resulted in severe population losses among non-European societies that lacked resistance to the Europeans' diseases. If couples need to live with some set of kin in order to make a living in noncommercial societies, it seems likely that couples in depopulated, noncommercial societies might have to live with whichever spouse's parents and other relatives are still alive. This interpretation seems to be supported by the cross-cultural evidence. Recently depopulated societies tend to have bilocal residence or frequent departures from unilocality, whereas societies that are not recently depopulated tend to have one pattern or another of unilocal residence.[10]

In hunter-gatherer societies, a few other circumstances may also favor bilocal residence. Bilocality tends to be found among those hunter-gatherers who have very small bands or unpredictable and low rainfall. Residential "choice" in these cases may be a question of adjusting marital residence to where the couple will have the best chance to survive or to find close relatives with whom to live and work.[11] Figure 18–2 illustrates the main predictors of the various marital residence patterns.

THE STRUCTURE OF KINSHIP

In noncommercial societies, kinship connections structure many areas of social life—from the kind of access an individual has to productive resources to the kind of political alliances formed between communities and larger territorial groups. In some societies, in fact, kinship connections have important bearing on matters of life and death.

Recall the social system described in Shakespeare's *Romeo and Juliet*. The Capulets and the Montagues were groups of kin engaged in lethal competition with each other, and the fatal outcome of Romeo and Juliet's romance was related to that competition. Although Romeo and Juliet's society had a commercial economy (but not, of course, an industrialized one), the political system of the city they lived in was a reflection of the way kinship was structured. Sets of kin of common descent lived together, and the various kin groups competed, and sometimes fought, for a prominent, or at least secure, place in the political hierarchy of the city-state.

If a preindustrial commercial society could be so structured by kinship, we can imagine how much more important kinship connections and kin groups are in many noncommercial societies that lack political mechanisms such as princes and councils of lords who try to keep the peace and initiate other activities on behalf of the community. It is no wonder that anthropologists often speak of the web of kinship as providing the main structure of social action in noncommercial societies.

If kinship is important, there is still the question of which set of kin a person affiliates with and depends on. After all, if every single relative were counted as equally important, there would be an unmanageably large number of people in each person's kinship network. Consequently, in most societies in which kinship connections are important, rules allocate each person to a particular and definable set of kin.

RULES OF DESCENT

Rules that connect individuals with particular sets of kin because of known or presumed common ancestry are called **rules of descent.** By the particular rule of descent operating in their society, individuals can know more or less immediately which set of kin to turn to for support and help.

There are only three known rules of descent that affiliate individuals with different sets of kin:

1. **Patrilineal descent,** the most frequent rule, affiliates an individual with kin of both sexes related to him or her *through men only.* As Figure 18–3 indicates, in patrilineal systems the children in each generation belong to the kin group of their father; their father, in turn, belongs to the group of his father; and so on. Although a man's sons and daughters are all members of the same descent group, affiliation with that group is transmitted only by the sons to their children.
2. **Matrilineal descent** affiliates an individual with kin of both sexes related to him or her *through women only.* In each generation, then, children belong to the kin group of their mother (see Figure 18–4). Although a woman's sons and daughters are all members of the same descent group, only her daughters can pass on their descent affiliation to their children.

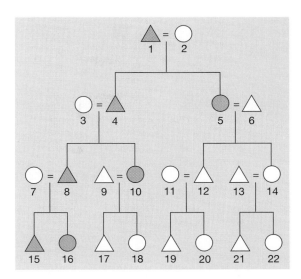

FIGURE 18–3 *Patrilineal Descent*

Individuals 4 and 5, who are the children of 1 and 2, affiliate with their father's patrilineal kin group, represented by the color purple. In the next generation, the children of 3 and 4 also belong to the purple kin group, since they take their descent from their father, who is a member of that group. However, the children of 5 and 6 do not belong to this patrilineal group, since they take their descent from their father, who is a member of a different group. That is, although the mother of 12 and 14 belongs to the purple patrilineal group, she cannot pass on her descent affiliation to her children, and since her husband (6) does not belong to her patrilineage, her children (12 and 14) belong to their father's group. In the fourth generation, only 15 and 16 belong to the purple patrilineal group, since their father is the only male member of the preceding generation who belongs to the purple patrilineal group. In this diagram, then, 1, 4, 5, 8, 10, 15, and 16 are affiliated by patrilineal descent; all the other individuals belong to other patrilineal groups.

3. **Ambilineal descent** affiliates an individual with kin related to him or her through men *or* women. In other words, some people in the society affiliate with a group of kin through their fathers; others, through their mothers. Consequently, the descent groups show both female and male genealogical links, as illustrated in Figure 18–5.

These three rules are usually, but not always, mutually exclusive. Most societies can be characterized as having only one rule of descent, but sometimes two principles are used to affiliate individuals with different sets of kin for different purposes. Some societies have, then, what is called **double descent** or

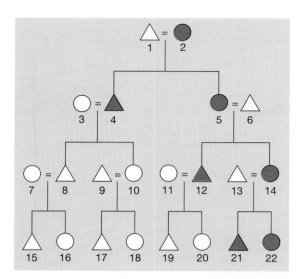

FIGURE 18–4 *Matrilineal Descent*

Individuals 4 and 5, who are the children of 1 and 2, affiliate with their mother's kin group, represented by the color green. In the next generation, the children of 5 and 6 also belong to the green kin group, since they take their descent from their mother, who is a member of that group. However, the children of 3 and 4 do not belong to this matrilineal group, since they take their descent from their mother, who is a member of a different group; their father, although a member of the green matrilineal group, cannot pass his affiliation on to them under the rule of matrilineal descent. In the fourth generation, only 21 and 22 belong to the green matrilineal group, since their mother is the only female member of the preceding generation who belongs. Thus, individuals 2, 4, 5, 12, 14, 21, and 22 belong to the same matrilineal group.

---

double unilineal descent, whereby an individual affiliates for some purposes with a group of matrilineal kin and for other purposes with a group of patrilineal kin. Thus, two rules of descent, each traced through links of one sex only, are operative at the same time. For example, if there is a patrilineal system and a matrilineal one, individuals would belong to *two* groups at birth: the matrilineal group of the mother *and* the patrilineal group of the father. Imagine combining Figures 18–3 and 18–4. Individuals 4 and 5 would belong to both the patrilineal group (purple on Figure 18-3) to which their father belongs and the matrilineal group (green on Figure 18-4) to which their mother belongs.

The way a society assigns names does not necessarily convey any information about a rule of descent. It is customary in North American society for children to have a last, or "family," name—usually their father's last name. All the people with the same

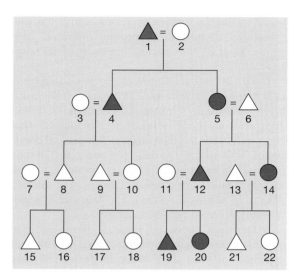

FIGURE 18–5 *Ambilineal Descent*

A hypothetical ambilineal group of kin is indicated by the color blue. Members 4 and 5 belong to this group because of a male link, their father (1); members 12 and 14 belong because of a female link, their mother (5); and members 19 and 20 belong because of a male link, their father (12). This is a hypothetical example because any combination of lineal links is possible in an ambilineal descent group.

---

last name do not conceive of themselves as descended from the same common ancestor; all Smiths do not consider themselves related. Nor do such people act together for any particular purpose. And many societies, even with rules of descent, do not give individuals the name of their kin group or of their father or mother. For example, among the patrilineal Luo of Kenya, babies were traditionally given names that described the circumstances of their birth (such as "born-in-the-morning"); their names did not include their father's or kin group's name. Only after the British established a colony in Kenya, and continuing after independence, did children get their father's personal name as a family name.

BILATERAL KINSHIP

Many societies, including our own, do not have lineal (matrilineal, patrilineal, or ambilineal) descent groups—sets of kin who believe they descend from a common ancestor. These are societies with **bilateral kinship.** *Bilateral* means "two-sided," and in this case it refers to the fact that one's relatives on both mother's and father's sides are equal in importance or, more usually, in unimportance. Kinship reckoning in bilateral societies does not refer to common descent but rather is horizontal, moving outward from close to more distant relatives rather than upward to common ancestors (see Figure 18–6).

The term **kindred** describes a person's bilateral set of relatives who may be called upon for some purpose. In our society, we think of the kindred as including the people we might invite to weddings, funerals, or some other ceremonial occasion; a kindred, however, is not usually a definite group. As anyone who has been involved in creating a wedding invitation list knows, a great deal of time may be spent deciding which relatives ought to be invited and which ones can legitimately be excluded. Societies with bilateral kinship differ in precisely how distant relatives have to be before they are lost track of or before they are not included in ceremonial activities. In societies such as our own, in which kinship is relatively unimportant, fewer relatives are included in the kindred. In other bilateral societies, however, where kinship connections are somewhat more important, more would be included.

The distinctive feature of bilateral kinship is that, aside from brothers and sisters, no two persons belong to exactly the same kin group. Your kindred contains close relatives spreading out on both your mother's and father's sides, but the members of your kindred are affiliated only by way of their connec-

tion to you (**ego,** or the focus). Thus, the kindred is an *ego-centered* group of kin. Because different people (except for brothers and sisters) have different mothers and fathers, your first cousins will have different kindreds, and even your own children will have a different kindred from yours. It is the ego-centered nature of the kindred that makes it difficult for it to serve as a permanent or persistent group. The only thing the people in a kindred have in common is the ego who brings them together. A kindred usually has no name, no common purpose, and only temporary meetings centered around the ego.[12] Furthermore, because everyone belongs to many different and overlapping kindreds, the society is not divided into clear-cut groups.

UNILINEAL DESCENT

Both matrilineal and patrilineal rules of descent are **unilineal descent** rules, in that a person is affiliated with a group of kin through descent links of one sex only—either males only or females only. Unilineal rules of descent affiliate an individual with a line of kin extending back in time and into the future. By virtue of this line of descent, whether it extends through males or females, some very close relatives are excluded. For example, in a patrilineal system, your mother and your mother's parents do not

---

FIGURE 18–6 *Bilateral Kinship*

In a bilateral system the kindred is ego-centered; hence, it varies with different points of reference (except for brothers and sisters). In any bilateral society, the kindred minimally includes parents, grandparents, aunts, uncles, and first cousins. So, if we look at the close kindred of the brother and sister 20 and 21 (enclosed by the solid line), it would include their parents (9 and 10), their aunts and uncles (7, 8, 11, 12), their grandparents (1, 2, 3, 4), and their first cousins (16–19, 22–25). But the kindred of the brother and sister 24 and 25 (shown by the dashed line) includes only some of the same people (3, 4, 10–12, 20–23); in addition, the kindred of 24 and 25 includes people not in the kindred of 20 and 21 (5, 6, 13–15, 26–29).

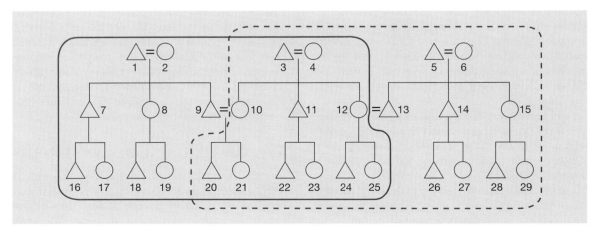

In societies with descent groups, ancestor worship is common. The patrilineal Dogon of Mali use carved wooden masks in ceremonies to honor their dead ancestors.

belong to your patrilineal group, but your father and his father (and their sisters) do. In your own generation in a matrilineal or patrilineal system, some cousins are excluded, and in your children's generation, some of your nieces and nephews are excluded.

However, although unilineal rules of descent exclude certain relatives from membership in one's kin group, just as practical considerations restrict the effective size of kinship networks in our own society, the excluded relatives are not necessarily ignored or forgotten. Indeed, in many unilineal societies they may be entrusted with important responsibilities. For example, when a person dies in a patrilineal society, some members of his or her mother's patrilineal descent group may customarily be accorded the right to perform certain rituals at the funeral.

Unlike bilateral kinship, unilineal rules of descent can form clear-cut, and hence unambiguous, groups of kin, which can act as separate units even after the death of individual members. Referring again to Figures 18–3 and 18–4, we can see that the individuals in the highlight color belong to the same patrilineal or matrilineal descent group without ambiguity; an individual in the fourth generation belongs to the

group just as much as one in the first generation. If we imagine that the patrilineal group has a name, say, the Hawks, then an individual knows immediately whether or not she or he is a Hawk. If the individual is not a Hawk, then he or she belongs to some other group, for each person belongs to only one line.

This fact is important if kin groups are to act as separate, nonoverlapping units. It is difficult for people to act together unless they know exactly who should get together. And it is easier for individuals to act together as a group if each one belongs to only one such group or line. Recall that in a bilateral system, not only is it sometimes unclear where the boundary of the kindred is, but one person belongs to many different kindreds—one's own and others' (children's, cousins', and so forth). Consequently, it is not surprising that a kindred gets together only temporarily for ceremonial occasions.

TYPES OF UNILINEAL DESCENT GROUPS

In a society with unilineal descent, people usually refer to themselves as belonging to a particular unilineal group or set of groups because they believe they share common descent in either the male (patrilineal) or female (matrilineal) line. These people form what is called a *unilineal descent group.* Several types of unilineal descent groups are distinguished by anthropologists: lineages, clans, phratries, and moieties.

LINEAGES. A **lineage** is a set of kin whose members trace descent from a common ancestor through known links. There may be **patrilineages** or **matrilineages,** depending on whether the links are traced through males only or through females only. Lineages are often designated by the name of the common male or female ancestor. In some societies, people belong to a hierarchy of lineages. That is, they first trace their descent back to the ancestor of a minor lineage, then to the ancestor of a larger and more inclusive major lineage, and so on.

CLANS. A **clan** (also sometimes called a **sib**) is a set of kin whose members believe themselves to be descended from a common ancestor, but the links back to that ancestor are not specified. In fact, the common ancestor may not even be known. Clans with patrilineal descent are called **patriclans;** clans with matrilineal descent are called **matriclans.** Clans often are designated by an animal or plant name, called a **totem,** which may have some special significance for the group and, at the very least, is a means of group identification. Thus, if someone says she or he belongs to the Bear, Wolf, or Turtle clan, others will know whether or not that person is a clan member. The word *totem* comes from the Ojibwa Indian word *ototeman,* "a relative of mine." In some societies, people have to observe taboos relating to their clan totem animal. For example, clan members may be forbidden to kill or eat their totem.

Although it may seem strange that an animal or plant should be a symbol of a kin group, animals as symbols of groups are familiar in our own culture. Football and baseball teams, for example, are often named for animals (Detroit Tigers, Baltimore Colts, Philadelphia Eagles, Chicago Bears). Voluntary associations, such as men's clubs, are sometimes called by the name of an animal (Elks, Moose, Lions). Entire nations may be represented by an animal; we speak, for instance, of the American Eagle and the British Lion.[13] Why humans so often choose animal names to represent groups is an intriguing question for which we have no tested answer as yet.

PHRATRIES. A **phratry** is a unilineal descent group composed of supposedly related clans or sibs. As with clans, the descent links in phratries are unspecified.

MOIETIES. When a whole society is divided into two unilineal descent groups, we call each group a **moiety.** (The word *moiety* comes from a French word meaning "half.") The people in each moiety believe themselves to be descended from a common ancestor, although they cannot specify how. Societies with moiety systems usually have relatively small populations (fewer than 9,000 people). Societies with phratries and clans tend to be larger.[14]

COMBINATIONS. Although we have distinguished several different types of unilineal descent groups, we do not wish to imply that all unilineal societies have only one type of descent group. Many societies have two or more types in various combinations. For example, some societies have lineages

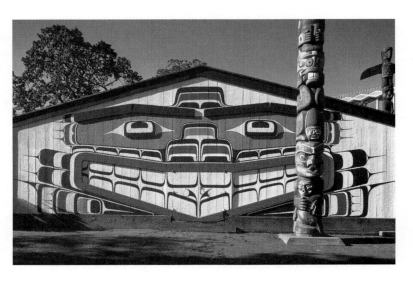

Many Northwest Pacific coast Indians construct totem poles representing the animal totems and human ancestors of their clans. Shown here are totem poles and a reconstructed house in Victoria, British Columbia.

and clans; others may have clans and phratries but no lineages; and still others may have clans and moieties but neither phratries nor lineages. Aside from the fact that a society that has phratries must also have clans (since phratries are combinations of clans), all combinations of descent groups are possible. Even if societies have more than one type of unilineal kin group—for example, lineages and clans—there is no ambiguity about membership. Small groups are simply subsets of larger units; the larger units include people who say they are unilineally related further back in time.

PATRILINEAL ORGANIZATION

Patrilineal organization is the most frequent type of descent system. The Kapauku Papuans, a people living in the central highlands of western New Guinea, are an example of a patrilineal society with many types of descent groups.[15] The hierarchy of groups to which the Kapauku are affiliated by virtue of the patrilineal descent system plays an extremely important part in their lives. Every Kapauku belongs to a patrilineage, to a patriclan that includes his or her lineage, and to a patriphratry that includes his or her clan.

The male members of a patrilineage—all the living males who can trace their actual relationship through males to a common ancestor—constitute the male population of a single village or, more likely, a series of adjoining villages. In other words, the lineage is a *territorial unit*. The male members of the lineage live together by virtue of a patrilocal rule of residence and a fairly stable settlement pattern. A son stays near his parents and brings his wife to live in or near his father's house; the daughters leave home and go to live with their husbands. If the group lives in one place over a long period, the male descendants of one man will live in the same territory. If the lineage is large, it may be divided into sublineages composed of people who trace their descent from one of the sons of the lineage ancestor. The male members of a sublineage live in a contiguous block within the larger lineage territory.

The members of the same patrilineage address each other affectionately, and within this group law and order are maintained by a headman. Killing within the lineage is considered a serious offense, and any fighting that takes place is done with sticks rather than lethal weapons such as spears. The sublineage headman tries to settle grievances within the sublineage as quickly and as peacefully as possible. If a sublineage mate commits a crime against out-siders, all members of the sublineage may be considered responsible and their property seized, or a member of the sublineage may be killed in revenge by the victim's kin.

The Kapauku also belong to larger and more inclusive patrilineal descent groups—clans and phratries. All the people of the same clan believe they are related to each other in the father's line, but they are unable to say how they are related. If a member of the patriclan eats the clan's plant or animal totem, it is believed that the person will become deaf. A Kapauku is also forbidden to marry anyone from his or her clan. In other words, the clan is exogamous.

Unlike the members of the patrilineage, the male members of the patriclan do not all live together. Thus, the lineage is the largest group of patrilineal kinsmen that is localized. The lineage is also the largest group of kinsmen that acts together politically. Among clan members there is no mechanism for resolving disputes, and members of the same patriclan (who belong to different lineages) may even go to war with one another.

The most inclusive patrilineal descent group among the Kapauku is the phratry, each of which is composed of two or more clans. The Kapauku believe that the phratry was originally one clan, but that in a conflict between brothers of the founding family the younger brother was expelled and he formed a new clan. The two resulting clans are viewed as patrilineally related, since their founders are said to have been brothers. The members of a phratry observe all the totemic taboos of the clans that belong to that phratry. Intermarriage of members of the same clan is forbidden, but members of the same phratry, if they belong to different clans, may marry.

The Kapauku, then, are an example of a unilineal society with many types of descent groups. They have lineages with demonstrated kinship links and two kinds of descent groups with unknown descent links (clans and phratries).

MATRILINEAL ORGANIZATION

Although societies with matrilineal descent seem in many respects like mirror images of their patrilineal counterparts, they differ in one important way. That difference has to do with who exercises authority. In patrilineal systems, descent affiliation is transmitted through males, and it is also the males who exercise authority. Consequently, in the patrilineal system, lines of descent and of authority converge. In a matrilineal system, however, although the line of descent passes through females, females rarely exercise authority in their kin groups. Usually males do. Thus, the lines of authority and descent do not converge.[16] Anthropologists do not completely understand why this is so, but it is an ethnographic fact. In any case, since males exercise authority in the kin group, an individual's mother's brother becomes an important authority figure, because he is the individual's closest male matrilineal relative in the parental generation. The individual's father does not belong to the individual's own matrilineal kin group and thus has no say in kin group matters.

The divergence of authority and descent in a matrilineal system has some effect on community organization and marriage. Most matrilineal societies practice matrilocal residence. Daughters stay at home after marriage and bring their husbands to live with them; sons leave home to join their wives. But the sons who are required to leave will be the ones who eventually exercise authority in their kin groups. This situation presents a problem. The solution that seems to have been arrived at in most matrilineal societies is that, although the males move away to live with their wives, they usually do not move too far away; indeed, they often marry women who live in the same village. Thus, matrilineal societies tend not to be locally exogamous—that is, members often marry people from inside the village—whereas patrilineal societies are often locally exogamous.[17]

The matrilineal organization on Truk, a group of small islands in the Pacific, illustrates the general

pattern of authority in matrilineal systems.[18] The Trukese have both matrilineages and matriclans. The matrilineage is a property-owning group whose members trace descent from a known common ancestor in the female line. The female lineage members and their husbands occupy a cluster of houses on the matrilineage's land. The property of the lineage group is administered by the oldest brother of the group, who allocates the productive property of his matrilineage and directs the work of the members. He also represents the group in dealings with the district chief and all outsiders, and he must be consulted on any matter that affects the group. There is also a senior woman of the lineage who exercises some authority, but only insofar as the activities of the women are concerned. She may supervise the women's cooperative work (they usually work separately from the men) and manage the household.

Within the nuclear family, the father and mother have the primary responsibility for raising and disciplining their children. When a child reaches puberty, however, the father's right to discipline or exercise authority over the child ceases. The mother continues to exercise her right of discipline, but her brother may interfere. A woman's brother rarely interferes with his sister's child before puberty, but after puberty he may exercise some authority, especially since he is an elder in the child's own matrilineage. On Truk, men rarely move far from their birthplace. As Ward Goodenough pointed out, "Since matrilocal residence takes the men away from their home lineages, most of them marry women whose lineage houses are within a few minutes' walk of their own."[19]

Although there are some differences between patrilineal and matrilineal systems, there are many similarities. In both types of systems there may be lineages, clans, phratries, and moieties, alone or in any combination. These kin groups, in either matrilineal or patrilineal societies, may perform any number of functions. They may regulate marriage; they may come to each other's aid economically or politically; and they may perform rituals together.

Now that we have learned something about matrilineal systems, the avunculocal pattern of residence, whereby married couples live with or near the husband's mother's brother, may become clearer. Although avunculocal residence is relatively rare, just about all avunculocal societies are matrilineal. As we have seen, the mother's brother plays an important role in decision making in most matrilineal societies. Aside from his brothers, who is a boy's closest male matrilineal relative? His mother's

Three female members of a Navajo matrilineal clan of the United States southwest.

New Perspectives on Gender

VARIATION IN RESIDENCE AND KINSHIP: WHAT DIFFERENCE DOES IT MAKE TO WOMEN?

When we say that residence and kinship have profound effects on people's lives, what exactly do we mean? We may imagine that it is hard for a woman in a patrilocal society to move at marriage into another village where her husband has plenty of relatives and she has few. But do we have evidence of that? Most ethnographies usually do not give details about people's feelings, but some do. For example, Leigh Minturn gives us the text of a letter that one new Rajput bride (who grew up in the village of Khalapur, India) sent to her mother shortly after she married into her husband's village. The letter was written when the bride had been gone six weeks, but she repeatedly asked if her mother, her father, her aunts had forgotten her. She begged to be called home and said her bags were packed. She described herself as "a parrot in a

cage" and complained about her in-laws. The bride's mother was not alarmed; she knew that such complaints were normal, reflections of her daughter's separation anxiety. Seven years later, when Minturn returned to India, the mother reported the daughter to be happy. Still, a few other brides did have more serious symptoms: ghost possession, 24- to 36-hour comas, serious depression, or suicide. What research has not told us is whether these serious symptoms are present more often in patrilocal, patrilineal societies than in other societies, particularly matrilocal, matrilineal societies. Conversely, do men have some symptoms in matrilocal, matrilineal societies that they do not have in patrilocal societies? We do not know.

What about the status of women? Some research suggests that matrilocality and matrilin-

eality enhance some aspects of women's status, but perhaps not as much as we might think. Even in matrilineal societies, men are usually the political leaders. The main effect of matrilocality and matrilineality appears to be that women control property, but they also tend to have more domestic authority in the home, more equal sexual restrictions, and more value placed on their lives. Alice Schlegel pointed out that women's status is not always relatively high in matrilineal societies, because they can be dominated by the husband or by brothers (because brothers play important roles in their kin groups). It is only when neither the husband nor the brother dominates that women may have considerable control over their own lives. Certainly the combination of matrilocality *and* matrilineality is better for women's status than patrilocality and patrilineality. Matrilocality and

brother. Going to live with mother's brother, then, provides a way of localizing male matrilineal relatives. But why should some matrilineal societies practice that form of residence? The answer may involve the prevailing type of warfare.

Avunculocal societies, in contrast with matrilocal societies, fight internally. Just as patrilocality may be a response to keep patrilineally related men home after marriage, so avunculocality may be a way of keeping related—in this case, matrilineally related—men together after marriage to provide for quick mobilization in case of surprise attack from nearby. Societies that already have strong, functioning matrilineal descent groups may, when faced with the outbreak of fighting close to home and high male mortality (which might make it difficult to trace descent through males), choose to practice avunculocality rather than switch to patrilocality.[20]

FUNCTIONS OF UNILINEAL DESCENT GROUPS

Unilineal descent groups exist in societies at all levels of cultural complexity.[21] Apparently however, they are most common in noncommercial food-producing, as opposed to food-collecting, societies.[22] Unilineal descent groups often have important functions in the social, economic, political, and religious realms of life.

REGULATING MARRIAGE. In unilineal societies, individuals are not usually permitted to marry within their own unilineal descent groups. In some, however, marriage may be permitted within more inclusive kin groups but prohibited within smaller kin groups. In a few societies, marriage within the kin group is actually preferred.

matrilineality might not enhance women's status because of the dominance of male matrilineal kin, but patrilocality and patrilineality are very likely to detract from women's status. Norma Diamond stated that even after the Chinese Communist revolution, which abolished the landholding estates of patrilineages and gave women access to education as well as jobs outside the home, male dominance continued. The mode of production and labor changed, but patrilocality did not. Women were still usually the in-marrying strangers, and members of the patrilineage became a work team on the collective farm. Diamond pointed out that those few women who became local leaders were likely to have atypical marriages that allowed them to live in the villages of their birth.

Residence and descent also predict societal attempts to control reproduction. According to Suzanne Frayser, patrilineal societies have several sexual and reproductive dilemmas. One dilemma is the contradiction between the importance of males in kinship and the women's role in reproduction. If patrilineal societies denigrate women too much, women may try to decrease their reproduction. If patrilineal societies exalt women too much, that exaltation may detract from the value of men. A second dilemma has to do with paternity, which is essential for patrilineal descent but harder than maternity to be certain of. Frayser argued that because kin group links are traced through males in patrilineal societies, they will do more to assure that the man a woman marries *is* the father. Frayser suggested that patrilineal societies therefore will be more restrictive about a woman's sexuality. Indeed, the results of her cross-cultural study indicate that patrilineal societies are more likely than other societies to prohibit premarital and extramarital sex for women, and they are more likely to make it very difficult for a woman to divorce her husband.

Sources: Leigh Minturn, *Sita's Daughters: Coming Out of Purdah: The Rajput Women of Khalapur Revisited* (New York: Oxford University Press, 1993), pp. 54–71; Martin King Whyte, *The Status of Women in Preindustrial Societies* (Princeton, NJ: Princeton University Press, 1978), pp. 132–34; Alice Schlegel, "The Status of Women," in Carol R. Ember and Melvin Ember, eds., *Cross-Cultural Research for Social Science* (Upper Saddle River, NJ: Prentice Hall, 1998), Prentice Hall/Simon & Schuster Custom Publishing; Norma Diamond, "Collectivization, Kinship, and the Status of Women in Rural China," in Rayna R. Reiter, *Toward an Anthropology of Women* (New York: Monthly Review Press, 1975); Suzanne G. Frayser, *Varieties of Sexual Experience* (New Haven, CT: HRAF Press, 1985), pp. 338–47.

But in general, the incest taboo in unilineal societies is extended to all presumed unilineal relatives. For example, on Truk, which has matriclans and matrilineages, a person is forbidden by the rule of descent group exogamy to marry anyone from her or his matriclan. The matrilineage is included within the matriclan, so the rule of descent group exogamy also applies to the matrilineage. Among the Kapauku, who have patriphratries, patriclans, and patrilineages, the largest descent group that is exogamous is the patriclan. The phratry may once have been exogamous, but the exogamy rule no longer applies to it. Some anthropologists have suggested that rules of exogamy for descent groups may have developed because the alliances between descent groups generated by such rules may be selectively favored under the conditions of life faced by most unilineal societies.

ECONOMIC FUNCTIONS. Members of a person's lineage or clan are often required to side with that person in any quarrel or lawsuit, to help him or her get established economically, to contribute to a bride price or fine, and to support the person in life crises. Mutual aid often extends to economic cooperation on a regular basis. The unilineal descent group may act as a corporate unit in land ownership. For example, house sites and farmland are owned by a lineage among the Trukese and the Kapauku. Descent group members may also support one another in such enterprises as clearing virgin bush or forest for farmland and providing food and other items for feasts, potlatches, curing rites, and ceremonial occasions, such as births, initiations, marriages, and funerals.

Money earned—either by harvesting a cash crop or by leaving the community for a time to work for cash wages—is sometimes viewed by the descent group as belonging to all. In recent times, however, young people in some places have shown an unwillingness to part with their money, viewing it as different from other kinds of economic assistance.

POLITICAL FUNCTIONS. The word *political,* as used by members of an industrialized society, generally does not apply to the vague powers that may be entrusted to a headman or the elders of a lineage or clan. But these persons may have the right to assign land for use by a lineage member or a clan member. Headmen or elders may also have the right to settle disputes between two members within a lineage, although they generally lack power to force a settlement. And they may act as intermediaries in disputes between a member of their own clan and a member of an opposing kin group.

Certainly one of the most important political functions of unilineal descent groups is their role in warfare—the attempt to resolve disputes within and without the society by violent action. In societies without towns or cities, the organization of such fighting is often in the hands of descent groups. The Tiv of central Nigeria, for instance, know very well at any given moment which lineages they will fight against, which lineages they will join as allies in case of a fight, which they will fight against using only sticks, and which must be attacked using bows and arrows.

RELIGIOUS FUNCTIONS. A clan or lineage may have its own religious beliefs and practices, worshiping its own gods or goddesses and ancestral spirits. The Tallensi of West Africa revere and try to pacify their ancestors. They view life as we know it as only a part of human existence; for them, life existed before birth and will continue after death. The Tallensi believe that the ancestors of their descent groups have changed their form but have retained their interest in what goes on within their society. They can show their displeasure by bringing sudden disaster or minor mishap and their pleasure by bringing unexpected good fortune. But people can never tell what will please them; ancestral spirits are, above all, unpredictable. Thus, the Tallensi try to account for unexplainable happenings by attributing them to the ever-watchful ancestors. Belief in the presence of ancestors also provides security; if their ancestors have survived death, so will they. The Tallensi religion is thus a descent-group religion. The Tallensi are not concerned with other people's ancestors; they believe it is only one's own ancestors who plague or protect one.[23]

DEVELOPMENT OF UNILINEAL SYSTEMS

Unilineal kin groups play very important roles in the organization of many societies. But not all societies have such groups. In societies that have complex systems of political organization, officials and agencies take over many of the functions that might be performed by kin groups, such as the organization of work and warfare and the allocation of land. But not all societies that lack complex political organization have unilineal descent systems. Why, then, do some societies have unilineal descent systems but others do not?

It is generally assumed that unilocal residence, patrilocal or matrilocal, is necessary for the development of unilineal descent. Patrilocal residence, if practiced for some time in a society, will generate a set of patrilineally related males who live in the same territory. Matrilocal residence over time will similarly generate a localized set of matrilineally related females. It is no wonder, then, that matrilocal and patrilocal residence are cross-culturally associated with matrilineal and patrilineal descent, respectively.[24]

But, although unilocal residence might be necessary for the formation of unilineal descent groups, it is apparently not the only condition required. For one thing, many societies with unilocal residence lack unilineal descent groups. For another, merely because related males or related females live together by virtue of a patrilocal or matrilocal rule of residence, it does not necessarily follow that the related people will actually view themselves as a descent group and function as such. Thus, it appears that other conditions are needed to supply the impetus for the formation of unilineal descent groups.

There is evidence that unilocal societies that engage in warfare are more apt to have unilineal descent groups than unilocal societies without warfare.[25] It may be, then, that the presence of fighting in societies lacking complex systems of political organization provides an impetus to the formation of unilineal descent groups. Unilineal descent groups provide individuals with unambiguous groups of persons who can fight or form alliances as discrete units.[26] There is no ambiguity about an individual's membership. It is perfectly clear whether someone belongs to a particular clan, phratry, or moiety. It is this feature of unilineal descent groups that enables them to act as separate and distinct units—mostly, perhaps, in warfare.

Bilateral systems, in contrast, are ego-centered; and every person, other than siblings, has a slightly different set of kin to rely on. Consequently, in bilateral societies it is often not clear to whom one can turn and which person has responsibility for aiding another. Such ambiguity, however, might not be a liability in societies without warfare or in societies with complex political systems that organize fighting on behalf of large populations.

AMBILINEAL SYSTEMS

Societies with ambilineal descent groups are far less numerous than unilineal or even bilateral societies. Ambilineal societies, however, resemble unilineal ones in many ways. For instance, the members of an ambilineal descent group believe that they are descended from a common ancestor, although frequently they cannot specify all the genealogical links. The descent group is commonly named and may have an identifying emblem or even a totem; land and other productive resources may be owned by the descent group; and myths and religious practices are often associated with the group. Marriage is often regulated by group membership, just as in unilineal systems, although kin group exogamy is not nearly as common as in unilineal systems. Moreover, ambilineal societies resemble unilineal ones in having various levels or types of descent groups. They may have lineages and higher orders of descent groups, distinguished (as in unilineal systems) by whether or not all the genealogical links to the supposed common ancestors are specified.[27]

The Samoans of the South Pacific are an example of an ambilineal society.[28] Samoa has two types of ambilineal descent groups, corresponding to what would be called clans and subclans in a unilineal society. Both groups are exogamous. Associated with each ambilineal clan are one or more chiefs. A group takes its name from the senior chief; subclans, of which there are always at least two, may take their names from junior chiefs.

The distinctiveness of the Samoan ambilineal system, compared with unilineal systems, is that because an individual may be affiliated with an ambilineal group through her or his father or mother (and her or his parents, in turn, could be affiliated with any of their parents' groups), there are a number of ambilineal groups to which that individual could belong. Affiliation with a Samoan descent group is optional, and a person may theoretically affiliate with any or all of the ambilineal groups to which she or he is related. In practice, however, a person is primarily associated with one group—the ambilineal group whose land he or she actually lives on and cultivates—although he or she may partici-

pate in the activities (house building, for example) of several groups. Because a person may belong to more than one ambilineal group, the society is not divided into separate kin groups, in contrast with unilineal societies. Consequently, the core members of each ambilineal group cannot all live together, as they could in unilineal societies, because each person belongs to more than one group and cannot live in several places at once.

Not all ambilineal societies have the multiple descent group membership that occurs in Samoa. In some ambilineal societies, a person may belong at any one time to only one group. In such cases, the society can be divided into separate, nonoverlapping groups of kin.

Why do some societies have ambilineal descent groups? Although the evidence is not clear-cut, it may be that societies with unilineal descent groups are transformed into ambilineal ones under special conditions, particularly in the presence of depopulation. We have already noted that depopulation may transform a previously unilocal society into a bilocal society. If that previously unilocal society also had unilineal descent groups, the descent groups may become transformed into ambilineal groups. If a society used to be patrilocal and patrilineal, for example, but some couples began to live matrilocally, then their children would be associated with a previously patrilineal descent group on whose land they may be living through their mother. Once this situation happens regularly, the unilineal principle may become transformed into an ambilineal principle.[29] Thus, ambilineal descent systems may have developed recently as a result of depopulation caused by the introduction of European diseases.

KINSHIP TERMINOLOGY

Our society, like all others, refers to a number of different kin by the same **classificatory term.** Most of us probably never stop to think about why we name relatives the way we do. For example, we call our mother's brother and father's brother (and often mother's sister's husband and father's sister's husband) by the same term—*uncle.* It is not that we are unable to distinguish between our mother's or father's brother or that we do not know the difference between **consanguineal kin** (blood kin) and **affinal kin** (kin by marriage, or what we call *in-laws*). Instead, it seems that in our society we do not usually find it necessary to distinguish between various types of uncles.

However natural our system of classification may seem to us, countless field studies by anthropologists have revealed that societies differ markedly in how they group or distinguish relatives. The kinship terminology used in a society may reflect its prevailing kind of family, its rule of residence and its rule of descent, and other aspects of its social organization. Kin terms may also give clues to prior features of the society's social system, if, as many anthropologists believe,[30] the kin terms of a society are very resistant to change. The major systems of kinship terminology are the Omaha system, the Crow system, the Iroquois system, the Sudanese system, the Hawaiian system, and the Inuit (Eskimo) system.

Because it is the most familiar to us, let us first consider the kinship terminology system employed in our own and many other commercial societies. But it is by no means confined to commercial societies. In fact, this system is found in many Inuit societies.

INUIT, OR ESKIMO, SYSTEM

The distinguishing features of the Inuit, or Eskimo, system (see Figure 18–7) are that all cousins are lumped together under the same term but are distinguished from brothers and sisters, and all aunts and uncles are lumped under the same terms but are distinguished from mother and father. In Figure 18–7 and in subsequent figures, the kin types that are referred to by the same term are colored and marked in the same way; for example, in the Inuit system, kin types 2 (father's brother) and 6 (mother's brother) are referred to by the same term (*uncle* in English). Note that in this system, in contrast to the others we will examine, no other relatives are generally referred to by the same terms used for members of the nuclear family—mother, father, brother, and sister.

The Inuit type of kinship terminology is not generally found where there are unilineal or ambilineal

descent groups; the only kin group that appears to be present is the bilateral kindred.[31] Remember that the kindred in a bilateral kinship system is an ego-centered group. Although relatives on both my mother's and my father's sides are equally important, my most important relatives are generally those closest to me. This is particularly true in our society, where the nuclear family generally lives alone, separated from and not particularly involved with other relatives except on ceremonial occasions. Because the nuclear family is most important, we would expect to find that the terminology for kin types in the nuclear family is different from the terminology for all other relatives. And the mother's and father's sides are equally important (or unimportant), so it makes sense that we use the same terms (*aunt, uncle,* and *cousin*) for both sides of the family.

OMAHA SYSTEM

The Omaha system of kin terminology is named after the Omaha of North America, but the system is found in many societies around the world, usually those with patrilineal descent.[32] Referring to Figure 18–8, we can see immediately which types of kin are lumped together in an Omaha system. First, father and father's brother (numbers 2 and 3) are both referred to by the same term. This way of classifying relatives contrasts markedly with ours, in which no term that applies to a member of the nuclear family (father, mother, brother, sister) is applied to any other relative. What could account for the Omaha system of lumping? One interpretation is that father and father's brother are lumped in this system because most societies in which this system is found have patrilineal kin groups. Both father and father's brother are in the parental generation of my patrilineal kin group and may behave

---

FIGURE 18–7 *Inuit (Eskimo) Terminology System*

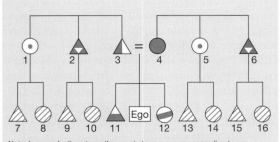

Note: In some Inuit systems the cousin term may vary according to sex. Kin types referred to by the same term are marked in the same way.

FIGURE 18–8 *Omaha Kinship Terminology System*

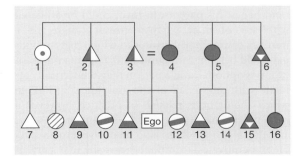

toward me similarly. My father's brother also probably lives near me, since patrilineal societies usually have patrilocal residence. The term for father and father's brother, then, might be translated "male member of my patrilineal kin group in my father's generation."

A second lumping, which at first glance appears similar to the lumping of father and father's brother, is that of mother and mother's sister (4 and 5), both of whom are called by the same term. But more surprisingly, mother's brother's daughter (16) is also referred to by this term. Why? If we think of the term as meaning "female member of my mother's patrilineage of *any* generation," then the term makes sense. Consistent with this view, all the male members of my mother's patrilineage of any generation (mother's brother, 6; mother's brother's son, 15) are also referred to by one term.

It is apparent, then, that relatives on the father's and the mother's sides are grouped differently in this system. For members of my mother's patrilineal kin group, I lump all male members together and all female members together regardless of their generation. Yet, for members of my father's patrilineal kin group, I have different terms for the male and female members of different generations. George Peter Murdock suggested that a society lumps kin types when there are more similarities than differences among them.[33]

Using this principle, and recognizing that societies with an Omaha system usually are patrilineal, I realize that my father's patrilineal kin group is the one to which I belong and in which I have a great many rights and obligations. Consequently, persons of my father's generation are likely to behave quite differently toward me than are persons of my own generation. Members of my patrilineal group in my father's generation are likely to exercise authority over me, and I am required to show them respect. Members of my patrilineal group in my own generation are those I am likely to play with as a child and to be friends with. Thus, in a patrilineal system, persons on my father's side belonging to different generations are likely to be distinguished. On the other hand, my mother's patrilineage is relatively unimportant to me (since I take my descent from my father). And because my residence is probably patrilocal, my mother's relatives will probably not even live near me. Thus, inasmuch as my mother's patrilineal relatives are comparatively unimportant in such a system, they become similar enough to be lumped together.

Finally, in the Omaha system, I refer to my male parallel cousins (my father's brother's son, 9, and my mother's sister's son, 13) in the same way I refer to my brother (number 11). I refer to my female parallel cousins (my father's brother's daughter, 10; and my mother's sister's daughter, 14) in the same way I refer to my sister (12). Considering that my father's brother and mother's sister are referred to by the same terms I use for my father and mother, this lumping of parallel cousins with **siblings** (brothers and sisters) is not surprising. If I call my own mother's and father's children (other than myself) "Brother" and "Sister," then the children of anyone whom I also call "Mother" and "Father" ought to be called "Brother" and "Sister" as well.

CROW SYSTEM

The Crow system, named after another North American culture, has been called the mirror image of the Omaha system. The same principles of lumping kin types are employed, except that the Crow system is associated with matrilineal descent,[34] so the individuals in my mother's matrilineal group (which is my own) are not lumped across generations, whereas the individuals in my father's matrilineal group are. Comparing Figure 18–9 with Figure 18–8, we find that the lumping and separating of kin types are much the same in both, except that the lumping across generations in the Crow system appears on the father's side rather than on the mother's side. In other words, I call both my mother and my mother's sister by the same term (since both are female members of my matrilineal descent group in my mother's generation). I call my father, my father's brother, and my father's sister's son by the same term (all male members of my father's matrilineal group in any generation). I call my father's sister and my father's sister's daughter by the same term (both female members of my father's matrilineal group).

FIGURE 18–9 *Crow Kinship Terminology System*

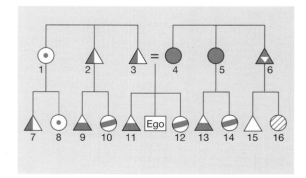

And I refer to my parallel cousins in the same way I refer to my brother and sister.

IROQUOIS SYSTEM

The Iroquois system, named after the Iroquois of North America, is similar to both the Omaha and Crow systems in the way in which I refer to relatives in my parents' generation (see Figure 18–10). That is, my father and my father's brother (2 and 3) are referred to by the same term, and my mother and my mother's sister (4 and 5) are referred to by the same term. However, the Iroquois system differs from the Omaha and Crow systems regarding my own generation. In the Omaha and Crow systems, one set of cross-cousins was lumped in the kinship terminology with the generation above. In the Iroquois system both sets of cross-cousins (mother's brother's children, 15 and 16; and father's sister's children, 7 and 8) are referred to by the same terms, distinguished by sex. That is, mother's brother's daughter and father's sister's daughter are both referred to by the same term. Also, mother's brother's son and father's sister's son are referred to by the same term. Parallel cousins always have terms different from those for cross-cousins and are sometimes, but not always, referred to by the same terms as one's brother and sister.

Like the Omaha and Crow systems, the Iroquois system has different terms for relatives on the father's and mother's sides. Such differentiation tends to be associated with unilineal descent, which is not surprising since unilineal descent involves affiliation with either mother's or father's kin. Why Iroquois, rather than Omaha or Crow, terminology occurs in a unilineal society requires explanation. One possible explanation is that Omaha or Crow is likely to occur in a developed, as opposed to a developing or decaying, unilineal system.[35] Another possibility is that Iroquois terminology emerges in societies that prefer marriage with both cross-cousins,[36] who are differentiated from other relatives in an Iroquois system.

SUDANESE SYSTEM

Unlike the Omaha, Crow, and Iroquois systems, the Sudanese system usually does not lump any relatives in the parents' and ego's generations. That is, the Sudanese system is usually a *descriptive system,* in which a different **descriptive term** is used for *each* of the relatives, as shown in Figure 18–11. What kinds of societies are likely to have such a system? Although societies with Sudanese terminology are likely to be patrilineal, they probably are different from most patrilineal societies that have Omaha or Iroquois terms. Sudanese terminology is associated with relatively great political complexity, class stratification, and occupational specialization. It has been suggested that under such conditions, a kinship system may reflect the need to make fine distinctions among members of descent groups who have different opportunities and privileges in the occupational or class system.[37]

The Omaha, Crow, Iroquois, and Sudanese systems, although different from one another and associated with somewhat different predictors, share one important feature: The terms used for the mother's and father's side of the family are not the same. If you imagine folding the kinship terminology diagrams in half, the two sides would not be the same. As we have seen in the Inuit system, however, the terms on the mother's and father's side of the family are *exactly* the same. This feature suggests that the two sides of the family are equally important or equally unimportant. The Hawaiian system also has the same terms on both sides, but kinship outside the nuclear family is more important.

HAWAIIAN SYSTEM

The Hawaiian system of kinship terminology is the least complex in that it uses the smallest number of terms. In this system, all relatives of the same sex in

FIGURE 18–10 *Iroquois Terminology System*

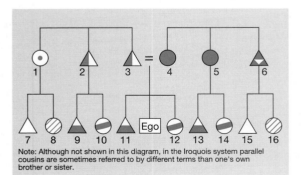

Note: Although not shown in this diagram, in the Iroquois system parallel cousins are sometimes referred to by different terms than one's own brother or sister.

FIGURE 18–11 *Sudanese Kinship Terminology System*

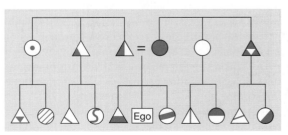

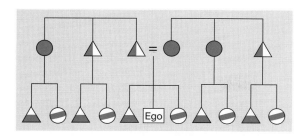

FIGURE 18–12 *Hawaiian Kinship Terminology System*

the same generation are referred to by the same term (see Figure 18–12). Thus, all my female cousins are referred to by the same term as my sister; all male cousins are referred to by the same term as my brother. Everyone known to be related to me in my parents' generation is referred to by one term if female (including my mother) and by another term if male (including my father).

The fact that societies with Hawaiian kin terminology tend not to have unilineal descent groups[38] helps explain why kinship terms are the same on both sides of the family. Why are the terms for mother, father, sister, and brother used for other relatives? Perhaps because societies with Hawaiian terminology are likely to have large extended families[39] to which every type of relative in Figure 18–12 may belong because of alternative (bilocal) residence patterns.[40] So, in contrast to our own society, many kin are very important, a fact that seems to be reflected in the practice of referring to other relatives with the same terms that are used for nuclear family members.

▦ SUMMARY

1. In our society, and in many other industrial societies, a newly married couple usually establishes a place of residence apart from parents or relatives (neolocal residence). But about 95 percent of the world's societies have some pattern of residence whereby the new couple settles within or very close to the household of the parents or some other close relative of the groom or bride.

2. The four major patterns in which married couples live with or near kinsmen are these:
   a. Patrilocal residence: The couple lives with or near the husband's parents (67 percent of all societies).
   b. Matrilocal residence: The couple lives with or near the wife's parents (15 percent of all societies).
   c. Bilocal residence: The couple lives with or near either the husband's parents or the wife's parents (7 percent of all societies).
   d. Avunculocal residence: The son and his wife settle with or near his mother's brother (4 percent of all societies).

3. In most societies in which kinship connections are important, a rule allocates each person to a particular and definable set of kin. The rules affiliating individuals with sets of kin are called rules of descent.

4. Rules of descent affiliate individuals with different sets of kin. There are only three known rules of descent:
   a. Patrilineal descent affiliates an individual with kin of both sexes related to him or her through men only. In each generation, then, children belong to the kin group of their father.
   b. Matrilineal descent affiliates an individual with kin related to her or him through women only. In each generation, then, children belong to the kin group of their mother.
   c. Ambilineal descent affiliates an individual with kin related to him or her through either men or women. Consequently, the descent groups show both female and male genealogical links.

5. Societies without lineal descent rules are bilateral societies. Relatives on both the mother's and father's sides of the family are of equal importance or, more usually, unimportance. Kindreds are ego-centered sets of kin who may be called together temporarily for some purpose.

6. With unilineal descent, patrilineal or matrilineal, people usually refer to themselves as belonging to a particular unilineal group or set of groups because they believe they share common descent in either the male or the female line. These people form what is called a unilineal descent group. There are several types:
   a. Lineages are sets of kin whose members trace descent from a common ancestor through known links.
   b. Clans are sets of kin who believe they are descended from a common ancestor but cannot specify the genealogical links.
   c. Phratries are groups of supposedly related clans.
   d. Moieties are said to exist when the whole society is divided into two unilineal descent groups without specified links to the supposed common ancestor of each.

7. Unilineal descent groups are most common in societies in the middle range of cultural complexity—that is, in noncommercial food-producing, as opposed to food-collecting, societies. In such societies, unilineal descent groups often have important functions in the social, economic, political, and religious realms of life.

8. Societies differ markedly in how they group or distinguish relatives under the same or different kinship terms. The major systems of terminology are the Inuit (Eskimo), Omaha, Crow, Iroquois, Sudanese, and Hawaiian systems.

GLOSSARY TERMS

affinal kin
ambilineal descent
avunculocal residence
bilateral kinship
bilocal residence
clan or sib
classificatory term
consanguineal kin
descriptive term
double descent or
    double unilineal
    descent
ego
kindred
lineage
matriclans

matrilineage
matrilineal descent
matrilocal residence
moiety
neolocal residence
patriclans
patrilineage
patrilineal descent
patrilocal residence
phratry
rules of descent
siblings
totem
unilocal residence
unilineal descent

CRITICAL QUESTIONS

1. What other things about our society would change if we practiced other than neolocal residence?

2. Why does kinship provide the main structure of social action in noncommercial societies?

3. Why might it be important for unilineal descent groups to be nonoverlapping in membership?

INTERNET EXERCISES

1. Read about kinship terminology in Medieval Western Europe at **http://kuhttp.cc.ukans.edu/kansas/orb/essays/text03.html**.

2. Many people who emigrate to another country become interested in identifying their ancestors. Tracing genealogies can be difficult, especially when naming systems are different from those you are used to. Look at h**ttp://www.geocities.com/Heartland/Plains/5100/na12.html** for a description of Norwegian naming and how it relates to genealogical reconstruction.

3. Learn more about kinship and social organization using the interactive Web site at **http://www.umanitoba.ca/faculties/arts/anthropology/tutor**. Use the tutorial to reinforce some of the concepts you may be having trouble with.

SUGGESTED READING

EMBER, M., AND EMBER, C. R. *Marriage, Family, and Kinship: Comparative Studies of Social Organization.* New Haven, CT: HRAF Press, 1983. A collection of reprinted cross-cultural and cross-species studies testing possible explanations of some aspects of human social organization. Relevant to this chapter are the studies of variation in marital residence and the development of unilineal descent.

MURDOCK, G. P. *Social Structure.* New York: Macmillan, 1949. A pioneering cross-cultural analysis of variation in aspects of social organization, including the family and marriage, kin groups, kinship terminology, the incest taboo and its extensions, and the regulation of sex.

PASTERNAK, B. "Family and Household: Who Lives Where, Why Does It Vary, and Why Is It Important?" In C. R. Ember and M. Ember, *Cross-Cultural Research for Social Science.* Upper Saddle River, NJ: Prentice Hall, 1998. Prentice Hall/Simon & Schuster Custom Publishing. The first part of this chapter, written especially for undergraduates, discusses the variation in marital residence practices.

PASTERNAK, B., EMBER, C. R., AND EMBER, M. *Sex, Gender and Kinship: A Cross-Cultural Perspective.* Upper Saddle River, NJ: Prentice Hall, 1997. An up-to-date review and discussion of cross-cultural studies of sex, gender, marriage, family and kinship. See particularly Chapter 12.

Associations and Interest Groups

CHAPTER OUTLINE

Nonvoluntary Associations

Voluntary Associations

Explaining Variation in Associations

amuel Johnson, the eighteenth-century English author, was once asked to describe James Boswell, his companion and biographer. "Boswell," he boomed, "is a very clubable man." Johnson did not mean that Boswell deserved to be attacked with bludgeons. He was referring to Boswell's fondness for all sorts of clubs and associations, a fondness he shared with many of his contemporaries. The tendency to form associations was not unique to eighteenth-century England. At all times and in all areas of the world, we find evidence of human beings' "clubability."

The notion of clubs may make us think of something extracurricular and not very important, but associations play very important roles in the economy and political life of many societies. In this chapter we examine the various kinds of associations formed in different societies, how these groups function, and what general purposes they serve. When we speak of **associations,** we mean different kinds of groups that are not based on kinship, as discussed in the preceding chapter, or on territory, which we take up in the next chapter. Associations, then, are nonkin and nonterritorial groups; and, although they vary, they also have several common characteristics: (1) some kind of formal, institutionalized structure; (2) the exclusion of some people; (3) members with common interests or purposes; and (4) members with a discernible sense of pride and feeling of belonging. Contemporary American society has an abundance of *interest groups*—to use the terminology of the political scientist—that display these general characteristics of associations. Such groups vary considerably in size and social significance, ranging from national organizations such as the Democratic and Republican parties to more local organizations such as college sororities and fraternities.

But societies differ considerably in the degree to which they have such associations and, if they do have them, in what kind they have. To make our discussion somewhat easier, we focus on two dimensions of how associations vary from one society to another. One is whether or not recruitment into the association is voluntary. In U.S. society, with the exception of the government's right to draft men into the military, just about all associations are voluntary—that is, people can choose to join or not join. But in many societies, particularly the more egalitarian ones, membership is nonvoluntary: All people of a particular category must belong.

MEMBERSHIP CRITERIA	RECRUITMENT	
	Voluntary	*Nonvoluntary*
Universally ascribed		Age-sets Most unisex associations
Variably ascribed	Ethnic associations Regional associations	Conscripted army
Achieved	Occupational associations Political parties Special interest groups	

TABLE 19–1 *Some Examples of Associations*

A second dimension of variation in associations is what qualifies a person for membership. There are two possible kinds of qualifications: those that are achieved and those that are ascribed. **Achieved qualities** are those a person acquires during his or her lifetime, such as superior skills in a sport or the skills required to be an electrician. **Ascribed qualities** are those determined for a person at birth, either because of genetic makeup (for instance, sex) or because of family background (ethnicity, place of birth, religion, social class). We speak of two kinds of ascribed qualities or characteristics: **universally ascribed qualities,** those that are found in all societies, such as age and sex; and **variably ascribed qualities,** those that are found only in some societies, such as ethnic, religious, or social class differences.

Table 19–1 gives these two dimensions of variation in associations—voluntary versus nonvoluntary recruitment and criteria for membership—and some kinds of associations that fit neatly into our classification. Some associations do not fit so neatly—for example, the criteria that qualify someone for Girl Scout membership include an interest in joining, an achieved quality, as well as biological sex, an ascribed characteristic.

NONVOLUNTARY ASSOCIATIONS

Although complex societies may have nonvoluntary associations, such associations are more characteristic of relatively unstratified or egalitarian societies. In relatively unstratified societies, associations tend to be based on the universally ascribed characteristics of age and sex. Such associations take two forms: age-sets and male or female (unisex) associations.

AGE-SETS

All societies use a vocabulary of age terms, just as they use a vocabulary of kinship terms. For instance, as we distinguish among *brother, uncle,* and *cousin,* so we differentiate *infant, adolescent,* and *adult. Age terms* refer to categories based on age, or age-grades. An **age-grade** is simply a category of persons who happen to fall within a particular culturally distinguished age range. **Age-set,** on the other hand, is the term for a group of persons of similar age and the same sex who move through some or all of life's stages together. For example, all the boys of a certain age range in a particular district might simultaneously become ceremonially initiated into "manhood." Later in life, the group as a whole might become "elders," and still later "retired elders." Entry into an age-set system is generally nonvoluntary and is based on the universally ascribed characteristics of sex and age.

Kinship forms the basis of the organization and administration of most noncommercial societies. In some noncommercial societies, however, age-sets crosscut kinship ties and form strong supplementary bonds. Two such societies are the Karimojong of East Africa and the Shavante of Brazil.

KARIMOJONG AGE-SETS. The Karimojong number some 60,000 people. Predominantly cattle herders, they occupy about 4,000 acres of semiarid country in northeastern Uganda. Their society is especially interesting because of its organization into combinations of age-sets and generation-sets. These groupings provide "both the source of political authority and the main field within which it is exercised."[1]

A Karimojong age-set comprises all the men who have been initiated into manhood within a span of about five to six years. A generation-set consists of a combination of five such age-sets, covering 25 to 30 years. Each generation-set is seen as "begetting" the one that immediately follows it, and at any one time two generation-sets are in existence. The senior unit—whose members perform the administrative, judicial, and priestly functions—is closed; the junior unit, whose members serve as warriors and police, continues to recruit. When all five age-sets

Some circumstances have changed, but the age-sets of the Nandi of Kenya still have importance. This young Nandi man (in a suit) is told by a traditional spiritual leader (in a skin cloak): "In the past, when our young warriors went out for the first time, we gave them spears and shields and told them to bring back wealth to the community. Today we give you a pen and paper and ask the same."

in the junior generation-set are established, that generation-set will be ready—actually impatient—to assume the status of its senior predecessor. Eventually, grumbling but realistic, the elders agree to a succession ceremony, moving those who were once in a position of obedience to a position of authority.

Once initiated, a boy has become a man, one with a clearly defined status and the ultimate certainty of exercising full authority together with his set partners. Indeed, a Karimojong is not expected to marry—and is certainly barred from starting a family—until he has been initiated. The initiation ceremony itself illustrates the essential political and social characteristics of the age-set system. Without the authority of the elders, the ceremony cannot be held; throughout the proceedings their authority is explicit. The father-son relationship of adjacent generation-sets is emphasized, for fathers are initiating their sons.

The Karimojong age system, then, comprises a cyclical succession of four generation-sets in a predetermined continuing relationship. The *retired generation-set* consists of elders who have passed on the mantle of authority, since most of the five age-sets within the retired generation-set are depleted, if not defunct. The *senior generation-set* contains the five age-sets that actively exercise authority. The *junior generation-set* is still recruiting members and, although obedient to elders, has some administrative powers. The *noninitiates* are starting a generation-set. Figure 19–1 illustrates the Karimojong age system.

SHAVANTE AGE-SETS. The Shavante inhabit the Mato Grasso region of Brazil. Right into the middle of the twentieth century they were hostile to Brazilians of European ancestry who tried to move into their territory. It was not until the 1950s that peaceful contact with the 2,000 or so Shavante was achieved. Although the Shavante practice some agriculture, they rely primarily on food collection. Wild roots, nuts, and fruits are their staple foods, and hunting is their passion.[2] The Shavante have villages, but they rarely stay in them for more than a few weeks at a time. Instead they make frequent community treks lasting 6 to 24 weeks to hunt or collect. They spend no more than four weeks a year at their gardens, which are located at least a day's journey from the villages.

Age-sets are an extremely important part of Shavante society, particularly for males. Boys emerge from the status of childhood when they are formally inducted into a named age-set and take up residence in the "bachelor hut." An induction ceremony takes

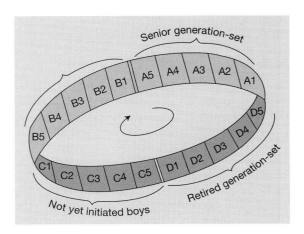

FIGURE 19–1

The Karimojong age system is composed of four distinct generation-sets (labeled A, B, C, and D in this diagram), which succeed each other cyclically. Each generation-set, in turn, is divided into five age-sets or potential age-sets. The senior generation-set (A) exercises authority. The junior age set (B), the warriors and policemen, is still recruiting. Generation-set D consists of retired age-sets. Noninitiated and not-yet-born boys constitute the potential age-sets C1–C5.

place every five years, and boys from seven to twelve years of age are inducted at the same time. The five-year period of residence in the bachelor hut is relatively free of responsibility. The boys' families provide food for them, and they go out hunting and collecting when they feel like it. But during their residence, the boys are instructed in hunting, weapon making, and ceremonial skills. At the end of the five years, an elaborate series of initiation ceremonies marks the boys' entry into a different status—that of "young men." The day they emerge from the bachelor hut for the last time, during the final rites of initiation, the whole age-set is married, each to a young girl, usually not yet mature, chosen by the boys' parents. Marriages cannot be consummated at this time, because the young men must wait until their wives are more mature. When the ceremonies are over, the young men make war clubs, for now they are thought of as the warriors of the community, and they earn the privilege of sitting in the evening village council. But they have no authority at this stage and few responsibilities.

The next stage is that of the "mature men," and when an age-set is inducted into this stage the members begin to experience some authority. It is in the mature men's council that important community decisions are made. This last status position

The Masai, who have age-sets, initiate boys in groups.

actually consists of five consecutive age-sets, because new age-sets are formed every five years and each one continues in existence until the death of its members. Among the mature men the oldest sets are considered senior to the younger ones. Members of the most junior mature men's age-set rarely talk in the council; they assert themselves more as they progress in the system.

In contrast to the Karimojong, who have age-sets just for males, the Shavante also have them for females. Shavante girls are inducted into an age-set when boys about their age enter the bachelor hut, but they belong to the age-set in name only. They do not participate in the bachelor hut, nor do they have their own equivalent; they are not initiated; and they cannot participate in the village council, which makes community decisions. About the only thing the age-set gives girls is occasional participation with males in a few ceremonies. For Shavante women, then, the age-set system does not function as an association.

UNISEX ASSOCIATIONS

Unisex, as used here, has quite a different meaning from its current connotation in our own society, where it signifies something that is suitable for both sexes. We use **unisex** to describe a type of association that restricts its membership to one sex, usually male. Sex as a qualification is directly related to the purpose of the unisex association. In many male unisex associations, this purpose is to strengthen the concept of male superiority and to offer men a refuge from females. In noncommercial societies, men's associations are similar to age-sets, except that there are only two sets, or stages—mature males, who are association members, and immature males, who are nonmembers. Like societies with age-sets, societies with male unisex associations are very

likely to have traumatic and dramatic male ceremonies initiating males into the group of "mature" men. We discuss these ceremonies further in the chapter on psychology and culture.

In most noncommercial societies, women have few associations perhaps because in such societies the men are dominant in the kinship, property, and political spheres of life. (There is also the possibility that anthropologists, most of whom were men, have given women's associations less attention than men's associations.) In some partly commercialized economies, such as in West Africa, women's associations are more common.[3] Unisex associations or clubs are also a feature of very industrialized societies. The Boy Scouts and the Kiwanis, the Girl Scouts and the League of Women Voters, are cases in point. Joining these clubs, however, is voluntary; in noncommercial and less complex societies, membership is more often nonvoluntary.

MAE ENGA BACHELOR ASSOCIATIONS. The Mae Enga are a subgroup of about 30,000 sedentary horticulturalists living in the New Guinea highlands. Anthropologists have paid a great deal of attention to their society because of its practice of sexual segregation—indeed, the strain of active hostility toward women that runs through its culture.[4] It is the custom for Mae men to live in a separate, communal house. Up to the age of 5, a young boy is permitted to live in his mother's house, although he is unconsciously aware of the "distance" between his father and mother. As he grows older, this awareness is made explicit by his father and elder clansmen. It is undesirable, he is told, to be so much in the company of women; it is better that he join the menfolk in their house and in their activities. As the boy grows up, the need to avoid contact with women is made abundantly clear to him. He is told that contact with menstrual blood or menstruating

New Perspectives on Gender

DO SEPARATE WOMEN'S ASSOCIATIONS INCREASE WOMEN'S STATUS AND POWER?

Some women's associations, like those of the Ijaw of southern Nigeria, are reported to have considerable power. Do women generally have more power where women create and join their own associations? We might assume that the existence of such organizations would increase the status of women overall, or at least lead to more equality with men. But it could also be argued the other way around, that "separate" does not generally lead to more equality; it may just increase separateness. As far as we know, researchers have not yet tried to assess the cross-cultural effect of women's associations on female status in various domains of life, but there has been one cross-cultural attempt to see if the presence of women's associations predicts various aspects of women's participation in the political process.

Marc Howard Ross looked at four aspects of women's political participation: (1) the degree of inequality between women's and men's participation in public or community decision making; (2) the degree to which women participate in politics privately; (3) the degree to which women have access to positions of authority; and (4) the degree to which women have separate associations that are under their exclusive control. It is this last domain that concerns us here. Does the presence of separate women's associations increase women's participation in public decision making and their access to positions of authority? Ross's cross-cultural data indicate that the answer is no. The presence of separate women's organizations *does not* generally increase the participation of women in public decision making, their access to positions of authority, or even their private participation in politics. This is not to say that women in organizations do not have influence. They do, but probably only or mainly within their organizations. The influence of women in their organiza-

tions, however, does not carry over into other political arenas.

Of course, we might need to consider other possible factors in future research. Perhaps women's participation in political arenas is more likely if female organizations control important economic resources. Such resources may give women more leverage politically. Also, some types of female organizations may have more power than others; for example, stand-alone organizations may have more power than those that are connected to male organizations. But it is also possible that adding these additional conditions would not change the basic finding: Separate female organizations—perhaps because they *are* separate—do not have any impact on women's participation in other political arenas.

Recently, people in the United States have started to discuss a related issue, the possible effects of female "separateness" on women's success. For example, do separate math and science classes for women lead to more equality between women and men in

women, if not countered by magic rites, can "pollute" a man. It can "corrupt his vital juices so that his skin darkens and wrinkles and his flesh wastes, permanently dull his wits, and eventually lead to a slow decline and death."[5]

Because Mae culture regards a woman as potentially unclean, to say the least, it enforces strict codes of male-female behavior. These codes are designed to safeguard male integrity, strength, and possession of crops and other property. So strict are these regulations that many young men are reluctant to marry. But the elders do try to impress upon the young men their duty to marry and reproduce. The men's association attempts to regulate the males' sexual re-

lationships. The association is said to have several purposes: to cleanse and strengthen its members; to promote their growth; to make them attractive to women; and, most important, to supervise contact between the sexes so that ultimately the "right" wives are procured for the men and the "right" children are born into the clan.

By the time he is 15 or 16, a Mae youth has joined the village bachelors' association. He agrees to take scrupulous care neither to copulate with a woman nor to accept food from her hands. As a club member, he will participate in the *sanggai* rituals. Bachelors, under the supervision of senior club members, go into seclusion, in a clubhouse deep in

academic performance, in obtaining advanced degrees in math and science, and in access to high-paying positions in those areas? It is well known that women are very underrepresented in the math and physical science professions in the United States. Only 11 percent of persons who hold doctorates in physics and 16 percent in computer science are women; but in the social sciences and humanities the numbers of men and women are approximately equal.

These differences could be mostly a result of social conditions that discourage females in various subjects and professions. Researchers have found that teachers of math and science pay more attention to boys. When boys give wrong answers, teachers are apt to challenge them; when girls give wrong answers, teachers tend to express sympathy. Boys are more likely to operate scientific equipment; girls are more likely to take notes. In the seventh grade, girls perform similarly to boys in math and science, but girls display less confidence in their abilities. By the time

they graduate from high school, women have taken fewer math and science courses, so they are at a disadvantage for continuing in those fields.

If the dampening effects on women are social, or mostly social, what can be done? Because current research suggests that girls do best in learning science and math without boys, some researchers have advocated separate math and science activities (classes and clubs). So, for example, voluntary girls' clubs (Operation SMART) have been set up in 240 locations to interest elementary and junior high school girls in science. A majority of the girls from those schools voluntarily attend. Moreover, many of them now say they want to go into science. Whether they stay in science, or how well they do if they stay, is not clear yet. But if these programs work, we would have to conclude that "separate" is more equal than "together."

The two situations we have described here do not seem to be parallel in their effects on women's status. Separate wo-

men's associations by themselves do not make for equality between the genders in political participation. But separate training for girls in math and science may make for more equality. What is different about the two situations? At least one thing is different. Separate women's associations are usually nonvoluntary; women more or less have to join because that's how the society structures what women can do. Separate training for females in math and science is usually voluntary; girls may opt for the separateness in order to acquire the skills and the confidence they need to move into arenas *open* to both genders. In other words, when achievement and not gender defines how far you can go, temporary separateness for women might increase the likelihood of gender equality in professions that do not have it now.

Sources: Marc Howard Ross, "Female Political Participation: A Cross-Cultural Explanation," *American Anthropologist,* 88 (1986): 843–58; "Women in Science '93: Gender and the Culture of Science," *Science,* April 16, 1993, 383–430.

the forest, to undergo "purification." During four days of "exercises," which are similar in purpose to those of a religious retreat, each youth observes additional prohibitions to protect himself from all forms of sexuality and impurity. For instance, pork is denied him (women have cared for the pigs), and he may not look at the ground during excursions into the forest, lest he see feminine footprints or pig feces. His body will be scrubbed, and his dreams discussed and interpreted. Finally, together with his club, now restored to purity and reprotected at least for a while against contamination, he will participate in organized dances and feasting with his chosen female partner.

The *sanggai* festivals afford the entire clan an opportunity to display its size, solidarity, and magnificence to its enemies, whom on other occasions it fights. Hostility toward women may not be surprising in view of the fact that a man's wife and mother come from neighboring clans (the Mae clan villages are exogamous) perpetually in conflict with his own. Male-female hostility, then, seems to reflect the broader, interclan hostility. The Mae have a succinct way of describing the situation: "We marry the people we fight."[6]

Men's houses, and occasionally women's, are found among many peoples, especially in Melanesia, Polynesia, Africa, and South America. Men's associations generally involve bachelors, although older married men will often come by to instruct the youngsters and pass on the benefits of their experience. In more militant days, men's houses acted as fortresses and arsenals—even as sanctuaries for fugitives. By and large, they serve to strengthen, certainly to symbolize, male power and solidarity. As do age-sets, men's clubs often provide ties that cut across and supplement kinship bonds. Hence, they permit a given group of men in a given society to act together toward the realization of mutually agreed-upon objectives, irrespective of kin relationships.

PORO AND SANDE. There is usually some secrecy in all associations, as in social life in general. In the examples we have discussed, many of the details of male initiation ceremonies usually are kept secret. But more secrecy seems to be required in the *Poro* and *Sande* associations of West Africa. The Poro and Sande associations exist in several cultural groups that speak Mande languages and are located in what is now Liberia, Sierra Leone, the Ivory Coast, and Guinea. In Guinea, the Poro and the Sande have been declared illegal, but in the other countries they are not only legal, they are an integral part of local political structure. Membership in them is public and nonvoluntary; all men in the community must belong to the Poro, and all women must belong to the Sande.[7]

Where the Poro and the Sande associations are legal, the community has two political structures—the "secular" and the "sacred." The secular structure consists of the town chief, neighborhood and kin group headmen, and elders. The sacred structure, or *Zo,* consists of the hierarchies of "priests" in the Poro and Sande associations. Among the Kpelle of Liberia, for example, the Poro and Sande Zo take turns in assuming responsibility for dealing with in-town fighting, murder, rape, incest, and disputes over land.

So in what sense are the Poro and Sande secret? If all adults belong to them, their membership and what they do can hardly be described as secret. Furthermore, anthropologists have not only written about these associations; some have even joined them. Beryl Bellman, who joined the Poro of the Kpelle,[8] suggested that what is "secret" about these associations is the necessity for members to learn to keep secrets, particularly about how people are initiated into membership. Only when people learn to keep secrets are they considered trustworthy for participation in political life.

The Poro leadership establishes the place where the initiates will undergo scarification and live in seclusion for about a year (formerly it was three or four years). The boys are taken out of town, where they engage in a mock battle with a *ngamu* (a member of the Poro masquerading as a forest devil) who incises marks on their necks, chests, and backs. These marks symbolize being killed and eaten by the devil; but then the initiates are "reborn." In the initiation "village" outside of town, the boys learn crafts, hunting, and the use of basic medicines. The children of the Zo are given special instruction so that they can take over the rituals from their fathers. Some are trained to perform as "devils." At the end of the year, the initiates are given Poro names, by which they will be known from then on. Secrecy is attached to events surrounding the initiates; everyone knows that the boys are not killed and eaten by the devil, but only some can speak of it. For example, women must say that the boys are in the devil's stomach; if they say otherwise, they might be killed in punishment.[9]

The initiation of females into the Sande (every seven years or so) also involves taking the initiates into the forest for a year (formerly three years). The girls not only undergo scarification; they also undergo a clitoridectomy, that is, the removal of the clitoris. Like the boys, the girls receive training in adult activities. In the years just before and during the Sande initiation, the women are responsible for the moral behavior of the community. Persons who commit crimes are first brought before the women. If a man is the accused, he is tried by the Poro Zo, but a portion of any fine is given to the women.[10]

The Poro and Sande Zo are held in great respect, and the devils are viewed with fear and awe for the powers they possess. Some authors suggest that fear of the Poro and the Sande strengthens the hands of secular political authority, because chiefs and landowners occupy the most powerful positions in the associations.[11]

Secret associations are common in many areas of the world—the Pacific, North and South America, as well as various parts of Africa—although they may be voluntary organizations in some places. In Africa, according to a recent cross-cultural study, secret associations are usually involved in political activities, as are the Poro and Sande. These activities punish persons who, according to the secret society, have committed some wrongs. The fact that the punished persons almost never seem to be members of the native elite or foreign rulers supports the observation about the Poro and Sande that they typically strengthen the hand of existing political authority.[12]

IJAW WOMEN'S ASSOCIATIONS. Among the Ijaw of southern Nigeria, only women in the northern part of this society are organized into associations. In one northern Ijaw village there are seven women's associations.[13] Once a married woman shows herself capable of supporting a household independent of her mother-in-law, which she does by engaging in marketing and trading, she has to belong to the women's association linked to her husband's patrilineage. Membership in such an association is nonvoluntary; all eligible women must join, and members are fined if they do not come to meetings or arrive late.

The women's associations act as mediators in disputes and impose punishments even in cases that have gone to court. For example, an association may impose fines for "crimes" such as defaming a woman's character or adultery. An association may also adopt rules for proper behavior. Judgments and rules are arrived at by consensus of all the women members. If a punished member does not accept a judgment, the other members might get together and taunt the woman or take some important item from her house and refuse to have anything to do with her.

Some of the larger associations also act as lending institutions, using their cash reserves from fines to lend to members or nonmembers at an interest rate of 50 percent or more. Even a male in debt to the association might be held captive in his own house until he pays his debt. It is no wonder, then, that few resist an association's judgment for long. Although it is not clear why women's associations such as the Ijaw's are common in West Africa, one of the factors that may have been important is the women's participation in marketing and trade, which allows

them to be financially independent of men. We shall see in the next section that women are increasingly forming voluntary self-help groups to improve themselves economically.

VOLUNTARY ASSOCIATIONS

Voluntary associations, such as the military associations of the Cheyenne of North America, may be found in some relatively simple societies. But voluntary associations tend to be more common in stratified and complex societies, presumably because stratified societies are composed of people with many different, and often competing, interests. We deal here with some examples of voluntary associations that are not familiar in American experience.

MILITARY ASSOCIATIONS

Military associations in noncommercial societies may be compared to our own American Legion or Veterans of Foreign War Posts. They all seem to exist to unite members through their common experiences as warriors, to glorify the activities of war, and to perform certain services for the community. Membership in such associations is usually voluntary and based on the achieved criterion of participation in war. Among the North American Plains Indians, military societies were common. The Cheyenne, for example, had military associations that were not ranked by age, but were open to any boy or man ready to go to war.[14]

In the beginning of the nineteenth century the Cheyenne had five military associations: the Fox,

Women sometimes have associations too. An N'jembe women's group in Gabon initiates young women into the group.

Dog, Shield, Elk (or Hoof Rattle), and Bowstring (or Contrary). The last-named association was annihilated by the Pawnee in the middle of the nineteenth century. Later, two new associations were established, the Wolf and Northern Crazy Dogs. Although the various associations may have had different costumes, songs, and dances, they were alike in their internal organization, each being headed by four leaders who were among the most important war chiefs.

When various Plains groups were confined to reservations, the military associations lost many of their old functions, but they did not entirely disappear. For example, among the Lakota, warrior societies continue to be an important part of social life because many men and women have engaged in military activity on behalf of the United States in World Wars I and II, in Korea and Vietnam, and in Desert Storm. Returning soldiers continue to be welcomed with traditional songs of honor and victory dances.[15]

REGIONAL ASSOCIATIONS

Regional associations bring together migrants from a common geographic background. Thus, they are often found in urban centers, which traditionally have attracted settlers from rural areas. In the United States, for example, migrants from rural Appalachia have formed associations in Chicago and Detroit. Many of these organizations have become vocal political forces in municipal government. Regional associations often form even when migrants have come from a considerable distance. For example, in the Chinatowns of the United States and Canada, there are many associations based on district of origin in China as well as on surname. The regional and family organizations are in turn incorporated into more inclusive ethnic associations, as we shall see later in this chapter.[16]

William Mangin described the role of regional associations in helping rural migrants adapt to

Research Frontiers

WHY DO STREET GANGS DEVELOP, AND WHY ARE THEY VIOLENT?

The street gangs of young people that we read and hear about so often are voluntary associations. They are a little like age-sets in that the members are all about the same age, but they are unlike age-sets in being voluntary and they do not "graduate" through life stages together. Nobody has to join, although there may be strong social pressure to join the neighborhood gang. Gangs have a clear set of values, goals, roles, group functions, symbols, and initiations. Street gangs are also often like military associations in their commitment to violence in the defense of gang interests.

Violent street gangs are found in many U.S. cities, particularly in poor neighborhoods. But poverty alone does not appear sufficient to explain the existence of gangs. For example, there is

plenty of poverty in Mexico, but gangs did not develop there. In Mexico there was a *palomilla* (age-cohort) tradition; age-mates hung out together and continued their friendship well into adulthood, but there were no gangs as we know them. Mexican American gangs did develop in the *barrios* of cities such as Los Angeles. When we realize that *most* youths in poor neighborhoods do not join gangs, it is clear that poor neighborhoods cannot explain gangs. It is estimated that only 3 to 10 percent of Mexican American young people join gangs.

But why do some young people join and not others? If we look at who joins a gang, it seems to be those children who are subject to the most domestic stress. The gang "joiners" are

likely to come from poor families, have several siblings, and have no father in the household. They seem to have had difficulty in school and have gotten into trouble early. What about gangs appeals to them? Most adolescents in this country have a difficult time deciding who they are and what kind of person they want to be, but young people who join gangs seem to have more identity problems. One 18-year-old said he "joined the gang for my ego to go higher," reflecting a low self-esteem. Those who are raised in female-centered households seem to be looking for a way to show how "masculine" they are. They look up to the tough male street gang members and want to act like them. But getting into a gang requires initiation. Most gangs have their own stylized rituals; for example, Mexican American gangs physi-

urban life in Lima, Peru.[17] During the 1950s, Mangin studied a group of migrants from the rural mountains, the *serranos* from Ancash. Typically these *serranos,* about 120,000 in number, lived in a slumlike urban settlement called a *barriada.* The *barriada* was not officially recognized by either the national government or the city authorities. Accordingly, it lacked all usual city services, such as water supply, garbage removal, and police protection. Its inhabitants had left their rural birthplaces for reasons typical of such population movements, wherever they occur. These reasons were social and economic; most were related to population and land pressure, but the higher expectations associated with the big city—better education, social mobility, wage labor—were also compelling considerations.

Typically also, the *serranos* from Ancash formed a regional association. Club membership was open to both sexes. Men generally controlled the executive positions, and club leaders were often men who had achieved political power in their hometowns. Women, who had relatively less economic and social freedom, nevertheless played an important part in club activities.

The *serrano* regional association performed three main services for its members. First, it lobbied the central government on matters of community importance—for example, the supplying of sewers, clinics, and similar public services. A club member had to follow a piece of legislation through the channels of government to make certain it was not forgotten or abandoned. Second, the *serrano* association assisted in acculturating newly arrived *serranos* to the urban life in Lima. The most noticeable rural traits—coca chewing, and hairstyle and clothing peculiarities—were the first to disappear, with the men generally able to adapt faster than the women. The association also provided opportunities for fuller contact with the national culture. And finally, the group organized social activities such as

cally beat the initiate, who must show bravery and courage. As happens in most initiation ceremonies, the gang initiate identifies even more strongly with the group afterward. So, belonging to a gang may make some youths feel as if they belong to something important. This is a kind of psychological adjustment, but is it adaptive? Does being in a gang help such youths survive in a neighborhood where young men are often killed? Or are gang members *less* likely to survive? We really don't know the answers to those questions.

Why did gangs develop in the United States and not in Mexico? Were there some things different about life for Mexican Americans in the cities of the United States? Life in the United States was more difficult in several respects. First, many Mexican immigrants had to settle for very low pay and housing in marginal areas of the city. Second, they were subject to a lot of social and job discrimination. Third, they were immersed in a new culture that differed in many ways from their own. The young people who were least able to cope with these stresses were probably most likely to join gangs. But what explains the culture of violence of these gangs? Some scholars have suggested that the need to show exaggerated "masculine" behavior is a response to the absence of male models in the household. The association of many young men who have this same need may explain the violence of gangs. If aggressiveness is part of the male role (for example, until recently only males were allowed to engage in military combat), then a young man who wants to exhibit his masculinity may be extremely aggressive.

We need much more research to uncover why gangs develop more often in some societies than in others, and why they often are violent. Are there places where aggressiveness is not so much part of the male role, and are they therefore less likely to have violent gangs?

Sources: James Diego Vigil, "Group Processes and Street Identity: Adolescent Chicano Gang Members," *Ethos,* 16 (1988): 421–45; James Diego Vigil, "Mexican Americans: Growing Up on the Streets of Los Angeles," in Melvin Ember, Carol R. Ember, and David Levinson, eds., *Portraits of Culture: Ethnographic Originals* (Upper Saddle River, NJ: Prentice Hall, 1998), Prentice Hall/Simon & Schuster Custom Publishing; Carol R. Ember and Melvin Ember, "Issues in Cross-Cultural Studies of Interpersonal Violence," *Violence and Victims,* 8 (1994): 217–33.

fiestas, acted as the clearinghouse for information transmitted to and from the home area, and supplied a range of other services to help migrants adapt to their new environment while retaining ties to their birthplace.

The functions of regional associations may change over time as social conditions change. For example, during the plantation period in Hawaii, many Filipino migrants joined hometown associations that served as mutual aid societies. As more and more Filipinos went to Hawaii, however, more people had kin to whom they could turn. The hometown associations continue to have some economic functions, such as assistance in times of emergency, serious illness, or death, and some scholarship aid, but meetings are infrequent and most members do not attend. Those members who are active seem to want the recognition and prestige that can be attained through leadership positions in the hometown association, which is much more than they can achieve in the wider Hawaiian arena.[18]

Although regional clubs may help to integrate their members into a more complex urban or changing environment, the presence of many such groups may increase divisiveness and rivalry among groups. In some areas the smaller groups have banded together and become quite powerful. For example, within each Chinatown of a major U.S. or Canadian city, the various regional and family associations formed a Chinese Benevolent Association. This larger association, usually controlled by the wealthiest Chinese merchants, acts to oversee business, settle disputes, and organize against discrimination from the outside.[19] Thus, by banding together, the regional and family associations formed ethnic associations.

ETHNIC ASSOCIATIONS

Various types of ethnic associations or interest groups are found in cities all over the world. Membership in these associations is based largely on ethnicity. Ethnic associations are particularly widespread in urban centers of West Africa. There, accelerated cultural change, reflected in altered economic arrangements, in technological advances, and in new urban living conditions, has weakened kinship relations and other traditional sources of support and solidarity.[20] Sometimes it is difficult to say whether a particular association is ethnic or regional in origin; it may be both.

Tribal unions are frequently found in Nigeria and Ghana. These are typical of most such associations in that they are extraterritorial—that is, they recruit members who have left their tribal locations; also, they have a formal constitution, and they have been formed to meet certain needs arising out of conditions of urban life. One such need is to keep

In most major cities with Chinatowns, as in San Francisco, many regional and family associations merged together to form larger associations, like Hop Sing Tong, a fraternal organization established in 1870 that acted to oversee business, settle disputes, and fight against discrimination.

members in touch with their traditional culture. The Ibo State Union, for example, in addition to providing mutual aid and financial support in case of unemployment, sickness, or death, performs the service "of fostering and keeping alive an interest in tribal song, history, language and moral beliefs and thus maintaining a person's attachment to his native town or village."[21] Some tribal unions collect money to improve conditions in their ancestral homes. Education, for example, is an area of particular concern. Others publish newsletters that report members' activities. Most unions have a young membership that exercises a powerful democratizing influence in tribal councils, and the organizations provide a springboard for those with national political aspirations.

West African occupational clubs also fall into the ethnic category. African versions of trade unions, organized along tribal as well as craft lines, their principal concern is the status and remuneration of their members as workers. The Motor Drivers' Union of Keta, in Ghana, was formed to fund insurance and legal costs, to contribute to medical care in case of accident or illness, and to help pay for funeral expenses.

Friendly societies differ from tribal unions in that their objectives are confined for the most part to mutual aid. Such a club was formed by the wives of Kru migrants in Freetown, Sierra Leone. Kru men normally go to sea, still a hazardous occupation. The club is classified into three grades. An admission fee permits entry into the lowest grade. Elevation to higher grades depends on further donations. At the death of a member or her husband, the family receives a lump sum commensurate with her status in the club.[22]

ROTATING CREDIT ASSOCIATIONS

A common type of mutual aid society is the *rotating credit association*. The basic principle is that each member of the group agrees to make a regular contribution, in money or in kind, to a fund, which is then handed over to each member in rotation.[23] The regular contributions promote savings by each member, but the lump sum distribution enables the recipient to do something significant with the money. These associations are found in many areas of East, South and Southeast Asia, Africa (particularly West Africa), and the West Indies.[24] They usually include a small number of people, perhaps between 10 or 30, so that rotations do not take that long. The associations are usually informal and may last only as long as one rotation.

How do these systems work? What prevents someone from quitting after getting a lump sum? Ethnographic evidence indicates that defaulting on regular contributions is so rare that participants consider it unthinkable. Once a person joins a rotating credit association, there is strong social pressure to continue paying regularly. If a person needs money for an emergency, the association can change the order of rotation. A person who joins does not have to fill out paperwork, as in a bank. All that is needed is a reputation for trustworthiness. There is often a social component to the association. Some have regular meetings with socializing and entertainment.[25]

The principle of a rotating credit association often has roots in traditional sharing systems. For example, among the Kikuyu, related women would work together to weed or harvest each other's fields in turn. When a person had special expenses, such as a funeral, there would be a contribution party and everyone who came would make a contribution. Nici Nelson describes a very successful rotating credit association that developed in a squatter area of Nairobi. The founding woman organized a group of women of similar economic status who came from the Kiambu district of Kenya. Early in 1971 the group had about 20 members, but expanded to about 30. In a few years the founder also started a land-buying cooperative. While the rotating credit association remained embedded in the cooperative, eventually it lost its usefulness as members became wealthy enough to have bank accounts of their own. It disbanded in the 1990s. At one point, men tried to join, but the women refused to allow it. One woman said: "They will take over and not let us speak in our own cooperative."[26]

In Ghana, despite 30 years of national banking institutions, most saving methods are still informal. In 1991 it was estimated that 55 percent of the money in the country was saved informally. Rotating credit associations flourish. Women are more likely to join rotating credit associations than men, and the associations or clubs tend to be sex-segregated. The club names often reflect their emphasis on mutual aid. One club in the Accra Makola Market has a name that translates as "Our Well-Being Depends on Others."[27] Most of the savings is used to provide capital for trading activities.

When people move far outside their homelands, they may make even more use of such associations. For example, rotating credit associations in Korea go back to 1633. In the Los Angeles area, Koreans are even more likely to use rotating credit associations, mostly to accumulate sums for business.[28]

MULTIETHNIC ASSOCIATIONS

Although many voluntary associations draw on people from the same regional or ethnic background, increasingly in the modern world voluntary groups draw members from many different backgrounds. For example, the Kafaina, or *Wok Meri* ("women's work"), associations in Papua New Guinea are savings and loan associations that link thousands of women from different tribal areas.[29] Originally, there were smaller groups that started as savings associations in particular localities, but links between groups developed as women who married out of a village encouraged a relative back home or in another village to start a "daughter" group. "Mother-daughter" visits between groups can last for three days, as one group hosts another and the groups exchange money. All money received from another group is placed in a netbag that is hidden and cannot be touched, so the savings grow over time. When a group accumulates a certain amount, a building the size of a men's house is built for the association and a very large ceremony is held.

Does the development of these women's associations translate into new power for women in their traditionally male-dominated societies? That has yet

---

The Kafaina women's savings and loan associations in New Guinea often encourage relatives to start "daughter" organizations. At a ceremony for the new organization, a "daughter" doll is displayed.

to happen (see the box "Do Separate Women's Associations Increase Women's Status and Power?"). Apparently frustrated by their exclusion from local politics, the women are increasingly participating in the Kafaina movement. They may have intergroup exchanges and they may now engage in public speaking, but so far their arena is still separate from the men's arena.

Just as the Kafaina women's associations seem to be a response to perceived deprivation, the formation of associations with multiethnic or regional membership is not unusual where colonialism or other political domination is recognized as a common problem. For example, in Alaska in the 1960s Native Americans felt threatened by proposals for economic development that they thought would threaten their subsistence resources. Many regional and ethnic associations formed during this crisis, but perhaps more significant from the point of view of achieving substantial compensation and titles to land was the formation of a pan-Alaska association called the Alaska Federation of Natives. What made the amalgamation possible? Like the leaders of multiethnic movements in many places, the leaders at the highest levels seem to have had a lot of things in common. They were educated, urban dwellers who worked at professional occupations. Perhaps most important, many of them had attended the same schools.[30]

Multiethnic and multiregional associations have often been involved in independence movements all over the world. Often, revolutionary political parties develop out of such associations and lead the efforts to gain independence. Why independence movements develop in some places but not in others is not yet understood.

OTHER INTEREST GROUPS

Societies such as the United States consist of people from many different ethnic backgrounds. Often there are voluntary ethnic and regional associations. But the majority of the voluntary associations in our own and other complex societies have members who belong because of common, achieved interests. These common interests include occupation (so we have trade unions and professional associations), political affiliation (as in national political parties and political action groups), recreation (sports and game clubs, fan clubs, music and theater groups), charities, and social clubs. The larger and more diversified the society, the more different kinds of associations there are. They bring together people with common interests, aspirations, or qualifications, and they provide opportunities to work for social causes, for self-improvement, or to satisfy a need for new and stimulating experiences. We join clubs and other interest groups because we want to achieve particular goals. Not the least of such goals is identification with a "corporate" group and through it the acquisition of status and influence.

Joining clubs is much more important in some societies than in others. Norway is an example of a society with a rich organizational life. Even in areas with small communities there are many different clubs. For example, Douglas Caulkins found that in the municipality of Volda, a town of about 7,000, there were 197 organizations. People were expected to be active in at least a couple of organizations, and these groups met regularly. In fact, there were so many meetings that organizations were expected to coordinate their calendars so that the meetings would not interfere with one another.[31] Why some societies, like Norway, have so much involvement with voluntary associations is not well understood. Nor do we understand what the consequences of such involvement may be. Norway happens to have a particularly low crime rate and it scores high on other indicators of social and economic health.[32] Does the complexity of its organizational life and its many overlapping involvements play a role in its social health? We don't know, because cross-cultural studies to test that possibility have not been done.

EXPLAINING VARIATION IN ASSOCIATIONS

Anthropologists are not content to provide descriptions of the structure and operation of human associations. They also seek to understand why different types of associations develop. For example, what may account for the development of age-set systems? S. N. Eisenstadt's comparative study of African age-sets led him to the hypothesis that when kinship groups fail to carry out functions important to the integration of society—such as political, educational, and economic functions—age-set systems arise to fill the void. Age-set systems may provide a workable solution to a society's need for functional divisions among its members, because age is a criterion that can be applied to all members of society in the allocation of roles.[33] But it is not at all clear why age-set systems arise to fill the void left by lack of kinship organization. Many societies have kin structures that are limited in scope, yet the majority of them have not adopted an age-set system.

B. Bernardi, in his critical evaluation of Nilo-Hamitic age-set systems, also suggested that age-set systems arise to make up for a deficiency in social organization.[34] But, in contrast with Eisenstadt, Bernardi specifically suggested why more social organization is necessary and what particular deficiencies in the previous form of organization should favor development of age-sets. He hypothesized that age-set systems arise in societies that have a history of territorial rivalry, lack central authority, and have only dispersed kin groups. When all three factors are present, he argued, the need for a mechanism of territorial integration is supplied by an age-set system.

One cross-cultural study suggests that territorial rivalry, as indicated by warfare, may favor the development of age-set systems, but this study found no evidence to support Bernardi's hypothesis that age-sets develop in societies that lack central authority and have only dispersed kin groups.[35] So it does not seem that age-set societies are deficient in political or kinship organization. An alternative explanation, which is consistent with the cross-cultural evidence, is that age-set systems arise in societies that have both frequent warfare and local groups that change in size and composition throughout the year. In such situations, men may not always be able to rely on their kinsmen for cooperation in warfare because the kinsmen are not always nearby. Age-sets, however, can provide allies *wherever* one happens to be.[36] This interpretation suggests that age-set systems arise *in addition to,* rather than as alternatives to, kin-based and politically based forms of integration.[37]

As for voluntary associations whose membership is variably ascribed—that is, determined at birth but not found in all persons of a given age-sex category—it is difficult to say exactly what causes them to arise. As already noted, there are suggestions that voluntary associations of all types become more numerous, and more important, as the society harboring them advances in technology, complexity, and scale. No definitive evidence is yet available to support this explanation, but the following trends seem to be sufficiently established to merit consideration.

First, there is urbanization. Developing societies are becoming urban, and as their cities grow, so does the number of people separated from their traditional kinship ties and local customs. It is not surprising, then, that the early voluntary associations should be mutual aid societies, established first to take over kin obligations in case of death and later broadening their benefits in other directions. In this respect, the recent associations of the developing African societies closely resemble the early English laboring-class associations. Those clubs also served to maintain the city migrant's contacts with former traditions and culture. The regional associations in Latin America resemble the regional associations of European immigrants in the United States. Such associations also seem to arise in response to the migrant's or immigrant's needs in the new home.

Second, there is an economic factor. Migrants and immigrants try to adapt to new economic conditions, and group interests in the new situations have to be organized, promoted, and protected.

Why, then, do variably ascribed associations tend to be replaced by clubs of the achieved category in highly industrialized societies? Perhaps the strong focus on specialization in industrialized societies is reflected in the formation of specialized groups. Possibly the emphasis on achievement in industrialized societies is another contributing factor. Perhaps, too, the trend toward uniformity, encouraged by mass marketing and the mass media, is progressively weakening the importance of regional and ethnic distinctions. The result seems to be that the more broadly based organizations are being replaced by more narrowly based associations that are more responsive to particular needs not being met by the institutions of mass society.

SUMMARY

1. Associations or interest groups have the following characteristics in common: (a) some kind of formal, institutional structure exists; (b) some people are excluded from membership; (c) membership is based on commonly shared interests or purposes; and (d) there is a clearly discernible sense of mutual pride and belonging. Membership varies according to whether or not it is voluntary and whether the qualities of members are universally ascribed, variably ascribed, or achieved.

2. Age-sets are nonvoluntary associations whose members belong because of universally ascribed characteristics—that is, groups of persons of similar age and sex who move through life's stages together. Entry into the system is usually by an initiation ceremony. Transitions to new stages are usually marked by succession rituals. Unisex associations restrict membership to one sex. In noncommercial societies membership in such associations (usually male) is generally nonvoluntary.

3. Regional and ethnic organizations are voluntary associations whose members belong because of variably ascribed characteristics. Both usually occur in societies where technological advance is accelerating, bringing with it economic and social complexity. Despite a variety of types, regional and ethnic associ-

ations have in common an emphasis on (a) helping members adapt to new conditions; (b) keeping members in touch with home-area traditions; and (c) promoting improved living conditions for members who have recently migrated to urban areas.

4. Associations whose members belong because of variably ascribed characteristics tend to be replaced in highly industrialized societies by associations whose membership is based on achieved qualities.

GLOSSARY TERMS

achieved qualities
age-grade
age-set
ascribed qualities
associations

unisex association
universally ascribed
    qualities
variably ascribed
    qualities

CRITICAL QUESTIONS

1. How could young people who might join gangs be encouraged not to?

2. What associations do you belong to and why?

3. Many formerly unisex associations have opened their membership to the opposite sex. What might be the results of this change?

INTERNET EXERCISES

1. Pick a hobby or interest of yours and see if you can find a Web site on the Internet for a voluntary organization devoted to that interest. What are the criteria for membership?

2. In complex societies, people with special interests usually join voluntary organizations. Check out one of the many organizations that anthropologists join: The American Anthropological Association at **http://www.ameranthassn.org**; the Society for Applied Anthropology at **http://www.saa.org**; or the Canadian Association for Physical Anthropology at **http://citd.scar.utoronto.ca/CAPA/capa.html**.

3. Using the World Wide Web, provide two examples and Web addresses of organizations that are devoted exclusively to ethnic groups.

SUGGESTED READING

ARDENER, S., AND BURMAN, S. *Money-Go-Rounds: The Importance of Rotating Savings and Credit Associations for Women* (Oxford/Washington, DC: Berg,

1995). Fifteen chapters explore rotating credit associations, particularly women's associations, in different parts of the world. Also included is a comparative, summary chapter.

CAULKINS, D. D. "Norwegians: Cooperative Individualists." In M. Ember, C. R. Ember, and D. Levinson, eds., *Portraits of Culture: Ethnographic Originals* (Upper Saddle River, NJ: Prentice Hall, 1998). Prentice Hall/Simon & Schuster Custom Publishing. This narrative of fieldwork in two coastal towns describes how the numerous voluntary organizations structure much of social life. Personal profiles illustrate the diversity of life-styles. Particular attention is paid to the role of women's organizations.

EISENSTADT, S. N. *From Generation to Generation: Age Groups and Social Structure.* New York: Free Press, 1956. A comparative and theoretical analysis of age groups in different societies. Chapters 2–5 give a detailed presentation of age groupings in a wide variety of societies.

RITTER, M. L. "The Conditions Favoring Age-Set Organization." *Journal of Anthropological Research,* 36 (1980): 87–104. Evaluates the various theories about the development of age-sets and presents a new theory, which is supported by cross-cultural evidence.

THOMPSON, R. H. "Chinatowns: Immigrant Communities in Transition." In M. Ember, C. R. Ember, and D. Levinson, eds., *Portraits of Culture: Ethnographic Originals* (Upper Saddle River, NJ: Prentice Hall, 1998). Prentice Hall/Simon & Schuster Custom Publishing. The author discusses how regional, familial, and ethnic associations have played important roles in the changes that have occurred in Chinatowns in the United States and Canada.

Political Life: Social Order and Disorder

For people in the United States, the phrase *political life* has many connotations. It may call to mind the various branches of government: the executive branch, from the president on the national level to governors on the state level to mayors on the local level; legislative institutions, from Congress to state legislatures to city councils; and administrative bureaus, from federal government departments to local agencies.

Political life may also evoke thoughts of political parties, interest groups, lobbying, campaigning, and voting. In other words, when people living in the United States think of political life, they may think first of "politics," the activities (not always apparent) that influence who is elected or appointed to political office, what public policies are established, how they get established, and who benefits from those policies.

But *political life* involves even more than government and politics in the United States and many other countries. Political life also involves ways of preventing or resolving troubles and disputes both within and outside the society. Internally, a complex society such as ours may employ mediation or arbitration to resolve industrial disputes, a police force to prevent crimes or track down criminals, and courts and a penal system to deal with lawbreakers as well as with social conflict in general. Externally, such a society may establish embassies in other nations and develop and utilize its armed forces both to maintain security and to support domestic and foreign interests.

By means of all these informal and formal political mechanisms, complex societies establish social order and minimize, or at least deal with, social disorder.

Formal governments have become more and more widespread around the world over the last 100 years, as powerful colonizing countries have imposed political systems upon others or as people less formally organized realized that they needed governmental mechanisms to deal with the larger world. But many societies known to anthropology did not have political officials or political parties or courts or armies. Indeed, the band or village was the largest autonomous political unit in 50 percent of the societies in the ethnographic record, as of the times they were first described. And those units were only informally organized; that is, they did not have individuals or agencies formally authorized to make and implement policy or resolve disputes. Does this mean they did not have political life? If we mean political life as we know it in our own society, then the answer has to be that they did not. But if we look beyond our formal institutions and mechanisms—if we ask what functions these institutions and mechanisms perform—we find that all societies have had political activities and beliefs to create and maintain social order and cope with social disorder.

Many of the kinds of groups we discussed in the three previous chapters, on families, descent groups, and associations, have political functions. But when anthropologists talk about *political organization* or *political life,* they are particularly focusing on activities and beliefs pertaining to *territorial groups.* Territorial groups, in whose behalf political activities may be organized, range from small communities, such as bands and villages, to large communities, such as towns and cities, to multilocal groups, such as districts or regions, entire nations, or even groups of nations.

As we shall see, the different types of political organization, as well as how people participate in politics and how they cope with conflict, are often strongly linked to variation in food-getting, economy, and social stratification.

VARIATION IN TYPES OF POLITICAL ORGANIZATION

Societies in the ethnographic record vary in *level of political integration*—that is, the largest territorial group on whose behalf political activities are organized—and in the degree to which political authority is centralized or concentrated in the integrated group. When we describe the political integration of particular societies, we focus on their traditional political systems. In many societies known to anthropology, the small community (band or village) was traditionally the largest territorial group on whose behalf political activities were organized. The authority structure in such societies did not involve any centralization; there was no political authority whose jurisdiction included more than one community. In other societies political activities were traditionally organized sometimes on behalf of a multilocal group, but there was no permanent authority at the top. And in still other societies political activities were often traditionally organized on behalf of multilocal territorial groups, and there was a centralized or supreme political authority at the top. In the modern world, every society has been incorporated into some larger, centralized political system.

Elman Service suggested that most societies can be classified into four principal types of political organization: bands, tribes, chiefdoms, and states.[1] Although Service's classification does not fit all societies, it is a useful way to show how societies vary in trying to create and maintain social order. We often use the present tense in our discussion, because that is the convention in ethnographic writing, but the reader should remember that most societies that used to be organized at the band, tribe, or chiefdom level are now incorporated into larger political entities. With a handful of exceptions, there are no politically autonomous bands or tribes or chiefdoms in the world any more.

BAND ORGANIZATION

Some societies were composed of fairly small and usually nomadic groups of people. Each of these groups is conventionally called a **band** and is politically autonomous. That is, in **band organization** the local group or community is the largest group that acts as a political unit. Because most recent food collectors had band organization, some anthropologists contend that this type of political organization characterized nearly all societies before the development of agriculture, or until about 10,000 years ago. But we have to remember that almost all of the described food-collecting societies are or were located in marginal environments; and almost all were affected by more dominant societies nearby.[2] So it is possible that what we call "band organization" may not have been typical of food collectors in the distant or prehistoric past.

Bands are typically small, with less than 100 people usually, often considerably less. Each small band occupies a large territory, so population density is low. Band size often varies by season, with the band breaking up or recombining according to the food resources available at a given time and place. Inuit bands, for example, are smaller in the winter, when food is hard to find, and larger in the summer, when there is sufficient food to feed a larger group.

Political decision making within the band is generally informal. The "modest informal authority"[3] that does exist can be seen in the way decisions affecting the group are made. Because the formal, permanent office of leader typically does not exist, decisions such as when camp has to be moved or how a hunt is to be arranged are either agreed upon by the community as a whole or made by the best-qualified member. Leadership, when it is exercised by an individual, is not the consequence of bossing or throwing one's weight about. Each band may have its informal **headman,** or its most proficient hunter, or a person most accomplished in rituals. There may be one person with all these qualities, or several persons, but such a person or persons will have gained status through the community's recognition of skill, good sense, and humility. Leadership, in other words, stems not from power but from influence, not from office but from admired personal qualities.

In Inuit bands, each settlement may have its headman, who acquires his influence because the other members of the community recognize his good judgment and superior skills. The headman's advice concerning the movement of the band and other community matters is generally heeded, but he possesses no permanent authority and has no power to impose sanctions of any kind. Inuit leaders are male, but men often consult their wives in private, and women who hunt seem to have more influence than those who do not.[4] In any case, leadership exists only in a very restricted sense, as among the Iglulik Inuit, for example:

> Within each settlement . . . there is as a rule an older man who enjoys the respect of the others and who decides when a move is to be made to another hunting center, when a hunt is to be started, how the spoils are to be divided, when the dogs are to be fed. . . . He is called *isumaitoq,* "he who thinks." It is not always the oldest man, but as a rule an elderly man who is a clever hunter or, as head of a large family, exercises great authority. He cannot be called a chief; there is no obligation to follow his counsel; but they do so in most cases, partly because they rely on his experience, partly because it pays to be on good terms with this man.[5]

A summary of the general features of band organization can be found in Table 20–1. Note, however, that there are exceptions to these generalizations. For example, not all known food collectors are organized at the band level or have all the features of a band type of society. Classic exceptions are the Native American societies of the Northwest Coast, who had enormous resources of salmon and other fish, relatively large and permanent villages, and political organization beyond the level of the typical band societies in the ethnographic record.

TRIBAL ORGANIZATION

When local communities mostly act autonomously but there are kinship groups (such as clans or lineages) or associations (such as age-sets) that can

TABLE 20–1   *Suggested Trends in Political Organization and Other Social Characteristics*

TYPE OF ORGANIZATION	HIGHEST LEVEL OF POLITICAL INTEGRATION	SPECIALIZATION OF POLITICAL OFFICIALS	PREDOMINANT MODE OF SUBSISTENCE	COMMUNITY SIZE AND POPULATION DENSITY	SOCIAL DIFFERENTIATION	MAJOR FORM OF DISTRIBUTION
Band	Local group or band	Little or none; informal leadership	Food collecting	Very small communities, very low density	Egalitarian	Mostly reciprocity
Tribe	Sometimes multilocal group	Little or none; informal leadership	Extensive (shifting) agriculture and/or herding	Small communities, low density	Egalitarian	Mostly reciprocity
Chiefdom	Multilocal group	Some	Extensive or intensive agriculture and/or herding	Large communities, medium density	Rank	Reciprocity and redistribution
State	Multilocal group, often entire language group	Much	Intensive agriculture and herding	Cities and towns, high density	Class and caste	Mostly market exchange

In many egalitarian societies, leadership shifts informally from one person to another. In much of New Guinea there is more competition for achieving "big" status. On Vanatinai the women compete as well as the men, so there are "big women" as well as "big men." Here a "big woman" paints the face of her cousin's widow for a feast honoring the dead man.

potentially integrate several local groups into a larger unit **(tribe),** we say that the society has **tribal organization.** Unfortunately, the term *tribe* is sometimes used to refer to an entire society; that is, an entire language group may be called a tribe. But a tribal type of political system does not usually permit the entire society to act as a unit; all the communities in a tribal society may be linked only occasionally for some political (usually military) purpose. Thus, what distinguishes tribal from band political organization is the presence in the former of some multilocal, but not usually societywide, integration. The multilocal integration, however, is *not permanent,* and it is *informal* in the sense that it is not headed by political officials. Frequently, the integration is called into play only when an outside threat arises; when the threat disappears, the local groups revert to self-sufficiency.[6] Tribal organization may seem fragile—and of course it usually is—but the fact that there are social ways to integrate local groups into larger political entities means that societies with tribal organization are militarily a good deal more formidable than societies with band organization.

Societies with tribal political organization are similar to band societies in their tendency to be egalitarian (see Table 20–1). At the local level, informal leadership is also characteristic. In those tribal societies where kinship provides the basic framework of social organization, the elders of the local kin groups tend to have considerable influence; where age-sets are important, a particular age-set is looked to for leadership. But, in contrast to band societies, societies with tribal organization generally are food producers. And because cultivation and animal husbandry are generally more productive than hunting and gathering, the population density of tribal societies is generally higher, local groups are larger, and the way of life is more sedentary than in hunter-gatherer bands.

KINSHIP BONDS. Frequently communities are linked to each other by virtue of belonging to the same kin group, usually a unilineal group such as a lineage or clan. A **segmentary lineage system** is one type of tribal integration based on kinship. A society with such a system is composed of segments, or parts, each similar to the others in structure and function. Every local segment belongs to a hierarchy of lineages stretching farther and farther back genealogically. The hierarchy of lineages, then, unites the segments into larger and larger genealogical groups. The closer two groups are genealogically, the greater their general closeness. In the event of a dispute between members of different segments, people related more closely to one contestant than to another take the side of their nearest kinsman.

The Tiv of northern Nigeria offer a classic example of a segmentary lineage system, one that happens to link all the Tiv into a single genealogical structure or tribe. The Tiv are a large society, numbering more than 800,000. Figure 20–1 is a representation of the Tiv lineage structure as described by Paul Bohannan. In the figure, there are four levels of lineages. Each of the smallest lineages, symbolized by *a* through *h,* is in turn embedded in more inclusive lineages. So minimal lineages *a* and *b* are together in lineage *1.* Lineages *1* and *2* are embedded in lineage *A.* Territorial organization follows lineage hierarchy. As shown in the bottom of the figure, the most closely related lineages have territories near each other. Minimal lineages *a* and *b* live next to each other; their combined territory is the territory of their higher-order lineage, *1.* Lineage *A* in turn has a territory that is differentiated from lineage *B.* All of Tivland is said to descend from one ancestor, represented by *I.*[7]

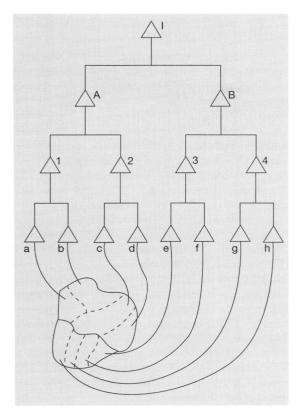

FIGURE 20–1 *Tiv Lineage Segments and Their Territories*

Source: Adapted from Paul Bohannan, "The Migration and Expansion of the Tiv," *Africa,* 24 (1954): 3.

Tiv lineage organization is the foundation of Tiv political organization. A look at Figure 20–1 helps to explain how. A dispute between lineages (and territories) *a* and *b* remains minor, since no more than "brother" segments are involved. But a dispute between *a* and *c* involves lineages 1 and 2 as well, with the requirement that *b* assist *a* and *d* support *c*. This process of mutual support, called **complementary opposition,** means that segments will unite only in a confrontation with some other group. Groups that will fight with each other in a minor dispute might coalesce at some later time against a larger group.

The segmentary lineage system was presumably very effective in allowing the Tiv to intrude into new territory and take land from other tribal societies with smaller descent groups. Individual Tiv lineage segments could call on support from related lineages when faced with border troubles. Conflicts within the society—that is, between segments—

especially in border areas, were often turned outward, "releasing internal pressure in an explosive blast against other peoples."[8]

Segmentary lineage systems may have military advantages even when they do not unite the entire society. A classic example is the Nuer of the Upper Nile region, who had tribal, but not societywide, organization because of their segmentary lineages. In the early 1800s the Nuer had a territory of about 8,700 square miles and the neighboring Dinka had ten times that much. But by 1890, the Nuer had cut a 100-mile swath through Dinka territory, increasing Nuer territory to 35,000 square miles. Even though the Nuer and Dinka were culturally very similar, the segmentary lineage organization of the Nuer seems to have given them a significant military advantage in their incursions into Dinka territory.[9]

A segmentary lineage system may generate a formidable military force, but the combinations of manpower it produces are temporary, forming and dissolving as the occasion demands.[10] Tribal political organization does not make for a political system that more or less permanently integrates a number of communities.

AGE-SET SYSTEMS. In the previous chapter we described age-set systems in general. Here we discuss how age-sets can function as the basis of a tribal type of political organization, as among the Karimojong of northeastern Uganda.[11]

The Karimojong age-set system has an important bearing on day-to-day tribal life. As herders, Karimojong adults are often separated from their usual settlements. Herders will meet, mingle for a while, then go their separate ways, but each may call upon other members of his age-set wherever he goes. The age-set system is important among the Karimojong because it immediately allocates to each individual a place in the system and thereby establishes for him an appropriate pattern of response. A quarrel in camp will be settled by the representatives of the senior age-set who are present, regardless of which section of the tribe they may belong to.

Among the Karimojong, political leaders are not elected from among the elders of a particular age-set, nor are they appointed; they acquire their positions informally. Usually a man's background, and the ability he has demonstrated in public debates over a period of time, will result in his being considered by the men of his neighborhood to be their spokesman. His function is to announce what course of action seems required in a particular situation, to initiate that action, and then to coordinate it after it has begun.

Most political leaders exercise their authority within the local sphere because the pastoral nature of the Karimojong economy, with its dispersed groups and movement from one feeding ground to another, offers no alternative. From time to time an elder may acquire the status of a prophet and be awarded respect and obedience on a tribal scale. He will be called upon to lead sacrifices (to avert misfortune), to undertake rainmaking (to bring prosperity), and so on. Yet even a prophet's prestige and authority do not warrant him a position of overlord or chief.[12]

CHIEFDOM ORGANIZATION

Whereas a tribe has some informal mechanism that can integrate more than one community, a **chiefdom** has some *formal* structure that integrates more than one community into a political unit. The formal structure could consist of a council with or without a chief, but most commonly there is a person—the **chief**—who has higher rank or authority than others. Most societies at the chiefdom level of organization contain more than one multicommunity political unit or chiefdom, each headed by a district chief or a council. There may also be more than one level of chief beyond the community, such as district chiefs and higher-level chiefs. Compared with tribal societies, societies with chiefdoms are more densely populated and their communities more permanent, partly as a consequence of their generally greater economic productivity (see Table 20–1).

The position of chief, which is sometimes hereditary and generally permanent, bestows high status on its holder. Most chiefdoms have social ranking and accord the chief and his family greater access to prestige. The chief may redistribute goods, plan and direct the use of public labor, supervise religious ceremonies, and direct military activities on behalf of the chiefdom. In South Pacific chiefdoms, the chiefs carried out most of these duties. In Fijian chiefdoms, for example, the chief was responsible for the redistribution of goods and the coordination of labor:

> [The chief] could summon the community's labor on his own behalf, or on behalf of someone else who requested it, or for general purposes. . . . Besides his right to summon labor he accumulated the greater proportion of the first fruits of the yam crop . . . and he benefited from other forms of food presentation, or by the acquisition of special shares in ordinary village distribution. . . . Thus, the paramount [chief] would collect a significant part of the surplus production of

the community and redistribute it in the general welfare.[13]

In contrast to leaders in tribal societies, who generally have to earn their privileges by their personal qualities, hereditary chiefs are said to have those qualities in their "blood." A high-ranking chief in Polynesia, that huge triangular area of islands in the South Pacific, inherited special religious power called *mana*. Mana sanctified his rule and protected him.[14] Chiefs in Polynesia had so much religious power that the missionaries could convert people to Christianity only after their chiefs had been converted.[15]

In most chiefdoms, the chiefs did not have the power to compel people to obey them; people would act in accordance with the chief's wishes because the chief was respected and often had religious authority. But in the most complex paramount chiefdoms, such as those of Hawaii and Tahiti, the chiefs seemed to have more compelling sanctions than the "power" of respect or mana. Substantial amounts of goods and services collected by the chiefs were used to support subordinates, including specialists, such as high priests, political envoys, and warriors who could be sent to quell rebellious factions.[16] When redistributions do not go to everybody—when chiefs are allowed to keep items for their own purposes—and when a chief begins to use armed force, the political system is on the way to becoming what we call a state.

STATE ORGANIZATION

A **state,** according to one more or less standard definition, is "an autonomous political unit, encompassing many communities within its territory and having a centralized government with the power to collect taxes, draft men for work or war, and decree and enforce laws."[17] States, then, have a complex, centralized political structure that includes a wide range of permanent institutions with legislative, executive, and judicial functions and a large bureaucracy. Central to this definition is the concept of legitimate force used to implement policies both internally and externally. In states, the government tries to maintain a monopoly on the use of physical force.[18] This monopoly can be seen in the development of formal and specialized instruments of social control: a police force, a militia, a standing army.

Just as a particular society may contain more than one band, tribe, or chiefdom, so may it contain more than one state. The contiguously distributed population speaking a single language may or may

Presenting kava, a special drink, to a chief in Fiji.

not be politically unified in a single state. Ancient Greece was composed of many city-states; so, too, was Italy until the 1870s. German speakers are also not politically unified; Austria and Germany are separate states, and Germany itself was not politically unified until the 1870s. We say that a society has **state organization** when it is composed of one or more political units that are states.

A state may include more than one society. Multisociety states often are the result of conquest or colonial control when the dominant political authority, itself a state, imposes a centralized government over a territory with many different societies and cultures, as the British did in Nigeria and Kenya. Nearly all of the multisociety states that emerged after World War II were the results of successful independence movements against colonial powers.[19] Most have retained their political unity despite the fact that they contain many different societies. For example, Nigeria remains unified despite a civil war; the eastern section called Biafra (mostly populated by people of Ibo culture) tried unsuccessfully 30 years ago to secede, and subsequently there has been serious conflict among some of the constituent societies. Multisociety or multiethnic states may also form voluntarily, in reaction to external threat.

Switzerland comprises cantons, each of which speaks mainly French, German, Italian, or Romansch; the various cantons confederated originally to shake off control by the Holy Roman Empire.

In addition to their strictly political features, state-organized societies are generally supported by intensive agriculture. The high productivity of the agriculture allows for the emergence of cities, a high degree of economic and other kinds of specialization, and market or commercial exchange. In addition, state societies usually have class stratification (see Table 20–1).

When states come into existence, people's access to scarce resources is radically altered. So, too, is their ability to *not* listen to leaders: You cannot refuse to pay taxes and go unpunished. Of course, the rulers of a state do not maintain the social order by force alone. The people must believe, at least to some extent, that those in power have a legitimate right to govern. If the people think otherwise, history suggests that those in power may eventually lose their ability to control. Witness the recent downfall of Communist parties throughout most of Eastern Europe and the former Soviet Union.

So force and the threat of force are not enough to explain the legitimacy of power, and the inequities

All governments, even state societies, ultimately depend on the people's sense of legitimacy. This toppled statue of Lenin symbolizes the recent breakup of the Soviet Union and the overthrow of the Communist party.

that occur commonly, in state societies. But then what does? There are various theories. The rulers of early states often claimed divine descent to buttress their legitimacy, but this claim is rare nowadays. Another theory is that if parents teach their children to accept all authority, such lessons may generalize to the acceptance of political authority. Some analysts think that people accept state authority for no good reason; the rulers are just able to fool them. Finally, some theorists think that states must provide people with real or rational advantages; otherwise people would not think that the rulers deserve to exercise authority. Legitimacy is not an all-or-none phenomenon; it varies in degree. Why it has varied, in different times and places, remains a classic question in the social sciences, including anthropology, as well as in philosophy and other humanistic disciplines.[20]

A state society can retain its legitimacy, or at least its power, for a long time. For example, the Roman Empire was a complex state society that dominated the Mediterranean and Near East for hundreds of years. It began as a city-state that waged war to acquire additional territory. At its height, the Roman Empire embraced more than 55 million people;[21] the capital city of Rome had a population of well

over a million.[22] The empire included parts of what are now Great Britain, France, Spain, Portugal, Germany, Rumania, Turkey, Greece, Armenia, Egypt, Israel, and Syria.

Another example of a state society was the kingdom of Nupe in West Africa, now part of the nation-state of Nigeria. As is characteristic of state societies, Nupe society was rigidly stratified. At the top of the social system was the king, or *etsu*. Beneath the king, members of the royal family formed the highest aristocratic class. Next in order were two other classes of nobility, the local chiefs and the military leaders. At the bottom were the commoners, who had neither prestige nor power and no share in political authority.

The Nupe king possessed ultimate authority in many judicial matters. Minor disputes and civil cases were handled by local village councils, but serious criminal cases were the prerogative of the king. Such cases, referred to as "crimes for the king," were brought before the royal court by the king's local representatives. The king and his counselors judged the cases and determined suitable punishments.

The most powerful influence of the state over the Nupe people was in the area of taxation. The king was given the power to impose taxes and collect them from every household. Payment was made either in money (cowrie shells originally and, later, British currency) or certain gifts, such as cloth, mats, and slaves. Much of the revenue collected was kept by the king, and the remainder was shared with his local representatives and lords. In return for the taxes they paid, the people received security—protection against invasion and domestic disorder.[23]

FACTORS ASSOCIATED WITH VARIATION IN POLITICAL ORGANIZATION

The kinds of political organization we call band, tribal, chiefdom, and state are points on a continuum of levels of political integration or unification, from small-scale local autonomy to large-scale regional unification. There also is variation in political authority, from a few temporary and informal political leaders to large numbers of permanent, specialized political officials, from the absence of coercive political power to the monopoly of public force by a central authority. These aspects of variation in political organization are generally associated with shifts from food collection to more intensive food production, from small to large communities, from low to high population densities, from an emphasis on reciprocity to redistribution to market exchange, and from egalitarian to rank to fully stratified class societies.

The associations just outlined, which seem to be confirmed by the available cross-cultural evidence, are summarized in Table 20–1. With regard to the relation between level of subsistence technology and political complexity, one cross-cultural study employing a small random sample of societies found that the greater the importance of agriculture in a society, the larger the population that is politically unified and the greater the number and types of political officials.[24] A massive cross-cultural survey reported a similar trend: The more intensive the agriculture, the greater the likelihood of state organization; conversely, societies with no more than local political institutions are likely to depend on hunting, gathering, and fishing.[25]

With regard to community size, the first of these studies also suggested that the larger the leading community, the wider the range of political officials in the society.[26] Robert Textor presented a similar finding: Societies with state organization tend to have cities and towns, whereas those with only local political organization are more likely to have communities with an average population of fewer than 200 persons.[27] Cross-cultural research also tends to

confirm that societies with higher levels of political integration are more likely to exhibit social differentiation, especially in the form of class distinctions.[28]

Does this evidence provide us with an explanation for why political organization varies? Clearly, the data indicate that several factors are associated with political development, but exactly why changes in organization occur is not yet understood. Although economic development may be a necessary condition for political development,[29] that relation does not fully explain why political organization should become more complex just because the economy can support it. Some theorists have suggested that competition between groups may be a more important reason for political consolidation. For example, Elman Service suggested competition as a reason why a society might change from a band level of political organization to a tribal level. Band societies are generally hunter-gatherers. With a changeover to agriculture, population density and competition between groups may increase. Service believed that such competition would foster the development of some informal organization beyond the community—namely, tribal organization—for offense and defense.[30] Indeed, as we saw in the chapters on residence and kinship and associations, both unilineal kinship groups and age-set systems seem to be associated with warfare.

Among agriculturalists, defensive needs might also be the main reason for switching from informal multivillage political organization to more formal chiefdom organization. Formally organized districts are probably more likely to defeat autonomous villages or even segmentary lineage systems.[31] In addition, there may be economic reasons for political development. With regard to chiefdoms, Service suggested that chiefdoms will emerge when redistribution between communities becomes important or when large-scale coordinated work groups are required. The more important these activities are, the more important—and hence more "chiefly"—the organizer and his family presumably become.[32] But redistribution is far from a universal activity of chiefs.[33]

Theory and research on the anthropology of political development have focused mostly on the high end of the scale of political complexity, and particularly on the origins of the first state societies. Those earliest states apparently rose independently of one another, after about 3500 B.C., in what are now southern Iraq, Egypt, northwestern India, northern China, and central Mexico. As we discussed in the chapter on origins of cities and states, several theories have been proposed to explain the earliest states, but no one theory seems to fit all the known archaeological sequences in early state formation.

THE SPREAD OF STATE SOCIETIES

For whatever reasons the earliest states developed, the state level of political development has come to dominate the world. Societies with states have larger communities and higher population densities than do band, tribal, and chiefdom societies. They also have armies that are ready to fight at almost any time. State systems that have waged war against chiefdoms and tribes have almost always won, and the result has usually been the political incorporation of the losers. For example, the British and, later, the U.S. colonization of much of North America led to the defeat and incorporation of many Native American societies.

The defeat and incorporation of the Native Americans was at least partly due to the catastrophic depopulations they suffered because of epidemic diseases, such as smallpox and measles, that European colonists introduced. Catastrophic depopulation was commonly the outcome of the first contacts between Euro-Americans and the natives of North and South America, as well as the natives of the far islands in the Pacific. People in the New World and the Pacific had not been exposed, and therefore were not resistant, to the diseases the Euro-Americans carried with them when they began to colonize the world. Before the expansion of Europeans, the people of the New World and the Pacific had been separated for a long time from the people and diseases on the geographically continuous landmass we separate into Europe, Africa, and Asia. Smallpox, measles, and the other former scourges of Europe had largely become childhood diseases that most individuals of European ancestry survived.[34]

Whether by depopulation, conquest, or intimidation, the number of independent political units in the world has decreased strikingly in the last 3,000 years, and especially in the last 200 years. Robert Carneiro estimated that in 1000 B.C., there may have been between 100,000 and 1 million separate political units in the world; today there are fewer than 200.[35] In the ethnographic record, about 50 percent of the 2,000 or so societies described within the last 150 years had only local political integration. That is, the highest level of political integration in one out of two fairly recent societies was the local community.[36] Thus, most of the decrease in the number of independent political units has occurred fairly recently.

But the recent secessions from the former Soviet Union and Yugoslavia and other separatist movements around the world suggest that ethnic rivalries may make for departures from the trend toward larger and larger political units. Ethnic groups that have been dominated by others in multinational states may opt for political autonomy, at least for a while. On the other hand, the separate nations of Western Europe are becoming more unified every day, both politically

State societies frequently try to expand by conquering other peoples, as the Spanish did in Mexico. This Aztec drawing depicts a 1530 Spanish battle in which a non-Aztec group fought together with the Spanish against another non-Aztec group.

and economically. So the trend toward larger and larger political units may be continuing, even if there are departures from it now and then.

Extrapolating from past history, a number of investigators have suggested that the entire world will eventually come to be politically integrated, perhaps as soon as the twenty-third century and no later than A.D. 4850.[37] Only the future will tell if this prediction will come true. And only the future will tell if further political integration in the world will occur peacefully—with all parties agreeing—or by force or the threat of force, as has happened so often in the past.

VARIATION IN POLITICAL PROCESS

Anthropologists are increasingly interested in the politics, or political processes, of the societies they study: who acquires influence or power, how they acquire it, and how political decisions are made. But even though we have descriptive accounts of politics in many societies, there is still little comparative or cross-cultural research on what may explain variation in politics.[38]

GETTING TO BE A LEADER

In those societies that have hereditary leadership, which is common in rank societies and in state societies with monarchies, rules of succession usually establish how leadership is inherited. Such leaders are often identifiable in some obviously visible way; they may be permanently marked or tattooed, as in chiefdoms in Polynesia, or they may wear elaborate dress and insignia, as in class-stratified societies (see the discussion of body adornment in the chapter on the arts). But for societies whose leaders are *chosen*, either as informal leaders or as political officials, we need a lot more research to understand why some kinds of people are chosen over others.

A few studies have investigated the personal qualities of leaders in tribal societies. One study, conducted among the Mekranoti-Kayapo of central Brazil, found that leaders, in contrast to followers, tend to be rated by their peers as higher on intelligence, generosity, knowledgeability, ambitiousness, and aggressiveness. Leaders also tend to be older and taller. And despite the egalitarian nature of Mekranoti society (at least with respect to sharing resources), sons of leaders are more likely than others to become leaders.[39]

Research in another Brazilian society, the Kagwahiv of the Amazon region, suggests another personal quality of leaders: They seem to have positive feelings about their fathers and mothers.[40] In many respects, studies of leaders in the United States show them to be not that different from their counterparts in Brazil. But there is one major difference. Mekranoti and Kagwahiv leaders are not wealthier than others; in fact, they give their wealth away. U.S. leaders are wealthier than others.[41]

"BIG MEN." In some egalitarian tribal societies, the quest for leadership seems quite competitive. In parts of New Guinea and South America, "big men" compete with other ambitious men to attract followers. Men who want to compete must show that they have magical powers, success in gardening, and bravery in war. But, most important, they have to collect enough goods to throw big parties at which the goods are given away. Big men have to work very hard to attract and keep their followings, for dissatisfied followers can always join other aspiring men.[42] The wives of big men are often leaders too. Among the Kagwahiv, for example, a headman's wife is usually the leader of the women in the community; she is responsible for much of the planning for feasts and often distributes the meat at them.[43]

Although the phenomenon of big men leaders is common throughout New Guinea, researchers are beginning to see variation in the type and extent of "bigmanship" in different areas of New Guinea. For example, in the southern Highlands, groups of men (not just big men) may engage in large-scale giveaways, so big men are not so different from ordinary men. In the northwestern Highlands, on the other hand, big men stand out from other men in striking ways. They make policy for groups of people and organize collective events, they have substantial access to pigs or to valuables acquired in exchanges, and they have control over a substantial amount of labor (more than one wife and fellow kin).[44]

We know that some big men are "bigger" than others, but how does a man get to be a big man? Among the Kumdi-Engamoi, a central Highlands group, a man who wants to be considered a *wua nium* (literally a "great-important-wealthy man") needs to have many wives and daughters, because the amount of land controlled by a man and how much can be produced on that land depend on the number of women in his family. The more wives he has, the more land he is given to cultivate. He must also be a good speaker. Everyone has the right to speak and give speeches, but to get to be known as a big man requires speaking well and forcefully and knowing when to sum up a consensus. It usually takes a man until his thirties or forties to acquire more than one wife and to make his name through exchanges. When a man wants to inaugurate an exchange, he needs to get shells and pigs from his family and relatives. Once he has achieved a reputation as a *wua nium,* he can keep it only if he continues to perform well, that is, if he continues to distribute fairly, make wise decisions, speak well, and conduct exchanges.[45]

"BIG WOMEN." In contrast to most of mainland New Guinea, the islands off the southeastern coast are characterized by matrilineal descent. But, like the rest of New Guinea, the islands also have a shifting system of leadership in which people compete for "big" status. Here, though, the people competing are women as well as men, and so there are "big women" as well as "big men." On the island of Vanatinai, for example, women and men compete with each other to exchange valuables.

Women lead canoe expeditions to distant islands to visit male as well as female exchange partners, women mobilize relatives and exchange partners to mount large feasts, and the women get to keep the ceremonial valuables exchanged, at least for a while.[46]

The prominence of women on Vanatinai may be linked to the disappearance of warfare—the colonial powers imposed peace; we call this "pacification." Interisland exchanges became frequent when war became rarer in the early twentieth century, giving women and men more freedom to travel. For men, but not women, war provided a path to leadership; champion warriors would acquire great renown and influence. It is not that women did not participate in war; they did, which is unusual cross-culturally, but a woman could not become a war leader. Now, in the absence of war, women have an opportunity through exchanges to become leaders, or "big women."

Research Frontiers

DEMOCRACY AND ECONOMIC DEVELOPMENT: HOW AND WHY ARE THEY RELATED?

The subsistence economies traditionally studied by anthropologists are becoming more and more commercialized as people increasingly produce goods and services for a market. And the pace of economic development is quickening, particularly in places that until recently lacked industrial wage labor, as their economies are increasingly integrated into the same world system. What effect, if any, does economic development have on political participation? Can we speculate about the future on the basis of comparative research?

Most of the comparative research on the relationship between economic development and political participation has been cross-national, comparing data on different countries. Some countries are more democratic than others, on the basis of such

characteristics as contested elections, an elected head of state, an elected powerful legislature, and the protection of civil liberties. In capitalist countries, more democracy is generally associated with higher levels of economic development, as measured by indicators such as per capita output; in countries that are not very industrialized, there is little democracy at the national level. Why should more democracy be associated with more economic development? The prevailing opinion is that economic development increases the degree of social equality in the country, and the more equality among interest groups, the more they demand participation in the political process, and hence the more democracy. Or, to put this theory another way, as the economy develops, the more what we might call the middle

and working classes can demand rewards and power, and therefore the less power the elite can retain.

What about the societies usually studied by anthropologists, what we call the cross-cultural or ethnographic record? We know that some of the highest levels of political participation occur in the least complex societies, such as foraging societies. Many adults in such societies have a say in decisions and leadership is informal; leaders can retain their roles only if people voluntarily go along with them. Concentrated power and less political participation are more likely in chiefdoms and states than in band and tribal societies. The more hierarchical chiefdoms and states usually depend on agriculture, particularly intensive agriculture, which can produce more goods and services per capita than foraging economies can. So the relationship between economic

In one respect, however, women have less of an opportunity to acquire influence now. There are local government councils now, but all the councillors are male. Why? Some women were nominated for the posts, but they withdrew in embarrassment because they could not speak English. Big men or big women do not automatically have a path to these new positions; it is mostly young males who know English and become the councillors. But this situation may change. With the opening of a government primary school in 1984, both girls and boys are learning English, so women in the future may be more likely to achieve leadership by becoming councillors.

POLITICAL PARTICIPATION

The political scientist Marc Ross conducted cross-cultural research on variation in degree of political participation. As Ross phrased the research ques-tion: "Why is it that in some polities there are relatively large numbers of persons involved in political life, while in others political action is the province of very few?"[47]

Political participation in preindustrial societies ranges from widespread to low or nonexistent. In 16 percent of the societies examined, there is widespread participation; decision-making forums are open to all adults. The forums may be formal (councils and other governing bodies) or informal. Next in degree of political participation are societies (37 percent) that have widespread participation by some but not all adults (men but not women, certain classes but not others). Next are societies (29 percent) that have some but not much input by the community. Finally, 18 percent of the societies have low or nonexistent participation, which means that leaders make most decisions, and involvement of the average person is very limited.

development and political participation in the ethnographic record is *opposite* to what we find cross-nationally. That is, the more economic development, the *less* political participation, in the societies studied by anthropologists. Why should this be so? It seems that social equality *decreases* with economic development in the ethnographic record (which does not include many industrialized societies). In that record, an economically developed society is likely to have features such as plowing, fertilizers, and irrigation, which make permanent cultivation of the fields and permanent communities possible. Such intensive agricultural activity is more conducive to concentrated wealth than is hunter-gatherer subsistence or shifting cultivation (horticulture). Thus, in the ethnographic record, the more economically developed societies have *more* social inequality and therefore *less* democracy.

The two sets of findings, the cross-national and the cross-cultural, are not that hard to reconcile. Social and economic inequality appears to work against democracy and extensive political participation. Social inequality increases with the switch from foraging to agriculture. But social inequality decreases with the switch from preindustrial agriculture to high (industrial) levels of economic development. Political participation decreases with the first switch and increases with the second, because social inequality first increases and then decreases.

So what does comparative research suggest about the future? If the middle and working classes feel they are not getting a fair return on their labor, their demands should increase. The elite may be willing to satisfy those increased demands; if they do, their power will be reduced. In either case, unless the elite try to retain their power at any cost, there should be more political participation and more democracy, at least in the long run.

Sources: Kenneth A. Bollen, "Liberal Democracy: Validity and Method Factors in Cross-National Measures," *American Journal of Political Science,* 37 (1993): 1207–30; Edward N. Muller, "Economic Determinants of Democracy," and Melvin Ember, Carol R. Ember, and Bruce Russett, "Inequality and Democracy in the Anthropological Record," pp. 133–155 and 110–130, respectively, in Manus I. Midlarsky, ed., *Inequality, Democracy, and Economic Development* (Cambridge, England: Cambridge University Press, 1997); pp 110–130. Marc Howard Ross, "Political Participation," in Carol R. Ember and Melvin Ember, eds., *Cross-Cultural Research for Social Science* (Upper Saddle River, NJ: Prentice Hall, 1998), Prentice Hall/Simon & Schuster Custom Publishing.

Degree of political participation seems to be high in small-scale societies, as well as in modern democratic nation-states, but not in between (feudal states and preindustrial empires). Why? In small-scale societies leaders do not have the power to force people to act; thus a high degree of political participation may be the only way to get people to go along with decisions. In modern democracies, which have many powerful groups outside the government—corporations, unions, and other associations are examples—the central authorities may only theoretically have the power to force people to go along; in reality, they rely mostly on voluntary compliance. For example, the U.S. government failed when it tried with force (Prohibition, 1920–1933) to stop the manufacture, transport, and sale of alcoholic beverages.

A high degree of political participation seems to have an important consequence. In the modern world, democratically governed states rarely go to war with each other. This does not mean that modern democracies are more peaceful in general; on the contrary, they are as likely to go to war as other kinds of political systems, but not so much with each other.[48] So, for example, the United States invaded three countries—Grenada, Panama, and Iraq—between 1980 and 1993 but no democracies. Similarly, it appears that more participatory, that is, more "democratic," political units in the ethnographic record fight with each other significantly less often than do less participatory political units, just as seems to be the case among modern nation-states.[49] Exactly why more participation or more democracy may lead to peace remains to be established; we explore the implications of the relationship in the chapter on applied anthropology and social problems.

RESOLUTION OF CONFLICT

As we noted in the beginning of this chapter, political life involves more than the making of policy, its administration, and its enforcement. Political life also involves the resolution of conflict, which may be accomplished peacefully by avoidance, community action, mediation or the negotiation of compromises, apology, appeal to supernatural forces, or adjudication by a third party. As we shall see, the procedures used usually vary with degree of social complexity; decisions by third parties are more likely in hierarchical societies.[50] But peaceful solutions are not always possible, and disputes may

erupt into violent conflict. When violence occurs within a political unit in which disputes are usually settled peacefully, we call such violence crime, particularly when committed by an individual. When the violence occurs between groups of people from separate political units—groups between which there is no procedure for settling disputes—we usually call such violence warfare. When violence occurs between subunits of a population that had been politically unified, we call it civil war.

PEACEFUL RESOLUTION OF CONFLICT

Most modern industrialized states have formal institutions and offices, such as police, district attorneys, courts, and penal systems, to deal with minor disputes and more serious conflicts that may arise in society. All these institutions generally operate according to **codified laws**—that is, a set of explicit, usually written, rules stipulating what is permissible and what is not. Transgression of the law by individuals gives the state the right to take action against them. The state has a monopoly on the legitimate use of force in the society, for it alone has the right to coerce subjects into agreement with regulations, customs, political edicts, and procedures.

Many societies lack such specialized offices and institutions for dealing with conflict. Yet, because all societies have peaceful, regularized ways of handling at least certain disputes, some anthropologists speak of the *universality of law.* E. Adamson Hoebel, for example, stated the principle as follows:

> Each people has its system of social control. And all but a few of the poorest of them have as a part of the control system a complex of behavior patterns and institutional mechanisms that we may properly treat as law. For, "anthropologically considered, law is merely one aspect of our culture—the aspect which employs the force of organized society to regulate individual and group conduct and to prevent redress or punish deviations from prescribed social norms."[51]

Law, then, whether informal as in simpler societies, or formal as in more complex societies, provides a means of dealing peacefully with whatever conflicts develop. That does not mean that conflicts are always resolved peacefully. But that also does not mean that people cannot learn to resolve their conflicts peacefully. The fact that there are societies with little or no violent conflict means that it may be possible to learn from them; it may be possible to discover how to avoid violent outcomes of conflicts. How come South Africa could move relatively peacefully from a society dominated by people from

Europe to one with government and civil rights shared by all groups? On the other hand, Bosnia had very violent conflict between ethnic groups and needed intervention by outside parties to keep the warring sides apart.[52]

AVOIDANCE. Violence can often be avoided if the parties to a dispute voluntarily avoid each other or are separated until emotions cool down. Anthropologists have frequently remarked that foragers are particularly likely to make use of this technique. People may move to other bands or move their dwellings to opposite ends of camp. Shifting horticulturalists may also split up when conflicts get too intense. Avoidance is obviously easier in societies, such as band societies, that are nomadic or seminomadic and in which people have temporary dwellings. And avoidance is more feasible when people live independently and self-sufficiently (for example, in cities and suburbs).[53] But even if conditions in such societies may make avoidance easier, we still need to know why some societies use avoidance more than confrontation as a way of resolving conflict.

COMMUNITY ACTION. Societies have found various ways of resolving disputes peacefully. One such way involves action by a group or the community as a whole; collective action is common in simpler societies that lack powerful authoritarian leaders.[54] Many Inuit societies, for example, frequently resolve disputes through community action. Within local groups, kinship ties are not particularly emphasized, and the family is regarded as autonomous in most matters. They believe that spirits, particularly if displeased, can determine much of a person's fate. Consequently, people carry out their daily tasks within a complex system of taboos. This system is so extensive that the Inuit, at least in the past, may have had no need for a formal set of laws.

Nevertheless, conflicts do arise and have to be resolved. Accordingly, *principles* act as guides to the community in settling trouble cases. An individual's failure to heed a taboo or to follow the suggestions of a shaman leads to expulsion from the group, because the community cannot accept a risk to its livelihood. A person who fails to share goods voluntarily will find them confiscated and distributed to the community, and he or she may be executed in the process. A single case of murder, as an act of vengeance (usually because of the abduction of a wife or as part of a blood feud), does not concern the community, but repeated murders do. Franz Boas gave a typical example:

There was a native of Padli by the name Padlu. He had induced the wife of a native of Cumberland Sound to desert her husband and follow him. The deserted husband, meditating revenge . . . visited his friends in Padli, but before he could accomplish his intention of killing Padlu, the latter shot him. . . . A brother of the murdered man went to Padli to avenge the death . . . but he also was killed by Padlu. A third native of Cumberland Sound, who wished to avenge the death of his relatives, was also murdered by him.

On account of these outrages the natives wanted to get rid of Padlu, but yet they did not dare to attack him. When the *pimain* (headman) of the Akudmurmuit learned of these events he started southward and *asked every man in Padli whether Padlu should be killed. All agreed;* so he went with the latter deer hunting . . . and . . . shot Padlu in the back.[55]

The killing of an individual is the most extreme action a community can take—we call it *capital punishment.* The community as a whole or a political official or a court may decide to administer such punishment, but capital punishment seems to exist in nearly all societies, from the simplest to the most complex.[56] It is often assumed that capital punishment deters crime. If it did, we would expect the abolition of capital punishment to be followed by an increase in homicide rates. But that does not seem to happen. A cross-national study indicated that the abolition of capital punishment tends to be followed by a *decrease* in homicide rates.[57]

NEGOTIATION AND MEDIATION. In many conflicts, the parties to a dispute may come to a settlement themselves by **negotiation.** There aren't necessarily any rules for how they will do so, but any solution is "good" if it restores peace.[58] Sometimes an outside or third party is used to help bring about a settlement between the disputants. We call it **mediation** when the outside party tries to help bring about a settlement, but that third party does not have the formal authority to force a settlement. Both negotiation and mediation are likely when the society is relatively egalitarian and it is important for people to get along.[59]

Among the Nuer of East Africa, a pastoral and horticultural people, disputes within the community can be settled with the help of an informal mediator called the "leopard-skin chief." This man is not a political chief but a mediator. His position is hereditary, has religious overtones, and makes its holder responsible for the social well-being of the district. Matters such as cattle stealing rarely come to the attention of the leopard-skin chief; the parties involved usually prefer to settle in their own private way. But if, for example, a murder has been committed, the culprit will go at once to the house of the leopard-skin chief. Immediately the chief cuts the culprit's arm so that blood flows; until the cut has been made the murderer may not eat or drink. If the murderer is afraid of vengeance by the slain man's family, he will remain at the house of the leopard-skin chief, which is considered sanctuary. Then, within the next few months, the chief attempts to mediate between the parties to the crime.

The chief elicits from the slayer's kin that they are prepared to pay compensation to avoid a feud, and he persuades the dead man's kin that they ought to accept compensation, usually in the form of cattle. During this period neither party may eat or drink from the same vessels as the other, and they may not, therefore, eat in the house of the same third person. The chief then collects the cattle—some 40 to 50 beasts—and takes them to the dead man's home, where he performs various sacrifices of cleansing and atonement.[60]

Throughout the process, the chief acts as a go-between. He has no authority to force either party to negotiate, and he has no power to enforce a solution once it has been arrived at. However, he is able to take advantage of the fact that because both disputants belong to the same community and are anxious to avoid a blood feud, they usually are willing to come to terms.

RITUAL RECONCILIATION—APOLOGY. The desire to restore a harmonious relationship may also explain ceremonial apologies. An apology is based on deference—the guilty party shows obeisance and asks for forgiveness. Such ceremonies tend to occur in recent chiefdoms.[61] Among the Fijians of the South Pacific, there is a strong ethic of harmony and mutual assistance, particularly within a village. When a person offends someone of higher status, the offended person and other villagers begin to avoid, and gossip about, the offender. If the offender is sensitive to village opinion, he or she will perform a ceremony of apology called *i soro*. One of the meanings of *soro* is "surrender." In the ceremony the offender keeps her or his head bowed and remains silent while an intermediary speaks, presents a token gift, and asks the offended person for forgiveness. The apology is rarely rejected.[62]

OATHS AND ORDEALS. Still another way of peacefully resolving disputes is through oaths and ordeals, both of which involve appeals to supernatural power. An **oath** is the act of calling upon a deity to bear witness to the truth of what one says. An **ordeal** is a means used to determine guilt or innocence by submitting the accused to dangerous or painful tests believed to be under supernatural control.[63]

Oaths, as one would expect, vary widely in content, according to the culture in which they are found. The Rwala Bedouin, for example, do the following:

> In serious disputes the judge requires the *msabba* oath, so called from the seven lines drawn with a saber on the ground. The judge first draws a circle with a saber, then its diameter; then he intersects with five vertical lines, inviting the witness to step inside and, facing south, to swear: "A false oath is the ruin of the descendants, for he who [swears falsely] is insatiable in his desire [of gain] and does not fear for his Lord."[64]

Scarcely is the oath finished when the witness jumps out of the circle and, full of rage, runs at his opponent, who has made him swear. The people at the trial have to hold him until he calms down.

A common kind of ordeal, found in almost every part of the world, is scalding. Among the Tanala of Madagascar, the accused person, having first had his hand carefully examined for protective covering, has to reach his hand into a cauldron of boiling water and grasp, from underneath, a rock suspended there. He then plunges his hand into cold water, has it bandaged, and is led off to spend the night under guard. In the morning his hand is unbandaged and examined. If there are blisters, he is guilty.

Oaths and ordeals have also been practiced in Western societies. Both were common in medieval Europe. Even today, in our own society, vestiges of oaths can be found: children can be heard to say, "Cross my heart and hope to die," and witnesses in courts of law are obliged to swear to tell the truth.

Why do some societies use oaths and ordeals? John Roberts suggested that they tend to be found in fairly complex societies in which political officials lack sufficient power to make and enforce judicial decisions or would make themselves unnecessarily vulnerable were they to attempt to do so. So the officials may use oaths and ordeals to let the gods decide guilt or innocence. When political officials gain more power, oaths and ordeals seem to decline or disappear.[65] In contrast, smaller and less complex societies probably have no need for elaborate mechanisms such as courts and oaths and ordeals to ascertain guilt. In such societies, everyone is aware of what crimes have been committed and who the guilty parties probably are.

ADJUDICATION, COURTS, AND CODIFIED LAW. We call it **adjudication** when a third party acting as judge makes a decision that the disputing parties have to accept. Judgment may be rendered by one person (a judge), a panel of judges, a jury, or a political agent or agency (a chief, a royal personage, a council). Courts are often open to an audience, but they need not be. Judges and courts may rely on codified law and stipulated punishments, but codified law is not necessary for decisions to be made. Our own society relies heavily on codified law and courts to resolve disputes peacefully, but courts often, if not usually, rely on precedent—that is, the outcomes of previous, similar cases. Codified laws and courts are not limited to Western societies. From the late seventeenth to the early twentieth centuries, for example, the Ashanti of West Africa had a complex political system with elaborate legal arrangements. The Ashanti state was a military-based empire possessing legal codes that resembled those of many ancient civilizations.[66]

The most effective sanction underpinning Ashanti law and its enforcement was the intense respect—almost religious deference—accorded the wishes of the ancestors and also the elders as custodians of the ancestral tradition. Ashanti law was based on a concept of natural law, a belief that there is an order of the universe whose principles lawmakers should follow in the decisions they make and in the regulations they design. Criminal and religious law were merged by the Ashanti. Crimes, especially homicide, cursing of a chief, cowardice, and sorcery, were regarded as sins against the ancestral spirits. In Ashanti court procedure, elders examined and cross-examined witnesses as well as parties to the dispute. There were also quasi-professional advocates, and appeals against a verdict could be made directly to a chief. Particularly noteworthy was the emphasis on intent when assessing guilt. Drunkenness constituted a valid defense for all crimes except murder and cursing a chief, and a plea of insanity, if proved, was upheld for all offenses.

Ashanti punishments could be severe. Physical mutilation, such as slicing off the nose or an ear—even castration in sexual offenses—was often employed. Fines were more frequent, however, and death sentences could often be commuted to banishment and confiscation of goods.

Why do some societies have codified systems and others do not? One explanation, advanced by E. Adamson Hoebel, A. R. Radcliffe-Brown, and others, is that in small, closely knit communities there is little need for formal legal guidelines because competing interests are minimal. Hence, simple societies need little codified law. There are relatively few matters to quarrel about, and the general will of the group is sufficiently well known and demonstrated frequently enough to deter transgressors.

This point of view is echoed in Richard Schwartz's study of two Israeli settlements. In one communal kibbutz, a young man aroused a good deal of community resentment because he had accepted an electric teakettle as a gift. It was the general opinion that he had overstepped the code about not having personal possessions, and he was so informed. Accordingly, he gave the kettle to the communal infirmary. Schwartz observed that "no organized enforcement of the decision was threatened, but had he disregarded the expressed will of

Many societies have adopted courts to resolve disputes, as here in Papua New Guinea.

New Perspectives on Gender

NEW COURTS ALLOW WOMEN TO ADDRESS GRIEVANCES IN PAPUA NEW GUINEA

In most societies in New Guinea, women did not traditionally participate in the resolution of disputes. And they could not bring actions against men. But when village courts were introduced, women began to go to court to redress offenses against them.

In colonial times, the introduced Western-style courts followed Western law, primarily Australian and British common law, not native customary law. After Papua New Guinea became an independent country, those courts remained in place. The lowest of the courts, called Local Courts, were located in town centers, often far from villages, so villagers rarely brought cases to them. But in 1973 a new kind of court was created. Called Village Courts, they were designed to settle local disputes in the villages, using a blend of customary law (relying on compromise) and Western law. In contrast to the Local Courts, magistrates in the Village Courts were not outsiders but were selected from the pool of traditional and local leaders who knew the local people.

When Richard Scaglion studied changes in village courts among the Abelam from 1977 to 1987, he noticed a shift toward the increased use of these courts by women. In 1977, most of the complainants were male, but by 1987 most of them were female. In a wider study of court cases over many regions of Papua New Guinea, Scaglion and Rose Whittingham found that most of the cases in which women were the plaintiffs were attempts to redress sex-related offenses (sexual jealousy, rape, incest, domestic disputes) committed by males. Most disputes in New Guinea villages are settled informally by self-help or by appeal to a "big man"; the courts are appealed to only as a last resort. But serious sex-related cases are unlikely to be settled informally but, rather, in the Village Court. Apparently women do not believe that they can get satisfaction informally. So they go to the Village Court, where they win some sort of punishment for the defendant in about 60 percent of the cases, just about the same rate that men achieve when they bring a case seeking punishment.

Culture change introduced from the outside often works against native peoples. But Papuan New Guinea women have benefited from the new Village Court system, particularly in redressing grievances against males. The traditional system for resolving disputes was largely male-dominated (women could not be plaintiffs) and so the possibility of taking disputes to the new courts has given women some measure of legal equality with men.

Sources: Richard Scaglion, "Legal Adaptation in a Papua New Guinea Village Court," *Ethnology* 29 (1990): 17–33; Richard Scaglion and Rose Whittingham, "Female Plaintiffs and Sex-Related Disputes in Rural Papua New Guinea," in S. Toft, ed., *Domestic Violence in Papua New Guinea. Monograph No. 3* (Port Moresby, Papua New Guinea: Law Reform Commission, 1985), pp. 120–33.

---

the community, his life . . . would have been made intolerable by the antagonism of public opinion."[67]

In this community, where people worked and ate together, not only did everyone know about transgressions, but a wrongdoer could not escape public censure. Thus, public opinion was an effective sanction. In another Israeli community, however, where individuals lived in widely separated houses and worked and ate separately, public opinion did not work as well. Not only were community members less aware of problems, but they had no quick way of making their feelings known. As a result, they established a judicial body to handle trouble cases.

Larger, more heterogeneous and stratified societies are likely to have more frequent disputes, which at the same time are less visible to the public. Individuals in stratified societies are generally not so dependent on community members for their well-being and hence are less likely to know of, or care about, others' opinions. It is in such societies that codified laws and formal authorities for resolving disputes develop—in order, perhaps, that disputes may be settled impersonally enough so that the parties can accept the decision and social order can be restored.

A good example of how more formal systems of law develop is the experience of towns in the American West during the gold-rush period. These communities were literally swamped by total strangers. The townsfolk, having no control (authority) over these intruders because the strangers had no local ties, looked for ways to deal with the troublesome cases that were continually flaring up. A first attempt at a solution was to hire gunslingers, who were also strangers, to act as peace officers or sheriffs, but this strategy usually failed. Eventually, towns succeeded in having federal authorities send in marshals backed by federal power.

Is there some evidence to support the theory that codified law is necessary only in larger, more complex societies? Data from a large, worldwide sample of societies suggest that codified law is associated with political integration beyond the local level. Murder cases, for example, are dealt with informally in societies that have only local political organization. In societies with multilocal political units, murder cases tend to be judged or adjudicated by specialized political authorities.[68] There is also some cross-cultural evidence that violence within a society tends to be less frequent when there are formal authorities (chiefs, courts) who have the power to punish murderers.[69] In general, adjudication or enforced decisions by outside authorities tend to occur in hierarchical societies with social classes and centralized power.[70]

Violent Resolution of Conflict

People are likely to resort to violence when regular, effective alternative means of resolving a conflict are not available. Some societies consider violence between individuals to be appropriate under certain circumstances; we generally do not and call it **crime.** When violence occurs between political entities such as communities, districts, or nations, we call it **warfare.** The type of warfare, of course, varies in scope and complexity from society to society. Sometimes a distinction is made among feuding, raiding, and large-scale confrontations.

Some scholars talk about a cultural pattern of violence. But are some cultures more violent than others? The answer seems to be yes. More often than not, societies with one type of violence have others. Societies with more war tend to have warlike sports, malevolent magic, severe punishment for crimes, high murder rates, feuding, and family violence. What might explain this tendency? One suggestion is that if war is frequent, the society may have to encourage boys to be aggressive, so that they can grow up to be effective warriors. But this socializing for aggression can spill over into other areas of life; high rates of crime and other violence may be inadvertent or unintended consequences of the encouragement of aggressiveness.[71]

INDIVIDUAL VIOLENCE. Although at first it may seem paradoxical, violent behavior itself is often used to try to control behavior. In some societies it is considered necessary for parents to beat children who misbehave. They don't consider this criminal behavior or child abuse; they consider it punishment (see our discussion of family violence in the chapter on applied anthropology and social problems). Similar views may attach to interpersonal behavior between adults. If a person trespasses on your property or hurts someone in your family, some societies consider it appropriate or justified to kill or maim the trespasser. Is this social control, or is it just lack of control? Most societies have norms about when such "punishment" is or is not appropriate, so the behavior of anyone who contemplates doing something wrong, as well as the behavior of the person wronged, is likely to be influenced by the "laws" of their society. For example, systems of individual self-help are characteristic of egalitarian societies.[72] How is this different from "community action," which earlier we classified under peaceful resolution of conflict? Because community action is explicitly based on obtaining a consensus, it is likely to lead to the ending of a particular dispute. Individual action, or self-help, particularly if it involves violence, is not.

FEUDING. **Feuding** is an example of how individual self-help may not lead to a peaceful resolution of conflict. Feuding is a state of recurring hostilities between families or groups of kin, usually motivated by a desire to avenge an offense—whether insult, injury, deprivation, or death—against a member of the group. The most common characteristic of the feud is that responsibility to avenge is carried by all members of the kin group. The killing of any member of the offender's group is considered appropriate revenge, because the kin group as a whole is regarded as responsible. Nicholas Gubser told of a feud within a Nunamiut Inuit community, caused by a husband's killing of his wife's lover, that lasted for decades. The Nunamiut take feuds seriously, as do many societies, especially when murder has been committed. Gubser described what happens when a man is killed:

> The closely related members of his kindred do not rest until complete revenge has been achieved. The immediate relatives of the deceased . . . recruit as much support from other relatives as they can. Their first action, if possible, is to kill the murderer, or maybe one of his closest kin. Then, of course, the members of the murderer's kindred are brought into the feud. These two kindreds may snipe at each other for years.[73]

Feuds are by no means limited to small-scale societies; they occur as frequently in societies with high levels of political organization.[74]

RAIDING. Raiding is a short-term use of force, planned and organized, to realize a limited objective. This objective is usually the acquisition of goods, animals, or other forms of wealth belonging to another, often neighboring community.

Raiding is especially prevalent in pastoral societies, in which cattle, horses, camels, or other animals are prized and an individual's own herd can be augmented by theft. Raids are often organized by temporary leaders or coordinators whose authority may not last beyond the planning and execution of the venture. Raiding may also be organized for the purpose of capturing people. Sometimes people are taken to marry—the capture of women to be wives or concubines is fairly common[75]—or to be slaves. Slavery has been practiced in about 33 percent of the world's known societies, and war has been one way of obtaining slaves either to keep or to trade for other goods.[76]

LARGE-SCALE CONFRONTATIONS. Both feuding and raiding usually involve relatively small numbers of persons and almost always an element of surprise. Because they are generally attacked without warning, the victims are often unable to muster an immediate defense. Large-scale confrontations, in contrast, involve a large number of persons and planning by both sides of strategies of attack and defense. Large-scale warfare is usually practiced among societies with intensive agriculture or industrialization. Only these societies possess a technology sufficiently advanced to support specialized armies, military leaders, strategists, and so on. But large-scale confrontations are not limited to state societies: they occur, for example, among the horticultural Dugum Dani of central New Guinea.

The military history of the Dani, with its shifting alliances and confederations, is reminiscent of that of Europe, although Dani battles involve far fewer fighters and less sophisticated weaponry. Among the Dani, long periods of ritual warfare are characterized by formal battles announced through a challenge sent by one side to the opposing side. If the challenge is accepted, the protagonists meet at the agreed-upon battle site to set up their lines. Fighting with spears, sticks, and bows and arrows begins at midmorning and continues either until nightfall or until rain intervenes. There may also be a rest period during the midday heat during which the two sides shout insults at each other or talk and rest among themselves.

The front line of battle is composed of about a dozen active warriors and a few leaders. Behind them is a second line, still within arrow range, composed of those who have just left the forward line or are preparing to join it. The third line, outside arrow range, is composed of noncombatants—males too

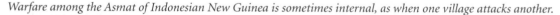

Warfare among the Asmat of Indonesian New Guinea is sometimes internal, as when one village attacks another.

old or too young to participate and those recovering from wounds. This third line merely watches the battle taking place on the grassy plain. On the hillsides far back from the front line, some of the old men help to direct ancestral ghosts to the battle by gouging a line in the ground that points in the direction of the battlefield.[77]

Yet, as total as large-scale confrontations may be, even warfare has cultural rules. Among the Dani, for instance, no fighting occurs at night, and weapons are limited to simple spears and bows and arrows. Similarly, in state societies, governments will sign "self-denying" pacts restricting the use of poison gas, germ warfare, and so forth. Unofficially, private arrangements are common. One has only to glance through the memoirs of national leaders of the two world wars to become aware of locally arranged truces, visits to one another's front positions, exchanges of prisoners of war, and so on.

EXPLAINING WARFARE

Most societies anthropology knows about have had warfare between communities or larger territorial groups. The vast majority of the societies in a recent cross-cultural study had at least occasional wars when they were first described, unless they had been pacified or incorporated by more dominant societies.[78] Yet relatively little research has been done on the possible causes of war and why it varies in type and frequency. For instance, why have some people fought a great deal, and others only infrequently? Why in some societies does warfare occur internally, within the society or language group?

We have answers, based on cross-cultural studies, to some of those questions. There is evidence that people in preindustrial societies go to war mostly out of fear, particularly a fear of expectable but unpredictable natural disasters (e.g., droughts, floods, locust infestations) that will destroy food resources. People may think they can protect themselves against such disasters ahead of time by taking things from defeated enemies. In any case, preindustrial societies with higher frequencies of war are very likely to have had a history of expectable but unpredictable disasters. The fact that chronic (annually recurring and therefore predictable) food shortages do not predict higher frequencies of war suggests that people go to war in an attempt to cushion the impact of the disasters they expect to occur in the future but cannot predict. Consistent with this tentative conclusion is the fact that the victors in war almost always take land or other resources from the defeated. And this is true for simpler as well as more complex preindustrial societies.[79] Might similar motives affect decisions about war and peace in the modern world?

We know that complex or politically centralized societies are likely to have professional armies, hierarchies of military authority, and sophisticated weapons.[80] But surprisingly, the frequency of warfare seems to be not much greater in complex societies than in simple band or tribal societies.[81] We have some evidence that warfare is unlikely to occur internally (within a society) if it is small in population (21,000 or fewer people) or territory; in a larger society there is a high likelihood of warfare within the society, between communities or larger territorial divisions.[82] In fact, complex societies, even if they are politically unified, are not less likely than simpler societies to have internal warfare.[83]

What about the idea that men in band and tribal societies may mostly go to war over women?[84] If this were true, those band and tribal societies with the most frequent wars should have shortages of women, and those with little or no war—less often than once in 10 years—should have more equal numbers of women and men. But the cross-cultural evidence clearly contradicts this theory. Band and tribal societies with more wars do not have fewer women.[85]

What, if anything, do we know about recent warfare between nation-states? Here we also have some surprising findings. Although many people think that military alliances lessen the chance of war, it turns out that nations formally allied with other nations have gone to war more often than nations lacking formal alliances. Also, trade relationships do not appear to lessen the chance of war. Rather, disputes between trading partners escalate to war more frequently than disputes between nations that do not trade much with each other. Finally, military equality between nations, particularly when preceded by a rapid military buildup, seems to increase rather than lessen the chance of war between those nations.[86]

Clearly, these findings contradict some traditional beliefs about how to prevent war. If alliances, trade, and military buildups do not make war less likely, what may? We have already noted that participatory ("democratic") political systems are less likely to go to war with each other than are authoritarian political systems. Later, in the chapter on applied anthropology and social problems, we discuss how the results of these studies may translate into policies that could minimize the risk of war in the world.

1. All societies have customs or procedures that, organized on behalf of territorial groups, result in decision making and the resolution of disputes. These ways of creating and maintaining social order and coping with social disorder vary from society to society.

2. Societies with a band type of political organization are composed of fairly small, usually nomadic groups. Each of these bands is politically autonomous, the band being the largest group that acts as a political unit. Authority within the band is usually informal. Societies with band organization generally are egalitarian hunter-gatherers. But band organization may not have been typical of food collectors in the distant past.

3. Societies with tribal organization are similar to those with band organization in being egalitarian. But in contrast with band societies, they generally are food producers, have a higher population density, and are more sedentary. Tribal organization is defined by the presence of groupings, such as clans and age-sets, that can integrate more than one local group into a larger whole.

4. The personal qualities of leaders in tribal societies seem to be similar to the qualities of leaders in the United States, with one major difference: United States leaders are wealthier than others in their society.

5. Chiefdom organization differs from tribal organization in having formal authority structures that integrate multicommunity political units. Compared with societies with tribal organization, societies with chiefdoms are more densely populated and their communities are more permanent. In contrast to "big men" in tribal societies, who generally have to earn their privileges by their personal qualities, chiefs generally hold their positions permanently. Most chiefdom societies have social ranking.

6. A state has been defined as a political unit composed of many communities and having a centralized government with the authority to make and enforce laws, collect taxes, and draft men for military service. In state societies, the government tries to maintain a monopoly on the use of physical force. In addition, states are generally characterized by class stratification, intensive agriculture (the high productivity of which presumably allows the emergence of cities), commercial exchange, a high degree of economic and other specialization, and extensive foreign trade. The rulers of a state cannot depend forever on the use or threat of force to maintain their power; the people must believe that the rulers are legitimate or have the right to govern.

7. Degree of political participation varies in the societies studied by anthropologists, just as among modern nation-states. Degree of political participation seems to be high in small-scale societies, as well as in modern democratic nation-states, but not in those in between, such as feudal states and preindustrial empires.

8. Many societies lack specialized offices and institutions for dealing with conflict. Yet all societies have peaceful, regularized ways of handling at least certain disputes. Avoidance, community action, and negotiation and mediation are more common in simpler societies. Ritual apology occurs frequently in chiefdoms. Oaths and ordeals tend to occur in complex societies in which political officials lack power to enforce judicial decisions. Adjudication is more likely in stratified, more complex societies. Capital punishment seems to exist in nearly all societies, from the simplest to the most complex.

9. People are likely to resort to violence when regular, effective alternative means of resolving a conflict are not available. Violence can occur between individuals, within communities, and between communities. Violence that occurs between political entities such as communities, districts, or nations is generally referred to as warfare. The type of warfare varies in scope and complexity from society to society. Preindustrial societies with higher warfare frequencies are likely to have had a history of unpredictable disasters that destroyed food supplies. More often than not, societies with one type of violence have others.

▉▉ GLOSSARY TERMS

adjudication	negotiation
band	oath
band organization	ordeal
chief	raiding
chiefdom	segmentary lineage
codified laws	system
complementary	state
opposition	state organization
crime	tribal organization
feuding	tribe
headman	warfare
mediation	

CRITICAL QUESTIONS

1. When, if ever, do you think the world will be politically unified, and why do you think so?

2. Why don't informal methods of social control work well in societies like our own? Why don't formal methods work better than they do?

3. What does research on war and violence suggest about how to minimize them?

INTERNET EXERCISES

1. Visit **http://jefferson.village.virginia.edu/vshadow2** and read some of the correspondence related to the Civil War in the United States (**http://jefferson.village.virginia.edu/vshadow2/letters.html**). Briefly describe your findings.

2. A political scientist, Rudy Rummel, has compiled data on genocide and more generally democide, by which he means the murder of any person or people by a government, including genocide, politicide, and mass murder. Go to his site **http://www2.hawaii.edu/~rummel**. What kinds of governments commit the most democide? Keep in mind that you have to add three zeros to most of his figures to see the number of people killed.

3. Learn about international criminal tribunals and their functions at **http://www.igc.apc.org/tribunal**. Briefly describe the functions of a tribunal.

SUGGESTED READING

FRY, D. P., AND K. BJÖRKQVIST, EDS. *Cultural Variation in Conflict Resolution: Alternatives to Violence.* Mahwah, NJ: Lawrence Erlbaum Associates, 1997. The case studies in this book show that alternatives to violence exist in many societies, indicating that violence is not inevitable. If conflicts are often resolved without violence, it should be possible to dis-

cover the principles of nonviolent conflict resolution, which people could learn and practice.

HAAS, J., ED. *The Anthropology of War.* Cambridge: Cambridge University Press, 1990. The contributors to this volume discuss war in general and in particular places, focusing on explanatory models of warfare, origins versus persistence of warfare, and causes versus effects of warfare in nonstate societies.

MCGLYNN, F., AND TUDEN, A., EDS. *Anthropological Approaches to Political Behavior.* Pittsburgh: University of Pittsburgh Press, 1991. A compilation of articles that discuss political processes in a variety of societies. The editors provide an overview of the central concerns of political anthropology and its different approaches.

ROSS, M. H. "Political Participation." In C. R. Ember and M. Ember, eds., *Cross-Cultural Research for Social Science* (Upper Saddle River, NJ: Prentice Hall, 1998). Prentice Hall/Simon & Schuster Custom Publishing. This chapter, written especially for undergraduates, discusses variation in political participation (decision making and demand making) in societies and nations. The author also discusses why political participation varies.

SCAGLION, R. "Law and Society." In C. R. Ember and M. Ember, eds., *Cross-Cultural Research for Social Science* (Upper Saddle River, NJ: Prentice Hall, 1998). Prentice Hall/Simon & Schuster Custom Publishing. Written especially for undergraduates, this chapter reviews some of the comparative research on law and summarizes two approaches to the study of law in anthropology—the rule-centered approach and the processual approach.

UPHAM, S., ED. *The Evolution of Political Systems: Sociopolitics in Small-Scale Sedentary Societies.* Cambridge: Cambridge University Press, 1990. The contributors to this volume offer different and sometimes contradictory ideas about political organization and change in sedentary societies. They explore fundamental questions such as how people come to give up local autonomy and equality for bigger, hierarchical political units.

Psychology and Culture

*V*isitors to another society often come to feel that the people there think differently, or have different reactions to situations, that they seem to have different **personalities**—distinctive ways of thinking, feeling, and behaving—compared with people back home. Stereotypes are born from these casual observations. Certain peoples are thought to be reserved, others authoritarian, still others hot-tempered. Although anthropologists generally reject such stereotypes because they are often based on hasty, even ethnocentric judgments, they do not reject the idea that there may be differences from society to society in some aspects of thinking, feeling, and behaving.

Consider the contrast in feelings and behavior between the Semai of central Malaya and the Yanomamö of the Brazil-Venezuela border, a contrast that clearly expresses differences in personality. The Semai are famous in Malaya for their timidity and have never been described as hostile or surly. When asked about anger, the Semai say, "We do not get angry."[1] The Yanomamö, on the other hand, are known for their aggression. They not only have chronic warfare between villages but frequently show aggression within a village. Shouting and threatening to obtain demands are frequent, as are wife beatings and bloody fights with clubs. Men are proud of their scars and sometimes shave their heads to display them.[2]

Even though there may be psychological differences between societies, there also are psychological similarities. After all, we are all human. People the world over cry or weep when a loved one dies, laugh or smile when something good happens, learn from mistakes, and have many of the same needs. Anthropologists who are interested in psychological differences between and within societies and in psychological similarities across the broad range of human societies call themselves *psychological anthropologists*. Psychologists who study people in two or more societies call themselves *cross-cultural psychologists*. Four main questions seem to characterize psychological anthropology: To what extent do all human beings develop psychologically in the same ways? If there are differences, what are they and what may account for them? How do people in different societies conceive of personality and psychological development? What kinds of cultural variation might be explained by psychological factors? This chapter discusses some of the attempts made by researchers to answer these questions.

THE UNIVERSALITY OF PSYCHOLOGICAL DEVELOPMENT

Anthropologists became interested in psychology in the early years of the twentieth century partly because they did not believe that human nature was completely revealed in Western societies, as psychologists then generally assumed. Only recently have many psychologists joined anthropologists in questioning the assumption that humans are exactly the same psychologically in all societies. The psychologist Otto Klineberg, for example, scolded his colleagues in 1974: "My contact with anthropology affected me somewhat like a religious conversion. How could psychologists speak of *human* attributes and *human* behavior when they knew only one kind of human being?"[3]

How can we know what is universal about human behavior and what is variable until we study all kinds of humans? Because humans the world over are the same species and share a very large proportion of their genes, we might assume that there is a good deal of similarity across societies in the way people develop psychologically from birth to maturity or in the way people think, feel, and behave. We have already discussed many universals—culture, language, marriage, the incest taboo—but here we discuss some that are related more to psychology. Donald Brown compiled a list of probable human universals in the psychological realm.[4] They include the ability to create taxonomies, make binary contrasts, order phenomena, use logical operators (e.g., *and, not, equals*), plan for the future, and have an understanding of the world and what it is about.

With regard to ideas about people, it seems universal to have a concept of the self or person, to recognize individual faces, to try to discern other persons' intentions from observable clues in their faces, utterances, and actions, and to imagine what others are thinking. With regard to emotions, people seem universally to be able to empathize with the feelings of others, facially communicate and recognize, as well as hide or mimic, the emotions of happiness, sadness, anger, fear, surprise, disgust, and contempt (see the box "Do Masks Show Emotion in Universal Ways?" in the chapter on the arts), smile when friendly, cry when in pain or unhappy, play for fun, show and feel affection for others, feel sexual attraction, envy, and jealousy, and have similar childhood fears (e.g., fear of strangers). Indeed, it seems that people in different cultures even conceive of love in much the same ways, despite love's reputation as something mysterious and culturally variable.[5]

What about psychological development? We saw in the chapter on communication and language that certain aspects of language acquisition appear to be universal across cultures. In what respects is psychological development the same the world over? In what respects is it different?

EARLY RESEARCH ON EMOTIONAL DEVELOPMENT

When Margaret Mead went to American Samoa in the mid-1920s, psychologists believed that adolescence was universally a period of "storm and stress" because of the physiological changes that occur at puberty. Mead's observations of, and interviews with, Samoan adolescent girls led her to doubt the idea that adolescence was necessarily a time of turmoil. Samoan girls apparently showed little evidence of emotional upheaval and rebelliousness, and therefore it was questionable whether psychological development in adolescence was the same in all societies.[6]

Bronislaw Malinowski, another early anthropologist, questioned the universality of an assumption about emotional development, in this case Freud's assumption that young boys universally see themselves, unconsciously, as sexual rivals of their fathers for possession of their mothers. Freud called these feelings the *Oedipus complex,* after the character in Greek mythology who killed his father and married his mother without knowing that they were his parents. Freud thought that all boys before the age of 7 or so would show hostility toward their fathers, but Malinowski disagreed on the basis of his fieldwork in the matrilineal Trobriand Islands.[7]

Malinowski suggested that young boys in nonmatrilineal societies may feel hostility toward the father not as a sexual rival but as the disciplinarian. Malinowski proposed this theory because he thought that the Oedipus complex works differently in matrilineal societies. Boys in matrilineal societies may feel more hostile toward their mother's brother—who is the main authority figure in the matrilineal kin group—than toward their father.

Derek Freeman criticized Mead's conclusions about Samoa,[8] and Melford Spiro challenged Malinowski's conclusions about the Trobriand Islanders.[9] Mead and Malinowski may or may not have been correct about the societies they studied, but the issues they raised remain crucial to the question of whether psychological development is similar across societies. To find out, we need research in *many* soci-

Adolescence in many societies is a time for developing work skills. An Asmat boy in Indonesian New Guinea is learning to carve, and an adult is supervising.

eties, not just a few. Only on the basis of extensive cross-cultural research will we be able to decide whether stages of emotional development can be affected by cultural differences.

For example, it is only recently that adolescence has been systematically studied cross-culturally. Alice Schlegel and Herbert Barry reported that adolescence is generally not a period of overt rebelliousness. The reason, they suggested, is related to the fact that most people in most societies live with or near (and depend on) close kin before and after they grow up. Only in societies like our own, where children leave home when they grow up, might adolescents be rebellious, possibly to prepare emotionally for going out on their own.[10] (See the box "Neolocality and Adolescent Rebellion: Are They Related?" in the chapter on marital residence and kinship.)

RESEARCH ON COGNITIVE DEVELOPMENT

One day the two of us went out for pizza. The pizza maker was laughing hilariously, and we asked what was so funny. He told us: "I just asked the guy ahead of you, 'How many slices do you want me to cut the pizza into, six or eight?' 'Six,' he said, 'I'm not very hungry.'" According to a theory of cognitive (intellectual) development suggested by Jean Piaget, the renowned Swiss psychologist, the "not very hungry" guy may not have acquired the concept of *conservation*, which characterizes a stage of thinking normally acquired by children between the ages of 7 and 11 in Western societies.[11] The pizza customer ahead of us, like many very young children, seemed not to understand that certain properties of an object, such as quantity, weight, and volume, remain constant even if the object is divided into small pieces or removed to a container of a different shape. They have not acquired the mental image of *reversibility*, the ability to imagine that if you put the pizza back together again it would be the same size whether you had cut it into eight or six slices. To the child or adult who has not acquired the ability to reverse actions mentally, eight slices may seem like more pizza than six slices, because eight is more than six.

Piaget's theory says that the development of thinking in humans involves a series of stages, each of which is characterized by different mental skills. To get to a higher stage of thinking, one has to pass through a lower stage. So Piaget's theory would predict that the pizza customer would not be able to think systematically about the possible outcomes of hypothetical situations, a defining feature of Piaget's *formal-operational* stage, because he had not acquired the notion of conservation and the other mental skills that characterize the previous, *concrete-operational* stage of cognitive development.

A four-and-a-half-year-old girl is being tested for conservation of area.

What does the evidence suggest about the universality of Piaget's supposed stages? And do people the world over get to each stage at the same age? The first stage of development, *sensorimotor,* has not been investigated in many societies, but the results of studies conducted so far are remarkably consistent. They support Piaget's notion that there is a predictable order in the sequence of stages.[12] And, on the basis of their reactions to the same conditions, babies in different places seem to think similarly. For example, a comparison of French babies and Baoulé babies in the Ivory Coast showed that the Baoulé babies, who had never seen objects such as red plastic tubes and paper clips, nevertheless tried to pass the clips through the tubes in the same way the French babies did. The two sets of babies even made the same kinds of errors.[13] And even though they have few toys, the Baoulé babies showed advances over French babies on such tasks as using instruments to increase the reach of the arm. But Baoulé babies are allowed to touch all kinds of objects, even things that Europeans consider dangerous.[14]

Most of the cross-cultural studies of Piaget's stages have focused on the transition between the second, *preoperational,* and third, *concrete-operational,* stages, particularly the attainment of the concept of conservation. The results of many of these studies are somewhat puzzling. Although older children are generally more likely to show conservation than younger children, it is not clear what to make of the apparent finding that the attainment of conservation is much delayed in many non-Western populations. Indeed, in some places most of the adults tested do not appear to understand one or more of the conservation properties.

Can this be true? Do people in different cultures differ that much in intellectual functioning, or is there some problem with the way conservation is measured? Is it possible that an adult who just brought water from the river in a large jug and poured it into five smaller containers does not know that the quantity of water is still the same? We may also be skeptical about the findings on the formal-operational stage. Most of the studies of formal-operational thinking have found little evidence of such thinking in non-Western populations. But people in nonliterate societies surely have formal-operational thinking if they can navigate using the stars, remember how to return to camp after a 15-mile trek, or identify how people are related to each other three and more generations back.

One reason to be skeptical about the apparent findings regarding delay of conservation and formal-operational thinking is that most of the cross-cultural psychologists have taken tests developed in our own and other Western countries to measure cognitive development elsewhere.[15] This procedure puts non-Westerners at a considerable disadvantage, because they are not as familiar as Westerners with the test materials and the whole testing situation. In tests of conservation, for example, researchers have often used strange-looking glass cylinders and beakers. Some researchers who have used natively familiar materials, however, have gotten different results. Douglass Price-Williams found no difference between Tiv, in West Africa, and European children in understanding the conservation of earth, nuts, and number.[16] Also, some researchers have retested children after brief training sessions and found that they improved substantially. It would seem, then, that children anywhere can acquire the concept of conservation if they have had preparatory life experiences or appropriate training.[17]

The results of tests elsewhere on formal-operational thinking may also be questionable. Such tests ask questions dealing with content that is taught here in science and mathematics classes. It should not be surprising, then, that schooled individuals usually do better than the nonschooled on tests of formal-operational thinking. Where compulsory schooling is lacking, we should not expect people to do well on tests of such thinking.[18]

In trying to find out what may be universal in emotional and cognitive development, researchers have discovered some apparent differences between societies. These differences, to which we now turn, need to be explored and explained.

CROSS-CULTURAL VARIATION IN PSYCHOLOGICAL CHARACTERISTICS

Thinking about personality differences seems to come easily to many North Americans. We like to talk about the psychology of those we know. We speculate why one friend is emotional, why another has a quick temper, why another is shy. We may also wonder why one friend is likely to remember faces and why another is a whiz at computers. We are interested in personality as an individual characteristic, and we emphasize the uniqueness of each individual. Indeed, because every person has a unique combination of genetic traits and life experiences, we can say that in some ways no person is like any

other person. But anthropologists are interested in approaching personality from a different perspective. Instead of focusing on the uniqueness of an individual, psychological anthropologists are interested in those aspects of personality that may be common in a population.

Why should we expect different societies to differ in some personality characteristics? It is generally agreed that our personalities are the result of an interaction between genetic inheritance and life experiences. But a considerable portion of one's life experiences, as well as one's genes, is shared with others. Parents undoubtedly exert a major influence on the way we grow up. Because family members share similar life experiences and genes, they may be somewhat similar in personality. But we have to consider why a particular family raises children the way it does. Much of the way parents rear children is influenced by their culture—by typical patterns of family life and by shared conceptions of the way to bring up children.

It is not easy to determine the extent to which members of a society share conceptions about child rearing. As we look at families in our own society, we see differences in upbringing that reflect different ideas about the "right" way to raise children. Indeed, some parents seem determined to bring up their children in unconventional ways in terms of our society. Still, in a study of unconventional California families, headed by single mothers, unmarried couples, or living in communes, researchers found that compared with parents in other societies, these so-called unconventional parents did not differ that much from conventional parents (married, living in nuclear families).[19] For example, even though unconventional California mothers breast-fed their children for a significantly longer period than conventional mothers did, both groups usually stopped breast-feeding after about a year, which is far below the worldwide average. In 70 percent of the world's societies, mothers typically breast-feed children for at least two years; last-born children may be weaned even later. In a few societies, such as the Chenchu of India, children typically were not weaned until they were 5 or 6 years old.[20] Both the unconventional and conventional California parents differed in other ways too, compared with parents in most other societies. In the California study, no parent, conventional or unconventional, was observed to carry a baby more than 25 percent of the time, but it is common in many preindustrial societies for babies to be held more than half the day.[21]

Our own cultural conceptions begin to become apparent only when we examine other societies and

One major difference in childrearing between the West and other places is the degree to which an infant is held by a caretaker during the day. In the United States and other Western countries, an infant spends much of the day in a crib, playpen, or stroller. This Bai baby from Yunnan Province in China spends a good deal of time in physical contact with the mother.

their patterns of child rearing. Consider how societies vary in how quickly parents respond to an infant's needs, in other words, the degree of "indulgence." In many aspects of indulgence—amount of time holding, feeding on demand, responding to crying—industrialized societies such as the United States tend to indulge babies less than do preindustrialized societies. In contrast to those preindustrial societies in which babies are held more than half the day, consider the United States, England, and the Netherlands, where babies may spend most of the day in cagelike devices such as playpens or cribs. It is estimated that babies are held or touched only 12 to 20 percent of their daytime hours in these countries and in Japan. The same pattern continues at nighttime. In preindustrial societies, babies are much more apt to be close to another person, usually sleeping with the mother in the same bed or, if not in the same bed, in the same room. During the day, babies are breast-fed in all preindustrial societies, usually on demand. In industrialized societies, bottle-feeding is common, and feeding is usually spaced out every few hours; in some preindustrial societies babies are fed 20 to 40 times a day. And in many preindustrial societies people respond very quickly to an infant's crying. For example, among the Efe of the Ituri Forest in central Africa, a 3-month-old infant who cries gets a response within 10 seconds 75 percent of the time. In the United

States, a caregiver deliberately *does not* respond at all about 45 percent of the time.[22]

The cross-cultural variation just described seems to reflect cultural attitudes toward child rearing. Parents in the United States say that they do not want their babies to be dependent and clingy; they want to produce independent and self-reliant children. Whether children become self-reliant because of our kind of child rearing is debatable,[23] but our attitudes about child rearing are certainly consistent with our practices.

Let us again consider the Yanomamö and the Semai. With respect to aggression, the two societies have very different ways of dealing with children. (The difference is not surprising, in view of the way adult behaviors and attitudes differ in the two societies.) Yanomamö boys are encouraged to be aggressive and are rarely punished for hitting either their parents or the girls in the village. One father, for example, lets his son Ariwari

beat him on the face and head to express his anger and temper, laughing and commenting on his ferocity. Although Ariwari is only about four years old, he has already learned that the appropriate response to a flash of anger is to strike someone with his hand or with an object, and it is not uncommon for him to give his father a healthy smack in the face whenever something displeases him. He is frequently goaded into hitting his father by teasing, being rewarded by gleeful cheers of assent from his mother and from the other adults in the household.[24]

Whereas the Yanomamö clearly and actively encourage aggression, the Semai communicate nonviolence in more subtle ways. They say, in fact, that they do not teach children. The Semai expect children to be nonviolent and are shocked when they are not. When a child loses her temper, an adult will simply cart her off and bring her home. The Semai do not physically punish a child's aggression, and this approach may be one of the most important teaching devices of all. With such teaching—by example—a child rarely sees an aggressive model and thus has no aggression to imitate.[25] In comparison with the ways Semai and Yanomamö parents treat their children, most North American parents are somewhere in the middle. Hardly any North American parents would encourage children to hit them in the face or encourage them to hit other children. Yet many probably use physical punishment sometimes, and many feel that boys especially should "stand up for themselves" if another child provokes a fight.

As these examples suggest, societies vary in how they raise children. We assume that the way children are reared determines in part the type of personality they will have in adulthood. In other words, different societies, with different customs of child rearing, will probably tend to produce different kinds of people. Other cultural differences also may produce differences in typical personality characteristics. As we will see, growing up in an extended family and going to school seem to affect personality development. We do not mean to suggest, however, that all personalities in a society are alike. An individual's uniqueness is derived from her or his distinctive genetic endowment and life experiences—and thus one personality will be at least somewhat different from another within the same culture or subculture.

Cultural anthropologists are interested in common or shared patterns of behavior, belief, feeling, and thinking. Psychological anthropologists are therefore often interested in those aspects of personality that are common or typically shared with others—other members of the society or other members of some subcultural group. Personality attributes are not all-or-nothing characteristics but usually need to be described or measured in terms of degree. So, for example, aggressiveness is not present or absent in a person, but is found to a greater or lesser degree in some people than in others. Similarly, when we say that a great deal of physical or verbal aggression is a characteristic personality trait in a particular society, we are making a relative judgment. When we compare ethnographic descriptions of the Yanomamö and Semai, we can be fairly certain that the Yanomamö typically display much more aggression than the Semai. If fieldworkers based their judgments on systematic comparisons of behavior, we could say how often aggressive behavior is exhibited in a culture, and we could calculate the *modal* frequency of aggression among individuals within a given period of time. That modal frequency could then be compared with the modal frequencies of such behavior in other societies.

Just as culture is never fixed or static, so typical personality characteristics are never static. Individuals often alter their behavior in adapting to changing circumstances. When enough individuals in a society have altered their own behavior or the way they bring up their children, typical personality characteristics will also have changed.

CHILD-REARING EXPLANATIONS

Many researchers have tried to discover if variation in child-rearing customs can account for observed psychological differences. **Socialization** is a term used by both anthropologists and psychologists to describe the development, through the influence of parents and other people, of patterns of behavior, and attitudes and values, in children that conform to cultural expectations. Parents and others often try to socialize children directly by rewarding certain behaviors and ignoring or punishing other behaviors. Socialization can be indirect or subtle as well as direct. In assigning tasks to children, parents are not only encouraging specific skills needed for adult life, but they may also be subtly communicating what kind of person they want their children to become. Whether children go to school may affect their psychological, particularly cognitive, development. Finally, parents may affect the psychological development of their children by the way they generally feel about them.

PARENTAL ACCEPTANCE AND REJECTION. In a classic study of personality, Cora Du Bois spent almost 18 months on the island of Alor in eastern Indonesia studying the native Alorese. To understand the Alorese personality, she broke new ground by asking specialists in various fields to assess and interpret her field data independently. These authorities were given no background briefing on Alorese culture or attitudes, nor were they permitted to see Du Bois's general ethnographic notes or interpretations. To a remarkable degree, their findings concurred with hers.[26]

An unfavorable picture of the typical Alorese personality emerged from this many-sided investigation. Alorese of both sexes were described by Du Bois and her colleagues as suspicious and antagonistic, prone to violent, emotional, and often jealous outbursts. They tended to be uninterested in the world around them, slovenly in workmanship, and indifferent to goals. Turning to the possible causal influences, Du Bois and her co-researchers focused on the experiences of the Alorese infant, particularly time gaps between breast-feedings. At the root of much of Alorese personality development, they suggested, is the mother's long absence from the baby during the day; she returns to agricultural work about ten days to two weeks after the birth. Women are the major food suppliers, working daily in the family gardens; men occupy themselves with commercial affairs, usually the trading of pigs, gongs, and kettledrums. The infant is left in the care of the father, an older sibling, or a grandparent, but it is deprived of the breast as well as the mother for most of the day. Substitute foods are given, but infants often spit them out, suggesting that they are not satisfactory. In Freudian terms, the infant experiences oral frustration and resultant anxiety. At the same time, the baby suffers bewildering switches in attention, from loving and petting to neglect and bad-tempered rejection. Thus, maternal neglect in infancy is viewed as being largely responsible for Alorese personality.

But how do we know that maternal neglect is really responsible for the seeming suspiciousness and outbursts of jealousy among the Alorese? Perhaps maternal neglect is responsible, but the cause or causes could also be any number of other conditions of Alorese life. For example, some critics have suggested that the high prevalence of debilitating diseases in Alor may be responsible for much of the behavior of the Alorese.[27] To be more certain that a particular aspect of child rearing produces certain effects on Alorese personality, we must compare the people of Alor with people in other societies. Do other societies with this kind of maternal neglect show the same pattern of personality traits? If they do, then the presumed association becomes more plausible. If they do not, then the interpretation is questionable.

Although subsequent researchers have not specifically followed up on the possible effects of time gaps between breast-feedings, Ruth and Robert Munroe studied the effects of more versus less

holding by the mother in infancy on Logoli children.[28] The Munroes had observational information on how often infants were held, and they were able to interview many of these individuals as children five years later. They were interested in seeing whether children who had been held more often by their mothers were more secure, trusting, and optimistic. So they designed a series of personality measures appropriate for young children. As a measure of optimism, they showed children smiling faces and nonsmiling faces and asked which they preferred. As measures of trust, they looked to see how long a child was willing to stay in a room with a stranger or play with new toys.

The results of the study suggest that children who were often held or carried by their mothers as infants are significantly more trusting and optimistic at age 5 than are other children. Somewhat to their surprise, the Munroes found that, although time held by other caregivers did not predict more trust and optimism, the sheer number of different people who had held the infant did predict more trust and optimism. Holding by the mother was important, but trust was even greater if the baby had been held by a large number of other persons. One possible explanation is that a highly trusting mother is likely to allow many others to hold the baby; by doing so she conveys trust to the baby.

What about the quality of parenting? Are there positive effects on personality when parents show love, warmth, and affection to their children and negative effects when parents are indifferent or hostile to their children? These questions are difficult to investigate cross-culturally because cultures

A father in Laos bathes his child. In societies where fathers and grandparents help to care for children, the children are less likely to be rejected by parents.

vary in the ways feeling is expressed. If love and affection are not expressed in the same ways, outsiders may misinterpret parental behavior. Nevertheless, Ronald Rohner and his colleagues did extensive work on the effects of parental acceptance and rejection on children after infancy. In a cross-cultural comparison of 101 societies, using measures based on ethnographic materials, Rohner found that children tend to be hostile and aggressive when they are neglected and not treated affectionately by their parents. In societies in which children tend to be rejected, adults seem to view life and the world as unfriendly, uncertain, and hostile.[29] Other studies have compared individuals in different cultures to see if the cross-cultural findings were supported. In general, they were. In addition to finding the world more unfriendly and hostile, individuals who think they were rejected are likely to have negative evaluations of themselves.[30]

Under what conditions is parental rejection likely in childhood? The Rohner study suggests that rejection is likely where mothers get no relief from child care; when fathers and grandparents play a role in child care, rejection is less likely. Food-collecting societies (those dependent on wild food resources) tend to show warmth and affection to their children. More complex societies are less likely to be affectionate to their children.[31] It is not clear why this should be, but perhaps parental rejection is more likely where parents have less leisure time. Less leisure time may make parents more tired and irritable and therefore have less patience with their children. As we noted in the chapter on economic systems, leisure time probably decreases as cultural complexity increases. More complex societies, which rely on intensive agriculture, also tend to have more economic uncertainty, as we noted in the chapter on getting food. Not only do they tend to have more risk of famines and food shortages, but they also tend to have social inequality. In societies with social classes, many families may not have enough food and money to satisfy their needs, and this factor can also produce frustration in the parents. Whatever the reasons for parental rejection, it seems to perpetuate itself: Children who were rejected tend to reject their own children.

TASK ASSIGNMENT. In our society, young children are not expected to help much with chores. If they do have chores, such as tidying up their rooms, they are not likely to affect the welfare of the family or its ability to survive. In contrast, in some societies known to anthropology young children, even 3- and 4-year-olds, are expected to help prepare food, care

for animals, and carry water and firewood, as well as clean. A child between 5 and 8 years of age may even be given the responsibility of caring for an infant or toddler for much of the day while the mother works in the fields.[32] What are the effects of such task assignment on personality development?

We now have evidence from more than 10 cultures that children who regularly babysit are more nurturant—that is, offer more help and support to others—than are other children, even when they are not babysitting. Some of this evidence comes from a project known as the Six Cultures study, in which different research teams observed children's behavior in Kenya (Nyansongo), Mexico, India, the Philippines, Okinawa, and the United States (New England).[33] Ruth and Robert Munroe collected data on children's behavior in four other cultures that show the same relationship between babysitting and nurturant behavior; the Munroes' data come from Kenya (Logoli), Nepal, Belize, and American Samoa.[34] Clearly, children who babysit infrequently are less attuned to others' needs than are children who babysit often.

Why might task assignment affect the behaviors of children? One possibility is that children learn certain behaviors during performance of the task,

---

Children learn from observation as well as by direct instruction from parents and teachers.

and these behaviors become habitual. For example, a responsible babysitter is supposed to offer help. Mothers might directly instruct the babysitter to make sure that happens. But there is probably also an intrinsic satisfaction in doing a job well. For example, it is pleasurable to see an infant smile and laugh, but it is unpleasant to hear a baby cry. We might therefore expect that a child who is assigned babysitting would learn for himself or herself that comforting a baby brings its own rewards.[35]

Children who are assigned many tasks may spend their day in different kinds of settings, and these settings may indirectly influence behavior. For example, children who are asked to do many household chores are apt to be around both adults and younger children. Children who are assigned few or no tasks are freer to play with their agemates. Some of the results of the Six Cultures project suggest that children tend to be more aggressive the more they associate with other children of the same age. In contrast, children tend to inhibit aggression when they are around adults more.[36] We have already noted that being around younger children may make older children more nurturant. So the kinds of tasks assigned to children may influence behavior not only because certain tasks require certain behaviors (for example, babysitting requires nurturance) but also because the kinds of tasks assigned will place children in different social contexts that may also affect how they behave.

SCHOOLING. Most researchers focus on the parents when they investigate how children are brought up. But in our own and other societies, children may spend a substantial part of their time in school from the age of 3 or so. What influence does school have on children's social behavior and on how they think as measured by tests? To investigate the effect of schooling, researchers have compared children or adults who have not gone to school with those who have. All of this research has been done in societies that do not have compulsory schooling; otherwise we could not compare the schooled with the unschooled. We know relatively little about the influence of school on social behavior. In contrast, we know more about how schooling influences performance on cognitive tests.

Schooling clearly predicts "superior" performance on many cognitive tests, and within the same society schooled individuals will generally do better than the unschooled on those tests. So, for example, nonschooled individuals in non-Western societies are not as likely as schooled individuals to perceive depth in two-dimensional pictures, do not perform

as well on tests of memory, are not as likely to classify items in certain ways, and do not display evidence of formal-operational thinking.[37] But schooling does not always produce superior performance on tests of inferential reasoning.[38]

Why does schooling have these effects? Although it is possible that something about schooling creates higher levels of cognitive thinking in some respects, there are other possible explanations. The observed differences may be due to the advantages that schoolchildren have because of their experiences in school, advantages that have nothing to do with general cognitive ability. For example, consider research that asks people to classify or group drawings of geometric shapes that belong together. Suppose a person is shown three cards—a red circle, a red triangle, and a white circle—and is asked which two are most alike. A person could choose to classify in terms of color or in terms of shape. In the United States, young children usually classify by color, and as they get older they classify more often by shape. Many psychologists assume that classification by color is more "concrete" and classification by shape or function is more "abstract." Unschooled adults in many parts of Africa sort by color, not by shape. Does this mean that they are classifying less abstractly? Not necessarily. It may just be that nonschooled Africans classify differently because they are likely to be unfamiliar with the test materials (drawings on paper, geometric shapes).

How can people classify "abstractly" (for example, by shape) if they have never had the experience of handling or seeing shapes that are drawn in two dimensions? Is it likely that they would classify things as triangles if they had never seen a three-pointed figure with straight sides? In contrast, consider how much time teachers in the United States spend drilling children on various geometric shapes. People who are familiar with certain materials may for that reason alone do better on cognitive tests that use those materials.[39]

A comparative study of Liberian rice farmers in West Africa and U.S. undergraduates also illustrates the point that choice of materials may influence research results. The comparison involved a set of materials familiar to the rice farmers, bowls of rice, and a set of materials familiar to the undergraduates, geometric cards. Rice farmers appeared to classify more "abstractly" than undergraduates when they were asked to classify rice, and undergraduates seemed to classify more "abstractly" than rice farmers when they classified geometric cards.[40]

Schooled individuals may also enjoy an advantage on many cognitive tests just because they are familiar

Current Issues

DO SCHOOLS TEACH VALUES?

In the United States there is controversy nowadays about the teaching of values. Many people think that the schools should teach values; others think that such teachings should be left to parents and family. But whether or not schools should explicitly teach values, research in different countries suggests that schools do, at least implicitly, teach values. They do not just teach content.

Joseph Tobin, David Wu, and Dana Davidson videotaped preschool classroom scenes in Japan, China, and the United States. In each country they asked children, teachers, parents, and school administrators to comment on the scenes in all three countries. We can get a feel for how different values are implicitly taught in each country by reviewing the comments.

When individuals in the United States viewed the Japanese tape, they were generally bothered by two things. One was the fact that children in Japan often did the same things simultaneously as a group. For example, the teacher showed what to fold first and subsequently to make an origami bird figure, and the children followed along. U.S. parents and teachers

said that children should have more choice in what to do and how to do it. The second thing that bothered people in the United States, as well as in China, was that the teacher in Japan appeared to ignore what we might consider "unruly" behavior by the children. For example, when children got restless during a group workbook activity, they would leave their seats, joke with friends, or go to the bathroom. In the tape, a particularly troublesome boy talked loudly, sometimes purposely hurt other children, and threw things around, but the teacher seemed to ignore these behaviors. People in the United States and China thought that the teacher should try to do something in such situations. In Japan, however, most of the teachers preferred not to call attention to, or single out, a troublesome child. Japanese teachers expect such a child eventually to behave more appropriately, and they encourage the other children to exert social pressure in that direction. In Lois Peak's words: "Learning to go to school in Japan is primarily defined as training in group life."

Most of the activities in the Chinese preschool were highly structured. For example, the first

task of the day was building with blocks, but in contrast to the style at the Japanese preschool, the children in China were expected to complete the task on their own and to do so in silence. If they spoke, the teacher reprimanded them. They used a picture as a guide to what to do. When they were done, the teachers checked their work. If they got it right, they took it apart and rebuilt it; if they got it wrong they were asked to correct it. An arithmetic lesson followed. Children then ate the lunch that was brought for them into the classroom. Teachers monitored the lunch to make sure that the children ate all their food and ate in silence. After an afternoon nap, the children listened to a patriotic story and then had relay races, which were followed by 15 minutes of free play. Supper was served at 5:00 P.M. and parents came at 6:00. In seeing the videotapes, Americans and Japanese were bothered by the rigidity and "overcontrol" of the children and by the lack of privacy in their communal bathroom.

In the U.S. preschool, in Honolulu, as in Japan, parents brought their children at different times, but some parents stayed with the child for as long

with tests and the way tests ask them to think of new situations. For example, consider the reaction of a nonschooled person in central Asia who was asked the following question by a Russian psychologist interested in measuring logical thinking: "In the Far North where there is snow, all bears are white. Novaya Zemlya is in the Far North and there is always snow there. What color are the bears there?" The

reply was, "We don't talk about what we haven't seen." Such a reply was typical of nonschooled individuals; they did not even try to answer the question because it was not part of their experience.[41] Clearly, we cannot judge whether people think logically if they do not want to play a cognitive game.

Much research needs to be done on exactly how and why schooling affects cognition. Is it important

as a half hour. Compared with the other preschools, the U.S. preschool emphasized individual participation and individualized activity. For example, "show and tell" was voluntary; sometimes only three kids decided to get up and talk. In an activity involving a feltboard, each child was asked to add something to the board. Much of the rest of the day was spent in "learning centers"; the teachers helped the children decide which center they would like to go to. Children started at one activity but could change if they wished. Even lunch was more individual. Each child took out her or his lunch box and took it to a big table where they all ate and talked animatedly. Many kids went home after lunch; those who stayed had naptime followed by relatively free play. The U.S. teacher, in contrast to the Japanese teacher, intervened when a child misbehaved, such as when one boy grabbed a block from another. Without raising her voice, the teacher asked the two children to talk to each other about the disagreement. She resorted to a "time-out" (a period of isolation) when the dispute was not settled by talking.

Even though they do not teach values explicitly, these preschools clearly convey values by how they deal with the children. First is the importance of the group versus the individual. In the U.S. preschool, most of the daily activities allowed individual choice of some kind; in both Japan and China, group activities predominated, although the Japanese preschool allowed flexible arrival times, more free play, and more freedom to talk or move about than the Chinese preschool. Second is the source of control. The Japanese teachers relied informally on the group to control the children's behavior. For example, after nine months the unruly boy sat by himself at lunch; the other children did not want to sit with him. In contrast, the Chinese teachers saw to it that the children behaved like others in the group by exerting strong control over the children's behavior. The U.S. teachers also intervened in response to unruly behavior.

Cultural values are not unchanging. Although many Japanese educational administrators thought that the Japanese preschool was quite "Japanese" in style, and therefore satisfactory, a considerable number of Japanese parents and teachers were critical of the school and said there were "better" schools in Japan that were more like the U.S. preschool. And some Japanese thought that more attention should be paid to the individual needs of troubled children. Some Chinese complained, when they saw the tapes of the Chinese school, that it was too "old-fashioned." Yet even they agreed that the amount of freedom displayed at the Japanese and U.S. schools was too much. And the Chinese stressed the importance of schools' not "spoiling" children, especially now that parents are not supposed to have more than one child.

Whether or not they consciously intend to, preschools in different countries do seem to socialize their children according to what is valued in the culture.

Sources: Joseph J. Tobin, David Y. H. Wu, and Dana H. Davidson, *Preschool in Three Cultures: Japan, China, and the United States* (New Haven, CT: Yale University Press, 1989); Lois Peak, *Learning to Go to School in Japan: The Transition from Home to Preschool* (Berkeley: University of California Press, 1991); Margaret Lock, "Japan: Glimpses of Everyday Life," in Melvin Ember, Carol R. Ember, and David Levinson, eds., *Portraits of Culture: Ethnographic Originals* (Upper Saddle River, NJ: Prentice Hall, 1998), Prentice Hall/Simon & Schuster Custom Publishing.

which specific things are taught? Is it important to be asked to attend to questions that are out of context? Is being literate a factor? This last question was the subject of research among the Vai of Liberia, who had a somewhat unusual situation in that schooling and literacy were not completely confounded. The Vai had an indigenous script learned outside of school. Thus, the researchers Sylvia Scribner and Michael Cole were able to see how Vai individuals who were literate but not formally schooled compared with others who were formally schooled (and literate) and those who were unschooled (and illiterate). They found some, but relatively minor, effects of literacy itself; cognitive test performance was much more affected by the number of years of schooling. Similar results come

Attending school has become customary in many parts of the world, as among the Baoulé of the Ivory Coast. Schooling seems to affect cognitive development, but we do not know exactly why or how.

from a study of the Cree of northern Ontario who have their own syllabic script learned outside of school.[42] These comparisons suggest that some other aspects of schooling are more important than literacy as determinants of cognitive performance.

By studying other societies where schooling is not universal, we may be better able to understand just what role schooling plays in cognitive and other development. That schooling makes for so much difference in cognitive performance raises the serious issue of how much of what we observe about child development in our society and in other Western societies is simply a function of what children are taught in school. After all, children who grow up in this society not only get older each year, they also go one year further in school. Schools are not just places to learn a particular curriculum. Children learn to interact with one another and with adults who are not parents and family. Therefore we might expect that schools not only shape cognition but also convey important cultural attitudes, values, and appropriate ways of behaving toward others (see the box "Do Schools Teach Values?").

GENERAL CULTURAL THEMES AS EXPLANATIONS

Many of the aspects of socialization we have discussed are fairly specific—customs such as how often a baby is held, whether children are encouraged to be aggressive, what kinds of tasks are assigned to children, and whether they attend formal schools. As we have suggested, many of these specific aspects of socialization may have important effects on how a person grows up psychologically. But children may also be influenced by more general themes or ideas prevalent in the culture. Earlier, for example, when we discussed various aspects of infant care—how often babies are held, how quickly they are responded to—we mentioned that many customs seem to be parts of a larger pattern, such as high or low indulgence. But what ideas underlie and possibly explain these larger patterns? One likely general theme in the United States is many parents' belief that the child should not grow up spoiled or dependent. Perhaps, then, there are general ideas or themes *behind* a culture's specific socialization patterns. These general themes may be expressed in a variety of ways.

CONCEPTS OF THE SELF. Anthropologists have begun to study different cultural ideas of personhood or concept of the "self." Many have concluded that the concept of self in many non-Western societies is quite different from the Western conception. Clifford Geertz described the Western conception of the person as "bounded, unique, . . . a dynamic center of awareness, emotion, judgment, and action organized into a distinctive whole."[43] He claimed, on the basis of his fieldwork in Java, Bali, and Morocco, that those societies have very different conceptions of a person, not only different from each other but quite different from the Western conception. For example, he said that the Balinese describe a person as having many different roles, like an actor who plays different characters. The unique characteristics of a person are not emphasized; what is emphasized are the "masks" people wear and the "parts" they play.

Geertz focused on the variation and uniquenesses in different cultures' conceptions of the self. But other scholars think that there are recognizable and predictable patterns in this variation. One of the most talked about patterns is the Western emphasis on the self as an autonomous individual and the non-Western emphasis on the relations a person has with others.[44] Labels used to describe such Western/non-Western cultural differences are "individualism" versus "holism" or "collectivism," "egocentric" versus "sociocentric," and the like. For example, the Japanese concept of self is often described as "relational" or "situational"; people exist in networks of relationships and the ideal person has the ability to shift easily from one social situation to another.[45]

There are two major objections to the idea that the Western sense of self should be contrasted with the non-Western. The first is that studies of other cultures have suggested other dimensions of variation besides "individualism" versus "collectivism." For example, the traditional Inuit concept *inummarik*, "a genuine person," seems to include a lifelong process of ecological involvement—interacting with animals and the environment as well as people.[46] A culture's concept of self, then, may include other dimensions besides individual versus collective. A second objection to the Western/non-Western contrast is that it may not be based on adequate evidence. As Melford Spiro pointed out, it is necessary to find out how a sample of individuals in a society actually view themselves. The ideal in the culture might be different from the actual.[47] For example, individuals even in the United States do not just describe themselves as autonomous. When Jane Wellenkamp and Douglas Hollan interviewed Americans about their feelings about the death of someone close, they got statements about autonomy (such as "I can stand on my own" and "At least you have yourself"), but they also got statements reflecting interdependence ("You realize that they're gone and that a part of you has gone with them").[48] This is not to say that the autonomy of the individual isn't important in the United States. It is. But individuals also realize that they are interdependent. How we actually think of ourselves may not be so different from how people in other societies think of themselves.

If a cultural theme such as individualism is important, societies may express or convey this theme in many ways. It may start right after birth, as when a baby is put in a crib or bassinet to sleep alone rather than with someone in the family. Young children may be given their "own" toys. They may go to preschool or daycare, where they are encouraged to make their own choices (see the box titled "Do Schools Teach Values?"). And schools for older children may require individual, not group, achievement. Does the theme of individualism have to be taught explicitly? Probably not, because it can be conveyed in so many different ways.

ADAPTATIONAL EXPLANATIONS

The cultural anthropologist seeks not only to establish connections between child-rearing customs and personality traits but also to learn why those customs differ in the first place. Some anthropologists believe that child-rearing practices are largely adaptive—that a society produces the kinds of personalities best suited to performance of the activities necessary for the survival of the society. As John Whiting and Irvin Child expressed it, "The economic, political and social organs of a society—the basic customs surrounding the nourishment, sheltering and protection of its members . . . seem a likely source of influence on child training practices."[49] The belief that child-rearing practices are adaptive does not mean that societies always produce the kinds of persons they need. Just as in the biological realm, where we see poor adaptations and extinctions of species and subspecies, so we may expect that societies sometimes produce personality traits that are maladapted to the requirements of living in that society. So we cannot assume that just because a trait is present it must be adaptive. We cannot come to that conclusion unless we carefully investigate whether the trait is beneficial or harmful.[50] But we do expect that most societies that have survived to be recorded have produced personality traits that are mostly adaptive.

Robert LeVine suggested an adaptational explanation for the frequent holding and feeding of infants and quick response of caretakers to them in preindustrial societies.[51] Only 1 percent of infants die in industrial societies in the first year of life, but typically more than 20 percent die in preindustrial societies. What can parents do? Parents often do not have access to modern medical care, but they can respond to a baby's fussing immediately if the baby is with them. Also, babies may be safer off the ground if there are cooking fires, dangerous insects, and snakes in the vicinity. When survival is not so much at issue, LeVine suggested, parents can safely leave babies more on their own.

Herbert Barry, Irvin Child, and Margaret Bacon cross-culturally investigated the possibility that child-training practices are adapted to the economic requirements of a society. Such requirements, they theorized, might explain why some societies strive to develop "compliant" (responsible, obedient, nurturant) children while others aim more for "assertiveness" (independence, self-reliance, and achievement).[52] The cross-cultural results indicated that agricultural and herding societies are likely to stress responsibility and obedience, whereas hunting-and-gathering societies tend to stress self-reliance and individual assertiveness. The investigators suggested that agricultural and herding societies cannot afford departures from established routine, because departures might jeopardize the food supply for long periods. Such societies are therefore likely to emphasize compliance with tradition. Departures from routine in a hunter-gatherer society cannot cause much damage to a food supply that has to be collected anew almost every day. So

hunter-gatherers can afford to emphasize individual initiative.

Although our own society relies on food production and has large stores of accumulated food, we seem more like hunter-gatherers in emphasizing individual initiative. Are we, then, exceptions to the Barry, Child, and Bacon findings? Not really. Hardly any of us are farmers (in the United States, only 2 percent of the total population is still on the farm), and most of us expect that we can "forage" in the supermarket or "store" just about anytime. Perhaps more important is the fact that our highly commercial economy, with most people dwelling in or near cities, requires us to compete to get jobs to make a living. In our kind of economy, then, individual initiative is important too. Consider the results of a cross-national comparison of eight countries in which the researchers asked parents what quality they most wanted their school-age children to have. Independence and self-reliance were seldom mentioned by parents in the more rural countries (Indonesia, Philippines, and Thailand) but were often mentioned in the more urban countries (Korea, Singapore, and the United States).[53]

Child-rearing practices may also be affected by household characteristics. Leigh Minturn and William Lambert reported, on the basis of data from the Six Cultures study, that children of families who live in cramped quarters tend to be punished more strongly for fighting with others than are children of families who have ample space. The more people living in a house, the less apt a parent is to permit disobedience.[54] This observation is consistent with the finding of a cross-cultural study, conducted by John Whiting, that societies with extended-family households are more likely than societies with nuclear families to severely punish aggression in children.[55]

Whether adults express aggression freely may be related to a society's economy and social environment. In a comparative study of personality differences between pastoralists and farmers in four societies in East Africa, Robert Edgerton found that pastoralists were more willing than farmers to express aggression openly. As a matter of fact, pastoralists seemed freer to express all kinds of emotion, including sadness and depression. Although farmers displayed reluctance to express overt aggression themselves, they were quite willing to talk about witchcraft and sorcery practiced by others. How can we explain these personality differences? Edgerton proposed that the life-style of farmers, who must spend their lives cooperating with a fixed set of neighbors, requires them to

People relying mostly on food production tend to stress responsibility and obedience in children. Young children in Iringa, Tanzania, work in the fields.

contain their feelings, particularly hostile feelings. (But these feelings may not go away, and so the farmers might "see them" in others.) Pastoralists, on the other hand, can more readily move away in conflict situations because they are not as dependent on a fixed set of individuals. Not only might they be able to express aggression more openly, but such aggression may even be adaptive. The pastoralists studied by Edgerton engaged frequently in raids and counterraids involving cattle stealing, and the most aggressive individuals may have had the best chance of surviving the skirmishes.[56]

Might the environment influence the way people in different societies think and perceive (interpret sensory information)? John Berry suggested that different perceptual and cognitive processes may be selected and trained for in societies that differ in their adaptational requirements.[57] Berry's particular focus was on what psychologists call *field independence* and *field dependence*.[58] Field independence means being able to isolate a part of a situation from the whole. The opposite perceptual style, field dependence, means that parts are not perceived separately; rather, the whole situation is focused on.

The contrast between field independence and field dependence may become clear if we look at some of the ways they are measured. In the rod-and-frame test, a person seated in a darkened room is asked to adjust a tilted luminous rod so that it is upright within a luminous frame. Individuals are considered field dependent if they adjust the rod to line up with the frame when the frame is tilted. Individuals are considered field independent if they adjust the rod to a truly upright position even though the frame is tilted. Field independence is also measured by the ability to see a simply drawn figure when it is included but somewhat hidden in a more complex picture.

Why should some societies produce people who are more field independent or dependent? Berry suggested that people who rely a lot on hunting must be field independent to be successful, because hunting requires the visual isolation of animals from their backgrounds. Hunters must also learn to visualize themselves in precise relationship to their surroundings so that they can find animals and get back home. In a comparative study of communities in four societies, Berry found that degree of reliance on hunting predicted field independence. The more a community relied on hunting, the more the individuals showed field independence on tests. Those communities more reliant on agriculture tested out to be more field dependent. How might hunters

develop field independence as a cognitive style? Different child training might be involved. In the United States and a few other societies, it has been found that children whose parents are very strict are less likely to develop field independence than are children whose parents are lenient.[59] It seems that emotional independence from parents is necessary for the perceptual style of field independence to develop. No matter what the precise mechanism is, we know from the Barry, Child, and Bacon study that hunter-gatherers are more likely to train children to be individualistic and assertive, and that agriculturalists and herders are more likely to train their children to be compliant. So hunter-gatherers may cause their children to develop field independence by stressing emotional independence in childhood.

Investigations have shown that there are gender differences in the United States and other (but not all) cultures in degree of field dependence versus independence.[60] Perhaps these differences reflect the fact that girls are more encouraged to be obedient and responsible and boys more to be independent and self-reliant. And perhaps, too, gender differences in field dependence versus independence may be related to the fact that girls work more in and around the home, close to others. If so, we might expect that girls who are more field dependent are also more likely to have a morality that stresses interpersonal concerns (see the box titled "Do Women Have a Different Morality?").

POSSIBLE GENETIC AND PHYSIOLOGICAL INFLUENCES

Some researchers have suggested that genetic or physiological differences between populations predispose them to have different personality characteristics. Daniel Freedman found differences in "temperament" in newborn babies of different ethnic groups; because he observed newborns, the differences between them were presumed to be genetic. Comparing Chinese and European American newborns with the families matched on income, number of previous children, and so on, Freedman found that European American babies cried more easily, were harder to console, and fought experimental procedures more. Chinese babies, on the other hand, seemed calmer and more adaptable. Navaho babies were similar to the Chinese, showing even more calmness.[61] Freedman also suggested that an infant's behavior can influence how the parents respond. A calm baby may encourage a calm parental response; a more active baby may encourage a

DO WOMEN HAVE A DIFFERENT MORALITY?

There is widespread agreement that as children mature they develop a sense of self that distinguishes themselves from others. But *what kind* of sense of self do they develop? Some researchers suggest that different cultures have different conceptions of the self. In particular, the West seems to emphasize the separateness of each person; other cultures emphasize the connection of the self to others.

Several psychologists, including Carol Gilligan, proposed that women, in contrast to men, are more likely to develop a sense of themselves that involves social interaction and connectedness. Gilligan proposed that women also tend to have a different sense of morality, one that is more apt to consider the feelings of others and the preservation of relationships. Men, she suggested, are more likely to emphasize rules or principles that are applied equally and impartially to individuals. Is there any substantial evidence for her claims about gender differences in morality?

Some studies have interviewed females and males and explicitly compared their statements about themselves and about solutions to moral dilemmas. The responses are coded for the degree to which the self is described as "autonomous" or as "connected" and the degree to which responses to moral dilemmas are couched in "justice" or "care" terms. "Well, you have to think about whether it is right . . . or whether it is wrong," is an example of a statement couched in justice terms. "I wanted them to get along . . . I didn't want anybody getting in fights or anything" is an example of a statement couched in "care" terms.

So far the research, conducted mostly in the United States among well-educated populations, suggests that, although women more often than men do tend to describe themselves as "connected" and more often display a "caring" morality, there is no absolute separation between the genders. Most people, regardless of gender, give "connected" and "autonomous" statements about themselves, and most people express "justice" and "care" concerns with regard to moral dilemmas. If there is a difference between the genders in a culture, it is only in tendency not in a completely different approach to morality.

Although moral development in childhood has been studied in several cultures, there is relatively little research that directly addresses the issues raised by Gilligan. To be sure, research by David Stimpson and his colleagues compared educated university students in Korea, China, Thailand, and the United States and found support for the idea that women were more concerned with affection, compassion, and sensitivity to the needs of others, as compared with men. But that study did not specifically ask for responses to moral dilemmas. Some other researchers suggest that the picture may be more complicated, because concepts of morality may vary quite a bit from the two types described by Gilligan. For example, Joan Miller found that middle-class Hindu Indians generally had a very strong sense of interpersonal morality compared with people in the United States. But the Hindu Indian morality was not based on individual concern for others; rather their responses to moral dilemmas were strongly influenced by considerations of *social duty*. And Miller found no gender differences in responses.

All we can conclude now is that the genders may have somewhat different moralities in *some* cultures. We need more research on how morality may vary by gender as well as by culture.

Sources: Carol Gilligan, *In a Different Voice: Psychological Theory and Women's Development* (Cambridge, MA: Harvard University Press, 1982); Nona Plessner Lyons, "Two Perspectives: On Self, Relationships, and Morality," and Carol Gilligan and Jane Attanucci, "Two Moral Orientations," in Carol Gilligan, Janie Victoria Ward, and Jill McLean Taylor, eds., *Mapping the Moral Domain: A Contribution of Women's Thinking to Psychological Theory and Education* (Cambridge, MA: Harvard University Press, 1988), pp. 22–45 and 73–86, respectively; David Stimpson, Larry Jensen, and Wayne Neff, "Cross-Cultural Gender Differences in Preference for a Caring Morality," *Journal of Social Psychology,* 132 (1992): 317–22; Joan G. Miller, "Cultural Diversity in the Morality of Caring: Individually Oriented versus Duty-Based Interpersonal Moral Codes," *Cross-Cultural Research,* 28 (1994): 3–39.

more active response.[62] So, in Freedman's view, babies' genetically determined behavior can lead to ethnic differences in adult personality and caretaking styles.

But we cannot rule out nongenetic explanations of babies' behavior. For example, the mother's diet or her blood pressure could affect the baby's behavior. And it may be that the baby can learn even in the womb. After all, babies in the womb apparently can hear and respond to sounds and to other stimuli. Therefore, it is possible that in societies in which pregnant women are calm, their babies may have learned calmness even before they were born. Last, we still do not know if the initial differences observed in newborn babies persist to become personality differences in adulthood.

Just as the diet of the mother, including the intake of alcohol and drugs, may affect the developing fetus, the diet of infants and children may also affect their intellectual development and their behavior. Studies have shown that malnutrition is associated with lower levels of activity, less attentiveness, lack of initiative, and low tolerance of frustration. Behavior of children can change with short-term nutrition supplements. For example, Guatemalan children who were given nutritional supplements were observed to have less anxiety, more exploratoriness, and greater involvement in games than children who were not given supplements.[63] The problem of malnutrition is not just a matter of nutrition. Other kinds of care may also be reduced. For example, caretakers of malnourished children may interact with them less than do caretakers of healthy children. As a malnourished child shows reduced activity, caretakers tend to respond to the child with lower frequency and less enthusiasm. Then the child withdraws from interaction, creating a potentially serious vicious cycle.[64]

Physiological (not necessarily genetic) differences between populations may also be responsible for some personality differences in adulthood. Research by Ralph Bolton suggests that a physiological condition known as hypoglycemia may be responsible for the high levels of aggression recorded among the Qolla of Peru.[65] (People with hypoglycemia experience a big drop in their blood sugar level after they ingest food.) Bolton found that about 55 percent of the males he tested in a Qolla village had hypoglycemia. Moreover, those men with the most aggressive life histories tended to be hypoglycemic. Whether hypoglycemia is induced by genetic or environmental factors or both, the condition can be alleviated by a change in diet.

MENTAL ILLNESS

So far in this chapter we have discussed cross-cultural universals and societal differences in "normal" behavior, but anthropologists have also been intrigued by questions about similarities and differences in *abnormal* behavior. Central to the study of abnormal behavior is how to define it. Is abnormality relative? That is, can what is normal in one society be abnormal in another? Or, alternatively, are there universals in abnormality cross-culturally?

In a very widely read book, Ruth Benedict suggested that abnormality was relative. In her view, behavior thought to be appropriate and normal in one society can be considered abnormal in another.[66] Many German officials, for instance, were regarded in every way as normal by their neighbors and co-workers during the period of Nazi control. Yet these officials committed acts of inhumanity so vicious that to many observers in other Western societies they appeared criminally insane. The Saora of Orissa, India, provide another example of behavior normal to one society that would be abnormal to another society. The Saora took for granted that certain of their womenfolk regularly were courted by lovers from the supernatural world, married them, and had children who were never seen, yet allegedly were suckled at night.[67] Behavior that is so alien to our own makes it no easy task for researchers to identify mental illness in other societies, let alone compare more complex and less complex societies on rates of mental disorder.

When Western anthropologists first started describing mental illness in non-Western societies, there seemed to be unique illnesses in different cultures. These are referred to as *culture-bound syndromes*. For example, a mental disorder called *pibloktoq* occurred among some Eskimo adults of Greenland, usually women, who became oblivious to their surroundings and acted in agitated, eccentric ways. They might strip themselves naked and wander across the ice and over hills until they collapsed of exhaustion. Another disorder, *amok,* occurred in Malaya, Indonesia, and New Guinea, usually among males. It was characterized by John Honigmann as a "destructive maddened excitement . . . beginning with depression and followed by a period of brooding and withdrawal [culminating in] the final mobilization of tremendous energy during which the 'wild man' runs destructively berserk."[68] *Anorexia nervosa,* the disorder involving aversion to food, may be unique to the relatively few societies that idealize slimness.[69]

Some scholars think that each society's views of personality and concepts of mental illness have to be understood in its own terms. Western understandings and concepts cannot be applied to other cultures. For example, Catherine Lutz suggested that the Western concept of depression cannot be applied to the Pacific island of Ifaluk. The people there have many words for thinking or feeling about "loss and helplessness," but all their words are related to a *specific* need for someone, such as when someone dies or leaves the island. Such thoughts and feelings of loss are considered perfectly normal, and there is no word in their language for general hopelessness or "depression."[70] Therefore Lutz questioned the applicability of the Western concept of depression as well as other Western psychiatric categories.

Other researchers are not so quick to dismiss the possible universality of psychiatric categories. Some think they have found a considerable degree of cross-cultural uniformity in conceptions of mental illness. Jane Murphy studied descriptions by Inuit and Yoruba, in Nigeria, of severely disturbed persons. She found that their descriptions not only were similar to each other but also corresponded to North American descriptions of schizophrenia. The Inuit word for "crazy" is *nuthkavihak*. They use this word when something inside a person seems to be out of order. *Nuthkavihak* people are described as talking to themselves, believing themselves to be animals, making strange faces, becoming violent, and so on. The Yoruba have a word, *were,* for people who are "insane." People described as *were* sometimes hear voices, laugh when there is nothing to laugh at, and take up weapons and suddenly hit people.[71]

Robert Edgerton found similarities in conceptions of mental illness in four East African societies. He noted not only that the four groups essentially agreed on the symptoms of psychosis but also that the symptoms they described were the same ones that are considered psychotic here.[72] Edgerton believed that the lack of exact translation in different cultures, such as the one pointed out by Lutz regarding Ifaluk, does not make comparison impossible. If researchers can come to understand another culture's views of personality *and* if the researchers can manage to communicate these views to people of other cultures, we can compare the described cases and try to discover what may be universal and what may be found only in some cultures.[73]

Some mental illnesses, such as schizophrenia and depression, seem so widespread that many researchers think they are probably universal. Consistent with this idea is the fact that schizophrenic individuals in different cultures seem to share the same patterns of distinctive eye movements.[74] Still, cultural factors may influence the risk of developing such diseases, the specific symptoms that are expressed, and the effectiveness of different kinds of treatment.[75] There may be some truly culture-bound (nearly unique) syndromes, but others thought at one time to be unique may be culturally varying expressions of conditions that occur widely. *Pibloktoq,* for example, may be a kind of hysteria.[76]

Biological but not necessarily genetic factors may be very important in the etiology of some of the widespread disorders such as schizophrenia.[77] With regard to hysteria, Anthony Wallace theorized that nutritional factors such as calcium deficiency may cause hysteria and that dietary improvement may account for the decline of this illness in the Western world since the nineteenth century.[78] By the early twentieth century, the discovery of the value of good nutrition, coupled with changes in social conditions, had led many people to drink milk, eat vitamin-enriched foods, and spend time in the sun. These changes in diet and activity increased their intake of vitamin D and helped them to maintain a proper calcium level. Concurrently, the number of cases of hysteria declined.

Regarding *pibloktoq,* Wallace suggested that a complex set of related variables may cause the disease. The Inuit live in an environment that supplies only a minimum amount of calcium. A diet low in calcium could result in two different conditions. One condition, rickets, would produce physical deformities potentially fatal in the Inuit hunting economy. Persons whose genetic makeup made them prone to rickets would be eliminated from the population through natural selection. A low level of calcium in the blood could also cause muscular spasms known as tetany. Tetany, in turn, may cause emotional and mental disorientation similar to the symptoms of *pibloktoq.* Such attacks last for only a relatively short time and are not fatal, so people who developed *pibloktoq* would have a far greater chance of surviving in the Arctic environment with a calcium-deficient diet than would those who had rickets.

Although researchers disagree about the comparability of mental illnesses among cultures, most realize that effective treatment requires understanding a culture's ideas about a mental illness—why it occurs, what treatments are believed to be effective, and how families and others respond to those afflicted.[79]

PSYCHOLOGICAL EXPLANATIONS OF CULTURAL VARIATION

We have been talking only about societal variation in psychological characteristics and the possible causes of that variation. But psychological anthropologists, as well as other social scientists, have also investigated the possible *consequences* of psychological variation, particularly how psychological characteristics may help us understand certain aspects of cultural variation. For example, David McClelland's research suggests that societies that develop high levels of achievement motivation (a personality trait) in individuals will be likely to experience high rates of economic growth. Economic decline, McClelland suggested, will follow a decline in achievement motivation.[80] Differences in achievement motivation may even have political consequences. For example, Robert LeVine, who studied achievement motivation in three Nigerian ethnic groups, noted that the entry of one of them, the Ibo, into higher education and into many emerging professions may have been resented by the traditionally more influential groups.[81] Soon after LeVine's book was published, the friction between the rival groups escalated into rebellion by the Ibo and the defeat of a separatist Ibo state named Biafra.

Psychological factors may also help us explain why some aspects of culture are statistically associated with others. Abram Kardiner originally suggested that cultural patterns influence personality development through child training and that the resulting personality characteristics in turn influence the culture. He believed that *primary institutions,* such as family organization and subsistence techniques, give rise to certain personality characteristics. Once the personality is formed, though, it can have its own impact on culture. In Kardiner's view, the *secondary institutions* of society, such as religion and art, are shaped by common—he called them *basic*—personality characteristics. Presumably, these secondary institutions have little relation to the adaptive requirements of the society. But they may reflect and express the motives, conflicts, and anxieties of typical members of the society.[82] Thus, if we can understand why certain typical personality characteristics develop, we might, for example, be able to understand why certain kinds of art are associated with certain kinds of social systems. Whiting and Child used the phrase **personality integration of culture** to refer to the possibility that an understanding of personality might help us explain

connections between primary and secondary institutions.[83] As examples of how personality may integrate culture, we turn to some suggested explanations for cultural preferences in games and for the custom of male initiation ceremonies.

In a cross-cultural study conducted by John Roberts and Brian Sutton-Smith, cultural preferences for particular types of games were found to be related to certain aspects of child rearing. The researchers suggested that these associations are a consequence of conflict generated in many people in a society by particular types of child-rearing pressures. Games of strategy, for example, are associated with child training that emphasizes obedience. Roberts and Sutton-Smith proposed that severe obedience training can create a conflict between the need to obey and the desire not to obey, a conflict that arouses anxiety. Such anxiety may or may not manifest itself against the person who instigates the anxiety. In any event, the conflict and the aggression itself can be played out on the miniature battlefields of games of strategy such as chess or the Japanese game of *go*. Similarly, games of chance may represent defiance of societal expectations of docility and responsibility. The general interpretation suggested by Roberts and Sutton-Smith is that players—and societies—initially become curious about games, learn them, and ultimately develop high involvement

Games of strategy, such as this game played in Mali, tend to occur where societies are hierarchical and where obedience is stressed.

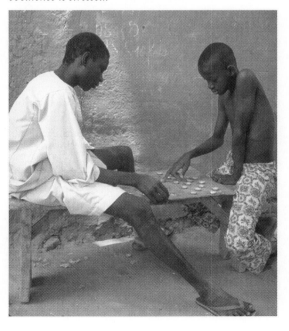

in them because of the particular kinds of psychological conflicts that are handled or expressed, but not necessarily resolved, by the games.[84]

The possible role of psychological processes in connecting different aspects of culture is also illustrated in cross-cultural work on initiation ceremonies for boys at adolescence. In the ceremonies, boys are subjected to painful tests of manhood, usually including genital operations, which indicate the boys' transition to adulthood. Roger Burton and John Whiting found that initiation ceremonies tend to occur in patrilocal societies in which infant boys initially sleep exclusively with their mothers. They suggest that initiation rites in such societies are intended to break a conflict in sex identity. The conflict is believed to exist because boys in these societies would initially identify with their mothers, who exercise almost complete control over them in infancy. Later, when the boys discover that men dominate the society, they will identify secondarily with their fathers. This sex-role conflict is assumed to be resolved by the initiation ceremony, which demonstrates a boy's manhood, thus strengthening the secondary identification.[85]

In the next two chapters we discuss cultural variation in religion and the arts. In doing so we refer to some psychological explanations. Some researchers feel that such explanations may help us understand why gods in some societies are viewed as mean, why artists in some societies prefer repetitive designs, and why strangers in some societies tend to be the "bad ones" in folktales. It is often assumed by psychological anthropologists that conceptions of gods and artistic creations are not constrained by any objective realities, so people are free to create them as they wish. In other words, people may tend to *project* their personalities—their feelings, their conflicts, their concerns—into these areas. This idea of projection underlies what psychologists call **projective tests.** In such tests, which presumably reveal personality characteristics, subjects are given stimuli that are purposely ambiguous. So, for example, in the Thematic Apperception Test (TAT), subjects are shown vague drawings and asked what they think is going on in them, what happened before, and how they think things will turn out. Because the test materials give few instructions about what to say, it is assumed that subjects will interpret the materials by projecting their own personalities. As we will see in subsequent chapters, some aspects of religion and the arts may be similar to TAT stories and may express or reflect the common personality characteristics of a society.

 **SUMMARY**

1. Psychological anthropologists are interested in the psychological differences and similarities between societies. Their research has focused mainly on four questions: Do all human beings develop psychologically in much the same ways? What may explain the apparent differences in personality characteristics from one society to another? How do people in different societies conceive of personality and psychological development? What kinds of cultural variation might be explained by psychological factors?

2. Early research in psychological anthropology was concerned mainly with how supposedly universal stages of emotional development seem to be affected by cultural differences. Some doubt has been cast on the idea that adolescence is necessarily a time of "storm and stress" and that the Oedipus complex, at least in the form stated by Freud, is universal.

3. Recent research on universals in psychological development has been concerned more with cognitive, or intellectual, development. In looking for universals, many researchers have discovered some apparent differences. But most of the tests used in research may favor people in Western cultures and those who attend formal schools.

4. To understand cross-cultural variation in psychological characteristics, many researchers have tried to discover if variation in child-rearing customs can account for the observed psychological differences.

5. *Socialization* is a term used by anthropologists and psychologists to describe the development, through the influence of parents and others, of patterns of behavior in children that conform to cultural expectations.

6. Socialization can be direct or indirect. Indirectly, the degree to which parents like children, the kinds of work children are asked to do, and whether children go to school may at least partly influence how children develop psychologically.

7. Anthropologists seek not only to establish connections between child-rearing customs and personality traits but also to learn why those customs originated. Some anthropologists believe societies produce the kinds of personality best suited to performance of the activities necessary for the survival of the society.

8. Anthropologists are also interested in mental illness. Some mental illnesses are believed to be more or less universal, but the ways they are expressed, their frequencies, and the outcomes of

treatment may vary from culture to culture. Furthermore, some syndromes may be unique to some cultures.

9. Psychological anthropologists are interested not only in the possible causes of psychological differences between societies but also in the possible consequences of psychological variation, particularly how psychological characteristics may help us understand statistical associations between various aspects of culture.

 GLOSSARY TERMS

personality
personality integration
  of culture

projective tests
socialization

 CRITICAL QUESTIONS

1. Do you think indulging children makes them more or less self-reliant as adults? Why do you think so?

2. What may explain adolescent rebelliousness?

3. Agriculturalists and foragers seem to have somewhat different personalities, so method of food-getting may be related to personality. Do you think there is a similar relationship between occupation and personality? If so, why?

INTERNET EXERCISES

1. Explore some Web pages on psychological anthropology. Try **http://www.colossus.hamilton.edu/academic/anthro/Raybeck.html**, or search for "psychological anthropology" on a Web search engine to find a course curriculum on psychological anthropology.

2. Mothering is more often talked about than fathering. Visit the Web site **http://www.apa.org/monitor/apr96/nurture2.html** and read an article summarizing how culture influences the parenting style of fathers. When you finish reading that article, use the search engine of the APA home page to check out other articles on fathering.

3. What are some of the rights of children that are contained in the The Convention on the Rights of the Child, a treaty on human rights for children (**http://www.unicef.org/crc/**)?

SUGGESTED READING

BURBANK, V. K. "Adolescent Socialization and Initiation Ceremonies." In C. R. Ember and M. Ember, eds., *Cross-Cultural Research for Social Science.* Upper Saddle River, NJ: Prentice Hall, 1998. Prentice Hall/Simon & Schuster Custom Publishing. A review of how and why socialization in adolescence varies, with a special focus on initiation ceremonies and gender differences.

HEWLETT, B. S. "Diverse Contexts of Human Infancy." In C. R. Ember and M. Ember, eds., *Cross-Cultural Research for Social Science.* Upper Saddle River, NJ: Prentice Hall, 1998. Prentice Hall/Simon & Schuster Custom Publishing. Examines North American and Western European biases in what is considered "normal" in infancy by cross-culturally examining the diverse practices regarding childbirth, infant care, and characteristics of infant caretakers.

MUNROE, R. H., MUNROE, R. L., AND WHITING, B. B., EDS. *Handbook of Cross-Cultural Human Development.* New York: Garland, 1981. A massive collection of papers, prepared especially for this volume, on many aspects of human development that have been investigated cross-culturally.

ROGOFF, B. *Apprenticeship in Thinking: Cognitive Development in Social Context.* New York: Oxford University Press, 1990. This book suggests that children's cognitive development is an apprenticeship, that the particular cognitive skills developed are rooted in the particular historical and cultural activities of the society.

SEGALL, M. H., DASEN, P. R., BERRY, J. W., AND POORTINGA, Y. H. *Human Behavior in Global Perspective: An Introduction to Cross-Cultural Psychology.* New York: Pergamon, 1990. An introduction to research in many societies around the world on the ways in which perception, cognition, motivation, and other aspects of human behavior are influenced by variable social and cultural factors.

WHITING, B. B., AND EDWARDS, C. P., in collaboration with C. R. Ember, G. M. Erchak, S. Harkness, R. L. Munroe, R. H. Munroe, S. B. Nerlove, S. Seymour, C. M. Super, T. S. Weisner, and M. Wenger. *Children of Different Worlds: The Formation of Social Behavior.* Cambridge, MA: Harvard University Press, 1988. On the basis of data collected in the Six Cultures project, the authors explore the ways in which age, gender, and culture affect the social behavior of children. Knowledge of the company children keep and of the proportion of time they spend with various categories of people makes it possible to predict important aspects of children's interpersonal behavior.

22

Religion and Magic

As far as we know, all societies have possessed beliefs that can be grouped under the term *religion*. These beliefs vary from culture to culture and from year to year. Yet, despite their variety, we shall define **religion** as any set of attitudes, beliefs, and practices pertaining to *supernatural power,* whether that power be forces, gods, spirits, ghosts, or demons.

In our society, we divide phenomena into the natural and the supernatural, but not all languages or cultures make such a neat distinction. Moreover, what is considered **supernatural**—powers believed to be not human or not subject to the laws of nature—varies from society to society. Some of the variation is determined by what a society regards as natural. For example, some illnesses commonly found in our society are believed to result from the natural action of bacteria and viruses. In other societies, and even among some people in our own society, illness is thought to result from supernatural forces, and thus it forms a part of religious belief.

Beliefs about what is, or is not, a supernatural occurrence also vary within a society at a given time or over time. In Judeo-Christian traditions, for example, floods, earthquakes, volcanic eruptions, comets, and epidemics were once considered evidence of supernatural powers intervening in human affairs. It is now generally agreed that they are simply natural occurrences—even though many still believe that supernatural forces may be involved. Thus, the line between the natural and the supernatural varies in a society according to what people believe about the causes of things and events in the observable world.

In many cultures, what we would consider religious is embedded in other aspects of everyday life. That is, it is often difficult to separate the religious or economic or political from other aspects of the culture. Such cultures have little or no specialization of any kind; there are no full-time priests, no purely religious activities. So the various aspects of culture we distinguish (for example, in the chapter titles of this book) are not separate and easily recognized in many societies, as they are in complex societies such as our own. However, it is sometimes difficult even for us to agree whether or not a particular custom of ours is religious. After all, the categorizing of beliefs as religious or political or social is a relatively new custom. The ancient Greeks, for instance, did not have a word for religion, but they did have many concepts concerning the behavior of their gods and their own expected duties to the gods.

When people's duties to their gods are linked with duty to their princes, it is difficult to separate religious from political ideas. As an example of our own difficulty in labeling a particular class of actions or beliefs as religious or social, consider our attitudes about wearing clothes. Is our belief that it is necessary to wear clothing, at least in the company of nonlovers, a religious principle, or is it something else? Recall that in Genesis, the wearing of clothes, or fig leaves, is distinctly associated with the loss of innocence: Adam and Eve, after eating the apple, covered their nakedness. Accordingly, when Christian missionaries first visited islands in the Pacific in the nineteenth century, they forced the native women to wear more clothes, particularly to cover their sexual parts. Were the missionaries' ideas about sex religious or social, or perhaps both?

THE UNIVERSALITY OF RELIGION

Religious beliefs and practices are found in all known contemporary societies, and archaeologists think they have found signs of religious belief associated with *Homo sapiens* who lived at least 60,000 years ago. People then deliberately buried their dead, and many graves contain the remains of food, tools, and other objects that were probably thought to be needed in an afterlife. Some of the artistic productions of modern humans after about 30,000 years ago may have been used for religious purposes. For example, sculptures of females with ample secondary sex characteristics may have been fertility charms. Cave paintings in which the predominant images are animals of the hunt may reflect a belief that the image had some power over events. Perhaps early humans thought that their hunting would be more successful if they drew images depicting good fortune in hunting. The details of religions practiced in the distant past cannot be recovered. Yet evidence of ritual treatment of the dead suggests that early people believed in the existence of supernatural spirits and tried to communicate with, and perhaps influence, them.

We may reasonably assume the existence of prehistoric religion and we have evidence of the universality of religion in historic times, so we can understand why the subject of religion has been the focus of much speculation, research, and theorizing. As long ago as the fifth century B.C., Herodotus made fairly objective comparisons among the religions of the 50 or so societies he traveled to from his home in

Greece. He noted many similarities among their gods and pointed out evidence of diffusion of religious worship. During the 2,500 years since Herodotus's time, scholars, theologians, historians, and philosophers have speculated about religion. Some have claimed superiority for their own forms of religion; others have derided the naive simplicity of others' beliefs; and some have expressed skepticism concerning all beliefs.

Speculation about which religion is superior is not an anthropological concern. What is of interest to anthropologists is why religion is found in all societies and how and why it varies from society to society. Many social scientists—particularly anthropologists, sociologists, and psychologists—have offered theories to account for the universality of religion. Most think that religions are created by humans in response to certain universal needs or conditions. Four such needs or conditions have been discussed: a need for intellectual understanding, reversion to childhood feelings, anxiety and uncertainty, and a need for community.

THE NEED TO UNDERSTAND

One of the earliest social scientists to propose a major theory of the origin of religion was Edward Tylor. In Tylor's view, religion originated in people's speculation about dreams, trances, and death. The dead, the distant, those in the next house, animals—all seem real in dreams and trances. Tylor thought that the lifelike appearances of these imagined persons and animals suggests a dual existence for all things—a physical, visible body and a psychic, invisible soul. In sleep, the soul can leave the body and appear to other people; at death, the soul permanently leaves the body. Because the dead appear in dreams, people come to believe that the souls of the dead are still around.

Tylor thought that the belief in souls was the earliest form of religion; **animism** is the term he used to refer to belief in souls.[1] But many scholars criticized Tylor's theory for being too intellectual and not dealing with the emotional component of religion. One of Tylor's students, R. R. Marett, felt that Tylor's animism was too sophisticated an idea to be the origin of religion. Marett suggested that **animatism**—a belief in impersonal supernatural forces (for example, the power of a rabbit's foot)—preceded the creation of spirits.[2] A similar idea is that when people believe in gods, they are *anthropomorphizing*—attributing human characteristics and motivations to nonhuman, particularly supernatural, events.[3] Anthropomorphizing may be an attempt to understand what is otherwise incomprehensible and disturbing.

REVERSION TO CHILDHOOD FEELINGS

Sigmund Freud believed that early humans lived in groups each of which was dominated by a tyrannical man who kept all the women for himself.[4] Freud postulated that, on maturing, the sons were driven out of the group. Later they got together to kill and eat the hated father. But then the sons felt enormous guilt and remorse, which they expressed (projected) by prohibiting the killing of a totem animal (the father-substitute). Subsequently, on ritual occasions, the cannibalistic scene was repeated in the form of a totem meal. Freud believed that these early practices gradually became transformed into the worship of deities or gods modeled after the father.

Freud's interpretation of the origin of religion is not accepted by most social scientists today. But there is widespread agreement with his idea that events in infancy can have long-lasting and powerful effects on beliefs and practices in adult life. Helpless and dependent on parents for many years, infants and children inevitably and unconsciously view their parents as all-knowing and all-powerful. When adults feel out of control or in need, they may unconsciously revert to their infantile and childhood feelings. They may then look to gods or magic to do what they cannot do for themselves, just as they looked to their parents to take care of their needs. As we shall see, there is evidence that feelings about the supernatural world parallel feelings in everyday life.

ANXIETY AND UNCERTAINTY

Freud thought that humans would turn to religion during times of uncertainty, but he did not view religion positively, believing that humans would eventually outgrow the need for religion. Others viewed religion more positively. Bronislaw Malinowski noted that people in all societies are faced with anxiety and uncertainty. They may have skills and knowledge to take care of many of their needs, but knowledge is not sufficient to prevent illness, accidents, and natural disasters. The most frightening prospect is death itself. Consequently, there is an intense desire for immortality. As Malinowski saw it, religion is born from the universal need to find comfort in inevitable times of stress. Through religious belief, people affirm their convictions that death is neither real nor final, that people are endowed with a personality that persists even after death. In religious ceremony, humans can commemorate and communicate with those who have died, and in these ways achieve some measure of comfort.[5]

Theorists such as William James, Carl Jung, Erich Fromm, and Abraham Maslow have viewed religion even more positively: Religion is not just a way of relieving anxiety; it is thought to be therapeutic. James suggested that religion provides a feeling of union with something larger than oneself,[6] and Jung suggested that it helps people resolve their inner conflicts and attain maturity.[7] Fromm proposed that religion helps provide people with a framework of values,[8] and Maslow argued that it provides people with a transcendental understanding of the world.[9]

Research Frontiers

THE USEFULNESS OF RELIGION: TABOOS AMONG NEW ENGLAND FISHERMEN

People who engage in risky activities may try to ensure their safety by carrying or wearing lucky charms. They believe the charms protect them by invoking the help of supernatural beings or forces. We might also believe we can protect ourselves by *not* doing some things. For example, baseball players on a hitting streak may choose *not* to change their socks or sweatshirt for the next game (to continue their luck). Or we obey a prohibition because we think that by doing so we can avoid supernatural punishment. For example, we may fast or give up certain foods for a period of time. Why? God knows!

Whether or not religious beliefs and practices can affect our success or reduce our risk, we may consider them useful or adaptive if they reduce our anxieties. And reducing anxiety might indirectly maximize our success. Doesn't an actor try to reduce his or her "stage fright" before a performance? Prohibitions (taboos) are perhaps particularly likely to be adaptive in this way. Consider some research on New England fishermen that suggests that their taboos, or "rituals of avoidance," may reduce anxiety.

John Poggie and Richard Pollnac interviewed a random sample of 108 commercial fishermen from three New England ports. They were trying to explain the number of taboos among the fishermen, as measured by asking them to describe all the superstitions related to fishing they could remember. The fishermen were often embarrassed when they talked about their ritual beliefs and practices. They would say they did not really believe in their taboos, but they admitted that they would not break them while fishing. The taboos prohibited saying or doing a certain thing, or something bad would happen. Most frequently mentioned were "Don't turn a hatch cover upside down," "Don't whistle on a boat," and "Don't mention the word *pig* on board." When the fishermen were asked what these taboos meant, they talked about personal safety and preventing bad luck.

The results of the study suggest that anxiety about personal danger while fishing is the main stimulus for the taboo behavior observed among the fishermen. For example, there are more taboos reported when the duration of exposure to danger is longer. Fishermen who go out just for the day report significantly fewer taboos than fishermen who go out for longer periods of time. And longer trips are clearly more dangerous because they are farther from shore. If there is a storm, the farther out you are, the more risk of disaster because you are exposed longer to rough seas. And it is more difficult to deal with illness, injury, breakdowns, and damage to the boat far from shore. Also consistent with the conclusion that the fishermen's taboos reduce anxiety is the fact that inshore fishermen (those who are after shellfish close to shore) report a significantly smaller number of taboos than offshore fishermen (who go out farther in trawlers).

On shore, the fishermen express some disbelief in the effectiveness of their taboos. (They *are* called "superstitions," you know!) But at sea it seems that the omnipresence of danger raises anxiety levels and discourages the fishermen from testing their disbelief. It won't hurt to practice the taboo at sea, they say, but it might hurt not to!

Sources: John J. Poggie, Jr., and Richard B. Pollnac, "Danger and Rituals of Avoidance among New England Fishermen," *MAST: Maritime Anthropological Studies,* 1 (1988): 66–78; John J. Poggie, Jr., Richard B. Pollnac, and Carl Gersuny, "Risk as a Basis for Taboos among Fishermen in Southern New England," *Journal for the Scientific Study of Religion,* 15 (1976): 257–62.

The Need for Community

All those theories of religion agree on one thing: Whatever the beliefs or rituals, religion may satisfy psychological needs common to all people. But some social scientists believe that religion springs from society and serves social, rather than psychological, needs. Émile Durkheim, a French sociologist, pointed out that living in society makes humans feel pushed and pulled by powerful forces. These forces direct their behavior, pushing them to resist what is considered wrong, pulling them to do what is considered right. These are the forces of public opinion, custom, and law. Because they are largely invisible and unexplained, people would feel them as mysterious forces and therefore come to believe in gods and spirits. Durkheim suggested that religion arises out of the experience of living in social groups; religious belief and practice affirm a person's place in society, enhance feelings of community, and give people confidence. He proposed that society is really the object of worship in religion.

Consider how Durkheim explained totemism, so often discussed by early religious theorists. He thought that nothing inherent in a lizard, rat, or frog, animal totems for some Australian aborigine groups, would be sufficient to make them *sacred*. The totem animal therefore must be a symbol. But a symbol of what? Durkheim noted that the people are organized into clans, and each clan has its own totem animal; the totem distinguishes one clan from another. So the totem is the focus of the clan's religious rituals and symbolizes both the clan and the clan's spirits. It is the clan with which people mostly identify, and it is the clan that is affirmed in ritual.[10]

Guy Swanson accepted Durkheim's belief that certain aspects or conditions of society generate the responses we call religious, but he thought that Durkheim was too vague about exactly what in society would generate the belief in spirits or gods. So what might? Swanson suggested that the belief in spirits derives from the existence of *sovereign groups* in a society. These are the groups that have independent jurisdiction (decision-making powers) over some sphere of life—the family, the clan, the village, the state. Such groups are not mortal; they persist beyond the lifetimes of their individual members. According to Swanson, then, the spirits or gods that people invent personify or represent the powerful decision-making groups in their society. Just like sovereign groups in a society, the spirits or gods are immortal and have purposes and goals that supersede those of an individual.[11]

VARIATION IN RELIGIOUS BELIEFS

There is no general agreement among scholars as to why people need religion, or how spirits, gods, and other supernatural beings and forces come into existence. (Any or all of the needs we have discussed, psychological or social, may give rise to religious belief and practice.) Yet there is general recognition of the enormous variation in the details of religious beliefs and practices. Societies differ in the kinds of supernatural beings or forces they believe in and the character of those beings. They also differ in the structure or hierarchy of those beings, in what the beings actually do, and in what happens to people after death. Variation exists also in the ways in which the supernatural is believed to interact with humans.

Types of Supernatural Forces and Beings

SUPERNATURAL FORCES. Some supernatural forces have no personlike character. As we discussed earlier, Marett referred to such religious beliefs as animatism. For example, a supernatural, impersonal force called **mana,** after its Malayo-Polynesian name, is thought to inhabit some objects but not others, some people but not others. A farmer in Polynesia places stones around a field; the crops are bountiful; the stones have mana. During a subsequent year the stones may lose their mana and the crops will be poor. People may also possess mana, as, for example, the chiefs in Polynesia were said to do. However, such power is not necessarily possessed permanently; chiefs who were unsuccessful in war or other activities were said to have lost their mana.

The word *mana* may be Malayo-Polynesian, but a similar concept is also found in our own society. We can compare mana to the power golfers may attribute to some but, unhappily not all, of their clubs. A ballplayer might think a certain sweatshirt or pair of socks has supernatural power or force, and that more runs or points will be scored when they are worn. A four-leaf clover has mana; a three-leaf clover does not.

Objects, persons, or places can be considered **taboo.** Anthony Wallace distinguished mana from taboo by pointing out that things containing mana are to be touched, whereas taboo things are not to be touched, for their power can cause harm.[12] Thus, those who touch them may themselves become taboo. Taboos surround food not to be eaten, places not to be entered, animals not to be killed, people not to be touched sexually, people not to be touched at all, and so on. An Australian aborigine could not normally kill and eat the animal that was his totem; Hebrew tribesmen were forbidden to touch a woman during menstruation or for seven days afterward.

SUPERNATURAL BEINGS. Supernatural beings fall within two broad categories: those of nonhuman origin, such as gods and spirits, and those of human origin, such as ghosts and ancestral spirits. Chief among the beings of nonhuman origin, **gods** are named personalities. They are often anthropomorphic—that is, conceived in the image of a person—although they are sometimes given the shapes of other animals or of celestial bodies, such as the sun or moon. Essentially, the gods are believed to have created themselves, but some of them then created, or gave birth to, other gods. Although some are seen as creator gods, not all peoples include the creation of the world as one of the acts of gods.

After their efforts at creation, many creator gods retire. Having set the world in motion, they are not interested in its day-to-day operation. Other creator gods remain interested in the ordinary affairs of human beings, especially the affairs of one small, chosen segment of humanity. Whether or not a society has a creator god, the job of running the creation is often left to lesser gods. The Maori of New Zealand, for example, recognize three important gods: a god of the sea, a god of the forest, and a god of agriculture. They call upon each in turn for help and try to get all three to share their knowledge of how

There's room in the world for all religions—those who believe in rocks, those who believe in trees, those who believe in clouds. . ."
(© 1984 by Sidney Harris)

the universe runs. The gods of the ancient Romans, on the other hand, specialized to a high degree. There were three gods of the plow, one god to help with the sowing, one for weeding, one for reaping, one for storing grain, one for manuring, and so on.[13]

Beneath the gods in prestige, and often closer to people, are multitudes of unnamed **spirits.** Some may be guardian spirits for people. Some, who become known for particularly efficacious work, may be promoted to the rank of named gods. Some spirits who are known to the people but never invoked by them are of the hobgoblin type. Hobgoblins delight in mischief and can be blamed for any number of small mishaps; other spirits take pleasure in deliberately working evil on behalf of people.

Many Native American groups believed in guardian spirits that had to be sought out, usually in childhood. For example, among the Sanpoil of northeastern Washington, boys and sometimes girls would be sent out on overnight vigils to acquire their guardians. Most commonly the spirits were animals, but they could also be uniquely shaped rocks, lakes, mountains, whirlwinds, or clouds. The vigil was not always successful. When it was, the guardian spirit appeared in a vision or dream, and always at first in human form. Conversation with the spirit would reveal its true identity.[14]

Ghosts and **ancestor spirits** are among the supernatural beings who were once human. The belief that ghosts or their actions can be perceived by the living is almost universal.[15] The near-universality of the belief in ghosts may not be difficult to explain. There are many cues in everyday experience that are associated with a loved one, and even after her or his death those cues might arouse the feeling that the dead person is still somehow present. The opening of a door or the smell of tobacco or cologne in a room may evoke the idea that the person is still present, if only for a moment. Then, too, loved ones live on in dreams. Small wonder, then, that most societies believe in ghosts. If the idea of ghosts is generated by these familiar associations, we might expect that ghosts in most societies would be close relatives and friends, not strangers—and they are.[16]

Although the belief in ghosts is nearly universal, the spirits of the dead do not play an active role in the life of the living in all societies. In his cross-cultural study of 50 societies, Swanson found that people are likely to believe in active ancestral spirits where descent groups are important decision-making units. The descent group is an entity that exists over time, back into the past as well as forward into the future, despite the deaths of individual members.[17] The dead feel concern for the fortunes, the prestige, and the continuity of their descent group as strongly as the living. As a Lugbara elder (in northern Uganda in Africa) put it, "Are our ancestors not people of our lineage? They are our fathers and we are their children whom they have begotten. Those that have died stay near us in our homes and we feed and respect them. Does not a man help his father when he is old?"[18]

THE CHARACTER OF SUPERNATURAL BEINGS

Whatever type they may be, the gods or spirits venerated in a given culture tend to have certain personality or character traits. They may be unpredictable or predictable, aloof from or interested in human affairs, helpful or punishing. Why do the gods and spirits in a particular culture exhibit certain character traits rather than others?

We have some evidence from cross-cultural studies that the character of supernatural beings may be related to the nature of child training. Melford Spiro and Roy D'Andrade suggested that the god-human relationship is a projection of the parent-child relationship, in which case child-training practices might well be relived in dealings with the supernatural.[19] For example, if a child was nurtured immediately by her parents when she cried or waved her arms about or kicked, she might grow up expecting to be nurtured by the gods when she attracted their attention by performing a ritual. On the other hand, if her parents often punished her, she would grow up expecting the gods to punish her if she disobeyed them. William Lambert, Leigh Minturn Triandis, and Margery Wolf, in another cross-cultural study, found that societies with hurtful or punitive child-training practices are likely to believe that their gods are aggressive and malevolent; societies with less punitive child training are more likely to believe that the gods are benevolent.[20] These results are consistent with the Freudian notion that the supernatural world should parallel the natural. It is worth noting in this context that some peoples refer to the god as their father and to themselves as his children.

STRUCTURE OR HIERARCHY OF SUPERNATURAL BEINGS

The range of social structures in human societies from egalitarian to highly stratified has its counterpart in the supernatural world. Some societies have gods or spirits that are not ranked; one god has about as much power as another. Other societies have gods or spirits that are ranked in prestige and power. For example, on the Pacific islands of Palau, which was a rank society, gods were ranked as people were. Each clan worshiped a god and a goddess that had names or titles similar to clan titles. Although a clan god was generally important only to the members of that clan, the gods of the various clans in a village were believed to be ranked in the same order that the clans were. Thus, the god of the highest-ranking clan was respected by all the clans of the village. Its shrine was given the place of honor in the center of the village and was larger and more elaborately decorated than other shrines.[21]

Although the Palauans did not believe in a high god or supreme being who outranked all the other gods, some societies do. Consider Judaism, Christianity, and Islam, which we call **monotheistic** religions. Although *monotheism* means "one god," most monotheistic religions actually include more than one supernatural being (e.g., demons, angels, the Devil). But the supreme being or high god, as the creator of the universe or the director of events (or both), is believed to be ultimately responsible for all events.[22] A **polytheistic** religion recognizes many important gods, no one of which is supreme.

Why do some societies have a belief in a high god and others do not? Recall Swanson's suggestion that people invent gods who personify the important decision-making groups in their society. He therefore hypothesized that societies with hierarchical political systems should be more likely to believe in a high god. In his cross-cultural study of 50 societies (none of which practiced any of the major world religions), he found that belief in a high god is strongly associated with three or more levels of "sovereign" (decision-making) groups. Of the 20 sample societies that had a hierarchy of three or more sovereign groups—for instance, family, clan, and chiefdom—17 possessed the idea of a high god. Of the 19 societies that had fewer than three levels of decision-making groups, only 2 had a high god.[23] Consistent with Swanson's findings, societies dependent on food production are more likely to have a belief in a high god than are food-collecting societies.[24] These results strongly suggest, then, that the realm of the gods parallels and may reflect the everyday social and political world.

INTERVENTION OF THE GODS IN HUMAN AFFAIRS

According to Clifford Geertz, it is when faced with ignorance, pain, and the unjustness of life that a person explains events by the intervention of the gods.[25] Thus, in Greek religion the direct intervention of Poseidon as ruler of the seas prevented Odysseus from getting home for ten years. In the Old Testament, the direct intervention of Yahweh caused the great flood that killed most of the people in the time of Noah. In other societies, people may search their memories for a violated taboo that has brought punishment through supernatural intervention.

In addition to unasked-for divine interference, there are numerous examples of requests for divine intervention, either for good for oneself and friends or for evil for others. Gods are asked to intervene in the weather and make the crops grow, to send fish to the fisherman and game to the hunter, to find lost things, and to accompany travelers and prevent accidents. They are asked to stop the flow of lava down the side of a volcano, to stop a war, or to cure an illness.

The gods do not intervene in all societies. In some they intervene in human affairs; in others, they are not the slightest bit interested; and in still others they interfere only occasionally. We have little research on why gods are believed to interfere in some societies and not in others. We do, however, have some evidence suggesting when the gods will take an interest in the morality or immorality of human behavior. Swanson's study suggests that the gods are likely to punish people for immoral behavior when there are considerable differences in wealth in the society.[26] His interpretation is that supernatural support of moral behavior is particularly useful where inequalities tax the ability of the political system to maintain social order and minimize social disorder. Envy of others' privileges may motivate some people to behave immorally; the belief that the gods will punish such behavior might deter it.

LIFE AFTER DEATH

In many societies, ideas about an afterlife are vague and seemingly unimportant, but many other peoples have very definite and elaborate ideas of what happens after death. The Lugbara see the dead

Most religions that we call monotheistic have other, minor supernatural beings. This painting by Blake (ca. 1805) portrays good and bad angels struggling over a child. Source: "The Good and Evil Angels struggling for Possession of a Child", © Tate Gallery/Art Resource.

as joining the ancestors of the living and staying near the family homesite. They retain an interest in the behavior of the living, both rewarding and punishing them. The Zuni of the southwestern United States think the dead join the past dead, known as the *katcinas,* in a katcina village at the bottom of a nearby lake. There they lead a life of singing and dancing and bring rain to the living Zuni. They are also swift to punish the priest who fails in his duty or the people who impersonate them in masks during the dance ceremonies.[27]

The Chamulas have merged the ancient Mayan worship of the sun and moon with the Spanish conquerors' Jesus and Mary. Their vision of life after death contains a blending of the two cultures. All souls go to the underworld, where they live a humanlike life except that they are incapable of sexual intercourse. After the sun travels over the world, it travels under the underworld, so that the dead have sunlight. Only murderers and suicides are punished, being burned by the Christ-sun on their journey.[28]

Many Christians believe that the dead are divided into two groups: The unsaved are sent to everlasting punishment and the saved to everlasting reward. Accounts differ, but hell is often associated with torture by fire, heaven with mansions. Several societies see the dead as returning to earth to be reborn. The Hindus use this pattern of reincarnation to justify one's caste in this life and to promise eventual release from the pain of life through the attainment of *nirvana,* or inclusion into the One. The afterworld in many religions may resemble the everyday world, but we still lack comparative studies that show exactly how.

VARIATION IN RELIGIOUS PRACTICES

Beliefs are not the only elements of religion that vary from society to society. There is also variation in how people interact with the supernatural. The manner of approach to the supernatural varies from supplication—requests, prayers, and so on—to manipulation. And societies vary in the kinds of religious practitioners they have.

WAYS TO INTERACT WITH THE SUPERNATURAL

How to get in touch with the supernatural has proved to be a universal problem. Wallace identified a number of ways used by people the world over, though not necessarily all together, including, but

not limited to, prayer (asking for supernatural help), physiological experience (doing things to the body and mind), simulation (manipulating imitations of things), feasts, and sacrifices.[29] Prayer can be spontaneous or memorized, private or public, silent or spoken. The Lugbara do not say the words of a prayer aloud, for doing so would be too powerful; they simply think about the things that are bothering them. The gods know all languages.

Doing things to the body or mind may involve drugs (hallucinogenics such as peyote or opiates) or alcohol; social isolation or sensory deprivation; dancing or running till exhausted; being deprived of food, water, and sleep; and listening to repetitive sounds such as drumming. Such behaviors may induce trances or altered states of consciousness.[30] Erika Bourguignon found that achieving these altered states, which she generally referred to as *trances,* is part of religious practice in 90 percent of the world's societies.[31] In some societies, trances are thought to involve the presence of a spirit or power inside a person that changes or displaces that person's personality or soul. These types are referred to as possession trances. Other types of trances may involve the journey of a person's soul, experiencing visions, or transmitting messages from spirits. Possession trances are especially likely in societies that depend on agriculture and have social stratification, slavery, and more complex political hierarchies. Nonpossession trances are most likely to occur in food-collecting societies. Societies with moderate levels of social complexity have both possession and nonpossession trances.[32]

Voodoo employs simulation, or the imitation of things. Dolls are made in the likeness of an enemy and then are maltreated in hopes that the original enemy will experience pain and even death. Simulation is often employed during **divination,** or getting the supernatural to provide guidance. Many people in our society have their fortunes read in crystal balls, tea leaves, Ouija boards, or cards. Or they may choose a course of action by a toss of a coin or a throw of dice. All are variations of methods used in other cultures.

Omar Moore suggested that among the Naskapi hunters of Labrador, divination is an adaptive strategy for successful hunting. The Naskapi consult the diviner every three or four days when they have no luck in hunting. The diviner holds a caribou bone over the fire, and the burns and cracks that appear in it indicate where the group should hunt. Moore, unlike the Naskapi, did not believe that the diviner really can find out where the animals will be; the cracks in the bones merely provide a way of randomly choosing where to hunt. Because humans are likely to develop customary patterns of action, they might be likely to look for game according to some plan. But game might learn to avoid hunters who operate according to a plan. Thus, any method of ensuring against patterning or predictable plans—any random strategy—may be advantageous. Divination by "reading" the bones would seem to be a random strategy. It also relieves any individual of the responsibility of deciding where to hunt, a decision that might arouse anger if the hunt failed.[33]

The eating of a sacred meal is found in many religions. For instance, Holy Communion is a simulation of the Last Supper. Australian aborigines, normally forbidden to eat their totem animal, have one totem feast a year at which they eat the totem. Feasts are often part of marriage and funeral ceremonies, as well as a fringe benefit of the sacrifice of food to the gods.

Some societies make sacrifices to a god in order to influence the god's action, either to divert anger or to attract goodwill. Characteristic of all sacrifices is that something of value is given up to the gods, whether it be food, drink, sex, household goods, or the life of an animal or person. Some societies feel that the god is obligated to act on their behalf if they make the appropriate sacrifice. Others use the sacrifice in an attempt to persuade the god, realizing there is no guarantee that the attempt will be successful.

Of all types of sacrifice, we probably think that the taking of human life is the ultimate. Nevertheless, human sacrifice is not rare in the ethnographic

Although all societies have religious beliefs and practices, these pictures hint at the range of variation: worshippers dressed in white in a Vietnam temple; a worshipper making offerings at the feet of a statue in an Indian temple; prayer time before a soccer game in Saudi Arabia; celebrants sharing food and drink with the dead at a cemetery in Peru.

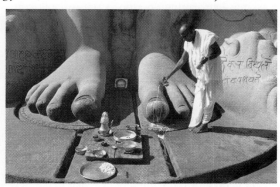

and historical records. Why have some societies practiced it? One cross-cultural study found that among preindustrial societies, those with full-time craft specialists, slavery, and the corvée are most likely to practice human sacrifice. The suggested explanation is that the sacrifice mirrors what is socially important: Societies that depend mainly on human labor for energy (rather than animals or machines) may think of a human life as an appropriate offering to the gods when people want something very important.[34]

MAGIC

All these modes of interacting with the supernatural can be categorized in various ways. One dimension of variation is how much people in society rely on pleading or asking or trying to persuade the supernatural to act on their behalf, as opposed to whether they believe they can compel the supernatural to help by performing certain acts. For example, prayer is asking; performing voodoo is presumably compelling. When people believe their action can compel the supernatural to act in some particular and intended way, anthropologists often refer to the belief and related practice as **magic.**

Magic may involve manipulation of the supernatural for good or for evil. Many societies have magical rituals designed to ensure good crops, the replenishment of game, the fertility of domestic animals, and the avoidance and cure of illness in humans. We tend to associate the belief in magic with societies simpler than our own. But as many as 80,000 people in the United States take magic seriously.[35] Many claim to be witches. An understanding of why magic appeals to some individuals but not others in our own society may help us explain why magic is an important part of religious behavior in many societies.

As we will see, the witch doctor and the shaman often employ magic to effect a cure. But the use of magic to bring about harm has evoked perhaps the most interest.

SORCERY AND WITCHCRAFT. Sorcery and witchcraft are attempts to invoke the spirits to work harm against people. Although the words *sorcery* and *witchcraft* are often used interchangeably, they are also often distinguished. **Sorcery** may include the use of materials, objects, and medicines to invoke supernatural malevolence. **Witchcraft** may be said to accomplish the same ills by means of thought and emotion alone. Evidence of witchcraft can never be found. This lack of visible evidence

makes an accusation of witchcraft both harder to prove and harder to disprove.

To the Azande of Zaire, in central Africa, witchcraft was part of everyday living. It was not used to explain events for which the cause was known, such as carelessness or violation of a taboo, but to explain the otherwise unexplainable. A man is gored by an elephant. He must have been bewitched, because he had not been gored on other elephant hunts. A man goes to his beer hut at night, lights some straw, and holds it aloft to look at his beer. The thatch catches fire and the hut burns down. The man has been bewitched, for huts did not catch fire on hundreds of other nights when he and others did the same thing. Some of the pots of a skilled potter break; some of the bowls of a skilled carver crack. Witchcraft. Other pots, other bowls treated exactly the same have not broken.[36]

The witch craze in Europe during the sixteenth and seventeenth centuries and the witch trials in 1692 in Salem, Massachusetts, remind us that the fear of others, which the belief in witchcraft presumably represents, can increase and decrease in a society within a relatively short period of time. Many scholars have tried to explain these witch hunts. One factor often suggested is political turmoil, which may give rise to widespread distrust and a search for scapegoats. In the case of Europe during the sixteenth and seventeenth centuries, small regional political units were being incorporated into national states, and political allegiances were in flux. In addition, as Swanson noted, the commercial revolution and related changes were producing a new social class, the middle class, and "were promoting the growth of Protestantism and other heresies from Roman Catholicism."[37] In the case of Salem, the government of the colony of Massachusetts was unstable and there was much internal dissension. In 1692, the year of the witchcraft hysteria, Massachusetts was left without an English governor, and judicial practices broke down. These extraordinary conditions saw the accusation of a single person for witchcraft become the accusation of hundreds and the execution of 20 people. Swanson suggested that the undermining of legitimate political procedures may have generated the widespread fear of witches.[38]

It is also possible that epidemics of witchcraft accusation, as in Salem as well as other New England and European communities, may be the result of real epidemics—epidemics of disease. The disease implicated in Salem and elsewhere is the fungus disease called ergot, which can grow on rye plants. (The rye flour that went into the bread that the

In 1692 there was an epidemic of witchcraft accusations in Salem, Massachusetts. Some scholars have suggested that ergot poisoning may have made people act and feel as if they were bewitched.

Salem people ate may have been contaminated by ergot.) It is now known that people who eat grain products contaminated by ergot suffer from convulsions, hallucinations, and other symptoms, such as crawling sensations in the skin. We also now know that ergot contains LSD, the drug that produces hallucinations and other delusions that resemble those occurring in severe mental disorders.

The presumed victims of bewitchment in Salem and other places had symptoms similar to victims of ergot poisoning today. They suffered from convulsions and the sensations of being pricked, pinched, or bitten. They had visions and felt as if they were flying through the air. We cannot know for sure that ergot poisoning occurred during those times when witchcraft accusations flourished. There is no direct evidence, of course, since the "bewitched" were not medically tested. But we do have some evidence that seems to be consistent with the ergot theory. Ergot is known to flourish on rye plants under certain climatic conditions—particularly a very cold winter followed by a cool, moist spring and summer. Tree-ring growth indicates that the early 1690s were particularly cold in eastern New England; and the outbreaks of witchcraft accusation in Europe seem to

have peaked with colder winter temperatures.[39] Interestingly, too, when witchcraft hysteria was greatest in Europe, Europeans were using an ointment containing a skin-penetrating substance that we now know produces hallucinations and a vivid sensation of flying.[40] It may not be cause for wonder, then, that our popular image of witches is one of people flying through the air on broomsticks.

But whether or not epidemics of witchcraft hysteria are due to epidemics of ergot poisoning or episodes of political turmoil or both, we still have to understand why so many societies in the ethnographic record believe in witchcraft and sorcery in the first place. Why do so many societies believe that there are ways to invoke the spirits to work harm against people? One possible explanation, suggested by Beatrice Whiting, is that sorcery or witchcraft will be found in societies that lack procedures or judicial authorities to deal with crime and other offenses. Her theory is that all societies need some form of social control—some way of deterring most would-be offenders and of dealing with actual offenders. In the absence of judicial officials who, if present, might deter and deal with antisocial behavior, sorcery may be a very effective social-control mechanism. If you misbehave, the person you mistreated might cause you to become ill or even die. The cross-cultural evidence seems to support this theory. Sorcery is more important in societies that lack judicial authorities than in those that have them.[41]

TYPES OF PRACTITIONER

Individuals may believe that they can directly contact the supernatural, but almost all societies also have part-time or full-time religious or magical practitioners. Research suggests there are four major types of practitioner: shamans, sorcerers or witches, mediums, and priests. As we shall see, the number of types of practitioner in a society seems to vary with degree of cultural complexity.[42]

THE SHAMAN. The **shaman** is usually a part-time male specialist who has fairly high status in his community and is often involved in healing.[43] Westerners often call shamans witch doctors because they don't believe that shamans can effectively cure people. Do shamans effectively cure? Actually, Westerners are not the only skeptics. A Native American named Quesalid from the Kwakiutl of the Northwest Coast didn't believe that shamanism was effective either. So he began to associate with the shamans in order to spy on them and was taken into their group. In his first lessons, he learned

> a curious mixture of pantomime, prestidigitation, and empirical knowledge, including the art of simulating fainting and nervous fits, . . . sacred song, the technique for inducing vomiting, rather precise notions of auscultation or listening to sounds within the body to detect disorders and obstetrics, and the use of "dreamers," that is, spies who listen to private conversations and secretly convey to the shaman bits of information concerning the origins and symptoms of the ills suffered by different people. Above all, he learned the *ars magna*. . . . The shaman hides a little tuft of down in the corner of his mouth, and he throws it up, covered with blood at the proper moment—after having bitten his tongue or made his gums bleed—and solemnly presents it to his patient and the onlookers as the pathological foreign body extracted as a result of his sucking and manipulations.[44]

His suspicions were confirmed, but his first curing was a success. The patient had heard that Quesalid had joined the shamans and believed that only he could heal him. Quesalid remained with the shamans for the four-year apprenticeship, during which he could take no fee, and he became increasingly aware that his methods worked. He visited other villages, competed with other shamans in curing hopeless cases and won, and finally seemed

convinced that his curing system was more valid than those of other shamans. Instead of denouncing the trickery of shamans, he continued to practice as a renowned shaman.[45]

After working with shamans in Africa, E. Fuller Torrey, a psychiatrist and anthropologist, concluded that they use the same mechanisms and techniques to cure patients as psychiatrists and achieve about the same results. He isolated four categories used by healers the world over:

1. **The naming process.** If a disease has a name—"neurasthenia" or "phobia" or "possession by an ancestral spirit" will do—then it is curable; the patient realizes that the doctor understands his case.
2. **The personality of the doctor.** Those who demonstrate some empathy, nonpossessive warmth, and genuine interest in the patient get results.
3. **The patient's expectations.** One way of raising the patient's expectations of being cured is the trip to the doctor; the longer the trip—to the Mayo Clinic, Menninger Clinic, Delphi, or Lourdes—the easier the cure. An impressive setting (the medical center) and impressive paraphernalia (the stethoscope, the couch, attendants in uniform, the rattle, the whistle, the drum, the mask) also raise the patient's expectations. The healer's training is important: The Ute has dreams analyzed; the Blackfoot has a seven-year training course; the American psychiatrist spends four years in medical school and three in hospital training and has diplomas on the wall. High fees also help to raise a patient's expectations. (The Paiute doctors always collect their fees before starting a cure; if they don't, it is believed that they will fall ill.)
4. **Curing techniques.** Drugs, shock treatment, conditioning techniques, and so on have long been used in many different parts of the world.[46]

Medical research suggests that psychological factors are sometimes very important in illness. Patients who believe that medicine will help them often recover quickly even if the medicine is only a sugar pill. Patients who "lose the will to live" may succumb to illness easily. Still, as pharmaceutical companies have discovered, many "folk medicines" collected in anthropological fieldwork do work.

Shamans may coexist with medical doctors. Don Antonio, a respected Otomi Indian shaman in central Mexico, has many patients, perhaps not as many

Healers commonly go into a trance to bring about a cure. This !Kung San healer is being held by others so he doesn't injure himself while he is in a trance.

as before modern medicine, but still plenty. In his view, when he was born God gave him his powers to cure, but his powers are reserved for removing "evil" illnesses (those caused by sorcerers). "Good" illnesses can be cured by herbs and medicine, and he refers patients with those illnesses to doctors; he believes that doctors are more effective than he could be in those cases. The doctors, however, do not seem to refer any patients to Don Antonio or other shamans![47]

SORCERERS AND WITCHES. In contrast with shamans, who have fairly high status, sorcerers and witches of both sexes tend to have very low social and economic status in their societies.[48] Suspected sorcerers and witches are usually feared because they are thought to know how to invoke the supernatural to cause illness, injury, and death. Because sorcerers use materials for their magic, evidence of sorcery can be found, and suspected sorcerers are often killed for their malevolent activities. Because witchcraft supposedly is accomplished by thought and emotion alone, it may be harder to prove that someone is a witch, but the difficulty of proving witchcraft has not prevented people from accusing and killing others for being witches.

MEDIUMS. **Mediums** tend to be females. These part-time practitioners are asked to heal and divine while in possession trances—that is, when they are thought to be possessed by spirits. Mediums are described as having tremors, convulsions, seizures, and temporary amnesia.

PRIESTS. **Priests** are generally full-time male specialists who officiate at public events. They have very high status and are thought to be able to relate to superior or high gods who are beyond the ordinary person's control. In most societies with priests, the people who get to be priests obtain their offices through inheritance or political appointment.[49] Priests are sometimes distinguished from other people by special clothing or a different hairstyle. The training of a priest can be vigorous and long, including fasting, praying, and physical labor, as well as learning the dogma and the ritual of his religion. Priests in the United States complete four years of theological school and sometimes serve first as apprentices under established priests. The priest does not receive a fee for his services but is supported by donations from parishioners or followers. Priests often have some political power as a result of their office—the chief priest is sometimes also the head of state or is a close adviser to the chief of state—and their material well-being is a direct reflection of their position in the priestly hierarchy.

It is the dependence on memorized ritual that both marks and protects the priest. If a shaman repeatedly fails to effect a cure, he will probably lose his following, for he has obviously lost the support of the spirits. But if a priest performs his ritual perfectly and the gods choose not to respond, the priest will usually retain his position and the ritual will preserve its assumed effectiveness. The nonresponse of the gods will be explained in terms of the people's unworthiness of supernatural favor.

PRACTITIONERS AND SOCIAL COMPLEXITY. More complex societies tend to have more types of religious or magical practitioners. If a society has only one type of practitioner, it is almost always a shaman; such societies tend to be nomadic or seminomadic food collectors. Societies with two types of practitioner (usually shaman-healers and priests) have agriculture. Those with three types of practitioner are agriculturalists or pastoralists with political integration beyond the community (the additional practitioner type tends to be either a sorcerer-witch or a medium). Finally, societies with all four types of practitioners have agriculture, political integration beyond the community, and social classes.[50]

RELIGION AND ADAPTATION

Following Malinowski, many anthropologists take the view that religions are adaptive because they reduce the anxieties and uncertainties that afflict all peoples. We do not really know that religion is the only means of reducing anxiety and uncertainty, or even that individuals or societies *have* to reduce their anxiety and uncertainty. Still, it seems likely that certain religious beliefs and practices have directly adaptive consequences. For example, the Hindu belief in the sacred cow has seemed to many to be the very opposite of a useful or adaptive custom. Their religion does not permit Hindus to slaughter cows. Why do the Hindus retain such a belief? Why do they allow all those cows to wander around freely, defecating all over the place, and not slaughter any of them? The contrast with our own use of cows could hardly be greater.

Marvin Harris suggested that the Hindu use of cows may have beneficial consequences that some other use of cows would not have. Harris pointed out that there may be a sound economic reason for not slaughtering cattle in India. The cows, and the males they produce, provide resources that could not easily be gotten otherwise. At the same time, their wandering around to forage is no strain on the food-producing economy.

The resources provided by the cows are varied. First, a team of oxen and a plow are essential for the many small farms in India. The Indians could produce oxen with fewer cows, but to do so they would have to devote some of their food production to the feeding of those cows. In the present system, they do not feed the cows, and even though poor nutrition makes the cows relatively infertile, males, which are castrated to make oxen, are still produced at no cost to the economy. Second, cow dung is essential as a cooking fuel and fertilizer. The National Council of Applied Economic Research estimated that an amount of dung equivalent to 45 million tons of coal is burned annually. Moreover, it is delivered practically to the door each day at no cost. Al-

ternative sources of fuel, such as wood, are scarce or costly. In addition, about 340 million tons of dung are used as manure—essential in a country obliged to derive three harvests a year from its intensively cultivated land. Third, although Hindus do not eat beef, cattle that die naturally or are butchered by non-Hindus are eaten by the lower castes, who, without the upper-caste taboo against eating beef, might not get this needed protein. Fourth, the hides and horns of the cattle that die are used in India's enormous leather industry. Therefore, because the cows do not themselves consume resources needed by people and it would be impossible to provide traction, fuel, and fertilizer as cheaply by other means, the taboo against slaughtering cattle may be very adaptive.[51]

RELIGIOUS CHANGE AS REVITALIZATION

The long history of religion includes periods of strong resistance to change as well as periods of radical change. Anthropologists have been especially interested in the founding of new religions or sects. The appearance of new religions is one of the things that may happen when cultures are disrupted by contact with dominant societies. Various terms have been suggested for these religious movements—cargo cults, nativistic movements, messianic movements, millenarian cults. Wallace suggested that they are all examples of **revitalization movements,** efforts to save a culture by infusing it with a new purpose and new life.[52] We turn to examples of such movements from North America and Melanesia.

THE SENECA AND THE RELIGION OF HANDSOME LAKE. The Seneca reservation of the Iroquois on the Allegheny River in New York State was a place of "poverty and humiliation" by 1799.[53] Demoralized by whiskey and dispossessed from their traditional lands, unable to compete with the new technology because of illiteracy and lack of training, the Seneca were at an impasse. In this setting, Handsome Lake, the 50-year-old brother of a chief, had the first of a number of visions. In them, he met with emissaries of the Creator who showed him heaven and hell and commissioned him to revitalize Seneca religion and society. This he set out to do for the next decade and a half. He used as his principal text the *Gaiwiio,* or "Good Word," a gospel that contains statements about the nature of religion and eternity and a code of conduct for the righteous. The *Gaiwiio* is interesting both for the influence of Quaker Christianity it clearly reveals[54] and for the way the new material was merged with traditional Iroquois religious concepts.

Current Issues

ONE APPEAL OF RELIGION MAY BE THE WISH FOR A BETTER WORLD

There are many religions in the United States today, and new sects, often derisively called cults, emerge regularly. Few of us realize that nearly all of the major churches or religions in the world began as minority sects or cults. Indeed, some of the most established and prestigious Protestant churches were radical social movements at first. For example, what we now know as the United Church of Christ, which includes the Congregational Church, was founded by radicals in England who wanted church governance to be in the hands of the local congregation. Many of these radicals became the people we call Pilgrims, who had to flee to the New World. But they were very fundamentalist in their beliefs too; for example, as late as the 1820s, Congregationalist-dominated towns in Connecticut prohibited celebrations of Christmas outside of church because they were not mentioned in the Bible. Nowadays, Congregationalists are among the most liberal Protestants.

We should not be surprised to learn that most of the various Protestant churches today, including some considered very conservative, began as militant sects that set out to achieve a better world. After all, that's why we call them "Protestant." At first, the rebellion was against Rome and the Catholic Church. Later, sects developed in opposition to church and government hierarchies. And remember that Christianity itself began as a radical group in the hinterland of the Roman Empire. So new sects or cults were probably always political and social, as well as religious, movements. Recall that the word *millennium,* as used in discussions of religious movements, refers to a wished-for or expected future time when human life and society will be perfect and free of troubles; the world will then be prosperous and happy and peaceful. Nowadays, the wish for a better world may or may not be religiously inspired. Some people who seek a more perfect world believe that humans alone must achieve it.

How should we categorize this wish for a better world? Should we call it "conservative" because the imagined world may have existed in the past? If the imagined world does not yet exist, is it "radical" to believe it can be achieved? Maybe the wish for a more perfect world is neither conservative nor radical. Maybe it is just that people who are not satisfied with the world as it is think that something can be done to improve things, with or without divine assistance. However it will come, the "millennium" will be different from now, and better.

Ideas about the millennium, and the origins of new cults and religions, might best be viewed then as human hopes: Which ones do people have? Do they vary from culture to culture, and why? Are some hopes universal? And how might they be achieved?

Sources: Rodney Stark, *The Future of Religion: Secularization, Revival and Cult Formation* (Berkeley: University of California Press, 1985); G. W. Trompf, ed., *Cargo Cults and Millenarian Movements: Transoceanic Comparisons of New Religious Movements* (Berlin: Mouton de Gruyter, 1990).

The first part of the "Good Word" has three main themes, one of which is the concept of an apocalypse. Handsome Lake offered many signs by which the faithful could recognize impending, cosmic doom. Great drops of fire would rain from the skies and a veil would be cast over the earth. False prophets would appear, witch women would openly cast spells, and poisonous creatures from the underworld would seize and kill those who had rejected the *Gaiwiio.* Second, the *Gaiwiio* emphasized sin. The great sins were disbelief in the "good way," drunkenness, witchcraft, and abortion. Sins had to be confessed and repented. Finally, the *Gaiwiio*

offered salvation. Salvation could be won by following a code of conduct, attending certain important traditional rites, and performing public confession.

The second part of the *Gaiwiio* sets out the code of conduct. This code seems to orient the Seneca toward advantageous Euro-American practices without separating them from their culture. The code has five main sections:

1. **Temperance.** All Seneca leaders were fully aware of the social disorders arising out of abuse of liquor. Handsome Lake went to great

lengths to illustrate and explain the harmfulness of alcohol.

2. **Peace and social unity.** Seneca leaders were to cease their futile bickering, and all were to be united in their approach to the larger society.

3. **Preservation of tribal lands.** Handsome Lake, fearing the piecemeal alienation of Seneca lands, was far ahead of his contemporaries in demanding a halt in land sales to non-Seneca.

4. **Proacculturation.** Though individual property and trading for profit were prohibited, the acquisition of literacy in English was encouraged so that people would be able to read and understand treaties and to avoid being cheated.

5. **Domestic morality.** Sons were to obey their fathers, mothers should avoid interfering with daughters' marriages, and husbands and wives should respect the sanctity of their marriage vows.

Handsome Lake's teaching seems to have led to a renaissance among the Seneca. Temperance was widely accepted, as were schooling and new farming methods. By 1801, corn yields had been increased tenfold, new crops (oats, potatoes, flax) had been introduced, and public health and hygiene had improved considerably. Handsome Lake himself acquired great power among his people. He spent the remainder of his life fulfilling administrative duties, acting as a representative of the Iroquois in Washington, and preaching his gospel to neighboring tribes. By the time of Handsome Lake's death in 1815, the Seneca clearly had undergone a dramatic rebirth, attributable at least in part to the new religion. Later in the century, some of Handsome Lake's disciples founded a church in his name that, despite occasional setbacks and political disputes, survives to this day.

Although many scholars believe cultural stress gives rise to these new religious movements, it is still important to understand exactly what the stresses are and how strong they have to become before a new movement emerges. Do different kinds of stresses produce different kinds of movements? And does the nature of the movement depend on the

---

A revitalization movement that became known as the Ghost Dance spread eastward from the Northwest in the 1870s to the 1890s. It was generally believed that if people did the dance correctly, ghosts would come to life with sufficient resources to allow the people to return to their old ways, and, as a result of some cataclysm, the whites would disappear. This painting depicts the Ghost Dance as practiced by the Sioux or Lakota.

cultural elements already present? Let us consider some theory and research on the causes of the millenarian cargo cults that began to appear in Melanesia from about 1885 on.

CARGO CULTS. The *cargo cults* can be thought of as religious movements "in which there is an expectation of, and preparation for, the coming of a period of supernatural bliss."[55] Thus, an explicit belief of the cargo cults was the notion that some liberating power would bring all the Western goods (cargo in pidgin English) the people might want. For example, around 1932, on Buka in the Solomon Islands, the leaders of a cult prophesied that a tidal wave would sweep away the villages and a ship would arrive with iron, axes, food, tobacco, cars, and arms. Work in the gardens ceased, and wharves and docks were built for the expected cargo.[56]

What may explain such cults? Peter Worsley suggested that an important factor in the rise of cargo cults and millenarian movements in general is the existence of oppression—in the case of Melanesia, colonial oppression. He suggested that the reactions in Melanesia took religious rather than political forms because they were a way of pulling together people who previously had no political unity and who lived in small, isolated social groups.[57] Other scholars, such as David Aberle, suggested that *relative deprivation* is more important than oppression in explaining the origins of cults; when people feel that they could have more, and they have less than what they used to have or less than others, they may be attracted to new cults.[58] Consistent with Aberle's general interpretation, Bruce Knauft's comparative study of cargo cults found that such cults were more important in Melanesian societies that had had *decreasing* cultural contact with the West, and presumably decreasing contact with valued goods, within the year prior to the cult's emergence.[59]

If the recent as well as distant past is any guide, we can expect religious belief and practice to be revitalized periodically, particularly during times of stress. Thus, we can expect the world to continue to have religious variation.

SUMMARY

1. Religion is any set of attitudes, beliefs, and practices pertaining to supernatural power. Such beliefs may vary within a culture as well as among societies, and they may change over time.

2. Religious beliefs are evident in all known cultures and are inferred from artifacts associated with *Homo sapiens* since at least 60,000 years ago.

3. Theories to account for the universality of religion suggest that humans create it in response to certain universal needs or conditions, including a need for understanding, reversion to childhood feelings, anxiety or uncertainty, and a need for community.

4. There are wide variations in religious beliefs. Societies vary in the number and kinds of supernatural entities in which they believe. There may be impersonal supernatural forces (e.g., mana and taboo), supernatural beings of nonhuman origin (gods and spirits), and supernatural beings of human origin (ghosts and ancestor spirits). The religious belief system of a society may include any or all such entities.

5. Gods and spirits may be unpredictable or predictable, aloof from or interested in human affairs, helpful or punishing. In some societies, all gods are equal in rank; in others, there is a hierarchy of prestige and power among gods and spirits, just as among the humans in those societies.

6. A monotheistic religion is one in which there is one high god, as the creator of the universe or the director of events (or both); all other supernatural beings are either subordinate to, or function as alternative manifestations of, this god. A high god is generally found in societies with a high level of political development.

7. Faced with ignorance, pain, and injustice, people frequently explain events by claiming intervention by the gods. Such intervention has also been sought by people who hope it will help them achieve their own ends. The gods are likely to punish the immoral behavior of people in societies that have considerable differences in wealth.

8. Various methods have been used to attempt communication with the supernatural. Among them are prayer, doing things to the body and mind, simulation, feasts, and sacrifices.

9. When people believe that their actions can compel the supernatural to act in a particular and intended way, anthropologists refer to the belief and related practice as magic. Sorcery and witchcraft are attempts to make the spirits work harm against people.

10. Almost all societies have part-time or full-time religious or magical practitioners. Recent cross-cultural research suggests that there are four major types of practitioner: shamans, sorcerers or witches, mediums, and priests. The number of types of practitioner seems to vary with degree of cultural

complexity: the more complex the society, the more types of practitioners.

11. The history of religion includes periods of strong resistance to change and periods of radical change. One explanation for this cycle is that religious practices always originate during periods of stress. Religious movements have been called revitalization movements—efforts to save a culture by infusing it with a new purpose and new life.

GLOSSARY TERMS

ancestor spirits
animatism
animism
divination
ghosts
gods
magic
mana
mediums
monotheistic
polytheistic

priests
religion
revitalization
   movements
shaman
sorcery
spirits
supernatural
taboo
witchcraft

CRITICAL QUESTIONS

1. How does your conception of God compare with supernatural beings in other religious systems?
2. What do you think is the future of religion?
3. Could any of the religious practices you know about be classified as magic? Are they associated with anxiety-arousing situations?

INTERNET EXERCISES

1. Religious differences often result in intolerance. Visit **http://www.religioustolerance.org**. Click on the Other Religions button or go to **http://www.religioustolerance.org/var_rel.htm** and read about one world religion you are not familiar with and one other religion.
2. A project at Harvard University on pluralism is designed to study the growing diversity of religions in the United States. Go to the site **http://www.fas.harvard.edu/~pluralism/** and click About the Project; then explore the slides in Images of America.
3. Explore a site that gives some information about different religions in the Canadian province of Newfoundland at **http://www.ucs.mun.ca/** **~hrollman/indexjava.html**. Compare at least two religious traditions.

SUGGESTED READING

CHILD, A. B., AND CHILD, I. L. *Religion and Magic in the Life of Traditional Peoples.* Englewood Cliffs, NJ: Prentice Hall, 1993. Based on a review of ethnographic data from all over the world, this book discusses the features common to traditional religions everywhere, as well as the factors that may account for variation in religion.

EMBER, M., EMBER, C. R., AND LEVINSON, D., EDS. *Portraits of Culture: Ethnographic Originals.* Upper Saddle River, NJ: Prentice Hall, 1998. Prentice Hall/Simon & Schuster Custom Publishing. Several chapters deal extensively with religious belief and practice as seen in a particular culture: G. Brandon, "African-Americans: Getting into the Spirit"; J. W. Dow, "Sierra Otomí: People of the Mexican Mountains"; W. K. Powers and M. N. Powers, "Lakota: A Study in Cultural Continuity"; S. B. Schaefer, "Huichol: Becoming a Godmother"; J. R. Sosa, "Maya: The Sacred in Everyday Life."

MALINOWSKI, B. *Magic, Science and Religion and Other Essays.* Garden City, NY: Doubleday, 1954. A classic collection of papers representing some of Malinowski's work on ritual and religious behavior and the nature of primitive cults, magic, and faith.

MATLOCK, J. G. "Universals and Variation in Religious Belief and Practice." In C. R. Ember and M. Ember, eds., *Cross-Cultural Research for Social Science.* Upper Saddle River, NJ: Prentice Hall, 1998. Prentice Hall/Simon & Schuster Custom Publishing. An up-to-date review of cross-cultural studies of religious diversity, suggesting how religious beliefs and practices change in response to changes in social and political organization and subsistence strategy.

MORRIS, B. *Anthropological Studies of Religion: An Introductory Text.* Cambridge: Cambridge University Press, 1987. A review of theories about the origin and persistence of religion.

SERED, S. S. *Priestess, Mother, Sacred Sister.* New York: Oxford University Press, 1994. This book discusses how and why women rather than men came to dominate the religion of some societies known to anthropology.

SWANSON, G. E. *The Birth of the Gods: The Origin of Primitive Beliefs.* Ann Arbor: University of Michigan Press, 1969. A pioneering cross-cultural study that explores the origins of religious beliefs and examines how various aspects of religion may be related to social and political organization.

The Arts

CHAPTER OUTLINE

Body Decoration and Adornment

Explaining Variation in the Arts

Viewing the Art of Other Cultures

Artistic Change and Culture Contact

Most societies do not have a word for art.[1] Perhaps that is because art, particularly in societies with relatively little specialization, is often an integral part of religious, social, and political life. Indeed, most of the aspects of culture we have already discussed—economics, kinship, politics, religion—are not easily separated from the rest of social life.[2]

Art appears in human history at least as far back as 28,000 years ago. We say that those earliest known carvings, beads, and cave paintings are art, but what do we mean by "art"? A stone spear point and a bone fish hook obviously require skill and creativity to make. But we do not call them art. Why do we feel that some things are art and others are not?

Some definitions of art emphasize its evocative quality. From the viewpoint of the person who creates it, art expresses feelings and ideas; from the viewpoint of the observer or participant, it evokes feelings and ideas. The feelings and ideas on each side may or may not be exactly the same. And they may be expressed in a variety of ways—drawing, painting, carving, weaving, body decoration, music, dance, story. An artistic work or performance is intended to excite the senses, to stir the emotions of the beholder or participant. It may produce feelings of pleasure, awe, repulsion, fear, but usually not indifference.[3]

But emphasizing the evocative quality of art may make it difficult to compare the art of different cultures because what is evocative in one culture may not be evocative in another. For example, a humorous story in one culture may not be funny in another. Thus, most anthropologists agree that art is more than an attempt by an individual to express or communicate feelings and ideas. There is also some cultural patterning or meaning; societies vary in their characteristic kinds and styles of art.[4]

Artistic activities are always in part cultural, involving shared and learned patterns of behavior, belief, and feeling. What are some of the ideas about art in our own culture? We tend to think that anything useful is not art. If a basket has a design that is not necessary to its function, we may possibly consider it art, especially if we keep it on a shelf; but the basket with bread on the table would probably not be considered art. The fact that such a distinction is not made in other societies strongly suggests that our ideas about art are cultural. Among Native Americans on the Northwest Coast, elaborately carved totem poles not only displayed the crests of the lineages of their occupants; they also supported the house.[5] The fact that artistic activities are partly cultural is evident when we compare how people in different societies treat the outsides of their houses. Most North Americans share the value of decorating the interiors of their homes with pictures—paintings, prints, or photographs hung on the walls. But they do not share the value of painting pictures on the outside walls of their houses, as Native Americans did on the Northwest Coast.

In our society, we also insist that to be considered art, a work must be unique. This aspect is clearly consistent with our emphasis on the individual. However, even though we require that artists be unique and innovative, the art they produce must still fall within some range of acceptable variation. Artists must communicate to us in a way we can relate to, or at least learn to relate to. Often, they must follow certain current styles of expression that have been set by other artists or by critics, if they hope to have their art accepted by the public. The idea that an artist should be original is a cultural idea; in some societies the ability to replicate a traditional pattern is more valued than originality.

So art seems to have several qualities: It expresses as well as communicates. It stimulates the senses, affects emotions, and evokes ideas. It is produced in culturally patterned ways and styles. It has cultural meaning. In addition, some people are thought to be better at it than others.[6] Art does not require some people to be full-time artistic specialists; many societies in the ethnographic record had no full-time specialists of any kind. But, although everyone in some societies may participate in some arts (dancing, singing, body decoration), it is usually thought that certain individuals have superior artistic skill.

To illustrate the cross-cultural variation that exists in artistic expression, we will consider first the art of body decoration and adornment.

BODY DECORATION AND ADORNMENT

In all societies, people decorate or adorn their bodies. The decorations may be permanent—scars, tattoos, changes in the shape of a body part. Or they may be temporary, in the form of paint or objects such as feathers, jewelry, skins, and clothing that are not strictly utilitarian. Much of this decoration seems to be motivated by aesthetic considerations, which, of course, vary from culture to culture. The actual form of the decoration depends on cultural traditions. Body ornamentation includes the pierced noses of some women in India, the elongated necks of the Mangebetu of central Africa, the tattooing of North American males, the body painting of the Caduveo of South America, and the variety of ornaments found in almost every culture.

However, in addition to satisfying aesthetic needs, body decoration or adornment may be used to delineate social position, rank, sex, occupation, local and ethnic identity, or religion within a society. Along with social stratification come visual means of declaring status. The symbolic halo (the crown) on the king's head, the scarlet hunting jacket of the English gentleman, the eagle feathers of the Native American chief's bonnet, the gold-embroidered jacket of the Indian rajah—each mark of high status is recognized in its own society. Jewelry in the shape of a cross or the Star of David indicates Christian or Jewish inclinations. Clothes may set apart the priest or the nun or the member of a sect such as the Amish.

The erotic significance of some body decoration is also apparent. Women draw attention to erogenous zones of the body by painting, as on the lips, and by attaching some object—an earring, a flower behind the ear, a necklace, bracelet, brooch, anklet, or belt. Men draw attention, too, by beards, tattoos, and penis sheaths (in some otherwise naked societies) that point upward. We have only to follow the fashion trends for women of Europe and North America during the past 300 years, with their history of pinched waists, ballooned hips, bustled rumps, exaggerated breasts, painted faces, and exposed bosoms, to realize the significance of body adornment for sexual provocation. Why some societies emphasize the erotic adornment of women and others emphasize it in men is not yet understood.

In many societies the body is permanently marked or altered, often to indicate a change in status. For example, in the Poro initiation ceremony practiced by the Kpelle of Liberia, newly circumcised boys spent a period of seclusion in the forest with the older men. They returned with scars down their backs, symbolic tooth marks indicative of their close escape from *ngamu*, the Great Masked Figure, which ate the child but disgorged the young adult.[7]

A need to decorate the human body seems universal. We have noted some of the various methods people have used to adorn themselves in different societies. We are also aware of body-decoration practices that raise questions to which we have no ready answers. What explains adornment of the body by permanent marking such as scarification, bound feet, elongated ears and necks, shaped heads,

Body tattooing sometimes is used to permanently mark status, as with chiefs in Polynesia. But in many places, like among the Dayak of Borneo, tattooing is more personal; people decorate their bodies however they wish.

pierced ears and septums, and filed teeth? (See the box "Politics and Art" for suggestions about the relationship between permanent body marking and politics.) Why do different societies adorn, paint, or otherwise decorate different parts of the body for sexual, or other, reasons? And what leads some members of our society to transfer body decoration to their animals? Why the shaped hair of the poodle, the braided manes of some horses, and diamond collars, painted toenails, coats, hats, and even boots for some pets?

EXPLAINING VARIATION IN THE ARTS

In our society we stress the freedom of the artist, so it may seem to us that art is completely free to vary. But our emphasis on uniqueness obscures the fact that different cultures not only use or emphasize different materials and have different ideas of beauty, but they also may have characteristic styles and themes. It is easy to see styles when we look at art that is different from our own; it is harder to see similarity when we look at the art of our own culture. If we look at dance styles, for example, we may think that the dance style of the 1940s is completely different from the dance style of the 1990s. It might take an outsider to notice that in our culture we still generally see couples dancing as a pair rather than in a group line or circle, as in dances we call "folk dances." And, in our culture, females and males dance together rather than separately. Furthermore, our popular music still has a beat or combination of beats and is made by many of the same kinds of instruments as in the past.

But where do these similarities in form and style come from? Much of the recent research on variation in the arts supports the idea that form and style in visual art, music, dance, and folklore are very much influenced by other aspects of culture. Some psychological anthropologists, as we saw in the chapter on psychology and culture, would go even further, suggesting that art, like religion, expresses the typical feelings, anxieties, and experiences of people in a culture. And the typical feelings and anxieties in turn are influenced by basic institutions such as child rearing, economy, social organization, and politics.

Consider how the physical form of art preferred by a society may reflect its way of life. For example, Richard Anderson pointed out that the art of traditionally nomadic people such as the !Kung, Inuit, and Australian aborigines is mostly carryable.[8] Song, dance, and oral literature are very important in those societies and are as portable as they can be. Those societies decorate useful objects that they carry with them—harpoons for the Inuit, boomerangs for the Australian aborigines, ostrich egg "canteens" for the !Kung San. But they don't have bulky things such as sculpture or elaborate costumes. And what about the presence of artists or art critics? Although some people in small-scale societies are more artistic than others, specialized artists,

Research Frontiers

POLITICS AND ART

Art is exceedingly variable cross-culturally. But that does not mean that the variability is unexplainable, not linkable to other aspects of human existence. The various findings described in this chapter indicate that much of art *is* linkable to other aspects of culture. Here we consider the possibility that even politics, that messy and sometimes volatile arena of human social life, may have reflections in art. For example, Christopher Steiner's article, "Body Personal and Body Politic," focuses on four forms of self-decoration—body painting, tattooing, masking, and "crowning." (A mask conceals the face and head of the wearer; a crown or other headdress draws attention to, or identifies, the wearer.) Steiner first discusses how body decoration reflects politics in the islands of

Melanesia and Polynesia (in the Pacific).

In Melanesia, political leadership is typically of the "big man" type. There is no fixed authority; big men gain influence by attracting followers, who may not follow for long. There are no political offices or permanent positions of authority. And of course there are no centralized chiefdoms and no hierarchy of influential or powerful people. The whole system is fragile and subject to change. In Polynesia, in contrast, there are permanent systems of authority, usually integrating large populations, with a chief or king at the top whose position is usually inherited. Leaders do not achieve their positions by personal action; they succeed to their positions by genealogical right. The system is permanent or nonshifting as well as hierarchical.

Now consider how body adornment may reflect politics in the two areas. Melanesians paint their bodies, and the painting is ephemeral. It disappears within a short time, or after the first wash, just as a big man's status may go up or down quickly, depending on what he has done lately for his followers. Polynesians decorate their bodies with tattoos, which are permanent, as are their systems of leadership. Just as the chief retains his status over time, so, too, a tattoo does not wash away. In Samoa, for example, tattoos distinguished the chiefly class from commoners. Bands and stripes were restricted to persons of high status; low-status persons could have tattoos only of solid black and only from waist to knees. Within the ruling class, the number of tattooed triangles down a man's leg indicated his

as well as critics or theoreticians of art, tend to be found only in societies with a complex, specialized division of labor.

VISUAL ART

Perhaps the most obvious way artistic creations reflect how we live is by mirroring the environment—the materials and technologies available to a culture. Stone, wood, bones, tree bark, clay, sand, charcoal, berries for staining, and a few mineral-derived ochers are generally available materials. In addition, depending on the locality, other resources are accessible: shells, horns, tusks, gold, copper, and silver. The different uses to which societies put these materials are of interest to anthropologists, who may ask, for example, why a people chooses to use clay and not copper when both items are available. Although we have no conclusive answers as yet, such questions have important rami-

fications. The way in which a society views its environment is sometimes apparent in its choice and use of artistic materials. Certain metals, for example, may be reserved for ceremonial objects of special importance. Or the belief in the supernatural powers of a stone or tree may cause a sculptor to be sensitive to that particular material.[9]

What is particularly meaningful to anthropologists is the realization that, although the materials available to a society may to some extent limit or influence what it can do artistically, the materials by no means determine what is done. Why does the artist in Japanese society rake sand into patterns, the artist in Navaho society paint sand, and the artist in Roman society melt sand to form glass? Moreover, even when the same material is used in the same way in different societies, the form or style of the work varies enormously from culture to culture.

A society may choose to represent objects or phenomena that are especially important to the people

relative rank. Because tattooing is permanent, it is a form of body decoration well suited to a society with inherited social stratification.

The traditional political systems of Africa ranged from centralized kingdoms (on the complex end of the continuum) to village-based or segmentary lineage systems in which leadership was ephemeral or secret (tied to secret societies). Masks that conceal identity are often used in the uncentralized systems; crowns or other headdresses indicating high status are frequent in the kingdoms. Among the uncentralized Ibo of eastern Nigeria, masks are often worn by the young men of a village when they criticize the behavior of the village elders. In the kingdom of Ngoyo, in western Zaire, the king's status is indicated by his special cap

as well as by his special three-legged stool.

If art may reflect politics on the cultural level, it may also do so on the psychological or individual level. Lewis Austin found that a person's preferences in visual (graphic) symbols can often be predicted from his or her political ideology. Experimental subjects from Japan and the United States were asked to locate themselves on a continuum from radical to conservative and to indicate their preferences in pairs of visual symbols—unbalanced versus balanced, uneven versus even, incomplete versus complete, varying versus uniform. So, for example, a set of bars, as in a bar graph, of the same height is even; bars of different heights are uneven. Conservatives preferred symbols that were orderly (bars side by side ordered from small to large versus unequal-sized bars

lying at angles to each other), passive (a flat line versus a squiggle or sine wave), and uniform (four squares versus three squares and a circle). In these terms, the Japanese subjects were generally more conservative than the American. But in each country artistic preferences varied in similar ways with political ideology.

If preferences in visual images have a metaphorical significance that is associated with political preferences, perhaps other style preferences—in clothing, furniture, architecture, and so on—also reflect political ideology. Only future research will tell.

Sources: Christopher B. Steiner, "Body Personal and Body Politic: Adornment and Leadership in Cross-Cultural Perspective," *Anthropos,* 85 (1990): 431–45; Lewis Austin, "Visual Symbols, Political Ideology, and Culture," *Ethos,* 5 (1977): 306–25.

The same materials may be used artistically in different societies. In Japan sand is raked into traditional patterns. In the southwestern United States, a Navaho creates a sand painting.

or elite. An examination of the art of the Middle Ages tells us something about the medieval preoccupation with theological doctrine. In addition to revealing the primary concerns of a society, the content of that society's art may also reflect the culture's social stratification. Authority figures may be represented in obvious ways. In the art of ancient Sumerian society, the sovereign was portrayed as being much larger than his followers, and the most prestigious gods were given oversized eyes. Also, differences in clothing and jewelry styles within a society usually reflect social stratification.

Certain possible relationships between the art of a society and other aspects of its culture have always been recognized by art historians. Much of this attention has been concentrated on the content of art, since European art has been representational for such a long time. But the style of the art may reflect other aspects of culture. John Fischer, for example, examined the stylistic features of art with the aim of discovering "some sort of regular connection between some artistic feature and some social situation."[10] He argued that the artist expresses a form of social fantasy. In other words, in a stable society artists will respond to those conditions in the society that bring them, and the society, security or pleasure.

Assuming that "pictorial elements in design are, on one psychological level, abstract, mainly unconscious representations of persons in the society,"[11] Fischer reasoned that egalitarian societies would tend to have different stylistic elements in their art

as compared with stratified societies. Egalitarian societies are generally composed of small, self-sufficient communities that are structurally similar and have little differentiation between persons. Stratified societies, on the other hand, generally have larger and more interdependent, and dissimilar, communities and great differences among persons in prestige, power, and access to economic resources. Fischer hypothesized, and found in a cross-cultural study, that certain elements of design were strongly related to the presence of social hierarchy. His findings are summarized in Table 23–1.

Repetition of a simple element, for example, tends to be found in the art of egalitarian societies,

TABLE 23–1 *Artistic Differences in Egalitarian and Stratified Societies*

EGALITARIAN SOCIETY	STRATIFIED SOCIETY
Repetition of simple elements	Integration of unlike elements
Much empty or "irrelevant" space	Little empty space
Symmetrical design	Asymmetrical design
Unenclosed figures	Enclosed figures

Source: Based on John Fischer, "Art Styles as Cultural Cognitive Maps," *American Anthropologist,* 63 (1961): 80–83.

which have little political organization and few authority positions. If each element unconsciously represents individuals within the society, the relative sameness of people seems to be reflected in the repetitiveness of design elements. Conversely, the combinations of different design elements in complex patterns that tend to be found in the art of stratified societies seem to reflect the high degree of social differentiation that exists in such societies.

According to Fischer, the egalitarian society's empty space in a design represents the society's relative isolation. Because egalitarian societies are usually small and self-sufficient, they tend to shy away from outsiders, preferring to find security within their own group. In contrast, the art of stratified societies is generally crowded. The hierarchical society does not seek to isolate individuals or communities within the group because they must be interdependent, each social level ideally furnishing services for those above it and help for those

beneath it. As Fischer suggested, we can, in general, discern a lack of empty space in the designs of societies in which security is not sought by avoiding strangers, but rather "security is produced by incorporating strangers into the hierarchy, through dominance or submission as the relative power indicates."[12]

Symmetry, the third stylistic feature related to type of society, is similar to the first. Symmetry may suggest likeness or an egalitarian society; asymmetry suggests difference and perhaps stratification. The fourth feature of interest here, the presence or absence of enclosures or boundaries—"frames" in our art—may indicate the presence or absence of hierarchically imposed rules circumscribing individual behavior. An unenclosed design may reflect free access to most property; in egalitarian societies, the fencing off of a piece of property for the use of only one person is unknown. In the art of stratified societies, boundaries or enclosures may reflect the idea

Symmetry and the repetition of design elements tend to be found in the art of unstratified societies, as in these Masai bead designs. Stratified societies are more likely to have asymmetry and different design elements, as in this Japanese painting.

Source: BCC17718 The Lady Fujitsubo watching Prince Genji departing in the moonlight, 1853, (colour woodblock print) by Ando or Utagawa Hiroshige (1797-1858). Private Collection/Bridgeman Art Library, London/New York.

of private property. Or they may symbolically represent the real differences in dress, occupation, type of food allowed, and manners that separate the different classes of people.

Studies such as Fischer's offer anthropologists new tools with which to evaluate ancient societies that are known only by a few pieces of pottery or a few tools or paintings. If art reflects certain aspects of a culture, then the study of whatever art of a people has been preserved may provide a means of testing the accuracy of the guesses we make about their culture on the basis of more ordinary archaeological materials. For example, even if we did not know from classical Greek writings that Athens became more and more socially stratified between 1000 B.C. and 450 B.C., we might guess that such a transformation had occurred because of the changes we can see over time in the way the Athenians decorated vases. Consistent with Fischer's cross-cultural findings, as Athens became more stratified, its vase painting became more complex, more crowded, and more enclosed.[13]

MUSIC

When we hear the music of another culture, we often don't know what to make of it. We may say it does not "mean" anything to us, not realizing that

Research Frontiers

DO MASKS SHOW EMOTION IN UNIVERSAL WAYS?

Anthropologists have documented how forms and styles in art vary from culture to culture. But with all this variation, it seems that certain forms of art may show emotion in universally similar ways. For example, research on masks from different cultures supports the conclusion that masks, like faces, tend to represent certain emotions in the same ways. Face masks are commonly used in rituals and performances. They not only hide the real face of the mask wearer but they often evoke powerful emotions in the audience—anger, fear, sadness, joy. You might think, because so many things vary cross-culturally, that the ways in which emotion is displayed and recognized in the face vary too. But apparently they do not. We now have some evidence that the symbolism used in masks is often universal.

The research on masks builds on work done by Ekman and Izard, who used photographs of individuals experiencing, or actors simulating, various emotions. Ekman and Izard showed photographs to members of different cultural groups and asked them to identify the emotions displayed in the photographs. A particular emotion was identified correctly by most viewers, whatever the viewer's native culture. The results for the viewers from less Westernized cultures paralleled the results for viewers from more Westernized cultures. Coding schemes were developed to enable researchers to compare the detailed facial positions of individual portions of the face (eyebrows, mouth, etc.) for different emotions. What exactly do we do when we scowl? We contract the eyebrows and lower the corners of the mouth; in geometric terms,

In this "Devil Dance" in Yare, Venezuela, males wearing masks try to get rid of the "devil" inside themselves. Like many masks around the world that are supposed to be frightening, these masks have sharp angular lines, such as the large ears.

the "meaning" of music has been programmed into us by our culture. In music as well as in art, our culture largely determines what we consider acceptable variation, what we say has "meaning" to us. Even a trained musicologist, listening for the first time to music of a different culture, will not be able to hear the subtleties of tone and rhythm that members of the culture hear with ease. This predicament is similar to that of the linguist who, exposed to a foreign language, cannot at first distinguish phonemes, morphemes, and other regular patterns of speech.

Not only do instruments vary, but music itself varies widely in style from society to society. For example, in some societies people prefer music with a regularly recurring beat; in others, they prefer changes in rhythm. There are also variations in singing styles. In some places it is customary to have different vocal lines for different people; in other places people all sing together in the same way.

Is variation in music, as in the other arts, related to other aspects of culture? On the basis of a cross-cultural study of more than 3,500 folk songs from a sample of the world's societies, Alan Lomax and his co-researchers found that song style seems to vary with cultural complexity. As we will see, these findings about variation in song style are similar to Fischer's findings about variation in art.

we make angles and diagonals on our faces. When we smile, we raise the corners of the mouth; we make it curved.

The psychologist Joel Aronoff and his colleagues compared two types of wooden face masks from many different societies—masks described as threatening (for example, designed to frighten off evil spirits) versus masks associated with nonthreatening functions (a courtship dance). As suspected, the two sets of masks had significantly different proportions of certain facial elements. The threatening masks had eyebrows and eyes facing inward and downward and a downward-facing mouth. The threatening masks also were more likely to have pointed heads, chins, beards, and ears, as well as projections from the face such as horns. In more abstract or geometrical terms, threatening features generally tend to be angular or diagonal, and nonthreatening features tend to be curved or rounded. A face with a pointed beard is threatening; a baby's face is not. The theory—originally suggested by Charles Darwin, the evolutionist—is that humans express and recognize basic emotions in uniform ways because all human faces are quite similar, skeletally and muscularly.

But is it the facial features themselves that convey threat or is it the design elements of angularity and diagonality that convey threat? To help answer this question, students in the United States were asked to associate adjectives with drawings of abstract pairs of design features (for example, a *V* shape and a *U* shape). Even with abstract shapes, the angular patterns were thought of as less "good," more "powerful," and "stronger" than the curved shapes.

We should not be surprised to discover that humans all over the world use their faces, and masks, to show emotions in the same ways. Aren't we all members of the same species? Our skin color may vary from dark to light. Our hair may be straight or wavy or kinky—or skimpy. We vary in the percentages of a lot of characteristics. But those are the characteristics we see. We are not so likely to notice the things about us (by far *most* of the things about us) that don't vary—such as how we show emotion in our faces. That's why a movie made in Hollywood or Beijing may evoke the same feelings wherever people see it. The universality of human emotion as expressed in the face becomes obvious only when we see faces (and masks) from elsewhere, showing emotions in ways that are unmistakable to us.

Thus, we become aware of universality (in masks as well as other cultural things) in the same way we become aware of variation—by exposure through reading and direct experience to the ways cultures do and do not vary.

Sources: Joel Aronoff, Andrew M. Barclay, and Linda A. Stevenson, "The Recognition of Threatening Facial Stimuli," *Journal of Personality and Social Psychology*, 54 (1988): 647–55; Joel Aronoff, Barbara A. Woike, and Lester M. Hyman, "Which Are the Stimuli in Facial Displays of Anger and Happiness? Configurational Bases of Emotion Recognition," *Journal of Personality and Social Psychology*, 62 (1992): 1050–66.

Just as in art and song, dance style seems to reflect societal complexity. In less complex societies, everyone participates in dances in much the same way, as among the Huli of New Guinea. In more complex societies, there tend to be leading roles and minor roles, as in a Japanese Geisha show.

Lomax and his co-researchers found some features of song style to be correlated with cultural complexity. (The societies classified as more complex tend to have higher levels of food-production technology, social stratification, and higher levels of political integration.) For example, wordiness and clearness of enunciation were found to be associated with cultural complexity. The association is a reasonable one: The more a society depends on verbal information, as in giving complex instructions for a job or explaining different points of law, the more strongly will clear enunciation in transmitting information be a mark of its culture. Thus, hunter-gatherer bands, in which people know their productive role and perform it without ever being given complex directions, are more likely than we are to base much of their singing on lines of nonwords, such as our refrain line "tra-la-la-la-la." Their songs are characterized by lack of explicit information, by sounds that give pleasure in themselves, by much repetition, and by relaxed, slurred enunciation.[14]

Examples of the progression from repetition or nonwords to wordy information are found within our society. The most obvious, and universal, example of a song made entirely of repetition is the relaxed lullaby of a mother repeating a comforting syllable to her baby while improvising her own tune. But this type of song is not characteristic of our society. Although our songs sometimes have single lines of nonwords, it is rare for an entire song to be made of them. Usually, the nonwords act as respites from information:

> Zippity do dah
> Zippety ay
> My o my
> What a wonderful day[15]

In associating variation in music with cultural complexity, Lomax found that elaboration of song parts also corresponds to the complexity of a society. Societies in which leadership is informal and temporary seem to symbolize their social equality by an *interlocked* style of singing. Each person sings independently but within the group, and no one singer is differentiated from the others. Rank societies, in which there is a leader with prestige but no real power, are characterized by a song style in which one "leader" may begin the song, but the others soon drown out his voice. In stratified societies, where leaders have the power of force, choral singing is generally marked by a clear-cut role for the leader and a secondary "answering" role for the others. Societies marked by elaborate stratification show singing parts that are differentiated and in which the soloist is deferred to by the other singers.

Lomax also found a relationship between **polyphony,** where two or more melodies are sung simultaneously, and a high degree of female participation in food-getting. In societies in which women's work is responsible for at least half of the food, songs are likely to contain more than one simultaneous melody, with the higher tunes usually sung by women. Moreover:

> Counterpoint was once believed to be the invention of European high culture. In our sample it turns out to be most frequent among simple producers, especially gatherers, where women supply the bulk of the food. Counterpoint and perhaps even polyphony may then be very old feminine inventions. . . . Subsistence complementarity is at its maximum among gatherers, early gardeners, and horticulturalists. It is in such societies that we find the highest occurrence of polyphonic singing.[16]

In societies in which women do not contribute much to food production, the songs are more likely to have a single melody and to be sung by males.[17]

In some societies, survival and social welfare are based on a unified group effort; in those cultures, singing tends to be marked by cohesiveness. That is, cohesive work parties, teams of gatherers or harvesters and kin groups who work voluntarily for the good of the family or community, seem to express their interconnectedness in song by blending both tone and rhythm.

Some variations in music may be explained as a consequence of variation in child-rearing practices. For example, researchers are beginning to explore child rearing as a way to explain why some societies respond to, and produce, regular rhythm in their music, whereas others enjoy free rhythm that has no regular beat but instead approximates the rhythm of speech. One hypothesis is that a regular beat in music is a simulation of the regular beat of the heart. For nine months in the womb, the fetus feels the mother's regular 80 or so heartbeats a minute. Moreover, mothers generally employ rhythmic tactics in quieting crying infants—patting their backs or rocking them. But the fact that children respond positively to an even tempo does not mean that the regular heartbeat is completely responsible for their sensitivity to rhythm. In fact, if the months in the womb were sufficient to establish a preference for rhythm, then every child would be affected in exactly the same manner by a regular beat, and all societies would have the same rhythm in their music.

Barbara Ayres suggested that the importance of regular rhythm in the music of a culture is related to the rhythm's *acquired reward value*—that is, its associations with feelings of security or relaxation. In a cross-cultural study of this possibility, Ayres found a strong correlation between a society's method of carrying infants and the type of musical rhythm the society produced. In some societies, the mother or an older sister carries the child, sometimes for two or three years, in a sling, pouch, or shawl, so that the child is in bodily contact with her for much of the day and experiences the motion of her rhythmic walking. Ayres discovered that such societies tend to have a regularly recurring beat in their songs. Societies in which the child is put into a cradle or is strapped to a cradleboard tend to have music based either on irregular rhythm or on free rhythm.[18]

The question of why some societies have great tonal ranges in music whereas others do not was also studied by Ayres, who suggested that this difference too might be explained by certain child-rearing practices. Ayres theorized that painful stimulation of infants before weaning might result in bolder, more exploratory behavior in adulthood, which would be apparent in the musical patterns of the culture. This hypothesis was suggested to her by laboratory experiments with animals. Contrary to expectations, those animals given electric shocks or handled before weaning showed greater than usual physical growth and more exploratory behavior when placed in new situations as adults. Ayres equated the range of musical notes (from low to high) with the exploratory range of animals and forcefulness of accent in music with boldness in animals.

The kinds of stress Ayres looked for in ethnographic reports were those that would be applied to all children or to all of one sex—for example, scarification; piercing of the nose, lips, or ears; binding, shaping, or stretching of feet, head, ears, or any limb; inoculation; circumcision; or cauterization. The results showed that in societies in which infants are stressed before the age of 2, music is marked by a wider tonal range than in societies in which children are not stressed or are stressed only at a later age. Also, a firm accent or beat is characteristic of music more often in societies that subject children to stress than in societies that do not.[19]

Cultural emphasis on obedience or independence in children is another variable that may explain some aspects of musical performance. In societies in which children are generally trained for compliance, cohesive singing predominates; when children are encouraged to be assertive, singing is mostly individualized. Moreover, assertive training of children is associated with a raspy voice or harsh singing. A raspy voice seems to be an indication of assertiveness and is most often a male voice quality. Interestingly enough, in societies in which women's work predominates in subsistence production, the women sing with harsher voices.

Other voice characteristics may also be associated with elements of culture. For example, sexual restrictions in a society seem to be associated with voice restrictions, especially with a nasalized or narrow, squeezed tone. These voice qualities are associated with anxiety and are especially noticeable in sounds of pain, deprivation, or sorrow. Restrictive sexual practices may be a source of pain and anxiety, and the nasal tone in song may reflect such emotions.[20]

If the cross-cultural results about music are valid, they should be able to explain change over time as well as variation within a society. Future research in a variety of societies may help test some of the theories of Lomax and Ayres.[21]

FOLKLORE

Folklore is a broad category including all the myths, legends, folktales, ballads, riddles, proverbs, and superstitions of a cultural group.[22] In general, folklore is transmitted orally, but it may also be written. Games are also sometimes considered folklore, although they may be learned by imitation as well as transmitted orally. All societies have a repertoire of stories that they tell to entertain each other and teach children. Examples of our folklore include fairy tales and the legends we tell about our folk heroes, such as George Washington's confessing that he chopped down the cherry tree. Folklore is not always clearly separable from the other arts, particularly music and dance; stories often are conveyed in those contexts.

Although some folklore scholars emphasize the traditional aspects of folklore and the continuity between the present and the past, more recently attention has been paid to the innovative and emergent aspects of folklore. In this view, folklore is constantly created by any social group that has shared experiences. So, for example, computer programmers may have their jokes and their own proverbs (for example, "Garbage in, garbage out!").[23] Jan Brunvand compiled a set of recently arisen *urban legends*. One such legend is "The Hook." The story, which has many versions, is basically about a young couple parked on Lover's Lane with the radio on. There is an announcement that a killer with an artificial hand is loose, so the girl suggests that they leave. The boy starts the car and drives her home. When he walks around the car to open her door, he finds a bloody hook attached to the door handle.[24] There are even legends on college campuses. What is the answer to the question of how long students should wait for a tardy professor? Students have an answer, ranging from 10 to 20 minutes. Is this a rule, or only a legend? Brunvand reported that he never found a regulation about how long to wait for the professor on any campus that tells this story![25]

Some folklore scholars are interested in universal or recurrent themes. Clyde Kluckhohn suggested that five themes occur in the myths and folktales of all societies: catastrophe, generally through flood; the slaying of monsters; incest; sibling rivalry, generally between brothers; and castration, sometimes actual but more commonly symbolic.[26] Edward Tylor, who proposed that religion is born from the human need to explain dreams and death, suggested that hero myths follow a similar pattern the world over—the central character is exposed at birth, is subsequently saved by others (humans or animals), and grows up to become a hero.[27] Joseph Campbell argued that hero myths resemble initiations—the hero is separated from the ordinary world, ventures forth into a new world (in this case, the supernatural world) to triumph over powerful forces, and then returns to the ordinary world with special powers to help others.[28]

Myths may indeed have universal themes, but few scholars have looked at a representative sample of the world's societies, and therefore we cannot be sure that current conclusions about universality are correct. Indeed, most folklore researchers have not been interested in universal themes but in the particular folktales told in specific societies or regions. For example, some scholars have focused on the "Star Husband Tale," a common Native American story. Stith Thompson presented 84 versions of this tale—his goal was to reconstruct the original version and pinpoint its place of origin. By identifying the most common elements, Thompson suggested that the basic story (and probably the original) is the following:

> Two girls sleeping out of doors wish that stars would be their husbands. In their sleep the girls are taken to the sky where they find themselves married to stars, one of which is a young man and the other an old man. The women are warned not to dig, but they disregard

the warning and accidentally open up a hole in the sky. Unaided they descend on a rope and arrive home safely.[29]

The tale, Thompson suggested, probably originated in the Plains and then spread to other regions of North America.

Alan Dundes has concentrated on the structure of folktales; he thinks that Native American folktales, including the "Star Husband Tale," have characteristic structures. One is a movement away from disequilibrium. Equilibrium is the desirable state; having too much or too little of anything is a condition that should be rectified as soon as possible. Disequilibrium, which Dundes calls *lack,* is indicated by the girls in the "Star Husband Tale" who do not have husbands. The lack is then corrected, in this case by marriage with the stars. This tale has another common Native American structure, says Dundes— a sequence of prohibition, interdiction, violation, and consequence. The women are warned not to dig, but they do—and as a consequence they escape for home.[30] It should be noted that the consequences in folktales are not always good. Recall the Garden of Eden tale. The couple are warned not to eat the fruit of a tree; they eat the fruit; they are cast out of their paradise. Similarly, Icarus in the Greek tale is warned not to fly too high or low. He flies too high; the sun melts the wax that holds his feathered wings, and he falls and drowns.

As useful as it might be to identify where certain tales originated, or what their common structures might be, many questions remain. What do the tales mean? Why did they arise in the first place? Why are certain structures common in Native American tales? We are still a long way from answering many of these questions, and trying to answer them is difficult. How does one try to understand the meaning of a tale?

It is easy for people to read different meanings into the same myth. For example, consider the myth the Hebrews told of a paradise in which only a man was present until Eve, the first woman, arrived and ate the forbidden fruit of knowledge. One might conclude that men in that society had some traditional grudge against women. If the interpreter were a psychoanalyst, he, or especially she, might assume that the myth reflected the male's deeply hidden fears of female sexuality. A historian might believe that the myth reflected actual historical events and that men were living in blissful ignorance until women invented agriculture—the effect of Eve's "knowledge" led to a life of digging rather than gathering.

It is clearly not enough to suggest an interpretation. Why should we believe it? We should give it serious consideration only if some systematic test seems to support it. For example, Michael Carroll suggested a Freudian interpretation of the "Star Husband Tale"—that the story represents repressed sentiments in the society. Specifically, he suggested that incestuous intercourse is the underlying concern of this myth, particularly the desire of a daughter to have intercourse with her father. He assumed that the stars symbolize fathers. Fathers, like stars, are high above, in children's eyes. Carroll predicted that if the "Star Husband Tale" originated on the Plains, and if it symbolizes intercourse, then the Plains tribes should be more likely than other tribes to have intercourse imagery in their versions of the tale. That seems to be the case. Analyzing 84 versions of the tale, Carroll found that Plains societies are the Native American tribes most likely to have imagery suggesting intercourse, including the lowering of a rope or ladder—symbolizing the penis—through a sky hole—symbolizing the vagina.[31]

Few studies have investigated why there is cross-cultural variation in the frequency of certain features in folktales. One feature of folktale variation that has been investigated cross-culturally is aggression. George Wright found that variation in child-rearing patterns predicted some aspects of how aggression is exhibited in folktales. Where children are severely punished for aggression, more intense aggression appears in the folktales. And in such societies, strangers are more likely than the hero or friends of the hero to be the aggressors in the folktales. It seems that where children may be afraid to exhibit aggression toward their parents or those close to them because of fear of punishment, the hero or his or her close friends in folktales are also not likely to be aggressive.[32]

Other kinds of fears may be reflected in folktales. A recent cross-cultural study found that unprovoked aggression is likely in folktales of societies that are subject to unpredictable food shortages. Why? One possibility is that the folktales reflect reality; after all, a serious drought may seem capricious, not possibly provoked by any human activity, brought on by the gods or nature "out of the blue." Curiously, however, societies with a history of unpredictable food shortages hardly mention natural disasters in their folktales, perhaps because disasters are too frightening. In any case, the capriciousness of unpredictable disasters seems to be transformed into the capricious aggression of characters in the folktales.[33]

Folklore, just like other aspects of art, may at least partly reflect the feelings, needs, and conflicts that people acquire as a result of growing up in their culture.

VIEWING THE ART OF OTHER CULTURES

Sally Price raised some critical questions about how Western museums and art critics look at the visual art of less complex cultures. Why is it that when artworks from Western or Oriental civilizations are displayed in a museum here, they carry the artist's name? In contrast, art from less complex cultures, often labeled "primitive art," tends to be displayed without the name of the artist; instead, it often is accompanied by a description of where it came from, how it was constructed, and what it may be used for. More words of explanation seem to accompany displays of unfamiliar art. Price suggested that the art pieces that we consider the most worthy require the least labeling, subtly conveying that the viewer needs no help to judge a real work of art.[34] In addition, art acquired from less complex cultures tends to be labeled by the name of the Westerner who acquired it. It is almost as if the fame of the collector, not the art itself, sets the value of such art.[35]

Just as the art from less complex cultures tends to be nameless, it also tends to be treated as timeless. We recognize that Western art and the art from classical civilizations change over time, which is why it must be dated, but the art from other places seems to be viewed as representing a timeless cultural tradition.[36] Do we know that the art of peoples with simpler technology changes less, or is this assumption a kind of ethnocentrism? Price, who has studied the art of the Saramakas of Suriname, points out that although Westerners think of Saramakan art as still representing its African ancestry, Saramakans themselves can identify shifts in their art styles over time. For example, they describe how calabashes used to be decorated on the outside, then the style changed to decorating the inside. They can also recognize the artist who made particular carved calabashes as well as identify those who were innovators of designs and techniques.[37]

Although it seems that individual artists can usually be recognized in any community, some societies do appear to be more "communal" than others in their art style. For example, let us compare the Puebloan peoples of the Southwest with native peoples of the Great Plains. Traditionally, women Puebloan potters did not sign their pots, and they largely followed their pueblo's characteristic style. In contrast, each Plains warrior stressed his individual accomplishments by painting representations of those accomplishments on animal hides. Either the warrior would do it himself or he would ask someone else to do it for him. These hides were worn by the warrior or displayed outside his tipi.[38]

When Westerners do notice changes over time in the art of less complex societies, it seems to be because they are concerned about whether the art represents traditional forms or is "tourist art." Tourist art is often evaluated negatively, perhaps because of its association with money. But famous Western artists often also worked for fees or were supported by elite patrons, and yet the fact that they were paid does not seem to interfere with our evaluation of their art.[39]

ARTISTIC CHANGE AND CULTURE CONTACT

It is unquestionably true that contact with the West did alter some aspects of the art of other cultures, but that does not imply that their art was changeless before. What kinds of things changed with contact? In some places, artists began to represent European contact itself. For example, in Australia, numerous rock paintings by aborigines portray sailing ships, men on horseback carrying pistols, and even cattle brands. With encouragement from Europeans, indigenous artists also began drawing on tree bark, canvas, and masonite to sell to Europeans. Interestingly, the art for sale mostly emphasizes themes displayed before contact and does not include representations of ships and guns.[40] As aboriginal populations were decimated by European contact, a lot of their traditional art forms disappeared, particularly legends and rock paintings that were associated with the sacred sites of each clan. The legends

described the creation of the sacred places, and art motifs with painted human or animal heroes marked the sites.[41]

In North America, contact between native groups produced changes in art even before the Europeans came. Copper, sharks' teeth, and marine shells were traded extensively in precontact times and were used in the artwork of people who did not have access to those materials locally. Ceremonies were borrowed between groups, and with the new ceremonies came changes in artistic traditions. Borrowing from other native groups continued after European contact. The Navaho, who are well known today for their rug weaving, were not weavers in the seventeenth century. They probably obtained their weaving technology from the Hopi and then began to weave wool and herd sheep. European contact also produced material changes in art; new materials including beads, wool cloth, and silver were introduced. Metal tools such as needles and scissors could now be used to make more tailored and more decorated skin clothing. In the Northwest, the greater availability of metal tools made it possible to make larger totem poles and house posts.[42]

After they were placed on reservations, virtually all Native Americans had to change their ways of making a living. Selling arts and crafts earned some of them supplementary income. Most of these crafts used traditional techniques and traditional designs, altered somewhat to suit European expectations. Outsiders played important roles in encouraging changes in arts and crafts. Some storekeepers became patrons to particular artists who were then able to devote themselves full time to their craft. Traders would often encourage changes such as new objects—for example, ashtrays and cups made of pottery. Scholars have played a role too. Some have helped artisans learn about styles of the past that had

---

Australian aborigines used to make rock paintings. Now they paint on other materials for the art market.

disappeared. For example, with the encouragement of anthropologists and others in the Santa Fe area, Maria and Julian Martinez of San Ildefonso Pueblo brought back a polished black-on-black pottery style originally produced by nearby ancient peoples.[43]

Some of the artistic changes that have occurred after contact with the West are partly predictable from the results of cross-cultural research on artistic variation. Remember that Fischer found that egalitarian societies typically had less complex designs and more symmetry than did stratified societies. With the loss of traditional ways of making a living and with the increase in wage labor and commercial enterprises, many Native American groups have become more socially stratified. Extrapolating from Fischer's results, we would predict that designs on visual art should become more complex and asymmetrical as social stratification increases. Indeed, if early reservation art (1870–1901) among the Shoshone-Bannock of southeastern Idaho is compared with their recent art (1973–1983), it is clear that the art has become more complex as social stratification has increased.[44] It could also be true that the art changed because the artists came to realize that more asymmetry and complexity would sell better to people who collect art.

SUMMARY

1. Not all societies have a word for art, but art universally seems to have several qualities. It expresses as well as communicates. It stimulates the senses, affects emotions, and evokes ideas. It is produced in culturally patterned ways and styles. It has cultural meaning. And some people are thought to be better at it than others.

2. All societies decorate or adorn the body, temporarily or permanently. But there is enormous cultural variation in the parts decorated and how. Body decoration may be used to delineate social position, sex, or occupation. It may also have an erotic significance, as for example, in drawing attention to erogenous zones of the body.

3. The materials used to produce visual art, the way those materials are used, and the natural objects the artist may choose to represent all vary from society to society and reveal much about a particular society's relation to its environment. Some studies indicate a correlation between artistic design and social stratification.

4. Like the visual arts, music is subject to a remarkable amount of variation from society to society. Some studies suggest correlations between musical styles and cultural complexity. Other research shows links between child-rearing practices and a society's preference for certain rhythmical patterns, tonal ranges, and voice quality.

5. Folklore is a broad category including all the myths, legends, folktales, ballads, riddles, proverbs, and superstitions of a cultural group. In general, folklore is transmitted orally, but it may also be written. Some anthropologists have identified basic themes in myths—catastrophe, slaying of monsters, incest, sibling rivalry, and castration. Myths may reflect a society's deepest preoccupations.

6. Art is always changing, but recent culture contact has had some profound effects on art in various parts of the world. With the decimation of many indigenous populations, many areas have lost some of their artistic traditions. But the art also changed as individuals began to sell arts and crafts.

GLOSSARY TERMS

folklore
polyphony

CRITICAL QUESTIONS

1. How innovative or original can a successful artist be?

2. What kind of art do you prefer, and why?

3. Do you think art made for tourists is inferior? Whatever you think, why do you think so?

INTERNET EXERCISES

1. Art changes over time. Go to a Native American art gallery online at **http://www.indart.com/ gallery/gallery.htm** and compare some of the art from before 1900 with that done more recently. What differences do you see?

2. Stories, folklore, and fairy tales are part of human societies. Societies have passed stories through generations. Read some of them at **http:// www.pitt.edu/~dash/water.html** and **http://www. pitt.edu/~dash/folktexts.html**. Summarize your view on the subject as it relates to this chapter.

3. Visit the Javanese Mask Collection at **http:// www.fmnh.org./exhibits/javamask/Javamask.htm**. Some of the masks are more frightening than others. Compare the features of those that are more or less frightening. Compare with what you find on Mongolian masks at **http://www.indart. com/gallery/gallery.htm**.

4. The Virtual Ceramic Exhibit at **http://www.uky.edu/Artsource/vce/VCEhome.html** offers numerous examples of ceramic art. Select at least three examples and summarize your findings.

◼◼ SUGGESTED READING

ANDERSON, R. L. *Calliope's Sisters: A Comparative Study of Philosophies of Art.* Englewood Cliffs, NJ: Prentice Hall, 1990. A comparison of the art of ten diverse societies in order to discover similarities and differences in their arts as well as how they think about art.

BAUMAN, R., ED. *Folklore, Cultural Performances, and Popular Entertainment.* New York: Oxford University Press, 1992. A collection of brief articles on popular expressive forms and practices. Covers basic concepts and provides an entrance into the literature.

LOMAX, A., ED. *Folk Song Style and Culture. American Association for the Advancement of Science Publication No. 88.* Washington, DC, 1968. A classic cross-cultural study of the stylistic elements of folk songs from societies around the world. The data compiled in this study, which was known as the Cantometrics Project, were used to test hypotheses about the relationship of song style to other aspects of culture.

MAQUET, J. *The Aesthetic Experience: An Anthropologist Looks at the Visual Arts.* New Haven, CT: Yale University Press, 1986. The author explores the universal and culturally varying components of the visual arts.

WADE, E. L., ED. *The Arts of the North American Indian: Native Traditions in Evolution.* New York: Hudson Hills Press, 1986. A large-format, beautifully illustrated introduction to the varieties of art in Native North American cultures.

Culture Change

Most of us are aware that "times have changed," especially when we compare our lives with those of our parents. Witness the recent changes in attitudes about sex and marriage, as well as the changes in women's roles. But such culture change is not unusual. Throughout history humans have replaced or altered customary behaviors and attitudes as their needs have changed. Just as no individual is immortal, no particular cultural pattern is impervious to change. Anthropologists, therefore, want to understand how and why culture change occurs.

Three general questions can be asked about culture change: What is the source of a new trait? Why are people motivated, unconsciously as well as consciously, to adopt it? And is the new trait adaptive? The source of the change may be inside or outside the society. That is, a new idea or behavior may originate within the society, or it may come from another society. With regard to motivation, people may adopt the new idea or behavior voluntarily, even if unconsciously, or they may be forced to adopt it. Finally, the outcome of culture change may or may not be beneficial. In this chapter, we first discuss the various processes of culture change in terms of the three dimensions of source, motivation, and outcome. Then we discuss some of the major types of culture change in the modern world. As we will see, these changes are associated largely with the expansion of Western societies over the last 500 years.

HOW AND WHY CULTURES CHANGE

Discoveries and inventions, which may originate inside or outside a society, are ultimately the sources of all culture change. But they do not necessarily lead to change. If an invention or discovery is ignored, no change in culture results. It is only when society accepts an invention or discovery and uses it regularly that we can begin to speak of culture change.

DISCOVERY AND INVENTION

The new thing discovered or invented, the innovation, may be an object—the wheel, the plow, the computer—or it may involve behavior and ideas—buying and selling, democracy, monogamy. According to Ralph Linton, a discovery is any addition to knowledge and an invention is a new application of knowledge.[1] Thus, a person might discover that children can be persuaded to eat nourishing food if the food is associated with an imaginary character who appeals to them. And then someone might exploit that discovery by inventing a character named Popeye who appears in a series of animated cartoons, acquiring miraculous strength in a variety of dramatic situations by devouring cans of spinach.

UNCONSCIOUS INVENTION. In discussing the process of invention, we should differentiate between various types of inventions. One type is the consequence of a society's setting itself a specific goal, such as eliminating tuberculosis or placing a person on the moon. Another type emerges less intentionally. This second process of invention is often referred to as *accidental juxtaposition* or *unconscious invention.* Linton suggested that some inventions, especially those of prehistoric days, were probably the consequences of literally dozens of tiny initiatives by "unconscious" inventors. These inventors made their small contributions, perhaps over many hundreds of years, without being aware of the part they were playing in bringing one invention, such as the wheel or a better form of hand ax, to completion.[2] Consider the example of children playing on a fallen log, which rolls as they walk and balance on it, coupled with the need at a given moment to move a slab of granite from a cave face. The children's play may have suggested the use of logs as rollers and thereby set in motion a series of developments that culminated in the wheel.

In reconstructing the process of invention in prehistoric times, however, we should be careful not to look back on our ancestors with a smugness born of our more highly developed technology. We have become accustomed to turning to the science sections of our magazines and newspapers and finding, almost daily, reports of miraculous new discoveries and inventions. From our point of view, it is difficult to imagine such a simple invention as the wheel taking so many centuries to come into being. We are tempted to surmise that early humans were less intelligent than we are. But the capacity of the human brain has been the same for perhaps 100,000 years; there is no evidence that the inventors of the wheel were any less intelligent than we are.

INTENTIONAL INNOVATION. Some discoveries and inventions arise out of deliberate attempts to produce a new idea or object. It may seem that such innovations are obvious responses to perceived needs. For example, during the Industrial Revolution there was a great demand for inventions that would increase productivity. James Hargreaves, in eighteenth-century England, is an example of an inventor who responded to an existing demand. Textile manufacturers were clamoring for such large quantities of spun yarn that cottage laborers, working with foot-operated spinning wheels, could not meet the demand. Hargreaves, realizing that prestige and financial rewards would come to the person who invented a method of spinning large quantities of yarn in a short time, set about the task and developed the spinning jenny.

But perceived needs and the economic rewards that may be given to the innovator do not explain why only some people innovate. We know relatively little about why some people are more innovative than others. The ability to innovate may depend in part on individual characteristics such as high intelligence and creativity. And creativity may be influenced by social conditions.

A study of innovation among Ashanti artist-carvers in Ghana suggests that creativity is more likely in some socioeconomic groups than in others.[3] Some carvers produced only traditional designs; others departed from tradition and produced "new" styles of carving. Two groups were found to innovate the most—the wealthiest and the poorest carvers. These two groups of carvers may tolerate risk more than the middle socioeconomic group. Innovative carving entails some risk because it may take more time and it may not sell. Wealthy carvers can afford the risk, and they may gain some prestige as well as income if their innovation is appreciated. The poor are not doing well anyway, and they have little to lose by trying something new.

WHO ADOPTS INNOVATIONS? Once someone discovers or invents something, there is still the question of whether the innovation will be adopted by others. Many researchers have studied the characteristics of "early adopters." Such individuals tend to be educated, high in social status, upwardly mobile, and, if they are property owners, have large farms and businesses. The individuals who most need technological improvements—those who are less well off—are generally the last to adopt innovations. The theory is that only the wealthy can afford to take the substantial risks associated with new ways of doing things. In periods of rapid technological change, therefore, the gap between rich and poor is likely to widen because the rich adopt innovations sooner, and benefit more from them, than the poor.[4]

Does this imply that the likelihood of adopting innovations is a simple function of how much wealth a possible adopter possesses? Not necessarily. Frank Cancian reviewed several studies and found that upper-middle-class individuals show more conservatism than lower-middle-class individuals. Cancian suggested that when the risks are unknown, the lower-middle-class individuals are more receptive to innovation because they have less to lose. Later on, when the risks are better known, that is, as more people adopt the innovation, the upper-middle class catches up to the lower-middle.[5] So the readiness to accept innovation, like the likelihood of creativity among Ashanti carvers, may not be related to socioeconomic position in a linear way.

The speed of accepting an innovation may depend partly on how new behaviors and ideas are

The idea of Santa Claus has diffused to many places, including Taiwan.

typically transmitted in a society. In particular, is a person exposed to many versus few "teachers"? If children learn most of what they know from their parents or from a relatively small number of elders, then innovation will be slow to spread throughout the society, and culture change is likely to be slow. Innovations may catch on more rapidly if individuals are exposed to various teachers and other "leaders" who can influence many in a relatively short time. And the more peers we have, the more we might learn from them.[6] Perhaps this is why the pace of change appears to be so quick today. In societies like our own, and increasingly in the industrializing world, it is likely that people learn in schools from teachers, from leaders in their specialties, and from peers.

COSTS AND BENEFITS. An innovation that is technologically superior is not necessarily going to be adopted. There are costs as well as benefits for both individuals and large-scale industries. Take the typewriter keyboard. The keyboard used most often on computers today is called the QWERTY keyboard (named after the letters on the left side of the line of keys below the row of number keys). It was actually invented for mechanical typewriters to slow typing speed down! Early typewriters had mechanical keys that jammed if the typist went too fast.[7] Computer keyboards don't have that problem, so an arrangement of keys that allowed faster typing would probably be better. Different keyboard configurations have been invented, but they haven't caught on. Most people probably would find it too hard or too time-consuming to learn a new style of typing, so the original style of keyboard persists.

In large-scale industries, technological innovations may be very costly to implement. A new product or process may require revamping a manufacturing or service facility and retraining workers. Before a decision is made to change, the costs of doing so are weighed against the potential benefits. If the market is expected to be large for a new product, the product is more likely be produced. If the market is judged small, the benefits may not be sufficient inducement to change. Companies may also judge the value of an innovation by whether it could be copied by competitors. If the new innovation is easily copyable, the inventing company may not find the investment worthwhile. Although the market may be large, the inventing company may not be able to hold onto market share if other companies could produce the product quickly without having to invest in research and development.[8]

DIFFUSION

The source of new cultural elements in a society may also be another society. The process by which cultural elements are borrowed from another society and incorporated into the culture of the recipient group is called **diffusion.** Borrowing sometimes enables a group to bypass stages or mistakes in the development of a process or institution. For example, Germany was able to accelerate its program of industrialization in the nineteenth century because it was able to avoid some of the errors made by its English and Belgian competitors by taking advantage of technological borrowing. Japan did the same somewhat later. Indeed, in recent years some of the earliest industrialized countries have fallen behind their imitators in certain areas of production, such as automobiles, televisions, cameras, and computers.

In a well-known passage, Linton conveyed the far-reaching effects of diffusion by considering the first few hours in the day of an American man in the 1930s. This man

> awakens in a bed built on a pattern which originated in the Near East but which was modified in northern Europe before it was transmitted to America. He throws back covers made from cotton, domesticated in India, or linen, domesticated in the Near East, or silk, the use of which was discovered in China. All of these materials have been spun and woven by processes invented in the Near East. . . . He takes off his pajamas, a garment invented in India, and washes with soap invented by the ancient Gauls. He then shaves, a masochistic rite which seems to have derived from either Sumer or ancient Egypt.
>
> Before going out for breakfast he glances through the window, made of glass invented in Egypt, and if it is raining puts on overshoes made of rubber discovered by the Central American Indians and takes an umbrella, invented in southeastern Asia. . . .
>
> On his way to breakfast he stops to buy a paper paying for it with coins, an ancient Lydian invention. . . . His plate is made of a form of pottery invented in China. His knife is of steel, an alloy first made in southern India, his fork a medieval Italian invention, and his spoon a derivative of a Roman original. . . . After his fruit (African watermelon) and first coffee (an Abyssinian plant) . . . he may have the egg of a species of bird domesticated in Indo-China, or thin strips of the flesh of an animal domesticated in Eastern Asia which have been salted and smoked by a process developed in northern Europe. . . .
>
> While smoking (an American Indian habit) he reads the news of the day, imprinted in characters invented

by the ancient Semites upon a material invented in China by a process invented in Germany. As he absorbs the accounts of foreign troubles he will, if he is a good conservative citizen, thank a Hebrew deity in an Indo-European language that he is 100 percent American.[9]

PATTERNS OF DIFFUSION. There are three basic patterns of diffusion: direct contact, intermediate contact, and stimulus diffusion.

1. **Direct contact.** Elements of a society's culture may be first taken up by neighboring societies and then gradually spread farther and farther afield. The spread of the use of paper (a sheet of interlaced fibers) is a good example of extensive diffusion by direct contact. The invention of paper is attributed to the Chinese Ts'ai Lun in A.D. 105. Within 50 years, paper was being made in many places in central China. While the art of papermaking was kept secret for about 500 years, paper was distributed as a commodity to much of the Arab world through the markets at Samarkand. But when Samarkand was attacked by the Chinese in 751, a Chinese prisoner was forced to set up a paper mill. Paper manufacture then spread to the rest of the Arab world; it was first manufactured in Baghdad in A.D. 793, Egypt about A.D. 900, and Morocco about A.D. 1100. Paper making was introduced as a commodity in Europe by Arab trade through Italian ports in the twelfth century. The Moors built the first European paper mill in Spain about 1150. The technical knowledge then spread throughout Europe with paper mills built in Italy in 1276, France 1348, Germany 1390, and England in 1494.[10] In general, the pattern of accepting the borrowed invention was the same in all cases. Paper was first imported as a luxury, then in ever-expanding quantities as a staple product. Finally, and usually within one to three centuries, local manufacture was begun.

2. **Intermediate contact.** Diffusion by intermediate contact occurs through the agency of third parties. Frequently, traders carry a cultural trait from the society that originated it to another group. As an example of diffusion through intermediaries, Phoenician traders spread the alphabet, which may have been invented by another Semitic group, to Greece. At times, soldiers serve as intermediaries in spreading a culture trait. European crusaders, such as the Knights Templar and the Knights of St. John, acted as intermediaries in two ways: they carried Christian culture to Muslim societies of North Africa and brought Arab culture back to Europe. In the nineteenth century, Western missionaries in all parts of the world encouraged natives to wear Western clothing. The result is that in Africa, the Pacific Islands, and elsewhere, native peoples can be found wearing shorts, suit jackets, shirts, ties, and other typically Western articles of clothing.

3. **Stimulus diffusion.** In stimulus diffusion, knowledge of a trait belonging to another culture stimulates the invention or development of a local equivalent. A classic example of stimulus diffusion is the Cherokee syllabic writing system created by a Native American named Sequoya so that his people could write down their language. Sequoya got the idea from his contact with Europeans. Yet he did not adopt the English writing system; indeed, he did not even learn to write English. What he did was utilize some English alphabetic symbols, alter others, and invent new ones. All the symbols he used represented Cherokee syllables and in no way echoed English alphabetic usage. In other words, Sequoya took English alphabetic ideas and gave them a new, Cherokee form. The stimulus originated with Europeans; the result was peculiarly Cherokee.

THE SELECTIVE NATURE OF DIFFUSION. Although there is a temptation to view the dynamics of diffusion as similar to a stone sending concentric ripples over still water, this would be an oversimplification of the way diffusion actually occurs. Not all cultural traits are borrowed as readily as the ones we have mentioned, nor do they usually expand in neat, ever-widening circles. Rather, diffusion is a selective process. The Japanese, for instance, accepted much from Chinese culture, but they also rejected many traits. Rhymed tonal poetry, civil-service examinations, and foot binding, which were favored by the Chinese, were never adopted in Japan. The poetry form was unsuited to the structure of the Japanese language; the examinations were unnecessary in view of the entrenched power of the Japanese aristocracy; and foot binding was repugnant to a people who abhorred body mutilation of any sort.

Not only would we expect societies to reject items from other societies that are repugnant, we would also expect them to reject ideas and technology that do not satisfy some psychological, social, or cultural need. After all, people are not sponges; they don't automatically soak up the things around them. If they did, the amount of cultural variation in the world would be extremely small, which is clearly not the case. Diffusion is also selective because cultural traits differ in the extent to which they can be communicated. Elements of material culture, such as mechanical processes and techniques, and other traits, such as physical sports and the like, are not especially difficult to demonstrate. Consequently, they are accepted or rejected on their merits. But the moment we move out of the material context, we encounter real difficulties. Linton explained the problem in these words:

> Although it is quite possible to describe such an element of culture as the ideal pattern for marriage . . . it is much less complete than a description of basketmaking. . . . The most thorough verbalization has difficulty in conveying the series of associations and conditioned emotional responses which are attached to this pattern [marriage] and which gave it meaning and vitality within our own society. . . . This is even more true of those concepts which . . . find no direct expression in behavior aside from verbalization. There is a story of an educated Japanese who after a long discussion on the nature of the Trinity with a European friend . . . burst out with: "Oh, I see now, it is a committee."[11]

Finally, diffusion is selective because the overt form of a particular trait, rather than its function or meaning, frequently seems to determine how the trait will be received. For example, the enthusiasm for bobbed hair (short haircuts) that swept through much of North America in the 1920s never caught on among the Native Americans of northwestern California. To many women of European ancestry, short hair was a symbolic statement of their freedom. To Native American women, who traditionally cut their hair short when in mourning, it was a reminder of death.[12]

In the process of diffusion, then, we can identify a number of different patterns. We know that cultural borrowing is selective rather than automatic, and we can describe how a particular borrowed trait has been modified by the recipient culture. But our current knowledge does not allow us to specify when one or another of these outcomes will occur, under what conditions diffusion will occur, and why it occurs the way it does.

ACCULTURATION

On the surface, the process of change called **acculturation** seems to include much of what we have discussed under the label of diffusion, since acculturation refers to the changes that occur when different cultural groups come into intensive contact. As in diffusion, the source of new cultural items is the other society. But more often than not, the term *acculturation* is used by anthropologists to describe a situation in which one of the societies in contact is much more powerful than the other. Thus, acculturation can be seen as a process of extensive cultural borrowing in the context of superordinate-subordinate relations between societies.[13] The borrowing may sometimes be a two-way process, but generally it is the subordinate or less powerful society that borrows the most. The concept of diffusion can then be reserved for the voluntary borrowing of cultural elements, in contrast with borrowing under external pressure, which characterizes acculturation. (*Assimilation* means that people from another culture have more or less completely adopted the dominant culture of the society.)

External pressure for culture change can take various forms. In its most direct form—conquest or colonialization—the dominant group uses force or the threat of force to bring about culture change in the other group. For example, in the Spanish conquest of Mexico, the conquerors forced many of the native groups to accept Catholicism. Although such direct force is not always exerted in conquest situations, dominated peoples often have little choice but to change. Examples of such indirectly forced change abound in the history of Native Americans in the United States. Although the federal government made few direct attempts to force people to adopt American culture, it did drive many native groups from their lands, thereby obliging them to give up many aspects of their traditional ways of life. In order to survive, they had no choice but to adopt many of the dominant society's traits. When Native American children were required to go to schools, which taught the dominant society's values, the process was accelerated.

A subordinate society may acculturate to a dominant society even in the absence of direct or indirect force. The dominated people may elect to adopt cultural elements from the dominant society in order to survive in their changed world. Or, perceiving that members of the dominant society enjoy more secure living conditions, the dominated people may identify with the dominant culture in the hope that by doing so they will be able to share some of its benefits. For example, in Arctic areas many Inuit and Lapp groups seemed eager to replace dog sleds with snowmobiles without any coercion.[14]

But many millions of people never had a chance to acculturate after contact with Europeans. They simply died, sometimes directly at the hands of the conquerors, but probably more often as a result of

When powerful governments restrict native populations to small parcels of land on reservations or force them to move, there is usually little choice but to change in the direction of the more powerful group's way of life. This painting by Robert Lindneux ("The Trail of Tears") depicts the forced removal of the Cherokee from their homeland in the southeastern United States.

the new diseases the Europeans brought with them. Depopulation because of measles, smallpox, and tuberculosis was particularly common in North and South America and on the islands of the Pacific. Those areas had previously been isolated from contact with Europeans and from the diseases of that continuous landmass we call the Old World—Europe, Asia, and Africa.[15]

The story of Ishi, the last surviving member of a group of Native Americans in California called the Yahi, is a moving testimonial to the frequently tragic effect of contact with Europeans. In the space of 22 years, the Yahi population was reduced from several hundred to near zero. The historical record on this episode of depopulation suggests that Euro-Americans murdered 30 to 50 Yahi for every Euro-American murdered, and perhaps 60 percent of the Yahi died in the ten years following their initial exposure to European diseases.[16]

Nowadays, many powerful nations—and not just Western ones—may seem to be acting in more humanitarian ways to improve the life of previously subjugated as well as other "developing" peoples. For better or worse, these programs, however, are still forms of external pressure. The tactic used may be persuasion rather than force, but most of the programs are nonetheless designed to bring about acculturation in the direction of the dominant societies' cultures. For example, the introduction of formal schooling cannot help but instill new values that may contradict traditional cultural patterns. And even health-care programs may alter traditional ways of life by undermining the authority of shamans and other leaders and by increasing population beyond the number that can be supported in traditional ways. Confinement to "reservations" or

other kinds of direct force are not the only ways a dominant society can bring about acculturation.

REVOLUTION

Certainly the most drastic and rapid way a culture can change is as a result of **revolution**—replacement, usually violent, of a country's rulers. Historical records, as well as our daily newspapers, indicate that people frequently rebel against established authority. Rebellions, if they occur, almost always occur in state societies, where there is a distinct ruling elite. They take the form of struggles between rulers and ruled, between conquerors and conquered, or between representatives of an external colonial power and segments of the native society. Rebels do not always succeed in overthrowing their rulers, so rebellions do not always result in revolutions. And even successful rebellions do not always result in culture change; the individual rulers may change, but customs or institutions may not. The sources of revolution may be mostly internal, as in the French Revolution, or partly external, as in the Russian-supported 1948 revolution in Czechoslovakia and the United States–supported 1973 revolution against President Allende in Chile.

The American War of Independence toward the end of the eighteenth century is a good example of a colonial rebellion, the success of which was at least partly a result of foreign intervention. The American rebellion was a war of neighboring colonies against the greatest imperial power of the time, Great Britain. In the nineteenth century and continuing into the middle and later years of the twentieth century, there would be many other wars of independence, in Latin America, Europe, Asia, and

Revolutionary leaders are often from high-status backgrounds. Here we see a depiction of Patrick Henry giving his famous speech to the aristocratic landowners in the Virginia Assembly on March 23, 1775. Urging the Virginians to fight the British, Henry said that the choice was "liberty or death."

Africa. We don't always remember that the American rebellion was the first of these anti-imperialist wars in modern times, and the model for many that followed. And just like many of the most recent liberation movements, the American rebellion was also part of a larger worldwide war, involving people from many rival nations. Thirty thousand German-speaking soldiers fought, for pay, on the British side; an army and navy from France fought on the American side. There were volunteers from other European countries, including Denmark, Holland, Poland, and Russia.

One of these volunteers was a man named Kosciusko from Poland, which at the time was being divided between Prussia and Russia. Kosciusko helped win a major victory for the Americans, and subsequently directed the fortification of what later became the American training school for army officers, West Point. After the war he returned to Poland and led a rebellion against the Russians, which was only briefly successful. In 1808 he published a *Manual on the Maneuvers of Horse Artillery,* which was used for many years by the American army. When he died he left money to buy freedom and education for American slaves. The executor of Kosciusko's will was Thomas Jefferson.

As in many revolutions, those who were urging revolution were considered "radicals." At a now famous debate in Virginia in 1775, delegates from each colony met at a Continental Congress. Patrick Henry put forward a resolution to prepare for defense against the British armed forces. The motion barely passed, by a vote of 65 to 60. Henry's speech is now a part of American folklore. He rose to declare that it was insane not to oppose the

British and that he was not afraid to test the strength of the colonies against Great Britain. Others might hesitate, he said, but he would have "liberty or death." The "radicals" who supported Henry's resolution included many aristocratic landowners, two of whom, George Washington and Thomas Jefferson, became the first and third occupants of the highest political office in what became the United States of America.[17]

Not all peoples who are suppressed, conquered, or colonialized eventually rebel against established authority. Why this is so, and why rebellions and revolts are not always successful in bringing about culture change, are still open questions. But some possible answers have been investigated. One historian who examined the classic revolutions of the past, including the American, French, and Russian revolutions, suggested some conditions that may give rise to rebellion and revolution:

1. *Loss of prestige of established authority,* often as a result of the failure of foreign policy, financial difficulties, dismissals of popular ministers, or alteration of popular policies. France in the eighteenth century lost three major international conflicts, with disastrous results for its diplomatic standing and internal finances. Russian society was close to military and economic collapse in 1917, after three years of World War I.
2. *Threat to recent economic improvement.* In France, as in Russia, those sections of the population (professional classes and urban workers) whose economic fortunes had only shortly before taken an upward swing were

"radicalized" by unexpected setbacks, such as steeply rising food prices and unemployment. The same may be said for the American colonies on the brink of their rebellion against Great Britain.

3. *Indecisiveness of government,* as exemplified by lack of consistent policy, which gives the impression of being controlled by, rather than in control of, events. The frivolous arrogance of Louis XVI's regime and the bungling of George III's prime minister, Lord North, with respect to the problems of the American colonies are examples.

4. *Loss of support of the intellectual class.* Such a loss deprived the prerevolutionary governments of France and Russia of any avowed philosophical support and led to their unpopularity with the literate public.[18]

The classic revolutions of the past occurred in countries that were industrialized only incipiently at best. For the most part, the same is true of the rebellions and revolutions in recent years; they have occurred mostly in countries we call *developing.* The evidence from a worldwide survey of developing countries suggests that rebellions have tended to occur where the ruling classes depended mostly on the produce or income from land, and therefore were resistant to demands for reform from the rural classes that worked the land. In such agricultural economies, the rulers are not likely to yield political power or give greater economic returns to the workers, because to do so would eliminate the basis (land ownership) of the rulers' wealth and power.[19]

Finally, a particularly interesting question is why revolutions sometimes, perhaps even usually, fail to measure up to the high hopes of those who initiate them. When rebellions succeed in replacing the ruling elite, the result is often the institution of a military dictatorship even more restrictive and repressive than the government that existed before. The new ruling establishment may merely substitute one set of repressions for another, rather than bring any real change to the nation. On the other hand, some revolutions have resulted in fairly drastic overhauls of societies.

The idea of revolution has been one of the central myths and inspirations of many groups both in the past and in the present. The colonial empire building of countries such as England and France created a worldwide situation in which rebellion became nearly inevitable. In numerous technologically underdeveloped lands, which have been exploited by more powerful countries for their natural resources and cheap labor, a deep resentment has often developed against the foreign ruling classes or their local clients. Where the ruling classes, native or foreign, refuse to be responsive to those feelings, rebellion becomes the only alternative. In many areas, it has become a way of life.

CULTURE CHANGE AND ADAPTATION

The chapter on the concept of culture discussed the general assumption that most of the customary behaviors of a culture are probably adaptive, or at least not maladaptive, in that environment. A custom is adaptive if it increases the likelihood that the people practicing it will survive and reproduce. Even though customs are learned and not genetically inherited, cultural adaptation may be otherwise like biological adaptation or evolution. The frequency of certain genetic alternatives is likely to increase over time if those genetic traits increase their carriers' chances of survival and reproduction. Similarly, the frequency of a new learned behavior will increase over time and become customary in a population if the people with that behavior are most likely to survive and reproduce. Thus, if a culture is adapted to its environment, culture change should also be adaptive—not always, to be sure, but commonly.

One of the most important differences between cultural evolution and genetic evolution is that individuals often can decide whether or not to accept and follow the way their parents behave or think, whereas they cannot decide whether or not to inherit certain genes. When enough individuals change their behavior and beliefs, we say that the culture has changed. Therefore, it is possible for culture change to occur much more rapidly than genetic change.

But it is not necessarily more adaptive to change rapidly, just because it is possible. Robert Boyd and Peter Richerson showed mathematically that when the environment is relatively stable and individual mistakes are costly, staying with customary modes of behavior (usually transmitted by parents) is probably more adaptive than changing.[20] But what happens when the environment, particularly the social environment, is changing? There are plenty of examples in the modern world: People have to migrate to new places for work; medical care leads to increased population so that land is scarcer; people have had land taken away from them and are forced to make do with less land; and so on.

It is particularly when circumstances change that individuals are likely to try ideas or behaviors that are different from those of their parents. Most people would want to adopt behaviors that are more suited to their present circumstances, but how do they know which behaviors are better? There are various ways to find out. One way is by experimenting, trying out various new behaviors. Another way is to evaluate the experiments of others. If a person who tries a new technique seems successful, we would expect that person to be imitated, just as we would expect people to stick with new behaviors they have personally tried and found successful. Finally, one might choose to do what most people in the new situation decide to do.[21]

Why one choice rather than another? In part, the choice may be a function of the cost or risk of the innovation. It is relatively easy, for example, to find out how long it takes to cut down a tree with an introduced steel ax, as compared with a stone ax. Not surprisingly, innovations such as a steel ax catch on relatively quickly because comparison is easy and the results clear-cut. But what if the risk is very great? Suppose the innovation involves adopting a whole new way of farming that you have never practiced before. You can try it, but you might not have any food if you fail. As we discussed earlier, risky innovations are likely to be tried only by those individuals who can afford the risk. Other people may then evaluate their success and adopt the new strategy if it looks promising. Similarly, if you migrate to a new area, say from a high-rainfall area to a drier one, it may pay to look around to see what most people in the new place do; after all, the people in the drier area probably have customs that are adaptive for that environment.

We can expect, then, that the choices individuals make may often be adaptive ones. But it is important to note that adopting an innovation from someone in one's own society or borrowing an innovation from another society is not always or necessarily beneficial, either in the short or the long run. First, people may make mistakes in judgment, especially when some new behavior seems to satisfy a physical need. Why, for example, have smoking and drug use diffused so widely even though they are likely to reduce a person's chances of survival? Second, even if people are correct in their short-term judgment of benefit, they may be wrong in their judgment about long-run benefit. A new crop may yield more than the old crop for five consecutive years, but the new crop may fail miserably in the sixth year because of lower than normal rainfall or

because the new crop depleted soil nutrients. Third, people may be forced by the more powerful to change, with few if any benefits for themselves.

Whatever the motives for humans to change their behavior, the theory of natural selection suggests that new behavior is not likely to become cultural or remain cultural over generations if it has harmful reproductive consequences, just as a genetic mutation with harmful consequences is not likely to become frequent in a population.[22] Still, we know of many examples of culture change that seem maladaptive—the switch to bottle-feeding rather than nursing infants, which may spread infection because contaminated water is used, or the adoption of alcoholic beverages, which may lead to alcoholism and early death. In the last few hundred years, the major stimulus to culture change, adaptive and maladaptive, has been the new social environment produced by the arrival of people from Western societies.

TYPES OF CULTURE CHANGE IN THE MODERN WORLD

Many of the cultural changes in the world from A.D. 1500 to the present have been caused, directly or indirectly, by the dominance and expansion of Western societies.[23] Thus, much of the culture change in the modern world has been externally induced, if not forced. This is not to say that cultures are changing now only because of external pressures; but externally induced changes have been the changes most frequently studied by anthropologists and other social scientists. Most of the external pressures have come from Western societies, but not all. Eastern societies, such as Japan and China, have also stimulated culture change. And the expansion of Islamic societies after the eighth century A.D. made for an enormous amount of culture change in the Near East, Africa, Europe, and Asia.

COMMERCIALIZATION

One of the most important changes resulting from the expansion of Western societies is the increasingly worldwide dependence on commercial exchange. The borrowed customs of buying and selling may at first be supplementary to traditional means of distributing goods in a society. But as the new commercial customs take hold, the economic base of the receiving society alters. Inevitably, this alteration is accompanied by other changes, which have broad social, political, and even psychological ramifications.

In examining contemporary patterns of change, however, we should bear in mind that commercialization has occurred in many parts of the world in the ancient past. The Chinese, Persians, Greeks, Romans, Arabs, Phoenicians, and Hindus were some of the early state societies that pushed commercial enterprises in other areas. We may cast some light on how and why some earlier cultures changed when we consider several questions: How, and why, does a contemporary society change from a subsistence to a commercial economic base? What are the resultant cultural changes? Why do they occur?

In general, the limited evidence available suggests that a previously noncommercial people may begin to sell and buy things simply in order to live, not just because they may be attracted by goods they can obtain only by commercial exchange. If the resources available to a group have been significantly reduced per person—because the group has been forced to resettle on a small "reservation" or because population has increased—the group may be likely to take advantage of any commercial opportunities

Research Frontiers

OBESITY, HYPERTENSION, AND DIABETES: HEALTH CONSEQUENCES OF MODERNIZATION?

Contact with the West first brought medical devastation to many populations previously unexposed to European illnesses. However, with the acceptance of modern medical care throughout much of the developing world, infant mortality has declined and life expectancies have gone up. These achievements have largely come about because of the control of major epidemic diseases, such as smallpox (now eradicated), cholera, yellow fever, syphilis, and tuberculosis, as well as the innoculation of children against childhood diseases. Improvements in medical health are by no means uniform. The AIDS epidemic, which we discuss in the next chapter, is spreading throughout much of the world. Overall deaths from infectious diseases may have declined, but other health problems have increased. As more people survive into older ages, problems of hypertension, heart disease, cancer, and diabetes increase. Some of the increase in these chronic diseases is due to the aging of populations, but much of it appears to be due to changes in life-style that accompany modernization.

A good deal of research has focused on the Samoans of the

When food is not plentiful, the "thrifty gene" helps people survive on less. But when the food supply becomes plentiful and reliable, people may become overweight, as in the Marquesas.

that become available, even if such opportunities require considerably more work time and effort.[24]

MIGRATORY LABOR. One way commercialization can occur is for some members of a community to move to a place that offers the possibility of working for wages. This happened in Tikopia, an island near the Solomon Islands in the South Pacific. In 1929, when Raymond Firth first studied the island, its economy was still essentially noncommercial—simple, self-sufficient, and largely self-contained.[25] Some Western goods were available but, with the exception of iron and steel in limited quantities, not sought after. Their possession and use were associated solely with Europeans. This situation changed dramatically with World War II. During the war, military forces occupied neighboring islands, and people from Tikopia migrated to those islands to find employment. In the period following the war, several large commercial interests extended their activities in the Solomons, thus creating a continued demand for labor. As a result, when Firth revisited Tikopia in 1952, he found the economic situation significantly altered.

South Pacific. As we noted in the chapter on food getting, the Samoans traditionally depended on root and tree crop horticulture. As did many other people in the modern world, Samoans increasingly moved to urban areas, worked for wages, and started buying most of their food. Researchers reported substantial increases, within a relatively short time, in rates of hypertension, diabetes, and obesity across a wide range of age groups. For example, in 1990 about two-thirds of American Samoans were severely overweight, up substantially from the situation in the 1970s. And Samoans from more rural areas show less hypertension and physiological signs of stress. Among the life-style changes thought to be responsible are less physical activity and changes in diet to low-fiber, high-calorie foods. Stress may also increase as more individuals buy material things and status goods without having the economic resources to support them.

What about genetic factors? Could some genetic predisposition be interacting with modernization to create obesity in the Samoan population? One possibility is referred to as the "thrifty" gene. The geneticist James Neel suggested that individuals who have very efficient metabolisms and who can store calories in fatty tissue are most apt to survive and reproduce in environments with frequent famines or chronic food shortages. In time, populations in such environments would have a high prevalence of individuals with "thrifty" genes. What happens though when such individuals no longer need to exercise much or have access to high-calorie foods? Neel suggested that adult-onset diabetes might result, a scenario that is consistent with the increase in diabetes in Samoa and other parts of Polynesia. It is also consistent with the increase in obesity and hypertension.

The "thrifty" gene theory does not just pertain to the Samoans and other Polynesian populations. Probably most human populations used to have to cope with food uncertainty in the past. If the food supply increases with modernization, but it is accompanied by a reduction in physical activity and a switch to high-calorie diets, then increases in obesity, diabetes, and hypertension may frequently accompany modernization. Understanding both biological and cultural factors is essential in helping populations adapt to conditions of urban life.

Sources: John S. Allen and Susan M. Cheer, "The Non-Thrifty Genotype," *Current Anthropology,* 37 (1996): 831–42; James R. Bindon and Douglas E. Crews, "Changes in Some Health Status Characteristics of American Samoan Men: Preliminary Observations from a 12-Year Follow-up Study," *American Journal of Human Biology,* 5 (1993): 31–37; James R. Bindon, Amy Knight, William W. Dressler, and Douglas E. Crews, "Social Context and Psychosocial Influences on Blood Pressure among American Samoans," *American Journal of Physical Anthropology,* 103 (1997): 7–18; Stephen T. McGarvey, "The Thrifty Gene Concept and Adiposity Studies in Biological Anthropology," *Journal of the Polynesian Society,* 103 (1994): 29–42; J. D. Pearson, Gary D. James, and Daniel E. Brown, "Stress and Changing Lifestyles in the Pacific: Physiological Stress Responses of Samoans in Rural and Urban Settings," *American Journal of Human Biology,* 5 (1993): 49–60; World Bank, *World Development Report 1995. Workers in an Integrating World.* (Oxford: Oxford University Press, 1995).

More than 100 Tikopians had left the island to work for varying periods. The migrants wanted to earn money because they aspired to standards of living previously regarded as appropriate only to Europeans. Already living conditions on Tikopia were changing. Western cooking and water-carrying utensils, mosquito nets, kerosene storm lamps, and so forth had come to be regarded as normal items in a Tikopia household.

The introduction of money into the economy of Tikopia not only altered the economic system but also affected other areas of life. Compared with the situation in 1929, land was under more intensive cultivation in 1952, with manioc and sweet potatoes supplementing the principal taro crop. Pressures on the food supply resulting from improved living standards and an increased population seem to have weakened the ties of extended kinship. For example, the nuclear families constituting the extended family (the land-holding and land-using unit in 1929) were not cooperating as much in 1952. In many cases, in fact, the land had actually been split up among the constituent nuclear families; land rights had become more individualized. People were no longer as willing to share with members of their extended family, particularly with respect to the money and goods acquired by working in the Solomons.

NONAGRICULTURAL COMMERCIAL PRODUCTION. Commercialization can also occur when a self-sufficient hunting or agricultural society comes to depend more and more on trading for its livelihood. Such a change is exemplified by the Mundurucú of the Amazon Basin, who largely abandoned general horticulture for commercial rubber production. A similar change may also be seen in the Montagnais of northeastern Canada, who came to depend increasingly on commercial fur trapping, rather than hunting, for subsistence. Robert Murphy and Julian Steward found that when modern goods from industrialized areas became available through trade, both the Mundurucú and the Montagnais devoted their energies to making specialized cash crops or other trade items. They did this to obtain other industrially made objects.[26] The primary socioeconomic change that occurred among the Mundurucú and the Montagnais was a shift from cooperative labor and community autonomy to individualized economic activity and a dependence on an external market.

Among the Mundurucú, for example, before close trading links were established, the native population and the Europeans had been in contact for some 80 years without the Mundurucú way of life being noticeably altered. The men did give up their independent military activities in order to perform as mercenaries for the Brazilians, but they continued to maintain their horticultural economy. Some trading took place with Brazilians, with the chief acting as agent for the village. Barter was the method of exchange. Traders first distributed their wares, ranging from cheap cottons to iron hatchets, trinkets, and so on; they returned about three months later to collect manioc, India rubber, and beans from the Mundurucú. At this time (1860), however, rubber was only a secondary item of commerce.

The rapidly growing demand for rubber from the 1860s onward increased the importance of Mundurucú-trader relationships. Traders now openly began to appoint agents, called *capitoes,* whose job it was to encourage greater rubber production. *Capitoes* were given economic privileges and hence power, both of which began to undercut the position of the traditional chief. In addition, the process of rubber collection itself began to alter Mundurucú social patterns by moving people away from their jungle-based communities.

Wild rubber trees are found only along rivers, which are often a considerable distance from the jungle habitat of the Mundurucú and can be exploited only during the dry season (late May to December). So the Mundurucú man who elected to gather rubber had to separate himself from his family for about half the year. Furthermore, rubber collecting is a solitary activity. Each tapper must work his territory, consisting of about 150 trees, daily, and he must live close to his trees because the work lasts all day. Therefore, the tapper usually lives alone or in a small group except during the rainy season, when he returns to his village.

At this stage in the commercialization process, the Mundurucú became increasingly dependent on goods supplied by the trader. Firearms were useless without regular quantities of powder and lead or shot; clothing required needles and thread for repairs. But these items could be earned only through increased rubber production, which in turn led to greater dependency on the outside world. Inevitably, the ability to work with traditional materials and the desire to maintain traditional crafts disappeared. Metal pots took the place of clay ones, and manufactured hammocks replaced homemade ones. Gradually the village agricultural cycle ceased to be adhered to by all in the community so that rubber production would not suffer. The authority of the traditional chiefs was weakened as that of the *capitoes* was enhanced.

The point of no return was reached when significant numbers of Mundurucú abandoned the villages for permanent settlements near their individual territories of trees. These new settlements lacked the unity, the sense of community, of former village life. Property was held by nuclear families and carefully maintained in the interest of productivity.

With the discovery of gold, many Mundurucú young men have recently turned to panning for gold in rivers. The required equipment is simple, and gold is easier to transport and trade than rubber. Because gold can be sold for cash, which is then used for purchases, trading relationships are no longer so important. Cash is now used to buy transistor radios, tape recorders, watches, bicycles, and new kinds of clothing, in addition to firearms, metal pots, and tools. With money as a medium of exchange, the traditional emphasis on reciprocity has declined. Even food may now be sold to fellow Mundurucú, a practice that would have been unthinkable in the 1950s.[27]

SUPPLEMENTARY CASH CROPS. A third way commercialization occurs is when people cultivating the soil produce a surplus above their subsistence requirements, which is then sold for cash. In many cases, this cash income must be used to pay rent or taxes. Under these circumstances, commercialization may be said to be associated with the formation of a peasantry. **Peasants** are rural people who produce food for their own subsistence, but they must also contribute or sell their surpluses to others, in towns and cities, who do not produce their own food.

Peasants first appeared with the emergence of state and urban civilizations about 5,000 to 6,000 years ago, and they have been associated with civilization ever since.[28] To say that peasants are associated with urban societies perhaps needs some qualification. The contemporary, highly industrialized urban society has little need of peasants. Their scale of production is small and their use of land "uneconomic." A highly industrialized society with a large population of non-food producers requires mechanized agriculture. As a result, the peasant has passed, or is passing, out of all but the most peripheral existence in industrial countries. It is the preindustrial city, and the social organization it represents, that generates and maintains peasants. They cultivate land; they furnish the required quantity of food, rent, and profit on which the remainder of society, particularly the people in the cities, depends.

Commercialization can occur when people begin to produce a cash crop such as coffee for sale, as in Thailand.

What changes does the development of a peasantry entail? In some respects there is little disturbance of the cultivator's (now peasant's) former way of life. The peasant still has to produce enough food to meet family needs, to replace what has been consumed, to cover a few ceremonial obligations (for example, the marriage of a child, village festivals, and funerals). But in other respects the peasant's situation is radically altered. For in addition to the traditional obligations—indeed, often in conflict with them—the peasant now has to produce extra crops to meet the requirements of a group of outsiders— landlords or officials of the state. These outsiders expect to be paid rent or taxes in produce or currency, and they are able to enforce their expectations because they control the military and the police.

Although no two peasant cultures are exactly alike, there are similarities in form. Peasants the world over are faced with the problem of balancing the demands of an external world against those of an internal society. Their response generally involves increasing production, curtailing domestic consumption, or both.

INTRODUCTION OF COMMERCIAL AND INDUSTRIAL AGRICULTURE. Commercialization can come about through the introduction of commercial agriculture. In commercial agriculture, *all* the cultivated commodities are produced for sale rather than for personal consumption. Along with this change, the system of agriculture may be industrialized. In other words, some of the production processes, such as plowing, weeding, irrigation, and harvesting, are done by machine. Commercial agriculture is, in fact, often as mechanized as any manufacturing industry. Land is worked for the maximum return it will yield, and labor is hired and fired just as impersonally as in other industries.

E. J. Hobsbawm noted some of the developments that accompanied the introduction of commercial agriculture in eighteenth-century England and in continental Europe somewhat later.[29] The close, near-familial relationship between farmer and farm laborer disappeared, as did the once-personal connection between landlord and tenant. Land came to be regarded as a source of profit rather than a way of life. Fields were merged into single units and enclosed, and local grazing and similar privileges were reduced. Labor was hired at market rates and paid in wages. Eventually, as the emphasis on large-scale production for a mass market increased, machines began to replace farmers.

The introduction of commercial agriculture brings several important social consequences. Gradually, a class polarization develops. Farmers and landlords become increasingly separated from laborers and tenants, just as in the town the employer becomes socially separated from the employees. Gradually, too, manufactured items of all sorts are introduced into rural areas. Laborers migrate to urban centers in search of employment, often meeting even less sympathetic conditions there than exist in the country.

The changeover to commercial agriculture may result in an improved standard of living in the short and long run. But sometimes the switch is followed by a decline in the standard of living if the market price for the commercial crop declines. For example, the changeover of the farmer-herders of the arid *sertão* region of northeastern Brazil after 1940 to the production of sisal (a plant whose fibers can be made into twine and rope) seemed to be a move that could provide a more secure living in their arid environment. But when the world price for sisal dropped and the wages of sisal workers declined, many workers were forced to curtail the caloric intake of their children. The poorer people were obliged to save their

The sale of woven crafts has been an old custom in Guatemala.

now more limited food supplies for the money earners, at the expense of the children.[30]

Commercialization can start in various ways: People can begin to sell and buy because they begin to work near home or away for wages, or because they begin to sell nonagricultural products, surplus food, or cash crops (crops grown deliberately for sale). One type of commercialization does not exclude another; all types can occur in any society. However commercialization begins, it seems to have predictable effects on traditional economics. The ethic of generalized reciprocity declines, particularly with respect to giving money away. (Perhaps because it is nonperishable and hideable, money seems more likely than other goods to be kept for one's immediate family rather than shared with others.) Property rights become individualized rather than collective when people begin to buy and sell. And even in societies that were previously egalitarian, commercialization usually results in more unequal access to resources and hence a greater degree of social stratification.

RELIGIOUS CHANGE

Of course, commercialization is not the only type of culture change in the modern world. The growing influence of Western societies has also led to religious change in many places. Often, the change has been brought about intentionally through the efforts of missionaries, who have been among the first Westerners to travel to interior regions and out-of-the-way places. Missionaries have not met with equal success in all parts of the world. In some places, large portions of the native population have converted to the new religion with great zeal. In others, missionaries have been ignored, forced to flee, or even killed. We do not fully understand why missionaries have been successful in some societies and not in others. Yet, in many parts of the world, Western missionary activity has been a potent force for all kinds of cultural, and particularly religious, change. One possible reason is that missionaries offer resources that enable natives to minimize economic and other risks in the new, Western-dominated social environment.[31]

But aside from the direct effects of missionary work, contact with Westerners has often produced religious change in more indirect ways. In some native societies, contact with Westerners has led to a breakdown of social structure and the growth of feelings of helplessness and spiritual demoralization. In the chapter on religion and magic, we discussed how revitalization movements have arisen as apparent attempts to restore such societies to their former confidence and prosperity. We now examine the process of conversion on the island of Tikopia,

as an example of religious change brought about by direct contact with missionaries.

CHRISTIANITY ON TIKOPIA. Tikopia was one of the few Polynesian societies to retain its traditional religious system into the first decades of the twentieth century. An Anglican mission was first established on the island in 1911. With it came a deacon and the founding of two schools for about 200 pupils. By 1929, approximately half the population had converted, and in the early 1960s almost all Tikopia gave at least nominal allegiance to Christianity.[32]

Traditional Tikopian belief embraced a great number of gods and spirits of various ranks who inhabited the sky, the water, and the land. One god in particular—the original creator and shaper of the culture—was given a place of special importance, but he was in no way comparable to the all-powerful God of Christianity. Unlike Christianity, Tikopian religion made no claim to universality. The Tikopian gods did not rule over all creation, only over Tikopia. It was thought that if one left Tikopia, one left the gods behind.

The people of Tikopia interacted with their gods and spirits primarily through religious leaders who were also the heads of descent groups. Clan chiefs presided over rituals centering in the everyday aspects of island life, such as house construction, fishing, planting, and harvesting. The chief was expected to intercede with the gods on the people's behalf, to persuade them to bring happiness and prosperity to the group. Indeed, when conditions were good it was assumed that the chief was doing

On the island of Tahiti, as in many Polynesian islands, missionaries were very successful in converting people to Christianity. If they could persuade the chiefs, they were likely to persuade many others to convert as well.

his job well. When disaster struck, the prestige of the chief often fell in proportion. Why did the Tikopia convert to Christianity? Firth suggested several contributing factors.

First, the mission offered the people the prospect of acquiring new tools and consumer goods. Although conversion alone did not provide such benefits, attachment to the mission was believed to make them more attainable. Later, it became apparent that education, particularly in reading and writing English, was helpful in getting ahead in the outside world. Mission schooling became valued and provided a further incentive for adopting Christianity.

Second, conversion may have been facilitated by the ability of chiefs, as religious and political leaders, to bring over entire kin groups to Christianity. Should a chief decide to transfer his allegiance to Christianity, the members of his kin group usually followed him, since social etiquette required that they do so. Such a situation actually developed in 1923 when Tafua, chief of the Faea district of Tikopia, converted to the new religion. He brought with him his entire group—nearly half the population of the island. The ability of the chiefs to influence their kin groups, however, was both an asset and a hindrance to missionary efforts, since some chiefs steadfastly resisted conversion.

A final blow to traditional Tikopian religion came in 1955, when a severe epidemic killed at least 200 people in a population of about 1,700. According

Research Frontiers

CULTURE CHANGE AND PERSISTENCE IN COMMUNIST CHINA

In the years since the 1949 Communist takeover in China, the central government has initiated a variety of changes in family life. Many of these changes were literally forced; people who resisted them were often resettled or jailed. Ancestor worship and lineage organization were attacked or declared illegal. Most private property was abolished, undermining family loyalties. Why participate in family activities if there could be no economic reward? Still, the actions of the central government did not completely change family life. Even coercion has its limits.

The government may have wanted to restrict the family and kinship, but its investments in public health and famine relief reduced mortality, thereby strengthening family ties. Fewer infants died, more children lived long enough to marry, old age became more common—all of these developments allowed people in all social classes to have larger and more complex networks of kin than were possible before 1949. To be sure, government policies undercut the power and authority of extended family patriarchs. But the new healthier conditions were conducive to large, multigenerational households with economic as well as social ties to other kin.

As China became more accessible to anthropologists and other researchers from abroad, many investigators came to study the variability and similarity in Chinese family life. Most of these studies focused on the dominant Han Chinese (the Han constitute about 95 percent of the total population of China); investigators have also studied many of the 55 "recognized" minority cultures in China. Burton Pasternak, a U.S. anthropologist, Janet Salaff, a Canadian sociologist, and Chinese sociologists studied four communities of Han who had moved outside the Great Wall to colonize the Inner Mongolian frontier. (Inner Mongolia is part of China.) The results of their study suggest that, despite strong pressures from the government, what changes or persists in a culture mainly reflects what is possible ecologically and economically. A tradition of intensive agriculture cannot persist in the absence of sufficient watering. The government's insistence on one child per family cannot withstand a family's need for more children.

Han farmers who crossed the Great Wall were searching for a better life. They found difficulties in climate and soil that forced many to return home. But many adjusted to the grasslands and remained. Some continued to depend on farming on the fringes of the grasslands. Others farther out on the grasslands became herders. The Han who switched to herding are now in many respects more like the native Mongol herders than like Han or Mongol farmers. The gender division of labor among the Han pastoralists became much

to Firth, "the epidemic was largely interpreted as a sign of divine discrimination," because three of the outstanding non-Christian religious leaders died.[33] Subsequently, the remaining non-Christian chiefs voluntarily converted to Christianity and so did their followers. By 1966, all Tikopia, with the exception of one rebellious old woman, had converted to the new faith.

Although many Tikopians feel their conversion to Christianity has been a unifying, revitalizing force, the changeover from one religion to another has not been without problems. Christian missionaries on Tikopia have succeeded in eliminating the traditional Tikopian population-control devices of abortion, infanticide, and male celibacy. It is very possible that the absence of these controls will continue to intensify population pressure. The island, with its limited capacity to support life, can ill afford this outcome. Firth summed up the situation Tikopian society must now face:

> In the history of Tikopia complete conversion of the people to Christianity was formerly regarded as a solution to their problems; it is now coming to be realized that the adoption and practice of Christianity itself represents another set of problems. As the Tikopia themselves are beginning to see, to be Christian Polynesians in the modern technologically and industrially dominated world, even in the Solomon Islands, poses as many questions as it supplies answers.[34]

sharper than among the Han farmers since men are often far away with the herds. Pastoralist children, not that useful in herding because mistakes can be very costly, are more likely than farm children to stay in school for a long time. Perhaps because of the greater usefulness of children on the farm, Han farm families have more children than Han pastoralists. But both groups have more than one child per family. Herdsmen are less likely than farmers to need cooperative labor, so Han pastoralists are more likely to live as a neolocal independent family than as a patrilocal extended family (which was traditional). In short, the adjustment of the Han to the grasslands seems to be explained more by ecological requirements than by ethnic traditions.

Although an increasing number of Han have become more like Mongols in their pastoral adaptations, many Mongols have adopted an urban way of life and moved away from their pastoral life. The Chinese government was initially responsible for encouraging non-Mongols to move into Inner Mongolia, particularly into its new capital, Huhhot. At the same time, many Mongols moved from the grasslands and into the capital city. Chinese government policy was intended to make each non-Han ethnic group a minority in its traditional land, but the government paradoxically also tried to encourage minority ethnic pride in their traditional culture. So the city of Huhhot is filled with images of the traditional herding culture in its buildings and monuments.

As described by the anthropologist William Jankowiak, who studied the Mongols in the capital city of Huhhot, the results were not what the Chinese government intended. In many ways, to be sure, the urban Mongols had abandoned their traditional culture and assimilated to the dominant Han culture. But we see the force of ecology more than the hand of tradition in the outcome. Many Mongols in the city no longer speak the Mongol language. Parents find it difficult to get children to speak Mongol when they live among Han. And the scarcity of housing makes it difficult for the Mongols to form an ethnic enclave, or even live near kin as they did in the past. In contrast to life in the rural areas, which revolves around kinship, city life requires interacting with strangers as well as relatives. Indeed, nonkin are often more important to you than kin. As one person said to Jankowiak, "We hide from our cousins but not our friends."

Sources: Deborah Davis and Stevan Harrell, eds., *Chinese Families in the Post-Mao Era* (Berkeley: University of California Press, 1993); Burton Pasternak, "Han: Pastoralists and Farmers on a Chinese Frontier," in Melvin Ember, Carol R. Ember, and David Levinson, eds., *Portraits of Culture: Ethnographic Originals* (Upper Saddle River, NJ: Prentice Hall, 1998); Prentice Hall/Simon & Schuster Custom Publishing; William R. Jankowiak, "Urban Mongols: Ethnicity in Communist China," in Ember, Ember, and Levinson, eds., *Portraits of Culture: Ethnographic Originals.*

Unfortunately, not all native peoples have made the transition to Christianity as painlessly as the Tikopia. In fact, in most cases the record is dismal. All too frequently, missionary activity tends to destroy a society's culture and self-respect. It offers nothing in return but an alien, repressive system of values ill suited to the people's real needs and aspirations. Phillip Mason, a critic of European evangelists in Africa, pointed out some of the psychological damage inflicted by missionary activity.[35] The missionaries repeatedly stressed sin and guilt; they used the color black to represent evil and the color white to signify good; and they showed hostility toward pagan culture. Most damaging of all was their promise that the African, provided she or he adopted the European's ways, would gain access both to the European's heaven and to European society. But no matter how diligently Africans attempted to follow missionary precepts or climb the socioeconomic ladder, they were soon blocked from entry into European homes, clubs, and even churches and seminaries.

POLITICAL AND SOCIAL CHANGE

In addition to commercialization and religious change brought about by the expansion of Western and other countries, political changes have often occurred when a foreign system of government has been imposed. But, as recent events in the former Soviet Union and South Africa indicate, dramatic changes in a political system can also occur more or less voluntarily. Perhaps the most striking type of political change in recent years is the spread of participatory forms of government—"democracy."

To political scientists, democracy is usually defined in terms of voting by a substantial proportion of the citizenry, governments brought to power by periodic contested elections, a chief executive either popularly elected or responsible to an elected legislature, and often also civil liberties such as free speech. Depending on which criteria are used, only 12 to 15 countries qualified as democracies as of the beginning of the twentieth century. The number decreased after World War I, as emerging democratic institutions were replaced in Russia, Italy, Germany, central Europe, Japan, and elsewhere. After World War II, despite all the rhetoric associated with the founding of the United Nations, the picture was not much different. Some members of the new North Atlantic Treaty Organization (NATO) were not democracies, and neither were many members of the wider Western alliance system, in Latin America, the Middle East, and Asia.

It was not until the 1970s and 1980s that people, not just political scientists, started noticing that democracy was becoming more common in the world. By the early 1990s, President George Bush

Democracy—contested elections with widespread voting—is spreading around the world. In this rural area of South Africa, people line up to vote.

and then-candidate Bill Clinton were talking about the spread of the "democratic peace." As of 1992, about half of the countries in the world had more or less democratic governments, and others were in transition to democracy.[36] Social scientists do not yet understand why this change is happening. But it is possible that the global communication of ideas has a lot to do with it. Authoritarian governments can censor their own newspapers and prevent group meetings, but they really cannot stop the movement of ideas via telephone lines and the Internet. The movement of ideas, of course, does not explain the acceptance of those ideas. Why democracy has recently diffused to more countries than ever before still requires explanation.

Another frequent type of culture change in the modern world is increasing social stratification. Because of economic change, some groups become more privileged and powerful than others. For example, it has been suggested that the introduction of new technology may generally make for an *increase* in degree of social stratification.[37] When the snowmobile began to be used for herding by the Lapps, those who for various reasons could participate in the "snowmobile revolution" gained economic, social, and political advantages. But those who could not acquire the new machines tended to become an economically and generally deprived class—without machines *or* reindeer.[38]

Western influence has also brought about changes in dress, music, art, and attitudes throughout the world. The appeal of "popular" music, for example, is more and more international, whether or not it originates in the West.

CULTURAL DIVERSITY IN THE FUTURE

Measured in terms of travel time, the world today is much smaller than it has ever been. It is possible now to fly halfway around the globe in the time it took people less than a century ago to travel to the next state. In the realm of communication, the world is even smaller. We can talk to someone on the other side of the globe in a matter of minutes, we can send that person a message (by fax or Internet) in seconds, and through television we can see live coverage of events in that person's country. More and more people are drawn into the world market economy, buying and selling similar things and, as a consequence, altering the patterns of their lives in sometimes similar ways. Although modern transportation and communication facilitate the rapid spread of some cultural characteristics to all parts of

the globe, it is highly unlikely that all parts will end up the same. Cultures are bound to retain some of their original characteristics or develop some distinctive new adaptations. Even though television has diffused around the world, local people prefer to watch local programming when it is available. And even when people all over the world watch the same program, they may interpret it in very different ways. People are not just absorbing the messages they get; they may resist them or rework them.[39]

Future research on contemporary culture change should increase our understanding of how and why various types of change are occurring. And if we can increase our understanding of culture change in the present, we should be better able to understand similar processes in the past. Another lead to understanding change in the past is the large number of cross-cultural correlations between a cultural variation and its presumed causes that have been discovered since the 1970s.[40] All cultures have changed over time. Therefore the variations we see are the products of change processes, and the discovered predictors of those variations may suggest how and why the changes occurred.

SUMMARY

1. Culture is always changing. Because culture consists of learned patterns of behavior and belief, cultural traits can be unlearned and learned anew as human needs change.

2. Discoveries and inventions, though ultimately the sources of all culture change, do not necessarily lead to change. Only when society accepts an invention or discovery and uses it regularly can culture change be said to have occurred. Some inventions are probably the result of dozens of tiny, perhaps accidental, initiatives over a period of many years. Other inventions are consciously intended. Why some people are more innovative than others is still only incompletely understood. There is some evidence that creativity and a readiness to adopt innovations may be related to socioeconomic position.

3. The process by which cultural elements are borrowed from another society and incorporated into the culture of the recipient group is called diffusion. Three patterns of diffusion may be identified: diffusion by direct contact, in which elements of a culture are first taken up by neighboring societies and then gradually spread farther and farther afield; diffusion by intermediate contact, in which third parties, frequently traders, carry a cultural trait from the society originating it to another group; and

stimulus diffusion, in which knowledge of a trait belonging to another culture stimulates the invention or development of a local equivalent.

4. Cultural traits do not necessarily diffuse; that is, diffusion is a selective, not automatic, process. A society accepting a foreign cultural trait is likely to adapt it in a way that effectively harmonizes it with the society's own traditions.

5. When a group or society is in contact with a more powerful society, the weaker group is often obliged to acquire cultural elements from the dominant group. This process of extensive borrowing in the context of superordinate-subordinate relations between societies is called acculturation. In contrast with diffusion, acculturation comes about as a result of some sort of external pressure.

6. Perhaps the most drastic and rapid way a culture can change is by revolution—a usually violent replacement of the society's rulers. Rebellions occur primarily in state societies, where there is a distinct ruling elite. However, not all peoples who are suppressed, conquered, or colonized eventually rebel or successfully revolt against established authority.

7. Even though customs are not genetically inherited, cultural adaptation may be somewhat similar to biological adaptation. Traits (cultural or genetic) that are more likely to be reproduced (learned or inherited) are likely to become more frequent in a population over time. And if culture is generally adapted to its environment, then culture change should also be generally adaptive.

8. Many of the cultural changes observed in the modern world have been generated, directly or indirectly, by the dominance and expansion of Western societies. One of the principal changes resulting from the expansion of Western culture is the increasing dependence of much of the world on commercial exchange—that is, the proliferation of buying and selling in markets, usually accompanied by the use of money as the medium of exchange. The borrowed custom of buying and selling may at first be supplementary to traditional means of distributing goods, but as the new commercial customs take hold, the economic base of the receiving society alters. Inevitably, this alteration is accompanied by other changes, which have broad social, political, and even psychological ramifications.

9. One way commercialization can occur is for members of a community to become migratory workers, traveling to a place nearby that offers the possibility of working for wages. Commercialization can also occur when a simple, self-sufficient hunting or agricultural society comes to depend more and more on trading for its livelihood. A third way commercialization occurs is when those cultivating the soil produce more than they require for subsistence. The surplus is then sold for cash. In many instances, this cash income must be used to pay rent or taxes; under such circumstances, commercialization may be said to be associated with the formation of a peasantry. A fourth way in which commercialization can come about is through the introduction of commercial agriculture, in which *all* the cultivated commodities are produced for sale rather than for personal consumption. Along with this change, the system of agriculture may be industrialized, with some of the production processes being done by machine.

10. The growing influence of Western societies has also led to religious change in many parts of the world. In many societies, such change has been brought about intentionally through the efforts of missionaries.

11. One of the most striking types of culture change in the modern world is the spread of democracies. Participatory political institutions are now found in a majority of the world's countries.

GLOSSARY TERMS

acculturation	peasants
diffusion	revolution

CRITICAL QUESTIONS

1. What kinds of cultural items might most easily be borrowed by another culture, and why do you think so?

2. The expansion of the West has had terrible consequences for many peoples. Have there been any beneficial consequences?

3. Why might an increasing understanding of cultural variation also provide an increasing understanding of culture change?

INTERNET EXERCISES

1. While some political entities are breaking apart, others are integrating. How is Europe changing politically and economically? Look at the Web site on the European Parliament and summarize what it does (**http://www.europarl.eu.int/**). Also look at the site on the single European currency at **http://europa.eu.int/euro/**. What are the implications of an integrated Europe?

2. In English, the word *man* has traditionally been used to refer to humans generally. Not too long ago, anthropology was usually defined as the study of man. Many have argued that such phraseology enhances gender stereotypes and discrimination, so they have tried to encourage changes in the way a society uses language. Go to **http://www. macarthur.uws.edu.au/HR/policies/nonsexis.htm** to see some suggestions for more neutral gender language.

3. One organization dedicated to helping avoid the destruction of other cultures is Cultural Survival. Go to their online journal, Active Voices, and read one or two articles. The site is at **http:// www.cs.org/index.html**.

4. Computers and the Internet are resulting in global culture change. Different groups of people, large and small, are able to present themselves to others around the world. Go to the site **http:// www.pitt.edu/~lmitten/indians** to find individual Native American Web sites. Look at one such site to see what they present about themselves.

▨ SUGGESTED READING

Bernard, H. R., and Pelto, P. J., eds. *Technology and Social Change,* 2nd ed. Prospect Heights, IL: Waveland Press, 1987. This volume is concerned with the effects of introduced Western technology on diverse cultures. Thirteen case studies were written especially for the volume; the editors provide concluding observations.

Bodley, J. H. *Victims of Progress,* 3rd ed. Mountain View, CA: Mayfield, 1990. An examination of the effects of industrial nations on tribal peoples. Emphasizes the imperialist and exploitative practices of expansionist nations, as well as the destructive consequences of imposed "progress."

Boyd, R., and Richerson, P. J. *Culture and the Evolutionary Process.* Chicago: University of Chicago Press, 1985. The authors develop mathematical models to analyze how genes and culture interact, under the influence of evolutionary processes, to produce the diversity we see in human cultures.

Ember, M., Ember, C. R., and Levinson, D., eds. *Portraits of Culture: Ethnographic Originals.* Upper Saddle River, NJ: Prentice Hall, 1998. Prentice Hall/Simon & Schuster Custom Publishing. Most of the mini-ethnographies in this series discuss the changes in culture that have occurred in recent times.

Goldstone, J. A. "The Comparative and Historical Study of Revolutions." *Annual Review of Sociology,* 8 (1982): 187–207. A review of theory and research on why revolutions have occurred, and why some succeeded, in the past and present.

Herbig, P. A. *The Innovation Matrix: Culture and Structure Prerequisites to Innovation.* Westport, CT: Quorum Books, 1994. A discussion of the factors that may enable some societies to adapt and change more quickly than others.

McNeill, W. H. *Plagues and Peoples.* Garden City, NY: Doubleday Anchor, 1976. A historian suggests that epidemics have crucially affected the history of various societies all over the world.

Rogers, E. M. *Diffusion of Innovations,* 3rd ed. New York: Free Press, 1983. This book examines the roles of information and uncertainty in the spread of innovations, how different categories of people adopt innovations at different rates, and how change agents affect the process. A large literature is reviewed and synthesized.

25

Applied Anthropology and Social Problems

The news on radio and television and in the newspapers makes us aware every day that social problems threaten people around the world. From war to crime and family violence, from AIDS to poverty and famine, the pursuit of happiness and even life itself are jeopardized for many people in many places.

Worldwide communication has increased our awareness of problems elsewhere, and we seem to be increasingly bothered by problems in our own society. For these two reasons, and perhaps also because we know more than we used to about human behavior, we may be more motivated to try to solve those problems. We call them "social" problems not only because a lot of people worry about them but also because they have social causes or consequences, and their possible treatments or solutions require at least some changes in social behavior. For example, AIDS may be caused by a family of viruses, but it is also a social problem because it is mostly transmitted by sexual contact with another person. Thus, the only ways to avoid it now—abstinence, "safe" sex—require changes in social behavior. The lives of millions are at risk because of this global social problem.

Anthropology and most of the other social sciences have long been concerned with social problems. One way in which this concern is expressed is through "basic research" that tests theories about the possible causes of social problems. The results of such tests could suggest solutions to the problems if the causes, once discovered, can be reduced or eliminated. Another way to be concerned with social problems is to participate in or evaluate programs intended to improve people's lives. **Applied** or **practicing anthropology** as a profession is explicitly concerned with making anthropological knowledge useful. Applied or practicing anthropologists may be involved in one or more phases of a program: assembling relevant knowledge, developing plans, assessing the likely social and environmental impact of particular plans, implementing the program, and monitoring the program and its effects.[1]

Clearly, theory testing and applied research may both be motivated by a desire to improve the quality of human life. But it is often difficult to decide if a particular project is basic or applied. For example, consider a study of the possible causes of war; its results may suggest how the risk of war might be reduced. Is such a study basic or applied research?

This chapter has two major parts. The first deals with applied or practicing anthropology. We discuss its history and types of application in the United States, the ethical issues involved in trying to improve people's lives, the difficulties in evaluating whether a program is beneficial, and the problems in instituting planned change. In the second part of the chapter we turn to the study of global social problems and how understanding the possible causes of these problems may suggest possible solutions. We focus on research done by anthropologists and other kinds of comparative researchers that may help us better understand the spread of AIDS, disasters, homelessness, crime, family violence, and war.

APPLIED AND PRACTICING ANTHROPOLOGY

Anthropologists care and worry about the people they study, just as they care and worry about family and friends back home. It is upsetting if most of the families in your place of fieldwork have lost many of their babies to diseases that could be eliminated by medical care. It is upsetting when outside political and economic interests threaten to deprive your fieldwork friends of their resources and pride. Anthropologists have usually studied people who are disadvantaged—by imperialism, colonialism, and other forms of exploitation—and so it is no wonder that we feel protective about these people, whom we have lived and shared with in the field.

But caring is not enough to improve others' lives. We may need basic research that allows us to understand how a condition might be successfully treated. A particular proposed "improvement" might actually not be an improvement; well-meaning efforts have sometimes produced harmful consequences. And even if we know that a change would be an improvement, there is still the problem of how to make it happen. The people to be affected may not want to change. Is it ethical to try to persuade them? And, conversely, is it ethical not to try? Applied anthropologists must take all of these matters into consideration in determining whether and how to act in response to a perceived need.

Applied anthropology in the United States developed out of anthropologists' personal experiences with disadvantaged people in other cultures.[2] Today anthropologists are also interested in studying and solving problems in our own society. Anthropologists who call themselves applied or practicing anthropologists are usually employed in nonacademic

A medical worker in rural Ethiopia vaccinates children. Medical care without a subsequent reduction in births can have harmful consequences because of the increase in population.

settings, working for government agencies, international development agencies, private consulting firms, public health organizations, medical schools, public interest law firms, community development agencies, charitable foundations, and even profit-seeking corporations (see the box "Anthropology and Business"). Indeed, there are more anthropologists working in nonacademic than in academic settings.[3] These practicing anthropologists often work on specific projects that aim to improve people's lives, usually by trying to change behavior or the environment; or the anthropologists monitor or evaluate efforts by others to bring about change.[4] Usually the problems and projects are defined by the employers or clients (the client is sometimes the "target" population), not by the anthropologists.[5] But anthropologists are increasingly called upon to participate in deciding exactly what improvements might be possible, as well as how to achieve them.

HISTORY AND TYPES OF APPLICATION

In 1934, John Collier, the head of the federal Bureau of Indian Affairs, got legislation passed that provided protections for Native Americans: Land could no longer be taken away, lost land was supposed to be restored, tribal governments would be formed, and loans would be made available to reservations. This opened the way toward recognition of the useful roles that anthropologists could play outside academic settings. Collier employed some anthropologists to aid in carrying out the new policies. At about the same time, the Soil Conservation Service also hired anthropologists to help with projects related to Native American land use.[6] But until

World War II, almost all of the few hundred anthropologists in the United States were still employed in colleges, universities, and museums, and applied anthropology was practically nonexistent.

Events in the 1940s encouraged more applied anthropology. In 1941, anthropologists founded the Society for Applied Anthropology and a new journal devoted to applied anthropology, now called *Human Organization*.[7] During World War II, anthropologists were hired in unprecedented numbers by the U.S. government to help in the war effort. Margaret Mead estimated that something like 295 of the 303 anthropologists in the United States at the time were in one way or another direct participants in the war effort.[8]

The government hired anthropologists to help improve morale, increase our understanding of enemies and allies, and prepare for military campaigns and occupation of the islands of Micronesia and other areas in and around the Pacific.[9] For example, applied anthropologists were called on for advice when perplexed U.S. military officials wanted to understand why their Japanese enemies refused to behave like "normal" people. One of the practices that most distressed military leaders was the tendency of Japanese soldiers to try to kill themselves rather than be taken prisoner. Certainly, U.S. prisoners of war did not behave in this manner. Eventually, in order to understand the Japanese code of honor, the military hired anthropologists as consultants to the Foreign Morale Analysis Division of the War Office's Information Department.

After working with the anthropologists, the U.S. military learned that a major reason for the "strange" behavior of the Japanese prisoners was their belief that to surrender in a wartime situation, even in the face of greatly superior odds, or to be taken prisoner, even when injured and unconscious and therefore unable to avoid capture, was a disgrace. The Japanese believed further that the U.S. soldiers killed all prisoners. Thus, it is hardly surprising that so many captured Japanese soldiers preferred honorable death by their own hand. Once the U.S. military learned what the Japanese thought, they made efforts to explain to them that they would not be executed if captured, with the result that far more Japanese surrendered. Some prisoners even gave military information to the Americans—not to act against their own country but to try and establish new lives for themselves, since the disgrace of being captured prevented them from resuming their former lives.[10]

Anthropologists were enthusiastic about helping the government during World War II because they were overwhelmingly committed to winning the war. The government, in its turn, seemed eager for anthropological advice. But in the postwar period there was an enormous increase in higher education as returning veterans and, later, baby boomers went to college, and U.S. anthropologists increasingly found employment in universities and colleges. Anthropology became less concerned with applied problems and more concerned with theory and basic research.

The situation changed from the late 1970s on when interest in applied anthropology began to flourish. Some have attributed the increased interest to a shift in priorities in the aftermath of the Vietnam War; others cite declining employment opportunities in colleges and universities. Anthropologists who work in applied fields come out of all subfields of anthropology, although most from ethnology. They may work on public and private programs at home and abroad to provide improvements in agriculture, nutrition, mental and physical health, housing, job opportunities, transportation, education, and the lives of women or minorities. A frequent type of applied work is the "social impact" study required in connection with many programs funded by government or private agencies. For example, archaeologists are hired to study, record, and preserve "cultural resources" that will be disturbed or destroyed by construction projects. Applied anthropologists who were trained in physical anthropology may work in the area of medicine, public health, and forensic investigations. And applied work in education and communication often utilizes the skills of linguists.[11]

ETHICS OF APPLIED ANTHROPOLOGY

Ethical issues always arise in the course of fieldwork, and anthropology as a profession has adopted certain principles of responsibility. Above all, an anthropologist's first responsibility is to those who are being studied; everything should be done to ensure that their welfare and dignity will be protected. Anthropologists also have a responsibility to those who will read about their research; research findings should be reported openly and truthfully.[12] But because applied anthropology often deals with planning and implementing changes in some target population, ethical responsibilities can become complicated. Perhaps the most important ethical question is: Will the change truly benefit the target population?

In May 1946, the Society for Applied Anthropology established a committee to draw up a specific code of ethics for professional applied anthropologists. After many meetings and revisions, a statement on ethical responsibilities was finally adopted in 1948, and in 1983, the statement was revised.[13] According to the code, the target community should be included as much as possible in the formulation of policy, so that people in the community may know in advance how the program will affect them. Perhaps the most important aspect of the code is the pledge not to recommend or take any action that is harmful to the interests of the community. The National Association of Practicing Anthropologists goes further: If the work the employer expects of the employee violates the ethical principles of the profession, the practicing anthropologist has the obligation to try to change those practices or, if change cannot be brought about, to withdraw from the work.[14]

Ethical issues are often complicated. Thayer Scudder described the situation of Gwembe Tonga villagers who were relocated after a large dam was built in the Zambezi Valley of central Africa. Economic conditions improved during the 1960s and early 1970s, as the people increasingly produced goods and services for sale. But then conditions deteriorated. By 1980, the villagers were in a miserable state; rates of mortality, alcohol drinking, theft, assault, and murder were up. Why? One reason was that they had cut back on producing their own food in favor of producing for the world market. Such a strategy works well when world market prices are high; however, when prices fall, so does the standard of living.[15] The situation described by Scudder illustrates the ethical dilemma

Applied Anthropology

ANTHROPOLOGY AND BUSINESS

It is only relatively recently that businesspeople have come to realize that anthropologists have useful knowledge to contribute, particularly with regard to the globalization of trade, the increase in international investments and joint ventures, and the spread of multinational corporations. What can anthropology offer? One of the most important contributions of anthropology is understanding how much culture can influence relationships between people of different cultures. For example, anthropologists know that communication is much more than the formal understanding of another language. People in some countries, such as the United States, expect explicit, straightforward verbal messages, but people in other countries are more indirect in their verbal messages. In Japan and China, for example, negative messages are less likely than messages expressing politeness and harmony. Many Eastern cultures have ways of saying no without saying the word.

It is also important to understand that different cultures may have different values. People in the United States place a high value on the individual, but as we discussed in the chapter on psychology and culture, the importance of relationships with others may take precedence over individual needs in other places. People in the United States emphasize the future, youth, informality, and competitiveness, but in other societies the emphases are often the opposite. In any business arrangement, perhaps no difference is as salient as the value a culture places on time. As we say, "Time is money." If a meeting is arranged and the other person is late, say, 45 minutes late, people from the United States consider it rude; but such a delay is well within the range of acceptable behavior in many South American countries.

Anthropologists have helped businesses become aware of their own "cultures" (sometimes referred to as *organizational cultures*). The organizational culture of a business may interfere with the acceptance of new kinds of workers, or it may interfere with changing business needs. If parts of that culture need to be changed, it is necessary first to identify what the culture involves and to understand how and why it developed the way it did. Anthropologists know how to identify cultural patterns on the basis of systematic observation and interviewing of individuals.

Applied Anthropologist Jill Kleinberg and clients.

for many applied anthropologists. As he said: "So how is it that I can still justify working for the agencies that fund such projects?" He points out that large-scale projects are almost impossible to stop. The anthropologist can choose to stand on the sidelines and complain or try to influence the project to benefit the target population as much as possible.[16]

The problem described by Scudder comes about in part because the anthropologist is not often

The anthropologist Jill Kleinberg studied six Japanese-owned firms in the United States to understand the impact of both the larger culture and the organizational culture of the workplace. All six firms employed both Japanese and Americans, although the Japanese dominated the managerial positions. The main goal of the study was to discover why there was considerable tension in the six firms. Kleinberg's first order of business was to interview people about their views of work and their jobs. She found clear differences between the Japanese and the American employees that seemed to reflect broader cultural differences. Americans wanted a clear definition of the job and its attached responsibilities, and they also wanted their job titles, authority, rights, and pay to match closely. The Japanese, on the other hand, emphasized the need to be flexible in their responsibilities as well as their tasks. They also felt that part of their responsibility was to help their co-workers. (See the box "Do Schools Teach Values?" in the chapter on psychology and culture, in which we discussed Japanese preschools and their emphasis on the good of the group.) Americans were uncomfortable because the Japanese managers did not indicate exactly what the workers were

supposed to do; even if there was a job description, the manager did not appear to pay attention to it. Americans were given little information, were left out of decision making, and were frustrated by the lack of opportunity to advance. The Japanese thought that the Americans were too hard to manage, too concerned with money and authority, and too concerned with their own interests.

Dissatisfaction is a problem in any business. Absenteeism, high turnover, and lack of incentive on the job all detract from job performance and business capability. Kleinberg recommended giving all employees more information about the company as well as conducting training sessions about cross-cultural differences in business cultures. She also recommended making the Japanese philosophy of management more explicit during the hiring process so that the company would be able to find Americans who were more comfortable with that philosophy. But she also suggested that the managerial structure be somewhat "Americanized" so that American employees could be more comfortable. Finally, she recommended that Americans be given more managerial positions and contact with their Japanese counterparts overseas. These

suggestions might not eliminate all problems, but they would increase mutual understanding and trust.

In a way, then, as Andrew Miracle notes, the work of the practicing anthropologist is similar to the shaman's in traditional societies. The people who call on shamans for help believe in their abilities to help, and the shaman tries to find ways to empower the client to think positively. To be sure, there are profound differences between a shaman and an applied anthropologist. Perhaps the most important is that the applied anthropologist uses research, not trance or magic, to effect an organizational cure. Like a shaman, however, the applied anthropologist must make an understandable diagnosis and help the client see the way to health and restored power.

Sources: Gary P. Ferraro, *The Cultural Dimension of International Business,* 2nd ed. (Englewood Cliffs, NJ: Prentice Hall, 1994); Jill Kleinberg, "Practical Implications of Organizational Culture Where Americans and Japanese Work Together," in Ann T. Jordan, ed., *Practicing Anthropology in Corporate America: Consulting on Organizational Culture, NAPA Bulletin No. 14* (Arlington, VA: American Anthropological Association, 1994); Andrew W. Miracle, "A Shaman to Organizations," in Carol R. Ember, Melvin Ember, and Peter N. Peregrine, eds., *Research Frontiers in Anthropology* (Upper Saddle River: Prentice Hall, 1998). Prentice Hall/Simon & Schuster Custom Publishing.

involved until after a decision is made to go ahead with a change program. This situation has begun to change as applied anthropologists are increasingly asked to participate in earlier stages of the planning process. Anthropologists are also increasingly asked to help in projects initiated by the affected party. Such requests may range from help in solving problems in corporate organizations to helping Native Americans with land claims. Since the project is consistent with the wishes of the affected population, the results are not likely to put the anthropologist into an ethical dilemma.

EVALUATING THE EFFECTS OF PLANNED CHANGE

The decision as to whether a proposed change would benefit the target population is not always easy to make. In certain cases, as when improved medical care is involved, the benefits offered to the target group would seem to be unquestionable—we all feel sure that health is better than illness. However, this may not always be true. Consider a public health innovation such as inoculation against disease. Although it would undoubtedly have a beneficial effect on the survival rate of a population, a reduction in the mortality rate might have unforeseen consequences that would in turn produce new problems. Once the inoculation program was begun, the number of children surviving would probably increase. But it might not be possible to increase the rate of food production, given the level of technology, capital, and land resources possessed by the target population. Thus, the death rate, because of starvation, might rise to its previous level and perhaps even exceed it. The inoculation program would not affect the death rate; it might merely change the causes of death. This example shows that even if a program of planned change has beneficial consequences in the short run, a great deal of thought and investigation have to be given to its long-term effects.

Debra Picchi raised questions about the long-term effects on the Bakairi Indians of a program by the National Brazilian Indian Foundation (FUNAI) to produce rice with machine technology.[17] The Bakairi of the Mato Grosso region largely practice slash-and-burn horticulture in gallery forests along rivers, with supplementary cattle raising, fishing, and hunting. In the early part of the twentieth century their population had declined to 150 people and they were given a relatively small reserve. Some of it was gallery forest, but a larger part was parched and infertile *(cerrado)*. When the Bakairi population began to increase, FUNAI introduced a scheme to plant rice on formerly unused *cerrado* land, using machinery, insecticides, and fertilizer. FUNAI paid the costs for the first year and expected that by the third year the scheme would be self-supporting. The project did not go so well because FUNAI did not deliver all the equipment needed and did not provide adequate advice. So only half the expected rice was produced. Still, it was more food than the Bakairi had previously, so the program should have been beneficial to them.

But there were negative side effects, not anticipated. Nutritionally, to be sure, the Bakairi are growing an additional starchy food. But use of the *cerrado* for agriculture reduces the area on which cattle can be grazed; cattle are an important source of high-quality protein. So the now-mechanized agriculture has reduced the availability of animal protein. The mechanization also makes the Bakairi more dependent on cash for fuel, insecticides, fertilizer, and repairs. But cash is hard to come by. Only some individuals can be hired—usually men with outside experience who have the required knowledge of machinery. So the cash earned in the now-mechanized agriculture goes mainly to a relatively small number of people. It is debatable whether the new inequalities of income provide long-term effects that are beneficial to the Bakairi.

These failures were not the fault of anthropologists—indeed, most instances of planned change by governments and other agencies usually have begun without the input of anthropologists at all. Applied anthropologists have played an important role in pointing out the problems with programs like these that fail to evaluate long-term consequences. Such evaluations are an important part of convincing governments and other agencies to ask for anthropological help in the first place. Ironically, failure experiences are learning experiences—applied anthropologists who study previous examples of planned change can often learn a great deal about what is likely or not likely to be beneficial in the long run.

The benefits of programs or applied efforts are sometimes obvious. For example, Haiti has experienced serious deforestation. The process began in colonial times when the Spanish exported wood and the French cleared forests to grow sugarcane, coffee, and indigo. After Haiti's independence, foreign lumber companies continued to cut and sell hardwood. Wood is needed by the local population for fuel and for construction, but rapid population increases have increased the demand for fuel and wood and the trees are rapidly diminishing. The loss of tree cover also speeds up erosion of topsoil. Forestry experts, environmentalists, and anthropologists all agree about the need to stop this trend. How to bring about the appropriate change is not so easy. The poorer people become, the more likely they are to cut down trees to sell.[18] After numerous reforestation projects failed, an anthropologist was asked to help design a program that would work. And it did (see the box "Bringing the Trees Back to Haiti").

Applied Anthropology

BRINGING THE TREES BACK TO HAITI

No one disagrees that Haiti needs to replace its rapidly disappearing trees. Not only are trees important for preventing soil erosion, but wood is needed for fuel and construction. Overpopulation has resulted in less and less land for poor farmers. As increasing numbers crowd into the cities, demand for charcoal increases. So poor people chop down the few remaining trees to sell for charcoal in the cities. Planners know that reforestation is needed, but traditional reforestation programs have failed miserably. Why?

Understanding why previous projects failed was the first step in helping Gerald Murray design an effective project. One problem seems to have been that previous projects were run through the government's Ministry of Agriculture. The seedling trees that were given away were referred to as "the state's trees." So, when project workers told farmers not to cut the new trees down so as to protect the environment, farmers took this statement to mean that the land on which the trees were planted might be considered government land, which the farmers could not care less about. In contrast, in the project

proposed by Murray, private voluntary organizations rather than the Haitian government were used to distribute trees. The farmers were told that they were the owners of the trees. That ownership included the right to cut the trees and sell the wood, just as they sell crops. In previous projects farmers were given heavy, hard-to-transport seedlings that took a long time to mature. They were told to plant in a large communal woodlot, an idea inconsistent with the more individualistic Haitian land tenure arrangements. In the new plan, the tree seedlings given away were fast-growing species that matured in as little as four years. In addition, the new seedlings were very small and could be planted quickly. Perhaps most important of all, the new trees could be planted in borders or interspersed with other crops, interfering little with traditional crop patterns.

To Murray's great surprise, by the end of two years, 2,500 Haitian households had planted 3 million seedlings. By the end of four years, 75,000 households had planted 20 million trees. Also, farmers were not rushing to cut down trees. Because growing

trees do not spoil, farmers were postponing their cutting and sales until they needed cash. So even though farmers were told that it was all right to cut trees down, a statement contrary to the message of previous reforestation projects, the landscape was filling up with trees.

Murray's lengthy participant observation and interviewing had helped him predict what might fit in with the Haitian farmers' needs. The idea that wood could be an important marketable cash crop was much more consistent with farmers' existing behavior—they already sold crops for cash when they needed it. The difference now was that instead of cutting down naturally grown wood, they were raising wood just as they raised other crops.

The more it becomes known that anthropologists can be helpful in implementing programs, the more often development and government agencies will turn to them for advice.

Source: From *Anthropological Praxis* by Robert Wulff and Shirley Fiske. Copyright © 1987 by Westview Press. Reprinted by permission of Perseus Books LLC.

DIFFICULTIES IN INSTITUTING PLANNED CHANGE

Whether a program of planned change can be successfully implemented depends largely on whether the targeted population wants the proposed change and likes the proposed program. Before an attempt can be made at cultural innovation, the innovators must determine whether the target population is

aware of the benefits of the proposed change. Lack of awareness can be a temporary barrier to solving the problem at hand. For example, health workers have often had difficulty convincing people that they were becoming ill because something was wrong with their water supply. Many people do not believe that disease can be transmitted by water. At other times, the target population is perfectly aware of the problem. A case in point involved Taiwanese women who were introduced to family-planning methods beginning in the 1960s. The women knew they were having more children than they wanted or could easily afford, and they wanted to control their birth rate. They offered no resistance—they merely had to be given the proper devices and instructions and the birth rate quickly fell to a more desirable, and more manageable, level.[19]

RESISTANCE BY THE TARGET POPULATION. Not all proposed change programs are beneficial to the target population. Sometimes resistance is rational. Applied anthropologists have pointed to cases where the judgment of the affected population has been better than that of the agents of change. One such example occurred during a Venezuelan government–sponsored program to give infants powdered milk. The mothers rejected the milk, even though it was free, on the grounds that it implied that the mothers' milk was no good.[20] But who is to say that the resistance was not in fact intuitively smart, reflecting an awareness that such a milk program would not benefit the children? Medical research now indicates quite clearly that mother's milk is far superior to powdered milk or formula. First, human milk best supplies the nutrients needed for human development. Second, it is now known that the mother, through her milk, is able to transmit antibodies (disease resistances) to the baby. And third, nursing delays ovulation and usually increases the spacing between births.[21]

The switchover to powdered milk and formula in many underdeveloped areas has been nothing short of a disaster, resulting in increased malnutrition and misery. For one thing, powdered milk must be mixed with water, but if the water and the bottles are not sterilized, more sickness is introduced. Then, too, if powdered milk has to be purchased, mothers without cash are forced to dilute the milk to stretch it. And if a mother feeds her baby formula or powder for even a short time, the process is tragically irreversible, for her own milk dries up and she cannot return to breast-feeding even if she wants to.

As the Venezuelan example suggests, individuals may be able to resist proposed medical or health projects because acceptance is ultimately a personal matter. Large development projects planned by powerful governments or agencies rarely are stoppable, but even they can be resisted successfully. Recently, the Kayapo of the Xingu River region of Brazil were able to cancel a plan by the Brazilian government to build dams along the river for hydroelectric power. The Kayapo gained international attention when some of their leaders appeared on

Breastfeeding is now known to be better for the health of the baby. In many countries, breastfeeding in public is perfectly acceptable, as among the Huastec of Mexico. In the United States, the embarrassment of breastfeeding in public may discourage some mothers from breastfeeding.

North American and European television and then successfully organized a protest in 1989 by members of several tribal groups. Their success seemed to come in part from their ability to present themselves to the international community as guardians of the rain forest—an image that resonated with international environmental organizations that supported their cause. Although to outsiders it might seem that the Kayapo want their way of life to remain as it was, the Kayapo are not opposed to all change. In fact, they want greater access to medical care, other government services, and manufactured goods from outside.[22]

But even if a project *is* beneficial to a population, it may still meet with resistance. Factors that may hinder acceptance can be divided roughly into three, sometimes overlapping, categories: *cultural, social,* and *psychological* barriers.

Cultural barriers are shared behaviors, attitudes, and beliefs that tend to impede the acceptance of an innovation. For example, members of different societies may view gift giving in different ways. Particularly in commercialized societies, things received for nothing are often believed to be worthless. When the government of Colombia instituted a program of giving seedling orchard trees to farmers in order to increase fruit production, the farmers showed virtually no interest in the seedlings, many of which proceeded to die of neglect. When the government realized that the experiment had apparently failed, it began to charge each farmer a nominal fee for the seedlings. Soon the seedlings became immensely popular and fruit production increased.[23] The farmers' demand for the seedlings may have increased because they were charged a fee and therefore came to value the trees. The market demand for fruit may also have increased. Other examples of cultural resistance to change, which we discuss more fully later in this chapter, are beliefs about sex that make it difficult for people to follow medical guidelines for safer sex.

It is very important for agents of change to understand what the shared beliefs and attitudes are. First, indigenous cultural concepts or knowledge can sometimes be used effectively to enhance educational programs. For instance, in a program in Haiti to prevent child mortality from diarrhea, change agents used the terminology for traditional native herbal tea remedies (*rafrechi,* or cool refreshment) to identify the new oral rehydration therapy, which is a very successful medical treatment. In native belief, diarrhea is a "hot" illness and appropriate remedies have to have cooling properties.[24] Second, even if indigenous beliefs are not helpful to the campaign, not paying attention to contrary beliefs can undermine the campaign. But uncovering contrary beliefs is not easy, particularly when they do not emerge in ordinary conversation (see the box "Exploring Why an Applied Project Didn't Work").

The acceptance of planned change may also depend on social factors. Research suggests that acceptance is more likely if the change agent and the target or potential adopter are similar socially. But change agents may have higher social status and more education than the people they are trying to influence. So change agents may work more with higher-status individuals because they are more likely to accept new ideas. If lower-status individuals also have to be reached, change agents of lower status may have to be employed.[25]

Finally, acceptance may depend on psychological factors—that is, how the individuals perceive both the innovation and the agents of change. In the course of trying to encourage women in the south-eastern United States to breast-feed rather than bottle-feed their infants, researchers discovered a number of reasons why women were reluctant to breast-feed their infants, even though they heard it was healthier. Many women did not have confidence that they would produce enough milk for their babies; they were embarrassed about breast-feeding in public; and their family and friends had negative attitudes.[26] In designing an educational program, change agents may have to address such psychological concerns directly.

DISCOVERING AND UTILIZING LOCAL CHANNELS OF INFLUENCE. In planning a project involving cultural change, the administrator of the project should find out what the normal channels of influence are in the population. In most communities, there are preestablished networks for communication, as well as persons of high prestige or influence who are looked to for guidance and direction. An understanding of such channels of influence is extremely valuable when deciding how to introduce a program of change. In addition, it is useful to know at what times, and in what sorts of situations, one channel is likely to be more effective in spreading information and approval than another.

An example of the effective use of local channels of influence occurred when an epidemic of smallpox broke out in the Kalahandi district of the state of Orissa in India. The efforts of health workers to vaccinate villagers against the disease were consistently resisted. The villagers, naturally suspicious and fearful of these strange men with their equally strange medical equipment, were unwilling to offer themselves, and particularly their babies, to the peculiar experiments the strangers wished to perform. Afraid of the epidemic, the villagers appealed for help to their local priest, whose opinions on such matters they trusted. The priest went into a trance, explaining that the illness was the result of the goddess Thalerani's anger with the people. She could be appeased, he continued, only by massive feasts, offerings, and other demonstrations of the villagers' worship of her. Realizing that the priest was the village's major opinion leader, at least in medical matters, the frustrated health workers tried to get the priest to convince his people to undergo vaccination. At first, the priest refused to cooperate with the strange men, but when his favorite nephew fell ill, he decided to try any means available to cure the boy. He thereupon went into another trance, telling the villagers that the goddess wished all her worshipers to be vaccinated. Fortunately, the people agreed, and the epidemic was largely controlled.[27]

Applied Anthropology

EXPLORING WHY AN APPLIED PROJECT DIDN'T WORK

When applied projects do not succeed, it is important for researchers to try to figure why. Part of the problem may be that the intended recipients' ideas about how things work may be very different from the researchers' ideas. Consider the following example. In Guatemala, village health-care workers were not only testing people for malaria but they were also offering free antimalarial drugs. Yet, surprisingly, a community survey found that only 20 percent of people with malaria symptoms took advantage of the free treatment. More surprisingly, most people with symptoms spent the equivalent of a day's wages to buy an injection that was not strong enough to be effective! Why? What was going on?

Finding the answer was not easy. First, researchers designed interviews to elicit folk concepts about illness. What kinds of illnesses are there? What are their causes? What are their symptoms, and how are different illnesses to be treated? They conducted interviews with a random sample of households to check on what illnesses people had and what they did about them. Then they asked people to consider different hypothetical scenarios (vignettes), with different types of people and different degrees of severity of illness, to find out what treatment they would choose. All of these methods were well thought out, but the answers still did not predict what people actually did when they thought they had malaria. Finally, the researchers devised precise comparisons of the kinds of pills passed out by health-care workers and the pills and ampules for injections sold by the drugstore. They compared them two at a time, varying dosages and brands. People did think that more pills were more effective, as indeed they were. But they thought that the colorfully wrapped store-bought pill was more effective than the equivalent white unwrapped free pill, even though it was not. They also thought that one store-bought ampule used for injections, for which they would pay a day's wages, was more effective than four pills of any kind! In fact, one ampule was equivalent to only one pill.

Applied researchers often use such trial-and-error methods to find out how to get the information they need. Methods that work in one field setting don't always work in others. To get the information needed, researchers must sometimes let the subjects structure their own answers. At other times, as in this case, they may have to make very specific

---

If channels of influence are not stable, using influential persons in a campaign can sometimes backfire. In the educational campaign in Haiti to promote the use of oral rehydration therapy, Mme. Duvalier, the first lady of Haiti at the time, lent her name to the project. Because there were no serious social or cultural barriers to the treatment and mothers reported that children took to the solutions well, success was expected. But in the middle of the campaign, Haiti became embroiled in political turmoil and the first lady's husband was overthrown. Some of the public thought that the oral rehydration project was a plot by the Duvaliers to sterilize children, and this suspicion fueled resistance.[28] As the box on "Bringing the Trees Back in Haiti" shows, even after the Duvalier regime, people in Haiti were suspicious of any government-sponsored program.

Applied anthropologists often advocate integrating indigenous healers into medical change programs. This idea may encounter considerable resistance by the medical profession and by government officials who view such healers negatively. But this strategy may be quite effective in more isolated areas where indigenous healers are the only sources of health care. If they are involved in medical change programs, indigenous healers are likely to refer patients to hospitals when they feel unable to cope with an illness, and the hospitals choose sometimes to refer patients to the healers.[29]

Other social groups and their attitudes can play important roles in shaping the outcome of the change program. Most often the people who are being helped have few privileges, little political and economic power, and low prestige.[30] Change or development is often regarded as a threat to those with more privilege. If those who do have power object to the new program, they may effectively sabotage it. The development agent, then, not only has to reckon

comparisons to get predictive answers. The people in the Guatemala study didn't believe that the free pills were strong enough to work, so they didn't use them. More research would be needed to uncover why they did not believe the free pills were effective. Was it because they were free? Was it because the store-bought drugs were more nicely packaged? Or was there a belief that injections work better than pills? That's what the research process is like; it always leads to new questions, particularly more general questions requiring more extensive or more comparative research.

For example, the Guatemala project revealed why a particular program was not successful in a particular area. But how widespread are the interfering beliefs? Are they found throughout Guatemala? Do they interfere with the introduction of other medicines? Are we dealing with problems that exist in other areas of Central and South America? Although we don't yet have answers to these more extensive questions, anthropologists have developed efficient methods for assessing variation in beliefs within and between cultures.

We now know that if we ask one or two informants, we cannot assume that the answer is cultural, but that doesn't mean that we need to ask hundreds of people. If a belief is cultural and therefore commonly held, asking 10 to 20 individuals the same question is sufficient to provide the researcher with a high probability that an answer is correct. (The agreement among respondents is called *cultural consensus*.) So, for example, Guatemalan respondents mostly agreed about which illnesses were contagious. But they disagreed a lot about whether a particular disease should be treated with a "hot" or a "cold" remedy. Using cultural-consensus methods, researchers can compare rural and urban residents, and they can also compare informants in different cultures. When we have more of these systematic comparisons, medical anthropologists and health practitioners may have a better understanding of how to implement medical care.

Sources: Susan C. Weller, "The Research Process," in Carol R. Ember, Melvin Ember, and Peter N. Peregrine eds., *Research Frontiers in Anthropology* (Upper Saddle River, NJ: Prentice Hall, 1998), Prentice Hall/Simon & Schuster Custom Publishing, and the research referred to therein; A. Kimball Romney, Susan C. Weller, and William H. Batchelder, "Culture as Consensus: A Theory of Culture and Informant Accuracy," *American Anthropologist*, 88 (1986): 313–38.

with the local community but may also have to persuade more powerful groups in the society that the new program should be introduced.

TOWARD COLLABORATIVE APPLIED ANTHROPOLOGY

Most large-scale programs of planned change originate with governments, international aid organizations, or other agencies. Even if the programs are well intentioned and even if the appropriate evaluations are made to ensure that the population will not be harmed, the population targeted for the change is usually not involved in the decision making. Some anthropologists, like Wayne Warry, think that applied anthropology should be more collaborative. Warry explains that he was asked by a Native Canadian elder whether he (Warry) would tolerate his own methods and interpretations if he were the native.[31] This question prompted him to involve himself in a project with Native Canadian collaborators, directed by the Mamaweswen Tribal Council. The project assesses health care needs and develops plans to improve local community health care. Funding is provided by the Canadian government as part of a program to transfer health care to the First Nations. Native researchers are conducting the surveys and workshops to keep the community informed about the project. The tribal council also reviews any publications and shares in any profits resulting from those publications.

Applied anthropologists may be increasingly asked to work on behalf of indigenous grass-roots organizations. As we saw in the chapter on associations, the developing world has seen a proliferation of such groups. In some cases these small groups and networks of such groups are starting to hire their own technical assistance.[32] When such organizations do the hiring, they control the decision making. There is increasing evidence that grass-roots organizations are the key to effective development. For example, Kenyan farmers who belong to grass-roots organizations produce higher farm yields than those farmers who do not belong, even though the latter group is exposed to more agricultural extension agents.[33] Grass-roots organizations can succeed where government or outside projects fail. We have plenty of instances of people effectively resisting projects. Their willingness to change, and their participation in the crucial decision making, may be mostly responsible for the success of a change project.

GLOBAL SOCIAL PROBLEMS: BASIC RESEARCH AND POSSIBLE SOLUTIONS

Some anthropologists as well as other social scientists think that it is time to attack the major social problems that afflict our world. The idea that we can solve social problems is based on two assumptions. We have to assume that it is possible to discover the causes of a problem. And we have to assume that we may be able to do something about the causes, once they are discovered, and thereby eliminate or reduce the problem.

Not everyone would agree with these assumptions. Some would say that our understanding of a social problem cannot ever be sufficient to suggest a solution guaranteed to work. To be sure, no understanding in science is perfect or certain; there is always some probability that even a well-supported explanation is wrong or incomplete. But the uncertainty of knowledge does not rule out the possibility of application. With regard to social problems, the possible payoff from even incomplete understanding could be a better and safer world. This possibility is what motivates many researchers who investigate social problems. After all, the history of the various sciences strongly supports the belief that scientific understanding can often allow humans to control nature, not just predict and explain it. Why should human behavior be any different?

So what do we know about some of the global social problems, and what policies or solutions are suggested by what we know?

AIDS

Epidemics of disease have killed millions of people within short periods of time throughout recorded history. The Black Death, bubonic plague, killed between 25 and 50 percent of the population of Europe, perhaps 75 million people, during the fourteenth century; an epidemic during the sixth century killed an estimated 100 million people in the Middle East, Asia, and Europe. Less noted in our history books, but also devastating, was the enormous depopulation that accompanied the expansion of Europeans into the New World and the Pacific from the 1500s on. Not only were people killed directly by European conquerors; millions also died from introduced diseases to which the natives had little or no resistance, diseases such as smallpox and measles that the Europeans brought with them but were no longer dying from.

The current state of medical science and technology may lull us into thinking that epidemics are a thing of the past. But the recent and sudden emergence of the disease we call **AIDS (acquired immune deficiency syndrome)** reminds us that new diseases, or new varieties of old diseases, can appear at any time. Like all other organisms, disease-causing organisms also evolve. The human immunodeficiency viruses (HIV) that presumably cause AIDS emerged only recently. Viruses and bacteria

Women parade to arouse awareness of AIDS in Eritrea.

are always mutating, and new strains emerge that are initially a plague on our genetic resistance and on medical efforts to contain them.

Millions of people around the world already have the symptoms of AIDS, and millions more are infected with HIV but do not know they are infected. By the year 2000, according to World Health Organization estimates, about 40 million adults and children will be infected and 15 million people will have AIDS.[34] Many millions will have died of AIDS by then. AIDS is a frightening epidemic not only because of its likely toll. It is also frightening because it takes a long time (on average, four years) after exposure for symptoms to appear. This means that many people who have been infected by HIV but do not know they are infected may continue unknowingly to transmit the viruses to others.[35]

Transmission occurs mostly via sexual encounters, through semen and blood. Drug users may also transmit HIV by way of contaminated needles. Mothers may transmit the virus to their babies in the womb. Transmission by blood transfusion has been virtually eliminated in this and other societies by medical screening of blood supplies. In many countries, however, there is still no routine screening of blood prior to transfusions.

Many people think of AIDS as only a medical problem that requires only a medical solution, without realizing that there are behavioral and cultural issues that need to be addressed as well. It is true that developing a vaccine or a drug to prevent people from getting AIDS and finding a permanent cure for those who have it will finally solve the problem of AIDS. But, for a variety of reasons, we can expect that the medical solution alone will not be sufficient, at least not for a while. First, to be effective worldwide, or even within a country, a vaccine has to be inexpensive and relatively easy to produce in large quantities; the same is true of any medical treatment for victims. Second, governments around the world have to be willing and able to spend the money and hire the personnel necessary to manage an effective program.[36] Third, future vaccination and treatment will require the people at risk to be willing to get vaccinated and treated, which is not always easy to arrange. Witness the fact that the incidence of measles is on the rise in the United States because many people are not having their children vaccinated.

There are now expensive drug treatments that significantly reduce the HIV load, but we do not know if an effective and inexpensive vaccine or treatment will be developed soon. In the meantime, the risk of HIV infection can be reduced only by changes in social, particularly sexual, behavior. But to persuade people to change their sexual behavior, it is necessary to find out exactly what they do sexually, and why they prefer what they do. The reasons for preferring some activity may make it difficult to change.

Research so far suggests that different sexual patterns are responsible for HIV transmission in different parts of the world. In the United States, England, northern Europe, Australia, and Latin America, the recipients of anal intercourse, particularly men, are the most likely individuals to acquire HIV infection; vaginal intercourse can also transmit the infection, usually from the man to the woman. In Africa, the most common mode of transmission is vaginal intercourse, and so women get infected more commonly in Africa than elsewhere.[35] Is it reasonable to expect that people can generally be persuaded to stop doing what they prefer to do?

As of now, there are only two known ways to reduce the likelihood of sexual HIV transmission. One way is to abstain from sexual intercourse; the other is to use condoms. Educational programs that teach how AIDS spreads and what you can do about it may reduce the spread somewhat. But such programs may fail where people have incompatible beliefs and attitudes about sexuality. For example, people in some central African societies believe that deposits of semen *after* conception are necessary for a successful pregnancy and generally enhance a woman's health and ability to reproduce. It might be expected then that people who have these beliefs about semen would choose not to use condoms; after all, condoms in their view are a threat to public health.[38] Educational programs may also emphasize the wrong message. Promiscuity may increase the risk of HIV transmission, so hardly anyone would question the wisdom of advertising to reduce the number of sexual partners. And, at least in the homosexual community in the United States, individuals report fewer sexual partners than in the past. What was not anticipated, however, was that individuals in monogamous relationships, who may feel safe, are *less* likely to use condoms or to avoid the riskiest sexual practices. Needless to say, sex with a regular partner who is infected is not safe![39]

The stigma associated with AIDS also hinders efforts to reduce its spread. Possible victims may be unwilling to find out if they have been infected. The stigma, in this and some other societies, is the widespread belief that homosexual men are particularly likely to get infected.[40] Of course, not everyone who gets infected has engaged in homosexual behavior. Indeed, the majority of people now infected with

AIDS in the world are heterosexual.[41] But the disease's association with homosexuality, and a general prejudice against homosexuals, may contribute to the spread of AIDS: Some of those infected will continue to transmit the infection because they are afraid to find out that they might be infected. Much of the stigma associated with AIDS derives also from people's misinformation about exactly how AIDS is transmitted; indeed, many people fear contact with AIDS victims, as if any kind of contact could result in infection. Fear that they will be shunned if they are known to have AIDS may also contribute to some persons' unwillingness to be tested.

To solve the problem of AIDS, we may hope that medical science will develop an effective and inexpensive vaccination or treatment that can be afforded by all. In the meantime, we can try to understand why people engage in certain risky sexual practices. Such understanding may allow us to design educational and other programs that would more successfully inhibit the spread of AIDS.

NATURAL DISASTERS AND FAMINE

Natural events such as floods, droughts, earthquakes, and insect infestations are usually but not always beyond human control, but their effects are not.[42] We call such events accidents or emergencies when only a few people are affected, but we call them disasters when large numbers of people or large areas are affected. The harm caused is not just a function of the magnitude of the natural event. Between 1960 and 1980, 43 natural disasters in Japan killed an average of 63 people per disaster. During the same period, 17 natural disasters in Nicaragua killed an average of 6,235 people per disaster. In the United States, between 1960 and 1976, the average flood or other environmental disturbance killed just one person, injured a dozen, and destroyed fewer than five buildings. These comparative figures demonstrate that climatic and other events in the physical environment become *disasters* because of events or conditions in the social environment.

If people live in houses that are designed to withstand earthquakes—if governing bodies require such construction and the economy is developed enough so that people can afford such construction—the effects of an earthquake will be minimized. If poor people are forced to live in deforested flood plains in order to be able to find land to farm (as in coastal Bangladesh), if the poor are forced to live in shanties built on precarious hillsides (like those of Rio de

Janeiro), the floods and landslides that follow severe hurricanes and rainstorms can kill thousands and even hundreds of thousands.

Thus, natural disasters can have greater or lesser effects on human life, depending on social conditions. And therefore disasters are also social problems, problems that have social causes and possible social solutions. Legislating safe construction of a house is a social solution. The 1976 earthquake in Tangsham, China, killed 250,000 people, mostly because they lived in top-heavy adobe houses that could not withstand severe shaking, whereas the 1989 earthquake in Loma Prieta, California, which was of comparable intensity, killed 65 people.

One might think that floods, of all disasters, are the least influenced by social factors. After all, without a huge runoff from heavy rains or snow melt, there cannot be a flood. But consider why so many people have died from Yellow River floods in China. (One such flood, in 1931, killed nearly 4 million people, making it the deadliest single disaster in history.) The floods in the Yellow River basin have occurred mostly because the clearing of nearby forests for fuel and farmland has allowed enormous quantities of silt to wash into the river, raising the riverbed and increasing the risk of floods that burst the dams that normally would contain them. The risk of disastrous flooding would be greatly reduced if different social conditions prevailed—if people were not so dependent on firewood for fuel, or if they did not have to farm close to the river, or if the dams were higher and more numerous.

Famines, episodes of severe starvation and death, often appear to be triggered by physical events such as a severe drought or a hurricane that kills or knocks down food trees and plants. But famines do not inevitably follow such an event. Social conditions can prevent a famine or increase the likelihood of one. Consider what is likely to happen in Samoa after a hurricane.[43] Whole villages that have lost their coconut and breadfruit trees, as well as their taro patches, pick up and move for a period of time to other villages where there are relatives and friends. The visitors stay and are fed until some of their cultivated trees and plants start to bear food again, at which point they return home. This kind of intervillage reciprocity probably could occur only in a society that has relatively little inequality in wealth. Nowadays, the central government or international agencies may also help out by providing food and other supplies.

Researchers point out that famine rarely results from just one bad food production season. During one bad season, people can usually cope by getting help from relatives, friends, and neighbors, or by switching to less desirable foods. The famine in the African Sahel in 1974 occurred after eight years of bad weather; a combination of drought, floods, and a civil war in 1983–84 contributed to the subsequent famine in the Sahel, Ethiopia, and Sudan.[44] Famine almost always has some social causes. Who has rights to the available food, and do those who have more food distribute it to those who have less? Cross-cultural research suggests that societies with individual property rights rather than shared rights are more likely to suffer famine.[45] Nonetheless, government assistance can lessen the risk of famine in societies with individual property.

Relief provided by government may not always get to those who need it the most. In India, for example, the central government provides help in time of drought to minimize the risk of famine. But the food and other supplies provided to a village may end up being unequally distributed, following the rules of social and gender stratification. Members of the local elite arrange to function as distributors and find ways to manipulate the relief efforts to their advantage. Lower-class and lower-caste families still suffer the most. Within the family, biases against females, particularly young girls and elderly women, translate into their getting less food. It is no wonder, then, that in times of food shortage and famine, the poor and other socially disadvantaged persons are especially likely to die.[46]

Thus, the people of a society may not all be equally at risk in case of disaster. In socially stratified societies, the poor particularly suffer. It is they who are likely to be forced to overcultivate, overgraze, and deforest their land, making it more susceptible to degradation. A society most helps those it values the most.

People in the past, and even recently in some places, viewed disasters as divine retribution for human immorality. For example, the great Flood described in the Old Testament was understood to be God's doing. But scientific research increasingly allows us to understand the natural causes of disasters, and particularly the social conditions that magnify or minimize their effects. To reduce the impact of disasters, then, we need to reduce the social conditions that magnify the effects of disasters. If humans are responsible for those social conditions, humans can change them. If earthquakes destroy houses that are too flimsy, we can build stronger houses. If floods caused by overcultivation and overgrazing kill defenseless people directly (or indirectly by stripping their soils), we can grow new forest cover and provide new job opportunites to flood plain farmers. If prolonged natural disasters or wars threaten famine, social distribution systems can lessen the risk. In short, we may not be able to do much about the weather or other physical causes of disasters, but we can do a lot—if we want to—about the social factors that make disasters disastrous.

INADEQUATE HOUSING AND HOMELESSNESS

In most nations of the world, the poor typically live in inadequate housing, in areas we call *slums*. In many of the developing nations of the world, where cities are growing very rapidly, squatter settlements emerge as people build dwellings (often makeshift) that are typically declared illegal, either because the land is illegally occupied or because the dwellings violate building codes. Squatter settlements are often located in degraded environments that are subject to flooding and mudslides or have inadequate or polluted water. The magnitude of the problem is made clear in some statistics. As of the 1980s, 40 percent of the population in Nairobi, Kenya, lived in unauthorized housing, and 67 percent of the people in five of El Salvador's major cities lived in illegal dwellings.[47]

But contrary to what some people have assumed, not all dwellers in illegal settlements are poor; all but the upper-income elite may be found in such settlements.[48] Moreover, although squatter settlements have problems, they are not chaotic and unorganized places, full of crime. Most of the dwellers are employed, aspire to get ahead, live in intact nuclear families, and help each other.[49] People live in such settlements because they cannot find affordable housing and they house themselves as best they can. Many researchers think that such self-help tendencies should be assisted to improve housing, because governments in developing countries can seldom afford costly public housing projects. But they could invest somewhat in infrastructure—sewers, water supplies, roads—and provide construction materials to those who are willing to do the work required to improve their dwellings.[50]

Housing in slum areas or shantytowns does provide shelter, minimal though it may be. But many people in many areas of the world have no homes at all. Even in countries such as the United States, which are affluent by world standards, large numbers of people are homeless. They sleep in parks, over steam vents, in doorways, subways, and cardboard boxes. In 1987 it was estimated that there were more than 1 million homeless people in the

Homelessness is widespread in the United States.

United States.[51] A congressionally funded study suggested that unless action were taken in the United States to provide affordable housing, there would be as many as 19 million homeless people by the end of this century.[52]

Who are the homeless, and how did they get to be homeless? We have relatively little research on these questions, but what we do have suggests differences in the causes of homelessness in different parts of the world. In the United States, unemployment and the shortage of decent low-cost housing appear to be at least partly responsible for the large number of homeless persons.[53] But there is also another factor: the deliberate policy to reduce the number of people hospitalized for mental illness and other disabilities. For example, from the mid-1960s to mid-1990s, New York State released thousands of patients from mental hospitals. Many of these ex-patients had to live in cheap hotels or poorly monitored facilities with virtually no support network. With very little income, they found it especially hard to cope with their circumstances. Ellen Baxter and Kim Hopper, who studied the homeless in New York City, suggest that one event is rarely sufficient to render a person homeless. Rather, poverty and disability (mental or physical) seem to lead to one calamity after another, and finally homelessness.[54]

Many people cannot understand why homeless individuals do not want to go to municipal shelters. But observations and interviews with the homeless suggest that violence pervades the municipal shelters, particularly the men's shelters. Many feel safer on the streets. Some private charities provide safe shelters and a caring environment. These shelters are filled, but the number of homeless that could be accommodated in them is small.[55] Even single-room-occupancy hotels are hardly better. Many of them are infested with vermin, the common bathrooms are filthy, and they, like the shelters, often are dangerous.[56]

Some poor individuals may be socially isolated, with few or no friends and relatives and little or no social contact. But a society with many such individuals does not necessarily have much homelessness. Socially isolated individuals, even mentally ill individuals, could still have housing, or so the experience of Melbourne, Australia, suggests. Universal health insurance pays for health care as well as the visits of medical practitioners to isolated and ill individuals, wherever they live. Disabled individuals receive a pension or sickness benefits sufficient to allow them to live in a room or apartment. And there is still a considerable supply of cheap housing in Melbourne. Research in Melbourne suggests that a severe mental disorder often precedes living in marginal accommodations—city shelters, commercial shelters, and cheap single rooms. About 50 percent of the individuals living in such places were diagnosed as previously having some form of mental illness; this percentage is similar to what seems to be the case for homeless people and people living in marginal accommodations in the United States.

The contrast between the United States and Australia makes it clear that homelessness is caused by social and political policies. Individuals with similar characteristics live in both Australia and the United States, but in the United States a larger percentage of them are homeless.[57]

Because homelessness cannot occur if everybody can afford housing, some people would say that homelessness can happen only in a society with great extremes in income. Recent statistics on income distribution in the United States clearly show that since the 1970s the rich have gotten much richer and the poor have gotten much poorer. The United States now has more income inequality than other industrialized countries, such as Japan and the Netherlands. In fact, the profile of inequality in the United States more closely resembles that of developing countries, such as India and Mexico.[58]

In the United States, and many other countries, most homeless persons are adults. Whereas adults are "allowed" to be homeless, public sensibilities in the United States appear to be outraged by the sight of children living in the streets; when authorities discover homeless children, they try to find shelters or foster homes for them. But many countries have "street children." It has been estimated that 80 million of the world's children live in the streets. Forty million of them live in Latin America, 20 million in Asia, 10 million in Africa and the Middle East, and 10 million elsewhere.[59]

Lewis Aptekar, who studied street children in Cali, Colombia, reported some surprises.[60] Whereas many of the homeless in the United States and Australia are mentally disabled, the street children in Cali, ranging in age from 7 to 16, are mostly free of mental problems; by and large they also test normally on intelligence tests. In addition, even though many street children come from abusive homes or never had homes, they usually seem happy and enjoy the support and friendship of other street children. They cleverly and creatively look for ways to get money, frequently through entertaining passersby.

Although the observer might think that the street children must have been abandoned by their families, in actuality most of them have at least one parent they keep in touch with. Street life begins slowly, not abruptly; children usually do not stay on the streets full time until they are about 13. Though street children in Cali seem to be in better physical and mental shape than their siblings who stay at home, they often are viewed as a "plague." The street children come from poor families and cope with their lives as best they can, so why are they not viewed with pity and compassion? Aptekar suggests that well-off families see the street children as a threat because a life independent of family may appeal to children, even those from well-off families, who wish to be free of parental constraint and authority.

Whether people become homeless, whether there are shantytowns, seems to depend on a society's willingness to share wealth and help those in need.

The street children of Cali may remind us that children as well as adults need companionship and care. Addressing physical needs without responding to emotional needs may get people off the streets, but it won't get them a "home."

FAMILY VIOLENCE AND ABUSE

In U.S. society we hear regularly about the abuse of spouses and children. Such abuse appears to be increasing—but is it? This seems to be a simple question, but it is not so simple to answer. We have to decide what we mean by abuse.

Is physical punishment of a child who does something wrong child abuse? Not so long ago, teachers in public schools in the United States were allowed to discipline children by hitting them with rulers or paddles, and many parents used switches or belts. Some people today might consider these practices to be child abuse, but were they abusive when they were generally accepted? Some would argue that abuse is going beyond what a culture considers appropriate behavior. Others would disagree and would focus on the violence and severity of parents' or teachers' behavior, not the cultural judgment of appropriateness. And abuse need not involve physical violence. It could be argued that verbal aggression and neglect may be just as harmful as physical aggression. Neglect presents its own problems of definition. People from other cultures might argue that we act abusively when we put an infant or child alone in a room to sleep.[61] Few would disagree about severe injuries that kill a child or spouse or require medical treatment; but other disciplinary behaviors are more difficult to judge.

To avoid having to decide what is or is not abuse, many researchers focus their studies on variation in the frequencies of specific behaviors. For example, one can ask which societies have physical punishment of children without calling physical punishment abusive.

More child abuse cases are reported today in the United States than a decade or two ago, but that does not necessarily mean that violence against children has increased. It may mean only that our awareness and intolerance of violence against children have increased. In fact, in a national interview survey of physical familial violence in the United States, most types of physical violence decreased in frequency between 1975 and 1985. That is, people talked about fewer family homicides, fewer severe assaults on husbands and wives, and fewer severe assaults on children. Despite these declines, however, the United States remains a society with a generally high rate of physical violence in families. In 1985 alone, one out of six couples had a violent assault episode and one out of ten children was severely assaulted by a parent. The risk of assault by a family member in the United States is much greater than the risk of assault by a stranger; for women it is more than 200 times as great.[62] In a comparison of 27 nations, the United States had the third highest rate of child murder.[63]

Cross-culturally, if one form of family violence occurs, others are also likely. So, for example, wife beating, husband beating, child punishment, and fighting among siblings are all significantly associated with each other. But the relationships between these types of family violence are not that strong, which means that they cannot be considered as different facets of the same phenomenon. Indeed, somewhat different factors seem to explain different forms of family violence.[64] We focus here on two forms of violence that are most prevalent cross-culturally: violence against children and violence against wives.

VIOLENCE AGAINST CHILDREN. Cross-culturally, many societies practice and allow infanticide. Frequent reasons for infanticide include illegitimacy, deformity of the infant, twins, too many children, or that the infant is unwanted. Infanticide is usually performed by the mother, but this does not mean that she is uncaring; it may mean that she cannot adequately feed or care for the infant or that it has a poor chance to survive. The reasons for infanticide are similar to those given for abortion. Therefore, it seems that infanticide may be performed when abortion does not work or when unexpected qualities of the infant (for example, deformity) force the mother to reevaluate her ability to raise the child.[65]

Physical punishment of children occurs in over 70 percent of the world's societies. But the fact that children are sometimes punished physically in most societies does not mean that most societies use physical punishment regularly.[66] Why is physical punishment used in some societies and not in others? Some studies suggest that physical punishment is more likely whenever the mother is virtually the only caretaker for the child. Physical punishment is unlikely when there are other caretakers, who may relieve the mother of some of the stresses associated with child care.[67] In addition, societies that are more complex economically and politically tend to rely much more on physical punishment than simpler societies. Why this is so is not yet clear. One suggestion is that complex societies are hierar-

Help for mothers is an important predictor of less physical punishment of children. A sister cares for her younger sibling in South India.

chical and tend to insist on complying with orders; they may use physical punishment in child rearing to ensure that children learn to comply.[68]

VIOLENCE AGAINST WIVES. In the United States, wives and husbands are equally likely to assault the other. Wife battering in the United States is considered a more serious social problem because wives are much more likely to be seriously injured than husbands.[69] Cross-culturally, wife beating is the most common form of family violence; it occurs at least occasionally in about 85 percent of the world's societies. In about half the societies, wife beating is sometimes serious enough to cause permanent injury or death.[70]

It is often assumed that wife beating will be common in societies in which males control economic and political resources. In a cross-cultural test of this assumption, David Levinson found that not all indicators of male dominance predict wife beating, but many do. Specifically, wife beating is most common when men control the products of family labor, when men have the final say in decision making in the home, when divorce is difficult for women, when remarriage for a widow is controlled by the husband's kin, and when women do not have any female work groups.[71] Similarly, in the United States, the more one spouse in the family makes the decisions and has the power, the more physical violence occurs in the family. Wife beating is even more likely when the husband controls the household and is out of work.[72]

Wife beating appears to be related to broader patterns of violence in adulthood. Societies that have violent methods of conflict resolution within communities, physical punishment of criminals, high frequency of warfare, and cruelty toward enemies generally have more wife beating.[73]

REDUCING THE RISK. What can be done to minimize family violence? First, we have to recognize that probably nothing can be done as long as people in a society do not acknowledge that there is a problem. If severe child punishment and wife beating are perfectly acceptable by almost everyone in a society, they are unlikely to be considered social problems that need solutions. In our own society many programs are designed to take abused children or wives away from the family situation or to punish the abuser. (Of course, in these situations the violence has already occurred and was serious enough to have been noticed.) Cross-culturally, at least with respect to wife beating, intervention by others seems to be successful only if the intervention occurs before violence gets serious. As one would expect, however, those societies most prone to a high rate of wife beating are the least likely to practice immediate intervention. More helpful perhaps, but admittedly harder to arrange, is the promotion of conditions of life that are associated with low family violence. Research so far suggests that promoting the equality of men and women and the sharing of child-rearing responsibilities may go a long way toward lessening incidents of family violence.[74]

CRIME

What is a crime in one society is not necessarily a crime in another. Just as it is difficult to decide what constitutes abuse, it is difficult to define crime. In one society, it may be a crime to walk over someone's land without permission; in another, there might not be any concept of personal ownership, and therefore no concept of trespassing. In seeking to understand variation in crime, it is not surprising that many researchers have preferred to compare those behaviors that are more or less universally considered crimes and that are reliably reported. For example, in a large-scale comparison of crime in 110 nations over a span of 70 years, Dane Archer and Rosemary Gartner concentrated on homicide rates. They argued that homicide is harder for the public to hide and for officials to ignore than are other crimes. A comparison of interviews about crime with police records suggests that homicide is the most reliably reported crime in official records.[75]

Nations not only have very different crime rates when we compare them at a given point in time; the rates also vary over time within a nation. In the last 600 years, homicide rates have generally declined in Western societies. In England, where homicide rates have been well documented for centuries, the chance of murder during the thirteenth and fourteenth centuries was 10 times higher than in England today. But beginning in the 1960s, homicide and other crime rates have surged upward in many Western countries.[76] Some of the lowest homicide rates around 1970 (the latest date for which we have some indicator for many nations) were found in Iran, Dahomey, Puerto Rico, New Zealand, Norway, England, and France. Some of the highest homicide rates were found in Iraq, Colombia, Burma, Thailand, Swaziland, and Uganda. Compared with other countries, the United States had a fairly high homicide rate; approximately three-fourths of the countries surveyed had lower homicide rates than the United States.[77]

One of the clearest findings to emerge from comparative studies of crime is that war is associated with higher rates of homicide. Archer and Gartner compared changes in homicide rates of nations before and after major wars. Whether a nation is defeated or victorious, homicide rates tend to increase after a war. This result is consistent with the idea that a society or nation legitimizes violence during wartime. During wartime, societies approve of killing the enemy; afterward, homicide rates may go up because inhibitions against killing have been relaxed.[78] Ted Gurr suggested that the long-term downtrend in crime in Western societies seems to be consistent with an increasing emphasis on humanistic values and nonviolent achievement of goals. But such goals may be temporarily suspended during wartime. In the United States, for example, surges in violent crime rates occurred during the 1860s and 1870s (during and after the Civil War), after World War I, after World War II, and during the Vietnam War.[79]

In the types of societies that anthropologists typically study, homicide statistics are not usually available; so cross-cultural studies of homicide usually measure homicide rates by comparing and rank ordering ethnographers' statements about the frequency of homicide. For example, the statement that murder is "practically unheard of" is taken to mean that the murder rate is lower than where it is reported that "homicide is not uncommon." Despite the fact that the data on cultural homicide rates are not quantitative, the cross-cultural results are consistent with the cross-national results; more war is usually associated with more homicide and assault, as well as with socially approved aggressive behaviors (as in aggressive games) and severe physical punishment for wrongdoing.[80] Our own recent cross-cultural study suggests that the more war a society has, the more socialization or training of aggression in boys it will have, and such socialization strongly predicts higher rates of homicide and assault.[81]

Capital punishment—execution of criminals—is severe physical punishment for wrongdoing. It is commonly thought that would-be murderers are deterred by the prospect of capital punishment. Yet cross-national research suggests otherwise. Instead of increasing after capital punishment is abolished, murder rates go down.[82] Why? Perhaps capital punishment, which is homicide committed by society, legitimizes violence just as war seems to do.

Research conducted in the United States suggests that juvenile delinquents (usually boys) are likely to come from broken homes, with the father absent for much of the time the boy is growing up. The conclusion often drawn is that father absence somehow increases the likelihood of delinquency and adult forms of physical violence. But other conditions that may cause delinquency are also associated with broken homes, conditions such as the stigma of not having a "regular" family and the generally low standard of living of such families. It is therefore important to conduct research in other societies, in which father absence does not occur in concert with these other factors, to see if father absence by itself is related to physical violence.

For example, in many polygynous societies, children grow up in a mother-child household; the father lives separately and is hardly ever around the child. Does the father-absence explanation of delinquency and violence fit such societies? The answer is apparently yes: Societies in which children are reared in mother-child households or the father spends little time in child care tend to have more physical violence by males than do societies in which fathers spend time with children.[83]

More research is needed to discover exactly what accounts for this relationship. It is possible, as some suggest, that boys growing up without fathers are apt to act "super-masculine," to show how "male" they are. But it is also possible that mothers who rear children alone often use physical punishment, and therefore are likely to provide an aggressive role model for the child. In addition, high male mortality in war predicts polygyny, as we saw in the chapter on marriage and the family; therefore boys in polygynous societies are likely to be exposed to a warrior tradition.[84]

Trying to act super-masculine, however, may be likely to involve violence *only* if aggression is an important component of the male gender role in society. If men were expected by society to be sensitive, caring, and nonviolent, boys who grew up without fathers might try to be super-sensitive and super-caring. So society's expectations for males probably shape how growing up in a mother-child

A society may encourage boys to play soldier, perhaps to prepare them to be courageous in combat later on. Cross-culturally, socialization for aggression strongly predicts homicide and assault.

household affects behavior in adolescence and later.[85]

One widely held idea is that poor economic conditions increase the likelihood of crime, but the relationship does not appear to be strong. Also, the findings are somewhat different for different types of crime. For example, hundreds of studies in this and other countries do not show a clear relationship between changes in economic well-being as measured by unemployment rates and changes in violent crime as measured by homicide. Homicide does not appear to increase in bad times. Property crimes, however, do increase with increases in unemployment. Violent crime does appear to be associated with one economic characteristic: Homicide is usually highest in nations with high income inequality. Why income inequality predicts homicide but downturns in the economy do not is something of a puzzle.[86]

The fact that property crime is linked to unemployment is consistent with the cross-cultural finding that theft (but not violent crime) tends to occur less often in egalitarian societies than in stratified ones. Societies with equal access to resources usually have distribution mechanisms that offset any differences in wealth. Hence theft should be less of a temptation and therefore less likely in an egalitarian society. Theft rates are higher in socially stratified societies despite the fact that they are more likely than egalitarian societies to have police and courts to punish crime. Societies may try to deter property and other crimes when the rates of such are high, but we do not know that these efforts actually reduce the rates.

So what does the available research suggest about how we might be able to reduce crime? The results so far indicate that homicide rates are highest in societies that socialize their boys for aggression. Such socialization is linked to war and other forms of socially approved violence—capital punishment, television and movie violence by heroes, violence in sports. The statistical evidence suggests that war is a cause of socialization for aggression, which in turn is a cause of high rates of violence. The policy implication of these results is that if we can reduce socialization for aggression, by reducing the risk of war and therefore the necessity to produce effective warriors, and if we can reduce other forms of socially approved violence, we may thereby reduce rates of violent crime. The reduction of inequalities in wealth may also help to reduce crime, particularly theft. And although it is not yet clear why, it appears that raising boys with a male role model around may reduce the likelihood of male violence in adulthood.

WAR

War is an unfortunate fact of life in most societies known to anthropology, judging by the cross-cultural research we referred to in the chapter on political life. Almost every society had at least occasional wars when it was first described, unless it had been pacified (usually by Western colonial powers).[87] Since the Civil War, the United States has not had any wars on its territory, but it is unusual in that respect. Before pacification, most societies had frequent armed combat between communities or larger units that usually spoke the same language. That is, most warfare was internal to the society or language group. Even some wars in modern times involved speakers of the same language; recall the wars between Italian states before the unification of Italy and many of the "civil" wars of the last two centuries. Although people in some societies might fight against people in other societies, such "external" wars were usually not organized on behalf of the entire society or even a major section of it.[88] That is, warfare in the ethnographic record did not usually involve politically unified societies. Finally, the absolute numbers of people killed may have been small, but this does not mean that warfare in nonindustrial societies was a trivial matter. Indeed, it appears that nonindustrial warfare may have been even more lethal *proportionately* than modern warfare, judging by the fact that wars killed 25 to 30 percent of the males in some nonindustrial societies.[89]

In the chapter on political life, we discussed the possibility that people in nonindustrial societies go to war mostly out of fear, particularly a fear of expectable but unpredictable natural disasters (droughts, floods, hurricanes, among ot'hers) that destroy food supplies. People with more of a history of such disasters have more war. It seems as if they go to war to protect themselves ahead of time from disasters, inasmuch as the victors in war almost always take resources (land, animals, other things) from the defeated, even when the victors have no current resource problems. Another factor apparently making for more war is teaching children to mistrust others. People who grow up to be mistrustful of others may be more likely to go to war than to negotiate or seek conciliation with "enemies." Mistrust or fear of others seems to be partly caused by threat or fear of disasters.[90]

Is warfare in and between modern state societies explainable in much the same way that nonindustrial warfare seems to be explainable? If the answer to that question turns out to be yes, it will certainly be a modified yes, because the realities of industrialized societies require an expanded conception of disasters. In the modern world, with its complex economic and political dependencies among nations, we may not be worried only about weather or pest disasters that could curtail food supplies. Possible curtailments of other resources—particularly oil—may also scare us into going to war. According to some commentators, the decision to go to war against Iraq after it invaded Kuwait in 1991 fits that theory of war.

But even if the "threat-to-resources" theory is true, we may be coming to realize (with the end of the Cold War) that war is not the only way to ensure access to resources. There may be a better way in the modern world, a way that is more cost-effective as well as more preserving of human life. If it is true that war is most likely when people fear unpredictable disasters of any kind, the risk of war should lessen when people realize that the harmful effects of disasters could be reduced or prevented by international cooperation. Just as we have the assurance of disaster relief within our country, we could have the assurance of disaster relief worldwide. That is, the fear of unpredictable disasters and the fear of others, and the consequent risk of war, could be reduced by the assurance ahead of time that the world would help those in need in case of disaster. Instead of going to war out of fear, we could go to peace by agreeing to share. The certainty of international cooperation could compensate for the uncertainty of resources.

Consider how Germany and Japan have fared in the half century since their "unconditional surrender" in World War II. They were forbidden to participate in the international arms race and could rely on others, particularly the United States, to protect them. Without a huge burden of armaments, Germany and Japan thrived. But countries that competed militarily, particularly the United States and the Soviet Union, declined economically. Doesn't that scenario at least suggest the wisdom of international cooperation, particularly the need for international agreements to assure worldwide disaster relief? Compared with going to war and its enormous costs, going to peace would be a bargain!

Recent research in political science and anthropology suggests an additional way to reduce the risk of war. Among the societies known to anthropology, studies indicate that people in more participatory—that is, more "democratic"—political systems rarely go to war with each other.[91] Thus, if authoritarian governments were to disappear from the world, because the powerful nations of the world stopped supporting them militarily and otherwise, the world could be more peaceful for this reason too.

Although democratically governed states rarely go to war with each other, they are not necessarily more peaceful in general. On the contrary, they are as likely to go to war as are other kinds of political systems, but not so much with each other. For example, the United States has gone to war with Grenada, Panama, and Iraq—all authoritarian states—but not with democratic Canada, with which the United States has also had disputes. The theory suggested by the cross-national and cross-cultural results is that democratic conflict resolution within a political system generalizes to democratic conflict resolution between political systems, if the systems are both democratic. If our participatory institutions and perceptions allow us to resolve our disputes peacefully, internally and externally, we may think that similarly governed people would also be disposed to settle things peacefully. Therefore, disputes between participatory political systems should be unlikely to result in war.

The understanding that participatory systems rarely fight each other, and knowing why they do not, would have important consequences for policy in the contemporary world. The kinds of military preparations believed necessary and the costs people would be willing to pay for them might be affected. On the one hand, understanding the relationship beween democracy and peace might encourage war making against authoritarian regimes to overturn them—with enormous costs in human life and otherwise. On the other hand, understanding the consequences of democracy might encourage us to assist the emergence and consolidation of more participatory systems of government in the countries of eastern Europe, the former Soviet Union, and elsewhere. In any case, the relationship between democracy and peace strongly suggests that it is counterproductive to support any undemocratic regimes, even if they happen to be enemies of our enemies, if we want to minimize the risk of war in the world.

MAKING THE WORLD BETTER

Many social problems afflict our world, not just the ones discussed in this chapter. We don't have the space to discuss the international trade in drugs and how it plays out in violence, death, and corruption. We haven't discussed the negative effects of environmental degradation—water and air pollution, global warming, ozone depletion, destruction of forests and wetlands. We haven't said anything about overpopulation, the energy crisis, and a host of other problems we should care and do something about, if we hope to make this a better world. What we have tried to do in this chapter is encourage positive thinking by suggesting how the results of scientific research could be applied to solving social problems.

We may know enough now that we can do something about our problems, and we will discover more on the basis of future research. Social problems are mostly of human making and therefore are susceptible to human unmaking. There may be difficulties, but we can overcome them if we want to.

▌SUMMARY

1. We may be more motivated now to try to solve social problems because worldwide communication has increased our awareness of them elsewhere, because we seem to be increasingly bothered by problems in our own society, and because we know more than we used to about various social problems that afflict our world.

2. Applied anthropology in the United States developed out of anthropologists' personal experiences with disadvantaged peoples. Applied, or practicing, anthropologists may be involved in one or more phases of a program that is designed to change peoples' lives: assembling relevant knowledge, constructing alternative plans, assessing the likely social and environmental impact of particular plans, implementing the program, and monitoring the program and its effects.

3. Today many anthropologists are finding employment outside of anthropology departments—in medical schools, health centers, development agencies, urban-planning agencies, and other public and private organizations.

4. The code of ethics for those who work professionally as applied anthropologists specifies that the target population should be included as much as possible in the formulation of policy, so that people in the community may know in advance how the program may affect them. But perhaps the most important aspect of the code is the pledge not to be involved in any plan whose effect will not be beneficial. It is often difficult to evaluate the effects of planned changes. Long-term consequences may be detrimental even if the changes are beneficial in the short run.

5. Even if a planned change will prove beneficial to its target population, the people may not accept it. And if the proposed innovation is not utilized by the intended target, the project cannot be considered a success. Target populations may reject or resist a proposed innovation for various reasons: because they are unaware of the need for the change; because they misinterpret the symbols used to explain the change or fail to understand its real purpose; because their customs and institutions conflict with the change; or because they are afraid of it. The target population may also resist the proposed change because they unconsciously or consciously know it is not good for them.

6. To be effective, change agents may have to discover and use the traditional channels of influence in introducing their projects to the target population.

7. The idea that we can solve global social problems is based on two assumptions. We have to assume that it is possible to discover the causes of a problem, and we have to assume that we will be able to do something about the causes once they are discovered and thereby eliminate or reduce the problem.

8. Until medical science develops an effective and inexpensive vaccine or treatment for AIDS, the risk of infection can be reduced only by changes in social, particularly sexual, behavior.

9. Disasters such as earthquakes, floods, and droughts can have greater or lesser effects on human life, depending on social conditions. Therefore disasters are partly social problems, with partly social causes and solutions.

10. Whether people become homeless, whether there are shantytowns, seem to depend on a society's willingness to share wealth and help those in need.

11. Promoting the equality of men and women and the sharing of child-rearing responsibilities may reduce family violence.

12. We may be able to reduce rates of violent crime if we can reduce socialization and training for aggression. To do that we would have to reduce the likelihood of war, the high likelihood of which predicts more socialization for aggression and other forms of socially approved aggression. The reduction of inequalities in wealth may also help to reduce crime, particularly theft. And raising boys with a male role model around may reduce the likelihood of male violence in adulthood.

13. People seem to be most likely to go to war when they fear unpredictable disasters that destroy food supplies or curtail the supplies of other necessities. Disputes between more participatory (more "democratic") political systems are unlikely to result in war. Therefore, the more democracy spreads in the world, and the more people all over the world are assured of internationally organized disaster relief, the more they might go to peace rather than to war to solve their problems.

GLOSSARY TERMS

applied anthropology
or practicing
anthropology

AIDS (acquired
immune deficiency
syndrome)

CRITICAL QUESTIONS

1. What particular advantages do anthropologists have in trying to solve practical problems?

2. Is it ethical to try to influence people's lives when they have not asked for help?

3. Do global problems require solutions by global agencies? If so, which?

INTERNET EXERCISES

1. On the World Wide Web, document at least three Web pages that are related to AIDS and discrimination. Summarize your findings. While doing the search, focus on the relations between AIDS and anthropology as demonstrated in this chapter.

2. Visit **http://www.newhorizons.org/announce_pbsrace.html**, a site that provides links to a number of race related issues. Explore at least three links and summarize your findings on how the issues surrounding race are perceived in the United States.

3. Explore the Web page for one professional society devoted to applied anthropology. Check out **http://www.telepath.com/sfaa/**, which is the page for the Society for Applied Anthropology. Read the Statement of Ethics at that site. The Applied Anthropology Computer Network (**http://www.oakland.edu/~dow/anthap.htm**) has frequently asked questions about applied anthropology. Find one question you are curious about and summarize the answer.

4. The United Nations has a Web site with information about natural and other disasters at **http://wwwnotes.reliefweb.int/**. Using the search button, look for information on one current famine. What can you find out about its causes, and what, if anything, is the international world doing about it?

SUGGESTED READING

APTEKAR, L. *Environmental Disasters in Global Perspective.* New York: G. K. Hall/Macmillan, 1994. This volume discusses various kinds of environmental disaster. It is one of a series of monographs, sponsored by the Human Relations Area Files, on the current state of cross-cultural and cross-national research on social problems around the world.

Others in the series include S. M. Albert and M. G. Cattell, *Old Age in Global Perspective: Cross-Cultural and Cross-National Views,* 1994; and I. Glasser, *Homelessness in Cross-Cultural Perspective,* 1994.

BODLEY, J. H. *Anthropology and Contemporary Human Problems,* 3rd ed. Mountain View, CA: Mayfield, 1995. This book discusses the problems of overconsumption, adaptation to environment, resource depletion, hunger and starvation, overpopulation, violence, and war.

EDDY, E. M., AND PARTRIDGE, W., eds. *Applied Anthropology in America,* 2nd ed. New York: Columbia University Press, 1987. A set of essays about the relevance of applied anthropology in American society. Provides an overview of how anthropology has contributed and can contribute to major policy issues confronting our nation.

EMBER, C. R., EMBER, M., AND PEREGRINE, P., eds. *Research Frontiers in Anthropology.* Upper Saddle River, NJ: Prentice Hall, 1998. Prentice Hall/Simon & Schuster Custom Publishing; and Ember, C. R., and Ember, M. *Cross-Cultural Research for Social Science.* Upper Saddle River, NJ: Prentice Hall, 1998. Prentice Hall/Simon & Schuster Custom Publishing. A number of chapters in these two series deal explicitly with the study of social problems, including M. G. Cattell and S. M. Albert, "Caring for the Elderly"; A. Cohen and P. Koegel, "Homelessness"; R. Dirks, "Hunger and Famine"; G. M. Erchak, "Family Violence"; R. Gartner, "Crime: Variations across Cultures and Nations"; P. C. Rosenblatt, "Human Rights Violations across Cultures"; M. H. Ross, "Ethnocentrism and Ethnic Conflict"; and M. D. Williams, "Racism: The Production, Reproduction, and Obsolescence of Social Inferiority."

FLUEHR-LOBBAN, C., ed. *Ethics and the Profession of Anthropology: Dialogue for a New Era.* Philadelphia: University of Pennsylvania Press, 1991. This edited volume contains historical and contemporary reviews of ethical issues regarding the profession of anthropology.

PODOLEFSKY, A., AND BROWN, P. J. *Applying Cultural Anthropology: An Introductory Reader.* Mountain View, CA: Mayfield, 1997. A selection of readings across a broad range of topics in cultural anthropology that are designed to show how anthropology is important in today's world. The selections show both the basic and applied elements in anthropological research.

VAN WILLIGEN, J. *Applied Anthropology: An Introduction,* rev. ed. Westport, CT: Bergin & Garvey Paperback, 1993. With numerous examples of applied projects, this survey of applied anthropology deals with ethics in the subdiscipline, applied research methods, social impact assessment, evaluation research, action anthropology, community development, and the role of cultural broker.

Glossary

Absolute Dating   a method of dating fossils in which the actual age of a deposit or specimen is measured. Also known as chronometric dating.

Acculturation   the process of extensive borrowing of aspects of culture in the context of superordinate-subordinate relations between societies; usually occurs as the result of external pressure.

Acheulian   a stone toolmaking tradition dating from 1.5 million years ago. Compared with the Oldowan tradition, Acheulian assemblages have more large tools created according to standardized designs or shapes. One of the most characteristic and prevalent tools in the Acheulian tool kit is the so-called handaxe, which is a teardrop-shaped bifacially flaked tool with a thinned sharp tip. Other large tools might have been cleavers and picks.

Achieved Qualities   those qualities a person acquires during her or his lifetime.

Adapid   a type of prosimian with many lemurlike features; appeared in the early Eocene.

Adaptive   a trait that enhances survival and reproductive success in a particular environment. Usually applied to biological evolution, the term is also often used by cultural anthropologists to refer to cultural traits that enhance reproductive success.

Affinal Kin   one's relatives by marriage.

Age-Grade   a category of persons who happen to fall within a particular, culturally distinguished age range.

Age-Set   a group of persons of similar age and the same sex who move together through some or all of life's stages.

AIDS (Acquired Immune Deficiency Syndrome)   a recent disease, almost always lethal, presumably caused by the HIV virus(es).

Allele   one member of a pair of genes.

Allen's Rule   the rule that protruding body parts (particularly arms and legs) are relatively shorter in the cooler areas of a species' range than in the warmer areas.

Ambilineal Descent   the rule of descent that affiliates an individual with groups of kin related to him or her through men *or* women.

Ancestor Spirits   supernatural beings who are the ghosts of dead relatives.

Animatism   a belief in supernatural forces.

Animism   a term used by Edward Tylor to describe a belief in a dual existence for all things—a physical, visible body and a psychic, invisible soul.

Anthropoids   one of the two suborders of primates; includes monkeys, apes, and humans.

Anthropological Linguistics   the anthropological study of languages.

Anthropology   the study of differences and similarities, both biological and cultural, in human populations. Anthropology is concerned with typical biological and cultural characteristics of human populations in all periods and in all parts of the world.

Applied Anthropology   the branch of anthropology that concerns itself with applying anthropological knowledge to achieve practical goals, usually in the service of an agency outside the traditional academic setting. Also called practicing anthropology.

^{40}Ar-^{39}Ar Dating Method   used in conjunction with potassium-argon dating, this method gets around the problem of needing different rock samples to estimate potassium and argon. A nuclear reactor is used to convert the ^{39}Ar to ^{39}K, on the basis of which the amount of ^{40}K can be estimated. In this way, both argon and potassium can be estimated from the same rock sample.

Arboreal   adapted to living in trees.

Archaeology   the branch of anthropology that seeks to reconstruct the daily life and customs of peoples who lived in the past and to trace and explain cultural changes. Often lacking written records for study, archaeologists must try to reconstruct history from the material remains of human cultures. See **Historical Archaeology.**

Ascribed Qualities   those qualities that are determined for a person at birth.

Association   an organized group not based exclusively on kinship or territory.

Atlatl   Aztec word for "spear-thrower."

Australopithecus   genus of Pliocene and Pleistocene hominids.

Australopithecus afarensis   a species of *Australopithecus* that lived 4 to 3 million years ago in East Africa and was definitely bipedal.

Australopithecus africanus   a species of *Australopithecus* that lived between about 3 and 2 million years ago.

Australopithecus aethiopicus   an early robust australopithecine.

Australopithecus anamensis   a species of *Australopithecus* that lived perhaps 4.2 million years ago.

Australopithecus boisei   an East African robust australopithecine species dating from 2.2 to 1.3 million years ago with somewhat larger cranial capacity than *A. africanus*. No longer thought to be larger than other australopithecines, it is robust primarily in the skull and jaw, most strikingly in the teeth. Compared with *A. robustus*, *A. boisei* has even more features that reflect a huge chewing apparatus.

Australopithecus robustus   a robust australopithecine species found in South African caves dating from about 1.8 to 1 million years ago. Not as large in the teeth and jaws as *A. boisei*.

Avunculocal Residence   a pattern of residence in which a married couple settles with or near the husband's mother's brother.

Balanced Reciprocity   giving with the expectation of a straightforward immediate or limited-time trade.

Balancing Selection a type of selection that occurs when a heterozygous combination of alleles is positively favored even though a homozygous combination is disfavored.

Band a fairly small, usually nomadic local group that is politically autonomous.

Band Organization the kind of political organization where the local group or band is the largest territorial group in the society that acts as a unit. The local group in band societies is politically autonomous.

Behavioral Ecology the study of how all kinds of behavior may be related to the environment. The theoretical orientation involves the application of biological evolutionary principles to the behavior (including social behavior) of animals, including humans. Also called sociobiology, particularly when applied to social organization and social behavior.

Berdache a male transvestite in some Native American societies.

Bergmann's rule the rule that smaller-sized subpopulations of a species inhabit the warmer parts of its geographical range and larger-sized subpopulations the cooler areas.

Bifacial Tool a tool worked or flaked on two sides.

Bilateral Kinship the type of kinship system in which individuals affiliate more or less equally with their mother's and father's relatives; descent groups are absent.

Bilocal Residence a pattern of residence in which a married couple lives with or near either the husband's parents or the wife's parents.

Biological Anthropology the study of humans as biological organisms, dealing with the emergence and evolution of humans and with contemporary biological variations among human populations. Also called physical anthropology.

Bipedalism locomotion in which an animal walks on its two hind legs.

Blade a thin flake whose length is usually more than twice its width. In the blade technique of toolmaking, a core is prepared by shaping a piece of flint with hammerstones into a pyramidal or cylindrical form. Blades are then struck off until the core is used up.

Brachiators animals that move through the trees by swinging hand over hand from branch to branch. They usually have long arms and fingers.

Bride Price a substantial gift of goods or money given to the bride's kin by the groom or his kin at or before the marriage. Also called bride wealth.

Bride Service work performed by the groom for his bride's family for a variable length of time either before or after the marriage.

Burin a chisel-like stone tool used for carving and for making such artifacts as bone and antler needles, awls, and projectile points.

Canines the cone-shaped teeth immediately behind the incisors; used by most primates to seize food and in fighting and display.

Cash Crop a cultivated commodity raised for sale rather than for personal consumption by the cultivator.

Caste a ranked group, often associated with a certain occupation, in which membership is determined at birth and marriage is restricted to members of one's own caste.

Catarrhines the group of anthropoids with narrow noses and nostrils that face downward. Catarrhines include monkeys of the Old World (Africa, Asia, and Europe) as well as apes and humans.

Cercopithecoids Old World monkeys.

Cerebral Cortex the "gray matter" of the brain; the center of speech and other higher mental activities.

Chief a person who exercises authority, usually on behalf of a multicommunity political unit. This role is generally found in rank societies and is usually permanent and often hereditary.

Chiefdom a political unit, with a chief at its head, integrating more than one community but not necessarily the whole society or language group.

Chromosomes paired rod-shaped structures within a cell nucleus containing the genes that transmit traits from one generation to the next.

Chronometric Dating see **Absolute Dating**

Civilization urban society, from the Latin word for "city-state."

Clan a set of kin whose members believe themselves to be descended from a common ancestor or ancestress but cannot specify the links back to that founder; often designated by a totem. Also called a sib.

Class a category of persons who have about the same opportunity to obtain economic resources, power, and prestige.

Classificatory Terms kinship terms that merge or equate relatives who are genealogically distinct from one another; the same term is used for a number of different kin.

Class Society a society containing social groups that have unequal access to economic resources, power, and prestige.

Cline the gradually increasing (or decreasing) frequency of a gene from one end of a region to another.

Codeswitching using more than one language in the course of conversing.

Codified Laws formal principles for resolving disputes impersonally in larger, more heterogeneous and stratified societies.

Cognates words or morphs that belong to different languages but have similar sounds and meanings.

Commercial Exchange see **Market Exchange.**

Commercialization the increasing dependence on buying and selling, with money usually as the medium of exchange.

Complementary Opposition the occasional uniting of various segments of a segmentary lineage system in opposition to similar segments.

Consanguineal Kin one's biological relatives; relatives by birth.

Core Vocabulary nonspecialist vocabulary.

Corvée a system of required labor.

Cretaceous geological epoch 135 to 65 million years ago, during which dinosaurs and other reptiles ceased to be the dominant land vertebrates and mammals and birds began to become important.

Crime violence not considered legitimate that occurs within a political unit.

Cro-Magnons humans who lived in western Europe about 35,000 years ago. Once thought to be the earliest specimens of modern-looking humans, or *Homo sapiens sapiens*. But it is now known that modern-looking humans appeared earlier outside of Europe; the earliest so far found lived in Africa.

Cross-Cousins children of siblings of the opposite sex. One's cross-cousins are father's sisters' children and mother's brothers' children.

Cross-Cultural Researcher an ethnologist who uses ethnographic data about many societies to test possible explanations of cultural variation.

Crossing-Over exchanges of sections of chromosomes from one chromosome to another.

Cultural Anthropology the study of cultural variation and universals.

Cultural Ecology the analysis of the relationship between a culture and its environment.

Cultural Relativism the attitude that a society's customs and ideas should be viewed within the context of that society's problems and opportunities.

Culture the set of learned behaviors, beliefs, attitudes, values, and ideals that are characteristic of a particular society or population.

Cuneiform wedge-shaped writing invented by the Sumerians around 3000 B.C.

Descriptive Linguistics see **Structural Linguistics.**

Descriptive Term kinship term used to refer to a genealogically distinct relative; a different term is used for each relative.

Dialect a variety of a language spoken in a particular area or by a particular social group.

Diffusion the borrowing by one society of a cultural trait belonging to another society as the result of contact between the two societies.

Directional Selection a type of natural selection that increases the frequency of a trait (the trait is said to be positively favored, or adaptive).

Diurnal active during the day.

Divination getting the supernatural to provide guidance.

DNA deoxyribonucleic acid; a long, two-stranded molecule in the genes that directs the making of an organism according to the instructions in its genetic code.

Domestication modification or adaptation of plants and animals for use by humans. When people plant crops, we refer to the process as cultivation. It is only when the crops cultivated and the animals raised have been modified—are different from wild varieties—that we speak of plant and animal domestication.

Dominant the allele of a gene pair that is always phenotypically expressed in the heterozygous form.

Double Descent a system that affiliates an individual with a group of matrilineal kin for some purposes and with a group of patrilineal kin for other purposes. Also called double unilineal descent.

Dowry a substantial transfer of goods or money from the bride's family to the bride.

Dryopithecus genus of ape from the later Miocene found primarily in Europe. It had thin tooth enamel and pointed molar cusps quite similar to those of the fruit-eating chimpanzees of today.

Egalitarian Society a society in which all persons of a given age-sex category have equal access to economic resources, power, and prestige.

Ego in the reckoning of kinship, the reference point or focal person.

Electron Spin Resonance Dating like thermoluminescence dating, this technique measures trapped electrons from surrounding radioactive material. The material to be dated is exposed to varying magnetic fields in order to obtain a spectrum of the microwaves absorbed by the tested material. Because no heating is required for this technique, electron spin resonance is especially useful for dating organic materials, such as bone and shell, that decompose if heated.

Endogamy the rule specifying marriage to a person within one's own (kin, caste, community) group.

Eocene a geological epoch 55 to 34 million years ago during which the first definite primates appeared.

Ethnocentric refers to judgment of other cultures solely in terms of one's own culture.

Ethnocentrism the attitude that other societies' customs and ideas can be judged in the context of one's own culture.

Ethnographer a person who spends some time living with, interviewing, and observing a group of people so that he or she can describe their customs.

Ethnographic analogy method of comparative cultural study that extrapolates to the past from recent or current societies.

Ethnography a description of a society's customary behaviors, beliefs, and attitudes.

Ethnohistorian an ethnologist who uses historical documents to study how a particular culture has changed over time.

Ethnology the study of how and why recent cultures differ and are similar.

Exogamy the rule specifying marriage to a person from outside one's own (kin or community) group.

Explanation an answer to a *why* question. In science, there are two kinds of explanation that researchers try to achieve—associations and theories.

Expressive Culture activities, such as art, music, dance, and folklore, that presumably express thoughts and feelings.

Extended Family a family consisting of two or more single-parent, monogamous, polygynous, or polyandrous families linked by a blood tie.

Extensive Cultivation a type of horticulture in which the land is worked for short periods and then left to regenerate for some years before being used again. Also called shifting cultivation.

Falsification showing that a theory seems to be wrong by finding that implications or predictions derivable from it are not consistent with objectively collected data.

Family a social and economic unit consisting minimally of a parent and a child.

Feuding a state of recurring hostility between families or groups of kin, usually motivated by a desire to avenge an offense against a member of the group.

Fieldwork firsthand experience with the people being studied and the usual means by which anthropological information is obtained. Regardless of other methods (e.g., censuses, surveys) that anthropologists may use, fieldwork usually involves participant observation for an extended period of time, often a year or more. See **Participant Observation.**

Fission-Track Dating a chronometric dating method used to date crystal, glass, and many uranium-rich materials contemporaneous with fossils or deposits that are from 20 to 5 billion years old. This dating method entails counting the tracks or paths of decaying uranium-isotope atoms in the sample and then comparing the number of tracks with the uranium content of the sample.

Folklore includes all the myths, legends, folktales, ballads, riddles, proverbs, and superstitions of a cultural group. Generally, folklore is transmitted orally, but it may also be written.

Food Collection all forms of subsistence technology in which food-getting is dependent on naturally occurring resources—wild plants and animals.

Food Production the form of subsistence technology in which food-getting is dependent on the cultivation and domestication of plants and animals.

Foragers people who subsist on the collection of naturally occurring plants and animals. Also referred to as hunter-gatherers.

Foramen Magnum hole in the base of the skull through which the spinal cord passes en route to the brain.

Fossils the hardened remains or impressions of plants and animals that lived in the past.

Fraternal Polyandry the marriage of a woman to two or more brothers at one time.

F-U-N Trio fluorine (F), uranium (U), and nitrogen (N) tests for relative dating. All three minerals are present in groundwater. The older a fossil is, the higher its fluorine or uranium content will be, and the lower its nitrogen content.

Gender Differences differences between females and males that reflect cultural expectations and experiences.

Gene chemical unit of heredity.

Gene Flow the process by which genes pass from the gene pool of one population to that of another through mating and reproduction.

Generalized Reciprocity gift giving without any immediate or planned return.

General-Purpose Money a universally accepted medium of exchange.

Genetic Drift the various random processes that affect gene frequencies in small, relatively isolated populations.

Genotype the total complement of inherited traits or genes of an organism.

Genus a group of related species; pl., *genera.*

Ghosts supernatural beings who were once human; the souls of dead people.

Gloger's Rule the rule that populations of birds and mammals living in warm, humid climates have more melanin (and therefore darker skin, fur, or feathers) than populations of the same species living in cooler, drier areas.

Gods supernatural beings of nonhuman origin who are named personalities; often anthropomorphic.

Group Marriage marriage in which more than one man is married to more than one woman at the same time; not customary in any known human society.

Group Selection natural selection of group characteristics.

Half-Life the time it takes for half of the atoms of a radioactive substance to decay into atoms of a different substance.

Headman a person who holds a powerless but symbolically unifying position in a community within an egalitarian society; may exercise influence but has no power to impose sanctions.

Heterozygous possessing differing genes or alleles in corresponding locations on a pair of chromosomes.

Hieroglyphics "picture writing," as in ancient Egypt and in Mayan sites in Mesoamerica (Mexico and Central America).

Historical Archaeology a specialty within archaeology that studies the material remains of recent peoples who left written records.

Historical Linguistics the study of how languages change over time.

Holistic refers to an approach that studies many aspects of a multifaceted system.

Hominids the group of hominoids consisting of humans and their direct ancestors. It contains at least two genera: *Homo* and *Australopithecus.*

Hominoids the group of catarrhines that includes both apes and humans.

Homo genus to which modern humans and their ancestors belong.

Homo erectus the first hominid species to be widely distributed in the Old World. The earliest finds are possibly 1.8 million years old. The brain (averaging 895–1040 cc) was larger than that found in any of the australopithecines or *H. habilis* but smaller than the average brain of a modern human.

Homo habilis early species belonging to our genus, *Homo,* with cranial capacities averaging about 630–640 cc, about 50 percent of the brain capacity of modern humans. Dating from about 2 million years ago.

Homo sapiens all living people belong to one biological species, *Homo sapiens,* which means that all human populations on earth can successfully interbreed. The first *Homo sapiens* may have emerged by 200,000 years ago.

Homo sapiens neanderthalensis a variety of early *Homo sapiens.*

Homo sapiens sapiens modern-looking humans, undisputed examples of which appeared about 50,000 years ago; may have appeared earlier.

Homozygous possessing two identical genes or alleles in corresponding locations on a pair of chromosomes.

Horticulture plant cultivation carried out with relatively simple tools and methods; nature is allowed to replace nutrients in the soil, in the absence of permanently cultivated fields.

Human Paleontology the study of the emergence of humans and their later physical evolution. Also called paleoanthropology.

Human Variation the study of how and why contemporary human populations vary biologically.

Hunter-gatherers people who collect food from naturally occurring resources, namely wild plants and animals. Also referred to as foragers.

Hylobates the family of hominoids that includes gibbons and siamangs; often referred to as the lesser apes (as compared with the great apes such as gorillas and chimpanzees).

Hypotheses predictions, which may be derived from theories, about how variables are related.

Hypoxia a condition of oxygen deficiency that often occurs at high altitudes. The percentage of oxygen in the air is the same as at lower altitudes, but because the barometric pressure is lower, less oxygen is taken in with each breath. Often, breathing becomes more rapid, the heart beats faster, and activity is more difficult.

Incest Taboo prohibition of sexual intercourse or marriage between mother and son, father and daughter, and brother and sister.

Incisors the front teeth; used for holding or seizing food and preparing it for chewing by the other teeth.

Indirect Dowry goods given by the groom's kin to the bride (or her father, who passes most of them to her) at or before her marriage.

Indirect Percussion a toolmaking technique common in the Upper Paleolithic. After shaping a core into a pyramidal or cylindrical form, the toolmaker can put a punch of antler or wood or another hard material into position and strike it with a hammer. Using a hammer-struck punch enabled the toolmaker to strike off consistently shaped blades.

Individual Selection natural selection of individual characteristics.

Insectivore the order or major grouping of mammals, including modern shrews and moles, that is adapted to feeding on insects.

Intensive Agriculture food production characterized by the permanent cultivation of fields and made possible by the use of the plow, draft animals or machines, fertilizers, irrigation, water-storage techniques, and other complex agricultural techniques.

^{40}K a radioactive isotope of potassium.

Kenyapithecus an apelike primate from the Middle Miocene found in East Africa. It had very thickly enameled teeth and robust jaws, suggesting a diet of hard, tough foods. Probably somewhat terrestrial.

Kindred a bilateral set of close relatives.

Kitchen Midden a pile of refuse, often shells, in an archaeological site.

Knuckle Walking a locomotor pattern of primates such as the chimpanzee and gorilla in which the weight of the upper part of the body is supported on the thickly padded knuckles of the hands.

Kula **Ring** a ceremonial exchange of valued shell ornaments in the Trobriand Islands, in which white shell armbands are traded around the islands in a counterclockwise direction and red shell necklaces are traded clockwise.

Laws (Scientific) associations or relationships that are accepted by almost all scientists.

Levalloisian Method a method that allowed flake tools of a predetermined size to be produced from a shaped core. The toolmaker first shaped the core and prepared a "striking platform" at one end. Flakes of predetermined and standard sizes could then be knocked off. Although some Levallois flakes date from as far back as 400,000 years ago, they are found more frequently in Mousterian toolkits.

Levirate a custom whereby a man is obliged to marry his brother's widow.

Lexical Content vocabulary or lexicon.

Lexicon the words and morphs, and their meanings, of a language; approximated by a dictionary.

Lineage a set of kin whose members trace descent from a common ancestor through known links.

Linguistics the study of language.

Lumbar Curve found only in hominids; the bottom part of the vertebral column forms a curve, causing the spinal column to be S-shaped (as seen from the side).

Magic the performance of certain rituals that are believed to compel the supernatural powers to act in particular ways.

Maladaptive a trait that diminishes the chances of survival and reproduction in a particular environment. Usually applied to biological evolution, the term is often used by cultural anthropologists to refer to behavioral or cultural traits that are likely to disappear because they diminish reproductive success.

Mana a supernatural, impersonal force that inhabits certain objects or people and is believed to confer success and/or strength.

Manumission the granting of freedom to a slave.

Market or Commercial Exchange transactions in which the "prices" are subject to supply and demand, whether or not the transactions occur in a marketplace. Also called commercial exchange.

Marriage a socially approved sexual and economic union usually between a man and a woman that is presumed, both by the couple and by others, to be more or less permanent, and that subsumes reciprocal rights and obligations between the two spouses and between spouses and their future children.

Matriclan a clan tracing descent through the female line.

Matrifocal Family a family consisting of a mother and her children.

Matrilineage a kin group whose members trace descent through known links in the female line from a common female ancestor.

Matrilineal Descent the rule of descent that affiliates an individual with kin of both sexes related to him or her through *women* only.

Matrilocal Residence a pattern of residence in which a married couple lives with or near the wife's parents.

Measure to describe how something compares with other things on some scale of variation.

Medium part-time religious practitioner who is asked to heal and divine while in a trance.

Meiosis the process by which reproductive cells are formed. In this process of division, the number of chromosomes in the newly formed cells is reduced by half, so that when fertilization occurs the resulting organism has the normal number of chromosomes appropriate to its species, rather than double that number.

Mesolithic   the archaeological period in the Old World beginning about 12,000 B.C. Humans were starting to settle down in semipermanent camps and villages, as people began to depend less on big game (which they used to have to follow over long distances) and more on relatively stationary food resources such as fish, shellfish, small game, and wild plants rich in carbohydrates, proteins, and oils.

Microlith   a small, razorlike blade fragment that was probably attached in a series to a wooden or bone handle to form a cutting edge.

Miocene   the geological epoch from 24 to 5.2 million years ago.

Mitosis   cellular reproduction or growth involving the duplication of chromosome pairs.

Moiety   a unilineal descent group in a society that is divided into two such maximal groups; there may be smaller unilineal descent groups as well.

Molars   the large teeth behind the premolars at the back of the jaw; used for chewing and grinding food.

Monogamy   marriage between only one man and only one woman at a time.

Monotheistic   believing that there is only one high god and that all other supernatural beings are subordinate to, or are alternative manifestations of, this supreme being.

Morph   the smallest unit of a language that has a meaning.

Morpheme   one or more morphs with the same meaning.

Morphology   the study of how sound sequences convey meaning.

Mousterian tool assemblage   named after the tool assemblage found in a rock shelter at Le Moustier in the Dordogne region of southwestern France. Compared with an Acheulian assemblage, the Middle Paleolithic (40,000–300,000 years ago) Mousterian has a smaller proportion of large core tools such as handaxes and cleavers and a bigger proportion of small flake tools such as scrapers. Flakes were often altered or "retouched" by striking small flakes or chips from one or more edges.

Mutation   a change in the DNA sequence, producing an altered gene.

Natural Selection   the outcome of processes that affect the frequencies of traits in a particular environment. Traits that enhance survival and reproductive success increase in frequency over time.

Negative Reciprocity   giving and taking that attempts to take advantage of another for one's own interest.

Neolithic   originally meaning "the new stone age," now meaning the presence of domesticated plants and animals. The earliest evidence of domestication comes from the Near East about 8000 B.C.

Neolocal Residence   a pattern of residence whereby a married couple lives separately, and usually at some distance, from the kin of both spouses.

Nocturnal   active during the night.

Nonfraternal Polyandry   marriage of a woman to two or more men who are not brothers.

Nonsororal Polygyny   marriage of a man to two or more women who are not sisters.

Normalizing Selection   the type of natural selection that removes harmful genes that arose by mutation.

Norms   standards or rules about acceptable behavior in a society. The importance of a norm usually can be judged by how members of a society respond when the norm is violated.

Nuclear Family   a family consisting of a married couple and their young children.

Oath   the act of calling upon a deity to bear witness to the truth of what one says.

Obsidian   a volcanic glass that can be used to make mirrors or sharp-edged tools.

Oldowan   the earliest stone toolmaking tradition, named after the tools found in Bed I at Olduvai Gorge, Tanzania; from about 2.5 million years ago. The stone artifacts include core tools and sharp-edged flakes made by striking one stone against another. Flake tools predominate. Among the core tools, so-called choppers are common.

Oligocene   the geological epoch 34 to 24 million years ago during which definite anthropoids emerged.

Omnivorous   eating both meat and vegetation.

Omomyid   a type of prosimian with many tarsier-like features that appeared in the early Eocene.

Operational Definition   a description of the procedure that is followed in measuring a variable.

Opposable Thumb   a thumb that can touch the tips of all the other fingers.

Optimal Foraging Theory   the theory that individuals seek to maximize the returns (in calories and nutrients) on their labor in deciding which animals and plants they will go after.

Ordeal   a means of determining guilt or innocence by submitting the accused to dangerous or painful tests believed to be under supernatural control.

Paleoanthropology   see **Human Paleontology.**

Paleocene   the geological epoch 65 to 55 million years ago.

Paleolithic   period of the early Stone Age, when flint, stone, and bone tools were developed and hunting and gathering were the means of acquiring food.

Parallel Cousins   children of siblings of the same sex. One's parallel cousins are father's brothers' children and mother's sisters' children.

Parapithecids   small monkeylike Oligocene primates found in the Fayum area of Egypt.

Participant-Observation   living among the people being studied—observing, questioning, and (when possible) taking part in the important events of the group. Writing or otherwise recording notes on observations, questions asked and answered, and things to check out later are parts of participant-observation.

Pastoralism   a form of subsistence technology in which food-getting is based directly or indirectly on the maintenance of domesticated animals.

Patriclan   a clan tracing descent through the male line.

Patrilineage   a kin group whose members trace descent through known links in the male line from a common male ancestor.

Patrilineal Descent the rule of descent that affiliates an individual with kin of both sexes related to him or her through *men* only.

Patrilocal Residence a pattern of residence in which a married couple lives with or near the husband's parents.

Peasants rural people who produce food for their own subsistence but who must also contribute or sell their surpluses to others (in towns and cities) who do not produce their own food.

Percussion Flaking a toolmaking technique in which one stone is struck with another to remove a flake.

Personality the distinctive way an individual thinks, feels, and behaves.

Personality Integration of Culture the theory that personality or psychological processes may account for connections between certain aspects of culture.

Phenotype the observable physical appearance of an organism, which may or may not reflect its genotype or total genetic constitution.

Phone a speech sound in a language.

Phoneme a sound or set of sounds that makes a difference in meaning to the speakers of the language.

Phonology the study of the sounds in a language and how they are used.

Phratry a unilineal descent group composed of a number of supposedly related clans (sibs).

Physical Anthropology See **Biological Anthropology.**

Platyrrhines the group of anthropoids that have broad, flat-bridged noses, with nostrils facing outward; these monkeys are currently found only in the New World (Central and South America).

Pleistocene a geological epoch that started 1.6 million years ago and, according to some, continues into the present. During this period, glaciers have often covered much of the earth's surface and humans became the dominant life form.

Pliocene the geological epoch 5.2 to 1.6 million years ago during which the earliest definite hominids appeared.

Polyandry the marriage of one woman to more than one man at a time.

Polygamy plural marriage; marriage to more than one spouse simultaneously.

Polygyny the marriage of one man to more than one woman at a time.

Polyphony two or more melodies sung simultaneously.

Polytheistic recognizing many gods, none of whom is believed to be superordinate.

Pongids hominoids whose members include both the living and extinct apes.

Postpartum Sex Taboo prohibition of sexual intercourse between a couple for a period of time after the birth of their child.

Potassium-Argon (K-Ar) Dating a chronometric dating method that uses the rate of decay of a radioactive form of potassium (^{40}K) into argon (^{40}Ar) to date samples from 5,000 to 3 billion years old. The K-Ar method dates the minerals and rocks in a deposit, not the fossils themselves.

Potlatch a feast among Northwest Coast Indians at which great quantities of food and goods are given to the guests in order to gain prestige for the host(s).

Practicing Anthropology see **Applied Anthropology.**

Prairie grassland with a high grass cover.

Prehensile adapted for grasping objects.

Prehistory the time before written records.

Premolars the teeth immediately behind the canines; used in chewing, grinding, and shearing food.

Pressure Flaking toolmaking technique whereby small flakes are struck off by pressing against the core with a bone, antler, or wood tool.

Priest generally a full-time specialist, with very high status, who is thought to be able to relate to superior or high gods beyond the ordinary person's access or control.

Primary Institutions the sources of early experiences, such as family organization and subsistence techniques, that presumably help form the basic, or typical, personality found in a society.

Primary Subsistence Activities the food-getting activities: gathering, hunting, fishing, herding, and agriculture.

Primate a member of the mammalian order Primates, divided into the two suborders of prosimians and anthropoids.

Primatologists persons who study primates.

Probability Value (p-value) the likelihood that an observed result could have occurred by chance.

Proconsul the best-known genus of proto-apes from the Early Miocene; found mostly in Africa.

Projective Tests tests that utilize ambiguous stimuli; test subjects must project their own personality traits in order to structure the ambiguous stimuli.

Propliopithecids apelike anthropoids dating from the early Oligocene, found in the Fayum area of Egypt.

Prosimians literally "premonkeys," one of the two suborders of primates; includes lemurs, lorises, and tarsiers.

Protolanguage a hypothesized ancestral language from which two or more languages seem to have derived.

Quadrupeds animals that walk on all fours.

Race in biology, *race* refers to a subpopulation or variety of a species that differs somewhat in gene frequencies from other varieties of the species. All members of a species can interbreed and produce viable offspring. Many anthropologists do not think that the concept of race is usefully applied to humans because humans do not fall into geographic populations that can be easily distinguished in terms of different sets of biological or physical traits. Thus, race in humans is largely a culturally assigned category.

Rachis the seed-bearing part of a plant. In the wild variety the rachis shatters easily, releasing the seeds. Domesticated grains have a tough rachis, which does not shatter easily.

Racism the belief, without scientific basis, that one race is superior to others.

Radiocarbon Dating a dating method that uses the decay of carbon-14 to date organic remains. It is reliable for dating once-living matter up to 50,000 years old.

Raiding a short-term use of force, generally planned and organized, to realize a limited objective.

Random Sample a sample in which all cases selected have had an equal chance to be included.

Rank Society a society that does not have very unequal access to economic resources or power, but with social groups that have unequal access to status positions and prestige.

Recessive   an allele phenotypically suppressed in the heterozygous form and expressed only in the homozygous form.

Reciprocity   giving and taking (not politically arranged) without the use of money.

Redistribution   the accumulation of goods (or labor) by a particular person or in a particular place and their subsequent distribution.

Relative Dating   a method of dating fossils that determines the age of a specimen or deposit relative to a known specimen or deposit.

Religion   any set of attitudes, beliefs, and practices pertaining to supernatural power, whether that power rests in forces, gods, spirits, ghosts, or demons.

Revitalization Movement   a new religious movement intended to save a culture by infusing it with a new purpose and life.

Revolution   A usually violent replacement of a society's rulers.

Rules of Descent   rules that connect individuals with particular sets of kin because of known or presumed common ancestry.

Sampling Universe   the list of cases to be sampled from.

Savanna   tropical grassland.

Secondary Institutions   aspects of culture such as religion, music, art, folklore, and games, which presumably reflect or are projections of the basic, or typical, personality in a society.

Secondary Subsistence Activities   activities that involve the preparation and processing of food either to make it edible or to store it.

Sedentarism   settled life.

Sediment   the dust, debris, and decay that accumulates over time.

Segmentary Lineage System   a hierarchy of more and more inclusive lineages; usually functions only in conflict situations.

Segregation   the random sorting of chromosomes in meiosis.

Sexual Dimorphism   a marked difference in size and appearance between males and females of a species.

Sexually Dimorphic   refers to a species in which males differ markedly from females in size and appearance.

Shaman   a religious intermediary, usually part-time, whose primary function is to cure people through sacred songs, pantomime, and other means; sometimes called witch doctor by Westerners.

Shifting Cultivation   see **Extensive Cultivation.**

Sib   see **Clan.**

Siblings   a person's brothers and sisters.

Sickle-Cell Anemia (Sicklemia)   a condition in which red blood cells assume a crescent (sickle) shape when deprived of oxygen, instead of the normal (disk) shape. The sickle-shaped red blood cells do not move through the body as readily as normal cells, and thus cause damage to the heart, lungs, brain, and other vital organs.

Sivapithecus   a genus of ape from the later Miocene known for its thickly enameled teeth, suggesting a diet of hard, tough, or gritty items. Found primarily in western and southern Asia and now thought to be ancestral to orangutans.

Slash-and-Burn   a form of shifting cultivation in which the natural vegetation is cut down and burned off. The cleared ground is used for a short time and then left to regenerate.

Slaves   a class of persons who do not own their own labor or the products thereof.

Socialization   a term used by anthropologists and psychologists to describe the development, through the direct and indirect influence of parents and others, of children's patterns of behavior (and attitudes and values) that conform to cultural expectations.

Society   a group of people who occupy a particular territory and speak a common language not generally understood by neighboring peoples. By this definition, societies do not necessarily correspond to nations.

Sociobiology   see **Behavioral Ecology.**

Sociolinguistics   the study of cultural and subcultural patterns of speaking in different social contexts.

Sorcery   the use of certain materials to invoke supernatural powers to harm people.

Sororal Polygyny   the marriage of a man to two or more sisters at the same time.

Sororate   a custom whereby a woman is obliged to marry her deceased sister's husband.

Special-Purpose Money   objects of value for which only some goods and services can be exchanged.

Speciation   the development of a new species.

Species   a population that consists of organisms able to interbreed and produce fertile and viable offspring.

Spirits   unnamed supernatural beings of nonhuman origin who are beneath the gods in prestige and often closer to the people; may be helpful, mischievous, or evil.

State   a political unit with centralized decision making affecting a large population. Most states have cities with public buildings; full-time craft and religious specialists; an "official" art style; a hierarchical social structure topped by an elite class; and a governmental monopoly on the legitimate use of force to implement policies.

Statistical Association   a relationship or correlation between two or more variables that is unlikely to be due to chance.

Statistically Significant   refers to a result that would occur very rarely by chance. The result (and stronger ones) would occur fewer than 5 times out of 100 by chance.

Status   a position of prestige in a society.

Steppe   grassland with a dry, low grass cover.

Stratigraphy   the study of how different rock formations and fossils are laid down in successive layers or strata. Older layers are generally deeper or lower than more recent layers.

Structural Linguistics   the study of how languages are constructed. Also called descriptive linguistics.

Subculture   the shared customs of a subgroup within a society.

Subsistence Technology   the methods humans use to procure food.

Supernatural   believed to be not human or not subject to the laws of nature.

Syntax   the ways in which words are arranged to form phrases and sentences.

Taboo a prohibition that, if violated, is believed to bring supernatural punishment.

Taxonomy the classification of extinct and living organisms.

Terrestrial adapted to living on the ground.

Theoretical Construct something that cannot be observed or verified directly.

Theories explanations of associations or laws.

Thermoluminescence Dating a dating technique that is well suited to samples of ancient pottery, brick, tile, or terra cotta, which (when they were made) were heated to a high temperature that released trapped electrons. Such an object continues over time to trap electrons from radioactive elements around it and the electrons trapped after manufacture emit light when heated, so the age of the object can be estimated by measuring how much light is emitted when the object is heated.

Totem a plant or animal associated with a clan (sib) as a means of group identification; may have other special significance for the group.

Tribal Organization the kind of political organization in which local communities mostly act autonomously but there are kin groups (such as clans) or associations (such as age-sets) that can temporarily integrate a number of local groups into a larger unit.

Tribe a territorial population in which there are kin or nonkin groups with representatives in a number of local groups.

Tundra treeless plains characteristic of sub-Arctic and Arctic regions.

Unifacial Tool a tool worked or flaked on one side only.

Unilineal Descent affiliation with a group of kin through descent links of one sex only.

Unilocal Residence a pattern of residence (patrilocal, matrilocal, or avunculocal) that specifies just one set of relatives that the married couple lives with or near.

Unisex Association an association that restricts its membership to one sex, usually male.

Universally Ascribed Qualities those ascribed qualities (age, sex) that are found in all societies.

Uranium-Series Dating a technique for dating *Homo sapiens* sites that uses the decay of two kinds of uranium (^{235}U and ^{238}U) into other isotopes (such as ^{230}Th—thorium). Particularly useful in cave sites. Different types of uranium-series dating use different isotope ratios.

Variable a thing or quantity that varies.

Variably Ascribed Qualities those ascribed qualities (such as ethnic, religious, or social-class differences) that are found only in some societies.

Vertical Clinging and Leaping a locomotor pattern characteristic of several primates, including tarsiers and galagos. The animal normally rests by clinging to a branch in a vertical position and uses its hind limbs alone to push off from one vertical position to another.

Warfare violence between political entities such as communities, districts, or nations.

Witchcraft the practice of attempting to harm people by supernatural means, but through emotions and thought alone, not through the use of tangible objects.

Notes

Chapter 1

1. Gail G. Harrison, "Primary Adult Lactase Deficiency: A Problem in Anthropological Genetics," *American Anthropologist,* 77 (1975): 812–35; William H. Durham, *Coevolution: Genes, Culture and Human Diversity* (Stanford, CA: Stanford University Press, 1991), pp. 228–37.
2. E. Chambers, *Applied Anthropology: A Practical Guide,* rev. ed. (Prospect Heights, IL: Waveland, 1989), as referred to in Gilbert Kushner, "Applied Anthropology," in William G. Emener and Margaret Darrow, eds., *Career Explorations in Human Services* (Springfield, IL: Charles C. Thomas, 1991).
3. Andrew W. Miracle, "A Shaman to Organizations," in Carol R. Ember, Melvin Ember, and Peter N. Peregrine, eds., *Research Frontiers in Anthropology* (Upper Saddle River, NJ: Prentice Hall, 1998), Prentice Hall/Simon & Schuster Custom Publishing; Kushner, "Applied Anthropology."
4. Leslie A. White, "The Expansion of the Scope of Science," in Morton H. Fried, ed., *Readings in Anthropology,* 2nd ed., vol. 1 (New York: Thomas Y. Crowell, 1968), pp. 15–24.
5. The exclamation point in the word *!Kung* signifies one of the clicking sounds made with the tongue by speakers of the !Kung language.
6. Edward T. Hall, *The Hidden Dimension* (Garden City, NY: Doubleday, 1966), pp. 144–53.

Chapter 2

1. Carl Sagan, "A Cosmic Calendar," *Natural History,* December 1975, 70–73.
2. Arthur O. Lovejoy, *The Great Chain of Being: A Study of the History of an Idea* (Cambridge, MA: Harvard University Press, 1964), pp. 58–63.
3. Quoted in ibid., p. 63.
4. Ibid., p. 183.
5. See Loren C. Eiseley, "The Dawn of Evolutionary Theory," in Loren C. Eiseley, *Darwin's Century: Evolution and the Men Who Discovered It* (Garden City, NY: Doubleday, 1958), reprinted in Louise B. Young, ed., *Evolution of Man* (New York: Oxford University Press, 1970), pp. 13–15; and Ernst Mayr, *The Growth of Biological Thought: Diversity, Evolution, and Inheritance* (Cambridge, MA: Belknap Press of Harvard University Press, 1982), pp. 171–75, 340–41.
6. Mayr, *The Growth of Biological Thought,* pp. 339–60.
7. Ernst Mayr, "The Nature of the Darwinian Revolution," *Science,* June 2, 1972, 981–89.
8. Alfred Russel Wallace, "On the Tendency of Varieties to Depart Indefinitely from the Original Type," *Journal of the Proceedings of the Linnaean Society,* August 1858, reprinted in Young, ed., *Evolution of Man,* p. 75.
9. Mayr, *The Growth of Biological Thought,* p. 423.
10. Darwin had a still longer title. It continued, *Or the Preservation of the Favoured Races in the Struggle for Life.* Darwin's notion of "struggle for life" is often misinterpreted to refer to a war of all against all. Although animals may fight with each other at times over access to resources, Darwin was referring mainly to their metaphorical "struggle" with the environment, particularly to obtain food.
11. Charles Darwin, *The Origin of Species,* excerpted in Young, ed., *Evolution of Man,* p. 78.
12. Quoted in Ashley Montagu's introduction to Thomas H. Huxley, "Man's Place in Nature," in Young, ed., *Evolution of Man,* pp. 183–84.
13. Robert N. Brandon. *Adaptation and Environment* (Princeton, NJ: Princeton University Press, 1990), pp. 6–7.
14. George C. Williams, *Natural Selection: Domains, Levels, and Challenges* (New York: Oxford University Press, 1992), p. 7.
15. John Maynard Smith, *Evolutionary Genetics* (New York: Oxford University Press, 1989), pp. 42–45.
16. Charles Devillers and Jean Chaline, *Evolution: An Evolving Theory* (New York: Springer-Verlag, 1993), pp. 22–23.
17. Bruce Alberts, Dennis Bray, Julian Lewis, Martin Raff, Keith Roberts, and James D. Watson, *Molecular Biology of the Cell* (New York: Garland, 1983), p. 185.
18. Ibid., pp. 99–103.
19. George Beadle and Muriel Beadle, *The Language of Life* (Garden City, NY: Doubleday, 1966), p. 216.
20. J. Claiborne Stephens, Mark L. Cavanaugh, Margaret I. Gradie, Martin L. Mador, and Kenneth K. Kidd, "Mapping the Human Genome: Current Status," *Science,* October 12, 1990, 237–50. The October 2, 1992, issue of *Science* contains several articles on the human genome as well as a map of the progress made as of then in investigating the X chromosome. Jonathan Friedlaender, "Update on the Human Genome Diversity Project," *Evolutionary Anthropology,* 2 (1993): 40 reports that physical anthropologists are working to make sure that human diversity is adequately represented in the project mapping the human genome.
21. Alberts et al., *Molecular Biology of the Cell,* pp. 107–11.
22. Paul Berg and Maxine Singer, *Dealing with Genes: The Language of Heredity* (Mill Valley, CA: University Science Books, 1992), p. 53.
23. Alberts et al., *Molecular Biology of the Cell,* pp. 107–11.
24. Ibid., p. 842.

25. Beadle and Beadle, *The Language of Life,* p. 123.
26. Alberts et al., *Molecular Biology of the Cell.*
27. Theodosius Dobzhansky, *Mankind Evolving: The Evolution of the Human Species* (New Haven, CT: Yale University Press, 1962), pp. 138–40.
28. Ibid., p. 139.
29. David P. Barash, *Sociobiology and Behavior* (New York: Elsevier, 1977).
30. J. R. Krebs and N. B. Davies, eds., *Behavioural Ecology: An Evolutionary Approach,* 2nd ed. (Sunderland, MA: Sinauer, 1984); J. R. Krebs and N. B. Davies, *An Introduction to Behavioural Ecology,* 2nd ed. (Sunderland, MA: Sinauer, 1987).
31. George B. Schaller, *The Serengeti Lion: A Study of Predator–Prey Relations* (Chicago: University of Chicago Press, 1972), cited in Edward O. Wilson, *Sociobiology: The New Synthesis.* (Cambridge, MA: Belknap Press of Harvard University Press, 1975), p. 504.
32. Wilson, *Sociobiology* (Cambridge, MA: Harvard University Press, 1975), quoted in Bobbi Low, "Behavioral Ecology, 'Sociobiology' and Human Behavior," in Carol R. Ember, Melvin Ember, and Peter N. Peregrine, eds., *Research Frontiers in Anthropology* (Upper Saddle River, NJ: Prentice Hall, 1998), Prentice Hall/Simon & Schuster Custom Publishing.
33. Low, "Behavioral Ecology, 'Sociobiology' and Human Behavior."
34. Donald T. Campbell, "Variation and Selective Retention in Socio-Cultural Evolution," in Herbert Barringer, George Blankstein, and Raymond Mack, eds., *Social Change in Developing Areas: A Re-Interpretation of Evolutionary Theory* (Cambridge, MA: Schenkman, 1965), pp. 19–49.
35. Henry W. Nissen, "Axes of Behavioral Comparison," in Anne Roe and George Gaylord Simpson, eds., *Behavior and Evolution* (New Haven, CT: Yale University Press, 1958), pp. 183–205.
36. Robert Boyd and Peter J. Richerson, *Culture and the Evolutionary Process* (Chicago: University of Chicago Press, 1985).
37. William H. Durham, *Coevolution: Genes, Culture, and Human Diversity* (Stanford, CA: Stanford University Press, 1991).

CHAPTER 3

1. The classic description of common primate traits is J. R. Napier and P. H. Napier, *A Handbook of Living Primates* (New York: Academic Press, 1967). See also Barbara B. Smuts, Dorothy L. Cheney, Robert M. Seyfarth, Richard W. Wrangham, and Thomas T. Struhsaker, eds., *Primate Societies* (Chicago: University of Chicago Press, 1987).
2. Simon K. Bearder, "Lorises, Bushbabies, and Tarsiers: Diverse Societies in Solitary Foragers," in Smuts et al., eds., *Primate Societies,* p. 14.
3. Alison F. Richard, *Primates in Nature* (New York: Freeman, 1985), pp. 22ff.
4. Robert D. Martin, "Strategies of Reproduction," *Natural History,* November 1975, 50. The opossum, which is not a primate but lives in trees and has many babies at one time, is a marsupial and has a pouch in which to keep the babies when they are very young.
5. H. F. Harlow et al., "Maternal Behavior of Rhesus Monkeys Deprived of Mothering and Peer Association in Infancy," *Proceedings of the American Philosophical Society,* 110 (1966): 58–66.
6. Nancy A. Nicolson, "Infants, Mothers, and Other Females," in Smuts et al., eds., *Primate Societies,* p. 339.
7. See J. Patrick Gray, *Primate Sociobiology* (New Haven, CT: HRAF Press, 1985), pp. 144–63, for a discussion of research that attempts to explain the variation among primates in the degree of male parental care.
8. Anne E. Russon, "The Development of Peer Social Interaction in Infant Chimpanzees: Comparative Social, Piagetian, and Brain Perspectives," in Sue Taylor Parker and Kathleen Rita Gibson, eds., *"Language" and Intelligence in Monkeys and Apes: Comparative Developmental Perspectives* (New York: Cambridge University Press, 1990), p. 379.
9. Phyllis Jay Dohlinow and Naomi Bishop, "The Development of Motor Skills and Social Relationships among Primates through Play," in Phyllis Jay Dohlinow, ed., *Primate Patterns* (New York: Holt, Rinehart & Winston, 1972), pp. 321–25.
10. D. S. Sade, "Some Aspects of Parent–Offspring and Sibling Relationships in a Group of Rhesus Monkeys, with a Discussion of Grooming," *American Journal of Physical Anthropology,* 23 (1965): 1–17; and Glenn Hausfater, Jeanne Altmann, and Stuart Altmann, "Long-Term Consistency of Dominance Relations among Female Baboons," *Science,* August 20, 1982, 752–54.
11. Elisabetta Visaberghi and Dorothy Munkenbeck Fragaszy, "Do Monkeys Ape?" in Parker and Gibson, eds., *"Language" and Intelligence in Monkeys and Apes,* p. 265; Michael Tomasello, "Cultural Transmission in the Tool Use and Communicatory Signaling of Chimpanzees," in ibid., pp. 304–305.
12. Jane van Lawick-Goodall, *In the Shadow of Man* (Boston: Houghton Mifflin, 1971), p. 242.
13. Visaberghi and Fragaszy, "Do Monkeys Ape?" pp. 264–65.
14. Robert Martin, "Classification and Evolutionary Relationships," in Steve Jones, Robert Martin, and David Pilbeam, eds., *The Cambridge Encyclopedia of Human Evolution* (Cambridge: Cambridge University Press, 1992), pp. 17–19; Glenn C. Conroy, *Primate Evolution* (New York: Norton, 1990), pp. 8–15.
15. This simplified chart of primate classification adapts information provided in Martin, "Classification and Evolutionary Relationships," p. 21.
16. G. A. Doyle and R. D. Martin, eds., *The Study of Prosimian Behavior* (New York: Academic Press, 1979); and Ian Tattersall, *The Primates of Madagascar* (New York: Columbia University Press, 1982).
17. Alison F. Richard, "Malagasy Prosimians: Female Dominance," in Smuts et al., eds., *Primate Societies,* p. 32.
18. Bearder, "Lorises, Bushbabies, and Tarsiers," p. 13.

19. Pierre Charles-Dominique, *Ecology and Behaviour of Nocturnal Primates,* trans. Robert D. Martin (New York: Columbia University Press, 1977), p. 258. See also Robert D. Martin and Simon K. Bearder, "Radio Bush Baby," *Natural History,* October 1979, 77–81; and Bearder, "Lorises, Bushbabies, and Tarsiers," pp. 18–22.

20. John MacKinnon and Kathy MacKinnon, "The Behavior of Wild Spectral Tarsiers," *International Journal of Primatology,* 1 (1980): 361–79.

21. Matt Cartmill, "Non-Human Primates," in Jones, Martin, and Pilbeam, eds., *The Cambridge Encyclopedia of Human Evolution,* p. 28; John G. Fleagle, *Primate Adaptation and Evolution* (San Diego: Academic Press, 1988), pp. 100–103.

22. Napier and Napier, *A Handbook of Living Primates,* pp. 32–33.

23. Richard, *Primates in Nature,* pp. 164–65.

24. Cartmill, "Non-Human Primates," p. 29; Anne Wilson Goldizen, "Tamarins and Marmosets: Communal Care of Offspring," in Smuts et al., eds., *Primate Societies,* p. 34. See also John F. Eisenberg, "Comparative Ecology and Reproduction of New World Monkeys," in Devra Kleinman, ed., *The Biology and Conservation of the Callitrichidae* (Washington, DC: Smithsonian Institution, 1977), pp. 13–22; and Robert W. Sussman and Warren G. Kinzey, "The Ecological Role of the Callitrichidae: A Review," *American Journal of Physical Anthropology,* 64 (1984): 419–49.

25. Eisenberg, "Comparative Ecology and Reproduction of New World Monkeys," pp. 15–17.

26. John G. Robinson, Patricia C. Wright, and Warren G. Kinzey, "Monogamous Cebids and Their Relatives: Intergroup Calls and Spacing," in Smuts et al., eds., *Primate Societies,* pp. 44–53; Carolyn Crockett and John F. Eisenberg, "Howlers: Variations in Group Size and Demography," in ibid., pp. 54–68; John G. Robinson and Charles H. Janson, "Capuchins, Squirrel Monkeys, and Atelines: Socioecological Convergence with Old World Primates," in ibid., pp. 69–82.

27. Sarah Blaffer Hrdy, *The Langurs of Abu: Female and Male Strategies of Reproduction* (Cambridge, MA: Harvard University Press, 1977), p. 18.

28. Ibid., pp. 18–19.

29. J. R. Napier, "Paleoecology and Catarrhine Evolution," in J. R. Napier and P. H. Napier, eds., *Old World Monkeys: Evolution, Systematics, and Behavior* (New York: Academic Press, 1970), pp. 80–82.

30. Linda Marie Fedigan, *Primate Paradigms: Sex Roles and Social Bonds* (Montreal: Eden Press, 1982), p. 11.

31. Ibid., pp. 123–24.

32. Phyllis C. Lee, "Home Range, Territory and Intergroup Encounters," in Robert A. Hinde, ed., *Primate Social Relationships: An Integrated Approach* (Sunderland, MA: Sinauer, 1983), p. 231.

33. Holger Preuschoft, David J. Chivers, Warren Y. Brockelman, and Norman Creel, eds., *The Lesser Apes: Evolutionary and Behavioural Biology* (Edinburgh: Edinburgh University Press, 1984).

34. C. R. Carpenter, "A Field Study in Siam of the Behavior and Social Relations of the Gibbon *(Hylobates lar)."*

Comparative Psychology Monographs, 16, no. 5 (1940): 1–212; David John Chivers, *The Siamang in Malaya* (Basel, Switzerland: Karger, 1974); and David J. Chivers, ed., *Malayan Forest Primates: Ten Years' Study in Tropical Rain Forest* (New York: Plenum, 1980).

35. H. D. Rijksen, *A Fieldstudy on Sumatran Orang Utans (Pongo Pygmaeus Abelii Lesson 1827): Ecology, Behaviour and Conservation* (Wageningen, Netherlands: H. Veenman and Zonen B.V., 1978), p. 22.

36. Dennis Normile, "Habitat Seen Playing Larger Role in Shaping Behavior," *Science,* March 6, 1998, 1454–455.

37. Biruté M. F. Galdikas, "Orangutan Adaptation at Tanjung Puting Reserve: Mating and Ecology," in David A. Hamburg and Elizabeth R. McCown, eds., *The Great Apes* (Menlo Park, CA: Benjamin/Cummings, 1979), pp. 220–23.

38. Dorothy L. Cheney and Richard W. Wrangham, "Predation," in Smuts et al., eds., *Primate Societies,* p. 236.

39. Rijksen, *A Fieldstudy on Sumatran Orang Utans,* p. 321.

40. Dian Fossey, *Gorillas in the Mist* (Boston: Houghton Mifflin, 1983), p. xvi.

41. Russell H. Tuttle, *Apes of the World: Their Social Behavior, Communication, Mentality, and Ecology* (Park Ridge, NJ: Noyes Publications, 1986), pp. 99–114.

42. George Schaller, *The Mountain Gorilla: Ecology and Behavior* (Chicago: University of Chicago Press, 1963). See also Schaller's *The Year of the Gorilla* (Chicago: University of Chicago Press, 1964).

43. Fossey, *Gorillas in the Mist,* p. 47.

44. A. H. Harcourt, "The Social Relations and Group Structure of Wild Mountain Gorillas," in Hamburg and McCown, eds., *The Great Apes,* pp. 187–92.

45. Jane Goodall, "My Life among Wild Chimpanzees," *National Geographic,* August 1963, pp. 272–308; and van Lawick-Goodall, *In the Shadow of Man.*

46. Geza Teleki, "The Omnivorous Chimpanzee," *Scientific American,* January 1973, 32–42.

47. Craig Stanford, "Chimpanzee Hunting Behavior and Human Evolution," in Carol R. Ember, Melvin Ember, and Peter N. Peregrine, eds., *Research Frontiers in Anthropology* (Upper Saddle River, NJ: Prentice Hall, 1998). Prentice Hall/Simon & Schuster Custom Publishing.

48. Ibid., pp. 35–41.

49. Normile, "Habitat Seen Playing Larger Role."

50. Tuttle, *Apes of the World,* pp. 266–69.

51. Morris Goodman, "Reconstructing Human Evolution from Proteins," in Jones, Martin, and Pilbeam, eds., *The Cambridge Encyclopedia of Human Evolution,* pp. 307–12.

52. T. H. Clutton-Brock and Paul H. Harvey, "Primate Ecology and Social Organization," *Journal of Zoology, London,* 183 (1977): 8–9.

53. L. C. Aiello, "Body Size and Energy Requirements," in Jones, Martin, and Pilbeam, eds., *The Cambridge Encyclopedia of Human Evolution,* pp. 41–44; Alison Jolly, *The Evolution of Primate Behavior,* 2nd ed. (New York: Macmillan, 1985), pp. 53–54.

54. Aiello, "Body Size and Energy Requirements."

55. Jolly, *The Evolution of Primate Behavior,* pp. 53–54.

56. Sue Taylor Parker, "Why Big Brains Are So Rare," in Parker and Gibson, eds., *"Language" and Intelligence in Monkeys and Apes,* p. 130.

57. Katharine Milton, "Distribution Patterns of Tropical Plant Foods as an Evolutionary Stimulus to Primate Mental Development," *American Anthropologist,* 83 (1981): 534–48; T. H. Clutton-Brock and Paul H. Harvey, "Primates, Brains and Ecology," *Journal of Zoology, London,* 190 (1980): 309–23.

58. Katharine Milton, "Foraging Behaviour and the Evolution of Primate Intelligence," in Richard W. Bryne and Andrew Whiten, eds., *Machiavellian Intelligence: Social Expertise and the Evolution of Intellect in Monkeys, Apes, and Humans* (Oxford: Clarendon Press, 1988), pp. 285–305.

59. Jolly, *The Evolution of Primate Behavior,* p. 119.

60. Clutton-Brock and Harvey, "Primate Ecology and Social Organization," p. 9.

61. John Terborgh, *Five New World Primates: A Study in Comparative Ecology* (Princeton, NJ: Princeton University Press, 1983), pp. 224–25.

62. Jolly, *The Evolution of Primate Behavior,* p. 120.

63. Ibid., p. 122.

64. Richard W. Wrangham, "An Ecological Model of Female-Bonded Primate Groups," *Behaviour,* 75 (1980): 262–300.

65. Female bonobo, or pygmy chimpanzees, engage in sexual intercourse nearly as often as human females. See Nancy Thompson-Handler, Richard K. Malenky, and Noel Badrian, "Sexual Behavior of *Pan paniscus* under Natural Conditions in the Lomako Forest, Equateur, Zaire," in Randall L. Susman, ed., *The Pygmy Chimpanzee: Evolutionary Biology and Behavior* (New York: Plenum, 1984), pp. 347–66. For a review of field research on pygmy chimpanzees, see Frances J. White, "*Pan paniscus* 1973 to 1996: Twenty-three Years of Field Research," *Evolutionary Anthropology,* 5 (1996): 11–17.

66. By male-female bonding we mean that at least one of the sexes is "faithful," that is, typically has intercourse with just one opposite-sex partner throughout at least one estrus or menstrual cycle or breeding season. Note that the bonding may not be monogamous; an individual may be bonded to more than one individual of the opposite sex. See Melvin Ember and Carol R. Ember, "Male–Female Bonding: A Cross-Species Study of Mammals and Birds," *Behavior Science Research,* 14 (1979): 37–41.

67. Ember and Ember, "Male–Female Bonding," p. 43; see also Carol R. Ember and Melvin Ember, "The Evolution of Human Female Sexuality: A Cross-Species Perspective," *Journal of Anthropological Research,* 40 (1984): 203–204.

68. Ember and Ember, "The Evolution of Human Female Sexuality," p. 207.

69. Ibid., pp. 208–209.

70. Frans de Waal and Frans Lanting, *Bonobo: The Forgotten Ape* (Berkeley: University of California Press, 1997).

71. Duane M. Rumbaugh, "Learning Skills of Anthropoids," in L. A. Rosenblum, ed., *Primate Behavior,* vol. 1 (New York: Academic Press, 1970), pp. 52–58.

72. Observation by others cited by Jolly, *The Evolution of Primate Behavior,* p. 53.

73. Alison C. Hannah and W. C. McGrew, "Chimpanzees Using Stones to Crack Open Oil Palm Nuts in Liberia." *Primates,* 28 (1987): 31–46.

74. "The First Dentist," *Newsweek,* March 5, 1973, 73.

75. Robert M. Seyfarth, Dorothy L. Cheney, and Peter Marler, "Monkey Response to Three Different Alarm Calls: Evidence of Predator Classification and Semantic Communication," *Science,* November 14, 1980, 801–803.

76. R. Allen Gardner and Beatrice T. Gardner, "Teaching Sign Language to a Chimpanzee," *Science,* August 15, 1969, 664–72.

77. Beatrice T. Gardner and R. Allen Gardner, "Two Comparative Psychologists Look at Language Acquisition," in K. E. Nelson, ed., *Children's Language,* vol. 2 (New York: Halsted Press, 1980), pp. 331–69.

78. Patricia Marks Greenfield and E. Sue Savage-Rumbaugh, "Grammatical Combination in *Pan paniscus:* Processes of Learning and Invention in the Evolution and Development of Language," in Parker and Gibson, eds., *"Language" and Intelligence in Monkeys and Apes,* pp. 540–78.

CHAPTER 4

1. Russell L. Ciochon and Dennis A. Etler, "Reinterpreting Past Primate Diversity," in Robert S. Corruccini and Russell L. Ciochon, eds., *Integrative Paths to the Past: Paleoanthropological Advances in Honor of F. Clark Howell* (Englewood Cliffs, NJ: Prentice Hall, 1994), pp. 33, 37–67.

2. Robert D. Martin, *Primate Origins and Evolution: A Phylogenetic Reconstruction* (Princeton, NJ: Princeton University Press, 1990), p. 42.

3. Alan Bilsborough, *Human Evolution* (New York: Blackie Academic & Professional, 1992), pp. 1–2.

4. Richard F. Kay, "Teeth," in Ian Tattersall, Eric Delson, and John van Couvering, eds., *Encyclopedia of Human Evolution and Prehistory* (New York: Garland, 1988), pp. 578, 571–78.

5. Bernard Wood, "Hominid Paleobiology: Recent Achievements and Challenges," in Corruccini and Ciochon, eds., *Integrative Paths to the Past,* pp. 153, 147–65.

6. Glenn C. Conroy, *Primate Evolution* (New York: Norton, 1990), pp. 76–77.

7. Bilsborough, *Human Evolution,* pp. 21–22.

8. Richard G. Klein, *The Human Career: Human Biological and Cultural Origins* (Chicago: University of Chicago, 1989), pp. 1–12.

9. Kenneth P. Oakley, "Analytical Methods of Dating Bones," in Don Brothwell and Eric Higgs, eds., *Science in Archaeology* (New York: Basic Books, 1963), p. 26.

10. W. Gentner and H. J. Lippolt, "The Potassium-Argon Dating of Upper Tertiary and Pleistocene Deposits," in Brothwell and Higgs, eds., *Science in Archaeology,* pp. 72–84.

11. Klein, *The Human Career,* pp. 15–17.

12. Bilsborough, *Human Evolution,* pp. 23–24; Frank H. Brown, "Geochronometry," in Tattersall, Delson, and

van Couvering, eds., *Encyclopedia of Human Evolution and Prehistory*, p. 225.

13. Robert L. Fleischer, P. B. Price, R. M. Walker, and L. S. B. Leakey, "Fission-Track Dating of Bed I, Olduvai Gorge," *Science*, April 2, 1965, 72–74.

14. Robert L. Fleischer and Howard R. Hart, Jr., "Fission-Track Dating: Techniques and Problems," in W. A. Bishop and J. A. Miller, eds., *Calibration of Hominid Evolution* (Toronto: University of Toronto Press, 1972), p. 474.

15. Fleischer et al., "Fission-Track Dating of Bed I, Olduvai Gorge."

16. John Kappelman, "The Attraction of Paleomagnetism," *Evolutionary Anthropology*, 2, no. 3 (1993): 89–99.

17. John G. Fleagle, "Anthropoid Origins," in Corruccini and Ciochon, eds., *Integrative Paths to the Past*, pp. 20, 17–35; Ciochon and Etler, "Reinterpreting Past Primate Diversity," p. 41; Matt Cartmill, "Explaining Primate Origins," in Carol R. Ember, Melvin Ember, and Peter N. Peregrine, eds., *Research Frontiers in Anthropology* (Upper Saddle River, NJ: Prentice Hall, 1998). Prentice Hall/Simon & Schuster Custom Publishing.

18. Conroy, *Primate Evolution*, pp. 49–53.

19. Ibid., p. 53.

20. Robert Sussman, "Primate Origins and the Evolution of Angiosperms," *American Journal of Primatology*, 23 (1991): 209–23.

21. Alison F. Richard, *Primates in Nature* (New York: Freeman, 1985), p. 31; and Matt Cartmill, "Rethinking Primate Origins," *Science*, April 26, 1974, 436–37.

22. Frederick S. Szalay, "The Beginnings of Primates," *Evolution*, 22 (1968): 32–33.

23. Cartmill, "Rethinking Primate Origins," pp. 436–43; for more recent statements by Cartmill, see his "New Views on Primate Origins," *Evolutionary Anthropology*, 1 (1992): 105–11, and his "Explaining Primate Origins."

24. Robert W. Sussman and Peter H. Raven, "Pollination by Lemurs and Marsupials: An Archaic Coevolutionary System," *Science*, May 19, 1978, 734–35.

25. Conroy, *Primate Evolution*, pp. 94–95.

26. Ibid., p. 99.

27. Fleagle, "Anthropoid Origins," pp. 22–23.

28. Conroy, *Primate Evolution*, p. 119.

29. Leonard Radinsky, "The Oldest Primate Endocast," *American Journal of Physical Anthropology*, 27 (1967): 358–88.

30. Ibid., p. 105; and Fleagle, "Anthropoid Origins," p. 21.

31. John P. Alexander, "Alas, Poor *Notharctus*," *Natural History*, August 1992, 55–59; Conroy, *Primate Evolution*, p. 111.

32. Martin, *Primate Origins and Evolution*, p. 46; Conroy, *Primate Evolution*, p. 46.

33. John G. Fleagle and Richard F. Kay, "The Paleobiology of Catarrhines," in Eric Delson, ed., *Ancestors: The Hard Evidence* (New York: Alan R. Liss, 1985), p. 25.

34. Fleagle, "Anthropoid Origins," pp. 44–45.

35. Ibid., p. 24.

36. Richard F. Kay, "Parapithecidae," in Tattersall, Delson, and van Couvering, eds., *Encyclopedia of Human Evolution and Prehistory*, p. 441.

37. Kay, "Parapithecidae," pp. 441–42; Conroy, *Primate Evolution*, p. 156.

38. John G. Fleagle, *Primate Adaptation* and *Evolution* (San Diego: Academic Press, 1988), pp. 334–35, 341.

39. Peter Andrews, "Propliopithecidae," in Tattersall, Delson, and van Couvering, eds., *Encyclopedia of Human Evolution and Prehistory*, pp. 486, 485–87.

40. Fleagle and Kay, "The Paleobiology of Catarrhines," pp. 25, 30; Conroy, *Primate Evolution*, pp. 160–61.

41. Fleagle, *Primate Adaptation and Evolution*, p. 339. See also John G. Fleagle and Richard F. Kay, "New Interpretations of the Phyletic Position of Oligocene Hominoids," in Russell L. Ciochon and Robert S. Corruccini, eds., *New Interpretations of Ape and Human Ancestry* (New York: Plenum, 1983), p. 205.

42. Fleagle, *Primate Adaptation and Evolution*, p. 363.

43. Conroy, *Primate Evolution*, pp. 248–49.

44. Ibid., p. 56.

45. Martin, *Primate Origins and Evolution*, p. 56.

46. David Begun, "Miocene Apes," in Carol R. Ember, Melvin Ember, and Peter N. Peregrine, eds., *Research Frontiers in Anthropology* (Upper Saddle River, NJ: Prentice Hall, 1998). Prentice Hall/Simon & Schuster Custom Publishing.

47. Conroy, *Primate Evolution*, pp. 206–11.

48. Begun, "Miocene Apes."

49. Peter Andrews, "*Proconsul*," in Tattersall, Delson, and van Couvering, eds., *Encyclopedia of Human Evolution and Prehistory*, p. 485.

50. Begun, "Miocene Apes."

51. Ibid.

52. Ibid.; and Jay Kelley, "The Evolution of Apes," in Steve Jones, Robert Martin, and David Pilbeam, eds., *The Cambridge Encyclopedia of Human Evolution* (New York: Cambridge University Press, 1992), pp. 225, 223–30.

53. E. Sue Savage-Rumbaugh, "Hominid Evolution: Looking to Modern Apes for Clues," in Duane Quiatt and Junichiro Itani, eds., *Hominid Culture in Primate Perspective* (Niwot: University Press of Colorado, 1994), pp. 7–49.

54. Conroy, *Primate Evolution*, pp. 185, 255.

55. Fleagle, *Primate Adaptation and Evolution*, p. 382.

56. Begun, "Miocene Apes."

57. Russell Ciochon, John Olsen, and Jamie James, *Other Origins: The Search for the Giant Ape in Human Prehistory* (New York: Bantam, 1990), pp. 99–102.

58. Begun, "Miocene Apes."

59. Ibid.

60. Fleagle, *Primate Adaptation and Evolution*, pp. 388–90.

61. Bilsborough, *Human Evolution*, p. 65.

62. Elwyn Simons, "The Primate Fossil Record," in Jones, Martin, and Pilbeam, eds., *The Cambridge Encyclopedia of Human Evolution*, p. 207.

63. Vincent M. Sarich and Allan C. Wilson, "Quantitative Immunochemistry and the Evolution of the Primate Albumins: Micro-Component Fixations," *Science*,

December 23, 1966, 1563–1566; Vincent M. Sarich, "The Origin of Hominids: An Immunological Approach," in S. L. Washburn and Phyllis C. Jay, eds., *Perspectives on Human Evolution,* vol. 1 (New York: Holt, Rinehart & Winston, 1968), pp. 99–121; and Roger Lewin, "Is the Orangutan a Living Fossil?" *Science,* December 16, 1983, 1222–23.

64. Jones, Martin and Pilbeam, eds., *The Cambridge Encyclopedia of Human Evolution,* p. 293; Martin, *Primate Origins and Evolution,* pp. 693–709.

65. The material referred to in this paragraph is drawn from Jones, Martin, and Pilbeam, eds., *The Cambridge Encyclopedia of Human Evolution,* pp. 8, 293–321.

CHAPTER 5

1. M. D. Rose, "Food Acquisition and the Evolution of Positional Behaviour: The Case of Bipedalism," in David J. Chivers, Bernard A. Wood, and Alan Bilsborough, eds., *Food Acquisition and Processing in Primates* (New York: Plenum, 1984), pp. 509–24.

2. Alan Bilsborough, *Human Evolution* (New York: Blackie Academic & Professional, 1992), pp. 64–65.

3. Kenneth Oakley, "On Man's Use of Fire, with Comments on Tool-Making and Hunting," in S. L. Washburn, ed., *Social Life of Early Man* (Chicago: Aldine, 1964), p. 186.

4. John D. Kingston, Bruno D. Marino, and Andrew Hill, "Isotopic Evidence for Neogene Hominid Paleoenvironments in the Kenya Rift Valley," *Science,* May 13, 1994, 955–59.

5. Gordon W. Hewes, "Food Transport and the Origin of Hominid Bipedalism," *American Anthropologist,* 63 (1961): 687–710.

6. Pat Shipman, "Scavenging or Hunting in Early Hominids: Theoretical Framework and Tests," *American Anthropologist,* 88 (1986): 27–43; Erik Trinkaus, "Bodies, Brawn, Brains and Noses: Human Ancestors and Human Predation," in Matthew H. Nitecki and Doris V. Nitecki, eds., *The Evolution of Human Hunting* (New York: Plenum, 1987), p. 115.

7. C. Owen Lovejoy, "The Origin of Man," *Science,* January 23, 1981, 341–50.

8. Sherwood Washburn, "Tools and Human Evolution," *Scientific American,* September 1960, 63.

9. David Pilbeam, *The Ascent of Man* (New York: Macmillan, 1972), p. 153.

10. Milford H. Wolpoff, "Competitive Exclusion among Lower Pleistocene Hominids: The Single Species Hypothesis," *Man,* 6 (1971): 602.

11. E. Sue Savage-Rumbaugh, "Hominid Evolution: Looking to Modern Apes for Clues," in Duane Quiatt and Junichiro Itani, eds., *Hominid Culture in Primate Perspective* (Niwot: University Press of Colorado, 1994), pp. 7–49.

12. M. H. Wolpoff, "*Ramapithecus* and Human Origins: An Anthropologist's Perspective of Changing Interpretations," in Russell L. Ciochon and Robert S. Corruccini, eds., *New Interpretations of Ape and Human Ancestry* (New York: Plenum, 1983), p. 666.

13. Adrienne L. Zihlman, "The Emergence of Human Locomotion: The Evolutionary Background and Environmental Context," in Toshisada Nishida, William C. McGrew, Peter Marler, Martin Pickford, and Frans B. M. de Waal, eds., *Topics in Primatology,* vol. 1, *Human Origins* (Tokyo: University of Tokyo Press, 1992), pp. 409–22.

14. D. Falk, "Enlarged Occipital/Marginal Sinuses and Emissary Foramina: Their Significance in Hominid Evolution," in Frederick E. Grine, ed., *Evolutionary History of the "Robust" Australopithecines* (New York: Aldine, 1988), pp. 85–96, as cited in ibid.

15. Zihlman, "The Emergence of Human Locomotion," p. 414.

16. Henry M. McHenry, "'Robust' Australopithecines, Our Family Tree, and Homoplasy," in Carol R. Ember, Melvin Ember, and Peter N. Peregrine, eds., *Research Frontiers in Anthropology* (Upper Saddle River, NJ: Prentice Hall, 1998). Prentice Hall/Simon & Schuster Custom Publishing. Philip V. Tobias, "The Craniocerebral Interface in Early Hominids: Cerebral Impressions, Cranial Thickening, Paleoneurobiology, and a New Hypothesis on Encephalization," in Robert S. Corruccini and Russell L. Ciochon, eds., *Integrative Paths to the Past: Paleoanthropological Advances in Honor of F. Clark Howell* (Englewood Cliffs, NJ: Prentice Hall, 1994), pp. 194–97.

17. Henry M. McHenry, "The Pattern of Human Evolution: Studies on Bipedalism, Mastication, and Encephalization," *Annual Review of Anthropology,* 11 (1982): 160–61.

18. Ibid., p. 162.

19. David Pilbeam and Stephen Jay Gould, "Size and Scaling in Human Evolution," *Science,* December 6, 1974, 899.

20. Theodosius Dobzhansky, *Mankind Evolving: The Evolution of the Human Species* (New Haven, CT: Yale University Press, 1962), p. 196.

21. Timothy G. Bromage and M. Christopher Dean, "Re-evaluation of the Age at Death of Immature Fossil Hominids," *Nature,* October 10, 1985, 525–27; B. Holly Smith, "Dental Development in *Australopithecus* and Early *Homo,*" *Nature,* September 25, 1986, 327–30.

22. Scott W. Simpson, "*Australopithecus afarensis* and Human Evolution," in Carol R. Ember, Melvin Ember, and Peter N. Peregrine, eds., *Research Frontiers in Anthropology* (Upper Saddle River, NJ: Prentice Hall, 1998). Prentice Hall/Simon & Schuster Custom Publishing.

23. Glenn C. Conroy, *Primate Evolution* (New York: Norton, 1990), p. 293.

24. Randall L. Susman, Jack T. Stern, Jr., and William L. Jungers, "Locomotor Adaptations in the Hadar Hominids," in Eric Delson, ed., *Ancestors: The Hard Evidence* (New York: Alan R. Liss, 1985), pp. 184–92. See also Rose, "Food Acquisition and the Evolution of Positional Behaviour."

25. Conroy, *Primate Evolution,* p. 274. See also Elizabeth Culotta, "New Hominid Crowds the Field," *Science,* August 18, 1995, 918; and John Noble Wilford, "The

Transforming Leap, from 4 Legs to 2," *New York Times,* September 5, 1995, pp. C1 ff.

26. Joshua Fischman, "Putting Our Oldest Ancestors in Their Proper Place," *Science,* September 30, 1994, 2011–2012.

27. Raymond Dart, "*Australopithecus africanus:* The Man-Ape of South Africa," *Nature,* 115 (1925): 195.

28. Bromage and Dean, "Re-evaluation of the Age at Death of Immature Fossil Hominids," pp. 525–27; Smith, "Dental Development in *Australopithecus* and Early *Homo,*" pp. 327–30.

29. Niles Eldredge and Ian Tattersall, *The Myths of Human Evolution* (New York: Columbia University Press, 1982), pp. 80–90.

30. Pilbeam, *The Ascent of Man,* p. 107.

31. Ralph L. Holloway, "The Casts of Fossil Hominid Brains," *Scientific American,* July 1974, 106–15.

32. Frederick S. Szalay and Eric Delson, *Evolutionary History of the Primates* (New York: Academic Press, 1979), p. 504.

33. C. Owen Lovejoy, Kingsbury Heiple, and Albert Bernstein, "The Gait of *Australopithecus,*" *American Journal of Physical Anthropology,* 38 (1973): 757–79.

34. Conroy, *Primate Evolution,* pp. 280–82.

35. Simpson, "*Australopithecus afarensis* and Human Evolution."

36. Donald C. Johanson and Maitland Edey, *Lucy: The Beginnings of Humankind* (New York: Simon & Schuster, 1981), pp. 17–18.

37. C. Owen Lovejoy, "Evolution of Human Walking," *Scientific American,* November 1988, 118–25.

38. William L. Jungers, "Relative Joint Size and Hominoid Locomotor Adaptations with Implications for the Evolution of Hominid Bipedalism," *Journal of Human Evolution,* 17 (1988): 247–65.

39. Donald C. Johanson and Tim D. White, "A Systematic Assessment of Early African Hominids," *Science,* January 26, 1979, 321.

40. Roger Lewin, "Fossil Lucy Grows Younger, Again," *Science,* January 7, 1983, 43–44.

41. Conroy, *Primate Evolution,* pp. 291–92; Simpson, "*Australopithecus afarensis* and Human Evolution."

42. Tim D. White, Donald C. Johanson, and William H. Kimbel, "*Australopithecus africanus:* Its Phyletic Position Reconsidered," *South African Journal of Science,* 77 (1981): 445–70; and Johanson and White, "A Systematic Assessment of Early African Hominids."

43. Bernard G. Campbell, *Humankind Emerging,* 4th ed. (Boston: Little, Brown, 1985), p. 202.

44. McHenry, "The Pattern of Human Evolution," p. 161.

45. Conroy, *Primate Evolution,* pp. 294–303.

46. McHenry, "'Robust' Australopithecines, Our Family Tree, and Homoplasy."

47. Szalay and Delson, *Evolutionary History of the Primates,* p. 504; Bernard A. Wood, "Evolution of Australopithecines," in Steve Jones, Robert Martin, and David Pilbeam, eds., *The Cambridge Encyclopedia of Human Evolution* (New York: Cambridge University Press, 1992), p. 236.

48. McHenry, "'Robust' Australopithecines, Our Family Tree, and Homoplasy."

49. Henry M. McHenry, "New Estimates of Body Weight in Early Hominids and Their Significance to Encephalization and Megadontia in 'Robust' Australopithecines," in Grine, ed., *Evolutionary History of the "Robust" Australopithecines,* pp. 133–48; William L. Jungers, "New Estimates of Body Size in Australopithecines," in ibid., pp. 115–25.

50. McHenry, "'Robust' Australopithecines, Our Family Tree, and Homoplasy."

51. Ibid.

52. Frederick E. Grine, "Evolutionary History of the 'Robust' Australopithecines: A Summary and Historical Perspective," in Grine, ed., *Evolutionary History of the "Robust" Australopithecines,* pp. 515–16.

53. Christopher Stringer, "Evolution of a Species," *Geographical Magazine,* 57 (1985): 601–607.

54. Wood, "Evolution of Australopithecines," p. 239.

55. Simpson, "*Australopithecus afarensis* and Human Evolution."

56. Conroy, *Primate Evolution,* p. 326.

57. McHenry, "'Robust' Australopithecines, Our Family Tree, and Homoplasy"; Tobias, "The Craniocerebral Interface in Early Hominids."

58. Simpson, "*Australopithecus afarensis* and Human Evolution."

59. Susman, "Fossil Evidence for Early Hominid Tool Use," *Science,* September 9, 1994, 1570.

60. Ibid.

61. "The First Tool Kit," *Science,* January 31, 1997, 623.

62. Louis S. B. Leakey, "Finding the World's Earliest Man," *National Geographic,* September 1960, 424.

63. J. Desmond Clark, *The Prehistory of Africa* (New York: Praeger, 1970), p. 68; Kathy Schick and Nicholas Toth, *Making Silent Stones Speak* (New York: Simon & Schuster, 1993), pp. 97–99.

64. Schick and Toth, *Making Silent Stones Speak,* pp. 153–70.

65. Ibid., p. 129.

66. Ibid., pp. 157–59.

67. Glynn Isaac, "The Archaeology of Human Origins: Studies of the Pleistocene in East Africa, 1971–1981," in Fred Wendorf and Angela E. Close, eds. *Advances in World Archaeology,* vol. 3 (Orlando, FL: Academic Press, 1984), p. 13.

68. John C. Whittaker, *Flintknapping: Making and Understanding Stone Tools* (Austin: University of Texas Press, 1994), pp. 283–285.

69. Reported in Schick and Toth, *Making Silent Stones Speak,* pp. 175–76.

70. John D. Speth, "Were Our Ancestors Hunters or Scavengers?" in Carol R. Ember, Melvin Ember, and Peter N. Peregrine, eds., *Research Frontiers in Anthropology* (Upper Saddle River, NJ: Prentice Hall, 1998). Prentice Hall/Simon & Schuster Custom Publishing.

71. Shipman, "Scavenging or Hunting in Early Hominids," 27–43. For the idea that scavenging may have been an important food-getting strategy even for protohominids, see Frederick S. Szalay, "Hunting-Scavenging Protohominids: A Model for Hominid Origins," *Man,* 10 (1975): 420–29.

72. John D. Speth and Dave D. Davis, "Seasonal Variability in Early Hominid Predation," *Science,* April 30, 1976, 441–45.

73. Glynn Isaac, "The Diet of Early Man: Aspects of Archaeological Evidence from Lower and Middle Pleistocene Sites in Africa," *World Archaeology,* 2 (1971): 289.

74. Richard Potts, *Early Hominid Activities at Olduvai* (New York: Aldine de Gruyter, 1988), pp. 253–58.

75. Ibid., pp. 278–81.

76. G. Philip Rightmire, "*Homo erectus,*" in Ian Tattersall, Eric Delson, and John van Couvering, eds., *Encyclopedia of Human Evolution and Prehistory* (New York: Garland, 1988), pp. 259–65.

77. C. C. Swisher III, G. H. Curtis, T. Jacob, A. G. Getty, A. Suprijo, and N. Widiasmoro, "Age of the Earliest Known Hominids in Java, Indonesia." *Science,* February 25, 1994, 1118–21.

78. Milford H. Wolpoff and Abel Nkini, "Early and Early Middle Pleistocene Hominids from Asia and Africa," in Delson, ed., *Ancestors,* pp. 202–205. See also G. Philip Rightmire, "The Tempo of Change in the Evolution of Mid-Pleistocene *Homo,*" in ibid., pp. 255–64.

79. G. Philip Rightmire, *The Evolution of Homo erectus: Comparative Anatomical Studies of an Extinct Human Species* (Cambridge: Cambridge University Press, 1990), pp. 12–14.

80. Swisher et al., "Age of the Earliest Known Hominids in Java, Indonesia."

81. Rightmire, "*Homo erectus.*"

82. Ibid.; and Tobias, "The Craniocerebral Interface in Early Hominids."

83. Robert G. Franciscus and Erik Trinkaus, "Nasal Morphology and the Emergence of *Homo erectus,*" *American Journal of Physical Anthropology,* 75 (1988): 517–27.

84. Craig S. Feibel and Francis H. Brown, "Microstratigraphy and Paleoenvironments," in Alan Walker and Richard Leakey, eds., *The Nariokotome* Homo erectus *Skeleton* (Cambridge, MA: Harvard University Press, 1993), p. 39.

85. Christopher B. Ruff and Alan Walker, "Body Size and Body Shape," in Walker and Leakey, eds., *The Nariokotome* Homo erectus *Skeleton,* pp. 235, 254.

86. David W. Phillipson, *African Archaeology,* 2nd ed. (Cambridge: Cambridge University Press, 1993), p. 57.

87. Schick and Toth, *Making Silent Stones Speak,* pp. 227, 233.

88. Ibid., pp. 231–33; Whittaker, *Flintknapping,* p. 27.

89. Schick and Toth, *Making Silent Stones Speak,* pp. 258–60; Whittaker, *Flintknapping,* p. 27.

90. Lawrence Keeley's analysis reported in Schick and Toth, *Making Silent Stones Speak,* p. 260; see that page for their analysis of tool use.

91. Russell Ciochon, John Olsen, and Jamie James, *Other Origins: The Search for the Giant Ape in Human Prehistory* (New York: Bantam, 1990), pp. 178–83. Geoffrey G. Pope, "Bamboo and Human Evolution," *Natural History,* October 1989, 49–57, as reported in ibid., p. 43.

92. F. Clark Howell, "Observations on the Earlier Phases of the European Lower Paleolithic," in *Recent Studies in Paleoanthropology, American Anthropologist,* special publication, April 1966, 111–40.

93. Richard G. Klein, "Reconstructing How Early People Exploited Animals: Problems and Prospects," in Nitecki and Nitecki, eds., *The Evolution of Human Hunting,* pp. 11–45; and Lewis R. Binford, "Were There Elephant Hunters at Torralba?" in ibid., pp. 47–105.

94. Leslie G. Freeman, "Torralba and Ambrona: A Review of Discoveries," in Corruccini and Ciochon, eds., *Integrative Paths to the Past,* pp. 597–637.

95. Isaac, "The Archaeology of Human Origins," pp. 35–36. Other evidence for deliberate use of fire comes from the Swartkans cave in South Africa and is dated 1 million to 1.5 million years ago; see C. K. Brain and A. Sillen, "Evidence from the Swartkrans Cave for the Earliest Use of Fire," *Nature,* December 1, 1988, 464–66.

96. Klein, *The Human Career,* p. 171.

97. Lewis R. Binford and Chuan Kun Ho, "Taphonomy at a Distance: Zhoukoudian, 'The Cave Home of Beijing Man'?" *Current Anthropology,* 26 (1985): 413–42.

98. Clark, *The Prehistory of Africa,* pp. 94–95.

99. Ibid., pp. 96–97.

100. Henry de Lumley, "A Paleolithic Camp at Nice," *Scientific American,* May 1969, pp. 42–50.

CHAPTER 6

1. Christopher Stringer, "Evolution of a Species," *Geographical Magazine,* 57 (1985): 601–607.

2. Ibid.

3. G. Philip Rightmire, "*Homo sapiens* in Sub-Saharan Africa," in Fred H. Smith and Frank Spencer, eds., *The Origins of Modern Humans: A World Survey of the Fossil Evidence* (New York: Alan R. Liss, 1984), p. 303.

4. Frank Spencer, "The Neandertals and Their Evolutionary Significance: A Brief Historical Survey," in Smith and Spencer, eds., *The Origins of Modern Humans,* pp. 1–50.

5. Erik Trinkaus, "Pathology and the Posture of the La Chapelle-aux-Saints Neandertal," *American Journal of Physical Anthropology,* 67 (1985): 19–41.

6. Christopher B. Stringer, "Neandertals," in Ian Tattersall, Eric Delson, and John van Couvering, eds., *Encyclopedia of Human Evolution and Prehistory* (New York: Garland, 1988), p. 370.

7. Erik Trinkaus and Pat Shipman, "Neandertals: Images of Ourselves," *Evolutionary Anthropology,* 1, no. 6 (1993): 198, 194–201.

8. Fred H. Smith, "Fossil Hominids from the Upper Pleistocene of Central Europe and the Origin of Modern Humans," in Smith and Spencer, eds., *The Origins of Modern Humans,* p. 187.

9. Erik Trinkaus, "Western Asia," in Smith and Spencer, eds., The *Origins of Modern Humans,* pp. 251–53.

10. See various chapters in Smith and Spencer, eds., *The Origins of Modern Humans.*

11. Wu Xinzhi and Wu Maolin, "Early *Homo sapiens* in China," in Wu Rukang and John W. Olsen, eds., *Paleoanthropology and Paleolithic Archaeology in the People's Republic of China* (Orlando, FL: Academic Press, 1985), pp. 91–106.

12. Lawrence Guy Strauss, "On Early Hominid Use of Fire," *Current Anthropology,* 30 (1989): 488–91.

13. Kathy D. Schick and Nicholas Toth, *Making Silent Stones Speak* (New York: Simon & Schuster, 1993), pp. 288–92.

14. Richard G. Klein, *The Human Career: Human Biological and Cultural Origins* (Chicago: University of Chicago Press, 1989), pp. 291–96.

15. Schick and Toth, *Making Silent Stones Speak,* pp. 288–92; John C. Whittaker, *Flintknapping: Making and Understanding Stone Tools* (Austin: University of Texas Press, 1994), pp. 30–31.

16. Klein, *The Human Career,* pp. 421–22.

17. Sally R. Binford and Lewis R. Binford, "Stone Tools and Human Behavior," *Scientific American,* April 1969, 70–84.

18. Paul R. Fish, "Beyond Tools: Middle Paleolithic Debitage Analysis and Cultural Inference," *Journal of Anthropological Research,* 37 (1981): 377.

19. Karl W. Butzer, "Geomorphology and Sediment Stratigraphy," in Ronald Singer and John Wymer, *The Middle Stone Age at Klasies River Mouth in South Africa* (Chicago: University of Chicago Press, 1982), p. 42.

20. David W. Phillipson, *African Archaeology,* 2nd ed. (Cambridge: Cambridge University Press, 1993), p. 63.

21. For the controversy about whether the inhabitants of the Dordogne Valley lived in their homesites year-round, see Lewis R. Binford, "Interassemblage Variability: The Mousterian and the 'Functional' Argument," in Colin Renfrew, ed., *The Explanation of Culture Change: Models in Prehistory* (Pittsburgh: University of Pittsburgh Press, 1973).

22. Schick and Toth, *Making Silent Stones Speak,* p. 292.

23. Richard G. Klein, "The Ecology of Early Man in Southern Africa," *Science,* July 8, 1977, 120.

24. Richard G. Klein, "Ice-Age Hunters of the Ukraine," *Scientific American,* June 1974, 96–105.

25. François Bordes, "Mousterian Cultures in France," *Science,* September 22, 1961, 803–10.

26. Thomas C. Patterson, *The Evolution of Ancient Societies: A World Archaeology* (Englewood Cliffs, NJ: Prentice Hall, 1981).

27. Phillipson, *African Archaeology,* 2nd ed., p. 64.

28. Richard G. Klein, "The Stone Age Prehistory of Southern Africa," *Annual Review of Anthropology,* 12 (1983): 38–39.

29. Lewis R. Binford, *Faunal Remains from Klasies River Mouth* (Orlando, FL: Academic Press, 1984), pp. 195–97. To explain the lack of complete skeletons of large animals, Klein (see note 28) suggests that the hunters may have butchered the large animals elsewhere because they could carry home only small cuts.

30. John Noble Wilford, "Ancient German Spears Tell of Mighty Hunters of Stone Age," *New York Times,* March 4, 1997, p. C6.

31. John E. Pfeiffer, *The Emergence of Man,* 3rd ed. (New York: Harper & Row, 1978), p. 155.

32. C. B. Stringer, J. J. Hublin, and B. Vandermeersch, "The Origin of Anatomically Modern Humans in Western Europe," in Smith and Spencer, eds., *The Origins of Modern Humans,* p. 107.

33. Singer and Wymer, *The Middle Stone Age at Klasies River Mouth in South Africa,* p. 149.

34. Günter Bräuer, "A Craniological Approach to the Origin of Anatomically Modern *Homo sapiens* in Africa and Implications for the Appearance of Modern Europeans," in Smith and Spencer, eds., *The Origins of Modern Humans,* pp. 387–89, 394; and Rightmire, "*Homo sapiens* in Sub-Saharan Africa," p. 320.

35. H. Valladas, J. L. Joron, G. Valladas, O. Bar-Yosef, and B. Vandermeersch, "Thermoluminescence Dating of Mousterian 'Proto-Cro-Magnon' Remains from Israel and the Origin of Modern Man," *Nature,* February 18, 1988, 614–16.

36. Stringer, Hublin, and Vandermeersch, "The Origin of Anatomically Modern Humans in Western Europe," p. 121.

37. For arguments supporting the single-origin theory, see the chapters by Günter Bräuer; F. Clark Howell; and C. B. Stringer et al., in Smith and Spencer, eds., *The Origins of Modern Humans.* For arguments supporting the multiregional theory, see the chapters by C. L. Brace et al.; David W. Frayer; Fred H. Smith; and Milford H. Wolpoff et al., in the same volume.

38. Erik Trinkaus, "The Neandertals and Modern Human Origins." *Annual Review of Anthropology,* 15 (1986): 193–218.

39. Ibid., p. 210.

40. Alan R. Templeton, "Gene Lineages and Human Evolution," *Science,* May 31, 1996, 1363. See also Francisco J. Ayala, "The Myth of Eve: Molecular Biology and Human Origins," *Science,* December 22, 1995, 1930–936; and his subsequent communication in *Science,* November 29, 1996, 1354.

41. F. H. Brown, "Methods of Dating," in Steve Jones, Robert Martin, and David Pilbeam, eds., *The Cambridge Encyclopedia of Human Evolution* (New York: Cambridge University Press, 1992), pp. 179, 470.

42. Frank Hole and Robert F. Heizer, *An Introduction to Prehistoric Archeology,* 3rd ed. (New York: Holt, Rinehart & Winston, 1973), pp. 252–54.

43. Brown, "Methods of Dating," pp. 180, 470.

44. Ibid., pp. 182–83; Henry P. Schwarcz, "Uranium-Series Dating and the Origin of Modern Man," in Henry P. Schwarcz, *The Origin of Modern Humans and the Impact of Chronometric Dating* (Princeton, NJ: Princeton University Press, 1993), pp. 12–26.

45. M. J. Aitken, *Thermoluminescence Dating* (London: Academic Press, 1985), pp. 1–4.

46. Ibid., pp. 191–202.

47. Ibid., pp. 4, 211–13.

48. Randall White, "Rethinking the Middle/Upper Paleolithic Transition," *Current Anthropology,* 23 (1982): 169–75.

49. Lawrence Guy Strauss, "Comment on White" [ibid.], *Current Anthropology,* 23 (1982): 185–86.

50. Patterson, *The Evolution of Ancient Societies.*

51. Bohuslav Klima, "The First Ground-Plan of an Upper Paleolithic Loess Settlement in Middle Europe and Its Meaning," in Robert J. Braidwood and Gordon R. Willey, eds., *Courses toward Urban Life: Archaeological Consideration of Some Cultural Alternatives,* Viking Fund Publications in Anthropology No. 32 (Chicago: Aldine, 1962), pp. 193-210.

52. Whittaker, *Flintknapping,* p. 33; Schick and Toth, *Making Silent Stones Speak,* pp. 293–99.

53. Whittaker, *Flintknapping,* p. 31.

54. Jacques Bordaz, *Tools of the Old and New Stone Age* (Garden City, NY: Natural History Press, 1970), p. 68.

55. Whittaker, *Flintknapping,* p. 33.

56. Phillipson, *African Archaeology,* 2nd ed., p. 60.

57. Bordaz, *Tools of the Old and New Stone Age,* p. 68.

58. We thank Robert L. Kelly (personal communication) for bringing this possibility to our attention. See also J. Desmond Clark, "Interpretations of Prehistoric Technology from Ancient Egyptian and Other Sources. Part II: Prehistoric Arrow Forms in Africa as Shown by Surviving Examples of the Traditional Arrows of the San Bushmen," *Paleorient,* 3 (1977): 136.

59. Robert Ascher, "Analogy in Archaeological Interpretation," *Southwestern Journal of Anthropology,* 17 (1961): 317–25.

60. S. A. Semenov, *Prehistoric Technology,* trans. M. W. Thompson (Bath, England: Adams & Dart, 1970), p. 103. For a more recent discussion of research following this strategy, see Lawrence H. Keeley, *Experimental Determination of Stone Tool Uses: A Microwear Analysis* (Chicago: University of Chicago Press, 1980).

61. Richard G. Klein, "Southern Africa before the Ice Age," in Robert S. Corruccini and Russell L. Ciochon, eds., *Integrative Paths to the Past: Paleoanthropological Advances in Honor of F. Clark Howell* (Englewood Cliffs, NJ: Prentice Hall, 1994), p. 508.

62. Olga Soffer, "Upper Paleolithic Adaptations in Central and Eastern Europe and Man-Mammoth Interactions," in Olga Soffer and N. D. Praslov, eds., *From Kostenki to Clovis: Upper Paleolithic–Paleo-Indian Adaptations* (New York: Plenum, 1993), pp. 38–40.

63. Phillipson, *African Archaeology,* 2nd ed., p. 74.

64. Virginia Morell, "The Earliest Art Becomes Older—and More Common," *Science,* March 31, 1995, 1908–909.

65. Peter J. Ucko and Andrée Rosenfeld, *Paleolithic Cave Art* (New York: McGraw-Hill, 1967).

66. Patricia C. Rice and Ann L. Paterson, "Cave Art and Bones: Exploring the Interrelationships," *American Anthropologist,* 87 (1985): 94–100. For similar results of a study of cave art in Spain, see Patricia C. Rice and Ann L. Paterson, "Validating the Cave Art–Archeofaunal Relationship in Cantabrian Spain," *American Anthropologist,* 88 (1986): 658–67.

67. Rice and Paterson, "Cave Art and Bones," p. 98.

68. Alexander Marshack, *The Roots of Civilization* (New York: McGraw-Hill, 1972).

69. Kim A. McDonald, "New Evidence Challenges Traditional Model of How the New World Was Settled," *Chronicle of Higher Education,* March 13, 1998, A22.

70. Ann Gibbons, "First Americans: Not Mammoth Hunters, but Forest Dwellers?" *Science,* April 19, 1995, 346–47; and A. C. Roosevelt et al., "Paleoindian Cave Dwellers in the Amazon: The Peopling of the Americas," *Science,* April 19, 1996, 373–84.

71. Joseph H. Greenberg and Merritt Ruhlen, "Linguistic Origins of Native Americans," *Scientific American,* November 1992, 94–99.

72. Christy G. Turner II, "Teeth and Prehistory in Asia," *Scientific American,* February 1989, as reported in ibid.

73. Emöke J. E. Szathmary, "Genetics of Aboriginal North Americans," *Evolutionary Anthropology,* 1 (1993): 202–20.

74. McDonald, "New Evidence Challenges Traditional Model of How the New World Was Settled."

75. Joe B. Wheat, "A Paleo-Indian Bison Kill," *Scientific American,* January 1967, 44–47.

76. Brian M. Fagan, *Ancient North America: The Archaeology of a Continent* (London: Thames and Hudson, 1991), p. 79.

77. John F. Hoffecker, W. Rogers Powers, and Ted Geobel, "The Colonization of Beringia and the Peopling of the New World," *Science,* January 1, 1993, 51.

78. J. D. Jennings, *Prehistory of North America* (New York: McGraw-Hill, 1968), pp. 72–88.

79. W. James Judge and Jerry Dawson, "Paleo-Indian Settlement Technology in New Mexico," *Science,* June 16, 1972, 1210–216.

80. Wheat, "A Paleo-Indian Bison Kill."

81. Brian M. Fagan, *People of the Earth: An Introduction to World Prehistory,* 6th ed. (Glenview, IL: Scott, Foresman, 1989), p. 221.

82. Wheat, "A Paleo-Indian Bison Kill."

83. Ibid.

84. Fagan, *People of the Earth,* p. 227.

85. Fagan, *Ancient North America,* p. 192.

86. Fagan, *People of the Earth,* p. 227.

CHAPTER 7

1. G. A. Harrison, James M. Tanner, David R. Pilbeam, and P. T. Baker, *Human Biology: An Introduction to Human Evolution, Variation, Growth, and Adaptability,* 3rd ed. (Oxford: Oxford University Press, 1988), pp. 209–12.

2. William H. Durham, *Coevolution: Genes, Culture, and Human Diversity* (Stanford, CA: Stanford University Press, 1991), pp. 122–23.

3. Harrison et al., *Human Biology,* pp. 205–206.

4. Ibid., pp. 205–208.

5. John Relethford, *The Human Species: An Introduction to Biological Anthropology* (Mountain View, CA: Mayfield, 1990), p. 94.

6. Harrison et al., *Human Biology,* pp. 198–200.

7. See Durham, *Coevolution,* pp. 154–225, for an extensive discussion of the relationship between genes and culture.

8. Joel M. Hanna, Michael A. Little, and Donald M. Austin, "Climatic Physiology," in Michael A. Little and Jere D. Haas, eds., *Human Population Biology: A Transdisciplinary Science* (New York: Oxford University

Press, 1989), pp. 133–36; Harrison et al., *Human Biology,* pp. 504–507.

9. D. F. Roberts, "Body Weight, Race, and Climate," *American Journal of Physical Anthropology,* 2 (1953): 553–58. Cited in Stanley M. Garn, *Human Races,* 3rd ed. (Springfield, IL: Charles C. Thomas, 1971), p. 73. See also D. F. Roberts, *Climate and Human Variability,* 2nd ed. (Menlo Park, CA: Cummings, 1978).

10. Roberts, "Body Weight, Race, and Climate."

11. Harrison et al., *Human Biology,* p. 505.

12. Alphonse Riesenfeld, "The Effect of Extreme Temperatures and Starvation on the Body Proportions of the Rat," *American Journal of Physical Anthropology,* 39 (1973): 427–59.

13. Ibid., pp. 452–53.

14. J. S. Weiner, "Nose Shape and Climate," *Journal of Physical Anthropology,* 4 (1954): 615–18; A. T. Steegman, Jr., "Human Adaptation to Cold," in Albert Damon, ed., *Physiological Anthropology* (New York: Oxford University Press, 1975), pp. 130–66. See also Clark Spenser Larsen, "Bare Bones Anthropology: The Bioarchaeology of Human Remains," in Carol R. Ember, Melvin Ember, and Peter N. Peregrine, eds., *Research Frontiers in Anthropology* (Upper Saddle River, NJ: Prentice Hall, 1998). Prentice Hall/Simon & Schuster Custom Publishing.

15. Harrison et al., *Human Biology,* pp. 308–10.

16. Anthony P. Polednak, "Connective Tissue Responses in Negroes in Relation to Disease," *American Journal of Physical Anthropology,* 41 (1974): 49–57. See also Richard F. Branda and John W. Eaton, "Skin Color and Nutrient Photolysis: An Evolutionary Hypothesis," *Science,* August 18, 1978, 625–26.

17. W. Farnsworth Loomis, "Skin-Pigment Regulation of Vitamin-D Biosynthesis in Man," *Science,* August 4, 1967, 501–506.

18. Peter W. Post, Farrington Daniels, Jr., and Robert T. Binford, Jr., "Cold Injury and the Evolution of 'White' Skin," *Human Biology,* 47 (1975): 65–80.

19. William A. Stini, *Ecology and Human Adaptation* (Dubuque, IA: Wm. C. Brown, 1975), p. 53.

20. Richard B. Mazess, "Human Adaptation to High Altitude," in Damon, ed., *Physiological Anthropology,* p. 168.

21. Lawrence P. Greksa and Cynthia M. Beall, "Development of Chest Size and Lung Function at High Altitude," in Little and Haas, eds., *Human Population Biology,* p. 223.

22. Ibid., p. 226.

23. A. Roberto Frisancho and Lawrence P. Greksa, "Development Responses in the Acquisition of Functional Adaptation to High Altitude," in Little and Haas, eds., *Human Population Biology,* p. 204.

24. Phyllis B. Eveleth and James M. Tanner, *Worldwide Variation in Human Growth,* 2nd ed. (Cambridge: Cambridge University Press, 1990), pp. 176–79.

25. Ibid., pp. 205–206.

26. Barry Bogin, *Patterns of Human Growth* (Cambridge: Cambridge University Press, 1988), pp. 105–106.

27. Harrison et al., *Human Biology,* p. 300.

28. Ibid., p. 198.

29. Rebecca Huss-Ashmore and Francis E. Johnston, "Bioanthropological Research in Developing Countries," *Annual Review of Anthropology,* 14 (1985): 482–83.

30. Harrison et al., *Human Biology,* pp. 385–86.

31. Reynaldo Martorell, "Interrelationships between Diet, Infectious Disease and Nutritional Status," in L. Greene and F. E. Johnston, eds., *Social and Biological Predictors of Nutritional Status, Physical Growth and Neurological Development* (New York: Academic Press, 1980), pp. 81–106.

32. Reynaldo Martorell, Juan Rivera, Haley Kaplowitz, and Ernesto Pollitt, "Long-Term Consequences of Growth Retardation during Early Childhood," paper presented at the VIth International Congress of Auxology, September 15–19, 1991, Madrid.

33. Thomas K. Landauer and John W. M. Whiting, "Infantile Stimulation and Adult Stature of Human Males," *American Anthropologist,* 66 (1964): 1007–28; S. Gunders and J. W. M. Whiting, "Mother–Infant Separation and Physical Growth," *Ethnology,* 7 (1968): 196–206; J. Patrick Gray and Linda D. Wolfe, "Height and Sexual Dimorphism of Stature among Human Societies," *American Journal of Physical Anthropology,* 53 (1980): 446–52; Thomas K. Landauer and John W. M. Whiting, "Correlates and Consequences of Stress in Infancy," in Ruth H. Munroe, Robert L. Munroe, and Beatrice B. Whiting, eds., *Handbook of Cross-Cultural Human Development* (New York: Garland, 1981), pp. 361–65.

34. Landauer and Whiting, "Infantile Stimulation and Adult Stature of Human Males"; Gunders and Whiting, "Mother–Infant Separation and Physical Growth"; Landauer and Whiting, "Correlates and Consequences of Stress in Infancy."

35. J. Patrick Gray and Linda Wolfe, "What Accounts for Population Variation in Height?" in Ember, Ember, and Peregrine, eds., *Research Frontiers in Anthropology.*

36. Landauer and Whiting, "Correlates and Consequences of Stress in Infancy," p. 369.

37. Eveleth and Tanner, *Worldwide Variation in Human Growth,* p. 205.

38. Thomas K. Landauer, "Infantile Vaccination and the Secular Trend in Stature," *Ethos,* 1 (1973): 499–503.

39. Arno Motulsky, "Metabolic Polymorphisms and the Role of Infectious Diseases in Human Evolution," in Morris, ed., *Human Populations, Genetic Variation, and Evolution,* p. 223.

40. Ibid., p. 226.

41. Ibid., p. 229.

42. Ibid., p. 230.

43. Ibid., p. 233.

44. Ibid.

45. Francis L. Black, "Why Did They Die?" *Science,* December 11, 1992, 1739–40.

46. James V. Neel, Willard R. Centerwall, Napoleon A. Chagnon, and Helen L. Casey, "Notes on the Effect of Measles and Measles Vaccine in a Virgin-Soil Population of South American Indians," *American Journal of Epidemiology,* 91 (1970): 418–29.

47. Relethford, *The Human Species,* pp. 425–27, referring to A. McElroy and P. R. Townsend, *Medical Anthropology* (North Scituate, MA: Duxbury Press, 1979).

48. Charles F. Merbs, "A New World of Infectious Disease," *Yearbook of Physical Anthropology,* 35 (1992): 16.

49. Durham, *Coevolution,* pp. 105–107.

50. Ibid.

51. Ibid., p. 107.

52. Harrison et al., *Human Biology,* p. 231.

53. For a review of the early research, see Durham, *Coevolution,* pp. 123–27. The particular form of malaria that is discussed is caused by the species *Plasmodium falciparum.*

54. See Lorena Madigral, "Hemoglobin Genotype, Fertility, and the Malaria Hypothesis," *Human Biology,* 61 (1989): 311–25, for a report of her own research and a review of earlier studies.

55. Ibid., pp. 124–45.

56. Motulsky, "Metabolic Polymorphisms and the Role of Infectious Diseases in Human Evolution," p. 238.

57. Jared Diamond, "Who Are the Jews?" *Natural History,* November 1993, 16.

58. Stephen Molnar, *Human Variation: Races, Types and Ethnic Groups,* 4th ed. (Upper Saddle River, NJ: Prentice Hall, 1998), p. 158.

59. Durham, *Coevolution,* p. 230.

60. Jane E. Brody, "Effects of Milk on Blacks Noted," *New York Times,* October 15, 1971, p. 15.

61. Durham, *Coevolution,* pp. 233–35.

62. Relethford, *The Human Species,* p. 127.

63. Robert D. McCracken, "Lactase Deficiency: An Example of Dietary Evolution," *Current Anthropology,* 12 (1971): 479–500; see also references to the work of F. J. Simoons as referred to in Durham, *Coevolution,* pp. 240–41.

64. McCracken, "Lactase Deficiency," p. 480.

65. Durham, *Coevolution,* pp. 263–69.

66. Jonathan Marks, "Black, White, Other: Racial Categories Are Cultural Constructs Masquerading as Biology," *Natural History,* December 1994, 33; Eugenia Shanklin, *Anthropology and Race* (Belmont, CA: Wadsworth, 1994), pp. 15–17.

67. Molnar, *Human Variation,* p. 19.

68. C. Loring Brace, David P. Tracer, Lucia Allen Yaroch, John Robb, Kari Brandt, and A. Russell Nelson, "Clines and Clusters versus 'Race': A Test in Ancient Egypt and the Case of a Death on the Nile." *Yearbook of Physical Anthropology,* 36 (1993): 17–19.

69. Alison S. Brooks, Fatimah Linda Collier Jackson, R. Richard Grinker, "Race and Ethnicity in America," *Anthro Notes* (National Museum of Natural History Bulletin for Teachers), 15, no. 3 (Fall 1993): 11.

70. Brace et al., "Clines and Clusters versus 'Race,'" p. 19.

71. Brooks, Jackson, and Grinker, "Race and Ethnicity in America," pp. 12–13.

72. Melvin D. Williams, "Racism: The Production, Reproduction, and Obsolescence of Social Inferiority," in Ember, Ember, and Peregrine, eds., *Research Frontiers in Anthropology.*

73. Saul S. Friedman, "Holocaust," in *Academic American* [now *Grolier*] *Encyclopedia,* vol. 10 (Princeton, NJ: Arete, 1980), p. 206.

74. Marc Howard Ross, "Ethnocentrism and Ethnic Conflict," in Ember, Ember, and Peregrine, eds., *Research Frontiers in Anthropology.*

75. Marks, "Black, White, Other," p. 32.

76. L. Carrington Goodrich, *A Short History of the Chinese People,* 3rd ed. (New York: Harper & Row, 1959), pp. 7–15.

77. Michael D. Coe, *The Maya* (New York: Praeger, 1966), pp. 74–76.

78. Elizabeth Bartlett Thompson, *Africa, Past and Present* (Boston: Houghton Mifflin, 1966), p. 89.

79. William H. McNeill, *Plagues and Peoples* (Garden City, NY: Doubleday/Anchor, 1976).

80. Motulsky, "Metabolic Polymorphisms and the Role of Infectious Diseases in Human Evolution," p. 232.

81. Ibid.

82. Otto Klineberg, *Negro Intelligence and Selective Migration* (New York: Columbia University Press, 1935); and Otto Klineberg, ed., *Characteristics of the American Negro* (New York: Harper & Brothers, 1944).

83. Arthur Jensen, "How Much Can We Boost IQ and Scholastic Achievement?" *Harvard Educational Review,* 29 (1969): 1–123.

84. M. W. Smith, "Alfred Binet's Remarkable Questions: A Cross-National and Cross-Temporal Analysis of the Cultural Biases Built into the Stanford-Binet Intelligence Scale and Other Binet Tests," *Genetic Psychology Monographs,* 89 (1974): 307–34.

85. Theodosius Dobzhansky, *Genetic Diversity and Human Equality* (New York: Basic Books, 1973), p. 11.

86. Ibid., pp. 14–15.

87. Research by Sandra Scarr and others reported in Robert Boyd and Peter J. Richerson, *Culture and the Evolutionary Process* (Chicago: University of Chicago Press, 1985), p. 56.

88. Theodosius Dobzhansky, *Mankind Evolving: The Evolution of the Human Species* (New Haven, CT: Yale University Press, 1962), p. 243.

89. J. B. S. Haldane, "Human Evolution: Past and Future," in Glenn L. Jepsen, Ernst Mayr, and George Gaylord Simpson, eds., *Genetics, Paleontology, and Evolution* (New York: Atheneum, 1963), pp. 405–18.

90. George Gaylord Simpson, *The Meaning of Evolution* (New York: Bantam, 1971), pp. 297–308.

CHAPTER 8

1. Naomi F. Miller, "The Origins of Plant Cultivation in the Near East," in C. Wesley Cowan and Patty Jo Watson, eds., *The Origins of Agriculture* (Washington, DC: Smithsonian Institution Press, 1992), pp. 41–42.

2. Gary W. Crawford, "Prehistoric Plant Domestication in East Asia," in Cowan and Watson, eds., *The Origins of Agriculture,* pp. 29–30; David W. Phillipson, *African Archaeology,* 2nd ed. (New York: Cambridge University Press, 1993), p. 118; Richard S. MacNeish, *The Origins of Agriculture and Settled Life* (Norman: University of Oklahoma Press, 1991), pp. 256, 268.

3. Kent V. Flannery, "The Research Problem," in Kent V. Flannery, ed., *Guila Naquitz: Archaic Foraging and Early Agriculture in Oaxaca, Mexico* (Orlando, FL:

Academic Press, 1986), pp. 6–8; Deborah Pearsall, "The Origins of Plant Cultivation in South America," in Cowan and Watson, eds., *The Origins of Agriculture*, p. 197; Bruce D. Smith, "Prehistoric Plant Husbandry in Eastern North America," in Cowan and Watson, eds., *The Origins of Agriculture*, p. 101.

4. Frank Hole, "Origins of Agriculture," in Steve Jones, Robert Martin, and David Pilbeam, eds., *The Cambridge Encyclopedia of Human Evolution* (New York: Cambridge University Press, 1992), p. 375.

5. Desmond Collins, "Later Hunters in Europe," in Desmond Collins, ed., *The Origins of Europe* (New York: Thomas Y. Crowell, 1976), pp. 88–125.

6. Chester S. Chard, *Man in Prehistory* (New York: McGraw-Hill, 1969), p. 171.

7. Grahame Clark, *The Earlier Stone Age Settlement of Scandinavia* (Cambridge: Cambridge University Press, 1975), pp. 101–61.

8. Erik B. Petersen, "A Survey of the Late Paleolithic and the Mesolithic of Denmark," in S. K. Kozlowski, ed., *The Mesolithic in Europe* (Warsaw: Warsaw University Press, 1973), pp. 94–96.

9. Lewis R. Binford, "Post-Pleistocene Adaptations," in Stuart Struever, ed., *Prehistoric Agriculture* (Garden City, NY: Natural History Press, 1971), pp. 45–49.

10. Kent V. Flannery, "The Origins of Agriculture," *Annual Review of Anthropology*, 2 (1973): 274.

11. Jack R. Harlan, "A Wild Wheat Harvest in Turkey," *Archaeology*, 20, no. 3 (June 1967): 197–201.

12. Kent V. Flannery, "The Origins and Ecological Effects of Early Domestication in Iran and the Near East," in Struever, ed., *Prehistoric Agriculture*, p. 59. Originally published in Peter J. Ucko and G. W. Dimbleby, eds., *The Domestication and Exploitation of Plants and Animals* (Chicago: Aldine, 1969).

13. James Mellaart, "Roots in the Soil," in Stuart Piggott, ed., *The Dawn of Civilization* (London: Thames & Hudson, 1961), pp. 41–64.

14. Donald O. Henry, *From Foraging to Agriculture: The Levant at the End of the Ice Age* (Philadelphia: University of Pennsylvania Press, 1989), pp. 214–15.

15. James A. Brown and T. Douglas Price, "Complex Hunter-Gatherers: Retrospect and Prospect," in T. Douglas Price and James A. Brown, *Prehistoric Hunter-Gatherers: The Emergence of Cultural Complexity* (Orlando, FL: Academic Press, 1985), pp. 435–41.

16. Henry, *From Foraging to Agriculture*, pp. 38–39, 209–10; Donald O. Henry, "Foraging, Sedentism, and Adaptive Vigor in the Natufian: Rethinking the Linkages," in Geoffrey A. Clark, ed., *Perspectives on the Past: Theoretical Biases in Mediterranean Hunter-Gatherer Research* (Philadelphia: University of Pennsylvania Press, 1991), pp. 365–68. See Deborah I. Olszewski, "Social Complexity in the Natufian? Assessing the Relationship of Ideas and Data," in ibid., pp. 322–40, for some questions about the degree of social complexity in Natufian sites.

17. Chester Gorman, "The Hoabinhian and After: Subsistence Patterns in Southeast Asia during the Late Pleistocene and Early Recent Periods," *World Archaeology*, 2 (1970): 315–16.

18. Kwang-Chih Chang, "The Beginnings of Agriculture in the Far East," *Antiquity*, 44, no. 175 (September 1970): 176. See also Gorman, "The Hoabinhian and After," pp. 300–19.

19. J. Desmond Clark, *The Prehistory of Africa* (New York: Praeger, 1970), pp. 171–72.

20. Phillipson, *African Archaeology*, 2nd ed., pp. 111–12.

21. Thomas C. Patterson, *America's Past: A New World Archaeology* (Glenview, IL: Scott, Foresman, 1973), p. 42.

22. Paul S. Martin, "The Discovery of America," *Science*, March 9, 1973, 969–74.

23. Donald K. Grayson, "Pleistocene Avifaunas and the Overkill Hypothesis," *Science*, February 18, 1977, 691–92. See also Larry G. Marshall, "Who Killed Cock Robin? An Investigation of the Extinction Controversy," Donald K. Grayson, "Explaining Pleistocene Extinctions: Thoughts on the Structure of a Debate," and R. Dale Guthrie, "Mosaics, Allelochemics and Nutrients: An Ecological Theory of Late Pleistocene Megafaunal Extinctions," in Paul S. Martin and Richard G. Klein, eds., *Quaternary Extinctions: A Prehistoric Revolution* (Tucson: University of Arizona Press, 1984), pp. 785–806, 807–23, 259–98.

24. Mark Nathan Cohen, *The Food Crisis in Prehistory: Overpopulation and the Origins of Agriculture* (New Haven, CT: Yale University Press, 1977), pp. 12, 85.

25. Ibid., p. 85; and Fekri A. Hassan, *Demographic Archaeology* (New York: Academic Press, 1981), p. 207. For the view that hunter-gatherers were very unlikely to have lived in tropical forests before agriculture, see Robert C. Bailey, Genevieve Head, Mark Jenike, Bruce Owen, Robert Rechtman, and Elzbieta Zechenter, "Hunting and Gathering in Tropical Rain Forest: Is It Possible?" *American Anthropologist*, 91 (1989): 59–82.

26. Mark Nathan Cohen, *Health and the Rise of Civilization* (New Haven, CT: Yale University Press, 1989), pp. 112–13.

27. David W. Frayer, "Body Size, Weapon Use, and Natural Selection in the European Upper Paleolithic and Mesolithic," *American Anthropologist*, 83 (1981): 57–73.

28. Cohen, *Health and the Rise of Civilization*, pp. 113–15.

29. Kent V. Flannery, "The Origins of the Village as a Settlement Type in Mesoamerica and the Near East: A Comparative Study," in Ruth Tringham, ed., *Territoriality and Proxemics* R1 (Andover, MA: Warner Modular, 1973), pp. 1–31.

30. Thomas C. Patterson, "Central Peru: Its Population and Economy," *Archaeology*, 24 (1971): 318–19.

31. Gregory A. Johnson, "Aspects of Regional Analysis in Archaeology," *Annual Review of Anthropology*, 6 (1977): 488–89. See also David R. Harris, "Settling Down: An Evolutionary Model for the Transformation of Mobile Bands into Sedentary Communities," in J. Friedman and M. J. Rowlands, eds., *The Evolution of Social Systems* (London: Duckworth, 1977), pp. 401–17.

32. Robert Sussman, "Child Transport, Family Size, and the Increase in Human Population Size during the

Neolithic," *Current Anthropology,* 13 (April 1972): 258–67; and Richard B. Lee, "Population Growth and the Beginnings of Sedentary Life among the !Kung Bushmen," in Brian Spooner, ed., *Population Growth: Anthropological Implications* (Cambridge, MA: MIT Press, 1972), pp. 329–42.

33. For some examples of societies that have practiced infanticide, see Harris, "Settling Down," p. 407.

34. Nancy Howell, *Demography of the Dobe !Kung* (New York: Academic Press, 1979); and Richard B. Lee, *The !Kung San: Men, Women, and Work in a Foraging Society* (Cambridge: Cambridge University Press, 1979).

35. Rose E. Frisch, "Fatness, Puberty, and Fertility," *Natural History,* October 1980, 16–27; and Howell, *Demography of the Dobe !Kung.*

36. Phillipson, *African Archaeology,* 2nd ed., pp. 60–61.

37. S. A. Semenov, *Prehistoric Technology,* trans. M. W. Thompson (Bath, England: Adams & Dart, 1970), pp. 63, 203–204; John C. Whittaker, *Flintknapping: Making and Understanding Stone Tools* (Austin: University of Texas Press, 1994), pp. 36–37.

38. Daniel Zohary, "The Progenitors of Wheat and Barley in Relation to Domestication and Agricultural Dispersal in the Old World," in Ucko and Dimbleby, eds., *The Domestication and Exploitation of Plants and Animals,* pp. 47–66.

39. Kent V. Flannery, "The Ecology of Early Food Production in Mesopotamia," *Science,* March 12, 1965, 1252.

40. Ibid., p. 1253. For the view that a high proportion of immature animals does not necessarily indicate domestication, see Stephen Collier and J. Peter White, "Get Them Young? Age and Sex Inferences on Animal Domestication in Archaeology," *American Antiquity,* 41 (1976): 96–102.

41. Hole, "Origins of Agriculture," p. 376; MacNeish, *The Origins of Agriculture and Settled Life,* pp. 127–28.

42. Juliet Clutton-Brock, "Domestication of Animals," in Jones, Martin, and Pilbeam, eds., *The Cambridge Encyclopedia of Human Evolution,* p. 384.

43. Frank Hole, Kent V. Flannery, and James A. Neely, *Prehistory and Human Ecology of the Deh Luran Plain. Memoirs of the Museum of Anthropology No. 1* (Ann Arbor: University of Michigan, 1969).

44. See Alan H. Simmons, Ilse Köhler-Rollefson, Gary O. Rollefson, Rolfe Mandel, and Zeidan Kafafi, "'Ain Ghazal: A Major Neolithic Settlement in Central Jordan," *Science,* April 1, 1988, 35–39.

45. James Mellaart, "A Neolithic City in Turkey," *Scientific American,* April 1964, 94–104.

46. K. C. Chang, "In Search of China's Beginnings: New Light on an Old Civilization," *American Scientist,* 69 (1981): 148–60; MacNeish, *The Origins of Agriculture and Settled Life,* pp. 159–63.

47. MacNeish, *The Origins of Agriculture and Settled Life,* pp. 267–68.

48. Ibid.; Hole, "Origins of Agriculture," p. 376.

49. Phillipson, *African Archaeology,* 2nd ed., p. 118.

50. Ibid.; MacNeish, *The Origins of Agriculture and Settled Life,* p. 314.

51. Clutton-Brock, "Domestication of Animals," p. 384.

52. Charles B. Heiser, Jr., *Of Plants and People* (Norman: University of Oklahoma Press, 1985), p. 21.

53. Flannery, "The Research Problem," pp. 6–8.

54. Ibid.

55. Ibid., pp. 8–9.

56. MacNeish, *The Origins of Agriculture and Settled Life,* pp. 37, 47; Hole, "Origins of Agriculture," p. 376.

57. Bruce D. Smith, *Rivers of Change* (Washington, DC: Smithsonian Institution Press, 1992), pp. 163, 287.

58. Nancy B. Asch and David L. Asch, "The Economic Potential of *Iva annua* and Its Prehistoric Importance in the Lower Illinois Valley," in Richard I. Ford, ed., *The Nature and Status of Ethnobotany. Anthropological Papers, Museum of Anthropology No. 67* (Ann Arbor: University of Michigan, 1978), pp. 301–42.

59. Smith, *Rivers of Change,* pp. 39, 274–75, 292; Smith, "Prehistoric Plant Husbandry in Eastern North America."

60. Smith, *Rivers of Change,* p. 6.

61. Ibid., p. 180.

62. Clutton-Brock, "Domestication of Animals," p. 385.

63. R. D. Crawford, "Turkey," in Ian L. Mason, *Evolution of Domesticated Animals* (New York: Longman, 1984), pp. 329–31.

64. Clutton-Brock, "Domestication of Animals," p. 385.

65. B. Müller-Haye, "Guinea Pig or Cuy," in Mason, *Evolution of Domesticated Animals,* p. 255.

66. Robert J. Wenke, *Patterns in Prehistory: Humankind's First Three Million Years,* 2nd ed. (New York: Oxford University Press, 1984), pp. 350, 397–98.

67. Flannery, "The Origins of the Village as a Settlement Type in Mesoamerica and the Near East," p. 1. There is evidence, however, that there could have been permanent communities as far back as 6000 B.C. in central Mexico, near what is now Mexico City; see Christine Niederberger, "Early Sedentary Economy in the Basin of Mexico," *Science,* January 12, 1979, pp. 131–42.

68. Richard S. MacNeish, "The Evaluation of Community Patterns in the Tehuacán Valley of Mexico and Speculations about the Cultural Processes," in Ruth Tringham, ed., *Ecology and Agricultural Settlements,* R2 (Andover, MA: Warner Modular, 1973), 1–27. Originally published in Peter J. Ucko, Ruth Tringham, and G. W. Dimbleby, eds., *Man, Settlement and Urbanism* (Cambridge, MA: Schenkman, 1972).

69. Jared Diamond, "Location, Location, Location: The First Farmers," *Science,* November 14, 1997, 1243–244.

70. Cited in MacNeish, *The Origins of Agriculture and Settled Life,* p. 6.

71. Robert J. Braidwood, "The Agricultural Revolution," *Scientific American,* September 1960, 130.

72. Robert J. Braidwood and Gordon R. Willey, "Conclusions and Afterthoughts," in Robert J. Braidwood and Gordon R. Willey, eds., *Courses toward Urban Life: Archeological Considerations of Some Cultural Alternatives. Viking Fund Publications in Anthropology No. 32* (Chicago: Aldine, 1962), p. 342.

73. Binford, "Post-Pleistocene Adaptations," pp. 22–49; and Flannery, "The Origins and Ecological Effects of Early Domestication in Iran and the Near East," pp. 50–70.

74. Gary A. Wright, "Origins of Food Production in Southwestern Asia: A Survey of Ideas," *Current Anthropology,* 12 (1971): 470.

75. Flannery, "The Research Problem," pp. 10–11.

76. Mark N. Cohen, "Population Pressure and the Origins of Agriculture," in Charles A. Reed, ed., *Origins of Agriculture* (The Hague: Mouton, 1977), pp. 138–41. See also Cohen, *The Food Crisis in Prehistory,* p. 279.

77. Roger Byrne, "Climatic Change and the Origins of Agriculture," in Linda Manzanilla, ed., *Studies in the Neolithic and Urban Revolutions. British Archaeological Reports International Series 349* (Oxford, 1987), pp. 21–34, referred to in Mark A. Blumler and Roger Byrne, "The Ecological Genetics of Domestication and the Origins of Agriculture," *Current Anthropology,* 32 (1991): 23–35. See also Henry, *From Foraging to Agriculture,* pp. 30–38; and Joy McCorriston and Frank Hole, "The Ecology of Seasonal Stress and the Origins of Agriculture in the Near East," *American Anthropologist,* 93 (1991): 46–69.

78. Henry, *From Foraging to Agriculture,* p. 41.

79. McCorriston and Hole, "The Ecology of Seasonal Stress."

80. Henry, *From Foraging to Agriculture,* p. 54.

81. John D. Speth and Katherine A. Spielmann, "Energy Source, Protein Metabolism, and Hunter-Gatherer Subsistence Strategies," *Journal of Anthropological Archaeology,* 2 (1983): 1–31.

82. Benjamin White, "Demand for Labor and Population Growth in Colonial Java," *Human Ecology,* 1, no. 3 (March 1973): 217–36. See also John D. Kasarda, "Economic Structure and Fertility: A Comparative Analysis," *Demography,* 8, no. 3 (August 1971): 307–18.

83. Carol R. Ember, "The Relative Decline in Women's Contribution to Agriculture with Intensification," *American Anthropologist,* 85 (1983): 285–304.

84. Melvin Konner and Carol Worthman, "Nursing Frequency, Gonadal Function, and Birth Spacing among !Kung Hunter-Gatherers," *Science,* February 15, 1980, 788–91.

85. Anna Curtenius Roosevelt, "Population, Health, and the Evolution of Subsistence: Conclusions from the Conference," in Mark Nathan Cohen and George J. Armelagos, eds., *Paleopathology at the Origins of Agriculture* (Orlando, FL: Academic Press, 1984), pp. 559–84. See also Mark Nathan Cohen and George J. Armelagos, "Paleopathology at the Origins of Agriculture: Editors' Summation," in the same volume, pp. 585–602; Mark N. Cohen, "The Significance of Long-Term Changes in Human Diet and Food Economy," in Marvin Harris and Eric B. Ross, eds., *Food and Evolution: Toward a Theory of Human Food Habits* (Philadelphia: Temple University Press, 1987), pp. 269–73; Mark N. Cohen, "Were Early Agriculturalists Less Healthy Than Food Collectors?" in Carol R. Ember, Melvin Ember, and Peter N. Peregrine, eds., *Research Frontiers in Anthropology* (Upper Saddle River, NJ: Prentice Hall, 1998). Prentice Hall/Simon & Schuster Custom Publishing. For evidence suggesting that the transition to food production was not generally associated with declining health, see James W. Wood, George R. Milner, Henry C. Harpending, and Kenneth M. Weiss, "The Osteological Paradox: Problems of Inferring Prehistoric Health from Skeletal Samples," *Current Anthropology,* 33 (1992): 343–70.

86. Roosevelt, "Population, Health, and the Evolution of Subsistence"; and Cohen and Armelagos, "Paleopathology at the Origins of Agriculture."

87. Alan H. Goodman and George J. Armelagos, "Disease and Death at Dr. Dickson's Mounds," *Natural History,* September 1985, 18. See also Alan H. Goodman, John Lallo, George J. Armelagos, and Jerome C. Rose, "Health Changes at Dickson Mounds, Illinois (A.D. 950–1300)," in Cohen and Armelagos, *Paleopathology at the Origins of Agriculture,* p. 300; Cohen, "Were Early Agriculturalists Less Healthy Than Food Collectors?"

88. Grahame Clark and Stuart Piggott, *Prehistoric Societies* (New York: Knopf, 1965), pp. 240–42.

89. Ibid., p. 235.

90. Colin Renfrew, "Trade and Culture Process in European Prehistory," *Current Anthropology,* 10 (April–June 1969): 156–57, 161–69.

91. *Webster's New World Dictionary, Third College Edition* (New York: Webster's New World, 1988).

CHAPTER 9

1. Robert J. Wenke, *Patterns in Prehistory: Humankind's First Three Million Years,* 3rd ed. (New York: Oxford University Press, 1990). See also Graham Connah, *African Civilizations: Precolonial Cities and States in Tropical Africa, an Archaeological Perspective* (Cambridge: Cambridge University Press, 1987); and Elman R. Service, *Origins of the State and Civilization: The Process of Cultural Evolution* (New York: Norton, 1975).

2. Kent V. Flannery, "The Cultural Evolution of Civilizations," *Annual Review of Ecology and Systematics,* 3 (1972): 399–426.

3. Ibid. See also Charles L. Redman, *The Rise of Civilization: From Early Farmers to Urban Society in the Ancient Near East* (San Francisco: Freeman, 1978), pp. 215–16.

4. Henry T. Wright and Gregory A. Johnson, "Population, Exchange, and Early State Formation in Southwestern Iran," *American Anthropologist,* 77 (1975): 267.

5. The discussion in the remainder of this section draws from ibid., pp. 269–74. See also Gregory A. Johnson, "The Changing Organization of Uruk Administration on the Susiana Plain," in Frank Hole, ed., *Archaeology of Western Iran* (Washington, DC: Smithsonian Institution Press, 1987), pp. 107–39.

6. Ibid., pp. 271–72.

7. Flannery, "The Cultural Evolution of Civilizations."

8. Service, *Origins of the State and Civilization,* p. 207.

9. Ibid.; and Flannery, "The Cultural Evolution of Civilizations."

10. This description of Sumerian civilization is based on Samuel Noel Kramer, *The Sumerians: Their History,*

Culture, and Character (Chicago: University of Chicago Press, 1963).

11. Jared Diamond, "The Accidental Conqueror," *Discover,* December 1989, 71–76.

12. Mary W. Helms, *Middle America* (Englewood Cliffs, NJ: Prentice Hall, 1975), pp. 34–36, 54–55. See also William T. Sanders, Jeffrey R. Parsons, and Robert S. Santley, *The Basin of Mexico: Ecological Processes in the Evolution of a Civilization* (New York: Academic Press, 1979).

13. Wenke, *Patterns in Prehistory;* and René Millon, "Teotihuacán," *Scientific American,* June 1967, 38–48.

14. René Millon, "Social Relations in Ancient Teotihuacán," in Eric R. Wolf, ed., *The Valley of Mexico: Studies in Pre-Hispanic Ecology and Society* (Albuquerque: University of New Mexico Press, 1976), pp. 215–20.

15. Millon, "Teotihuacán," pp. 38–44.

16. Helms, *Middle America,* pp. 61–63; see also Muriel Porter Weaver, *The Aztecs, Maya, and Their Predecessors,* 3rd ed. (San Diego: Academic Press, 1993).

17. Richard E. Blanton, "The Rise of Cities," in Jeremy A. Sabloff, ed., *Supplement to the Handbook of Middle American Indians,* vol. 1 (Austin: University of Texas Press, 1981), p. 397. See also Joyce Marcus, "On the Nature of the Mesoamerican City," in Evon Z. Vogt and Richard M. Leventhal, eds., *Prehistoric Settlement Patterns: Essays in Honor of Gordon R. Willey* (Albuquerque: University of New Mexico Press, 1983), pp. 195–242.

18. Richard Blanton, "The Origins of Monte Albán," in C. Cleland, ed., *Cultural Continuity and Change* (New York: Academic Press, 1976), pp. 223–32; and Richard Blanton, *Monte Albán: Settlement Patterns at the Ancient Zapotec Capital* (New York: Academic Press, 1978).

19. B. L. Turner, "Population Density in the Classic Maya Lowlands: New Evidence for Old Approaches," *Geographical Review,* 66, no. 1 (January 1970): 72–82. See also Peter D. Harrison and B. L. Turner II, eds., *Pre-Hispanic Maya Agriculture* (Albuquerque: University of New Mexico Press, 1978).

20. Stephen D. Houston, "The Phonetic Decipherment of Mayan Glyphs," *Antiquity,* 62 (1988): 126–35.

21. Robert J. Wenke, *Patterns in Prehistory: Humankind's First Three Million Years,* 2nd ed. (New York: Oxford University Press, 1984), p. 289.

22. Ibid., pp. 305–20.

23. K. C. Chang, "In Search of China's Beginnings: New Light on an Old Civilization," *American Scientist,* 69 (1981): 148–60.

24. Kwang-Chih Chang, *The Archaeology of Ancient China* (New Haven, CT: Yale University Press, 1968), pp. 235–55.

25. Wenke, *Patterns in Prehistory,* 2nd ed., p. 404.

26. Brian M. Fagan, *People of the Earth: An Introduction to World Prehistory,* 6th ed. (Glenview, IL: Scott, Foresman, 1989), pp. 428–30.

27. Melvin L. Fowler, "A Pre-Columbian Urban Center on the Mississippi," *Scientific American,* August 1975, 92–101.

28. For a more complete review of the available theories, see various chapters in Ronald Cohen and Elman R. Service, eds., *Origins of the State: The Anthropology of Political Evolution (Philadelphia: Institute for the Study of Human Issues, 1978);* see also Chapter 1 in Melinda A. Zeder, *Feeding Cities: Specialized Animal Economy in the Ancient Near East* (Washington, DC: Smithsonian Institution Press, 1991).

29. Karl Wittfogel, *Oriental Despotism: A Comparative Study of Total Power* (New Haven, CT: Yale University Press, 1957).

30. Robert M. Adams, "The Origin of Cities," *Scientific American,* September 1960, 153. See also Henry T. Wright, "The Evolution of Civilizations," in David J. Meltzer, Don D. Fowler, and Jeremy A. Sabloff, eds., *American Archaeology Past and Future* (Washington, DC: Smithsonian Institution Press, 1986), pp. 323–65.

31. Paul Wheatley, *The Pivot of the Four Quarters* (Chicago: Aldine, 1971), p. 291.

32. Adams, "The Origin of Cities," p. 153.

33. Robert McC. Adams, *Heartland of Cities: Surveys of Ancient Settlement and Land Use on the Central Floodplain of the Euphrates* (Chicago: University of Chicago Press, 1981), p. 244.

34. Ibid., p. 243; and Service, *Origins of the State and Civilization,* pp. 274–75.

35. Robert L. Carneiro, "A Theory of the Origin of the State," *Science,* August 21, 1970, 733–38. See also William T. Sanders and Barbara J. Price, *Mesoamerica* (New York: Random House, 1968), pp. 230–32.

36. Marvin Harris, *Cultural Materialism: The Struggle for a Science of Culture* (New York: Random House, 1979), pp. 101–102. See also Wenke, *Patterns in Prehistory,* 3rd ed.

37. T. Cuyler Young, Jr., "Population Densities and Early Mesopotamian Urbanism," in Peter J. Ucko, Ruth Tringham, and G. W. Dimbleby, eds., *Man, Settlement and Urbanism* (Cambridge, MA: Schenkman, 1972), pp. 827–42.

38. Sanders and Price, *Mesoamerica,* p. 141.

39. Richard E. Blanton, Stephen A. Kowalewski, Gary Feinman, and Jill Appel, *Ancient Mesoamerica: A Comparison of Change in Three Regions* (New York: Cambridge University Press, 1981), p. 224. For the apparent absence of population pressure in the Teotihuacán Valley, see Elizabeth Brumfiel, "Regional Growth in the Eastern Valley of Mexico: A Test of the 'Population Pressure' Hypothesis," in Kent V. Flannery, ed., *The Early Mesoamerican Village* (New York: Academic Press, 1976), pp. 234–50. For the Oaxaca Valley, see Gary M. Feinman, Stephen A. Kowalewski, Laura Finsten, Richard E. Blanton, and Linda Nicholas, "Long-Term Demographic Change: A Perspective from the Valley of Oaxaca, Mexico," *Journal of Field Archaeology,* 12 (1985): 333–62.

40. Wright and Johnson, "Population, Exchange, and Early State Formation in Southwestern Iran," p. 276. Carneiro, however, argued the opposite: that the population grew just before the states emerged in southwestern Iran—see Robert L. Carneiro, "The Circumscription Theory: Challenge and Response,"

American Behavioral Scientist, 31 (1988): 506–508. Whether or not population declined, Frank Hole has suggested that climate change around that time may have forced local populations to relocate, some to centers that became cities; see his "Environmental Shock and Urban Origins," in Gil Stein and Mitchell S. Rothman, eds., *Chiefdoms and Early States in the Near East: The Organizational Dynamics of Complexity* (Madison, WI: Prehistory Press, 1994).

41. Karl Polanyi, Conrad M. Arensberg, and Harry W. Pearson, eds., *Trade and Market in the Early Empires* (New York: Free Press, 1957), pp. 257–62; and William T. Sanders, "Hydraulic Agriculture, Economic Symbiosis, and the Evolution of States in Central Mexico," in Betty J. Meggers, ed., *Anthropological Archaeology in the Americas* (Washington, DC: Anthropological Society of Washington, 1968), p. 105.

42. Wright and Johnson, "Population, Exchange, and Early State Formation in Southwestern Iran," p. 277.

43. William L. Rathje, "The Origin and Development of Lowland Classic Maya Civilization," *American Antiquity,* 36 (1971): 275–85.

44. For a discussion of how political dynamics may play an important role in state formation, see Elizabeth M. Brumfiel, "Aztec State Making: Ecology, Structure, and the Origin of the State," *American Anthropologist,* 85 (1983): 261–84.

45. Richard A. Kerr, "Sea-Floor Dust Shows Drought Felled Akkadian Empire," *Science,* January 16, 1998, 325–26.

46. "The Last of the Cahokians," *Science,* April 19, 1996, 351.

47. Robert L. Wilkinson, "Yellow Fever: Ecology, Epidemiology, and Role in the Collapse of the Classic Lowland Maya Civilization," *Medical Anthropology,* 16 (1995): 269–94.

CHAPTER 10

1. Ralph Linton, *The Cultural Background of Personality* (New York: Appleton-Century-Crofts, 1945), p. 30.

2. See, for example, Dorothy Holland and Naomi Quinn, eds., *Cultural Models in Language and Thought* (Cambridge: Cambridge University Press, 1987), p. 4.

3. Edward Sapir, "Why Cultural Anthropology Needs the Psychiatrist," *Psychiatry,* 1 (1938): 7–12; cited by Pertti J. Pelto and Gretel H. Pelto, "Intra-Cultural Diversity: Some Theoretical Issues," *American Ethnologist,* 2 (1975): 1.

4. Pelto and Pelto, "Intra-Cultural Diversity," pp. 14–15.

5. Barry Hewlett, "Diverse Contexts of Human Infancy," in Carol R. Ember and Melvin Ember, eds., *Cross-Cultural Research for Social Science* (Upper Saddle River, NJ: Prentice Hall, 1998). Prentice Hall/Simon & Schuster Custom Publishing.

6. Horace Miner, "Body Rituals among the Nacirema," *American Anthropologist,* 58 (1956): 504–505 (reproduced by permission of the American Anthropological Association from *American Anthropologist,* 58: 504–505, 1956). Although Miner is not a foreign visitor, he wrote this description in a way that shows

how these behaviors might be seen from an outside perspective.

7. Richard B. Lee, "Population Growth and the Beginnings of Sedentary Life among the !Kung Bushmen," in Brian Spooner, ed., *Population Growth: Anthropological Implications* (Cambridge, MA: MIT Press, 1972), pp. 329–42.

8. For a more complete discussion, see Elizabeth M. Zechenter, "In the Name of Culture: Cultural Relativism and the Abuse of the Individual," *Journal of Anthropological Research,* 53 (1997): 325–27 (319–47). See also additional essays in the special issue of the *Journal of Anthropological Research,* 53, no. 3 (1997), "Universal Human Rights versus Cultural Relativity," Terence Turner and Carole Nagengast, eds.

9. Elvin Hatch, "The Good Side of Relativism," *Journal of Anthropological Research,* 53 (1997): 371–81.

10. Émile Durkheim, *The Rules of Sociological Method,* 8th ed., trans. Sarah A. Soloway and John H. Mueller, ed. George E. Catlin (New York: Free Press, 1938 [originally published 1895]), p. 3.

11. Solomon Asch, "Studies of Independence and Conformity: A Minority of One against a Unanimous Majority," *Psychological Monographs,* 70 (1956): 1–70.

12. Edward T. Hall, *The Hidden Dimension* (Garden City, NY: Doubleday, 1966), pp. 159–60.

13. Ibid., p. 120.

14. John W. M. Whiting, "Effects of Climate on Certain Cultural Practices," in Ward H. Goodenough, ed., *Explorations in Cultural Anthropology: Essays in Honor of George Peter Murdock* (New York: McGraw-Hill, 1964), pp. 511–44.

15. Charles Wagley, "Cultural Influences on Population: A Comparison of Two Tupi Tribes," in Patricia J. Lyon, ed., *Native South Americans: Ethnology of the Least Known Continent* (Boston: Little, Brown, 1974), pp. 377–84.

16. Roger Brown, *Social Psychology* (New York: Free Press, 1965), pp. 549–609.

17. Michael Chibnik, "The Evolution of Cultural Rules," *Journal of Anthropological Research,* 37 (1981): 256–68.

18. Indeed, some of the cultures we cite may have been quite different before as well as after the time referred to. For example, the !Kung hunter-gatherers of southern Africa probably were not only hunter-gatherers in the past. There is evidence that the !Kung of the Kalahari Desert have switched from hunting and gathering to herding animals, and back again, many times in the past. See Carmel Schrire, "An Inquiry into the Evolutionary Status and Apparent Identity of San Hunter-Gatherers," *Human Ecology,* 8 (1980): 9–32.

CHAPTER 11

1. Julian H. Steward, "The Concept and Method of Cultural Ecology," in Julian H. Steward, *Theory of Culture Change* (Urbana: University of Illinois Press, 1955), pp. 30–42.

2. Andrew P. Vayda and Roy A. Rappaport, "Ecology: Cultural and Noncultural," in James H. Clifton,

ed., *Introduction to Cultural Anthropology* (Boston: Houghton Mifflin, 1968), pp. 477–97. For a selection of recent studies in human ecology, see Daniel G. Bates and Susan H. Lees, eds., *Case Studies in Human Ecology* (New York: Plenum, 1996).

3. Ibid., p. 493.

4. See Roy A. Rappaport, "Ritual Regulation of Environmental Relations among a New Guinea People," *Ethnology,* 6 (1967): 17–30.

5. Sherry B. Ortner, "Theory in Anthropology since the Sixties," *Comparative Studies in Society and History,* 26 (1984): 141–42.

6. Stephen K. Sanderson, "Expanding World Commercialization: The Link between World-Systems and Civilizations," in Stephen K. Sanderson, ed., *Civilizations and World Systems: Studying World-Historical Change* (Walnut Creek, CA: AltaMira Press, 1995), pp. 261–72.

7. William Roseberry, "Political Economy," *Annual Review of Anthropology,* 17 (1988): 163; see also Eric R. Wolf, "San José: Subcultures of a 'Traditional' Coffee Municipality," and Sidney W. Mintz, "Canamelar: The Subculture of a Rural Sugar Plantation Proletariat," in Julian H. Steward, Robert A. Manners, Eric R. Wolf, Elena Padilla Seda, Sidney W. Mintz, and Raymond L. Scheele, *The People of Puerto Rico* (Urbana: University of Illinois Press, 1956), pp. 171–264.

8. Roseberry, "Political Economy," p. 164; see also Eleanor Leacock, "The Montagnais 'Hunting Territory' and the Fur Trade," *American Anthropological Association Memoir 78* (1954): 1–59.

9. Roseberry, "Political Economy," p. 166; see also André Gunder Frank, *Capitalism and Underdevelopment in Latin America: Historical Studies of Chile and Brazil* (New York: Monthly Review Press, 1967).

10. Roseberry, "Political Economy," pp. 166–67; see also Immanuel Wallerstein, *The Modern World-System* (New York: Academic Press, 1974).

11. William Irons, "Natural Selection, Adaptation, and Human Social Behavior," in Napoleon A. Chagnon and William Irons, eds., *Evolutionary Biology and Human Social Behavior: An Anthropological Perspective* (North Scituate, MA: Duxbury, 1979), pp. 10–12. For a mathematical model and a computer simulation suggesting that group selection is likely in cultural evolution, see Robert Boyd and Peter J. Richerson, "Group Selection among Alternative Evolutionarily Stable Strategies," *Journal of Theoretical Biology,* 145 (1990): 331–42.

12. Irons, "Natural Selection, Adaptation, and Human Social Behavior."

13. Bobbi S. Low, "Behavioral Ecology, 'Sociobiology' and Human Behavior," in Carol R. Ember, Melvin Ember, and Peter N. Peregrine, eds., *Research Frontiers in Anthropology* (Upper Saddle River, NJ: Prentice Hall, 1998). Prentice Hall/Simon & Schuster Custom Publishing.

14. Ibid.

15. James Clifford, "Introduction: Partial Truths," in James Clifford and George E. Marcus, eds., *Writing Culture: The Poetics and Politics of Ethnography* (Berkeley: University of California Press, 1986), p. 3.

16. Clifford Geertz, "Thick Description: Toward an Interpretative Theory of Culture," and "Deep Play: Notes on the Balinese Cockfight," in Clifford Geertz, *The Interpretation of Cultures: Selected Essays* (New York: Basic Books, 1973), pp. 3–30, 412–53; see also discussion of Geertz in George E. Marcus and Michael M. J. Fischer, *Anthropology as Cultural Critique: An Experimental Moment in the Human Sciences* (Chicago: University of Chicago Press, 1986), pp. 26–29.

17. For discussion of this position, see Marcus and Fischer, *Anthropology as Cultural Critique,* pp. x, 180–81.

18. Dan Sperber, *On Anthropological Knowledge: Three Essays* (Cambridge: Cambridge University Press, 1985), p. 34.

19. Carl G. Hempel, *Aspects of Scientific Explanation* (New York: Free Press, 1965), p. 139.

20. John W. M. Whiting, "Effects of Climate on Certain Cultural Practices," in Ward H. Goodenough, ed., *Explorations in Cultural Anthropology: Essays in Honor of George Peter Murdock* (New York: McGraw-Hill, 1964), pp. 511–44.

21. Ernest Nagel, *The Structure of Science: Problems in the Logic of Scientific Explanation* (New York: Harcourt, Brace & World, 1961), pp. 88–89.

22. Ibid., pp. 83–90.

23. Ibid., p. 85. See also Garvin McCain and Erwin M. Segal, *The Game of Science,* 5th ed. (Pacific Grove, CA: Brooks/Cole, 1988), pp. 75–79.

24. McCain and Segal, *The Game of Science,* pp. 62–64.

25. Peter Caws, "The Structure of Discovery," *Science,* December 12, 1969, 1378.

26. McCain and Segal, *The Game of Science,* p. 114.

27. Ibid., pp. 56–57, 131–32.

28. Whiting, "Effects of Climate on Certain Cultural Practices," pp. 519–20.

29. McCain and Segal, *The Game of Science,* pp. 67–69.

30. Hubert M. Blalock, Jr., *Social Statistics,* 2nd ed. (New York: McGraw-Hill, 1972), pp. 15–20; and David H. Thomas, *Refiguring Anthropology: First Principles of Probability and Statistics* (Prospect Heights, IL: Waveland Press, 1986), pp. 18–28. See also Melvin Ember, "Taxonomy in Comparative Studies," in Raoul Naroll and Ronald Cohen, eds., *A Handbook of Method in Cultural Anthropology* (Garden City, NY: Natural History Press, 1970), pp. 701–703.

31. For examples, see George P. Murdock, "Ethnographic Atlas: A Summary," *Ethnology,* 6 (1967): 109–236; and George P. Murdock and Douglas R. White, "Standard Cross-Cultural Sample," *Ethnology,* 8 (1969): 329–69.

32. Sets of the HRAF in paper or microfiche format, and now in electronic format, are found in almost 300 universities and research institutions around the world. HRAF Collections, *Ethnography: User's Guide* (New Haven, CT: Human Relations Area Files, 1997).

33. Cultural lag occurs when change in one aspect of culture takes time to produce change in another aspect. For the original definition of this concept, see William F. Ogburn, *Social Change* (New York: Huebsch, 1922), pp. 200–80.

34. H. Russell Bernard, *Research Methods in Cultural Anthropology,* 2nd ed. (Walnut Creek, CA.: Alta Mira Press, 1994), p. 137.

35. James L. Peacock, *The Anthropological Lens: Harsh Light, Soft Focus* (Cambridge: Cambridge University Press, 1986), p. 54.
36. Robert Lawless, Vinson H. Sutlive, Jr., and Mario D. Zamora, eds., *Fieldwork: The Human Experience* (New York: Gordon and Breach, 1983), pp. xi–xxi; Peacock, *The Anthropological Lens,* pp. 54–65.
37. Bernard, *Research Methods,* pp. 180–202.

CHAPTER 12

1. Helen Keller, *The Story of My Life* (New York: Dell, 1974 [originally published 1902]), p. 34.
2. Paul Ekman and Dachner Keltner, "Universal Facial Emotions of Emotion: An Old Controversy and New Findings," in Ullica Segerstråle and Peter Molnar, eds. *Nonverbal Communication: Where Nature Meets Culture* (Mahwah, NJ: Lawrence Erlbaum, 1997), p. 32.
3. Karl von Frisch, "Dialects in the Language of the Bees," *Scientific American,* August 1962, 78–87.
4. Robert M. Seyfarth and Dorothy L. Cheney, "How Monkeys See the World: A Review of Recent Research on East African Vervet Monkeys," in Charles T. Snowdon, Charles H. Brown, and Michael R. Petersen, eds., *Primate Communication* (New York: Cambridge University Press, 1982), pp. 242, 246.
5. C. F. Hockett and R. Ascher, "The Human Revolution," *Current Anthropology,* 5 (1964): 135–68.
6. Madhusree Mukerjee, "Field Notes: Interview with a Parrot," *Scientific American,* April 1996, 28.
7. E. S. Savage-Rumbaugh, "Language Training of Apes," in Steve Jones, Robert Martin, and David Pilbeam, eds., *The Cambridge Encyclopedia of Human Evolution* (Cambridge: Cambridge University Press, 1992), pp. 138–41.
8. Jane H. Hill, "Apes and Language," *Annual Review of Anthropology,* 7 (1978): 94.
9. Jane H. Hill, "Do Apes Have Language?" in Carol R. Ember, Melvin Ember, and Peter N. Peregrine, eds., *Research Frontiers in Anthropology* (Upper Saddle River, NJ: Prentice Hall, 1998). Prentice Hall/Simon & Schuster Custom Publishing.
10. Hockett and Ascher, "The Human Revolution," pp. 135–68.
11. T. S. Eliot, "The Love Song of J. Alfred Prufrock," in *Collected Poems, 1909–1962* (New York: Harcourt, Brace & World, 1963).
12. See Noam Chomsky, *Reflections on Language* (New York: Pantheon, 1975).
13. Wayne M. Senner, "Theories and Myths on the Origins of Writing: A Historical Overview," in Wayne M. Senner, ed., *The Origins of Writing* (Lincoln: University of Nebraska Press, 1989), pp. 1–26.
14. Franklin C. Southworth and Chandler J. Daswani, *Foundations of Linguistics* (New York: Free Press, 1974), p. 312. See also Franz Boas, "On Grammatical Categories," in Dell Hymes, ed., *Language in Culture and Society: A Reader in Linguistics and Anthropology* (New York: Harper & Row, 1964 [originally published 1911]), pp. 121–23.
15. Derek Bickerton, "Creole Languages," *Scientific American,* July 1983, 116–22.

16. Ibid., p. 122.
17. Brent Berlin, *Ethnobiological Classification: Principles of Categorization of Plants and Animals in Traditional Societies* (Princeton, NJ: Princeton University Press, 1992); Terence E. Hays, "Sound Symbolism, Onomatopoeia, and New Guinea Frog Names," *Journal of Linguistic Anthropology,* 4 (1994): 153–74.
18. Lila R. Gleitman and Eric Wanner, "Language Acquisition: The State of the State of the Art," in Eric Wanner and Lila R. Gleitman, eds., *Language Acquisition: The State of the Art* (Cambridge: Cambridge University Press, 1982), pp. 3–48; Ben G. Blount, "The Development of Language in Children," in Ruth H. Munroe, Robert L. Munroe, and Beatrice B. Whiting, eds., *Handbook of Cross-Cultural Human Development* (New York: Garland, 1981), pp. 379–402.
19. Roger Brown, "The First Sentence of Child and Chimpanzee," in Thomas A. Sebeok and Jean Umiker-Sebeok, eds., *Speaking of Apes* (New York: Plenum, 1980), pp. 93–94.
20. Peter A. de Villiers and Jill G. de Villiers, *Early Language* (Cambridge, MA: Harvard University Press, 1979), p. 48; see also Wanner and Gleitman, eds., *Language Acquisition.*
21. Bickerton, "Creole Languages," p. 122.
22. David Crystal, *Linguistics* (Middlesex, England: Penguin, 1971), p. 168.
23. Ibid., pp. 100–101.
24. Maria Barinaga, "Priming the Brain's Language Pump," *Science,* January 31, 1992, 535.
25. Adrian Akmajian, Richard A. Demers, and Robert M. Harnish, *Linguistics: An Introduction to Language and Communication,* 2nd ed. (Cambridge, MA: MIT Press, 1984), p. 136.
26. Robert L. Munroe, Ruth H. Munroe, and Stephen Winters, "Cross-Cultural Correlates of the Consonant-Vowel (CV) Syllable," *Cross-Cultural Research,* 30 (1996): 60–83; Melvin Ember and Carol R. Ember, "Cross-Language Predictors of Consonant-Vowel Alternation" (paper submitted for publication). The theory about the effect of baby-holding on consonant-vowel alternation is an extension of the theory that regular baby-holding encourages a preference for regular rhythm in music; see Barbara C. Ayres, "Effects of Infant Carrying Practices on Rhythm in Music," *Ethos,* 1 (1973): 387–404.
27. E. Sapir and M. Swadesh, "American Indian Grammatical Categories," in Hymes, ed., *Language in Culture and Society,* p. 103.
28. Akmajian, Demers, and Harnish, *Linguistics,* pp. 164–66.
29. Geoffrey Chaucer, *The Prologue to the Canterbury Tales, the Knightes Tale, the Nonnes Prestes Tale,* ed. Mark H, Liddell (New York: Macmillan, 1926), p. 8. Our modern English translation is based on the glossary in this book.
30. Akmajian, Demers, and Harnish, *Linguistics,* p. 356.
31. Philip Baldi, *An Introduction to the Indo-European Languages* (Carbondale: Southern Illinois University Press, 1983), p. 3.
32. Ibid., p. 12.

33. Paul Friedrich, *Proto-Indo-European Trees: The Arboreal System of a Prehistoric People* (Chicago: University of Chicago Press, 1970), p. 168.

34. Ibid., p. 166.

35. Marija Gimbutas, "An Archaeologist's View of PIE* in 1975," *Journal of Indo-European Studies,* 2 (1974): 293–95. See also Susan N. Skomal and Edgar C. Polomé, eds., *Proto-Indo-European: The Archaeology of a Linguistic Problem* (Washington, DC: Washington Institute for the Study of Man, 1987).

36. David Anthony, Dimitri Y. Telegin, and Dorcas Brown, "The Origin of Horseback Riding," *Scientific American,* December 1991, 94–100.

37. Colin Renfrew, *Archaeology and Language: The Puzzle of Indo-European Origins* (London: Jonathan Cape, 1987).

38. Joseph H. Greenberg, "Linguistic Evidence Regarding Bantu Origins," *Journal of African History,* 13 (1972): 189–216; see also D. W. Phillipson, "Archaeology and Bantu Linguistics," *World Archaeology,* 8 (1976): 71.

39. Phillipson, "Archaeology and Bantu Linguistics," p. 79.

40. Peter Trudgill, *Sociolinguistics: An Introduction to Language and Society,* rev. ed. (New York: Penguin, 1983), p. 34.

41. John J. Gumperz, "Speech Variation and the Study of Indian Civilization," *American Anthropologist,* 63 (1961): 976–88.

42. Trudgill, *Sociolinguistics,* p. 35.

43. John J. Gumperz, "Dialect Differences and Social Stratification in a North Indian Village," in *Language in Social Groups: Essays by John J. Gumperz,* selected and introduced by Anwar S. Dil (Stanford, CA: Stanford University Press, 1971), p. 45.

44. Uriel Weinreich, *Languages in Contact* (The Hague: Mouton, 1968), p. 31.

45. But see Sarah Grey Thomason and Terrence Kaufman, *Language Contact, Creolization, and Genetic Linguistics* (Berkeley: University of California Press, 1988), for a discussion of how grammatical changes due to contact may be more important than was previously assumed.

46. Colin Renfrew, "World Linguistic Diversity," *Scientific American,* January 1994, 116–23.

47. Brent Berlin and Paul Kay, *Basic Color Terms: Their Universality and Evolution* (Berkeley: University of California Press, 1969).

48. Ibid.

49. Ibid., pp. 5–6.

50. Ibid., p. 104; Stanley R. Witkowski and Cecil H. Brown, "Lexical Universals," *Annual Review of Anthropology,* 7 (1978): 427–51.

51. Marc H. Bornstein, "The Psychophysiological Component of Cultural Difference in Color Naming and Illusion Susceptibility," *Behavior Science Notes,* 8 (1973): 41–101.

52. Melvin Ember, "Size of Color Lexicon: Interaction of Cultural and Biological Factors," *American Anthropologist,* 80 (1978): 364–67.

53. Ibid.

54. Cecil H. Brown, "Folk Botanical Life-Forms: Their Universality and Growth," *American Anthropologist,* 79 (1977): 317–42.

55. Cecil H. Brown, "Folk Zoological Life-Forms: Their Universality and Growth," *American Anthropologist,* 81 (1979): 791–817.

56. Stanley R. Witkowski and Harold W. Burris, "Societal Complexity and Lexical Growth," *Behavior Science Research,* 16 (1981): 143–59.

57. Ibid.

58. Cecil H. Brown and Stanley R. Witkowski, "Language Universals," Appendix B in David Levinson and Martin J. Malone, eds., *Toward Explaining Human Culture: A Critical Review of the Findings of Worldwide Cross-Cultural Research* (New Haven, CT: HRAF Press, 1980), p. 379.

59. Cecil H. Brown, "World View and Lexical Uniformities," *Reviews in Anthropology,* 11 (1984): 106.

60. Harry Hoijer, "Cultural Implications of Some Navaho Linguistic Categories," in Hymes, ed., *Language in Culture and Society,* p. 146.

61. Karen E. Webb, "An Evolutionary Aspect of Social Structure and a Verb 'Have'," *American Anthropologist,* 79 (1977): 42–49; see also Floyd Webster Rudmin, "Dominance, Social Control, and Ownership: A History and a Cross-Cultural Study of Motivations for Private Property," *Behavior Science Research,* 22 (1988): 130–60.

62. Edward Sapir, "Conceptual Categories in Primitive Languages," paper presented at the autumn meeting of the National Academy of Sciences, New Haven, CT, 1931, published in *Science,* 74 (1931): 578; see also John B. Carroll, ed., *Language, Thought, and Reality: Selected Writings of Benjamin Lee Whorf* (New York: Wiley, 1956), pp. 65–86.

63. Richard Wardhaugh, *An Introduction to Sociolinguistics,* 2nd ed. (Oxford: Blackwell, 1992), p. 221.

64. J. Peter Denny, "The 'Extendedness' Variable in Classifier Semantics: Universal Features and Cultural Variation," in Madeleine Mathiot, ed., *Ethnolinguistics: Boas, Sapir and Whorf Revisited* (The Hague: Mouton, 1979), p. 97.

65. Paul Friedrich, *The Language Parallax* (Austin: University of Texas Press, 1986).

66. Alexander Z. Guiora, Benjamin Beit-Hallahmi, Risto Fried, and Cecelia Yoder, "Language Environment and Gender Identity Attainment," *Language Learning,* 32 (1982): 289–304.

67. John A. Lucy, *Grammatical Categories and Cognition: A Case Study of the Linguistic Relativity Hypothesis* (Cambridge: Cambridge University Press, 1992), p. 46.

68. Ibid., pp. 85–148.

69. Dell Hymes, *Foundations in Sociolinguistics: An Ethnographic Approach* (Philadelphia: University of Pennsylvania Press, 1974), pp. 83–117.

70. John L. Fischer, "Social Influences on the Choice of a Linguistic Variant," *Word* 14 (1958): 47-56; Wardhaugh, *An Introduction to Sociolinguistics,* research summarized in chapter 7, pp. 160–91.

71. Trudgill, *Sociolinguistics,* pp. 41–42.

72. Clifford Geertz, *The Religion of Java* (New York: Free Press, 1960), pp. 248–60; see also J. Joseph Errington, "On the Nature of the Sociolinguistic Sign: Describing the Javanese Speech Levels," in

Elizabeth Mertz and Richard J. Parmentier, eds., *Semiotic Mediation: Sociocultural and Psychological Perspectives* (Orlando, FL: Academic Press, 1985), pp. 287–310.

73. Roger Brown and Marguerite Ford, "Address in American English," *Journal of Abnormal and Social Psychology,* 62 (1961): 375–85.

74. Wardhaugh, *An Introduction to Sociolinguistics,* pp. 313–14.

75. Janet S. Shibamoto, "The Womanly Woman: Japanese Female Speech," in Susan U. Philips, Susan Steele, and Christine Tanz, eds., *Language, Gender, and Sex in Comparative Perspective* (Cambridge: Cambridge University Press, 1987), p. 28.

76. Robin Lakoff, "Language and Woman's Place," *Language in Society,* 2(1973): 45–80; Robin Tolmach Lakoff, "Why Can't a Woman Be Less Like a Man?" in Robin Tolmach Lakoff, ed., *Talking Power: The Politics of Language in Our Lives* (New York: Basic Books, 1990), pp. 198–214.

77. Wardhaugh, *An Introduction to Sociolinguistics,* pp. 322–23; Janet Holmes, *An Introduction to Sociolinguistics* (London: Longman, 1992), pp. 172–73; Trudgill, *Sociolinguistics,* pp. 87–88.

78. Mary R. Haas, "Men's and Women's Speech in Koasati," *Language,* 20 (1944): 142–49.

79. Elinor Keenan, "Norm-Makers, Norm-Breakers: Uses of Speech by Men and Women in a Malagasy Community," in Richard Bauman and Joel Sherzer, eds., *Explorations in the Ethnography of Speaking,* 2nd ed. (New York: Cambridge University Press, 1989), pp. 125–43.

80. Holmes, *An Introduction to Sociolinguistics,* pp. 176–81.

81. Wardhaugh, *An Introduction to Sociolinguistics,* pp. 98–104.

82. Monica Heller, "Introduction," in Monica Heller, ed., *Codeswitching: Anthropological and Sociolinguistic Perspectives* (Berlin: Mouton de Gruyter, 1988), p. 1.

83. Wardhaugh, *An Introduction to Sociolinguistics,* p. 107, citing an example from C. Pfaff, "Constraints on Language Mixing," *Language,* 55 (1979): 291–318.

84. Ibid., p. 108.

85. Susan Gal, "The Political Economy of Code Choice," in Heller, ed., *Codeswitching,* pp. 249–55.

86. Ron Scollon and Suzanne B. K. Scollon, *Narrative, Literacy and Face in Interethnic Communication* (Norwood, NJ: ABLEX, 1981), pp. 11–36.

CHAPTER 13

1. Carol R. Ember, "Myths about Hunter-Gatherers," *Ethnology,* 17 (1978): 439–48.

2. Susan Kent, ed. *Cultural Diversity among Twentieth-Century Foragers: An African Perspective* (Cambridge: Cambridge University Press, 1996).

3. Carmel Schrire, ed., *Past and Present in Hunter-Gatherer Studies* (Orlando, FL: Academic Press, 1984); Fred R. Myers, "Critical Trends in the Study of Hunter-Gatherers," *Annual Review of Anthropology,* 17 (1988): 261–82.

4. The discussion of the Australian aborigines is based on Richard A. Gould, *Yiwara: Foragers of the Australian Desert* (New York: Scribner's, 1969).

5. Victoria K. Burbank, *Fighting Women: Anger and Aggression in Aboriginal Australia* (Berkeley: University of California Press, 1994), p. 23. For a description of daily life, see Victoria K. Burbank, "Australian Aborigines: An Adolescent Mother and Her Family," in Melvin Ember, Carol R. Ember, and David Levinson, eds., *Portraits of Culture: Ethnographic Originals* (Upper Saddle River, NJ: Prentice Hall, 1998). Prentice Hall/Simon & Schuster Custom Publishing.

6. Material is drawn from Ernest S. Burch, Jr., "The North Alaskan Eskimos: A Changing Way of Life," in Melvin Ember, Carol R. Ember, and David Levinson, eds., *Portraits of Culture: Ethnographic Originals* (Upper Saddle River, NJ: Prentice Hall, 1998), Prentice Hall/Simon & Schuster Custom Publishing; and Ernest S. Burch, Jr., *The Eskimos* (Norman: University of Oklahoma Press, 1988).

7. Data from Robert B. Textor, comp., *A Cross-Cultural Summary* (New Haven, CT: HRAF Press, 1967); and Elman R. Service, *The Hunters,* 2nd ed. (Englewood Cliffs, NJ: Prentice Hall, 1979).

8. Gisli Palsson, "Hunters and Gatherers of the Sea," in Tim Ingold, David Riches, James Woodburn, eds., *Hunters and Gatherers 1: History, Evolution and Social Change* (New York: St. Martin's Press, 1988), pp. 189–204.

9. George P. Murdock and Caterina Provost, "Factors in the Division of Labor by Sex: A Cross-Cultural Analysis," *Ethnology,* 12 (1973): 207.

10. Richard B. Lee, "What Hunters Do for a Living, or, How to Make Out on Scarce Resources," in Richard B. Lee and Irven DeVore, eds., *Man the Hunter* (Chicago: Aldine, 1968), pp. 30–48; and Irven DeVore and Melvin J. Konner, "Infancy in Hunter-Gatherer Life: An Ethological Perspective," in N. F. White, ed., *Ethology and Psychiatry* (Toronto: Ontario Mental Health Foundation and University of Toronto Press, 1974), pp. 113–41.

11. C. R. Ember, "Myths about Hunter-Gatherers."

12. Frederick D. McCarthy and Margaret McArthur, "The Food Quest and the Time Factor in Aboriginal Economic Life," in C. P. Mountford, ed., *Records of the Australian-American Scientific Expedition to Arnhem Land. Volume 2: Anthropology and Nutrition* (Melbourne: Melbourne University Press, 1960).

13. Richard B. Lee, *The !Kung San: Men, Women, and Work in a Foraging Society* (Cambridge: Cambridge University Press, 1979), pp. 256–58, 278–80.

14. Dennis Werner, "Trekking in the Amazon Forest," *Natural History,* November 1978, 42–54.

15. Data from Textor, comp., *A Cross-Cultural Summary.*

16. This section is based largely on Raymond Hames, "Yanomamö: Varying Adaptations of Foraging Horticulturalists," in Melvin Ember, Carol R. Ember, and David Levinson, eds., *Portraits of Culture: Ethnographic Originals* (Upper Saddle River, NJ: Prentice Hall, 1998). Prentice Hall/Simon & Schuster Custom Publishing.

17. Napoleon Chagnon, *Yanomamö: The Fierce People,* 3rd ed. (New York: Holt, Rinehart & Winston, 1987) p. 60.
18. This section is based mostly on Melvin Ember's fieldwork on the islands of American Samoa in 1955–1956.
19. Douglas L. Oliver, *Ancient Tahitian Society. Volume 1: Ethnography* (Honolulu: University of Hawaii Press, 1974), pp. 252–53.
20. Seth S. King, "Some Farm Machinery Seems Less Than Human," *New York Times,* April 8, 1979, p. E9.
21. Ernestine Friedl, *Vasilika: A Village in Modern Greece* (New York: Holt, Rinehart & Winston, 1962).
22. Gerald Cannon Hickey, *Village in Vietnam* (New Haven, CT: Yale University Press, 1964), pp. 135–65.
23. Carol R. Ember, "The Relative Decline in Women's Contribution to Agriculture with Intensification," *American Anthropologist,* 85 (1983): 289.
24. Data from Textor, comp., *A Cross-Cultural Summary;* Robert Dirks, "Hunger and Famine," in Carol R. Ember, Melvin Ember, and Peter N. Peregrine, eds., *Research Frontiers in Anthropology* (Upper Saddle River, NJ: Prentice Hall, 1998). Prentice Hall/Simon & Schuster Custom Publishing; Ellen Messer, "Hunger Vulnerability from an Anthropologist's Food Systems Perspective," in Emilio F. Moran, ed. *Transforming Societies, Transforming Anthropology* (Ann Arbor: University of Michigan Press, 1996), p. 244.
25. Ibid.
26. Peggy F. Barlett, "Industrial Agriculture," in Stuart Plattner, ed., *Economic Anthropology* (Stanford, CA: Stanford University Press, 1989), pp. 253–91.
27. U.S. Bureau of the Census, *Statistical Abstract of the United States: 1993,* 113th ed. (Washington, DC: U.S. Government Printing Office, 1993).
28. Susan H. Lees and Daniel G. Bates, "The Origins of Specialized Nomadic Pastoralism: A Systemic Model," *American Antiquity,* 39 (1974): 187–93.
29. Fredrik Barth, *Nomads of South Persia* (Oslo: Universitetsforlaget, 1964; Boston: Little, Brown, 1968).
30. Ian Whitaker, *Social Relations in a Nomadic Lappish Community* (Oslo: Utgitt av Norsk Folksmuseum, 1955); and T. I. Itkonen, "The Lapps of Finland," *Southwestern Journal of Anthropology,* 7 (1951): 32–68.
31. Robert Paine, *Herds of the Tundra* (Washington, DC: Smithsonian Institution Press, 1994).
32. Data from Textor, comp., *A Cross-Cultural Summary.*
33. Dirks, "Hunger and Famine."
34. Data from Textor, comp., *A Cross-Cultural Summary.*
35. Lewis R. Binford, "Mobility, Housing, and Environment: A Comparative Study," *Journal of Anthropological Research,* 46 (1990): 119–52; see also Bobbi Low, "Human Responses to Environmental Extremeness and Uncertainty," in Elizabeth Cashdan, ed., *Risk and Uncertainty in Tribal and Peasant Economies* (Boulder, CO: Westview Press, 1990), pp. 242–43.
36. The few food collectors in cold areas relying primarily on hunting have animals (dogs, horses, reindeer) that can carry transportable housing; see Binford, "Mobility, Housing, and Environment."
37. Robert C. Bailey, Genevieve Head, Mark Jenike, Bruce Owen, Robert Rectman, and Elzbieta Zechenter, "Hunting and Gathering in Tropical Rain Forest: Is It Possible?" *American Anthropologist,* 91 (1989): 59–82.
38. Data from Textor, comp., *A Cross-Cultural Summary.*
39. Daniel H. Janzen, "Tropical Agroecosystems," *Science,* December 21, 1973, 1212–18. For an argument supporting the "weeding" explanation, see Robert L. Carneiro, "Slash-and-Burn Cultivation among the Kuikuru and Its Implications for Settlement Patterns," in Yehudi Cohen, ed., *Man in Adaptation: The Cultural Present* (Chicago: Aldine, 1968).
40. Ester Boserup, *The Conditions of Agricultural Growth: The Economics of Agrarian Change under Population Pressure* (Chicago: Aldine, 1965).
41. Janzen, "Tropical Agroecosystems."

CHAPTER 14

1. E. Adamson Hoebel, *The Law of Primitive Man* (New York: Atheneum, 1968 [originally published 1954]), pp. 46–63.
2. James Woodburn, "An Introduction to Hadza Ecology," in Richard B. Lee and Irven DeVore, eds., *Man the Hunter* (Chicago: Aldine, 1968), pp. 49–55.
3. Eleanor Leacock and Richard Lee, "Introduction," in Eleanor Leacock and Richard Lee, eds., *Politics and History in Band Societies* (Cambridge: Cambridge University Press, 1982), p. 8.
4. Rada Dyson-Hudson and Eric Alden Smith, "Human Territoriality: An Ecological Reassessment," *American Anthropologist,* 80 (1978): 21–41; Elizabeth Andrews, "Territoriality and Land Use among the Akulmiut of Western Alaska," in Ernest S. Burch, Jr., and Linda J. Ellanna, *Key Issues in Hunter-Gatherer Research.* (Oxford: Berg, 1994), pp. 65–92.
5. Robert F. Murphy, *Headhunter's Heritage: Social and Economic Change among the Mundurucú* (Berkeley: University of California Press, 1960), pp. 69, 142–43.
6. Not all pastoralists have individual ownership. For example, the Tungus of northern Siberia have kin group ownership of reindeer. See John H. Dowling, "Property Relations and Productive Strategies in Pastoral Societies," *American Ethnologist,* 2 (1975): 422.
7. Fredrik Barth, *Nomads of South Persia* (Oslo: Universitetsforlaget, 1964; Boston: Little, Brown, 1968), p. 124.
8. Dowling, "Property Relations and Productive Strategies in Pastoral Societies," pp. 419–26.
9. Gerald W. Creed, "Bulgaria: Anthropological Corrections to Cold War Stereotypes," in Melvin Ember, Carol R. Ember, and David Levinson, eds., *Portraits of Culture: Ethnographic Originals* (Upper Saddle River, NJ: Prentice Hall, 1998). Prentice Hall/Simon & Schuster Custom Publishing.
10. John H. Bodley, *Victims of Progress,* 3rd ed. (Mountain View, CA: Mayfield, 1990), pp. 77–93; Edwin N. Wilmsen, ed., *We Are Here: Politics of Aboriginal Land Tenure* (Berkeley: University of California Press, 1989), pp. 1–14.
11. Bodley, *Victims of Progress,* pp. 79–81.
12. Ibid., pp. 86–89.

13. Elman R. Service, *The Hunters,* 2nd ed. (Englewood Cliffs, NJ: Prentice Hall, 1979), p. 10.

14. Elizabeth Marshall Thomas, *The Harmless People* (New York: Knopf, 1959), p. 22.

15. Lisa Groger, "Of Men and Machines: Cooperation among French Family Farmers," *Ethnology,* 20 (1981): 163–75.

16. Stuart Plattner, "Marxism," in Stuart Plattner, ed., *Economic Anthropology* (Stanford, CA: Stanford University Press, 1989), pp. 379–96.

17. Jerald Hage and Charles H. Powers. *Post-Industrial Lives: Roles and Relationships in the 21st Century* (Newbury Park, CA: Sage, 1992).

18. Robert L. Carneiro, "Slash-and-Burn Cultivation among the Kuikuru and Its Implications for Settlement Patterns," in Yehudi Cohen, ed., *Man in Adaptation: The Cultural Present* (Chicago: Aldine, 1968), cited in Marshall Sahlins, *Stone Age Economics* (Chicago: Aldine, 1972), p. 68.

19. Marvin Harris, *Cows, Pigs, Wars and Witches: The Riddles of Culture* (New York: Random House, Vintage, 1975), pp. 127–28.

20. Sahlins, in *Stone Age Economics,* p. 87, introduced North American anthropology to Alexander Chayanov and coined the phrase *Chayanov's rule.*

21. Alexander V. Chayanov, *The Theory of Peasant Economy,* D. Thorner, B. Kerblay, and R. E. F. Smith, eds. (Homewood, IL: Richard D. Irwin, 1966), p. 78; for a discussion of Chayanov's analysis, see E. Paul Durrenberger, "Chayanov's Economic Analysis in Anthropology," *Journal of Anthropological Research,* 36 (1980): 133–48.

22. Michael Chibnik, "The Economic Effects of Household Demography: A Cross-Cultural Assessment of Chayanov's Theory," in Morgan D. MacLachlan, ed., *Household Economies and Their Transformations,* Monographs in Economic Anthropology No. 3 (Lanham, MD: University Press of America, 1987), pp. 74–106; Durrenberger, "Chayanov's Economic Analysis," also finds some support in an analysis of three northern Thailand groups. For a critique of the equation of Chayanov's rule with Chayanov's analysis, see Nicola Tannenbaum, "The Misuse of Chayanov: 'Chayanov's Rule' and Empiricist Bias in Anthropology," *American Anthropologist,* 86 (1984): 927–42.

23. Sahlins, *Stone Age Economics,* pp. 101–48.

24. David C. McClelland, *The Achieving Society* (New York: Van Nostrand, 1961).

25. Julian H. Steward and Louis C. Faron, *Native Peoples of South America* (New York: McGraw-Hill, 1959), pp. 122–25.

26. Beatrice B. Whiting and Carolyn P. Edwards, *Children of Different Worlds: The Formation of Social Behavior* (Cambridge, MA: Harvard University Press, 1988), p. 164.

27. Moni Nag, Benjamin N. F. White, and R. Creighton Peet, "An Anthropological Approach to the Study of the Economic Value of Children in Java and Nepal," *Current Anthropology,* 19 (1978): 295–96.

28. Whiting and Edwards, *Children of Different Worlds,* pp. 97–107.

29. Patricia Draper and Elizabeth Cashdan, "Technological Change and Child Behavior among the !Kung," *Ethnology,* 27 (1988): 348.

30. Nicholas Blurton Jones, Kristen Hawkes, and James F. O'Connell, "The Global Process and Local Ecology: How Should We Explain Differences between the Hadza and the !Kung?" in Susan Kent, *Cultural Diversity among Twentieth-century Foragers* (Cambridge: Cambridge University Press, 1996), p. 166–69.

31. Nag, White, and Peet, "Anthropological Approach to the Study of the Economic Value of Children in Java and Nepal," p. 293; see also Candice Bradley, "The Sexual Division of Labor and the Value of Children," *Behavior Science Research,* 19 (1984–1985): 160–64.

32. Carol R. Ember, "The Relative Decline in Women's Contribution to Agriculture with Intensification," *American Anthropologist,* 85 (1983): 291–97.

33. Monica Wilson, *Good Company: A Study of Nyakyusa Age Villages* (Boston: Beacon Press, 1963 [originally published 1951]).

34. Stanley H. Udy, Jr., *Work in Traditional and Modern Society* (Englewood Cliffs, NJ: Prentice Hall, 1970), pp. 35–37.

35. Marshall D. Sahlins, *Moala: Culture and Nature on a Fijian Island* (Ann Arbor: University of Michigan Press, 1962), pp. 50–52.

36. Leopold Pospisil, *The Kapauku Papuans of West New Guinea* (New York: Holt, Rinehart & Winston, 1963), p. 43.

37 Udy, *Work in Traditional and Modern Society,* pp. 35–39.

38. Eric Alden Smith, "Anthropological Applications of Optimal Foraging Theory: A Critical Review," *Current Anthropology,* 24 (1983): 626.

39. Kim Hill, Hillard Kaplan, Kristen Hawkes, and A. Magdalena Hurtado, "Foraging Decisions among Aché Hunter-Gatherers: New Data and Implications for Optimal Foraging Models," *Ethology and Sociobiology,* 8 (1987): 17–18.

40. Andrew Sih and Katharine A. Milton, "Optimal Diet Theory: Should the !Kung Eat Mongongos?" *American Anthropologist,* 87 (1985): 395–401.

41. Christina H. Gladwin, "A Theory of Real-Life Choice: Applications to Agricultural Decisions," in Peggy F. Barlett, ed., *Agricultural Decision-Making: Anthropological Contributions to Rural Development* (New York: Academic Press, 1980), pp. 45–85.

42. Michael Chibnik, "The Statistical Behavior Approach: The Choice between Wage Labor and Cash Cropping in Rural Belize," in Peggy P. Barlett, ed., *Agricultural Decision Making: Anthropological Contributions to Rural Development* (New York: Academic Press, 1980) pp. 87–114.

43. Karl Polanyi, "The Economy as Instituted Process," in Karl Polanyi, Conrad Arensberg, and Harry W. Pearson, eds., *Trade and Market in the Early Empires* (New York: Free Press, 1957), pp. 243–70.

44. Sahlins, *Stone Age Economics,* pp. 188–96.

45. Lorna Marshall, "Sharing, Talking and Giving: Relief of Social Tensions among !Kung Bushmen," *Africa,* 31 (1961): 239–41.

46. The // sign in the name for the G//ana people symbolizes a click sound not unlike the sound we make when we want a horse to move faster.

47. Elizabeth A. Cashdan, "Egalitarianism among Hunters and Gatherers," *American Anthropologist,* 82 (1980): 116–20.

48. Hillard Kaplan and Kim Hill, "Food Sharing among Aché Foragers: Tests of Explanatory Hypotheses," *Current Anthropology,* 26 (1985): 223–46; Hillard Kaplan, Kim Hill, and A. Magdalena Hurtado, "Risk, Foraging and Food Sharing among the Aché," in Elizabeth Cashdan, ed., *Risk and Uncertainty in Tribal and Peasant Economies* (Boulder, CO: Westview Press, 1990), pp. 107–43.

49. Raymond Hames, "Sharing among the Yanomamö. Part I. The Effects of Risk," in Cashdan, ed., *Risk and Uncertainty in Tribal and Peasant Economies,* pp. 89–105.

50. Kaplan, Hill, and Hurtado, "Risk, Foraging and Food Sharing among the Aché."

51. Bruce Winterhalder, "Open Field, Common Pot: Harvest Variability and Risk Avoidance in Agricultural and Foraging Societies," in Cashdan, ed., *Risk and Uncertainty in Tribal and Peasant Economies,* pp. 67–87.

52. Kathleen A. Mooney, "The Effects of Rank and Wealth on Exchange among the Coast Salish," *Ethnology,* 17 (1978): 391–406.

53. Asen Balikci, *The Netsilik Eskimo* (Garden City, NY: Natural History Press, 1970), quoted in Mooney, "The Effects of Rank and Wealth on Exchange among the Coast Salish," p. 392.

54. Mooney, "Effects of Rank and Wealth on Exchange among the Coast Salish," p. 392.

55. Marshall, "Sharing, Talking and Giving," p. 242.

56. Thomas S. Abler, "Iroquois: The Tree of Peace and the War Kettle," in Melvin Ember, Carol R. Ember, and David Levinson, eds., *Portraits of Culture: Ethnographic Originals* (Upper Saddle River, NJ: Prentice Hall, 1998). Prentice Hall/Simon & Schuster Custom Publishing.

57. Nadine Peacock and Robert Bailey, "Efe: Investigating Food and Fertility in the Ituri Rain Forest," in Melvin Ember, Carol R. Ember, and David Levinson, eds., *Portraits of Culture: Ethnographic Originals* (Upper Saddle River, NJ: Prentice Hall, 1998). Prentice Hall/Simon & Schuster Custom Publishing.

58. James L. Gibbs, Jr., "The Kpelle of Liberia," in James L. Gibbs, Jr., ed., *Peoples of Africa* (New York: Holt, Rinehart & Winston, 1965), p. 223. But in other societies the food provided a work party may exceed the value of the labor provided, or there may not be any subsequent reciprocation of labor. Thus, an exchange of food for labor may not always be balanced. See Mahir Saul, "Work Parties, Wages, and Accumulation in a Voltaic Village," *American Ethnologist,* 10 (1983): 77–96.

59. Caroline Humphrey and Stephen Hugh-Jones, "Introduction: Barter, Exchange and Value," in Caroline Humphrey and Stephen Hugh-Jones, eds., *Barter, Exchange and Value: An Anthropological Approach* (New York: Cambridge University Press, 1992).

60. Richard E. Blanton, "Variation in Economy," in Carol R. Ember and Melvin Ember, eds., *Cross-Cultural Research for Social Science* (Upper Saddle River, NJ: Prentice Hall, 1998). Prentice Hall/Simon & Schuster Custom Publishing; C. A. Gregory, *Gifts and Commodities* (New York: Academic Press, 1982).

61. J. P. Singh Uberoi, *The Politics of the Kula Ring: An Analysis of the Findings of Bronislaw Malinowski* (Manchester: University of Manchester Press, 1962).

62. Bronislaw Malinowski, "Kula: The Circulating Exchange of Valuables in the Archipelagoes of Eastern New Guinea," *Man,* 51, no. 2 (1920): 97–105; and Uberoi, *Politics of the Kula Ring.*

63. Jerry W. Leach, "Introduction," in Jerry W. Leach and Edmund Leach, eds., *The Kula: New Perspectives on Massim Exchange* (Cambridge: Cambridge University Press, 1983), pp. 12, 16.

64. Annette B. Weiner, *Women of Value, Men of Renown: New Perspectives in Trobriand Exchange* (Austin: University of Texas Press, 1976), pp. 77–117.

65. Sahlins, *Stone Age Economics,* p. 195.

66. Ibid., pp. 196–204.

67. Frederic L. Pryor, *The Origins of the Economy: A Comparative Study of Distribution in Primitive and Peasant Economies* (New York: Academic Press, 1977), pp. 204, 276.

68. Andrew P. Vayda, Anthony Leeds, and David B. Smith, "The Place of Pigs in Melanesian Subsistence," in Viola E. Garfield, ed., *Symposium: Patterns of Land Utilization, and Other Papers,* Proceedings of the Annual Spring Meeting of the American Ethnological Society, 1961 (Seattle: University of Washington Press, 1962), pp. 69–74.

69. Philip Drucker, "The Potlatch," in George Dalton, ed., *Tribal and Peasant Economies: Readings in Economic Anthropology* (Garden City, NY: Natural History Press, 1967), pp. 481–93.

70. Harris, *Cows, Pigs, Wars and Witches,* p. 120.

71. Kenneth D. Tollefson, "Tlingit: Chiefs Past and Present," in Melvin Ember, Carol R. Ember, and David Levinson, eds., *Portraits of Culture: Ethnographic Originals* (Upper Saddle River, NJ: Prentice Hall, 1998). Prentice Hall/Simon & Schuster Custom Publishing.

72. Andrew P. Vayda, "Pomo Trade Feasts," in George Dalton, ed., *Tribal and Peasant Economies: Readings in Economic Anthropology* (Garden City, NY: Natural History Press, 1967), pp. 494–500.

73. John Beattie, *Bunyoro: An African Kingdom* (New York: Holt, Rinehart & Winston, 1960).

74. R. C. Thurnwald, "Pigs and Currency in Buin: Observations about Primitive Standards of Value and Economics," *Oceania,* 5 (1934): 125.

75. Pryor, *Origins of the Economy,* pp. 284–86.

76. Elman R. Service, *Primitive Social Organization: An Evolutionary Perspective* (New York: Random House, 1962), pp. 145–46.

77. Harris, *Cows, Pigs, Wars and Witches,* pp. 118–21.

78. Stuart Plattner, "Introduction," in Stuart Plattner, ed., *Markets and Marketing,* Monographs in Economic Anthropology No. 4 (Lanham, MD: University Press of America, 1985), p. viii.

79. Pryor, *Origins of the Economy,* pp. 31–33.
80. Thurnwald, "Pigs and Currency in Buin," p. 122.
81. Plattner, "Introduction," p. xii.
82. Pryor, *Origins of the Economy,* pp. 153–83; James Stodder, "The Evolution of Complexity in Primitive Exchange," *Journal of Comparative Economics,* 20 (1995): 205, finds that monetary trade is more likely with capital-intensive agriculture.
83. Pryor, *Origin of the Economy,* pp. 109–11.
84. Brian L. Foster, "Ethnicity and Commerce," *American Ethnologist,* 1 (1974): 437–47.
85. Pryor, *Origins of the Economy,* pp. 125–48.
86. See, for example, Eric Wolf, "Types of Latin American Peasantry: A Preliminary Discussion," *American Anthropologist,* 57 (1955): 452–71; and Pedro Carrasco, "The Civil-Religious Hierarchy in Mesoamerican Communities: Pre-Spanish Background and Colonial Development," *American Anthropologist,* 63 (1961): 483–97.
87. Waldemar R. Smith, *The Fiesta System and Economic Change* (New York: Columbia University Press, 1977); and Marvin Harris, *Patterns of Race in the Americas* (New York: Walker, 1964).
88. Ibid.

CHAPTER 15

1. In an analysis of many native societies in the New World, Gary Feinman and Jill Neitzel argue that egalitarian and rank societies ("tribes" and "chiefdoms," respectively) are not systematically distinguishable. See their "Too Many Types: An Overview of Sedentary Prestate Societies in the Americas," in Michael B. Schiffer, ed., *Advances in Archaeological Method and Theory* (Orlando, FL: Academic Press, 1984), vol. 7, p. 57.
2. Morton H. Fried, *The Evolution of Political Society: An Essay in Political Anthropology* (New York: Random House, 1967), p. 33.
3. Christopher Boehm, "Egalitarian Behavior and Reverse Dominance Hierarchy," *Current Anthropology,* 34 (1993): 230–31.
4. Michael G. Smith, "Pre-Industrial Stratification Systems," in Neil J. Smelser and Seymour Martin Lipset, eds., *Social Structure and Mobility in Economic Development* (Chicago: Aldine, 1966), p. 152.
5. See, for example, the description of a Kwakiutl group called the Nimpkish in Donald Mitchell, "Nimpkish: Complex Foragers on the Northwest Coast of North America," in Melvin Ember, Carol R. Ember, and David Levinson, eds., *Portraits of Culture: Ethnographic Originals* (Upper Saddle River, NJ: Prentice Hall, 1998). Prentice Hall/Simon & Schuster Custom Publishing.
6. Philip Drucker, *Cultures of the North Pacific Coast* (San Francisco: Chandler, 1965), pp. 56–64.
7. Elman R. Service, *Profiles in Ethnology,* 3rd ed. (New York: Harper & Row, 1978), p. 249.
8. Marshall Sahlins, *Social Stratification in Polynesia* (Seattle: University of Washington Press, 1958), pp. 80–81.

9. Laura Betzig, "Redistribution: Equity or Exploitation?" in Laura Betzig, Monique Borgerhoff Mulder, and Paul Turke, eds., *Human Reproductive Behavior* (Cambridge: Cambridge University Press, 1988), pp. 49–63.
10. W. Lloyd Warner and Paul S. Lunt, *The Social Life of a Modern Community* (New Haven, CT: Yale University Press, 1941).
11. Robert S. Lynd and Helen Merrell Lynd, *Middletown* (New York: Harcourt, Brace, 1929); and Robert S. Lynd and Helen Merrell Lynd, *Middletown in Transition* (New York: Harcourt, Brace, 1937).
12. John A. Brittain, *Inheritance and the Inequality of Material Wealth* (Washington, DC: Brookings Institution, 1978).
13. Stephen Richard Higley, *Privilege, Power, and Place: The Geography of the American Upper Class* (Lanham, MD: Rowman & Littlefield, 1995), pp. 1–47.
14. Michael Argyle, *The Psychology of Social Class* (New York: Routledge, 1994).
15. Donald J. Treiman and Harry B. G. Ganzeboom, "Cross-National Comparative Status-Attainment Research," *Research in Social Stratification and Mobility,* 9 (1990): 117; David L. Featherman and Robert M. Hauser, *Opportunity and Change* (New York: Academic Press, 1978), pp. 4, 481.
16. Reeve Vanneman and Lynn Weber Cannon, *The American Perception of Class* (Philadelphia: Temple University Press, 1987), pp. 283–84.
17. Hugo G. Nutini, *The Wages of Conquest: The Mexican Aristocracy in the Context of Western Aristocracies* (Ann Arbor: University of Michigan Press, 1995), pp. 323–24.
18. Stanley R. Barrett, *Paradise: Class, Commuters, and Ethnicity in Rural Ontario* (Toronto: University of Toronto Press, 1994), pp. 17, 41.
19. Ibid., pp. 17–19, 34–35.
20. Ibid., p. 155.
21. Argyle, *Psychology of Social Class,* pp. 36–37, 178.
22. Ibid., p. 19.
23. Ibid.
24. Ruth Leger Sivard, *World Military and Social Expenditures 1993,* 15th ed. (Washington, DC: World Priorities, 1993).
25. Morton Klass, "Is There 'Caste' Outside of India?" in Carol R. Ember and Melvin Ember, eds., *Cross-Cultural Research for Social Science* (Upper Saddle River, NJ: Prentice Hall, 1998). Prentice Hall/Simon & Schuster Custom Publishing.
26. John Ruskin, "Of Kings' Treasures," in John D. Rosenberg, ed., *The Genius of John Ruskin: Selections from His Writings* (New York: Braziller, 1963), pp. 296–314.
27. See Oscar Lewis, with the assistance of Victor Barnouw, *Village Life in Northern India* (Urbana: University of Illinois Press, 1958).
28. Gerald D. Berreman, "Caste in India and the United States," *American Journal of Sociology,* 66 (1960): 120–27.
29. U.S. Bureau of the Census. *Statistical Abstract of the United States: 1993,* 113th ed. (Washington, DC: U.S. Government Printing Office, 1993), p. 463.

30. Lois Benjamin, *The Black Elite: Facing the Color Line in the Twilight of the Twentieth Century* (Chicago: Nelson-Hall, 1991); see also Melvin D. Williams, "Racism," in Carol R. Ember, Melvin Ember, and Peter N. Peregrine, eds., *Research Frontiers in Anthropology,* (Upper Saddle River, NJ: Prentice Hall, 1998). Prentice Hall/Simon & Schuster Custom Publishing.

31. Nicholas D. Kristof, "Japan's Invisible Minority: Better Off Than in Past, but Still Outcasts," *New York Times International*, November 30, 1995, p. A18.

32. For more information about caste in Japan, see Gerald D. Berreman, *Caste in the Modern World* (Morristown, NJ: General Learning Press, 1973), and "Race, Caste and Other Invidious Distinctions in Social Stratification," *Race*, 13 (1972): 403–14b.

33. Nicholas D. Kristof, "Japan's Invisible Minority: Burakumin," *Britannica Online*, December 1997.

34. For more information about caste in Rwanda, see Berreman, *Caste in the Modern World,* and "Race, Caste and Other Invidious Distinctions in Social Stratification."

35. "Book of the Year (1995): World Affairs: RWANDA," and "Book of the Year (1995): Race and Ethnic Relations: Rwanda's Complex Ethnic History," *Britannica Online,* December 1997.

36. Orlando Patterson, *Slavery and Social Death: A Comparative Study* (Cambridge, MA: Harvard University Press, 1982), pp. vii–xiii, 105.

37. Frederic L. Pryor, *The Origins of the Economy: A Comparative Study of Distribution in Primitive and Peasant Economies* (New York: Academic Press, 1977), p. 219.

38. Euripides, "The Trojan Women," in Edith Hamilton, trans., *Three Greek Plays,* (New York: Norton, 1937), p. 52.

39. S. F. Nadel, *A Black Byzantium: The Kingdom of Nupe in Nigeria* (London: Oxford University Press, 1942). The Nupe abolished slavery at the beginning of the twentieth century.

40. Pryor, *Origins of the Economy,* pp. 217–47.

41. Kent V. Flannery, "The Cultural Evolution of Civilizations," *Annual Review of Ecology and Systematics*, 3 (1972): 399–426.

42. Data from Robert B. Textor, comp., *A Cross-Cultural Summary* (New Haven, CT: HRAF Press, 1967).

43. Ibid.

44. Gerhard Lenski, *Power and Privilege: A Theory of Social Stratification* (Chapel Hill: University of North Carolina Press, 1984 [first published 1966]), pp. 308–18.

45. Treiman and Ganzeboom, "Cross-National Comparative Status-Attainment Research," p. 117; Phillips Cutright, "Inequality: A Cross-National Analysis," *American Sociological Review,* 32 (1967): 564.

46. Sahlins, *Social Stratification in Polynesia.*

47. Ibid., p. 4.

48. Marshall D. Sahlins, *Stone Age Economics* (Chicago: Aldine, 1972).

49. Lenski, *Power and Privilege.*

50. Antonio Gilman, "The Development of Social Stratification in Bronze Age Europe," *Current Anthropology,* 22 (1990): 1–23.

51. See Fried, *Evolution of Political Society,* pp. 201–201; and Michael J. Harner, "Scarcity, the Factors of Production, and Social Evolution," in Steven Polgar, ed., *Population, Ecology, and Social Evolution* (The Hague: Mouton, 1975), pp. 123–38.

52. C. K. Meek, *Land Law and Custom in the Colonies* (London: Oxford University Press, 1940), pp. 149–50.

CHAPTER 16

1. Lila Leibowitz, *Females, Males, Families: A Biosocial Approach* (North Scituate, MA: Duxbury, 1978), pp. 43–44.

2. Alice Schlegel, "Gender Issues and Cross-Cultural Research," *Behavior Science Research,* 23 (1989): 266; Cynthia Fuchs Epstein, *Deceptive Distinctions: Sex, Gender, and the Social Order* (New York: Russell Sage Foundation, 1988), pp. 5–6; Janet Saltzman Chafetz, *Gender Equity: An Integrated Theory of Stability and Change,* Sage Library of Social Research No. 176 (Newbury Park, CA: Sage, 1990), p. 28.

3. Sue-Ellen Jacobs and Christine Roberts, "Sex, Sexuality, Gender and Gender Variance," in Sandra Morgen, ed., *Gender and Anthropology: Critical Reviews for Research and Teaching* (Washington, DC: American Anthropological Association, 1989), pp. 438–62.

4. William A. Stini, "Evolutionary Implications of Changing Nutritional Patterns in Human Populations," *American Anthropologist,* 73 (1971): 1019–30.

5. David W. Frayer and Milford H. Wolpoff, "Sexual Dimorphism," *Annual Review of Anthropology,* 14 (1985): 431–32.

6. For reviews of theories and research on sexual dimorphism and possible genetic and cultural determinants of variation in degree of dimorphism over time and place, see Frayer and Wolpoff, "Sexual Dimorphism"; and J. Patrick Gray, *Primate Sociobiology* (New Haven, CT: HRAF Press, 1985), pp. 201–209, 217–25.

7. Judith K. Brown, "A Note on the Division of Labor by Sex," *American Anthropologist,* 72 (1970): 1074.

8. Among the Aché hunter-gatherers of Paraguay, women collect the type of honey produced by stingless bees (men collect other honey); this division of labor is consistent with the compatibility theory. See Ana Magdalena Hurtado, Kristen Hawkes, Kim Hill, and Hillard Kaplan, "Female Subsistence Strategies among the Aché Hunter-Gatherers of Eastern Paraguay," *Human Ecology,* 13 (1985): 23.

9. George P. Murdock and Caterina Provost, "Factors in the Division of Labor by Sex: A Cross-Cultural Analysis," *Ethnology,* 12 (1973): 213; Bryan Byrne, "Access to Subsistence Resources and the Sexual Division of Labor among Potters," *Cross-Cultural Research,* 28 (1994): 225–50.

10. Douglas R. White, Michael L. Burton, and Lilyan A. Brudner, "Entailment Theory and Method: A Cross-Cultural Analysis of the Sexual Division of Labor," *Behavior Science Research,* 12 (1977): 1–24.

11. Carol C. Mukhopadhyay and Patricia J. Higgins, "Anthropological Studies of Women's Status Revisited:

1977–1987," *Annual Review of Anthropology,* 17 (1988): 473.

12. Brown, "Note on the Division of Labor by Sex," pp. 1073–78; and White, Burton, and Brudner, "Entailment Theory and Method," pp. 1–24.

13. Sara B. Nerlove, "Women's Workload and Infant Feeding Practices: A Relationship with Demographic Implications," *Ethnology,* 13 (1974): 201–14.

14. Nancy E. Levine, "Women's Work and Infant Feeding: A Case from Rural Nepal," *Ethnology,* 27 (1988): 231–51.

15. Madeleine J. Goodman, P. Bion Griffin, Agnes A. Estioko-Griffin, and John S. Grove, "The Compatibility of Hunting and Mothering among the Agta Hunter-Gatherers of the Philippines," *Sex Roles,* 12 (1985): 1199–209.

16. John J. Macionis, *Sociology,* 4th ed. (Englewood Cliffs, NJ: Prentice Hall, 1993), p. 362.

17. Margaret Mead, *Sex and Temperament in Three Primitive Societies* (New York: Mentor, 1950 [originally published 1935]), pp. 180–84.

18. W. H. R. Rivers, *The Todas* (Oosterhout, N.B., The Netherlands: Anthropological Publications, 1967 [originally published 1906]), p. 567.

19. Melvin Ember and Carol R. Ember, "The Conditions Favoring Matrilocal versus Patrilocal Residence," *American Anthropologist,* 73 (1971): 573, table 1.

20. Alice Schlegel and Herbert Barry III, "The Cultural Consequences of Female Contribution to Subsistence," *American Anthropologist,* 88 (1986): 142–50.

21. Ester Boserup, *Woman's Role in Economic Development* (New York: St. Martin's Press, 1970), pp. 22–25; see also Schlegel and Barry, "Cultural Consequences of Female Contribution to Subsistence," pp. 144–45.

22. Boserup, *Woman's Role in Economic Development,* pp. 22–25.

23. Ibid., pp. 31–34.

24. Carol R. Ember, "The Relative Decline in Women's Contribution to Agriculture with Intensification," *American Anthropologist,* 85 (1983): 286–87; data from Murdock and Provost, "Factors in the Division of Labor by Sex," p. 212; Candice Bradley, "Keeping the Soil in Good Heart: Weeding, Women and Ecofeminism," in Karen Warren, ed., *Ecofeminism: Multidisciplinary Perspectives* (Bloomington: Indiana University Press, 1995).

25. Ember, "Relative Decline in Women's Contribution to Agriculture with Intensification," pp. 287–93.

26. Ember and Ember, "Conditions Favoring Matrilocal versus Patrilocal Residence," pp. 579–80.

27. Ibid., p. 581; see also Peggy R. Sanday, "Toward a Theory of the Status of Women," *American Anthropologist,* 75 (1973): 1684.

28. Nerlove, "Women's Workload and Infant Feeding Practices," pp. 207-14.

29. Schlegel and Barry, "Cultural Consequences of Female Contribution to Subsistence," 142–50.

30. Ember, "Relative Decline in Women's Contribution to Agriculture with Intensification," pp. 288–89.

31. Martin K. Whyte, "Cross-Cultural Codes Dealing with the Relative Status of Women," *Ethnology,* 17 (1978): 217.

32. Martha C. Nussbaum, "Introduction," in Martha C. Nussbaum and Jonathan Glover, *Women, Culture, and Development: A Study of Human Capabilities* (Oxford: Clarendon Press, 1995), p. 2, based on data from *Human Development Report* (New York: United Nations Development Programme, 1993).

33. Whyte, "Cross-Cultural Codes"; and David B. Adams, "Why There Are So Few Women Warriors," *Behavior Science Research,* 18 (1983): 196–212.

34. Judith K. Brown, "Economic Organization and the Position of Women among the Iroquois," *Ethnohistory,* 17 (1970): 151–67.

35. Peggy R. Sanday, "Female Status in the Public Domain," in Michelle Z. Rosaldo and Louise Lamphere, eds., *Woman, Culture, and Society* (Stanford, CA: Stanford University Press, 1974), pp. 189–206; and William T. Divale and Marvin Harris, "Population, Warfare, and the Male Supremacist Complex," *American Anthropologist,* 78 (1976): 521–38.

36. Naomi Quinn, "Anthropological Studies on Women's Status," *Annual Review of Anthropology,* 6 (1977): 189–90.

37. Susan Brandt Graham, "Biology and Human Social Behavior: A Response to van den Berghe and Barash," *American Anthropologist,* 81 (1979): 357–60.

38. Dennis Werner, "Chiefs and Presidents: A Comparison of Leadership Traits in the United States and among the Mekranoti-Kayapo of Central Brazil," *Ethos,* 10 (1982): 136–48; and Ralph M. Stogdill, *Handbook of Leadership: A Survey of Theory and Research* (New York: Macmillan, 1974), cited in ibid.; see also W. Penn Handwerker and Paul V. Crosbie, "Sex and Dominance," *American Anthropologist,* 84 (1982): 97–104.

39. Patricia Draper, "!Kung Women: Contrasts in Sexual Egalitarianism in Foraging and Sedentary Contexts," in Rayna R. Reiter, ed., *Toward an Anthropology of Women* (New York: Monthly Review Press, 1975), p. 103.

40. Dennis Werner, "Child Care and Influence among the Mekranoti of Central Brazil," *Sex Roles,* 10 (1984): 395–404.

41. Marc H. Ross, "Female Political Participation: A Cross-Cultural Explanation," *American Anthropologist,* 88 (1986): 843–58.

42. This description is based on the fieldwork of Elizabeth and Robert Fearnea (1956–1958), as reported in M. Kay Martin and Barbara Voorhies, *Female of the Species* (New York: Columbia University Press, 1975), pp. 304–31.

43. Elsie B. Begler, "Sex, Status, and Authority in Egalitarian Society," *American Anthropologist,* 80 (1978): 571–88.

44. Ibid. See also Whyte, "Cross-Cultural Codes Dealing with the Relative Status of Women," pp. 229–32.

45. Martin K. Whyte, *The Status of Women in Preindustrial Societies* (Princeton, NJ: Princeton University Press, 1978), pp. 95–120. For a similar view, see Quinn, "Anthropological Studies on Women's Status."

46. Whyte, *Status of Women in Preindustrial Societies,* pp. 124–29, 145; see also Sanday, "Toward a Theory of the Status of Women."

47. Whyte, *Status of Women in Preindustrial Societies,* pp. 129–30.

48. Brown, "Economic Organization and the Position of Women among the Iroquois."

49. Whyte, *Status of Women in Preindustrial Societies,* pp. 135–36.

50. Ibid., p. 135.

51. Quinn, "Anthropological Studies on Women's Status," p. 85; see also Mona Etienne and Eleanor Leacock, eds., *Women and Colonization: Anthropological Perspectives* (New York: Praeger, 1980), pp. 19–20.

52. Chafetz, *Gender Equity,* pp. 11–19.

53. Mead, *Sex and Temperament in Three Primitive Societies,* p. 206.

54. Nancy McDowell, "Mundugumor: Sex and Temperament Revisited," in Melvin Ember, Carol R. Ember, and David Levinson, eds., *Portraits of Culture: Ethnographic Originals* (Upper Saddle River, NJ: Prentice Hall, 1998). Prentice Hall/Simon & Schuster Custom Publishing.

55. Beatrice B. Whiting and Carolyn P. Edwards, "A Cross-Cultural Analysis of Sex Differences in the Behavior of Children Aged Three through Eleven," *Journal of Social Psychology,* 91 (1973): 171–88.

56. Eleanor E. Maccoby and Carol N. Jacklin, *The Psychology of Sex Differences* (Stanford, CA: Stanford, University Press, 1974).

57. For a more extensive discussion of behavior differences and possible explanations of them, see Carol R. Ember, "A Cross-Cultural Perspective on Sex Differences," in Ruth H. Munroe, Robert L. Munroe, and Beatrice B. Whiting, eds., *Handbook of Cross-Cultural Human Development* (New York: Garland, 1981), pp. 531–80.

58. Whiting and Edwards, "Cross-Cultural Analysis of Sex Differences in the Behavior of Children Aged Three through Eleven."

59. For references to this research, see Ember, "Cross-Cultural Perspective on Sex Differences," p. 559.

60. J. Z. Rubin, F. J. Provenzano, and R. F. Haskett, "The Eye of the Beholder: Parents' Views on the Sex of New Borns," *American Journal of Orthopsychiatry,* 44 (1974): 512–19.

61. For a discussion of this evidence, see Lee Ellis, "Evidence of Neuroandrogenic Etiology of Sex Roles from a Combined Analysis of Human, Nonhuman Primate and Nonprimate Mammalian Studies," *Personality and Individual Differences,* 7 (1986): 525–27; Ember, "Cross-Cultural Perspective on Sex Differences," pp. 531–80.

62. For example, Ellis, in "Evidence of Neuroandrogenic Etiology of Sex Roles," considers the evidence for the biological view of aggression "beyond reasonable dispute."

63. For a discussion of other possibilities see Ember, "Cross-Cultural Perspective on Sex Differences."

64. Ronald P. Rohner, "Sex Differences in Aggression: Phylogenetic and Enculturation Perspectives," *Ethos,* 4 (1976): 57–72.

65. Beatrice B. Whiting and John W. M. Whiting (in collaboration with Richard Longabaugh), *Children of Six Cultures: A Psycho-Cultural Analysis* (Cambridge, MA: Harvard University Press, 1975); see also Beatrice B. Whiting and Carolyn P. Edwards, *Children of Different Worlds: The Formation of Social Behavior* (Cambridge, MA: Harvard University Press, 1988), p. 273.

66. Carol R. Ember, "Feminine Task Assignment and the Social Behavior of Boys," *Ethos,* 1 (1973): 424–39.

67. Whiting and Edwards, "Cross-Cultural Analysis of Sex Differences in the Behavior of Children Aged Three through Eleven," pp. 175–79; see also Maccoby and Jacklin, *The Psychology of Sex Differences.*

68. Victoria Katherine Burbank, *Fighting Women: Anger and Aggression in Aboriginal Society* (Berkeley: University of California Press, 1994).

69. David R. Heise, "Cultural Patterning of Sexual Socialization," *American Sociological Review,* 32 (1967): 726–39.

70. Clellan S. Ford and Frank A. Beach, *Patterns of Sexual Behavior* (New York: Harper, 1951), p. 191.

71. Oscar Lewis, *Life in a Mexican Village: Tepoztlan Revisited* (Urbana: University of Illinois Press, 1951), p. 397.

72. Reynolds Farley, *The New American Reality: Who We Are, How We Got Here, Where We Are Going,* (New York: Russell Sage Foundation, 1996), p. 60.

73. Gwen J. Broude and Sarah J. Greene, "Cross-Cultural Codes on Twenty Sexual Attitudes and Practices," *Ethnology,* 15 (1976): 409–29.

74. Clyde Kluckhohn, "As an Anthropologist Views It," in A. Deutsch, ed., *Sex Habits of American Men* (Englewood Cliffs, NJ: Prentice Hall, 1948), p. 101.

75. Morton Hunt, *Sexual Behavior in the 1970s* (Chicago: Playboy Press, 1974), pp. 254–57; Tamar Lewin, "Sex in America: Faithfulness in Marriage Is Overwhelming," *New York Times (National),* October 7, 1994, pp. A1, A18.

76. Gwen J. Broude, "Extramarital Sex Norms in Cross-Cultural Perspective," *Behavior Science Research,* 15 (1980): 184.

77. Ford and Beach, *Patterns of Sexual Behavior,* p. 114.

78. Ibid., p. 69.

79. Ibid., p. 76.

80. John Morris, *Living with Lepchas: A Book about the Sikkim Himalayas* (London: Heinemann, 1938), p. 191.

81. Ruth M. Underhill, *Social Organization of the Papago Indians* (New York: Columbia University Press, 1938), pp. 117, 186.

82. Mahmud M. 'Abd Allah, "Siwan Customs," *Harvard African Studies,* 1 (1917): 7, 20.

83. Raymond C. Kelly, "Witchcraft and Sexual Relations: An Exploration in the Social and Semantic Implications of the Structure of Belief," paper presented at the annual meeting of the American Anthropological Association, Mexico City, 1974.

84. Data from Robert B. Textor, comp., *A Cross-Cultural Summary* (New Haven, CT: HRAF Press, 1967).

85. William N. Stephens, "A Cross-Cultural Study of Modesty," *Behavior Science Research,* 7 (1972): 1–28.

86. Gwen J. Broude, "Cross-Cultural Patterning of Some Sexual Attitudes and Practices," *Behavior Science Research,* 11 (1976): 243.

87. Dennis Werner, "A Cross-Cultural Perspective on Theory and Research on Male Homosexuality," *Journal of Homosexuality,* 4 (1979): 345–62; see also Dennis Werner, "On the Societal Acceptance or Rejection of Male Homosexuality," M.A. thesis, Hunter College of the City University of New York, 1975, p. 36.

88. Werner, "Cross-Cultural Perspective on Theory and Research on Male Homosexuality," p. 358.

89. Data from Textor, comp., *A Cross-Cultural Summary.*

90. Alice Schlegel, "Status, Property, and the Value of Virginity," *American Ethnologist,* 18 (1991): 719–34.

CHAPTER 17

1. William N. Stephens, *The Family in Cross-Cultural Perspective* (New York: Holt, Rinehart & Winston, 1963), p. 5.

2. George Peter Murdock, *Social Structure* (New York: Macmillan, 1949), p. 8.

3. Stephens, *The Family in Cross-Cultural Perspective,* pp. 170–71.

4. E. Kathleen Gough, "The Nayars and the Definition of Marriage," *Journal of the Royal Anthropological Institute,* 89 (1959): 23–34; N. Prabha Unnithan, "Nayars: Tradition and Change in Marriage and Family," in Melvin Ember, Carol R. Ember, and David Levinson, eds., *Portraits of Culture: Ethnographic Originals* (Upper Saddle River, NJ: Prentice Hall, 1998). Prentice Hall/Simon & Schuster Custom Publishing.

5. Unnithan, "Nayars."

6. E. Adamson Hoebel, *The Cheyennes: Indians of the Great Plains* (New York: Holt, Rinehart & Winston, 1960), p. 77.

7. E. E. Evans-Pritchard, "Sexual Inversion among the Azande," *American Anthropologist,* 72 (1970): 1428–34.

8. Denise O'Brien, "Female Husbands in Southern Bantu Societies," in Alice Schlegel, ed., *Sexual Stratification: A Cross-Cultural View* (New York: Columbia University Press, 1977), pp. 109–26; see also Regina Smith Oboler, "Is the Female Husband a Man? Woman/Woman Marriage among the Nandi of Kenya," *Ethnology,* 19 (1980): 69–88.

9. Regina Smith Oboler, "Nandi: From Cattle-Keepers to Cash-Crop Farmers," in Melvin Ember, Carol R. Ember, and David Levinson, eds., *Portraits of Culture: Ethnographic Originals* (Upper Saddle River, NJ: Prentice Hall, 1998). Prentice Hall/Simon & Schuster Custom Publishing.

10. Murdock, *Social Structure,* pp. 7–8.

11. Ibid., pp. 9–10.

12. See, for example, Ralph Linton, *The Study of Man* (New York: Appleton-Century-Crofts, 1936), pp. 135–36.

13. Melvin Ember and Carol R. Ember, "Male-Female Bonding: A Cross-Species Study of Mammals and Birds," *Behavior Science Research,* 14 (1979): 37–56.

14. Nelson H. Graburn, *Eskimos without Igloos* (Boston: Little, Brown, 1969), pp. 188–200.

15. Bronislaw Malinowski, *The Sexual Life of Savages in Northwestern Melanesia* (New York: Halcyon House, 1932), p. 77.

16. Ibid., p. 88.

17. John W. M. Whiting, *Becoming a Kwoma* (New Haven, CT: Yale University Press, 1941), p. 125.

18. Elman R. Service, *Profiles in Ethnology,* 3rd ed. (New York: Harper & Row, 1978).

19. Robert A. LeVine and Barbara B. LeVine, "Nyansongo: A Gusii Community in Kenya," in Beatrice B. Whiting, ed., *Six Cultures* (New York: Wiley, 1963), p. 65.

20. Ibid.

21. For an extensive discussion of the symbolism of Rotuman weddings, see Alan Howard and Jan Rensel, "Rotuma: Interpreting a Wedding," in Melvin Ember, Carol R. Ember, and David Levinson, eds., *Portraits of Culture: Ethnographic Originals* (Upper Saddle River, NJ: Prentice Hall, 1998). Prentice Hall/Simon & Schuster Custom Publishing.

22. Alice Schlegel and Rohn Eloul, "A New Coding of Marriage Transactions," *Behavior Science Research,* 21 (1987): 119.

23. Alice Schlegel and Rohn Eloul, "Marriage Transactions: Labor, Property, and Status," *American Anthropologist,* 90 (1988): 295, table 1. We used the data to calculate the frequency of various types of economic transaction in a worldwide sample of 186 societies.

24. Oboler, "Nandi."

25. Charles O. Frake, "The Eastern Subanun of Mindanao," in George P. Murdock, ed., *Social Structure in Southeast Asia,* Viking Fund Publications in Anthropology No. 29 (Chicago: Quadrangle, 1960), pp. 51–64.

26. Margaret Mead, *Growing Up in New Guinea* (London: Routledge & Kegan Paul, 1931), pp. 206–208.

27. Schlegel and Eloul, "Marriage Transactions," pp. 298–99.

28. Frederic L. Pryor, *The Origins of the Economy: A Comparative Study of Distribution in Primitive and Peasant Economies* (New York: Academic Press, 1977), pp. 363–64.

29. Ibid.

30. Robert F. Spencer, "Spouse-Exchange among the North Alaskan Eskimo," in Paul Bohannan and John Middleton, eds., *Marriage, Family and Residence* (Garden City, NY: Natural History Press, 1968), p. 136.

31. Schlegel and Eloul, "Marriage Transactions," pp. 296–97.

32. Ibid.

33. Ibid.

34. A. R. Radcliffe-Brown, *The Andaman Islanders: A Study in Social Anthropology* (London: Cambridge University Press, 1922), p. 73.

35. Jack Goody, "Bridewealth and Dowry in Africa and Eurasia," in Jack Goody and S. H. Tambiah, eds., *Bridewealth and Dowry* (Cambridge: Cambridge University Press, 1973), pp. 17–21.

36. Pryor, *Origins of the Economy,* pp. 363–65; Schlegel and Eloul, "Marriage Transactions," pp. 296–99.

37. Research is reported in Steven J. C. Gaulin and James S. Boster, "Dowry as Female Competition," *American Anthropologist,* 92 (1990): 994–1005. The first theory discussed herein is associated with Ester Boserup, *Woman's Role in Economic Development* (New York:

St. Martin's Press, 1970). The second is put forward by Gaulin and Boster.

38. Schlegel and Eloul, in "Marriage Transactions," following Goody, "Bridewealth and Dowry in Africa and Eurasia," p. 20.

39. Fredrik Barth, *Nomads of South Persia* (Boston: Little, Brown, 1961), pp. 18–19; as reported in (and coded as indirect dowry by) Schlegel and Eloul, "New Coding of Marriage Transactions." p. 131.

40. Russell Middleton, "Brother-Sister and Father-Daughter Marriage in Ancient Egypt," *American Sociological Review*, 27 (1962): 606.

41. William H. Durham, *Coevolution: Genes, Culture, and Human Diversity* (Stanford, CA: Stanford University Press, 1991), pp. 293–94, citing research by K. Hopkins, "Brother-Sister Marriage in Roman Egypt," *Comparative Studies of Society and History*, 22 (1980): 303–54.

42. Edward Westermarck, *The History of Human Marriage* (London: Macmillan, 1894).

43. Yonina Talmon, "Mate Selection in Collective Settlements," *American Sociological Review*, 29 (1964): 492.

44. Ibid., p. 504.

45. Arthur Wolf, "Adopt a Daughter-in-Law, Marry a Sister: A Chinese Solution to the Problem of the Incest Taboo," *American Anthropologist*, 70 (1968): 864.

46. Arthur P. Wolf and Chieh-shan Huang, *Marriage and Adoption in China, 1845–1945* (Stanford, CA: Stanford University Press), 1980, pp. 159, 170, 185.

47. Hilda Parker and Seymour Parker, "Father-Daughter Sexual Abuse: An Emerging Perspective," *American Journal of Orthopsychiatry*, 56 (1986): 53–49.

48. Melvin Ember, "On the Origin and Extension of the Incest Taboo," *Behavior Science Research*, 10 (1975): 249-81; Durham, *Coevolution*, pp. 341–57.

49. For a discussion of mechanisms that might lead to sexual aversion, see Seymour Parker, "The Precultural Basis of the Incest Taboo: Toward a Biosocial Theory," *American Anthropologist*, 78 (1976): 285–305; see also Seymour Parker, "Cultural Rules, Rituals, and Behavior Regulation," *American Anthropologist*, 86 (1984): 584–600.

50. Sigmund Freud, *A General Introduction to Psychoanalysis* (Garden City, NY: Garden City Publishing, 1943 [originally published in German in 1917]).

51. Bronislaw Malinowski, *Sex and Repression in Savage Society* (London: Kegan Paul, Trench, Trubner, 1927).

52. Quoted in Leslie A. White, *The Science of Culture: A Study of Man and Civilization* (New York: Farrar, Straus, & Cudahy, 1949), p. 313.

53. Gay Elizabeth Kang, "Exogamy and Peace Relations of Social Units: A Cross-Cultural Test," *Ethnology* 18 (1979): 85–99.

54. Curt Stern, *Principles of Human Genetics*, 3rd ed. (San Francisco: Freeman, 1973), pp. 494–95, as cited in Ember, "On the Origin and Extension of the Incest Taboo," p. 256. For a recent review of the theory and evidence, see Durham, *Coevolution*.

55. Eva Seemanova, "A Study of Children of Incestuous Matings," *Human Heredity*, 21 (1971): 108–28, as cited in Durham, *Coevolution*, pp. 305–309.

56. Durham, *Coevolution*, pp. 305–309.

57. Ibid., pp. 346–52.

58. Raymond Firth, *We, the Tikopia* (Boston: Beacon Press, 1957), pp. 287–88, cited (somewhat differently) in Durham, *Coevolution*, pp. 349–50.

59. A mathematical model of early mating systems suggests that people may have noticed the harmful effects of inbreeding once populations began to expand as a result of agriculture; people therefore may have deliberately adopted the incest taboo to solve the problem of inbreeding. See Ember, "On the Origin and Extension of the Incest Taboo." For a similar suggestion, see Durham, *Coevolution*, pp. 331–39.

60. William J. Goode, *The Family*, 2nd ed. (Englewood Cliffs, NJ: Prentice Hall, 1982), pp. 61–62.

61. Clellan S. Ford, *Smoke from Their Fires* (New Haven, CT: Yale University Press, 1941), p. 149.

62. Howard and Rensel, "Rotuma."

63. Susan Schaefer Davis, "Morocco: Adolescents in a Small Town," in Ember, Ember, and Levinson, eds., *Portraits of Culture*, 1998.

64. W. J. Goode, *World Revolution and Family Patterns* (New York: Free Press, 1970), p. 210.

65. Sherwood G. Lingenfelter, "Yap: Changing Roles of Men and Women," in Ember, Ember, and Levinson, eds., *Portraits of Culture*.

66. Ember, "On the Origin and Extension of the Incest Taboo," p. 262, table 3.

67. Annette Busby, "Kurds: A Culture Straddling National Borders," in Ember, Ember, and Levinson, eds., *Portraits of Culture*, 1994.

68. Ember, "On the Origin and Extension of the Incest Taboo," pp. 260–69; see also Durham, *Coevolution*, pp. 341–57.

69. Murdock, *Social Structure*, p. 29.

70. Waldemar Bogoras, "The Chukchee," pt. 3. *Memoirs of the American Museum of Natural History*, 2 (1909); cited in Stephens, *The Family in Cross-Cultural Perspective*, p. 195.

71. Douglas Oliver, *A Solomon Island Society* (Cambridge, MA: Harvard University Press, 1955), pp. 352–53.

72. Ibid., pp. 223–24; quoted in Stephens, *The Family in Cross-Cultural Perspective*, p. 58.

73. Margaret Mead, *Sex and Temperament in Three Primitive Societies* (New York: New American Library, 1950 [originally published 1935]), p. 101.

74. The discussion of these customs is based on Stephens, *The Family in Cross-Cultural Perspective*, pp. 63–67.

75. Philip L. Kilbride and Janet C. Kilbride, "Polygyny: A Modern Contradiction?" in Philip L. Kilbride and Janet C. Kilbride, *Changing Family Life in East Africa: Women and Children at Risk* (University Park: Pennsylvania State University Press, 1990), pp. 202-206.

76. Linton, *The Study of Man*, p. 183.

77. John W. M. Whiting, "Effects of Climate on Certain Cultural Practices," in Ward H. Goodenough, ed., *Explorations in Cultural Anthropology: Essays in Honor of George Peter Murdock* (New York: McGraw-Hill, 1964), pp. 511–44.

78. Ibid., p. 518.

79. Ibid., pp. 516–17.

80. Melvin Ember, "Warfare, Sex Ratio, and Polygyny," *Ethnology,* 13 (1974): 197–206. Bobbi Low, in "Marriage Systems and Pathogen Stress in Human Societies," *American Zoologist,* 30 (1990): 325–39, has suggested that a high incidence of disease also may reduce the prevalence of "healthy" men. In such cases it may be to a woman's advantage to marry a "healthy" man even if he is already married, and it may be to a man's advantage to marry several unrelated women to maximize genetic variation (and disease resistance) among his children.

81. Melvin Ember, "Alternative Predictors of Polygyny," *Behavior Science Research,* 19 (1984–1985): 1–23. The statistical relationship between late age of marriage for men and polygyny was first reported by Stanley R. Witkowski, "Polygyny, Age of Marriage, and Female Status," paper presented at the annual meeting of the American Anthropological Association, San Francisco, 1975.

82. Ember, "Warfare, Sex Ratio, and Polygyny," pp. 202–205.

83. Ember, "Alternative Predictors of Polygyny." For other predictors of polygyny, see Douglas R. White and Michael L. Burton, "Causes of Polygyny: Ecology, Economy, Kinship, and Warfare," *American Anthropologist,* 90 (1988): 871–87; and Low, "Marriage Systems and Pathogen Stress in Human Societies."

84. Allan D. Coult and Robert W. Habenstein, *Cross Tabulations of Murdock's World Ethnographic Sample* (Columbia: University of Missouri Press, 1965); George Peter Murdock, "World Ethnographic Sample," *American Anthropologist* 59 (1957): 664–87.

85. Melvyn C. Goldstein, "When Brothers Share a Wife," *Natural History,* March 1987, p. 39.

86. Stephens, *The Family in Cross-Cultural Perspective,* p. 45.

87. L. R. Hiatt, "Polyandry in Sri Lanka: A Test Case for Parental Investment Theory," *Man,* 15 (1980): 583–98.

88. Goldstein, "When Brothers Share a Wife," pp. 39–48. Formerly, in feudal Tibet, a class of serfs who owned small parcels of land also practiced polyandry. Goldstein suggested that a shortage of land would explain their polyandry too. See Melvyn C. Goldstein, "Stratification, Polyandry, and Family Structure in Central Tibet," *Southwestern Journal of Anthropology,* 27 (1971): 65–74.

89. For example, see Myron L. Cohen, *House United, House Divided: The Chinese Family in Taiwan* (New York: Columbia University Press, 1976).

90. Burton Pasternak, *Introduction to Kinship and Social Organization* (Englewood Cliffs, NJ: Prentice Hall, 1976), p. 96.

91. Coult and Habenstein, *Cross Tabulations of Murdock's World Ethnographic Sample.*

92. Margaret Mead, *Coming of Age in Samoa* (New York: Morrow, 1928), quoted in Stephens, *The Family in Cross-Cultural Perspective,* pp. 134–35.

93. Ibid., p. 135.

94. M. F. Nimkoff and Russell Middleton, "Types of Family and Types of Economy," *American Journal of Sociology,* 66 (1960): 215–25.

95. Burton Pasternak, Carol R. Ember, and Melvin Ember, "On the Conditions Favoring Extended Family Households," *Journal of Anthropological Research,* 32 (1976): 109–23.

96. Jean Libman Block, "Help! They've *All* Moved Back Home!" *Woman's Day,* April 26, 1983, pp. 72–76.

CHAPTER 18

1. Allan D. Coult and Robert W. Habenstein, *Cross Tabulations of Murdock's World Ethnographic Sample* (Columbia: University of Missouri Press, 1965); George Peter Murdock, "World Ethnographic Sample," *American Anthropologist,* 59 (1957): 664–87.

2. Percentages calculated from Coult and Habenstein, *Cross Tabulations of Murdock's World Ethnographic Sample.*

3. Laura Bohannan and Paul Bohannan, *The Tiv of Central Nigeria* (London: International African Institute, 1953).

4. Melvin Ember, "The Emergence of Neolocal Residence," *Transactions of the New York Academy of Sciences,* 30 (1967): 291–302.

5. Melvin Ember and Carol R. Ember, "The Conditions Favoring Matrilocal versus Patrilocal Residence," *American Anthropologist,* 73 (1971): 571–94. See also William T. Divale, "Migration, External Warfare, and Matrilocal Residence," *Behavior Science Research,* 9 (1974): 75–133.

6. Ember and Ember, "Conditions Favoring Matrilocal versus Patrilocal Residence," pp. 583–85; and Divale, "Migration, External Warfare, and Matrilocal Residence," p. 100.

7. Ember and Ember, "Conditions Favoring Matrilocal versus Patrilocal Residence." For a different theory— that matrilocal residence precedes, rather than follows, the development of purely external warfare— see Divale, "Migration, External Warfare, and Matrilocal Residence."

8. See Mary W. Helms, "Miskitos: Adaptations to Colonial Empires, Past and Present," in Melvin Ember, Carol R. Ember, and David Levinson, eds., *Portraits of Culture: Ethnographic Originals* (Upper Saddle River, NJ: Prentice Hall, 1998). Prentice Hall/Simon & Schuster Custom Publishing. See also Ember and Ember, "Conditions Favoring Matrilocal versus Patrilocal Residence."

9. Elman R. Service, *Primitive Social Organization: An Evolutionary Perspective* (New York: Random House, 1962), p. 137.

10. Carol R. Ember and Melvin Ember, "The Conditions Favoring Multilocal Residence," *Southwestern Journal of Anthropology,* 28 (1972): 382–400.

11. Carol R. Ember, "Residential Variation among Hunter-Gatherers," *Behavior Science Research,* 9 (1975): 135–49.

12. J. D. Freeman, "On the Concept of the Kindred," *Journal of the Royal Anthropological Institute,* 91 (1961): 192–220.

13. George Peter Murdock, *Social Structure* (New York: Macmillan, 1949), pp. 49–50.

14. Carol R. Ember, Melvin Ember, and Burton Pasternak, "On the Development of Unilineal Descent," *Journal of Anthropological Research,* 30 (1974): 84–89.

15. Leopold Pospisil, *The Kapauku Papuans of West New Guinea* (New York: Holt, Rinehart & Winston, 1963).

16. David M. Schneider, "The Distinctive Features of Matrilineal Descent Groups," in David M. Schneider and Kathleen Gough, eds., *Matrilineal Kinship* (Berkeley: University of California Press, 1961), pp. 1–35.

17. Ember and Ember, "Conditions Favoring Matrilocal versus Patrilocal Residence," p. 581.

18. David M. Schneider, "Truk," in Schneider and Gough, eds., *Matrilineal Kinship,* pp. 202–33.

19. Ward H. Goodenough, *Property, Kin, and Community on Truk* (New Haven, CT: Yale University Press, 1951), p. 145.

20. Melvin Ember, "The Conditions That May Favor Avunculocal Residence," *Behavior Science Research,* 9 (1974): 203–209.

21. Coult and Habenstein, *Cross Tabulations of Murdock's World Ethnographic Sample.*

22. Data from Robert B. Textor, comp., *A Cross-Cultural Summary* (New Haven, CT: HRAF Press, 1967).

23. Meyer Fortes, *The Web of Kinship among the Tallensi* (New York: Oxford University Press, 1949).

24. Data from Textor, comp., *A Cross-Cultural Summary.*

25. Ember, Ember, and Pasternak, "On the Development of Unilineal Descent."

26. The importance of warfare and competition as factors in the formation of unilineal descent groups is also suggested by Service, *Primitive Social Organization;* and Marshall D. Sahlins, "The Segmentary Lineage: An Organization of Predatory Expansion," *American Anthropologist,* 63 (1961): 332–45.

27. William Davenport, "Nonunilinear Descent and Descent Groups," *American Anthropologist,* 61 (1959): 557–72.

28. The description of the Samoan descent system is based on Melvin Ember's 1955–1956 fieldwork. See also his "The Nonunilinear Descent Groups of Samoa," *American Anthropologist,* 61 (1959): 573–77; and Davenport, "Nonunilinear Descent and Descent Groups."

29. Ember and Ember, "Conditions Favoring Multilocal Residence."

30. See, for example, Murdock, *Social Structure,* pp. 199–222.

31. Reported in Textor, comp., *A Cross-Cultural Summary.*

32. The association between the Omaha system and patrilineality is reported in Textor, comp., *A Cross-Cultural Summary.*

33. Murdock, *Social Structure,* p. 125.

34. The association between the Crow system and matrilineality is reported in Textor, comp., *A Cross-Cultural Summary.*

35. See Leslie A. White, "A Problem in Kinship Terminology," *American Anthropologist,* 41 (1939): 569–70.

36. Jack Goody, "Cousin Terms," *Southwestern Journal of Anthropology,* 26 (1970): 125–42.

37. Burton Pasternak, *Introduction to Kinship and Social Organization* (Englewood Cliffs, NJ: Prentice Hall, 1976), p. 142.

38. Reported in Textor, comp., *A Cross-Cultural Summary.*

39. Ibid.

40. This conjecture is based on our unpublished cross-cultural research.

CHAPTER 19

1. Neville Dyson-Hudson, *Karimojong Politics* (Oxford: Clarendon Press, 1966), p. 155. This section draws from this source.

2. This section is based on David Maybury-Lewis, *Akwe-Shavante Society* (Oxford: Clarendon Press, 1967).

3. Nancy B. Leis, "Women in Groups: Ijaw Women's Associations," in Michelle Z. Rosaldo and Louise Lamphere, eds., *Woman, Culture, and Society* (Stanford, CA: Stanford University Press, 1974), pp. 223–42.

4. M. J. Meggitt, "Male-Female Relationships in the Highlands of Australian New Guinea," *American Anthropologist,* 66 (special issue, 1964): 204–24.

5. Ibid., p. 207. For why men in some societies may fear sex with women, see Carol R. Ember, "Men's Fear of Sex with Women: A Cross-Cultural Study," *Sex Roles,* 4 (1978): 657–78.

6. Meggitt, "Male-Female Relationships in the Highlands of Australian New Guinea," p. 218.

7. Beryl L. Bellman, *The Language of Secrecy: Symbols and Metaphors in Poro Ritual* (New Brunswick, NJ: Rutgers University Press, 1984), pp. 8, 25–28, 33.

8. Ibid., p. 8.

9. Ibid., pp. 8, 80–88.

10. Ibid., pp. 33, 80; also Caroline H. Bledsoe, *Women and Marriage in Kpelle Society* (Stanford, CA: Stanford University Press, 1980), p. 67.

11. Kenneth Little, "The Political Function of the Poro," *Africa,* 35 (1965): 349–65; and 36 (1966): 62–71; Bledsoe, *Women and Marriage in Kpelle Society,* pp. 68–70.

12. Karen Paige Ericksen, "Male and Female Age Organizations and Secret Societies in Africa," *Behavior Science Research,* 23 (1989): 234–64.

13. Leis, "Women in Groups."

14. E. Adamson Hoebel, *The Cheyennes: Indians of the Great Plains* (New York: Holt, Rinehart & Winston, 1960).

15. William K. Powers and Marla N. Powers, "Lakota: A Study in Cultural Continuity," in Melvin Ember, Carol R. Ember, and David Levinson, eds., *Portraits of Culture: Ethnographic Originals* (Upper Saddle River, NJ: Prentice Hall, 1998). Prentice Hall/Simon & Schuster Custom Publishing.

16. Richard H. Thompson, "Chinatowns: Immigrant Communities in Transition," in Melvin Ember, Carol R. Ember, and David Levinson, eds., *Portraits of Culture: Ethnographic Originals* (Upper Saddle River, NJ: Prentice Hall, 1998). Prentice Hall/Simon & Schuster Custom Publishing.

17. William P. Mangin, "The Role of Regional Associations in the Adaptation of Rural Migrants to Cities in

Peru," in Dwight B. Heath and Richard N. Adams, eds., *Contemporary Cultures and Societies of Latin America* (New York: Random House, 1965), pp. 311–23.

18. Jonathan Y. Okamura, "Filipino Hometown Associations in Hawaii," *Ethnology,* 22 (1983): 341–53.

19. Thompson, "Chinatowns."

20. See Kenneth Little, *West African Urbanization* (New York: Cambridge University Press, 1965); and Claude Meillassoux, *Urbanization of an African Community* (Seattle: University of Washington Press, 1968).

21. Kenneth Little, "The Role of Voluntary Associations in West African Urbanization," *American Anthropologist,* 59 (1957): 582.

22. Ibid., p. 583.

23. Shirley Ardener, "Women Making Money Go Round: ROSCAs Revisited," in Shirley Ardener and Sandra Burman, *Money-Go-Rounds: The Importance of Rotating Savings and Credit Associations for Women* (Oxford/Washington, DC: Berg, 1995), p. 1.

24. Shirley Ardener "The Comparative Study of Rotating Credit Associations," in Ardener and Burman, *Money-Go-Rounds,* appendix. (Originally published in 1964.)

25. See the many chapters in Ardener and Burman, *Money Go-Rounds,* for examples of these principles.

26. Nici Nelson, "The Kiambu Group: A Successful Women's ROSCA in Mathare Valley, Nairobi (1971 to 1990)," in Ardener and Burman, *Money-Go-Rounds,* pp. 49–69. Quote on page 58.

27. Ellen Bortei-Doku and Ernest Aryeetey, "Mobilizing Cash for Business: Women in Rotating *Susu* Clubs in Ghana, in Ardener and Burman, *Money Go-Rounds,* pp, 83, 77–94.

28. Ivan Light and Zhong Deng, "Gender Differences in ROSCA Participation within Korean Business Households in Los Angeles," in Ardener and Burman, *Money-Go-Rounds,* pp. 217–40.

29. Wayne Warry, "Kafaina: Female Wealth and Power in Chuave, Papua New Guinea," *Oceania,* 57 (1986): 4–21.

30. Alexander M. Ervin, "Styles and Strategies of Leadership during the Alaskan Native Land Claims Movement: 1959–71," *Anthropologica,* 29 (1987): 21–38.

31. D. Douglas Caulkins, "Norwegians: Cooperative Individualists," in Melvin Ember, Carol R. Ember, and David Levinson, eds., *Portraits of Culture: Ethnographic Originals* (Upper Saddle River, NJ: Prentice Hall, 1998). Prentice Hall/Simon & Schuster Custom Publishing.

32. Raoul Naroll, *The Moral Order: An Introduction to the Human Situation* (Beverly Hills, CA: Sage, 1983), pp. 74–75.

33. S. N. Eisenstadt, "African Age Groups," *Africa,* 24 (1954): 102.

34. B. Bernardi, "The Age-System of the Nilo-Hamitic Peoples," *Africa,* 22 (1952): 316–32.

35. Madeline Lattman Ritter, "The Conditions Favoring Age-Set Organization," *Journal of Anthropological Research,* 36 (1980): 87–104.

36. Ibid.

37. For an explanation of age-sets among North American Plains Indians, see Jeffery R. Hanson, "Age-Set Theory and Plains Indian Age-Grading: A Critical Review and Revision," *American Ethnologist,* 15 (1988): 349–64.

CHAPTER 20

1. Elman R. Service, *Primitive Social Organization: An Evolutionary Perspective* (New York: Random House, 1962).

2. Carmel Schrire, "Wild Surmises on Savage Thoughts," in Carmel Schrire, ed., *Past and Present in Hunter Gatherer Studies* (Orlando, FL: Academic Press, 1984), pp. 1–25; see also Eleanor Leacock and Richard Lee, "Introduction," in Eleanor Leacock and Richard Lee, eds., *Politics and History in Band Societies* (Cambridge: Cambridge University Press, 1982), p. 8.

3. Service, *Primitive Social Organization,* p. 109.

4. Jean L. Briggs, "Eskimo Women: Makers of Men," in Carolyn J. Matthiasson, *Many Sisters: Women in Cross-Cultural Perspective* (New York: Free Press, 1974), pp. 261–304.

5. Therkel Mathiassen, *Material Culture of the Iglulik Eskimos* (Copenhagen: Glydendalske, 1928), as quoted in E. M. Weyer, *The Eskimos: Their Environment and Folkways* (New Haven, CT: Yale University Press, 1932), p. 213.

6. Service, *Primitive Social Organization,* pp. 114–15.

7. Paul Bohannan, "The Migration and Expansion of the Tiv," *Africa,* 24 (1954): 3.

8. Marshall D. Sahlins, "The Segmentary Lineage: An Organization of Predatory Expansion," *American Anthropologist,* 63 (1961): 342.

9. Raymond C. Kelly, *The Nuer Conquest: The Structure and Development of an Expansionist System* (Ann Arbor: University of Michigan Press, 1985), p. 1.

10. Sahlins, "The Segmentary Lineage," p. 345.

11. Neville Dyson-Hudson, *Karimojong Politics* (Oxford: Clarendon Press, 1966), chapters 5 and 6.

12. Ibid.

13. Marshall Sahlins, *Moala: Culture and Nature on a Fijian Island* (Ann Arbor: University of Michigan Press, 1962), pp. 293–94.

14. Marshall D. Sahlins, "Poor Man, Rich Man, Big-Man, Chief: Political Types in Melanesia and Polynesia," *Comparative Studies in Society and History,* 5 (1963): 295.

15. Marshall Sahlins, "Other Times, Other Customs: The Anthropology of History," *American Anthropologist,* 85 (1983): 519.

16. Sahlins, "Poor Man, Rich Man, Big-Man, Chief," p. 297.

17. Robert L. Carneiro, "A Theory of the Origin of the State," *Science,* August 21, 1970, p. 733.

18. See Max Weber, *The Theory of Social and Economic Organization,* trans. A. M. Henderson and Talcott Parsons (New York: Oxford University Press, 1947), p. 154.

19. Hakan Wiberg, "Self-Determination as an International Issue," in I. M. Lewis, ed., *Nationalism and Self-Determination in the Horn of Africa* (London: Ithaca Press, 1983), pp. 43–65.

20. For an extensive review of the various theories about legitimacy, see Ronald Cohen, "Introduction," in

Ronald Cohen and Judith D. Toland, eds., *State Formation and Political Legitimacy,* vol. 1, *Political Anthropology* (New Brunswick, NJ: Transaction Books, 1988), pp. 1–3.

21. M. I. Finley, *Politics in the Ancient World* (Cambridge: Cambridge University Press, 1983).

22. Jerome Carcopino, *Daily Life in Ancient Rome: The People and the City at the Height of the Empire,* edited with bibliography and notes by Henry T. Rowell, translated from the French by E. O. Lorimer (New Haven, CT: Yale University Press, 1940), pp. 18–20.

23. Our discussion of Nupe is based on S. F. Nadel, "Nupe State and Community," *Africa,* 8 (1935): 257–303.

24. Melvin Ember, "The Relationship between Economic and Political Development in Nonindustrialized Societies," *Ethnology,* 2 (1963): 228–48.

25. Data from Robert B. Textor, comp., *A Cross-Cultural Summary* (New Haven, CT: HRAF Press, 1967).

26. Ember, "Relationship between Economic and Political Development in Nonindustrialized Societies."

27. Data from Textor, comp., *A Cross-Cultural Summary.*

28. Raoul Naroll, "Two Solutions to Galton's Problem," *Philosophy of Science,* 28 (January 1961): 15–39. See also Marc H. Ross, "Socioeconomic Complexity, Socialization, and Political Differentiation: A Cross-Cultural Study," *Ethos,* 9 (1981): 217–47.

29. Ember, "Relationship between Economic and Political Development in Nonindustrialized Societies," pp. 244–46.

30. Service, *Primitive Social Organization;* see also David P. Braun and Stephen Plog, "Evolution of 'Tribal' Social Networks: Theory and Prehistoric North American Evidence," *American Antiquity,* 47 (1982): 504–25; Jonathan Haas, "Warfare and the Evolution of Tribal Polities in the Prehistoric Southwest," in Jonathan Haas, ed., *The Anthropology of War* (New York: Cambridge University Press, 1990), pp. 171–89.

31. Allen Johnson and Timothy Earle, *The Evolution of Human Societies: From Foraging Group to Agrarian State* (Stanford, CA: Stanford University Press, 1987), p. 158; Robert L. Carneiro, "Chiefdom-Level Warfare as Exemplified in Fiji and the Cauca Valley," in Haas, ed., *The Anthropology of War,* pp. 190–211.

32. Service, *Primitive Social Organization,* pp. 112, 145.

33. Gary Feinman and Jill Nietzel, "Too Many Types: An Overview of Sedentary Prestate Societies in the Americas," in Michael B. Schiffer, ed., *Advances in Archaeological Method and Theory,* vol. 7 (Orlando, FL: Academic Press, 1984), pp. 39–102.

34. William H. McNeill, *Plagues and Peoples* (Garden City, NY: Doubleday Anchor, 1976).

35. Robert L. Carneiro, "Political Expansion as an Expression of the Principle of Competitive Exclusion," in Ronald Cohen and Elman R. Service, eds., *Origins of the State: The Anthropology of Political Evolution* (Philadelphia: Institute for the Study of Human Issues, 1978), p. 215.

36. Data from Textor, comp., *A Cross-Cultural Summary.*

37. Carneiro, "Political Expansion as an Expression of the Principle of Competitive Exclusion." See also

Hornell Hart, "The Logistic Growth of Political Areas," *Social Forces,* 26 (1948): 396–408; Raoul Naroll, "Imperial Cycles and World Order," *Peace Research Society Papers No.* 7, Chicago Conference (1967): 83–101; and Louis A. Marano, "A Macrohistoric Trend toward World Government," *Behavior Science Notes,* 8 (1973): 35–40.

38. For a review of the descriptive literature until the late 1970s, see Joan Vincent, "Political Anthropology: Manipulative Strategies," *Annual Review of Anthropology,* 7 (1978): 175–94.

39. Dennis Werner, "Chiefs and Presidents: A Comparison of Leadership Traits in the United States and among the Mekranoti-Kayapo of Central Brazil," *Ethos,* 10 (1982): 136–48.

40. Waud H. Kracke, *Force and Persuasion: Leadership in an Amazonian Society* (Chicago: University of Chicago Press, 1979), p. 232.

41. Werner, "Chiefs and Presidents."

42. Sahlins, "Poor Man, Rich Man, Big-Man, Chief," pp. 285–303.

43. Kracke, *Force and Persuasion,* p. 41.

44. Rena Lederman, "Big Men, Large and Small? Towards a Comparative Perspective," *Ethnology,* 29 (1990): 3–15.

45. Ernest Brandewie, "The Place of the Big Man in Traditional Hagen Society in the Central Highlands of New Guinea," in Frank McGlynn and Arthur Tuden, eds., *Anthropological Approaches to Political Behavior* (Pittsburgh: University of Pittsburgh Press, 1991), pp. 62–82.

46. Maria Lepowsky, "Big Men, Big Women and Cultural Autonomy," *Ethnology,* 29 (1990): 35–50.

47. Marc Howard Ross, "Political Organization and Political Participation: Exit, Voice, and Loyalty in Preindustrial Societies," *Comparative Politics,* 21 (1988): 73. The discussion in this section draws mostly from ibid., pp. 73–89 and from Marc Howard Ross, "Political Participation," in Carol R. Ember and Melvin Ember, eds., *Cross-Cultural Research for Social Science* (Upper Saddle River, NJ: Prentice Hall, 1998). Prentice Hall/Simon & Schuster Custom Publishing.

48. For studies of international relations that support these conclusions, see footnotes 2 and 3 in Carol R. Ember, Melvin Ember, and Bruce Russett, "Peace between Participatory Polities: A Cross-Cultural Test of the 'Democracies Rarely Fight Each Other' Hypothesis," *World Politics,* 44 (1992): 573–99.

49. Ibid.

50. Richard Scaglion, "Law and Society," in Carol R. Ember and Melvin Ember, eds., *Cross-Cultural Research for Social Science* (Upper Saddle River, NJ: Prentice Hall, 1998). Prentice Hall/Simon & Schuster Custom Publishing.

51. E. Adamson Hoebel, *The Law of Primitive Man* (New York: Atheneum, 1968 [originally published 1954]), p. 4, quoting S. P. Simpson and Ruth Field, "Law and the Social Sciences," *Virginia Law Review,* 32 (1946): 858.

52. Douglas Fry and Kaj Björkqvist, *Cultural Variation in Conflict Resolution: Alternatives to Violence* (Mahwah, NJ: Lawrence Erlbaum Associates, 1997).

53. Donald Black, *The Social Structure of Right and Wrong* (San Diego: Academic Press, 1993), pp. 79–83.

54. Ross, "Political Organization and Political Participation."

55. Franz Boas, *Central Eskimos. Bureau of American Ethnology Annual Report No. 6* (Washington, DC, 1888), p. 668.

56. Keith F. Otterbein, *The Ultimate Coercive Sanction: A Cross-Cultural Study of Capital Punishment* (New Haven, CT: HRAF Press, 1986), p. 107.

57. Dane Archer and Rosemary Gartner, *Violence and Crime in Cross-National Perspective* (New Haven, CT: Yale University Press, 1984), pp. 118–39.

58. Scaglion, "Law and Society"; Black, *The Social Structure of Right and Wrong,* pp. 83-86.

59. Ibid.

60. E. E. Evans-Pritchard, "The Nuer of the Southern Sudan," in M. Fortes and E. E. Evans-Pritchard, eds., *African Political Systems* (New York: Oxford University Press, 1940), p. 291. The discussion of the Nuer follows this source.

61. Letitia Hickson, "The Social Contexts of Apology in Dispute Settlement: A Cross-Cultural Study," *Ethnology,* 25 (1986): 283–94.

62. Ibid.; and Klaus-Friedrich Koch, Soraya Altorki, Andrew Arno, and Letitia Hickson, "Ritual Reconciliation and the Obviation of Grievances: A Comparative Study in the Ethnography of Law," *Ethnology,* 16 (1977): 279.

63. John M. Roberts, "Oaths, Autonomic Ordeals, and Power," in Clellan S. Ford, ed., *Cross-Cultural Approaches: Readings in Comparative Research* (New Haven, CT: HRAF Press, 1967), p. 169.

64. Alois Musil, *The Manners and Customs of the Rwala Bedouins. American Geographical Society Oriental Exploration Studies No. 6* (New York, 1928), p. 430, as cited in Roberts, "Oaths, Autonomic Ordeals, and Power," pp. 169–70.

65. Roberts, "Oaths, Autonomic Ordeals, and Power," p. 192.

66. Hoebel, *The Law of Primitive Man,* chapter 9.

67. Richard D. Schwartz, "Social Factors in the Development of Legal Control: A Case Study of Two Israeli Settlements," *Yale Law Journal,* 63 (February 1954): 475.

68. Textor, comp., *A Cross-Cultural Summary.*

69. Wilfred T. Masumura, "Law and Violence: A Cross-Cultural Study," *Journal of Anthropological Research,* 33 (1977): 388–99.

70. Scaglion, "Law and Society"; Black, *The Social Structure of Right and Wrong,* pp. 83-86; Katherine S. Newman, *Law and Economic Organization: A Comparative Study of Preindustrial Societies* (Cambridge, MA: Cambridge University Press, 1983), p. 131.

71. Carol R. Ember and Melvin Ember, "War, Socialization, and Interpersonal Violence: A Cross-Cultural Study," *Journal of Conflict Resolution,* 38 (1994): 620–46.

72. Newman, *Law and Economic Organization,* p. 131.

73. Nicholas J. Gubser, *The Nunamiut Eskimos: Hunters of Caribou* (New Haven, CT: Yale University Press, 1965), p. 151.

74. Keith F. Otterbein and Charlotte Swanson Otterbein, "An Eye for an Eye, a Tooth for a Tooth: A Cross-Cultural Study of Feuding," *American Anthropologist,* 67 (1965): 1476.

75. Douglas R. White, "Rethinking Polygyny: Co-Wives, Codes, and Cultural Systems," *Current Anthropology* (1988): 529–58.

76. Orlando Patterson, *Slavery and Social Death: A Comparative Study* (Cambridge, MA: Harvard University Press, 1982), pp. 345–52.

77. Karl Heider, *The Dugum Dani* (Chicago: Aldine, 1970), pp. 105–11. See also Karl Heider, *Grand Valley Dani: Peaceful Warriors* (New York: Holt, Rinehart & Winston, 1979), pp. 88–99.

78. Melvin Ember and Carol R. Ember, "Cross-Cultural Studies of War and Peace: Recent Achievements and Future Possibilities," in S. P. Reyna and R. E. Downs, eds., *Studying War: Anthropological Perspectives* (New York: Gordon & Breach, 1992), pp. 188–189.

79. Carol R. Ember and Melvin Ember, "Resource Unpredictability, Mistrust, and War: A Cross-Cultural Study," *Journal of Conflict Resolution,* 36 (1992): 242–62. See also Melvin Ember, "Statistical Evidence for an Ecological Explanation of Warfare," *American Anthropologist,* 84 (1982): 645–49. For a discussion of how Dani warfare seems to be motivated mainly by economic considerations, see Paul Shankman, "Culture Contact, Cultural Ecology, and Dani Warfare," *Man,* 26 (1991): 299–321.

80. Keith Otterbein, *The Evolution of War* (New Haven, CT: HRAF Press, 1970).

81. Ember and Ember, "Resource Unpredictability, Mistrust, and War." See also Otterbein, *The Evolution of War;* and Colin K. Loftin, "Warfare and Societal Complexity: A Cross-Cultural Study of Organized Fighting in Preindustrial Societies," Ph.D. dissertation, University of North Carolina, Chapel Hill, 1971.

82. Carol R. Ember, "An Evaluation of Alternative Theories of Matrilocal versus Patrilocal Residence," *Behavior Science Research,* 9 (1974): 135–49.

83. Keith F. Otterbein, "Internal War: A Cross-Cultural Study," *American Anthropologist,* 70 (1968): 283. See also Marc H. Ross, "Internal and External Conflict and Violence," *Journal of Conflict Resolution,* 29 (1985): 547–79.

84. William T. Divale and Marvin Harris, "Population, Warfare, and the Male Supremacist Complex," *American Anthropologist,* 78 (1976): 521–38; see also Ann Gibbons, "Warring over Women," *Science,* August 20, 1993, pp. 987–88.

85. Ember and Ember, "Resource Unpredictability, Mistrust, and War," pp. 251–52.

86. J. David Singer, "Accounting for International War: The State of the Discipline," *Annual Review of Sociology,* 6 (1980): 349–67.

CHAPTER 21

1. Robert K. Dentan, *The Semai: A Nonviolent People of Malaya* (New York: Holt, Rinehart & Winston, 1968), pp. 55–56.

2. Napoleon A. Chagnon, *Yanomamö: The Fierce People,* 3rd ed. (New York: CBS College Publishing, 1983).

3. Quoted in Otto Klineberg, "Foreword," in Marshall H. Segall, *Cross-Cultural Psychology: Human Behavior in Global Perspective* (Monterey, CA: Brooks/Cole, 1979), p. v.

4. Donald E. Brown, *Human Universals* (Philadelphia: Temple University Press, 1991).

5. Carmella C. Moore, "Is Love Always Love?" *Anthropology Newsletter,* November 1997, pp. 8–9; see also A. Kimball Romney, Carmella C. Moore, and Craig D. Rusch, "Cultural Universals: Measuring the Semantic Structure of Emotion Terms in English and Japanese," *Proceedings of the National Academy of Sciences, U.S.A.,* 94 (1997): 5489–494.

6. Margaret Mead, *Coming of Age in Samoa,* 3rd ed. (New York: Morrow, 1961 [originally published 1928]).

7. Bronislaw Malinowski, *Sex and Repression in Savage Society* (Cleveland, OH: World, 1968; London: Kegan Paul, Trench, Trubner, 1927).

8. Derek Freeman, *Margaret Mead and Samoa: The Making and Unmaking of an Anthropological Myth* (Cambridge, MA: Harvard University Press, 1983). For reasons to be skeptical about Freeman's criticism, see Melvin Ember, "Evidence and Science in Ethnography: Reflections on the Freeman-Mead Controversy," *American Anthropologist,* 87 (1985): 906–909.

9. Melford E. Spiro, *Oedipus in the Trobriands* (Chicago: University of Chicago Press, 1982).

10. Alice Schlegel and Herbert Barry III, *Adolescence: An Anthropological Inquiry* (New York: Free Press, 1991), p. 44.

11. Jean Piaget, "Piaget's Theory," in Paul Mussen, ed., *Carmichael's Manual of Child Psychology,* vol. 1, 3rd ed. (New York: Wiley, 1970), 703–32.

12. John W. Berry, Ype H. Poortinga, Marshall H. Segall, and Pierre R. Dasen, *Cross-Cultural Psychology: Research and Applications* (New York: Cambridge University Press, 1992), p. 40.

13. Ibid., pp. 40–41.

14. Pierre R. Dasen and Alastair Heron, "Cross-Cultural Tests of Piaget's Theory," in Harry C. Triandis and Alastair Heron, eds., *Handbook of Cross-Cultural Psychology,* vol. 4, *Developmental Psychology* (Boston: Allyn & Bacon, 1981), pp. 305–306.

15. Carol R. Ember, "Cross-Cultural Cognitive Studies," *Annual Review of Anthropology,* 6 (1977): 33–56; and Barbara Rogoff, "Schooling and the Development of Cognitive Skills," in Triandis and Heron, eds., *Handbook of Cross-Cultural Psychology,* vol. 4, *Developmental Psychology,* pp. 233–94.

16. Douglass Price-Williams, "A Study Concerning Concepts of Conservation of Quantities among Primitive Children," *Acta Psychologica,* 18 (1961): 297–305.

17. Marshall H. Segall, Pierre R. Dasen, John W. Berry, and Ype H. Poortinga, *Human Behavior in Global Perspective: An Introduction to Cross-Cultural Psychology* (New York: Pergamon, 1990), p. 149.

18. Rogoff, "Schooling and the Development of Cognitive Skills," pp. 264–67.

19. Thomas S. Weisner, Mary Bausano, and Madeleine Kornfein, "Putting Family Ideals into Practice: Pronaturalism in Conventional and Nonconventional California Families," *Ethos,* 11 (1983): 278–304.

20. John W. M. Whiting and Irvin L. Child, *Child Training and Personality: A Cross-Cultural Study* (New Haven, CT: Yale University Press, 1953), pp. 69–71.

21. Weisner, Bausano, and Kornfein, "Putting Family Ideals into Practice," p. 291; Barry S. Hewlett, "Diverse Contexts of Human Infancy," in Carol R. Ember and Melvin Ember, eds., *Cross-Cultural Research for Social Science* (Upper Saddle River, NJ: Prentice Hall, 1998). Prentice Hall/Simon & Schuster Custom Publishing.

22. See the research cited in Hewlett, "Diverse Contexts of Human Infancy."

23. Ibid.

24. Chagnon, *Yanomamö,* p. 115.

25. Dentan, *The Semai,* p. 61.

26. Cora Du Bois, *The People of Alor: A Social-Psychological Study of an East Indian Island* (Minneapolis: University of Minnesota Press, 1944).

27. Victor Barnouw, *Culture and Personality,* 4th ed. (Homewood, IL: Dorsey, 1985), p. 118.

28. Ruth H. Munroe and Robert L. Munroe, "Infant Experience and Childhood Affect among the Logoli: A Longitudinal Study," *Ethos,* 8 (1980): 295–315.

29. Ronald P. Rohner, *They Love Me, They Love Me Not: A Worldwide Study of the Effects of Parental Acceptance and Rejection* (New Haven, CT: HRAF Press, 1975), pp. 97–105.

30. See studies reported in Ronald P. Rohner and Evelyn Rohner, eds., "Special Issue on Worldwide Tests of Parental Acceptance-Rejection Theory: An Overview," *Behavior Science Research,* 15 (1980): v–88; also Zdenek Matejcek, "Perceived Parental Acceptance-Rejection and Personality Organization among Czech Elementary School Children," *Behavior Science Research,* 18 (1983): 259–68.

31. Rohner, *They Love Me, They Love Me Not,* pp. 112–16.

32. Beatrice B. Whiting and John W. M. Whiting, in collaboration with Richard Longabaugh, *Children of Six Cultures: A Psycho-Cultural Analysis* (Cambridge, MA: Harvard University Press, 1975), p. 94. See also Ruth H. Munroe, Robert L. Munroe, and Harold S. Shimmin, "Children's Work in Four Cultures: Determinants and Consequences," *American Anthropologist,* 86 (1984): 369–79.

33. Beatrice B. Whiting and Carolyn Pope Edwards, in collaboration with Carol R. Ember, Gerald M. Erchak, Sara Harkness, Robert L. Munroe, Ruth H. Munroe, Sara B. Nerlove, Susan Seymour, Charles M. Super, Thomas S. Weisner, and Martha Wenger, *Children of Different Worlds: The Formation of Social Behavior* (Cambridge, MA: Harvard University Press, 1988), p. 265.

34. Munroe, Munroe, and Shimmin, "Children's Work in Four Cultures," pp. 374–76; see also Carol R. Ember, "Feminine Task Assignment and the Social Behavior of Boys," *Ethos,* 1 (1973): 424–39.

35. Whiting and Whiting, *Children of Six Cultures,* p. 179.

36. Ibid., pp. 152-63; and Carol R. Ember, "A Cross-Cultural Perspective on Sex Differences," in Ruth H.

Munroe, Robert L. Munroe, and Beatrice B. Whiting, eds., *Handbook of Cross-Cultural Human Development* (New York: Garland, 1981), p. 560.

37. Ember, "Cross-Cultural Cognitive Studies"; and Rogoff, "Schooling and the Development of Cognitive Skills."

38. Rogoff, "Schooling and the Development of Cognitive Skills," p. 285.

39. For how school experiences may improve particular cognitive skills, rather than higher levels of cognitive development in general, see Barbara Rogoff, *Apprenticeship in Thinking: Cognitive Development in Social Context* (New York: Oxford University Press, 1990), pp. 46–49.

40. Marc H. Irwin, Gary N. Schafer, and Cynthia P. Feiden, "Emic and Unfamiliar Category Sorting of Mano Farmers and U.S. Undergraduates," *Journal of Cross-Cultural Psychology,* 5 (1974): 407–23.

41. A. R. Luria, *Cognitive Development: Its Cultural and Social Foundations* (Cambridge, MA: Harvard University Press, 1976), p. 108; quoted in Rogoff, "Schooling and the Development of Cognitive Skills," p. 254.

42. Sylvia Scribner and Michael Cole, *The Psychology of Literacy* (Cambridge, MA: Harvard University Press, 1981); J. W. Berry and J. Bennett, "Syllabic Literacy and Cognitive Performance among the Cree," *International Journal of Psychology,* 24 (1989): 429–50, as reported in Berry, Poortinga, Segall, and Dasen, *Cross-Cultural Psychology, Research and Applications,* pp. 123–24.

43. Clifford Geertz, "'From the Native's Point of View': On the Nature of Anthropological Understanding," in Richard A. Shweder and Robert A. LeVine, eds., *Culture Theory: Essays on Mind, Self, and Emotion* (New York: Cambridge University Press, 1984), pp. 123–36.

44. Although Melford Spiro does not believe that this Western/non-Western pattern exists, the reader is referred to his article for the many references to the works of those who do. "Is the Western Conception of the Self 'Peculiar' within the Context of the World Cultures?" *Ethos,* 21 (1993): 107–53.

45. Jane M. Bachnik, "The Two 'Faces' of Self and Society in Japan," *Ethos,* (1992): 3–32.

46. Arlene Stairs, "Self-Image, World-Image: Speculations on Identity from Experiences with Inuit," *Ethos,* 20 (1992): 116-26.

47. Spiro, "Is the Western Conception of the Self 'Peculiar'"?

48. Research reported in Douglas Hollan, "Cross-Cultural Differences in the Self," *Journal of Anthropological Research,* 48 (1992): 289–90.

49. Whiting and Child, *Child Training and Personality,* p. 310.

50. Robert B. Edgerton, *Sick Societies: Challenging the Myth of Primitive Harmony* (New York: Free Press, 1992), p. 206.

51. Robert A. LeVine, "Human Parental Care: Universal Goals, Cultural Strategies, Individual Behavior," in Robert A. LeVine, Patrice M. Miller, and Mary Maxwell West, eds., *Parental Behavior in Diverse Societies* (San Francisco: Jossey-Bass, 1988), pp. 4–6; see also discussion in Hewlett, "Diverse Contexts of Human Infancy."

52. Herbert Barry III, Irvin L. Child, and Margaret K. Bacon, "Relation of Child Training to Subsistence Economy," *American Anthropologist,* 61 (1959): 51–63. For a somewhat different analysis of the data used in the Barry, Child, and Bacon study, see Llewellyn Hendrix, "Economy and Child Training Reexamined," *Ethos,* 13 (1985): 246–61.

53. Lois Wladis Hoffman, "Cross-Cultural Differences in Childrearing Goals," in LeVine, Miller, and West, eds., *Parental Behavior in Diverse Societies,* pp. 101–103.

54. Leigh Minturn and William W. Lambert, *Mothers of Six Cultures: Antecedents of Child Rearing* (New York: Wiley, 1964), p. 289.

55. John W. M. Whiting, "Cultural and Sociological Influences on Development," in *Growth and Development of the Child in His Setting* (Maryland Child Growth and Development Institute, 1959), pp. 5–9.

56. Robert B. Edgerton, *The Individual in Cultural Adaptation: A Study of Four East African Peoples* (Berkeley: University of California Press, 1971).

57. John W. Berry, *Human Ecology and Cognitive Style* (New York: Wiley, 1976).

58. Herman A. Witkin, "A Cognitive Style Approach to Cross-Cultural Research," *International Journal of Psychology,* 2 (1967): 233–50.

59. J. L. M. Dawson, "Cultural and Physiological Influences upon Spatial-Perceptual Processes in West Africa," *International Journal of Psychology,* 2 (1967): 115–28, 171–85; and John W. Berry, "Ecological and Cultural Factors in Spatial Perceptual Development," *Canadian Journal of Behavioural Science,* 3 (1971): 324–36.

60. Carol R. Ember, "Universal and Variable Patterns of Gender Difference," in Carol R. Ember and Melvin Ember, eds., *Cross-Cultural Research for Social Science* (Upper Saddle River, NJ: Prentice Hall, 1998). Prentice Hall/Simon & Schuster Custom Publishing.

61. Daniel G. Freedman, "Ethnic Differences in Babies," *Human Nature* (January 1979): 36–43.

62. Ibid., pp. 40–41. For a discussion of possible genetic influences on the social environment, see Sandra Scarr and Kathleen McCartney, "How People Make Their Own Environments: A Theory of Genotype-Environment Effects," *Child Development,* 54 (1983): 424–35.

63. See P. R. Dasen, J. W. Berry, and N. Sartorius, eds., *Health and Cross-Cultural Psychology: Toward Applications* (Newbury Park, CA: Sage, 1988), pp. 116–18, for references to research, particularly by D. E. Barrett, "Malnutrition and Child Behavior: Conceptualization, Assessment and an Empirical Study of Social-Emotional Functioning," in J. Brozek and B. Schürch, eds., *Malnutrition and Behavior: Critical Assessment of Key Issues* (Lausanne, Switzerland: Nestlé Foundation, 1984), pp. 280–306.

64. Dasen, Berry, and Sartorius, eds., *Health and Cross-Cultural Psychology,* pp. 117–18, 126–28.

65. Ralph Bolton, "Aggression and Hypoglycemia among the Qolla: A Study in Psychobiological Anthropology," *Ethnology,* 12 (1973): 227–57.

66. Ruth Benedict, *Patterns of Culture* (New York: Mentor, 1959 [originally published 1934]).

67. Verrier Elwin, *The Religion of an Indian Tribe* (London: Oxford University Press, 1955); cited in Barnouw, *Culture and Personality,* p. 356.

68. John J. Honigmann, *Personality in Culture* (New York: Harper & Row, 1967), p. 406.

69. Arthur Kleinman, *Rethinking Psychiatry: From Cultural Category to Personal Experience* (New York: Macmillan, 1988), p. 3.

70 Catherine Lutz, "Depression and the Translations of Emotional Worlds," in Arthur Kleinman and Byron Good, eds., *Culture and Depression: Studies in the Anthropology and Cross-Cultural Psychiatry of Affect and Disorder* (Berkeley: University of California Press, 1985), pp. 63–100.

71. Jane Murphy, "Abnormal Behavior in Traditional Societies: Labels, Explanations, and Social Reactions," in Munroe, Munroe, and Whiting, eds., *Handbook of Cross-Cultural Human Development,* p. 813.

72. Robert B. Edgerton, "Conceptions of Psychosis in Four East African Societies," *American Anthropologist,* 68 (1966): 408–25.

73. Edgerton, *Sick Societies,* pp. 16–45.

74. J. S. Allen, A. J. Lambert, F. Y. Attah Johnson, K. Schmidt, and K. L. Nero, "Antisaccadic Eye Movements and Attentional Asymmetry in Schizophrenia in Three Pacific Populations," *Acta Psychiatrica Scandinavia,* 94 (1996): 258–65.

75. Kleinman, *Rethinking Psychiatry,* pp. 34–52; Berry, Poortinga, Segall, and Dasen, *Cross-Cultural Psychology,* pp. 357–64.

76. Honigmann, *Personality in Culture,* p. 401.

77. Kleinman, *Rethinking Psychiatry,* p. 19.

78. Anthony F. C. Wallace, "Mental Illness, Biology and Culture," in F. L. K. Hsu, ed., *Psychological Anthropology,* 2nd ed. (Cambridge, MA: Schenkman, 1972), pp. 363–402.

79. Kleinman, *Rethinking Psychiatry,* pp. 167–85.

80. David C. McClelland, *The Achieving Society* (New York: Van Nostrand, 1961).

81. Robert A. LeVine, *Dreams and Deeds: Achievement Motivation in Nigeria* (Chicago: University of Chicago Press, 1966), p. 2.

82. Abram Kardiner, with Ralph Linton, *The Individual and His Society* (New York: Golden Press, 1946 [originally published 1939]), p. 471.

83. Whiting and Child, *Child Training and Personality,* pp. 32–38.

84. John M. Roberts and Brian Sutton-Smith, "Child Training and Game Involvement," *Ethnology,* 1 (1962): 178.

85. Roger V. Burton and John W. M. Whiting, "The Absent Father and Cross-Sex Identity," *Merrill-Palmer Quarterly of Behavior and Development,* 7, no. 2 (1961): 85–95. See also Robert L. Munroe, Ruth H. Munroe, and John W. M. Whiting, "Male Sex-Role Resolutions," in Munroe, Munroe, and Whiting, eds.,

Handbook of Cross-Cultural Human Development, pp. 611–32; for a recent review of cross-cultural research on initiation, see Victoria K. Burbank, "Adolescent Socialization and Initiation Ceremonies," in Ember and Ember, eds., *Cross-Cultural Research for Social Science.*

CHAPTER 22

1. Edward B. Tylor, "Animism" (originally published 1871), in William A. Lessa and Evon Z. Vogt, eds., *Reader in Comparative Religion: An Anthropological Approach,* 4th ed. (New York: Harper & Row, 1979), pp. 9–18.

2. R. R. Marett, *The Threshold of Religion* (London: Methuen, 1909).

3. Stewart Elliott Guthrie, *Faces in the Clouds: A New Theory of Religion* (New York: Oxford University Press, 1993).

4. Sigmund Freud, *Moses and Monotheism,* trans. Katherine Jones (New York: Vintage Books, 1967 [originally published 1939]); Christopher Badcock, *Essential Freud* (Oxford: Basil Blackwell, 1988), pp. 126–27, 133–36.

5. Bronislaw Malinowski, "The Group and the Individual in Functional Analysis," *American Journal of Sociology,* 44 (1939): 959; Bronislaw Malinowski, "Magic, Science, and Religion," in *Magic, Science, and Religion and Other Essays* (Garden City, NY: Doubleday, 1948), pp. 50–51.

6. William James, *The Varieties of Religious Experience: A Study in Human Nature* (New York: Modern Library, 1902).

7. Carl G. Jung, *Psychology and Religion* (New Haven, CT: Yale University Press, 1938).

8. Erich Fromm, *Psychoanalysis and Religion* (New Haven, CT: Yale University Press, 1950).

9. Abraham H. Maslow, *Religions, Values, and Peak-Experiences* (Columbus: Ohio State University Press, 1964).

10. Émile Durkheim, *The Elementary Forms of the Religious Life,* trans. Joseph W. Swain (New York: Collier Books, 1961 [originally published 1912]).

11. Guy E. Swanson, *The Birth of the Gods: The Origin of Primitive Beliefs* (Ann Arbor: University of Michigan Press, 1969), pp. 1–31.

12. Anthony Wallace, *Religion: An Anthropological View* (New York: Random House, 1966), pp. 60-61.

13. Annemarie De Waal Malefijt, *Religion and Culture: An Introduction to Anthropology of Religion* (New York: Macmillan, 1968), p. 153.

14. Verne F. Ray, *The Sanpoil and Nespelem: Salishan Peoples of Northeastern Washington* (New Haven, CT: HRAF Press, 1954), pp. 172–89.

15. Paul C. Rosenblatt, R. Patricia Walsh, and Douglas A. Jackson. *Grief and Mourning in Cross-Cultural Perspective* (New Haven, CT: HRAF Press, 1976), p. 51.

16. Ibid., p. 55.

17. Swanson, *The Birth of the Gods,* pp. 97-108; see also Dean Sheils, "Toward a Unified Theory of Ancestor

Worship: A Cross-Cultural Study," *Social Forces,* 54 (1975): 427–40.

18. John Middleton, "The Cult of the Dead: Ancestors and Ghosts," in William A. Lessa and Evon Z. Vogt, eds., *Reader in Comparative Religion: An Anthropological Approach,* 3rd ed. (New York: Harper & Row, 1971), p. 488.

19. Melford E. Spiro and Roy G. D'Andrade, "A Cross-Cultural Study of Some Supernatural Beliefs," *American Anthropologist,* 60 (1958): 456–66.

20. William W. Lambert, Leigh Minturn Triandis, and Margery Wolf, "Some Correlates of Beliefs in the Malevolence and Benevolence of Supernatural Beings: A Cross-Societal Study," *Journal of Abnormal and Social Psychology,* 58 (1959): 162–69. See also Ronald P. Rohner, *They Love Me, They Love Me Not: A Worldwide Study of the Effects of Parental Acceptance and Rejection* (New Haven, CT: HRAF Press, 1975), p. 108.

21. H. G. Barnett, *Being a Palauan* (New York: Holt, Rinehart & Winston, 1960), pp. 79–85.

22. Swanson, *The Birth of the Gods,* p. 56.

23. Ibid., pp. 55-81; see also William D. Davis, "Societal Complexity and the Nature of Primitive Man's Conception of the Supernatural," Ph.D. dissertation, University of North Carolina, Chapel Hill, 1971.

24. Robert B. Textor, comp., *A Cross-Cultural Summary* (New Haven, CT: HRAF Press, 1967); see also Ralph Underhill, "Economic and Political Antecedents of Monotheism: A Cross-Cultural Study," *American Journal of Sociology,* 80 (1975): 841–61.

25. Clifford Geertz, "Religion as a Cultural System," in Michael Banton, ed., *Anthropological Approaches to the Study of Religion. Association of Social Anthropologists of the Commonwealth Monograph No. 3* (New York: Praeger, 1966), pp. 1–46.

26. Swanson, *The Birth of the Gods,* pp. 153–74.

27. Ruth Bunzel, "The Nature of Katcinas," in Lessa and Vogt, eds., *Reader in Comparative Religion,* 3rd ed., pp. 493–95.

28. Gary H. Gossen, "Temporal and Spiritual Equivalents in Chamula Ritual Symbolism," in Lessa and Vogt, eds., *Reader in Comparative Religion,* 4th ed., pp. 116–28.

29. Wallace, *Religion: An Anthropological View,* pp. 52–67.

30. Michael Winkelman, "Trance States: A Theoretical Model and Cross-Cultural Analysis," *Ethos,* 14 (1986): 178-83.

31. Erika Bourguignon, "Introduction: A Framework for the Comparative Study of Altered States of Consciousness," in Erika Bourguignon, *Religion, Altered States of Consciousness, and Social Change* (Columbus: Ohio State University Press, 1973), pp. 3–35.

32. Erika Bourguignon and Thomas L. Evascu, "Altered States of Consciousness within a General Evolutionary Perspective: A Holocultural Analysis," *Behavior Science Research,* 12 (1977): 197–216. See also Winkelman, "Trance States," pp. 196–98.

33. Omar Khayyam Moore, "Divination: A New Perspective," *American Anthropologist,* 59 (1957): 69–74.

34. Dean Sheils, "A Comparative Study of Human Sacrifice," *Behavior Science Research,* 15 (1980): 245–62.

35. M. Adler, *Drawing Down the Moon* (Boston: Beacon Press, 1986), p. 418, as referred to in T. M. Luhrmann, *Persuasions of the Witch's Craft: Ritual Magic and Witchcraft in Present-Day England* (Oxford: Basil Blackwell, 1989), pp. 4–5.

36. E. E. Evans-Pritchard, "Witchcraft Explains Unfortunate Events," in Lessa and Vogt, eds., *Reader in Comparative Religion,* 4th ed., pp. 362–66.

37. Swanson, *The Birth of the Gods,* p. 150. See also H. R. Trevor-Roper, "The European Witch-Craze of the Sixteenth and Seventeenth Centuries," in Lessa and Vogt, eds., *Reader in Comparative Religion,* 3rd ed., pp. 444–49.

38. Swanson, *The Birth of the Gods,* pp. 150–51.

39. Linnda R. Caporael, "Ergotism: The Satan Loosed in Salem?" *Science,* April 2, 1976, pp. 21–26; Mary K. Matossian, "Ergot and the Salem Witchcraft Affair," *American Scientist,* 70 (1982): 355–57; and Mary K. Matossian, *Poisons of the Past: Molds, Epidemics, and History* (New Haven, CT: Yale University Press, 1989), pp. 70–80. For possible reasons to dismiss the ergot theory, see Nicholas P. Spanos, "Ergotism and the Salem Witch Panic: A Critical Analysis and an Alternative Conceptualization," *Journal of the History of the Behavioral Sciences,* 19 (1983): 358–69.

40. Michael Harner, "The Role of Hallucinogenic Plants in European Witchcraft," in Michael Harner, ed., *Hallucinogens and Shamanism* (New York: Oxford University Press, 1972), pp. 127–50.

41. Beatrice B. Whiting, *Paiute Sorcery. Viking Fund Publications in Anthropology No. 15* (New York: Wenner-Gren Foundation, 1950), pp. 36–37. See also Swanson, *The Birth of the Gods,* pp. 137–52, 240–41.

42. Michael Winkelman, "Magico-Religious Practitioner Types and Socioeconomic Conditions," *Behavior Science Research,* 20 (1986): 17–46.

43. Ibid., pp. 28–29.

44. Claude Lévi-Strauss, "The Sorcerer and His Magic," in Claude Lévi-Strauss, *Structural Anthropology,* trans. Claire Jacobsen and Brooke Grundfest Schoepf (New York: Basic Books, 1963), p. 169.

45. Franz Boas, *The Religion of the Kwakiutl. Columbia University Contributions to Anthropology,* vol. 10, pt. 2 (New York: Columbia University, 1930), pp. 1–41. Reported in Lévi-Strauss, *Structural Anthropology,* pp. 169–73.

46. E. Fuller Torrey, *The Mind Game: Witchdoctors and Psychiatrists* (New York: Emerson Hall, n.d.).

47. James Dow, *The Shaman's Touch: Otomi Indian Symbolic Healing* (Salt Lake City: University of Utah Press, 1986), pp. 6–9, 125.

48. Winkelman, "Magico-Religious Practitioner Types and Socioeconomic Conditions," pp. 27–28.

49. Ibid., p. 27.

50. Ibid., pp. 35–37.

51. Marvin Harris, "The Cultural Ecology of India's Sacred Cattle," *Current Anthropology,* 7 (1966): 51–63.

52. Wallace, *Religion,* p. 30.

53. Anthony Wallace, *The Death and Rebirth of the Seneca* (New York: Knopf, 1970), p. 239.

54. The Quakers, long-time neighbors and trusted advisers of the Seneca, took pains not to interfere with Seneca religion, principles, and attitudes.

55. Peter Worsley, *The Trumpet Shall Sound: A Study of "Cargo" Cults in Melanesia* (London: MacGibbon & Kee, 1957), p. 12.

56. Ibid., pp. 11, 115.

57. Ibid., p. 122.

58. David Aberle, "A Note on Relative Deprivation Theory as Applied to Millenarian and Other Cult Movements," in Lessa and Vogt, eds., *Reader in Comparative Religion*, 3rd ed., pp. 528–31.

59. Bruce M. Knauft, "Cargo Cults and Relational Separation," *Behavior Science Research*, 13 (1978): 185–240.

CHAPTER 23

1. Jacques Maquet, *The Aesthetic Experience: An Anthropologist Looks at the Visual Arts* (New Haven, CT: Yale University Press, 1986), p. 9.

2. Richard L. Anderson, *Art in Small-Scale Societies*, 2nd ed. (Englewood Cliffs, NJ: Prentice Hall, 1989), p. 21.

3. Robert P. Armstrong, *The Powers of Presence* (Philadelphia: University of Pennsylvania Press, 1981), pp. 6-9; see also Anderson, *Art in Small-Scale Societies*, p. 11.

4. Richard L. Anderson, *Calliope's Sisters: A Comparative Study of Philosophies of Art* (Englewood Cliffs, NJ: Prentice Hall, 1990), p. 278; Richard L. Anderson, "Do Other Cultures Have 'Art'?" *American Anthropologist*, 94 (1992): 926–29.

5. Edward Malin, *Totem Poles of the Pacific Northwest Coast* (Portland, OR: Timber Press, 1986), p. 27.

6. Anderson, *Art in Small-Scale Societies*, p. 11.

7. James L. Gibbs, Jr., "The Kpelle of Liberia," in James L. Gibbs, Jr., ed., *Peoples of Africa* (New York: Holt, Rinehart & Winston, 1965), p. 222.

8. Anderson, *Calliope's Sisters*, pp. 225–26.

9. James J. Sweeney, "African Negro Culture," in Paul Radin, ed., *African Folktales and Sculpture* (New York: Pantheon, 1952), p. 335.

10. John Fischer, "Art Styles as Cultural Cognitive Maps," *American Anthropologist*, 63 (1961): 80.

11. Ibid., p. 81.

12. Ibid., p. 83.

13. William W. Dressler and Michael C. Robbins, "Art Styles, Social Stratification, and Cognition: An Analysis of Greek Vase Painting," *American Ethnologist*, 2 (1975): 427–34.

14. Alan Lomax, ed., *Folk Song Style and Culture. American Association for the Advancement of Science Publication No. 88* (Washington, DC, 1968), pp. 117–28.

15. ©1945 Walt Disney Music Company; words by Ray Gilbert, music by Allie Wrubel.

16. Lomax, *Folk Song Style and Culture*, pp. 166–67.

17. Ibid., pp. 167–69.

18. Barbara C. Ayres, "Effects of Infant Carrying Practices on Rhythm in Music," *Ethos*, 1 (1973): 387–404.

19. Barbara C. Ayres, "Effects of Infantile Stimulation on Musical Behavior," in Lomax, ed., *Folk Song Style and Culture*, pp. 211–21.

20. Edwin Erickson, "Self-assertion, Sex Role, and Vocal Rasp," in Lomax, ed., *Folk Song Style and Culture*, pp. 190–97.

21. For a study of variation in music within India that does not support some of Lomax's findings, see Edward O. Henry, "The Variety of Music in a North Indian Village: Reassessing Cantometrics," *Ethnomusicology*, 20 (1976): 49–66.

22. Alan Dundes, *Folklore Matters* (Knoxville: University of Tennessee Press, 1989), p. viii.

23. Richard Bauman, "Folklore," in Richard Bauman, ed., *Folklore, Cultural Performances, and Popular Entertainments: A Communications-Centered Handbook* (New York: Oxford University Press, 1992), pp. 29–40.

24. Jan Harold Brunvand, *The Baby Train: And Other Lusty Urban Legends* (New York: Norton, 1993), p. 14.

25. Ibid., p. 296.

26. Clyde Kluckhohn, "Recurrent Themes in Myths and Mythmaking," in Alan Dundes, ed., *The Study of Folklore* (Englewood Cliffs, NJ: Prentice Hall, 1965), pp. 158–68.

27. As discussed in Robert A. Segal, *Joseph Campbell: An Introduction* (New York: Garland, 1987), pp. 1–2.

28. Joseph Campbell, *The Hero with a Thousand Faces* (New York: Pantheon, 1949), p. 30, as quoted in Segal, *Joseph Campbell*, p. 4.

29. Stith Thompson, "Star Husband Tale," in Dundes, ed., *The Study of Folklore*, p. 449.

30. Alan Dundes, "Structural Typology in North American Indian Folktales," in Dundes, ed., *The Study of Folklore*, pp. 206–15. Dundes's analysis of the "Star Husband Tale" is reported in Frank W. Young, "A Fifth Analysis of the Star Husband Tale," *Ethnology*, 9 (1970): 389–413.

31. Michael Carroll, "A New Look at Freud on Myth," *Ethos*, 7 (1979): 189–205.

32. George O. Wright, "Projection and Displacement: A Cross-Cultural Study of Folktale Aggression," *Journal of Abnormal and Social Psychology*, 49 (1954): 523-28.

33. Alex Cohen, "A Cross-Cultural Study of the Effects of Environmental Unpredictability on Aggression in Folktales," *American Anthropologist*, 92 (1990): 474–79.

34. Sally Price, *Primitive Art in Civilized Places* (Chicago: University of Chicago Press, 1989), pp. 82–85.

35. Ibid., pp. 102–103.

36. Ibid., pp. 56–67.

37. Ibid., p. 112.

38. John Anson Warner, "The Individual in Native American Art: A Sociological View," in Edwin L. Wade, ed., *The Arts of the North American Indian: Native Traditions in Evolution* (New York: Hudson Hills Press, 1986), pp. 172–75.

39. Price, *Primitive Art in Civilized Places*, pp. 77–81.

40. Robert Layton, *Australian Rock Art: A New Synthesis* (Cambridge: Cambridge University Press, 1992), pp. 93–94.

41. Ibid., pp. 31, 109.

42. J. C. H. King, "Tradition in Native American Art," in Wade, ed., *The Arts of the North American Indian*, pp. 74–82.

43. Warner, "The Individual in Native American Art," pp. 178–86.

44. Elizabeth Bryant Merrill, "Art Styles as Reflections of Sociopolitical Complexity," *Ethnology* 26 (1987): 221–230.

CHAPTER 24

1. Ralph Linton, *The Study of Man* (New York: Appleton-Century-Crofts, 1936), p. 306.

2. Ibid., pp. 310–11.

3. Harry R. Silver, "Calculating Risks: The Socioeconomic Foundations of Aesthetic Innovation in an Ashanti Carving Community," *Ethnology,* 20 (1981): 101–14.

4. Everett M. Rogers, *Diffusion of Innovations,* 3rd ed. (New York: Free Press, 1983), pp. 263–69.

5. Frank Cancian, "Risk and Uncertainty in Agricultural Decision Making," in Peggy F. Barlett, ed., *Agricultural Decision Making: Anthropological Contributions to Rural Development* (New York: Academic Press, 1980), pp. 161–202.

6. Barry S. Hewlett and L. L. Cavalli-Sforza, "Cultural Transmission among Aka Pygmies," *American Anthropologist,* 88 (1986): 922–34; L. L. Cavalli-Sforza and M. W. Feldman, *Cultural Transmission and Evolution: A Quantitative Approach* (Princeton, NJ: Princeton University Press, 1981).

7. Thomas W. Valente, *Network Models of the Diffusion of Innovations* (Cresskill, NJ: Hampton Press, 1995), p. 21.

8. Wesley Cohen, "Emprical Studies of Innovative Activity," in Paul Stoneman, ed., *Handbook of the Economics of Innovation and Technological Change* (Oxford: Blackwell, 1995), pp. 182–264.

9. Linton, *The Study of Man,* pp. 326–27. ©1936, renewed 1964; reprinted by permission of Prentice Hall, Inc.

10. "Printing, Typography, and Photoengraving: History of Prints: Origins in China: Transmission of Paper to Europe (12th century)" *Britannica Online,* February 1998; "Paper." *Academic American Encyclopedia* (Princeton, NJ: Areté, 1980).

11. Linton, *The Study of Man,* pp. 338–39.

12. George M. Foster, *Traditional Cultures and the Impact of Technological Change* (New York: Harper & Row, 1962), p. 26.

13. John H. Bodley, *Victims of Progress,* 3rd ed. (Mountain View, CA: Mayfield, 1990), p. 7.

14. Pertti J. Pelto and Ludger Müller-Wille, "Snowmobiles: Technological Revolution in the Arctic," in H. Russell Bernard and Pertti J. Pelto, eds., *Technology and Social Change,* 2nd ed. (Prospect Heights, IL, Waveland Press, 1987), pp. 207–43.

15. Bodley, *Victims of Progress,* pp. 38–41.

16. Theodora Kroeber, *Ishi in Two Worlds* (Berkeley: University of California Press, 1967), pp. 45–47.

17. The historical information we refer to comes from a book by Allan Nevins, *The American States during and after the Revolution* (New York: Macmillan, 1927). For how radical the American Revolution was, see Gordon S. Wood, *The Radicalism of the American Revolution* (New York: Knopf, 1992).

18. Crane Brinton, *The Anatomy of Revolution* (Englewood Cliffs, NJ: Prentice Hall, 1938).

19. Jeffrey M. Paige, *Agrarian Revolution: Social Movements and Export Agriculture in the Underdeveloped World* (New York: Free Press, 1975).

20. Robert Boyd and Peter J. Richerson, *Culture and the Evolutionary Process* (Chicago: University of Chicago Press, 1985), p. 106.

21. Ibid., p. 135.

22. Donald T. Campbell, "Variation and Selective Retention in Socio-Cultural Evolution," in Herbert Barringer, George Blankstein, and Raymond Mack, eds., *Social Change in Developing Areas: A Re-Interpretation of Evolutionary Theory* (Cambridge, MA: Schenkman, 1965), pp. 19–49. See also Boyd and Richerson, *Culture and the Evolutionary Process;* and William H. Durham, *Coevolution: Genes, Culture and Human Diversity* (Stanford, CA: Stanford University Press, 1991).

23. William H. McNeill, *A World History* (New York: Oxford University Press, 1967), pp. 283–87.

24. See, for example, Daniel R. Gross, George Eiten, Nancy M. Flowers, Francisca M. Leoi, Madeline Lattman Ritter, and Dennis W. Werner, "Ecology and Acculturation among Native Peoples of Central Brazil," *Science,* November 30, 1979, 1043–1050.

25. The description of Tikopia is based on Raymond Firth, *Social Change in Tikopia* (New York: Macmillan, 1959), chapters 5, 6, 7, and 9, passim.

26. Most of this discussion is based on Robert F. Murphy and Julian H. Steward, "Tappers and Trappers: Parallel Process in Acculturation," *Economic Development and Cultural Change,* 4 (July 1956): 335–55.

27. S. Brian Burkhalter and Robert F. Murphy, "Tappers and Sappers: Rubber, Gold and Money among the Mundurucú," *American Ethnologist,* 16 (1989): 100–116.

28. Eric Wolf, *Peasants* (Englewood Cliffs, NJ: Prentice Hall, 1966), pp. 3–4.

29. E. J. Hobsbawm, *Age of Revolution* (New York: Praeger, 1970).

30. Daniel R. Gross and Barbara A. Underwood, "Technological Change and Caloric Costs: Sisal Agriculture in Northeastern Brazil," *American Anthropologist,* 73 (1971): 725–40.

31. Daniel O. Larson, John R. Johnson, and Joel C. Michaelsen, "Missionization among the Coastal Chumash of Central California: A Study of Risk Minimization Strategies," *American Anthropologist,* 96 (1994): 263–99.

32. Discussion is based on Raymond Firth, *Rank and Religion in Tikopia* (Boston: Beacon Press, 1970).

33. Ibid., p. 387.

34. Ibid., p. 418.

35. Phillip Mason, *Prospero's Magic* (London: Oxford University Press, 1962).

36. Bruce Russett, with the collaboration of William Antholis, Carol R. Ember, Melvin Ember, and Zeev Maoz, *Grasping the Democratic Peace: Principles for a*

Post–Cold War World (Princeton, NJ: Princeton University Press, 1993), pp. 10–11, 14, 138.

37. H. Russell Bernard and Pertti J. Pelto, "Technology and Anthropological Theory: Conclusions," in Bernard and Pelto, eds., *Technology and Social Change,* p. 367.

38. Pelto and Müller-Wille, "Snowmobiles," p. 237.

39. Conrad Phillip Kottak, "The Media, Development, and Social Change," in Emilio F. Moran, *Transforming Societies, Transforming Anthropology* (Ann Arbor: University of Michigan Press, 1996), pp. 136, 153.

40. Carol R. Ember and David Levinson, "The Substantive Contributions of Worldwide Cross-Cultural Studies Using Secondary Data," *Behavior Science Research,* special issue, "Cross-Cultural and Comparative Research: Theory and Method," 25 (1991): 79–140.

CHAPTER 25

1. Gilbert Kushner, "Applied Anthropology," in William G. Emener and Margaret Darrow, eds., *Career Explorations in Human Services* (Springfield, IL: Charles C. Thomas, 1991), pp. 46–61.

2. Margaret Mead, "The Evolving Ethics of Applied Anthropology," in Elizabeth M. Eddy and William L. Partridge, eds., *Applied Anthropology in America* (New York: Columbia University Press, 1978), pp. 426–29.

3. Barbara Frankel and M. G. Trend, "Principles, Pressures and Paychecks: The Anthropologist as Employee," in Carolyn Fluehr-Lobban, ed., *Ethics and the Profession of Anthropology: Dialogue for a New Era* (Philadelphia: University of Pennsylvania Press, 1991), p. 177.

4. Robert A. Hackenberg, "Scientists or Survivors? The Future of Applied Anthropology under Maximum Uncertainty," in Robert T. Trotter II, ed., *Anthropology for Tomorrow: Creating Practitioner-Oriented Applied Anthropology Programs* (Washington, DC: American Anthropological Association, 1988), p. 172.

5. Kushner, "Applied Anthropology."

6. William L. Partridge and Elizabeth M. Eddy, "The Development of Applied Anthropology in America," in Eddy and Partridge, eds., *Applied Anthropology in America,* 2nd ed. (New York: Columbia University Press, 1987), pp. 25–26.

7. Ibid., pp. 31–40.

8. Margaret Mead, "Applied Anthropology: The State of the Art," in Anthony F. C. Wallace, J. Lawrence Angel, Richard Fox, Sally McLendon, Rachel Sady, and Robert Sharer, eds., *Perspectives on Anthropology 1976, American Anthropological Association Special Publication No. 10* (Washington, DC: American Anthropological Association, 1977), p. 149.

9. Partridge and Eddy, "The Development of Applied Anthropology," pp. 31–40.

10. George M. Foster, *Applied Anthropology* (Boston: Little, Brown, 1969), p. 200.

11. Partridge and Eddy, "The Development of Applied Anthropology," p. 52.

12. "Appendix C: Statements on Ethics: Principles of Professional Responsibility, Adopted by the Council of the American Anthropological Association, May 1971" (as amended through May 1976), and "Appendix I: Revised Principles of Professional Responsibility, 1990," in Fluehr-Lobban, ed., *Ethics and the Profession of Anthropology,* pp. 239–42, 274–79.

13. "Appendix A: Report of the Committee on Ethics, Society for Applied Anthropology," and "Appendix F: Professional and Ethical Responsibilities, SfAA," in ibid., pp. 239–42, 262–64.

14. "Appendix H: National Association of Practicing Anthropologists' Ethical Guidelines for Practitioners, 1988," in ibid., pp. 270–73.

15. Thayer Scudder, "Opportunities, Issues, and Achievements in Development Anthropology since the Mid-1960s: A Personal View," in Eddy and Partridge, eds., *Applied Anthropology in America,* 2nd ed., pp. 184–210.

16. Ibid., p. 204ff.

17. Debra Picchi, "The Impact of an Industrial Agricultural Project on the Bakairi Indians of Central Brazil," *Human Organization* 50 (1991): 26–38; for a more general description of the Bakairi, see Debra Picchi, "Bakairi: The Death of an Indian," in Melvin Ember, Carol R. Ember, and David Levinson, eds., *Portraits of Culture: Ethnographic Originals* (Upper Saddle River, NJ: Prentice Hall, 1998). Prentice Hall/Simon & Schuster Custom Publishing.

18. Gerald F. Murray, "The Domestication of Wood in Haiti: A Case Study in Applied Anthropology," in Aaron Podolefsky and Peter J. Brown, *Applying Cultural Anthropology: An Introductory Reader,* 3rd ed. (Mountain View, CA: Mayfield, 1997), p. 131.

19. Arthur H. Niehoff, *A Casebook of Social Change* (Chicago: Aldine, 1966), pp. 255–67.

20. Foster, *Applied Anthropology,* pp. 8–9.

21. Derrick B. Jelliffe and E. F. Patrice Jelliffe, "Human Milk, Nutrition, and the World Resource Crisis," *Science,* May 9, 1975, 557–61.

22. William H. Fisher, "Megadevelopment, Environmentalism, and Resistance: The Institutional Context of Kayapó Indigenous Politics in Central Brazil," *Human Organization,* 53 (1994): 220–32.

23. Foster, *Applied Anthropology,* pp. 122-23.

24. Jeannine Coreil, "Lessons from a Community Study of Oral Rehydration Therapy in Haiti," in John van Willigen, Barbara Rylko-Bauer, and Ann McElroy, eds., *Making Our Research Useful: Case Studies in the Utilization of Anthropological Knowledge* (Boulder, CO: Westview Press, 1989), pp. 149–50.

25. Everett M. Rogers, *Diffusion of Innovations,* 3rd ed. (New York: Free Press, 1983), pp. 321–31.

26. Carol A. Bryant and Doraine F. C. Bailey, "The Use of Focus Group Research in Program Development," in John van Willigen and Timothy L. Finan, eds., *Soundings: Rapid and Reliable Research Methods for Practicing Anthropologists, NAPA Bulletin No. 10* (Washington, DC: American Anthropological Association, 1990), p. 32, pp. 24–39.

27. Niehoff, *A Casebook of Social Change,* pp. 219–24.

28. Coreil, "Lessons from a Community Study of Oral Rehydration Therapy in Haiti," p. 155.

29. Dennis M. Warren, "Utilizing Indigenous Healers in National Health Delivery Systems: The Ghanaian Experiment, in van Willigen, Rylko-Bauer, and McElroy, eds., *Making Our Research Useful*, pp. 159–78.

30. Ward H. Goodenough, *Cooperation in Change* (New York: Russell Sage Foundation, 1963), p. 416.

31. Wayne Warry, "Doing unto Others: Applied Anthropology, Collaborative Research and Native Self-Determination," *Culture*, 10 (1990): 61–62.

32. Julie Fisher, "Grassroots Organizations and Grassroots Support Organizations: Patterns of Interaction," in Emilio F. Moran, ed., *Transforming Societies, Transforming Anthropology* (Ann Arbor: University of Michigan Press, 1996), p. 57.

33. Ibid., p. 91; Data from Kenya referred to in Clare Oxby, "Farmer Groups in Rural Areas of the Third World," *Community Development Journal*, 18 (1983): 50–59.

34. As reported in Steve Jones, Robert Martin, and David Pilbeam, eds., *The Cambridge Encyclopedia of Human Evolution* (Cambridge: Cambridge University Press, 1992), p. 420.

35. Ralph Bolton, "Introduction: The AIDS Pandemic, A Global Emergency," *Medical Anthropology*, 10 (1989): 93–104.

36. Ibid.

37. Joseph Carrier and Ralph Bolton, "Anthropological Perspectives on Sexuality and HIV Prevention," *Annual Review of Sex Research* 2 (1991): 49–75; B. Schoepf, "Women, AIDS, and Economic Crisis in Central Africa," *Canadian Journal of African Studies*, 22 (1988): 625, cited in Carrier and Bolton, "Anthropological Perspectives on Sexuality and HIV Prevention."

38. Schoepf, "Women, AIDS, and Economic Crisis in Central Africa," pp. 637–38.

39. Ralph Bolton, "AIDS and Promiscuity: Muddled in the Models of HIV Prevention," *Medical Anthropology*, 14 (1992): 145–223.

40. Douglas A. Feldman and Thomas M. Johnson, "Introduction," in Douglas A. Feldman and Thomas M. Johnson, eds., *The Social Dimensions of AIDS: Method and Theory* (New York: Praeger, 1986), p. 2.

41. Tony Barnett and Piers Blaikie, *AIDS in Africa: Its Present and Future Impact* (London: Belhaven, 1992), p. 4.

42. The discussion in this section draws extensively from Lewis Aptekar, *Environmental Disasters in Global Perspective* (New York: G. K. Hall/Macmillan, 1994).

43. Information collected during Melvin Ember's fieldwork in American Samoa (1955–1956).

44. John W. Mellor and Sarah Gavian, "Famine: Causes, Prevention, and Relief, *Science*, January 30, 1987, 539–44.

45. Robert Dirks, "Starvation and Famine," *Cross-Cultural Research*, 27 (1993): 28–69.

46. William I. Torry, "Morality and Harm: Hindu Peasant Adjustments to Famines," *Social Science Information*, 25 (1986): 125–60.

47. Jorge Hardoy and David Satterthwaite, "The Legal and the Illegal City," in Lloyd Rodwin, ed., *Shelter, Settlement, and Development* (Boston: Allen & Unwin, 1987), pp. 304–38.

48. Lloyd Rodwin and Bishwapriya Sanyal, "Shelter, Settlement, and Development: An Overview," in Rodwin, ed., *Shelter, Settlement, and Development*, pp. 3–31.

49. William Mangin, "Latin American Squatter Settlements: A Problem and a Solution," *Latin American Research Review*, 2 (1967): 65–98.

50. Rodwin and Sanyal, 'Shelter, Settlement, and Development"; for a critique of self-help programs, see Peter M. Ward, "Introduction and Purpose," in Peter M. Ward, ed., *Self-Help Housing: A Critique* (London: Mansell, 1982), pp. 1–13.

51. Alex Cohen and Paul Koegel, "Homelessness," in Carol R. Ember, Melvin Ember, and Peter Peregrine eds., *Research Frontiers in Anthropology* (Upper Saddle River, NJ: Prentice Hall, 1998). Prentice Hall/Simon & Schuster Custom Publishing.

52. Gregg Barak, *Gimme Shelter: A Social History of Homelessness in Contemporary America* (New York: Praeger, 1991), p. 4.

53. Cohen and Koegel, "Homelessness."

54. Ellen Baxter and Kim Hopper, *Private Lives/Public Spaces: Homeless Adults on the Streets of New York City* (New York: Community Service Society of New York, 1981), pp. 30–33, pp. 50–74.

55. Ibid.

56. Cohen and Koegel, "Homelessness."

57. Helen Herrman, "A Survey of Homeless Mentally Ill People in Melbourne, Australia," *Hospital and Community Psychiatry*, 41 (1990): 1291–292.

58. Barak, *Gimme Shelter*, pp. 63-65.

59. Lewis Aptekar, "Are Colombian Street Children Neglected? The Contributions of Ethnographic and Ethnohistorical Approaches to the Study of Children," *Anthropology and Education Quarterly*, 22 (1991): 326.

60. Ibid., pp. 326–49. See also Lewis Aptekar, *Street Children of Cali* (Durham, NC: Duke University Press), 1988.

61. Jill E. Korbin, "Introduction," in Jill E. Korbin, ed., *Child Abuse and Neglect: Cross-Cultural Perspectives* (Berkeley: University of California Press, 1981), p. 4.

62. Murray A. Straus, "Physical Violence in American Families: Incidence Rates, Causes, and Trends," in Dean D. Knudsen and JoAnn L. Miller, eds., *Abused and Battered: Social and Legal Responses to Family Violence* (New York: Aldine de Gruyter, 1991), pp. 17–34.

63. Raoul Naroll, *The Moral Order: An Introduction to the Human Situation* (Beverly Hills, CA: Sage, 1983), p. 247.

64. David Levinson, *Family Violence in Cross-Cultural Perspective* (Newbury Park, CA: Sage, 1989), pp. 11–12, 44.

65. Leigh Minturn and Jerry Stashak, "Infanticide as a Terminal Abortion Procedure," *Behavior Science Research*, 17 (1982): 70–85. Using a sociobiological orientation, a study by Martin Daly and Margo Wilson (*Homicide* [New York: Aldine de Gruyter, 1988], pp. 43–59) also suggests that infanticide is largely due to the difficulty of raising the infant successfully.

66. Levinson, *Family Violence in Cross-Cultural Perspective*, pp. 26–28.

67. Ruth H. Munroe and Robert L. Munroe, "Household Structure and Socialization Practices," *Journal of Social Psychology*, 111 (1980): 293–94; and Ronald P. Rohner, *The Warmth Dimension* (Beverly Hills, CA: Sage, 1986), as referred to in Levinson, *Family Violence in Cross-Cultural Perspective*, pp. 54–55.

68. L. R. Petersen, G. R. Lee, and G. J. Ellis, "Social Structure, Socialization Values, and Disciplinary Techniques: A Cross-Cultural Analysis," *Journal of Marriage and the Family*, 44 (1982): 131–42, as cited in Levinson, *Family Violence in Cross-Cultural Perspective*, p. 63.

69. Straus, "Physical Violence in American Families," p. 17.

70. Levinson, *Family Violence in Cross-Cultural Perspective*, p. 31.

71. Ibid., p. 71.

72. Richard J. Gelles and Murray A. Straus, *Intimate Violence* (New York: Simon & Schuster, 1988), pp. 78–88.

73. Gerald M. Erchak, "Family Violence," in Carol R. Ember and Melvin Ember, eds., *Cross-Cultural Research for Social Science* (Upper Saddle River, NJ: Prentice Hall, 1998). Prentice Hall/Simon & Schuster Custom Publishing; Levinson, *Family Violence in Cross-Cultural Perspective*, pp. 44–45.

74. Levinson, *Family Violence in Cross-Cultural Perspective*, pp. 104–107.

75. Dane Archer and Rosemary Gartner, *Violence and Crime in Cross-National Perspective* (New Haven, CT: Yale University Press, 1984), p. 35.

76. Ted Robert Gurr, "The History of Violent Crime in America: An Overview," in Ted Robert Gurr, ed., *Violence in America*, vol. 1, *The History of Crime* (Newbury Park, CA: Sage, 1989), pp. 11–12.

77. The comparison described here is based on data we retrieved from the extensive appendix in Archer and Gartner, *Violence and Crime in Cross-National Perspective*.

78. Archer and Gartner, *Violence and Crime in Cross-National Perspective*, pp. 63–97.

79. Ted Robert Gurr, "Historical Trends in Violent Crime: Europe and the United States," in Gurr, ed., *Violence in America*, vol. 1, *The History of Crime*, pp. 47-48.

80. Elbert W. Russell, "Factors of Human Aggression," *Behavior Science Notes*, 7 (1972): 275–312; William Eckhardt, "Primitive Militarism," *Journal of Peace Research*, 12 (1975): 55–62; Richard G. Sipes, "War, Sports and Aggression: An Empirical Test of Two Rival Theories," *American Anthropologist*, 75 (1973): 64–86.

81. Carol R. Ember and Melvin Ember, "War, Socialization and Interpersonal Violence: A Cross-Cultural Study," *Journal of Conflict Resolution*, 38 (1994): 620–46.

82. Archer and Gartner, *Violence and Crime in Cross-National Perspective*, pp. 118–39.

83. Margaret Bacon, Irvin L. Child, and Herbert Barry III, "A Cross-Cultural Study of Correlates of Crime," *Journal of Abnormal and Social Psychology*, 66 (1963): 291–300; Beatrice B. Whiting, "Sex Identity Conflict and Physical Violence," *American Anthropologist*, 67 (1965): 123–40.

84. Ember and Ember, "War, Socialization and Interpersonal Violence," p. 625.

85. Carol R. Ember and Melvin Ember, "Issues in Cross-Cultural Studies of Interpersonal Violence," *Violence and Victims*, 8 (1993): 217–33, 227.

86. Colin Loftin, David McDowall, and James Boudouris, "Economic Change and Homicide in Detroit, 1926–1979," in Gurr, ed., *Violence in America*, vol. 1, *The History of Crime*, pp. 163–77; H. Krahn, T. F. Hartnagel, and J. W. Gartrell, "Income Inequality and Homicide Rates: Cross-National Data and Criminological Theories," *Criminology*, 24 (1986): 269–95, as referred to in Daly and Wilson, *Homicide*, pp. 287–88; Rosemary Gartner, "Crime: Variations across Cultures and Nations," in Carol R. Ember and Melvin Ember, *Cross-Cultural Research for Social Science* (Upper Saddle River, NJ: Prentice Hall, 1998). Prentice Hall/Simon & Schuster Custom Publishing.

87. Carol R. Ember and Melvin Ember, "Violence in the Ethnographic Record: Results of Cross-Cultural Research on War and Aggression," in David Frayer and Debra Martin, eds., *Troubled Times: Osteological and Archaeological Evidence of Violence* (Langhorne, PA: Gordon and Breach, 1997), pp. 1–20.

88. Most of the discussion in this section comes from Melvin Ember and Carol R. Ember, "Cross-Cultural Studies of War and Peace: Recent Achievements and Future Possibilities," in S. P. Reyna and R. E. Downs, eds., *Studying War: Anthropological Perspectives* (New York: Gordon and Breach, 1992), pp. 204–206.

89. Mervyn Meggitt, *Blood Is Their Argument: Warfare among the Mae Enga Tribesmen of the New Guinea Highlands* (Palo Alto, CA: Mayfield, 1977), p. 201.

90. For the cross-cultural results suggesting the theory of war described here, see Carol R. Ember and Melvin Ember, "Resource Unpredictability, Mistrust, and War: A Cross-Cultural Study," *Journal of Conflict Resolution*, 36 (1992): 242–62.

91. For the results on political participation and peace in the ethnographic record, see Carol R. Ember, Melvin Ember, and Bruce Russett, "Peace between Participatory Polities: A Cross-Cultural Test of the 'Democracies Rarely Fight Each Other' Hypothesis," *World Politics*, 44 (1992): 573–99. For the results on political participation and peace in the modern world, see the references in that essay.

Photo Credits

Chapter opener and box textiles: The Graham Collection

Chapter 1: 1 Robert Frerck/Odyssey Productions 5 Irven DeVore/Anthro-Photo 6 Mary G. Hodge 9 Terence Hays 10 Anita Spring 12 Photo Researchers, Inc. 13 William Strode/Woodfin Camp & Associates

Chapter 2: 16 E.R. Degginger/Animals Animals/Earth Scenes 17 Adam Jones/Photo Researchers, Inc. 22 *(left)* Photo Researchers, Inc.; *(right)* M.W. Tweedie/Photo Researchers, Inc. 30 *(top)* David C. Fritts/Animals Animals/Earth Scenes; *(bottom)* Alan Carey/Photo Researchers, Inc.

Chapter 3: 33 Kennan Ward Photography/Corbis-Bettman 38 *(top)* Photo Researchers, Inc.; *(bottom)* Sygma 40 *(left)* Wardene Weisser/Bruce Coleman, Inc.; *(right)* Animals Animals/Earth Scenes 41 Bruce Coleman, Inc. 42 K&K Ammann/Bruce Coleman, Inc. 43 Photo Researchers, Inc. 44 Michael K. Nichols/National Geographic Society

Chapter 4: 51 The Natural History Museum of London 57 The Natural History Museum of London 60 Russell C. Ciochon, University of Iowa, and Stephen Nash 64 Russell L. Ciochon, University of Iowa

Chapter 5: 68 John Reader/Science Photo Library/Photo Researchers, Inc. 72 Nancy Burson with Richard Carling and David Krumlich/Burndy Library/Dibner Institute 76 John Reader/Science Photo Library/Photo Researchers, Inc. 77 Tom McHugh/Photo Researchers, Inc. 85 Russell L. Ciochon, University of Iowa

Chapter 6: 91 Photo Researchers, Inc. 93 John Reader/Science Photo Library/Photo Researchers, Inc. 97 Kenneth Garrett/National Geographic Society 105 Jack Unruh/National Geographic Society 106 Sygma 107 Kenneth Garrett/National Geographic Society

Chapter 7: 113 Lawrence Migdale/PIX 117 Ettagale Blauer/Laure Communiations 118 Alison Wright/Panos Pictures 120 The Image Bank 125 *(top)* Animals Animals/Earth Scenes; *(bottom)* Irven DeVore/Anthro-Photo 130 James L. Stanfield/National Geographic Society 131 Jeff Greenberg/Photo Researchers, Inc.

Chapter 8: 134 Wolfgang Kaehler Photography 136 Jonathan Blair/Woodfin Camp & Associates 140 Irven DeVore/Anthro-Photo 146 American Museum of Natural History 148 Runk/Schoenberger/Grant Heilman Photography, Inc. 154 Robert Osti/Courtesy of *Scientific American*

Chapter 9: 157 Photo Researchers, Inc. 162 *(top)* The Granger Collection; *(bottom)* Paolo Koch/Photo Researchers, Inc. 163 Frerck/Odyssey Productions 170 Wolfgang Kaehler/Corbis-Bettmann

Chapter 10: 172 George Holton/Photo Researchers, Inc. 174 Stephen McBrady/PhotoEdit 176 *(left)* N. Martin Haudrich/Photo Researchers, Inc.; *(right)* James L. Stanfield/National Geographic Society 179 Chuck Savage/The Stock Market 180 *(left)* C. Seghers/Photo Researchers, Inc.; *(center)* Renee Lynn/Photo Researchers, Inc.; *(right)* Joseph Nettis/Photo Researchers

Chapter 11: 189 John Reader/Science Photo Library/Photo Researchers, Inc. 191 Kal Muller/Woodfin Camp & Associates 192 Jason Laure/Laure Communications 199 *(left)* Bildarchiv Okapia/Photo Researchers, Inc.; *(right)* Victor Englebert/Photo Researchers Inc. 202 Wolfgang Kaehler/Wolfgang Kaehler Photography 203 Ken Heyman/Woodfin Camp & Associates

Chapter 12: 208 Carolyn Watson 209 Robert Frerck/Odyssey Productions 211 Susan Kuklin/Science Source/Photo Researchers, Inc. 214 Lawrence Migdale/PIX 219 North Wind Picture Archives 226 *(left)* Rhoda Sidney/Monkmeyer Press; *(right)* Renata Hiller/Monkmeyer Press

Chapter 13: 232 Penny Tweedle/Corbis-Bettmann 234 George Holton/Photo Researchers, Inc. 239 Melvin Ember/Carol & Melvin Ember 241 Mike Yamashita/Woodfin Camp & Associates 243 Tiziana and Gianni Baldizzone/Corbis-Bettmann 247 Richard T. Nowitz/ Corbis-Bettmann

Chapter 14: 249 Comstock 254 David R. Frazier Photolibrary, Inc. 258 John Roberts/The Stock Market 259 Devore/Anthro-Photo 260 Jim Bradenburg/Minden Pictures 262 Flip Nicklin/Minden Pictures 266 Jose Azel/Woodfin Camp & Associates 269 Wendy Stone/Odyssey Productions 271 Dana Hyde/Photo Researchers, Inc.

Chapter 15: 274 David R. Frazier Photo Library, Inc. 275 Eastcott/Momatiuk/Woodfin Camp & Associates 278 Wendy Stone/Odyssey Productions 279 The Ritz-Carlton 285 Fumiko Asia Hi/New York Times Permissions

Chapter 16: 291 Wolfgang Kaehler Photography 292 Robert Harbison 293 Photo Researchers, Inc. 296 Terence Hays 300 Ann Mohs/Sto:Lo Nation 304 Photo Researchers, Inc. 308 Penny Tweedle/Panos Pictures

Chapter 17: 311 Robert Frerck/Odyssey Productions 314 Christine Osborne/Corbis-Bettmann 318 Francoise de Mulder/Corbis-Bettmann 321 North Wind Picture Archives 323 Alan Howard 324 Vic Bider/PhotoEdit 326 Nick Wheeler/Corbis-Bettmann 329 Woodfin Camp & Associates

Chapter 18: 334 Bruce Paton/Panos Picures 336 Photo Researchers, Inc. 344 Jason Laure/Laure Communications 345 Woodfin Camp & Associates 347 Luc Novovitch/Gamma-Liaison, Inc.

Chapter 19: 357 Ask Images/Art Directors & TRIP Photo Library 359 LeonOboler 361 Adrian Arbib/Anthro-Photo 365 Sylvia Grandadam/Photo Researchers, Inc. 368 Bernard Wong 370 Wayne Warry

Chapter 20: 374 Brian Brake/Photo Researchers, Inc. 378 Maria Lepowsky 381 Katz/Anthro-Photo 382 Reuters/Corbis-Bettmann 384 The Granger Collection 391 David Austen/Woodfin Camp & Associates 394 BIOS (A. Compost)/Peter Arnold, Inc.

Index

 A

Abelam, 284, 392
Aberle, David, 437
Abnormal behavior, 415–16
Aborigines, Australian, 276, 320–21, 442
Abortion, 308
Accidental juxtaposition, 457
Acculturation, culture change and, 461
Aché, 261, 276
Acheulian tool tradition, 85, 87
Achieved qualities, 358
Adams, David, 302
Adapids, 56, 60
Adaptive customs, 269–70, 272
Adjudication, conflict resolution by, 391
Adolescent rebellion, neolocality and, 336
Aegyptopithecus, 61
Affinal kinship, 349
Africa:
    domestication of plants/animals in, 147
    pre-agricultural developments in, 138
    sub-Saharan, city-states in, 165
African Americans, 284
Afterlife, 427–28
Age-grade, 359
Age-sets, 359–61
    tribal organization and, 379
Agribusiness, 328
Agriculture. *See also* Food production
    climate change and, 151
    commercialization/mechanization, 328–29, 470
    gender patterns, 297–98
    intensive, 326–29
    women's contribution to, 10
Agta, 295
AIDS (acquired immune deficiency syndrome), 490–92
Akkadian empire, fall of, 167
Algaze, Guillermo, 160–61
Ali Kosh, 144–45
Alleles, 24
Allen's rule, 116, 117
Allman, J., 59
Alorese, 404–5
Altered states of consciousness, 428
Altruism, 280
Alvarez, Louis, 21
Amazon rain forest, 268
Ambilineal descent, 339
Ambilineal systems, 349
Ambrona, fossil finds at, 87
Americas, pre-agricultural developments in, 138
Amok, 415
Ancestor spirits, 425–26
Anderson, Richard, 442

Andrews, Peter, 86
Animatism, 422
Animism, 422
Anorexia nervosa, 415
Anthropoids, 38, 40–44
    emergence of, 60–61
    Fayum Oligocene, 60–61
    hominoids, 42–44
    Miocene, 61–64
    New World monkeys, 41
    Old World monkeys, 41–42
    variability of, 30, 40–44
Anthropological linguistics, 7–8
Anthropology, 2–14. *See also* Theoretical orientations
    anthropological curiosity, 3
    business and, 482–83
    fields of, 3–9
    holistic approach in, 3
    relevance of, 11–13
    scope of, 2
    specialization in, 8–11
Anthropomorphizing, 422
Apache Indians, 270
Apes. *See* Great Apes
Apidium, 61
Apology, conflict resolution by, 390
Applied anthropology, 2, 10, 11, 268, 271, 479–502
    endangered primates, 37
    ethics of, 481–84
    global issues, 490–501
        AIDS, 490–92
        crime, 497–99
        family violence/abuse, 495–97
        housing/homelessness, 493–95
        natural disasters/famines, 492–93
        war, 499–500
    historical background, 480–81
    planned change, 484–90
        collaborative approach, 489–90
        difficulties in instituting, 485–89
Aptekar, Lewis, 495
Arapesh, 284, 303, 326
Arboreal, primates as, 34
Arboreal theory of primate origins, 57–58
Archaeology, 5–7
Archer, Dane, 497
Ardipithecus, 75
Argon-argon (Ar-Ar) dating method, 55–56
Aristotle, 17
Aronoff, Joel, 447
Arranged marriages, 322–23
Art, in Upper Paleolithic cultures, 101, 105–6
Arts, 440–55
    body decoration/adornment, 440–41
    culture contact and changes in, 453–54

    folklore, 450–52
    of less complex cultures, 452–53
    music, 446–50
    politics and, 442–43
    variation in, 441–52
    visual, 443–46
Aryans, 127
Asch, Solomon, 268
Ascribed qualities, 358
Ashanti, 391, 458
Assimilation, 461
Associations, 281, 358–73
    age sets, 359–61
    defined, 358
    ethnic, 368–69
    military, 365–66
    multiethnic, 370
    nonvoluntary, 358–65
    regional, 366–68
    rotating credit, 369–70
    statistical, 283
    unisex, 361–65
    variation in, 371–72
    voluntary, 365–72
Athapaskan Indians, 270, 317
Atlatls, 104
Australopithecines, 72–73, 74–80
    in East Africa, 74–75
Australopithecus, 69, 75
Australopithecus aethiopicus, 75
Australopithecus afarensis, 74, 77–78
Australopithecus africanus, 74, 76–77, 79–80
Australopithecus anamensis, 74
Australopithecus boisei, 75, 78–80
Australopithecus ramidus, 75
Australopithecus robustus, 75, 78–80
Avoidance, conflict resolution by, 389
Avunculocal residence, 333, 345–46
Ayres, Barbara, 450
Azande, 301, 330
Aztecs, 254

B

Bachelor associations, 361–65
Bacon, Margaret, 412, 413
Bailey, Robert, 123
Bakairi, 484
Balanced reciprocity, 263
Balancing selection, 114, 123
Balikci, Asen, 263
Bands/band organization, 376–77, 378
Bantu languages, 308
Baoulé, 401
Barrett, Stanley, 282
Barriada, 367
Barry, Herbert, 336, 400, 412, 413
Barth, Fredrik, 251–52

Fertile Crescent, 143–44, 149, 150
Feuding, conflict resolution by, 393–94
Field dependence/independence, 413
Fieldwork, 289, 291
Fijians, 121, 380, 390
Fire, *Homo erectus* and, 87–88
Firth, Raymond, 467
Fischer, John, 313, 444, 445, 446
Fish, Paul, 96
Fission-track dating method, 56
Flannery, Kent, 137, 149–50, 244–45
Folklore, 450–52
Folsom toolmaking, 109–10
Food collection, 320–24
  by Australian aborigines, 320–21
  collectors' characteristics, 323–24
  environmental restraints on, 331–33
  by Inuit, 321–23
  land ownership and, 251
  technology and, 255–56
Food production, 135–56, 324–31
  domestication of plants and animals,
    141–49
  horticulture, 324–26
  intensive agriculture, 326–29
  origin of, 244–45
  pastoralism, 329–31
  preagricultural developments, 96–97,
    136–41
    Africa, 138
    Americas, 138
    broad-spectrum food collecting,
      138–40
    Europe, 136–37
    Near East, 137–38
    sedentarism, 140–41
    Southeast Asia, 138
  reasons for development of, 149–51
  rise of, consequences of, 151–55
    accelerated population growth,
      151–52
    declining health, 152–54
    elaboration of material possessions,
      154–55
  spread/intensification of, 245–46
Foragers, 320
Foramen magnum, 76
Forced labor, 258
Ford, Clellan, 322
Ford, Marguerite, 314
Formal-operational stage, 401
Fossils, 3–4
  dating of
    absolute/chronometric methods,
      55–56
    relative methods, 55
  formation of, 52–53
  information provided by, 53–54
Founder principle, 114–15
Fouts, Roger, 298
Frank, André Gunder, 279
Fraternal polyandry, 328
Frayser, Suzanne, 347
Freedman, Daniel, 413, 415
Freeman, Derek, 291, 400
Frequency distribution, 269
Freud, Sigmund, 320, 400, 422
Fried, Morton, 276

Friedl, Ernestine, 326
Friedrich, Paul, 308
Friendly societies, 369
Frisch, Karl von, 297
Fromm, Erich, 423
Funeral rituals, in Middle Paleolithic
  era, 97
F-U-N trio, 55

 G

Gaiwiio, 434
G//ana, 262
Gangs, 366–67
Garber, Paul, 59
Gardner, Beatrice T., 48
Gardner, R. Allen, 48
Gartner, Rosemary, 497
Geertz, Clifford, 280, 411, 426–27
Gender differences, 292
  in behavior, misconceptions
    about, 306
  division of labor, 258–59, 293–95
  field dependence/independence, 413
  morality, 414
  political leadership, 298–301
  relative contributions to subsistence,
    295–98
  relative status of women, 301, 303
  role assignments, 293–95
  speech/language, 314, 322
  warfare and, 299, 302
Gender stratification, 301
Gene flow, 115
Generalized reciprocity, 261–63
General-purpose money, 267–68
Genes, 24–26
Genetic drift, 114–15
Genetic engineering, 28–29, 131
Genetic recombination, 26
Genotypes, 24
Ghana, 128
Ghosts, 425–26
Gibbons, 42, 48
Gift exchanges, 263, 318
Gigantopithecus, 62–63, 64
Gilligan, Carol, 414
Gimbutas, Marija, 308
Gladwin, Christina, 261
Gloger's rule, 118
Gods, 425
  intervention in human affairs, 426–27
Goldstein, Melvyn, 328
Goodenough, Ward, 345
Gorillas, 43, 48
Gould, Richard, 321
Gould, Stephen Jay, 20
Grammar
  cultural influences, 311
  in structural linguistics, 302
Grant, Peter, 21
Gray, J. Patrick, 120
Great Apes, 42–44, 63–64
Greece, 326–27
  slavery in, 285–86
Greenberg, Joseph, 107, 308

Grimm, Jakob, 307
Group marriage, 326
Group selection, 280
Group size, primate variability and,
  46–47
Grubb, Henry, 128, 129
Guatemala, 488–89
Guber, Nicholas, 394
Guiora, Alexander, 312
Gumperz, John, 309
Gunders, Shulamith, 119
Gurr, Ted, 497
Gusii, 316, 321
Gwembe Tonga, 481–82

 H

Hadar, fossil finds at, 74, 77–78
Hadza, 259, 277
Haiti, 484–85, 488
Half-life, 55
Hall, Edward, 268
Hames, Raymond, 324
Handsome Lake, 434–36
Haplorhines, 40
Hardin, Garrett, 252
Hargreaves, James, 458
Harlow, Harry, 36–37
Harris, Marvin, 166, 434
Hausa, 327
Hawaiian kinship terminology
  system, 353
Hays, Terrence E., 9
Headman, 376
Health, food production and, 152–54
Height, human variation in, 119–20
Henry, Patrick, 463
Heredity, 23–26
  genes and, 24–26
Herodotus, 421–22
Herrnstein, Richard, 128, 130
Herskovits, Melville, 264
Heterozygous organisms, 24
Hewes, Gordon, 71
Hickey, Gerald, 327
Hieroglyphics, 163
High-altitude adaptation, 118–19
Hindus, 428, 434
Historical archaeology, 5
Historical linguistics, 7, 305–8
Historical research, 292
HIV (human immunodeficiency virus),
  490–91
Hobsbawm, E.J., 470
Hoebel, E. Adamson, 388–89, 391
Hoijer, Harry, 311
Holistic approach, 3
Hollan, Douglas, 411
Homelessness, 493–95
Homesites
  Middle Stone Age, 96
  Upper Paleolithic, 102
Homestead Act (1862), 253
Hominids, 42, 44
  australopithecines, 74–80
  early cultures of, 81–83

Kwakiutl Indians, 277, 322–23
Kwashiorkor, 270, 327
Kwoma, 316

L

Labor
    division of, 258–59
    forced, 258
    incentives, 256–57
    organization, 260
Lactase deficiency, 124–25
Laetoli, fossil finds at, 74, 77–78
Lake Turkana, fossil finds at, 74, 81, 85
Lakoff, Robin, 314
Lakota Indians, 366
Lamarck, Jean Baptiste, 18
Lambert, William, 412, 426
Landauer, Thomas, 119, 120
Land ownership, 250–55
    communal, 252–53
Language, 48–49
Languages. See also Speech
    children's acquisition of, 301–2
    core vocabulary, 311
    creole, 299–301
    culture and, 309–12,
    endangered, 300
    families of, 307–8
    grammar, 302, 311
    historical linguistics, 305–8
    lexical content, 310
    linguistic divergence, 308–9
    morphology, 304–5
    origins, 299
    phonology, 302–4
    sexism and, 315–16
    structural linguistics, 302–5
    symbolic quality, 262
    syntax, 305
Lapps, 276, 330, 461
La Venta, fossil finds at, 158
Laws, 281
Leacock, Eleanor, 279
Leakey, Louis, 81
Leakey, Mary, 81
Lee, Richard, 141
Lee, Richard B., 322
Leeds, Anthony, 265
Le Moustier, fossil finds at, 94–96, 97
Lemur-like prosimians, 39
Lenski, Gerhard, 288, 289
Lepcha, 307
Leroi-Gourhan, André, 103
Lese, 123, 263
Lesu, 307
Levalloisian method, 94–95
LeVine, Robert, 412, 417
Levirate marriage, 325
Lévi-Strauss, Claude, 321
Lexical content, 310
Lexicon, 304
Lichter, Daniel, 331
Lieblich, A., 129
Lineages, 343

Linguistics
    divergence processes, 308–9
    historical, 305–8
    structural, 302–5
Linnaeus, Carolus, 18
Linton, Ralph, 327, 457, 459, 461
Lomax, Alan, 447–48
Loris-like prosimians, 40
Lotstein, Deborah, 123
Lovejoy, C. Owen, 71
Low, Bobbi, 28, 280
Lucy, 77
Lucy, John, 312
Lugbara, 426, 427–28
Lumbar curve, 77
Lunt, Paul, 279
Luo, 269, 304, 305–6, 326, 340
Lutz, Catherine, 416
Lyell, Charles, 19
Lynd, Helen, 279
Lynd, Robert, 279

M

Maboko Island, fossil finds at, 63
MacNeish, Richard, 149
Macrobius, 17
Mae Enga, 361–64
Magic, 430–32
Maglemosian culture, 136–37
Maize, 147–48
Maladaptive customs, 270
Malaria theory of sickle-cell anemia, 123–24
Male-female bonding, 47–48
Male-male marriages, 313
Malinowski, Bronislaw, 320, 400, 422, 434
Mana, 424
Mangebetu, 441
Mangin, William, 366
Manumission, 286
Manus, 317
Maori, 302, 425
Marett, R.R., 422, 424
Market exchange, 267–71
Market foraging, 329
Marmosets, 41
Marriage
    economic aspects, 317–19
    forms of, 326–28
    incest taboo, 319–22
    marking onset of, 316–17
    mate choice, 322–26
    Nayar exception, 312–13
    rare forms of, 313
    residence patterns, 333–38
    sex within, 307
    universality of, 312, 313–15
Marshack, Alexander, 106
Marshall, Lorna, 261–62
Martin, Robert, 52, 57
Martinez, Julian, 454
Martinez, Maria, 454
Martorell, Reynaldo, 119
Masai, 323

Masks, 446–47
Maslow, Abraham, 423
Mason, Phillip, 474
Material possessions, food production and, 154–55
Matriclans, 343
Matrifocal families, 329
Matrilineages, 343
Matrilineal descent, 339, 344–46
Matrilineal societies, 298–99
Matrilocal residence, 333
    patrilocal residence vs., 335–37
Mayr, Ernst, 20
Mbuti Pygmies, 119, 255, 277, 301, 331
McClelland, David, 417
McCracken, Robert, 125
McDowell, Nancy, 304
McHenry, Henry, 78–79
Mead, Margaret, 264, 291, 303–4, 326, 329, 336, 337, 400, 480
Measurement, 286–87
Mediation, conflict resolution by, 389–90
Medical anthropologists, 9
Mediums, 433
Meek, C.K., 289
Meiosis, 24
    crossing-over of chromosomes in, 26
    segregation of chromosomes in, 26
Mekong Delta, 327–28, 331
Mekranoti-Kayapo, 385
Melanin, 26, 118
Memes, 30
Mende, 301
Mendel, Gregor, 23–24
Mental illness, 415–16. See also Psychological development
Merina dialect, 314
Merwe, N.J. van der, 153
Mesoamerica, cities and states in, 163–64
Mesolithic period, 135. See also Food production
    technology in, 141
Message sealings, 159
Messenger RNA, 25–26
Mexico, domestication of plants/animals in, 147–48
Microliths, 103, 141
Middle Paleolithic culture, 94–97
    funeral rituals, 97
    getting food, 96–97
    homesites, 96
    time line, 95
    tool assemblages, 94–96
Middle Stone Age, 94
Middleton, Russell, 330
Migratory labor, commercialization and, 467–68
Military associations, 365–66
Miller, Joan, 414
Milton, Katherine, 46
Mintz, Sidney, 279
Miocene epoch, anthropoids of, 61
    early Miocene, 62–63
    late Miocene, 64
    middle Miocene, 63–64
Miracle, Andrew, 483
Miskito, 337
Mitochondrial DNA (mtDNA), 100

Mitosis, 24
Modal response, 268, 269
Mode, 268
Modern humans. *See* Homo sapiens
   sapiens
Modern synthesis theory of evolution,
   20–21
Moieties, 343
Molars, 35
Molecular clock, 65
Money, 267–69, 270
Monkeys
   cercopithecine, 42
   colobine, 41–42
   New World, 41
   Old World, 41–42
Monogamy, 326
Monotheism, 426
Montagnais-Naskapi Indians, 279, 468
Monte Albán, 164
Monte Verde, 107, 108
Moore, Omar, 428
Morality, gender differences and, 414
Morgan, Lewis Henry, 264
Morphemes, 304
Morphology, 302, 304–5
Morphs, 304
Motulsky, Arno, 120, 121
Mousterian tool assemblage, 94–96
Multiethnic associations, 370
Multilingualism, 315–17
Multiregional theory, 98
Mundugumor, 303
Mundurucu, 251, 468
Munroe, Robert, 316, 405, 406
Munroe, Ruth, 316, 405, 406
Murdock, George Peter, 328, 333
Murphy, Jane, 416
Murphy, Robert, 468
Murray, Charles, 128, 130
Murray, Gerald, 485
Music, 446–50
Muslim society, 301, 307, 326
Mutations, 26–27, 114
Myths, 451–52
Myxomatosis, 120–21

 N

Naftulians, 137–38
Nandi, 313
Napier, John, 81
Nariokotome, fossil finds at, 85
Naskapi, 428–29
National Association of Practicing
   Anthropologists, 481
National Brazilian Indian Foundation
   (FUNAI), 484
Native Americans, 384, 440, 451, 453,
   454, 461, 480. *See also* specific tribes
Natufians, 151
Natural selection, 19–23, 277
   of behavioral traits, 27–31
   observed examples of, 22–23
   types of, 114
Navaho Indians, 270, 302, 307, 311,
   413, 453

Nayar, 312–13
Neandertals, 92–93
Neander Valley, 92
Near East
   domestication in, 143–46
     Ali Kosh, 144–45
     Catal Hüyük, 145–46
   preagricultural developments, 137–38
Neel, James, 467
Negative reciprocity, 265
Negotiation, conflict resolution by,
   389–90
Nelson, Nici, 369–70
Neolithic era, 141
Neolithic revolution, 135
Neolocal residence, 333, 335
   adolescent rebellion and, 336–37
Newman, Katherine, 280
New World
   domestication of plants/animals in,
     147–49
   monkeys, 41, 61
Ngatatjara, 321
Nile Valley, cities/states in, 165
Nimkoff, M.F., 330
Nirvana, 428
Nissen, Henry, 30
Nocturnal lemurs, 39
Nonfraternal polyandry, 328
Nonsororal polygyny, 327
Nonvoluntary associations, 358–65
Normalizing selection, 114, 122
Norms, 267
North America, domestication of
   plants/animals in, 148
Nuclear families, 329
Nuer, 379
Nupe, 286–87, 382–83
Nyakyusa, 259

 O

Oaths, conflict resolution through,
   390–91
Oaxaca, fossil finds at, 147
Obsidian, 145, 155
Oedipus complex, 400
Olduvai Gorge
   fission-track dating at, 56
   fossil finds at, 78, 81–83, 85
Old World monkeys, 41–42
Oligocene epoch, anthropoids of, 60–61
Olsen, John, 62
Olsen-Chubbuck site, fossil finds at,
   110–11
Omaha kinship terminology system,
   350–51, 352
Omnivorous, primates as, 34–35
Omomyids, 56, 60
One-parent families, 329, 330–31
Open class systems, 278–83
Operational definition, 286
Opposable thumbs, 35
Optimal foraging theory, 260–61
Orangutans, 42–43, 48
Ordeals, conflict resolution through,
   390–91

Organizational cultures, 482
*Origin of Species by Means of Natural
   Selection, The* (Darwin), 19
Orokaiva, 302
Owens Valley Paiute, 251

 P

Palauans, 252, 426
Paleoanthropology, 3
Paleocene epoch, 56, 57
Paleomagnetic dating method, 56
Panter-Brick, Catherine, 123
Papago, 307–8
Papua New Guinea, 264, 269, 392
Parallel cousins, 323–24
Paranthropus, 78
Parapithecids, 61
Parental acceptance/rejection, 404–6
Parker, Hilda, 320
Parker, Seymour, 320
Participant-observation, 289
Pasternak, Burton, 472
Pastoralism, 251–52, 255, 329–31
Paterson, Ann, 105
Patriclans, 343
Patrilineages, 343
Patrilineal descent, 339, 344
Patrilocal residence, 333
   matrilocal residence *vs.,* 335–37
Peacock, Nadine, 123
Peak, Lois, 408
Peasant economies, 269
Peasants, 469
"Peking man," 85
Peninj River, fossil finds at, 87
Percussion flaking, 81
Personalities, 399. *See also* Psychological
   development
   genetic influences, 413, 415
   physiological influences, 413, 415
   sex differences, 303–6
Personality integration of culture, 417
Pfeifer, John, 97
Phenotypes, 24
Phonemes, 303
Phones, 302
Phonology, 302–4
Phratries, 343, 344
Physical anthropology, 3–5
Piaget, Jean, 401
Pibloktoq, 415, 416
Picchi, Debra, 484
Pidgin languages, 299–300
Pilbeam, David, 71
Pithecanthropus erectus. See Homo erectus
Pit houses, 137
Plato, 17
Platyrrhines, 40, 41
Play, social learning and, 37
Plesiadapiforms, 56
Pliocene epoch, 76
Plotinus, 17
Political economy, 278–79
Political leadership, 385–87
   gender differences and, 298–301
Political life, 375

Tell es-Sawwan, fossil finds at, 158
Templeton, Alan, 99
Teotihuacán, 163–64
Tepoztlan, 307
Terborgh, John, 46
Terrestrial monkeys, 41
Territorial groups, 375
Testing of explanations, 285–88
    measurement, 286–87
    operationalization, 286
    sampling, 287
    statistical evaluation, 287–88
Tests of significance, 288
Thematic Apperception Test (TAT), 418
Theoretical constructs, 283
Theoretical orientations, 277–83
    behavioral ecology, 279–80
    cultural ecology, 277–78
    interpretive approaches, 280–81
    political economy, 278–79
Theories, 283–85
    alternative, evaluating, 284
    falsification of, 284
    generating, 285
    provability of, 283–85
Thermoluminescence dating, 99–100
Thomas, Elizabeth, 255
Thompson, Stith, 451
Tibetans, 328
Tikopia, 467–68, 471–74
Tiv, 318, 334, 348, 377–79, 402
Tobias, Philip, 81
Tobin, Joseph, 408
Toda, 296, 328
Tonga, 327
Tool assemblages
    Mousterian, 94–96
    post-Acheulian, 96
Tools/toolmaking, 48
    Acheulian, 85, 87
    early hominid life-styles and, 81
    in Middle Paleolithic cultures, 94–96
    in New World, 108–10
    in Upper Paleolithic cultures, 102–4
Toralba, fossil finds at, 87
Torrey, E. Fuller, 432
Totems, 343
Trade, emergence of states and, 167
Trances, 428
Triandis, Leigh Minturn, 346, 412, 426
Tribal organization, 377–80
Tribal unions, 368–69
Trobriand Islanders, 263–65, 316, 400
Trukese, 345, 347
Tsembaga, 277–78
Tundras, 136
Tupari Indians, 121
Turner, Christy, 107
Tutsi, 285, 323
Tuzin, Donald, 284
Twa, 323
Tylor Edward B., 321, 422, 451

 U

Ucko, Peter, 105
Unconscious invention, 457
Unifacial tools, 81
Uniformitarianism, 19
Unilineal descent, 341–49
    descent groups, 342–44, 346–48
    matrilineal organization, 344–46
    patrilineal organization, 344
    systems, development of, 348–49
Unilocal residence, 335
Unisex associations, 361–65
Universally ascribed qualities, 358
Untouchables, 283–84
Upper Paleolithic cultures, 100–106
    art, 101, 105–6
    homesites, 102
    tools, 102–4
Uranium-series dating, 99
Urbanization, voluntary associations
    and, 371–72
Urban legends, 450–51
Uruk period, 159
    imperialism/colonialism in, 160–61
Usufruct, 250

 V

Vai, 409–10
Values, schooling and, 408–9
Vanatinai, 386–87
Variability, natural selection and, 19,
    26–27
Variables, 281
Variably ascribed qualities, 358
Vayda, Andrew, 265, 277
Venuses, 106
Vertical clinging/leaping, of lemurs, 39
Violence, conflict resolution by, 393–96
Visual arts, 443–46
Visual predation theory, 58
Voluntary associations, 365–72
Voodoo, 428

 W

Wallace, Alfred Russel, 19
Wallace, Anthony, 416, 424, 428
Wallerstein, Immanuel, 279
Wankas, 168–69
War, development of states and, 166
Warfare, 393, 499–500
    explanations for, 394–96
    gender roles and, 299, 302
Warry, Wayne, 489
Washburn, Sherwood, 71
Washington, George, 463

Washoe, 48
Watson, James, 24
Weidenreich, Franz, 85, 86
Weiss, Harvey, 167
Wellenkamp, Jane, 411
Werner, Dennis, 300
Westermarck, Edward, 319, 320
Whitaker, Ian, 330
White, Leslie A., 11, 321
White, Tim, 77
Whiting, Beatrice, 305, 431
Whiting, John, 119, 120, 281, 283–86,
    288, 305, 327, 411, 412, 418
Whittingham, Rose, 392
Whorf, Benjamin Lee, 312, 315
Whyte, Martin, 301, 303
Wilberforce, Bishop, 19
Willey, Gordon, 149
Wilson, Allan, 65
Wilson, Edward O., 28
Witchcraft, 430–32, 433
Within-culture comparisons, 290, 292
Wolf, Arthur, 320
Wolf, Eric, 279
Wolf, Margery, 426
Wolfe, Linda, 120
Wolpoff, Milford, 71
Women. *See also* Gender; Sex differences
    contributions to agriculture, 10
    effects of imperialism on, 168–69
    electoral success, 300
    relative status, 301, 303
    residence/kinship, 346–47
    violence against, 496–97
Women's associations, 362–63
    Ijaw, 365
Wood, Bernard, 86
Wright, George, 452
Wright, Henry, 159, 167
Wright, Sewall, 114
Wright effect, 114
Wu, David, 408

 Y

Yanomamö, 14, 121, 262, 276, 324–25,
    399, 403–4
Yoruba, 327, 416
Yucatec Mayan language, 312

 Z

Zawi Chemi Shanidar, fossil finds at,
    143
Zechenter, Elizabeth, 265
Zihlman, Adrienne, 72
Zo, 364
Zuni Indians, 428

Index to the Notes

Cohen, Myron L., 542:89
Cohen, Ronald, 544–45:20
Cohen, Wesley, 552:8
Collier, Stephen, 525:40
Collins, Desmond, 524:5
Connah, Graham, 526:1
Conrad, Phillip Kottak, 553:39
Conroy, Glenn C., 513:14; 516:18, 19, 25,
    26, 28, 32, 43, 44, 47, 54; 517:23, 25;
    518:34, 41, 45, 56
Coreil, Jeannine, 553:24; 554:28
Coult, Allan D., 542:1, 2, 84, 91; 543:21
Crawford, Gary W., 523:2
Creed, Gerald W., 533:9
Crockett, Carolyn, 514:26
Crystal, David, 530:22, 23
Cutright, Phillips, 537:45

 D

Daly, Martin, 554:65; 555:86
Dart, Raymond, 518:27
Darwin, Charles, 512:10, 11
Dasen, Pierre R., 547:14; 548:63, 64
Davenport, William, 543:27
Davis, Susan Schaefer, 541:63
Dawson, J.L.M., 548:59
Denny, J. Peter, 531:64
Dentan, Robert K., 546:1; 547:25
Devillers, Charles, 512:16
DeVilliers, Peter A., 530:20
DeVore, Irven, 532:10
Diamond, Jared, 523:57; 525:69; 527:11
Dirks, Robert, 554:45
Divale, William T., 538:35; 542:5–7;
    546:84
Dobzhansky, Theodosius, 513:27, 28;
    517:20; 523:85, 86, 88
Dohlinow, Phyllis Jay, 513:9
Dow, James, 550:47
Dowling, John H., 533:6, 8
Doyle, G.A., 513:16
Draper, Patricia, 534:29; 538:39
Dressler, William W., 551:13
Drucker, Philip, 535:69; 536:6
Du Bois, Cora, 547:26
Dundes, Alan, 551:22, 30
Durham, William H., 512:1; 513:37;
    521:2, 7; 523:49–51, 53, 59, 61, 65;
    541:41, 56, 57
Durkheim, Émile, 528:10; 549:10
Durrenberger, E. Paul, 534:21
Dyson-Hudson, Rada, 533:4; 543:1;
    544:11, 12

 E

Eckhardt, William, 555:80
Edgerton, Robert B., 548:50, 56;
    549:72, 73
Eisenberg, John F., 514:24, 25
Eisenstadt, S.N., 544:33
Eisley, Loren C., 512:5
Ekman, Paul, 530:2
Eldredge, Niles, 518:29

Eliot, T.S., 530:11
Ellis, Lee, 539:61, 62
Elwin, Verrier, 549:67
Ember, Carol R., 515:67; 526:83; 532:1,
    11; 533:23; 534:32; 538:24, 25, 30;
    539:57, 59, 63, 66; 542:10, 11; 543:5,
    14, 25; 545:48, 49; 546:71, 79, 82;
    547:15; 548:37, 60; 553:40; 555:81,
    84, 85, 87, 90, 91
Ember, Melvin, 515:66–69; 529:30;
    530:26; 531:52, 53; 533:18; 538:19,
    25–27; 540:13; 541:48, 59, 66, 68;
    542:4–8, 80–83; 543:17, 20, 28, 29,
    545:24, 26, 29; 546:78, 79, 81, 85;
    547:8
Epstein, Cynthia Fuchs, 537:2
Erchak, Gerald M., 555:73
Ericksen, Karen Paige, 543:12
Erickson, Edwin, 551:20
Ervin, Alexander M., 544:30
Euripides, 537:38
Evans-Pritchard, E.E., 540:7; 546:60;
    550:36
Eveleth, Phyllis B., 522:24, 25, 37

 F

Fagan, Brian M., 521:76, 84–86; 527:26
Falk, D., 517:14
Farley, Reynolds, 539:72
Featherman, David L., 536:15
Fedigan, Linda Marie, 514:30, 31
Feibel, Craig S., 519:84
Feinman, Gary M., 527:39; 536:1; 545:33
Feldman, Douglas A., 554:40
Finley, M.I., 545:21
Firth, Raymond, 541:58; 552:25, 32–34
Fischer, John L., 531:70, 551:10–12
Fischman, Joshua, 518:26
Fish, Paul, 520:18
Fisher, Julie, 554:32, 33
Fisher, William H,, 553:22
Flannery, Kent V., 523:3; 524:10, 12, 29;
    525:39, 40, 53–55; 526:2, 3, 7, 75;
    537:41
Fleagle, John G., 516:17, 27, 33–35, 38,
    40–42, 55, 60
Fleischer, Robert L., 515:10; 516:13–15
Ford, Clellan S., 539:70, 77–79; 541:61
Fortes, Meyer, 543:23
Fossey, Dian, 514:40, 43
Foster, Brian L., 536:84
Foster, George M., 552:12; 553:10, 20, 23
Fowler, Melvin L., 527:27
Frake, Charles O., 540:25
Franciscus, Robert G., 519:83
Frank, André Gunder, 529:9
Frankel, Barbara, 553:3
Frayer, David W., 520:37; 524:27; 537:5, 6
Freedman, Daniel G., 548:61, 62
Freeman, Derek, 547:8
Freeman, J.D., 542:12
Freeman, Leslie G., 519:94
Freud, Sigmund, 541:50; 549:4
Fried, Morton, 536:2; 537:51
Friedl, Ernestine, 533:21
Friedlander, Jonathan, 512:20

Friedman, Saul S., 523:73
Friedrich, Paul, 531:33, 34, 65
Frisancho, A. Roberto, 522:23
Frisch, Karl von, 530:3
Frisch, Rose E., 525:35
Fromm, Erich, 549:8
Fry, Douglas, 545:52

 G

Gal, Susan, 532:85
Galdikas, Biruté M.F., 514:37
Gardner, Beatrice T., 515:77
Gardner, R. Allen, 515:76
Gartner, Rosemary, 555:86
Gaulin, J.C., 540:37
Geertz, Clifford, 529:16; 531:72; 548:43;
    550:25
Gelles, Richard J., 555:72
Gentner, W., 515:10
Gibbons, Ann, 521:70
Gibbs, James L., Jr., 535:58; 551:7
Gilman, Antonio, 537:50
Gimbutas, Marija, 531:35
Gladwin, Christina H., 534:41
Gleitman, Lila R., 530:18
Goldstein, Melvyn, 542:85, 88
Goodall, Jane, 514:45
Goode, William J., 541:60, 64
Goodenough, Ward H., 543:19; 554:30
Goodman, Alan H., 526:87
Goodman, Madeline J., 538:15
Goodman, Morris, 514:51
Goodrich, L. Carrington, 523:76
Goody, Jack, 540:35; 543:36
Gorman, Chester, 524:17
Gossen, Gary H., 550:28
Gough, E. Kathleen, 540:4
Gould, Richard A., 532:4
Graburn, Nelson H., 540:14
Graham, Susan Brandt, 538:37
Gray, J. Patrick, 513:7; 522:33, 35; 537:6
Grayson, Donald K., 524:23
Greenberg, Joseph H., 521:71; 531:38
Greksa, Lawrence P., 522:21, 22
Grine, Frederick E., 518:52
Groger, Lisa, 534:15
Gross, Daniel R., 552:24, 30
Gubser, Nicholas J., 546:73
Guiora, Alexander Z., 531:66
Gumperz, John J., 531:41, 43
Gunders, S., 522:33, 34
Gurr, Ted Robert, 555:76, 79
Guthrie, R. Dale, 524:23
Guthrie, Stewart Elliott, 549:3

 H

Haas, Jonathan, 545:30
Haas, Mary R., 532:78
Hackenberg, Robert A., 553:4
Hage, Jerald, 534:17
Haldane, J.B.S., 523:89
Hall, Edward T., 512:6, 528:6
Hames, Raymond, 532:16; 535:49

GRANT OF LICENSE:

In consideration of your payment of the license fee, which is part of the price you paid for this product, and your agreement to abide by the terms and conditions of this Agreement, the Company grants to you:

• For the data disk - a nonexclusive right to use and display the copy of the enclosed data disk (hereinafter the DATA).

• For the program disk: a nonexclusive, nontransferable, permanent license to use and display the copy of the enclosed software program (hereinafter the PROGRAM) on a single computer (i.e., with a single CPU) at a single location so long as you comply with the terms of this Agreement.

The Company reserves all rights not expressly granted to you under this Agreement. Together, the PROGRAM AND THE DATA ARE CALLED THE SOFTWARE.

OWNERSHIP OF SOFTWARE:

You own only the magnetic or physical media (the enclosed disk) on which the SOFTWARE is recorded or fixed, but the Company retains all the rights, title, and ownership to the SOFTWARE recorded on the original disk copy(ies) and all subsequent copies of the SOFTWARE, regardless of the form or media on which the original or other copies may exist. This license is not a sale of the original SOFTWARE or any copy to you.

RESTRICTIONS ON COPYING, USE AND TRANSFER:

This SOFTWARE and the accompanying printed materials and user manual (the Documentation) are the subject of copyright and are licensed to you only.

• For the PROGRAM: You may not copy the documentation or the PROGRAM except that you may make a single copy of the PROGRAM for backup or archival purposes only.

You may not network the PROGRAM or otherwise use it on more than one computer or computer terminal at the same time. You may physically transfer the PROGRAM from one computer to another provided that the PROGRAM is used on only one computer at a time. You may not distribute copies of the PROGRAM DISK or Documentation to others. You may not reverse engineer, disassemble, decompile, modify, adapt, translate, or create derivative works based on the PROGRAM or the Documentation without the prior written consent of the Company.

The enclosed PROGRAM may not be transferred to any one else without the prior written consent of the Company. Any unauthorized transfer of the PROGRAM shall result in the immediate termination of this Agreement.

• For the DATA: You may not sell or license copies of the DATA or the documentation to others, and you may not transfer or distribute it, except to instructors and students in your school who are users of the Company textbook that accompanies this SOFTWARE.

You may be held legally responsible for any copying or copyright infringement which is caused or encouraged by your failure to abide by the terms of these restrictions.

TERMINATION:

This license is effective until terminated. This license will terminate automatically without notice from the Company and become null and void if you fail to comply with any provisions or limitations of this license. Upon termination, you shall destroy the Documentation and all copies of the SOFTWARE. All provisions of this Agreement as to warranties, limitation of liability, remedies or damages, and our ownership rights shall survive termination.

(continued on next page)

GRANT OF LICENSE: *(continued from previous page)*

MISCELLANEOUS:
THIS AGREEMENT SHALL BE CONSTRUED IN ACCORDANCE WITH THE LAWS OF THE UNITED STATES OF AMERICA AND THE STATE OF NEW YORK, APPLICABLE TO CONTRACTS MADE IN NEW YORK, AND SHALL BENEFIT THE COMPANY, ITS AFFILIATES AND ASSIGNEES.

ACKNOWLEDGMENT:
YOU ACKNOWLEDGE THAT YOU HAVE READ THIS AGREEMENT, UNDERSTAND IT, AND AGREE TO BE BOUND BY ITS TERMS AND CONDITIONS. YOU ALSO AGREE THAT THIS AGREEMENT IS THE COMPLETE AND EXCLUSIVE STATEMENT OF THE AGREEMENT BETWEEN YOU AND THE COMPANY AND SUPERSEDES ALL PROPOSALS OR PRIOR AGREEMENTS, ORAL, OR WRITTEN, AND ANY OTHER COMMUNICATIONS BETWEEN YOU AND THE COMPANY OR ANY REPRESENTATIVE OF THE COMPANY RELATING TO THE SUBJECT MATTER OF THIS AGREEMENT.

Should you have any questions concerning this agreement or if you wish to contact the Company for any reason, please contact in writing: Executive Manager, New Media, Humanities and Social Sciences Division, Prentice Hall, 1 Lake Street, Upper Saddle River, New Jersey 07458.

INSTALLATION INSTRUCTIONS

INSTALLATION WINDOWS 3.1
Insert disk in CD-ROM drive. Open Program Manager and select Run from the File menu. Type x:\autorun and press Enter (with x being the letter for your CD-ROM drive).

INSTALLATION WINDOWS 95
Insert disk in CD-ROM drive. If your Windows Autorun feature is active, it will start the set-up menu. Select an option. Run from Hard Drive will install the program. Run from CD will play program directly from CD-ROM. If the Autorun feature does not work, then click on the Start button, select Run, and type x:\autorun and press Enter (with x being the letter for your CD-ROM drive).

INSTALLATION MACINTOSH
Insert disk in CD-ROM drive. Open the CD and double-click on the Exploring Anthropology icon.

MINIMUM SYSTEM REQUIREMENTS

WINDOWS
- 486/33 MHz CPU or higher
- Windows 3.1x, Windows 95
- 640x480 resolution, 256 colors
- 8MB RAM (12MB recommended)
- 13MB hard disk space for installation (0MB if running from CD)
- 2x CD-ROM drive
- Sound card

MACINTOSH
- 68030 or faster processor (Power Macintosh recommended)
- System 7.5.1 or later
- 8MB RAM (12MB recommended)
- Color monitor with 640x480 resolution and 256 colors
- 2x CD-ROM drive